MERGERS, ACQUISITIONS, AND OTHER RESTRUCTURING ACTIVITIES

An Integrated Approach to Process, Tools, Cases, and Solutions

---

ELEVENTH EDITION

DONALD M. DEPAMPHILIS, PH.D.
Emeritus Professor of Finance
College of Business Administration
Loyola Marymount University
Los Angeles, California

Academic Press is an imprint of Elsevier
525 B Street, Suite 1800, San Diego CA 92101, USA
50 Hampshire Street, 5th Floor, Cambridge, MA 02139, USA
The Boulevard, Langford Lane, Kidlington, Oxford, OX5 1GB, UK

Library of Congress Cataloging-in-Publication Data
9780128197820

For information on all Academic Press publications, visit our website at *www.elsevierdirect.com*.

Publisher: Katey Birtcher
Senior Editorial Project Manager: Susan Ikeda
Content Development Manager: Lynsey Gathercole
Publishing Services Manager: Shereen Jameel
Project Manager: Nadhiya Sekar
Design Direction: Ryan cook

Printed in the United States of America
22 23 24 25 10 9 8 7 6 5 4 3 2

Dedication

I would like to express my gratitude for my wife, Cheryl, and my daughter, Cara, whose patience made the completion of this book possible; for my brother, Mel, who encouraged me to undertake this book; and for the blessings of my beautiful grandchildren, Max and Hannah.

Dedication

Contents

II
The mergers and acquisitions process: Phases 1 through 10

4. Planning: developing business and acquisition plans—phases 1 and 2 of the acquisition process

5. Implementation: search through closing—phases 3 to 10 of the acquisition process

6. Postclosing integration: mergers, acquisitions, and business alliances

III
Mergers and acquisitions valuation and modeling

7. Mergers and acquisitions cash flow valuation basics

8. Relative, asset-oriented, and real-option valuation basics

9. Financial modeling basics

18. Alternative exit and restructuring strategies: bankruptcy, reorganization, and liquidation

19. Cross-border mergers and acquisitions: analysis and valuation

About the Author

Dr. Donald DePamphilis has managed through closing more than 30 transactions, including acquisitions, divestitures, joint ventures, minority investments, licensing, and supply agreements in a variety of different industries. These industries include financial services, software, metals manufacturing, business consulting, health care, automotive, communications, and real estate. He earned a BA in economics from the University of Pittsburgh and an MA and a PhD in economics from Harvard University.

He is currently Emeritus Professor of Finance at Loyola Marymount University in Los Angeles, where he has taught mergers and acquisitions (M&As), corporate restructuring, deal making, financial analysis, financial modeling, and micro- and macroeconomics (to both business and nonbusiness majors) to undergraduate, MBA, and Executive MBA students. In addition, he has taught corporate governance and executive leadership to Executive MBA students.

Dr. DePamphilis has also served as an instructor in the Loyola Marymount University International Executive Education Program, teaching corporate restructuring tactics and strategies in a global context. He has served as chair of the Student Investment Fund at Loyola Marymount University's College of Business and has been a member of the graduate business program curriculum committee. He has also directed curriculum development and faculty recruitment efforts in specific teaching modules within the University's Executive MBA program.

Dr. DePamphilis is the recipient of the Loyola Marymount University Executive MBA Leadership Achievement Award and has represented the University on the Los Angeles Council of Economic Advisors serving Mayor Eric Garcetti on matters relating to the economy.

Dr. DePamphilis has lectured on M&A and corporate restructuring, financial analysis, and economics at the University of California, at Irvine; Chapman University; and Concordia University. As a visiting professor, he taught M&As and corporate restructuring strategies at the Antai School of Management, Shanghai Jiao Tong University, in Shanghai, China. He has also served as a teaching fellow in economics at Harvard University.

The author has more than 25 years of experience in businesses ranging in size from small privately owned firms to Fortune 100 companies in various industries and with varying degrees of responsibility. Previously, he served as vice president of Electronic Commerce for Experian Corporation, vice president of Business Development at TRW Information Systems and Services, senior vice president of Planning and Marketing at PUH Health Systems, director of Corporate Business Planning at TRW, and chief economist for National Steel Corporation (formerly a Fortune 100 company).

He also served as Director of Banking and Insurance Economics for Chase Econometric Associates providing consulting services to dozens of clients in private industry and the government and as an economic analyst for United California Bank. While at United California Bank, he developed a complex, interactive econometric forecasting and simulation model of the US economy, which was used in both internal and external bank forecasts and in conducting simulations of alternative economic outcomes based on differing assumptions. Dr. DePamphilis has also spoken to numerous industry trade associations and customer groups and to Los Angeles community and business groups. He is a graduate of the TRW and National Steel Corporation Executive Management programs.

Dr. DePamphilis has authored numerous articles, chapters in books, and books on M&A. He has published in the areas of business planning and development, marketing, and economics in peer-reviewed academic journals as well as business and trade publications. His books include the highly popular, award-winning *Mergers, Acquisitions, and Other Restructuring Activities*, now in its eleventh edition; *Mergers and Acquisitions Basics: All You Need to Know*; and *Merger and Acquisition Basics: Negotiation and Deal Structuring*. *Mergers, Acquisitions, and Other Restructuring Activities* has been translated into Chinese (now in its second edition) and Russian and has been used in more than 150 universities worldwide. The seventh edition was voted the 2014 Textbook Excellence Award (Texty) in the business book category by the Text and Academic Authors Association. For more details, see http://blog.taaonline.net/2014/02/2014-taa-textbook-award-winners-announced/.

Dr. DePamphilis has served as a consultant in product and personal liability, patent infringement, and business valuation litigation, including but not limited to providing expert analysis and depositions in cases primarily related to M&As. He has also served in an advisory capacity on matters of acquisition target selection, negotiation support, and business valuation.

The author has been a board member of the National Council of Orange County (California), Economics Club of Pittsburgh, Economic Council of Western Pennsylvania, and Hospital Council of Western Pennsylvania. He has also been active in the Rotary Club and Junior Achievement.

Please forward any comments you may have about this book to the author at dondepam@pacbell.net. Your suggestions about ways in which this text may be improved are welcome.

Preface

> Success is how we measure what we do for ourselves. Significance is how we measure what we do for others.
>
> —Donald M. DePamphilis

To the reader

In a world in transition from global economic integration to a return of nationalism and regionalism, it is reasonable to expect turmoil and rising uncertainty. After World War II, we saw the rapid disintegration of the remaining vestiges of colonialism. In the 1950s and 1960s, the European Coal and Steel Community emerged, laying the groundwork for the eventual formation of the European Union. We also saw the Bretton Woods Agreement, the Marshall Plan, and the emergence of the dollar as a reserve currency spur economic growth. Throughout this period, the spread of democracy encouraged the expansion of international trade, and the number of people living in poverty fell sharply worldwide. In the decades that followed, living standards in much of the world improved as barriers to trade and capital flows continued to fall.

But shortly after the beginning of the 21st century, cracks began to appear. Much of the global growth was fueled by mounting indebtedness: governments to finance expanding welfare programs, corporations to buy back stock and hype financial returns, and households to satisfy their immediate desires. As long as lenders believed borrowers would repay what they owed, the economic prosperity continued. But growth based largely on faith is tenuous. When this confidence began to crumble, the global financial system first tottered and then almost collapsed in what became known as the "great recession" in 2008 and 2009.

Hoping to revive the world economy, monetary authorities pumped money into their economies at a voracious clip in a policy known as "quantitative easing." Interest rates were pushed ever lower. In some countries, interest rates on government debt and later corporate debt turned negative. With the cost of borrowing at historically low levels, the volume of borrowing exploded. Many countries saw their outstanding debt exceed substantially their annual gross domestic product (GDP).

Even though equity markets soared as investors sought higher financial returns, the economic recovery began to stall. Why? The world was awash in debt. Governments believed that they could continue to finance their spending without consequences by borrowing at near-zero or even negative interest rates. The low rates also spurred corporations to borrow excessively.

But all this borrowing had an insidious side. The low rates allowed government's share of total resources as measured by GDP to balloon as spending could be financed by selling debt directly to central banks. Thus, resources shifted from the private sector to the generally less productive public sector. The availability of inexpensive debt also enabled so-called "zombie" corporations to remain afloat when they would otherwise have gone bankrupt. The shift of resources away from those that are more productive to those that are less inevitably slows productivity and subsequently economic growth. Moreover, tariffs were used to promote national interests, igniting trade wars and disrupting supply chains. With the cost and availability of imports from traditional trading partners uncertain, firms scrambled to secure new sources of supply. Foreign investment slowed as confidence in formerly attractive investment opportunities waned. Finally, the coronavirus pandemic in early 2020 plunged the global economy into the deepest recession since the Great Depression of the 1930s, setting the stage for a slow and uneven recovery. And the new Biden Administration muddled the outlook for US foreign policy.

Against this backdrop of uncertain global economic growth, the rise in protectionism, and changing trading and investment patterns, the nature of both domestic and cross-border mergers and acquisitions (M&As) is likely to change. Although it does not promise easy answers to the changing nature of corporate restructuring activities, this book does offer insight into how executives can manage in these turbulent times. It does so by discussing the practical applications of all aspects of the corporate restructuring process from takeovers and joint ventures (JVs) to divestitures and spin-offs and equity carve-outs to reorganizing businesses inside and outside the protection of the bankruptcy court.

This book is unique as the most current and comprehensive text on M&A and corporate restructuring supported by cutting-edge academic research spread throughout its 19 chapters. It is *current* in that it includes many of the most up-to-date and notable deals, precedent-setting judicial decisions, government policies and regulations, and trends affecting M&As, as well as strategies and tactics used in takeovers. This edition is *comprehensive* as nearly all aspects of M&As and corporate restructuring are explored from planning to target selection and valuation to negotiation and integration, illustrated by case studies involving deals announced or completed during the past several years. And it is *cutting edge* with conclusions and insights documented by almost 1000 empirical studies published in leading peer-reviewed journals, with more than one-third having been published just since 2019.

The highlights of the new edition are listed here:

- **New cases:** Nearly **90%** of the 40 case studies are new and involve transactions announced or completed since **2019.** These cases represent friendly, hostile, highly leveraged, and cross-border deals in 10 different industries, involving public and private firms as well as firms experiencing financial distress. All end-of-chapter case studies begin with a "Case study objectives" section indicating what the reader should learn from the case study and include discussion questions and solutions available in the online instructors' manual to measure student comprehension.
- **Latest research:** This edition focuses on the most recent and relevant academic studies, some of which contain surprising insights changing the way we view this subject matter. Recent research has significant implications for academicians, students, M&A practitioners, and government policy makers shedding new light on current developments and trends in the ever-changing M&A market.
- **New content**: In addition to a chapter on valuing and modeling leveraged buyouts, each chapter contains fresh information and insights on the changing market for M&As. This *new content* is highlighted by chapter in the following discussion.

The M&A environment

Chapter 1 provides an overview of M&As and updates the growing body of academic research documenting that acquirers on average realize positive financial returns for their shareholders. The chapter also addresses the implications for M&As of the 2020 COVID-19 pandemic, the new Biden administration in the United States, alternative takeover strategies, improving borrowing capacity, the impact of default risk on postmerger performance, deal completion rates throughout merger waves, and unconventional arbitrage strategies. The section on socially responsible investments in the context of M&As has been expanded to address how such investment affects the behavior of family-owned firms, institutional investors, deal completion rates, target selection, cost of capital, leverage, dividend policy, public image, target premiums, and firm value. The chapter also updates acquirer long-term postmerger performance and how M&As contribute to productivity and social welfare.

Additional new content includes a discussion of how media attention and supply-chain knowledge affect acquirer announcement date returns, factors affecting bondholder and arbitrageur excess returns, how synergy is created and limited by coordination costs, and behavioral explanations of excess financial returns. How diversification impacts firm value, the role of acquirer characteristics in generating higher announcement date returns, and the superior long-term performance of private versus public bidders are also addressed. Finally, the limitations of statistical analysis underlying academic research and how they can bias estimates of the payoffs of M&As for shareholders, bondholders, and society are explained in detail.

Chapter 2 addresses M&A regulatory matters. New content includes a discussion of corporate governance in the context of managing stakeholder interests, how monopolies hurt consumers, and when monopoly breakups can be worse than the problem. Novel content also includes the impact of labor laws and collective bargaining on deal completion rates, time to completion, synergy realization, and postmerger innovation, as well as the impact of social media on price discovery. The impact of the Sarbanes-Oxley Act on poorly governed firms and the implications for M&As of the European Union's new data protection and copyright laws for M&As are also addressed. New regulatory powers affecting foreign investment and antitrust guidelines for mergers involving complementary products and input suppliers are reviewed, as well as US restrictions on foreign acquisitions and recent legislation to preclude foreign firms from listing on public exchanges under certain circumstances.

Other new material includes an examination of director trading patterns before acquisition announcements and the impact of board gender and racial diversity on board performance. The chapter also includes analyses of the 2019 revisions to the "Volcker Rule" and the potential for government-insured banks to invest along with their customers in speculative investments, as well as new Public Company Accounting Oversight Board rules. Issues of price stickiness in evaluating horizontal mergers, the usefulness of insider trading information, and factors affecting the extent of risk disclosure in public reporting are detailed. Finally, the chapter describes how competition or antitrust policies can reduce acquirer returns and the efficiency of the takeover market.

Chapter 3 deals with takeover tactics and defenses and has been expanded to include a more thorough discussion of the role of the board of directors, lead independent directors, activist investors, institutional blockholders, short sellers, management incentive systems, and class action lawsuits in promoting good corporate governance. Other new content includes how bidders determine purchase prices through the "price discovery process," how short sellers impact the bidding process, bidder conflicts of interests arising in determining offer prices, and the impact of CEO relative pay on acquisition premiums. The chapter also highlights tactics used by target firms to reduce the likelihood of takeover, alternatives to breakup fees, how CEO tenure affects M&A decision making, and how politically connected CEOs can impact a firm's financing costs. Finally, how dual-class shareholders affect management entrenchment, the impact of protectionist antitakeover legislation on firm value, the declining role of board executive committees, and the impact of activist investors on the ability of equity analysts to monitor firm performance are discussed in greater detail.

The M&A process

Chapter 4 introduces the 10 steps of the M&A process with a focus on the role of business and acquisition plans and now addresses how firms use mission and vision statements to communicate both tactically and strategically to all stakeholders. Updated applications of SWOT (strengths, weaknesses, opportunities, and threats) analyses are provided as are insights into how "search frictions" can create inefficient mergers. New applications of "war gaming" and scenario planning to develop new insights into how to achieve competitive advantage and assess risks are illustrated. Finally, the discussion of diversification is expanded to include exploratory versus exploitative strategies.

Chapter 5 speaks to M&A process execution issues from target selection to negotiation to closing and postclosing evaluation. It focuses on how "big data," data analytics, artificial intelligence (AI), blockchains, and smart contracting tools can impact the M&A process. New content discusses the application of AI to business and strategy development, search and screening, opportunity selection, negotiation, valuation, premerger planning, and postmerger organizational structure, as well as how blockchain technology is changing the way deals are done. The pros and cons of implementing these new technologies in the M&A process are discussed in detail, as well as the low success rates in implementing certain types of "big data" strategies.

Additional content describes the role of "reputational capital" and corporate social responsibility indices in target selection and in performing initial due diligence. The chapter now includes a more detailed discussion of factors affecting deal completion rates such as the importance of identifying differences (similarities) between the target and acquirer during due diligence. Finally, the chapter also discusses the reliability of audited data and how so-called "reference points" can be used during negotiations.

Chapter 6 addresses postmerger integration and includes new discussions of alternative postclosing integration models for cross-border deals, reducing stakeholder stress levels, and complications arising for premerger integration planning if national security concerns are present. The chapter also addresses how to link the integration of research and development, marketing, and sales functions, as well as the way in which trust promotes improved performance in international strategic alliances. New subject matter also includes a discussion of the importance of what people actually do and the way they do it in making organizational changes while preserving critical cultural differences between the acquirer and target firms. Finally, the chapter highlights the effectiveness of co-managed as opposed to acquirer-supervised postmerger integration work teams and the role of target managers in transferring proprietary knowledge.

M&A valuation and modeling

Chapter 7 focuses on discounted cash flow valuation. Updated content includes changes in the accounting treatment of operating leases, historical trends in interest rates and their implications for calculating the capital asset pricing model, and the implications of negative interest rates and "black swan" events (e.g., pandemics) for cash flow valuation. Suggestions are made as to how to adjust present value calculations for these factors. Additional new content includes an assessment of the impact of conservative accounting practices on the cost of capital, how to estimate the implied cost of capital using index options, and valuing "unicorns."

Chapter 8 introduces the basics of relative valuation methods and documents how real-options awareness can contribute to higher firm value. The chapter also addresses the impact of real options on takeover premiums, how Monte Carlo analysis can be used to obtain more accurate real-option values, and the application of real options to infrequently traded assets. Other new content speaks to the ways in which misleading accounting measures can skew firm valuation and which valuation methodologies finance professionals use in practice.

Chapter 9 covers the basics of M&A modeling. New content describes the implications of the new treatment of operating leases for model building and common forecasting methods. The chapter also speaks to the relevance of establishing comparable financial statements between target and acquirer firms in making better takeover decisions and the importance of analyzing cash flows to identify the manipulation of accrual-based earnings.

Chapter 10 describes the challenges of buying and selling private firms and addresses in more detail the relative cost of reverse mergers versus initial public offerings (IPOs), the revival of blank check companies (special-purpose acquisition corporations), and how earnings quality may be manipulated in reverse mergers. Furthermore, new content includes the implications of overpricing of "unicorns," the impact of excess control rights on target overpayment risk, and how ownership structure affects stock market returns.

Deal structuring and financing strategies

Chapter 11 addresses legal and payment considerations and has been updated to include how the COVID-19 pandemic impacts deal structuring, a more rigorous discussion of factors affecting the choice of stock versus cash as a form of payment, and how time pressure affects the choice of tactics employed in the deal-structuring process.

Chapter 12 speaks to tax and accounting aspects of deals and now addresses the implications of the new Biden Administration tax policies for M&As. In addition, Financial Accounting Standards Board (FASB) rule changes impacting the treatment of operating leases, the impact of tax inversions on abnormal financial returns, and how effective tax rates affect M&A decisions are explained. New content also speaks to the need for standardized financial reporting across countries as well as for environmental, social, and governance risks; the role of differential tax rates on the choice of a restructuring strategy; and the impact of the Tax Cuts and Jobs Act on M&As and the business startup rate. Revisions in 2019 made to the 2017 Tax Cuts and Jobs Act and how earnings restatements impact share prices also are addressed.

Chapter 13 addresses M&A financing issues and now includes a discussion of the impact of restrictive loan covenants on M&A premiums and target selection, IPOs and equity carve-outs as sources of M&A financing, financing-related synergy, and improving debt capacity as a takeover motive. New content also includes an analysis of how private equity fund managers are compensated, possible manipulation of returns reported by private equity fund managers, the impact of class action lawsuits against "club" bidding, and how negative interest rates affect risk taking. The chapter also addresses determinants of private equity takeover premiums, hedge fund performance, deleveraging via sale-lease back deals, how marketing communication can be used to offset the negative effects of leverage on firm value, an expanded discussion of leverage buyout (LBO) target selection criteria, and the impact of buyouts on employment.

Subjects such as the relative performance of venture versus private equity–backed IPOs, the impact of LBOs on credit spreads, and how the growth in private financing has affected the number of IPOs are examined. The section discussing capital structure theory and practice includes an illustration of how capital structure can impact excess acquirer financial returns, the role of institutional investors in corporate capital structure decisions, and how employee bankruptcy rights can impact LBO leverage. How the replacement of the London Interbank Offered Rate (LIBOR) financing rate by Secured Overnight Financing Rate will affect M&A financing is analyzed, as is the impact of mutual funds on the growth of private market financing and the frequency of IPOs.

Chapter 14 discusses how to value highly leveraged transactions via commonly used methods (cost of capital method and adjusted present value) and provides a template for doing so. New content includes an assessment of the impact of accounting standards on LBO valuation and modeling and the effects of negative interest rates on risk taking in these types of financing structures.

Chapter 15 illustrates the application of sophisticated financial models to M&A deal structuring, valuation, and financing of stock and asset deals. New content includes a discussion of synergies that increase a firm's borrowing capacity; FASB rule changes impacting the treatment of operating leases; and how to use firm financial statements to predict future revenue, profit, and cash flow. New content also includes a more detailed discussion of how to apply the concept of minimum and maximum offer prices. How bidder pro forma forecasts affect deal completion rates and the magnitudes of acquisition premiums are described, as are ways in which productivity gains in horizontal mergers can be reflected in financial models. The chapter also addresses the role of confirmation bias in estimating synergy, the pending phase-out of LIBOR (widely used in M&A models in calculating swap rates), modeling firm adjustment from actual to target capital structures, and the effects of aggressive asset management on projecting firm cash flows. The potential effects of the 2017 Tax Cuts and Jobs Act on financial models such as how to adjust a target's capital spending to reflect the full expensing of certain capital assets also are examined.

Alternative business and restructuring strategies

Chapter 16 addresses alternatives to M&As and has been expanded to include a discussion of how to choose the correct business alliance strategy, the relevance of antitrust immunity to business alliances, and how national security concerns and protectionism affects alliance formation. New content also includes how bondholders as well as shareholders often benefit from business alliances, the ways cultural and governance differences impact cross-border alliances, how alliances can be viewed as real options, partner selection, and how control strategies impact international JV performance. The role of JV experience in the partner selection process and choosing the right governance mechanism are explored. Other new topics include cultural diversity and the rate of innovation in multinational corporation subsidiaries involved in strategic alliances and the impact of cultural and institutional similarity in achieving alliance performance objectives.

Chapter 17 deals with non–M&A-related corporate restructuring. Fresh content involves an expanded discussion of factors impacting the size of premiums. These include financial market considerations; acquirer, target, and deal characteristics; and media pessimism about a deal. The chapter also includes a discussion on the timing of asset sales and the impact of corporate innovation on the likelihood of takeover.

Chapter 18 speaks to bankruptcy issues and now includes such topics as the impact of the 2020 pandemic on bankruptcy, the high cost of reorganization and the novel use of textual data, credit spreads, combining accounting and market-based data, and the application of AI deep-learning models to improve bankruptcy prediction accuracy. New content also includes a discussion of wealth transfers when failed firms are acquired out of bankruptcy and the Small Business Reorganization Act of 2019.

Finally, Chapter 19 focuses on factors affecting cross-border deals and how to value them. New content centers on the decline in globalism because of growing protectionism, the sidelining of the World Trade Organization, the rise in regionalism and bilateralism, and the implications for cross-border deals. The chapter discusses in detail how to navigate the growing complexities of international transactions amid ongoing China–US trade friction, disruption in global supply chains, "black swan" events such as the 2020 pandemic, escalating national security concerns, and rising populism across the globe. The chapter details the nature of tariffs and nontariff barriers, winners and losers, the impact on supply chains, unintended consequences, and how to develop M&A strategies to succeed in this new environment.

Other new content pertains to the determinants of cross-border takeover premiums and addresses whether governance concerns are a strong motive for initiating cross-border deals. Moreover, the chapter now addresses how acquirer size and prior experience can attenuate the negative effects of significant cultural differences in cross-border M&As, how investor protection laws affect value creation, and the impact of investor protection laws on LBO financing. Factors affecting ownership stakes, country entry strategies, risk management, and the impact of competitive markets on takeovers are also discussed in greater detail.

New topics pertaining to financial returns include the following: the impact of foreign takeovers on financial returns to rivals, how acquirer returns are affected by deal complexity, the long-term performance of African takeovers, and the ways in which emerging-market formal and informal institutions impact firm valuation. How cross-border M&As fill institutional voids and improve human rights, how strong property rights attract foreign investment, and ways in which cultural and religious differences affect cross-border M&As are analyzed in detail. Finally,

tax issues arising in international deals, how international JV boards manage uncertainty, and how to adjust valuation formulas for real and nominal taxable earnings are among the fresh content covered in this chapter.

Updated ancillary materials: Both online student and instructor PowerPoint slide presentations have been updated to reflect recent research, trends, and new chapter content. Located below each slide, instructor PowerPoint presentations also contain suggested topics and key points to be made by the instructor. The student PowerPoint slides are structured to serve as student study guides.

The textbook contains more than 300 end-of-chapter discussion and review questions, problems, and exercises that give readers the opportunity to test their knowledge. Many of the exercises enable students to find their own solutions based on different assumptions using Excel-based spreadsheet models available on the companion site to this textbook. In addition to Excel-based customizable M&A valuation and structuring software, PowerPoint presentations, and due diligence materials, the companion site (https://www.elsevier.com/books-and-journals/book-companion/9780128150757) also contains a Student Study Guide.

This book is intended for students in courses on M&A, corporate restructuring, business strategy, management, and entrepreneurship. This book works well at both the undergraduate and graduate levels. The text also should interest financial analysts, CFOs, operating managers, investment bankers, and portfolio managers. Others who may have an interest include bank lending officers, venture capitalists, regulators, human resource managers, entrepreneurs, and board members.

To the instructor

This text is an attempt to provide organization to a topic that is inherently complex because of the diverse matter and the breadth of disciplines that must be applied to complete most transactions. Consequently, the discussion of M&A is not easily divisible into highly focused chapters. Efforts to compartmentalize the topic often result in the reader's not understanding how seemingly independent topics are integrated. Understanding M&A involves an understanding of a full range of topics, including management, finance, economics, business law, financial and tax accounting, organizational dynamics, and the role of leadership.

This book provides a novel paradigm for discussing the complex and dynamically changing world of M&A. The book is organized into five parts according to the context in which topics occur in the M&A process: M&A environment, M&A process, M&A valuation and modeling, deal structuring and financing strategies, and alternative business and restructuring strategies. See Exhibit 1 for the organizational layout of the book.

This book equips the instructor with the information needed to communicate with students having different levels of preparation. The generous use of examples and recent business cases makes the text suitable for distance learning and self-study programs as well as for large, lecture-focused courses. The extensive use of end-of-chapter discussion questions, problems, and exercises (with answers available in the Online Instructors' Manual) offers instructors the opportunity to test the students' progress in mastering the material. Prerequisites for this text include familiarity with basic accounting, finance, economics, and management concepts.

Each chapter begins with a vignette intended to illustrate a key point or points described in more detail as the chapter unfolds. Hundreds of examples, case studies, tables, and figures illustrate the application of key concepts. Exhibits and diagrams summarize otherwise-diffuse information and the results of numerous empirical studies substantiating key points made in each chapter. Each chapter concludes with a series of 10 discussion questions and recent integrative end-of-chapter business cases intended to stimulate critical thinking and test the reader's understanding of the material. Many chapters also include a series of practice problems and exercises to facilitate learning the chapter's content.

Please email the publisher at educate@elsevier.com (within North America), emea.textbook@elsevier.com (in Europe, Middle East, and Africa), apa.stbooks@elsevier.com (in Asia), and sandt.anz@elsevier.com (in Australia and New Zealand) for access to the online manual. Please include your contact information (name, department, college, address, email, and phone number) along with your course information, including course name and number, annual enrollment, ISBN, book title, and author. All requests are subject to approval by the company's representatives.

Additional information is available on the Instructor Site: https://educate.elsevier.com/9780128150757 and Companion Site: https://www.elsevier.com/books-and-journals/book-companion/9780128150757.

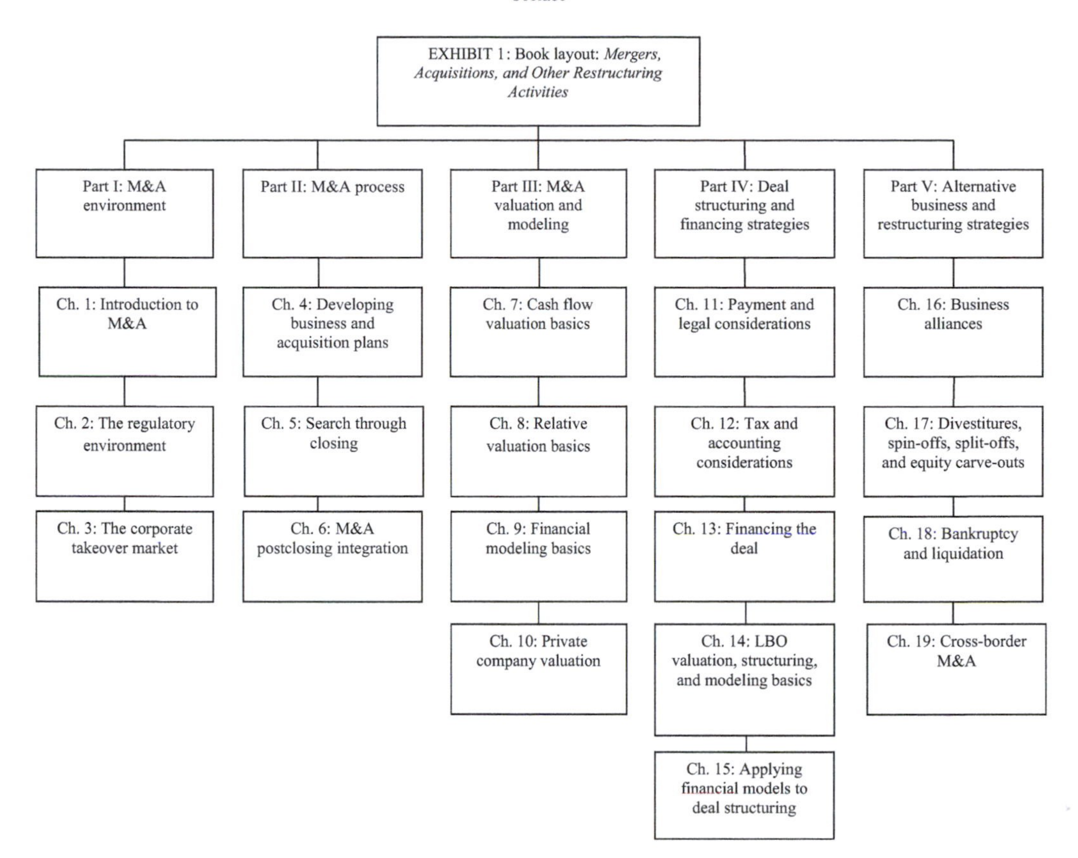
EXHIBIT 1: Book layout: *Mergers, Acquisitions, and Other Restructuring Activities*
Part I: M&A environment
Ch. 1: Introduction to M&A
Ch. 2: The regulatory environment
Ch. 3: The corporate takeover market
Part II: M&A process
Ch. 4: Developing business and acquisition plans
Ch. 5: Search through closing
Ch. 6: M&A postclosing integration
Part III: M&A valuation and modeling
Ch. 7: Cash flow valuation basics
Ch. 8: Relative valuation basics
Ch. 9: Financial modeling basics
Ch. 10: Private company valuation
Part IV: Deal structuring and financing strategies
Ch. 11: Payment and legal considerations
Ch. 12: Tax and accounting considerations
Ch. 13: Financing the deal
Ch. 14: LBO valuation, structuring, and modeling basics
Ch. 15: Applying financial models to deal structuring
Part V: Alternative business and restructuring strategies
Ch. 16: Business alliances
Ch. 17: Divestitures, spin-offs, split-offs, and equity carve-outs
Ch. 18: Bankruptcy and liquidation
Ch. 19: Cross-border M&A

Acknowledgments

I would like to express my sincere appreciation for the many helpful suggestions received from a number of anonymous reviewers and the many resources of Academic Press/Butterworth-Heinemann/Elsevier. Specifically, I would like to thank Alan Cherry, Ross Bengel, Patricia Douglas, Jeff Gale, Jim Healy, Charles Higgins, Michael Lovelady, John Mellen, Jon Saxon, David Offenberg, Chris Manning, Maria Quijada, Warren Miller, Chris Kohler, Jake Feldman, and Burcu Dincergok for their constructive comments. I would also like to thank Scott Bentley, executive editor at Academic Press/Butterworth-Heinemann/Elsevier; Katey Birtcher, publisher at Elsevier; and Susan Ikeda, senior editorial project manager, for their ongoing support and guidance.

Praise for various editions

"*Mergers, Acquisitions, and Other Restructuring Activities* by Donald DePamphilis is an outstanding book. Simply put, it is the most comprehensive M&A book on the market and ideal for anyone wishing to have a global view of this important phenomenon. The book's value lies in drawing on multiple academic disciplines to inform the reader's understanding of M&A supported by foundational academic research to support key insights. The rigor of this approach, together with the liberal use of a wide variety of notable and up-to-date cases, makes the book an invaluable asset to anyone seeking to further their understanding of M&A."

– Duncan Angwin, Lancaster University

"A comprehensive guide to corporate restructuring processes, with a focus on the strategic and financial considerations involved in M&A and other restructuring activity. A must read!"

– Satu Teerikangas, University of Turku and University College London

"DePamphilis has masterfully covered in one book all relevant managerial, strategic, financial, accounting, legal and tax aspects of M&A in an easily understood roadmap for any M&A transaction, large or small. With totally up-to-date material, he provides the crucial information that is necessary in today's rapidly changing M&A world."

– Lloyd Levitin, Professor of Clinical Finance and Business Economics, University of Southern California

"After teaching M&A for ten years, I was relieved when last semester I finally switched to DePamphilis' text. His single book replaced numerous other sources that I had to use before. His academic rigor is combined with his deep personal experience as a deal maker, and thus the textbook is highly valuable to both newcomers and those who have been involved in transactions for many years."

– Viktoria Dalko, Global Professor of Finance, Harvard University Extension School

"*Mergers, Acquisitions, and Other Restructuring Activities*, Sixth Edition, delivers an essential understanding of the corporate restructuring processes by combining insights from many case studies with academic rigor. The book points out how M&A can create value as well as the ways it can lead to value destruction. In addition to the state-of-the-art valuation techniques, it also explains the regulatory corporate governance framework for both the United States and Europe. It's an excellent text, and I highly recommend it."

– Luc Renneboog, Professor of Corporate Finance, CentER, Tilburg University

"Great textbook that in a simple and straightforward manner combines the latest insights from academia with contemporary industry practices. It fits perfect in a class of MBA students or executives. I will for sure use it next time I teach M&A."

– Karin Thorburn, DnB NOR Professor of Finance, Norwegian School of Economics and Business Administration

"*Mergers, Acquisitions, and Other Restructuring Activities* is quite simply an outstanding text. Don DePamphilis delivers a comprehensive guide to the M&A process from start to finish. . . . In sum, this book is a comprehensive, up-to-date, outstanding text."

– Scott C. Linn, R.W. Moore Chair in Finance and Economic Development, The University of Oklahoma

"This is a truly comprehensive text and does a wonderful job at supplying the underlying motives and theory as well as the critical 'in practice' elements that many books lack. It spans all types of M&A and restructuring transactions and covers all the relevant knowledge from the academic research to the practical legal, accounting, and regulatory details. The book is up-to-date and teaches the state-of-the-art techniques used today. It contains numerous cases and spreadsheet support that enable the reader to put into practice everything that is covered. The combination of great writing and active case learning make this book the best I have seen in the M&A and restructuring arena."

– Matthew T. Billett, Associate Professor of Finance, Henry B. Tippie Research Fellow, University of Iowa

"I am happy to recommend the Fifth Edition of *Mergers, Acquisitions, and Other Restructuring Activities*. Having used prior editions of Don DePamphilis' text, I can affirm that this edition builds on a firm foundation of coverage, real-world examples, and readability. My students have consistently responded favorably to prior editions of the book. In this edition, I was delighted to discover that Don is expanding his coverage of family-owned businesses, already a strength in his earlier editions that were distinguished by their coverage of the valuation of privately held businesses. Additional attention is paid to restructuring, bankruptcy, and liquidation as well as risk management, which are clearly topics of interest to every business person in today's economic climate."

– Kent Hickman, Professor of Finance, Gonzaga University

"The fifth edition is one of the most comprehensive books on mergers and acquisitions. The text combines theories, valuation models, and real-life cases to give business students an overall insight into the M&A deal process. The up-to-date real-life examples and cases provide opportunities for readers to explore and to apply theories to a wide variety of scenarios such as cross-border transactions, highly levered deals, firms in financial distress, and family-owned businesses. The chapter on restructuring under bankruptcy and liquidation both inside and outside the protection of the bankruptcy court is timely and most useful in light of today's economic crisis. Overall, this is an excellent book on mergers, acquisitions, and corporate restructuring activities."

– Tao-Hsien Dolly King, Rush S. Dickson Professor of Finance, Associate Professor, Department of

Finance, The Belk College of Business, University of North Carolina at Charlotte

"*Mergers, Acquisitions, and Other Restructuring Activities* is an interesting and comprehensive look at the most important aspects of M&A and corporate restructuring—from strategic and regulatory considerations and M&A deal process, through several chapters on M&A valuation and deal structuring, to other types of restructuring activities. It not only provides a road map for the M&A and other corporate restructuring transactions, but also highlights the key things to watch for. The book is clearly written with extensive but easy-to-follow case examples and empirical findings and cases to illustrate the points in the text. It is a book by an expert, and for M&A instructors and students as well as practitioners."

– Qiao Lui, Faculty of Business and Economics, The University of Hong Kong

"I am delighted with Don DePamphilis' *Mergers, Acquisitions, and Other Restructuring Activities*, Fifth Edition. It is a clear, comprehensive, and thorough discussion of the issues involving all restructuring activities. The use of mini-cases throughout each chapter both highlights and clarifies key elements of aspects of the decision-making process. The end-of-chapter discussion questions are ideally complemented with the problem set questions to challenge readers' understanding of the covered concepts. I am impressed with the current reflection of market conditions throughout the text and the extent of the recent changes to provide greater understanding for students. I expect to find that the students are also impressed with its the clarity and structure when I introduce this edition to my course. I recommend it to any professor covering mergers, acquisitions, bankruptcies, or other restructuring . . . to cover limited topics, or as a text for a complete course on restructuring."

– John F. Manley, Professor of Finance, Hagan School of Business, Iona College

"Mergers and acquisitions continue to be amongst the preferred competitive options available to the companies seeking to grow and prosper in the rapidly changing global business scenario. In the Fifth Edition of his path-breaking book, the author and M&A expert Dr. DePamphilis illustrates how mergers, acquisitions, and other forms of restructuring can help a company grow and prosper in the highly complex and competitive corporate takeover marketplace. Interspersed with most relevant and up-to-date M&A case studies . . . , this book deals with the multifarious aspects of corporate restructuring in an integrated manner . . . a lucid style. . . . Every effort has been made to deal with the intricacies of the subject by offering comprehensive coverage of the latest methods and techniques . . . of both public and private companies.

"The book provides practical ways of dealing with M&As even in an economic downturn with a chapter on corporate restructuring under bankruptcy and liquidation. With the greatly enlarged and up-to-date material on varied aspects of the subject, the book provides a plethora of real-world examples that will go a long way in making the subject easy, stimulating, and interesting to both academicians and practitioners alike."

– Donepudi Prasad, ICFAI Business School, Hyderabad, India

"Professor DePamphilis has made significant, important, and very timely updates in the Fifth Edition of his text. He incorporates contemporary events, such as the credit crunch and the latest accounting rules in the West, plus M&A issues in emerging markets including family businesses. He also readdresses corporate governance, a topic that will become increasingly important in Business Schools the world over in M&A. This text has become, and will increasingly become, the definitive comprehensive and thorough reference on the subject."
– Jeffrey V. Ramsbottom, Visiting Professor, China Europe International Business School, Shanghai

"I think the Fifth Edition of *Mergers, Acquisitions, and Other Restructuring Activities* does a comprehensive job of covering the M&A field. As in the previous edition, the structure is divided into five parts. These are logical and easy to follow, with a nice blend of theory, empirical research findings, and practical issues. I especially like two chapters—the chapter on bankruptcy and liquidation is extremely relevant in today's economic conditions, and the chapter on private equity and hedge funds is interesting because M&A activities by these players are not well-documented in the literature. Overall, I believe that MBA students would find the book useful both as a textbook in class and as a reference book for later use."
– Raghavendra Rau, Purdue University and Barclays Global Investors

"This book is truly outstanding among the textbooks on takeovers, valuation, and corporate restructuring for several reasons: the DePamphilis book not only gives a very up-to-date overview of the recent research findings on takeovers around the world, but also offers nearly 100 recent business cases. The book treats all the valuation techniques in depth and also offers much institutional detail on M&A and LBO transactions. Not just takeover successes are analyzed, but also how financially distressed companies should be restructured. In short, the ideal textbook for any M&A graduate course."
– Luc Renneboog, Professor of Corporate Finance, Tilburg University, The Netherlands

"The Fifth Edition of *Mergers, Acquisitions, and Other Restructuring Activities* by Professor Donald DePamphilis is an excellent book. Among its many strengths, I could easily identify three features that stand out. First, it is up to date, covering the recent knowledge published in most of the academic journals. Second, it offers comprehensive coverage of the subject matter, including chapters on the U.S. institutional, legal, and accounting environment; on technical aspects; valuation techniques; and strategic issues. Third, it is practical by including Excel Spreadsheet Models and a large number of real cases. These three aspects along with the . . . end-of-chapter discussion and review questions, problems, and exercises make this book one of the best choices for the subject."
– Nickolaos G. Travlos, The Kitty Kyriacopoulos Chair in Finance, and Dean, ALBA Graduate Business School, Greece

"It is difficult to imagine that his fourth edition could be improved on, but Dr. DePamphilis has done just that. This edition is clearer, better organized, and contains a wealth of vitally important new material for these challenging times. I especially recommend the new chapter on liquidation for members of boards of directors who face extreme circumstances. This is a remarkably useful book for readers at any level—students, instructors, company executives, as well as board members. Bravo Don!"
– Wesley B. Truitt, Adjunct Professor, School of Public Policy, Pepperdine University

"The book is an excellent source for both academicians and practitioners. In addition to detailed cases, it provides tools contributing to value creation in M&A. A must book for an M&A course."
– Vahap Uysal, Assistant Professor of Finance, Price College of Business, University of Oklahoma

"An impressive detailed overview of all aspects of mergers and acquisitions. Numerous recent case studies and examples convince the reader that all the material is very relevant in today's business environment."
– Theo Vermaelen, Professor of Finance, INSEAD

"The DePamphilis text is an excellent textbook that provides a full end-to-end view of the process with the appropriate level of detail. I have reviewed many M&A texts, and this text provides an excellent process view rather than just a series of topics."
–Stephen G. Morrissette, University of Chicago

PART I

The mergers and acquisitions environment

The statement that the only constant in life is change is often intended to encourage us to embrace change as an ordinary part of life. Yet change is just that . . . change. It is not inherently good or bad! In some instances, it should be encouraged, but other types of change should be simply accepted. Still other forms of change should be resisted. Moreover, change is not spontaneous but rather triggered by a change agent, something that either promotes or enables change to happen. Mergers and acquisitions (M&As) are examples of such agents.

No matter how we feel about change, it seems to be accelerating because of the quickening pace of technological change and a growing social and political reaction to the conventional wisdom of recent decades. The inescapable conclusion is that factors contributing to a firm's competitive advantage today may be irrelevant tomorrow, causing firms once dominant in their chosen markets to fall by the wayside.

Part I describes how change often can be triggered by mergers, acquisitions, and corporate restructuring in the context in which they occur. The three chapters in this section of the book provide an overview of M&As, common tactics and defenses, financial returns to both acquirer and target shareholders, a discussion of important regulations impacting M&As, and the key role of the many participants in the takeover and restructuring process.

Chapter 1 addresses the basic vocabulary of M&As, common reasons why they happen, and how they occur in a series of somewhat predictable waves. Alternatives to M&As and the skills required by those involved in the M&A process, from investment bankers to lenders to regulatory authorities, are discussed in detail. The chapter also discusses whether M&As benefit shareholders, bondholders, and society, with conclusions grounded in the most recent academic studies. The chapter closes with an extensive discussion of corporate social responsibility and how it can (or should) impact M&As.

The labyrinth of regulations impacting the M&A process are covered in Chapter 2, including recent changes in US federal and state securities and antitrust laws as well as environmental, labor, and benefit laws that add to the increasing complexity of completing deals. The implications of the growing role of privacy considerations and copyright protections both in the United States and around the globe are also considered in describing how future deals involving certain types of firms are likely to be done. The chapter addresses the question of whether the United States has a "monopoly problem" and, if so, what can (or should) be done. The implications of cross-border deals, which offer a new set of regulatory challenges, also are explored here and throughout this book.

Chapter 3 speaks to corporate governance from the perspective of protecting and managing stakeholder interests rather than as a singular focus on shareholders. The chapter addresses the question of whether shareholder wealth maximization, historically considered the primary focus of the firm, is compatible with an expanded definition of governance. The chapter reviews common takeover tactics used as part of an overall bidding strategy, the motivation behind such tactics, and the defenses used by target firms to deter or delay such practices. Bidding strategies are discussed for both friendly and hostile business takeovers, as are the role of hostile deals in disciplining underperforming management, improving corporate governance practices, and reallocating assets to those who can use them more effectively. This chapter also addresses the growing role activists are taking in promoting good corporate governance and in disciplining incompetent or entrenched managers.

CHAPTER

1

An introduction to mergers, acquisitions, and other restructuring activities

OUTLINE

Mergers, Acquisitions, and Other Restructuring Activities, Eleventh Edition
https://doi.org/10.1016/B978-0-12-819782-0.00001-0

TABLE 1.1 Common theories of what causes mergers and acquisitions

Theory	Motivation
Operating synergy Economies of scale Economies of scope Complementary resources	Improve operating efficiency through economies of scale or scope by acquiring a customer, supplier, or competitor or to enhance technical or innovative skills or to gain access to scarce resources.
Financial synergy	Lower cost of capital; increase borrowing capacity.
Diversification New products and current markets New products and new markets Current products and new markets	Position the firm in higher-growth products or markets.
Strategic realignment Technological change Regulatory and political change	Acquire capabilities to adapt more rapidly to environmental changes than could be achieved if they were developed internally.
Hubris (managerial overconfidence)	Acquirers believe their valuation of the target is more accurate than the market's, causing them to overpay by overestimating synergy.
Buying undervalued assets (Q-ratio)	Acquire assets more cheaply when the market value of equity of existing companies is less than the cost of buying or building the assets.
Managerialism (agency problems)	Increase the size of a company to increase the power and pay of managers.
Tax considerations	Obtain unused net operating losses and tax credits and asset write ups and substitute capital gains for ordinary income.
Market power	Actions taken to boost selling prices above competitive levels by affecting either supply or demand.
Misvaluation	Investor overvaluation of acquirer's stock encourages M&As using stock.

are often lower for larger firms. Whereas economies of scale focus on the cost advantage associated with a higher level of production for one good, economies of scope focus on the average total cost of producing multiple products.

Economies of scale refer to the reduction in average total costs for a firm producing a single product for a given scale of plant because of the decline in average fixed costs per unit as production increases. Fixed costs include depreciation of equipment, amortization of capitalized software, maintenance spending, and obligations such as interest and lease payments; union, customer, and vendor contracts; and taxes. These costs are fixed because they cannot be altered in the short run. Variable costs are those that change with output levels. Thus for a given scale or amount of fixed expenses, the dollar value of fixed expenses per unit of output and per dollar of revenue decreases as output and sales increase.

To illustrate the profit improvement from economies of scale, consider the merger of Firm B into Firm A. Firm A has a plant producing at half of its capacity, enabling Firm A to shut down Firm B's plant that is producing the same product and move the production to its own facility. Consequently, Firm A's profit margin improves from 6.25% before the merger to 14.58% after the merger. Why? The additional output transferred from Firm B is mostly profit because it adds nothing to Firm A's fixed costs (Table 1.2).[4]

Economies of scale also affect variable costs such as a reduction in purchased material prices caused by an increase in bulk purchases and lower production line setup costs from longer production runs. Merged firms often negotiate lower purchase prices from suppliers because they order in quantities much larger than they had separately. Suppliers are willing to cut prices because they also realize economies of scale as their plant utilization increases. Setup costs include personnel costs incurred in changing from producing one product to another, materials used in this process, and the time lost while the production line is down.[5]

[4] The profit improvement is overstated as variable costs per unit are constant at $2.75. In reality, average variable costs rise as output increases, reflecting equipment downtime caused by maintenance, increased overtime pay, additional shifts requiring new and often less productive employees, and disruptions to production resulting from the logistical challenges of maintaining adequate supplies of raw materials. In addition, the example excludes the cost of financing the transaction and any shutdown costs incurred in closing Firm B's plant.

[5] Assume a supplier's initial setup costs are $3000 per production run to produce an order of 2500 units. Setup costs per unit produced are $1.20. If the order is doubled to 5000 units, setup costs per unit are cut in half to $0.60 per unit. Suppliers may be willing to pass some of these savings on to customers to get the larger order.

CHAPTER

1

An introduction to mergers, acquisitions, and other restructuring activities

OUTLINE

Mergers, Acquisitions, and Other Restructuring Activities, Eleventh Edition
https://doi.org/10.1016/B978-0-12-819782-0.00001-0

If you give a man a fish, you feed him for a day. If you teach a man to fish, you feed him for a lifetime. —*Lao Tze*

Inside mergers and acquisitions: the growing popularity of digital payments drives a record-setting deal in the electronics payments industry

KEY POINTS

- Mergers between competitors generally offer the most synergy but often face the greatest regulatory scrutiny.
- Acquirer shares often fall when investors think the buyer paid too much, is excessively leveraged due to the deal, or new shares will dilute current owners.
- Realizing anticipated synergy on a timely basis often is elusive.

Consumers routinely insert credit and debit cards into card readers to make purchases, unaware of the complex infrastructure underlying this process.[1] Key participants in this transaction clearing process include the cardholder, merchant, payment processor, issuing bank (i.e., cardholder bank), and card association or franchisor (e.g., Visa and MasterCard). Payment processors provide merchants with equipment to accept cards and provide customer service involved in card acceptance and earn fees for each transaction processed. Serving as middlemen between merchants and banks, they act as a single point of contact for card authorization (recovering funds from the card-issuing bank and paying all issuer fees on behalf of the merchant) and as an intermediary in the event of card claims and refunds.

The growth in online purchases put traditional in-store processors under substantial pressure to reduce costs in the wake of declining transactions at brick-and-mortar retailers. Processors are further challenged by rising competition from technology start-ups that charge lower fees. The combination of downward pressure on fees and lethargic growth in the number of in-store transactions has constrained revenue and profit improvement.

To address these issues, payment processors have sought global scale through M&As. During the 5 years ending in 2019, six major deals were completed, the largest of which was Fidelity National Information Services' (FIS')

[1] Transaction data are passed from the card reader to a payments processor and then through the bank network to the card-issuing bank for approval. The issuing bank then sends an approval through the card network to the processor before it ends up back at the retailer's terminal. All this is done in seconds.

takeover of Worldpay in 2019 for $35 billion. Serving clients in 130 countries, FIS handles back-office functions for money managers, and Worldpay dominates retail payment online processing in 146 countries. Together, FIS and Worldpay can offer their services to the others' customers while eliminating duplicate operations.

Under the terms of the deal, Worldpay shareholders received 0.9287 FIS shares and $11 in cash for each Worldpay share, representing a 32% premium to Worldpay's average share price immediately before the announcement date. Upon the news, Worldpay shares jumped 10% as investors bought the shares to capture the premium. Worldpay's share price rose to just below the offer price as investors fretted the deal may not receive regulatory approval. FIS shares fell 0.7% because of the potential dilution of current FIS shareholders from the issuance of new FIS shares and concerns that it may have overpaid.

Chapter overview

As change agents, mergers and acquisitions (M&As) initiate and enable change that ushers in the new at the expense of the old ways of doing things. Change agents disrupt the status quo, sometimes creating social and political backlash. Socially responsible corporate behavior requires boards and managers to protect and manage the interests of all stakeholders in the firm, ranging from customers to employees to shareholders to communities and lenders. Given their interdependence, achieving a proper balance among such interests requires managing the trade-offs implicit in dealing with disparate stakeholder groups.

Our intent in this chapter is to describe what M&As are, why they occur, and the extent to which M&As are being conducted responsibly. As such, this chapter provides insights into why M&As happen, why they cluster in waves, and the strategies used to restructure firms. The chapter addresses how these factors could change in the future. The roles and responsibilities of the primary participants in the M&A process also are discussed in detail as are the implications of socially responsible M&As.

A firm that attempts to acquire or merge with another company is called an acquiring company, acquirer, or bidder. The target company is the firm being solicited by the acquiring company. *Takeovers* and *buyouts* are generic terms for a change in the controlling ownership interest of a corporation. A review of this chapter (including practice questions and answers) is available in the file folder entitled Student Study Guide on the companion website for this book: https://www.elsevier.com/books-and-journals/book-companion/9780128197820.

Why do M&As happen?

Despite decades of research, there is little consensus about the primary determinants of M&As.[2] Research has focused on aggregate data, which may conceal important size, sector, and geographic differences. Some analysts argue markets are efficient because decisions are made rapidly in response to new data, but others see markets adjusting more slowly to changing conditions. Still others contend that microeconomic factors are more important determinants of M&As than macroeconomic considerations. Table 1.1 lists some of the more prominent theories about why M&As happen. Of these, anticipated synergy is most often cited in empirical studies as the primary motivation.[3] The various theories are discussed in greater detail in the remainder of this section.

Synergy

Synergy is the value realized from the incremental cash flows generated by combining two businesses. If the market values of two firms are $100 million and $75 million, respectively, and their combined market value is $200 million, the implied value of synergy is $25 million. Although synergy may improve combined firm performance, growing *coordination costs* (e.g., increased communication, information processing, and joint decision making) may worsen performance because of greater complexity. As firms become more complex, such costs may limit the expected benefits of synergy. The two basic types of synergy are *operating* and *financial*.

Operating synergy

Operating synergy consists of economies of scale and scope, as well as the acquisition of complementary resources such as technologies, skills, and materials. Economies of scale and scope explain why average total costs

[2] Fuller et al., 2018

[3] Ferreira et al., 2014

TABLE 1.1 Common theories of what causes mergers and acquisitions

Theory	Motivation
Operating synergy Economies of scale Economies of scope Complementary resources	Improve operating efficiency through economies of scale or scope by acquiring a customer, supplier, or competitor or to enhance technical or innovative skills or to gain access to scarce resources.
Financial synergy	Lower cost of capital; increase borrowing capacity.
Diversification New products and current markets New products and new markets Current products and new markets	Position the firm in higher-growth products or markets.
Strategic realignment Technological change Regulatory and political change	Acquire capabilities to adapt more rapidly to environmental changes than could be achieved if they were developed internally.
Hubris (managerial overconfidence)	Acquirers believe their valuation of the target is more accurate than the market's, causing them to overpay by overestimating synergy.
Buying undervalued assets (Q-ratio)	Acquire assets more cheaply when the market value of equity of existing companies is less than the cost of buying or building the assets.
Managerialism (agency problems)	Increase the size of a company to increase the power and pay of managers.
Tax considerations	Obtain unused net operating losses and tax credits and asset write ups and substitute capital gains for ordinary income.
Market power	Actions taken to boost selling prices above competitive levels by affecting either supply or demand.
Misvaluation	Investor overvaluation of acquirer's stock encourages M&As using stock.

are often lower for larger firms. Whereas economies of scale focus on the cost advantage associated with a higher level of production for one good, economies of scope focus on the average total cost of producing multiple products.

Economies of scale refer to the reduction in average total costs for a firm producing a single product for a given scale of plant because of the decline in average fixed costs per unit as production increases. Fixed costs include depreciation of equipment, amortization of capitalized software, maintenance spending, and obligations such as interest and lease payments; union, customer, and vendor contracts; and taxes. These costs are fixed because they cannot be altered in the short run. Variable costs are those that change with output levels. Thus for a given scale or amount of fixed expenses, the dollar value of fixed expenses per unit of output and per dollar of revenue decreases as output and sales increase.

To illustrate the profit improvement from economies of scale, consider the merger of Firm B into Firm A. Firm A has a plant producing at half of its capacity, enabling Firm A to shut down Firm B's plant that is producing the same product and move the production to its own facility. Consequently, Firm A's profit margin improves from 6.25% before the merger to 14.58% after the merger. Why? The additional output transferred from Firm B is mostly profit because it adds nothing to Firm A's fixed costs (Table 1.2).[4]

Economies of scale also affect variable costs such as a reduction in purchased material prices caused by an increase in bulk purchases and lower production line setup costs from longer production runs. Merged firms often negotiate lower purchase prices from suppliers because they order in quantities much larger than they had separately. Suppliers are willing to cut prices because they also realize economies of scale as their plant utilization increases. Setup costs include personnel costs incurred in changing from producing one product to another, materials used in this process, and the time lost while the production line is down.[5]

[4] The profit improvement is overstated as variable costs per unit are constant at $2.75. In reality, average variable costs rise as output increases, reflecting equipment downtime caused by maintenance, increased overtime pay, additional shifts requiring new and often less productive employees, and disruptions to production resulting from the logistical challenges of maintaining adequate supplies of raw materials. In addition, the example excludes the cost of financing the transaction and any shutdown costs incurred in closing Firm B's plant.

[5] Assume a supplier's initial setup costs are $3000 per production run to produce an order of 2500 units. Setup costs per unit produced are $1.20. If the order is doubled to 5000 units, setup costs per unit are cut in half to $0.60 per unit. Suppliers may be willing to pass some of these savings on to customers to get the larger order.

TABLE 1.2 Economies of scale[a]

Period 1: Firm A (premerger)	Period 2: Firm A (postmerger)
Assumptions: Price = \$4 per unit of output sold Variable costs = \$2.75 per unit of output Fixed costs = \$1,000,000 Firm A is producing 1,000,000 units of output per year Firm A is producing at 50% of plant capacity	Assumptions: Firm A acquires Firm B, which is producing 500,000 units of the same product per year Firm A closes Firm B's plant and transfers production to Firm A's plant Price = \$4 per unit of output sold Variable costs = \$2.75 per unit of output Fixed costs = \$1,000,000
Profit = Price × Quantity − Variable costs − Fixed costs $= \$4 \times 1,000,000 - \$2.75 \times 1,000,000 - \$1,000,000$ $= \$250,000$	Profit = Price × Quantity − Variable costs − Fixed costs $= \$4 \times 1,500,000 - \$2.75 \times 1,500,000 - \$1,000,000$ $= \$6,000,000 - \$4,125,000 - \$1,000,000$ $= \$875,000$
Profit margin (%) $= \$250,000/\$4,000,000 = 6.25$	Profit margin(%) $= \$875,000/\$6,000,000 = 14.58$
Fixed costs per unit $= \$1,000,000/\$1,000,000 = \$1.00$	Fixed cost per unit $= \$1,000,000/1,500,000 = \$.67$

[a]Contribution to profit of additional 500,000 units = \$4 × 500,000 − \$2.75 ×5 00,000 = \$625,000.
Margin per unit sold at fixed cost per unit of \$1.00 = \$4.00 − \$2.75 − \$1.00 = \$0.25.
Margin per unit sold at fixed cost per unit of \$.67 = \$4.00 − \$2.75 − \$0.67 = \$0.58.

Economies of scope refers to the reduction in average total costs by producing multiple products (or services) from a single location rather than from separate locations. An example of *production-related economies of scope* is a mobile phone handset maker deciding to add a new line of phones. The cost would be lower if the manufacturer uses the same facility because it can use existing equipment, workforce, warehousing, and distribution. Common examples of *overhead- and sales-related economies of scope* include having a single department (e.g., accounting) support multiple product lines and a sales force selling multiple related products rather than a single product. In addition, lower distribution costs can be achieved by transporting a number of products to a single location rather than a single product. Other examples include the savings realized by using specific skills or an asset currently used in producing a product to produce multiple products.

Complementary resources such as technical assets, know-how, and skills are those possessed by one firm that could be used by another to fill gaps in or augment its capabilities. The merger between Pharmacia and Monsanto gave Pharmacia access to Monsanto's COX-2 inhibitors and Monsanto access to the other's genomics expertise. The merger allowed for expanded in-house clinical research and development and accelerated getting products to market.

Financial synergy

Financial synergy refers to the reduction in the acquirer's cost of capital due to a merger. This could occur if the merged firms have relatively uncorrelated cash flows, realize cost savings from lower securities' issuance costs, or are better able to finance investment opportunities with internally generated funds. Sometimes referred to as *coinsurance*, the imperfect correlation of business unit cash flows allows resources to be transferred from cash-rich units to cash-poor units as needed. As such, multi-product firms with less correlated business unit cash flows may be less risky than firms whose business unit cash flows are correlated. Target firms, unable to finance their investment opportunities, are said to be financially constrained, and they may view access to additional financing provided by an acquirer's unused borrowing capacity[6] or excess cash balance as a form of financial synergy.

Diversification

Buying firms beyond a company's current lines of business is called *diversification*. Diversification may create financial synergy that reduces the cost of capital as noted earlier. Alternatively, it may allow a firm to shift from

[6] Borrowing capacity refers to the ability of a firm to borrow additional money without materially impacting its cost of borrowing or violating loan covenants on existing debt.

TABLE 1.3 Product—market matrix

	Markets	
Products	Current	New
Current	Lower growth and lower risk	Higher growth and higher risk (related diversification)
New	Higher growth and higher risk (related diversification)	Highest growth and highest risk (unrelated diversification)

its core product line(s) to those having higher growth prospects. The new product lines or target markets may be related or unrelated to the firm's current products or markets. The product—market matrix illustrated in Table 1.3 identifies a firm's primary diversification options.

A firm facing slower growth in its current markets may accelerate growth through related diversification by selling its current products in new markets. IBM acquired web-based human resource software maker Kenexa to move its existing software business into the fiercely competitive but fast-growing market for delivering business applications via the internet.

A firm also may attempt to achieve higher growth by acquiring new products with which it is relatively unfamiliar and then selling them in familiar and less risky current markets.[7] Retailer J.C. Penney's $3.3 billion acquisition of the Eckerd Drugstore chain (a drug retailer) and Johnson & Johnson's $16 billion acquisition of Pfizer's consumer health care products line are examples of such related diversification. In each instance, the firm assumed additional risk by selling new products but into markets in which it had significant experience: J.C. Penney in consumer retail markets and J&J in retail health care markets.

There is considerable evidence that acquisitions resulting in unrelated diversification more often result in lower financial returns when they are announced than nondiversifying acquisitions.[8] Firms that operate in a number of largely unrelated industries are called *conglomerates*. Their prices often trade at a discount to shares of focused firms or to their value if broken up and sold as individual businesses. This *conglomerate discount* sometimes values such firms 15% lower than more focused firms in the same industry.

Investors often perceive conglomerates as riskier because management has difficulty understanding these firms and may underinvest in attractive opportunities. Also, outside investors may have trouble in valuing the various parts of highly diversified firms. Likewise, investors may be reluctant to invest in firms whose management appears intent on diversifying to build "empires" rather than to improve performance. The larger the difference between conglomerates whose share prices trade below more focused firms, the greater the likelihood these diversified firms will engage in restructuring that increases their focus.[9]

Other researchers find evidence that the most successful mergers in developed countries are those that focus on deals that promote the acquirer's core business, largely reflecting their familiarity with such businesses. Related acquisitions may even be more likely to generate higher financial returns than unrelated deals because related firms are more likely to realize cost savings due to overlapping functions. Also, cross-border deals are more likely to be completed when the degree of relatedness between the acquiring and target firms is high.[10]

The conglomerate discount is not universally true. About 30% of US publicly traded firms between 1976 and 2015 offered products in at least two or more distinct Standard Industrial Classifications. Of these diversified firms, 43% traded at a premium compared with the sum of the market value of their individual businesses, with the remainder trading at or below their breakup value.[11]

[7] Friberg (2020) describes a methodology for evaluating the impact on risk of intra-industry diversification.

[8] Akbulut and Matsusaka, 2010

[9] Hovakimian, 2016

[10] Lim and Lee, 2016

[11] Xiao and Xu, 2019. Siraj et al. (2020) argue that highly diversified firms in cyclical industries whose operating unit cash flows are positive and uncorrelated can command a valuation premium because they are better able to withstand economic fluctuations.

Strategic realignment

Firms use M&As to adjust to such factors as regulatory changes and technological innovation. Industries subject to significant deregulation in recent years—financial services, health care, utilities, media, telecom, defense—have been at the center of M&A activity because deregulation breaks down artificial barriers and stimulates competition. Deregulation often sparks a flurry of M&A activity resulting in fewer competitors in the industry. Technological advances create new products and industries and force a restructuring of existing ones. Tablet computers reduced the demand for desktop and notebook computers, and e-readers reduced the popularity of hardback books. Services such as WhatsApp and Microsoft's Skype erode a major source of mobile phone company revenue: voice and text messaging. Cloud computing allows firms to outsource their information technology operations.

Hubris and the "winner's curse"

Overconfident CEOs may pay more than the target is worth. Having overpaid, such acquirers may feel remorse—experiencing what is called the "winner's curse." The presence of multiple bidders may contribute to overpaying as CEOs get caught up in the excitement of an auction. Moreover, overconfident CEOs tend to view their firms as undervalued. When such firms have substantial cash holdings, these CEOs are prone to avoid external financing as too costly and use this cash to overinvest and engage in excessive M&A activity.[12]

Buying undervalued assets: the Q-ratio

The *Q*-ratio is the ratio of the market value of the acquirer's stock to the replacement cost of its assets. Firms can invest in new assets or obtain them by buying a company with a market value less than what it would cost to replace the assets (i.e., *Q*-ratio <1).

Managerialism (agency problems)

Agency problems arise when the interests of managers and shareholders differ. Managers may make acquisitions to add to their prestige, to build their influence, to increase compensation, or for self-preservation. Such mismanagement can persist when a firm's shares are widely held because the cost of such negligence is spread across a large number of shareholders.

Tax considerations

Acquirers of firms with accumulated losses and tax credits may use them to offset future profits. However, the taxable nature of the transaction often plays a more important role in determining whether a merger takes place than do any tax benefits accruing to the acquirer. Why? A properly structured deal allows the target shareholders to defer any capital gain until the acquirer's stock received in exchange for their shares is sold.[13] Taxes also are an important factor motivating firms to move their corporate headquarters to low-cost countries.

Market power

The market power theory suggests that firms merge to improve their ability to set product prices by reducing output or by colluding. Moreover, increased market power among firms supplying widely used inputs, such as oil and natural gas, across a broad spectrum of industries can be particularly harmful to society. Why? Such price increases are pervasive and tend to compound as they are passed up the various levels of production.[14] However, recent studies conclude that increased merger activity is much more likely to contribute to improved operating efficiency than to increased market power (see "Payoffs for Society?" section).

[12] Aktas et al., 2019

[13] Todtenhaupt et al. (2020) estimate a 1 percentage point increase in the US capital gains tax rate can reduce the number of M&As by 1%, resulting in a loss of government tax revenue and potential corporate efficiencies.

[14] Basso and Ross, 2019

Misvaluation

Absent full information, investors may incorrectly value a firm, especially for smaller firms receiving little financial media coverage.[15] If a firm's shares are overvalued (undervalued), they are likely to decline (rise) in the long run to their true value as investors more accurately value such shares based on new information. Opportunistic acquirers may profit by buying undervalued targets for cash at a price below their actual value or by using overvalued equity (even if the target is overvalued) as long as the target is less overvalued than the bidding firm's stock. Overvalued shares enable the acquirer to purchase a target firm in a share for share exchange by issuing fewer shares, reducing the dilution of current acquirer shareholders in the combined companies.[16]

Misvaluation contributes to market inefficiencies: the winning bidder may not be the one with the greatest synergy, and the purchase price paid may exceed the target's true value. Acquirers using their overvalued stock to bid for a target can outbid others whose offers are limited to the extent of their potential synergy with the target firm. If the acquirer's purchase price is based more on its overvalued shares than on perceived synergy, it is unlikely to create as much value for shareholders than a bidder basing their offer solely on synergy. Such instances are rare, occurring in about 7% of deals, and the magnitude of the inefficiency on average is small.[17] However, even if the buyer fails to acquire the target, their presence bids up the price paid, thereby potentially causing the winning bidder to overpay for the target. The effects of misvaluation are short-lived because the overvaluation of an acquirer's share price often is reversed in 1 to 3 years as investors' enthusiasm about potential synergies wanes.[18]

M&A waves

The domestic volume and value of M&As tend to display periods of surging growth only to later recede.[19] European waves follow those in the United States with a lag. Cross-border deals tend to follow cyclical patterns similar to domestic merger waves. Understanding M&A waves can help buyers and sellers properly time and structure their deals.

Why do M&A waves occur?

US M&As have clustered in multiyear waves since the late 1890s. One explanation is that merger waves occur when firms react to industry "shocks," such as from deregulation, new technologies, distribution channels, substitute products, or unpredictable events such as the 2020 global pandemic. Another explanation is based on misvaluation and suggests that managers use overvalued stock to buy the assets of lower-valued firms. For M&As to cluster in waves, goes the theory, valuations of many firms must increase at the same time. Managers whose stocks are believed to be overvalued move concurrently to acquire firms whose stock prices are valued less. For this theory to be correct, the method of payment would have to be stock.

In fact, the empirical evidence shows that less stock is used to finance takeovers during merger waves. Because M&A waves typically correspond to an improving economy, managers confident about their stocks' future appreciation are more inclined to use debt to finance takeovers[20] because they believe their shares are currently undervalued. Thus the shock argument seems to explain M&A waves better than the misvaluation theory.[21]

[15] Li, 2020. Hossain and Javakhadze (2020) document how acquirer executives with strong ties to journalists are able to gain more favorable media coverage by managing the reporting of takeovers.

[16] Consider an acquirer who offers the target firm shareholders $10 for each share he or she owns. If the acquirer's current share price is $10, the acquirer would have to issue one new share for each target share outstanding. If the acquirer's share price is valued at $20, only 0.5 new shares would have to be issued, and so forth. Consequently, the initial dilution of the current acquirer's shareholders' ownership stake in the new firm is less the higher the acquirer's share price compared with the price offered for each share of target stock outstanding.

[17] Li et al., 2018

[18] Akbulut, 2013

[19] Maksimovic et al., 2013

[20] Malmendier et al., 2011

[21] Garcia-Feijoo et al., 2012

Domestic merger waves

M&As commonly occur during periods of sustained high rates of economic growth, low or falling interest rates, and a rising stock market. Historically, each merger wave has differed in terms of a specific development (e.g., a new technology), industry focus (e.g., rail or oil), deregulation, and type of deal (i.e., horizontal, vertical, conglomerate, strategic, or financial).

Firms pursuing attractive deals early pay lower prices for targets than followers. Late in the cycle, purchase prices escalate as more bidders enter the takeover market, leading many buyers to overpay. Reflecting this "herd mentality," deals completed late in M&A waves tend to show lower acquirer returns than those announced before an upsurge in deal activity[22] and are less likely to be completed.[23] Another reason deals undertaken late in the cycle underperform is that monetary policy is generally tightening, resulting in higher postacquisition financing costs and less shareholder wealth creation.[24]

Cross-border merger waves

Similar to domestic mergers, cross-border mergers cluster by industry and by time period. Both are triggered by similar factors; but, unlike domestic M&A waves, deals completed later in the cross-border cycle show higher acquirer financial returns. Also, returns tend to be much higher than deals completed outside of waves. Postmerger operating performance is also better for within-wave cross-border deals. This superior performance is even greater if the target country is different from the acquirer's country in terms of culture, economic development, geographic location, capital market maturity, and legal system.

The superior performance of cross-border acquirers doing deals later in the cycle may reflect their ability to learn from prior deals made in the target country. Earlier deals establish comparable transaction values that may be used for valuation of the target firm, thereby limiting the acquirer's risk of overpaying. If in these prior deals investors have rewarded acquirers by bidding up their share prices, investors are more likely to applaud similar future deals as long as the acquirer does not overpay. Empirical evidence supports this notion in that firms are more (less) likely to undertake cross-border deals in the same country if they observe positive (negative) stock price reactions to previous comparable deals.[25]

Understanding corporate restructuring activities

Corporate restructuring falls into two categories: operational and financial. *Operational restructuring* involves changing a firm's asset structure by acquiring new businesses, the outright sale or spin-off of product lines, or downsizing by closing facilities. *Financial restructuring* describes changes in a firm's capital structure, such as share repurchases or adding debt either to lower the company's overall cost of capital or as part of a takeover defense. The focus in this book is on business combinations and breakups rather than on operational downsizing and financial restructuring. Business combinations include mergers, consolidations, acquisitions, or takeovers and can be friendly or hostile.

Mergers and consolidations

Mergers can be described from a legal perspective and an economic perspective. The implications of each are discussed next.

A legal perspective

A *merger* is a combination of two or more firms, often comparable in size, in which only one continues to exist legally. A *statutory* or *direct merger* is one in which the acquiring or surviving company assumes automatically the assets and liabilities of the target in accordance with the statutes of the state in which the combined companies

[22] Duchin et al., 2013

[23] Fuad et al., 2019

[24] Adra et al., 2020

[25] Xu, 2017

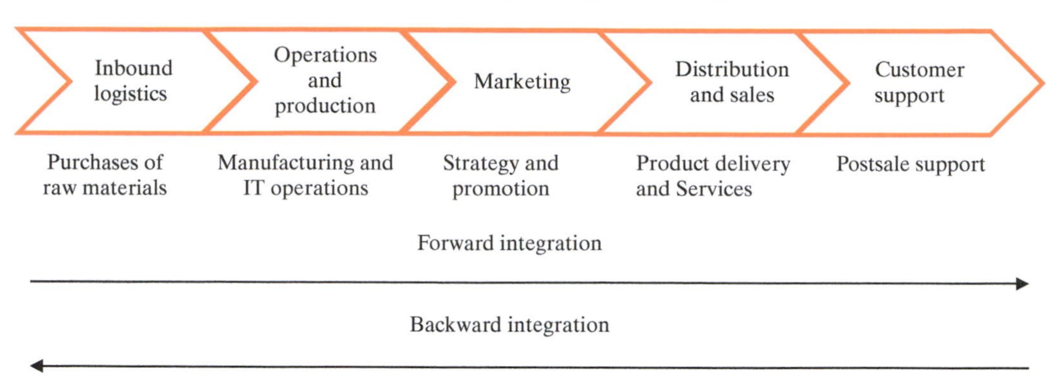

FIGURE 1.1 The corporate value chain. *IT*, Information technology.

will be incorporated. A *subsidiary merger* involves the target's becoming a subsidiary of the parent. To the public, the target firm may be operated under its brand name, but it will be owned and controlled by the acquirer. A *statutory consolidation*—which involves two or more companies joining to form a new company—is technically not a merger. All legal entities that are consolidated are dissolved during the formation of the new company, which usually has a new name. Shareholders in the firms typically exchange their shares for shares in the new company.

An economic perspective

Business combinations may also be defined depending on whether the merging firms are in the same (horizontal) or different industries (conglomerate) and on their positions in the corporate value chain (vertical). Figure 1.1 illustrates the stages of the value chain. A value chain in the basic steel industry may distinguish between raw materials, such as coal or iron ore, steel making and rolling operations, and distribution. Similarly, an oil and gas industry value chain would separate exploration activities from production, refining, and marketing.

In a vertical merger, companies that do not own operations in each major segment of the value chain "backward integrate" by acquiring a supplier or "forward integrate" by buying a distributor. When paper manufacturer Boise Cascade acquired Office Max, an office products distributor, the $1.1 billion transaction represented forward integration. PepsiCo backward integrated through a $7.8 billion purchase of its two largest bottlers.

Acquisitions, divestitures, spin-offs, split-offs, carve-outs, and leveraged buyouts

An *acquisition* occurs when a firm buys a controlling interest in another firm, a legal subsidiary of another firm, or selected assets of another firm. They may involve the purchase of another firm's assets or stock, with the acquired firm continuing to exist as a legally owned subsidiary. A *leveraged buyout (LBO)* is the acquisition of a firm financed primarily by debt with the assets of the acquired firm used to secure the debt; a management buyout (MBO) is an LBO in which the target firm's existing management remains with the firm after the buyout, often owning an equity stake in the firm. Firms with high insider ownership are more likely to select an MBO rather than an LBO.[26]

In contrast, a *divestiture* is the sale of all or substantially all of a company or product line to another party for cash or securities. A *spin-off* is a transaction in which a parent creates a new legal subsidiary and distributes shares in the subsidiary to its shareholders as a stock dividend, with the spun-off subsidiary now independent of the parent. A *split-off* is similar to a spin-off, in that a firm's subsidiary becomes an independent firm and the parent firm does not generate any new cash. However, unlike a spin-off, the split-off involves an offer to exchange parent stock for stock in the parent firm's subsidiary. An *equity carve-out* involves the parent issuing a portion of its stock or a subsidiary's to the public.

Failing firms sometimes seek protection from creditors from the bankruptcy court. The purpose is to reorganize *inside bankruptcy*; alternatively, the firm's managers may negotiate with creditors *outside of bankruptcy* court in an attempt to restructure the firm at an overall lower cost. Figure 1.2 provides a summary of the various forms of corporate restructuring.

[26] Mittoo et al., 2020

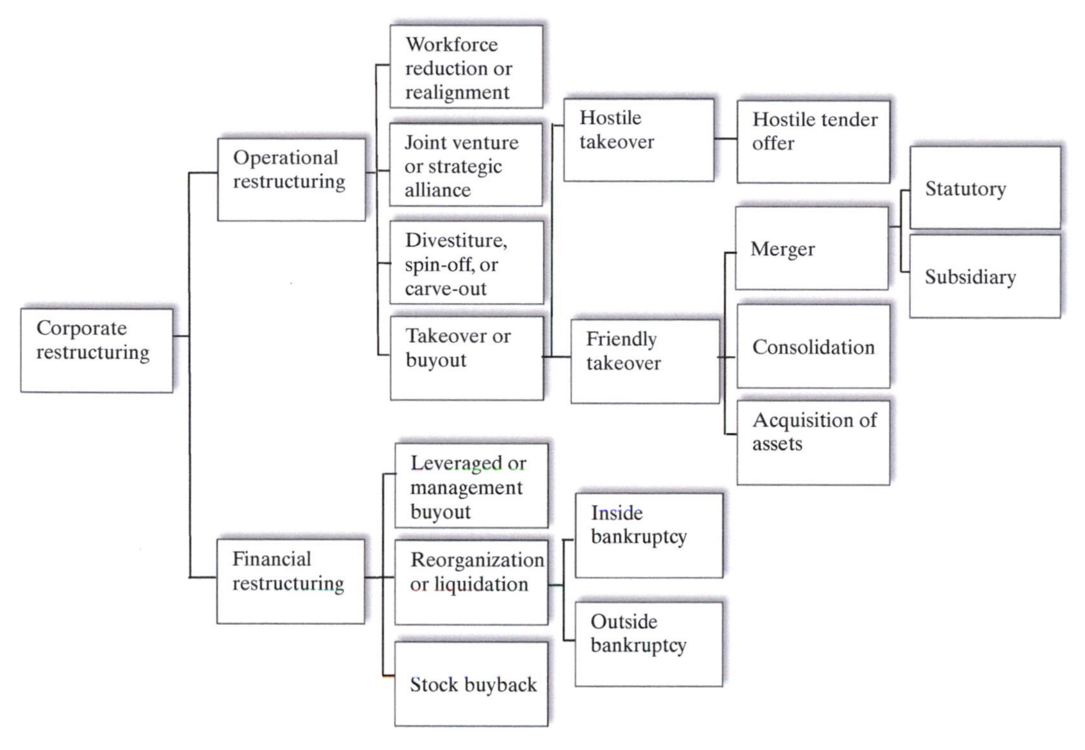

FIGURE 1.2 The corporate restructuring process.

Alternative takeover strategies

The term *takeover* is used when one firm assumes control of another. In a *friendly takeover*, the target's board and management recommend shareholder approval. To gain control, the acquirer usually must offer a premium to the target's current stock price. For example, French telecommunications giant Altice paid $34.90 per share of US cable company Cablevision in cash, 22% higher than Cablevision's closing stock price the day before the deal was announced. The excess of the offer price over the target's premerger share price is called a *purchase* or *acquisition premium* and varies widely by country.[27] The premium reflects the perceived value of a controlling interest, the value of synergies, and any overpayment for the target. Overpayment is the amount an acquirer pays in excess of the present value of future cash flows, including synergy.[28] The size of the premium varies widely over time and across industries, reflecting different expected growth rates.

A formal proposal to buy shares in another firm made directly to its shareholders, usually for cash or securities or both, is called a *tender offer*. Tender offers most often result from friendly negotiations (i.e., *negotiated tender offers*) between the boards of the acquirer and the target firm. Cash tender offers may be used because they can represent a faster alternative to mergers.[29] Those that are unwanted by the target's board are referred to as *hostile tender offers*. *Self-tender offers* are used when a firm seeks to repurchase its stock.

[27] A more accurate representation of the purchase price premium paid to target firm shareholders would reflect the run-up in the target's share price in advance of the deal's announcement date plus the price offered for the target shares in excess of the target's share price immediately prior to the announcement date.

[28] Analysts often attempt to determine the premium paid for a controlling interest (i.e., control premium) and the amount of value created due to operating synergies. An example of a pure control premium is a conglomerate willing to pay a price above the prevailing market price for a target to gain a controlling interest, even though operating synergies are limited. The acquirer believes it will recover the control premium by making better management decisions for the target firm.

[29] Speed is important to acquirers if there are other potential bidders for the target firm. Cash tender offers may be completed more rapidly since no target shareholder meeting is required, the length of regulatory review is less, and their higher shareholder approval requirements can be achieved through so-called short-form mergers (Offenberg et al., 2015).

A *hostile takeover* occurs when the offer is unsolicited, the approach was contested by the target's management, and control changed hands. The acquirer may attempt to circumvent management by offering to buy shares directly from the target's shareholders and by buying shares on a public stock exchange (i.e., an open market purchase). Friendly takeovers are often consummated at a lower purchase price than hostile deals, which may trigger an auction for the target firm. Acquirers often prefer friendly takeovers because the postmerger integration process is usually more expeditious when both parties are cooperating fully, and customer and employee attrition is less. Most transactions tend to be friendly, with hostile takeovers usually comprising less than 5% of the value of total deals.

The role of holding companies in mergers and acquisitions

A holding company is a legal entity having a controlling interest in one or more companies. The key advantage is the ability to gain effective control[30] of other companies at a lower cost than if the firm were to acquire 100% of the target's shares. Effective control sometimes can be achieved by owning as little as 30% of the voting stock of another firm when the bylaws require approval of major decisions by a majority of votes cast rather than a majority of the voting shares outstanding. This is particularly true when the target company's ownership is highly fragmented, with few shareholders owning large blocks of stock, and shareholder voting participation is limited. Effective control generally is achieved by acquiring less than 100% but usually more than 50% of another firm's equity, leaving the holding company with minority shareholders who may not always agree with the strategic direction of the firm. Also, holding company shareholders may be subject to an onerous tax burden, with corporate earnings potentially subject to triple taxation.[31]

The role of employee stock ownership plans in M&As

Employee stock ownership plans (ESOPs) are trust funds that invest in the securities of the firm sponsoring the plan. Designed to attract and retain employees, ESOPs are defined contribution[32] employee pension plans that invest at least 50% of the plan's assets in the sponsor's common shares. The plans may receive the employer's stock or cash, which is used to buy the sponsor's stock. The sponsor can make tax-deductible contributions of cash, stock, or other assets into the trust.[33] The plan's trustee is charged with investing the trust assets, and the trustee often can sell, mortgage, or lease the assets. Stock acquired by the ESOP is allocated to accounts for individual employees based on some formula and vested over time. ESOP participants must be allowed to vote their allocated shares at least on major issues such as selling the company.

If a subsidiary cannot be sold at what the parent firm believes is a reasonable price and liquidation would be disruptive to customers, the parent may divest the subsidiary to employees through a shell corporation. A shell corporation, as defined by the US Securities and Exchange Commission in 2005, is one with "no or nominal operations, and with no or nominal assets or assets consisting solely of cash and cash equivalents."[34]

The shell sets up the ESOP, which borrows the money to buy the subsidiary; the parent guarantees the loan. The shell operates the subsidiary, and the ESOP holds the stock. As income is generated from the subsidiary, tax-deductible contributions are made by the shell to the ESOP to service the debt. As the loan is repaid, the shares are allocated to employees who eventually own the firm. ESOPs may be used by employees in LBOs to buy the

[30] One firm is said to have effective control when it has been achieved by buying voting stock, it is not likely to be temporary, there are no legal restrictions on control (e.g., from a bankruptcy court), and there are no powerful minority shareholders.

[31] Subsidiaries of holding companies pay taxes on their operating profits. The holding company then pays taxes on dividends received from its subsidiaries. Finally, holding company shareholders pay taxes on dividends they receive from the holding company.

[32] Employee contributions are set as a percentage of salary, and the value of their pensions depends on the performance of the sponsoring firm's shares.

[33] Cash contributions made by the sponsoring firm for both interest and principal payments on bank loans to ESOPs are tax deductible. Dividends paid on stock contributed to ESOPs also are deductible if they are used to repay ESOP debt. The sponsoring firm could use tax credits equal to 0.5% of payroll if contributions in that amount were made to the ESOP. Finally, lenders must pay taxes on only half of the interest received on loans made to ESOPs owning more than 50% of the sponsoring firm's stock.

[34] Shell corporations often are created with the sole intent of merging with a privately held company, after selling their operations and assets to another firm, or as a result of the bankruptcy process.

shares of owners of privately held firms. This is common when the owners have most of their net worth tied up in their firms. ESOPs also provide an effective antitakeover defense because employees who also are shareholders tend to vote against bidders for fear of losing their jobs.

Business alliances as alternatives to M&As

In addition to M&As, businesses may combine through joint ventures (JVs), strategic alliances, minority investments, franchises, and licenses. The term *business alliance* is used to refer to all forms of business combinations other than M&As.

Joint ventures are business relationships formed by two or more parties to achieve common objectives. Although the JV is often a legal entity, such as a corporation or partnership, it may take any organizational form desired by the partners. Each JV partner continues to exist as a separate entity; JV corporations have their own management reporting to a board of directors. In early 2020, US auto company General Motors and South Korea's battery maker LG Chem announced the formation of a JV to build a battery factory in the United States.

A *strategic alliance* generally does not create a separate legal entity and may be an agreement to sell each firm's products to the other's customers or to co-develop a technology, product, or process. Such agreements may be legally binding or informal. To compete more effectively against Amazon.com, the leader in retailing and cloud computing, Walmart Inc. and Microsoft Corp signed a 5-year agreement in 2018 to use Microsoft's cloud computing capabilities to expedite customer shopping.

Minority investments, those involving less than a controlling interest, require little management time for those willing to be passive investors. Such investments are frequently made in firms that have attractive growth opportunities but lack the resources to pursue them. Investors often receive representation on the board or veto rights in exchange for their investment. A minority investor can effectively control a business by having veto rights to changes in strategy, certain capital expenditures, key management promotions, management salary increases, the amount and timing of dividends, and when the business would be sold.

Licenses enable firms to extend their brands to new products and markets by permitting others to use their brand names or to gain access to a proprietary technology. Firms with highly recognizable brand names can find such deals extremely profitable. For example, global consumer products powerhouse Nestle, disappointed with the growth of its own coffee products, acquired the rights to market, sell, and distribute Starbucks' packaged coffees and teas outside the United States for an upfront payment of $7.2 billion in early 2019.

A *franchise* is a form of a license agreement granting a privilege to a dealer from a manufacturer or franchise service organization to sell the franchiser's products or services in a given area. Under a franchise agreement, the franchiser may offer the franchisee consultation, promotional assistance, and financing in exchange for a share of the franchise's revenue. Franchises are common in fast food services and retailing, where a successful business model can be easily replicated.

The attraction of these M&A alternatives is the opportunity for each partner to gain access to the other's skills, products, and markets at a lower overall cost. Disadvantages include limited control, profit sharing, and the potential loss of secrets to competitors.

Participants in the mergers and acquisitions process

In addition to the acquirer and target firms, the key participants in the M&A process include providers of specialized services, regulators, institutional investors and lenders, activist investors, and M&A arbitrageurs. Each participant plays a distinctly different role.

Providers of specialized services

This category includes investment banks, lawyers, accountants, proxy solicitors, and public relations personnel. Negotiations typically involve teams of people with varied specialties because teams have access to a wider variety of expertise and can react more rapidly to changing negotiating strategies than can a single negotiator.

Investment banks

Investment banks provide advice and deal opportunities; screen potential buyers and sellers; make initial contact with a seller or buyer; and offer negotiation, valuation, and deal-structuring guidance. The "universal or top-tier banks" (e.g., Goldman Sachs) also maintain broker–dealer operations, serving wholesale and retail clients in brokerage and advisory roles, to support financing mega-transactions.

Investment bankers derive significant income from so-called *fairness opinion letters*—signed third-party statements certifying the appropriateness of the price of a proposed deal involving a tender offer, merger, asset sale, or LBO. They often are developed as legal protection for members of the boards of directors against possible shareholder challenges of their decisions.[35] Researchers have found that fairness opinion letters reduce the risk of lawsuits associated with M&A transactions and the size of the premium paid for targets if they result in acquirers' performing more rigorous due diligence and deal negotiation.[36]

Factors impacting the selection of investment banks by acquirers and targets include track record, bank size and market share, access to funding, prior relationships, and acquirer and target deal experience. These factors are considered in more detail next.

Acquirer and target firms focus far more on a bank's track record in generating high financial returns for their clients than on its size or market share.[37] Smaller advisors may generate higher returns for their clients than the mega-investment banks because of proprietary industry knowledge.[38] Advisor size and market share do matter in certain situations. Contrary to earlier studies that report a negative or weak relationship between bidder advisor size and bidder returns, bidders using top-tier investment banks as advisors report a 1% improvement in returns in deals involving public targets.[39] Top-tier investment banks are better able to assist in funding large deals because of their current relationships with lenders and broker networks.

About 50% of deals are advised by top-tier investment banks, which appear more helpful in improving both short- and long-term financial performance for acquirers who have limited access to funds. High financing costs force such firms to be more careful in making acquisitions and to hire top-tier advisors to identify synergies.[40]

Longstanding investment banking relationships do matter. Investment banks are more likely to use their best bankers to support deals involving their most valued clientele, causing financial returns on deals to vary widely within the same bank.[41] Frequent acquirers are more likely to use the same investment advisor if they have had good prior outcomes. Investment banking relationships are significant for inexperienced acquirers, who are more likely to hire financial advisors with whom they have had a longstanding underwriting relationship for new equity issues.[42] After the takeover of a target firm, some acquirers choose the target's former investment bank in future deals even though no prior relationship existed. Why? The service provided by the advisor to the target is perceived as high, the advisor is reputable, and the target's management is retained by the combined firms.[43]

In recent years, active acquirers have been relying more on their internal staffs to perform what has traditionally been done by outside investment bankers. The trend is driven by a desire to control costs, keep deals confidential, and move quickly when needed.

Lawyers

Lawyers help structure deals, evaluate risk, negotiate the tax and financial terms, and arrange financing. Specific tasks include drafting the purchase agreement and related documents, providing opinion of counsel letters to the

[35] Typically limited to "change of control" transactions, fairness opinions include a range of values for a firm. The proposed purchase price is considered "fair" if it falls within the range. Problems with fairness opinions include the potential conflicts of interest with investment banks that receive large fees. Often, the investment bank that brings the deal to a potential acquirer is the same one that writes the fairness opinion.

[36] Kisgen et al., 2009

[37] Bao et al., 2011

[38] Graham et al., 2017

[39] Golubov et al., 2011

[40] Guo et al., 2020

[41] Liu et al., 2019

[42] Francis et al., 2014. Chen et al. (2021) argue that prior underwriting activities with acquirers enable investment banks to have a better understanding of the firm's business, enabling them to be more effective in assisting acquirers throughout the takeover process and to charge lower M&A advisory fees.

[43] Bhattacharya et al., 2019

lender, performing due diligence activities, and defending against lawsuits. The choice of legal counsel in deal making often is critical. They can negotiate cheaper and faster deals, can protect low-premium deals from serious legal challenges, and are more effective in multijurisdictional litigation cases.[44]

Accountants

Accountants provide advice on financial structure, perform financial due diligence, and help create the optimal deal tax structure. Accountants also prepare financial statements and perform audits. Many agreements require that the targets' books and records be prepared in accordance with generally accepted accounting principles.

Proxy solicitors

Proxy contests are attempts to change the management control or policies of a firm by gaining the right to cast votes on behalf of other shareholders. Proxy solicitors are hired by acquirers to compile mailing lists of shareholder addresses and to track thousands of votes cast. The target's management may also hire proxy solicitors to design strategies for convincing their shareholders to support the board. Likewise, proxy solicitors can be used by institutional investors to determine how they should vote on an issue. With 97% market share, Institutional Shareholder Services and Glass Lewis are the leading US proxy solicitor firms. As of mid-2020, proxy solicitors have a legal obligation to disclose material conflicts of interest and to provide more timely information.

Regulators

Regulations affecting M&As exist at all levels of government and involve security, antitrust, environmental, racketeering, employee benefits laws, and data privacy. Others are industry specific, such as public utilities, insurance, banking, broadcasting, telecommunications, defense contracting, and transportation. State antitakeover statutes place limitations on how and when a hostile takeover may be implemented. Moreover, approval at both the state and federal levels may be required for deals in certain industries. Cross-border transactions may be even more complicated because it may be necessary to obtain approval from regulatory authorities in all countries in which the acquirer and target companies do business.

Institutional investors and lenders

These financial intermediaries pool funds provided by others and invest or lend funds to finance the purchase of a wide array of assets, from securities to real property to corporate takeovers. They include insurance companies, pension funds, and mutual funds; private equity, hedge funds, and venture capital funds; sovereign wealth funds; and angel investors. Commercial banks also are important; however, recent legislation relegates their role to lending rather than investing money deposited with the bank.

Institutional ownership of US firms has grown dramatically during the past 30 years. In the late 1980s, institutional investors owned about 30% of the average publicly traded firm, with individual investors owning the remainder. By 2015, institutions accounted for about two-thirds of the average firm's shares.[45] Institutional investors whose portfolio turnovers are low and that tend to concentrate their investments in large firms contribute to higher valuations, superior governance practices, and better long-term performance of the firms in which they invest.[46] Why? They provide ongoing monitoring of board and management performance.

Institutional investors are more likely to own stock in both acquiring and target firms than retail investors. As such, they may have access to better and more current information than other investors, and they can be more influential in lobbying both acquirer and target board members and management. Shareholders owning stock in both the target and acquirer have an ability to offset losses on one side of the transaction with gains on the other side. Cross-ownership increases the chances of two firms merging, reduces deal premiums, and decreases the completion of unattractive deals (i.e., those whose share prices tend to fall when they are announced). Moreover, postdeal long-term performance tends to be positive.[47]

[44] Krishnan et al., 2017

[45] Blume et al., 2017

[46] Borochin et al., 2017

[47] Brooks et al., 2017

Hedge funds (more than other institutional investors) tend to purchase shares in firms both before and immediately after the deal announcement date. Often having more information than other institutional investors, they can make better investment decisions. Deals with many institutional investors often display substantial positive financial returns. [48]

Insurance, pension, and mutual funds

Risk-averse and subject to substantial regulation, these institutions invest in assets whose risk and return characteristics match their obligations to their customers. For example, an insurance company offers to mitigate risk for its customers in exchange for an insurance premium. The main source of profit for insurance companies is the sale of insurance products, but they also make money by investing premium income. Employers establish pension funds to provide pensions for employees when they retire. Typically, pension funds are managed by a financial advisor for the company and its employees, although some larger corporations operate their pension funds in house. Mutual funds are pools of money professionally managed for the benefit of investors.

Commercial banks

Traditionally, commercial banks have accepted checking, savings, and money market accounts and lend these funds to borrowers. This model has evolved into one in which banks sell many of the loans they originate to others for whom buying, selling, and collecting loan repayments is their primary business. Commercial banks also derive profits from fees charged for various types of services offered to depositors and fees charged for underwriting and other investment banking services.

Hedge, private equity, and venture capital funds

These funds assume higher levels of risk than other types of institutional investors and usually are limited partnerships in which the general partner has made a substantial personal investment. They are distinguished by their investment strategies, lockup periods (i.e., the length of time investors are required to commit funds), and the liquidity of their portfolios. Hedge fund investment strategies include trading a variety of financial instruments—debt, equity, options, futures, and foreign currencies—as well as higher-risk strategies, such as corporate restructurings (e.g., LBOs) and credit derivatives (e.g., credit default swaps). Because of their shorter lockup periods, hedge funds focus on investments that can be readily converted into cash. In contrast, private equity funds often make highly illiquid investments[49] in private companies and hold such investments for 5 years or more; they attempt to control risk by being actively involved in managing the firm in which they have invested. Venture capitalists are a significant source of funds for financing both start-ups and acquisitions.

Sovereign wealth funds

Sovereign wealth funds are government-backed entities that invest foreign currency reserves. Through such funds, countries with huge quantities of US dollars often reinvest the money in US Treasury securities. These funds are increasingly taking equity positions in foreign firms.

Angel investors

Such investors are wealthy individuals banding together in "investment clubs" or networks to identify deals, pool money, and share expertise. Some angel groups imitate professional investment funds, some affiliate with universities, and others engage in for-profit philanthropy. The angel investor market tends to be informal and less professional than the venture capital market. They fund early-stage start-ups (often without revenue) and serve as mentors and sometimes as outside directors for entrepreneurs.

Activist investors

Institutions often play the role of activist investors to alter the policies of companies in which they invest and to discipline inept corporate management. Institutions having a long-term investment horizon have been shown to

[48] Ismail et al., 2019

[49] Nadauld et al. (2019) document how private equity investors address the illiquidity of their investments by selling their ownership stakes in secondary markets but only at a substantial discount from net asset value.

contribute to a firm's financial performance because of their more active monitoring of management decisions.[50] Activism has become more important in recent years by replacing the historic role of hostile takeovers in disciplining underperforming managers or changing corporate strategies.[51]

Mutual funds and pension funds

Although regulations restrict their ability to discipline corporate managers, institutional investors with huge portfolios can be effective in demanding governance changes.[52] Corporate governance is the system of rules, processes, and practices that control a firm. These institutions may challenge management on such issues as takeover defenses, CEO severance benefits, and employee stock option accounting. Voting against management, though, can be problematic because some mutual funds manage retirement plans and, increasingly, provide a host of outsourcing services—from payroll to health benefits—for their business clients. Mutual funds may own stock, on behalf of their clients, in these same firms.

Activists also are finding that they may avoid the expense of a proxy fight simply by threatening to vote in certain ways on supporting a CEO or a management proposal. This may mean a "no" vote, although in some instances, the only option is to vote in the affirmative or abstain. Abstaining is a way to indicate dissatisfaction with a CEO or a firm's policy without jeopardizing future underwriting or M&A business for the institution.

Hedge funds and private equity firms

Hedge funds and private equity firms have had more success as activist investors than other institutional investors. They are successful about two-thirds of the time in their efforts to change a firm's strategic, operational, or financial strategies, often generating attractive financial returns for shareholders.[53] They seldom seek control (with ownership stakes averaging about 9%) and are often nonconfrontational. Not subject to the same regulations as mutual funds and pension funds, hedge funds can hold concentrated positions in a small number of firms. Moreover, they are not limited by the same conflicts of interests that afflict mutual funds and pension funds.

M&A arbitrageurs

After a bid announcement, the target's share price often trades at a small discount to the actual bid, reflecting the risk that the deal may not be completed. Merger arbitrage refers to an investment strategy that attempts to profit from this spread. Arbitrageurs buy the stock and make a profit on the difference between the bid price and the target's current stock price if the deal is completed. Others may "short" the stock after it increases, betting that the proposed merger will not be completed and the target's share price will drop to its pre-announcement level.

To illustrate, assume a target firm's shares are selling at $6 per share and an acquirer announces an offer to pay $10 per share. Because the outcome is uncertain, the target's share price will rise to less than $10; assume $9.[54] Other investors may bet the merger will not be completed and sell the stock short (i.e., sell borrowed shares—paying interest to the share owner based on the value of the shares when borrowed—hoping to buy them back at a lower price) at $9 and buy it back at $6.[55]

In a cash-financed merger, arbitrageurs seeking to buy the target firm's shares provide liquidity to the target's shareholders that want to sell on the announcement day or shortly thereafter. Arbitrageurs may actually reduce liquidity for the acquirer's stock in a share for share merger because they immediately "short" the acquirer shares.

[50] Andriosopoulos, 2015

[51] Denes et al., 2016

[52] Mutual funds, to achieve diversification, are limited in the amount they can invest in any one firm's outstanding stock. State regulations often restrict the share of a life insurance or property casualty company's assets that can be invested in stock to as little as 2%.

[53] Clifford (2008) and Klein and Zur (2009) found that hedge fund activism generates an approximate 7% higher financial return to shareholders than normal around the announcement that the hedge fund is initiating some form of action.

[54] The target's share price rises by $4–$10 if investors were certain the deal would get done. Because it rises only to $9, investors are implicitly stating that there is a 75% (i.e., $3/$4) probability that the merger will be completed.

[55] Jiang et al. (2019) discuss an unconventional arbitrage strategy in which speculators take a long position in an acquirer's shares when the announced takeover is viewed as value-destroying with the expectation that they can use their position to break up the deal and profit from the subsequent rise in the acquirer's share price.

The downward pressure that arbitrageur short selling puts on the acquirer's share price at the time the deal is announced makes it difficult for others to sell without incurring a loss from the pre-announcement price.

Excess financial returns (i.e., above what would be expected for the risk assumed) to arbitrage funds reflect the number of deals available and the degree of competition among funds to invest in those deals, the age of the fund, the arbitrage spread reflecting prevailing economic conditions, and fund size. The age of the fund is a proxy for experience, whereas fund size reflects economies of scale. As fund size increases, financial returns diminish, other things being equal, because fund managers have difficulty in investing funds productively.[56]

The impact of protectionism on M&As

Government policies that restrict imports (or promote exports) for the benefit of a domestic economy are called protectionist. Examples include tariffs, nontariff barriers, quotas, and subsidies. See Chapter 19 for a more detailed discussion of this topic.

A tariff is a tax intended to protect domestic jobs from foreign competition, shelter emerging industries, promote national security, or retaliate against foreign protectionist practices. So-called nontariff barriers include import licensing; packaging and labeling requirements; and plant, food, and animal inspections. Other examples include local content requirements, anti-dumping laws, and environmental impact restrictions that serve to increase the cost of imported products.[57] Whereas a tariff is a tax levied on imported products, quotas limit the amount of a good that can be imported. Subsidies are benefits granted to a business by the government in the form of a cash payment, tax deduction, or some other tax incentive to boost a nation's exports.[58]

Protectionism in its various forms promotes the inefficient use of resources by discouraging takeovers of inefficient domestic firms by more efficient foreign firms and impacts the types of mergers undertaken.[59] Tariffs can encourage cross-border horizontal mergers (i.e., between competitors) and discourage vertical mergers (i.e., between customers and suppliers). Foreign firms are inclined to acquire competitors in countries protected by tariffs as their products are not subject to tariff barriers. In contrast, tariffs on imports of raw materials and intermediate products from countries whose exports are subject to tariffs make cross-border vertical deals less attractive.

The impact of the 2020 coronavirus pandemic on M&As

The immediate impact was that deal terms on completed deals often included holding back a portion of the purchase price, lengthy due diligence became the norm, financing for large deals dried up, share exchanges became more common, and many negotiated deals did not get done. For example, aerospace and industrial components manufacturers Woodward Inc. and Hexcel Corp. mutually agreed to cancel their merger announced in early 2020, citing the need to focus on their core operations. And bankruptcies nearly doubled, concentrated in the mining, oil and gas, and retail sectors. LBOs waned early in the year as private equity firms focused on "nursing" their portfolio of businesses through the pandemic-induced recession. However, sitting on a cash hoard of $2.7 trillion according to data provider Prequin, buyout firms renewed their pursuit of buying assets at distressed prices using funds borrowed at record low interest rates by year end. Strategic buyers that did undertake M&A pursued targets in COVID-resistant sectors, such as technology and health care.

The longer-term impact depends on the pace and sustainability of the global economic recovery and the resiliency of world trade and capital markets. Restrictions are likely to make capital and labor flow across national borders more difficult. Regulators worldwide will tighten rules for foreign investments to protect "national assets" viewed

[56] Rzakhanov and Jetley, 2020

[57] Grundke and Moser, 2019

[58] In 2020, the European Union proposed greater regulatory scrutiny of foreign firms receiving subsidies from their home countries. This could imperil foreign acquisition of European Union assets.

[59] Srinivasan, 2020

as critical to domestic security.[60] And countries will become more self-sufficient in the production of items considered in the national interest, such as medical equipment and supplies. Supply chains will look far different from what they are today as businesses diversify sourcing. The net effect of these factors could be to reduce the number of cross-border deals and increase interest in domestic firms. These topics are discussed in more detail elsewhere in this book.

The implications of M&As for shareholders, bondholders, and society

Current finance textbooks generally view shareholder wealth maximization as the primary purpose of the corporation. Implicit in this statement is that the interests of other stakeholder groups such as customers, employees, lenders, and communities must be considered adequately if a corporation is to achieve this objective. Why? Because the failure to do so contributes to a firm's share price underperformance and potentially to its eventual demise.

What follows is an extensive discussion of the academic literature which generally measures the success or failure of M&As based on their ability (or inability) to create shareholder wealth. A more detailed discussion of whether M&As contribute to societal well-being when all stakeholders are considered is deferred until the end of the chapter.

The limitations of statistical analysis

Every year dozens of academic articles are published in widely respected journals analyzing the effects of M&As on financial returns for shareholders, bondholders, and society. Such studies do not "prove" that certain independent variables explain returns but rather suggest that they are statistically significant (i.e., their correlation is not due to chance) for the sample and time period selected. In many academic studies, about one-quarter (or less) of the total variation in financial returns is explained by the independent variables used. The remaining variance is unexplained, thus making the results of such studies problematic at best because the exclusion of relevant variables can bias (or invalidate) the results.[61]

An independent variable that is statistically significant in a regression model[62] that explains a low percentage of the variation in the dependent variable can be a proxy for a variable that should have been included in the equation. Thus the included variable is not the true determinant of, for example, acquirer returns but rather is simply correlated with the excluded variable, which is the true determinant.

Can we reach reasonable conclusions based on available research? Yes, if the results found in many studies using different time periods, data sets, and methodologies are consistent and if the explicit (and implicit) assumptions underlying the results make sense.

Most M&As create shareholder value!

On average, the sum of target and acquirer shareholders' gains around the deal's announcement date is positive and statistically significant (i.e., not due to chance).[63] Although most of the gain accrues to target shareholders because they usually have the greatest bargaining leverage, acquirer shareholders often experience financial gains in excess of what would have been realized in the absence of a takeover. And, as explained later, there is evidence that acquirer announcement-date financial returns may be significantly understated.

In the years after a takeover, it is less clear if acquirer shareholders continue to benefit from the deal. As time passes, other factors impact performance, making it difficult to determine the extent to which a change in performance is due to an earlier acquisition.

[60] The Indian government in 2020 announced it would require investments from countries with contiguous borders to obtain government consent to minimize "opportunistic takeovers." And both the United States and China announced late in 2020 export controls on items considered critical to their national well-being.

[61] In reviewing academic studies, the author suggests the reader pay particular attention to *adjusted* R squares (usually found in tables at the back of the article), which measure percentage of variation explained by variables that actually affect the dependent variable. In contrast, unadjusted R square provides the percentage of variation as if all independent variables in the model affect the dependent variable.

[62] Regression models involve quantifying the relationship among variables. Fluctuations in the so-called dependent variable (some measure of financial returns) are explained by selecting a set of factors (i.e., independent variables) whose variation is believed to explain changes in the dependent variable.

[63] Mulherin et al., 2017

Researchers use a variety of approaches to measure the impact of takeovers on shareholder value.[64] The two most common are *premerger event returns* and *postmerger accounting returns*. So-called event studies examine abnormal stock returns to the shareholders of both acquirers and targets around the announcement of an offer (the "event"). Event studies presume that investors can accurately assess the likely success or failure of M&As realizing expected synergy around the deal's announcement date.[65] However, there is ample reason to question this presumption because investor reactions on the announcement date differ widely depending on the justification for the deal.[66] Furthermore, the results of these studies vary widely depending on the listing status,[67] size of the acquirer and target firms, and the form of payment. Empirical studies of postmerger returns often use accounting measures to gauge the impact on shareholder value in the years immediately after a takeover.

To assess value creation potential, we look at abnormal financial returns to the following constituencies: acquirer and target shareholders, bondholders, and for society (i.e., the sum of acquirer and target shareholders). These are addressed in the following sections.

Premerger returns to shareholders

Positive *abnormal* or *excess* shareholder returns may be explained by such factors as improved efficiency, pricing power, market share gains, and tax benefits. They are abnormal in that they exceed what an investor would normally expect to earn for accepting a certain level of risk. If an investor expects to earn a 10% return on a stock but actually earns 15% because of a takeover, the abnormal or excess return to the shareholder would be 5%.[68]

Returns high for target shareholders

Average abnormal returns to target shareholders during the 2000s averaged 25.1% as compared with 18.5% during the 1990s.[69] This upward trend may reflect bidders' willingness to offer higher premiums in friendly takeovers to preempt other bidders, the increasing sophistication of takeover defenses, federal and state laws requiring bidders to notify target shareholders of their intentions before completing the deal, and the decline in the number of publicly listed firms during the past 2 decades.[70] Although relatively infrequent, returns from hostile tender offers generally exceed those from friendly mergers, which are characterized by less contentious negotiated settlements and the absence of competing bids.

Sometimes returns to target shareholders on the announcement date can be negative. Why? Because investors are sensitive to the size of the actual offer price relative to the expected offer price.[71] When the announced offer price is below expectations, investors often express their disappointment by selling their shares. Selling pressure can be particularly intense when the run-up in share prices before the bid is fueled largely by speculators hoping to profit from a sizable jump in the stock. When it becomes clear that their expectations will not be realized, speculators try to lock in any profits they have by selling their shares.

[64] In an analysis of 88 empirical studies between 1970 and 2006, Zola and Meier (2008) identify 12 different approaches to measuring the impact of takeovers on shareholder value. Of these studies, 41% use the event study method to analyze premerger returns, and 28% use long-term accounting measures to analyze postmerger returns.

[65] Bargeron et al., 2014

[66] De Groote et al. (2020) argue that differences in initial investor assessments of takeover announcements are often driven more by perceptions than reality. To illustrate, they document differences between announcement date returns to synergistic and thematic takeovers, with the former showing higher abnormal returns than the latter. However, such differences tend to converge shortly after the announcement date. Why? Thematic takeovers (e.g., acquisition of an emerging technology) take longer for investors to understand.

[67] Whether a deal involves listed (on a public stock exchange) or unlisted (privately held) firms often makes a difference in the financial returns to shareholders because the majority of firms engaging in takeovers involve a private acquirer, private target, or both.

[68] Abnormal returns are calculated by subtracting the actual return from a benchmark indicating investors' required returns, often the capital asset pricing model or the S&P 500 stock index.

[69] See table 11 in Netter et al. (2011).

[70] According to the Center for Research in Security Prices, the number of publicly listed firms has fallen from more than 7400 in 1996 to about half that in 2017 because of companies staying private longer, bankruptcies, and M&As (Wursthorn et al., 2018).

[71] Ang et al., 2015

Rival firms in the same industry as the target firm also show significant abnormal announcement date returns. This reflects investor anticipation that such firms are likely to become targets themselves as the industry consolidates.

Although media coverage of M&As impacts the magnitude of announcement date returns by expanding awareness of a proposed tie-up, the media's attitude toward an announced business combination can also be predictive. Media outlets may have access to undisclosed information that when released helps investors more accurately assess the success or failure of a deal. Pessimistic media attention about a deal correlates highly with much lower acquirer announcement date returns as well as subpar postmerger performance.[72] Announcement returns also are higher when macro indicators are released because media attention is greater.[73]

Returns to acquirer shareholders are positive on average

Recent research, involving large samples of tens of thousands of public and private firms over lengthy time periods including US, foreign, and cross-border deals, documents that acquirer shareholder returns are generally positive around the deal announcement date.[74] Before 2009, event studies showed average negative acquirer returns of about 1% in cash and stock deals involving large public firms and deals in which the primary payment was stock.

After 2009, M&As showed average positive and statistically significant abnormal returns of about 1% for acquirers, and stock deals no longer destroy value.[75] Why? The Dodd-Frank reform act that passed in 2010, although aimed primarily at financial institutions, has improved monitoring and governance systems for all US listed firms. This has been achieved through new mandatory disclosure rules, refining executive compensation plans, granting more powers to shareholders, and strengthening executive and director accountability.

Earlier studies usually dealt with public firms and largely ignored deals involving private acquirers, private targets, or both, which comprise more than four-fifths of total deals. Although deals involving public companies are declining in line with the shrinking number of public firms, public transactions represent a large percentage of the total dollar volume of deals.

Studies including private targets and acquirers display average acquirer shareholder positive abnormal returns of about 1% to 1.5%. If deals involving public companies and takeovers of public firms financed primarily with stock are removed from the academic studies, acquirer returns would on average increase even more.

The earlier studies also fail to explain why tens of thousands of M&As are reported annually worldwide and why the number and size of M&As continues to grow. If M&As did not on average generate positive acquirer returns, we would have to argue counterintuitively that managers are incapable of learning from their own and others' past failures.

Pre-2009 studies also understate average acquirer returns because they are based on relatively small samples of mostly large public firms, use problematic methodologies, fail to capture the pre-announcement rise in acquirer share prices, and fail to adjust for distortions of a few large transactions. Nor do they account for premerger pay for performance programs even though bidders with high pay for performance plans tend to pay lower premiums and realize higher returns than firms that do not have such plans.[76]

Furthermore, commonly used sampling methods bias sample selection toward larger publicly traded firms making such samples unrepresentative of most firms involved in M&As.[77] And studies focusing on publicly traded firms are likely to suffer from increasingly small sample bias as the number of such firms continues to drop, having fallen by more than 50% over the past several decades.

Deal success (or failure) should be viewed in the context of a business strategy

Business strategies tend to drive M&A outcomes and consolidated financial returns,[78] and announcement date returns vary widely, often reflecting the differing motives for mergers.[79]

[72] Yang et al., 2019

[73] Saunders et al., 2020

[74] Yilmaz et al., 2016; Erel et al., 2012; Netter et al., 2011; Ellis et al., 2011

[75] Alexandridis et al., 2017

[76] Krolikowski, 2016

[77] Moeller et al., 2005; Jansen et al., 2014

[78] Jurich et al., 2019

[79] Wang, 2018

Event studies assume that investors at the time of the deal's announcement can accurately assess potential synergy even though investors lack access to the necessary information to make an informed decision. If event return studies understate synergy, they tend to understate actual financial returns to the acquirer when combined with the target firm. What follows are illustrations of how corporate strategies can generate attractive acquirer returns even though individual M&As can be viewed as destroying shareholder value when viewed in isolation. Also, note the differing motives for undertaking deals.

Google was criticized as having overpaid in 2006 when it acquired YouTube for $1.65 billion. Google's business strategy was to increase usage of its search engine and websites to attract advertising revenue. Today YouTube is by far the most active site featuring videos on the internet and has attracted substantial additional web activity for its parent. Viewed independently from the Google business strategy, YouTube may not exhibit attractive financial returns, but as part of a larger strategy, it has been wildly successful.

Event studies do not take into account the potential beneficial impact of defensive acquisitions (i.e., those made to prevent a competitor from acquiring a firm).[80] Facebook's eye-popping $21.8 billion acquisition in 2014 of WhatsApp with its meager $20 million in annual revenue was in part justified because it kept this rapidly growing mobile messaging business away from Google. Although not yet a big moneymaker, WhatsApp had more than 2 billion users by late 2020, making it the second most user active business owned by Facebook. Combining its WhatsApp and Messenger services, Facebook has dominant market share everywhere but China.[81]

Amazon.com's $13.7 billion buyout of grocer Whole Foods in 2017 may show negative returns if viewed as separate from Amazon's corporate strategy but can exhibit very positive financial returns if viewed in the context of creating more brand loyalty. It does not matter where Amazon.com makes money throughout its diverse array of businesses but only that it does make enough to satisfy investors.

Disney was severely criticized as overpaying when it acquired Pixar for $7.3 billion in 2006, Marvel Entertainment in 2009 for $4 billion, and Lucasfilm for $4 billion in 2012. Disney's business strategy has been to nurture strong brands and grow creative content. The acquisition of the successful film animation studio Pixar reinvigorated Disney's animation and production studio business and prevented Pixar from being acquired by a rival. Marvel Entertainment provided the firm with numerous iconic brands. Lucasfilm added the Star Wars franchise to Disney's growing film library. When combined with Disney's creative skills and global distribution, the growth in Disney's film library pushed the firm to record box-office revenues in 2019.

Disney blunted efforts by telecom conglomerates to enter the content market in 2019 by acquiring Fox's entertainment assets for a whopping $71 billion. With enough proprietary material, Disney launched its wildly popular streaming service (Disney Plus) in late 2019. By late 2020, Disney Plus had well over 50 million subscribers.

Postmerger returns to shareholders

The objective of examining postmerger performance measures such as cash flow and operating profit is to determine how performance changed as a result of a deal. Most studies focus on the 3-year period after closing. With the passage of time, it is increasingly difficult to isolate the target's impact on the combined firms because of the growing number of other factors that could affect performance. Yet, as we shall see, this short time span may also bias significantly the results of many postmerger performance studies.

A comprehensive literature survey of postmerger performance studies before 2019 concluded that average acquirer performance in the years after a deal tends to decline.[82] A more recent study found that although M&As frequently create acquirer shareholder value around the announcement date, the initial wealth creation is often not sustainable.[83] However, these findings may be problematic because of certain limitations, such as excessively short postmerger sample periods, failure to identify acquirer motives, situational differences, definitional issues, and technical differences. Other shortcomings of such studies include not knowing what would have happened had these deals not been done and a focus on public acquirers. Each of these deficiencies is discussed next.

[80] Acquirers may rationally overpay when the cost of overpaying is less than the cost incurred in losing the target to a competitor.

[81] In 2020, Facebook was sued by the US Federal Trade Commission and 48 states on the grounds that its actions were anticompetitive in that they prevented the emergence of rivals. See Chapter 2 for more details.

[82] Renneboog and Vansteenkiste, 2019

[83] Rao and Mishra, 2020

Most postmerger studies presume that 3 years is sufficient to assess the direction of long-term postmerger operating performance. In fact, many business strategies take far longer to implement fully. For example, Disney's strategy to build a dominant film library involved multiple deals and took more than a decade to complete. The individual takeovers represented building blocks needed to execute the corporation's strategy. On their own, they may have created little value; but collectively, they made Disney the media powerhouse it is today.

Different acquirers have different motives. Facebook's takeover of WhatsApp was a defensive move. Google's acquisition of YouTube and Amazon's takeover of Whole Foods were in part intended to drive additional consumer traffic to their websites, generating additional product sales and advertising revenue. In each instance, individual takeovers may show only modest (or even negative) financial returns, but corporate consolidated financial returns are much higher than they would have been had the deals not been done. Moreover, acquirers who focus on long-term value creation are willing to devote the resources needed to achieve their objectives. Such acquirers often outperform those with a shorter-term focus.[84]

Postmerger performance is affected by the acquirer's situation when the deal was undertaken. In looking at longer-term performance, it is important to consider the level of default risk associated with the bidder around the announcement date.[85] Although the announcement date financial returns may be similar between financially distressed and nondistressed acquirers, long-term returns tend to be highly negative for the former.[86] Acquirers whose management has significant familiarity with the target's suppliers or customers tend to integrate efficiently both firms generating on average a 3.8% increase in postmerger accounting returns and a 12% decline in the amount of goodwill written off compared with acquirers with limited knowledge of target supply chains.[87]

Another study illustrates how the definition of financial performance can affect conclusions. In a large study evaluating the immediate versus intermediate effects of M&As on firm value, researchers using the ratio of the enterprise value to earnings before interest, taxes, and depreciation (EBITDA) concluded that firm value increases in the year in which the deal is completed but declines within 3 years.[88] Using cash flow from operations, which include changes in working capital and capital outlays, shows a sustained increase in firm value relative to cash flow postclosing. Therefore the acquirer's postmerger performance deterioration could simply reflect how operating performance is measured.

Technical differences matter. Dutta and Jog (2009) do not find evidence of any systematic long-term deterioration in acquirer financial performance. They attribute findings of such deterioration to the choice of benchmarks, differing methodologies, and statistical techniques.

Although postmerger studies can compare the performance of an acquirer to their peers, they are unable to compare how well the acquirer would have done without the acquisition. Would Facebook have been able to dominate the messaging business if Google had acquired WhatsApp? Would Disney have had sufficient creative talent to dominate the movie production business had a competitor acquired Pixar? Would Google continue to show double-digit annual increases in advertising revenue if it had not acquired YouTube?

Private bidders experience greater postacquisition operating performance improvements compared to public bidders. And the number of private bidders far exceeds the number of public buyers, although the dollar value of public takeovers tends to be larger. Private bidders exhibit positive operating performance following acquisitions, whereas postmerger performance for public bidders is mostly negative. Specifically, private bidders increase their return on assets by 3% to 8% in the 3 years after the completion of the deal, but public bidders see a modest decline in their Return on Assets (ROA) of between 0% and 2%.[89]

[84] Breuer et al. (2020) in a study of 38,153 M&A deals from 54 countries from 2000 to 2015 document that acquirers with a longer-term focus outperform significantly those with a shorter-term orientation.

[85] Chen et al., 2019

[86] Bruyland et al., 2019

[87] Fich and Nguyen, 2020

[88] Bianconi et al., 2019. Enterprise value reflects both the value of equity and debt less cash holdings. The researchers conjecture that enterprise value grows faster than EBITDA because investors anticipating higher cash flow bid up share prices faster than EBITDA increases. EBITDA reflects historical depreciation and amortization expense and as such is likely to change more slowly than enterprise value. EBITDA is also a poor proxy for operating cash flow because it fails to reflect the increase in working capital and capital expenditures (both of which are deductions from cash flow) in subsequent years as the combined firm's revenues grow.

[89] Golubov and Xiong (2020) argue that managers in private firms are more likely to have a controlling (or near controlling) interest in their firms than managers in public firms. Private firm managers are more likely to pay lower takeover premiums and manage postmerger assets more efficiently by achieving greater cost control than those in public firms, which tend to engage in empire building.

Acquirer returns vary by acquirer, target, and deal characteristics

Abnormal returns to acquirer shareholders are largely situational, varying according to the size of the acquirer, the type and size of the target, the form of payment, and firm-specific characteristics (Table 1.4).

Smaller acquirers tend to realize higher M&A returns

Managers at large firms tend to overpay more than those at smaller firms because large-firm executives having been involved in more deals may be subject to hubris. In addition, incentive systems at larger firms may focus on growth rather than performance, thereby encouraging senior managers to focus on large, difficult-to-integrate takeovers. Finally, managers of large firms may pursue larger, more risky investments (e.g., unrelated acquisitions) in an attempt to support the firm's overvalued share price.

CEOs of small firms tend to own a larger percentage of the firm's outstanding shares than CEOs of larger firms. On average, whereas CEOs of small firms own 7.4% of their firm's stock, those of larger firms own on average 4.5%. Consequently, small company CEOs may be more risk-averse in negotiating M&As. Regardless of the reason, research shows that, whereas large public acquirers tend to destroy shareholder wealth, small acquirers create wealth.[90]

Acquirer returns are often positive for privately owned or subsidiary targets

US acquirers of private firms or subsidiaries of publicly traded firms often realize positive abnormal returns of 1.55% to 2.6% around the announcement date. Acquirers pay less for private firms or subsidiaries of public companies because of limited information and the limited number of bidders for such firms. Because these targets may be acquired at a discount from their true value, acquirers can realize a larger share of the combined value of the firms.[91]

Relatively small deals may generate higher returns

Acquirer announcement returns tend to be three times larger for acquisitions involving small targets than for those involving large targets.[92] High-tech firms realize attractive returns by acquiring small, but related, target firms to fill gaps in their product offerings.[93] Larger deals tend to be riskier for acquirers[94] and experience consistently lower postmerger performance, possibly reflecting the challenges of integrating large target firms and realizing projected synergies. There are exceptions: firms making large acquisitions show less negative or more positive returns in slower growing than in faster growing sectors.[95] In slow-growth industries, integration may be less disruptive than in faster-growing industries, which may experience a slower pace of new product introductions and upgrade efforts.

Form of payment impacts acquirer returns

Pre-2009, studies often found that announcement date returns to acquirer shareholders were negative when the acquirer and target are publicly traded and the form of payment consists mostly of stock. Why? Public acquirers tend to issue stock when they believe their shares are overvalued because they can issue fewer new shares, resulting in less earnings dilution.

Investors treat such decisions as signals that the stock is overvalued and sell their shares when the new equity issue is announced, causing the firm's share price to decline. Moreover, acquirers using overvalued stock tend to overpay for target firms, making it difficult to recover the premium paid by realizing synergy.[96] The combination of these factors, so the argument goes, made most stock deals unattractive for acquirer shareholders. Although

[90] Regardless of how they were financed (i.e., stock or cash) or whether they were public or private targets, acquisitions made by smaller firms had announcement returns of 1.55%, higher than a comparable acquisition made by a larger firm (Moeller et al., 2004).

[91] Moeller et al., 2004. Similar results were found in an exhaustive study of UK acquirers (Draper et al., 2006) making bids for private firms or subsidiaries of public firms, in which the positive abnormal returns were attributed to the relative illiquidity of such businesses.

[92] Vijn and Yang, 2013

[93] Frick et al., 2002

[94] Hackbarth et al., 2008; Alexandridis et al., 2011

[95] Rehm et al., 2012

[96] Fu et al., 2013

TABLE 1.4 Acquirer returns differ by characteristics of the acquirer, target, and deal

Characteristic	Empirical support
Type of target: Acquirer returns on US buyouts are often positive when the targets are privately owned (or are subsidiaries of public companies) and slightly negative when the targets are large publicly traded firms (i.e., so-called "listing effect") regardless of the country. Cross-border deals are generally positive except for those involving large public acquirers, which are often zero to negative.	Netter et al. (2011) Capron and Shen (2007) Faccio et al. (2006) Draper and Paudyal (2006) Moeller et al. (2005) Barbopoulos et al. (2013) Erel et al. (2012) Ellis et al. (2011) Chari et al. (2004) Yilmaz et al. (2016)
Form of payment: acquirer returns on Equity-financed acquisitions of large public firms often negative and less than cash-financed deals in the United States Equity-financed acquisitions of public or private firms frequently more than all-cash-financed deals in EU countries Equity-financed deals involving private firms (or subsidiaries of public firms) often exceed significantly cash deals Cross-border deals financed with equity often negative	Fu et al. (2013) Schleifer et al. (2003) Megginson et al. (2003) Netter et al. (2011) Officer et al. (2009) Chang (1998) Ellis et al. (2011) Vijh et al. (2013) Offenberg (2009)
Acquirer or target size Smaller acquirers often realize higher returns than larger acquirers. Relatively small deals often generate higher acquirer returns than larger ones. Acquirer returns may be lower when the size of the acquisition is large relative to the buyer (i.e., >30% of the buyer's market value).	Gorton et al. (2009) Moeller et al. (2005) Moeller et al. (2004) Hackbarth et al. (2008) Frick et al. (2002) Rehm et al. (2012)
Firm-specific characteristics: acquirer returns higher because of deal-making experience Postmerger integration skills Specific industry or proprietary knowledge Knowledge of target's supply chain Knowledge of target's patents	Hu et al. (2019) Golubob et al. (2015) Deboldt et al. (2019) Fich et al. (2020) Kim et al. (2020)

acquirers may be able to convince target firm shareholders to accept overvalued shares, there appears to be little evidence according to one recent study that they can do so frequently.[97]

Whereas the value of acquirer shares can be ambiguous, the value of cash is not. Acquirers using cash are less inclined to overpay because it can be more obvious to investors. Such acquirers often exhibit better long-term share price performance than do those using stock.[98] Investors interpret the use of cash as a signal that the acquirer's stock is undervalued and bid up the acquirer's share price.

Post-2009, acquirer returns, as noted previously, have improved significantly.[99] Cash deals often show positive returns and stock deals no longer destroy value. The magnitude of the decline in acquirer shares (and in turn investor wealth) in stock deals appears to be overstated. The majority of the decline in acquirer shares on the announcement date may be related more to merger arbitrage activity than to investors believing the shares are overvalued. About 60% of the sharp decline in acquirer shares on the announcement date may reflect short selling as arbitrageurs buy the target's shares and short the acquirer's.[100]

The decline in acquirer share prices in stock-financed deals is more likely with transactions in which the acquirer is subject to high rather than low investor scrutiny.[101] Because deals can be highly complex and vary depending on terms and conditions, investors may not be paying sufficient attention to the extent of the acquirer's stock

[97] Eckbo et al., 2018

[98] Akbulut, 2013

[99] Alexandridiss et al., 2017

[100] Liu and Wu, 2014; Kryzanowski et al., 2019

[101] Adra et al., 2018

overvaluation. When investor attention is low as reflected in tepid trading volume, the acquirer's share price may not decline to its true value. The acquirer's share price may continue to decline after acquisition as investors recognize the full extent of the overvaluation.

Why would target shareholders accept overvalued acquirer shares? Because in share exchanges the requirement to pay capital gains taxes is deferred until target shareholders sell their shares, the takeover may be too big for the acquirer to finance with cash, and overvaluation may not be obvious. Moreover, target firm shareholders may believe the synergy resulting from the merger is enough to offset the potential for the overvalued acquirer shares to decline.[102] Also, the acquirer shares may reduce the combined firms' leverage with the lessening of default risk reducing the overvaluation of acquirer shares.[103]

Firm-specific characteristics may outweigh deal-specific factors

Acquirer characteristics can explain to a greater extent than deal-specific factors (e.g., form and timing of payment) the variation in acquirer financial returns.[104] Although a growing literature over the past 3 decades has identified a number of determinants of acquirer performance, the overall variation in acquirer returns remains largely unexplained.

Well-managed acquirers achieve higher abnormal returns[105] and better postmerger performance when the target is related rather than unrelated.[106] Related acquirers are better able to exploit an innovative target's patents and expertise.[107] Highly active acquirers display M&A performance superior to those making fewer deals because in-house knowledge enables better deal screening, due diligence, and valuation.[108] Moreover, acquirers realize higher positive returns when they have significant growth opportunities and buy firms with poor growth prospects by diverting target resources to more attractive projects.[109]

Other factors impacting acquirer financial returns include a firm's time-tested postmerger integration process, specific industry or proprietary knowledge, and effective corporate governance.[110] In addition, firms whose management is highly familiar with a target firm's supply chain often are better able to more accurately value the target.[111] Finally, dividend paying acquirers exhibit greater discipline by buying targets more likely to contribute to free cash flow earlier than takeovers involving non-dividend paying acquirers. Why? Dividend payers require additional cash flow to sustain their dividends.[112]

Payoffs for bondholders

M&As have little impact on abnormal returns to acquirer or target bondholders except in special situations when wealth transfers between bond and stockholders occur. The limited impact on bondholder wealth is due to the relationship between leverage and operating performance.[113] How M&As affect bondholder wealth reflects, in part, the

[102] Di Guili, 2013
[103] Vermaelen and Xu, 2014
[104] Golubov et al., 2015
[105] Chen et al., 2017
[106] Cui and Leung, 2020
[107] Kim et al., 2020
[108] De Bodt et al., 2019 Hu et al., 2019
[109] Davis et al., 2017
[110] Thraya et al., 2019a
[111] Fich and Nguyen, 2020
[112] Glambosky et al., 2020
[113] Renneboog et al., 2007

extent to which an increase in leverage that raises the potential for default is offset by the discipline imposed on management to improve operating performance.[114]

M&As can impact target firm bondholders when credit quality is low, when poison puts are present, and when the target tenders for its bonds (i.e., a public offer to all bondholders to purchase their bonds at a specific price and time). M&As can also trigger a wealth transfer from bond to stockholders when financial institutions are "dual holders," takeovers are financed with cash, acquirers have large cash balances, and boards increase dividend payouts after pressure from activists. These special cases are discussed next.

Target firm bondholders, whose debt is below investment grade, experience positive abnormal returns if the acquirer has a higher credit rating.[115] Furthermore, when loan covenants for firms subject to takeover include poison puts allowing bondholders to sell their bonds to the company at a fixed price, bondholders often experience positive abnormal returns when a change of control takes place.[116]

Another special case occurs when financial institutions hold both equity and debt positions in a firm. Sometimes called "dual holders," such institutions have an incentive to accept smaller equity premiums when the value of the debt position is likely to increase by an amount greater than the equity premium. A takeover resulting in a lower debt-to-equity ratio often causes the value of the target's debt to appreciate significantly if the firm was previously viewed as highly leveraged before the takeover bid.[117]

Deals financed with cash on the balance sheet or by new borrowing can reduce the value of acquirer debt. When cash is used, less risky cash assets are substituted for more risky assets owned by the target raising default risk. When cash is obtained through new borrowing, the new debt is often senior in liquidation to existing acquirer debt, thereby increasing the default risk associated with pre-acquisition acquirer debt.[118]

The impact on acquirer bondholders can be even more pronounced when acquirers have large pre-acquisition cash balances that serve as a cushion against default. Why? Large cash balances tend to encourage value-destroying takeovers because management tends to overpay in the presence of such balances.[119] Finally, target bondholder returns decline when activists initiate an action to force the firm's board to increase cash dividends. The increase reduces cash available to make interest and principal repayments.[120]

Payoffs for society

M&As promote economic growth by introducing dynamic change, productivity improvement,[121] and innovation.[122] M&As create value for society when we sum abnormal financial returns to acquiring and target firm shareholders. Value is created by M&As when more efficient firms acquire less efficient ones. Even greater value is created when risk-taking bidders with limited investment opportunities acquire risk-averse targets with attractive growth opportunities and redeploy the assets to more productive uses.[123]

Empirical studies show that M&As result in improved productivity and lower product prices than would have been the case without the deal.[124] Why? After a takeover, acquirers have a strong incentive to increase the target's

[114] The empirical evidence is ambiguous. A study by Billett et al. (2004) shows slightly negative abnormal returns to acquirer bondholders regardless of the acquirer's bond rating. However, they also find that target firm holders of below-investment-grade bonds earn average excess returns of 4.3% or higher around the merger announcement date, when the target firm's credit rating is less than the acquirer's and when the merger is expected to decrease the target's risk or leverage. A study of European deals finds positive returns to acquirer bondholders of 0.56% around the announcement date of the deal (Renneboog et al., 2006).

[115] Chen et al., 2020

[116] Billett et al., 2010

[117] Bodnaruk et al., 2016

[118] Li, 2018

[119] Poldolski et al., 2016

[120] Jory et al., 2017

[121] Arocena et al., 2020

[122] Fang et al., 2019

[123] Hegde et al., 2017

[124] Arocena et al.; 2020; J. Xu, 2017

operating efficiency to recover any premium paid. Society benefits as a result of the additional output and employment, as well as wages and salaries in the long run that would not have been realized otherwise.

If employment levels are reduced in the short run because of takeovers, economic theory predicts higher wages and salaries owing to improved worker productivity. Over time employment levels rise in line with increasing firm output. The combination of increasing employment and wages in the long run boosts societal aggregate income and wealth. But the differences between theory and reality can be stark. M&As can result in short-term job loss. Communities can be ravaged as plants are shuttered or moved elsewhere. The projected long-term increase in aggregate income ignores the income redistribution from less to more productive workers and the potential for social discord. In view of these impacts, where should the firm's responsibilities lie? This question is addressed next.

M&As and corporate socially responsible investing

Socially responsible firms are those that recognize their obligation to society as well as to the firm. The discussion of corporate socially responsible (CSR) investing has coalesced around two schools of thought. The "shareholder view" argues that a firm's only social responsibility is to maximize shareholder value that benefits customers by providing products they desire, employees with higher wages, and communities with more jobs and tax revenue. And profits earned provide money to make corporate socially responsible investments. The "stakeholder view" suggests that CSR activities ranging from corporate philanthropy to ethical behavior to being a good steward of the environment contribute to firm profitability.[125]

The two views are not inconsistent! To maximize shareholder value, firms must consider the interests of *all* stakeholders. In addition to those previously mentioned, firms must repay lenders, operate in a legal and ethical way, and enable suppliers to earn returns needed to remain solvent. Every year thousands of firms are forced into bankruptcy or merged with other firms because they failed to achieve the right balance among stakeholder interests.

Corporate socially responsible investing and value creation

Recent evidence on the impact CSR investment (including M&As) has on firm profitability and value is mixed, ranging from negative to positive under certain circumstances.[126] Recognizing that firms create jobs, income, and tax revenue, CSR advocates posit that CSR outlays can contribute to firm value by promoting a firm's brand,[127] attracting workers who share the firm's corporate values,[128] and attracting socially conscious investors.

But conflicts may emerge when firms try to balance maximizing shareholder value and CSR investing.[129] Conflicts between shareholders and managers arise as some CSR expenditures are wasteful and degrade shareholder wealth, as they are intended to obtain support from other stakeholder groups in management's effort to improve their compensation. However, agency conflicts can be lessened if firms spending more on CSR-related projects are able to pay sufficient dividends to satisfy their shareholders.[130] Firms with well-connected board members often are

[125] Ni (2020) argues that the broader stakeholder view instills more ethical business practices and reduces the likelihood that managers will manipulate earnings to limit the board's ability to monitor their activities.

[126] Noting a lack of consensus, Lin et al. (2019) document a negative correlation between "socially responsible" firms and financial performance. They argue such firms are less focused on profitability, which contributes to subpar financial performance and reduces their ability to make future CSR investments. Glozer and Morsing (2020) discuss how firms' CSR marketing literature often is inconsistent with their actions. Franco et al. (2020) argue that CSR spending improves performance only if it establishes significant relationships between firms and their stakeholders. Globner (2019) and Chen et al. (2019a) conclude that CSR spending is in the best interests of long-term shareholders when block shareholders monitor such spending to mitigate agency conflicts. Ting (2020) concludes that CSR spending improves the performance of larger but not smaller firms. Guidi et al. (2020) document less favorable announcement date returns when so-called "sin" firms are acquired (compared with "non-sin" takeovers), although the reaction varies by country and culture.

[127] Bardos et al., 2020

[128] Sheikh, 2018

[129] Abeysekera et al. (2019) show that family-owned firms are more inclined to avoid CSR investing than non—family-owned companies because of the family's concentration of wealth in the firm.

[130] Benlemlih, 2019

better able to resolve such conflicts because they have access to information about what is working at other firms engaging in CSR spending.[131]

Firms subject to public controversy may engage in symbolic rather than substantive CSR spending to improve their public image, as such spending represents a low-cost way of enhancing public image and can be implemented rapidly (e.g., charitable giving). And symbolic CSR spending is often greeted favorably by shareholders because it deflects from controversy.[132] Similarly, overconfident CEOs may use CSR spending to improve their public image after having completed an underperforming acquisition.[133]

The attributes of CSR firms often are hard to quantify because they relate to such intangibles as a firm's reputation and culture. Consequently, CSR ratings (analogous to credit ratings) have been developed to evaluate a firm's performance in terms of its social, ethical, and environmental behavior. [134] Such ratings appear to have an impact on M&A activities.

Deal completion rates, premiums, postmerger performance, and borrowing costs

CSR spending to resolve environmental issues may improve acquirer reputations and raise deal completion rates because they are more likely to get community support and regulatory approval.[135] Also, bidders often pay higher purchase premiums for targets with high CSR ratings, which provide a summary measure of the target's corporate culture and reputation as perceived by others. This can be important in understanding cultural compatibility and in conducting initial due diligence.[136] And postmerger performance is higher when the target's CSR spending was greater than the acquirer's before the takeover, perhaps reflecting more effective postmerger governance and culture.[137] Finally, "socially irresponsible" targets receive lower takeover premiums, especially when it is widely reported in the media.[138]

Although CSR ratings have both a social and environmental dimension, the former seems to be more valued in cross-border deals. Such deals tend to be more complex than domestic deals because they involve different cultures, legal systems, and governance practices. CSR ratings provide a measure of how reliable the target's historical financial statements are likely to be and the extent to which the target's board and management has engaged in ethical behavior.[139]

There also is evidence that CSR can help offset the negative impact (i.e., higher borrowing costs and bankruptcy potential) of high leverage on firm performance. Why? Customers who otherwise would be reluctant to buy from a highly leveraged firm because of the potential for deteriorating customer service, on-time delivery, and product quality are willing to buy from firms they view as socially responsible. Moreover because high-CSR firms are able to raise prices, they often exhibit more stable cash flows and thus are better able to withstand price-cutting by competitors.[140] Therefore high-CSR acquirers may be able to increase leverage at lower overall borrowing costs than they would have otherwise.[141]

[131] Amin et al., 2020

[132] Li et al., 2019

[133] Gul et al., 2020

[134] Reputation Institute provides CSR scores for firms by tracking consumers' perceptions of company governance, positive influence on society, and treatment of employees.

[135] Arouri et al., 2019

[136] Gomes, 2019; Krishnamurti et al., 2020

[137] Tampakoudis and Anagnostopoulou, 2020

[138] Maung et al., 2020

[139] Gomes and Marsat, 2019. Boubaker et al. (2020) find evidence that high CSR firms are less likely to experience financial distress.

[140] Bae et al., 2019

[141] Sheikh (2019) argues that CSR spending often is reduced in highly leveraged firms in highly competitive markets because they are under pressure to invest more in investments perceived to more likely increase firm value.

Local and international considerations

What is considered appropriate socially responsible investing and the impetus for such spending differs from one country (or local community) to another. CSR investments need not replicate what is already provided in countries (or communities) with broad social safety nets. When voids exist in areas such as health care and education, CSR investments need to be customized to meet local or country-specific stakeholder needs. There appears to be a causal link between firms with high institutional ownership and spending on environmental and socially responsible investment. And the extent to which institutional investors drive such investment tends to be greatest in countries that view CSR spending as important.[142]

The implications of the Biden administration for M&As

The administration could have a far-reaching impact on domestic and international M&As through its tax policies, reintroduction of regulations cut by the Trump administration, expanded regulation of the health care and energy industries, and changes to foreign policy. Restoring US participation in the Paris climate accord and a revival of the Iran nuclear deal will be high on the agenda, but policies toward China are less likely to change.

The Biden tax plan targets both individuals and corporations by either eliminating tax benefits or implementing new tax liabilities. Higher corporate and capital gains taxes will reduce target firm valuations and financial returns by reducing cash flow and profits. When combined with state taxes, the Biden tax hikes would push the United States back toward the high end of industrialized countries' corporate rates, making it harder for US firms to compete with foreign rivals based in countries with lower tax rates. Some US firms could reincorporate abroad. Labor costs will rise because of expanded labor protections, mandated paid time off, and higher minimum wages. A move to convert independent contractors to employees could negatively impact small businesses relying on outside contractors.

Industries benefitting from the Biden administration include renewable energy as recipients of higher government subsidies; trains and buses, reflecting greater interest in public transportation; and electric vehicles to curb carbon emissions. Expansion of Obamacare should help insurers and hospitals, which stand to receive billions of dollars in subsidies. Drug makers would be hurt by having to negotiate drug prices with Medicare and by price controls. Other industry losers include major carbon emitters, such as coal, oil and natural gas, and airline travel. Large-cap technology and health care companies will face heightened antitrust scrutiny. Increased carbon taxes, limits on drilling both offshore and on federal land, and incentives for using renewable energy could threaten the oil giants and drive more mergers or asset sales.

Some things to remember

M&As represent only one way of executing business plans. Alternatives include "go it alone" strategies and the various forms of business alliances. Which method is chosen depends on management's desire for control, willingness to accept risk, and the range of opportunities present at a particular moment in time. M&As generally reward significantly target shareholders and, to a lesser extent, acquirer shareholders, with some exceptions. M&As also tend to improve productivity and societal wealth in the long run but can be highly disruptive in the short term. The traditional view that the objective of each firm is to maximize shareholder value is consistent with the view that firms must address the needs of all stakeholders. Why? To maximize shareholder value, firms cannot ignore the long-term interests of any major stakeholder group. To do so invites failure.

Chapter discussion questions

1.1 Discuss why mergers and acquisitions occur.
1.2 What is the role of the investment banker in the M&A process?
1.3 In your judgment, what are the motivations for two M&As currently in the news?

[142] Park et al., 2019

1.4 What are the arguments for and against corporate diversification through acquisition? Which do you support and why?

1.5 What are the primary differences between operating synergy and financial synergy?

1.6 At a time when natural gas and oil prices were at record levels, oil and natural gas producer Andarko Petroleum announced the acquisition of two competitors, Kerr-McGee Corp. and Western Gas Resources, for $16.4 billion and $4.7 billion in cash, respectively. The acquired assets complemented Andarko's operations, providing the scale and focus necessary to cut overlapping expenses and concentrate resources in adjacent properties. What do you believe were the primary forces driving Andarko's acquisition? How will greater scale and focus help Andarko cut costs? What are the assumptions implicit in your answer to the first question?

1.7 Mattel, a major US toy manufacturer, virtually gave away The Learning Company (TLC), a maker of software for toys, to rid itself of a disastrous acquisition. Mattel, which had paid $3.5 billion for TLC, sold the unit to an affiliate of Gores Technology Group for rights to a share of future profits. Was this a related or unrelated diversification for Mattel? Explain your answer.

1.8 AOL acquired Time Warner in a deal valued at $160 billion. Time Warner was at the time the world's largest media company, whose major business segments included cable networks, magazine publishing, book publishing, direct marketing, recorded music and music publishing, and film and TV production and broadcasting. AOL viewed itself as the world leader in providing interactive services, web brands, internet technologies, and electronic commerce services. Would you classify this business combination as a vertical, horizontal, or conglomerate transaction?

1.9 Pfizer, a leading pharmaceutical company, acquired drug maker Pharmacia for $60 billion, betting that size is what mattered in the new millennium. Pfizer was finding it difficult to sustain the double-digit earnings growth demanded by investors, caused by the skyrocketing costs of developing and commercializing new drugs. Expiring patents on a number of so-called blockbuster drugs intensified pressure to bring new drugs to market. In your judgment, what were the primary motivations for Pfizer's desire to acquire Pharmacia? Categorize these in terms of the primary motivations for M&As discussed in this chapter.

1.10 Dow Chemical, a leading chemical manufacturer, acquired Rohm and Haas Company, a maker of paints, coatings, and electronic materials, for $15.3 billion. Although Dow has competed profitably in the plastics business for years, this business has proved to have thin margins and to be highly cyclical. Because of the deal, Dow would be able to offer less cyclical and higher-margin products. Would you consider this related or unrelated diversification? Explain your answer. Would you consider this a cost-effective way for the Dow shareholders to achieve better diversification of their investment portfolios?

Answers to these Chapter Discussion Questions are available in the Online Instructor's Manual for instructors using this book.

End-of-chapter case study: Occidental petroleum outbids Chevron in high-stakes energy deal

Case study objectives

To illustrate how

Being the first bidder does not ensure a successful takeover of a target firm.
Disciplined bidders often do not participate in bidding contests for target firms.
The target may not view the highest bid as the best bid.
The way in which a deal is financed is sometimes a tactic to avoid shareholder votes.

The profit performance of firms engaged in shale oil and gas production has suffered in recent years. New wells, in some instances, are producing less than older ones. Therefore investors are pressuring firms to slow the pace of investment in new wells and to return more cash to shareholders through buybacks and higher dividends.

Before the onset of the 2020 global pandemic, larger energy firms with access to greater financial resources showed interest in shale oil and gas extraction in areas such as the Permian Basin of Texas and New Mexico. The huge shale oil and gas deposits in the Permian Basin are capable of producing for decades as a result of lower-cost fracking technology. As a result of the growth of oil output in this region, US daily production rose to 12 million barrels, more than that of Russia and Saudi Arabia.

Against this backdrop, mega energy company Chevron Corp (Chevron) announced that it had reached an agreement to buy Anadarko Petroleum Corp (Anadarko) on April 12, 2019, in a cash and stock deal valued at $33 billion. Immediately after Chevron's announced deal with Anadarko, Occidental Petroleum Corp (Occidental) blasted publicly Anadarko's board for reaching a deal with Chevron without seeking other bids.

Seizing the moment, Occidental made a counteroffer less than 2 weeks later valued at $38 billion, split 50/50 between cash and stock. The Occidental bid pitted it against Chevron, a firm four times its size. Even though the Occidental bid was superior on paper, Anadarko favored the deal with Chevron. Questions swirled around the Occidental proposal. Would Occidental's shareholders approve such a pricy deal that was predicated on continued high oil prices? Could the already highly leveraged firm finance the cash component of its offer?

There was ample reason for Anadarko's board to be concerned about Occidental's bid. And Occidental shareholders expressed concern that the firm was indeed paying too much and that the firm would not be able to achieve its cost of capital on the investment. This opposition was manifest in Occidental's annual shareholder meeting when the board was reelected with less than 70% of the votes cast as opposed to the normal 95%.

The diminished support was viewed as a protest against the firm's decision to avoid a shareholder vote. Investors were skeptical that Occidental could integrate successfully a much larger firm. Moody's Investors Service estimated that the assumption of Anadarko's debt and additional borrowings to cover the offer would add almost $40 billion in new debt to Occidental. Moody's put the company's debt rating under review for downgrade.

Occidental addressed the first concern by submitting a revised offer consisting of 78% cash and 22% stock. Under the new offer, each Anadarko shareholder would receive $59 in cash and 0.2934 share of Occidental stock per each share they held. This compared to the initial bid consisting of $38 in cash and 0.6094 share of Occidental common. The new offer entailed far less equity and did not require approval by Occidental shareholders.[143]

To address the second issue, Occidental secured a $10 billion investment from Berkshire Hathaway's Warren Buffett consisting of 100,000 shares of Occidental preferred stock, paying an 8% annual dividend and a warrant[144] to purchase $5 billion in Occidental common stock. In addition, Occidental negotiated an agreement with French oil firm Total SA (Total) to acquire all of its non-US assets for $8.5 billion, including its US Gulf of Mexico offshore wells and reserves as well as its liquefied natural gas project in Mozambique.

Under pressure from its shareholders to accept the bid after these two issues had been resolved, Anadarko brushed aside Chevron's $65 per share cash and stock bid, accepting Occidental's revised $76 per share offer. Anadarko's board secured Occidental's position as the largest shale oil and gas producer in the Permian Basin.

Recognizing that there were other attractive targets in the Permian, Chevron's board reasoned that if it paid too much it would be difficult to earn the financial returns its investors required. In withdrawing its bid, Chevron collected a $1 billion termination fee it had negotiated as part of its earlier deal with Anadarko and promised to return the cash to its shareholders through share buybacks and dividend increases.

On May 4, 2019, the day Anadarko announced it had accepted Occidental's revised bid, its shares jumped 11.6% to close at $71.40, well above the $65 per share offered by Chevron. Investors punished Occidental by driving its shares down by 6.4% to $62 while rewarding Chevron for its discipline by boosting its share by 3.1% to $118.28 per share.

What made Anadarko so valuable to Occidental and Chevron? Chevron needs to replenish its dwindling oil and gas reserves. Anadarko seemed to satisfy that need. In recent years, Chevron had displayed remarkable restraint in managing its spending on oil and gas exploration, preferring to return cash to shareholders through share buybacks and dividends. Anadarko was attractive to Chevron because of its large position in the Permian Basin, the overlap between the two firms' deep-water operations in the Gulf of Mexico, and its liquid natural gas project in southern Africa. The takeover of Anadarko would also have allowed Chevron to achieve substantial economies of scale in the Permian Basin.

Occidental's interest in Anadarko represented a big bet on the future of shale oil and gas and that energy prices would remain high long enough for the firm to recoup its investment. A deal would add nearly a quarter million

[143] State statutes usually require shareholder approval by both the bidder and target firms in a merger. However, no acquirer shareholder vote is required if the form of payment is cash, the authorized number of new acquirer shares issued is less than 20% of the firm's outstanding shares, or the number of shares previously is sufficient to complete the deal. Public stock exchanges require acquirer shareholder approval if the number of new shares issued exceeds 20% of the acquirer's outstanding shares.

[144] Similar to options, warrants grant holders the right but not the obligation to buy (or sell) a security at a certain price before they expire. Unlike options that are issued by third parties, warrants are issued by a company. And unlike options that are based on the value of existing shares, warrants are dilutive to shareholders because they involve the issuance of new shares when they are converted into common shares.

acres to Occidental's holdings in the lucrative Permian shale basin, double its global production to 1.4 million barrels of oil and gas per day, and enable access to shale fields in Colorado and Wyoming. Occidental's interest in the deal is that it will be positioned to reduce costs significantly and expand its footprint in the booming Permian Basin, an area where it is already one of the largest operators. The deal would allow Occidental to achieve substantial operating savings in the region. However, the plunge in oil prices and the global recession in 2020 raise serious doubts about Occidental's ability to support its increased leverage due to the takeover.

Discussion questions

1. Is the highest bid necessarily the best bid? Explain your answer.
2. Speculate as to why Chevron did not increase its initial offer price after Occidental's initial bid. Revised bid?
3. When, if ever, is it appropriate for a board to prevent shareholder votes on matters involved in selling a firm?
4. What were the motivations for Chevron and Occidental to be interested in acquiring Anadarko? Be specific. What were the key assumptions implicit in both firms' efforts to take control of Anadarko?
5. What does the reaction of investors tell you about how they felt about Occidental's takeover of Anadarko? Be specific.

Answers to these questions are found in the Online Instructor's Manual available to instructors using this book.

CHAPTER

2

The regulatory environment

OUTLINE

Mergers, Acquisitions, and Other Restructuring Activities, Eleventh Edition
https://doi.org/10.1016/B978-0-12-819782-0.00002-2

I am not a product of my circumstances. I am a product of my decisions. —***Stephen Covey***

Inside mergers and acquisitions: AT&T's merger with Time Warner withstands regulatory scrutiny

KEY POINTS

- To illustrate how regulators and the courts see horizontal and vertical mergers in a wholly different context and
- To illustrate how vertical mergers between distributors and content providers can potentially increase competition rather than stifle it.

The US Department of Justice (DOJ) lost its court appeal in 2019 as it attempted to upend the $85.4 billion merger between AT&T and Time Warner, with the court ruling the bid legal and imposing no restrictions. The case has implications for vertical takeovers common among tech and telecom firms. Unlike those between direct competitors, vertical mergers involve firms at different stages of the supply chain. The merger allows AT&T, one of the largest internet, cable, and wireless providers in the United States, to become a major content provider. As a wholly owned AT&T subsidiary, Time Warner was renamed WarnerMedia, a video-streaming giant whose content includes HBO shows, Cartoon Network, and major box office hits.

The DOJ argued AT&T could use access to HBO or CNN to convince consumers to leave their current broadband providers. It could also charge other cable providers more to access those channels, or it could simply stop carrying competitor content. The appeals court noted that Netflix and Hulu allow consumers a range of alternatives to WarnerMedia. The court saw Time Warner and AT&T in businesses that did not compete: whereas one owns distribution, the other owns content carried via the distributor.

By ruling in favor of the merger between AT&T and Time Warner, the DC Circuit Court of Appeals rejected the government's contention that the merger would increase excessively AT&T's bargaining leverage over content providers and therefore violate antitrust law. With the merger, the court reasoned that consumers have more freedom to choose, not less. If AT&T did leave Time Warner subscribers with fewer channels and higher prices, they could cancel their subscriptions and switch to other providers. Interestingly, AT&T became disenchanted with the performance of its media businesses, spinning off and merging WarnerMedia with Discovery Inc. in mid-2021.

Chapter overview

Which deals are likely to require regulatory approval? What criteria will regulators use to review proposed transactions? How are regulatory concerns often resolved? These questions and many others are addressed by focusing on the key elements of the regulatory process and its implications for mergers and acquisitions (M&As). In addition to antitrust and securities laws, the labyrinth of environmental, labor, benefit, and foreign laws that affect M&As is also discussed. Table 2.1 provides a summary of applicable legislation and specific regulations discussed in this chapter. A chapter review is available (including practice questions and answers) in the file folder titled Student Study Guide contained on the companion site to this book (https://www.elsevier.com/books-and-journals/book-companion/9780128197820).

Understanding federal securities laws

When the acquirer or target has publicly traded securities, the firms are subject to federal securities laws.[1] Passed in the 1930s, these laws reflected the loss of confidence in the securities markets following the 1929 stock market crash.

Securities Act of 1933

This legislation requires that securities offered to the public be registered with the government to protect investors by making issuers disclose all material facts regarding the security issue. Registration requires that the facts represented in the registration statement and prospectuses are accurate. The law makes providing inaccurate or misleading statements in the sale of securities to the public subject to a fine, imprisonment, or both.

Securities Exchange Act of 1934

This Act extended disclosure requirements to include securities already trading on the national exchanges and established the Securities and Exchange Commission (SEC). The SEC is intended to protect investors from fraud by requiring accurate financial disclosure by firms offering stocks, bonds, and other securities to the public. In 1964, coverage was expanded to include securities traded on the Over-the-Counter (OTC) Market. The Act covers proxy solicitations by a firm or shareholders. The 2010 Dodd-Frank Act strengthened SEC enforcement powers by allowing the SEC to impose financial penalties against any person rather than just entities. Companies and individuals are informed by the SEC when investigations uncovering violations have been completed in a letter (so-called Wells Notices) outlining the violations and impending enforcement actions.

Reporting requirements

Companies having to file periodic reports with the SEC are those for which any of the following are true: the firm has assets of more than $10 million and whose securities are held by more than 499 shareholders, it is listed on any of the major US or international stock exchanges, or its shares are quoted on the OTC Bulletin Board. Even if both parties to a transaction are privately owned, an M&A transaction is subject to federal securities laws if a portion of the purchase price is going to be financed by an initial public offering of securities.

Section 13: periodic reports

Form 10K documents the firm's financial activities during the prior year and includes the income statement, the balance sheet, the statement of retained earnings, and the statement of cash flows. Form 10K also includes a relatively detailed description of the business, the markets served, major events and their impact on the business, key competitors, and competitive market conditions. Form 10Q is a succinct quarterly update of such information.

An 8K is a public declaration of material events to shareholders or the SEC. If an acquisition or divestiture is deemed significant,[2] an 8K must be submitted to the SEC within 15 days of the event. Form 8K describes the assets acquired or disposed, the type and amount of payment, and the identity of those for whom the assets

[1] Note that a private company can be subject to the same reporting requirements if it merges with a public shell company in a reverse merger in which the private company becomes a publicly traded entity.

[2] Acquisitions and divestitures are usually deemed significant if the equity interest in the acquired assets or the amount paid or received exceeds 10% of the total book value of the assets of the registrant and its subsidiaries.

TABLE 2.1 Laws Affecting Mergers and Acquisitions

Law	Intent
Federal Securities Laws	
Securities Act (1933)	Prevents the public offering of securities without a registration statement; defines minimum data reporting requirements and noncompliance penalties
• Regulation D	Rules pertaining to exemptions from registration requirements
• Regulation FD	All material disclosures of nonpublic information made by public firms must be disclosed to the general public
• Regulation CF	Rules pertaining to equity crowdfunding
Securities Exchange Act (1934)	Established the Securities and Exchange Commission (SEC) to regulate securities trading; empowers the SEC to revoke the registration of a security if the issuer violates any provision of the act
• Section 13	Defines content and frequency of SEC filings as well as events triggering them
• Section 14	Defines disclosure requirements for proxy solicitation
• Section 16(a)	Defines what insider trading is and who is an insider
• Section 16(b)	Defines investor rights with respect to insider trading
Williams Act (1968)	Regulates tender offers
• Section 13D	Defines disclosure requirements
Sarbanes–Oxley Act (2002)	Reforms regulations governing disclosure, governance, auditing, analyst reports, and insider trading
Jumpstart Our Business Startups Act (JOBS Act) (2012)	Intended to reduce reporting requirements for so-called "emerging companies"
Federal Antitrust Laws	
Sherman Act (1890)	Made "restraint of trade" illegal; establishes criminal penalties for anticompetitive behaviors
• Section 1	Makes mergers creating monopolies illegal
• Section 2	Applies to firms dominant in their served markets to prevent them from "unfairly" restraining trade
Clayton Act (1914)	Outlawed such practices as price discrimination, exclusive contracts, and tie-in contracts; created civil penalties for illegally restraining trade
Celler–Kefauver Act of 1950	Amended the Clayton Act to cover asset as well as stock purchases
Federal Trade Commission Act (1914)	Established a federal antitrust enforcement agency; made it illegal to engage in deceptive business practices
Hart–Scott–Rodino Antitrust Improvement Act (1976)	Requires a waiting period before a transaction can be completed and sets regulatory data submission requirements
• Title I	Defines what must be filed
• Title II	Defines who must file and when
• Title III	Enables state attorneys general to file triple damage suits on behalf of injured parties
Other Legislation Affecting M&As	
Dodd-Frank Wall Street Reform and Consumer Protection Act (2010)	Reforms executive pay; introduces new hedge/private equity fund SEC registration requirements; increases Federal Reserve and SEC authority; gives the government authority to liquidate systemically risky firms; enables government regulation of consumer financial products; and makes it illegal for federal employees and regulators to engage in insider trading. Limits bank security trading under the "Volcker rule"
Revisions to Dodd-Frank Act in 2018	Increased the asset threshold from $50 billion to $250 billion for banks to be declared "systemically risky." Banks with assets less than $10 billion not subject to the "Volcker rule"
Revisions to Dodd-Frank Act in 2019	The types of security trades subject to regulatory review was narrowed substantially

TABLE 2.1 Laws Affecting Mergers and Acquisitions—cont'd

Law	Intent
State antitakeover laws	Define conditions under which a change in corporate ownership can take place; may differ by state
State antitrust laws	Similar to federal antitrust laws; states may sue to block mergers, even those not challenged by federal regulators
Exon-Florio Amendment to the Defense Protection Act of 1950	Establishes Committee on Foreign Investment in the United States (CFIUS) to review the impact of foreign direct investment (including M&As) on national security
Foreign Investment National Security Act of 2007	CFIUS review powers expanded to include cross-border deals in energy, technology, shipping, and transportation
Foreign Investment Risk Review Modernization Act of 2018	CFIUS powers amended to include review of noncontrolling interests in "critical technologies"
US Foreign Corrupt Practices Act	Prohibits payments to foreign officials in exchange for new business or retaining existing contracts
Holding Foreign Companies Accountable Act	Prevents foreign firms listing on public exchanges if they fail to meet US audit standards
Industry-specific regulations	Banking, communications, railroads, defense, insurance, and public utilities
Environmental laws (federal and state)	Define disclosure requirements
Labor and benefit laws (federal and state)	Define disclosure requirements
Applicable foreign laws	Cross-border deals subject to jurisdictions of countries in which the bidder and target firms have operations

were acquired. Form 8K also must identify who is financing the purchase and the financial statements of the acquired business.

Section 14: proxy solicitations

When proxy contests involve corporate control, the act requires that materials contain the names and interests of all participants to be filed with the SEC in advance of voting. If the deal involves either acquirer or target shareholder approval, any materials distributed to shareholders must conform to the SEC rules for proxy materials.

Insider trading regulations

Insider trading involves individuals who buy or sell securities based on knowledge not publicly available. "Insiders" are corporate officers, directors, and any other person having access to material nonpublic information about a firm's securities. Inside information is useful in predicting future financial returns on a firm's stock.[3] And director trading conveys valuable information about the quality of subsequent acquisitions.[4] To blunt the usefulness of such information, the Sarbanes–Oxley Act (SOA) of 2002 requires insiders to disclose changes in ownership within 2 business days of the transaction. The SEC is required to post the filing on the internet within 1 business day after the filing is received.

The SEC is responsible for investigating insider trading. Individuals found guilty of engaging in such trading may be subject to penalties and forfeiture of any profits. In 2010, the Dodd-Frank Act granted the Commodity Futures Trading Commission authority to investigate insider trading in commodities used in interstate commerce and made it illegal for federal employees to engage in insider trading. The Act also allows the SEC to compensate those providing information on insider trading activities (so-called whistleblowers) up to 30% of the damages assessed in the successful prosecution of insider trading cases.

[3] Drobetz et al., 2020

[4] Hossain et al., 2019

The effectiveness of insider trading legislation is limited by the difficulty in defining what it is. Although the rate at which insiders buy target firm shares slows before takeover announcements, they reduce the pace at which they sell shares by even more, causing holdings to increase.[5] Even the tone of a spin-off prospectus can enable insiders to buy more shares at a lower price if it conceals the true upside potential known only to insiders.[6]

To limit litigation, firms restrict when insiders can trade in the firm's securities. Corporate policies specify certain time periods when insiders can trade their stock. During these *blackout periods*, insiders cannot trade their shares without corporate approval. Nevertheless, employees engaging in insider trading find ways to avoid these restrictions.

On December 7, 2016, the US Supreme Court ruled that prosecutors in insider trading cases do not always have to show that money or something of value changed hands. The Supreme Court concluded that offering information to a relative is the same as trading on the information by the tipster followed by a gift of the proceeds generated. Simply proving a tipster and trader were related was enough to initiate a lawsuit alleging insider trading.

The more difficult issues (pertaining to cases about trading among friends and professional acquaintances) were addressed in an August 22, 2017, ruling by the Second Circuit Court of Appeals. The ruling substantially broadened the application of insider trading laws, concluding that the government needs to prove only that a gift of inside information to anybody knowing they are going to trade on that information is illegal.

Jumpstart Our Business Startups Act (JOBS Act)

The 2012 JOBS Act mandated changes to Rule 506 of the SEC's Regulation D (Reg D), which governed private placement of securities exemptions, to permit both accredited and non-accredited investors to invest in private companies through licensed broker-dealers or websites registered with the SEC. The JOBS Act is intended to reduce reporting requirements for firms with less than $1 billion in annual revenue and fewer than 2000 shareholders. For qualifying firms, the SEC requires only 2 years of audited financial statements in IPO registration documents, a less detailed disclosure of executive compensation, and no requirement for SOA Section 404(b), which deals with internal controls and financial reporting.

The Williams Act: regulation of tender offers

Passed in 1968, the Williams Act consists of amendments to the Securities Act of 1934 intended to protect target shareholders from fast takeovers in which they do not have enough time to assess adequately an acquirer's offer. The Williams Act requires more disclosure by the bidding company, establishing a minimum period during which a tender offer must remain open, and authorizing targets to sue bidding firms. The disclosure requirements of the Williams Act apply to anyone, including the target, asking shareholders to accept or reject a takeover bid.

Sections 13(D) and 14(D) of the Williams Act apply to all types of tender offers: those negotiated with the target firm, those undertaken by a firm to repurchase its own stock (i.e., self-tender offers), and hostile tender offers.[7]

Sections 13(D) and 13(G): ownership disclosure requirements

Section 13(D) of the Williams Act is intended to regulate "substantial share" or large deals and provides an early warning for a target's shareholders and management of a pending bid. Any person or firm acquiring 5% or more of the stock of a public firm must file a Schedule 13(D) with the SEC within 10 days of reaching that percentage threshold. Section 13(D) also requires that derivatives, such as options, warrants, or rights convertible into shares within 60 days, must be included in determining whether the threshold has been reached.

Schedule 13(D) requires the inclusion of the identities of acquirers, their occupations, their sources of financing, and the purpose of the acquisition. If the purpose is to take control of the target firm, the acquirer must reveal its business plan. The plans could include the breakup of the firm, suspending dividends, a recapitalization of the firm, the intention to merge it with another firm, or simply the accumulation for investment purposes only.

[5] If insiders normally buy 100 shares and sell 50 shares each month, the normal increase in their holdings would be 50. However, if their purchases drop to 90 and sales to 30 each month, their holdings rise by 60 shares.

[6] Choi, 2020

[7] The courts have ruled that a tender offer is characterized by either of the following conditions: (a) a bidder announcing publicly the intent to purchase a substantial block of another firm's stock to gain control or (2) the actual purchase of a substantial portion of another firm's shares in the open market or through a privately negotiated block purchase of the firm's shares.

Under Section 13(G), any stock accumulated by related parties, such as affiliates, brokers, or investment bankers working on behalf of the person or firm, are counted toward the 5% threshold. This prevents an acquirer from avoiding filing by accumulating more than 5% of the target's stock through a series of related parties. Institutional investors, such as registered brokers and dealers, banks, and insurance companies, can file a Schedule 13(G)—a shortened version of Schedule 13(D)—if the securities were acquired in the normal course of business.

Section 14(D): rules governing the tender offer process

Although Section 14(D) of the Williams Act relates to public tender offers only, it applies to acquisitions of any size. The 5% notification threshold also applies.

- **Obligations of the acquirer.** An acquirer must disclose its intentions, business plans, and any agreements between the acquirer and the target firm in a Schedule 14(D)-1. This schedule is called a tender offer statement. The commencement date of the tender offer is defined as the date on which the tender offer is published, advertised, or submitted to the target. Schedule 14(D)-1 must contain the identity of the target company and the type of securities involved; the identity of the person, partnership, syndicate, or corporation that is filing; and any past contracts between the bidder and the target company. The schedule also must include the source of the funds used to finance the tender offer, its purpose, and any other information material to the transaction.
- **Obligations of the target firm.** The management of the target company cannot advise its shareholders how to respond to a tender offer until it has filed a Schedule 14(D)-9 with the SEC within 10 days after the tender offer's start date. This schedule is called a tender offer solicitation/recommendation statement.
- **Shareholder rights: 14(D)-4 to 14(D)-7.** The tender offer must remain open for a minimum of 20 trading days. The firm making the tender offer may get an extension of the 20-day period if it believes that there is a better chance of getting the shares it needs. The firm must purchase the shares tendered at the offer price, at least on a pro rata or proportional basis, unless the firm does not receive the total number of shares it requested under the tender offer. The tender offer also may be contingent on the approval of the DOJ and the Federal Trade Commission (FTC). The law also requires that when a new bid for the target is made from another party, the target firm's shareholders must have an additional 10 days to consider the bid.
- **The "best price" rule: 14(D)-10.** To avoid discrimination, the "best price" rule requires all shareholders holding the same class of security be paid the same price in a tender offer. If a bidder increases what it is offering to pay for the remaining target firm shares, it must pay the higher price to those who have already tendered their shares.[8]

The Sarbanes—Oxley Act of 2002

Section 302 of the SOA requires quarterly certification of financial statements and disclosure controls and procedures for CEOs and CFOs. Section 404 requires most public companies to certify annually that their internal control system is operating successfully and to report material weaknesses in internal controls to analysts when making earnings forecasts.

The legislation, in concert with new listing requirements at public stock exchanges, requires a greater number of directors on the board who do not work for the company (i.e., independent directors). The SOA also requires board audit committees to have at least one financial expert, while the full committee must review financial statements every quarter after the CEO and CFO certify them. The SOA also provides for greater transparency or visibility into a firm's financial statements and greater accountability.

Empirical studies of the SOA's effectiveness give mixed results. Monitoring costs imposed by the SOA have been a factor in many small firms' going private since the introduction of the legislation. The overall costs of corporate boards soared post-SOA because of sharply higher director compensation. However, shareholders of large, poorly governed firms that are required to overhaul their existing governance systems under the SOA may benefit as new shareholder protections are put in place.[9]

[8] Acquirers often initiate two-tiered tender offers, in which target shareholders receive a higher price if they tender their shares in the first tier than those submitting shares in the second tier. The "best price" rule requires all shareholders tendering their shares in the first tier be paid the price offered for shares in the second tier.

[9] Chourou et al., 2019

In some instances, the SOA's requirements appear to be redundant. New York Stock Exchange listing requirements far exceed SOA's auditor-independence requirements. Companies must have board audit committees consisting of at least three independent directors and a written charter describing its responsibilities in detail. Moreover, the majority of all board members must be independent, and nonmanagement directors must meet periodically without management. Board compensation and nominating committees must consist of independent directors. Shareholders must be able to vote on all stock option plans.

The SOA also created a quasi-public oversight agency, the Public Company Accounting Oversight Board (PCAOB), which registers auditors and defines and enforces compliance with SOA mandates through periodic audits. In a public rebuke of "big four" accounting firm KPMG in early 2019, PCAOB found serious deficiencies in nearly half of the more than 100 audits scrutinized during the 2016 and 2017 reviews. PCAOB audits have proved to be particularly effective in increasing data reliability in international M&A deals.[10]

Historically, the auditor's letter in an annual report has been largely a pass/fail exercise. To achieve greater disclosure, independent auditors are required as of December 15, 2020, under a new PCAOB rule to reveal "critical audit matters" they uncovered during the audit process. The new rule highlights significant audit concerns that need to be considered in investor valuation of public firms and require further investigation by potential acquirers.

Fair disclosure

On August 7, 2018, Tesla Inc. (Tesla) Chairman and CEO Elon Musk used Twitter to announce "Am considering taking Tesla private at $420 (per share). Funding secured." The firm's stock immediately soared. Did he violate US SEC rules? Not for using social media,[11] but he was sued by the SEC for violating the Fair Disclosure Rule for "false and misleading" statements that could have prevented him from running a public firm. In late 2018, Musk settled with the SEC by stepping down as chairman of Tesla for 3 years (but remaining as chief executive) and paying a fine of $20 million.

Although social media has the power to disseminate information rapidly and to validate rumors based on the "wisdom of crowds" (i.e., groups are presumed smarter than individuals), it can also promote false speculation. Merger rumors accompanied by increased tweet volume can distort price by increasing (decreasing) merger values well above (below) their true value, with the distortion persisting for as long as 8 weeks before being reversed. In fact, only about 10% to 30% of such rumors materialize.[12]

The SEC adopted Regulation FD (Fair Disclosure) on August 15, 2000, to address the selective release of information by publicly traded firms. Regulation FD requires public firms to disclose material nonpublic information given to some investors to be released to the general public. Critics warned that less information would be provided by managers concerned about litigation. In fact, there has been an increase in voluntary disclosure.[13]

Understanding antitrust (competition) legislation

Known as competition laws in many countries, federal antitrust laws exist to prevent corporations from assuming so much market power that they can limit their output and raise prices. The DOJ and FTC have the primary responsibility for enforcing federal antitrust laws. The challenge for regulators is to apply laws in ways to discourage monopolistic practices without reducing gains in operational efficiency that may accompany M&As. Although national laws usually do not affect firms outside their domestic political boundaries, there are two exceptions: antitrust laws and laws applying to bribing foreign government officials.

[10] Kim et al., 2020

[11] Known as the Reed Hastings Rule, the SEC determined using social media as a means of disclosing material information appropriate as long as investors are alerted and access is not restricted.

[12] Jia et al., 2020

[13] Albring et al., 2020

The Sherman Act

Passed in 1890, the Sherman Act makes illegal all contracts, combinations, and conspiracies that restrain trade "unreasonably." Examples include agreements to fix prices, rig bids, allocate customers among competitors, or monopolize any part of interstate commerce. Section I of the Sherman Act prohibits new business combinations resulting in monopolies or in a significant concentration of pricing power in a single firm. Section II applies to firms that already are dominant in their targeted markets. The act applies to all transactions and businesses involved in interstate commerce or, if the activities are local, all transactions and business "affecting" interstate commerce. Most states have comparable statutes.

The Clayton Act

Passed in 1914, the Clayton Act was created to outlaw certain practices not prohibited by the Sherman Act and to help government stop a monopoly before it developed. Section 5 of the act made price discrimination between customers illegal unless it could be justified by cost savings associated with bulk purchases. Tying of contracts—in which a firm refuses to sell certain important products to a customer unless the customer agrees to buy other products from the firm—also was prohibited. Section 7 prohibits one company from buying the stock of another company if their combination results in reduced competition. Interlocking directorates also were made illegal when the directors were on the boards of competing firms.

Unlike the Sherman Act, the Clayton Act is a civil statute. The Clayton Act allows private parties that were injured by an antitrust violation to sue in federal court for three times their actual damages to encourage private lawsuits. Such lawsuits augment public antitrust law enforcement resources. If the plaintiff wins, the costs are borne by the party that violated the prevailing antitrust law in addition to the criminal penalties imposed under the Sherman Act.

Acquirers soon learned how to circumvent the original statutes of the Clayton Act of 1914, which applied to the purchase of stock. They simply would acquire the assets, rather than the stock, of a target firm. Under the Celler–Kefauver Act of 1950, the Clayton Act was amended to give the FTC the power to prohibit asset as well as stock purchases.

The Federal Trade Commission Act of 1914

This act created the FTC, consisting of five full-time commissioners appointed by the president for a 7-year term. The commissioners have a support staff of economists, lawyers, and accountants to assist in the enforcement of antitrust laws.

The Hart–Scott–Rodino Antitrust Improvements Act of 1976

Acquisitions involving companies of a specific size cannot be completed until certain information is supplied to the federal government and a specified waiting period has elapsed. The premerger notification allows the FTC and the DOJ time to challenge acquisitions believed to be anticompetitive before they are completed.

Figure 2.1 illustrates the premerger notification and review process. In step 1, parties to a deal meeting certain size requirements file with both the FTC and DOJ but only one agency conducts the review. In step 2, deals are assigned to the agency having more expertise with the industry involved and resources available to conduct the review. The

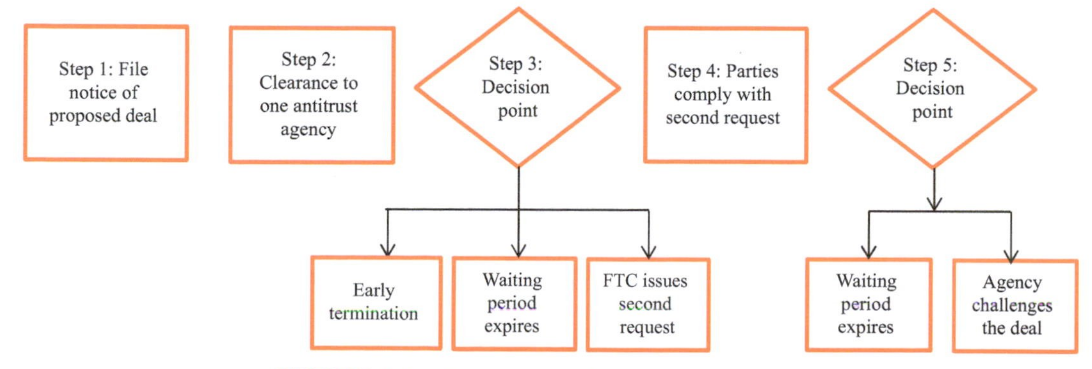

FIGURE 2.1 **The prenotification and review process.**

agency must decide in step 3 to issue an "early termination" of the waiting period or allow the waiting period to elapse, in either case allowing the deal to close. If the agency requests more information in a "second request," the parties are allowed additional time to comply (step 4).

Upon receiving additional data, the agency must decide to challenge the deal by filing a preliminary injunction in federal court pending an administrative trial or if not to simply let the waiting period expire. Although a challenge stops the deal from closing, it may still be approved if the filing parties make changes to the proposed merger acceptable to regulators.

Failing to get approval can be costly: termination fees paid to target shareholders if required by the contract, use of company resources during due diligence, legal and consulting fees, management distraction, and so on. One study finds that the failure to get antitrust regulatory approval results in a reduction in acquirer shareholder value of about 2.8%. Lobbying before deal announcements to take advantage of political connections makes sense, and such efforts are frequently associated with more favorable review outcomes, especially in horizontal deals.[14] Table 2.2 provides a summary of 2020 prenotification filing requirements.

TABLE 2.2 Regulatory Prenotification Filing Requirements Effective February 27, 2020

	Williams Act	Hart–Scott–Rodino Act
Required filing	Schedule 13(D) within 10 days of acquiring 5% stock ownership in another firm Ownership includes stock held by affiliates or agents of the bidder Schedule 14(D)-1 for tender offers Disclosure required even if 5% accumulation not followed by a tender offer	HSR filing is necessary when: **1.** Size-of-transaction test: The buyer purchases assets or securities >$94 million. **2.** Size-of-parties test:[a] The buyer or seller has annual net sales or assets ≥$188 million and the other party has net sales or assets ≥$18.8 million. **3.** If the acquisition value >$376 million, a filing is required regardless of whether (2) is met. Thresholds in (1)–(3) are adjusted annually by the increase in gross domestic product.
File with whom	Schedule 13(D) Six copies to the Securities and Exchange Commission One copy via registered mail to the target's executive office One copy via registered mail to each public exchange on which the target stock is traded Schedule 14(D)-1 10 copies to SEC One copy hand-delivered to the target's executive offices One copy hand delivered to other bidders One copy mailed to each public exchange on which the target stock is traded (each exchange also must be phoned)	Premerger Notification Office of the Federal Trade Commission Director of Operations of the Department of Justice Antitrust Division
Time period	Tender offers must stay open a minimum of 20 business days Begins on date of publication, advertisement, or submission of materials to target Unless the tender offer has been closed, shareholders may withdraw tendered shares up to 60 days after the initial offer	Review or waiting period: 30 days (15 days for cash tender offers) Target must file within 15 days of bidder's filing Period begins for all cash offers when bidder files; for cash or stock bids, period begins when both bidder and target have filed Regulators can request a 20-day extension

[a]The "size-of-parties" test measures the size of the "ultimate parent entity" of the buyer and seller. The ultimate parent entity is the entity that controls the buyer and seller and is not itself controlled by anyone else.

[14] Fidrmuc et al., 2018

Title I: what must be filed?

Title I of the act gives the DOJ the power to request internal corporate records if it suspects potential antitrust violations. Information requirements include background data on the "ultimate parent entity"[15] of the acquiring and target parents, a description of the deal, and all background studies relating to the transaction.

Title II: who must file and when?

In 2020, to comply with the size-of-transaction test, deals in which the buyer purchases voting securities or assets valued in excess of $94 million must be reported under the Hart–Scott–Rodino (HSR) Act. However, according to the size-of-parties (a reference to the acquirer and target firms) test, transactions valued at less than this figure may still require filing if the acquirer or the target firm has annual net sales or total assets of at least $188 million and the other party has annual net sales or total assets of at least $18.8 million. These thresholds are adjusted upward by the annual rate of increase in gross domestic product. A filing is required if the transaction value exceeds $376 million without regard to whether the size-of-parties test is met.

Bidding firms must execute an HSR filing at the same time they make an offer to a target firm. The target also is required to file within 15 days following the bidder's filing. Filings consist of information on the operations of the two companies and their financial statements. The waiting period begins when both the acquirer and target have filed. The FTC or the DOJ may request a 20-day extension of the waiting period for transactions involving securities and 10 days for cash tender offers. If the acquiring firm believes there is little likelihood of anticompetitive effects, it can request early termination. In practice, only about 20% of transactions require HSR filings; of these, only about 4% are challenged by the regulators.

If regulators suspect anticompetitive effects, they will file a lawsuit to obtain a court injunction to prevent completion of the proposed deal. A government lawsuit can result in huge legal expenses and use of management time. Even if the FTC's lawsuit is overturned, the benefits of the merger often have disappeared by the time the lawsuit has been decided. Potential customers and suppliers are less likely to sign lengthy contracts with the target firm during the period of trial. New investment in the target is limited, and employees and communities where the target's operations are located are subject to uncertainty.

Recognizing the possible cost of litigating an FTC injunction to prevent Fidelity Title's proposed takeover of Stewart Title, the two firms announced in late 2019 that they had mutually agreed to call off the deal. Fidelity was contractually bound to pay Stewart a $50 million reverse takeover fee (i.e., payments made by acquirers when a deal is not completed). Presumably, Fidelity had calculated that the cumulative cost of contesting this matter would exceed the amount of the fee paid to Stewart.

How does HSR affect state antitrust regulators?

Title III expands the powers of state attorneys general to initiate triple damage suits on behalf of individuals in their states injured by violations of the antitrust laws.

Procedural rules

A DOJ antitrust lawsuit is adjudicated in the federal courts. When the FTC initiates the action, it is heard before an administrative law judge at the FTC. The FTC then votes whether to accept or reject the judge's rulings. The FTC's decision can be appealed in the federal circuit courts. As an alternative to litigation, a company may seek to negotiate a voluntary settlement of its differences with the FTC. Such settlements usually are negotiated during the review process and are called consent decrees.

The consent decree

A typical consent decree may consist of both structural and behavioral remedies. *Structural remedies* require the party or parties seeking regulatory approval to sell assets or businesses in areas where they compete directly. *Behavioral remedies* attempt to regulate future conduct of the relevant party or parties (e.g., regulating the prices that a party may charge) and require significant monitoring by regulators to ensure compliance.

[15] The ultimate parent entity is the firm at the top of the chain of ownership if the actual buyer is a subsidiary.

In mid-2018, German chemical firm Bayer agreed to a *structural remedy* involving the sale of agricultural businesses to a competitor to get US regulatory approval to complete its $66 billion takeover of US-based Monsanto. US regulators reasoned that the sale offered customers an alternative to Bayer for certain agricultural chemicals. Google's 2021 takeover of wearable tech firm Fitbit required certain behavioral remedies to gain EU approval. Google would not use Fitbit data for targeted advertising, keep the two firms' databases separate, and require users' approval to use Fitbit fitness data in its search engine.

If a potential acquisition is likely to be challenged by the regulatory authorities, an acquirer may seek to negotiate a consent decree in advance of the deal. In the absence of a consent decree, a buyer often requires that an agreement of purchase and sale includes a provision allowing the acquirer to back out of the transaction if it is challenged by regulators.

Antitrust guidelines for horizontal mergers

Understanding an industry begins with analyzing its market structure. *Market structure* may be defined in terms of the number of firms in an industry; their concentration, cost, demand, and technological conditions; and ease of entry and exit. Intended to clarify the provisions of the Sherman and Clayton acts, the DOJ issued in 1968 largely quantitative guidelines, presented in terms of market share percentages and concentration ratios. *Concentration ratios* were defined in terms of the market shares of the industry's top four or eight firms.

Since then, the guidelines have been revised to reflect the role of both quantitative and qualitative data. Qualitative data include factors such as the enhanced efficiency resulting from a combination of firms, the financial viability of potential merger candidates, and the ability of US firms to compete globally.

In 1992, both the FTC and the DOJ announced new guidelines indicating they would challenge mergers creating or enhancing market power even if there are measurable efficiency benefits. *Market power* is defined as the ability of the combined firms to profitably maintain prices above competitive levels. These guidelines were revised in 1997 to reflect the regulatory authorities' willingness to recognize that improvements in efficiency could more than offset the effects of increases in market power. In 2010, the guidelines were updated to give regulators more leeway to challenge mergers. However, they also raised the thresholds for determining if a merger would cause anticompetitive concentration. In general, horizontal mergers are most likely to be challenged by regulators. Vertical mergers—those involving customer–supplier relationships—are considered much less likely to result in anticompetitive effects unless they deprive other firms access to an important resource.

As part of the review process, regulators consider customers and the prospect for price discrimination, market definition, market share and concentration, unilateral effects, coordinated effects, ease of entry, realized efficiencies, potential for business failure, and partial acquisitions. These factors are considered next.

Targeted customers and the potential for price discrimination

Price discrimination occurs when sellers can improve profits by raising prices to some targeted customers but not to others. For such discrimination to exist, there must be evidence that certain customers are charged higher prices even though the cost of doing business with them is no higher than selling to other customers, who are charged lower prices. Furthermore, customers charged higher prices must have few alternative sources of supply.

Market definition

Markets are defined by regulators solely in terms of the customers' ability and willingness to substitute one product for another in response to a price increase. The market may be geographically defined, with scope limited by such factors as transportation costs, tariff and nontariff barriers, exchange rate volatility, and so on.

Market share and concentration

The number of firms in a market and their respective shares determine market concentration. Such ratios measure how much of the total output of an industry is produced by the "*n*" largest firms in the industry. To account for the distribution of firm size, the FTC measures concentration using the Herfindahl–Hirschman Index (HHI), which is calculated by summing the squares of the market shares for each firm competing in the market. For example, a market consisting of five firms with market shares of 30%, 25%, 20%, 15%, and 10%, respectively, would have an HHI of 2,250 ($30^2 + 25^2 + 20^2 + 15^2 + 10^2$). Note that an industry consisting of five competitors with market shares of 70%, 10%, 5%, 5%, and 5%, respectively, will have a much higher HHI score of 5075, because the process of squaring the market shares gives the greatest weight to the firm with the largest market shares.

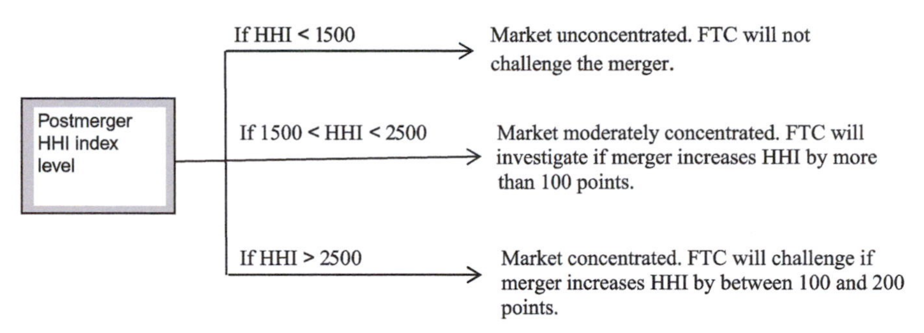

FIGURE 2.2 **Federal Trade Commission (FTC) actions at various market share concentration levels. *HHI*, Herfindahl–Hirschman Index.** *Adapted from FTC Merger Guidelines, www.ftc.gov.*

The HHI ranges from 10,000 for an almost pure monopoly to approximately 0 in the case of a highly competitive market. The index gives more weight to the market shares of larger firms to reflect their relatively greater pricing power. The FTC scoring system described in Figure 2.2 is one factor in determining if the FTC will challenge a proposed deal.

Increased concentration is often driven by technological innovation and the need for consolidation in the face of intensifying global competition. Mergers offer economies of scale and scope that increase efficiency and innovation[16] and in some instances preserve jobs at firms too weak to remain competitive on their own. Reflecting these factors, there appears to be little evidence of a widespread decline in the degree of competition in the United States despite the increase in market concentration during the past 20 years. Although economy-wide this may be true, the impact of an increase in concentration in a given industry can be ambiguous: it can be a result of intensified competition (as argued earlier) or contribute to increased pricing power for the remaining firms in the industry.[17]

The notion that increased concentration contributes to market power presumes that product demand is relatively unresponsive (i.e., inelastic) to higher prices. The level of elasticity varies by industry: lowest for products that represent a small fraction of customer income and have few substitutes and highest when the opposite is true. For horizontal mergers in oligopolistic industries in which demand is relatively elastic, product prices change slowly (they are said to be "sticky") and total output postmerger is comparable to premerger levels. Why? Large price increases can result in more than proportional decreases in product demand and revenue for the combined firms. Thus, regulators in horizontal mergers monitoring the likelihood of a postmerger decline in output levels need to evaluate the response of product demand to higher prices in the presence of "sticky" product prices.[18]

Unilateral effects

A merger between two firms selling differentiated products may reduce competition by enabling the merged firms to profit by raising the price of one or both products above the premerger level. Also, a merger between competitors prevents buyers from negotiating lower prices by playing one seller against the other. Finally, in markets involving undifferentiated products, a firm, having merged with a large competitor, may restrict output to raise prices.

Coordinated effects

After a merger with a competitor, a firm may coordinate its output and pricing decisions with the remaining firms in the industry. Such actions could include a simple understanding of what a firm would do under certain circumstances. If the firm with dominant market share was to reduce output, others may follow suit, with the intent of raising product prices.[19]

[16] Horizontal mergers can stimulate innovation by eliminating research and development (R&D) overlap and by better aligning projects with the combined firms' goals (Denicolo et al., 2018). Haucap et al. (2019) argue that innovation can be hurt in highly R&D-intensive industries, such as pharmaceuticals, when firms within the industry merge.

[17] Binns and Bietti (2020) argue that third-party personal data tracking, in which a firm tracks data from users of other services and resells it, can contribute to market power by increasing an individual firm's access to data not provided by its own customers.

[18] Esfahani, 2019

[19] Porter (2020) provides a detailed discussion of the theory of mergers and coordinated effects.

Ease of entry

Ease of entry is defined as entry that would be timely, likely to occur, and sufficient to counter the competitive effects of a combination of firms that temporarily increases market concentration. Barriers to entry—such as proprietary technology or knowledge, patents, government regulations, exclusive ownership of natural resources, or huge investment requirements—can limit the number of new competitors that enter a market. Excessive entry barriers may hinder innovation because of a reduced need to do so because of the limited threat of competition. However, defining what is excessive is highly subjective.

Efficiencies

Increases in efficiency resulting from M&As can enhance the combined firms' ability to compete and result in lower prices, improved quality, better service, or innovation. For example, the reduction in the number of major US airlines from six to three over the past 2 decades has been widely viewed as procompetitive, having had little impact on nominal fares while fostering increased traffic and capacity.[20] Efficiencies are difficult to verify because they will be realized after the merger has taken place. A reduction in the average fixed cost per unit of output due to economies of scale is an example of a verifiable efficiency.

Alternative to imminent failure

Regulators also consider the likelihood that a firm would fail if not allowed to merge with another firm. The regulators must weigh the potential cost of the failing firm, such as the loss of jobs, against any potential increase in market power resulting from a merger.

Partial acquisitions

Regulators may also review acquisitions of minority positions involving competing firms if it is determined that the partial acquisition results in the effective control of the target firm. A partial acquisition can lessen competition by giving the acquirer the ability to influence the competitive conduct of the target firm in that the acquirer may have the right to appoint members of the board of directors. The minority investment also may blunt competition if the acquirer gains access to nonpublicly available competitive information. In April 2020, the FTC sued cigarette maker Altria to unwind its 2018 $12.8 billion minority stake in e-cigarette producer Juul Labs, arguing that the former rivals collaborated to reduce competition.

Antitrust guidelines for vertical mergers

Firms may vertically integrate with their distributors or suppliers to realize competitive advantages. Although historically rare, vertical mergers may become a concern to regulators if an acquisition by a supplier of a customer prevents the supplier's competitors from having access to the customer. Alternatively, the acquisition by a customer of a supplier could be challenged if it prevents the customer's competitors from having access to the supplier. New guidelines released in mid-2020 indicate that regulators will also evaluate the potential impact on competition of vertical mergers if they provide a firm (acquiring either a distributor or supplier) with data on their competitors, which could be used to harm competitors.

On November 20, 2017, AT&T's $85 billion planned takeover of Time Warner Inc. was blocked by the US DOJ, which expressed concern that the combination would lead to higher prices for traditional pay-TV and limit the expansion of low-cost streaming services, threatening AT&T's DirecTV business. Although the case was ultimately dismissed, vertical mergers involving competitors dominant in their respective markets are more likely in the future to result in regulatory scrutiny.

Antitrust guidelines for mergers involving complementary products

Complementary products are those commonly used together (e.g., shoes and shoelaces). Selling them together often produces efficiencies such as sharing common distribution channels, skill sets, supply chains, and so on. To take advantage of efficiencies, suppliers often engage in "tying and bundling" practices. A *tying arrangement* is one in which a seller requires the purchase of one product to buy a complementary product. However, the amount

[20] Carlton et al., 2019

of the purchase of the complementary product is not defined at the time of the sale. A bundled sale is one in which the purchase of a product requires a specific amount of the complementary product to be purchased at the time of the sale.

Mergers involving complementary products (e.g., one firm produces jet engines and the other avionics) can produce anticompetitive conditions when the products can only be purchased together as a "bundle." If the merged firms own the intellectual property rights to the technology underlying the products, they can limit the development of substitute products by refusing to license the technology. When the products are critical to customers, they are forced to buy from the merged firms. Consequently, prices charged often are higher than they would have been if substitutes were available. Antitrust law has been violated when the intent of the merger was primarily to deter entry of rivals that invest in substitute products. The end result of the merger often is higher prices and lower research and development (R&D) spending.[21]

Antitrust guidelines for collaborative efforts

Collaborative efforts are horizontal agreements among competitors such as joint ventures, business arrangements in which businesses pool resources. Sometimes called "buffer JVs," such entities can reduce direct competition between partners since they are also each competing against the JV products. By having the JV raise prices, restrict output, or both, the partners can raise prices or restrict output of their own products.[22] Regulators are less likely to block a collaborative effort if (1) the participants continue to compete through independent operations, (2) the financial interest in the effort by each participant is relatively small, (3) each participant's ability to control the effort is limited, (4) safeguards prevent information sharing, and (5) the duration of the effort is short.

Antitrust guidelines for monopsonies

A monopsony is a large buyer whose purchases account for most of a market's sales. The resulting market power allows the monopsonist to demand that its suppliers lower their prices. When mergers of competing buyers boost the market power of the combined firms, regulators use the same framework they would use to evaluate the market power of a merger among sellers in which the combined firms would be able to boost selling prices. That is, do sellers have a sufficient number of alternative buyers? When there are few alternative buyers such that the resulting lower selling prices will weaken suppliers, regulators may rule that market power of the monopsonist will harm sellers.[23] But not all increased concentration among buyers is detrimental to sellers. For example, a merger among buyers may lower prices paid by the merged firms because sellers realize lower shipping and marketing costs per unit when they can increase quantities sold to a single customer. Sellers also may realize lower equipment setup costs and longer production runs when selling to fewer buyers.

Revisions to intellectual property guidelines

On January 12, 2017, US regulators issued new guidelines reflecting recent Supreme Court rulings that a patent holder is not violating antitrust law by simply refusing to allow competitors to use the patent. Also, prices charged for granting others the right to use intellectual property are subject to the "rule of reason."[24]

[21] Etro, 2019

[22] Chen and Ross, 2020

[23] Loertscher and Marx (2019a and 2019b) argue that without cost synergies, mergers among suppliers harm buyers regardless of buyer power.

[24] The "rule of reason" is a legal doctrine developed to apply the Sherman Antitrust Act. It states that an attempt should be made to weigh the aspects of potentially restrictive business practices that support competition against its anticompetitive effects in order to determine whether the practice should be prohibited. For example, price fixing is illegal per se but monopoly is not. The combination of two firms resulting in dominant market share may be acceptable if it can be shown that the combination will result in improved operating efficiency.

When are antitrust regulators most likely to intervene?

Regulatory authorities are more likely to intervene when market concentration is high. The likelihood of antitrust intervention in horizontal mergers is less when foreign import competition is high, industry entry barriers are low, existing competitors have the capacity to increase supply, and mergers are motivated by efficiency gains.[25]

Trends in enforcement efforts

Enforcement efforts ebb and flow with changes in presidential administrations and political and economic philosophies. During the decade ending in 2010, combinations among direct competitors often were approved as a means of achieving greater operating efficiency. In the most recent decade, enforcement efforts were targeted in concentrated industries such as telecommunications, airlines, and media. Despite continued growth in the number and dollar value of M&As during the past 30 years, antitrust enforcement has fallen, with DOJ complaints against firms in 2018 more than 60% below their early-1980s levels.[26]

How business platform strategies complicate antitrust enforcement

A *platform strategy* allows a firm to create value by expediting transactions between consumers and producers. Businesses create large, scalable networks of users that can be accessed on demand (e.g., Facebook, Apple, Google/YouTube, Alibaba, and Uber). Successful platforms build strong barriers to entry for potential competitors in the form of extensive networks or installed user bases and operate at a scale that offers extremely low user acquisition and retention costs. Current antitrust law does not easily address market dominance in such cases. The current law focuses on how a proposed M&A impacts output and prices and in turn consumer welfare to determine if it is anticompetitive. But that framework does not apply easily to businesses that grow through platform strategies.

Amazon.com is the premier example of how a successful platform strategy contributes to market dominance. It has done so by building a highly scalable infrastructure to support a growing volume of users while driving down infrastructure expenses per dollar of revenue.

This infrastructure can be used to dominate specific and related lines of business. Amazon is in a variety of seemingly unrelated lines of business ranging from a delivery and logistics network and an auction house to a major book publisher, a TV and film producer, and a hardware manufacturer to a leading supplier of cloud services and a grocery business. The common element is that each line of business generates data on consumer- and business-buying behaviors, which can be used to determine pricing strategies, achieve optimal inventory management, and anticipate future product offerings in various markets.

The end result of successful platform strategies is that they tend to concentrate market power. As such, a business may be able to stifle innovation of new products that could threaten their own product offering and to raise prices with relative ease. Note that de facto price increases can be achieved by lowering product quality without actually raising selling prices.[27] Firms competing on the basis of achieving platform dominance in multiple markets may choose to vertically integrate by owning valuable content, which can be sold across markets. Such firms also can restrict competitor access to this content.

If platform strategies do indeed lead to natural monopolies,[28] regulators are faced with few alternatives. One option is to let online competitors govern the marketplace. Antitrust regulators can help sustain competition by limiting the extent to which a firm's platform is used in other markets, banning vertical integration by such firms, and by moving aggressively to limit predatory pricing (i.e., selling products below cost to drive out competitors).[29] Another option is for regulators to approve business combinations involving platform businesses that increase efficiency through economies of scale to achieve savings that can be passed on to customers. Regulators can then treat such businesses as utilities and regulate what they can charge their customers and the services they may offer.

[25] Gao et al., 2017

[26] Institute for Mergers, Acquisitions, and Alliances: https://imaa-institute.org/mergers-and-acquisitions-statistics

[27] Chen and Gayle, 2019

[28] A natural monopoly is one that results from high fixed costs or start-up costs of operating a business in a specific industry. Such industries are characterized by very high entry barriers, such as utilities.

[29] Although predatory pricing (selling below cost) is illegal, it is extremely difficult to win predatory pricing lawsuits because the court needs to prove that the alleged predator can in fact raise prices and recover its losses.

Impact of antitrust actions on firm value

Share prices of firms accused of potential antitrust violations drop initially, but they recover quickly if the concessions required to satisfy regulators are seen as minimal.[30] Antitrust legislation establishing clearer guidelines is viewed as positive by investors. Why? Such laws reduce the discretion (and implicitly the perceived arbitrariness) given to regulators.

Failure to comply with local antitrust regulations can be exceedingly expensive. For example, Google was fined $5.1 billion in 2019 by the European Union for abusing its dominance of the Android mobile device operating system. In 2017 and in 2018, the European Union had fined the firm $2.7 billion for favoring its shopping service over competitors.

Does the United States have a monopoly problem?

The growing backlash in recent years against "big business," particularly Amazon, Google, and Facebook, has sparked bipartisan support for revamping US antitrust laws. This threatens to overturn decades of consensus in Washington to allow markets to determine competitive conditions.[31] Some argue that certain tech firms have grown too ubiquitous, intrusive, and powerful. But should current laws be changed or simply more rigorously enforced? If they are changed, how is it done so as not to destroy the benefits these tech firms provide?

Although "big tech" has taken center stage in the antitrust debate, government regulators also have others in their sights: financial services, health care providers, drug companies, telecom, and media firms. For example, the DOJ in late 2020 blocked Visa's purchase of Plaid Inc., arguing it would allow Visa to unlawfully maintain a monopoly in online debit cards, resulting in higher prices, greater entry barriers, and less innovation.

Monopoly power (seller-side market power)

A monopoly is a single firm dominating a market and selling a product having few substitutes. This allows the firm to raise selling prices by restricting output and to produce inferior-quality products to realize profits higher than they would have been in a more competitive market. Such positions are sustainable when barriers to entry are high.

But are all monopolies harmful? So-called *natural monopolies* arise when firms have patents or make products that are so specialized that only a single firm can produce them. Moreover, given the high fixed costs of the utility business, it is most efficient for a single firm to supply water or electricity in a specific area. Still other monopolies emerge when one firm (e.g., Alphabet/Google) satisfies consumer demands better than its competitors.

Monopsony power (buyer-side market power)

In contrast to a monopoly (i.e., a dominant supplier selling to multiple buyers), a monopsony is a single (or dominant) buyer buying from multiple sellers. The monopolist forces prices up by restricting output, and the monopsonist forces prices down by limiting its purchases. Although it is clear how consumers are hurt by increasing prices, the impact on consumers is less clear when suppliers are forced to lower their prices.

The DOJ challenged the proposed merger between Anthem Healthcare Services and Cigna Insurance, alleging the resulting monopsony power in the health care services market would reduce payments to doctors and other providers and ultimately reduce service quality. Although consumers would benefit from lower-cost health care, they would be hurt if the merger resulted in lower-quality services. In 2018, the FTC required global health care firm Grifols S.A. to divest blood collection centers in three US cities, arguing that Grifols and Biotest US were the only buyers in these markets. The FTC reasoned that without the divestitures, Grifols would be able to exercise buyer-side market power by reducing fees paid to donors. Consumers could be hurt if this resulted in a reduced supply of blood.

Do current antitrust laws need to be changed?

Under current law, it is not enough to show that a firm has the power to raise prices. Regulators must demonstrate that a firm is engaging in anticompetitive practices, such as restricting competitor access to scarce resources and distribution channels, and that consumers are being harmed by such practices.

[30] Gunter et al., 2016

[31] Markets can correct monopoly problems through future innovation. After 13 years and tens of millions of dollars spent investigating IBM's mainframe business, the case was dropped in 1982. Within a few years, IBM's alleged market power was undercut by the introduction of personal computers.

Does the way regulators measure harm need to change? Instead of charging higher prices, tech firms often give away their services for free in exchange for selling personal data that consumers voluntarily provide. Large tech firms have gained dominant positions in digital search, social media, and providing easy access to millions of products because they have satisfied a market need better than anyone else.

But such firms may use their dominance to direct business to their own products and stifle innovation among firms that might otherwise have emerged as competitors.[32] In late 2020, the DOJ alleged that Alphabet (Google) monopolizes internet search by negotiating exclusionary contracts with cell phone makers, wireless carriers, and computer makers (who receive billions of dollars from Google) to make Google their default search engine. Such agreements, the government argues, are anticompetitive because they effectively preclude other search engines from gaining significant market share. Also in 2020, the FTC and 48 states' attorneys general filed antitrust lawsuits alleging Facebook was violating antitrust law by buying up competitors such as WhatsApp and Instagram, depriving consumers of alternative choices. If successful, these lawsuits could result in Facebook's divesting these two businesses.

For the past 4 decades, the courts and regulators have generally not acted unless they were certain consumers would be hurt. Some argue this contributed to an "unholy alliance" between business and government, with government often picking winners and losers. Others argue for preserving the current antitrust policy but enforcing it more rigorously. Still others argue for breaking up businesses having too much power. There is little consensus. Even if the current antitrust laws do not change, the extent to which they are enforced may. Whatever happens, the implications for M&As are likely to be far-reaching.

Do antitrust laws contribute to management–shareholder conflicts?

Potentially, there is evidence that such policies may contribute to fewer takeovers because of uncertainty about gaining regulatory approval or achieving adequate financial returns if required to divest key target product lines. The reduction in the threat of takeover seems most pronounced in countries with vigorous law enforcement and in industries that are relatively concentrated. The diminishing threat of takeover allows incompetent managers to become entrenched. Such entrenchment often is associated with corporate funds being invested to promote the managers' rather than the shareholders' interests. For example, entrenched managers may engage in "empire building" through acquisitions (to justify increasing their compensation), often leading to lower acquirer returns in such deals.[33]

M&A implications of the Dodd-Frank Wall Street Reform and Consumer Protection Act (including 2018 revisions)

Comprehensive in scope, the Dodd-Frank Act of 2010 substantially changed federal regulation of financial services firms as well as some nonfinancial public companies. The Act's objectives included restoring public confidence in the financial system and preventing future financial crises that threaten the viability of financial markets.

Its provisions range from giving shareholders a say on executive compensation to greater transparency in the derivatives markets to new powers granted to the Federal Deposit Insurance Corporation (FDIC) to liquidate financial firms whose failure would threaten the US financial system. Although the implications of the legislation are far-reaching, the focus in this book is on aspects of the act impacting corporate governance directly, the environment in which M&As and other restructuring activities take place, and participants in the restructuring process. The act's provisions (and 2018 revisions) having the greatest impact on M&As and restructuring are summarized in Table 2.3.

On May 24, 2018, President Trump signed into law revisions to the Dodd-Frank Act of 2010 intended to free smaller banks from being classified as "too big to fail" in an effort to revitalize bank lending. Smaller banks will no longer be subject to the more stringent capital and liquidity requirements, leverage and lending limits, mandatory risk committees and resolution plans, and annual stress tests applied to large banks.

The new legislation raised to $250 billion the asset threshold for banks to be subject to the more stringent regulatory oversight as "systemically important financial institutions."[34] The new law also exempts small banks with

[32] Katz, 2020

[33] Dissanaike et al., 2020

[34] On October 31, 2018, the US Federal Reserve, the nation's largest regulator of financial institutions, recommended extending this relief to banks with total assets exceeding $700 billion.

TABLE 2.3 Selected Dodd-Frank Wall Street Reform and Consumer Protection Act Provisions (Including 2018 Revisions)

Provision	Requirements
Governance and Executive Compensation[a]	
Say on pay	In a nonbinding vote on the board, shareholders may vote on executive compensation packages every 2 or 3 years.
Say on golden parachutes	Proxy statements seeking shareholder approval of acquisitions, mergers, or sale of substantially all of the company's assets must disclose any agreements with executive officers of the target or acquirer with regard to compensation.
Institutional investor disclosure	Institutional managers (e.g., mutual funds, pension funds) must disclose annually their positions on pay and on golden parachutes (i.e., executive termination pay) voting.
Clawbacks	Public companies are required to develop and disclose mechanisms for recovering incentive-based compensation paid during the 3 years before earnings restatements.
Broker discretionary voting	Public stock exchanges are required to prohibit brokers from voting shares without direction from owners in the election of directors, executive compensation, or any other significant matter as determined by the Securities and Exchange Commission (SEC).
Compensation Committee independence	SEC will define rules requiring stock exchanges to prohibit listing any issuer that does not comply with independence requirements governing compensation of committee members and consultants.
Systemic Regulation and Emergency Powers	
Financial Stability Oversight Council	To mitigate systemic risk, the Council, consisting of 10 voting members and chaired by the Secretary of the Treasury, monitors US financial markets to identify domestic or foreign banks and some nonbank firms whose default or bankruptcy would risk the financial stability of the United States.
New Federal Reserve (Fed) bank and nonbank holding company supervision requirements	Applies to bank and nonbank holding companies with consolidated assets exceeding $250 billion must: • Submit plans for their rapid and orderly dissolution in the event of failure. • Provide periodic reports about their credit exposure. • Limit their credit exposure to any unaffiliated company to 25% of its capital. • Conduct semiannual "stress tests" to determine capital adequacy. • Provide advance notice of intent to purchase voting shares in financial services firms.
Limitations on leverage	For bank holding companies whose assets exceed $250 billion, the Fed may require the firm to maintain a debt-to-equity ratio of no more than 15 to 1.
Limits on size	The size of any single bank cannot exceed 10% of deposits nationwide. The limitation does not apply for mergers involving troubled banks.
Capital requirements	Bank capital requirements are to be left to the regulatory agencies and should reflect the perceived risk of bank or nonbank institutions.
Savings and loan regulations	Fed gains supervisory authority over all savings and loan holding companies and their subsidiaries.
Federal Deposit Insurance Corporation (FDIC)	The FDIC may guarantee obligations of solvent insured depository institutions if the Fed and the Systemic Risk Council determine that financial markets are illiquid (i.e., investors cannot sell assets without incurring a significant loss).
Orderly liquidation authority	The FDIC may seize and liquidate a financial services firm whose failure threatens the financial stability of the United States, to ensure the speedy disposition of the firm's assets and to ensure that losses are borne by shareholders and bondholders while losses of public funds are limited.[b]
Capital Markets	
Office of Credit Ratings	Proposes rules for internal controls, independence, transparency, and penalties for poor performance, making it easier for investors to sue for "unrealistic" ratings. Office conducts annual audits of rating agencies.
Securitization	Issuers of asset-backed securities must retain an interest of at least 5% of the collateral underlying any security sold to third parties.
Hedge and private equity fund registration	Advisers to private equity and hedge funds with $\geq$$100 million in assets under management must register with the SEC as investment advisers; those with <$100 million will be subject to state registration. Registered advisors provide reports and be subject to periodic examinations.

Continued

TABLE 2.3 Selected Dodd-Frank Wall Street Reform and Consumer Protection Act Provisions (Including 2018 Revisions)—cont'd

Provision	Requirements
Clearing and trading of over-the-counter (OTC) derivatives	Commodity Futures Trading Commission and SEC will mandate central clearing of certain OTC derivatives on a central exchange and the real-time public reporting of volume and pricing data as well as the parties to the transaction.
Financial Institutions	
Volcker rule	Prohibits insured depository institutions and their holding companies from buying and selling securities with their own money (so-called proprietary trading) or sponsoring or investing in hedge funds or private equity funds. Banks are not permitted to serve as a general partner or in some way gain control of such funds. Underwriting and market-making activities are exempt. Proprietary trading may occur outside the United States as long as the bank does not own or control the entity. Banks whose assets are <$10 billion are not subject to the Volcker rule. In late 2019, the rule was revamped to create a presumption of compliance for security trades held longer than 60 days.
Consumer Financial Protection Bureau	Creates an agency to write rules governing all financial institutions offering consumer financial products, including banks, mortgage lenders, and credit card companies as well as "pay day" lenders. The authority applies to banks and credit unions with assets >$10 billion and all mortgage-related businesses. Although institutions with <$10 billion have to comply, they are supervised by their current regulators.
Federal Insurance Office	The office monitors all aspects of the insurance industry (other than health insurance and long-term care), coordinates international insurance matters, consults with states regarding insurance issues of national importance, and recommends insurers that should be treated as systemically important.

[a]See Chapter 3 for more details.
[b]See Chapter 17 for more details.

assets under $10 billion from the Volcker rule ban on proprietary trading.[35] Banks with between $100 billion and $250 billion in assets will still face periodic stress tests, but they will be exempt from other tougher standards as of 2020. The legislation will leave fewer than 10 US banks subject to the most restrictive federal oversight.

The Volcker rule was further weakened in late 2019 to make it easier for banks to "make markets" (i.e., buy and sell securities for their customers). The original Volcker rule forbade FDIC insured banks from engaging in speculation while allowing banks to make markets by buying and selling securities for their customers. The challenge was to tell the difference between speculative trading and that undertaken to satisfy customers.

The solution was to focus on outcomes rather than intent. If traders stayed within certain limits on profits and losses on trading, their trading would be presumed to be market making. Trading activity generating larger profits and losses would be considered speculative, and traders would have to justify their trades to regulators. Moreover, regulators agreed to narrow the definition of trades that would be subject to regulatory review, excluding about one-fourth of the trades originally covered under the Volcker rule.

M&A implications of privacy, data protection, and copyright regulations

New rules on how personal information can be used and copyrighted material displayed online are likely to create new legal liabilities for firms collecting and reselling consumer data and posting and sharing copyrighted material. Acquirers must understand how these new rules will impact the targets they pursue. Firms thinking about putting themselves or units using customer generated data up for sale must take steps to minimize potential liabilities. These regulations and their implications are discussed next.

Data protection regulations

Effective May 24, 2018, the EU countries adopted new data protection rules known as the General Data Protection Regulation (GDPR). The new rules allow consumers access to their personal data held by firms and give them the option to have their data deleted. The GDPR applies to firms processing personal data with a presence in the

[35] *Proprietary trading* refers to banks making speculative investments for their own profit rather than relying on earning commissions and fees by trading on the behalf of clients.

European Union, as well as those outside the European Union offering goods or services to EU residents or monitoring their behavior.

France's data protection agency was among the first to impose penalties for violating the new law when in 2019 it fined Google $57 million for not providing consumers sufficient transparency into how their personal data were being used. The GDPR will have an impact beyond EU borders because Brazil, Japan, and South Korea are expected to follow the EU's lead, with the European Union ready to limit access to its market if countries do not comply with its standards.

In contrast, the United States currently lacks a single data protection law comparable to the GDPR. Rather, US privacy legislation has been adopted on sector-by-sector basis.[36] Unlike the European Union, the United States relies on a combination of legislation, regulation, and self-regulation rather than simply government regulation. Why? Free speech is guaranteed explicitly in the US Constitution, but privacy is only an implicit right as interpreted by the US Supreme Court.

The ad hoc regulatory approach in the United States could change because of the implementation of the California Consumer Privacy Act (CCPA) on January 1, 2020. And the California law could become a model for similar laws in other states. The CCPA gives consumers the right to request data that businesses have collected about them, to object to sale of their data, to receive their data in a portable format, and to ask businesses to delete such data. Personal data are defined in broad categories such as biometric data, psychometric information, browsing and search history, and geolocation data. Rather than having a patchwork of individual state laws, firms using consumer data extensively argue that data protection is better achieved through a federal law rather than state by state, which can result in inconsistent regulation.

The proliferation of data protection laws creates new challenges for firms engaged in cross-border as well as domestic takeovers. Noncompliant acquirers must incur the expense of installing the systems and processes to gain regulatory approval and to avoid hefty fines. Data-related liabilities can arise years after a target firm has been acquired, necessitating more comprehensive and intrusive due diligence to minimize potential liabilities. For global tech firms such as Facebook and Google, inconsistent data privacy laws require modifications of their systems to account for the idiosyncrasies of each country's laws. The same applies to firms wishing to do business in multiple states within the United States. Finally, increasing limitations of how personal data are used for various types of marketing programs could limit future profitability of target firms whose business models are dependent on their customers' data.

Failure to comply with local data protection laws can be very expensive. For example, Facebook was fined by the US FTC in late 2019 $5 billion for mishandling user data. This constituted the largest such fine in the FTC's history.

Copyright regulation

Known as Article 13, the EU's new copyright rules require websites to sign licensing agreements with musicians, authors, and publishers to post their work online. The intent is to force tech firms to remove unlicensed copyrighted material from their websites proactively rather than waiting for complaints. Critics say the law would result in censorship and limit data sharing. Supporters argue it would protect innovators and force companies to pay for content they share online. Although initially targeting Facebook and Google, the new law could increase the frequency of lawsuits and fines for any firm engaging in posting and sharing information. The law requires Google and other websites with more than 5 million unique monthly visitors to make their "best effort" to receive authorization from the owners of copyrighted content or to take steps to keep such material from being shared.

In the past, website operators have enjoyed protection from liability when a user posts unlicensed content. They were required to remove the material after it was brought to their attention. Now they must be proactive; otherwise, they can be legally liable. This new exposure could be costly for sites dependent on user-generated content such as Wikipedia.

EU member countries have until June 2021 to implement Article 13.

[36] Examples include the Fair Credit Reporting Act of 1970, the Fair Debt Collections Act of 1977, the Video Privacy Protection Act of 1988, the Cable TV Protection and Competition Act of 1992, and the 1996 Health Insurance Portability and Accountability Act.

State regulations affecting M&As

In the United States, laws affecting takeovers differ among states. This complicates compliance with all such laws when deals involve multiple state jurisdictions. These are discussed next.

State antitakeover laws

Such laws, supporters argue, improve the likelihood that target firm bids will be more reflective of the target's true value, protect minority shareholders, and ultimately generate higher returns for target shareholders. More accurate target valuations reflect the potential for competing bids and more time for allowing shareholders to consider such bids.

Critics argue that such laws increase barriers to takeovers and the potential for management entrenchment. They also argue that such laws can contribute to overbidding by the acquirer because of increased competition among bidders. Others contend increased takeover protection is a zero-sum game benefitting target shareholders at the expense of acquirer shareholders by transferring gains from bidders to targets.

With 68% of all Fortune 500 companies as of 2019 incorporated in Delaware, the state's corporate law has a substantial influence on publicly traded firms. The next most popular state is Nevada with 15%. Delaware corporate law generally defers to the judgment of business managers and board directors in accordance with the so-called "business judgment rule." This rule acknowledges that the daily operation of a business is inherently risky and controversial and, as such, states that the board of directors should be allowed to make decisions without fear of being prosecuted. The rule further assumes that it is unreasonable to expect those managing a company to make the right decisions all the time.

If the courts believe a board acted rationally, there should be no legal repercussions against managers and directors. The major exception is in change-of-control situations. Here, managers are subject to an enhanced business judgment test. This requires a target board to show there are reasonable grounds to believe that a danger to corporate viability exists and that the adoption of defensive measures is reasonable.

Although Delaware law is the norm for many companies, firms incorporated in other states often are subject to corporate law that may differ from Delaware law. What follows is a discussion of commonalities across the states.

States regulate corporate charters. *Corporate charters* define the rights and responsibilities of shareholders, boards of directors, and managers. However, states are not allowed to pass any laws that impose restrictions on interstate commerce or conflict in any way with federal laws. State laws affecting M&As tend to apply only to firms incorporated in the state or that conduct a substantial amount of their business within the state. These laws often contain *fair price provisions*, requiring that all target shareholders of a successful tender offer receive the same price as those tendering their shares. In an attempt to prevent highly leveraged transactions, some state laws include *business combination provisions*, which may specifically rule out the sale of the target's assets for a specific period.[37]

Other common characteristics of state antitakeover laws include cash-out and control-share provisions. *Cash-out provisions* require a bidder whose purchases of stock exceed a stipulated amount to buy the remainder of the target stock on the same terms granted those shareholders whose stock was purchased at an earlier date. By forcing acquirers to purchase 100% of the stock, potential bidders lacking substantial financial resources are eliminated from bidding. *Share-control provisions* require that a bidder obtains prior approval from shareholders holding large blocks of target stock once the bidder's purchases of stock exceed some threshold level. The latter provision can be troublesome to an acquiring company when the holders of the large blocks of stock tend to support target management.

State antitrust and securities laws

State laws are often similar to federal laws. Under federal law, states have the right to sue to block mergers even if the DOJ or FTC does not challenge them. State "blue sky" laws are designed to protect individuals from investing in fraudulent security offerings.

[37] These provisions limit leveraged buyouts from using the proceeds of asset sales to reduce indebtedness.

Restrictions on direct foreign investment in the United States

The Committee on Foreign Investment in the United States (CFIUS) operates under the authority of the Exon-Florio amendment (Section 721 of the Defense Production Act of 1950). CFIUS includes representatives from many government agencies to ensure that all national security issues are considered in the review of foreign acquisitions of US businesses.

The president can block the acquisition of a US corporation based on recommendations made by CFIUS if there is credible evidence that the foreign entity might take action that threatens national security. In 2007, CFIUS was amended under the Foreign Investment National Security Act to cover critical infrastructure such as cross-border transactions involving energy, technology, shipping, and transportation.

Effective August 13, 2018, the Foreign Investment Risk Review Modernization Act expanded CIFIUS's review authority beyond those in which foreign investors had a controlling interest in a US business. Now, CIFIUS's jurisdiction covers noncontrolling deals including "critical technologies" in industries such as defense, energy, telecommunications, and financial services and deals involving "sensitive personal data" on US citizens. Such data include financial, insurance, and health care information.

The new legislation was prompted by complaints that foreign entities were using joint ventures with US firms or minority interests in such ventures to gain access to technology and proprietary information critical to US national security. It covers foreign entities owning a minority position in an acquirer that buys a controlling or minority interest in certain US firms. The statute also gives CFIUS the authority to initiate its own investigations instead of waiting for a buyer to seek regulatory approval.

In early 2018, CFIUS recommended against the sale of US-based global payment service MoneyGram to China's Alibaba affiliate Ant Financial (and the Trump Administration agreed) over concerns about how personal data about US citizens would be used. Also, in 2018, the Trump Administration blocked Singapore-based semiconductor manufacturer Broadcom from acquiring US-based Qualcom, a leader in the development of 5G networks. The administration argued that the takeover would reduce Qualcom's R&D investment in such networks, ceding the future development of this technology to Chinese firms.

Restrictions on foreign acquisitions by US acquirers

The US Treasury's Office of Foreign Asset Control (OFAC) enforces US sanctions against countries and individuals for activities such as foreign aggression, terrorism, and narcotics sales. It currently monitors sanctions impacting 22 countries, including Cuba, Iran, Russia, and Venezuela. During 2019, OFAC initiated 26 enforcement actions (of which six were M&A related) and collected $1.3 billion in penalties, both all-time highs. Acquirers must determine if the target does business in or with any OFAC-prohibited jurisdiction or person. When violations have occurred, remedial actions post-takeover include terminating contracts, disciplining employees, compliance procedures, and ongoing auditing. Both controlling and minority investors with stakes in US-sanctioned firms can be subject to fines.

The US Foreign Corrupt Practices Act

The Foreign Corrupt Practices Act of 1977 prohibits individuals, firms, and foreign subsidiaries of US firms from paying anything of value to foreign government officials in exchange for new business or retaining existing contracts. Even though many nations have laws prohibiting bribery of public officials, enforcement tends to be lax.

Of the 38 countries signing the 1997 Anti-Bribery Convention of the Organization for Economic Cooperation and Development, more than half have no enforcement mechanisms, according to a 2010 study by Transparency International. The US law permits "facilitation payments" to foreign officials if small amounts of money are required to gain export approval. Such payments are considered legal according to US law and the laws of countries where such payments are considered routine.

Microsoft agreed to pay $16.6 million to the US SEC in late 2019 to settle charges that it violated the Foreign Corrupt Practices Act in Hungary, Saudi Arabia, Thailand, and Turkey. The firm paid an $8.75 million criminal fine stemming from its bribing Hungarian government officials to purchase Microsoft site licenses for government agencies that were recorded as if they were purchased at a discount.

The Holding Foreign Companies Accountable Act

Passed in 2020, this law bars the listing of securities of foreign firms on any US stock exchange if they have failed to comply with the US Public Accounting Oversight Board's audits for 3 consecutive years. And the act would also require public companies to disclose whether they are owned or controlled by a foreign government.

Specific industry regulation

In addition to the DOJ and the FTC, a variety of other agencies monitor activities (including M&As) in certain industries, such as commercial banking, railroads, defense, and cable TV.

Banking

Currently, three agencies review banking mergers. The Office of the Comptroller of the Currency has responsibility for transactions in which the acquirer is a national bank. The FDIC oversees mergers in which the acquiring bank or the bank resulting from combining the acquirer and the target will be a federally insured state-chartered bank that operates outside the Federal Reserve System. The third agency is the Board of Governors of the Federal Reserve System (the Fed). It has the authority to regulate mergers in which the acquirer or the resulting bank will be a state bank that is also a member of the Fed.

The Dodd-Frank legislation eliminated the Office of Thrift Supervision and transferred the responsibility for regulating savings and loan associations, credit unions, and savings banks (collectively referred to as *thrift institutions*) to other regulators. The Fed will supervise savings and loan holding companies and their subsidiaries, the FDIC will gain supervisory authority of all state savings banks, and the Office of the Comptroller of the Currency will supervise all federal savings banks.

M&A transactions involving financial institutions resulting in substantial additional leverage or in increased industry concentration will also come under the scrutiny of the Financial Stability Oversight Council created by the Dodd-Frank Act to monitor systemic risk. The Council is empowered to limit bank holding companies deemed systemically risky (or a nonbank financial firm regulated by the Fed) from merging, acquiring, or consolidating with another firm. The council may require the holding company to divest certain assets if it is thought to constitute a threat to the financial stability of US financial markets. Under current legislation, the size of any single bank or nonbank cannot exceed 10% of deposits nationwide. However, this constraint may be relaxed for mergers involving failing banks.

Communications

The Federal Communications Commission (FCC) is charged with regulating interstate and international communication by radio, television, wire, satellite, and cable. The FCC is responsible for the enforcement of such legislation as the Telecommunications Act of 1996 intended to reduce regulation while promoting lower prices and higher-quality services.

One of the FCC's first major actions under the Trump Administration was to relax media ownership restrictions, allowing TV broadcasters to own newspapers in the same market and two of the top four stations in a city. The new rules implemented on November 15, 2017, could lead to mergers among broadcasters, who have long argued that consolidation was necessary to compete with cable and internet companies for local advertising dollars.

On December 15, 2017, the FCC rescinded the so-called "net neutrality rules" that were introduced in early 2015. The rescission enables internet broadband providers, such as AT&T, Comcast, and Verizon, to determine what content they can provide and at what price. The providers can now block or slow down data transmission speeds and seek payments in exchange for faster access on their internet networks.

The FCC argued that state and local governments cannot create their own net neutrality rules since internet services crossed state lines and were subject to the so-called "commerce clause."[38] Supporters of the net neutrality rules, such as Google's parent Alphabet Inc. and Facebook Inc., contend that eliminating the rules would stifle internet

[38] The "commerce clause" refers to Article 1, Section 8, Clause 3 of the U.S. Constitution, which gives Congress the power "to regulate commerce … among the …states. …"

innovation. In 2018, California introduced state-level net neutrality rules and was sued by the FCC. In late 2019, a federal appeals court ruled that although the federal government could eliminate net neutrality regulations at the national level, it could not prevent the states from developing their own rules. As of early 2020, California, New Jersey, Oregon, Vermont, and Washington have already enacted legislation or adopted resolutions protecting net neutrality. And 34 states and the District of Columbia have introduced legislation and resolutions.

Railroads

The Surface Transportation Board (STB), the successor to the Interstate Commerce Commission (ICC), governs mergers of railroads. Under the ICC Termination Act of 1995, the STB determines if a merger should be approved by assessing the impact on public transportation, the areas currently served by the carriers involved in the proposed transaction, and the burden of the total fixed charges resulting from completing the transaction.

Defense

During the 1990s, the US defense industry underwent consolidation, consistent with the Department of Defense's (DOD) philosophy that it is preferable to have three or four highly viable defense contractors than a dozen weaker firms. Although defense industry mergers are technically subject to current antitrust regulations, the DOJ and FTC have assumed a secondary role to the DOD. Efforts by a foreign entity to acquire national security-related assets also must be reviewed by the CFIUS.

Other regulated industries

Historically, the insurance industry was regulated largely at the state level. Under the Dodd-Frank Act, the Federal Insurance Office was created within the US Treasury to monitor all non—health care—related aspects of the insurance industry. As a "systemic" regulator, its approval will be required for all acquisitions of insurance companies whose sizes and interlocking business relationships could have repercussions on the US financial system. The acquisition of more than 10% of a US airline's outstanding shares is subject to approval of the Federal Aviation Administration. Public utilities are highly regulated at the state level. Like insurance companies, their acquisition requires state government approval.

Environmental laws

Failure to comply with environmental laws can result in huge potential liabilities. These laws require full disclosure of hazardous materials and the extent to which they are being released into the environment. Such laws include the Clean Water Act (1974), the Toxic Substances Control Act of 1978, the Resource Conservation and Recovery Act (1976), and the Comprehensive Environmental Response, Compensation, and Liability Act (Superfund) of 1980. Additional reporting requirements were imposed in 1986 with the passage of the Emergency Planning and Community Right to Know Act (EPCRA). In addition to EPCRA, several states also passed "right-to-know" laws such as California's Proposition 65.

Labor and benefit laws

These laws govern such areas as employment discrimination, immigration law, sexual harassment, age discrimination, drug testing, and wage and hour laws. Labor and benefit laws include the Family Medical Leave Act, the Americans with Disabilities Act, and the Worker Adjustment and Retraining Notification Act (WARN). WARN governs notification before plant closings and requirements to retrain workers.

Employee benefit plans frequently represent one of the biggest areas of liability to a buyer. The greatest liabilities often are found in defined pension benefit plans, postretirement medical plans, life insurance benefits, and deferred compensation plans. Such liabilities arise when reserves on the seller's balance sheet do not reflect fully future obligations. The liability from improperly structured benefit plans grows with each new round of legislation, starting with the passage of the Employee Retirement Income and Security Act of 1974.

Laws affecting employee retirement and pensions were strengthened by additional legislation, including the Multi-Employer Pension Plan Amendments Act of 1980, the Retirement Equity Act of 1984, the Single Employer Pension Plan Amendments Act of 1986, the Tax Reform Act of 1986, and the Omnibus Budget Reconciliation acts of 1987, 1989, 1990, and 1993. Buyers and sellers also must be aware of the Unemployment Compensation Act of 1992, the Retirement Protection Act of 1994, and Statements 87, 88, and 106 of the Financial Accounting Standards Board.[39]

The Pension Protection Act of 2006 places a potentially increasing burden on acquirers of targets with underfunded pension plans. The legislation requires employers with defined benefit plans to make sufficient contributions to meet a 100% funding target and erase funding shortfalls over 7 years. Furthermore, the legislation requires employers with so-called "at-risk" plans to accelerate contributions. "At-risk" plans are those whose pension fund assets cover less than 70% of future pension obligations.

Cross-border transactions

With more than 150 merger regulatory bodies globally, deals involving firms in different countries are complicated by having to cope with many regulatory authorities in specific countries or regions. More regulators mean more scrutiny and longer delays in completing deals. This creates significant costs to acquirer and target shareholders, such as legal compliance, restructuring business operations required by foreign regulators, greater uncertainty about deal closing, and the potential loss of merger related synergies.

Changes in the European Union in 2013 are among the most far-reaching revisions affecting cross-border deals within major trading blocs. The review process, outlined in Article 101 of the Treaty on the Functioning of the European Union (TFEU), which prohibits anticompetitive practices in 27 countries, has been greatly simplified. Certain agreements, such as technology transfers, between firms whose combined market share is less than 20% between competitors and less than 30% between noncompetitors are exempt from TFEU review. In 2020, the European Union proposed greater regulatory scrutiny of foreign acquirers receiving significant home country subsidies. And in 2021, the European Union introduced bills that, if enacted, will levy fines on global big-tech revenue or even break them up to stop anticompetitive abuses. The United Kingdom also is considering similar legislation to curb alleged big-tech competition abuses.

Established in 2001, the International Competition Network (ICN) attempts to promote cooperation among "competition law" (antitrust) authorities globally. The ICN announced updated protocols on April 5, 2019, intended to streamline the enforcement process while preventing countries from using local antitrust laws to favor domestic companies over foreign competitors. Despite having 132 countries as members, the effectiveness of the new protocols may be limited in that individual nations must opt in to be bound by the framework, and some major economies such as China are not yet ICN members.

When regulations differ among countries, not only is the cost of takeovers affected but also the pattern of M&As as businesses engage in "regulatory arbitrage." Firms may be encouraged to acquire targets in countries with less stringent antitrust, environmental, and labor protections than those prevailing in their own countries.[40]

Some things to remember

Current laws require that securities offered to the public must be registered with the government and that target firm shareholders receive enough information and time to assess the value of an acquirer's offer. Federal antitrust laws exist to prevent individual corporations from assuming too much market power. Numerous state regulations affect M&As, such as state antitakeover and antitrust laws. A number of industries are also subject to regulatory approval at the federal and state levels. Finally, gaining regulatory approval in cross-border transactions can be nightmarish because of the potential for the inconsistent application of antitrust laws, reporting requirements, fee structures, and legal jurisdictions.

[39] Sherman, 2018

[40] Farooq et al. (2019) found that collective bargaining mechanisms can offset the tendency of stringent country labor laws to discourage M&As and that collective bargaining improves deal completion rates, reduces time to completion, and increases synergy realization. Why? Collective bargaining can reduce tension between the acquirer and target employees by providing a forum for mediating disputes as they arise and by offering alternatives for employees, including reassignment, early retirement, and retraining.

Chapter discussion questions

2.1 What factors do US antitrust regulators consider before challenging a transaction?
2.2 What are the obligations of the acquirer and target firms according to the Williams Act?
2.3 Discuss the pros and cons of federal antitrust laws.
2.4 When is a person or firm required to submit a Schedule 13(D) to the SEC? What is the purpose of such a filing?
2.5 Give examples of the types of actions that may be required by the parties to a proposed merger subject to an FTC consent decree.
2.6 Ameritech and SBC Communications received permission from the FCC to combine to form the nation's largest local telephone company. The FCC gave its approval, subject to conditions requiring that the companies open their markets to rivals and enter new markets to compete with established local phone companies in an effort to reduce the cost of local phone calls and give smaller communities access to appropriate phone service. SBC had considerable difficulty in complying with its agreement with the FCC. Over an 18-month period, SBC paid the US government $38.5 million for failing to provide rivals with adequate access to its network. The government noted that SBC failed to make available its network in a timely manner, meet installation deadlines, and notify competitors when their orders were filled. Comment on the fairness and effectiveness of using the imposition of heavy fines to promote government-imposed outcomes rather than free market–determined outcomes.
2.7 In an effort to gain approval of their proposed merger from the FTC, top executives from Exxon Corporation and Mobil Corporation argued that they needed to merge because of the increasingly competitive world oil market. Falling oil prices during much of the late 1990s put a squeeze on oil industry profits. Moreover, giant state-owned oil companies pose a competitive threat because of their access to huge amounts of capital. To offset these factors, Exxon and Mobil argued that they had to combine to achieve substantial cost savings. Why were the Exxon and Mobil executives emphasizing efficiencies as a justification for this merger?
2.8 How important is properly defining the market segment in which the acquirer and target companies compete in determining the potential increase in market power if the two firms are permitted to combine? Explain your answer.
2.9 Comment on whether antitrust policy can be used as an effective means of encouraging innovation. Explain your answer.
2.10 The SOA has been very controversial. Discuss the arguments for and against the SOA. Which side do you find more convincing and why?

Answers to these Chapter Discussion Questions are available in the Online Instructor's Guide for instructors using this book.

End-of-chapter case study: behavioral remedies as an alternative to structural remedies in addressing anticompetitive practices

Case study objectives

To illustrate

- Antitrust issues in forming joint ventures among competitors
- Differences between structural and behavior remedies
- How behavioral remedies may be used in lieu of structural remedies

In a consent decree, M&A-related antitrust issues are usually resolved through the sale of assets or businesses in markets where the buyer and target compete directly (structural remedies), by regulating their future conduct through continued monitoring to ensure compliance (behavioral remedies), or some combination. Normally, anticompetitive concerns arise in transactions involving only two parties. However, when the buyer is a joint venture, more than two parties often are involved. This was the case when a Texas area petrochemical plant was acquired by a JV whose partners were also direct competitors. Regulators saw immediately the potential for anticompetitive practices.

Having been closed because of unpaid liens, the M&G Resins petrochemical plant, which was supposed to produce more than 1 million tons per year of plastic used to make soda bottles, was forced into bankruptcy by its creditors in early 2018. To exit the protection of the bankruptcy court, the federal bankruptcy court judge approved the purchase of the plant by a joint venture for about $1.125 billion. Named Corpus Christi Polymers (CCP), the JV consists of firms from Mexico, Thailand, and Taiwan. Still under construction at the time of the purchase, the plant was about 80% complete. Upon completion, it will be the largest plastics manufacturing facility in the United States.

The JV owners include Alpek S.A.B. (Alpek), Indorama Ventures Holdings LP (Indorama), and Far Eastern Investment Limited (Far Eastern). The JV had acquired the plant's assets and intellectual property. Under the terms of the agreement, the partners would finance the completion of the plant. Alpek, headquartered in Mexico, is the largest producer of polystyrene in North America. Thailand-based Indorama is one of the world's leading petrochemical producers. Far Eastern is a wholly owned subsidiary of Far Eastern New Century (FENC), one of the top five polyethylene terephthalate (PET) producers in the world.

After more than 9 months, the Federal Trade Commission (FTC) approved the deal in late January 2019, subject to extensive behavioral remedies. Because DAK, FENC, and Indorama were three of the four PET resin producers in North America that jointly controlled more than 90% of the market, the FTC was concerned that these firms and the JV could collude to set price or manipulate PET prices by restricting production. When fully operational, the JV would have the capacity to supply almost one-fourth of PET in North America. The JV could also provide, so the FTC thought, a conduit for exchanging information among the three partners that could be used to set pricing.

To limit the potential for anticompetitive behavior, ownership stakes of each partner could not exceed one-third of the outstanding shares. In addition, the JV had to offer any unused production capacity to the other owners or to third parties to prevent the owners from affecting price by limiting JV output. Moreover, the JV owners were required to submit in writing an explanation of all communications with other owners that pertained to the JV. JV owners could not hire away key JV personnel and former JV board members, which could have affected adversely the operation of the JV.

The FTC appointed an outsider to monitor the JV's compliance to these requirements. The behavioral remedies also required that the JV would have to notify the FTC for approval to make substantive governance changes to operations. These remedies would remain in force for 20 years, twice as long as the period usually applied in merger consent decrees.

In this instance, the FTC did not require the owners to sell assets to create other competitors as would normally be required had structural remedies been employed. The concern was that such sales could materially weaken the competitiveness of the JV owners. The FTC's consent decree underscores that the FTC is in some instances willing to use only behavioral remedies if the forced sale of assets threatens to weaken other competitors in the marketplace. This case also reflects the FTC's desire to preserve jobs because the owners bought this facility out of bankruptcy. If it could not be sold, it may have been liquidated with the proceeds going to pay the lien holders.

Critics express concern that behavioral remedies are difficult to enforce. In this instance, such concerns were mitigated by using an independent monitor and substantive reporting requirements, limiting the exchange of competitive data, and having the remedies in place for a long time. Although regulators continue to favor the use of structural remedies, behavioral remedies are used when they appear to be the best way to maintain competition.

Discussion questions

1. What is antitrust policy, and why is it important? What does the often-used phrase "anticompetitive practices" mean? Be specific.
2. What is a consent decree? If a consent decree cannot be negotiated successfully, what alternatives are available to the parties involved?
3. What antitrust guidelines are generally followed by regulators in dealing with collaborative arrangements such as joint ventures?
4. Speculate as to the effectiveness of behavioral remedies. Are they likely to be enforceable in the long term? Explain your answer.
5. If the firm being acquired is likely to fail if prevented from doing so, antitrust regulators often approve the deal under what is known as the "failing firm" doctrine. Do you believe that this is a good practice if the resulting merger raises the potential for anticompetitive practices?

Solutions to these case study questions are found in the Online Instructor's Manual available to instructors using this book.

CHAPTER

3

The corporate takeover market: common takeover tactics, antitakeover defenses, and corporate governance

OUTLINE

Mergers, Acquisitions, and Other Restructuring Activities, Eleventh Edition
https://doi.org/10.1016/B978-0-12-819782-0.00003-4

Treat a person as he is, and he will remain as he is. Treat him as he could be, and he will become what he should be. —***Jimmy Johnson***

Inside mergers and acquisitions: proxy fights—to support a takeover or simply to gain influence?

KEY POINTS

- The true motivation for proxy contests is often unclear.
- Proxy fights often are more sound and fury with little lasting effect.

Gannett Co. (Gannett) retained control of its entire board in a proxy fight with Digital First Media (Digital) that ended in mid-May 2019. Financed by hedge funds, Digital had argued that Gannett had been mismanaged and should be sold. After a hotly contested fight to change the composition of Gannett's board, shareholders had elected all of Gannett's nominees, receiving significantly more support than the three nominees proposed by Digital.

Gannett viewed the outcome as a vote of confidence from shareholders in its migration to digital media. In contrast, Digital called the result a win for the entrenched Gannett board.

The dispute between Gannett's board and Digital had started months earlier. Digital had urged Gannett, the largest publisher in the United States by circulation, to undertake a strategic review after Digital made an unsolicited $1.4 billion offer for the firm in January 2019. Gannett rejected the bid, arguing that it undervalued the firm. Gannett also argued publicly that Digital would be unable to finance the all-cash bid. To enlist employee support, the firm highlighted Digital's reputation for aggressive cost cutting. In response, Digital sought to replace three Gannett directors in an effort to gain more board support for its offer.

Both Gannett and Digital lobbied leading proxy advisory services to support their candidates. One such firm recommended that Gannett shareholders support one of Digital's nominees and five of Gannett's.[1] Two other advisory services recommended that Gannett's shareholders support all of Gannett's nominees. The advisory services also cast doubt on Digital's ability to finance their bid and argued that it would be foolish to change the board during a difficult digital transformation period. Digital, they argued, was more interested in achieving representation on the board to gain influence over a competitor. Gannett widely publicized the support the proxy advisory services had given to its slate of nominees.

Despite 5 months of turmoil, the value of Gannett's shares changed very little. Immediately after the announcement that Gannett's nominees had been reelected, the firm's shares rose slightly by 0.7% to $8.93. The firm's share price had jumped more than 26% to $11.82 after Digital's takeover announcement in January, but it had since drifted lower to around $8.75 as confidence that the takeover would actually happen waned.

[1] Proxy advisory firms advise investors how to vote their shares on governance issues. Hedge funds, mutual funds, pension funds, and other institutional investors pay such firms for their advice.

Chapter overview

On August 19, 2019, the business lobbying group, The Business Roundtable, composed of leading US CEOs, announced that it promises "to deliver value to all (stakeholders) . . . for the future success of our companies, our communities, and our country." With this statement of the Purpose of a Corporation, the Business Roundtable codified the need for satisfying or exceeding customer expectations, investing in employees, treating suppliers fairly, and supporting the communities in which businesses have operations.

This statement is largely aspirational in nature. And lacking in performance metrics, it also is largely subjective. Is the long-standing objective of the firm of maximizing shareholder value (as stated in most current finance and economics textbooks) at odds with the Business Roundtable's statement? How do we know when a firm is delivering value to all stakeholders? Can (or should) all stakeholders be treated equally? If not, what are the trade-offs involved? And how do we measure value and over what time period?

These questions are among the many that are addressed in this chapter that are relevant to managing the mergers and acquisitions (M&A) takeover process. The market in which transfers of control between buyers and sellers takes place is sometimes called the *corporate takeover market*. It serves two important functions in a free market economy: allocating resources and disciplining failing corporate managers. Ideally, corporate resources are transferred to those who can manage them more efficiently. Replacing inept managers helps to promote good corporate governance and in turn a firm's financial performance.

Significant attention is paid in this chapter to the pivotal role of the board of directors in promoting good corporate governance and in overseeing the M&A process. Common takeover strategies ranging from friendly to hostile buyouts and tactics, including bear hugs, proxy contests, and tender offers, are discussed in detail. The chapter also addresses how bidding strategies are developed and how common pitfalls are resolved. Activist investment strategies as an alternative to takeovers also are analyzed. Finally, this chapter addresses the advantages and disadvantages of alternative defenses used in change-of-control battles.

A chapter review (including practice questions) is available in the file folder titled Student Study Guide contained on the companion site to this book (https://www.elsevier.com/books-and-journals/book-companion/9780128197820).

Corporate governance: protecting and managing stakeholder interests

Is the traditional view of the primary objective of the firm of maximizing shareholder wealth still relevant today? The answer is a resounding yes! Efforts to maximize shareholder value are affected by the interests of other stakeholders. And most big companies incorporate other stakeholder concerns in their decision making. Failure to do so is a sure path to an underperforming share price and potentially to bankruptcy.

Critics of the shareholder maximization goal argue, often quite legitimately, that firms can do a better job in addressing stakeholder interests. Although considering the interests of all stakeholders is laudable, doing so in practice is complicated. Why? The interests of stakeholders often are conflicting, resulting in trade-offs that a firm's board and management must make. It will always be true that some stakeholders will be treated less well than others. To paraphrase Ben Franklin, you can please some of the stakeholders all the time, all the stakeholders some of the time, but you can't please all the stakeholders all the time. How corporations balance stakeholders' interests is called *corporate governance*: the rules and processes by which a business is controlled and operated. Corporate governance is about leadership and accountability, and it involves all factors internal and external to the firm that interact to protect the interests of corporate stakeholders. Failure to achieve this balance can derail efforts to maximize shareholder value as disputes arise among constituents over control, strategies, and how cash flow will be used. The challenge is to negotiate disputes between disparate groups to achieve mutually acceptable outcomes.

Disputes among constituent groups generally fall into two categories: vertical and horizontal. Whereas vertical disputes result from direct disagreements between managers and shareholders, horizontal disputes are those between other stakeholder groups. Vertical disputes arise when managers, as agents of shareholders, make decisions to increase their wealth and power, which may not be in the best interests of shareholders. Such disputes are generally referred to as agency conflicts and are discussed extensively throughout this book.

Horizontal disputes arise when nonmanagerial stakeholders have conflicting goals, such as different classes of shareholders, creditors versus equity holders, short-term versus long-term investors, large customers and suppliers versus smaller ones, and so on. Although how to deal with such disputes is beyond the scope of this book, the sheer number and diversity of potential disputes underscores the complexity of managing a corporation in the 21st century.

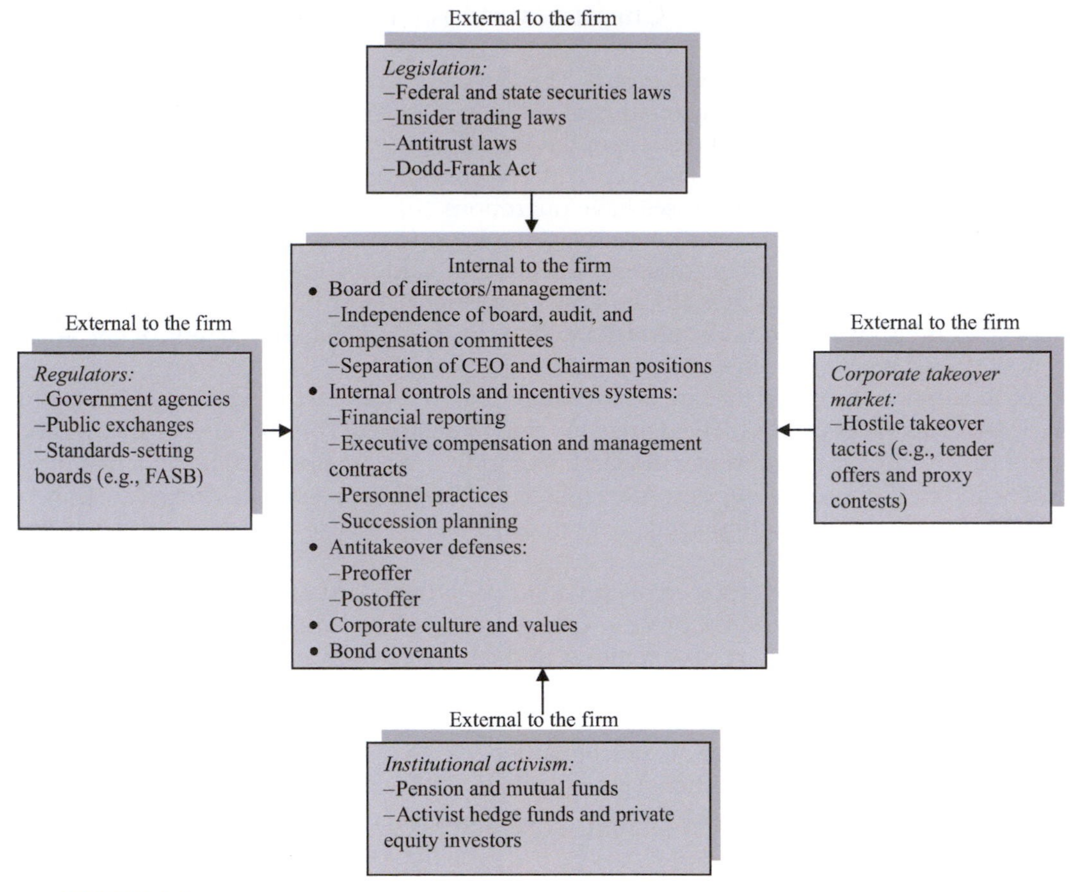

FIGURE 3.1 Factors affecting corporate governance. *FASB*, Financial Accounting Standards Board.

TABLE 3.1 Alternative models of corporate governance

Market model applicable when:	Control model applicable when:
Capital markets are highly liquid	Capital markets are illiquid
Equity ownership is widely dispersed	Equity ownership is heavily concentrated
Board members are largely independent	Board members are largely "insiders"
Ownership and control are separate	Ownership and control overlap
Financial disclosure is high	Financial disclosure is limited
Shareholders focus more on short-term gains	Shareholders focus more on long-term gains

Figure 3.1 illustrates the factors affecting governance, including the corporate takeover market. When capital markets are liquid, investors discipline bad managers by selling their shares (i.e., the market model). When capital markets are illiquid, bad managers are disciplined by those owning large blocks of stock in the firm (i.e., the control model). Table 3.1 summarizes the characteristics of these two common models of corporate governance.

Factors internal to the firm

Governance is affected by the effectiveness of the firm's board, internal controls and incentive systems, takeover defenses, culture, and bond covenants.

The board of directors and management

Boards differ among countries and consist of two basic types: unitary (single) and two-tier (dual) structures. A *unitary board* consists of company managers and independent directors. An *independent (or outside) director* is someone who has not worked for the firm in the past, is not a current manager, does not stand to benefit financially beyond what is paid to other board directors, and is not predisposed to the firm's current business practices. A *two-tier board* consists of a management board composed of company executives, including the CEO, who runs the firm's operations, and a supervisory board composed only of independent directors. Overseeing the management board, the supervisory board is responsible for strategic decisions and contains other stakeholders, such as employees.

Whereas the United States and the United Kingdom have mandated unitary board structures, Germany and Austria use the two-tiered board structure. In other countries, such as France, firms are permitted to switch between the two types of structures. What follows is more descriptive of a unitary board structure. For such boards, the primary duties are to advise the CEO and monitor firm performance. The board hires, fires, and sets CEO pay and is expected to oversee strategy, management, and financial reports to shareholders. So-called *inside directors* may be employees, founding family members, or affiliated with the firm through a banking relationship, a law firm, or a customer or supplier representative. Their value lies in their substantial organizational knowledge. The risk is the potential for conflicts of interest.

The role of independent directors

Some argue that boards should consist mostly of directors independent of or from outside of the firm because of their objectivity. Although their lack of specific firm knowledge may inhibit informed decisions, they reduce monitoring costs by limiting self-serving actions of insiders. Firm value is positively affected by outsider-dominated boards.[2] Boards controlled by outside directors show higher returns when targets are public, given the greater availability of information on public firms.[3]

Acquisitive boards benefit from independent directors with past experience in making successful acquisitions.[4] Moreover, outside directors with an extensive network of contacts[5] and diverse views are better able to advise CEOs in making difficult takeover decisions, such as cross-border M&As.[6] Outside directors with experience in the industry in which the firm competes tend to have the greatest impact on firm value in companies with large investment programs (particularly research and development [R&D]) and excess cash balances. Why? Investment decisions made by industry experts are more likely to boost firm value. However, prior industry experience is less helpful in dynamically changing industries in which the future looks less like the past.[7]

In the United States, the role of the *lead independent director* has become increasingly important among public firms. Such directors are charged with approving meeting agendas, chairing nonmanagement directors' meetings, and serving as a contact point for institutional investors. They also have the authority to call board meetings. Firms with dual CEO–chairman roles, multiple takeover defenses, and large cash holdings often select an independent lead director to reduce the perception of potential agency conflicts. Investors seem to value such directors as their announcement is associated with a 0.7% positive abnormal financial return.[8]

Leadership structure

The chairman and the CEO can either be held by one person (so-called CEO duality or unified leadership) or by different individuals. Does the form of leadership structure affect firm performance? Yes, but only in certain circumstances. With CEO duality, decision making can be faster. But it also is possible for an assertive CEO to limit board efforts to discipline management. Whether leadership structure impacts a firm's performance depends on the quality of leadership, firm size and complexity, the need for rapid decision making, and the effectiveness of external monitoring.

[2] Armstrong et al., 2015

[3] Dahya et al., 2017. Concentrated ownership can lead to less independent boards in common-law countries where shareholder protections are stronger than in civil law countries (Pérez-Calero et al., 2019).

[4] Field et al., 2017

[5] Basuil et al., 2017

[6] Datta et al., 2020

[7] Drobetz et al., 2018

[8] Lamoreaux et al., 2019

CEO duality, when the CEO is highly skilled, can contribute to lower acquisition premiums because of the CEO's takeover experience, negotiating ability, and industry contacts.[9] Moreover, powerful and knowledgeable CEOs in founder and CEO-duality firms can have a positive impact on firm value. For example, information technology firms in which proprietary knowledge is highly concentrated in founders and top management tend to have higher firm values than their peers.[10] Unified leadership tends to be most beneficial for small, relatively simple businesses and for those competing in dynamically changing markets in which nimble decision making is critical for long-term performance.[11]

The concentration of power in one individual can negatively impact firm performance because institutional investors and equity analysts find it difficult to monitor the firm's decision making.[12] The challenges are compounded in the presence of activist investors, because their potential impact increases the level of uncertainty for equity analysts attempting to predict firm performance.[13]

Behavioral and demographic characteristics of CEOs and board members

The quality of CEO and board decisions also is affected by risk aversion and CEO age; however, the effects of the gender and racial board makeup are unclear, as discussed next.

CEO acquisition decisions tend to mirror their personal stock portfolio trading patterns because they may reflect the willingness of CEOs to accept risk. CEOs engaging in relatively conservative trading practices tend to be more successful at avoiding value-destroying M&As than do CEOs whose personal portfolios exhibit high levels of trading activity.[14]

Younger CEOs tend to be more acquisitive than older ones. CEO compensation often reflects firm size, with CEOs of smaller firms earning less than those in larger companies. This creates an incentive for CEOs to pursue deals earlier in their careers, recognizing the potential for future large increases in compensation. Furthermore, CEOs who are underpaid relative to their peers tend to pay larger acquisition premiums in an effort to increase the size of their firms to justify earning higher salaries.[15]

Despite extensive research on the gender and racial composition of boards, the literature is ambiguous as to the impact on board decision making.[16] Some studies show that gender differences can impact firm outcomes. For example, boards with more women directors tend to be less acquisitive and to pay lower premiums when takeovers occur, perhaps reflecting less hubris than men.[17] Another study finds that gender diversity of boards is associated with a lower divestiture rate and greater financial returns on divestitures, but greater racial diversity is associated with lower returns. Why? When backgrounds and opinions are diverse, achieving consensus can become ponderous, contributing to missed opportunities.[18]

Trends in board composition and leadership structure

Although it continues to be common for one person to be CEO and chairman, boards are increasingly composed of independent directors. In the early 1990s, 40% of boards were composed of individuals affiliated with the firm. In recent years, more than 90% of boards have only one or two non-independent directors. Despite this trend, more independent boards are not a panacea because underperforming managers are no more likely to be removed today than in the past. And having more independent directors does not seem to lower CEO pay.[19]

With 20% of Fortune 500 companies' directors on more than one board, the demands on directors' time are substantial. The most talented directors, often on multiple boards, may spend the bulk of their time on boards of the

[9] Ghannam et al., 2019

[10] Chiu et al., 2020

[11] Georgen et al., 2020

[12] Hsu et al., 2020

[13] Flugum and Howe, 2020

[14] Leung et al., 2017

[15] Lee et al., 2019.

[16] Kirsch, 2018

[17] Chen et al., 2019

[18] Kolev and McNamara, 2020

[19] Guthrie et al., 2012

most highly regarded firms that may add to their reputations. And they may be distracted by major issues arising on such boards. Thus they may be less effective on other boards on which they serve.[20] Firms whose directors are busy with outside directorships are often associated with lower profitability.[21] When directors are more focused on a few boards, they are more productive. Firms whose directors serve on relatively few boards are associated with higher profitability, market-to-book ratios, and a greater willingness of board members to serve on committees.[22]

Shareholders appear to be comfortable with the combined role of chairman and CEO. According to Institutional Shareholder Services, only 6% of the 372 proposals to separate the roles at S&P 500 companies during the decade ending in 2016 were approved by shareholders. Perhaps shareholder reticence to eliminate CEO duality reflects the tendency of firm performance to be higher in firms having CEO duality and a reputation for protecting shareholder rights. In firms with weak governance, CEO duality seems to harm firm performance. Therefore simply separating the two functions without having a board that is actively protecting shareholder interests is unlikely to increase shareholder value.

Board performance, size, selection, and compensation

The oft-used adage that information is power is certainly true in the boardroom. Well-connected CEOs often have access to information not readily available to others, giving them greater control over board agendas and the ability to achieve consensus among board members. Access to better information also makes it more difficult to remove underperforming CEOs who claim they have a more accurate view of future competitive trends and that continued reliance of their business strategy will result in eventual success.[23]

Political connections matter. Acquirers whose board members or senior managers include former politicians and regulators are more likely to receive regulatory approval, realize higher announcement date returns, and exhibit superior postmerger operating performance than those that do not.[24] Investors think such acquirers may receive more favorable treatment by regulators and be able to acquire more synergistic targets, such as direct competitors. Former politicians and regulators can be helpful in navigating the regulatory process, gaining access to decision makers for purposes of lobbying, and in receiving government contracts.

According to a 2017 survey by the National Association of Corporate Directors, boards of companies with market capitalizations of at least $10 billion average about 10.9 members, about half of their average size during the 1970s. Smaller boards tend to be more effective, because each member can wield more influence since their vote represents a larger percentage of the total board, thereby effectively reducing the power of the CEO. Smaller boards also are more likely to replace a CEO because of poor performance. Because of smaller boards' perceived effectiveness in promoting good governance and achieving consensus rapidly, firms often downsize their boards when uncertainty over government economic policy increases.[25]

Boards may be slow to dismiss incompetent managers due to cronyism. For publicly traded firms, dismissing high-profile CEOs reflects negatively on the board that hired the CEO, raising investor concerns about board competence. Such concerns could impact the firm's future cost of financing and may help explain why CEOs often seem to be compensated for M&A deals that create as well as destroy value.[26]

How board members themselves are selected may be problematic: based more on their public profile[27] than on past performance. Also, prior acquisition experience may contribute less to cross-border deal success than having board members with different organizational and country experience.[28]

Directors receive different types of compensation: stock, stock options, and fees paid to attend meetings. Director stock ownership is positively related to future corporate performance.[29] Directors on boards of larger

[20] Masulis and Zhang, 2019

[21] Ferris et al., 2020

[22] Hauser, 2018

[23] Guo et al., 2019a

[24] Ferris et al., 2016. Pham (2019) argues that politically connected firms' cost of equity is less sensitive to rising economic policy uncertainty.

[25] Ongsakul et al., 2020

[26] Fich et al., 2015

[27] CEOs of firms viewed as socially responsible are more likely to be selected to serve on outside boards.

[28] Wang, 2019

[29] Bhagat and Bolton, 2014

firms tend to be paid more. Firms with greater growth opportunities pay a larger percentage of director compensation in the form of equity, presumably to better align director interests with those of the firm's shareholders.[30]

When a CEO's compensation is dependent on equity, shareholders are more confident that acquisitions are likely to enhance firm value. Equity-based compensation becomes less important in the presence of large block holders, who closely monitor firm performance.[31]

In the end, too much emphasis is placed on form over substance in achieving effective governance. Form focuses on the size and distribution of the board between independent and non-independent directors and whether the chairman and CEO positions are held by different individuals. Substantive improvement in governance often comes more from the integrity of board members and senior managers and the willingness of board members to remain engaged in the ongoing activities of the business.

The key to effective boards

Board makeup has many facets: skills, gender, age, ethnicity, educational background, and breadth of experience. And the combined effect of different sources of diversity appears to be more important in how boards achieve consensus than any single factor.

Board diversity can result in better board decisions and firm performance when it stimulates more diverse thinking, when nimble decision making is not required, and when consensus is possible. Board diversity appears to have less impact on moderating firm risk when the majority of board members have been in place for a long time because they may be less likely to disagree with strong CEOs because of their close personal relationships.[32]

Another recent study finds that some firms select directors with many different skills to their boards, but other firms focus on a few particular skills. Firms whose directors' skills tend to be highly concentrated tend to outperform those whose directors have more diverse skills. Why? Firms whose boards have highly diverse skill sets may lack common ground, thereby making consensus building more challenging.[33]

Board structure may also affect the link between board diversity and firm performance. Board demographic diversity is positively related to the performance of standalone businesses but negatively related to boards whose members may serve on multiple boards. Such so-called interlocking directorates are generally legal under current US antitrust regulations unless the firms are direct competitors. In some emerging countries, board members may serve on multiple firms within the same industry. Such directors may be more focused on the goals of the group than on those of a single standalone firm.[34]

Target board's advisory role in takeover bids

Target boards often recommend shareholders vote against takeover proposals unless the premium is widely recognized as exceeding the fair value of the firm's shares. If the premium is very high (or very low) shareholders will have greater confidence in making their own decisions, and the board's position is largely ignored. If the adequacy of the premium is unclear, the influence of the board's recommendation can be substantial. Whether the board will be ignored by target shareholders depends on its credibility as measured by the independence of its members and their industry-related expertise, as well as the uncertainty among industry analysts about the true value of target shares.[35]

The declining importance of executive committees

Representing a subset of board members, executive committees have historically played a very influential role in board decision making because they can exert board authority in between board meetings. Although they can be more responsive in addressing "crisis" conditions, their existence may hinder information sharing with the full board. With improving telecommunications, executive committees have declined in importance and are found in

[30] Lahlou et al., 2017

[31] Feito-Ruiz et al., 2017

[32] Bernile et al., 2018

[33] Adams et al., 2018

[34] Aggarwal et al., 2019

[35] Levit, 2017

only about one-fifth of publicly traded firms. Because of their potential for insulating senior management from board monitoring, firms with executive committees are valued less in the stock market and show less CEO turnover.[36]

Internal controls and incentive systems

Critical to aligning shareholder and managerial interests, internal controls help prevent fraud and encourage legal compliance. Financial, legal, and auditing functions, as well as hiring and firing policies, within the firm are examples of internal controls. Compensation, consisting of base pay, bonuses, and stock options, typically underpins incentive systems. Management contracts formally stipulate responsibilities, term of employment, basic compensation arrangements, change-in-control provisions, and severance packages.

Financial incentive systems may create abuses as well as positive behaviors. To rectify management abuses, the Dodd–Frank Act of 2010 gives public firm shareholders the right to vote on executive compensation. Under the so-called "say on pay" rules, such votes must occur at least once every 3 years. The Dodd–Frank Act also requires public firms to develop ways for recovering (so-called "clawbacks") compensation based on executive misconduct.

Compensation plans take many forms. A pure performance-based plan is one in which the CEO makes money only if the shareholders make money. In 2018, Tesla awarded CEO Elon Musk 12 sets of stock options that vest only when the firm hits certain market value, revenue, and profit milestones. The options could be worth as much as $55 billion. Alternatively, managers can own a significant portion of the firm's outstanding stock, or the manager's ownership of the firm's stock comprises a substantial share of his or her personal wealth.[37]

Incentive programs tend to improve acquirer abnormal returns around deal announcement dates and have had an even greater positive impact after the Sarbanes–Oxley Act (SOA) in 2002, which makes senior management more accountable for their actions. Senior managers at firms with high pay for performance incentive plans tend to pay 23.3% lower average merger premiums to public target firm shareholders than firms with more modest incentive plans.[38]

Although management contracts can guarantee pay for failure, they enable firms to attract and retain the best talent and encourage the pursuit of value-enhancing investments by aligning compensation with long-term firm performance and specifying severance packages. Contracts also extend CEO on-the-job tenure. Long-tenured CEOs are more prudent, more likely to buy private firms (which can often be acquired at a discount to their true value), and more likely to acquire targets they understand, such as domestic firms in the same industry.[39]

Although the CEO is motivated by performance-based incentive plans, her or his subordinates are motivated by both performance and promotion-based incentives. Firms that promote from within and encourage subordinates to "compete" for the CEO spot tend to be more acquisitive and induce managers to work harder and pursue M&As that add to shareholder value.[40]

Antitakeover defenses

A firm's board and management may use defenses to negotiate a higher purchase price with a bidder or to protect their current position within the firm. The range of defensive actions is detailed later in this chapter.

Corporate culture and values

Good governance also depends on an appropriate employee culture. Setting the right tone comes from senior management's behavior being consistent with what they demand from employees. A firm's culture is often viewed by management as a valuable asset; as such, their desire to preserve the culture can impact investment policy. Such firms tend to make acquisitions that are on average one-third the size of those made by other firms, enabling their

[36] Vafeas and Vlittis, 2019

[37] An alternative to concentrating ownership in management is for one or more shareholders who are not managers to accumulate a large block of voting shares. These block holders may be more aggressive in monitoring management and more receptive to takeovers, thereby increasing the risk to managers that they will be ousted for poor performance. Block holders can include hedge funds, mutual funds, pension funds, and other corporations. Benamraoui et al. (2019) and Lou et al. (2020) argue that these "outside" (i.e., nonmanagement and nondirector block holders) block holders are a key determinant of future firm performance.

[38] Krolikowski, 2015

[39] Zhou et al., 2020

[40] Nguyen et al., 2020

culture to be dominant in defining the behavior of the employees of the combined firms.[41] When a firm's employment practices are problematic, resulting in litigation and negative media attention, the CEO experiences a loss of reputation and a loss of board seats in subsequent elections because investors view such developments as poor corporate governance.[42]

Bond covenants

Covenants forbid the issuer from undertaking certain actions, such as dividend payments, or require the issuer to meet specific requirements, such as periodic information reporting. Covenants can motivate managers to pursue relatively low-risk investments, such as capital expenditures, and avoid higher-risk investments, such as research and development spending.

Factors external to the firm

Federal and state legislation, the court system, regulators, activist investors, and the corporate takeover market play key roles in maintaining good corporate governance practices.

Legislation and the legal system

The 1933 and 1934 Securities Acts created the Securities and Exchange Commission (SEC), charged with writing and enforcing securities' regulations. The US Congress has since transferred some enforcement tasks to public stock exchanges operating under SEC oversight.[43] Under the SOA, the SEC oversees the Public Company Accounting Oversight Board, whose task is to develop and enforce auditing standards. State legislation also has a significant impact on governance practices by requiring corporate charters to define the role of boards and managers with respect to shareholders.

Stronger investor protections, such as laws and regulations increasing investor access to accurate financial data, limit managerial misuse of corporate resources as proxy contests, takeovers, or investor-initiated lawsuits transfer control to those more able to manage the firm.[44] Class action lawsuits filed during the 2 years before a merger announcement increase the prospect that a firm will become a takeover target as investors overreact to the negative news driving down the firm's market value.[45]

Regulators

The SEC, Federal Trade Commission, and Department of Justice can discipline firms through formal investigations and lawsuits as outlined in Chapter 2. In 2003, the SEC approved new listing standards that would put many lucrative, stock-based pay plans to a shareholder vote. The 2010 Dodd–Frank Act requires listed firms to have fully independent compensation committees and promotes more detailed salary transparency for key managers. However, the regulatory drive for greater transparency, rather than restraining outsized salary increases, may be fueling the upward spiral because of how boards set CEO compensation. Boards look at CEO salaries at comparable firms, pegging salaries at levels above those offered by peer firms to attract or retain the best talent.

Activist investors

Although pension funds, private equity investors, and mutual funds tend to be long-term investors, hedge funds engage in both short- and long-term investing. Activist investors target about one in seven publicly traded firms worldwide.[46] Activist investors can enhance firm value by forcing removal of inept executives, introducing compensation-based incentive plans, changing board makeup, divesting failing assets, and increasing a firm's focus.[47]

[41] Bargeron et al., 2015

[42] Unsal and Brodmann, 2020

[43] The SEC itself has delegated certain responsibilities for setting accounting standards to the not-for-profit Financial Accounting Standards Board.

[44] Larrain et al., 2017

[45] Basnet et al., 2020

[46] Kim et al., 2015

[47] Gantchev et al., 2020

Hedge funds play a significant role as activist investors in the takeover market through merger arbitrage: buying target shares and selling short acquirer shares. Desirous of realizing a quick profit, short sellers are stock traders who sell borrowed shares with the expectation they will decline in value, allowing them to buy them back at a profit.

Shareholders of public firms may submit proposals to be voted on at annual meetings, but such proposals are usually not binding. The firm's board can accept or reject the proposal even if approved by a majority of shareholders. Only 30% of proposals receiving majority support are implemented within 1 year of the vote.[48] Nonbinding proposals approved by shareholders pertaining to takeover defenses, executive compensation, and so on are more likely to be implemented if there is an activist investor likely to threaten a proxy fight.

Directors take notice when shareholders express their discontent through shareholder votes, even when such votes are nonbinding. Directors facing dissent are more likely to depart boards, though those not leaving often are moved to less prominent positions on the board and receive fewer offers from other firms for board positions.[49]

In 2019, Japan's Takeda Pharmaceutical acquired Ireland-based Shire Pharmaceutical for $60 billion in a deal involving a 60% premium. Although Takeda shareholders did support the deal, 52% of the firm's investors voted in favor of a measure requiring management to return much of their performance-related pay if the deal did not meet promised results. The measure did not satisfy the required two-thirds threshold and as such was not binding. However, the message was clear: shareholders would hold management and the board accountable.

Accounting for one-third of activist investments, hedge funds demonstrated announcement date returns of 7% to 8% between 2001and 2016 on investments in target firms, consistent with those returns observed in earlier periods.[50] The most successful hedge funds were those willing to take minority positions in large targets mired in complicated situations. Such firms had a demonstrated track record of either changing the composition of the target's board or getting the board to change direction by using proxy contests, lawsuits, overcoming strong defenses, and replacing board members.[51]

When institutions hold their investments for long periods, they play an important role in promoting good governance and in combating managers' tendency to focus on short-term performance. As long-term investors with significant ownership stakes in the firm, they can communicate directly with management to influence decision making and when necessary threaten to sell their shares or initiate proxy fights. They may impact decisions ranging from investment projects to dividend payouts to accounting practices.

Long-term activist investors can improve governance by initiating or supporting shareholder proposals, improve board quality by influencing the election of board members, and affect executive turnover. By convincing the board to lower takeover defenses, they also are able to lessen management entrenchment. By helping management to prioritize investments better, long-term investors can reduce unproductive investments.[52] In late 2019, AT&T relented to pressure from activist investor Elliot Management by announcing a 3-year plan that included adding two new board members, selling off up to $10 billion worth of noncore businesses, and paying off debt incurred in the Time Warner takeover.

In contrast to long-term activist investors, short sellers seek a quick profit by making managerial misconduct public. Their actions can discourage managers from undertaking value-destroying deals by forcing an acquirer's share price lower through public criticism. They quicken the rate at which the true price of a firm's stock can be discovered by accelerating the incorporation of negative information into stock prices.[53]

When confronted with significant short-selling pressure, board members and managers are faced with the prospect of losing their jobs and receiving less equity-based pay, thereby weakening their resolve to resist the bid. Moreover, it is difficult for the target board to argue that the bid undervalues the firm when shareholders are selling. Anticipating this pressure, bidders may reduce their bids. Although short selling can result in a lower bid, it often raises the probability that the bid will be accepted.[54] Short sellers are more effective than analyst coverage because they have their own capital at stake and are less prone to conflicts of interest.[55]

[48] Ertimur et al., 2010

[49] Aggarwal et al., 2019

[50] Von Lilienfeld-Toal and Schnitzler, 2020

[51] Krishnan et al., 2016

[52] Harford et al., 2018

[53] Chague et al., 2019

[54] Ordóñez-Calafí and Thanassoulis, 2020

[55] Chang et al., 2019

Activist investors can be effective in forcing managers to sell their firms, because their interests coincide with a target firm's shareholders. Bidders want to buy target firm shares as cheaply as possible, but activist investors want the highest price possible. Not surprisingly, bidders often find it difficult to win proxy battles, with activist investors frequently able to force target firm managers to sell to another party at a price higher than the original bid.[56]

The corporate takeover market

Changes in corporate control can occur because of a hostile or friendly takeover or because of a proxy contest initiated by activist investors. The threat of a takeover seems to have at least a modest impact on motivating managers interested in retaining their positions to improve performance.[57] The disciplining effect of a takeover threat can be reinforced when it is paired with a large shareholding by an institutional investor. Moreover, firms whose management has a more short-term than long-term focus are more likely to be subject to takeover bids.[58]

The *management entrenchment theory* suggests that managers use takeover defenses to ensure their longevity with the firm. And such managers tend to be less skilled as measured by their inability to achieve excess financial returns.[59] Although relatively rare in the United States, hostile takeovers and the threat of such takeovers have historically been useful for maintaining good corporate governance by removing bad managers and installing better ones. An alternative viewpoint is the *shareholder interest's theory,* which suggests that management resistance to takeovers is a good bargaining strategy to increase the purchase price to the benefit of shareholders.

Understanding alternative takeover tactics

Implementing a friendly takeover is described briefly in the following section and in detail in Chapter 5. Hostile takeover tactics are described extensively in the following sections.

Friendly takeovers are most common

In friendly takeovers, a negotiated settlement is possible without the acquirer resorting to aggressive tactics. The acquirer and target reach an agreement on the key issues early in the process, such as the long-term business strategy, how they will operate in the short term, and who will be in key executive positions. Often, a *standstill agreement* is negotiated in which the acquirer agrees not to make any further investments in the target's stock for a specific period. This permits negotiations without the threat of more aggressive tactics, such as those discussed in the following sections.

Hostile takeovers are more a threat than a reality

If initial efforts to take control of a target firm are rejected, an acquirer may choose to adopt more aggressive tactics, including the bear hug, the proxy contest, and the tender offer. However, relatively few deals reach this stage. During the 5 years ending 2019, 137 (or about 0.4%) of more than 34,500 deals involving US firms were considered hostile.[60]

Why are hostile deals rare? Arguably, firms are more efficient today than in the 1980s when highly diversified firms offered the likes of such corporate raiders as Carl Icahn and T. Boone Pickens opportunities to reap huge profits by selling them in pieces. The proliferation of takeover defenses has made hostile takeovers more problematic and expensive. Nonetheless, hostile takeovers are relatively rare, making headlines more because they are so infrequent and therefore newsworthy. However, the threat of an unsolicited offer turning hostile increases the likelihood the target firm's management will negotiate a settlement.

[56] Corum et. Levit., 2019

[57] Wang and Wu, 2020

[58] Tunyi et al., 2019

[59] Mishra, 2020

[60] Culpan, December 19, 2019

The bear hug: limiting the target's options

A *bear hug* is an offer to buy the target's shares at a substantial premium to its current share price and often entails mailing a letter containing the proposal to the target's CEO and board without warning and demanding a rapid decision. It usually involves a public announcement to put pressure on the board. Directors voting against the proposal may be subject to shareholder lawsuits alleging they are not working in the best interests of their shareholders. When the bid is made public, the company is likely to attract additional bidders. Institutional investors and arbitrageurs add to the pressure by lobbying the board to accept the offer. By accumulating target shares, they make purchases of blocks of stock by the bidder easier.

Proxy contests in support of a takeover or to gain influence

Activist shareholders often initiate a proxy fight for a variety of reasons: to remove management because of poor performance, promote the spin-off of a business unit or the outright sale of the firm, force a cash distribution to shareholders, or eliminate takeover defenses.[61] Proxy fights enable such shareholders to replace board members with those more willing to support their positions. Corporate bylaws usually stipulate who can nominate board members, to avoid frivolous nominations. Apple Inc.'s bylaws state that only a group of no more than 20 shareholders who collectively own at least 3% of Apple's stock can nominate a director.

Arguing the firm had become uncompetitive, activist investor Nelson Peltz narrowly lost in his effort to gain a seat on the board of consumer products giant Proctor & Gamble (P&G). P&G spent more than $100 million to encourage shareholders to vote against Mr. Peltz, stating that he was not right for the board. Mr. Peltz's Trian fund spent an estimated $25 million on his campaign. Recognizing the degree of shareholder discontent, P&G decided to add him to the board in light of his having lost by 0.1% of the more than 2 billion votes cast. Although Peltz lost the proxy battle, he won the war by making it clear to P&G's board and management that they would have to make many of the changes he was promoting.

Implementing a proxy contest

When the bidder is also a shareholder, the proxy process may begin with the bidder attempting to call a special shareholder meeting. Or the bidder may put a proposal to replace the board at a regular shareholder meeting. Before the meeting, the bidder opens an aggressive public relations campaign, with direct solicitations sent to shareholders and a media campaign to convince them to support their proposals. The target often responds with its own campaign. When shareholders receive the proxies, they may choose to sign and send them directly to a designated collection point, such as a brokerage house.

The impact of proxy contests on shareholder value

Despite a low success rate, proxy fights can result in positive returns to shareholders after a management change, subsequent firm restructuring, expectations of a future change in control, and cash payouts by firms with excess cash balances.[62] When management wins by a wide margin, firm value often declines because little changes.[63]

The hostile tender offer

A *hostile tender offer* circumvents the target's board and management by making the offer directly to the target's shareholders. Although boards discourage unwanted bids initially, they are more likely to relent to a hostile tender offer.[64] Such offers are undertaken for several reasons: (1) as a last resort if the bidder cannot get the target's board and management to yield, (2) to preempt another firm from making a bid for the target, and (3) to close a transaction quickly if the bidder believes that time is critical. A common hostile takeover strategy involves acquiring a

[61] Faleye, 2004

[62] Faleye, 2004

[63] Listokin, 2009

[64] In a study of 1018 tender offers in the United States between 1962 and 2001, Bhagat et al. (2005) found that target boards resisted tender offers about one-fifth of the time. In a study of 49 countries, Rossi and Volpin (2004) found that only about 1% of 45,686 M&A deals between 1990 and 2002 were opposed by target boards.

controlling interest in the target and later completing the combination through a merger. This strategy is described in detail later in this chapter.

Pretender offer tactics: toehold bidding strategies

Toehold investments involve taking a less than controlling interest in a target firm. Bidders do so to amass shares at a price less than the eventual offer price. Such purchases are secretive to avoid increasing the average price paid. For public firms, investments exceeding 5% of the target's shares must be made public. Bidders achieve leverage with the voting rights associated with the stock purchased and can sell this stock if the takeover attempt is unsuccessful. After a toehold position has been made, the bidder may attempt to call a special stockholders meeting to replace the board or remove takeover defenses.[65]

Although rare in friendly takeovers, these actions are commonplace in hostile transactions, comprising about half of all such takeovers. In friendly deals, bidders are concerned about alienating a target firm's board; however, in hostile deals, the target firm would have rejected the initial bid anyway. The frequency of toehold bidding has declined since the early 1990s in line with the widespread adoption of takeover defenses and a decline in the frequency of hostile deals. Acquirers with a toehold investment in the target firm before a takeover represent about 5.4% of public firms and 1.4% of private firms. The average toehold investment is about 31% of the target's shares (higher in hostile but lower in friendly ones).[66]

The value of a toehold investment is greatest when one potential bidder has access to significantly less information than competing bidders. After the toehold investment is made, the more informed bidders can make offers giving the toehold investor a better idea of what constitutes a reasonable bid. The incentive for one bidder to make a toehold investment early in the bidding process is less if other bidders are also having difficulty in obtaining accurate information. Furthermore, the value of the toehold investment as a means of gaining information is less when the number of potential bidders is large, because some bidders with poor information may make excessive offers for the target based on hubris.[67]

Implementing a tender offer

Tender offers can be for cash, stock, debt, or some combination. Unlike mergers, tender offers frequently use cash as the form of payment. Deals involving securities take longer to complete because of the need to comply with SEC and state registration requirements and to obtain shareholder approval. If the offer involves a share exchange, it is referred to as an *exchange offer*. Whether cash or securities, the offer made to target shareholders may be extended for a specific period and may be unrestricted (any-or-all offer) or restricted to a certain percentage or number of the target's shares.

Tender offers restricted to purchasing less than 100% of the target's shares may be oversubscribed. For example, if the tender offer is for 70% of the target's outstanding shares and 90% of the target's stock is offered, the bidder may prorate the purchase of stock by buying only 63% (i.e., 0.7×0.9) of the stock tendered by each shareholder. Tender offers for publicly firms are usually successful, although the success rate is lower if it is contested.

Federal securities laws impose reporting, disclosure, and antifraud requirements on acquirers who initiate tender offers. After the tender offer has been made, the acquirer cannot purchase any target shares other than the number specified in the offer. Section 14(D) of the Williams Act requires that any individual or entity making a tender offer resulting in owning more than 5% of any class of equity must file a Schedule 14(D)-1 with the SEC.

Multitiered offers

A bid can be either a one- or two-tiered offer. In a *one-tiered offer*, the acquirer announces the same offer to all target shareholders, which provides the potential to purchase control of the target quickly and discourages other bidders from disrupting the deal. In a *two-tiered offer*, the acquirer offers to buy some shares at one price and more at a lower price at a later date. The form of payment in the second tier may be less attractive, consisting of securities rather than cash. The intent of the two-tiered approach is to incent target shareholders to tender their shares early in the process

[65] When such a meeting can be called is determined by the firm's articles of incorporation, governed by the laws of the state in which the firm is incorporated. A copy of a firm's articles of incorporation can usually be obtained from the Office of the Secretary of State of the state where the firm is incorporated.

[66] Betton et al., 2009

[67] Povel et al., 2014

to receive a more attractive price. Because shareholders tendering their shares in the first tier enable the acquirer to obtain a controlling interest, their shares are worth more than those choosing to sell in the second tier.

When the bidder has a controlling interest in the target (usually 50.1%), the bidder may initiate a *back-end merger*. This is done by calling a special shareholder meeting seeking approval for a merger, in which minority shareholders are required to accede to the majority vote.

Alternatively, the bidder may operate the target firm as a partially owned subsidiary, later merging it into a newly created wholly owned subsidiary. Many state statutes require equal treatment for all tendering shareholders as part of two-tiered offers and give target shareholders *appraisal rights*[68] that allow those not tendering shares in the first or second tier to ask the state court to determine a "fair value" for the shares.[69] State statutes may also contain *fair-price provisions*, in which all target shareholders, including those in the second tier, receive the same price and redemption rights, enabling target shareholders in the second tier to redeem their shares at a price similar to that paid in the first tier.

The major disadvantage of owning less than 100% of the target's voting shares is the potential for dissatisfied minority shareholders owning blocks of stock to disrupt efforts to implement important management decisions. Also, the acquirer will incur the cost of providing financial statements to both majority and minority shareholders.

Comparative success rates

Friendly deals are the most common takeover tactic used, for good reason. According to Thomson Reuters, success rates among hostile bids and proxy contests are relatively low. For the 25-year period ending in 2016, about 40% of hostile takeover attempts resulted in a completed deal. Proxy contests that actually went to a shareholder vote concluded in a victory for the challenger approximately 26% of the time during the 5 years ending in 2016. If we include settlements between the company's board and activist groups, those initiating the proxy fight won roughly 57% of the time during the same period. The success of proxy contests has paralleled the growth in activist hedge funds, which have grown from less than $100 million in assets under management in 2000 to more than $140 billion in 2016.[70]

Other tactical considerations

Successful takeovers depend on the size of the offer price premium; the board's composition; and the makeup, sentiment, and investment horizon of the target's current shareholders. Other factors include the target's bylaws and the target's ability to add takeover defenses.

The importance of premium, board composition, and investor sentiment

The target's board will find it more difficult to reject offers exhibiting substantial premiums to the target's current share price. The composition of the target's board also influences what the board does, because one dominated by independent directors may be more likely to negotiate the best price for shareholders by soliciting competing bids than to protect itself and current management. The final outcome of a hostile takeover also is dependent on the composition of the target's ownership, how shareholders feel about management's performance, and how long they intend to hold the stock. Firms held predominately by short-term investors (i.e., <4 months) are more likely to receive a bid exhibiting a lower average premium of as much as 3% when acquired. Firms held by short-term investors have a weaker bargaining position with the bidder because of the limited loyalty of such shareholders.[71]

[68] In 2015, Delaware's Court of Chancery had 43 appraisal lawsuits filed, up from 16 the prior year. The majority of the plaintiffs settled for a small increase in the value of their target shares. Although appraisal rights can be abused by opportunistic target shareholders in an effort to gain more than fair value for their shares, such instances appear to be relatively rare (Kalodimos et al., 2017).

[69] The minority shares may be subject to a "minority discount" because they are worth less to the bidder than those acquired in the process of gaining control.

[70] Bartlett et al., 2017

[71] Gaspara et al., 2005

To assess these factors, an acquirer compiles lists of stock ownership by category: management, officers, employees, and institutions such as pension and mutual funds. This information can be used to estimate the target's *float*—total outstanding shares less shares held by insiders. The larger the share of stock held by insiders such as corporate officers, family members, and employees, the smaller the number of shares that are likely to be easily purchased by the bidder, because these types of shareholders are less likely to sell their shares.

Finally, an astute bidder will analyze the target firm's bylaws for provisions potentially adding to the cost of a takeover.[72] Such provisions could include a staggered board, the inability to remove directors without cause, or supermajority voting requirements for approval of mergers. These and other measures are detailed later in this chapter.

Contract considerations

To heighten the chance of a successful takeover, the bidder will include provisions in a *letter of intent* (LOI) to discourage the target firm from disavowing preliminary agreements. The LOI is a preliminary agreement between two companies intending to merge, stipulating areas of agreement between the parties as well as their rights and limitations. It may contain features protecting the buyer; among the most common is the *no-shop agreement*, prohibiting the target from seeking other bids or making public information not readily available.

Contracts often grant the target and acquirer the right to withdraw from the agreement. This usually requires the payment of *breakup* or *termination fees*, sums paid to the acquirer or target to compensate for their expenses. Expenses could include legal and advisory expenses, management time, and the costs associated with opportunities that may have been lost to the bidder while involved in trying to close this deal.

Termination fees are used more frequently for targets than acquirers because targets have greater incentives to break contracts and seek other bidders. Such fees give the target firm some leverage with the bidder. Averaging about 3% of the purchase price and found in about two-thirds of M&As, such fees result in about a 4% higher premium paid to target firms.[73] Although termination fees increase the target's cost to withdraw from a deal, there is little evidence that large fees discourage targets from accepting other bids.[74] Breakup fees paid by the bidder to the target firm are called *reverse breakup fees* and have become more common in recent years as buyers, finding it difficult to finance deals, have backed out of signed agreements. The *stock lockup*, an option granted to the bidder to buy the target firm's stock at the first bidder's initial offer, is another form of protection for the bidder. It is triggered whenever the target firm accepts a competing bid. Because the target may choose to sell to a higher bidder, the stock lockup arrangement usually ensures that the initial bidder will make a profit on its purchase of target stock.

As an alternative to breakup fees, bidders may seek promises from the biggest shareholders of a target company to support the deal. Such commitments are known as *irrevocables*. The intent is to signal potential bidders that the proposed deal already has major target shareholder support. In the United Kingdom, regulators began discouraging the use of breakup fees in an attempt to get higher offer prices for target firm shareholders. Usually irrevocables are negotiated in secret 12 to 48 hours ahead of a deal announcement. Such arrangements often include a caveat that allows shareholders to drop their backing if an alternative bid arises that is much higher than the bid they initially supported.

Developing a bidding strategy

Tactics used in a bidding strategy represent a series of decision points, with objectives and options clearly stated. A poor strategy can be costly to CEOs, who may lose their jobs.[75] CEOs who are disciplined bidders are less likely to be replaced than those who are not.[76] Common bidding-strategy objectives include winning control of the target, minimizing the control premium, minimizing transaction costs, and facilitating postacquisition integration.

[72] Unlike charters, which are recorded in the Office of the Secretary of State in the state where the firm is incorporated, corporate bylaws generally are held by the firm along with other corporate records and may be available through the firm's website or by requesting a copy directly from the firm.

[73] Jeon et al., 2011

[74] Neyland et al., 2018

[75] Lehn et al. (2006) found that 47% of acquiring-firm CEOs were replaced within 5 years.

[76] Jacobsen, 2014

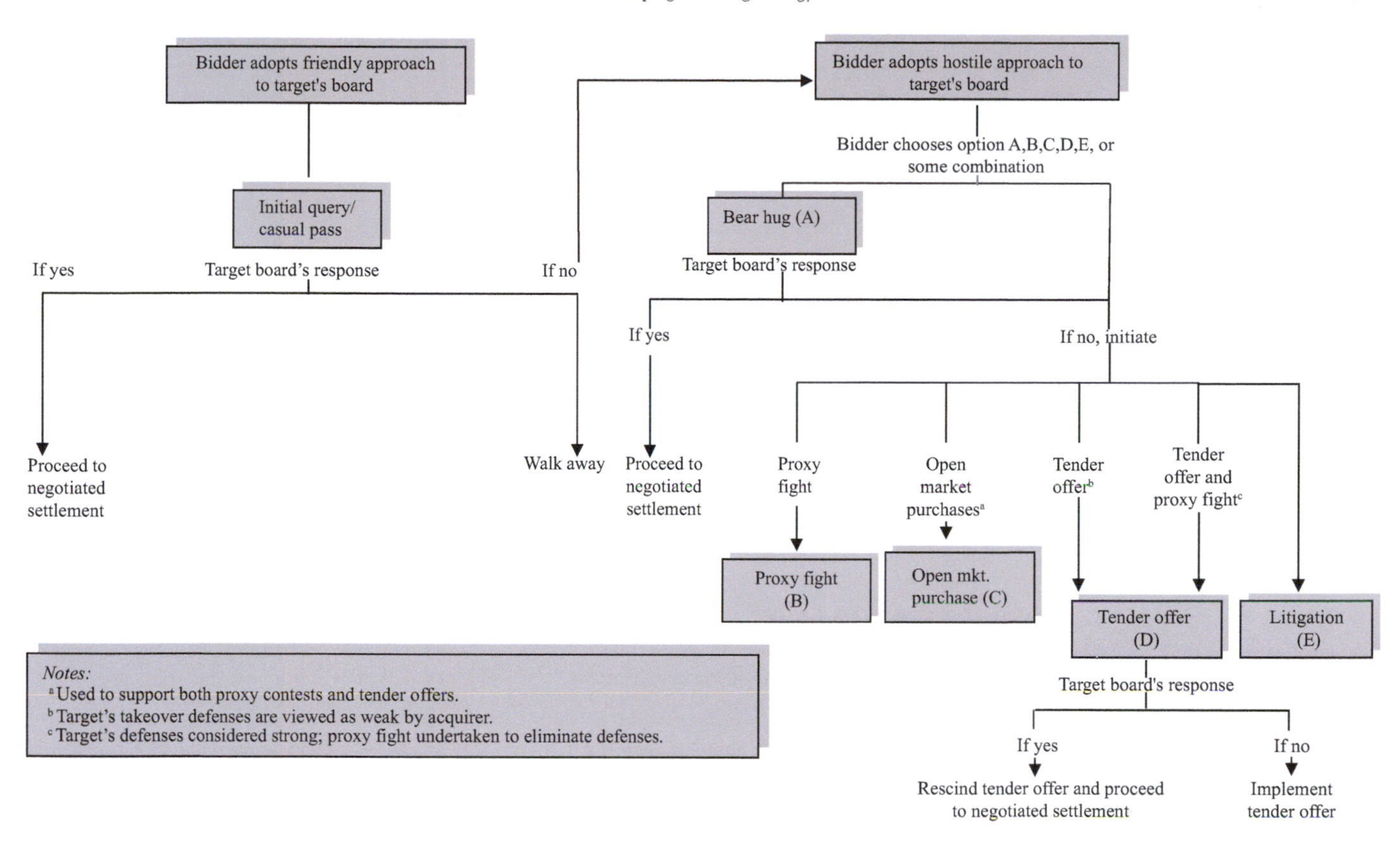

FIGURE 3.2 Alternative takeover tactics.

If minimizing the purchase price and transaction costs while maximizing cooperation between the two parties is critical, the bidder may choose the "friendly" approach. This reduces the loss of key personnel, customers, and suppliers while control is changing hands. Friendly takeovers avoid an auction environment, which may raise the target's purchase price. Amicable deals facilitate premerger integration planning and increase the pace at which the firms can be integrated after closing.

Reading Figure 3.2 from left to right, we see that the bidder initiates contact informally through an intermediary (sometimes called a *casual pass*) or through a more formal inquiry. If rejected, the bidder's options are to walk away or become aggressive. In the latter case, the bidder may undertake a bear hug, hoping that pressure from large institutional shareholders and arbs will nudge the target toward a negotiated settlement. If that fails, the bidder may accumulate enough shares in the open market from institutional investors to call a special shareholder meeting or initiate a proxy battle to install new board members receptive to a takeover or to dismember the target's defenses.

Although generally less expensive than tender offers (which include a premium to the target's current share price), proxy campaigns are expensive, with an average cost of $6 million, not including possible litigation costs.[77] In extreme cases, the costs of proxy battles can exceed $100 million.[78] If the target's defenses are weak, the bidder may forego a proxy contest and initiate a tender offer for the target's stock. If the target's defenses appear formidable, the bidder may implement a proxy contest and a tender offer concurrently.

Litigation often is used to pressure the target's board to relent to the bidder's proposal or remove defenses and is most effective if the firm's defenses appear to be onerous. The bidder may initiate litigation that accuses the target's board of not giving the bidder's offer sufficient review, or the bidder may argue that the target's defenses are not in the best interests of the target's shareholders. Table 3.2 summarizes common bidder objectives and the advantages and disadvantages of the various tactics that may be used to achieve these objectives.

[77] Gantchev, 2013

[78] In late 2017, P&G spent more than $100 million to thwart activist investor Nelson Peltz's effort to gain a board seat. Mr. Peltz's firm Trian is rumored to have spent as much as $25 million.

TABLE 3.2 Advantages and disadvantages of alternative takeover tactics

Common bidder strategy objectives

- Gain control of target firm
- Minimize the size of the control premium
- Minimize transactions costs
- Facilitate postacquisition integration

Tactic	*Advantages*	*Disadvantages*
Casual pass (i.e., informal inquiry)	• May learn target is receptive to deal	• Gives advance warning
Bear hug offer (i.e., letter to target board forcefully proposing takeover)	• Raises pressure on target to negotiate a deal	• Gives advance warning
Open market purchases (i.e., acquirer buys target shares on the public market)	• May lower cost of transaction • Create profit if target agrees to buy back bidder's toehold position • May discourage other bidders	• Can result in a less than controlling interest • Limits on amount one can purchase without disclosure • Some shareholders could hold out for higher price • Could suffer losses if takeover attempt fails • Could alienate target management and make a friendly takeover more difficult
Proxy contest (i.e., effort to obtain target shareholder support to change target board or dismantle target defenses)	• Less expensive than tender offer • May obviate need for tender offer	• Relatively low probability of success if target stock is widely held • Adds to transactions costs
Hostile tender offer (i.e., direct offer to target shareholders to buy shares not supported by target's board or management)	• Pressures target shareholders to sell stock • Bidder not bound to purchase tendered shares unless desired number of shares tendered	• Tends to be the most expensive tactic • Disrupts postmerger integration because of the potential loss of key target managers, customers, and suppliers
Litigation (i.e., lawsuits accusing target board of improper conduct)	• Puts pressure on the target board	• Expense

Activist investors: gaining influence without control

An increasingly important threat to corporate boards and management is the activist investor. They are shareholders who influence managerial and board decisions by exercising or threatening to exercise their voting rights. Unlike hostile takeovers, an activist investor does not want control of the firm but rather to purchase enough shares to gain the attention of other investors by making their grievances well known. After this has been achieved, the investor will promote a particular agenda designed to change a firm's behavior to increase firm value.

Companies have become more proactive by determining where they are vulnerable and how they might minimize risk. Firms may spin off or divest underperforming businesses or increase dividends to reduce excess cash on the balance sheet or to borrow to undertake share buybacks. Company management is now more inclined to talk to activists in an effort to keep the discussions out of the media so as not to impact the firm's reputation or share price.

Activist investors who succeed in achieving their objectives do so by gaining a seat(s) on the board of the target company, giving them access to proprietary information and an opportunity to express their opinions at board meetings. Allowing such representation avoids highly public proxy fights. Unlike their predecessors, active investors in recent years are less interested in short-term gains and more interested in agitating for a specific long-term goal: a change in business strategy, higher dividends, or a change in the makeup of the firm's board.

Although some efforts are successful, others go horribly wrong. TPG-Axon was able to push out Sand Ridge Energy's CEO, Tom Ward. In contrast, William Ackman, in attempting to remove Target Corporation's CEO, ended up selling his stake at a loss of almost $500 million.

Banks having an ongoing interest in lending to firms have traditionally supported management in shareholder votes.[79] In contrast, pension funds often build their reputations on serving investor interests and can influence the voting behavior of small investors.[80] And mutual funds often reap substantial revenue by providing administrative services to the firms in which they invest, such as providing back-office operations for 401(k) pension plans. This creates a potential conflict of interest: do fund managers vote shares to support management or in the best interests of those investing in funds managed by the mutual fund?

Institutional voting power is heavily concentrated among three index fund managers (Blackrock, State Street Global Investors, and Vanguard), which on average currently hold 25% of all shares voted in corporate elections. These holdings are expected to increase in the future, exacerbating potential conflicts of interest.[81] For example, mutual funds whose directors also are on boards of firms in which the funds have made investments tend to more often support management in proxy votes than funds that do not have such connections.[82]

Critics argue that activist investors seek to limit shareholder rights by noting their potential adverse impact on firm value when they force a board and management to focus on short-term decisions, often at the expense of long-term performance. For example, forcing a board to pay dividends to reduce cash on the balance sheet or to borrow to repurchase shares may limit the firm's ability to pursue future high-growth opportunities. However, the empirical evidence does not seem to support these claims. On average, firms' operating performance measured by return on assets improved relative to their industry peers during the 5 years after the activist's investment.[83]

Understanding alternative takeover defenses

Managers who focus on sustaining long-term value, even at the expense of the firm's current profitability, are less likely to face takeover than managers pursuing current profitability at the expense of shareholder value.[84] However, in practice, even the best managers strain investor patience because the implementation of their strategy is taking longer than expected. As such, managers often argue that they need to have sufficient takeover defenses in place to gain the time necessary for their corporate strategies to be deemed successful by investors.

Takeover defenses are designed to slow down an unwanted offer or to force a suitor to raise the bid to get the target's board to rescind the defense. They can be grouped in two categories: those put in place before receiving an offer (preoffer) and those implemented after receipt of an offer (postoffer). Given the number of alternative defenses, it is critical to understand that no individual defense is suitable for all firms at all times because the relative costs and benefits of specific defenses depend on the firm's unique circumstances. Table 3.3 shows the most commonly used preoffer and postoffer defenses.

Preoffer defenses

Preoffer defenses are used to delay a change in control, giving the target firm time to erect additional defenses after the unsolicited offer has been received. Such defenses generally fall into three categories: poison pills,[85] shark repellents, and golden parachutes. Table 3.4 summarizes the advantages and disadvantages of preoffer defenses.

[79] Dahiya et al. (2020) find that activist's efforts resulting in a reduction in a firm's assets (caused by a divestiture or spinoff) increase the risk associated with bank loans by reducing the firm's liquidation value in bankruptcy.

[80] Gine et al., 2017

[81] Bebchuk and Hirst, 2019

[82] Calluzzo and Kedia, 2020. Note that this pattern also could reflect better informed decisions.

[83] Bebchuk et al., 2015

[84] Tunyi et al., 2019

[85] Poison pills could be viewed as postoffer defenses because they can be implemented after an offer has been made.

TABLE 3.3 Alternative preoffer and postoffer takeover defenses

Preoffer defenses	Postoffer defenses
Poison pills[a]: • Flip-over rights plans • Flip-in rights plans • Blank check preferred stock plans	**Greenmail** (bidder's investment purchased at a premium to what bidder paid as inducement to refrain from any further activity)
Shark repellents (implemented by changing bylaws or charter):	**Standstill agreements** (often used in conjunction with an agreement to buy bidder's investment)
Strengthening the board's defenses • Staggered or classified board elections • "For cause" provisions	
Limiting shareholder actions with respect to: • Calling special meetings • Consent solicitations • Advance notice provisions • Supermajority rules	
Other shark repellents • Anti-greenmail provisions • Fair-price provisions • Dual-class recapitalization • Reincorporation	
Golden parachutes (change-of-control payments)	**White knights**
	Employee stock ownership plans
	Leveraged recapitalization
	Share repurchase or buyback plans
	Corporate restructuring
	Litigation

[a]Although many different types of poison pills are used, only the most common forms are discussed in this text. Note also that the distinction between preoffer and postoffer defenses is murky because, increasingly, poison pill plans are put in place immediately after the announcement of a bid. Pills can be adopted without a shareholder vote because they are issued as a dividend, and the board has the exclusive authority to issue dividends.

Poison pills (shareholder rights plans and blank check preferred stock)

A *poison pill* involves a board issuing rights to current shareholders, other than of an unwanted investor, to buy the firm's shares at an exercise price below their current market value. Because they are issued as a dividend and the board usually has the exclusive authority to declare dividends, a pill can be adopted without a shareholder vote and implemented either before or after a hostile bid.

If a specified percentage (usually 10%–20%) of the target's common stock is acquired by a hostile investor, each right entitles the holder to purchase common stock or some fraction of participating preferred stock of the target firm (a "flip-in pill").[86] If a merger, consolidation, sale of at least some percentage (usually 50%) of the target's assets, or announced tender offer occurs, the rights holder may purchase acquirer common shares (a "flip-over pill"). Both the flip-in and flip-over pills entitle their holders upon paying the exercise price to buy shares having a value on the date the pill is triggered equal to some multiple (often two times) the right's exercise price. Rights are redeemable at any

[86]The fraction of a preferred share is intended to give the shareholder about the same dividend, voting, and liquidation rights as would one common share and should approximate the value of one common share.

TABLE 3.4 Advantages and disadvantages of preoffer takeover defenses

Type of defense	Advantages for target firm	Disadvantages for target firm
Poison Pills: Raising the Cost of Acquisitions		
Flip-over pills (rights to buy stock in the acquirer, activated with 100% change in ownership)	• Dilutes ownership position of current acquirer shareholders • Rights redeemable by buying them back from shareholders at nominal price	• Ineffective in preventing acquisition of <100% of target (bidders could buy controlling interest only and buy remainder after rights expire) • Subject to hostile tender contingent on target board's redemption of pill • Makes issuer less attractive to white knights
Flip-in pills (rights to buy target stock, activated when acquirer purchases <100% change in ownership)	• Dilutes target stock regardless of amount purchased by potential acquirer • Not given to investor who activated the rights • Rights redeemable at any point before triggering event	• Not permissible in some states because of discriminatory nature • No poison pill provides any protection against proxy contests
Shark Repellents: Strengthening the Board's Defenses		
Staggered or classified boards	Delays assumption of control by a majority shareholder	May be circumvented by increasing size of board, unless prevented by charter or bylaws
Limitations on when directors can be removed	"For cause" provisions narrow range of reasons for removal	Can be circumvented unless supported by a supermajority requirement for repeal
Shark Repellents: Limiting Shareholder Actions		
Limitations on calling special meetings	Limits ability to use special meetings to add board seats and remove or elect new members	States may require a special meeting if a certain percentage of shareholders requests a meeting
Limiting consent solicitations	Limits ability of dissatisfied shareholders to expedite a proxy contest process	May be subject to court challenge
Advance-notice provisions	Gives board time to select its own slate of candidates and to decide an appropriate response	May be subject to court challenge
Supermajority provisions	May be applied selectively to events such as hostile takeovers	Can be circumvented unless a supermajority of shareholders is required to change provision
Other Shark Repellents		
Anti-greenmail provision	Eliminates profit opportunity for raiders	Eliminates greenmail as a takeover defense
Fair-price provisions	Increases the cost of a two-tiered tender offer	Raises the cost to a white knight unless waived by typically 95% of shareholders
Dual-class recapitalization or supervoting stock	Concentrates control by giving "friendly" shareholders more voting power than others	Difficult to implement because requires shareholder approval and only useful when voting power can be given to pro-management shareholders
Reincorporation	Takes advantage of most favorable state antitakeover statutes	Requires shareholder approval; time-consuming to implement unless subsidiary established before takeover solicitation
Golden parachutes	Emboldens target management to negotiate for a higher premium and raises the cost of a takeover to the hostile bidder	Negative public perception; makes termination of top management expensive; cost not tax deductible; subject to nonbinding shareholder vote

time by the board (usually at $0.01 per right), expire after some period (sometimes up to 10 years), and trade on public exchanges.

The flip-in pill discourages hostile investors from buying a minority stake, because it dilutes their ownership interest as more target shares are issued. If the hostile investor buys a 20% interest in the firm and the number of target shares doubles, the investor's ownership stake is reduced to 10%. The value of the investor's investment also decreases as other shareholders buy more shares at a deeply discounted price. Efforts by the hostile investor to sell shares at what she or he paid are thwarted by the willingness of other shareholders, having acquired shares at a much lower price, to sell below the price paid by the hostile investor.

The cost of completing the takeover rises as the number of shares that must be acquired in a cash offer increases or the number of acquirer shares issued in a share exchange rises (thereby diluting current acquirer shareholders). Similarly, the flip-over poison pill dilutes the acquirer's current shareholders and depresses the value of their investment as more acquirer shares are issued at below their current market value.

Netflix adopted a poison pill, having both flip-in and flip-over rights, in response to a 9.98% investment stake in the firm by investor Carl Icahn. Each shareholder, except Icahn, received a right for each common share held as of November 12, 2012, to buy one one-thousandth of a new preferred share at an exercise price of $350 per right if an investor buys more than 10% of the firm without board approval. If triggered, each flip-in right entitled its holder to purchase, by paying the right's exercise price, a number of shares of Netflix common stock having a market value of twice the exercise price (i.e., $700).

At the time of the issue, Netflix common stock traded at $76 per share. Each right would be convertible into 9.2 common shares—(2 × $350)/$76—if the pill was triggered. If the firm was merged into another firm or it was to sell more than 50% of its assets, each flip-over right would entitle the holder to buy a number of common shares of the acquirer at the then-market value at twice the exercise price after payment of the $350 exercise price.

Poison pill proponents argue that it prevents a raider from acquiring a substantial portion of the firm's stock without board permission. Because the board generally has the power to rescind the pill, bidders are compelled to negotiate with the target's board, which could result in a higher offer price. Pill defenses may be most effective when used with staggered board defenses because a raider would be unable to remove the pill without winning two successive elections.[87] Detractors argue that pill defenses simply entrench management.

Landmark legal precedents have strengthened takeover defenses. In 2011, the Delaware Chancery Court deferred to managerial discretion as long as the board is found to be upholding its fiduciary responsibilities to the firm's shareholders.[88] The ruling allows target boards to use a poison pill as long as the board deems it justified, and it is far-reaching because Delaware law governs most US publicly traded firms. In 2014, the Delaware state court legitimized the use of the two-tiered poison pill to discriminate against activist investors by limiting the ownership stake in a company of a specific investor.[89]

Blank check preferred stock is a class of preferred shares over which the firm's board has the authority to determine voting rights, dividends, and conversion rights without shareholder approval. The most common reason for a firm to have such stock is to discourage an unwanted takeover of the firm. Normally, a firm must amend its articles of incorporation to create such stock. After this is done, the board now has the power to issue a class of preferred shares that can be converted to a substantial number of voting shares intended to increase the cost of a takeover. Other reasons for blank check preferred stock are to allow the board to quickly raise capital or as an equity contribution used in the formation of a business alliance.

Shark repellents

Shark repellents are takeover defenses achieved by amending either a *corporate charter* or *corporation bylaws*.[90] They predate poison pills as a defense, and their success in slowing down takeovers and making them more expensive has been mixed. Their primary role is to make it more difficult to gain control of the board through a proxy fight at an

[87] Bebchuk et al., 2002

[88] After having revised its hostile offer for Airgas twice, Air Products asked the Delaware Court on February 10, 2010, to invalidate Airgas's poison pill. On February 15, 2011, the court ruled that the board has the right to prevent shareholders from voting on the takeover offer as long as it is acting in good faith.

[89] In 2014, the Delaware state court blocked efforts by hedge fund mogul Daniel Loeb to remove a poison pill at legendary auction house Sotheby. Loeb argued that the poison pill plan unfairly discriminated against his firm. The pill specifically limited him to no more than 10% of Sotheby's shares while letting passive (long-term) investors hold as much as 20% of Sotheby's shares without triggering the pill. Sotheby argued, and the court concurred, that it had adopted the plan to protect shareholders from coercive takeover tactics.

[90] The charter gives the corporation its legal existence and consists of the *articles of incorporation*, a document filed with a state government by the founders of a corporation, and a *certificate of incorporation*, a document received from the state after the articles have been approved. The corporation's powers thus derive from the laws of the state and from the provisions of the charter. Rules governing the internal management of the corporation are described in the corporation's bylaws, which are determined by the corporation's founders.

annual or special meeting. Shark repellents necessitate a shareholder vote because they require amendments to a firm's charter. Although there are many variations of shark repellents, the most typical are staggered board elections, restrictions on shareholder actions, anti-greenmail provisions, differential voting rights (DVR) shares, and debt-based defenses.

Strengthening the board's defenses

Corporate directors are elected at annual shareholder meetings by a vote of the holders of a majority of shares who are present and entitled to vote. The mechanism for electing directors differs among corporations, with voting shares being cast either through a straight vote or cumulatively. With *straight voting*, shareholders may cast all their votes for each member of the board of directors, virtually ensuring that the majority shareholder(s) will elect all of the directors. For example, assume that a corporation has four directors up for election and has two shareholders, one owning 80 shares (i.e., the majority shareholder) and one owning 20 shares (i.e., the minority shareholder). With each share having one vote, the majority shareholder will always elect the director for whom he or she casts his or her votes.

In *cumulative voting* systems, the number of votes each shareholder has equals the number of shares owned times the number of directors to be elected. The shareholder may cast all of these votes for a single candidate or for any two or more candidates. With cumulative voting, all directors are elected at the same time. Using the same example, the majority shareholder will have 320 votes (80×4), and the minority shareholder will have 80 votes (20×4). If the minority shareholder casts all of her votes for herself, she is assured of a seat because the majority shareholder cannot outvote the minority shareholder for all four board seats.[91]

In states where cumulative voting is mandatory, companies can distribute the election of directors over a number of years to make it harder for a dissatisfied minority shareholder to gain control of the board. The *staggered* or *classified board election* divides the firm's directors into different classes. Only one class is up for reelection each year. A 12-member board may have directors divided into four classes, with each director elected for a 4-year period. In the first year, the three directors in what might be called "class 1" are up for election; in the second year, "class 2" directors are up for election; and so on. A shareholder, even one who holds the majority of the stock, would have to wait for three election cycles to gain control of the board. Moreover, the size of the board is limited by the firm's bylaws to preclude the dissident shareholder from adding board seats to take control of the board.

For-cause provisions specify the conditions (e.g., fraud, regulatory noncompliance) for removing a member of the board of directors. This narrows the range of permissible reasons and limits the flexibility of dissident shareholders in contesting board seats.

Limiting shareholder actions

The board can restrict shareholders' ability to gain control of the firm by bypassing the board. Limits can be set on their ability to call special meetings, engage in consent solicitations, and use supermajority rules (explained later). Firms frequently rely on the conditions under which directors can be removed (i.e., the "for cause" provision discussed earlier) and a limitation on the number of board seats as defined in the firm's bylaws or charter.[92]

Restricting the circumstances when shareholders can call special meetings limits their opportunity to introduce a new slate of directors or to push for a rescission of certain defenses, such as a poison pill. A firm's bylaws often require that a new slate of directors can be nominated only at its annual meeting and restrict the ability of shareholders to call special meetings. This allows shareholders wishing to replace directors who are up for reelection only one opportunity to do so at the annual meeting.

In some states, shareholders may take action, without a special shareholder meeting, to add to the number of seats on the board, remove specific board members, or elect new members. These states allow dissatisfied shareholders to obtain support for their proposals simply by obtaining the written consent of shareholders. Called *consent solicitation*, this process requires firms to comply with the disclosure requirements applicable to proxy contests. Shareholders

[91] Although there are many possible combinations, if the majority shareholder was to cast 81 votes for each of three seats, she would have only 77 votes remaining (i.e., 320 − 243) for the last seat. As the number of directors increases, it becomes easier for the minority shareholder to win a seat (or seats) because the majority shareholder's votes must be spread over more directors to block the minority shareholder.

[92] In 2020, the SEC voted to require shareholders to hold $25,000 of a firm's stock for 1 year, up from $2000 previously, to submit shareholder resolutions. That threshold falls to $15,000 after 2 years of ownership and to $2000 after 3 years to minimize costly "nuisance" submissions.

vote by responding to a mailing, thus circumventing the delays inherent in setting up a meeting to conduct a shareholder vote.[93]

Corporate bylaws may include *advance-notice provisions* requiring shareholder proposals and board nominations to be announced well in advance, sometimes as long as 2 months, of an actual vote, to buy time for management. *Supermajority rules* require a higher level of approval than is standard to amend the charter for transactions such as M&As. Such rules are triggered when an "interested party" acquires a specific percentage of shares (e.g., 5% −10%). Supermajority rules may require that as much as 80% of the shareholders must approve a proposed merger or a simple majority of all shareholders except the potential acquirer.

Other shark repellents

Other shark repellent defenses include anti-greenmail provisions, fair-price provisions, DVR shares, reincorporation, and golden parachutes. These are discussed next.

Anti-greenmail provisions

Dubbed "greenmail," bidders in the 1980s profited by taking an equity position in a firm, threatening takeover, and subsequently selling their shares back to the firm at a premium over what they paid for them. Many firms have since adopted charter amendments, called *anti-greenmail provisions*, restricting the firm's ability to repurchase shares at a premium.

Fair-price provisions

Requirements that any acquirer pay minority shareholders at least a fair market price for their stock are called *fair-price provisions*. The fair market price may be expressed as some historical multiple of the company's earnings or as a specific price equal to the maximum price paid when the buyer acquired shares in the company.[94]

Dual-class recapitalization

A firm may create more than one class of stock to separate the performance of individual operating subsidiaries, compensate subsidiary management, maintain control, or prevent hostile takeovers. The process of creating another class of stock is called a *dual-class recapitalization* and involves separating shareholder voting rights from cash flow rights.

Voting rights indicate the degree of control shareholders have over how a firm is managed, whereas cash flow rights are rights to receive dividends. Shares with different voting rights, DVR shares, may have multiple voting rights (so-called supervoting shares), fractional voting rights, or no voting rights. DVR shares may have 10 to 100 times the voting rights of another class of stock or a fraction of a voting right per share (e.g., a shareholder might be required to hold 100 DVR shares to cast one vote). Shares without voting rights but having cash flow rights may pay a dividend higher than those with voting rights. After being approved by shareholders, the new class of stock is issued as a pro rata stock dividend or an exchange offer in which the new class of stock is offered for one currently outstanding.

Dual-class structures tend to concentrate voting power because supervoting shares are issued as a pro rata dividend; later, shareholders are given the option of exchanging their supervoting shares for shares offering higher dividends, with managers retaining their supervoting shares. In dual-class structures, the largest shareholder owns, on average, about 23% of the firm's equity and about 58% of the voting rights.[95]

Investors tend to show less interest in shares in which the separation between ownership and control is great.[96] Some studies find that firm value is reduced as controlling shareholders erect excessive takeover defenses, create

[93] Whereas the winning vote in a proxy fight is determined as a percentage of the number of votes actually cast, the winning vote in a consent solicitation is determined as a percentage of the number of shares outstanding. A dissatisfied shareholder may find it easier to win a proxy contest because many shareholders simply do not vote.

[94] In two-tiered tender offers, the fair-price provision forces the bidder to pay target shareholders who tender their stock in the second tier the same terms offered to those tendering their stock in the first tier.

[95] Baulkaran, 2014

[96] Cumming et al., 2019

agency conflicts, and avoid higher-risk value—enhancing investments.[97] Other studies document an increase in firm value when the firm moves from a single- to a dual-class capital structure because controlling shareholders have more time to focus on longer-term strategies, are subject to less short-term pressure, and are more inclined to pursue higher-risk growth opportunities.[98]

Dual-class structures can create agency costs when controlling shareholders receive benefits not available to other shareholders. For example, controlling shareholders can invest the firm's cash in other firms in which they have an interest.[99] When control is concentrated, insiders can create weaker boards, allowing the insiders to entrench themselves. Dual-class firm managers can manipulate earnings to conceal the full extent of the benefits they receive from having control. Acquirers in which control is concentrated also tend to overpay for target firms as managers engage in empire building.[100]

The degree to which controlling shareholders can extract benefits varies with the strength of corporate governance. Firms with dual-class structures and with strong shareholder rights protections often exhibit increasing firm value. Why? The shareholder protections limit the ability of those with supervoting shares to exploit other classes of shareholders. Such firms allow shareholders to call special meetings, act by written consent, have no poison pill, have no staggered board, and offer shareholders cumulative voting rights.[101] The elimination of the dual-class structure dilutes the voting power of controlling shareholders (whose high vote shares lose their multiple voting rights), making the firm vulnerable to shareholders seeking a change in the control of the firm through proxy contests. The firm's market value often increases after the elimination of the dual-class structure for US firms.[102] Similar findings have been documented in the United Kingdom.[103]

The New York Stock Exchange has allowed firms to go public with dual-class structures since the 1980s. As of 2019, 15% of the firms on US exchanges had dual-class shares. This compares to about 1% in 2005. Other major indices exclude dual-class firms. FTSE Russell excludes firms whose free float (i.e., shares outstanding less restricted shares) comprises less than 3% of total voting power. S&P Dow Jones excludes all dual-class firms, and MSCI reduces the weight such firms have in its indices. Limitations on the inclusion of firms in these indices means shareholders in dual-class firms will not benefit from the trend toward passive investment in stock indices.[104]

Reincorporation

A target may change the state or country where it is incorporated to one where the laws are more favorable for implementing takeover defenses by creating a subsidiary in the new state and later merging with the parent. Several factors need to be considered in selecting a location for incorporation, such as how the courts have ruled in lawsuits alleging breach of corporate director fiduciary responsibility in takeovers as well as the laws pertaining to certain takeover tactics and defenses. Reincorporation requires shareholder approval.

Golden parachutes (change-of-control payouts)

Employee severance packages, triggered when a change in control takes place, are called *golden parachutes*, which cover only a few dozen employees and terminate after a change in control. They can vary substantially with some including a lump-sum payment, but others contain stock grants, options, health insurance, pension plans, consultancy arrangements, and even use of corporate jets.[105] They are designed to raise the bidder's acquisition cost rather than to gain time for the board. Such packages may serve the interests of shareholders by making senior management more willing to accept an acquisition.[106]

[97] Gompers et al., 2010

[98] Jordan et al., 2016

[99] Caixe et al., 2019

[100] Thraya et al., 2019

[101] Li et al., 2017

[102] Lauterbach et al., 2015

[103] Braggion et al., 2019

[104] Dual-class firms circumvent index restrictions by adding "sunset" provisions or by phasing out supervoting shares after a certain number of years following the firm's initial public offering.

[105] Maskara et al., 2017

[106] Fich et al., 2016

Golden parachutes are often associated with a reduction in firm value around their adoption date. They may increase the chance of a takeover but destroy firm value by encouraging CEOs to accept deals not in the best interests of the firm's shareholders. For instance, the target's CEO may accept overvalued acquirer shares to close the deal and trigger payout of the golden parachute even though such shares are likely to decline in value.[107]Actual payouts to management, such as accelerated equity awards, pensions, and other deferred compensation after a change in control, may significantly exceed the value of golden parachutes.[108] Tax considerations and legislation affect corporate decisions to implement such compensation packages.[109]

Postoffer defenses

When an unwanted suitor has approached a firm, a variety of additional defenses can be introduced. These include greenmail to dissuade the bidder from continuing the pursuit; defenses designed to make the target less attractive, such as restructuring and recapitalization strategies; and efforts to place an increasing share of the company's ownership in friendly hands by establishing employee stock ownership plans (ESOPs) or seeking white knights. Table 3.5 summarizes the advantages and disadvantages of these postoffer defenses.

TABLE 3.5 Advantages and disadvantages of postoffer takeover defenses

Type of defense	Advantages for target firm	Disadvantages for target firm
Greenmail	Encourages raider to go away (usually accompanied by a standstill agreement)	Reduces risk to raider of losing money on a takeover attempt; unfairly discriminates against nonparticipating shareholders; generates litigation; triggers unfavorable tax issues and bad publicity
Standstill agreement	Prevents raider from returning for a specific time period	Increases amount of greenmail paid to get raider to sign standstill; provides only temporary reprieve
White knights	May be a preferable to the hostile bidder	Involves loss of target's independence
Employee stock ownership plans (ESOPs)	Alternative to white knight and highly effective if used in conjunction with certain states' antitakeover laws	Employee support not guaranteed; ESOP cannot overpay for stock because transaction could be disallowed by federal law
Recapitalizations	Makes target less attractive to bidder and may increase target shareholder value if incumbent management is motivated to improve performance	Increased leverage reduces target's borrowing capacity
Share buyback plans	Reduces number of target shares available for purchase by bidder, arbs, and others who may sell to bidder	Cannot self-tender without Securities and Exchange Commission filing after the hostile tender is underway; reduction in the shares outstanding may facilitate bidder's gaining control
Corporate restructuring	Going private may be an attractive alternative to the bidder's offer for target shareholders and for incumbent management	Going private, sale of attractive assets, making defensive acquisitions, or liquidation may reduce target's shareholder value versus bidder's offer
Litigation	May buy time for target to build defenses and increases takeover cost to the bidder	May have negative impact on target shareholder returns

[107] Bebechuk et al., 2014

[108] Offenberg et al., 2012

[109] The 1986 Tax Act imposed penalties on these types of plans if they create payments that exceed three times the employee's average pay over the previous 5 years and treats them as income and thus not tax deductible by the paying corporation. More recently, the Dodd—Frank bill of 2010 gives shareholders the opportunity to express their disapproval of golden parachutes through a nonbinding vote.

Greenmail

Greenmail consists of a payment to buy back shares at a premium price in exchange for the acquirer's agreement not to initiate a hostile takeover. In exchange for the payment, the potential acquirer is required to sign a *standstill agreement*, specifying the amount of stock, if any, the investor can own and the circumstances under which the raider can sell such stock.[110]

White knights and white squires

A target may seek another firm or *white knight* willing to acquire the target on terms more favorable than those of other bidders. Fearing a bidding war, the white knight often demands protection in the form of a *lockup*. This may involve giving the white knight options to buy stock in the target that has not yet been issued at a fixed price or to acquire specific target assets at a fair price. Such lockups make the target less attractive to other bidders. So-called *white squires* are investors willing to support a firm's board and management in the event of an unwanted takeover attempt. Unlike a white knight, which agrees to acquire the entire firm, the white squire is willing to purchase a large block of stock often at a favorable price, an attractive dividend yield, and for a seat on the board.

Employee stock ownership plans

ESOPs are trusts that hold a firm's stock as an investment for its employees' retirement program. They can be quickly set up, with the firm either issuing shares directly to the ESOP or having an ESOP purchase shares on the open market. The stock held by an ESOP is likely to be voted in support of management in the event of a hostile takeover attempt.

Leveraged recapitalization

Recapitalizing involves issuing new debt to buy back stock or to finance a dividend payment or both. Although debt is a means of forcing managers to focus on operating performance, it can allow them to become entrenched. The additional debt reduces the firm's borrowing capacity, making it less attractive to a bidder. The payment of a dividend or a stock buyback may persuade shareholders to support the target's management in a proxy contest or hostile tender offer.[111] Recapitalization may require shareholder approval, depending on the company's charter and the laws of the state in which it is incorporated.[112]

Share repurchase or buyback plans

Share buybacks are used to reward shareholders,[113] signal undervaluation, fund ESOPs, satisfy option plans, adjust capital structure, ward off takeovers, and when there are few attractive investment options. When used as a takeover defense, share buybacks reduce the number of shares that could be purchased by the potential buyer or arbitrageurs. What remains are shares held by those who are less likely to sell, namely individual investors.[114]

Share repurchase announcements may actually increase the probability a firm will be taken over, especially if the firm appears vulnerable to a takeover because of weak defenses or poor governance. Why? Because such firms' share

[110] Courts view greenmail as discriminatory because not all shareholders are offered the opportunity to sell their stock back to the target firm at an above-market price. Nevertheless, courts in some states (e.g., Delaware) have found it appropriate if done for valid business reasons. Such reasons could include the need for the firm to stay focused on implementing its business strategy. Courts in other states (e.g., California) have favored shareholder lawsuits, contending that greenmail breaches fiduciary responsibility.

[111] The primary differences between a leveraged recapitalization and a leveraged buyout are the firm remains a public company and that management does not take an equity stake in the firm in a leveraged recapitalization.

[112] Shareholders benefit from a dividend or capital gain resulting from a stock repurchase. The increased interest expense shelters some of the firm's taxable income and may encourage management to improve the firm's performance. Thus current shareholders may benefit more from this defense than from a hostile takeover.

[113] Alderson et al. (2019) argue that although share repurchases reduce assets available to bondholders in bankruptcy and transfer wealth from bondholders to shareholders, share buybacks signal management's belief that the firm's shares are undervalued, benefitting bondholders as firm value increases.

[114] Share buybacks make firm ownership less concentrated as large shareholders such as institutional investors, perhaps showing a greater preference for liquidity, appear to be more likely to participate in buybacks than individual shareholders (Golbe et al., 2013).

prices often underperform before buybacks, and share buyback announcements call attention to their likely undervaluation.

Corporate restructuring

Restructuring involves taking the company private, selling assets, undertaking an acquisition, or even liquidating the firm. "Going private" entails the management team's purchase of the bulk of a firm's public shares. This may create a win–win situation for shareholders, who receive a premium for their stock, and for management, who retain control. Alternatively, the target may make itself unattractive by divesting assets the bidder wants, with the proceeds financing share buybacks or a special shareholder dividend. A target also may undertake a so-called *defensive acquisition* to reduce excess cash balances and its current borrowing capacity. A firm may choose to liquidate the company, pay off creditors, and distribute the remaining proceeds to shareholders as a *liquidating dividend*. This makes sense if the liquidating dividend exceeds what the shareholders would have received from the bidder.

Litigation

More than 90% of large deals experience at least one lawsuit, often a class action lawsuit. Lawsuits may involve alleged antitrust concerns, violations of securities laws, target undervaluation, inadequate bidder disclosure, and fraudulent behavior. Targets seek a court injunction to stop a takeover until the court has decided the merits of the allegations. By preventing a bidder from buying more stock, the target is gaining time to erect more defenses.

Litigation seldom prevents a takeover, but it may uncover information about the bidder through the "discovery" process that leads to more substantive litigation. Most lawsuits are settled before going to court. Bidders may sue targets to obtain shareholder mailing lists or to have takeover defensives removed.

Although there is considerable evidence that litigation generally negatively impacts firm value, class action lawsuits may deter managers from empire building. Acquirers in states in which federal court rulings have reduced class action lawsuits have tended to acquire larger targets, followed by lower returns, especially those with weak corporate governance.[115]

The impact of takeover defenses on shareholder value

Statistical outcomes are heavily dependent on the size and quality of the sample and the testing methodology used. Small changes in sample size and the application of different statistical tests can lead to very different conclusions.[116]

Takeover defenses and target firm shareholder financial returns

Considerable research during the past 2 decades suggests that takeover defenses on average have a slightly negative impact on target firm shareholder value. However, there is evidence that the conclusions of these studies may be problematic. Why? Because variables sometimes appear to be relevant because they are proxies for variables excluded from the analysis.

Recent research demonstrates that the results of these studies change significantly when other factors are considered. These factors include the presence of other state antitakeover laws, a firm's previous defenses, and court decisions.[117] Other studies document specific situations in which staggered boards and poison pills can add to firm value. Some studies question whether takeover defenses even matter to shareholder value because of offsetting factors.

This section is intended to wade through the numerous recent studies addressing these issues. Empirical studies finding a negative relationship between firm value and takeover defenses support the notion that management acts in its own interests (management entrenchment theory), but those finding a positive relationship support the idea that management acts in the best interests of shareholders (shareholders' interests theory).

[115] Chung et al., 2020. In 1999, a US Ninth Circuit Court of Appeals ruling made it more difficult to implement class action lawsuits in states under its jurisdiction.

[116] Cohen et al., 2017

[117] Karpoff et al., 2018

Management entrenchment theory

The creation of a detailed "management entrenchment index"[118] revealed that during the 1990s, firms scoring lower on the index (i.e., exhibiting lower levels of entrenchment) had larger positive returns than firms with higher scores.[119] The close correlation between a firm's entrenchment and abnormal returns disappeared in the 2000s because investors had already bid up the prices of those firms that had removed takeover defenses in the 1990s and penalized those that had not.[120] Another large study concluded that managers at firms protected by takeover defenses are less subject to takeover and are more likely to engage in "empire-building" acquisitions that destroy firm value.[121]

Still another study found that firms moving from staggered board elections to annual elections of directors experience an abnormal return of 1.8%, reflecting investor expectations that the firm is more likely to be subject to a takeover. More recently, a study found a close positive correlation between the number of takeover defenses in place and director compensation. This suggests that directors who propose such defenses directly benefit to the extent they are insulated from activists and hostile takeovers.[122]

The negative impact of takeover defenses on firm value is most pronounced after judicial approval of such defenses in the 1985 landmark Delaware Supreme Court decision of *Moran v. Household*. The court case validated the use of poison pills, giving boards the sole right to adopt such measures. The court ruling also granted boards broader powers to adopt other types of takeover defenses, as long as they were reasonable, and wide legal discretion to reject unsolicited takeover bids. Following the ruling, firms experienced an average 5% reduction in their market value immediately after the announcement that they had adopted a poison pill. Even in the absence of a poison pill, firms adopting other measures restricting shareholder rights exhibited a decline in firm value of 1.7%.[123]

Moran v. Household reinforced another Delaware Court ruling involving *Unocal v. Mesa Petroleum*, also in 1985, legitimizing the two-tiered tender offer. The effect of these two cases was to weaken the disciplinary impact of hostile takeover threats by giving boards the legal authority to reject unsolicited takeover bids. Delaware court decisions shape laws in other states. In fact, many states have adopted Delaware's poison pill statutes, and not a single state has invalidated the use of poison pills.[124]

Protectionist antitakeover legislation, often in the name of national security, also can contribute to entrenching management. France's Alstrom Decree passed in 2014 stipulated that five industry sectors, accounting for 30% of all publicly traded French firms, allows the government to veto M&A deals targeting firms in these sectors if the bidder is foreign.[125]

Shareholder interests theory

It is widely held that the *Moran v. Household* and *Unocal v. Mesa Petroleum* cases and the spread of poison pills contributed to management entrenchment. However, there is evidence that the opposite has occurred. Poison pills since these cases were litigated have contributed to larger takeover premiums but have had little impact on deal completion rates.[126]

Takeover defenses may not reduce deal completion rates, but they can discourage opportunistic bidders seeking buyouts at "bargain" prices. Therefore the bids that are received by target firms with defenses in place are likely to be

[118] Bebchuk et al. (2005) created a management entrenchment index in an effort to assess which of 24 provisions tracked by the Investor Responsibility Research Center had the greatest impact on shareholder value. The index includes staggered boards, limits to shareholder bylaw amendments, supermajority requirements for mergers, supermajority requirements for charter amendments, poison pills, and golden parachutes.

[119] Cain et al., 2017

[120] Bebchuk et al., 2010

[121] Masulis et al., 2007

[122] Souther, 2016

[123] Cremers et al., 2014

[124] In 1995, additional Delaware court rulings validated other types of poison pills. These cases include *Unitrin, Inc. v. American General Corp.* and *Moore Corp. v. Wallace Computer Services Inc.*

[125] Frattaroli, 2020

[126] Heron et al., 2015

higher than they would have been had the firm been defenseless.[127] The degree of resistance to a takeover attempt enables target firm shareholders to realize higher premiums than they might have otherwise.[128]

Takeover defenses may also allow a firm's senior management to communicate potentially negative information to investors on a more timely basis because of their feeling somewhat protected from takeover threats. The gradual release of negative information can allow the firm's share price to adjust in a more orderly manner rather than to crash when the accumulated information is released to surprised shareholders.[129]

An empirical study spanning 1978 to 2015 finds no evidence that staggered boards have a negative impact on firm value and under certain circumstances can have a significant positive impact.[130] Staggered boards, so goes the argument, can create value by enabling management to focus on long-term value-enhancing investments such as R&D. Making it easier to remove board members can disrupt the firm's commitment to such investments.[131] Furthermore, firms with substantial takeover defenses can create shareholder value by reducing the focus on short-term results in the presence of large blockholders monitoring firm performance.[132]

Still another study questions whether takeover defenses have much of an impact on shareholder value. Competition for takeovers, the authors reason, is now more likely to take place in private through a controlled auction process in which targets contact potential bidders. Moreover, takeover premiums have not declined over time. The researchers conclude that these findings are consistent with the shareholder interests' hypothesis, which suggests that target boards and managers are more likely to negotiate aggressively on behalf of shareholders.[133] This conclusion is supported by another study that finds that takeover bids are most often rejected because they are of low quality, and target management's primary motive is to negotiate higher bids to increase shareholder value.[134]

Leveraged recapitalizations and target firm financial returns

How investors react to the announcement of a leveraged recapitalization depends on how they assess the motives of the firm's board and management. The shares of firms managed by poor-performing managers often display decidedly negative financial returns when they announce substantial additional borrowing in the wake of a takeover attempt. Financial returns are even more negative if the potential acquirer later withdraws the offer. Investors reason that they are now stuck with bad management and a highly leveraged firm. Shareholders of target firms with high-performing managers realize less negative and often positive returns if the offer is withdrawn as investors anticipate that existing management will enhance value by more than the premium offered by the potential acquirer.[135]

Leveraged recapitalization is a defensive tactic more common in countries with liquid capital markets (providing easy access to inexpensive capital) and significant investor protections than in countries with poorly developed capital markets and investor safeguards. Abnormal returns tend to be negative for such firms around the announcement of additional borrowing and become more negative if the takeover proposal is withdrawn.[136]

Takeover defenses and public offerings

Takeover defenses can create greater initial public offering (IPO) value if investors believe the firm can attract, retain, and motivate effective managers and employees. Such defenses give the new firm time to implement its business plan and to upgrade employee skills. The firm's IPO value is likely to be higher when it has strong takeover

[127] Goktan et al., 2012

[128] Dimopoulos et al. (2015) estimate that in about three-fourths of deals involving only one bidder the acquisition price paid is determined largely by the degree of target resistance.

[129] Bhargavi et al., 2016

[130] Cremers et al., 2017; Amihud et al., 2017

[131] Bebchuk et al. (2017) dispute the findings of Cremers et al. (2017).

[132] Drobetz and Momtaz, 2020

[133] Liu et al., 2018

[134] Bates et al., 2017

[135] Jandik et al., 2015

[136] Jandik et al., 2017

defenses and large customers, dependent suppliers, and strategic partners.[137] Why? Because takeover defenses tend to strengthen the firm's business relationships with its customers, suppliers, and other strategic partners because they increase the likelihood that commitments negotiated with the firm will be sustained.

Some things to remember

Corporate takeovers facilitate the allocation of resources and promote good governance by disciplining underperforming managers. Other factors external to the firm—such as federal and state legislation, the court system, regulators, and institutional activism—also serve important roles in maintaining good governance practices. Governance also is affected by the professionalism of the firm's board of directors as well as by the effectiveness of the firm's internal controls and incentive systems, takeover defenses, and corporate culture.

Chapter discussion questions

Answers to these Chapter Discussion Questions are available in the Online Instructor's Manual for instructors using this book.

3.1 What are the management entrenchment and the shareholders' interests' hypotheses? Which seems more realistic in your judgment? Explain your answer.

3.2 What are the advantages and disadvantages of the friendly versus hostile approaches to a corporate takeover? Be specific.

3.3 What are the primary advantages and disadvantages of common takeover defenses?

3.4 How may golden parachutes for senior management help a target firm's shareholders? Are such severance packages justified in your judgment? Explain your answer.

3.5 How might recapitalization as a takeover defense help or hurt a target firm's shareholders? Explain your answer.

3.6 Anheuser-Busch (AB) rejected InBev's all-cash offer price of $65 per share, saying it undervalued the company, despite the offer's representing a 35% premium to AB's preannouncement share price. InBev refused to raise its offer while repeating its strong preference for a friendly takeover. Speculate as to why InBev refused to raise its initial offer price. Why do you believe that InBev continued to prefer a friendly takeover? What do you think InBev should have done to pressure the AB board to accept the offer?

3.7 What do you believe are the primary factors a target firm's board should consider when evaluating a bid from a potential acquirer?

3.8 If you were the CEO of a target firm, what strategy would you recommend to convince institutional shareholders to support your position in a proxy battle with the bidding firm?

3.9 AB reduced its antitakeover defenses in 2006, when it removed its staggered board structure. Two years earlier, it did not renew its poison pill provision. Speculate as to why the board acquiesced in these instances. Explain how these events may have affected the firm's vulnerability to a takeover.

3.10 In response to Microsoft's efforts to acquire the firm, the Yahoo board adopted a "change in-control" compensation plan. The plan stated that if a Yahoo employee's job is terminated by Yahoo without cause (i.e., the employee is performing his or her duties appropriately) or if an employee leaves voluntarily because of a change in position or responsibilities within 2 years after Microsoft acquires a controlling interest in Yahoo, the employee will receive 1 year's salary. Yahoo notes that the adoption of the plan is an effort to ensure that employees are treated fairly if Microsoft wins control. Microsoft views the tactic as an effort to discourage a takeover. With whom do you agree and why?

End-of-chapter case study: new technologies drive value chain consolidation

Case study objectives

To illustrate

[137] Johnson et al., 2015.

- Common tactics employed in hostile takeovers
- Common takeover defenses and how they are used as a negotiating tool
- How multiple bidders impact purchase prices

The move to 5G wireless technology has not only sparked increased interest in chipmakers but also in firms supplying critical components used in fabricating semiconductors. Such suppliers count the likes of behemoths Intel and Samsung among their customers. Their sheer size gives them substantial negotiating leverage over their suppliers. Consequently, suppliers are taking steps to achieve the scale necessary to produce the increasingly sophisticated products demanded by chipmakers while holding prices at competitive levels.

On January 28, 2019, Entegris Inc. (Entegris), a provider of products used to purify, protect, and transport critical materials used in semiconductor chip fabrication, announced that it had reached a share for share exchange deal structured as a merger of equals with Versum Materials Inc. (Versum). The deal valued Versum, a provider of specialty materials for semiconductor makers, at $4.3 billion. Entegris argued that the combination of the two firms would create a specialty materials firm with greater product breadth and world-class research and development capabilities. However, the deal also had an unintended side effect.

The announcement caught the attention of Germany's Merck KGaA, a family-owned leader in health care and performance materials, which entered the fray in early February with an unsolicited all-cash $4.8 billion offer to buy Versum. After being rebuffed several times by Versum, Merck implemented a hostile tender offer in late February worth $5.5 billion.

Versum argued that synergy with Entegris was greater than with Merck; Merck countered that the Versum board was not acting in the best interests of its shareholders. Versum's board announced on February 28, 2019, a rights plan giving all shareholders the right to purchase common stock at a heavily discounted price, triggered if a bidder bought more than 12.5% of the firm's shares. Versum's board could redeem the rights at $0.01 per right at any time. Any person or group owning more than 12.5% of the firm's stock before the plan was introduced would be exempt. The plan was structured such that it would not be triggered by the merger agreement to combine Versum and Entegris.

Merck threatened a proxy contest to change the board's makeup to include members favorable to their offer and willing to rescind the rights plan. Both Merck and Versum solicited shareholders to support the list of directors they were supporting. Under increasing shareholder pressure, Versum's board entered into negotiation with Merck. The two firms jointly announced on April 12, 2019, that they had reached an agreement in which Merck would buy all outstanding Versum shares at $53 per share payable in cash. The deal valued Versum at $5.8 billion; Merck would also assume Versum's $700 million in outstanding debt. The deal was expected to be immediately accretive to Merck's earnings per share and to create $85 million in annual synergies by the third full year after closing.

Merck's revised bid constituted a 10.4% increase from its initial bid and a 28% premium to Versum's closing price of $41.40 on February 26, the day before Merck announced its initial bid. According to the agreement with Versum, Entegris had 1 week to decide to submit a counterproposal but decided not to do so and walked away with a $143 million termination fee paid by Merck as the new owner of Versum. Shareholder reaction was swift. Merck shares fell by 1.95% to $21.93; Versum shares traded up slightly at $51.95. Entegris's shares rose by 2.79% to $40.37. The contest for Versum was over in less than 1 month, a product of hard bargaining by both parties.

Discussion questions

1. Describe the takeover tactics used by Merck. Why were they employed, and were they effective?
2. What takeover defenses were employed by Versum in this case? Why were they used, and were they effective?
3. Discuss the arguments for and against hostile corporate takeovers.
4. What is the true purchase price Merck agreed to pay for Versum?
5. Why do the shares of acquiring companies tend to perform better when cash is used to make the acquisition rather than equity?
6. What does the reaction of investors to Merck's takeover of Versum and Entegris deciding not to revise its bid tell you about how they viewed the outcome?

Answers to these questions are found in the Online Instructor's Manual available to instructors using this book.

PART II

The mergers and acquisitions process
Phases 1 through 10

Developing appropriate growth strategies and the proper execution of such strategies become critical in achieving and sustaining a competitive edge. But what worked in the past can change quickly with changing consumer tastes and the introduction of new technologies. Exploiting such changes requires that firms remain nimble in their decision making, showing a willingness to radically realign their businesses when required.

Part II of this book discusses how business strategies are developed and how management may choose to implement such strategies. Mergers and acquisitions (M&As) in this text are not viewed as business strategies but rather a means of implementing them. Business strategies define a firm's vision and long-term objectives and how it expects to achieve these ends. M&As simply represent one means of executing the strategy selected from a range of alternative implementation strategies, including "going it alone," partnering, or acquiring another firm.

Chapters 4 through 6 discuss the 10 phases typical of the M&A process. Each is discussed in detail in the context in which it occurs. Although not all M&As unfold in exactly the same way, the process outlined in this section serves as a roadmap for executing deals. This process is sufficiently flexible to be applicable to divesting a business because the selling process involves activities common to takeovers: the identification of potential buyers, approaching such buyers, valuation, negotiating deals, and so on.

Chapter 4 focuses on how to develop a business strategy and how to select the appropriate strategy from a range of reasonable alternatives. If an acquisition is deemed the best way of realizing that strategy, the chapter details how to develop an acquisition plan. An intelligent acquisition plan defines the necessary tactics, a realistic timeline, and the roles and responsibilities of those charged with getting the deal done.

Chapter 5 deals with identifying targets, making initial contact, and developing the necessary legal documents before beginning due diligence and formal negotiations. Although initial valuations provide a starting point, the actual purchase price is determined during the negotiation period. The chapter also addresses in detail how new technologies, such as artificial intelligence and blockchain, are changing the way M&As are done.

Chapter 6 discusses the critical role that postmerger integration plays in successful M&As. Particular emphasis is given to preintegration planning and how it contributes to realizing synergy in a timely manner. The chapter also addresses the common obstacles arising during the postclosing integration effort and how to overcome such challenges.

CHAPTER

4

Planning: developing business and acquisition plans

phases 1 and 2 of the acquisition process

OUTLINE

Mergers, Acquisitions, and Other Restructuring Activities, Eleventh Edition
https://doi.org/10.1016/B978-0-12-819782-0.00004-6

If you don't know where you are going, any road will get you there. —*Lewis Carroll*, **Alice's Adventures in Wonderland**

Inside M&As: when cost cutting alone is not a sustainable strategy

KEY POINTS

- Aggressive cost cutting can show substantial short-term benefits.
- But sustaining the resulting profit improvement often requires substantial investment in product development and marketing.

On paper, the strategy seemed simple: acquire a firm with excessive operating expenses and aggressively reduce costs to improve profit margins. To sustain profit improvement, repeat the process. Several critical assumptions were implicit in this strategy: the firm's existing product offering (the so—called legacy offering) would continue to satisfy customers, and there would be additional attractive acquisition targets. What follows is a discussion of the old adage that what can go wrong often does.

The food industry was abuzz when little-known Brazilian investment company 3G Capital spent billions to acquire Burger King, Kraft, and Heinz more than 10 years ago. With the backing of several other major shareholders, 3G pursued relentlessly its signature cost—cutting strategy, resulting in mass layoffs and improved productivity. However, initial success was short-lived because the investment company failed to adapt to changing consumer tastes.

Such well-respected investors as Berkshire Hathaway's Warren Buffet and hedge fund manager William Ackman publicly expressed their admiration for 3G's business acumen in improving profit margins. However, 3G lost its magic in recent years. The limitations of aggressive cost cutting were evident in early 2019 when the Kraft Heinz Company had to write down the value of its Kraft and Oscar Mayer brands by $15 billion. Forced to slash its dividend, the firm saw its shares crash by more than 28%.

The firm's critics were quick to point out that 3G had underinvested in developing brands to boost current profits at the expense of future growth. The firm failed to anticipate the pace at which consumers were turning away from traditional brands to pursue healthier products. Millennials proved to be less loyal to the legacy brands and instead focused on consuming natural and organic ingredients. Packaged foods were out of favor with consumers, which has hurt the big brands the most: Kraft Heinz, General Mills, and Mondelez.

3G's business strategy had been to require a full accounting for all line-item expenses and assigning a manager to each major company-wide expense category (e.g., travel expenses) whose responsibility was to keep detailed track of how and why each item was being used. At the beginning of a budget cycle, each cost-category manager started with a budget of zero and had to justify each expense item that was subject to a cap. The process (commonly called zero-based budgeting) ignored totally the prior year's budget.

The firm's strategy had credibility in 2013 when it partnered with Warren Buffet to acquire H.J. Heinz Company. Two years later, Heinz was merged with Kraft Foods Group Inc. 3G was able to boost profits quickly by closing factories and cutting thousands of jobs. But by the end of 2017, the firm's profits began to vanish as savings from the merger shrank.

As a result of their budgeting process, 3G assumed the savings would be sufficient to fund investments needed to sustain revenue growth. However, shrinking financial returns reflected the inadequacy of anticipated savings in the wake of a dramatic shift in consumer tastes.

3G had historically depended on acquisitions to boost profit growth following the application of zero-based budgeting. In recent years, the firm has been unable to close large deals, sometimes because of the unwillingness of a potential target firm to accept the imposition of the 3G cost-cutting culture. And during the next several years, the firm lost half of its value as investors waited for the next big move.

Competitors such as Kellogg, Mondelez, and Campbell Soup also applied zero-based budgeting and achieved savings that eliminated some of their attractiveness as potential 3G targets. 3G now readily admits that although aggressive cost cutting boosts margins in the short term, they are not sustainable without additional spending to develop and market new products.

Despite 3G's shift in 2018 to spending as much as $300 million on developing and marketing new products, reducing out-of-stock items, and negotiating better shelf space in the major supermarket chains, profits continued to fall in its major operating units. Indeed, short-term profit gains had come at the expense of longer-term performance. 3G had failed to understand fully the transitory nature of the key assumptions underlying their strategy.

Chapter overview

In the media business, content is king! With its portfolio already overflowing with well-known franchise characters, The Walt Disney Company gained control of even more content by buying most of 21st Century Fox's entertainment assets in December 2017. Through Fox's stake in the Hulu video streaming service, Disney assumed majority control of one of Netflix's main competitors. This massive infusion of content by acquisition is intended to power Disney's planned direct-to-consumer streaming services' strategy.

Disney used acquisitions to accumulate the content needed to achieve its vision of becoming the preeminent entertainment company on the globe. This was achievable through a well-planned and disciplined acquisition program. The underlying business strategy served as a road map for identifying additional acquisitions to fuel future growth.

This chapter focuses on the first two phases of the acquisition process—building the business and acquisition plans—and on the tools commonly used to evaluate, display, and communicate information to key constituencies both inside the corporation (e.g., board of directors, management, and employees) and outside (e.g., customers, stockholders, and lenders). Phases 3 to 10 are discussed in Chapter 5. Subsequent chapters detail the remaining phases of the mergers and acquisitions (M&A) process. A review of this chapter (including practice questions and answers) is available in the file folder entitled Student Study Guide, and a listing of Common Industry Information Sources is contained on the companion site to this book (https://www.elsevier.com/books-and-journals/book-companion/9780128197820).

The role of planning in M&As

The acquisition process envisioned here can be separated into two stages: planning and implementation. The *planning* stage comprises developing business and acquisition plans. The *implementation* stage (discussed in Chapter 5) includes the search, screening, contacting the target, negotiation, integration planning, closing, integration, and evaluation activities.

Key business planning concepts

A planning-based M&A process starts with a business plan (or business model) and a merger or acquisition plan, which drive all subsequent phases of the acquisition process. The *business plan* articulates a mission (what the organization is today) and vision (what it is to become) for the firm and a *business strategy* for realizing that vision for all of the firm's stakeholders. *Stakeholders* are a firm's constituents: customers, shareholders, employees, suppliers, lenders, regulators, and communities.

Although the objective of the firm is to maximize shareholder value, this is most likely achieved when the interests of all major stakeholder groups are considered. Overlooking the interests of one group can easily derail the most well-thought-out strategies. The business strategy is oriented to the long term and usually cuts across organizational lines to affect many different functional areas. It typically provides relatively little detail.

With respect to business strategy, it is important to distinguish between corporate-level and business-level strategies. *Corporate-level strategies* are set by the management of a diversified or multiproduct firm and generally cross business unit organizational lines. They entail decisions about financing the growth of certain businesses, operating others to generate cash, divesting some units, and pursuing diversification. *Business-level strategies* are set by the management of a specific operating unit within the corporate organizational structure. They may involve a unit's attempting to achieve a low-cost position in the markets it serves, differentiating its product offering, or narrowing its focus to a specific market niche.

The *implementation strategy* refers to the way in which the firm chooses to execute the business strategy. The *merger or acquisition plan* is a specific type of implementation strategy and describes in detail the motivation for the acquisition and how and when it will be achieved. *Functional strategies* describe in detail how each major function within the firm (e.g., manufacturing, marketing, human resources) will support the business strategy.

American heavyweight boxing champion Mike Tyson wryly noted, "Everyone has a plan until you get punched in the mouth." To be prepared for the unexpected, *contingency plans* are needed: actions taken as an alternative to the firm's current business strategy. The selection of which alternative to pursue may be contingent on certain events called *trigger points* (e.g., failure to realize revenue targets). When the trigger points are reached, the firm faces a number of alternatives, sometimes referred to as *real options*: abandoning, delaying, or accelerating an investment strategy. Unlike the strategic options discussed later in this chapter, real options are decisions made after an investment has been made.

The M&A process

Some argue that a structured process only delays responding to opportunities, both anticipated and unanticipated. *Anticipated opportunities* are those identified as a result of the planning process: understanding the firm's external operating environment, assessing internal resources, reviewing a range of options, and articulating a clear vision of the future for the business and a realistic strategy for achieving that vision. *Unanticipated opportunities* may emerge as new information becomes available. Having a well-designed business plan does not delay pursuing opportunities; rather, it provides a way to evaluate the opportunity, rapidly and substantively, by determining the extent to which it supports realization of the business plan.

Figure 4.1 illustrates the 10 phases of the M&A process described in this and subsequent chapters. These phases fall into two sets of activities: pre- and postpurchase decision activities. Negotiation, with its four concurrent and

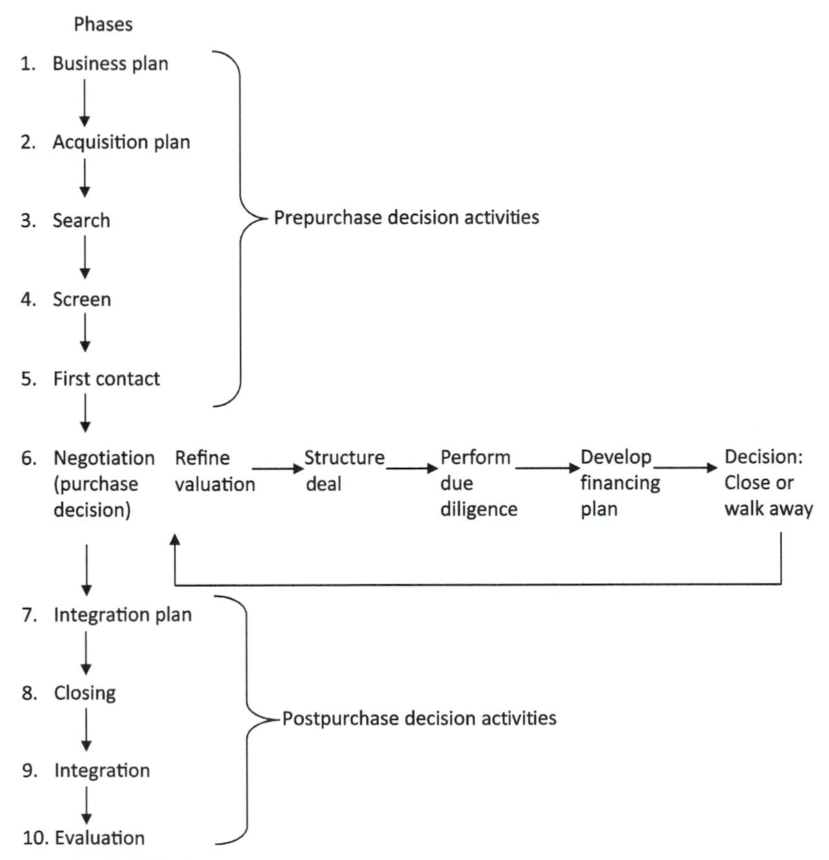

FIGURE 4.1 Flow diagram for the mergers and acquisitions process.

interrelated activities, is the crucial phase of the acquisition process. The decision to purchase or walk away is determined as a result of continuous iteration through the four activities that make up the negotiation phase.

The phases of the M&A process are summarized as follows:

- Phase 1: business plan—Develop a strategic plan for the entire business.
- Phase 2: acquisitions plan—Develop the acquisition plan supporting the business plan.
- Phase 3: search—Search actively for acquisition candidates.[1]
- Phase 4: screen—Screen and prioritize potential candidates.
- Phase 5: first contact—Initiate contact with the target.
- Phase 6: negotiation—Refine valuation, structure the deal, perform due diligence, and develop the financing plan.
- Phase 7: integration plan—Develop a plan for integrating the acquired business.
- Phase 8: closing—Obtain the necessary approvals, resolve postclosing issues, and execute the closing.
- Phase 9: integration—Implement the postclosing integration.
- Phase 10: evaluation—Conduct the postclosing evaluation of the acquisition.

Prepurchase activities involve "getting to yes" with the target's board and management. Postpurchase activities for strategic M&As involve combining the businesses to realize anticipated synergies. Decisions made at each phase involve certain trade-offs. To identify these, we must focus on the context in which the deal occurs and the deal's stakeholders.[2]

How fast (slow) the acquirer should go depends on the context of the deal. What are industry conditions? Is the deal friendly or hostile? Is the target's business related or unrelated to the acquirer? For example, industries undergoing rapid change require more time to perform due diligence. However, too much time spent analyzing the industry can mean that others will have time to formulate competing bids for the target firm. Friendly deals can result in smoother postmerger integration but may result in the acquirer's paying a higher premium to "buy" the target's cooperation. Hostile deals may result in a faster takeover but may result in a disruptive postmerger integration. Related deals often result in larger potential synergies but may entail a lengthy regulatory review process.

Deal stakeholders include shareholders, board members and top managers, advisors (investment bankers, accountants, and lawyers), customers, employees, lenders, and communities. The interests of any one group must be balanced against those of other groups.

In theory, acquisitions should only be done if they increase firm value; in practice, agency problems can create motives for doing deals that are not in the best interests of shareholders. Board members and top managers must be committed to making the deal happen so as to provide the necessary resources. However, hubris and excessive emotional attachment to the target can result in overpayment. Advisors assist in making better, faster decisions, but they also add significantly to total deal costs. Communicating intentions to customers and employees may reduce attrition, but it invites leakage of key information to competitors. Lenders must be convinced that the deal makes sense so they are willing to finance the transaction. And communities must understand how a deal impacts them.

The resolution of conflicting stakeholder interests comes from the board's and senior management's commitment to premerger planning. Long-range planning to anticipate issues that might arise and developing contingency plans to resolve such issues means that decisions can be made more rapidly as circumstances change. Senior managers must remain engaged throughout the deal process so that they are aware of the benefits and costs of available options and be willing to make the difficult decisions when the need arises.[3]

[1] When combined, phases 3 and 4 are sometimes referred to as "deal sourcing."

[2] Meglio et al., 2017

[3] Welch et al. (2020) provides a summary of research on the prepurchase phases of the M&A process.

Phase 1: building the business plan or model

A well-designed business plan results from eight key activities, summarized next. The process of developing a business plan requires addressing a number of detailed questions corresponding to each of these activities.[4]

The first activity is the *external analysis* undertaken to determine where a firm might compete—that is, which industry or market(s) appear to be most attractive in terms of potential growth and profitability—and how to compete—that is, what it takes to earn competitive financial returns in the markets the firm finds attractive. This is followed by the *internal analysis* of the firm's strengths and weaknesses relative to competitors in these markets. The combination of these two activities—the external and internal analyses—is often called *SWOT analysis* because it determines the **s**trengths, **w**eaknesses, **o**pportunities, and **t**hreats associated with a business. After this analysis has been completed, management has a clearer understanding of emerging opportunities and threats to the firm and of the firm's primary internal strengths and weaknesses. Information gleaned from the external and internal analyses drives the development of business, implementation, and functional strategies.

The third activity is to define a *mission and vision statement* summarizing where and how the firm has chosen to compete, based on the external analysis, as well as management's operating experience and values. Fourth, *objectives* are set, and quantitative financial and nonfinancial metrics are developed. Having completed these steps, the firm is ready to *select a business strategy* likely to achieve the objectives, subject to constraints identified in the self-assessment. The business strategy defines, in general terms, how the business intends to compete (i.e., through cost leadership, differentiation, or increased focus).

Next, an *implementation strategy* articulates how to implement the business strategy. The firm may choose to act independently, partner with others, or acquire or merge with another firm. This is followed by development of a *functional strategy* that defines the roles, responsibilities, and resource requirements of each major functional area within the firm needed to support the business strategy.

The final activity is to establish *strategic controls* to monitor actual performance to plan, implement incentive systems, and take corrective actions as necessary. Bonus plans and other incentive mechanisms to motivate all employees to achieve their individual objectives on or ahead of schedule are put in place. When significant deviations from the implementation plan occur, the firm may take corrective actions (e.g., cutting output or costs) included in certain contingency plans. Let's look at each of these eight activities in greater detail.

External analysis

What makes a market attractive? And what does a firm in that market have to do to earn the rate of return required by its shareholders? Answers to these questions can be obtained by modifying Michael Porter's well-known "Five Forces" model. The basic model suggests that profit is determined in an industry or market by the relative bargaining power or influence of a firm's customers, suppliers, and current competitors; the potential for new entrants; and the availability of close product substitutes. The basic model can be modified to include other considerations such as labor, government regulation, and global exposure.

The intensity of competition determines the potential to earn abnormal profits (i.e., those in excess of what would be expected for the degree of assumed risk). In general, competition among firms is likely to be more intense when entry barriers are low, exit barriers are high, competitors use a common technology, switching costs are low, there are many substitutes, there are many competitors who are comparable in size, and market growth is slowing.

More intense rivalry often puts downward pressure on selling prices as firms compete for market share, add to marketing expenses, and boost prices for inputs. Firms are further constrained in their ability to raise selling prices when there are close product substitutes. The end result is that greater competition squeezes profit margins, potentially eliminating a firm's ability to earn "abnormal financial" returns.[5]

How a firm selects target industries or markets depends on the firm's selection criteria and how it ranks the relative importance of each criterion as well as the risk tolerance and imagination of a firm's board and management.

[4] Extensive checklists can be found in Porter (1985). Answering these types of questions requires gathering substantial economic, industry, and market information.

[5] See the End-of-chapter case study in Chapter 9 for an illustration of how the "Five Forces" model can be used to understand an industry's or market's competitive dynamics.

Examples of selection criteria include market size and growth rate, profitability, cyclicality, price sensitivity of customers, amount of regulation, degree of unionization, and existence of entry and exit barriers.

An industry may be defined as a collection of markets; and markets, as a series of customers (either individuals or businesses) exhibiting common needs and characteristics. Markets can be subdivided into a series of subsegments by applying a process called *market segmentation.* For example, a firm may segment markets until it finds customers whose buying decisions are based primarily on price, quality, or service.

Viewing the automotive industry as consisting of the new and used car markets as well as the after-market for replacement parts is a simple example of market segmentation. Markets may be further subdivided by examining cars by makes, model years, type of powertrain (combustion, hybrid, and electric), and so on. The automotive industry could also be defined regionally (e.g., New England, North America, Europe) or by country. Each subdivision, whether by product or geographic area, defines a new market within the automotive industry.

Another example is the cloud computing industry, which consists of firms providing customers remote access in three discrete markets: software, infrastructure, and platform services. The software services market consists of such firms as Salesforce and Workday providing customers on-demand licensing of their software applications for a fee. The infrastructure services market allows companies to rent on-demand operating systems, servers, and storage services from such competitors as Microsoft, Google, and Amazon.com. The platform market, consisting of the likes of Google, Amazon.com, and Salesforce, offers templates for customers to create software to meet their specific needs.

The factors affecting each component of the modified Five Forces model and how they may impact profit (and cash flow) are discussed in more detail next.

Bargaining power of customers

The relative bargaining power of customers depends on their primary buying criteria (i.e., quality or reliability, service, convenience, or some combination), price sensitivity or elasticity, switching costs, their number and average size, and availability of substitutes. A customer whose primary buying criterion is product quality and reliability may be willing to pay a premium for a BMW because it is perceived to have higher relative quality. Customers are highly price-sensitive in industries characterized by largely undifferentiated products and low switching costs.[6] Customers are likely to have considerable bargaining power when they are large compared with suppliers. Customers having substantial bargaining power can force selling prices down, negotiate favorable credit terms, and squeeze supplier margins.

Bargaining power of suppliers

Suppliers in this context include material, services, and capital. Their bargaining power is impacted by switching costs, differentiation, their number and average size compared with the customer, and the availability of substitutes. When the cost of changing suppliers is high, their products are highly differentiated, they are few in number and large relative to their customers, and there are few substitutes, suppliers are able to boost their selling prices. Suppliers also can impose more stringent credit terms and lengthen delivery schedules.

Degree of competitive rivalry

The intensity of competition among current competitors is determined by the industry growth rate, industry concentration, degree of differentiation and switching costs, scale and scope economies, excess capacity, and exit barriers. If an industry is growing rapidly, existing firms have less need to compete for market share based on aggressive pricing. If an industry is highly concentrated, firms can more easily coordinate their pricing activities, unlike fragmented industries in which price competition is intense.[7]

If the cost of switching from one supplier to another is minimal because of low perceived differentiation, customers are likely to switch based on relatively small differences in price. In industries in which production volume is important, companies may compete aggressively for market share to realize economies of scale. Moreover, firms in industries exhibiting substantial excess capacity often reduce prices to fill unused capacity. Finally,

[6] Switching costs are highest when customers must pay penalties to exit long-term supply contracts or when buyers would have to undergo an intensive learning process to buy from a different supplier.

[7] In some instances, intense competition can arise even when the industry is highly concentrated. Firms may compete largely on the basis of price when their product or service offerings are largely undifferentiated to gain market share. Such a market structure is called an *oligopoly.*

competition may be intensified in industries in which it is difficult for firms to exit because of barriers such as large unfunded pension liabilities and single-purpose assets.

Potential new entrants

The likelihood of new entrants is affected by scale economies, first-mover advantage, legal barriers (e.g., patents), limited access to distribution channels, and product differentiation. Competitors within an industry characterized by low barriers to entry have limited pricing power. Attempts to raise prices, resulting in abnormally large profits, attracts new competitors, thereby adding to the industry's productive capacity. In contrast, high entry barriers give existing competitors significant pricing power. Barriers to new entrants include situations in which the large-scale operations of current competitors give them a potential cost advantage because of economies of scale. The "first-mover advantage" (i.e., being an early competitor in an industry) may also create entry barriers because first movers achieve widespread brand recognition, establish industry standards, develop exclusive relationships with key suppliers and distributors, and create large installed user bases.[8] Finally, legal constraints, such as copyrights and patents, may inhibit the entry of new firms.

Availability of substitute products

The potential for substitute products is affected by relative prices, performance, quality, and service, as well as the willingness of customers to switch. The selling price of one product compared to a close substitute—called the *relative price*—determines the threat of substitution, along with the performance of competing products, perceived quality, and switching costs. Potential substitutes could come from current or potential rivals and include those that are similar to existing products and those performing the same function—for example, a tablet computer rather than a hardcover book. In general, when substitutes are close to existing products, switching costs are low, and customers are willing to switch, substitutes limit price increases for current products by reducing the demand for product offerings of existing industry competitors and potentially their profit margins.

Bargaining power of the labor force

Labor's bargaining power is affected by the degree of unionization, management–labor harmony, and availability of critical skills. Labor's share of total operating expenses can range from very low in automated manufacturing industries to very high in nonmanufacturing industries. Work stoppages create opportunities for competitors to gain market share. Customers are forced to satisfy their product and service needs elsewhere. Although the loss of customers may be temporary, it may become permanent if the customer finds that another firm's product is superior.

The degree of government regulation

Governments may choose to regulate industries that are highly concentrated, are natural monopolies (e.g., utilities), or provide a potential risk to the public. Regulatory compliance adds significantly to an industry's operating costs and creates barriers to both entering and exiting an industry. However, incumbent competitors can benefit from the creation of entry barriers caused by regulation because it can limit the number of new entrants.

Global exposure

Global exposure refers to the extent to which an industry or market is affected by export and import competition. The automotive industry is a global industry in which participation requires having assembly plants and distribution networks in major markets worldwide. Global exposure introduces the firm to the impact of currency risk on profit repatriation and political risk, such as the confiscation of the firm's properties. An industry exposure to foreign competition also restrains the ability to pass on cost increases to customers.

Internal analysis

The primary objective is to determine the firm's strengths and weaknesses. What are they, compared with the competition? Can the firm's critical strengths be easily duplicated and surpassed by the competition? Can they be used to gain advantage in the firm's chosen market? Can competitors exploit the firm's key weaknesses? These questions must be answered objectively for the information to be useful in formulating a viable strategy.

Ultimately, competing successfully means doing a better job than competitors of satisfying the needs of the firm's targeted customers. A self-assessment identifies the strengths or competencies—so-called *success factors*—necessary

[8] Flor and Moritzen (2020) relate first-mover advantage to firms having important patents.

TABLE 4.1 Hypothetical Facebook SWOT matrix

Strengths	Weaknesses
Brand recognition Global scale with 2.57 billion monthly active users as of 12/31/19 User engagement (time spent online) Extensive user database attractive to advertisers Integrated website and applications widens user appeal Ability to monetize increasing mobile traffic through Instagram	Privacy issues Dependence on display ads, which have lower user "click-through" rate Dependence on advertising for >80% of revenue Aging user demographics Lack of website customization limits user personalization Poor protection of user information
Opportunities	**Threats**
Increasing use of Facebook through mobile devices Expansion in emerging nations Diversifying revenue sources Continuing shift of traditional to online advertising Adding new features and functions to enable customization Expanded "graph search" advertising[a]	Increasing user privacy concerns and potential government regulation Accelerating the shift toward accessing internet through mobile devices, including wearable technology such as Google Glass Alterative social networks (e.g., Twitter, Tumblr, LinkedIn, Pinterest, and Google+) compete for users and advertisers Lack of website customization Highly competitive ad market putting downward pressure on ad rates Increased frequency of identity theft

[a]Graph Search is a search engine that allows Facebook users to look up anything shared with them throughout their history on Facebook.

to compete successfully in the firm's chosen or targeted market. These may include high market share compared with the competition, product line breadth, cost-effective sales distribution channels, age and geographic location of production facilities, relative product quality, price competitiveness, research and development (R&D) effectiveness, customer service effectiveness, corporate culture, and profitability.

Recall that the combination of the external and internal analyses just detailed can be summarized as a SWOT analysis to determine the strengths and weaknesses of a business as well as the opportunities and threats confronting a business. The results of a SWOT analysis can be displayed on a SWOT matrix. Based on this analysis, firms can select how to prioritize opportunities and threats and how to focus corporate resources to exploit opportunities or to reduce vulnerabilities. This information helps management set a direction in terms of where and how the firm intends to compete, which is then communicated to the firm's stakeholders in the form of a mission and vision statement and a set of quantifiable objectives.

Table 4.1 illustrates a hypothetical SWOT analysis for Facebook. It is not intended to be a comprehensive list of perceived strengths, weaknesses, opportunities, and threats. Rather, it is provided only for illustrative purposes. Facebook's management using similar information may have opted to acquire mobile message service WhatsApp for an eye-popping $21.8 billion to adapt to the shift of internet users to mobile devices and to preclude competitors such as Google from acquiring this explosively growing mobile messaging firm.

Mark Zuckerberg has stated his vision for Facebook is to make the world more open and connected. How? By giving people the power to share whatever they want and to be connected to whatever they want no matter where they are. Although Facebook dominates the social network space in which users are able to share everything they want others to know, Facebook also wants to dominate how people communicate.

The opportunity is to build the best and most ubiquitous mobile product, a platform where every app that is created can support social interaction, and to build Facebook into one of the world's most valuable companies. The threat is that others such as Google may acquire the business propelling them to the forefront of the mobile communications space.

The acquisition of WhatsApp in early 2014 illustrates Mark Zuckerberg's understanding that people want to communicate in different ways: sometimes broadly through Facebook and sometimes narrowly through WhatsApp's mobile messaging capability. Because Facebook's efforts to penetrate the mobile messaging market have failed, the firm needed a means of doing so. WhatsApp appeared to be the answer. With the WhatsApp acquisition not yet closed, Facebook acquired startup Oculus VR (virtual reality), the maker of VR headsets, in mid-2014 for $2 billion. To increase user time spent online (a Facebook strength), the deal was a bet that VR can turn social networking into an immersive, 3D experience. This deal also represented an investment for Facebook in wearable hardware that "reimagines" how people will one day interact with information and other types of content.[9]

[9]See Fernandes (2019) for additional illustrations of the application of SWOT analysis.

Other tools that help answer these questions range from scenario planning to business war games to a combination of both methodologies. *Business war games* are used to anticipate how current competitors might react to actions a firm might take to achieve a competitive advantage. *Scenario planning* is a process of envisioning the future based on different possible outcomes. By combining these two methodologies, managers gain insight into the actions of both current and possible future competitors and how to develop a business strategy to exploit prospective opportunities and defend against emerging threats.[10]

Defining the mission and vision statements

Broadly speaking, a *mission* describes why an organization exists and describes what it does, for whom, and the resulting benefit created. For example, Pfizer Corp views its mission as innovating ("what they do") every day to make the world a healthier place for everyone ("why and for whom"). Coca-Cola's mission states that the firm strives to refresh the world by offering uniquely different tastes ("what they do") and to inspire moments of optimism and happiness among their customers ("why and for whom").

A *vision* statement describes what an organization wants to become. In 2019, Pfizer announced a major change in its vision from one of becoming a diversified pharmaceutical company to one focused solely on patent-protected drugs when it merged its off-patent drug business with generic drug maker Mylan Labs. Coca-Cola's current vision is to become a full beverage company by diversifying into related products. Examples include the introduction of mini cans of full-calorie soda and the 2018 $5.1 billion acquisition of Costa Coffee.

Whereas the mission describes the present, the vision talks about the future. Such statements are important because they help all stakeholders better understand what the firm's purpose is and where it hopes to go in the future. Mission and vision statements often contain a section identifying a firm's values defining what are acceptable behaviors and attitudes.

Mission and vision statements often vary in length and detail and can include references to the firm's targeted markets, reflecting the fit between the corporation's primary strengths and competencies and how it is able to satisfy customer needs better than the competition. Such statements should define the product offering broadly enough to allow for the introduction of new products derived from the firm's core competencies. Distribution channels—how the firm chooses to sell its products—could be identified, as could target customer groups.

Narrowly defined mission and vision statements can make it difficult to ascertain opportunities and threats to the core business that do not fall neatly within the firm's view of itself and the future. Mission and vision statements should not be tied to a specific product or service the firm currently produces. If railroads had defined their missions more broadly as establishing a strong market share in the transportation industry rather than limiting their positions to the rail business, they may have retained the preeminent position in the transportation industry they once enjoyed. That is, by defining their positions narrowly around existing products and services, railroads failed to see alternative forms of transportation emerging in time to be proactive. Although a narrow definition of mission and vision puts boundaries on the range of opportunities a firm could pursue, defining them too broadly creates a range of outcomes too large to analyze effectively and resource to pursue.

Table 4.2 provides an example of a succinct statement of purpose, mission, vision, and values for Newmont Mining. It is for illustration only and not intended to be an example of an ideal statement of corporate intentions. According to this statement, Newmont Mining exists to create value and improve the well-being of stakeholders in a way that protects the environment and satisfies the firm's societal obligations. Although the firm focuses on gold mining, the mission statement is general enough and related to its core competence in mineral extraction so that the firm can diversify into other forms of mining if appropriate.

The mission answers the questions posed earlier: what it is (a mining company), for whom does it exist (for all stakeholders), and what is the benefit of the firm's existence (industry leading shareholder returns, safety record, and a reputation for being socially responsible and a good steward of the environment)? Newmont's vision is to be recognized as exceptional in performing the three key elements stated in its mission statement, with its guiding principles identified in its value section. Although few in number, these values and principles make it clear to stakeholders how the firm intends to operate in areas it finds fundamental to its business.

[10] Schwarz et al., 2019

TABLE 4.2 Newmont mining: purpose, mission, vision, and values (2019)

Purpose: Our purpose is to create value and improve lives through sustainable and responsible mining.

Mission: We transform mineral resources into shared value for our stakeholders and lead the industry in shareholder returns, safety, social responsibility, and environmental stewardship.

Vision: We will be recognized and respected for exceptional economic, environmental, and social performance.

Values

Safety: We take care of our safety, health, and wellness by recognizing, assessing, and managing risk and choosing safer behaviors at work and home to reach our goal of zero harm.
Integrity: We behave ethically and respect each other and the customs, cultures, and laws wherever we operate.
Sustainability: We serve as a catalyst for local economic development through transparent and respectful stakeholder engagement and as responsible stewards of the environment.
Inclusion: We create an inclusive environment where employees have the opportunity to contribute, develop, and work together to deliver our strategy.
Responsibility: We deliver on our commitments, demonstrate leadership, and have the courage to speak up and challenge the status quo.

Setting strategic or long-term business objectives

A business objective is what must be accomplished within a specific period. Good business objectives are measurable and have a set time frame in which to be realized. They include revenue growth rates, minimum acceptable financial returns, and market share; these and others are discussed in more detail later. A good business objective might state that the firm seeks to increase revenue from the current $1 billion to $5 billion by a given year. A poorly written objective would simply state the firm seeks to increase revenue substantially.

Common business objectives

Financial objectives typically include the firm seeking to achieve a rate of *return* that will equal or exceed the return required by its shareholders, lenders, or the combination of the two (cost of capital) by a given year. The firm may set a *size objective,* seeking to achieve some critical mass, defined in terms of sales volume, to realize economies of scale by a given year. *Accounting-related growth objectives* include seeking to grow earnings per share (EPS), revenue, or assets at a specific annual growth rate. *Valuation-related growth objectives* may be expressed in terms of the firm's price-to-earnings ratio, book value, cash flow, or revenue.

Diversification objectives are those where the firm desires to sell current products in new markets, new products in current markets, or new products in new markets. The firm may set an objective to derive 25% of its revenue from new products by a given year. It is also common for firms to set *flexibility objectives:* production facilities and distribution capabilities that can be shifted rapidly to exploit new opportunities. *Technology objectives* may reflect a firm's desire to possess capabilities in core technologies.

Selecting the appropriate corporate and business-level strategies

Each level of strategy serves a specific purpose. Implementation (also known as investment) strategies are necessarily more detailed than corporate-level strategies and provide specific guidance for a firm's business units.

The different strategy levels can be illustrated by looking at Alphabet, the holding company containing Google and other businesses. Alphabet determines the firm's corporate strategy and allocates funds to its various business units. Google, by far the largest and most profitable business unit, gets the majority of corporate resources. Each business unit has its own strategy consistent with the corporate strategy. As Alphabet's largest subsidiary, Google's business unit strategy involves making investments necessary to drive more people to use the internet more frequently and in more diverse ways. Other Alphabet business units include R&D operation X Development, biotech firm Calico, thermostat maker Nest, and venture capital unit GV.

By investing in diverse activities, Alphabet is seeking to bolster sales and profits in new markets by promoting the association of the Google brand with quality and innovation. Furthermore, increased penetration of additional markets increases the amount of information it collects on users of their services, enhancing its marketing data base(s) used to improve the effectiveness of firms advertising on Google websites.

The strategy is driven by a combination of factors external and internal to Google. The inherent utility of the internet for both consumers and business will continue to drive usage worldwide (factors external to Google). However, the usefulness of the internet is enhanced by improved search techniques proprietary to Google (factors internal to Google). Google has implemented this strategy in the past by internally developing new products and services (e.g., the driverless car technology, which requires constant communication with cloud servers via the internet) or through acquisition (e.g., Motorola for its smartphone software and intellectual property patents, and Nest for its innovative presence in the residential and commercial heating and cooling niche).

Corporate-level and business unit–level strategies as well as implementation strategies are discussed in more detail next.

Corporate-level strategies

Corporate-level strategies may include all or some of the business units that are either wholly or partially owned by the corporation. They usually fall into the following categories: growth, diversification, operational restructuring, and financial restructuring.

A *growth strategy* focuses on accelerating the firm's consolidated revenue, profit, and cash flow growth and may be implemented in many different ways. For example, CEO Satya Nadella's corporate-level growth strategy for Microsoft is oriented around cloud computing, mobile platforms, content, and productivity software.

A *diversification strategy* involves a decision at the corporate level to enter new related or unrelated businesses. Relatedness may be defined in terms of the degree to which a target firm's products and served markets are similar to those of the acquirer. Diversification can be further segmented into *exploratory* (e.g., developing new expertise) or *exploitative* (e.g., reinforcing existing capabilities) strategies in related or unrelated industries. The former offers the potential to penetrate new high growth markets, whereas the latter confines the firm to a narrow range of knowledge. Exploratory deals in related industries in related industries show superior performance to those in unrelated industries.[11]

An *operational restructuring strategy* usually refers to the outright or partial sale of companies or product lines, downsizing by closing unprofitable or nonstrategic facilities, obtaining protection from creditors in bankruptcy court, or liquidation. Such strategies also are referred to as turnaround or defensive strategies.

A *financial restructuring strategy* describes actions by the firm to change its capital structure. The motivation for this strategy may be better use of excess cash through share-repurchase programs, reducing the firm's cost of capital by increasing leverage, or increasing management's control by acquiring shares through a management buyout.

Business-level strategies

A firm should choose its business strategy from among the range of reasonable options that enables it to achieve its stated objectives in an acceptable period, subject to resource constraints. These include limitations on the availability of management talent and funds. Business strategies fall into one of four basic categories: price or cost leadership, product differentiation, focus or niche strategies, and hybrid strategies. These are discussed next.

Price or cost leadership strategy

This strategy is designed to make a firm the cost leader in its market by constructing efficient production facilities, controlling overhead expenses, and eliminating marginally profitable customer accounts. It is predicated on the experience curve and the product life cycle theories, both popularized by the Boston Consulting Group.

The *experience curve* states that as the cumulative historical volume of a firm's output increases, cost per unit of output decreases geometrically as the firm becomes more efficient in producing that product. The firm with the largest historical output should also be the lowest-cost producer, so this theory suggests. This implies that the firm should enter markets as early as possible and reduce product prices aggressively to maximize market share.[12]

The *product life cycle* characterizes a product's evolution in four stages: embryonic, growth, maturity, and decline. Strong sales growth and low barriers to entry characterize the first two stages. Over time, however, entry becomes more costly as early entrants into the market accumulate market share and experience lower per-unit production costs as a result of experience curve effects. New entrants have poorer cost positions thanks to their small market shares compared with earlier entrants, and they cannot catch up to the market leaders as overall market growth

[11] Zhang et al., 2020

[12] The experience curve works best for commodity-type industries, in which scale can lead to reductions in per-unit production costs, such as PC or cell phone handset manufacturing. The strategy of continuously driving down production costs makes most sense for the existing industry market share leader because it may be able to improve its cost advantage by pursuing market share more aggressively through price cutting.

TABLE 4.3 Hybrid strategies

	Cost leadership	Product differentiation
Niche focus approach	Cisco Systems WD-40	Coca-Cola McDonalds
Multimarket approach	Walmart Oracle	Google Microsoft

slows. During the later phases, slowing market growth and falling product prices force unprofitable firms to close or to consolidate with other firms.[13]

Product differentiation strategy

Differentiation covers a range of strategies in which the product offered is seen by customers to be slightly different from other product offerings in the marketplace. Brand image is one way to accomplish differentiation. Another is to offer customers a range of features or functions. For example, many banks issue MasterCard or Visa credit cards, but each bank tries to differentiate its card by offering a higher credit line or a lower interest rate or annual fee or a rewards programs. Apple Computer has used innovative technology to stay ahead of competitors, most recently with cutting-edge capabilities of its newer iPads and iPhones.

Focus (or niche) strategy

Firms adopting this strategy concentrate their efforts by selling a few products or services to a single market and compete primarily by understanding their customers' needs better than competitors. The firm seeks to carve out a niche with respect to a certain group of customers, a narrow geographic area, or a particular use of a product. Examples include regional airlines, airplane manufacturers (e.g., Boeing), and major defense contractors (e.g., Lockheed Martin).

Hybrid strategy

A hybrid strategy involves some combination of the three strategies just discussed (Table 4.3). For example, Coca-Cola pursues both a differentiated and highly market-focused strategy. The company derives the bulk of its revenues by focusing on the worldwide soft drink market, and its main product is differentiated in that consumers perceive it to have a distinctly refreshing taste. Fast-food industry giant McDonalds pursues a differentiated strategy, competing on the basis of providing fast food of a consistent quality in a clean, comfortable environment at a reasonable price.

Blue ocean strategy

Proponents of this strategy argue that instead of competing with others in your own industry, a firm should strive to create unique products for new markets and to profit from these new markets or "blue oceans." Apple Inc.'s record of introducing highly innovative products is perhaps the best example of this strategy. The firm has a record of innovating new products that consumers did not even know they wanted but who learned to find them "cool" and indispensable. Firms that compete in traditional markets are said to work in "red ocean" conditions, in which businesses fight for a share of an existing market. In contrast, "blue ocean" opportunities offer the prospect of a market free of competitors. Why? They are unique.

Platform strategy

A platform strategy connects independent parties with the objective of expediting transactions. They include firms ranging from telephone services to computer operating systems. The objective is to garner as many users as possible such that a firm can supply multiple products and services to its user base.

[13] Knowing the firm's stage of the product life cycle can help project future cash flow growth, which is necessary for valuation purposes. During the high-growth phase, firms in the industry normally have high investment requirements, and operating cash flow is normally negative. During the mature and declining growth phases, investment requirements are lower, and cash flow becomes positive.

For instance, the Microsoft Windows operating system served as a "platform" to support sales to its huge user base of additional products such as Microsoft Office that worked best on the firm's proprietary operating system. Similarly, mobile phone companies compete in part of the basis of geographic network coverage. Those offering national (rather than simply regional) coverage could acquire more customers to whom they could sell other services and content. The sheer size of Microsoft's user base and Verizon's network coverage created huge entry barriers for potential competitors.

Platform strategies are most effective when they are readily scalable to accommodate ever larger numbers of users. Platforms can create "communities" in which users can communicate and make transactions. Amazon.com, Google, Facebook, Uber,[14] Airbnb, Pinterest, and Alibaba are examples of highly scalable platform companies. The key to their success is the ability to attract users cost effectively, connect buyers and sellers, and provide the payment systems to consummate transactions.

Platform strategies do not involve owning production operations but rather they provide value in connecting consumers and businesses. This contrasts with the more traditional businesses, which have a clearly delineated supply chain consisting of suppliers, production, distribution, and customer service. Supply chain–driven companies create value by producing and delivering goods and services they sell through owned or independent distributors. Examples include manufacturers such as auto and farm equipment makers General Motors and John Deere; subscription businesses such as Netflix and HBO, which create or license their content; and resellers such as Walmart, Costco, and Target.

Selecting an implementation strategy

After a firm has determined its business strategy, it must decide the best means of implementation. Typically, a firm has five choices: implement the strategy based solely on internal resources (the solo venture, go it alone, or build

TABLE 4.4 Strategy implementation

Basic options	Advantages	Disadvantages
Solo venture or build (organic growth)	• Control	• Capital and expense[a] requirements • Speed
Partner (shared growth and shared control) • Marketing–distribution alliance • Joint venture • License • Franchise	• Limits capital and expense investment requirements • May be precursor to acquisition	• Lack of or limited control • Potential for diverging objectives • Potential for creating a competitor
Invest (e.g., minority investments in other firms)	• Limits initial capital or expense requirements	• High risk of failure • Lack of control • Time
Acquire or merge	• Speed • Control	• Capital and expense requirements • Potential earnings dilution
Swap assets	• Limits use of cash • No earnings dilution • Limits tax liability if basis in assets swapped remains unchanged	• Finding willing parties • Reaching agreement on assets to be exchanged

[a]Expense investment refers to expenditures made on such things as application software development, database construction, research and development, training, and advertising to build brand recognition, which (unlike capital expenditures) usually are expensed in the year in which the monies are spent.

[14] Uber views itself as a platform company in that it provides a software app linking passengers with drivers. On December 20, 2017, the European Union ruled that Uber was not a platform company but rather a transportation firm and should be regulated as one.

approach), partner with others, invest, acquire, or swap assets. There is little evidence that one strategy is consistently superior to another. Not surprisingly, if one strategy consistently outpaced others, it would be adopted by all firms. Table 4.4 compares the advantages and disadvantages of these options.

In theory, choosing among alternative options should be based on selecting the one with the highest net present value (NPV). In practice, many other considerations are at work such as intangible factors and the plausibility of underlying assumptions.

The role of intangible factors

Although financial analyses are conducted to evaluate the various strategy implementation options, the ultimate choice may depend on a firm's board and management desires, risk profile, and hubris. The degree of control offered by the various alternatives is often the central issue senior management must confront.

Although the solo venture and acquisition options offer the highest degree of control, they can be the most expensive and risky, although for very different reasons. Typically, a build strategy will take longer to realize objectives, and it may have a significantly lower current value than the alternatives—depending on the magnitude and timing of cash flows generated from the investments. Gaining control through acquisition can also be expensive because of the premium the acquirer normally has to pay to gain a controlling interest in another firm.

The joint venture may be a practical alternative to either a build or acquire strategy; it gives a firm access to skills, product distribution channels, proprietary processes, and patents at a lower initial expense than might otherwise be required. Asset swaps may be an attractive alternative to the other options, but in most industries, they are generally very difficult to establish unless the physical characteristics and use of the assets are substantially similar and the prospects for realizing economies of scale and scope are attractive.[15]

Analyzing assumptions

The option with the highest net present value may be problematic if the premise on which the strategy is based is faulty. It is critical to understand the key assumptions underlying the chosen strategy as well as those underlying alternative strategies. This forces senior management to make choices based on a discussion of the reasonableness of the assumptions associated with each option rather than simply the numerical output of computer models.

Functional strategies

Such strategies generally are developed by functional areas. They require concrete actions for each function or business group, depending on the company's organization. It is common to see separate plans with specific goals and actions for the marketing, manufacturing, R&D, engineering, and financial and human resources functions. Such strategies should include clearly defined objectives, actions, timetables, resources required, and identification of the individual responsible for ensuring that the actions are completed on time and within budget.

Specific functional strategies might read as follows:

- Set up a product distribution network in the northeastern United States that is capable of handling a minimum of 1 million units of product annually by 12/31/20XX. (Individual responsible: Oliver Tran; estimated budget: $5 million.)
- Develop and execute an advertising campaign to support the sales effort in the northeastern United States by 10/31/20XX. (Individual responsible: Maria Gomez; estimated budget: $0.5 million.)
- Hire a logistics manager to administer the distribution network by 9/15/20XX. (Individual responsible: Patrick Petty; estimated budget: $250,000.)
- Acquire a manufacturing company with sufficient capacity to meet the projected demand for the next 3 years by 6/30/20XX at a purchase price not to exceed $250 million. (Individual responsible: Chang Lee.)

Perhaps an application software company is targeting the credit card industry. Here is an example of how the company's business mission, vision, business strategy, implementation strategy, and functional strategies are related.

[15] In 2016, French drug maker Sanofi agreed to transfer its animal health care business in exchange for $5.2 billion and Boehringer Ingleheim's consumer health care business. In 2011, Starbucks assumed 100% ownership of restaurants in major Chinese provinces from its joint venture partner Maxim's Caterers in exchange for Maxim's assuming full ownership of the joint venture's restaurants in Hong Kong and Macau.

- *Mission*: We provide remittance processing software to banks and other credit card-issuing organizations to improve their customer service and profitability.
- *Vision*: To be recognized by our customers as the leader in providing accurate, high-speed, high-volume transactional software for processing credit card remittances by 20XX.
- *Business Strategy*: Upgrade our current software by adding the necessary features and functions to differentiate our product and service offering from our primary competitors and satisfy projected customer requirements by 20XX.
- *Implementation Strategy*: Purchase a software company at a price not to exceed $400 million that is capable of developing "state-of-the-art" remittance processing software by 12/31/20XX. (Individual responsible: Daniel Stuckee.)
- *Functional Strategies:* Support the Implementation Strategy. (Note: Each requires a completion date, budget, and individual responsible for implementation.)

  R&D: Develop new applications for remittance processing software.

  Marketing and sales: Assess the impact of new product offerings on revenue generated from current and new customers.

  Human resources: Determine appropriate staffing requirements.

  Finance: Identify and quantify potential cost savings generated from improved productivity as a result of replacing existing software with the newly acquired software and from the elimination of duplicate personnel in our combined companies.

  Legal: Ensure that all target company customers have valid contracts and that these contracts are transferable without penalty. Also, ensure that we will have exclusive and unlimited rights to use the remittance processing software.

  Tax: Assess the tax impact of the acquisition on our cash flow.

Strategic controls

Strategic controls include both incentive and monitoring systems. *Incentive systems* involve bonus, profit-sharing, or other performance-based payments made to motivate both acquirer and target company employees to work to implement the business strategy for the combined firms. Incentives include *retention bonuses* for key employees of the target firm if they remain with the combined companies for a specific period after deal completion. *Monitoring systems* are implemented to track the actual performance of the combined firms against the business plan. They may be accounting-based and monitor financial measures such as revenue, profits, and cash flow; or they may be activity-based and monitor variables that drive financial performance such as customer retention, average revenue per customer, employee turnover, and revenue per employee.

The business plan as a communication document

The business plan is an effective means of communicating with key stakeholders. External communication of a firm's business plan when it is different from the industry norm can improve the firm's share price by enabling investors to better understand what the firm is trying to do and to minimize confusion among industry analysts. A good business plan should be short, focused, and supported with the appropriate financial data. There are many ways to develop such a document. Exhibit 4.1 outlines the key features that should be addressed in a good business plan—one that is so well reasoned and compelling that decision makers accept its recommendations.

The executive summary must communicate succinctly and compellingly what is being proposed, why it is being proposed, how it is to be achieved, and by when. It must also identify the major resource requirements and risks associated with the critical assumptions underlying the plan. The executive summary is often the first and only portion of the business plan that is read by a time-constrained CEO, lender, or venture capitalist. As such, it may represent the first and last chance to catch the attention of the key decision maker. Supporting documentation should be referred to in the business plan text but presented in the appendices.

Phase 2: building the M&A implementation plan

If a firm decides to execute its business strategy through an acquisition, it will need an acquisition plan. The steps of the acquisition planning process are discussed next.

EXHIBIT 4.1

Typical Business Unit –Level Business Plan Format

1. *Executive summary:* In a few pages, describe what is proposed, why, how it will be accomplished, by what date, critical assumptions, risks, and resource requirements.
2. *Industry or market definition:* Define the industry or market in which the firm competes in terms of size, growth rate, product offering, and other pertinent characteristics.
3. *External analysis:* Describe industry or market competitive dynamics such as factors affecting customers, competitors, potential entrants, product or service substitutes, and suppliers and how they interact to determine profitability and cash flow. Discuss the major opportunities and threats that exist because of the industry's competitive dynamics. Information accumulated in this section should be used to develop the assumptions underlying revenue and cost projections in building financial statements.
4. *Internal analysis:* Describe the company's strengths and weaknesses and how they compare with the competition. Identify strengths and weaknesses critical to the firm's targeted customers and explain why. These data can be used to develop cost and revenue assumptions underlying the firm's projected financial statements.
5. *Business mission or vision statements:* Describe what the firm does, its purpose, what it intends to become, and how it wishes to be perceived by its stakeholders.
6. *Quantified strategic objectives* (including completion dates): Indicate both financial goals (e.g., rates of return, sales, cash flow, share price) and nonfinancial goals (e.g., market share; being perceived by customers or investors as number 1 in the targeted market in terms of market share, product quality, price, innovation).
7. *Business strategy:* Identify how the vision and objectives will be achieved (e.g., become a cost leader, adopt a differentiation strategy, focus on a specific market, or some combination). Show how the chosen business strategy satisfies a key customer need or builds on a major strength possessed by the firm.
8. *Implementation strategy:* From a range of reasonable options (i.e., solo venture or "go it alone" strategy; partner via a joint venture or less formal business alliance, license, or minority investment; or acquire –merge), indicate which option would enable the firm to best implement its chosen business strategy. Indicate why the chosen implementation strategy is superior to alternative options.
9. *Functional strategies:* Identify plans, individuals responsible, and resources required by major functional areas, including manufacturing, engineering, sales and marketing, research and development, finance, legal, and human resources.
10. *Business plan financials and valuation:* Provide projected annual income, balance sheet, and cash flow statements for the firm, and estimate the firm's value based on the projected cash flows. State key forecast assumptions.
11. *Risk assessment:* Evaluate the potential impact on valuation by changing selected assumptions one at a time. Briefly identify contingency plans that would be undertaken if critical assumptions prove inaccurate. Identify specific events that would cause the firm to pursue a contingency plan.

The acquisition plan is a specific type of implementation strategy that focuses on tactical or short-term issues rather than strategic or longer-term issues. It includes management objectives, a resource assessment, a market analysis, senior management's guidance regarding management of the acquisition process, a timetable, and the name of the individual responsible for making it all happen. These and the criteria to use when searching acquisition targets are codified in the first part of the planning process; after a target has been identified, several additional steps must be taken, including contacting the target, developing a negotiation strategy, determining the initial offer price, and developing financing and integration plans. See Chapter 5 for more details.

Acquisition plan development should be directed by the "deal owner," typically a high-performing manager. Senior management should, early in the process, appoint the deal owner to this full- or part-time position. It can be someone in the firm's business development unit with substantial deal-making experience. Often, it is the individual who will be responsible for the operation and integration of the target, with an experienced deal maker playing a supporting role. The first steps in the acquisition planning process are undertaken before selecting the target firm and involve documenting the necessary plan elements.

Observing the outcome of previous deals in the same industry can be useful in planning an acquisition. Researchers have identified a positive correlation between premerger planning involving an analysis of past M&As and postmerger performance.[16]

Plan objectives

The acquisition plan's objectives should be consistent with the firm's strategic objectives. Financial and nonfinancial objectives should support realization of the business plan objectives. As is true with business plan objectives, the acquisition plan objectives should be quantified and include a date when such objectives are expected to be realized.

Financial objectives could include a minimum rate of return or profit, revenue, and cash flow targets to be achieved within a specified period. Minimum return targets may be higher than those specified in the business plan, which relate to shareholder required returns. The required return for the acquisition may reflect a substantially higher level of risk associated with the amount and timing of the expected cash flows resulting from the acquisition.

Nonfinancial objectives address the motivations for a deal that support the financial returns stipulated in the business plan.[17] They could include obtaining rights to specific products, patents, copyrights, or brand names; providing growth opportunities in the same or related markets; and developing new distribution channels in the same or related markets. Other examples include obtaining more production capacity in strategically located facilities; adding R&D capabilities; and acquiring access to proprietary technologies, processes, and skills.[18] Because these objectives identify the factors that determine whether a firm will achieve its desired financial returns, they provide more guidance than financial targets.

Acquirers relying on key nonfinancial objectives that drive firm value are more likely to realize larger announcement date financial returns than those that do not.[19] Why? Firms whose managers are focused on financial returns can lose sight of the factors that drive returns. Firms using so-called "value-based management" measure their performance against value drivers and are more likely to realize desired financial returns. Table 4.5 illustrates how acquisition plan objectives can be linked with business plan objectives.

Resource and capability evaluation

Early in the acquisition process, it is important to determine the maximum amount of the firm's available resources senior management will commit to a deal. This information is used when the firm develops target selection criteria before undertaking a search for target firms. Financial resources available to the acquirer include those provided by internally generated cash flow in excess of normal operating requirements plus funds from the equity and debt markets. When the target firm is known, the potential financing pool includes funds provided by the internal cash flow of the combined companies in excess of normal operating requirements, the capacity of the combined firms to issue equity or increase leverage, and proceeds from selling assets not required to execute the acquirer's business plan.

Financial theory suggests that an acquiring firm will always be able to attract sufficient funding for an acquisition if it can demonstrate that it can earn its cost of capital. In practice, senior management's risk tolerance plays an important role in determining what the acquirer believes it can afford to spend on a merger or acquisition. Three basic types of risk confront senior management considering an acquisition. How they are perceived can determine the available resources management will be willing to commit to making an acquisition.

Operating risk addresses the ability of the buyer to manage the acquired company. Generally, it is higher for M&As in markets unrelated to the acquirer's core business. *Financial risk* refers to the buyer's willingness and ability to leverage a transaction as well as the willingness of shareholders to accept dilution of near-term earnings per share

[16] Francis et al., 2014

[17] Gan et al. (2020) argue that the inclusion of nonfinancial performance measures in executive performance packages are more likely to align their behavior with long-term firm performance and increase firm value than simply to rely on equity-based compensation.

[18] DePamphilis, 2001

[19] Knauer et al., 2018

TABLE 4.5 Examples of linkages between business and acquisition plan objectives

Business plan objective	Acquisition plan objective
Financial: The firm will • Achieve rates of return that will equal or exceed its cost of equity or capital by 20XX. • Maintain a debt-to-total capital ratio of x%.	*Financial returns*: The target firm should have • A minimum return on assets of x%. • A debt-to-total capital ratio $\leq y$%. • Unencumbered assets[a] of $z million. • Cash flow in excess of operating requirements of $x million.
Size: The firm will be the number one or two market share leader by 20XX. • Achieve revenue of $x million by 20XX	*Size*: The target firm should be at least $x million in revenue.
Growth: The firm will achieve through 20XX annual average • Revenue growth of x% • Earnings per share growth of y% • Operating cash flow growth of z%	*Growth*: The target firm should • Have annual revenue, earnings, and operating cash flow growth of at least x%, y%, and z%, respectively. • Provide new products and markets resulting in $z by 20XX. • Possess excess annual production capacity of x million units.
Diversification: The firm will reduce earnings variability by x%.	*Diversification*: The target firm's earnings should be largely uncorrelated with the acquirer's earnings.
Flexibility: The firm will achieve flexibility in manufacturing and design.	*Flexibility*: The target firm should use flexible manufacturing techniques.
Technology: The firm will be recognized by its customers as the industry's technology leader.	*Technology*: The target firm should own important patents, copyrights, and other forms of intellectual property.
Quality: The firm will be recognized by its customers as the industry's quality leader.	*Quality*: The target firm's product defects must be less than x per million units manufactured.
Service: The firm will be recognized by its customers as the industry's service leader.	*Warranty record*: The target firm's customer claims per million units sold should be not greater than x.
Cost: The firm will be recognized by its customers as the industry's low-cost provider.	*Labor costs*: The target firm should be nonunion and not subject to significant government regulation.
Innovation: The firm will be recognized by its customers as the industry's innovation leader.	*R&D capabilities*: The target firm should have introduced new products accounting for at least x% of total revenue in the last 2 years.

[a]*Unencumbered assets are those that are not being used as collateral underlying current loans. As such, they may be used to collateralize additional borrowing to finance an acquisition.*

(EPS). To retain a specific credit rating, the acquiring company must maintain certain levels of financial ratios, such as debt-to-total capital and interest coverage.[20] Senior management could also gain insight into how much EPS-dilution equity investors may be willing to tolerate through informal discussions with Wall Street analysts and an examination of comparable deals financed by issuing stock. *Overpayment risk* involves the dilution of EPS or a reduction in its earnings growth rate resulting from paying significantly more than the economic value of the acquired company.[21]

[20] A firm's incremental debt capacity can be approximated by comparing the relevant financial ratios with those of comparable firms in the same industry that are rated by the credit rating agencies. The difference represents the amount the firm, in theory, could borrow without jeopardizing its current credit rating. Suppose the combined acquirer and target firms' interest coverage ratio is 3, and the combined firms' debt-to-total capital ratio is 0.25. Assume further that other firms within the same industry with comparable interest coverage ratios have debt-to-total capital ratios of 0.5. Consequently, the combined acquirer and target firms could increase borrowing without jeopardizing their combined credit rating until their debt-to-total capital ratio equals 0.5.

[21] To illustrate the effects of overpayment risk, assume that the acquiring company's shareholders are satisfied with the company's projected increase in EPS of 20% annually for the next 5 years. The company announces it will be acquiring another firm and that "restructuring" expenses will slow EPS growth next year to 10%. Management argues that savings resulting from merging the two companies will raise the combined EPS growth rate to 30% in the second through fifth year of the forecast. The risk is that the savings cannot be realized in the time assumed by management and the slowdown in earnings extends well beyond the first year..

EXHIBIT 4.2

Examples of Management Guidance Provided to the Acquisition Team

1. Determining the criteria used to evaluate prospective candidates (e.g., size, price range, current profitability, growth rate, geographic location, and cultural compatibility)
2. Specifying acceptable methods for finding candidates (e.g., soliciting board members; analyzing competitors; contacting brokers, investment bankers, lenders, law firms, and the trade press)
3. Establishing roles and responsibilities of the acquisition team, including the use of outside consultants, and defining the team's budget
4. Identifying acceptable sources of financing (e.g., equity issues, bank loans, unsecured bonds, seller financing, or asset sales)
5. Establishing preferences for an asset or stock purchase and form of payment
6. Setting a level of tolerance for goodwill (i.e., the excess of the purchase price over the fair market value of acquired assets less acquired liabilities)
7. Indicating the degree of openness to partial rather than full ownership
8. Specifying willingness to launch an unfriendly takeover
9. Setting affordability limits (expressed as a maximum price to after-tax earnings, earnings before interest and taxes, or cash flow multiple or maximum dollar amount)
10. Indicating any desire for related or unrelated acquisitions.

Management guidance

To ensure that the process is consistent with management's risk tolerance, management must provide guidance to those responsible for finding and valuing the target as well as negotiating the deal. Upfront participation by management will help dramatically in the successful implementation of the acquisition process. Exhibit 4.2 provides examples of the more common types of management guidance that might be found in an acquisition plan.

Timetable

A timetable recognizes all of the key events that must take place in the acquisition process. Each event should have beginning and ending dates and performance to plan milestones along the way and should identify who is responsible for ensuring that each milestone is achieved. The timetable of events should be aggressive but realistic. The timetable should be sufficiently aggressive to motivate all involved to work as expeditiously as possible to meet the plan's management objectives while avoiding overoptimism that may demotivate individuals if uncontrollable circumstances delay reaching certain milestones.

Exhibit 4.3 recaps the typical acquisition planning process. The first two elements are discussed in this chapter; the remaining items are the subject of the next chapter.

Some things to remember

The success of an acquisition depends greatly on the focus, understanding, and discipline inherent in a thorough and viable business planning process. An acquisition is only one of many options available for implementing a business strategy. The decision to pursue an acquisition often rests on the desire to achieve control and a perception that the acquisition will result in achieving the desired objectives more rapidly than other options. After a firm has decided that an acquisition is critical to realizing the strategic direction defined in the business plan, a merger or acquisition plan should be developed.

Chapter discussion questions

4.1 How does planning facilitate the acquisition process?
4.2 What is the difference between a business plan and an acquisition plan?

EXHIBIT 4.3

Acquisition Plan For the Acquiring Firm

1. *Plan objectives*: Identify the specific purpose of the acquisition. Include what goals are to be achieved (e.g., cost reduction, access to new customers, distribution channels or proprietary technology, expanded production capacity) and how the achievement of these goals will better enable the acquiring firm to implement its business strategy.
2. *Timetable*: Establish a timetable for completing the acquisition, including integration if the target firm is to be merged with the acquiring firm's operations.
3. *Resource and capability evaluation*: Evaluate the acquirer's financial and managerial capability to complete an acquisition. Identify affordability limits in terms of the maximum amount the acquirer should pay for an acquisition.
4. *Management guidance*: Specify the acquirer's preferences for a "friendly" takeover; controlling interest; using stock, debt, cash, or some combination; and so on.
5. *Search plan*: Develop criteria for identifying target firms and explain plans for conducting the search, why the target ultimately selected was chosen, and how you will make initial contact with the target firm (see Chapter 5 for more details).
6. *Negotiation strategy*: Identify key buyer and seller issues. Recommend a deal structure (i.e., terms and conditions) addressing the primary needs of all parties involved. Comment on the characteristics of the deal structure. Such characteristics include the proposed acquisition vehicle (i.e., the legal structure used to acquire the target firm; see Chapter 11 for more details), the postclosing organization (i.e., the legal framework used to manage the combined businesses following closing), and the form of payment (i.e., cash, stock, or some combination). Other characteristics include the form of acquisition (i.e., whether assets or stock are being acquired) and tax structure (i.e., whether it is a taxable or a nontaxable transaction; see Chapter 12 for more detail). Indicate how you might "close the gap" between the seller's price expectations and the offer price. These considerations are discussed in more detail in Chapter 5.
7. *Determine initial offer price*: Provide projected 5-year income, balance sheet, and cash flow statements for the acquiring and target firms individually and for the consolidated acquirer and target firms with and without the effects of synergy. (Note that the projected forecast period can be longer than 5 years if deemed appropriate.)
8. Develop a preliminary minimum and maximum purchase price range for the target. List key forecast assumptions.
9. Identify an initial offer price, the composition (i.e., cash, stock, debt, or some combination) of the offer price, and why you believe this price is appropriate in terms of meeting the primary needs of both target and acquirer shareholders. The appropriateness of the offer price should reflect your preliminary thinking about the deal structure (see Chapters 11 and 12 for a detailed discussion of the deal-structuring process).
10. *Financing plan*: Determine if the proposed offer price can be financed without risking the combined firm's creditworthiness or seriously eroding near-term profitability and cash flow. For publicly traded firms, pay particular attention to the near-term impact of the acquisition on the EPS of the combined firms (see Chapter 15).
11. *Integration plan*: Identify integration challenges and possible solutions (see Chapter 6 for more details). For financial buyers, identify an "exit strategy." Highly leveraged transactions are discussed in more detail in Chapter 13.

4.3 What are the advantages and disadvantages of using an acquisition to implement a business strategy compared with a joint venture?

4.4 Why is it important to understand the assumptions underlying a business or an acquisition plan?

4.5 Why is it important to get senior management involved early in the acquisition process?

4.6 In your judgment, which of the elements of the acquisition plan discussed in this chapter are the most important and why?

4.7 After having acquired the OfficeMax superstore chain, Boise Cascade announced the sale of its paper and timber products operations to reduce its dependence on this cyclical business. Reflecting its new emphasis on distribution, the company changed its name to OfficeMax, Inc. How would you describe the OfficeMax vision and business strategy implicit in these actions?

4.8 Dell Computer is one of the best-known global technology companies. In your opinion, who are Dell's primary customers? Current and potential competitors? Suppliers? How would you assess Dell's bargaining power with respect to its customers and suppliers? What are Dell's strengths and weaknesses versus those of its current competitors?

4.9 Discuss the types of analyses inside General Electric that may have preceded its announcement that it would spin off its consumer and industrial business to its shareholders.

4.10 Ashland Chemical, the largest US chemical distributor, acquired chemical manufacturer Hercules Inc. for $3.3 billion. This move followed Dow Chemical Company's purchase of Rohm & Haas. The justification for both acquisitions was to diversify earnings and offset higher oil costs. How will this business combination offset escalating oil costs?

Answers to these discussion questions are found on the online instructors' site available for this book.

End-of-chapter case study: Newmont becomes global leader in the gold-mining industry

Case study objectives

To illustrate how

- Industry consolidation often drives mergers and acquisitions
- Firms use acquisitions to augment their existing capabilities and resources
- Gaining regulatory approval often requires concessions on a wide array of issues

Gold-mining companies had been out of favor for almost 10 years with institutional investors disenchanted with industry consolidation that took place at the height of the commodity cycle, leaving many firms laden with debt. With the world's economically accessible reserves dwindling, gold-mining firms needed to find more gold deposits to ensure continued production. With the lackluster pace of discovery of new reserves, companies looked to M&As as an alternative way of replenishing their resources.

M&As among gold-mining companies heated up in 2018. Barrick Gold (Barrick) and Randgold Resources (Randgold) announced a merger in September 2018 followed by a November tie-up of Pan American Silver and Tahoe Resources. In January 2019, Newmont Mining Corp. (Newmont) announced that it had reached an agreement to merge with Canada's Goldcorp Inc. The next month, Barrick made a hostile bid to acquire Newmont but was rebuffed, as the offer was considered insufficient by the Barrick board.

Newmont's takeover of Goldcorp created the largest gold mining firm on the globe. The new firm will be named Newmont Goldcorp. According to Newmont CEO Gary Goldberg, the $10 billion all-stock purchase of Canada-based Goldcorp provided access to substantial new reserves, efficient operations, mines in safe areas, and continued investment in Canada. The latter observation was critical to getting regulatory approval.

The Newmont deal was a stark contrast to rival Barrick's takeover of Randgold. Barrick intended to reduce its presence in Canada and increase the firm's exposure to more risky geographic areas. But whereas Barrick's share price soared after announcing its transaction, Newmont's stock plunged almost 9% after its takeover announcement. The deals negotiated by each company displayed sizable differences in their strategies as they confronted the challenges of growing future revenue and profits.

For years, both firms had competed to be the global leader in gold mining. Newmont had achieved that coveted position with the Goldcorp acquisition. Newmont declared publicly that it is targeting annual production at an unprecedented 7 million ounces of gold. Gold mining is a capital-intensive business with substantial fixed costs in an industry that is often subject to wide swings in the price of gold. Profitability tends to soar when revenue rises well above fixed expenses because little additional capital or labor is needed to produce more gold. However, falling gold prices can result in sizable losses.

By holding production at 7 million ounces annually, Newmont hopes to sustain its ability to pay the highest dividend in the industry. In contrast, Toronto-based Barrick, having just completed its $6 billion takeover of Randgold, downplayed planned production levels and instead focused on ways to improve operating cash flow. The firm also immediately conducted layoffs at its offices in Toronto.

Both firms are facing the challenges of developing and operating new mines. With the rising cost of finding new reserves, risk mitigation has become paramount. And the two firms are taking different approaches. Newmont stressed its combination with Goldcorp as creating a company in stable geographic areas: about half of the firm's operations are in Australia, Canada, and the United States, and the remainder are mainly in Latin America. Barrick's acquisition of Randgold meant it was acquiring a firm whose operations were centered in Africa, with mines concentrated in Cote D'Ivoire, the Democratic Republic of Congo, and Mali. Although generally viewed as higher risk, they potentially offer much higher returns commensurate with the hazards involved.

What seems to have peaked investor interest in Barrick's deal was that it appointed Randgold's CEO Mark Bristow to lead the combined companies. He has a track record of operating successfully mines located in politically risky areas and of being a cost cutter. In contrast, Goldberg, also considered a good operator, planned to retire at the end of 2019.

Barrick has been widely criticized for reducing its presence in Canada. Recognizing the potential regulatory minefield after the invective directed at Barrick, Newmont extolled the benefits of the merger to Canada to gain regulatory approval. Newmont argued that combining with Goldcorp ensures that Canada's gold industry will participate in a world-leading natural resources firm. Furthermore, Newmont plans to preserve jobs in Canada by designating Goldcorp's current Vancouver headquarters as Newmont Goldcorp's North American regional office, overseeing the firm's properties in Canada and the United States.

Newmont stated publicly it will honor all of Goldcorp's commitments to indigenous communities. Newmont Goldcorp's board would appoint Canadian citizens as board members in proportion to Goldcorp's investor ownership in the new company. Newmont Goldcorp would be listed both on the New York and Toronto Stock Exchanges. The firm promised to provide employment and pay higher wages for highly skilled jobs at Canadian mines and to continue contributions to charities in communities in which the firm operates.

The terms of the Newmont deal are that Newmont will exchange 0.328 of a share for each of Goldcorp's outstanding common shares, resulting in a 17% premium based on the company's 20-day volume-weighted average share price. Newmont shareholders will own 65% of the combined businesses and Goldcorp shareholders the rest. The deal valued Goldcorp's equity at $10 billion, and the firm's enterprise value was $12.5 billion. Annual pretax synergy was estimated at $100 million, and the deal would be accretive during the first full year of operation after closing.

Newmont closed the Goldcorp acquisition in late 2019 after receiving regulatory approval. Newmont shareholder support for the deal was overwhelming. The deal creates the world's largest gold producer by market value, output, and reserves, supplanting Barrick for the top spot. Goldcorp investors had approved the deal earlier in 2019.

Newmont Goldcorp has laid out ambitious plans for itself as stated publicly in its vision for the firm: "We will be recognized and respected for exceptional economic, environmental and social performance." This implies accountability to all stakeholders, ranging from shareholders to the natural resources the firm manages to the communities in which it operates. Exceptional shareholder financial returns, the board and management reasons, can be realized and sustained only if the firm is a good steward of natural resources and contributes to the public well-being. Well-being is not only measured in terms of job creation but also in terms of helping to satisfy unmet public needs. Good citizenship is good business!

Discussion questions

1. If you were managing the firm, how would you be guided by Newmont's corporate vision, business strategy, and implementation strategy?
2. What external and internal factors are driving the merger between Newmont and Goldcorp?
3. In the context of M&A, synergy represents the incremental cash flows generated by combining two businesses. Identify the potential synergies you believe could be realized in combining Newmont and Goldcorp. Speculate as to what might be some of the challenges limiting the timely realization of these synergies.
4. Why did Newmont's shares fall and Goldcorp's rise immediately after the deal's announcement? Speculate as to why Goldcorp's share price did not rise by the full amount of the premium.
5. What alternative implementation strategies could Newmont have pursued? Speculate as to why they may have chosen to acquire rather than an alternative implementation strategy. What are the key risks involved in the takeover of Goldcorp?

Answers to these questions are found in the Online Instructor's Manual available for instructors using this book.

CHAPTER

5

Implementation: search through closing

phases 3 to 10 of the acquisition process

OUTLINE

Mergers, Acquisitions, and Other Restructuring Activities, Eleventh Edition
https://doi.org/10.1016/B978-0-12-819782-0.00005-8

A man that is very good at making excuses is probably good at nothing else. —***Ben Franklin***

Inside M&A: Salesforce.com makes a big bet to move beyond its core customer relationship management business

KEY POINTS

- "Big data" and artificial intelligence–driven data analytics are reshaping the focus of software firms.
- To fill gaps in their product offering, software firms are paying what appear to be excessive premiums to make acquisitions.

Software firms' customers are demanding "big data" capabilities.[1] This requires such companies to provide applications that facilitate managing large databases and correcting, organizing, and presenting data in a manner that satisfies customer needs. The next step is to apply artificial intelligence (AI) software[2] to the customer's data to identify appropriate decisions. Responding to its customers, Salesforce.com (Salesforce) agreed to acquire data analytics firm Tableau Software (Tableau) in mid-2019 in an all-stock deal valued at $15.7 billion. The deal represented a nearly 50% premium to Tableau's closing price immediately before the announcement date.

Tableau is not a cloud company; rather, its products run primarily in on-premises data centers. Tableau will complement Salesforce's 2018 $6.5 billion acquisition of MuleSoft, whose products are designed to develop specific software applications and then to ensure they work with other software applications. MuleSoft's products work with firms that do not have all their data in the cloud for data privacy reasons such as in the health care industry.

Salesforce's core business is to provide customers online access to customer relationship management (CRM) software.[3] As a platform provider, Salesforce is motivated to make these types of acquisitions to provide additional services to its clients. The firm's business strategy is to expand its capability as a "service on demand" platform provider to help its customers make sense out of their data.[4] Salesforce sees synergy between its Einstein AI tools

[1] "Big data" commonly refers to the availability of very large data sets available for analysis.

[2] AI in this context refers to machines performing tasks formerly done by humans.

[3] CRM software gives marketing, sales, and service departments a common view of their customers and access to the tools to display and interpret the data. CRM allows the storage and management of prospect and customer information, including contact information, accounts, leads, and sales opportunities in a single location.

[4] A platform provider is a business offering either services (e.g., Amazon offering easy access to products) or applications (e.g., Salesforce's application-specific cloud computing service). Such firms allow their customers to develop, run, and manage applications without having to build the infrastructure themselves.

and Tableau's business intelligence software. Tableau's software helps firms display data by enabling them to build databases, graphs, and maps from data, and Einstein helps customers make decisions based on the data. Salesforce's objective is to add new and retain existing subscribers to sustain its subscription-driven revenue stream.

Investors were distressed by the size of the premium paid for Tableau and the potential earnings dilution resulting from the flood of new Salesforce shares to finance the deal. When announced, Salesforce's stock fell 5.3%, whereas Tableau's shares rose 33.7%. To justify the lofty premium paid, Salesforce must execute flawlessly to realize anticipated synergy.

Chapter overview

Big data, data analytics, AI, block chains, and smart contracting are tools that are increasingly being applied to various aspects of the mergers and acquisitions (M&A) process. To what extent do they offer promising solutions to challenging problems? To what extent are they overhyped? These are among the questions addressed in this chapter, which presumes that a firm has developed a viable business plan that requires an acquisition to implement its business strategy.

Whereas Chapter 4 addressed the creation of business and acquisition plans (phases 1 and 2), this chapter focuses on phases 3 to 10 of the M&A process, including search, screening, first contact, negotiation, integration planning, closing, integration implementation, and evaluation. A chapter review (including practice questions and answers) is contained in the file folder entitled Student Study Guide on the companion site to this book (https://www.elsevier.com/books-and-journals/book-companion/9780128197820). The companion site also contains a comprehensive due diligence question list.

Phase 3: the search process

Search frictions are the direct and indirect costs associated with target selection. Direct costs include the resources devoted to and the time required to complete the process. Indirect costs could include actual merger gains being less than what could have been realized had a more appropriate target been selected.[5] To minimize such costs, public acquirers often use investment banks to augment their internal resources in conducting target searches. But hiring investment banks can be expensive. Increasingly, companies—even midsize firms—are moving investment banking "in house." Rather than use brokers or so-called "finders"[6] as part of their acquisition process, they are identifying potential targets, doing valuation, and performing due diligence on their own. This reflects efforts to save on investment banking fees, which can easily be more than $5 million plus expenses on a $500 million transaction.[7]

Initiating the process

The first step in searching for acquisition candidates is to establish a small number of primary selection criteria, including the industry and the size of the transaction. Deal size is best defined by the maximum purchase price a firm is willing to pay, expressed as a maximum price-to-earnings, book, cash flow, or revenue ratio, or a maximum purchase price stated in terms of dollars. It also may be appropriate to limit the search to a specific geographic area.

Consider a private acute care hospital holding company that wants to buy a skilled nursing facility within 50 miles of its largest hospital in Allegheny County, Pennsylvania. Management believes it cannot afford to pay

[5] Larkin and Lyandres, 2020

[6] A *broker* has a fiduciary responsibility to the buyer or the seller and is not permitted to represent both parties. Compensation is paid by the client to the broker. A *finder* introduces both parties but represents neither party. The finder has no fiduciary responsibility to either party and is compensated by either one or both parties.

[7] The Lehman formula was a widely used fee structure; in it, broker or finder fees would be equal to 5% of the first $1 million of the purchase price, 4% of the second, 3% of the third, 2% of the fourth, and 1% of the remainder. Today, fee structures are usually negotiated and consist of a basic fee paid regardless of whether the deal is consummated, an additional fee paid on closing, and an "extraordinary" fee paid under unusual circumstances that may delay the closing (e.g., gaining antitrust approval). Fees vary widely, but 1% of the total purchase price plus reimbursement of expenses is often considered reasonable. For small deals, the Lehman formula may apply.

more than $45 million for the facility. Its primary selection criteria could include an industry (skilled nursing), a location (Allegheny County, PA), and a maximum price (five times cash flow, not to exceed $45 million). Similarly, a Texas-based maker of patio furniture with operations in the southwestern United States seeks to expand its sales in California. The firm is seeking to purchase a patio furniture maker for no more than $100 million. Its primary criteria include an industry (outdoor furniture), a geographic location (California, Arizona, and Nevada), and a maximum purchase price (10 times operating earnings, not to exceed $100 million).

If confidentiality is not an issue, a firm may advertise its interest in acquiring a particular type of firm in the *Wall Street Journal* or the trade press. Although likely to generate interest, it is less likely to produce good prospects. Rather, it often results in many responses from those interested in getting a free valuation of their own company or from brokers claiming that their clients fit the buyer's criteria as a ruse to convince you that you need the broker's services. More often, confidentiality is important to acquirers desiring to avoid having multiple bidders for a firm or to create angst among their own employees, customers, and suppliers as well as those of the potential target. Consequently, firms try to avoid making their search efforts public.

Commonly used information sources

The next step is to search available computerized databases using the selection criteria. Common databases and directory services include Disclosure, Dun & Bradstreet, Standard & Poor's Corporate Register, and Capital IQ. Firms also may query their law, banking, and accounting firms to identify other candidates. Investment banks, brokers, and leveraged buyout firms are also fertile sources of potential candidates, although they are likely to require a finder's fee. Yahoo! Finance and EDGAR Online enable analysts to obtain data quickly about competitors and customers. These sites provide easy access to a variety of documents filed with the Securities and Exchange Commission. The usefulness of such publicly available information in the search process tends to be greater when a potential target's product lines are substantially similar to the acquirer's.[8] Exhibit 5.1 provides a comprehensive listing of alternative information sources.

Data reliability

Publicly traded firms and those wishing to borrow require independent auditing firms to determine the accuracy of their financial statements. However, auditors may be willing to overlook certain flaws in client data if they are concerned about losing the client. On average, audit firms experience a drop in future client and revenue growth after detecting a "material weakness" in a firm's financial reporting system.[9]

Finding reliable information about privately owned firms is a major problem. Sources such as Dun & Bradstreet and Experian may only provide fragmentary data. Publicly available information may offer additional details. For example, surveys by trade associations or the US Census Bureau often include industry-specific average sales per employee. A private firm's sales can be estimated by multiplying this figure by an estimate of the firm's workforce, which may be obtained by searching the firm's product literature, website, or trade show speeches or even by counting the number of cars in the parking lot during each shift.

Less obvious data sources

Credit rating agencies—independent firms that assign a rating to a firm's ability to repay its debt—assess the viability of both publicly traded and privately owned firms. Acquirers are less likely to overpay because of access to financial information used by the rating agencies. Rated targets receive lower premiums and generate higher acquirer postmerger returns than nonrated firms.[10]

The initial public offering (IPO) market can also provide information about private firms. The resulting price to sales, profit, or cash flow multiples associated with the IPO can be applied to similar private firms to estimate their fair market value. The information in the IPO market disseminated by media and analyst coverage raises the likelihood that private firms in the same industry as the firm undergoing an IPO will be acquired.[11]

Who owns the firm also can represent an important source of information when key information on the firm is not publicly available. Firms, either partially or wholly owned by private equity investors, may command a higher

[8] Bernard et al., 2020

[9] Maurer, August 12, 2019

[10] Jory et al., 2017

[11] Wu and Reuer, 2020

EXHIBIT 5.1

Information Souces on Individual Companies

Securities and Exchange Commission Filings (Public Companies Only)

10-K: provides information on a company's annual operations, competitors, market conditions, legal proceedings, risk factors, and other related data
10-Q: updates investors about the company's operations each quarter.
S-1: filed when a company wants to register new stock; can contain information about the company's operating history and business risks
S-2: filed when a company is completing a material transaction, such as a merger; provides substantial detail underlying the terms and conditions of the transaction, the events surrounding the transaction, and justification for the merger or acquisition
8-K: filed when a company faces a "material event," such as a merger
Schedule 14A: a proxy statement; gives details about the annual meeting and biographies of company officials and directors, including stock ownership and pay

Websites

Corporate Social Responsibility Index: www.reputationinstitute.com
Financial Accounting Standards Board: www.fasb.org
International Accounting Standards Board: www.iasc.org
American Institute of Certified Public Accountants: www.aicpa
Current deal-related stories: www.nytimes.com/pages/business/dealbook/index.html
Current deal-related stories: www.reuters.com/finance/deals/mergers
M&A deal terms: www.bvresources.com/products/factset-mergerstat
Businesses for sale: www.bizbuysell.com
Financial data: www.capitaliq.com
Securities and Exchange Commission company filings: www.edgar-online.com
Financial data: www.factset.com
Industry and company financial data: http://finance.yahoo.com
Company reports: www.hoovers.com
Legal, news and business documents: www.lexisnexis.com
Social network for business professionals: https://dealstream.com
Information on security regulations and enforcement actions: www.sec.gov
Information on antitrust laws and premerger review: www.ftc.gov
Recent corporate press releases: http://www.businesswire.com/portal/site/home/my-business-wire
Current M&A trends and developments: https://www.pwc.com/us/en/washington-national-tax/newsletters/mergers-and-acquisitions.html

Organizations

Reputation Institute: provides corporate social responsibility index
Value Line Investment Survey: information on public companies
Directory of Corporate Affiliations: corporate affiliations
Lexis/Nexis: database of general business and legal information
Thomas Register: organizes firms by products and services
Frost & Sullivan: industry research
Findex.com: financial information
Competitive Intelligence Professionals: information about industries
Dialog Corporation: industry databases
Wards Business Directory of US and public companies
Predicasts: provides databases through libraries
Business Periodicals Index: business and technical article index
Dun & Bradstreet Directories: information about private and public companies
Experian: information about private and public companies
Nelson's Directory of Investment Research: Wall Street Research Reports
Standard & Poor's Publications: industry surveys and corporate records
Harris Infosource: information about manufacturing companies
Hoover's Handbook of Private Companies: information on large private firms
Washington Researchers: information on public and private firms, markets, and industries
The Wall Street Journal Transcripts: Wall Street research reports
Directory of Corporate Affiliations (published by Lexis-Nexis Group)

premium, especially if the private equity firm has a reputation for improving the performance of firms in which they invest.[12]

Phase 4: the screening process

Screening is a refinement of the search process. It begins by pruning the initial list of potential candidates created using the primary criteria discussed earlier. Because relatively few primary criteria are used, the initial list may be lengthy. It can be shortened using secondary selection criteria; however, too many criteria can excessively shorten the list. The best screening criteria are generally those that are measurable and for which data are current. The following selection criteria include examples often used in the screening process.

- *Market segment*: A market segment is a group of customers who share one or more characteristics in common. A lengthy list of candidates can be shortened by identifying a subsegment of a target market. For example, a manufacturer of flat rolled steel coils wishes to move up the value chain by acquiring a steel fabricated products company. Although the primary search criterion could be to search for US-based steel fabricating firms (i.e., the steel manufacturer's target market), a secondary criterion could stipulate segmenting the steel fabrication products market further to include only those fabricators making steel tubing.
- *Product line*: A product line is a group of products sold by one company under the same logo or brand. Assume a well-known maker of men's sports apparel wishes to diversify into women's sports apparel. The primary search criteria would be to search for makers of women's sports apparel, and the secondary criterion could be a specific type of apparel.
- *Profitability*: Profitability should be defined in terms of the percentage return on sales, assets, or total investment. This allows a more accurate comparison among candidates of different sizes. A firm with operating earnings of $5 million on sales of $100 million may be less attractive than a firm with $3 million in operating income on sales of $50 million because the latter firm may be more efficient.
- *Degree of leverage*: Debt-to-equity or debt-to-total capital ratios are used to measure leverage or indebtedness. The acquirer may not want to purchase a firm whose debt burden may cause the combined company's leverage ratios to jeopardize its credit rating.
- *Market share*: The acquiring firm may be interested only in firms that are number 1 or 2 in market share in the targeted industry or in firms whose market share is some multiple (e.g., 2 × the next-largest competitor).[13]
- *Cultural compatibility*: Insights into a firm's culture can be obtained from public statements about the target's vision for the future and its governance practices as well as its reputation as a responsible corporate citizen. Examining employee demographics reveals much about the diversity of a firm's workforce. Finally, an acquirer needs to determine whether it can adapt to the challenges of dealing with foreign firms, such as different languages and customs.
- *Age of CEO or controlling shareholder*: For public firms, CEOs are more inclined to support an offer to buy their firms if they are at or close to retirement age. Why? Because target firm CEOs are unlikely to find a position with the acquirer and have less to lose because they are about to retire.[14] For privately owned firms, the age of the founder often is an important determinant of when a firm is likely to be willing to sell.
- *Target reputation:* Acquirers often avoid targets with dissimilar reputations. Firms viewed as environmentally green avoid acquiring firms that are viewed as polluters.[15] Acquirers may evaluate potential targets by using a Corporate Social Responsibility index provided by the Boston-based Reputation Institute, which scores firms by tracking consumer perceptions.

[12] Tang et al., 2018

[13] Firms having substantially greater market share than their competitors often are able to achieve lower cost positions than their competitors because of economies of scale and experience curve effects.

[14] Jenter et al., 2015

[15] Boone et al., 2019

Phase 5: first contact

After a list of attractive targets has been compiled, the acquirer turns to the next phase of the acquisition process, first contact. For each target firm, develop an approach strategy in which the acquirer identifies reasons the target should consider an acquisition proposal. Such reasons could include the need for capital, a desire by the owner to "cash out," and succession planning issues.

Research efforts should extend beyond publicly available information and include interviews with customers, suppliers, ex-employees, and trade associations in an effort to understand better the strengths, weaknesses, and objectives of potential target firms. Insights into management, ownership, performance, and business plans help provide a compelling rationale for the proposed acquisition and heighten the prospect of obtaining the target firm's interest. Of course, the downside of interviews is that the acquirer's interest in a target could become public.

Contact strategies

How initial contact is made depends on the size of the company, whether the potential acquirer has direct contacts with the target, whether the target is publicly or privately held, and the acquirer's time frame for completing a deal. If time permits, there is no substitute for developing a personal relationship with the sellers, especially if the firm is privately held. A rapport often makes it possible to acquire a firm not thought to be for sale. Personal relationships must be formed at the highest levels within a privately held target firm. Founders often have great flexibility in negotiating a deal that "feels right" rather than simply holding out for the highest possible price. In contrast, personal relationships can go only so far when negotiating with a public company that has a fiduciary responsibility to its shareholders to get the best price. If time is a critical factor, acquirers may not have the luxury of developing personal relationships with the seller. Under these circumstances, a more expeditious approach must be taken.

For small companies with which the buyer has no personal relationships, initiate contact through a vaguely worded letter expressing interest in a joint venture (JV) or marketing alliance. During the follow-up phone call, be prepared to discuss options with the seller. Get to the point quickly but indirectly. Identify yourself, your company, and its strengths. Demonstrate your understanding of the contact's business and how an informal partnership could make sense. Be able to explain the benefits of your proposal to the contact. If the opportunity arises, propose a range of options, including an acquisition. Listen carefully to the contact's reaction. If the contact is willing to entertain the notion of an acquisition, request a face-to-face meeting.[16]

Whenever possible, use a trusted intermediary to make contact, generally at the highest level possible in the target firm. In some instances, the appropriate contact is the most senior manager, but it could be a disaffected large shareholder. Intermediaries include members of the acquirer's board or the firm's outside legal counsel, accounting firm, lender, broker or finder, or investment banker. Intermediaries can be less intimidating than if you take a direct approach. When firms have a common board member, empirical research suggests that the likelihood of a deal closing is greater, and the duration of the negotiation is usually shorter.[17]

Common connections enable both parties to gather information about the other more easily, which tends to promote trust. Still, a high degree of familiarity between board members and management of the acquirer and target firms can lower announcement date acquirer financial returns if it causes cronyism, resulting in less objective analysis. In the presence of significant social ties, there is a greater likelihood that the target's CEO and a larger fraction of the target's preacquisition board will remain on the board of the combined firms after the merger.[18]

Firms sharing a lender in common with a potential acquirer have a higher likelihood of becoming a takeover target than firms that do not. The common lender can serve as an intermediary through which the potential acquirer contacts the potential bidder. When such takeovers are announced, the announcement date return for the combined firms is higher than for firms without this connection. Also, borrowing costs for the bidder tend to be lower presumably because the lender is highly familiar with both parties. Although having a common lender is generally positive

[16] To ensure confidentiality, choose a meeting place that provides sufficient privacy. Create a written agenda for the meeting after soliciting input from all participants. The meeting should start with a review of your company and your perspective on the outlook for the industry. Encourage the potential target firm to provide information on its own operations and its outlook for the industry. Look for areas of consensus. After the meeting, send an email to the other party highlighting what you believe was accomplished and then await their feedback.

[17] Renneboog and Zhao, 2013

[18] Ishii and Xuan, 2014

for bidders, this often is not true for target shareholders, with the average target receiving lower acquisition premiums.[19]

For public companies, discretion is critical because of the target's concern about being "put into play"—that is, it may be an attractive investment opportunity for other firms. Even rumors of an acquisition can have adverse consequences for the target, as customers and suppliers express concern about a change of ownership, and key employees leave, concerned about an uncertain future. A change in control could imply variation in product or service quality, reliability, and the level of service provided under product warranty or maintenance contracts. Suppliers worry about possible disruptions in their production schedules as the transition to the new owner takes place. Employees worry about possible layoffs or changes in compensation.[20]

If the resources are available, it is critical to talk simultaneously to as many potential targets as possible. Why? So that a prospective acquirer seldom feels pressure to do a specific deal. In practice, continuously comparing opportunities and ranking them according to their overall attractiveness enables buyers to maintain price discipline and avoid overpaying.

Discussing value

Neither the buyer nor the seller has any incentive to be the first to provide an estimate of value. It is difficult to back away from a number put on the table by either party should new information emerge. Getting a range may be the best you can do. Discussing values for recent acquisitions of similar businesses is one way to get a range. Another is to agree to a formula for calculating the purchase price, which may be defined in terms of a price to current year operating earnings' multiple, enabling both parties to perform due diligence to reach a consensus on the actual current year's earnings for the target firm. The firm's current year's earnings are then multiplied by the previously agreed-on price-to-earnings multiple to estimate the purchase price.

Preliminary legal transaction documents

Typically, parties to M&A transactions negotiate a confidentiality agreement, a term sheet, and a letter of intent (LOI) early in the process. These are explained next.

Confidentiality agreement

All parties to the deal usually want a confidentiality agreement (also called a nondisclosure agreement), which is generally mutually binding—that is, covering all parties to the deal. In negotiating the agreement, the buyer requests as much audited historical data and supplemental data as the seller is willing to provide. The prudent seller requests similar information about the buyer to assess the buyer's financial credibility. The agreement should cover only information that is not publicly available and should have a reasonable expiration date.[21]

Term sheet

Term sheets outline areas of agreement and are often used as the basis for a more detailed LOI. Typically two to four pages long, they stipulate the purchase price (often as a range), what is being acquired (i.e., assets or stock), limitations on the use of proprietary data, a no-shop provision preventing the seller from sharing the terms of the buyer's bid with other potential buyers, and a termination date. Many deals skip the term sheet and go directly to an LOI.

Letter of intent

Not all parties to the deal may want an LOI. Although the LOI can be useful in identifying areas of agreement, the rights of all parties to the transaction, and certain protective provisions, it may delay the signing of a definitive purchase agreement. This delay could also result in some legal risk to either the buyer or the seller if the deal is not consummated. Public companies that sign an LOI for a transaction that is likely to have a "material" impact on the buyer or seller need to announce the LOI publicly to comply with securities law.

[19] Fee et al., 2019

[20] Competitors will do what they can to fan these concerns in an effort to persuade current customers to switch and potential customers to defer buying decisions; key employees will be encouraged to defect to the competition.

[21] The confidentiality agreement can be negotiated independently or as part of the term sheet or letter of intent.

The LOI stipulates the reason for the agreement and major terms and conditions. It also indicates the responsibilities of both parties while the agreement is in force, an expiration date, and how all fees associated with the transaction will be paid. Major terms and conditions include a deal structure outline, such as the payment of cash or stock for certain assets and the assumption of certain target company liabilities. The letter may also include an agreement that selected personnel of the target will not compete with the combined companies for some period if they leave. Another condition may indicate that a certain portion of the purchase price will be allocated to the noncompete agreement.[22]

The LOI may express the offer price as a specific dollar figure, as a range, or as a multiple of some measure of value, such as operating earnings or cash flow. The LOI also specifies the types of data to be exchanged and the duration and extent of the initial due diligence. Legal, consulting, and asset transfer fees (i.e., payments made to governmental entities when ownership changes) may be paid for by the buyer or the seller, or shared.

A well-written LOI contains language limiting the extent to which the agreement binds the two parties. Price or other provisions are generally subject to closing conditions, such as the buyers having full access to all of the seller's records; having completed due diligence; having obtained financing; and having received approval from boards of directors, stockholders, and regulatory bodies. Other standard conditions include requiring signed employment contracts for key target firm executives and the completion of all necessary M&A documents. Failure to satisfy any of these conditions will invalidate the agreement. The LOI should also describe the due diligence process in some detail, stipulating how the buyer should access the seller's premises, the frequency and duration of such access, and how intrusive such activities should be.

Phase 6: negotiation

It is during this phase that the actual purchase price paid for the acquired business is determined, and often it will be quite different from the initial target company valuation. How people negotiate often reflects their frame of reference. For example, the seller may demand an offer price based on its 52-week high share price despite having a much lower current share price. Buyers often base purchase price premium calculations on the value of recently sold comparable firms, resulting in a valuation much different from the seller's. A behavioral bias is introduced into the negotiations when one party or both becomes "anchored" to certain reference points.[23] Getting to a successful outcome when participants lack objectivity requires flexibility on the part of the negotiators and a willingness and ability to offer deal terms that can overcome such biases.

A successful outcome for a negotiation is usually defined as achieving a negotiator's primary goals. Such outcomes reflect the relative leverage a party has in the negotiation and their willingness to accept preclosing risk (i.e., the risk of failing to satisfy closing conditions that postpone or prevent deal completion) and postclosing risk (i.e., vulnerability to potential liabilities following closing).[24] Other factors impacting the likelihood of achieving successful outcomes include competition (if any) among multiple bidders and the skill of the negotiators.[25]

The emphasis in negotiation should be on problem solving rather than simply stating positions and making demands. In most successful negotiations, parties to the deal search jointly for solutions to problems. All parties must be willing to make concessions that satisfy their own needs as well as the highest-priority needs of the others involved in the negotiation. The negotiation phase consists of four iterative activities that may begin at different times but tend to overlap (Fig. 5.1). Due diligence starts when the target is willing to allow it and, if permitted, runs throughout the negotiation process. Another activity is refining the initial valuation as new data are uncovered during due diligence, enabling the buyer to understand the target's value better. A third activity is deal structuring, which involves meeting the most important needs of both parties by addressing issues of risk and reward. The final activity, the financing plan, provides a reality check for the buyer by defining the maximum amount the buyer can expect to finance and pay for the target company. These activities are detailed next.

[22] Such an allocation of the purchase price is in the interests of the buyer because the amount of the allocation can be amortized over the life of the agreement. As such, it can be taken as a tax-deductible expense. However, it may constitute taxable income for the seller.

[23] Smith et al., 2019; Ma et al., 2019

[24] For a discussion of how leverage can be used to achieve negotiation objectives, see Wiltermuth et al.(2018).

[25] According to Bloomberg Law, mega deals (those valued at >$10 billion) failed to close about 16% of the time in 2019 as compared with about 2% of deals valued at less than $1 billion. Why? Larger deals tend to involve complex financing, more regulatory scrutiny, and extensive due diligence.

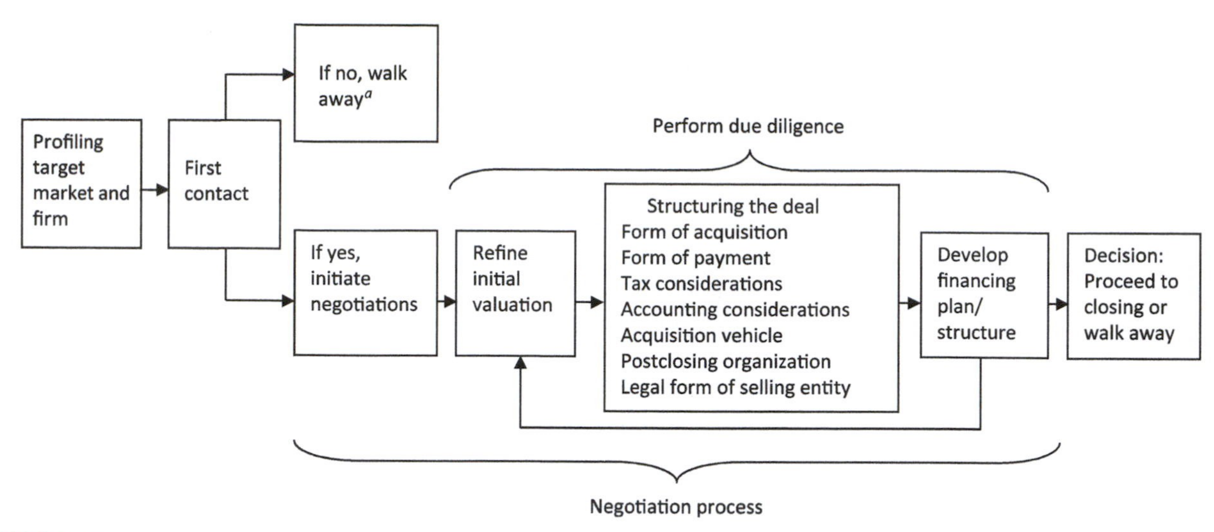

FIGURE 5.1 Viewing negotiation as a process. [a]Alternatively, the potential buyer could adopt a more hostile approach, such as initiating a tender offer to achieve a majority stake in the firm or a proxy contest to change the composition of the target's board to eliminate defenses.

Refining valuation

The starting point for negotiation is to update the preliminary target valuation based on new information. A buyer usually requests at least 3 to 5 years of historical financial data. Although it is desirable to examine data audited in accordance with generally accepted accounting principles (GAAP), such data may not be available for small, privately owned companies. Moreover, startup firms are unlikely to have any significant historical data. Historical data should be normalized: adjusted for nonrecurring gains, losses, or expenses.[26] Such adjustments allow the buyer to smooth out irregularities to understand the dynamics of the business. Each major expense category should be expressed as a percentage of revenue. By observing year-to-year changes in these ratios, trends in the data are more discernible.

Deal structuring

This process involves identifying and satisfying as many as possible of the highest-priority objectives of the parties involved. It begins with each party determining its initial negotiating position, potential risks, options for managing risk, and what might trigger either party to "walk away." Deal structuring also entails understanding potential sources of disagreement—from simple arguments over basic facts to substantially more complex issues, such as the form of payment and legal, accounting, and tax structures. It requires identifying conflicts of interest that influence the outcome of discussions. For example, when a portion of the purchase price depends on the long-term performance of the acquired business, its management—often the former owner—may not behave in the acquirer's best interests.

Decisions made throughout the deal-structuring process influence various aspects of the deal, including how ownership is determined, how assets are transferred, how ownership is protected (i.e., governance), and how risk is apportioned among parties to the deal. Other aspects of the process include the type, number, and complexity of the documents required for closing; the types of approvals required; and the time needed to complete the transaction. These decisions will influence how the combined companies will be managed, the amount and timing of resources committed, and the magnitude and timing of current and future tax liabilities.

The deal-structuring process can be viewed as comprising a number of interdependent components. These include the acquisition vehicle, postclosing organization, legal form of the selling entity, form of payment, form of acquisition, and tax and accounting considerations.

[26] Nonrecurring gains (losses) can result from the sale of land, equipment, product lines, patents, or software. Nonrecurring expenses include severance payments, employee signing bonuses, and settlements of litigation.

The *acquisition vehicle* refers to the legal structure (e.g., corporation or partnership) used to acquire the target company. The *postclosing organization* is the organizational and legal framework (e.g., corporation or partnership) used to manage the combined businesses after the completion of the transaction. The *legal form of the selling entity* refers to whether the seller is a C or Subchapter S Corporation, a limited liability company, or a partnership.

The *form of payment* may be cash, common stock, debt, or some combination. Some portion of the payment may be deferred or dependent on the future performance of the acquired entity. The *form of acquisition* reflects what is being acquired (e.g., stock or assets) and how ownership is being transferred. *Tax considerations* involve determining when a deal is immediately taxable to target shareholders or when taxes owed can be deferred. As a general rule, a transaction is taxable if remuneration paid to the target company's shareholders is primarily something other than the acquirer's stock, and it is nontaxable (i.e., tax-deferred) if what they receive is largely acquirer stock. Finally, *accounting considerations* refer to the impact of financial reporting requirements on the earnings volatility of business combinations because of the potential for asset revaluation to fair market value as new information becomes available. Fair market value is what a willing buyer and seller, having access to the same information, would pay for an asset.[27]

Conducting due diligence

Due diligence is an exhaustive review of records and facilities and typically continues throughout the negotiation phase. Although some degree of protection is achieved through a well-written contract, legal documents should never be viewed as a substitute for conducting formal due diligence. Remedies for violating contract representations (claims) and warranties (statements of fact) often require litigation, with the outcome uncertain. Due diligence may help to avoid the need for costly litigation by enabling the acquirer to identify and value target liabilities and to adjust the purchase price paid at closing accordingly.[28]

Table 5.1 lists online information sources helpful in conducting due diligence.[29] Although it is most often associated with buyers, both sellers and lenders conduct due diligence.

An expensive and exhausting process, due diligence is highly intrusive, and it places considerable demands on managers' time and attention. Frequently, the buyer wants as much time as possible, whereas the seller wants to limit the length and scope. Due diligence rarely works to the advantage of the seller because a long and detailed due diligence is likely to uncover items the buyer will use as a reason to lower the purchase price. Consequently, sellers may seek to terminate due diligence before the buyer thinks it is appropriate.[30]

Acquirer and target firms choosing a common auditor to perform due diligence reduces potential conflicts of interest and deal uncertainty. When common auditors are used, both the acquiring and target firms split the auditor's fees, reducing the potential for the auditor to show favoritism to the party paying them the most. Auditors representing both parties can ensure that data and accounting standards are applied consistently, leading to less uncertainty. Common auditors face greater litigation risk because they may be sued for earnings misreporting by either the acquirer or target. The reduction in deal uncertainty results in higher announcement date returns, lower target premiums, and greater return on assets postclosing.[31]

The components of due diligence

Due diligence consists of three primary reviews, which often occur concurrently. The *strategic and operational review* conducted by senior managers asks questions that focus on the seller's management team, operations, and sales and marketing strategies. The *financial review*, directed by financial and accounting personnel, focuses on the quality, timeliness, and completeness of the seller's financial statements. High-quality financial statements are those

[27] Changes in the value of assets and liabilities can result in one-time gains or losses recorded on the income statement, thereby contributing to swings in earnings. For a more detailed discussion of how to structure M&A transactions, see DePamphilis (2010b).

[28] Even if the acquirer were to win its lawsuit, receiving remuneration for breach of contract may be impossible if the seller declares bankruptcy, disappears, or moves assets to offshore accounts.

[29] A detailed preliminary acquirer due diligence question list is provided on the companion site to this book.

[30] If the target firm succeeds in reducing the amount of information disclosed to the target firm, it can expect to be required to make more representations and warranties in the legally binding purchase agreement.

[31] Chircop et al., 2017

TABLE 5.1 Convenient information sources for conducting due diligence

Website	Content
Securities and Exchange Commission	Financial Information/Security Law Violations
• www.sec.gov http://www.sec.gov/litigation.shtml	• Public filings for almost 10 years available through the Edgar database • Enforcement actions
US Patent Office	Intellectual property rights information
• www.uspto.gov • www.uspto.gov/patft/index.html	• Search patent database if you have the patent number
Federal Communications Commission	Regulates various commercial practices
• www.fcc.gov • http://www.fcc.gov/searchtools.html	• General information • Access to database of individuals sanctioned for illegal practices
US and States Attorneys General Offices	Information on criminal activities
• http://www.naag.org/ag/full_ag_table.php	• Listing of states attorneys general
Better Business Bureau	
• http://search.bbb.org/search.html	• Compiles Consumer Complaints Database
Paid services	Information on:
• US Search (www.ussearch.com) • KnowX (www.knowx.com)	• Criminal violations • Liens and bankruptcies • Credit history • Litigation

recorded in a consistent manner over time, are not subject to frequent or significant one-time adjustments, and whose earnings are sustainable. The financial review also confirms that the anticipated synergies are real and can be achieved within a reasonable time frame. A *legal review*, which is conducted by the buyer's legal counsel, deals with corporate records, financial matters, management and employee issues, tangible and intangible assets of the seller, and material contracts and obligations of the seller, such as litigation and claims.[32]

Learning from our differences

Often the focus in performing due diligence is on identifying similarities between the two firms to identify redundant personnel and overlapping functions, enabling the acquirer to quantify cost-related synergy. While such effort is critical, identifying major differences can be equally important. Differences in organizational structure, processes, routines, and skill sets can either enhance or jeopardize postmerger integration efforts.

Although acquirer and target functional departments may appear to align well in terms of complementary skills, those charged with due diligence must dig deeper to determine how well functions within the target (and acquirer) work together. Is there adequate communication and information sharing? Do those in the research and development (R&D) functions have the skill sets needed to support new products and services the marketing and sales department believes are wanted by customers? Focusing on cross-functional relationships in a detailed way in terms of daily interaction can uncover not only potential problems but also behaviors that should be encouraged to realize greater synergy.[33]

Buyer, seller, and lender due diligence

Buyers use due diligence to validate assumptions underlying their preliminary valuation and to uncover new sources of value and risk. Key objectives include identifying and confirming sources of value or synergy and

[32] The interview process provides invaluable sources of information. By asking the same questions of a number of key managers, the acquirer is able to validate the accuracy of its conclusions.

[33] Haapanen et al., 2019

TABLE 5.2 Identifying potential sources of value

Potential source of value	Examples	Potential impact
Operating Synergy		
• Eliminating functional overlap	• Reduce duplicate overhead positions	• Improved margins
• Productivity improvement	• Increased output per employee	• Same
• Purchasing discounts	• Volume discounts on raw material purchases	• Same
• Working capital management	• Reduced days in receivables because of improved collection of accounts receivable	• Improved return on total assets
	• Fewer days in inventory because of improved inventory turns	• Same
• Facilities management		
Economies of scale	• Increased production in underused facilities	• Same
Economies of scope	• Data centers, research and development functions, call centers, and so on; support multiple product lines or operations	• Same
• Organizational realignment	• Reducing the number of layers of management	• Reduced bureaucratic inertia
Financial Synergy		
• Increased borrowing capacity	• Target has little debt and many unencumbered assets	• Increased access to financing
• Increased leverage	• Access to lower-cost source of funds	• Lower cost of capital
Marketing–Product Synergy		
• Access to new distribution channels	• Increased sales opportunities	• Increased revenue
• Cross-selling opportunities	• Selling acquirer products to target customers and vice versa	• Same
• Research and development	• Cross-fertilization of ideas	• More innovation
• Product development	• Increased advertising budget	• Improved market share
Control		
• Opportunity identification	• Acquirer identifies opportunities not seen by target's management	• New growth opportunities
• More proactive management style	• More decisive decision making	• Improved financial returns

mitigating real or potential liability by looking for fatal flaws that reduce value. From the perspective of the buyer's attorney, the due diligence review represents an opportunity to learn about the target firm to allocate risk properly among the parties to the negotiation, unearth issues that reduce the likelihood of closing, and assist their client in drafting the reps and warranties for the acquisition agreement. Table 5.2 categorizes potential sources of value from synergy that may be uncovered or confirmed during due diligence and the impact these may have on operating performance.

Although the bulk of due diligence is performed by the buyer on the seller, the prudent seller should also perform due diligence on the buyer and on its own personnel and operations. By investigating the buyer, the seller can determine whether the buyer has the financial wherewithal to finance the purchase. When the seller is to receive buyer shares, it is prudent to evaluate the accuracy of the buyer's financial statements to determine if earnings have been stated accurately by looking at the buyer's audited statements before agreeing to the form of payment. Buyers have an incentive to overstate their pre-deal earnings to inflate their share price to reduce the number of new shares they must issue to buy the target firm.

As part of its internal due diligence, a seller often requires its managers to sign affidavits attesting to the truthfulness of what is being represented in the contract that pertains to their areas of responsibility. The seller hopes to mitigate liability stemming from inaccuracies in the seller's representations and warranties made in the definitive agreement of purchase and sale.

If the acquirer is borrowing to buy a target firm, the lender(s) will want to perform its own due diligence independent of the buyer's effort. Multiple lender investigations, often performed concurrently, can be quite burdensome to the target firm's management and employees. Sellers should agree to these activities only if confident the transaction will be consummated.

Protecting customer data

The year 2018 saw the implementation of the European Union's general data protection regulation and passage of California's Consumer Privacy Act (that took effect on January 1, 2020). Both increased the liabilities associated with the misuse of personal data. Both laws allow consumers to access their personal data held by businesses, to object to the data being sold, and to demand that it be deleted. The impact of the EU legislation is expected to be far-reaching because it represents 27 countries, and other countries are expected to conform to EU privacy standards to gain access to the EU markets. Similarly, the legislation passed in California could serve as a template for similar laws in other states.

The US Federal Trade Commission and EU regulatory bodies can hold an acquirer responsible for lax data security at an acquired firm. The new laws require more due diligence to limit possible infractions. However, evaluating accurately a target's data security practices can be daunting because data issues may arise years after a deal closes.

Due diligence questions to consider range from whether a target has received a regulatory inquiry concerning data privacy and security[34] to past litigation to the target's ability to track and resolve complaints submitted by consumers to it and the government. The target firm should have an appropriate written information security program and mechanism for resolving issues. Moreover, the target's policies and procedures should comply with the required legal standards.[35]

The rise of the virtual data room

After the 2020 pandemic, more of the deal process will be conducted via videoconferencing with drones used to confirm the existence and location of tangible assets listed on a firm's balance sheet. Although smaller deals will still involve presentations and the exchange of data in conference rooms, increasingly more deals will use the virtual data room, an online site used for storage and distribution of documents during the due diligence process in a secure environment at any time and from any location.

Developing the financing plan

The last of the four negotiation phase activities is to develop the consolidated balance sheet, income, and cash flow statements. Unlike the projections of cash flow made to value the target, these statements should include the expected cost of financing the transaction. Developing the financing plan is a key input in determining the purchase price because it places a limitation on the amount the buyer can offer the seller. The financing plan is appended to the acquirer's business and acquisition plans and is used to obtain financing for the deal (see Chapter 13).

Defining the purchase price

The three commonly used definitions of purchase price are total consideration, total purchase price or enterprise value, and net purchase price. Each serves a different purpose.

Total consideration

In the purchase agreement, the total consideration consists of cash (C), stock (S), new debt (ND) issues, or some combination of all three paid to the seller's shareholders. It is a term commonly used in legal documents to reflect the different types of remuneration received by target company shareholders. Note that payment can include both financial and nonfinancial assets such as real estate. Nonfinancial compensation sometimes is referred to as payment in

[34] During the 2020 pandemic, working from home became increasingly common and created a new set of data security challenges. The proliferation of data-protection regulations has increased dramatically the potential liability for misusing personal data.

[35] For items to consider in conducting a target data and security review, see the acquirer due diligence question list on the website accompanying this textbook.

kind. The debt counted in the total consideration is what the target company shareholders receive as payment for their stock, along with any cash or acquirer stock.

Each component should be viewed in present value terms; therefore the total consideration is itself expressed in present value terms (PV_{TC}). The present value of cash is its face value. The stock component of the total consideration is the present value (PV_S) of future dividends or net cash flows or the acquiring firm's stock price per share times the number of shares to be exchanged for each outstanding share of the seller's stock. New debt issued by the acquiring company as part of the compensation paid to shareholders can be expressed as the present value (PV_{ND}) of the cumulative interest payments plus principal discounted at some appropriate market rate of interest (see Chapter 7).

Total purchase price or enterprise value[36]

The total purchase price (PV_{TPP}) or enterprise value of the target firm consists of the total consideration (PV_{TC}) plus the market value of the target firm's debt (PV_{AD}) assumed by the acquiring company. The enterprise value is sometimes expressed as the total purchase price plus net debt.[37] The enterprise value of the firm often is quoted in the media as the purchase price because it is most visible to those not familiar with the details. The enterprise value paid for US-based Cablevision in late 2015 by French telecom giant Altice was $17.7 billion, consisting of $8.1 billion in assumed Cablevision debt plus $9.6 billion paid for Cablevision equity.

The enterprise value is important to analysts and shareholders alike because it approximates the total investment[38] made by the acquiring firm. It is an approximation because it does not necessarily measure liabilities the acquirer is assuming that are not visible on the target firm's balance sheet. Nor does it reflect the potential for recovering a portion of the total consideration paid to target company shareholders by selling undervalued or redundant assets. These considerations are reflected in the net purchase price, discussed next.

Net purchase price

The net purchase price (PV_{NPP}) is the total purchase price plus other assumed target firm liabilities (PV_{OAL})[39] less the proceeds from the sale of discretionary or redundant target assets (PV_{DA}) [40] on or off the balance sheet. PV_{OAL} are those assumed liabilities not fully reflected on the target's balance sheet or in the estimation of the economic value of the target firm. The net purchase price is the most comprehensive measure of the actual price paid for the target firm. It includes all known cash obligations assumed by the acquirer as well as any portion of the purchase price that is recovered through the sale of assets. The various definitions of price can be summarized as follows:

$$\text{Total consideration} = PV_{TC} = C + PV_S + PV_{ND}$$

$$\text{Total purchase price or enterprise value} = PV_{TPP} = PV_{TC} + PV_{AD}$$

$$\text{Net purchase price} = PV_{NPP} = PV_{TPP} + PV_{OAL} - PV_{DA}$$

$$= (C + PV_S + PV_{ND} + PV_{AD}) + PV_{OAL} - PV_{DA}$$

[36] In Chapter 7, enterprise value used for valuation purposes is defined in more detail. The discussion of enterprise value here is discussed as it is normally defined in the popular media.

[37] Net debt includes the market value of debt assumed by the acquirer less cash and marketable securities on the books of the target firm.

[38] Total investment equals what the acquirer pays the shareholders plus assumed liabilities such as long-term debt.

[39] If the target's balance sheet reserves reflected all known future obligations and there were no potential off-balance-sheet liabilities, there would be no need to adjust the purchase price for assumed liabilities other than for short- and long-term debts assumed by the acquiring company. In practice, reserves are often inadequate to satisfy pending claims. Common examples include underfunded or underreserved employee pension and health care obligations and uncollectable receivables.

[40] *Discretionary assets* are those not required to operate the target and can be sold to recover some portion of the purchase price. Such assets include land valued at its historical cost. Other examples include cash balances in excess of normal working capital needs and product lines or operating units considered nonstrategic by the buyer. The sale of discretionary assets is not considered in the calculation of the value of the target because economic value is determined by future operating cash flows before consideration is given to how the transaction will be financed.

Although the total consideration is most important to the target's shareholders as a measure of what they receive in exchange for their stock, the acquirer's shareholders often focus on the total purchase price or enterprise value as the actual amount paid for the target's equity plus the value of assumed debt. However, the total purchase price tends to ignore other adjustments that should be made to determine actual or pending "out-of-pocket" cash spent by the acquirer. The net purchase price reflects adjustments to the total purchase price and is a much better indicator of whether the acquirer overpaid for the target firm.[41]

Phase 7: developing the integration plan

Acquirers should begin planning postmerger integration well before closing to avoid disruptions alienating employees, customers, and suppliers.

Contract-related issues

Integration planning involves addressing human resource, customer, and supplier issues that overlap the change of ownership. The responsibilities of the buyer and seller in resolving these "transitional issues" should be negotiated before closing and included in the purchase agreement to make the transition from the seller to the buyer as smooth as possible. For example, the agreement may stipulate how target employees will be paid and their benefit claims processed.[42]

Prudent buyers should include assurances in the purchase agreement to limit their postclosing risk. Most seller representations and warranties made to the buyer refer to the past and present condition of the seller's business. They pertain to items such as the ownership of securities; real and intellectual property; current levels of receivables, inventory, and debt; pending lawsuits, worker disability, and customer warranty claims; and an assurance that the target's accounting practices are in accordance with GAAP.

Although "reps and warranties" apply primarily to the past and current state of the seller's business, they do have future implications. If a seller claims there are no lawsuits pending and a lawsuit is filed shortly after closing, the buyer may seek to recover damages from the seller.

Buyers and sellers also may insist that certain conditions be satisfied before closing can take place. Common closing conditions include employment contracts, agreements not to compete, financing, and regulatory and shareholder approval. Finally, buyers and sellers should make the final closing contingent on receiving approval from the appropriate regulatory agencies and shareholders (if needed) of both companies before any money changes hands.

Earning trust

Decisions made before closing affect postclosing integration activity.[43] Successfully integrating firms require getting employees in both firms to work to achieve common objectives. This comes about through building credibility and trust, not through superficial slogans and empty promises. Trust comes from cooperation, keeping commitments, and experiencing success.

[41] The application of the various definitions of the purchase price is addressed in more detail in Chapter 9.

[42] If the number of employees is small, this may be accommodated easily by loading the acquirer's payroll computer system with the necessary salary and personal information before closing or by having a third-party payroll processor perform these services. For larger operations or where employees are dispersed geographically, the target's employees may continue to be paid for a specific period using the target's existing payroll system. Employee health care and disability claims tend to escalate just before a transaction closes as employees, whether they leave or stay with the new firm, file more health and disability claims for longer periods after downsizing. The sharp increase in such expenses for the acquirer and should be addressed in the merger agreement. For example, all claims incurred within a specific number of days before closing but not submitted by employees until after closing will be reimbursed by the seller. Alternatively, such claims may be paid from an escrow account containing a portion of the purchase price.

[43] Benefits packages, employment contracts, and retention bonuses to keep key employees typically are negotiated before the closing. Contractual covenants and conditions also affect integration. Earnouts, which are payments made to the seller based on the acquired business's achieving certain profit or revenue targets, can limit the buyer's ability to integrate the target effectively into the acquirer's operations.

Choosing the integration manager and other critical decisions

The buyer should designate an integration manager possessing excellent interpersonal and project management skills. The buyer must also determine what is critical to continuing the acquired company's success during the first 12 to 24 months after the closing.[44] Critical activities include identifying key managers, vendors, and customers and determining what is needed to retain them. Preclosing integration planning activities should determine the operating standards required for continued operation of the businesses: executive compensation, labor contracts, billing procedures, product delivery times, and quality metrics. Finally, there must be a communication plan for all stakeholders that can be implemented immediately following closing.

Phase 8: closing

Closing entails obtaining all necessary shareholder, regulatory, and third-party consents (e.g., customer and vendor contracts) and completing the definitive purchase agreement.

Gaining the necessary approvals

The buyer's legal counsel is responsible for ensuring that the transaction is in compliance with securities, antitrust, and state corporation laws. Care must be exercised to ensure that all filings required by law have been made with the Federal Trade Commission and the Department of Justice. Finally, many deals require approval by the acquirer and target firm shareholders. See Chapter 11 for when shareholder approval is required.

Assigning customer and vendor contracts

In a purchase of assets, many customer and vendor contracts cannot be assigned to the buyer without receiving written approval from the other parties. Although often a formality, both vendors and customers may attempt to negotiate more favorable terms. Licenses must be approved by the licensor, which can be a major impediment to a timely closing.

Completing the M&A agreement

The acquisition or merger or purchase agreement is the foundation of the closing documents. It indicates all of the rights and obligations of the parties both before and after the closing.

Deal provisions

In an asset or stock purchase, deal provisions define the form of payment, how it will be paid, and the assets or shares to be acquired. In a merger, the agreement defines the number (or fraction) of acquirer shares to be exchanged for each target share.

Price

The purchase price or total consideration may be fixed at the time of closing, subject to future adjustment, or it may be contingent on future performance. For asset transactions, it is common to exclude cash on the target's balance sheet from the deal. The price paid for noncurrent assets, such as plant and intangible assets, will be fixed, but the price for current assets will depend on their levels at closing following an audit.

If acquirer stock is part of the total consideration, the terms of the common or preferred stock (including liquidation preferences, dividend rights, redemption rights, voting rights, transferability restrictions, and registration rights) must be negotiated. Part of this process may include whether the shares should be valued at signing or at closing, as well as how to limit upside and downside risk due to share value fluctuations.

[44] Wu et al. (2020) argue that much can be learned by examining recent peer M&As.

If promissory notes are part of the deal consideration, negotiators must determine the interest rate, principal payments, and maturity date, as well as the events triggering default and when the seller can accelerate note repayment if the terms of the note are breached. If an earnout is involved, milestones to be met and the size of payments made must be determined. If the purchase price is subject to a working capital adjustment after completion of a postclosing audit, agreement must be reached on an appropriate definition of working capital.

Escrow and holdback clauses

To protect the buyer from losses if the seller's claims and obligations are not satisfied or if risks continue postclosing, a portion of the purchase price might be withheld. Pending litigation, patent approvals, or warranty claims are common reasons for holdbacks. The portion of the purchase price withheld is put into an escrow account held by a third party. If part of the consideration consists of acquirer equity, the acquirer and target must agree on whether the escrow will be all cash, all stock, or some combination.

Go shop provisions

Such provisions allow a target firm to seek competing offers after it has received a firm bid. They are usually in force for 1 to 2 months, give the first bidder the opportunity to match any better offer the target might receive, and include a termination fee paid to the initial bidder if the target accepts another offer. Target firms whose merger agreements contain such provisions are more likely to receive higher initial bid premiums and announcement date abnormal financial returns.[45] Why? The initial bid is likely to be at the higher end of the acquirer's range to discourage potential bidders.

Allocation of price

The buyer often tries to allocate as much of the purchase price as possible to depreciable assets (e.g., fixed assets, customer lists, and noncompete agreements), enabling them to depreciate or amortize these upwardly revised assets and reduce future taxable income. However, such an allocation may constitute taxable income to the seller. Both parties should agree on how the purchase price should be allocated in an asset transaction before closing, eliminating the chance that conflicting positions will be taken for tax reporting purposes.

Payment mechanism

Payment may be made at closing by wire transfer or cashier's check, or the buyer may defer the payment of a portion of the purchase price by issuing a promissory note to the seller. The buyer may agree to put the unpaid portion of the purchase price in escrow or to a holdback allowance, thereby facilitating the settlement of claims that might be made in the future.[46]

Assumption of liabilities

The seller retains liabilities not assumed by the buyer. In instances such as environmental liabilities, unpaid taxes, and underfunded pension obligations, the courts may go after the buyer and the seller. In contrast, the buyer assumes all known and unknown liabilities in a merger or share purchase.

Representations and warranties

Reps and warranties are claims made as "statements of fact" by buyers and sellers. As currently used, the terms are virtually indistinguishable from one another. They serve three purposes: disclosure, termination rights, and indemnification rights.

- *Disclosure*: Contract reps and warranties should provide for full disclosure of all information covering areas of greatest concern to both parties. These include financial statements, corporate organization, capitalization, absence of undisclosed liabilities, current litigation, contracts, title to assets, taxes and tax returns, no violation of laws or regulations, employee benefit plans, labor issues, and insurance coverage.

[45] Gogineni et al., 2017

[46] The escrow account involves the buyer's putting a portion of the purchase price in an account held by a third party, whereas the holdback allowance generally does not.

- *Termination rights*: Reps and warranties serve to allocate risk by serving as a closing condition. At closing, representations such as those concerning the state of the business and financial affairs are again reviewed for accuracy. If there has been a material change in the target's business or financial affairs between signing and closing, the bidder has the right to terminate the transaction.
- *Indemnification rights*: Often in transactions involving private firms, certain representations will extend beyond closing. They serve as a basis for indemnification, that is, the buyer is compensated for costs incurred subsequent to closing.

Covenants

Covenants are agreements by the parties about actions they agree to take or refrain from taking between signing and closing. The seller must conduct business in the "usual and customary" manner and seek approval for all expenditures considered out of the ordinary such as one-time dividend payments or sizeable increases in management compensation. In contrast to reps and warranties, covenants do not relate to a point in time but rather to future behavior between signing and closing. Although they usually expire at closing, covenants sometimes survive closing. Typical examples include a buyer's covenant to register stock that it is issuing to the seller and to complete the dissolution of the firm after closing in an asset sale.

Covenants may be either negative (restrictive) or positive (requirement to do something). Negative covenants may restrict a party from the payment of dividends or the sale of an asset without the permission of the buyer between signing and closing. Positive covenants may require the seller to continue to operate its business in a way that is consistent with its past practices. Many purchase agreements include the same language in both representations and covenants.

Employment and benefits

Many deals involve targets that have used stock options to motivate employees. To minimize unwanted employee turnover, acquirers address in the agreement how outstanding stock options issued by the seller will be treated. Often unvested (not yet conferred) options will be accelerated as a result of the deal such that option holders can buy target firm shares at a price defined by the option contract and sell the shares to the acquirer at a profit. In other instances, unvested options are accelerated only if the holder is terminated as a result of the change in control. Terms of any new employment agreements with seller management must also be spelled out in the agreement. It must also be determined who will pay severance if any target employees are terminated at or shortly after closing.

Closing conditions

The satisfaction of negotiated conditions determines whether a party to the agreement must consummate the deal. Among the most important is the *bring-down provision*, requiring that representations made at the signing are still true as of the closing date. Other examples include obtaining all necessary legal opinions, the execution of other agreements (e.g., promissory notes), and the absence of any "material adverse change" in the condition of the target company.

Material adverse change (MAC) clauses are commonly found in M&A contracts and enable the buyer to withdraw from a contract without penalty. Unless stipulated, the challenge is to determine what constitutes a material adverse change and how long it would last. M&A agreements preceding the 2020 COVID-19 pandemic require a buyer seeking to invoke a MAC clause by citing the effects of the virus to demonstrate both that the crisis had a material adverse impact on the seller's financial condition and that the harm would persist for a significant period.

Indemnification

In effect, indemnification is the reimbursement of the other party for a loss incurred after closing for which they were not responsible. The definitive agreement requires the seller to indemnify or absolve the buyer of liability in the event of misrepresentations or breaches of warranties or covenants. Similarly, the buyer usually agrees to indemnify the seller.[47]

[47] At least 1 full year of operation and a full audit are necessary to identify claims. Some claims (e.g., environmental) extend beyond the survival period of the indemnity clause. Neither party can submit claims to the other until some minimum threshold, usually the number or dollar size of claims, has been exceeded.

Other closing documents

Closing may be complicated by the complexity of other documents. In addition to the definitive agreement, the more important documents include patents, licenses, royalty agreements, trade names, and trademarks; labor and employment agreements; leases; mortgages, loan agreements, and lines of credit; stock and bond commitments; and supplier and customer contracts. Other documents could include distributor and sales representative agreements, stock option and employee incentive programs, and health and other benefit plans. Complete descriptions of all foreign patents, facilities, and investments; insurance policies, coverage, and claims pending; intermediary fee arrangements; litigation pending for and against each party; and environmental compliance issues resolved or on track to be resolved often are part of the closing documents. Furthermore, the seller's corporate minutes of the board of directors and any other significant committee information, as well as articles of incorporation, bylaws, stock certificates, and corporate seals, are part of the final documentation.[48]

Financing contingencies

Most purchase agreements contain a financing contingency. The buyer is not subject to the terms of the contract if funding to complete the deal cannot be found. Breakup fees can be useful to ensure that the buyer will attempt aggressively to obtain financing. The seller may require the buyer to put a nonrefundable deposit in escrow to be forfeited if the buyer is unable to obtain financing to complete the deal.[49]

Phase 9: implementing postclosing integration

The postclosing integration activity is widely viewed as among the most important phases of the acquisition process and is discussed in detail in Chapter 6. What follows is a discussion of those activities required immediately after closing, which fall into five categories.

Communication plans

Such plans should address employee, customer, and vendor concerns. Employees need to understand how their compensation might change. They may find a loss of specific benefits palatable if offset by other benefits or better working conditions. Customers want reassurance there will be no deterioration in product quality or delivery time during the transition to new ownership. Vendors want to know how the change in ownership will affect their sales to the new firm. To accomplish these ends, acquirer managers can be sent to address employee groups (on site, if possible). Senior managers also should contact key customers and vendors (preferably in person or at least by telephone) to provide the needed reassurances.

Employee retention

Retaining middle-level managers should be a top priority during postmerger integration. Senior managers of the target company whom the buyer chooses to retain are asked to sign employment agreements as a condition of closing. Although senior managers provide overall direction for the firm, middle-level managers execute the firm's daily operations. Bonuses, stock options, and enhanced sales commission schedules are commonly put in place to keep such managers.

Satisfying cash flow requirements

Talking to managers after closing often reveals areas in which maintenance has been deferred. Receivables thought collectable may have to be written off. Production may be disrupted as employees of the acquired firm find it difficult to adapt to new practices or if inventory levels cannot support customer delivery times. Finally,

[48] Sherman, 2006

[49] Most deals involving privately owned firms do not involve breakup fees, termination fees, or liquidated damage provisions because such sellers are viewed as highly motivated. If the seller refuses to sell the business after having signed an agreement to do so, the buyer has a breach of contract lawsuit that it can bring against the seller.

customer attrition may be high because competitors use the change in ownership as an opportunity to woo them away with various incentives.

Using "best practices"

The combined firms often realize synergies by using the "best practices" of both the acquirer and target firms. In some areas, neither company may be using what its customers believe to be the preeminent practices in the industry. Management should look beyond its own operations to adopt the practices of other companies in the same or other industries.

Cultural issues

Corporate cultures reflect the set of beliefs and behaviors of the management and employees of a corporation. Some firms are paternalistic, and others are "bottom-line" oriented. Some empower employees, whereas others believe in highly centralized control. Some promote problem solving within a team environment; others encourage individual performance. Inevitably, different corporate cultures impede postacquisition integration efforts. The key to success is taking the time to explain to all of the new firm's employees what behaviors are expected and why and to tell managers that they should "walk the talk."

Phase 10: conducting a postclosing evaluation: stop, assess, and learn

The purpose of this phase is to determine if the acquisition is meeting expectations, undertake corrective actions if necessary, and identify what was done well and what should be done better in future deals.

Do not change performance benchmarks

When the acquisition is operating normally, evaluate the actual performance to that projected in the acquisition plan. Success should be defined in terms of actual to plan performance. Too often, management simply ignores the performance targets in the acquisition plan and accepts less than plan performance to justify the acquisition. This may be appropriate if circumstances beyond the firm's control caused a change in the operating environment.

Ask the difficult questions

The types of questions asked vary with the time elapsed since the closing. After 12 months, what has the buyer learned about the business? Were the original valuation assumptions reasonable? If not, what did the buyer not understand about the target company and why? What did the buyer do well? What should have been done differently? What can be done to ensure that the same mistakes are not made in future acquisitions? After 24 months, is the business meeting expectations? If not, what can be done to put the business back on track? Is the cost of fixing the business offset by expected financial returns? Are the right people in place to manage the business for the long term? After 36 months, does the acquired business still appear attractive? If not, should it be divested? If yes, when should it be sold and to whom?

Learn from mistakes

Highly acquisitive companies can benefit by centralizing resources at the corporate level to support acquisitions made throughout the firm. Despite evidence that abnormal financial returns to frequent acquirers tend to decline on average, such firms learn from experience through repetitive deals, especially when the acquirer's CEO remains the same and the successive deals are related.[50] Learning tends to be more rapid when acquisitions are frequent, recent, and focused in the same markets or products.[51] And firms also can improve their ability to successfully negotiate

[50] Aktas et al., 2013

[51] Chao, 2017

and complete takeovers by observing the behavior of acquirers of their divested units.[52] However, experienced acquirers need to be aware that hubris often can derail acquisitions because "confidence tends to increase faster than competence" among serial acquirers.[53]

The application of technology to the M&A process

Recent survey data suggest that firms are increasingly applying technology to the M&A process.[54] These technologies offer, but by no means guarantee, the potential to expedite the process, reduce risk, and improve strategic decision making.[55] However, the implementation of new technologies often fails to deliver what has been promised by vendors.[56]

The focus in this section is on AI and blockchain networks, two technologies that have the potential to change fundamentally how the M&A process detailed in Chapter 4 is managed. What follows is a discussion of how these technologies can be applied to this process to improve efficiency, accuracy, and security, as well as their limitations. The challenge is to separate reality from hype. Discussed in more detail in the following pages, Table 5.3 lists some of the ways these technologies can affect how takeovers are executed.

Artificial intelligence

There is no universally accepted definition of AI, making it difficult to discuss AI and related concepts.[57] Consequently, this section defines how certain terms often used interchangeably with AI are defined in this book.

Frequently described as the identification and interpretation of patterns in raw data, *data analysis or analytics* relies on the application of statistics, computer programing, and model building to uncover insights helpful in decision making.[58] The term "big data" is defined by the size of the data set available for analysis. *AI* involves machines performing tasks representative of human intelligence: planning, sound and object recognition, language comprehension, and problem solving. *General AI* includes all the characteristics of human intelligence. *Narrow AI* exhibits some facet(s) of human intelligence but is lacking in other areas (e.g., a machine that is great at recognizing images but nothing else). AI has been around for more than 6 decades, becoming more popular in recent years because of the advent of big data sets, advanced algorithms, and improved computing power and storage.[59]

Early AI applications involved the development of "expert systems" making decisions based on a database of knowledge provided by human experts. More recently, AI applied to having machines learn directly from the data. *Machine learning* trains a machine to perform certain tasks without programming it to do so. "Training" involves feeding huge amounts of data to an algorithm and allowing it to improve the accuracy of its predictions.[60]

Deep learning is one of many approaches to machine learning.[61] It imitates the brain in which neurons having discrete layers connect to other neurons, with each layer responsible for a task. Deep learning methods are better

[52] Doan et al., 2018

[53] Schriber and Degischer, 2020

[54] Deloitte's *The State of the Deal M&A Trends 2019* survey of 1000 executives at corporations and private equity firms indicated that almost two-thirds of those surveyed are using new M&A technology tools.

[55] Merendino et al., 2019

[56] Tabesh et al. (2019) note that recent survey results show high dissatisfaction rates among firms attempting to implement big data strategies.

[57] For an overview of AI, see López-Robles et al. (2019).

[58] For a discussion of big data analytics applications in business, see Corte-Real et al. (2019).

[59] Duan et al., 2019

[60] For example, humans might identify pictures containing a specific image. The algorithm then builds a model that can accurately identify a picture as containing that image as well as a human could.

[61] Other approaches include decision tree learning, inductive logic programming, clustering, reinforcement learning, and Bayesian networks.

TABLE 5.3 How new technologies impact the mergers and acquisitions (M&A) process

Artificial intelligence applications	M&A process phase	Blockchain networks and smart contracting applications
Threat and opportunity assessment; strategy selection	Business plan	
Resource requirements and risk assessment	Acquisition plan	
Target identification	Search	
Target prioritization	Screen	
Providing background information on key target board members and management	First contact	
	Negotiation	
Cash flow projections	Refining initial valuation	
Expedited workflow and document review	Deal structuring	Contract review and security; cryptocurrencies as a potential form of payment
Expedited workflow, document and data analysis[a]; highlighting irregularities in contracts, spreadsheets, manufacturing processes, and so on	Due diligence	Enhanced integrity and security of historical data stored in blockchain networks; facilitates data review
Target workforce assessment; survey results validation	Integration plan	
Confirms document accuracy and completeness	Closing	Guarantees payment when closing conditions satisfied Increases confidence in earnout agreement
Tracks progress to plan, identifies new synergy opportunities, prioritizes investments, and assists in renegotiating customer and vendor contracts	Integration	
Monitors target performance to business plan and to similar deals	Evaluation	

[a] *Artificial intelligence enables analysis of both structured (e.g., accounting statements) and unstructured data (e.g., data gathered from social media, customer surveys, and weather reports).*

able to use so-called "structured data" such as 10K financial statements, which are more easily accessible and manipulated than "unstructured data." The latter ranges from data gathered from social media to customer survey results to weather information. According to business research firm Gartner Inc., about 80% of business data is unstructured, consisting of nonfinancial data such as contracts, social media comments, and emails.

In the M&A process, AI is applied currently to the most labor-intensive activities. Because AI systems learn the more they are applied, firms engaging in M&As can increase their effectiveness by standardizing the various steps involved in takeovers. To convert physical documents to machine readable form (i.e., digitize), optical character recognition software can be used to increase the amount of data that can be reviewed. AI has the potential to streamline the M&A process from end to end, particularly in business and acquisition strategy development, search and screening, due diligence, negotiation and related activities, premerger integration planning, and postmerger integration. These are discussed next.

AI applications in business and acquisition strategy development

AI tools enable firms to comingle proprietary third-party databases, including economic, demographic, patent, and financial data, to make predictions and gain new insights. This may assist firms in anticipating attractive opportunities and potential threats in support of the SWOT analysis described in Chapter 4. AI software may also assist in determining whether a firm should pursue opportunities on its own, partner with others, or make an acquisition based on an analysis of the firm's available resources and competencies. In this manner, AI can be used to develop and validate business and acquisition strategies.[62]

[62] Acuña-Carvajal et al., 2019

AI applications in search and screening

Often referred to as "deal sourcing," AI models can assist in identifying target firms whose characteristics best match the acquirer's selection criteria. Choosing a target firm or its assets for possible acquisition frequently involves analyzing volumes of granular data. Models using both structured and unstructured data may provide insights into patterns not observable in the output of financial spreadsheet models.[63] Machines can review volumes of disparate data to identify outlier patterns, which are called to the attention of analysts for further review.

AI software can help prioritize the relative attractiveness of prospective targets to reduce the number to be contacted. How? The software identifies the primary sources of synergy. And such tools provide insight into the factors impacting financial and operating performance. AI also can assist in evaluating nebulous areas such as a firm's reputation from the viewpoint of its customers, vendors, and competitors. AI makes possible comprehensive reviews of websites such as LinkedIn, Indeed, Vault, Yelp, and Glassdoor to provide a more thorough understanding of a target firm's reputation with its customers and identify potential issues.

AI applications in performing due diligence

Traditionally, only about 5% of documents are fully reviewed doing due diligence. The lack of a complete review can result in important information being overlooked. Enter AI! AI programs collect the needed documents and identify, analyze, and classify the information to be reviewed, analyzed, and organized. With the appropriate software, lawyers can review systematically numerous contracts to identify nonstandard features. Such contracts are then flagged for more detailed review. Financial analysts can predict more accurately which target firm customers are dissatisfied and are likely to leave amid the usual turmoil after a change in control. And senior managers can assess the target's operating efficiency by comparing machine run times and on-time delivery metrics with the acquirer's and industry-wide metrics.

AI applications in negotiation

AI systems can assist in the drafting of legal documents by reviewing similar documents and identifying differences with those provided by the target firm. Such systems are trained by providing the algorithm with examples of similar provisions found in M&A agreements such as confidentiality agreements, noncompete clauses, patent infringement, governance, dispute resolution, indemnification, and change in control provisions. AI does not replace the need for lawyers but focuses their time on reviewing what appear to be nonstandard documents.

AI also can assist in refining the initial target valuation based on information uncovered doing due diligence. For example, AI software can review customer and vendor contracts to identify what percentage are expiring within the next 6 months, 1 year, and so on, enabling analysts to more accurately construct the magnitude and timing of projected cash flows.

AI applications in premerger integration planning

Understanding target firm employee work patterns and attitudes as well as customer perceptions of the target firm has historically been revealed through the use of surveys. These data often are helpful in identifying the best way to retain talent and maintain employee morale while minimizing customer attrition after closing. So-called *augmented AI*, a way of applying human-generated data (e.g., survey data) with patterns recognized by machines, can be used to validate survey results. How? AI software can be used to surface current and historical patterns of what employees and customers think of the target firm using volumes of social media and publicly available information. When the AI survey results are consistent with human-created data, the planning team can proceed to develop action plans to resolve issues expected to arise during the postclosing integration period.

Another application is in assessing the target firm's talent pool by identifying the number of employees with certain types of degrees or certifications and length of work experience. Comparisons can be made between the target's and acquirer's compensation systems to determine what changes might have to be made and the impact on the combined firm's cost structure.

[63] For a discussion of how AI models can be applied to identify M&A opportunities, see Aaldering et al. (2019).

AI applications in postmerger integration

AI can be used to monitor integration programs by tracking project scheduling, resource requirements and availability, and deviations from plan, and by suggesting corrective actions.

For postmerger integration, AI tools help identify new synergy opportunities, postintegration challenges, prioritization of investment opportunities, and how to deal with customers and suppliers when renegotiating contracts. AI is useful in training target firm employees in new operating procedures and practices. And AI systems can help motivate employees at both the acquirer and target firms by responding to employee information requests about compensation, human resource policies, and the combined firms' business strategy. Such systems can also automate customer service capabilities by responding to customer inquiries.

Blockchain technology and smart contracts

As a shared ledger that can automatically record and verify transactions, blockchain technology[64] can change the way deals are done. *Smart contracts* are lines of software code in a blockchain network in the database of each network participant defining the conditions to which all parties to the contract have agreed. When the conditions are satisfied, the actions required by the contract are executed. Because the smart contract is resident on each network participant's database, they all must get the same result when the contract's terms are executed.

Public blockchain such as Bitcoin, do not require trusted third parties to complete transactions but rather only that we trust the software. *Private block chains*, those residing within an enterprise, are decentralized ledgers using a variety of methods for validating and recording transactions. Private blockchain networks allow only prevalidated individuals or groups of individuals to access the ledger and view and enter data. A hidden benefit of blockchain for data analytics is its role in improving data quality: validating and standardizing data.

The first significant use of blockchain technology was the cryptocurrency Bitcoin. Blockchain technology is currently applied to conducting transactions in monetary assets (e.g., currency, securities, and remittances) and real property (e.g., land and car registrations), as well as addressing contractual issues (e.g., licensing, registration, wills, IP registration) and for verifying credentials (e.g., passport, driver's licenses, birth registries).

Users of blockchain networks have cryptographic identities, similar to an email address. To access your email, you need a password. With a cryptographic identity your public key is like your email address, and your private key is like your password. Software, known as wallets, signs transactions by creating a one-time digital signature with your cryptographic identity. This is then broadcast to the network, indicating your ownership of an account and allowing you to conduct transactions on the blockchain.

Blockchain applications to negotiation, due diligence, and deal closing

Smart contracting has many potential applications in critical areas of the M&A process. For example, to reach agreement, an acquirer may have to structure a payment as an earnout. When a seller agrees to an earnout, they can be confident that after predetermined goals have been satisfied, their accounts will automatically be credited with previously agreed upon sums of money. Private block chains resident on an enterprise's system provide enhanced data security and data reliability, expediting the due diligence process. Block chains also facilitate deal closing. After contract conditions have been satisfied, payment is automatically transferred from the buyer's escrow account to the seller's account. Buyers can be assured that they are receiving what they think they purchased without assuming hidden liabilities.

Cryptocurrency as a potential form of payment

Cryptocurrencies are digital monies using cryptography to make transactions secure, verify the transfer of funds, and control the creation of additional units. Users trade Bitcoin, for example, over a network of decentralized computers, eliminating intermediaries such as governments, commercial banks, and central banks. Bitcoin enables users to avoid transaction fees incurred if the banking system had been used to complete transactions and to eliminate currency conversion costs in international transactions, all done in relative secrecy. Bitcoin is difficult to counterfeit and may enable immediate verifiable payment in M&A deals.

[64] A blockchain is a distributed database of electronic records maintained not by a central authority but by a network of users on computer servers. Consisting of records, called blocks, linked and secured using cryptography, a blockchain is an open ledger that can record transactions between parties. Copies of the entire system can be kept simultaneously on millions of computers located anywhere. When a new entry is made, the entire ledger is updated on every server. Any change to an old entry requires everyone to agree to make the change on their servers, making historical data reliable. After being created and accepted by block chain users, a record can never be altered or disappear.

But obstacles to using cryptocurrencies are high. Acquisition and liquidation costs represent barriers to using them as a form of payment. The lack of price stability undermines confidence in using this form of payment in M&As without some type of a collar arrangement within which the value of the purchase price can fluctuate. Alternatively, cryptocurrencies if traded on a futures exchange could be hedged against loss of value by buying a futures contract locking in the current price, although this would add to transaction costs. There also are concerns about security, with several instances of theft of Bitcoin by hackers. Other issues include the general lack of regulation and transparency. Government taxing authorities, concerned with the accuracy of the sale price reported for tax purposes, might be quick to audit those involved in Bitcoin-financed M&A deals. Money laundering also is a potential concern to governments. Monies obtained from criminal activities can be used to buy Bitcoin, which could then be used to acquire a legitimate business.

Could there be a role for cryptocurrency as a form of payment in M&As? Yes, if concerns about security, volatility, and transparency are overcome. Until then, cash and securities will be the primary form of payment in M&As. Although cryptocurrencies could either revolutionize financial markets or become a quaint footnote in history books, they do merit watching.

Separating hype from reality

Too often vendors engage in hyperbole to promote the "next big thing." Its potential appears limitless, and its true limitations are hidden. AI and block chain networks are no exception.

Artificial intelligence

Machine learning requires volumes of high-quality data, is heavily dependent on past data points and patterns, often reproduces human biases, and tends to be complicated for senior managers to understand. Each of these factors is considered next.

For machine learning to provide reliable results, there needs to be sufficient historical examples of the phenomenon for the empirical analysis to identify the factors that consistently predict its occurrence. Problems with data quality, so the argument goes, can be overcome by analyzing massive amounts of data. Although software can sift through reams of data to identify patterns, it is not always clear that they are real or simply an anomaly in the data.[65] Moreover, additional data are most useful when they reflect different examples, allowing the software to identify potentially different patterns. The data analyzed may come from multiple sources outside an organization from vendors interested in selling their data and data mining services. The reliability of such data may be problematic.[66] Furthermore, the management of the target firm is likely to balk at handing over voluminous amounts of data during due diligence.

AI has been most successful when trained to achieve specific objectives such as the identification of irregularities in contracts, spreadsheets, manufacturing processes, and so on. But AI is less likely to anticipate new technologies, products, and markets if they are truly revolutionary rather than evolutionary and offer few historical examples with which to train the software.

If unchecked, AI can reproduce human biases.[67] For example, using AI to analyze the composition of a firm's workforce to address issues of diversity can inject racial, gender, and ethnic prejudices into the analysis. Moreover, having access to better information about the external environment does not necessarily lend itself to better decision making. Analytical tools can appear to executive decision makers as "black boxes." When executives don't understand how conclusions were reached, they tend to have less confidence in them. And boards and senior managers may simply do nothing despite new information.

Achieving competitive advantage and avoiding business failure still require the ability to use data better than the competition.[68] Some researchers argue that it is not the technologies that are so important but rather the diffusion of the knowledge of how to apply these methods throughout the organization that can help firms achieve their goals.[69]

[65] Ghosh, February 16, 2019

[66] Safhi et al., 2019

[67] Ma, 2019

[68] Amankwah-Amoah et al., 2019

[69] Mikalef et al., 2019

There is little evidence at the time of this writing that the application of AI improves firm value. One recent study concludes that although the use of diverse social media data made possible by AI can add to firm value, the impact seems greater for small- to intermediate-size enterprises and less for larger firms.[70] Larger, more diverse firms seem to require greater effort to integrate this information, often limiting the potential value of data analytics.[71] Seventy percent of firms report minimal or no gains so far from their AI initiatives.[72] A 2020 survey by the Boston Consulting Group shows similar results, noting that firms have yet to determine which tasks are best done by machines and which should be left to humans.

Blockchain technology

As is true of AI, block chain technology is difficult for board members and senior managers to understand. The proliferation of esoteric jargon adds to their confusion. Furthermore, although cryptosecurity has proved effective thus far in these networks, they are by no means immune from hackers. Also, block chain system speeds may be inadequate to meet growing demand. In addition, block chain technologies are not yet standardized, making establishing connections between businesses difficult because of different architectures. As of 2019, many firms were still investigating the applicability of block chain technology in relatively small projects.[73] Although the technology currently lacks general acceptance, it offers great promise.

Business acceptance of these new technologies

Although AI and block chain technologies have made impressive strides in recent years, how fast they will be adopted in implementing M&As is problematic.[74] Larger acquirers are likely to embrace these new technologies relatively rapidly because of their ability to marshal the necessary resources. For these technologies to be used effectively, a firm must build a culture of trust in their output at all levels of management. For smaller firms, the prudent approach is to use narrowly focused vendor-supplied AI tools to assist in contract drafting and review of the target's documents to gain experience and contain costs.

Can AI replace human judgment (the ability to assess a situation and reach a logical conclusion) in decision making? Not in the foreseeable future. Determining the benefits of an expected outcome requires human understanding of the situation; as such, it is not a prediction problem. AI software examines text, images, and sounds; compares them with similar data in its database; and makes predictions as to what the data are.[75] But in our current environment in which the pace of change is accelerating, AI systems will be confronted with a growing range of possible and potentially inconsistent outcomes based on ever-larger historical databases.

Just because we can do something does not mean we should!

AI and block chain technologies do have a role in M&As, largely around automating time-consuming tasks and enhancing data security. However, machines are increasingly being allowed to make decisions. This raises fundamental ethical and social questions. Can we trust the results of models we don't really understand? Does the machine learn certain biases from the data patterns existing in massive historical databases? Are decisions made by machines consistent with our values? These concerns mean we must find the appropriate balance between regulating AI innovation while not eliminating its benefits. Just because machines enable us to do things more quickly does not mean that it improves the quality of our decisions.

Some things to remember

The first phase of the M&A process defines the business plan. If an acquisition is necessary to implement the business strategy, an acquisition plan is developed during the second phase. The next phase consists of the search for

[70] Dong et al., 2020

[71] For a detailed discussion of factors contributing to the effective use of big data, see Surbakti et al. (2019).

[72] Ransbotham et al., October 15, 2019

[73] Morkunas et al., 2019

[74] See Hughes et al. (2019) for a detailed discussion of the challenges facing acceptance of these new technologies.

[75] For example, AI software can be trained to determine whether or not the image in a photo is a dog or cat and its breed if it is shown enough images of different dogs and cats.

acquisition candidates, with screening being a refinement of the search activity. How the potential acquirer initiates first contact depends on the urgency of completing a deal, target size, and access to target contacts. The negotiation phase consists of refining valuation, deal structuring, conducting due diligence, and developing a financing plan. Integration planning must be done before closing. The postclosing integration stage entails communicating effectively with stakeholders, retaining key employees, resolving cash flow needs, and realizing synergies. Although commonly overlooked, the postclosing evaluation is critical if a firm is to learn from past mistakes.

Chapter discussion questions

5.1 Identify at least three criteria that might be used to select a manufacturing firm as a potential acquisition candidate. A financial services firm? A high-technology firm?

5.2 Identify alternative ways to make "first contact" with a potential acquisition target. Why is confidentiality important? Under what circumstances might a potential acquirer make its intentions public?

5.3 What are the differences between total consideration, total purchase price or enterprise value, and net purchase price? How are these different concepts used?

5.4 What is the purpose of the buyer's and the seller's performing due diligence?

5.5 Why is preclosing integration planning important?

5.6 In a rush to complete its purchase of health software producer HBO, McKesson did not perform adequate due diligence but instead relied on representations and warranties in the agreement of sale and purchase. Within 6 months after closing, McKesson announced that it would have to reduce revenue by $327 million and net income by $191.5 million for the preceding 3 fiscal years to correct for accounting irregularities. The company's stock fell by 48%. If HBO's financial statements had been declared to be in accordance with GAAP, would McKesson have been justified in believing that HBO's revenue and profit figures were 100% accurate? Explain your answer.

5.7 Find a transaction currently in the news. Speculate as to what criteria the buyer may have used to identify the target company as an attractive takeover candidate. Be specific.

5.8 Fresenius, a German manufacturer of dialysis equipment, acquired APP Pharmaceuticals for $4.6 billion. The deal includes an earnout, under which Fresenius would pay as much as $970 million if APP reaches certain future financial targets. What is the purpose of the earnout? How does it affect the buyer and the seller?

5.9 Material adverse change clauses (MACs) allow parties to the contract to determine who will bear the risk of adverse events between the signing of an agreement and the closing. MACs are frequently not stated in dollar terms. How might MACs affect the negotiating strategies of the parties to the agreement during the period between signing and closing?

5.10 Mattel acquired The Learning Company (TLC), a leading developer of software for toys, in a stock-for-stock transaction valued at $3.5 billion. Mattel had determined that TLC receivables were overstated, a $50 million licensing deal had been prematurely put on the balance sheet, and TLC brands were becoming outdated. TLC also had substantially exaggerated the amount of money put into R&D for new software products. Nevertheless, driven to become a big player in children's software, Mattel closed on the transaction, aware that TLC's cash flows were overstated. After restructuring charges associated with the acquisition, Mattel's consolidated net loss was $82.4 million on sales of $5.5 billion. Mattel's stock fell by more than 35% to end the year at about $14 per share. What could Mattel have done to better protect its interests?

Answers to these Chapter Discussion Questions are available in the Online Instructor's Manual for instructors using this book.

End-of-chapter case study: Roche acquires Spark Therapeutics in move to replenish drug pipeline

Case study objectives

To illustrate how

- Firms use acquisitions to augment or replace their existing capabilities and resources
- Success sometimes requires an acquirer to be able to discern the "next big thing"

- The real value in a target firm often is its intellectual property and its employees
- Assessing the success or failure of mergers often requires many years

Big drug firms generate profits by investing in R&D in the hope that they can discover new breakthrough solutions to medical problems. The process tends to be lengthy, often spanning many years, and fraught with risk as relatively few experimental drugs actually reach the commercial stage. Governments grant patent protection for a limited period to enable firms to recover their investment plus a financial return sufficient to compensate for risk.

Absent continuous R&D reinvestment, existing products are subject to competition from generic drug manufacturers when patent protection expires. Big pharmaceutical companies have the option of reinvesting in their own R&D operations or partnering with or acquiring smaller biotech firms with drugs at various stages of development.[76] With patent protection expiring for many of their primary cash-generating drugs, big pharmaceutical companies are aggressively pursuing biotech firms to help replenish their "drug pipelines."

Having become commercially viable in recent years, gene therapy, a protocol in which defective genes are replaced by healthy ones, shows great promise for curing a variety of inherited illnesses. Advances in manufacturing, better product safety and efficacy, and a favorable regulatory environment make gene therapy a high-growth investment opportunity.

A key milestone was achieved in 2017 when US-based Spark Therapeutics (Spark) secured Federal Drug Administration approval for treating an inherited retinal disease. Since then, more applications have been identified, with more drug companies placing big bets that gene therapy will become a major contributor to revenue and profit growth.

The growth potential of gene therapy was not lost on Swiss multinational health care company Roche Holdings AG (Roche). Roche announced on February 25, 2019, that it had reached an all-cash agreement to buy Spark for $114.50 per share. The $4.8 billion purchase price represented a premium of 122% over Spark's closing market value on February 22, 2019, immediately before the announcement. The premium size reflects a possible bidding war with Pfizer and Novartis, both of which have partnerships with Spark to develop drugs. Spark will operate as a wholly owned subsidiary within Roche Pharmaceuticals.

By focusing on treatments for rare, inherited diseases, Roche expects to be able to command some of the highest prices in medicine. For example, Spark's blindness therapy Luxturna is priced at $850,000 per patient. Roche is counting on new medicines, including gene therapies, to help compensate for patent losses on the firm's $21 billion per year cancer medicines. The Spark deal gives Roche a proven platform for commercializing gene therapies.

Although Spark's primary drug offering, Luxturna, thus far has been a money loser, the firm does have royalty income from a deal with Pfizer. With the Spark deal, Roche could become more competitive in the hemophilia treatment market if Spark's gene therapies prove effective.

Even with the acquisition, Roche will not be first to market. Novartis has targeted gene therapy as an area of focus, giving it the lead on Roche. Novartis's spinal muscular atrophy (SMA) medicine gained approval in 2019. In contrast, Spark's top drug only started phase 3 trials in late 2019.

In addition to being late to market with new gene therapy drugs, a risk to Roche is that its current sales of Hemlibra to treat hemophilia A, a genetic disorder that prevents blood from clotting, may be cannibalized. Roche is betting that Hemlibra and gene therapy are more complementary than substitutes. Furthermore, with Spark, Roche enters a crowded hemophilia gene therapy market because other firms also have gene therapies under development. Roche anticipates that the market will be large enough for multiple firms.

Discussion questions

1. What external and internal factors drove the merger between Roche and Spark Therapeutics?
2. What options other than an acquisition could Roche have pursued? Speculate as to why they chose to acquire rather than to pursue other alternatives.
3. What are the major assumptions implicit in Roche's takeover strategy? Be specific.

[76] Although both produce medicines, the main difference between biotech and pharmaceutical firms is that whereas the former produce medicines from living organisms, the latter's products generally are based on chemicals..

4. Speculate as to why Roche chose to operate Spark as a wholly owned subsidiary. What are the advantages and disadvantages in operating the business independently from the parent?

Solutions to these case study discussion questions are found in the Online Instructor's Manual available to instructors using this book.

CHAPTER

6

Postclosing integration

mergers, acquisitions, and business alliances

OUTLINE

https://doi.org/10.1016/B978-0-12-819782-0.00006-X

Whether you think you can, or you think you can't—you're right. —*Henry Ford*

Inside M&As: setting postmerger integration goals and tactics before closing

KEY POINTS

- Successful postmerger integration requires clearly stated goals and tactics to be set before closing the deal.
- Failure to move quickly to implement the highest priority changes can impair postmerger performance and brand for years.
- Protracted integration reduces the acquirer's ability to recover the premium paid for the target because of the loss of disaffected customers, employees, and suppliers.

Postintegration problems mounted as Dollar Tree Inc. (Dollar Tree) announced a $2.73 billion accounting write-off as it marked down the value of its Family Dollar chain acquired in 2015 for almost $9 billion. The takeover was completed only after a prolonged bidding war with discount store leader Dollar General Corp (Dollar General). The impetus for the takeover had been to achieve the scale needed to compete effectively against rivals Dollar General and Walmart Inc. Increased scale, so the argument goes, would enable the firm to spread its overhead over more sales and to gain negotiating leverage with suppliers. From the outset, Family Dollar sales lagged behind competitors', undercutting parent Dollar Tree's financial performance. Although Dollar Tree shares have appreciated 20% since the deal closed in mid-2015, the firm has underperformed other stores in its market segment. Segment leader Dollar General has seen its share price soar more than 50% during the same period.

Impatient with Dollar Tree's failure to improve performance, activist investor Starboard Value LP acquired a 1.7% stake in Dollar Tree in early 2019. The hedge fund immediately pushed for the sale of Family Dollar, a board shakeup, and increasing prices above a dollar on selected products in an effort to boost profitability.

Family Dollar's issues predate its acquisition by Dollar Tree, but the situation seemed to worsen because of continued neglect by management. Family Dollar's lackluster sales compared with those of their competitors reflected the deteriorating condition of its stores, shoddy product selection, and high worker turnover. Family Dollar failed to benefit from the growth in its market segment during the decade after the 2008–2009 recession as consumers shifted spending to discount stores.

Pressured by investors, Dollar Tree raised its prices on certain items above $1 in early June 2019, hoping customers could be persuaded to pay a little more for higher quality products. Dollar Tree also announced plans to renovate 1000 Family Dollar stores, close up to 390 Family Dollar stores, and convert about 200 to Dollar Tree outlets, leaving Dollar Tree with fewer than 8000 Family Dollar stores and about 7000 Dollar Tree locations by the end of 2019.

Dollar Tree was slow to exploit the differences between its customers and Family Dollar's. Whereas Dollar Tree stores are in suburban areas, Family Dollar targets urban locations. But this puts Family Dollar in direct competition with industry leader Dollar General. Dollar Tree intends to expand Family Dollar's market share in rural America, taking business away from independent grocers and other retailers that have closed stores in those areas in recent years.

Dollar Tree has failed to differentiate Family Dollar from its primary competitor, Dollar General, in urban areas. Dollar General's stores tend to be more attractive and offer a wider variety of products. Although Family Dollar's stores look and feel a lot like Dollar General, they often are in a state of disrepair. Family Dollar's continued problems have impaired its brand, leading to severe asset write-offs, confirming that Dollar Tree overpaid substantially for the firm.

Although store renovations to provide a new look may boost sales, it will be some time before the brand can recover. The bidding war with Dollar General may have prevented Dollar Tree from doing adequate planning before closing, causing the firm to be too distracted to focus on the proper priorities. Dollar Tree may be experiencing "buyer's remorse" for some time to come.

Chapter overview

As demographics change, product life cycles shorten, and the role of technology accelerates, decisions about when and how to integrate a target become more complex. Should the target firm be fully, partially, or not at all integrated into the acquirer's operations? Whether and when integration happens and the pace at which it occurs depend on the intent of the acquirer, the terms of the deal, and external factors beyond the control of either the buyer or seller.

For our purposes here, assume that integration is the goal of the acquirer immediately after the transaction closes. The factors critical to a successful postmerger integration include careful premerger planning, candid and continuous communication, adopting the right pace for combining the businesses, appointing an integration manager and team with clearly defined goals and lines of authority, and making the difficult decisions early in the process. This chapter concludes with a discussion of how to overcome some of the obstacles encountered in integrating business alliances. A chapter review (consisting of practice questions and answers) is available in the file folder titled "Student Study Guide" on the companion site to this book (https://www.elsevier.com/books-and-journals/book-companion/9780128197820).

The degree of integration varies by type of acquirer and deal

Deciding if and when to integrate an acquisition often depends on the type of acquirer—financial or strategic—which differs primarily in terms of how long they intend to retain the business. *Financial buyers*—those who buy a business for eventual resale—tend not to integrate the acquired business into another entity. Rather than manage the business, they are inclined to monitor management and intervene only if there is a significant deviation between actual and projected performance. Sometimes financial buyers will "roll up" a fragmented industry by buying a firm within the industry and subsequently use it as a platform for acquiring additional businesses. In either case—whether the financial buyer manages the acquired firm as a standalone operation or uses it to consolidate an industry—the objective is the same: take the business public through an initial public offering (IPO), sell to a strategic buyer, or sell to another financial buyer. In contrast, *strategic buyers* want to make a profit by managing the acquired business for an extended period. How they manage the business postmerger can range from operating the target as a separate subsidiary to partially or wholly integrating the acquired business into the parent.

Transformational deals involve acquiring new markets, products, distribution channels, and operations, resulting in a strategic realignment of the acquirer. Such deals are challenging to integrate because they involve combining different corporate cultures as well as new technologies, production methodologies, and selling strategies. They often are undertaken to move the acquirer away from a maturing to a higher-growth industry; as such, value creation relies more on revenue than cost synergies. Usually less challenging during integration are *consolidating acquisitions* involving companies in the same industry, with much of the value creation realized through cost reduction and improving efficiency. They tend to be less difficult than transformational deals because the acquirer has greater operational and customer familiarity.

Acquisitions of small companies are sometimes referred to *bolt-on transactions* and generally involve buyouts of new technologies, products, or intellectual property. Finally, *standalone transactions* are those in which the target is kept separate from the acquirer's organization. This may be done to preserve the target's culture, in accordance with the terms of the negotiated contract (e.g., earnouts); to minimize the parent's vulnerability to potential target liabilities; or simply because the buyer expects to sell the unit within a relatively short period.

The role of integration in successful acquisitions

Rapid integration is more likely to result in a merger that achieves the acquirer's expectations. Why? Integration done quickly (and sensibly) generates the returns expected by shareholders and minimizes employee turnover and customer attrition. The pace of integration has improved in recent years with much of the postmerger integration process being completed in 6 months or less.[1] The greatest improvement areas are leadership selection, stakeholder communication, and execution. The sooner key positions are filled and reporting relationships established, the faster

[1] PriceWaterhouseCoopers, 2017

people can focus on integration. Frequent communication with customers and employees reduces anxiety by setting expectations. Finally, quickly implementing the desired policies and practices accelerates synergy realization.

This does not mean that restructuring ends entirely within this time period. Integration may continue in terms of plant sales or closures for years after closing. Almost half of acquirers either sell or close target firms' plants within 3 years of closing. And within 5 years, plant divestitures and closures increase by an additional 9% to 10%.[2] In some countries, employee protections preclude the rapid elimination of jobs, slowing the acquirer's ability to realize synergies and often increasing the cost of reducing the workforce because of large payouts to terminated employees required by law.

Realizing projected financial returns

Rapid integration helps realize projected financial returns. Suppose a firm's current market value of $100 million accurately reflects the firm's future cash flows discounted at its cost of capital. Assume an acquirer is willing to pay a $25 million premium for this firm over its current market value, believing it can recover the premium by realizing cost savings resulting from integrating the two firms. The amount of cash the acquirer will have to generate to recover the premium will increase the longer it takes to integrate the target company. If the cost of capital is 10% and integration is completed by the end of the first year, the acquirer will have to earn $27.5 million by the end of the first year to recover the premium plus its cost of capital: $\$25 + (\$25 \times 0.10)$. If integration is not completed until the end of the second year, the acquirer will have to earn an incremental cash flow of $30.25 million—$\$27.5 + (\$27.5 \times 0.10)$—and so on.

The impact of employee turnover

Some loss of managers is intentional after a takeover to eliminate redundancies and incompetent executives. Target firm CEOs commonly are replaced, with their departure often associated with an improvement in the firm's operating performance.[3] Other managers, often those the acquirer would like to retain, frequently quit during the integration turmoil, making it difficult to recover any premium paid.

The cost of employee turnover does not stop with the loss of key employees. The loss of current employees results in recruitment and training costs to replace those who depart. Moreover, the loss of employees is likely to reduce the morale and productivity of those who remain. To minimize unwanted employee turnover, acquirers often raise significantly target firm employee compensation to retain employees following takeovers. In friendly deals, employee commitment to the takeover can increase by involving key employees from both acquirer and target firms on implementation teams from preplanning through postmerger integration.[4]

Acquisition-related customer attrition

During normal operations, a business can expect a certain level of churn in its customer list. Depending on the industry, normal churn as a result of competitive conditions can be anywhere from 20% to 40%. A newly merged company will experience a loss of another 5% to 10% of its existing customers as a direct result of a merger, reflecting uncertainty about on-time delivery and product quality and more aggressive postmerger pricing by competitors.[5]

[2] Maksimovic et al., 2012

[3] Demirtas, 2016

[4] Degbey et al., 2020

[5] A McKinsey study found that, on average, merged firms grew four percentage points less than their peers during the 3 years after closing. Moreover, 42% of the sample actually lost ground. Only 12% of the sample showed revenue growth significantly ahead of their peers (Bekier et al., 2001).

Rapid integration does not mean doing everything at the same pace

Although rapid integration may quicken synergy realization, it also contributes to employee and customer attrition. Intelligent integration involves managing these tradeoffs by quickly implementing projects offering immediate payoff and deferring those resulting in the greatest short-term revenue loss. Acquirers often postpone integrating data processing and customer service call centers to maintain on-time delivery and high-quality customer service.

Integration is a process, not an event

Integrating a business into the acquirer's operations involves six major steps: premerger planning, resolving communication issues, defining the new organization, developing staffing plans, integrating functions, and building a new culture. Some activities are continuous and unending. For instance, communicating with all major stakeholder groups and developing a new corporate culture are largely ongoing activities, spanning the integration period and beyond. Table 6.1 outlines this sequence of activities common to effective postmerger integration efforts.

There is no "one size fits all" formula that ensures that the integration effort will achieve anticipated synergy and strategic goals. The degree of integration as well as formal and informal coordination mechanisms[6] can vary widely. For acquirers and targets in the same industry, extensive integration is most beneficial in mature industries; limited integration is much more appropriate in growing and declining industries.[7] Formal coordination mechanisms are most beneficial in declining industries; in growing industries, only informal coordination mechanisms are valuable.[8] Cross-border deals can be particularly challenging to integrate because of the need to balance sensitivity

TABLE 6.1 Viewing merger integration as a process

Integration planning	Developing communication plans	Creating a new organization	Developing staffing plans	Functional integration	Building a new corporate culture
Premerger planning: select the appropriate integration strategy • Refine valuation • Resolve transition issues • Negotiate contractual assurances	Stakeholders: • Employees • Customers • Suppliers • Investors • Lenders • Communities (including regulators)	Learn from the past Business needs drive structure	Determine personnel requirements for the new organization Determine resource availability Establish staffing plans and timetables Develop compensation strategy Create needed information systems	Revalidate due diligence data Conduct performance benchmarking Integrate functions: • Operations • Information technology • Finance • Sales • Marketing • Purchasing • Research and development • Human resources • Legal	Identify cultural issues through corporate profiling Integrate through shared: • Goals • Standards • Services • Space

[6] *Formal coordination* mechanisms refer to departmental structures, centralization of authority, standard written policies and procedures, and strategic and operational plans. Informal mechanisms consist of communication among department managers, work teams, and a culture based on shared objectives and values.

[7] Mature industries reflect slowing demand and intensifying competition. Economies of scale and increased price competition force smaller rivals to exit the industry, leading to industry concentration. As a result, management structures become formal with clearly defined rules to achieve discipline as firms become larger and more complex.

[8] When markets are expanding rapidly, postmerger organizations need to be informal to adapt to changing industry conditions. In declining industries, competition intensifies, often requiring firms to either consolidate or diversify.

to the local culture while applying the best management methods throughout the combined firms.[9] Local cultural differences constitute a greater challenge to realizing synergy than differences between acquirer and target corporate cultures in cross-border deals because acquirers can only influence corporate culture.[10]

Premerger integration planning

Premerger integration planning should coincide with the onset of due diligence.[11] During this period, the acquirer is accumulating information about the target generally not available publicly. This enables the acquirer to more accurately assess potential synergy, a reasonable timetable for realizing synergy, and costs that are likely to be incurred during postmerger integration.

The planning activity involves prioritizing the critical actions that must be completed to combine the businesses. Planning enables the acquirer to refine its original estimate of the value of the target and deal with postclosing transition issues in the merger agreement. It also gives the buyer an opportunity to insert into the agreement the appropriate reps and warranties as well as closing conditions that facilitate the postmerger integration process. The planning process creates a postmerger integration organization to expedite the integration process after the closing.

Planning should also consider how to capture synergies without destroying target firm proprietary skills and knowledge. This is often best achieved by retaining and motivating target firm managers to play a key role in identifying and accessing knowledge in their organization.[12]

Planning may be complicated in cross-border deals where national security concerns arise as a result of recent legislation. The Foreign Investment Risk Review Modernization Act (FIRRMA) of 2018 gives the Committee on Foreign Investment in the United States (CFIUS) greater authority to review foreign investments. Discussing corporate intentions ahead of time with CFIUS will be critical when there is a possibility of national security concerns. What was formerly voluntary now for some deals is required under FIRRMA to notify CFIUS even if a deal is being contemplated (see Chapter 2 for more details). If CFIUS identifies possible risks to national security, it may require certain departments or functions be kept separate even after other functions have been fully integrated. CFIUS also may limit sharing access to intellectual property and product development activities, thereby preventing the complete integration of research and development (R&D), engineering, and information technology (IT) functions.

Putting the postmerger integration organization in place before closing

To minimize potential confusion, it is critical to get the integration manager involved in the process as early as possible—ideally, well before the negotiation process begins. Doing so makes it more likely that the strategic rationale for the deal remains well understood by those involved in conducting due diligence and postmerger integration. A key responsibility of the integration manager is to set the pace of the integration: knowing when to apply pressure to accelerate the process without demotivating those involved in the integration. Too slow a pace can make it difficult for the acquirer to earn back any premium paid; too fast a pace can dishearten managers as they begin to feel that goals are unrealistic.

A postmerger integration organization with clearly defined goals and responsibilities should be in place before the deal closes. For friendly mergers, the organization—including supporting teams—should consist of individuals from both the acquirer and target with a vested interest in the newly formed company. During a hostile takeover, of course, it can be problematic to assemble such a team, given the lack of cooperation that may exist between the parties to the transaction. The acquirer will find it difficult to access needed data and to involve the target's management in the planning process before the transaction closes.

[9] Tsui-Auch et al. (2019) discuss the pros and cons of alternative postmerger integration strategies based on Walmart's experience in Mexico, Germany, and Japan.

[10] Wang et al., 2020

[11] Generally, due diligence begins during negotiation. When the seller has substantial leverage, due diligence may be postponed until after an agreement is signed. But the agreement is contingent on the buyer conducting adequate due diligence, the terms of which are described in the sales agreement.

[12] Colman, 2020

If the plan is to integrate the target firm into one of the acquirer's business units, it is critical to place responsibility for integration in that business unit. Personnel from the business unit should be well represented on the due diligence team to ensure they understand how best to integrate the target to realize synergies expeditiously.

The postmerger integration organization: composition and responsibilities

The postmerger integration organization should consist of a management integration team (MIT) and work teams focused on implementing a specific portion of the integration plan. Senior managers from the two merged organizations serve on the MIT, which is charged with realizing synergies identified during the preclosing due diligence. Involving senior managers from both firms captures the best talent and signals employees that decision makers agree. The MIT's emphasis during integration should be on activities that create the greatest value for shareholders. Exhibit 6.1 summarizes the key tasks the MIT must perform to realize anticipated synergies.

The MIT should give teams not only the responsibility but also the authority and resources to get the job done. To be effective, the work teams must have access to accurate information; receive candid, timely feedback; and be kept informed of the overall integration effort to avoid becoming too narrowly focused. Work teams that are co-managed by representatives from both the acquirer and target often prove more effective than those in which an acquiring firm manager supervises the team's activities.[13] This structure allows for the use of the best managerial talent in both firms and can promote cross-fertilization of ideas.

Developing communication plans for key stakeholders

Before announcing an acquisition, the acquirer should prepare a communication plan targeted at major stakeholder groups. Managers should communicate clearly, proactively, and interactively to all those affected by the postmerger integration effort to distinguish between decisions made as a consequence of the integration and decisions taken as a result of other considerations.[14] Managers should be aware that the postmerger integration process is embedded within a series of processes unrelated to the integration effort such as corporate investments, new product introductions, facility closures, and new marketing programs. As such, it is easy for stakeholders to confuse change related to other activities with the integration effort, which contributes to stress levels and disaffection. Each stakeholder group is discussed next.

EXHIBIT 6.1

Key Management Integration Team Responsibilities

1. Build a master schedule of what should be done by whom and by what date.
2. Determine the required economic performance for the combined entity.
3. Establish work teams to determine how each function and business unit will be combined (e.g., structure, job design, and staffing levels).
4. Focus the organization on meeting ongoing business commitments and operational performance targets during the integration process.
5. Create an early warning system consisting of performance indicators to ensure that both integration activities and business performance stay on plan.
6. Monitor and expedite key decisions.
7. Establish a rigorous communication campaign to support aggressively the integration plan. Address both internal constituencies (e.g., employees) and external constituencies (e.g., customers, suppliers, and regulatory authorities).

[13] Birollo and Teerikangas, 2019

[14] Rouzies et al., 2019

Employees: addressing the "me" issues immediately

Employees need to understand early on what is expected of them and why. Acquirer efforts to explain the justification for the takeover and its implications for employees of both the acquirer and target firms can be disruptive by challenging current practices and beliefs. And how employees feel emotionally about a takeover can determine its ultimate success.

Without their acceptance, employees can resist integration efforts either openly or passively. The latter is perhaps the most insidious because employees can appear to be cooperating but in fact are not. They are either slow to respond to requests for information or behavioral changes or do not respond at all. Passive resistance undermines the rapid integration.

Acquirer and target employees are interested in any information pertaining to the merger and how it will affect them, often in terms of job security, working conditions, and total compensation. For example, if the acquirer expects to improve worker productivity or reduce benefits, it is critical to explain that the long-term viability of the business requires such actions because of increasing market competition.

Target firm employees often represent most of its value, particularly for technology and service-related businesses. The CEO should lead the effort to communicate to employees at all levels through on-site meetings or via teleconferencing. Communication to employees should be frequent; it is better to report that there is no change than to remain silent.

Deteriorating job performance and absence from work are clear signs of workforce anxiety. Many companies find it useful to create a single information source accessible to all employees, whether it is an individual whose job is to answer questions or a menu-driven automated phone system programmed to respond to commonly asked questions. The best way to communicate in a crisis, however, is through regularly scheduled employee meetings. Press releases should be coordinated with the public relations department to ensure that the same information is released concurrently to all employees. Email systems, voicemail, or intranets may be used to facilitate employee communications. In addition, personal letters, question-and-answer sessions, newsletters, and videotapes are highly effective ways to deliver messages.

Customers: undercommitting and overdelivering

Attrition can be minimized if the newly merged firm commits to customers that it will maintain or improve product quality, on-time delivery, and customer service. Such assurances are more credible if the merged firms dedicate a customer service team to each major customer. Each team's responsibilities would include all communications with the customer and the resolution of issues that might arise while minimizing the amount of change each customer experiences. The firm must communicate to customers realistic benefits associated with the merger. From the customer's perspective, the merger can increase the range of products or services offered or provide lower selling prices because of economies of scale and new applications of technology.

Suppliers: developing long-term vendor relationships

The new company should seek long-term relationships rather than simply ways to reduce costs. Aggressive negotiation may win high-quality products and services at lower prices in the short run, but that may be transitory if the new company is a large customer of the supplier and if the supplier's margins are squeezed continually. The supplier's product or service quality will suffer, and the supplier eventually may exit the business.

Investors: maintaining shareholder loyalty

The new firm must be able to present to investors a vision of the future. In a share exchange, target shareholders become shareholders in the newly formed company. Loyal shareholders tend to provide a more stable ownership base and may contribute to lower share price volatility.

All firms attract particular types of investors—some with a preference for high dividends and others for capital gains—who may clash over their preferences, as America Online's acquisition of Time Warner in January 2000 illustrates. The combined market value of the two firms lost 11% in the 4 days after the announcement: investors fretted over what had been created, and there was a selling frenzy that involved investors who bought Time Warner for its stable growth and America Online for its meteoric growth rate of 70% per year.

Communicating with stakeholders through social media can be an efficient and timely means of allaying fears arising when deal insiders have more information than outsiders. For example, disclosing acquisition announcements on Twitter tends to weaken negative market reaction around the announcement date.[15] Using social media to keep investors abreast of postmerger integration progress can reduce acquirer share price volatility during this period of uncertainty.

Lenders: maintaining sound banking relationships

Acquirers must get permission from the target's lenders to assume target debt. Additional borrowing to finance the deal cannot violate loan covenants on debt held by the acquirer or target firms in order not to allow lenders to immediately demand repayment of any outstanding balances. Many loan agreements have "cross-default" clauses such that if a borrower is in default with one lender, other lenders can also demand repayment. Lenders are most likely satisfied if the combined firms have substantial liquid assets that can be used to collateralize existing debt and predictable cash flow in excess of what is needed to keep the new company operating.

Communities: building strong, credible relationships

Good working relationships with communities are simply good public relations. Companies should communicate plans to build or keep plants, stores, or office buildings in a community as soon as they can be confident that these actions will be implemented. Such steps often translate into new jobs and increased tax collections for the community.

Creating a new organization

Despite the requirement to appoint dozens of managers—including heads of key functions, groups, and even divisions—creating a new top management team must be given first priority.

Establishing a structure

Building reporting structures requires knowing the target company's prior organization, its effectiveness, and the future business needs of the new firm. Prior organization charts provide insights into how individuals from both companies will interact within the new company because they reveal the past experience and future expectations of individuals with regard to reporting relationships. The focus at this point goes beyond simply job titles but identifying what people actually do and how they do it. This enables those involved in integration planning to better identify ways to improve productivity, eliminate job overlap or redundancy, and achieve cost reduction without reducing the operational performance of the combined organizations. Such information also helps to identify important shared values and which cultural differences between the acquirer's and target's organizations are critical to preserve and which are not.[16] The next step is to create a structure that meets the business needs of the new firm. Common structures include functional, product, and divisional organizations. In a *functional organization*, people are assigned to specific departments, such as accounting, engineering, and marketing. In a *product organization*, functional specialists are grouped by product line, and each has its own accounting, sales, and marketing staffs. *Divisional organizations*, in which groups of products are combined into divisions, are the most common and have their own management teams and tend to be highly decentralized.

The popularity of decentralized versus centralized management structures varies with the economy. During recessions, when top management is under pressure to cut costs, companies tend to move toward centralized management structures, only to decentralize when the economy recovers. Highly decentralized authority can retard the pace of integration because there is no single authority to resolve issues. In a centralized structure, senior management can dictate policies governing all aspects of the combined companies, centralize all types of functions that provide support to operating units, and resolve issues among the operating units.

Still, centralized control can destroy value if policies imposed by the headquarters are inappropriate for the operating units—such as those imposing too many rigid controls, focusing on the wrong issues, hiring or promoting the wrong managers, or establishing inappropriate performance metrics. Moreover, centralized companies often have multiple layers of management and centralized functions providing services to the operating units. The parent companies pass on the costs of centralized management and support services to the operating units, and these costs often outweigh the benefits.

[15] Mazboudi et al., 2017

[16] Sarala et al., 2019

The benefits of rapid postmerger integration suggest a centralized management structure initially with few management layers. The distance between the CEO and division heads, measured in terms of intermediate positions, has decreased in recent years, but the span of a CEO's authority has widened. This does not mean all integration activities should be driven from the top. When integration is complete, the new company may move to a more decentralized structure in view of the potential costs of centralized corporate organizations.

Developing staffing plans

Staffing plans should be formulated early in the integration process, providing an opportunity to include key personnel from both firms in the integration effort. Other benefits include the increased likelihood of retaining employees with key skills and talents, maintaining corporate continuity, and team building. Figure 6.1 presents the logical sequencing of staffing plans and the major issues addressed in each segment.

Personnel requirements

The appropriate organizational structure is one that meets the current functional requirements of the business and is flexible enough to be expanded to satisfy future requirements. Before establishing the organizational structure, the integration team should agree on the specific functions needed to run the combined businesses and project each function's personnel requirements based on a description of the function's ideal structure to achieve its objectives.

Employee availability

Employee availability refers to the number of each type of employee needed by the new firm. The skills of the current workforce should be compared with the current and future requirements of the new company. The local labor pool can be a source of new hires to augment the existing workforce. Data should be collected on the educational levels, skills, and demographic composition of the local workforce as well as prevailing wage rates by skill category.

Staffing plans and timetable

A detailed staffing plan can be developed after the preceding steps are completed. Gaps in the firm's workforce that need to be filled via outside recruitment can be readily identified. The effort to recruit externally should be tempered by its potentially adverse impact on current-employee morale. Filling needed jobs should be prioritized and phased in over time in recognition of the time required to fill certain types of positions and the impact of major hiring programs on local wage rates in communities with a limited availability of labor.

Compensation plans

Merging compensation plans must be done in compliance with prevailing regulations and sensitivity. Total compensation consists of base pay, bonuses or incentive plans, benefits, and special contractual agreements. Bonuses may take the form of a lump sum of cash or stock paid to an employee for meeting or exceeding these targets.

Special contractual agreements may consist of noncompete agreements, in which key employees, in exchange for an agreed-on amount of compensation, agree not to compete against the new firm if they leave. Such agreements are not without costs to the firm. Although they can protect an employer's intellectual capital and contribute to employee retention, managers whose options in the job market are limited may go to extreme lengths to avoid dismissal by limiting discretionary investment, such as R&D spending, to improve earnings. Such decisions can

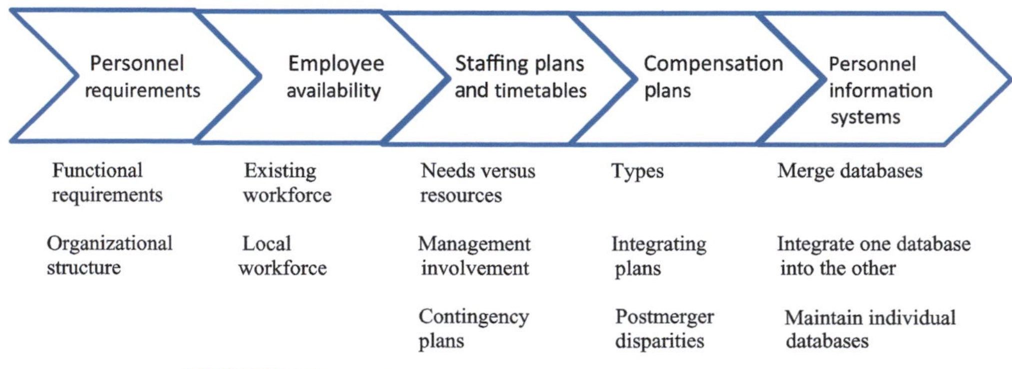

FIGURE 6.1 Staffing strategy sequencing and associated issues.

limit the firm's future product innovation and long-term profitability.[17] Other types of special agreements include severance packages for senior management and retention bonuses for employees if they agree to stay with the new company for a specific period.[18]

Personnel information systems

The acquiring company may choose to merge all personnel data into a new database, merge one corporate database into another, or maintain the separate personnel databases of each business. A single database enables authorized users to access employee data more readily, plan more efficiently for future staffing requirements, and conduct workforce analyses. Maintenance expenses associated with a single database also may be lower. The decision to keep personnel databases separate may reflect plans to divest the unit in the future.

Functional integration

So far, you have learned about the steps involved in *planning* the integration process. Now let's look at functional integration—the actual execution of the plans. The MIT must determine the extent to which the firms' operations and support staffs are to be centralized or decentralized. The focus should be IT, manufacturing operations, sales, marketing, finance, purchasing, R&D, and the requirements to staff these functions. Successful mergers and acquisitions (M&As) are often those in which a substantial amount of management time is spent in integrating the two firms' functional departments, because this is where integration plans are implemented.[19]

Revalidating due diligence data

Data collected during due diligence should be reviewed immediately after closing. Pressure to complete the transaction often results in a haphazard preclosing due diligence review. For example, to compress the time devoted to due diligence, sellers often allow buyers access only to senior managers. For similar reasons, site visits by the buyer often are limited to those with the largest number of employees, so risks and opportunities that might exist at other sites remain undiscovered. The buyer's legal and financial reviews are conducted only on the largest customer and supplier contracts, promissory notes, and operating and capital leases. Receivables are evaluated, and physical inventory is counted using sampling techniques. The effort to determine whether intellectual property has been properly protected is often spotty.

Benchmarking performance

Benchmarking important functions, such as the acquirer and target manufacturing and IT operations, is a useful starting point for determining how to integrate these activities. Standard benchmarks include the International Standards Organization's (ISO) 9000 Quality Systems—Model for Quality Assurance in Design, Development, Production, Installation, and Servicing. Other benchmarks that can be used include the US Food and Drug Administration's Good Manufacturing Practices and the Department of Commerce's Malcolm Baldrige Award.

Resetting synergy expectations

Companies that are most successful in realizing incremental value after integration often are those that use their pre-deal estimates of synergy as baseline estimates (i.e., the minimum they expect to achieve) and actively seek new synergy opportunities during integration. Such firms are four times more likely to characterize their deals as being more highly successful than executives of acquiring firms that do not reset their synergy expectations. Additional value is often realized by making fundamental operational changes or from providing customers with new products or services that were envisioned during the due diligence process.[20]

[17] Chen et al., 2018

[18] In 2014, Facebook's $3 billion acquisition of virtual reality headset company, Oculus, included $700 million in retention bonuses to retain the services of the founder and other key personnel.

[19] Teerikangas et al., 2017

[20] Agrawal et al., 2011

Integrating manufacturing operations

The objective should be to reevaluate overall capacity, the potential for future cost reductions, the age and condition of facilities, the adequacy of maintenance budgets, and compliance with environmental and safety laws. The integration should consider carefully whether target facilities that duplicate manufacturing capabilities are potentially more efficient than those of the buyer. As part of the benchmarking process, the operations of both the acquirer and the target should be compared with industry standards to evaluate their efficiency properly.

Efficiency may be evaluated in terms of the following processes: production planning, materials ordering, order entry, and quality control. The production planning and materials ordering functions need to coordinate activities because the amount and makeup of the materials ordered depend on the accuracy of sales projections. Order entry may offer significant opportunities for cost savings. Companies that produce in anticipation of sales, such as automakers, often carry large finished-goods inventories; others, such as PC makers, often build only when an order is received, to minimize working capital. Finally, the efficiency of quality control can be measured as the percentage of products that have to be reworked because of their failure to meet quality standards.

Plant consolidation begins with adopting a set of common standards for all manufacturing activities. These include the time between production runs, cost per unit of output, and scrap rates. Vertical integration can be achieved by focusing on different stages of production. Different facilities specialize in the production of selected components, which are then shipped to other facilities to assemble the finished product. Finally, a company may close certain facilities whenever there is excess capacity.

Integrating information technology

If the buyer intends to operate the target company independently, the information systems of the two companies may be kept separate as long as communications links between them can be established. If the buyer intends to integrate the target, though, the process can be daunting.

Academic research suggests that the successful integration of the acquirer's and target's IT systems requires an extensive investigation of the target's IT function during due diligence. This heightens the probability that the combined firm's IT functions will better support the firm's business strategy.[21] Examples include the acquirer's efforts to improve manufacturing efficiency, procurement, order entry, and customer service.

Cybercrime (i.e., criminal activities carried out by means of computers or the internet) represents a major challenge in postmerger integration of IT systems. Poor cybersecurity protection at either the acquirer or target firms can create significant vulnerability because IT defense systems may be down or because of employee error due to confusion as to how the two systems work together. Culture clash can slow cooperation in integrating systems, and frustrated employees may steal proprietary information.[22]

Integrating finance

Some target companies will be operated as standalone operations with separate finance functions, but others will be completely merged, including finance functions, with the acquirer's operations. International acquisitions involve companies in geographically remote areas that operate largely independent of the parent. Considerable effort is needed to ensure that the buyer can monitor financial results from a distance, even if the parent has its representative on site. The acquirer should also establish a budgeting process and signature approval levels to control spending at remote locations.

Integrating sales

Sales force integration, which eliminates duplicate sales representatives and related support expenses, such as travel and entertainment expenses, training, and management, may result in significant cost savings. A single sales force may also minimize customer confusion by allowing customers to deal with a single person when buying multiple products. Whether the sales forces of the two firms are integrated or operated independently depend on their size, the nature of their products and markets, and their geographic location. A small sales force may be combined with the larger sales force if they sell similar products and serve similar markets. The sales forces may be kept separate if the products they sell require in-depth understanding of the customers' needs and a detailed knowledge of the product.

[21] Baker and Niederman, 2013

[22] Moskowitz, 2017

It is common for firms that sell complex products such as robotics or enterprise software to employ a particularly well-trained and sophisticated sales force that uses a "consultative selling" approach. This entails the firm's sales force working with the customer to develop a solution tailored to their specific needs and may require keeping the sales forces of merged firms separate. Sales forces in globally dispersed businesses often are kept separate to reflect the uniqueness of their markets, while support activities (e.g., training) are centralized.

Integrating marketing

Achieving consistent messaging in advertising and promotional campaigns may be the greatest challenge facing the integration of the marketing function. Steps to ensure consistency, however, should not confuse the customer by radically changing a product's image or how it is sold. The location and degree of integration of the marketing function depend on the global nature of the business, the diversity or uniqueness of product lines, and the pace of change in the marketplace. A business with operations worldwide may be inclined to decentralize marketing in the local countries to increase awareness of local laws and cultural patterns.

Integrating purchasing

Managing the new firm's purchasing function aggressively can reduce the total cost of goods and services purchased by the merged companies. A merger creates uncertainty among both companies' suppliers, particularly if they might have to compete against each other for business with the combined firms. Many offer cost savings and new partnership arrangements, given the merged organization's greater bargaining power to renegotiate contracts. The new company may choose to realize savings by reducing the number of suppliers. As part of the premerger due diligence, both the acquirer and the target should identify a short list of their most critical suppliers, with a focus on those accounting for the largest share of purchased materials expenses.

Integrating research and development

Often, the buyer and seller R&D organizations are working on duplicate projects or projects not germane to the buyer's long-term strategy. Senior managers and the integration team must define future areas of R&D collaboration and set priorities for future R&D research.

Barriers to R&D integration abound. Some projects require considerably more time to produce results than others. Another obstacle is that some personnel stand to lose in terms of titles and power if they collaborate. Finally, the acquirer's and the target's R&D financial return expectations may differ. The acquirer may wish to give R&D a higher or lower priority in the combined operation of the two companies. A starting point for integrating R&D is to have researchers from both companies share their work with each other and colocate.

Integrating acquirer and target R&D functions should be done in concert with efforts to integrate marketing and sales functions. Given their close proximity to the customers, marketing and sales personnel need to work closely with those in the R&D functions in developing new products and services that customers want. The likelihood that new product launches are successful is increased dramatically if personnel in these disparate functions in the acquirer and target firms cooperate. This may be accomplished by interspersing R&D and marketing and sales personnel from both the target and acquiring firms on the marketing and R&D integration teams.

Integrating human resources

Such departments have traditionally been centralized, responsible for evaluating management, conducting employee surveys, developing staffing plans, and providing training. They may be used to evaluate the strengths and weaknesses of potential target firm workforce, integrate the acquirer's and target's management teams, implement pay and benefit plans, communicate information about acquisitions, and, with the support of legal counsel, ensure compliance with applicable labor laws.[23] Because of a perceived lack of responsiveness, the trend in recent years has been to move the human resources (HR) function to the operating unit, where hiring and training may be done more effectively. Despite this trend, the administration of benefit plans, management of HR information systems, and organizational development often remains centralized because of their complexity and requirements for specialized expertise.

[23] See Chapter 2 for a more details. For example, the week following its merger with Sprint in 2020, T-Mobile announced that it would be laying off 400 employees as part of its compliance with the WARN Act, which requires advance notice of layoffs for employers of more than 100 people.

Integrating legal

Whereas large companies usually have in-house legal functions, smaller firms choose to keep a law firm on retainer. Legal counsel deals with issues ranging from lawsuits from customers, suppliers, and employees to ensuring compliance with prevailing laws and regulations. Legal departments tend to be centralized because of their specialized expertise and cost.

Building a new corporate culture

In general, acquirer and target firms that are similar require a higher level of integration and a greater loss of target firm autonomy than those that are dissimilar. When firms are very dissimilar, the loss of autonomy often is resisted by target firm employees. As such, they may be unwilling to cooperate with the acquirer's employees. This can hinder dramatically the integration process if the acquirer cannot gain adequate control of key operations and resources. This resistance may be overcome by creating a unified culture after closing.

Corporate culture is a common set of values, traditions, and beliefs that influence management and employee behavior within a firm. There is a body of research arguing that leaving the evolution of a firm's culture to chance can incur many tangible and intangible costs.[24] See Table 6.2 for a listing of the characteristics of high-performing corporate cultures.

Cultural differences can instill creativity in the new company or create a contentious environment. Corporate culture also can be a source of competitive advantage if it can be changed to reinforce the firm's desired business strategy. Postmerger integration can be a time for senior managers to diagnose the target's culture and to decide strategies for modifying the new firm's culture to be compatible with that desired for the combined firms. But this is far easier said than done because it is often unobservable core beliefs held by employees that drive their observable behaviors.

Actions speak louder than words

Tangible symbols of culture include statements hung on walls containing the firm's mission and principles as well as status associated with the executive office floor and designated parking spaces. Intangible forms include the behavioral norms communicated through implicit messages about how people are expected to act. Because they represent the extent to which employees and managers actually "walk the talk," these messages are often far more influential in forming and sustaining corporate culture than the tangible symbols.

Employees, customers, and other constituencies can see the extent to which management values integrity if their actions support their words. Management that blames their firm's poor performance on factors beyond their control often is viewed as untruthful. In contrast, management willing to take responsibility for a firm's underperformance often is viewed by investors as willing to take the needed corrective actions. As such, investors reward such firms by bidding up their share prices and penalize others whose management is viewed as deceitful.[25]

TABLE 6.2 Characteristics of high-performing corporate cultures

Leaders who are admired and build organizations that excel at achieving results and at taking care of their people and customers
Clear and compelling vision, mission, goals, and strategy
Clear roles, responsibilities, success criteria, and a strong commitment to engaging, empowering, and developing people
Positive, can-do work environment
Open, candid, straightforward, and transparent communication
Teamwork, collaboration, and involvement
Constant improvement and state-of-the-art knowledge and practices
Willingness to change, adapt, learn from successes and mistakes, take reasonable risk, and try new things

Adapted from Warrick (2016).

[24] Warrick, 2017

[25] Chance et al., 2015

Trust is undermined after a merger, in part by the ambiguity of the new organization's identity. As ambiguity abates and acceptance of a common culture grows, trust can be restored, especially among those who identified closely with their previous organization. Firms whose cultures are "employee friendly," in which workers trust management and feel well-treated, tend to show higher market values than those that are not. This should not be surprising because satisfied employees tend to be more productive, and the cost of employee turnover is lower.[26]

Collaborative cultures

With the pace of change not only accelerating but also becoming increasingly complex, an acquirer may choose to focus on developing a culture in which employees expect to participate on teams, share ideas, and assist others in achieving their goals. Steve Jobs is credited with saying "Great things in business are never done by one person; they are done by a team of people." Although the results of such efforts often are significant, so are the potential pitfalls. The fuzzy reporting relationships and the need to get input and acceptance by other team members often slow decision making to a crawl. Collaborative efforts can frustrate the firm's most productive members because of the demands on their time to attend meetings, respond to emails, and help others. Such employees can eventually experience "burn-out" and leave the company.

Identifying cultural issues through profiling

The first step in building a new corporate culture is to develop a cultural profile of both the acquirer and acquired companies through employee surveys and interviews and by observing management styles and practices. Sometimes it is difficult to identify the root causes of observable behaviors. As such, it may be helpful to work backward by hypothesizing what is driving such behaviors to understand their origin. The information is then used to show the similarities and differences between the two cultures as well as their comparative strengths and weaknesses and to diagnose potential problems that need changing.

The relative size and maturity of the acquirer and target firms can have major implications for cultural integration. Start-up companies typically are highly informal in terms of dress and decision making. Compensation may be largely stock options and other forms of deferred income. Benefits, beyond those required by state and federal law, and "perks" such as company cars are largely nonexistent. Company policies frequently do not exist, are not in writing, or are drawn up only as needed. Internal controls covering employee expense accounts are often minimal. In contrast, larger, mature companies are often more highly structured, with well-defined internal controls, compensation structures, benefits packages, and employment policies in place because the firms have grown too large and complex to function in an orderly manner.

When senior management reviews the information in the cultural profile, it must decide which characteristics of both cultures to emphasize. The most realistic expectation is that employees in the new company can be encouraged to adopt a shared vision, a set of core values, and behaviors deemed important by senior management. Anything more is probably wishful thinking: a company's culture evolves over a long period, but getting to the point where employees wholly embrace management's desired culture may take years at best or never be achieved.

Overcoming cultural differences

Cultural differences can be very difficult to overcome because they may have become entrenched in an organization over many years. For example, in a firm in which the CEO for the past decade had been very directive and intolerant of dissent, employees may be reluctant to share their ideas. Consequently, efforts to change the culture can take many years.

Sharing common goals, standards, services, and space can be a highly effective way to integrate disparate cultures. Common goals drive different units to cooperate. At the functional level, setting exact timetables for new product development can drive different operating units to collaborate as project teams strive to introduce the product by the target date. At the corporate level, incentive plans spanning many years can focus all operating units to pursue the same goals. Although it is helpful in the integration process to have common goals, individuals must still have specific goals to minimize the tendency of some to underperform while benefiting from the performance of others.

Shared standards and practices enable one unit to adopt the "best practices" found in another. Standards include operating procedures, technological specifications, ethical values, internal controls, employee performance

[26] Fauver et al., 2018; Khan et al. (2020) emphasize the importance of reward systems and policies being perceived by all employees as fair to encourage acceptance of a new corporate culture.

measures, and reward systems throughout the combined companies. Some functional services can be centralized and shared by multiple departments or operating units. Commonly centralized services include accounting, legal, public relations, internal audit, and IT. The most common way to share services is to use a common staff. Alternatively, a firm can create a support services unit and allow operating units to purchase services from it or to buy similar services outside the company.

Mixing offices or even locating acquired company employees in space adjacent to the parent's offices is a highly desirable way to improve communication and idea sharing. Common laboratories, computer rooms, and lunchrooms also facilitate communication and cooperation.

Changing culture when employees work remotely

Peer pressure and daily modeling of appropriate behaviors to change cultures are most effective when employees are on-site. With employees increasingly working remotely, they must be reminded frequently of the mission, vision, and guiding principles of the combined organizations via email and videoconferencing. But this alone is insufficient to instill the desired level of passion that can come from the daily interaction of employees at a single location. Enthusiasm comes from giving employees challenging work, bonuses, and kudos when appropriate.

Digital tools and change management

Programs designed to change corporate culture often fail because of employee opposition or a lack of management commitment. Success rates tend to be higher if "digital tools" are properly applied to accelerate and simplify the ability of an organization to adopt a new set of desired behaviors.[27] Such tools offer the prospect for immediate feedback, personalizing communication to the employee's experience, building shared purpose, and communicating progress.

Immediate feedback involves offering employees the right information when they can actually use it to adjust their behavior to what is desired by the corporation. For example, establishing a short messaging system (SMS) can keep widely dispersed employees informed about new products, customer developments, and market changes.

Personalizing communications makes information more important to the user because it can show how the individual fits in the overall organization and how her or his actions contribute to achieving corporate goals. This requires limiting broadcast messages throughout the corporation and increasing focus on directly communicating information relevant to a specific employee's function such as finance, HR, engineering, marketing, and so on.

Building shared purpose is especially challenging in organizations that are widely dispersed geographically. Giving employees in all regions access to the same databases, activities conducted by other team members, and online opinion forums facilitates information flow. Shared information and commentary can help employees to understand what is expected and how others are adapting to the new cultural behaviors.

Communicating progress toward corporate goals can help employees see the "fruit" of their collective effort by tracking the firm's progress against key corporate goals. When employees see progress, it creates a sense of success, confidence in current business strategies, and greater acceptance of desired corporate behaviors.

Integrating business alliances

Business alliances also must pay close attention to integration activities. Unlike M&As, alliances usually involve shared control. Successful implementation requires maintaining a good working relationship between venture partners. When this is not possible, the alliance is destined to fail. The breakdown in the working relationship is often a result of an inadequate integration.

Robert Porter Lynch suggests six integration mechanisms to apply to business alliances: leadership, teamwork and role clarification, control by coordination, policies and values, consensus decision making, and resource commitments.[28] These are discussed next.

[27] Ewenstein et al., 2015

[28] Lynch, 1993

Leadership

Although the terms *leadership* and *management* often are used interchangeably, there are critical differences. A leader sets direction and makes things happen, whereas a manager ensures that things continue to happen. Leadership involves vision, drive, and selling skills; management involves communication, planning, delegating, coordinating, and making choices. Successful alliances require both sets of skills. The leader must provide direction, values, and behaviors to create a culture that focuses on the alliance's strategic objectives as its top priority. Managers foster teamwork in the shared control environment of the business alliance.

Teamwork and role clarification

Teamwork is the underpinning that makes alliances work and engenders trust and discipline. Teams reach across functional lines, often consisting of diverse experts or lower-level managers. The team provides functional managers with flexible staffing to augment their own specialized staff. They tend to create better coordination and communication at lower levels of the alliance as well as between partners in the venture. Because teams represent individuals with possibly conflicting agendas, they may foster rather than resolve conflict.[29]

Coordination

Alliances do not lend themselves to control through mandate; rather, in an alliance, control is best exerted through coordination. The best alliance managers are those who coordinate activities through effective communication. When problems arise, the manager's role is to manage the decision-making process, not necessarily to make the decision.

Policies and values

Alliance employees need to understand how decisions are made, what has highest priority, who will be held accountable, and how rewards will be determined. When people know where they stand and what to expect, they are better able to deal with uncertainty. This level of clarity can be communicated through policies and procedures that are well understood by joint venture or partnership employees.

Consensus decision making

Consensus decision making does not mean that decisions are based on unanimity; rather, decisions are based on the premise that all participants have had an opportunity to express their opinions and are willing to accept the final decision. Operating decisions must be made within a reasonable timeframe. The formal decision-making structure varies with the type of legal structure. Joint ventures often have a board of directors and a management committee that meet quarterly and monthly, respectively. Projects normally are governed by steering committees. Many alliances are started to take advantage of complementary skills or resources available from alliance participants. The alliance can achieve its strategic objective only if all parties to the alliance provide the resources they agreed to commit.

Integrating family-owned firms

The integration process described in this chapter deals with the challenges of combining public firms. Although there are significant similarities when acquiring a family-owned or privately owned firm, the acquirer often is confronted with a range of issues not necessarily found in public firms.

[29] Robson et al. (2019) discuss the link between trust and performance in international strategic alliances.

The acquirer is not just buying a company but also a long history of strong ties between individuals with extensive shared experiences. In such situations, the pace of integration often is much slower than in public firms because the buildup of respect and trust may take much longer.[30] The integrating mechanisms discussed in the previous section for business alliances often apply to integrating family or privately owned firms.

Chapter 10 describes the hurdles associated with such businesses, including primitive internal controls and reporting systems, limited product and customer diversification, and employee interests and time horizons differing from those in public firms. As such, a prudent acquirer may choose to discount the offer price from what they believe to be the true value of the target in recognition of the daunting challenges associated with integrating successfully nonpublic firms.

Some things to remember

Managers in M&As that are successfully integrated often demonstrate leadership by communicating a clear vision, set of values, and priorities to all stakeholder groups. Successful integration efforts are those that are well planned, appoint an integration manager and a team with clearly defined lines of authority, and make the tough decisions early in the process. The focus must be on issues with the greatest near-term impact.

Chapter discussion questions

6.1 Why is the integration phase of the acquisition process considered so important?
6.2 Why should acquired companies be integrated quickly?
6.3 Why is candid and continuous communication so important during the integration phase?
6.4 What messages might be communicated to the various audiences or stakeholders of the new company?
6.5 Cite examples of difficult decisions that should be made early in the integration process.
6.6 When Daimler Benz acquired Chrysler Corporation, it announced that it could take 6 to 8 years to integrate fully the combined firm's global manufacturing operations and certain functions such as purchasing. Speculate as to why it might take that long.
6.7 In your judgment, are acquirers more likely to under- or to overestimate anticipated cost savings? Explain your answer.
6.8 Cite examples of expenses you believe are commonly incurred in integrating target companies. Be specific.
6.9 A common justification for mergers of competitors is the potential cross-selling opportunities it would provide. Comment on the challenges that might be involved in making such a marketing strategy work.
6.10 Billed as a merger of equals, Citibank and Travelers resorted to a co-CEO arrangement when they merged. Why do you think they adopted this arrangement? What are the advantages and disadvantages of such an arrangement?

Answers to these Chapter Discussion Questions are available in the Online Instructor's Manual for instructors using this book.

End-of-chapter case study: culture clash—AT&T buys Time Warner

Case study objectives

To illustrate how

- The challenges of integrating firms with profoundly different corporate cultures
- The likelihood of multiple subcultures existing within diversified firms
- The compromises that must be made to retain creative talent, promote cooperation, and achieve aggressive cost-cutting targets

[30] Meier et al., 2014.

Having received court approval in early 2019 to merge with Time Warner in an $85 billion deal over US Department of Justice DOJ objections, AT&T was finally able to integrate aggressively Time Warner's operations. As a wholly owned subsidiary of AT&T, Time Warner was renamed WarnerMedia, a video-streaming giant whose content includes HBO shows, Cartoon Network, and major box office hits. With legal challenges behind them, AT&T's management was about to move to an even more daunting task: melding disparate, complex, and long-standing corporate cultures while engaging in aggressive cost cutting.

Changing the name of Time Warner to WarnerMedia was symbolic because it was intended to communicate to all stakeholders that past behaviors were about to change. Newly appointed WarnerMedia CEO, John Stankey, stated publicly that he wanted WarnerMedia to resemble other media firms, in which there is more cross-pollination between units. This, of course, would be made more difficult because it was to occur against a backdrop of aggressive cost cutting.

Layoffs were expected as HBO and Turner Entertainment combined and Warner Bros. integrated Turner's animation business. The key was to retain critical talent while streamlining the business's cost structure. The two efforts are often incompatible because retention of the most talented staff often requires increased compensation and perks.

For years, Time Warner executives tried to change its culture, characterized by businesses operating more as independent fiefdoms than part of a larger firm. But its efforts were met with limited success. AT&T was betting that it, as an outside catalyst, it would be able to shake up that culture. How? By undertaking a radical reorganization, which resulted in departures of high-profile Time Warner executives and putting previously shelved plans into action. AT&T had to succeed in altering Time Warner's past behavior if it was to compete successfully against the likes of Netflix Inc., Walt Disney Co., and Comcast Corp.

The reorganization consisted of combining Time Warner's different networks and entertainment businesses in a manner that promised greater creativity and innovation. The new structure effectively broke up Turner, with some assets folded into Warner Bros. and the rest combined with HBO in a new unit called WarnerMedia Entertainment and Direct-to-Consumer.

Other parts of Turner Broadcasting were to be merged with different units as part of the reorganization. Turner's sports operation is now part of WarnerMedia News and Sports. The new company intends to put businesses whose content is centered on children, such as the Cartoon Network and Boomerang channels, under the same management. Turner Classic Movies will also be housed at Warner Bros. By combining Turner's animation with Warner Bros.' DC Entertainment, AT&T is looking to create a new global children's programming and videogame behemoth.

While promoting greater cooperation and innovation, a reorganization of this scale often requires substantial upfront costs, as employees must be moved and collocated with their peers and facilities must be renovated to accommodate new operational requirements. The reorganization also resulted in AT&T's bringing in new management to replace former managers. For example, outsider Robert Greenblatt, former chairman of entertainment at Comcast's NBCUniversal, would run WarnerMedia Entertainment. His philosophy was to manage the new business with a shared vision and set of goals.

This extensive reorganization was to be accomplished while improving sharply the firm's operating cash flow. Why? AT&T had to satisfy the debt service requirements on more than $170 billion on its balance sheet. The firm was projecting annual cost savings of $1.5 billion and an additional $1 billion in revenue-related synergies (i.e., incremental merchandise sales and content licensing fees). The consolidation of several units within WarnerMedia was expected to lead to significant staff reductions to achieve these targets. The cost cutting is likely to be greatest at Turner, which accounted for as much operating income at Time Warner as HBO and Warner Bros. combined. Additional layoffs would add substantially to employee termination expenses and potentially contribute to lower productivity because they can demotivate those who remain.

The pace of the reorganization caught many by surprise because it was announced only a week after AT&T won its court battle against the DOJ. AT&T had been operating WarnerMedia assets since June 2018 when the deal closed while the government sought to overturn a district court verdict that cleared the transaction. AT&T had agreed to leave Time Warner's workforce alone until the litigation was completed. With the DOJ issue resolved, AT&T moved rapidly to improve the firm's cash flow because principal and interest payments were coming due, and much had to be accomplished if the firm had any hope of earning back the premium paid for Time Warner.

Critics of the reorganization worried that the Time Warner culture that allowed HBO to make highly acclaimed content would be gone. WarnerMedia's culture when it was part of Time Warner had been characterized by dispersed control, lavish parties, and a host of perks, benefits that former Time Warner employees would be reluctant to surrender. In contrast, AT&T's serious business-like environment in which authority was highly centralized was foreign to long-time Time Warner employees. It is likely to be some time before many former Time Warner employees are comfortable in the new environment. Those that aren't can be expected to leave.

Creating an effective corporate-wide culture is complicated. Time Warner had grown through numerous acquisitions, each of which with its own distinctive culture. By the late 1990s, three distinct corporate cultures existed: HBO, Turner cable networks, and Warner Bros. studios. HBO rarely acquired shows from Warner Bros. Efforts by Turner to collaborate with HBO on streaming-TV initiatives were fruitless. Despite efforts at the corporate level to promote cooperation among its businesses, little progress was made.

Notwithstanding owning Time Warner in mid-2018, AT&T could do little to deal with its rapidly changing environment because of the government's efforts to unwind the deal on antitrust grounds. For example, the companies were unable to coordinate efforts to combat customer attrition because of cable TV "cord cutting."

Although specific initiatives could not be undertaken until legal issues were resolved, AT&T established brainstorming groups called "workstreams" in which cross-functional groups of employees could address subjects such as marketing and program content. More than 100 employees from Warner Bros, Turner, and HBO analyzed problems and identified possible solutions. A particularly important idea emerged from one of the workstream groups that involved a subscription streaming-video service to compete with Netflix. The service would be driven by HBO, which would access content from the rest of the firm's film and TV libraries.

Despite its blend of distribution channels and attractive content, AT&T was unable to fulfill its vision of becoming a leading media firm spinning off its Time Warner assets to Discovery Inc. in 2021, just 3 years after having completed the takeover. Why? The media landscape had changed too rapidly as consumers shifted from "pay TV" to streaming content from any device. Despite its formidable resources, AT&T could not move quickly enough to overcome the substantial cultural differences between AT&T and Time Warner, while shifting its focus to meet changing competitive market conditions.

Discussion questions

1. What is corporate culture? Why is it important?
2. Should the success or failure of the Time Warner acquisition be judged based on Time Warner operated as a standalone business or as part of implementing AT&T's larger media strategy? Explain your answer.
3. What key external and internal factors are likely to impact AT&T's postmerger integration of Time Warner?
4. What is the key premise on which AT&T's business strategy is based, and why does AT&T believe that cultural differences between the two firms can be overcome? Be specific.
5. If AT&T can fully integrate Time Warner into its operations, do you believe the firm can compete successfully with Netflix? Explain your answer.
6. Why is it often considered critical to integrate the target business quickly? Be specific.

Answers to these questions are found in the Online Instructor's Manual for instructors using this book.

PART III

Mergers and acquisitions valuation and modeling

When abnormally low interest rates persist, central bank policy options are limited, bank margins squeezed, pension funds underfunded, savers penalized, irresponsible risk taking promoted, resources misallocated, and asset valuations inflated. The implications are daunting. With central bank policies continuing to dominate financial markets, traditional valuation and financial modeling methods are subject to severe limitations. The following chapters represent a cautionary tale about how we as analysts should not fall prey to a mechanical acceptance of purely quantitative methods without injecting a substantial amount of judgment.

Chapter 7 explains the economic implications of near-zero or negative interest rates in the context of asset valuation. The chapter begins with a primer on constructing valuation cash flows, calculating discount rates, and commonly used discounted cash flow (DCF) methods. These include the zero-growth, constant-growth, and variable-growth methods. How to value nonoperating assets also is discussed, as are the implications for valuation of changes in US tax laws in 2017. Alternatives to DCF techniques are discussed in Chapter 8, including relative valuation, asset-oriented, and replacement-cost methods. Implicit in the DCF approach to valuation is that management has no flexibility once an investment decision has been made. In practice, management can accelerate, delay, or abandon investments as circumstances change. This flexibility may be reflected in the value of the target firm by adjusting present value for the value of so-called *real options*.

Chapter 9 discusses how to build financial models in the context of mergers and acquisitions (M&As). Such models are helpful in answering questions pertaining to valuation, financing, and deal structuring. (Deal structuring is discussed in detail in Chapters 11 and 12.) Such models may be particularly helpful in determining a range of values for a target firm reflecting different sets of assumptions. Moreover, such models are powerful tools during M&A negotiations, allowing participants to evaluate rapidly the attractiveness of different proposals. (Chapter 15 discusses in detail how complex models are used in deal negotiations.) This chapter also addresses how to include limitations on interest expense deductibility imposed by the Tax Cuts and Jobs Act of 2017.

Finally, Chapter 10 addresses the challenges of valuing privately held firms, which represent the vast majority of firms involved in M&As, and how to adjust purchase prices for illiquidity and noncontrolling interests as well as for the value of control. The process sometimes used to take private firms public and "early stage" investment in emerging businesses are also discussed.

CHAPTER

7

Mergers and acquisitions cash flow valuation basics

OUTLINE

Mergers, Acquisitions, and Other Restructuring Activities, Eleventh Edition
https://doi.org/10.1016/B978-0-12-819782-0.00007-1

Remember, if you need a hand, you'll find it at the end of your arm. —***Audrey Hepburn***

Inside M&As: valuation methods and outcomes in M&A appraisal cases

KEY POINTS

- Dissenting shareholders may have their shares valued by an independent appraiser.
- Recent rulings suggest that courts are more likely to rely on the negotiated deal price as the best estimate of fair value rather than on appraisals.
- Courts have ruled about half of the time that fair value exceeded the deal price; the rest of the time, petitioners had to settle for a valuation at the deal price or lower.

Target firm shareholders need not accept an acquirer's offer price for their shares; instead, they can pursue litigation, hoping to receive a higher price. Because many publicly traded firms are headquartered in Delaware, a large percentage of appraisal rights cases are tried in the Delaware Court of Chancery under Section 262 of the Delaware General Corporation Law. Section 262 allows dissenting shareholders to petition the court to determine fair value for their shares.

After rising since 2006, shareholder appraisal petitions filed yearly with the Delaware Court peaked at 76 in 2016, falling to a low of 26 in 2018. Only 34 of the 433 petitions filed between 2006 and 2018 went to trial. In half of the cases, the court ruled that fair value was above the deal price, with the remaining rulings concluding that fair value was at or below the deal price. For the 16 cases in which a positive premium was awarded, the average premium was 47%.[1]

For deals involving an auction and no participant duress or conflicts of interest, the court ruled consistently that the deal price was the fair value of the dissenters' shares when financial buyers were involved. For strategic buyers in which synergy plays a large role in determining deal price, the court's decisions have varied because strategic buyers are able to make higher offers than financial buyers. In general, when the deal process is viewed as appropriate, the court relies on deal price in financial buyer transactions and the deal price less synergies for strategic buyers.

When the deal price has been compromised, the court consistently relies on the appraised value based on discounted cash flow (DCF), comparable companies, or recent comparable deals regardless of the type of buyer. Over the period from 2006 to 2018, 59% of the appraisal opinions relied on DCF analysis, and 38% relied on deal price in determining fair value. In the remaining instances, the court had no opinion. However, Delaware courts have expressed concerns about the subjectivity of DCF analyses, noting their use of many inputs and the potential for large differences in valuation.

Chapter overview

This chapter provides a review of basic finance concepts, including measuring risk and return, the capital asset pricing model (CAPM), the weighted average cost of capital (WACC), the effects of operating and financial leverage on risk and return, and the implications of near-zero or negative interest rates. How to construct free cash flow to equity (equity cash flow) or to the firm (enterprise cash flow) are discussed in detail as are the conditions in which it is appropriate to use each definition.

[1] Marcus et al., 2019

The advantages and disadvantages of alternative discounted cash flow methods and when they should be applied also are described. In addition, how to select the appropriate discount rate, forecast period, account for the cash impact of deferred taxes, handle contingent liabilities, and the treatment of noncontrolling interests and nonoperating assets are explained. Other valuation methods are discussed in Chapter 8. Despite the reduction in the US corporate tax rate in 2017, this book uses the pre-2017 combined state and local tax rate of 40% because of the uncertainty of future tax rates given the pandemic-induced growth of government deficits. This chapter concludes with a series of discussion questions, practice problems, and a short case study. A review of this chapter is available in the file folder titled "Student Study Guide" in the companion website to this book (https://www.elsevier.com/books-and-journals/book-companion/9780128197820).

Economic implications of negative interest rates

Negative rates imply investors have a greater desire to preserve capital.[2] Such rates have substantial implications for how the economy operates by disrupting traditional financial institutions and reducing monetary policy effectiveness. In addition, negative yields inadequately compensate investors for risk, erode savers' ability to save, sustain firms that otherwise would go bankrupt, and discourage business investment. These considerations are discussed next.

Low or negative yields make it impractical for pension funds and insurance companies to purchase long-term debt whose principal plus accrued interest is sufficient to meet their long-term obligations. Negative yields can also discourage bank lending as profit margins on loans shrink. Why? Banks often are unable to pass along higher deposit rates by raising lending rates.

Rather than reward investors for holding relatively risk-free assets, negative yields encourage investors to hoard cash outside the banking system or seek increasingly higher-risk nonbank investments. This reduces the effectiveness of monetary policy, whose impact is transmitted primarily through the banking system. Monetary authorities in individual countries must push their interest rates lower in line with easier policies in other countries or see their currencies appreciate, thereby making their exports less competitive and imports more expensive.

The search for yield boosts the price of risky assets, forcing their yields lower. Spreads between high-yield debt and risk-free assets are squeezed below historical levels, ensuring that investors are not rewarded for assumed risk. And low interest rates crimp the ability to amass savings using low-risk assets. Although less saving stimulates consumer spending, it undermines saving for retirement, creating a potential future financial crisis among retirees as they seek to invest in higher-risk assets. As investors pile into risky assets, firms that would have gone bankrupt at higher interest rates are able to borrow to meet their cash flow needs. Referred to as "zombie" firms, they continue to use resources that could be better used by others. Finally, as shrinking yields pump up asset prices, valuing accurately assets using common valuation methodologies becomes increasingly difficult, reducing management's confidence in their ability to assess the true financial return on investments. The resulting uncertainty limits new investments or contributes to unproductive investments that waste resources.

Estimating required financial returns

Investors require a minimum rate of return that must be at least equal to what the investor can receive on alternative investments exhibiting a comparable level of perceived risk.

Cost of equity and the capital asset pricing model

The cost of equity (k_e) is the rate of return required to induce investors to purchase a firm's equity. It is a return to shareholders after corporate taxes have been paid but before personal taxes. It may be estimated using the CAPM, which measures the relationship between expected risk and return. Presuming investors require higher rates of return for accepting higher levels of risk, the CAPM states that the expected return on an asset is equal to a risk-free rate of return plus a risk premium.

[2] Arslanalp et al., 2019

A risk-free rate of return is one for which the expected return is free of default risk.[3] Other types of risk remain, such as the reinvestment rate (i.e., the rate of return that can be earned at the end of the investor's holding period), the potential loss of principal if the security is sold before its maturity date (market risk), and the loss of purchasing power due to inflation (inflation risk). Despite widespread agreement on the use of US Treasury securities as assets that are free of default risk, analysts differ over whether a short- or long-term Treasury rate should be applied.

Which rate should be used depends on how long the investor intends to hold the investment. An investor who anticipates holding an investment for 5 or 10 years should use either a 5- or 10-year Treasury bond rate.[4] In this book, a 10-year Treasury bond rate is used as the risk-free rate because it is most appropriate for a strategic or long-term acquirer.

Estimating market risk premiums

The market risk, or equity premium, is the additional return in excess of the risk-free rate investors require to purchase a firm's equity. The risk premium is what the investor demands as compensation for buying a risky asset and is the only factor the basic CAPM model uses to approximate the incremental risk of adding a stock to a diversified portfolio. Although the risk premium should be forward-looking, obtaining precise estimates of future market returns is difficult. Analysts often look to historical data despite results that vary based on the time periods selected and whether returns are calculated as arithmetic or geometric averages. CAPM relates the cost of equity (k_e) to the risk-free rate of return and market risk premium as follows:

$$\text{CAPM}: k_e = R_f + \beta\left(R_m - R_f\right) \tag{7.1}$$

in which

R_f = risk-free rate of return
β = beta (See the section of this chapter titled "Risk Assessment.")[5]
R_m = expected rate of return on equities
$R_m - R_f$ = 5.5% (i.e., risk premium equal to the difference between the return on a diversified portfolio of stocks and the risk-free rate)[6]

Despite its intuitive appeal, studies show that actual returns on risky assets frequently differ significantly from those returns predicted by the CAPM.[7] Because the CAPM measures a stock's risk relative to the overall market and ignores returns on assets other than stocks, some analysts use *multifactor models*.[8] Studies show that of the variables improving the CAPM's accuracy, firm size tends to be among the more important.[9] The size premium serves as a proxy for smaller firms being subject to higher default risk and generally being less liquid than large-capitalization firms. Table 7.1 provides estimates of the adjustment to the cost of equity to correct for firm size based on actual data since 1963.

[3] *Default risk* refers to the degree of certainty that an investor will receive the nominal value of her or his investment plus accumulated interest according to the terms of the agreement with the borrower.

[4] A 3-month Treasury bill rate is not free of risk for a 5- or 10-year period because interest and principal received at maturity must be reinvested at 3-month intervals, resulting in considerable reinvestment risk.

[5] Statistically, a beta measures the variation of an individual stock's return with the overall market as a percent of the variation of the overall market (i.e., the covariance of a stock's return to a broadly defined market index/variance of the broadly defined index).

[6] Fernandez et al. (2018) found that the median and average equity risk premium for about three-fourths of the 59 countries surveyed fell within a range of 5.0% to 7.0%. In the United States, the survey documented a median and average equity risk premium in 2018 used by those surveyed of 5.2% and 5.4%, respectively.

[7] For a summary of the extensive literature discussing CAPM's shortcomings, see Fernandez (2014).

[8] Such models adjust the CAPM by adding other risk factors that determine asset returns, such as firm size, bond default premiums, the bond term structure, and inflation. Fama and French (2015) argue that a five-factor model captures the effects of size, value (market-to-book ratio), profitability, and firm investment better than models using fewer factors but fails to capture the low returns on small stocks whose firms invest heavily despite low profitability. For a discussion of how to judge the efficacy of asset pricing models, see Fama et al. (2018).

[9] Shapovalova et al. (2011)

TABLE 7.1 Size premium estimates

Market value ($000,000)	Percentage points added to CAPM estimate	Book value ($000,000)	Percentage points added to CAPM estimate
>21,889	0	>11,977	0
7,450–21,889	1.4	4467–11,977	1.1
3,024–7,450	2.4	1298–4467	2.1
1,766–3,024	3.4	977–1298	3.2
712–1,766	4.5	402–977	3.9
191–712	5.3	72–402	4.7
<191	7.2	<72	5.6

CAPM, Capital asset pricing model.
Source: Size premium estimates calculated by collapsing Center for Research in Security Prices (CRSP) deciles size premia data available in Grabowski et al. (2017) into seven categories. Pratt et al. (2010) found that small firms displayed a higher premium whether size is measured by market value, book value, or some other performance measure (e.g., operating profit).

Equation 7.1 can be rewritten to reflect an adjustment for firm size as follows:

$$\text{CAPM} : k_e = R_f + \beta\left(R_m - R_f\right) + \text{FSP} \tag{7.2}$$

in which FSP = firm size premium.

Applying CAPM in a near-zero (or negative) interest rate environment

After being stable at about 2% for more than a century, global real interest rates on government debt (i.e., nominal interest rates less expected inflation) have trended sharply lower during the past 3 decades.[10] Exacerbated by the search for both safety and liquidity since the financial crisis of 2008 and 2009, both nominal and real interest rates in many developed countries have been at or near historical lows (and in some instances negative).

Are low interest rates more reflective of anemic global economic growth or central bank policies or both? Some argue that the low interest rate environment is more a result of weak financial market conditions caused by expectations of lackluster economic growth as central banks exert only limited control of short-term interest rates and little influence on long-term interest rates. Others argue that the continuing low interest rate environment reflects the highly aggressive liquidity injections by central banks during this period.

If we believe low interest rates reflect primarily financial market factors such as anemic or uncertain global economic growth, historically low or negative risk-free rates do not bias target firm valuations. Why? Historically low risk-free rates will be offset partially by increasing risk premiums on stocks, keeping the magnitude of the cost of equity stable. If the expected return on stocks remains the same, equity premiums must widen as risk-free rates decline.[11]

To illustrate how changes in the risk-free rate are offset partly by changes in the risk premium, consider the following. Assuming the risk-free rate is −0.5%, the expected return on all stocks is 6%, and the target firm's beta is 1.2, the cost of equity using CAPM is 7.3%, that is, cost of equity = -0.005 + 1.2(0.06 – (−0.005). The cost of equity is little changed at 7.1%, that is, cost of equity = 0.005 + 1.2(0.06 – 0.005) if we use the same assumptions except for a positive 0.5% risk-free rate.

If we believe that interest rates are depressed by central bank policies and do not reflect financial market conditions, application of the CAPM can result in an underestimate of the cost of equity and target firm overvaluation. To minimize this bias, the risk-free rate should be the expected future risk-free rate because the CAPM is predicated on future cash flows and their associated risk. However, any estimation of future interest rates is problematic.

[10] Del Negro et al., 2019

[11] Duarte and Rosa (2015) concluded that increases in the equity risk premium in recent years were a result of declining risk-free interest rates.

A practical alternative is to use an historical average of an appropriate long-term risk-free rate over several decades to capture more than one interest rate cycle. Nonetheless, using an historical average as a proxy for future rates is subjective because of the difficulty determining the appropriate length of the historical time period and may overstate the cost of equity.[12] European respondents to a recent survey indicated they used a risk-free rate higher than their country's 10-year government bond rate. Estimates varied between 1.5% and 3%.[13]

In summary, current low interest rates reflect both sluggish growth and central bank policies. It is doubtful the relative importance of each factor can be determined, because they are interdependent. That is, many central banks continue to aggressively inject liquidity into the financial markets because of slow economic growth, and growth is slow in part because of these bank policies.[14] Without compelling evidence that adjusting CAPM for the current low interest rates provides more reliable estimates, the author recommends using the basic two-factor CAPM, adjusted for firm size if such data are available, to estimate the cost of equity.

Accounting conservatism: too much of a good thing?

A current debate within the accounting and finance community concerns conservative accounting practices and their impact on a firm's cost of equity capital. Proponents argue that such practices reduce information risk (e.g., earnings revisions), the information imbalance between senior management and investors, and earnings manipulation. This in turn lowers a firm's cost of equity. Critics counter that such practices contribute to "earnings surprises" and potentially missed investment opportunities. And recognizing losses on a timely basis can increase the cost of equity by reducing investor earnings expectations for a firm. Yes, conservative accounting can lower the cost of equity, but it should not be overdone.[15]

Pretax cost of debt

Interest is the cost of borrowing and is tax deductible by the firm; in bankruptcy, bondholders are paid before shareholders as the firm's assets are liquidated. Therefore, debt is generally cheaper than equity. Default risk is the likelihood the firm will fail to repay interest and principal when required. Interest paid by the firm on its current debt can be used as an estimate of the current cost of debt if nothing has changed since the firm last borrowed.

When conditions have changed, the analyst must estimate the cost of debt reflecting current market interest rates and default risk. To do so, analysts use the yield to maturity (YTM)[16] of the company's long-term, option-free bonds. This requires knowing the price of the security and its coupon value and face value.[17]

In general, the cost of debt is estimated by calculating the YTM on each of the firm's outstanding bond issues. A weighted average YTM is then computed, with the estimated YTM for each issue weighted by its percentage of total debt outstanding. In Table 7.2, Microsoft's weighted average YTM on the bulk of its long-term debt on January 24, 2011, was 2.4%. The source for the YTM for each debt issue was found in the Financial Industry Regulatory Authority's (FINRA) Trace database: www.finra.org/marketdata.[18]

[12] Using an historical average risk-free rate with today's equity premiums instead of the lower actual current rate may tend to overstate the cost of equity as equity premiums are already high due in part to the uncertainty created by the artificially low interest rate environment. To avoid this bias, the analyst should use the average risk-free rate and equity risk premium over the same historical period in applying CAPM.

[13] Fernandez et al., 2018

[14] Low interest rates can discourage business spending because of difficulty in assessing investment risk, expectations of future slow growth and deflationary pressures, speculative bubbles and capital misallocation, and consumers deferring spending to save more for retirement.

[15] Khalifa et al., 2019

[16] YTM is the internal rate of return on a bond held to maturity, assuming payment of principal and interest, which takes into account the capital gain on a discount bond or capital loss on a premium bond.

[17] YTM is not appropriate for valuing short-term bonds because their term to maturity often is much less than the duration of the company's cash flows. YTM is affected by the bond's cash flows and not those of the firm's; therefore, it is distorted by corporate bonds, which also have conversion or call features, because their value will affect the bond's value but not the value of the firm's cash flows.

[18] FINRA is the largest independent regulator for all securities firms in the United States. For access to financial market data and a more detailed discussion of FINRA, see http://cxa.marketwatch.com/finra/MarketData/CompanyInfo/default.aspx.

TABLE 7.2 Weighted average yield to maturity of Microsoft's long-term debt

Coupon rate (%)	Maturity	Book value (face value in $ millions)	Percentage of total debt	Price (% of par)	Yield to maturity (%)
0.88	9/27/2013	1250	0.25	99.44	1.09
2.95	6/1/2014	2000	0.40	104.27	1.63
4.20	6/1/2019	1000	0.20	105.00	3.50
5.20	6/1/2039	750	0.15	100.92	5.14
		5000	1.00		2.40

YTM represents the most reliable estimate of a firm's cost of debt if the firm's debt is investment grade[19] because the difference between the expected and promised rate of return[20] is small. YTM is a good proxy for actual future returns on investment-grade debt because the potential for default is low. Non–investment-grade debt (rated less than BBB by Standard & Poor's and Baa by Moody's) represents debt with significant default risk. The expected YTM is calculated based on the current market price of the non–investment-grade bond, the probability of default, and the expected recovery rate after default.[21]

When such data are unavailable, the average YTM for a number of similarly rated bonds of other firms can be used. Such bonds include a so-called *default premium,* which reflects the compensation that lenders require over the risk-free rate to buy non–investment-grade debt. For nonrated firms, the analyst could use the cost of debt for rated firms whose debt-to-equity ratios, interest coverage ratios, and operating margins are similar to those of the nonrated firm.[22]

Cost of preferred stock

Preferred stock is similar to long-term debt, in that its dividend is generally constant, and preferred stockholders are paid after debt holders but before common shareholders if the firm is liquidated. Because preferred stock is riskier than debt but less risky than common stock in bankruptcy, the cost to the company to issue preferred stock should be less than the cost of equity but greater than the cost of debt. The cost of preferred stock exceeds that of debt because, with debt, investors are certain to receive the principal if they hold such bonds until maturity.

Viewing preferred dividends as paid in perpetuity, the cost of preferred stock (k_{pr}) can be calculated as dividends per share of preferred stock (d_{pr}) divided by the market value of the preferred stock (PR) (see the section of this chapter titled "Zero-Growth Valuation Model"). If a firm pays a $2 dividend on its preferred stock, whose market value is $50, the firm's cost of preferred stock is 4% (i.e., $2 ÷ $50). The cost of preferred stock can be generalized as follows:

$$k_{pr} = \frac{d_{pr}}{PR} \tag{7.3}$$

[19] Investment-grade bonds are those whose credit quality is considered among the most secure by independent bond-rating agencies: BBB or higher by Standard & Poor's and Baa or higher by Moody's Investors Service.

[20] The promised rate of return assumes that the interest and principal are paid on time.

[21] Titman et al. (2011), pp. 144–147

[22] Much of this information can be found in local libraries in such publications as Moody's Company Data; Standard & Poor's *Descriptions*, the *Outlook*, and *Bond Guide*; and Value Line's *Investment Survey*. In the United States, the FINRA TRACE database also is an excellent source of interest rate information.

Cost of capital

The WACC is the broadest measure of the firm's cost of funds and represents the return that a firm must earn to induce investors to buy its common stock, preferred stock, and bonds. The WACC[23] is calculated using a weighted average of the firm's cost of equity (k_e), cost of preferred stock (k_{pr}), and pretax cost of debt (i):

$$WACC = k_e \frac{E}{D+E+PR} + i(1-t)\frac{D}{D+E+PR} + k_{pr}\frac{PR}{D+E+PR} \quad (7.4)$$

in which

E = the market value of common equity
D = the market value of debt
PR = the market value of preferred stock
t = the firm's marginal tax rate

A portion of interest paid on borrowed funds is recoverable by the firm because of the tax deductibility of interest. For every dollar of taxable income, the tax owed is equal to \$1 multiplied by t. Because each dollar of interest expense reduces taxable income by an equivalent amount, the actual cost of borrowing is reduced by $(1 - t)$. Therefore, the after-tax cost of borrowed funds to the firm is estimated by multiplying the pretax interest rate, i, by $(1 - t)$.

Note the weights $[E/(D + E + PR)]$, $[D/(D + E + PR)]$, and $[PR/(D + E + PR)]$ associated with the cost of equity, preferred stock, and debt, respectively, reflect the firm's target capital structure or capitalization. They are targets because they represent the capital structure the firm hopes to achieve. Market rather than book values are used because the WACC measures the cost of issuing debt, preferred stock, and equity securities, which are issued at market value.

The use of the target capital structure avoids the circular reasoning associated with using the current market value of equity to construct the WACC, which is subsequently used to estimate the firm's current market value. Non—interest-bearing liabilities, such as accounts payable, are excluded from the estimation of the cost of capital for the firm to simplify the calculation of WACC.[24] Estimates of industry betas, cost of equity, and WACC are provided by firms such as Ibbotson Associates, Value Line, Standard & Poor's, and Bloomberg.

Cost of capital with limited interest deductibility

The Tax Cuts and Jobs Act of 2017 reduced the top US corporate tax rate from 35% to 21% beginning in 2018. The marginal US corporate rate is now 26%, consisting of the 21% maximum federal rate plus an average 5% state and local tax rate. Furthermore, net interest expense deductions are capped at 30% of earnings before interest and taxes (EBIT) after 2022.

To incorporate the capping of the tax deductibility of net interest expense into the calculation of WACC, separate total debt into that portion whose interest is tax deductible and the portion whose interest is not.[25] The cost of equity, preferred stock, and debt are denoted by k_e, k_{pr}, and i, respectively. Equation 7.4 can be rewritten as follows:

$$WACC = K_e\, \{E/(D_1+D_2+E+PR)\} + i(1-t)\, \{D_1/(D_1+D_2+E+PR)\} + i\{D_2/(D_1+D_2+E+PR)\} + kp_r\, \{PR/(D_1+D_2+E+PR)\} \quad (7.5)$$

[23] Note that Equation 7.4 calculates WACC assuming the firm has one type of common equity, long-term debt, and preferred stock. This is for illustrative purposes only because a firm may not have any preferred stock and may have many different types of common stock and debt of various maturities.

[24] The cost of capital associated with such liabilities (k_{cl}) is included in the price paid to vendors for purchased products and services and affects cash flow through its inclusion in operating expenses (e.g., the price paid for raw materials). When a firm's current liabilities (CLs) are large, Equation 7.4 could be modified as follows: $WACC = k_e [E/(D + E + PR + CL)] + i (1 - t) [D/(D + E + PR + CL)] + k_{pr} [PR/(D + E + PR + CL)] + k_{cl} [CL/(D + E + PR + CL)]$. Accruals are interest-free and accounts and notes payable have a capital cost approximated by the firm's short-term cost of funds. Because the market and book value of current liabilities are usually similar, book values can be used in calculating the capital cost of current liabilities.

[25] Assume i = \$100 million, D (total debt) = \$2000 million, and EBIT = \$200 million. Tax-deductible interest expense = 0.3 × \$200 million = \$60 million. Tax-deductible debt (D_1) = (\$60/\$100) × \$2000 million = \$1200 million. Non—tax-deductible debt (D_2) = \$2000 million - \$1200 million = \$800 million.

in which

E = the market value of common equity
D_1 = the market value of debt whose interest is tax deductible
D_2= the market value of debt whose interest is not tax deductible
PR = the market value of preferred stock
t = the firm's marginal tax rate

If the firm's net interest expense is expected to be less than or equal to 30% of EBIT, all interest expense is tax deductible, and D_2 in Equation 7.5 is zero. Illustrations in the remainder of this chapter use a marginal tax rate of 40% (reflecting the pre-2017 federal corporate tax rate of 35% plus a 5% state and local tax rate) because the magnitude of the cap on the deductibility of interest could fluctuate periodically with changes in the political parties in power. Changes in the cap do not change the methodology for calculating WACC shown in Equation 7.5.

Risk assessment

Risk is the degree of uncertainty associated with an investment's expected returns. It consists of two components: (1) diversifiable, or nonsystematic, risk (i.e., firm-specific strikes and lawsuits) and (2) nondiversifiable, or systematic, risk (i.e., inflation and war) affecting all firms. Firm-specific risk can be eliminated by investors selecting a portfolio of stocks whose cash flows are uncorrelated.

Estimating beta

Beta (β) is a measure of nondiversifiable risk, or how a firm's financial return changes because of a change in the general stock market's return. Although all stocks are impacted by stock market fluctuations, the extent of the impact on each stock will differ, resulting in wide variation in the magnitude of beta from one stock to the next. Betas are commonly estimated by regressing the percent change in the total return on a specific stock with that of a broadly defined stock market index such as the S&P 500 index. The resulting beta estimated for an individual security incorporates both the security's volatility and its correlation with the overall stock market.

Volatility measures the magnitude of a security's fluctuations relative to the overall stock market, and *correlation* measures the direction. When $\beta = 1$, the stock is as risky as the market; when $\beta < 1$, the stock is less risky; and when $\beta > 1$, the stock is riskier than the market.

The CAPM states that all risk is measured from the perspective of a marginal or incremental investor who is well diversified. Investors are compensated only for risk that cannot be eliminated through diversification (i.e., nondiversifiable, or systematic, risk).[26] Estimates of public company betas may be obtained at abg-analytics.com/stock-betas.shtml finance.yahoo.com, and reuters.com. Alternatively, a firm's beta may be calculated based on the betas of a sample of similar firms at a moment in time, as described in the next section.

Effects of financial and operating leverage on beta

Leverage represents the additional increase (decrease) in profit when a firm's revenue exceeds (falls short of) its fixed expenses and the variable expenses incurred to realize the incremental revenue.[27] Fixed expenses related to a firm's operating activities do not vary with output and include depreciation, rent, and obligations such as employee and vendor contracts that do not vary with production. Fixed expenses related to a firm's financing activities include interest and lease expenses and principal repayments on debt.

Operating leverage refers to how a firm combines fixed and variable expenses (i.e., its ratio of fixed expenses to total costs). It is measured in terms of the increase in operating income caused by an increase in revenue. Operating

[26] Beta in this context applies to the application of CAPM to public firms, where the marginal investor is assumed to be fully diversified. For private firms in which the owner's net worth is disproportionately tied up in the firm, analysts sometimes calculate a total beta, which reflects both systematic and nonsystematic risk. See Chapter 10.

[27] Recall that operating profits equals total revenue less fixed and variable costs. If revenue and fixed and variable costs are $100, $50, and $25 million (variable costs are 25% of revenue), respectively, the firm's operating profits are $25 million. If revenue doubles to $200 million, the firm's profit rises to $100 million (i.e., $200 − $50 − $50).

leverage tends to be greatest in high fixed-cost industries such that fixed costs constitute most of the firm's total costs. After the firm has increased revenue by the amount necessary to cover its fixed expenses, most of each dollar of additional revenue goes to increasing operating profit. Financial leverage describes the way in which a firm combines debt and equity to finance its operations, often measured by its debt-to-equity ratio.

In the absence of debt, the β is called an unlevered β, denoted β_u. β_u is determined by the firm's operating leverage and by the type of industry in which the firm operates (e.g., cyclical or noncyclical). If a firm borrows, the unlevered beta must be adjusted to reflect the risk that the firm may not be able to repay the debt when due. By borrowing, the firm is able to invest more in its operation without increasing equity, resulting in a proportionately larger return to equity holders. The resulting beta is called a leveraged or levered β, denoted β_l. Both operating and financial leverage increase the volatility of a firm's profits and financial returns.

Table 7.3 illustrates the effects of operating leverage on financial returns. The three cases reflect the same level of fixed expenses but varying levels of revenue and the impact on financial returns. The illustration assumes in case 1 that the firm's total costs is 80% of revenue and that fixed expenses comprise 60% of the total costs. Note the volatility of the firm's return on equity resulting from fluctuations of 25% in the firm's revenue in cases 2 and 3.

Table 7.4 shows how financial leverage increases the volatility of a firm's financial returns. This is because equity's share of total capital declines faster than the decline in net income as debt's share of total capital increases. The three cases in the table reflect varying levels of debt but the same EBIT. Between case 1 and case 3, net income declines by one-fourth, and equity declines by half, magnifying the impact on returns.

TABLE 7.3 How operating leverage affects financial returns[a]

	Case 1	Case 2: revenue increases by 25%	Case 3: revenue decreases by 25%
Revenue	100	125	75
Fixed	48	48	48
Variable[b]	32	40	24
Total cost of sales	80	88	72
Earnings before taxes	20	37	3
Tax liability at 40%	8	14.8	1.2
After-tax earnings	12	22.2	1.8
Firm equity	100	100	100
Return on equity (%)	12	22.2	1.8

[a]All figures are in millions of dollars unless otherwise noted.
[b]In case 1, variable costs represent 32% of revenue. Assuming this ratio is maintained, variable costs in cases 2 and 3 are estimated by multiplying total revenue by 0.32.

TABLE 7.4 How financial leverage affects financial returns[a]

	Case 1: no debt	Case 2: 25% debt to total capital	Case 3: 50% debt to total capital
Equity	100	75	50
Debt	0	25	50
Total capital	100	100	100
Earnings before interest and taxes	20	20	20
Interest at 10%	0	2.5	5
Income before taxes	20	17.5	15
Less income taxes @ 40%	8	7.0	6
After-tax earnings	12	10.5	9
After-tax returns on equity (%)	12	14	18

[a]All figures are in millions of dollars unless otherwise noted.

If a firm's stockholders bear all the risk from operating and financial leverage and interest paid on debt is tax deductible, then leveraged and unleveraged betas can be calculated as follows for a firm whose debt-to-equity ratio is denoted by D/E:

$$\beta_1 = \beta_u[1 + (1 - t)(D/E)] \tag{7.6}$$

and

$$\beta_u = \beta_1[1 + (1 - t)(D/E)] \tag{7.7}$$

Shareholders view risk as the potential for a firm not to earn sufficient future cash flow to satisfy their minimum required returns. Equation 7.6 implies that increases in a firm's leverage, denoted by D/E, will increase risk, as measured by the firm's levered beta because the firm's interest payments represent fixed expenses that must be paid before payments can be made to shareholders. This increased risk is offset somewhat by the tax deductibility of interest, which increases after-tax cash flow available for shareholders. Thus, the levered beta will increase with an increase in leverage and decrease with an increase in tax rates.

In summary, β_u is determined by the characteristics of the industry in which the firm competes and the firm's degree of operating leverage. The value of β_l is determined by the same factors and the degree of the firm's financial leverage. Our objective is to estimate a beta reflecting the relationship between future risk and return. Estimating beta using historical data assumes the historical relationship will hold in the future.

An alternative to using historical data is to estimate beta using a sample of similar firms and applying Equations 7.6 and 7.7. Referred to as the "bottoms-up" approach, this three-step process suggests that the target firm's beta reflects the business risk (cyclicality and operating leverage only) of the average firm in the industry better than its own historical risk–return relationship. Step 1 requires selecting firms with similar cyclicality and operating leverage (i.e., firms usually in the same industry). Step 2 involves calculating the average unlevered beta for firms in the sample to eliminate the effects of their current financial leverage on their betas. Finally, in step 3, we relever the average unlevered beta using the debt-to-equity ratio and the marginal tax rate of the target firm to reflect its capital structure and tax rate.

Network equipment and storage company Brocade Communications Systems' beta estimated using historical data is 0.88, and its current debt-to-equity ratio is 0.256. Assume analysts believe that the firm's levered beta estimated in this manner is too low. Using a representative data networking and storage industry sample, the firm's levered beta is estimated to be 1.50 using the "bottoms-up" methodology (Table 7.5).

Using Equations 7.6 and 7.7, the effects of different amounts of leverage on the cost of equity also can be estimated.[28] The process is as follows:

TABLE 7.5 Estimating Brocade Communications Systems' (Brocade) beta using the "bottoms-up" approach

Step 1: Select a sample of firms having similar cyclicality and operating leverage.			Step 2: Compute the average of the firms' unlevered betas.	Step 3: Relever average unlevered beta using Brocade's debt-to-equity ratio.
Firm	Levered beta[a]	Debt-to-equity ratio[a]	Unlevered beta[b]	Brocade relevered beta[c]
EMC	1.62	0.301	1.37	NA
Sandisk	1.44	0.285	1.23	NA
Western Digital	1.51	0.273	1.30	NA
NetApp Inc.	1.83	0.254	1.59	NA
Terredata	1.12	0.149	1.03	NA
			1.30	1.50

[a]Yahoo! Finance. Beta estimates are based on the historical relationship between the firm's share price and a broadly defined stock index.
[b]$\beta_u = \beta_l / [1 + (1 - t)(D/E)]$, in which β_u and β_l are unlevered and levered betas, respectively; the marginal tax rate is 0.4. For example, the unlevered beta for EMC = $\beta_u = 1.62/[1+(1-.4).301] = 1.37$
[c]$\beta_l = \beta_u [1 + (1 - t)(D/E)]$. Using Brocade's debt-to-equity ratio of 0.256 and marginal tax rate of 0.4, Brocade's relevered beta = $1.30[1 + (1 - 0.4)0.256] = 1.50$.
NA, Not applicable.

[28] The re-estimation of a firm's beta to reflect a change in leverage requires that we first deleverage the firm to remove the effects of the firm's current level of debt on its beta and then releverage the firm using its new level of debt to estimate the new levered beta.

EXHIBIT 7.1

Estimating the Impact of Changing Debt Levels on the Cost Of Equity

Assume that a target's current or preacquisition debt-to-equity ratio is 25%, the current levered beta is 1.05, and the marginal tax rate is 0.4. After the acquisition, the debt-to-equity ratio is expected to rise to 75%. What is the target's postacquisition levered beta?

Answer: Using Equations 7.6 and 7.7:

$$\beta_u = \beta_l/[1+(1-t)(D/E)*] = 1.05/[1+(1-0.4)\ (0.25)] = 0.91$$

$$\beta_l = \beta_u[1+(1-t)(D/E)**] = 0.91/[1+(1-0.4)\ (0.75)] = 1.32$$

in which $(D/E)^*$ and $(D/E)^{**}$ are, respectively, the target's preacquisition and postacquisition debt-to-equity ratios and β_l^* is the target's preacquisition beta.

1. Determine a firm's current equity β^* and $(D/E)^*$.
2. Estimate the unlevered beta to eliminate the effects of the firm's current capital structure: $\beta_u = \beta^*/[1 + (1 - t)(D/E)^*]$
3. Estimate the firm's levered beta: $\beta_l = \beta_u\ [1 + (1 - t)(D/E)^{**}]$.
4. Estimate the firm's cost of equity for the new levered beta.

in which β^* and $(D/E)^*$ represent the firm's current beta and the market value of the firm's debt-to-equity ratio before additional borrowing takes place, respectively. $(D/E)^{**}$ is the firm's debt-to-equity ratio after additional borrowing occurs, and t is the firm's marginal tax rate.

In an acquisition, an acquirer may anticipate increasing the target firm's debt level after closing. To determine the impact on the target's beta of the increased leverage, the target's levered beta, which reflects its preacquisition leverage, must be converted to an unlevered beta, reflecting the target firm's operating leverage and the cyclicality of the industry in which the firm competes. To measure the increasing risk associated with new borrowing, the resulting unlevered beta is then used to estimate the levered beta for the target firm (Exhibit 7.1).

Calculating free cash flows

Common definitions of cash flow used for valuation are free cash flow to the firm (FCFF), or enterprise cash flow, and free cash flow to equity investors (FCFE), or equity cash flow. Referred to as valuation cash flows, they are constructed by adjusting generally accepted accounting principles (GAAP) cash flows for noncash factors.

Free cash flow to the firm (enterprise cash flow)

FCFF is the cash available to satisfy all investors holding claims against the firm's resources. Claim holders include common stockholders, lenders, and preferred stockholders. Consequently, enterprise cash flow is calculated before the sources of financing are determined and is not affected by the firm's financial structure.[29]

FCFF is calculated by adjusting operating EBIT as follows:

$$\text{FCFF} = \text{EBIT}\ (1 - \text{Tax rate}) + \text{Depreciation and amortization} - \text{Gross capital expenditures} - \Delta\ \text{Net working capital} \quad (7.8)$$

[29] In practice, the financial structure may affect the firm's cost of capital and therefore its value because of the potential for bankruptcy (see Chapter 18).

Only cash flow from operating and investment activities, but not from financing, is included because this is what is available to pay those providing funds to the firm. The tax rate is the marginal rate. Net working capital is current operating assets (excluding cash balances above that required to meet normal operations) less current operating liabilities.[30] Depreciation and amortization expenses are not actual cash outlays and are added to operating income in calculating cash flow.

Selecting the right tax rate

The correct tax rate is the firm's marginal rate (i.e., the rate paid on each additional dollar of earnings) or its effective tax rate (i.e., taxes due divided by taxable income). The effective rate is usually less than the marginal rate due to the use of tax credits to reduce actual taxes paid or accelerated depreciation to defer tax payments. After tax credits have been used and the ability to defer taxes has been exhausted, the effective rate can exceed the marginal rate in the future.

Effective rates lower than the marginal rate may be used in the early years of cash flow projections if the current favorable tax treatment is likely to continue into the foreseeable future, and eventually the effective rates may be increased to the firm's marginal tax rate. It is critical to use the marginal rate in calculating after-tax operating income in perpetuity. Otherwise, the implicit assumption is that taxes can be deferred indefinitely.

Dealing with operating leases

Before 2019, firms did not have to record operating leases on the balance sheet; instead, the lease charge was recorded as an expense on the income statement, and future lease commitments were recorded in footnotes to the firm's financial statements. Beginning in 2019, the Financial Accounting Standards Board requires firms paying to lease real estate, office equipment, aircraft, or similar items to show leases on the balance sheet. Leasing is likely to get a boost from the 2017 Tax Cuts and Jobs Act, which caps interest expense.

Free cash flow to equity investors (equity cash flow)

FCFE is cash flow available for returning cash through dividends or share repurchases to current common equity investors or for reinvesting in the firm after the firm satisfies all obligations. These include debt payments, capital expenditures, changes in net working capital, and preferred dividend payments. FCFE can be defined as follows:

$$\begin{aligned}\text{FCFE} = {} & \text{Net income} + \text{Depreciation and amortization} - \text{Gross capital expenditures} - \Delta\,\text{Net working capital} \\ & + \text{New debt and preferred equity issues} - \text{Principal repayments} - \text{Preferred dividends}\end{aligned} \quad (7.9)$$

Exhibit 7.2 summarizes the key elements of enterprise cash flow (Equation 7.8) and equity cash flow (Equation 7.9). Note that equity cash flow reflects operating, investment, and financing activities, whereas enterprise cash flow excludes cash flow from financing.

Applying discounted cash flow methods

DCF methods provide estimates of firm value at a moment in time, which do not need to be adjusted if the intent is to acquire a small portion of the company. However, if the intention is to obtain a controlling interest, a control premium must be added to determine the purchase price.[31]

Enterprise discounted cash flow model (enterprise or FCFF method)

The enterprise valuation, or FCFF, approach discounts after-tax free cash flow from operations the weighted average cost of capital to obtain the estimated enterprise value. The enterprise value (often referred to as firm value)

[30] Negative net working capital is unlikely to be sustainable and should be set to zero.

[31] A controlling interest is considered more valuable to an investor than a noncontrolling interest because the investor has the right to approve important decisions affecting the business.

EXHIBIT 7.2

Defining Valuation Cash Flows: Equity and Enterprise Cash Flows

Free cash flow to common equity investors (equity cash flow: FCFE)

FCFE = {Net income + Depreciation and amortization − Δ Working capital}[a] − Gross capital expenditures[b] + {New preferred equity issues − Preferred dividends + New debt issues − Principal repayments}[c]

⇨ Cash flow (after taxes, debt repayments and new debt issues, preferred dividends, preferred equity issues, and all reinvestment requirements) available for paying dividends and/or repurchasing common equity.

Free cash flow to the firm (enterprise cash flow: FCFF)

FCFF = {Earnings before interest and taxes (1 − Tax rate) + Depreciation and amortization − Δ Working capital}[a] − Gross capital expenditures[b]

⇨ Cash flow (after taxes and reinvestment requirements) available to repay lenders and/or pay common and preferred dividends and repurchase equity.

[a] Cash from operating activities.
[b] Cash from investing activities.
[c] Cash from financing activities.

represents the sum of investor claims on the firm's cash flows from all those holding securities, including long-term debt, preferred stock, common shareholders, and noncontrolling shareholders. Because it reflects all claims, it is a much more accurate estimate of a firm's takeover value than the market value of a firm's equity. For example, in addition to buying a target firm's equity, an acquirer would generally have to assume responsibility for paying off the target firm's debt and preferred stock.

Because the enterprise DCF model estimates the present value of cash flows, the enterprise value also can be estimated as the market value of the firm's common equity plus long-term debt, preferred stock, and noncontrolling interest less cash and cash equivalents. The firm's common equity value can be determined by subtracting the market value of the firm's debt and other investor claims on cash flow, such as preferred stock and noncontrolling interest, from the enterprise value.[32] The enterprise method is used when information about the firm's debt repayment schedules or interest expense is limited.

Equity discounted cash flow model (equity or FCFE method)

The equity valuation, or FCFE, approach discounts the after-tax cash flows available to the firm's shareholders at the cost of equity. This approach is more direct than the enterprise method when the objective is to value the firm's equity. The enterprise, or FCFF, method and the equity, or FCFE, method are illustrated in the following sections of this chapter using three cash flow growth scenarios: zero-growth, constant-growth, and variable-growth rates.

The zero-growth valuation model

This model assumes that free cash flow is constant in perpetuity. The value of the firm at time zero (P_0) is the discounted or capitalized value of its annual cash flow.[33] The subscript FCFF or FCFE refers to the definition of cash flow used in the valuation.

[32] Equity estimates derived this way equal the value of equity determined by discounting the cash flow available to the firm's shareholders at the cost of equity if assumptions about cash flow and discount rates are consistent.

[33] The present value of a constant payment in perpetuity is a diminishing series as it represents the sum of the PVs for each future period. Each PV is smaller than the preceding one; therefore, the perpetuity is a diminishing series that converges to 1 divided by the discount rate.

EXHIBIT 7.3

The Zero-Growth Valuation Model

1. What is the enterprise value of a firm whose annual $FCFF_0$ of $1 million is expected to remain constant in perpetuity and whose cost of capital is 12% (see Equation 7.10)?

$$P_{0,FCFF} = \$1/0.12 = \$8.3 \text{ million}$$

2. Calculate the weighted average cost of capital (see Equation 7.4) and the enterprise value of a firm whose capital structure consists only of common equity and debt. The firm desires to limit its debt to 30% of total capital.[a] The firm's marginal tax rate is 0.4, and its beta is 1.5. The corporate bond rate is 8%, and the 10-year US Treasury bond rate is 5%. The expected annual return on stocks is 10%. Annual FCFF is expected to remain at $4 million indefinitely.

$$k_e = 0.05 + 1.5\,(0.10 - 0.05) = 0.125 \times 100 = 12.5\%$$

$$WACC = 0.125 \times 0.7 + 0.08 \times (1 - 0.4) \times 0.3$$
$$= 0.088 + 0.014 = 0.102 = 10.2\%$$

$$P_{0,FCFF} = \$4/0.102 = \$39.2 \text{ million}$$

[a] If the analyst knows a firm's debt-to-equity ratio (D/E), it is possible to calculate the firm's debt-to-total capital ratio $[D/(D+E)]$ by dividing (D/E) by ($1 + D/E$) because $D/(D+E) = (D/E)/(1 + D/E) = [(D/E)/(D+E)/E] = (D/E) \times (E/D+E) = D/(D+E)$.

FCFF, Free cash flow to the firm.

$$P_{0,FCFF} = FCFF_0/WACC \tag{7.10}$$

in which $FCFF_0$ is free cash flow to the firm at time 0 and WACC is the cost of capital.

$$P_{0,FCFE} = FCFE_0/k_e \tag{7.11}$$

in which $FCFE_0$ is free cash flow to common equity at time 0 and k_e is the cost of equity.

Although simplistic, the zero-growth method is easily understood by all parties to the deal. There is little evidence that complex methods provide consistently better valuation estimates because of their requirement for more inputs and assumptions. This method often is used to value commercial real estate transactions and small, privately owned businesses (Exhibit 7.3).

The constant-growth valuation model

The constant-growth model is applicable for firms in mature markets, characterized by a somewhat predictable rate of growth. Examples include beverages, cosmetics, personal care products, prepared foods, and cleaning products.

To project growth rates, extrapolate the industry's growth rate over the past 5 to 10 years. The constant-growth model assumes that cash flow grows at a constant rate, g, which is less than the required return, k_e. The assumption that k_e is greater than g is a necessary mathematical condition for deriving the model. In this model, next year's cash flow to the firm ($FCFF_1$), or the first year of the forecast period, is expected to grow at the constant rate of growth, g.[34] Therefore, $FCFF_1 = FCFF_0\,(1 + g)$:

$$P_{0,FCFF} = FCFF_1/(WACC - g) \tag{7.12}$$

$$P_{0,FCFE} = FCFE_1/(k_e - g) \tag{7.13}$$

in which $FCFE_1 = FCFE_0\,(1 + g)$.

This simple valuation model also provides an estimate of the risk premium component of the cost of equity as an alternative to relying on historical information, as is done in the capital asset-pricing model. This model was

[34] Note that the zero-growth model is a special case of the constant-growth model for which g = 0.

EXHIBIT 7.4

The Constant-Growth Model

1. Determine the enterprise value of a firm whose projected free cash flow to the firm (enterprise cash flow) *next* year is $1 million, WACC is 12%, and expected annual cash flow growth rate is 6% (see Equation 7.12).

$$P_{0,FCFF} = \$1/(0.12 - 0.06) = \$16.7 \text{ million}$$

2. Estimate the equity value of a firm whose cost of equity is 15% and whose free cash flow to equity holders (equity cash flow) in the *prior* year is projected to grow 20% this year and then at a constant 10% annual rate thereafter. The prior year's free cash flow to equity holders is $2 million.

$$P_{0,FCFE} = [(\$2.0 \times 1.2)(1.1)]/(0.15 - 0.10) = \$52.8 \text{ million}$$

WACC, Weighted average cost of capital.

developed originally to estimate the value of stocks in the current period (P_0) using the level of expected dividends (d_1) in the next period. It estimates the present value (PV) of dividends growing at a constant rate forever. Assuming the stock market values stocks correctly and that we know P_0, d_1, and g, we can estimate k_e. Therefore,

$$P_0 = d_1/(k_e - g) \text{ and } k_e = (d_1 / P_0) + g \quad (7.14)$$

For example, if d_1 is $1, g is 10%, and $P_0 = \$10$, then k_e is 20%. See Exhibit 7.4 for an illustration of how to apply the constant-growth model.[35]

The variable-growth (supernormal or nonconstant) valuation model

Many firms experience periods of high growth followed by a period of slower, more stable growth. Examples include cellular phone, personal computer, and cable TV firms. Such firms experienced double-digit growth rates for periods of 5 to 10 years because of low penetration early in the product's life cycle. As the market becomes saturated, growth slows to a rate more in line with the overall growth of the economy or the general population.

The PV of such firms is equal to the sum of the PV of the discounted cash flows during the high-growth period plus the discounted value of the cash flows generated during the stable-growth period. The discounted value of the cash flows generated during the stable-growth period is often called the terminal, sustainable, horizon, or continuing-growth value.

The terminal value may be estimated using the constant-growth model.[36] Free cash flow during the first year beyond the *n*th or final year of the forecast period, $FCFF_{n+1}$, is divided by the difference between the assumed cost of capital and the expected cash flow growth rate beyond the *n*th-year forecast period. The terminal value is the PV in the *n*th year of all future cash flows beyond the *n*th year. To convert the terminal value to its value in the current year, use the discount rate used to convert the *n*th-year value to a present value.

Small changes in assumptions can result in dramatic swings in the terminal value and firm valuation. Table 7.6 illustrates the sensitivity of a terminal value of $1 million to different spreads between the cost of capital and the stable growth rate. Note that, using the constant-growth model formula, the terminal value declines dramatically

[35] Launhardt and Miebs (2019) discuss ways of estimating the cost of capital using equity index options.

[36] The use of the constant-growth model provides consistency because the discounted cash flow methodology is used during both the variable- and stable-growth periods.

TABLE 7.6 Impact of changes in assumptions on a terminal value of $1 million

Difference between cost of capital and cash flow growth rate	Terminal value ($ millions)
3%	33.3[a]
4%	25.0
5%	20.0
6%	16.7
7%	14.3

[a]$1.0/0.03.

as the spread between the cost of capital and expected stable growth for cash flow increases by 1 percentage point.[37]

Using the definition of free cash flow to the firm, $P_{0,\text{FCFF}}$ can be estimated using the variable-growth model as follows:

$$P_{0,\text{FCFF}} = \sum_{t=1}^{n} \frac{\text{FCFF}_0(1+g_t)^t}{(1+\text{WACC})^t} + \frac{P_n}{(1+\text{WACC})^n} \tag{7.15}$$

in which

$$P_n = \frac{\text{FCFF}_n(1+g_m)}{\text{WACC}_m - g_m}$$

FCFF_0 = FCFF in year 0
WACC = weighted average cost of capital through year n
WACC_m = cost of capital assumed beyond year n (Note: WACC > WACC_m.)
P_n = value of the firm at the end of year n (terminal value)
g_t = growth rate through year n
g_m = stabilized or long-term growth rate beyond year n (Note: $g_t > g_m$.)

Similarly, the value of the firm to equity investors can be estimated using Equation 7.16 with projected FCFE discounted using the firm's cost of equity.

The cost of capital differs between the high-growth and stable-growth periods when applying the variable-growth model. High-growth rates usually are associated with increased levels of uncertainty. A high-growth firm may have a beta above 1, but when the growth rate stabilizes, we can assume the beta should be near 1. A reasonable approximation of the discount rate to be used during the stable-growth period is to adopt the industry average cost of capital.

Equation 7.16 can be modified to use the growing-annuity model[38] to approximate the high-growth and terminal periods. This formulation requires fewer computations if the number of annual cash flow projections is large. As such, $P_{0,\text{FCFF}}$ also can be estimated as follows:

$$P_{0,\text{FCFF}} = \frac{\text{FCFF}_0(1+g)}{\text{WACC} - g}\left[1 - \left(\frac{1+g}{1+\text{WACC}}\right)^n\right] + \frac{P_n}{(1+\text{WACC})^n} \tag{7.16}$$

Exhibit 7.5 illustrates how to apply the variable-growth and growing annuity models.

[37] Terminal value also may be estimated using price-to-earnings, price-to-cash flow, or price-to-book ratios to value the target as if it were sold at the end of a specific number of years. At the end of the forecast period, the terminal year's earnings, cash flow, or book value is projected and multiplied by a multiple appropriate for that year.

[38] Ross et al. (2009), pp. 238–240.

EXHIBIT 7.5

The Variable-Growth Valuation Model

Estimate the enterprise value of a firm (P_0) whose free cash flow is projected to grow at a compound annual average rate of 35% for the next 5 years. Growth is expected to slow to a more normal 5% annual rate. The current year's cash flow to the firm is $4 million. The firm's weighted average cost of capital during the high-growth period is 18% and 12% beyond the fifth year. The firm's cash in excess of normal operating balances is zero. Using Equation 7.16 the PV of cash flows during the high-growth five-year forecast period (PV_{1-5}) is calculated as follows:

$$PV_{1-5} = \frac{\$4.00 \times 1.35}{1.18} + \frac{\$4.00 \times (1.35)^2}{(1.18)^2} + \frac{\$4.00 \times (1.35)^3}{(1.18)^3} + \frac{\$4.00 \times (1.35)^4}{(1.18)^4} + \frac{\$4.00 \times (1.35)^5}{(1.18)^5}$$

$$= \frac{\$5.40}{1.18} + \frac{\$7.29}{(1.18)^2} + \frac{\$9.84}{(1.18)^3} + \frac{\$13.29}{(1.18)^4} + \frac{\$17.93}{(1.18)^5}$$

$$= \$4.58 + \$5.24 + \$5.99 + \$6.85 + \$7.84 = \$30.50$$

Calculation of the terminal value (PV_{TV}) is as follows:

$$PV_{TV} = \frac{[\$4.00 \times (1.35)^5 \times 1.05]/(0.12 - 0.05)}{(1.18)^5}$$

$$= \frac{\$18.83/0.07}{2.29} = \$117.60$$

$$P_{0,FCFF} = P_{1-5} + PV_{TV} = \$30.50 + \$117.60 = \$148.10$$

Using the growing annuity model [see Eq. (7.16)], the PV of free cash flow to the firm is estimated as follows:

$$PV = \frac{\$4.00 \times 1.35}{0.18 - 0.35} \times \left\{1 - [(1.35/1.18)]^5\right\} + \frac{[\$4.00 \times (1.35) \times 1.05]^5/(0.12 - 0.05)}{(1.18)^5}$$

$$= \$30.50 + \$117.60$$

$$= \$148.10$$

Determining the duration of the high-growth period

Projected growth rates for sales, profit, and cash flow can be calculated based on the historical experience of the firm or industry or surveying security analyst projections.[39] Recent research suggests that Wall Street analyst forecasts tend to be more accurate in projecting financial performance than simply looking at past performance.[40]

The high-growth period should be longer when the current growth rate of a firm's cash flow is much higher than the stable-growth rate and the firm's market share is small. For example, if the industry is expected to grow at 5% annually and the target firm, which has a negligible market share, is growing at three times that rate, it may be appropriate to assume a high-growth period of 5 to 10 years. If the terminal value constitutes more than 75% of the total PV, the annual forecast period should be extended beyond 5 years to at least 10 to reduce its impact on the total market value. Sales and profitability tend to revert to normal levels within 5 to 10 years.[41]

Determining the stable or sustainable growth rate

The stable growth rate generally is less than or equal to the overall growth rate of the industry in which the firm competes or the general economy. Stable growth rates above these levels implicitly assume the firm's cash flow eventually will exceed that of its industry or the economy. For multinational firms, the stable growth rate should not exceed the projected growth rate for the world economy or a particular region of the world.

[39] The availability of analysts' projections is likely to decline in the future as global investment firms are moving rapidly to align their practices with the European Union regulation titled Markets in Financial Instruments Directive (MiFID). Investment firms have historically offered their customers "free" research reports in exchange for a minimum amount of trading volume. MiFID makes such practices unacceptable. With customers unwilling to pay for research, firms are reducing the number of industry analysts and the availability of research.

[40] Khimich, 2017

[41] Palepu et al., 2004

Determining the appropriate discount rate

Choosing the right discount rate is critical to accurately valuing the target. Surveys show that many acquirers use a single firm-wide WACC to value target firms because of its simplicity. This is problematic when the acquirer has many lines of business and fails to use the WACC associated with each line of business.[42] The correct discount rate is the target's cost of capital if the acquirer is merging with a higher-risk business. However, either the acquirer's or the target's cost of capital may be used if the two firms are equally risky and based in the same country.

The impact of "black swan" events such as coronavirus

Catastrophic incidents such as pandemics impact valuation by increasing the uncertainty associated with future cash flows and can be incorporated by either adjusting projected cash flow growth rates, discount rates, or both. An important assumption is the expected duration of such events. Because investors often overreact, an analyst may reduce the projected cash flow growth rate during the early years and increase the rate during the outer years of the forecast period to reflect a "rebound effect." Alternatively, the discount rate can be raised in the early years and reduced near the end of the forecast period.[43]

Valuing unicorns

Unicorns are privately held start-up companies with a market value exceeding $1 billion. Examples include ride sharing firm Uber, space travel company SpaceX, and fintech firm Robin Hood. They are usually big money losers, with their current valuation based totally on the perceived potential of a valuable proprietary technology or novel product or service offering. Given the uniqueness of the business, there often are no comparable companies with which to compare the unicorn and few metrics with which to value it. Thus, valuation is dependent almost totally on projected financials based on highly speculative assumptions. One way of determining the reasonableness of a unicorn's current valuation is to determine the profit required to support its $1-billion-plus value. For example, if you believe a business could earn $150 million in profit in 10 years, its future value assuming a multiple of 12 would be $1.8 billion. Discounting at 8%, PV would be $834 million, well below its current $1-billion-plus valuation.[44]

Using the enterprise method to estimate equity value

A firm's common equity value often is calculated by estimating its enterprise value, adding the value of nonoperating assets, and then deducting nonequity claims on cash flows. Such claims include long-term debt, deferred taxes, unfunded pension liabilities, preferred stock, employee options, and noncontrolling interests. What follows is a discussion of how to value nonequity claims and nonoperating assets. This approach is especially useful when a firm's capital structure (i.e., debt-to–total capital ratio) is expected to remain stable.

Determining the market value of long-term debt

The current value of a firm's debt generally is independent of its enterprise value for financially healthy companies. This is not true for financially distressed firms and for hybrid securities.

Financially stable firms

If the debt repayment schedule is unknown, the market value of debt may be estimated by treating the book value of the firm's debt as a conventional coupon bond, in which interest is paid annually or semiannually and the principal is repaid at maturity. The coupon is the interest on all of the firm's debt, and the principal at maturity is a weighted average of the maturity of all of the debt outstanding. The weighted average principal at maturity is the sum of the amount of debt outstanding for each maturity date multiplied by its share of total debt outstanding.

[42] Kruger et al., 2015

[43] See Chapter 14 for a discussion of how to calculate present value when the discount rate varies.

[44] This calculation assumes implicitly that cumulative cash flows during the 10 years net to zero.

The estimated current market value of the debt is calculated as the sum of the annuity value of the interest expense per period plus the PV of the principal (Exhibit 7.6).[45]

The book value of debt may be used unless interest rates have changed since the debt was incurred or default risk is high. If interest rates have risen since the debt was issued, the value of existing bonds falls as the higher interest rates on the newly issued bonds pay more than older ones. In these situations, value each bond issued by the firm separately by discounting cash flows at yields to maturity for similarly rated debt with similar maturities issued by comparable firms. Book value also may be used for floating-rate debt because its market value is unaffected by fluctuations in interest rates.[46]

Financially distressed firms

For such firms, the value of debt and equity reflect the risk of the firm's cash flows. As such, debt and equity are not independent. And the calculation of a firm's equity value cannot be estimated by subtracting the market value of the firm's debt from its enterprise value. One solution is to estimate the firm's enterprise value using two scenarios: one in which the firm is able to return to financial health and one in which the firm deteriorates. For each scenario, calculate the firm's enterprise value and deduct the book value of the firm's debt and other nonequity claims. Weight each scenario by the probability the analyst attaches to each scenario, such that the resulting equity value estimate represents the expected value of the scenarios.

Hybrid securities (convertible bonds and preferred stock)

Convertible bonds and stock represent conventional debt and preferred stock plus a call option to convert them to shares of common equity at a stipulated price per share. Because the value of the debt reflects the value of common equity, it is not independent of the firm's enterprise value and therefore cannot be deducted from the firm's enterprise value to estimate equity value. One approach to valuing such debt and preferred stock is to assume that all of it will be converted into equity when a target firm is acquired. This makes sense when the offer price for the target exceeds the price per share at which the debt can be converted. See Table 15.12 in Chapter 15 for an illustration of this method.

Determining the cash impact of deferred taxes

Deferred tax assets and liabilities arise when the tax treatment of an item is temporarily different from its financial accounting treatment. Such taxes may result from uncollectible accounts receivable, warranties, options expensing, pensions, leases, net operating losses, depreciable assets, and inventories. A deferred tax asset is a future tax benefit. Deductions not allowed in the current period may be realized in a future period. A deferred tax liability represents the increase in taxes payable in future years. The excess of accelerated depreciation taken for tax purposes over straight-line depreciation, often used for financial reporting, reduces the firm's current tax liability but increases future tax liabilities when spending on plant and equipment slows. The amount of the deferred tax liability equals the excess of accelerated over straight-line depreciation times the firm's marginal tax rate.

To estimate a firm's equity value, the PV of net deferred tax liabilities (i.e., deferred tax assets less deferred tax liabilities) is deducted from the firm's enterprise value.[47] The use of net deferred tax liabilities is appropriate because deferred tax liabilities often are larger than deferred tax assets for firms in the absence of net operating losses (NOLs). The impact on free cash flow of a change in deferred taxes can be estimated as the difference between a firm's marginal and effective tax rates multiplied by the firm's EBIT.

For example, the effective tax rate for 5 years increases the deferred tax liability to the firm during that period as long as the effective rate is below the marginal rate. The deferred tax liability at the end of the fifth year is estimated by adding to the current cumulated deferred tax liability the additional liability for each of the next 5 years. This

[45] The only debt that must be valued is the debt outstanding on the valuation date. Future borrowing is irrelevant if we assume that investments financed with future borrowings earn their cost of capital. As such, net cash flows would be sufficient to satisfy interest and principal payments associated with these borrowings.

[46] In the United States, the current market value of a firm's debt can be determined using the FINRA TRACE database. For example, Home Depot Inc.'s 5.40% fixed coupon bond maturing on March 1, 2016, was priced at $112.25 on September 5, 2010, or 1.1225 times par value. Multiply the book (par) value of debt, which for Home Depot was $3,040,000, by 1.1225 to determine its market value of $3,412,400 on that date.

[47] Alternatively, noncurrent deferred taxes may be valued separately, with deferred tax assets added to and deferred tax liabilities subtracted from the firm's enterprise value.

EXHIBIT 7.6

Estimating Common Equity Value by Deducting the Market Value of Debt, Preferred Stock, Deferred Taxes From the Enterprise Value

Operating income, depreciation, working capital, and capital spending are expected to grow 10% annually during the next 5 years and 5% thereafter. The book value of the firm's debt is $300 million, with annual interest expense of $25 million and term to maturity of four years. The debt is an "interest only" note, with a repayment of principal at maturity. The firm's annual preferred dividend expense is $20 million. The market yield on preferred stock issued by similar firms is 11%. Pension and healthcare obligations are fully funded. The firm's current cost of debt is 10%. The firm's weighted average cost of capital is 12%. Because it is already at the industry average, it is expected to remain at that level beyond the fifth year.

Because of tax deferrals, the firm's current effective tax rate of 25% is expected to remain at that level for the next 5 years. The firm's current net deferred tax liability is $300 million. The projected net deferred tax liability at the end of the fifth year is expected to be paid off in 10 equal amounts during the following decade. The firm's marginal tax rate is 40%, and it will be applied to the calculation of the terminal value. What is the value of the firm to common equity investors?

Financial data (in $ million)

	Current Year	Year 1	Year 2	Year 3	Year 4	Year 5
EBIT	$200	$220	$242	$266.2	$292.8	$322.1
EBIT (1 − t)	$150	$165	$181.5	$199.7	$219.6	$241.6
Depreciation (straight line)	$8	$8.8	$9.7	$10.7	$11.7	$12.9
Δ Net working capital	$30	$33	$36	$39.9	$43.9	$48.3
Gross capital spending	$40	$44	$48.4	$3.2	$58.6	$64.4
FCFF	$88	$96.8	$106.5	$117.3	$128.8	$141.8

$$P_{0,FCFF} = \frac{\$88.00(1.10)}{0.12-0.10} \times \left[1-\left(\frac{1.10}{1.12}\right)\right]^5 + \frac{\$93.50^b \times 1.05/(0.12-0.05)}{(1.12)^5}$$

$$= \$416.98 + \$795.81$$

$$= \$1212.80$$

$$PV_D(\text{Debt})^c = \$25 \times \frac{1-1/(1.04)^4}{0.10} + \frac{\$300}{(1.10)^4}$$

$$= \$25(3.17) + \$300(0.683)$$

$$= \$79.25 + \$204.90$$

$$= \$284.15$$

$$PV_{PFD}(\text{preferred stock})^d = \frac{\$20.11}{0.11} = \$181.82$$

Deferred tax liability by end of year 5 = $300 + ($220+ $242+ 266.20+ $292.80+ $322.10)(0.40− 0.25) = $501.47

$$PV_{DEF}\ (\text{deferred taxes}) = \frac{\$501.47}{10} \times \frac{1-[1/(1.12)]^{10}/1.12^5}{0.12}$$

$$= \frac{\$50.15 \times 5.65}{1.76} = \$160.99$$

$$P_{0,FCFE} = \$1,212.80 - \$284.15 - \$181.82 - \$160.99 = \$585.84$$

[a] See Equation 7.16, for consistency.
[b] The terminal value reflects the recalculation of the fifth-year after-tax operating income using the marginal tax rate of 40% and applying the constant-growth model. Fifth-year free cash flow equals $322.1(1 − 0.4) + $12.9 − $48.3 − $64.4 = $93.5.
[c] The PV of debt is calculated using the PV of an annuity for 4 years and a 10% interest rate plus the PV of the principal repayment at the end of 4 years. The firm's current cost of debt of 10% is higher than the implied interest rate of 8% ($25/$300) on the loan currently on the firm's books. This suggests that the market rate of interest has increased since the firm borrowed the $300 million "interest only" note.
[d] The market value of preferred stock (PV_{PFD}) is equal to the preferred dividend divided by the cost of preferred stock.

EBIT, Earnings before interest and taxes; *FCFF*, free cash flow to the firm.

liability is the sum of projected EBIT times the difference between the marginal and effective tax rates. Assuming tax payments on the deferred tax liability at the end of the fifth year will be spread equally over the following 10 years, the PV of the tax payments during that 10-year period is then estimated and discounted back to the current period (see Exhibit 7.6).

Determining the cash impact of unfunded pension liabilities

Deduct the PV of such liabilities from the enterprise value to estimate the firm's equity value. Publicly traded firms are required to identify the PV of unfunded pension obligations; if not shown on the firm's balance sheet, such data can be found in the footnotes to the balance sheet.[48]

Determining the cash impact of employee options

Key employees often receive compensation in the form of options to buy a firm's common stock at a stipulated price (i.e., exercise price). After being exercised, these options impact cash flow as firms attempt to repurchase shares to reduce earnings-per-share dilution resulting from the firm's issuance of new shares to those exercising their options. The PV of these future cash outlays to repurchase stock should be deducted from the firm's enterprise value.[49]

Determining the cash impact of other provisions and contingent liabilities

Provisions (i.e., reserves) for future layoffs caused by restructuring are recorded on the balance sheet in undiscounted form because they represent cash outlays to be made in the near term. Such provisions should be deducted from the enterprise value because they are equivalent to debt. Contingent liabilities, whose future cash outlays depend on certain events, are shown not on the balance sheet but, rather, in footnotes. Examples include pending litigation and loan guarantees. Because such expenses are tax deductible, estimate the PV of future after-tax cash outlays discounted at the firm's cost of debt and deduct from the firm's enterprise value.

Determining the market value of noncontrolling interests

A firm owning less than 100% of another business is shown on the firm's consolidated balance sheet. That portion not owned by the firm is shown as a noncontrolling interest. For valuation purposes, the noncontrolling interest has a claim on the assets of the majority-owned subsidiary and not on the parent firm's assets. If the less-than-wholly-owned subsidiary is publicly traded, value the noncontrolling interest by multiplying it by the market value of the subsidiary. If the subsidiary is not publicly traded and you as an investor in the subsidiary have access to its financials, value the subsidiary by discounting the subsidiary's cash flows at the cost of capital appropriate for the industry in which it competes. The resulting value of the noncontrolling interest also should be deducted from the firm's enterprise value.

Valuing nonoperating assets

Assets not used in operating the firm also may contribute to firm value and include excess cash balances, investments in other firms, and unused or underused assets. Their value should be added to the firm's enterprise value to determine the total value of the firm.

[48] If the unfunded liability is not shown in the footnotes, they should indicate where it is shown.

[49] Options represent employee compensation and are tax deductible for firms. Accounting rules require firms to report the PV of all stock options outstanding based on estimates provided by option-pricing models (see Chapter 8) in the footnotes to financial statements.

Cash and marketable securities

Excess cash balances are cash and short-term marketable securities held in excess of the target firm's minimum operating cash balance. What constitutes the minimum cash balance depends on the firm's cash conversion cycle, which reflects the firm's tendency to build inventory, sell products on credit, and later collect accounts receivable.

The length of time cash is tied up in working capital is estimated as the sum of the firm's inventory conversion period plus the receivables collection period less the payables deferral period.[50] To finance this investment in working capital, a firm must maintain a minimum cash balance equal to the average number of days its cash is tied up in working capital times the average dollar value of sales per day. The inventory conversion and receivables collection periods are calculated by dividing the dollar value of inventory and receivables by average daily sales. The payments deferral period is estimated by dividing payables by the firm's average cost of sales per day. Exhibit 7.7 shows how to estimate minimum and excess cash balances.

Although excess cash balances are added to the PV of operating assets, cash deficiencies are subtracted from the value of operating assets to determine the value of the firm. This reflects the acquirer's investment in more working capital to make up any deficiency. This method may not work for firms that manage working capital aggressively, so receivables and inventory are very low relative to payables. An alternative is to compare the firm's cash balance percent of revenue with the industry average. If the cash balance exceeds the industry average, the firm has excess cash balances, assuming the average firm in the industry has no excess cash. For example, if the industry average cash holdings as a percent of revenue is 5% and the target firm has 8%, the target holds excess cash equal to 3% of its annual revenue.

EXHIBIT 7.7

Estimating Minimum and Excess Cash Balances

Prototype Incorporated's current inventory, accounts receivable, and accounts payables are valued at $14 million, $6.5 million, and $6 million, respectively. Projected sales and cost of sales for the coming year total $100 million and $75 million, respectively. Moreover, the value of the firm's current cash and short-term marketable securities is $21,433,000. What minimum cash balance should the firm maintain? What is the firm's current excess cash balance?

$$\frac{\$14,000,000}{\$100,000,000/365}+\frac{\$6,500,000}{\$100,000,000/365}-\frac{\$6,000,000}{75,000,000/365}$$

$$= 51.1\ days + 23.7\ days - 29.2\ days = 45.6\ days$$

$$\text{Minimum cash balance} = 45.6\ \text{days} \times \$100,000,000/365 = \$12,493,151$$

$$\text{Excess cash balance} = \$21,433,000 - \$12,493,151 = \$8,939,849$$

[50] The inventory conversion period is the average time in days required to produce and sell finished goods. The receivables collection period is the average time in days required to collect receivables. The payables deferral period is the average time in days between the purchase of and payment for materials and labor.

Investments in other firms

Such investments, for financial reporting purposes, may be classified as noncontrolling passive investments, noncontrolling active investments, or majority investments. These investments are valued individually and added to the firm's enterprise value to determine the total firm value.

Unused and undervalued assets

Target firm real estate may have a market value in excess of its book value. A firm may have an overfunded pension fund. Intangible assets such as patents and licenses may have substantial value. In the absence of a predictable cash flow stream, their value may be estimated using the Black–Scholes model (see Chapter 8) or the cost of developing comparable technologies.

Patents, service marks, and trademarks

A patent without a current application may have value to an external party, which can be determined by a negotiated sale or license to that party. When a patent is linked to a specific product, it is normally valued based on the "cost avoidance" method. This method uses after-tax royalty rates paid on comparable patents multiplied by the projected future stream of revenue from the products whose production depends on the patent discounted to its PV at the cost of capital. Products and services, which depend on a number of patents, are grouped together as a single portfolio and valued as a group using a single royalty rate applied to a declining percentage of the future revenue. Trademarks are the right to use a name, and service marks are the right to use an image associated with a company, product, or concept. Their value is name recognition reflecting the firm's longevity, cumulative advertising expenditures, the effectiveness of its marketing programs, and the consistency of perceived product quality.

Overfunded pension plans

Defined benefit pension plans require firms to hold financial assets to meet future obligations. Shareholders have the legal right to assets in excess of what is needed. If such assets are liquidated and paid out to shareholders, the firm has to pay taxes on their value. The after-tax value of such funds may be added to the enterprise value.

Some things to remember

DCF methods are widely used to estimate the firm value. To do so, GAAP cash flows are adjusted to create enterprise and equity cash flow for valuation purposes. A common way of estimating equity value is to deduct the market value of nonequity claims from its enterprise value and to add the market value of nonoperating assets.

Chapter discussion questions

7.1 What is the significance of the weighted average cost of capital? How is it calculated? Do the weights reflect the firm's actual or target debt-to–total capital ratio?
7.2 What does a firm's β measure? What is the difference between an unlevered and a levered β?
7.3 Under what circumstances is it important to adjust the CAPM model for firm size? Why?
7.4 What are the primary differences between FCFE and FCFF?
7.5 Explain the conditions under which it makes the most sense to use the zero-growth and constant-growth DCF models. Be specific.
7.6 Which DCF valuation methods require the estimation of a terminal value? Why?
7.7 Do small changes in the assumptions pertaining to the estimation of the terminal value have a significant impact on the calculation of the total value of the target firm?
7.8 How would you estimate the equity value of a firm if you knew its enterprise value and the present value of all nonoperating assets, nonoperating liabilities, and long-term debt?

7.9 Why is it important to distinguish between operating and nonoperating assets and liabilities when valuing a firm?

7.10 Explain how you would value a patent under the following situations: a patent with no current application, a patent linked to an existing product, and a patent portfolio.

Answers to these Chapter Discussion Questions are available in the Online Instructor's Manual for instructors using this book.

Practice problems and answers

7.11 ABC Incorporated shares are currently trading for $32 per share. The firm has 1.13 billion shares outstanding. The market value of its debt is $2 billion. The 10-year Treasury bond rate is 6.25%. ABC earned a AAA rating from the major credit-rating agencies. The current interest rate on AAA corporate bonds is 6.45%. The historical risk premium over the risk-free rate of return is 5.5%. The firm's beta is estimated to be 1.1, and its marginal tax rate, including federal, state, and local taxes, is 40%.

a. What is the cost of equity? *Answer:* 12.3%
b. What is the after-tax cost of debt? *Answer:* 3.9%
c. What is the weighted average cost of capital? *Answer:* 11.9%

7.12 HiFlyer Corporation currently has no debt. Its tax rate is 0.4, and its unlevered beta is estimated to be 2.0. The 10-year bond rate is 6.25%, and the historical risk premium is 5.5%. Next year, HiFlyer expects to borrow up to 75% of its equity value to fund growth.

a. Calculate the firm's current cost of equity. *Answer:* 17.25%
b. Estimate the firm's cost of equity after the firm increases its leverage to 75% of equity. *Answer:* 22.2%

7.13 Abbreviated financial statements for Fletcher Corporation are given in Table 7.7. Year-end working capital in 2009 was $160 million, and the firm's marginal tax rate was 40% in both 2010 and 2011. Estimate the following for 2010 and 2011:

a. Free cash flow to equity. *Answer*: $16.4 million in 2010 and −$26.8 million in 2011
b. Free cash flow to the firm. *Answer*: $44.4 million in 2010 and $1.2 million in 2011

7.14 In 2011, No Growth Inc.'s EBIT was $220 million. The firm was expected to generate this level of operating income indefinitely. The firm had depreciation expenses of $10 million that year. Capital spending totaled $20 million during 2011. At the end of 2010 and 2011, working capital totaled $70 million and $80 million, respectively. The firm's combined marginal tax rate was 40%, and its outstanding debt had a market value of $1.2 billion. The 10-year Treasury bond rate is 5%, and the borrowing rate for companies exhibiting levels of creditworthiness similar to No Growth is 7%. The historical risk premium for stocks is 5.5%. No Growth's beta

TABLE 7.7 Abbreviated financial statements for Fletcher Corporation (in $ million)

	2010	2011
Revenues	$600	$690
Operating expenses	520	600
Depreciation	16	18
Earnings before interest and taxes	64	72
Less interest expense	5	5
Less taxes	23.6	26.8
Equals: net income	35.4	40.2
Addendum:		
Year-end working capital	150	200
Principal repayment	25	25
Capital expenditures	20	10

was estimated to be 1.0. The firm had 2.5 million common shares outstanding at the end of 2011. No Growth's target debt–to–total capital ratio is 30%.

a. Estimate free cash flow to the firm in 2011. *Answer:* $112 million
b. Estimate the firm's weighted average cost of capital. *Answer:* 8.61%
c. Estimate the enterprise value of the firm at the end of 2011, assuming that it will generate the value of free cash flow estimated in (a) indefinitely. *Answer:* $1,300.8 million
d. Estimate the value of the equity of the firm at the end of 2011. Answer: $100.8 million
e. Estimate the value per share at the end of 2011. *Answer:* $40.33

7.15 Carlisle Enterprises, a specialty pharmaceutical manufacturer, has been losing market share for 3 years because several key patents have expired. Free cash flow to the firm is expected to decline rapidly as more competitive generic drugs enter the market. Projected cash flows for the next 5 years are $8.5 million, $7 million, $5 million, $2 million, and $0.5 million. Cash flow after the fifth year is expected to be negligible. The firm's board has decided to sell the firm to a larger pharmaceutical company that is interested in using Carlisle's product offering to fill gaps in its own product offering until it can develop similar drugs. Carlisle's weighted average cost of capital is 15%. What purchase price must Carlisle obtain to earn its cost of capital?

Answer: $17.4 million

7.16 Ergo Unlimited's current year's free cash flow to equity is $10 million. It is projected to grow at 20% per year for the next 5 years. It is expected to grow at a more modest 5% beyond the fifth year. The firm estimates that its cost of equity is 12% during the next 5 years and will drop to 10% after that. Estimate the firm's current market value.

Answer: $358.3 million

7.17 In the year when it intends to go public, a firm has revenues of $20 million and net income after taxes of $2 million. The firm has no debt, and revenue is expected to grow at 20% annually for the next 5 years and 5% annually thereafter. Net profit margins are expected to remain constant throughout. Annual capital expenditures equal depreciation, and the change in working capital requirements is minimal. The average beta of a publicly traded company in this industry is 1.50, and the average debt-to-equity ratio is 20%. The firm is not expected to borrow in the foreseeable future. The Treasury bond rate is 6%, and the marginal tax rate is 40%. The risk premium on stocks is 5.5%. Reflecting slower growth beyond the fifth year, the discount rate is expected to decline to the industry average cost of capital of 10.4%. Estimate the value of the firm's equity.

Answer: $63.41 million

7.18 The information in Table 7.8 is available for two different common stocks: Company A and Company B.

a. Estimate the cost of equity for each firm. *Answer:* Company A = 15.45%; Company B = 12.2%
b. Assume that the companies' growth will continue at the same rates indefinitely. Estimate the per-share value of each company's common stock. *Answer*: Company A = $13.42; Company B = $61.00

7.19 You have been asked to estimate the beta of a high-technology firm that has three divisions with the characteristics shown in Table 7.9.

a. What is the beta of the equity of the firm? *Answer:* 1.52
b. If the risk-free return is 5% and the spread between the return on all stocks is 5.5%, estimate the cost of equity for the software division. *Answer*: 16%

TABLE 7.8 Common stocks

	Company A	Company B
Free cash flow per share in the current year ($)	1.00	5.00
Growth rate in cash flow per share (%)	8	4
Beta	1.3	0.8
Risk-free return (%)	7	7
Expected return on all stocks (%)	13.5	13.5

TABLE 7.9 High-technology company

Division	Beta	Market value ($ million)
Personal computers	1.60	100
Software	2.00	150
Computer mainframes	1.20	250

c. What is the cost of equity for the entire firm? *Answer*: 13.4%

d. FCFE in the current year for the entire firm is $7.4 million and for the software division is $3.1 million. If the total firm and the software division are expected to grow at the same 8% rate into the foreseeable future, estimate the market value of the firm and of the software division. *Answer*: PV (total firm) = $147.96; PV (software division) = $41.88

7.20 Financial Corporation wants to acquire Great Western Inc. Financial and has estimated the enterprise value of Great Western at $104 million. The market value of Great Western's long-term debt is $15 million, and cash balances in excess of the firm's normal working capital requirements are $3 million. Financial estimates the PV of certain licenses that Great Western is not currently using to be $4 million. Great Western is the defendant in several outstanding lawsuits. Financial Corporation's legal department estimates the potential future cost of this litigation to be $3 million, with an estimated present value of $2.5 million. Great Western has 2 million common shares outstanding. What is the adjusted equity value of Great Western per common share?

Answer: $46.75/share

Solutions to these Practice Problems are available in the Online Instructor's Manual for instructors using this book.

End-of-chapter case study: did United Technologies overpay for Rockwell Collins?

Case study objectives

To illustrate

- A methodology for determining if an acquirer overpaid for a target firm
- How sensitive discounted cash flow valuation is to changes in key assumptions
- The limitations of discounted cash flow valuation methods

United Technologies (UT) acquired Rockwell Collins (Rockwell) $30 billion, including $7 billion in assumed Rockwell debt, in late 2017. Rockwell shareholders received $140 per share. The purchase price consisted of $93.33 in cash plus $46.67 in UT stock and represented an 18% premium to Rockwell's closing share price the day before the announcement. UT's aerospace business will be combined with Rockwell to create a new business to be called Collins Aerospace Systems. UT anticipates about $500 million annually in cost savings by the fourth year after closing.

Rockwell's free cash flow to the firm (FCFF) is projected to be $750 million in 2017, which is expected to grow at 7% annually through 2022 and 2% thereafter. The firm's beta is 1.22 and average borrowing cost is 4.8%. The equity risk premium is 5 percentage points. The 10-year Treasury bond rate is 2.2%. The debt-to-equity ratio is 1.39. The firm's cost of capital in the years beyond 2022 is expected to be half of one percentage point below its level during the 2018 to 2022 period. The firm's marginal tax rate is 40%, and there is no cap on the tax deductibility of net interest expense.

An analyst was asked if UT overpaid for Rockwell. She reasoned that to answer this question, she would have to estimate the standalone value of Rockwell and the present value of synergy. The upper limit on the purchase price should be the sum of the standalone value plus the PV of synergy. If the actual purchase price exceeded the upper limit, the firm would have overpaid for the Rockwell. In effect, UT would have transferred all the value created by combining the two firms (i.e., anticipated synergy) to Rockwell shareholders.

Discussion questions

1. Estimate the firm's cost of equity and after-tax cost of debt.
2. Estimate the firm's weighted average cost of capital. (Hint: The debt-to-total capital ratio is equal to the debt-to-equity ratio divided by 1 plus the debt-to-equity ratio.)
3. What is the WAAC beyond 2022?
4. Use the discounted cash flow method to determine the standalone value for Rockwell Collins. Show your work.
5. Assuming the free cash flows from synergy will remain level in perpetuity, estimate the after-tax present value of anticipated synergy.
6. What is the maximum purchase price United Technologies should pay for Rockwell Collins? Did United Technologies overpay?
7. How might your answer to Question 5 change if the discount rate during the first 5 years and during the terminal period is the same as estimated in Question 2?
8. What are the limitations of the discounted cash flow method used in this case study?

Solutions to these case discussion questions are available in the Online Instructor's Manual for instructors using this book.

CHAPTER

8

Relative, asset-oriented, and real-option valuation basics

OUTLINE

Mergers, Acquisitions, and Other Restructuring Activities, *Eleventh Edition*
https://doi.org/10.1016/B978-0-12-819782-0.00008-3

Happiness is a personal choice. We can be angry about the things we do not have or happy about the things we do. —***Nick Vujicic***

Inside M&As: real options can provide management with substantial strategic flexibility

KEY POINTS

- Discounted cash flow and relative-valuation methods suggest that after an investment decision has been made, management cannot change the outcome.
- In practice, management often has considerable flexibility to accelerate, delay, or abandon the original investment as new information is obtained.

Investment decisions, including mergers and acquisitions (M&As), often contain implied options: the ability to accelerate growth by adding to the initial investment (i.e., expand), delay the timing of the initial investment (i.e., delay), or walk away (i.e., abandon). Real options differ from strategic options because they represent alternative management choices after an investment is made. Real options tend to be difficult to value and often are based on problematic assumptions. If a firm's management adds the value of an option to expand to its initial investment in a target firm, it may persuade the board to make an acquisition that would not otherwise have been made. The following deal illustrates how this flexibility may be exercised in the context of M&As.

In early 2020, Japanese conglomerate Hitachi Ltd completed its acquisition of 80.1% of Swiss-based robotics manufacturer ABB Inc.'s electric power grid division for $6.4 billion ($11 billion including net debt). Both Hitachi's and ABB's boards and management were under considerable pressure to change strategic direction: Hitachi because of the grim outlook for nuclear power and ABB because of an activist investor.

As part of the deal, ABB retained a 19.9% stake in its former power business and had a put option to sell its ownership position to Hitachi in 2022 at a predetermined price. The divestiture was applauded by activist investor Cevian Capital, which became a major ABB shareholder in 2015 and had pushed the board and management to break up the firm. Initially, ABB's CEO had resisted a breakup, arguing that the firm was substantially undervalued. However, after an exhaustive strategic review, he relented.

Immediately after the announcement in early 2019, investors expressed their belief that Hitachi had overpaid for the business by selling their shares and depressing the firm's market value by more than one percent. In contrast, ABB's investors greeted the announcement enthusiastically by driving its share price up by 1.5% on the news of a share repurchase and the firm's increased focus.

There is no guarantee that Hitachi can generate the returns its investors require within a reasonable period. If it is successful, Hitachi can accelerate investment in the business (i.e., pursue an option to expand); if the financial results are disappointing, Hitachi can pursue a range of options, including delaying future investment or divesting the business (i.e., pursue delay or abandon options). The abandon option could entail a variety of alternatives, including the outright sale of the unit or an equity carve-out or spin-off. ABB also has several real options available to it. If Hitachi is able to improve the power division's financial performance, ABB can choose not to exercise its put option and participate in the unit's value creation. However, if the unit's performance flounders, ABB can "put" its ownership share to Hitachi.

Chapter overview

This chapter is a continuation of the discussion of methodologies often employed to estimate the true or *intrinsic value* of an asset. Chapter 7 discussed how discounted cash flow (DCF) methods could be used to estimate the intrinsic value of mergers and acquisitions. This chapter addresses alternative methods of valuation, including relative-valuation (i.e., market-based) methods, asset-oriented methods, real-options analysis, and replacement cost. The chapter concludes with a summary of the strengths and weaknesses of the alternative valuation methods (including discounted cash flow) and when it is appropriate to apply each methodology. Because each valuation method reflects different assumptions, data requirements, and biases, the most accurate valuation estimate often is a weighted average of multiple approaches. A review of this chapter is available in the file folder titled "Student Study Guide" on the companion site to this book (https://www.elsevier.com/books-and-journals/book-companion/9780128197820).

Relative-valuation methods

Relative valuation involves valuing assets based on how similar assets are valued in the marketplace. Such methods assume a firm's market value can be approximated by a value indicator for comparable companies, comparable transactions, or comparable industry averages. Value indicators could include the firm's earnings, operating cash flow, EBITDA (i.e., earnings before interest and taxes, depreciation, and amortization), sales, and book value.

This approach often is described as market-based because it reflects the amounts investors are willing to pay for each dollar of earnings, cash flow, sales, or book value at a moment in time. As such, it reflects theoretically the collective wisdom of investors. Because of the requirement for positive current or near-term earnings or cash flow, this methodology is meaningful only for companies with a positive, stable earnings or cash flow stream.

If comparable companies are available, the market value of a target firm, MV_T, can be estimated by solving the following equation:

$$MV_T = (MV_C / VI_C) \times VI_T \quad (8.1)$$

in which

MV_C = market value of comparable company C
VI_C = value indicator for comparable company C
VI_T = value indicator for target firm T
(MV_C/VI_C) = market value multiple for the comparable company

For example, if the price-to-earnings (P/E) ratio or multiple for the comparable firm is 10 (i.e., MV_C/VI_C) and after-tax earnings of the target are \$2 million (VI_T), the market value of the target at that time is \$20 million (MV_T).

Relative valuation is used because it is simple to calculate, requires relatively few assumptions, is easy to explain, and reflects current market demand and supply conditions. The relationship expressed in Equation 8.1 is used to estimate the target's value in all relative-valuation and asset-oriented methods discussed in this chapter, except the replacement cost method.

The analyst must follow certain guidelines in applying relative-valuation methods. First, when using multiples (e.g., MV_C/VI_C), it is critical to ensure that the multiple is defined in the same way for all comparable firms. For example, in using a P/E ratio, earnings may be defined as trailing (i.e., prior), current, or projected.[1] Also, the numerator and the denominator of the multiple must be defined in the same way. If the numerator in the P/E ratio is defined as price per share, the denominator must be calculated as earnings per share. Second, the analyst must examine the distribution of the multiples of the firms being compared and eliminate outliers, those whose values are substantially different from others in the sample.

The comparable-companies method

This approach requires that the analyst identify firms substantially similar to the target firm. A comparable firm is one whose profitability, potential growth rate in earnings or cash flows, and perceived risk are similar to those of the firm to be valued. By defining comparable companies broadly, it is possible to use firms in other industries. As such, a computer hardware manufacturer can be compared to a telecom firm as long as they are comparable in terms of profitability, growth, and risk. Consequently, if the firm to be valued has a 15% return on equity (i.e., profitability), expected earnings or cash flow growth rates of 10% annually (i.e., growth), and a beta of 1.3 or debt-to-equity ratio of 1 (i.e., risk), the analyst must find a firm with similar characteristics in either the same industry or another industry.

In practice, analysts often look for comparable firms that are in the same industry and similar in terms of such things as markets served, product offering, degree of leverage, and size.[2] To determine if the firms selected are comparable, estimate the correlation between the operating income or revenue of the target firm and those of comparable firms. If the correlation is positive and high, the firms are comparable.[3] However, even when companies appear to be

[1] Forte et al. (2020) conclude that P/E ratios reflecting estimated future earnings provided more accurate estimates of bank equity values than those based on historical earnings.

[2] Smaller firms, other things equal, are more prone to default than larger firms, which generally have a larger asset base and more diversified revenue. As such, comparable firms should also be similar in size.

[3] Similarly, if the firm has multiple product lines, collect comparable firms for each product line and estimate the correlation coefficient between sales of the firm's product lines and those of comparable firms.

TABLE 8.1 Valuing Total SA using comparable integrated oil companies

	Target valuation based on following multiples (MV_C/VI_C)				
Comparable company	**Trailing P/E[a]**	**Forward P/E[b]**	**Price/sales**	**Price/book**	**Average**
	Col. 1	Col. 2	Col. 3	Col. 4	Cols. 1–4
Exxon Mobil Corp. (XOM)	168.56	9.12	4.64	6.97	
British Petroleum (BP)	207.69	9.55	4.45	8.87	
Chevron Corp. (CVX)	136.30	9.01	5.79	7.49	
Royal Dutch Shell (RDS-B)	194.23	8.22	3.22	5.19	
ConocoPhillips (COP)	9.02	11.71	1.43	1.50	
Eni SpA (E)	12.90	14.01	.57	1.12	
PetroChina Co. (PTR)	9.21	8.20	.50	1.04	
Oil & Natural Gas Corp. (ONGC)	11.40	7.11	1.71	1.82	
Average multiple (MV_C/VI_C)	93.66	9.62	2.79	4.25	
Total SA Value Indicators in Dollars Per Share (VI_T)	$1.77	$8.93	$76.60	$41.45	
Equals estimated market value of target ($Billions)[c]	$165.78	$85.87	$213.62	$176.16	$160.36

[a]Trailing 52-week averages.
[b]Projected 52-week averages.
[c]Billions of dollars. Average multiple (MV_C/VI_C) × Total SA value indicator expressed in dollars per share (VI_T). For example, using the price-to-trailing earnings multiple multiplied by Total SA trailing earnings per share = 93.66 × $1.77 = $165.78 billion.

similar, valuations can differ from one period to the next. For example, the announcement of a pending acquisition may boost the share prices of competitors as investors anticipate takeover bids for these firms. The impact of such events abates with the passage of time. Accordingly, comparisons made at different times can provide distinctly different results. By taking an average of multiples over many months, these differences may be minimized. Note that valuations derived using the comparable-companies method do not include a purchase price premium.

Table 8.1 shows how to apply the comparable-companies method to value French oil and gas company Total SA Total is a geographically diversified integrated oil and gas company; as such, it has economic and political risks and growth characteristics similar to other globally diversified integrated oil and gas companies. The estimated value of the total based on the average of the comparable companies' estimates calculated using the four different market multiples is $160.36 billion versus its actual March 14, 2014, market capitalization of $144.59 billion.

Changes in fundamentals affecting multiples include a firm's ability to grow earnings and cash flow through reinvestment in the firm as well as the risk associated with its earnings and cash flows. Firms with lower earnings and cash flow generation potential, lower growth prospects, and higher risk should trade at multiples less than firms with higher earnings and cash flow generation capability, higher growth prospects, and less risk. Therefore, an analyst needs to understand why one firm's multiple is less than a comparable firm's before concluding that it is under- or overvalued. For example, a firm with a P/E ratio of 10 may not be more expensive than a comparable firm with a P/E ratio of 8 if the former's growth prospects, profitability, and reinvestment rate are higher those of the latter.

Recent comparable transactions method

This method, also referred to as the *precedent-transactions method*, is used to estimate the value of the target based on purchase prices of recently acquired comparable companies. P/E, sales, cash flow, EBITDA, and book-value ratios are calculated using the purchase price for the recent comparable deal. Earnings, sales, cash flow, EBITDA, and book value for the target are subsequently multiplied by these ratios to estimate the target's market value. The estimated value of the target firm obtained using recent comparable transactions already reflects a purchase price premium, unlike the comparable-companies approach to valuation.

The obvious limitation to this method is the difficulty in finding truly comparable, recent transactions. Recent deals can be found in other industries as long as they are similar to the target firm in terms of profitability, expected

EXHIBIT 8.1

Valuing a Target Company Using the Same- or Comparable-Industries Method

As of March 17, 2014, Applied Materials Inc. (AMAT) had projected earnings per share for the coming year of $1.07.[a] The industry average forward price-to-earnings (P/E) ratio for 51 companies was 24.05.[b] Estimate the firm's intrinsic price per share (see Equation 8.1).

$$MV_T = (MV_{IND}/VI_{IND}) \times VI_T = 24.05 \times \$1.07$$

$$= \$25.73 \text{ per share } (3/17/2014 \text{ actual price} = \$18.98)$$

in which

MV_T = market value per share of the target company

MV_{IND}/VI_{IND} = market value per share of the average firm in the industry divided by a value indicator for that average firm in the industry (e.g., industry average forward P/E ratio)

VI_T = value indicator for the target firm (e.g., projected earnings per share)

[a] Thomson Reuters I/B/E/S Consensus Estimates Report for 2014 based on a survey of industry analysts taken on March 3, 2014.
[b] Source: http://people.stern.nyu.edu/adamodar/New_Home_Page/datafile/pedata.html

earnings and cash flow growth, and perceived risk. Table 8.1 could be used to illustrate how the recent comparable transaction method may be applied simply by replacing the data in the column headed "Comparable company" with data for "Recent comparable transactions."

Same- or comparable-industries method

Using this approach, the target's net income, revenue, cash flow, EBITDA, and book value are multiplied by the ratio of the market value of shareholders' equity to net income, revenue, cash flow, EBITDA, or book value for the average company in the target firm's industry or a comparable industry (Exhibit 8.1). Such information can be obtained from Standard & Poor's, Value Line, Moody's, Dun & Bradstreet, and Wall Street analysts. The primary advantage of this technique is the ease of use. Disadvantages include the presumption that industry multiples are actually comparable. The use of the industry average may overlook the fact that companies, even in the same industry, can have drastically different expected growth rates, returns on invested capital, and debt-to–total capital ratios.

Enterprise value to EBITDA method

In recent years, analysts have increasingly valued firms by multiplying the EV/EBITDA multiple based on comparable companies or recent transactions by the target firm's EBITDA. If the multiple for a sample of comparable firms or recent transactions is 8 and the target's EBITDA is $10 million, the value of the target is $80 million.

In this chapter, enterprise value is viewed from the perspective of the liability, or "right-hand," side of the balance sheet.[4] As such, the enterprise value consists of the sum of the market values of long-term debt (MV_D), preferred equity (MV_{PF}), common equity (MV_{FCFE}), and noncontrolling interest excluding cash. Other long-term liabilities often are ignored, and cash is assumed to be equal to cash and short-term marketable securities on the balance sheet.[5]

Cash and short-term marketable securities are deducted from the firm's enterprise value because interest income from such cash is not counted in the calculation of EBITDA. The inclusion of cash would overstate the EV/EBITDA multiple. Furthermore, cash is a nonoperating asset whose value is implicitly included in the market value of equity because it is owned by the shareholders. This multiple is commonly expressed as follows:

$$EV/EBITDA = [MV_{FCFE} + MV_{PF} + (MV_D - Cash)]/EBITDA \tag{8.2}$$

[4] In Chapter 7, enterprise value was discussed from the perspective of the asset, or "left-hand," side of the balance sheet as the PV of cash flows from operating assets and liabilities available for lenders and common and preferred shareholders (i.e., free cash flow to the firm). Thus defined, enterprise value was adjusted for the value of nonoperating assets and liabilities to estimate the value of common equity.

[5] Ignoring the firm's pension and health care obligations makes sense only if they are fully funded.

in which (MV_D − Cash) is often referred to as net debt.

Many consider the enterprise value a more accurate measure of firm value than equity value because it reflects the obligation of the acquirer to pay off assumed liabilities. The enterprise value-to-EBITDA valuation method is useful because more firms are likely to have negative earnings rather than negative EBITDA. Furthermore, net or operating income can be significantly affected by the way the firm chooses to calculate depreciation (e.g., straight line versus accelerated). Such problems do not arise with EBITDA, which is estimated before deducting depreciation and amortization expense. Finally, the multiple can be compared with firms having different levels of leverage than for other measures of earnings because the numerator represents the total value of the firm irrespective of its distribution between debt and equity and the denominator measures earnings before interest.

A shortcoming of EBITDA as a value indicator is that it provides a good estimate of the firm's assets already in place but ignores the impact of new investment on future cash flows. This is not a problem as long as the firm is not growing. Despite this limitation, EBITDA is more often used than a multiple based on free cash flow to the firm (FCFF) because FCFF is frequently negative because of increases in working capital and capital spending in excess of depreciation. EBITDA multiples are most often used for mature businesses, for which most of the value comes from the firm's existing assets. Exhibit 8.2 shows how to construct EV/EBITDA multiples.

Adjusting relative-valuation methods for firm growth rates

Assume that firm A and firm B are direct competitors and have P/E ratios of 20 and 15, respectively. Which is the cheaper firm? It is not possible to answer this question without knowing how fast the earnings of the two firms are growing and what rate of return can be earned on reinvested funds. Adjusting relative-valuation methods may be helpful even though reinvestment rates of return are not considered.

The most common adjustment is the price-to-earnings to growth (PEG) ratio, calculated by dividing the firm's P/E ratio by the expected growth rate in earnings. The comparison of a firm's P/E ratio with its projected earnings is helpful in identifying stocks of firms that are under- or overvalued. Firms with P/E ratios less than their projected growth rates may be considered undervalued, whereas those with P/E ratios greater than their projected growth rates may be viewed as overvalued. Note that growth rates do not increase multiples unless financial returns improve. Investors are willing to pay more for each dollar of future earnings only if they expect to earn a higher future rate of return.[6]

The PEG ratio can be helpful in selecting the most attractive acquisition target from among a number of potential targets. Attractiveness is defined as the target that is most undervalued. Undervaluation is the extent to which a firm's current share price exceeds the firm's intrinsic share price estimated using the PEG ratio. Whereas the PEG ratio uses P/E ratios, other ratios may be used, such as price to cash flow, EBITDA, revenue, and the like.

Equation 8.3 gives an estimate of the implied market value per share for a target firm (MV_T) based on the PEG ratio for comparable companies.

$$\frac{MV_C/VI_C}{VI_{CGR}} = A$$

and

$$MV_T = A \times VI_{TGR} \times VI_T \tag{8.3}$$

in which

A = PEG ratio—that is, market price—to—value indicator ratio (MV_C/VI_C) for comparable firms relative to the growth rate of the value indicator (VI_{CGR}) for comparable firms

VI_T = value indicator for the target firm

VI_{TGR} = projected growth rate of the value indicator for the target firm. Because this method uses an equity multiple (e.g., price per share/net income per share), consistency suggests that the growth rate in the value indicator should be expressed on a per-share basis. Therefore, if the value indicator is net income per share, then the growth in the value indicator should be the growth rate for net income per share and not net income.

[6] Investors may be willing to pay considerably more for a stock whose PEG ratio is greater than 1 if they believe the future increase in earnings will result in future financial returns that significantly exceed the firm's cost of equity.

EXHIBIT 8.2

Calculating Enterprise-Value-To-EBITDA Multiples

AT&T Inc. and Verizon Communications Inc. are US-based leading telecommunications companies. As of December 31, 2013, the market value of AT&T's common equity was $171.4 billion, and Verizon's was $193.2 billion. Neither firm had preferred stock outstanding. Per investment research firm Morningstar Inc., the weighted-average maturity dates are 16 years for AT&T's debt and 14 years for Verizon's. Market rate of interest for AT&T (rated A- by S&P) was 3.87% and for Verizon (rated BBB+ by S&P) was 4.45% for debt with those maturity dates at that time. AT&T's and Verizon's 2013 income, balance sheet, and cash flow statements are shown in the following table.

Financial statements

	AT&T	Verizon
Income statement (2013)	($Billions)	
Revenue	128.7	120.6
Cost of sales	51.5	44.9
Other expenses	46.8	43.7
Earnings before interest and taxes (EBIT)	30.4	32.0
Net interest expense	3.9	2.7
Earnings before taxes	26.5	29.3
Taxes	9.2	5.7
Minority interest		12.0
Net income	17.3	11.6
Balance sheet (12/31/2013)		
Cash	9.3	54.1
Other current assets	19.8	16.9
Long-term assets	254.6	203.1
Total assets	283.7	274.1
Current liabilities	35.0	27.1
Long-term debt	69.2	89.7
Other long-term liabilities	88.6	118.5
Total liabilities	192.8	235.3
Shareholders' equity	90.9	38.8
Equity + Total liabilities	283.7	113.20
Cash flow (2013)		
Net income	17.3	11.6
Depreciation	18.4	16.6
Change in working capital	−2.2	10.7
Investments	−23.1	−14.8
Financing	−13.2	26.5
Change in cash balances	−2.8	50.6

Source: Edgar Online.

Which firm has the higher enterprise-value-to-EBITDA ratio? (*Hint*: Use Equation 8.2.)

Answer: AT&T

Market value of existing debt

PV_D(PV of AT&T's long-term debt)[a]

$$= \$3.9 \times \frac{1 - 1/(1.0387)^{16}}{0.0387} + \frac{\$69.2}{(1.0387)^{16}}$$

$$= \$3.9 \times 11.76 + \$37.69 = \$83.55 \text{ billion}$$

PV_D(PV of Verizon's long-term debt)[b]

$$= \$2.7 \times \frac{1 - 1/(1.0445)^{14}}{0.0445} + \frac{\$89.7}{(1.0445)^{14}}$$

$$= \$2.7 \times 10.26 + \$48.76 = \$76.46 \text{ billion}$$

Enterprise-to-EBITDA ratio

(Market value of equity + Market value of debt − Cash)/(EBIT + Depreciation):[c]

AT&T: ($171.40 + $83.55 − $9.30)/($30.40 + $18.40) = 5.03

Verizon: ($193.20 + $76.46 − $54.10)/($32.00 + $16.60) = 4.44

[a]The present value (PV) of AT&T's debt is calculated using the PV of an annuity formula for 16 years and a 3.87% market rate of interest plus the PV of the principal repayment of $69.2 billion at the end of 16 years. Note that only annual interest expense of $3.9 billion is used in the calculation of the PV of the annuity payment because the debt is treated as a balloon note.

[b]The PV of Verizon's debt is calculated using the PV of an annuity formula for 14 years and a 4.45% market interest rate plus the PV of the principal repayment of $89.7 billion at the end of 14 years. Interest expense is $2.7 billion.

[c]A firm's financial statements may include depreciation in the cost of sales. Enterprise value to earnings before interest, taxes, and depreciation (EBITDA) may be calculated by adding EBIT from the income statement and depreciation shown on the cash flow statement.

EXHIBIT 8.3

Applying the PEG Ratio

An analyst is asked to determine whether Johnson and Johnson Inc. (JNJ) or Pfizer Inc. (PFE) is a more attractive takeover target. One measure of their attractiveness is to compare their current valuation to projected earnings growth. JNJ and PFE have projected annual earnings-per-share growth rates of 7.9% and 4.8%, respectively. JNJ's and PFE's current earnings per share for 2014 are $5.32 and $3.34, respectively. The share prices as of March 19, 2014, were $90.95 and $29.70 for JNJ and PFE, respectively. The industry average price-to-earnings (P/E) ratio and projected 5-year growth rate at that time were 19.7% and 11.6%, respectively. Which firm is a more attractive takeover target as of this date? (*Hint*: Use Equation 8.3.)

Industry average PEG ratio : $19.7/11.6 = 1.6983$[a]

JNJ : Implied intrinsic share price $= 1.6983 \times 7.9 \times \$5.32 = \$71.38$

PFE : Implied intrinsic share price $= 1.6983 \times 4.8 \times \$3.34 = \$27.23$

Answer: Both firms, according to their respective PEG ratio estimates of their intrinsic values compared to their actual prices, are overvalued at a moment in time. The percentage difference between the actual share price and implied intrinsic share prices for JNJ and PFE is 27.4% [i.e., ($90.95 − $71.38)/$71.38] and 9.1% [i.e., ($29.70 − $27.23)/$27.23], respectively. JNJ is much more overvalued than PFE according to this methodology. Because PEG ratios do not explicitly account for risk and the earnings reinvestment rate, the extent of the overvaluation may be misleading. In practice, the PEG ratio estimate simply provides an additional data point in any evaluation of the overall attractiveness of a potential target firm.

[a] Solving $MV_T = A \times VI_{TGR} \times VI_T$ using the target's PEG ratio, in which MV_T is the market value of the target firm, VI_T is the target's value indicator, and VI_{TGR} is VI_T 's growth rate, provides the firm's share price in period T because this formula is an identity. An industry average PEG ratio may be used to estimate the firm's intrinsic value if the target firm and the average industry firm exhibit the same relationship between P/E ratios and earnings growth rates.

PEG, Price-to-earnings to growth.

Data sources:
Industry earnings growth rates and price-to-earnings ratios: http://pages.stern.nyu.edu/~adamodar/New_Home_Page/datafile/pedata.html

Individual firm data: Thomson Reuters I/B/E/S *Consensus Estimates Report for 2014* based on a survey of industry analysts taken on March 3, 2014.

PEG ratios are useful for comparing firms whose expected growth rates are positive and different. This method implies a zero value for firms that are not growing and a negative value for those whose growth rates are negative. Firms that are not growing are not likely to increase in market value, whereas those exhibiting negative growth are apt to show declining firm values.[7] Exhibit 8.3 illustrates how to apply the PEG ratio.

Value driver–based valuation

In the absence of earnings, factors that drive firm value commonly are used to value start-up companies and initial public offerings (IPOs), which often have little or no earnings history. Measures of profitability and cash flow are the result of these value drivers. Value drivers exist for each major function within the firm, including sales, marketing, and distribution; customer service; operations and manufacturing; and purchasing.

Micro value drivers are those that impact specific functions within the firm. Examples for sales, marketing, and distribution include product quality measures, such as part defects per 100,000 units sold, on-time delivery, the number of multiyear subscribers, and the ratio of product price to some measure of perceived quality. Customer service drivers include average telephone wait time, billing errors as a percent of total invoices, and the time required correcting such errors. Operational value drivers include the average collection period, inventory turnover, and

[7] As a means of selecting attractive takeover targets, the PEG ratio can be calculated for each firm and the firms ranked from lowest (most undervalued) to highest (most overvalued) in terms of their PEG ratios. Although helpful in determining the most attractive acquisition targets (i.e., most undervalued), this ranking does not indicate the extent to which a firm is under- or overvalued compared with its current share price and why.

units produced per manufacturing employee hour. Purchasing value drivers include average payment period, on-time vendor delivery, and the quality of purchased materials and services.

Macro value drivers are more encompassing than micro value drivers because they affect all aspects of the firm. Examples include market share, customer satisfaction as measured by survey results, total asset turns, revenue per employee, and "same-store sales" in retailing.

Using value drivers to value businesses is straightforward. First, the analyst identifies the key drivers of firm value. Second, the market value for comparable companies is divided by the value driver selected for the target to calculate the dollars of market value per unit of value driver. Third, this figure is multiplied by the same value driver for the target company.

Assume that the key macro value driver in an industry is market share. How investors value market share is estimated by dividing the market leader's market value by its market share. If the market leader has a market value and market share of $300 million and 30%, respectively, the market is valuing each percentage point of market share at $10 million (i.e., the market multiple based on points of market share as an indicator of value $[MV_C/VI_C]$ is $300 million ÷ 30). If the target company in the same industry has a 20% market share, an estimate of the market value of the target company (MV_T) is $200 million (i.e., $MV_T = [MV_C/VI_C] \times VI_T =$ $10 million × 20 points of market share).

Similarly, the market value of comparable companies could be divided by other known value drivers. Examples include the number of unique visitors or page views per month for an internet content provider, magazine subscribers, cost per hotel room for a hotel chain, and the number of households with TVs in a specific geographic area for a cable TV company.

In a sign of how profitable financial services can be despite collapsing fees, US financial services behemoth Morgan Stanley paid $2,500 per customer in its $13 billion takeover of E-trade in March 2020. A few months earlier, Charles Schwab had acquired TDAmeritrade for $26 billion or $2167 per customer.

The major advantage of this approach is its simplicity. Its major disadvantage is the implied assumption that a single value driver or factor is representative of the total value of the business. The bankruptcy of many dot-com firms between 2000 and 2002 illustrates how this valuation technique can be misused.

Fun with numbers and other accounting tricks

The accuracy of relative-valuation methods is critically dependent on the reliability of the value indicator or performance metric. In contrast, DCF measures rely on many assumptions creating the potential for offsetting errors to result in a reasonable estimate of value. The issue was apparent in 2019 when office space leasing firm WeWork, ride sharing firm Lyft, and exercise equipment company Peloton Interactive used accounting gimmicks to show they were profitable despite having reported huge losses the prior year. How? By deducting only certain costs from the calculation of contribution margin[8] such as rent, marketing expenses, and compensation paid in the form of stock to employees.[9] These firms hoped to point investors to metrics that show the underlying health of the business while setting aside expenses that they think will moderate over time as revenue grows. This may make sense if indeed variable costs moderate as revenue grows because of increased operating efficiencies and purchasing economies. In practice, operating expenses can escalate faster than revenue growth. WeWork's leasing contracts contained escalation clauses in which rents are scheduled to rise in future years; marketing expenses surged for Lyft in its effort to gain market share from Uber, and Peloton's stock-related compensation quickened as it sought to attract and retain talent.

Asset-oriented methods

Discussed next are methods that value firms based on tangible book, breakup, and liquidation values.

[8] Contribution margin is selling price per unit of output less the variable cost of producing each unit. It is the contribution of a product to covering a firm's fixed expenses. Anything in excess of fixed expenses is pretax profit.

[9] Public firms are permitted to provide investors with performance measures that do not conform fully with generally accepted accounting principles to show how management views the business. However, financial measures cannot mislead investors.

EXHIBIT 8.4

Valuing Companies Using Tangible Book Value

Ingram Micro Inc. and its subsidiaries distribute information technology products worldwide. The firm's market price per share on March 20, 2014, was $29.83. Ingram's projected 5-year average annual net income growth rate is 11.2%, its beta is 0.90, and after-tax profit margin is 1.03%. The firm's shareholders' equity as of December 31, 2013, was $3.95 billion, and goodwill was $0.89 billion. Ingram has 155 million (0.155 billion) shares outstanding. The following firms represent Ingram's primary competitors.

Ingram's tangible book value per share (VI_T) = ($3.95 − $0.89)/0.155 = $19.74

The industry average ratio (MV_{IND}/VI_{IND}) = (2.10 + 2.70 + 1.72)/3 = 2.17

Ingram's implied value per share = MV_T = (MV_{IND} / VI_{IND}) × VI_T = 2.17 × $19.74 = $42.84

Based on the implied intrinsic value per share, Ingram was undervalued on March 20, 2014, when its share price was $29.83.

Data Source: Yahoo! Finance.

	Market value/tangible book value	Beta	Projected 5-year net income growth rate (%)	Net profit margin (%)
Tech Data	2.10	.99	11.15	1.44
United Stationers Inc.	2.70	1.36	13.11	2.42
PC Connections	1.72	.82	18.75	1.61

Tangible book value (shareholders' equity less goodwill) method

Book value is a much-maligned value indicator because book asset values rarely reflect actual market values. The value of land frequently is understated, whereas inventory often is overstated if it is old or obsolete. Moreover, book value may be higher for highly acquisitive firms than for other firms in the same industry that choose not to grow through acquisition.

Because of the way acquisitions are recorded for financial reporting purposes (see Chapter 12), takeovers often result in the creation of goodwill. Goodwill reflects the value of intangible factors such as a strong brand name, patents and other proprietary technologies, and synergy anticipated by the buyer when the acquisition was completed. Because acquirers may overpay, the book value of goodwill may overstate its actual value to the firm in generating future operating profits and cash flow. For these reasons, it is important to estimate *tangible book value* (i.e., book value less goodwill) in estimating an industry average multiple based on book value.[10]

Book values generally do not mirror actual market values for manufacturing companies, but they may be more accurate for distribution firms, whose assets are largely inventory with high turnover rates. Examples of such companies include pharmaceutical distributor Bergen Brunswick and personal computer supplier Ingram Micro.[11] Exhibit 8.4 provides an estimate of Ingram Micro's intrinsic share price on March 20, 2014, based on data for firms similar to Ingram in terms of risk (measured by beta), expected growth, and profitability.

Breakup value

Breakup value is the price of the firm's assets sold separately less liabilities and expenses incurred in dividing up the firm. If the breakup value exceeds the going concern value, shareholder value is maximized by splitting up the firm.

[10] The importance of this adjustment is evident in comparing highly diversified businesses with more focused competitors. When goodwill is deducted from the more acquisitive firms, market-to-book ratios tend to be similar to other firms in the same industry (Custodio, 2014).

[11] Book value is also widely used for valuing financial services companies, where tangible book value consists mostly of liquid assets.

EXHIBIT 8.5

Calculating the Breakup Value of JPMorgan Chase

Line of Business	Services provided by line of business	Industry market multiple	After-tax earnings ($ billions)	Fair market value of equity ($ billions)	Average June 2012 price-to-earnings ratio for large:
Investment bank	Advisory, underwriting, and market making	13.3×	6.8	90.4	Investment banks (e.g., Goldman Sachs)
Retail financial services	Consumer and residential mortgage lending	13.2×	1.7	22.4	Diversified financial services firms (e.g., American Express)
Card services and auto	Credit card, auto, and student loans	13.2×	4.5	59.4	Diversified financial services firms (e.g., American Express)
Commercial banking	Middle-market lending, term lending, and corporate client banking	11.1×	2.4	26.6	Money-center banks, excluding JPMorgan Chase (e.g., Citigroup Inc.)
Treasury and securities services	Global corporate cash management services	11.1×	1.2	13.3	Money center banks, excluding JPMorgan Chase (e.g., Citigroup Inc.)
Asset management	Private banking, retail and institutional investment management	17.2×	1.6	27.5	Mutual funds (e.g., T. Rowe Price)
Private equity	Corporate overhead and private equity activities	13.2×	0.6	7.9	Private equity firms (e.g., KKR)
Total fair market value				247.5	

Sources: JPMorgan Chase 2011 10K and Yahoo Finance.

Media conglomerate News Corp announced its decision to divide into two independent units: entertainment and publishing. Estimated after-tax earnings for the entertainment unit and publishing unit for the fiscal year ending June 2012 were $3.1 and $0.5 billion, respectively. If valued at Disney Corporation's P/E ratio of 17, the entertainment businesses were worth $52.7 billion at that time; if valued at newspaper conglomerate Gannett Inc.'s 7.3 P/E ratio, the publishing businesses were worth $3.7 billion. The resulting estimated breakup value of $56.4 billion versus its market value on July 7, 2012, of $50.4 billion suggested the firm was undervalued by 11.9%.

Exhibit 8.5 illustrates the estimation of the breakup value of JPMorgan Chase. Value is determined for each of the firm's lines of business by multiplying its 2011 reported net income by the average June 2012 P/E multiple for the industry in which the business competes and then summing each operation's value to determine the firm's total equity value. Reflecting the impact of highly publicized trading losses, the firm's July 6, 2012, market capitalization of $129.4 billion suggested that it was undervalued by as much as 91%.

Liquidation value

The terms *liquidation* and *breakup value* often are used interchangeably. However, there are subtle distinctions. Liquidation may be involuntary, as a result of bankruptcy, or voluntary, if a firm is viewed by its owners as worth more in liquidation than as a going concern. Liquidation and breakup strategies are explored further in Chapters 17 and 18.

Analysts may estimate the liquidation value of a target company to determine a firm's minimum value. It is particularly appropriate for financially distressed firms. Analysts often assume the assets can be sold in an orderly

EXHIBIT 8.6

Calculating Liquidation Value

Limited Options Corporation has declared bankruptcy, and the firm's creditors have asked the trustee to estimate its liquidation value assuming orderly sale conditions. This example does not take into account legal fees, taxes, management fees, and contractually required employee severance expenses. These expenses can make up a substantial percentage of the proceeds from liquidation.

Balance sheet item	Book value ($ millions)	Orderly sale value ($ millions)
Cash	100	100
Receivables	500	450
Inventory	800	720
Equipment (after depreciation)	200	60
Land	200	300
Total assets	1800	1630
Total liabilities	1600	1600
Shareholders' equity	200	30

fashion, often defined as 9 to 12 months. Under these circumstances, high-quality receivables often can be sold for 80% to 90% of their book value. Inventories might realize 80% to 90% of their book value, depending on the condition and the degree of obsolescence. The value of inventory may also vary, depending on whether it consists of finished, intermediate, or raw materials. More rapid liquidation might reduce the value of inventories to 60% to 65% of their book value. The liquidation value of equipment varies widely, depending on its age, condition, and purpose.

To determine liquidation value, review inventories in terms of obsolescence, receivables for collectability, equipment in terms of age and utility, and real estate for current market value. Equipment, such as computers, with a zero book value may have a significant useful life. Land can be a source of value because it frequently is undervalued on GAAP balance sheets. Prepaid assets, such as insurance premiums, can be liquidated, with a portion of the premium recovered. The liquidation value is reduced dramatically if the assets have to be liquidated in "fire sale" conditions (i.e., assets are sold at deeply discounted prices). See Exhibit 8.6.

The replacement-cost method

Replacement cost is the cost to replace a firm's assets at current market prices. Equity value is determined by deducting the present value (PV) of the firm's liabilities. Valuing the assets separately in terms of what it costs to replace them may understate the firm's true value because synergies created when the assets are used in combination are overlooked. The value of an automotive company that assembles cars on an assembly line consisting of a series of robots reflects the value of the final product of the assembly line (i.e., assembled cars) rather than the sum of the replacement cost of each of the machines. Moreover, this approach should not be used if the firm has significant intangible assets because of the difficulty in valuing such assets.

The weighted-average valuation method

No valuation method is universally accepted as the best measure of a firm's value, although some may be more appropriate in certain situations. When to use the various valuation methodologies discussed in this book is explained in Table 8.3 at the end of this chapter. Unless there is a compelling reason to apply a specific methodology, the weighted-average method of valuation represents a compromise position.[12]

This approach involves calculating the expected value (EXPV) or weighted average of a range of potential outcomes. The weights, which must sum to 1, reflect the analyst's relative confidence in the various methodologies used to value a business. Assuming that an analyst is equally confident in the accuracy of both methods, the expected value of a target firm valued at $12 million using discounted cash flow and $15 million using the comparable-companies method can be written as follows:

$$EXPV = 0.5 \times \$12 + 0.5 \times \$15 = \$13.5 \text{ million}$$

Neither valuation method includes a purchase price premium. Thus, a premium will have to be added to the expected value to obtain a reasonable purchase price for the target firm. With the exception of the recent-transactions method, the individual valuation estimates comprising the weighted-average estimate do not reflect a purchase premium.

Exhibit 8.7 illustrates a practical way of calculating the expected value of the target firm, including a purchase premium, using estimates from multiple valuation methods. In the example, the purchase price premium associated with the estimate provided by the recent-comparable-transactions method is applied to estimates provided by the other valuation methodologies.

EXHIBIT 8.7

Weighted Average Valuation of Alternative Methodologies

An analyst has estimated the value of a company using multiple valuation methodologies. The discounted cash flow value is $220 million, the comparable-transactions value is $234 million, the P/E–based value is $224 million, and the breakup value is $200 million. The analyst has greater confidence in certain methods than others. The purchase price paid for the recent comparable transaction included a 20% premium over the value of the firm at the time of the takeover announcement. Estimate the weighted-average firm value using all valuation methodologies and the weights or relative importance the analyst assigns to each method.

Estimated value ($ millions) Col. 1	**Estimated value including 20% premium ($ millions) Col. 2**	**Relative weight (as determined by analyst) Col. 3**	**Weighted average ($ millions) Col. 2 × Col. 3**
220	264.0	30	79.2
234	234.0[a]	40	93.6
224	268.8	20	53.8
200	240.0	10	24.0
		1.00	250.6

[a]Note that the comparable-recent-transactions estimate already contains a 20% purchase price premium.
P/E, Price-to-earnings.

[12] Liu et al. (2002) provide empirical support for using multiple valuation methods to estimate firm value.

Real-options analysis

An *option* is the right, but not the obligation, to buy, sell, or use property for a period in exchange for a specific amount of money. Those traded on financial exchanges, such as puts and calls, are called *financial options*. A *real option* is a choice that results from business opportunities involving real assets.[13]

Examples of real options include licenses, copyrights, trademarks, and patents, as well as the right to buy land, commercial property, and equipment. Such assets can be valued as call options if their current value exceeds the difference between the asset's current value and some preset level. If a business has an option to lease office space at a fixed price, the value of that option increases as lease rates for this type of office space increase. The asset can be valued as a put option if its value increases as the value of the underlying asset falls below a predetermined level. To illustrate, if a business has an option to sell an office building at a preset price, its value increases as the value of the office building declines. Unlike financial options, real options are generally not traded in markets.

Real options reflect management's ability to adopt and later revise investment decisions. They can impact substantially the value of an investment in a single project and should be considered when valuing such investments. However, real options can be costly to obtain (e.g., the right to extend a lease or purchase property), complex to value, and dependent on problematic assumptions. As such, they should not be pursued unless the firm has the resources to exploit the option and they add significantly to the value of the firm.

Identifying real options embedded or implied in M&A decisions

Investment decisions, including M&As, often contain "embedded or implied options." These include the ability to accelerate growth by adding to the initial investment (i.e., expand), delay the timing of the initial investment (i.e., delay), or walk away from the project (i.e., abandon).

Pharmaceutical firms seeking to acquire the next "blockbuster" drug frequently use an option to expand strategy as part of their M&A deals. British drug maker AstraZeneca acquired a 55% stake in Acerta Pharma for $4 billion in 2016 with the option to buy the remainder of Acerta for $3 billion. The buyout of the balance of Acerta was contingent on receipt of regulatory approval in the United States and Europe of certain drugs and the achievement of specified sales targets establishing the commercial value of the new drugs. Firms with options that could be realized in combination with a target firm often are willing to pay higher purchase price premiums reflecting the expected value of the real option.[14]

Valuing real options for M&As

Three ways to value real options are discussed in this book. The first is to use discounted cash flow, relative-valuation, or asset-oriented methods and ignore alternative real options by assuming their value is zero. The second is to value the real options in the context of a decision tree, an expanded timeline that branches into alternative paths whenever an event can have multiple outcomes. The decision tree branches at points called *nodes* and is most useful whenever the investment is subject to a small number of probable outcomes and can be made in stages. The third method involves the valuation of the real option as a put or call, assuming that the underlying asset has the characteristics of a financial option. A widely used method for valuing a financial option is the Black-Scholes model, which is typically applied to "European options," those that can be exercised only at the expiration date of the option.[15]

Valuing real options using a decision tree framework

Table 8.2 shows how real options may affect the net present value (NPV) of an acquisition in which management has identified two cash flow scenarios (i.e., a successful and an unsuccessful acquisition). Each pair of cash flow

[13] For an extensive review of 164 real option research papers published between 2004 and 2015, see Trigeorgis et al. (2018).

[14] Barbopoulos et al., 2019

[15] A more flexible method is the binomial valuation model used to value so-called American options, which may be exercised at any time before expiration. Although the binomial model allows for changing key assumptions over time, it requires many inputs, making it far more complex and problematic than the Black-Sholes approach.

TABLE 8.2 The impact of real options on valuing mergers and acquisitions

	Year 0	Year 1	Year 2	Year 3	Year 4	Year 5	Year 6	Year 7	Year 8	Year 9
First branch: option for immediate investment or acquisition										
Enterprise cash flows				Projected target firm cash flows						
• Successful case	−300	30	35	40	45	50	55	60	65	
• Unsuccessful case	−300	−5	−5	−5	−5	−5	−5	−5	−5	
Weighted cash flows										
• Successful case (60%)	0	18	21	24	27	30	33	36	39	
• Unsuccessful case (40%)	0	−2	−2	−2	−2	−2	−2	−2	−2	
Expected enterprise cash flow	−300	16	19	22	25	28	31	34	37	
Expected NPV years 1–8 at 15%										−166
Expected terminal value at 13%; sustainable growth rate = 5%										159
Expected total NPV										−7
Second branch: option to abandon (divest or liquidate)										
Enterprise cash flows				Projected target firm cash flows						
• Successful case	−300	30	35	40	45	50	55	60	65	
• Unsuccessful case	−300	−5	−5	−5	−5	−5	−5	−5	−5	
Weighted cash flows										
• Successful case (60%)	0	18	21	24	27	30	33	36	39	
• Unsuccessful case (40%)	0	−2	−2	150	0	0	0	0	0	
Expected enterprise cash flow	−300	16	19	174	27	30	33	36	39	
Expected NPV years 1–6 at 15%%										−75
Expected terminal value at 13%; sustainable growth rate = 5%										167
Expected total NPV										92
Third branch: option to delay investment or acquisition										
Enterprise cash flows				Projected target firm cash flows						
• Successful case	0	−300	35	40	45	50	55	60	65	70
• Unsuccessful case	0	−300	0	0	0	0	0	0	0	0
Weighted cash flows										
• Successful case (60%)	0	0	21	24	27	30	33	36	39	42
• Unsuccessful case (40%)	0	0	0	0	0	0	0	0	0	0
Expected enterprise cash flow	0	−300	21	24	27	30	33	36	39	42
Expected NPV at 15%										−146
Expected terminal value at 13%; sustainable growth rate = 5%										180
Expected total NPV										34

Note: The net present value (NPV) for the delay option is discounted at the end of year 1, whereas the other options are discounted from year 0 (i.e., the present).

scenarios is associated with different options: the option to acquire, delay, or abandon the acquisition. Each outcome is shown as a "branch" on a tree. Each branch shows the cash flows and probabilities of each scenario displayed as a timeline. The probability of realizing the "successful" cash flow projections is assumed to be 60%, and that of realizing the "unsuccessful" projections is 40%. The expected enterprise cash flow of the target firm is the sum of the

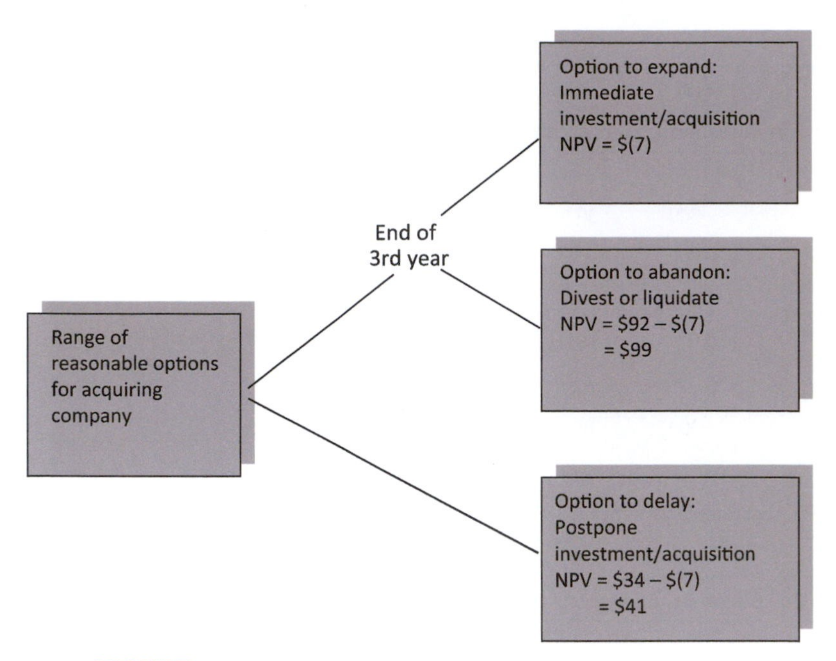

FIGURE 8.1 Real-options decision tree. *NPV*, Net present value.

future cash flows of the "successful" and "unsuccessful" scenarios multiplied by the estimated probability associated with each scenario. The target firm is assumed to have been acquired for $300 million, and the NPV is estimated using a 15% discount rate. The terminal value assumes a 5% growth rate. With an NPV of −$7 million, the immediate-investment option suggests that the acquisition should not be undertaken.

Recognizing that the target could be sold or liquidated, the expected NPV is $92 million, implying the acquisition should be undertaken. This assumes the target is sold or liquidated at the end of the third year after its acquisition for $152 million. Note that the cash flow in year 3 is $150 million, reflecting the difference between $152 million and the −$2 million in operating cash flow during the third year. The expected NPV with the option to delay is estimated at $34 million. Note that the investment is made after a 1-year delay only if the potential acquirer feels confident that competitive market conditions will support the projected "successful" scenario cash flows. Consequently, the "unsuccessful" scenario's cash flows are zero.

Figure 8.1 summarizes the results provided in Table 8.2 in a decision tree framework. Of the three options considered, valuing the target (including the value of the cash flows) with the option to abandon appears to be the most attractive investment strategy based on NPV. The values of the abandon and delay options are estimated as the difference between each of their NPVs and the "immediate investment or acquisition" NPV.

Valuing real options using the Black-Scholes model

Options for assets whose cash flows have large variances and a long time before they expire are typically more valuable than those with smaller variances and less time remaining. The greater variance and time to expiration increase the chance that the factors affecting cash flows will change a project from one with a negative NPV to one with a positive NPV. If the values of certain variables are known, we can use the Black-Scholes model to establish a theoretical option price. The limitations of the Black-Scholes model include the difficulty in estimating key assumptions (particularly risk), its assumptions that interest rates and risk are constant, that it can be exercised only on the expiration date, and that taxes and transactions costs are minimal. The basic Black-Scholes formula for valuing a call option is as follows:

$$C = SN(d_1) - Ee^{-Rt}N(d_2) \tag{8.4}$$

in which

C = theoretical call option value

$d_1 = \frac{ln(S/E)+[R+(1/2)\sigma^2]t}{\sigma\sqrt{t}}$

$d_2 = d_1 - \sigma\sqrt{t}$
S = stock price or underlying asset price
E = exercise or strike price
R = risk-free interest rate corresponding to the life of the option
σ^2 = variance (a measure of risk) of the stock's or underlying asset's return
t = time to expiration of the option
$N(d_1)$ and $N(d_2)$ = cumulative normal probability values of d_1 and d_2

The term Ee^{-Rt} is the PV of the exercise price when continuous discounting is used. The terms $N(d_1)$ and $N(d_2)$, which involve the cumulative probability function, are the terms that take risk into account. $N(d_1)$ and $N(d_2)$ measure the probability that the value of the call option will pay off and the probability that the option will be exercised, respectively. These two values are Z-scores from the normal probability function, and they can be found in many statistics books in cumulative normal distribution function tables for the standard normal random variable.

The variance (i.e., risk) used in the Black-Scholes model can be estimated in a number of ways.[16] First, risk could be estimated as the variance in the stock prices of similar firms. The average variance in the share prices of US oil services companies could be used as the variance in valuing a real option associated with the potential purchase of an oil services firm.[17] Second, the variance of cash flows from similar prior investments can be used. A pharmaceutical company may use the variance associated with the cash flows of previously developed comparable drugs in valuing an option to invest in a new drug. A third method is to use commonly available software to conduct Monte Carlo simulation analyses.[18]

Assuming that the necessary inputs (e.g., risk) can be estimated, a real option can be valued as a put or call option. The NPV of an investment can be adjusted for the value of the real option as follows:

$$\text{Total NPV} = \text{Present value} - \text{Investment} + \text{Option value} \tag{8.5}$$

Option to expand

To value a firm with an option to expand, the analyst must define the potential value of the option. For example, suppose a firm has an opportunity to enter a new market. The analyst must project cash flows that accrue to the firm if it enters the market. The cost of entering the market becomes the option's exercise price, and the PV of the expected cash flows resulting from entering the market becomes the value of the firm or underlying asset. The PV is likely to be less than the initial entry costs, or the firm would already have entered the market. The variance of the firm's value can be estimated by using the variances of the market values of publicly traded firms that currently participate in that market. The option's life is the length of time during which the firm expects to achieve a competitive advantage by entering the market now. Exhibit 8.8 illustrates how to value an option to expand.

Option to delay

The underlying asset is the project to which the firm has exclusive rights. The current value is the PV of expected cash flows from undertaking the project now. The variance of cash flows from similar past projects or acquisitions can be used to estimate the variance for the project under consideration. A firm exercises an option to delay when it decides to postpone investing in a project. The exercise price is the cost of making the initial investment.

The option to delay expires whenever the exclusive rights to the project end. Because the option eventually expires, excess profits associated with having the option disappear as other competitors emerge to exploit the

[16] For a discussion of alternative ways of determining real option values for infrequently traded assets, see Guja and Chandra (2019).

[17] In another example, if an acquirer of an oil company recognizes that, in buying the target, it would have a call option (real option to expand) to develop the firm's oil reserves at a later date, it could choose to value separately the target as a stand-alone entity and the option to develop the firm's reserves at some time in the future. The variance in world oil prices may be used as a proxy for the risk associated with an option to develop the reserves.

[18] Monte Carlo simulations approximate the probability of certain outcomes by running multiple trial runs (i.e., simulations) using random variables, those whose possible numerical values are the result of random or indeterminate factors. Guj et al. (2019) argue that Monte Carlo analysis, which relies on the probability distribution of individual variables rather than aggregated cash flow volatility, can produce more accurate real-option values.

EXHIBIT 8.8

Valuing an Option to Expand Using the Black-Scholes Model

AJAX is negotiating to acquire Comet. Based on its projections of Comet's cash flows as a stand-alone business, AJAX cannot justify paying more than $150 million for Comet. However, Comet is insisting on a price of $160 million. AJAX believes that if it applies its technology to Comet's operations, the firm's cash flow growth rate could be accelerated significantly.

By buying Comet, AJAX is buying an option to expand in a market in which it is not participating currently. The cost of modernizing Comet's manufacturing operations requires an initial investment of $100 million. The PV of the expected cash flows from making this investment today is $80 million. Consequently, based on this information, paying the higher purchase price cannot be justified by making the investment now.

However, if Comet could be first to market with a new product offering, it could dominate the market. Although the new products would be expensive to produce in small quantities, the cost of production is expected to fall as larger volumes are sold, making Comet the low-cost manufacturer. Moreover, because of patent protection, AJAX believes that it is unlikely that competitors will be able to develop a superior technology for at least 10 years.

An analysis of similar investments in the past suggests that the variance of the projected cash flows is 20%. The option is expected to expire in 10 years, reflecting the time remaining on AJAX's patent. The current 10-year Treasury bond rate (corresponding to the expected term of the option) is 6%. Does the value of the option to expand, expressed as a call option, justify paying Comet's asking price of $160 million (see Equation 8.4)?

Solution

Value of the asset (present value (PV) of cash flows from retooling Comet's operations) = $80 million
Exercise price (PV of the cost of retooling Comet's operations) = $100 million
Variance of the cash flows = 0.20
Time to expiration = 10 years
Risk-free interest rate = 0.06

$$d_1 = \frac{ln(\$80/\$100) + [0.06 + (1/2)0.2]10}{\sqrt{0.2}\sqrt{10}} = \frac{-0.2231 + 1.600}{0.4472 \times 3.1623} = \frac{1.3769}{1.4142} = 0.9736$$

$$d_2 = 0.9736 - 1.4142 = -0.4406$$

$$C = \$80(0.8340) - \$100(2.7183)^{-.06\times10}(0.3300)$$
$$= \$66.72 - \$18.11 = \$48.61 \text{ (value of the call option)}$$

The net present value of the investment in retooling Comet's operations, including the value of the call option, is $28.61 million: i.e., $80 – ($100 + $48.61). Including the value of the option, AJAX could pay Comet up to $178.61 million (i.e., $150 million + $28.61 million). It does make sense for AJAX to exercise its option to retool Comet's operations, and AJAX can justify paying Comet its $160 million asking price.

Note: Z-values for d_1 and d_2 are found in cumulative standardized normal distribution $N(d)$ tables.

opportunity. This opportunity cost associated with delaying implementation of an investment is similar to an adjustment made to the Black-Scholes model for stocks that pay dividends. The payment of a dividend is equivalent to reducing the value of the stock because such funds are not reinvested in the firm. For a project whose expected cash flows are spread evenly throughout the option period, each year the project is delayed, the firm will lose one year of profits that it could have earned. Thus, the annual cost of delay is $1/n$, in which n is the time period for which the option is valid. If cash flows are not spread evenly, the cost of delay may be estimated as the projected cash flow for the next period as a percent of the current present value (Exhibit 8.9). Equation 8.4 may be modified to reflect these considerations.

$$C = SN(d_1)e^{-DYt} - Ee^{-Rt}N(d_2) \tag{8.6}$$

in which

$d_1 = \frac{ln(S/E) + [R - DY + (1/2)\sigma^2]t}{\sigma\sqrt{t}}$
$d_2 = d_1 - \sigma\sqrt{t}$
DY = dividend yield or opportunity cost

EXHIBIT 8.9

Valuing an Option to Delay Using the Black-Scholes Model

Aztec Corp. seeks to acquire Pharmaceuticals Unlimited, which has a new cancer-fighting drug recently approved by the Food and Drug Administration. Although current market studies indicate that the new drug's market acceptance will be slow because of competing drugs, it is believed that the drug will have meteoric growth potential in the long term as new applications are identified. The research and development (R&D) and commercialization costs associated with exploiting new applications are expected to require an upfront investment of $60 million. However, Aztec can delay this investment until it is more confident of the new drug's actual growth potential.

Pharmaceuticals Unlimited's R&D efforts give it a 5-year time period before competitors will have similar drugs on the market. However, if the higher growth for the new drug does not materialize, Aztec estimates that the net present value (NPV) for Pharmaceuticals Unlimited to be $(30) million. That is, if the new cancer-fighting drug does not realize its potential, it makes no sense for Aztec to make the acquisition.

Cash flows from previous drug introductions have exhibited a variance equal to 50% of the PV of the cash flows. Simulating alternative growth scenarios for this new drug provides an expected value of $40 million. The 5-year Treasury bond rate (corresponding to the expected term of the option) is 6%. Despite the negative NPV associated with the acquisition, does the existence of the option to delay, valued as a call option, justify Aztec's acquiring Pharmaceuticals Unlimited (see Equation 8.6)?

Solution

Value of the asset (present value (PV) of projected cash flows for the new drug) = $40 million
Exercise price (investment required to develop the new drug fully) = $60 million
Variance of the cash flows = 0.5
Time to expiration (t) = 5 years
Risk-free interest rate = 0.06
Dividend yield or opportunity cost (cost of delay = 1/5) = 0.2

$$d_1 = \frac{ln(\$40/\$60) + [0.06 - 0.2 + (1/2)0.5]5}{\sqrt{0.5}\sqrt{5}}$$

$$= \frac{-0.4055 + 0.5500}{0.7071 \times 2.2361} = \frac{0.1445}{1.5811} = 0.0914$$

$$d_2 = 0.0914 - 1.5811 = -1.4897$$

$$C = \$40(0.5359)2.7183^{-0.2\times5} - \$60(0.0681)(2.7183)^{-0.06\times5}$$

$$= \$40(0.5359)0.3679 - \$60(0.0681)0.7408$$

$$= 7.89 - 3.03 = \$4.86 \text{ million (value of the call option)}$$

The modest $4.86 million value of the call option is insufficient to offset the negative NPV of $30 million associated with the acquisition. Consequently, Aztec should not acquire Pharmaceuticals Unlimited.

Note: Z-values for d_1 and d_2 are found in cumulative standardized normal distribution $N(d)$ tables.

Option to abandon

For a project with a remaining life of n years, the value of continuing the project should be compared to its value in liquidation or sale (i.e., abandonment). The project should be continued if its value exceeds the liquidation or sale value. Otherwise, the project should be abandoned. The option to abandon is equivalent to a put option (i.e., the right to sell an asset for a predetermined price at or before a stipulated time). The Black-Scholes formula for valuing a call option can be rewritten to value a put option (P) as follows (see Equation 8.4):

$$P = S\{1 - N(d_2)\}e^{-Rt} - E\{1 - N(d_1)\}e^{-DYt} \quad (8.7)$$

in which

P = theoretical put option value

$d_1 = \frac{ln(S/E) + [R - DY + (1/2)\sigma^2]t}{\sigma\sqrt{t}}$

$d_2 = d_1 - \sigma\sqrt{t}$

Exhibit 8.10 illustrates how the abandonment or put option can be applied.

EXHIBIT 8.10

Valuing an Option to Abandon Using the Black-Scholes Model

BETA agreed to buy a 30% ownership stake in Bernard Mining for $225 million to finance the development of new mining operations. The mines are expected to have an economically useful life of 35 years. BETA estimates that the present value (PV) of its share of the cash flows would be $210 million, resulting in a negative net present value (NPV) of $15 million (i.e., $210 million − $225 million). To induce BETA to make the investment, Bernard Mining gave BETA a put option enabling it to sell its share (i.e., abandon its investment) to Bernard at any point during the next 5 years for $175 million.

In evaluating deal terms, BETA needs to value the put option, whose PV will vary depending on when it is exercised. BETA estimates the variance in the PVs of future cash flows to be 20% based on the variance of the share prices of publicly traded similar mining companies. Because the value of the mines diminishes over time as reserves are depleted, the PV of the investment will diminish over time because of fewer years of cash flows remaining. The dividend yield or opportunity cost is estimated to be 1 divided by the number of years of profitable reserves remaining. The risk-free rate of return is 4%. Is the value of the put option sufficient to justify making the investment despite the negative net present value of the investment without the inclusion of the option value (see Equation 8.7)?

Solution

Present or expected value of BETA's 30% share of Bernard = $210 million
Exercise price of put option = $175 million
Time to expiration of put option = 5
Variance = 20%
Dividend yield (1/35) = 0.029

$$d_1 = \frac{ln(\$210/\$175) + [0.04 - 0.029 + (1/2)0.2]5}{\sqrt{0.2}\sqrt{5}}$$

$$= \frac{0.1823 + 0.5550}{0.4472 \times 2.2361} = \frac{0.7373}{1.0} = 0.7373$$

$$d_2 = 0.7373 - 1.000 = -0.2627$$

$$P = \$210 \times (1 - 0.6026) \times 2.7183^{-0.04\times 5}$$

$$- \$175 \times (1 - 0.7673) \times 2.7183^{-0.029\times 5}$$

$$= \$210 \times 0.3974 \times 0.8187 - \$175 \times 0.2327 \times 0.8650 = \$33.10$$

The value of the put option represents the value created by reducing risk associated with the investment. This additional value justifies the investment, because the sum of the NPV of $(15) million and the put option of $33.10 million gives a total NPV of $18.10 million.

Note: Z-scores for d_1 and d_2 are found in cumulative standardized normal distribution $N(d)$ tables.

Determining when to use the different approaches to valuation

Table 8.3 summarizes the appropriate application of each valuation method, including discounted cash flow discussed in Chapter 7, as well as the relative-valuation, asset-oriented, replacement-cost, and real-options methods discussed in this chapter. If a controlling interest is desired, a control premium (except for the recent-transactions method) must be added to the estimated firm value to determine the purchase price.

Valuing initial public offerings

Traditionally, firms undertaking IPOs hire investment bankers to implement the process. Known as underwriting, the investment bank assesses the risk of the shares to be issued and helps to determine what price represents their true economic value. Quantitative factors used to value the shares include the application of comparable-company multiples to a firm's projected earnings, revenue, cash flow, or other performance metrics. Competitors' multiples are used, or those from firms in other industries that are similar in terms of margin, growth, and risk can be used. Qualitative factors include an assessment of the credibility of financial projections provided in the IPO's prospectus and factors such as a firm's new products or proprietary technology as well as management quality.

After an initial estimate of value has been determined, investment bankers initiate a "road show." This consists of presentations made by the firm's management to solicit orders from potential investors ranging from pension to mutual funds. Institutional investors may express a specific price or range to receive an early allocation of the shares.

TABLE 8.3 When to use various valuation methodologies

Methodology	When to use this methodology
Discounted cash flow	• The firm is publicly traded or private with identifiable cash flows. • A start-up has some history to facilitate cash flow forecasts. • An analyst has a long time horizon. • An analyst has confidence in forecasting the firm's cash flows. • Current or near-term earnings or cash flows are negative but are expected to turn positive in the future. • A firm's competitive advantage is expected to be sustainable. • The magnitude and timing of cash flows vary significantly.
Comparable companies	• There are many firms exhibiting similar growth, return, and risk characteristics. • An analyst has a short-term time horizon. • Prior, current, or near-term earnings or cash flows are positive. • An analyst has confidence that the markets are, on average, right. • Sufficient information to predict cash flows is lacking. • Firms are cyclical. For P/E ratios, use normalized earnings (i.e., earnings averaged throughout the business cycle). • Growth rate differences among firms are large; use the PEG ratio.
Comparable transactions	• Recent transactions of similar firms exist. • An analyst has a short-term time horizon. • An analyst has confidence the markets are, on average, right. • Sufficient information to predict cash flows is lacking.
Same or comparable industry	• Firms within an industry or a comparable industry are substantially similar in terms of profitability, growth, and risk. • An analyst has confidence the markets are, on average, right. • Sufficient information to predict cash flows is lacking.
Replacement-cost approach	• An analyst wants to know the current cost of replicating a firm's assets. • The firm's assets are easily identifiable, tangible, and separable. • The firm's earnings or cash flows are negative.
Tangible book value	• The firms' assets are highly liquid. • The firm is a financial services or product distribution business. • The firm's earnings and cash flows are negative.
Breakup value	• The sum of the value of the businesses or product lines composing a firm are believed to exceed its value as a going concern.
Liquidation value	• An analyst wants to know asset values if they were liquidated today. • Assets are separable, tangible, and marketable. • Firms are bankrupt or subject to substantial financial distress. • An orderly liquidation is possible.
Real options (contingent claims)	• Additional value can be created if management has a viable option to expand, delay, or abandon an investment. • Assets not currently generating cash flows have the potential to do so. • Assets have characteristics most resembling financial options. • The asset owner has some degree of exclusivity (e.g., a patent).

P/E, Price-to-earnings; *PEG,* price-to-earnings to growth.

Such expressions of interest help confirm the value estimates suggested by applying relative-valuation methods. If investors believe the IPO risky because of insufficient historical data or lack of interest in the shares, the IPO share price may be issued at below what is believed to be its true value. Underpricing helps to compensate investors for the risk they are assuming, encouraging them to participate in the IPO.

All IPOs are not underwritten by investment bankers. Music streaming firm Spotify's 2018's IPO was directly listed on the New York Stock Exchange; as such, it did not involve any solicitation of orders before the IPO. Institutional investors were able to purchase shares on a private secondary market in which more than 8 million shares were sold to institutional and accredited investors with a net worth of at least $1 million, providing an early indication of the value of the shares. The direct listing helped Spotify shareholders sell shares before the public listing, reduced pent-up demand, and lessened potential volatility.

What do valuation professionals do in practice?

The capital budgeting process describes how firms determine which projects to undertake based on various investment rules. The primary decision rule is ranking projects by their NPVs. The basis for NPV analysis is the conversion of projected cash flows to a PV by discounting these future cash flows using a discount rate often based on the capital asset pricing model (CAPM). The finance literature argues that NPV results in better investment decisions compared with alternative methodologies such as internal rate of return (IRR)[19] or payback period.[20] However, past survey results suggest corporate chief financial officers are equally likely to use NPV techniques as they are IRR analyses. Large-company CFOs rely heavily on the CAPM to estimate their cost of capital. Investment bankers also are likely to use NPV methods and CAPM calculations in estimating the weighted-average cost of capital as illustrated in their fairness opinion documents for M&As.

Private equity firms often diverge from mainstream academic finance in how they value businesses. They rely primarily on IRR and exit multiples (i.e., what they hope to sell the business for at the end of the forecast period) derived from comparable company analyses to evaluate investments. Private equity investors tend not to calculate a weighted average cost of capital (WACC) but rather to develop their own target rate of return (often 20%–25%) that exceeds the standard WACC calculation. The target rates, is set above the WACC rate because buyout firms subtract their fees from these target rates, so they must be high enough that limited partners can still earn their desired rate of return. Private equity investors tend to use a 5-year forecast horizon (consistent with their expected holding period) in their IRR calculations.[21]

Unlike CFOs and private equity investors, few venture capital firms (VCs) use NPV to evaluate investment opportunities. This is particularly true of VCs focusing on emerging companies, which generally lack any significant performance history. Instead, VCs calculate "cash on cash" returns to determine the relative attractiveness of investments. Such returns equal how much cash the VC expects to receive upon exiting the investment divided by how much it initially invests; unlike IRR, it is not dependent on when the exit occurs.[22]

Some things to remember

Relative-valuation and asset-oriented methods offer alternatives to DCF estimates. Because no single approach ensures accuracy, analysts often choose to use a weighted average of several valuation methods to increase their level of confidence in the final estimate. Real options refer to management's ability to revise corporate investment decisions after they have been made.

Chapter discussion questions

8.1 Does the application of the comparable-companies valuation method require the addition of an acquisition premium? Why or why not?

8.2 Which is generally considered more accurate, the comparable-companies method or the recent-transactions method? Explain your answer.

8.3 What key assumptions are implicit in using the comparable-companies valuation method? The recent-comparable-transactions method?

8.4 Explain the primary differences between the income (discounted cash flow), market-based, and asset-oriented valuation methods.

8.5 Under what circumstances might it be more appropriate to use relative-valuation methods rather than the DCF approach? Be specific.

8.6 PEG ratios allow for the adjustment of relative-valuation methods for the expected growth of the firm. How might this be helpful in selecting potential acquisition targets?

[19] IRR is a discount rate that makes the NPV of all cash flows equal to zero in a DCF analysis.

[20] The amount of time it takes to recover the cost of an investment.

[21] Gompers et al., 2016

[22] Gompers et al., 2020

8.7 How is the liquidation value of a firm calculated? Why is the assumption of orderly liquidation important?
8.8 What are real options, and how are they applied in valuing acquisitions?
8.9 Give examples of pre- and postclosing real options. Be specific.
8.10 Conventional DCF analysis does not incorporate the effects of real options into the valuation of an asset. How might an analyst incorporate the potential impact of real options into conventional DCF valuation methods?

Answers to these Chapter Discussion Questions are available in the Online Instructor's Manual for instructors using this book.

Practice problems and answers

8.11 BigCo's chief financial officer is trying to determine a fair value for PrivCo, a nonpublicly traded firm that BigCo is considering acquiring. Several of PrivCo's competitors, including Ion International and Zenon, are publicly traded. Ion and Zenon have P/E ratios of 20 and 15, respectively. Moreover, Ion and Zenon's shares trade at a multiple of earnings before interest, taxes, depreciation, and amortization (EBITDA) of 10 and 8, respectively. BigCo estimates that next year PrivCo will achieve net income and EBITDA of $4 million and $8 million, respectively. To gain a controlling interest in the firm, BigCo expects to have to pay at least a 30% premium to the firm's market value. What should BigCo expect to pay for PrivCo?

a. Based on P/E ratios? *Answer*: $91 million
b. Based on EBITDA? *Answer*: $93.6 million

8.12 LAFCO Industries believes that its two primary product lines, automotive and commercial aircraft valves, are becoming obsolete rapidly. Its free cash flow is diminishing quickly as it loses market share to new firms entering its industry. LAFCO has $200 million in debt outstanding. Senior management expects the automotive and commercial aircraft valve product lines to generate $25 million and $15 million, respectively, in earnings before interest, taxes, depreciation, and amortization next year. The operating liabilities associated with these two product lines are minimal. Senior management also believes that it will not be able to upgrade these product lines because of declining cash flow and excessive current leverage. A competitor to its automotive valve business last year sold for 10 times EBITDA. Moreover, a company similar to its commercial aircraft valve product line sold last month for 12 times EBITDA. Estimate LAFCO's breakup value before taxes.

Answer: $230 million

8.13 Siebel Incorporated, a nonpublicly traded company, has 2009 after-tax earnings of $20 million, which are expected to grow at 5% annually into the foreseeable future. The firm is debt free, capital spending equals the firm's rate of depreciation, and the annual change in working capital is expected to be minimal. The firm's beta is estimated to be 2.0, the 10-year Treasury bond is 5%, and the historical risk premium of stocks over the risk-free rate is 5.5%. Publicly traded Rand Technology, a direct competitor of Siebel's, was sold recently at a purchase price of 11 times its 2009 after-tax earnings, which included a 20% premium over its current market price. Aware of the premium paid for the purchase of Rand, Siebel's equity owners would like to determine what it might be worth if they were to attempt to sell the firm in the near future. They chose to value the firm using the discounted–cash-flow and comparable–recent-transactions methods. They believe that either method provides an equally valid estimate of the firm's value.

a. What is the value of Siebel using the DCF method? *Answer:* $229.1 million
b. What is the value using the comparable–recent-transactions method? *Answer*: $220 million
c. What would be the value of the firm if we combine the results of both methods? *Answer*: $224.5 million

8.14 Titanic Corporation reached an agreement with its creditors to voluntarily liquidate its assets and use the proceeds to pay off as much of its liabilities as possible. The firm anticipates that it will be able to sell off its assets in an orderly fashion, realizing as much as 70% of the book value of its receivables, 40% of its inventory, and 25% of its net fixed assets (excluding land). However, the firm believes that the land on which it is located can be sold for 120% of book value. The firm has legal and professional expenses associated with the liquidation process of $2.9 million. The firm has only common stock outstanding. Using Table 8.4, estimate the amount of cash that would remain for the firm's common shareholders after all assets have been liquidated.

Answer: $1.3 million

TABLE 8.4 Titanic Corporation balance sheet

Balance sheet item	Book value of assets ($)	Liquidation value
Cash	10	
Accounts receivable	20	
Inventory	15	
Net fixed assets excluding land	8	
Land	6	
Total assets	59	
Total liabilities	35	
Shareholders' equity	24	

8.15 Best's Foods is seeking to acquire the Heinz Baking Company, whose shareholders' equity and goodwill are $41 million and $7 million, respectively. A comparable bakery was recently acquired for $400 million, 30% more than its tangible book value (TBV). What was the tangible book value of the recently acquired bakery? How much should Best's Foods expect to pay for the Heinz Baking Company? Show your work.

Answer: The TBV of the recently acquired bakery = $307.7 million, and the likely purchase price of Heinz = $44.2 million.

8.16 Delhi Automotive Inc. is the leading supplier of specialty fasteners for passenger cars in the US market, with an estimated 25% share of this $5 billion market. Delhi's rapid growth in recent years has been fueled by high levels of reinvestment in the firm. Although this has resulted in the firm's having "state-of-the-art" plants, it also has resulted in the firm's showing limited profitability and positive cash flow. Delhi is privately owned and has announced that it is going to undertake an IPO in the near future. Investors know that economies of scale are important in this high–fixed-cost industry and understand that market share is an important determinant of future profitability. Thornton Auto Inc., a publicly traded firm and market share leader, has an estimated market share of 38% and an $800 million market value. How should investors value the Delhi IPO? Show your work.

Answer: $526.3 million

8.17 Photon Inc. is considering acquiring one of its competitors. Photon's management wants to buy a firm it believes is most undervalued. The firm's three major competitors, AJAX, BABO, and COMET, have current market values of $375 million, $310 million, and $265 million, respectively. AJAX's FCFE is expected to grow at 10% annually, and BABO's and COMET's FCFEs are projected to grow by 12% and 14% per year, respectively. AJAX, BABO, and COMET's current year FCFE are $24 million, $22 million, and $17 million, respectively. The industry average price-to-FCFE ratio and growth rate are 10% and 8%, respectively. Estimate the market value of each of the three potential acquisition targets based on the information provided. Which firm is the most undervalued? Which firm is most overvalued? Show your work.

Answer: AJAX is most overvalued, and COMET is most undervalued.

8.18 Acquirer Incorporated's management believes that the most reliable way to value a potential target firm is by averaging multiple valuation methods, because all methods have their shortcomings. Consequently, Acquirer's chief financial officer estimates that the value of Target Inc. could range, before an acquisition premium is added, from a high of $650 million using DCF analysis to a low of $500 million using the comparable-companies relative-valuation method. A valuation based on a recent comparable transaction is $672 million. The CFO anticipates that Target Inc.'s management and shareholders would be willing to sell for a 20% acquisition premium based on the premium paid for the recent comparable transaction. The CEO asks the CFO to provide a single estimate of the value of Target Inc. based on the three estimates. In calculating a weighted average of the three estimates, she gives a value of 0.5 to the recent-transactions method, 0.3 to the DCF estimate, and 0.2 to the comparable-companies estimate. What is the weighted-average estimate she gives to the CEO?

Answer: $690 million

8.19 An investor group wants to purchase a firm whose primary asset is ownership of the exclusive rights to develop a parcel of undeveloped land sometime during the next 5 years. Without considering the value of the option to develop the property, the investor group believes the NPV of the firm is $(10) million. However, to convert the property to commercial use (i.e., exercise the option), the investors have to invest $60 million immediately in infrastructure improvements. The primary uncertainty associated with the property is how rapidly the surrounding area will grow. Based on their experience with similar properties, the investors estimate that the variance of the projected cash flows is 5% of NPV, which is $55 million. Assume the risk-free rate of return is 4%. What is the value of the call option the investor group would obtain by buying the firm? Is it sufficient to justify the acquisition of the firm? Show your work.

Answer: The value of the option is $13.47 million. The investor group should buy the firm because the value of the option more than offsets the $(10) million NPV of the firm if the call option were not exercised.

8.20 Acquirer Company's management believes that there is a 60% chance that Target Company's FCCF will grow at 20% per year during the next 5 years from this year's level of $5 million. Sustainable growth beyond the fifth year is estimated at 4% per year. However, they also believe that there is a 40% chance that cash flow will grow at half that annual rate during the next 5 years and then at a 4% rate thereafter. The discount rates are estimated to be 15% during the high-growth period and 12% during the sustainable-growth period. What is the expected value of Target Company?

Answer: $94.93 million
Solutions to these Practice Problems are available in the Online Instructor's Manual for instructors using this book.

End-of-chapter case study: did British American Tobacco overpay for Reynolds American?

Case study objectives

To illustrate

- The application of relative-valuation methods
- The limitations of such methods
- How to approximate the value of synergy
- The role key assumptions play in establishing the credibility of any valuation

British American Tobacco (BAT) completed its buyout of the 57.8% of Reynolds American Inc. (Reynolds) that it did not already own on July 25, 2017, for $49.4 billion in cash and stock for full control of the firm. Including assumed debt of $12.6 billion, the enterprise value of the deal totaled $62 billion. The deal took place at a time when both firms were struggling to gain market share and to find acceptable alternatives to cigarettes.

BAT agreed to pay $29.44 in cash and 0.5260 BAT shares for each Reynolds share outstanding. The purchase price represented a 26% premium over Reynolds's share price on October 20, 2016, the day before BAT's first offer was made public. Reynolds had rejected the initial offer made in November 2016, although the two parties continued to negotiate. The merger gives BAT products direct access to the US cigarette market.

The deal values 100% of Reynolds at about $85.5 billion ($49.4 billion/0.578) and marks the return of BAT to the highly regulated US cigarette market after a 12-year hiatus. BAT exited the United States in 2004 when it merged its subsidiary Brown & Williamson with R.J. Reynolds to form Reynolds American.

BAT's share price dropped after the announcement of the Reynolds takeover. Investors fretted about the total purchase price, the debt required to finance the cash portion of the deal, and Reynold's debt assumed by BAT. BAT anticipates annual pretax cost savings of at least $400 million within 2 years after closing. Failure to realize these savings in a timely manner can significantly impact the PV of synergy. Also, it is unclear if the full cost of realizing these synergies has been deducted from the projected savings.

The outlook for the industry remains problematic. The merger was completed one day after the World Health Organization released a report on tobacco companies' efforts to weaken anti-smoking laws worldwide. The UK public health charity Action on Smoking and Health (ASH) worried publicly that the creation of an even bigger tobacco firm would feed a growing tobacco epidemic in poor countries.

TABLE 8.5 Reynolds American valuation data

	12-month trailing P/E ratio	12-month forward P/E ratio
	Col. 1	Col. 2
Primary competitors		
Philip Morris International	24.27	22.83
Imperial Brands	20.23	19.40
Swedish Match AB	17.98	16.05
Altria Group	18.35	17.78
Scandinavian Tobacco Company	21.28	20.64
Reynolds American (Dollars Per Share)	4.26	4.64

P/E, Price-to-earnings.

Today, tobacco companies remain profitable, having weathered the lawsuits and regulations of the 1990s and by expanding sales in emerging countries. They seem to presume that growth in these markets will continue for the foreseeable future and that the attrition among smokers in the United States will slow to a crawl.

One way of determining if BAT overpaid for Reynolds is to estimate Reynolds's standalone value plus the PV of anticipated synergy. This estimate represents the maximum amount BAT should pay for Reynolds and still be able to earn its cost of capital. Any payment in excess of the maximum purchase price means that BAT is destroying shareholder value by, in effect, transferring more value than would be created to the target firm shareholders.

Table 8.5 provides data enabling an analyst to value Reynolds on a standalone basis using the comparable-company method. The choice of valuation multiples is subjective in that it is unclear which best mirror the standalone value of Reynolds. Abnormally low interest rates at the time of the merger announcement could have resulted in artificially high valuation multiples. Also, the competitors selected vary in size, profitability, and growth rates.

Discussion questions

1. Based on the information provided in Table 8.5, what do you believe is a reasonable standalone value for Reynolds? (Hint: Use the comparable-company valuation method to derive a single point estimate of standalone value.) Show your work.
2. Does your answer to question 1 include a purchase price premium?
3. What are the key limitations of the comparable-companies valuation methodology?
4. In estimating the value of anticipated cost savings, should an analyst use Reynolds marginal tax rate of 40% or its effective tax rate of 22%? Explain your answer.
5. What is the 2018 after-tax present value of the $400 million pretax annual cost savings expected to start in 2019? Assume the appropriate cost of capital is 10% and that the savings will continue in perpetuity. Show your work.
6. What are the key assumptions underlying the valuation of Reynolds? Include both the valuation of Reynolds as a standalone business and synergy value.
7. What is the maximum amount BAT could have paid for Reynolds and still earned its cost of capital? Recall that BAT acquired the remaining 57.8% of Reynolds that it did not already own. Did BAT overpay for Reynolds, based on the information given in the case? Explain your answer. (Hint: Use your answers to questions 1 and 5.)

Solutions to these questions are provided in the Online Instructor's Guide accompanying this manual.

CHAPTER

9

Financial modeling basics

OUTLINE

Mergers, Acquisitions, and Other Restructuring Activities, Eleventh Edition
https://doi.org/10.1016/B978-0-12-819782-0.00009-5

There are two kinds of forecasters: the ones who don't know and the ones who don't know they don't know. —*John Kenneth Galbraith*

Inside M&As: the role of financial models in the M&A process

KEY POINTS

- Establish corporate "baseline" standalone valuation estimates.
- Address valuation, deal structuring, and financing issues.
- Enable the rapid consideration of alternative scenarios by changing key assumptions.

Financial models constitute a highly useful tool in all aspects of the mergers and acquisitions (M&A) process from strategy development to target valuation to postmerger performance monitoring. An important application is valuing the target's cash flows, which typically involve identifying the key determinants of cash flow, projecting pro forma financial statements, and converting projected cash flows to a present value. This provides a baseline standalone value[1] for the target representing the minimum price a buyer can expect to pay in the absence of extenuating circumstances. Estimates of synergy plus the minimum price denote the maximum value the acquirer should pay for the target. If the purchase price exceeds the theoretical maximum price, the total value of synergy would be transferred to the target firm's shareholders. The actual price paid will often fall between the minimum and maximum price estimates.

Nexstar Media Group Inc.'s (Nexstar) $4.1 billion takeover of the Tribune Media Company (Tribune) in 2019 to create the largest owner of local TV stations in the United States illustrates some of the many applications of financial modeling in the M&A process. Having long been interested in Tribune, Nexstar was able to outbid private equity firm Apollo Global Management LLC. Nexstar's financial projections made it clear that, in an industry beset by threats from Netflix and other streaming services, increased scale mattered. Nexstar has pursued a hybrid business strategy (cost leadership and differentiation) focused on providing excellent local content in combination with growing scale to enable the firm to attract advertisers through competitive pricing. Nexstar had chosen to implement its business strategy through acquisitions.

Before making a bid, Nexstar's financial analysts churned out numerous pro forma financial statements to value Tribune on a standalone basis. Each scenario reflected changes to key assumptions. Estimated pretax cost synergies exceeded $20 million annually, and incremental revenue was expected to grow within a few years after closing to $160 million per year. This information helped Nexstar's board establish the opening offer price for Tribune. And financial models updated to include new information uncovered during due diligence enabled the firm to revise its bids accordingly throughout the negotiation process.

Investors lauded the deal, with Tribune shares jumping 10% to $44.29 and Nexstar's rising by 3.8% to $85.78 immediately after the deal's announcement. Investors viewed the transaction as giving Nexstar more leverage in negotiating retransmission feeds from pay-TV providers.

Chapter overview

This chapter discusses the basics of applying financial modeling to firm valuation and assists readers in understanding the power (and limitations) of models in analyzing real-world situations. Building on the basics of financial modeling outlined in this chapter, Chapter 15 discusses the important role such models play in valuing and structuring M&As using a substantially more complex, interactive model.

[1] The standalone value of a firm is its market value based on its total revenue and all costs, assets, and liabilities required to support that revenue.

This chapter begins with an overview of what financial modeling entails, why it is important, the data requirements of such models, and common financial model linkages. A simplified methodology for using a financial model to value a firm is discussed as are common sources of inputs to models. The case study at the end of the chapter titled "Life Technologies Undertakes a Strategic Review" illustrates how financial models can be used to estimate firm value, identify the key determinants of firm value, and simulate alternative outcomes to facilitate management decision making. The spreadsheets and formulas for the model described in this chapter are available in a Microsoft Excel file titled "Target Firm Valuation Model" on the companion site to this book (https://www.elsevier.com/books-and-journals/book-companion/9780128197820). A review of this chapter is also available in the file folder titled "Student Study Guide" on the companion site to this book.

What is financial modeling?

Financial modeling is the creation of a mathematical representation of the financial and operational characteristics of a business. Applications involving financial modeling include business valuation, management decision making, capital budgeting, financial statement analysis, and determining the firm's cost of capital. Their real value comes from forcing the model builder to think about the important relationships among the firm's financial statements and to focus on the key determinants of value creation and the assumptions underlying forecasts. Often referred to as "simulation," financial models provide a useful means of assessing alternative options and associated risks and of identifying how firm value is affected by different events. To estimate firm value, financial modeling requires the analyst to forecast cash flow. How this may be done and the accompanying challenges are addressed next.

Financial modeling data requirements

The quality of a model's output depends on the reliability of data used to build the model and the credibility of the assumptions underlying projections. Thus analysts must understand on what basis numbers are reported. Are they based on generally accepted accounting principles (GAAP) or pro forma financial statements?

Generally accepted accounting principles and international standards

US public companies prepare their financial statements in accordance with GAAP, established by the Financial Accounting Standards Board (FASB). GAAP is a rules-based system, with instructions for situations the FASB has anticipated. In contrast, *international accounting standards* (IAS) offers more generalized guiding principles. GAAP and IAS currently exhibit significant differences. Although the way financial data is recorded often differs by country, GAAP-based reporting is used throughout this book.

GAAP financial statements

A firm's financial statements consist of an income statement, balance sheet, and cash flow statement. The *income statement* measures a firm's financial performance over a specific time period, displaying revenue and expenses from both operating and nonoperating activities. Operating revenues and expenses are derived from the firm's normal operations; nonoperating revenues and expenses result from activities such as the sale of assets or employee termination expenses associated with a facility closure.

The *balance sheet* provides data on what a firm owns (i.e., its assets), what it owes (i.e., its liabilities), and its value to its shareholders (i.e., shareholders' equity) at a moment in time. Assets are resources that generate future cash flows for shareholders. Liabilities are the firm's financial obligations. Shareholders' equity is the value of the business to its owners after all financial obligations have been satisfied.

A *cash flow statement* summarizes the firm's cash inflows and outflows from operating, investing, and financing activities. Cash flows from operations arise from the firm's normal operations such as revenues and actual cash expenses after taxes. Cash from investing activities arises from the acquisition or disposition of current or fixed assets. Finally, cash inflows from financing activities include the issuance of additional shares or new borrowing; cash outflows include share repurchases, principal repayments, and dividend payouts.

EXHIBIT 9.1

Accounting Discrepancy Red Flags

1. The source of the revenue is questionable. Examples include revenue from selling to an affiliated party or selling something to a customer in exchange for something other than cash.
2. Income is inflated by nonrecurring gains. Gains on the sale of assets may be inflated by an artificially low book value of the assets sold.
3. Deferred revenue shows a large increase. Deferred revenue increases as a firm collects money from customers in advance of delivering its products and is reduced as the products are delivered. A jump in this item could mean the firm is having trouble delivering its products.
4. Reserves for bad debt are declining as a percentage of revenue. This implies the firm may be boosting revenue by not reserving enough to cover losses from uncollectable accounts.
5. Growth in accounts receivable exceeds substantially the increase in revenue or inventory. This may mean that a firm is having difficulty in selling its products (i.e., inventories are accumulating) or that it is having difficulty collecting what it is owed.
6. The growth in net income is much different from the growth in cash from operations. Because it is more difficult to "manage" cash flow than net income (often distorted because of improper revenue recognition), this could indicate that net income is being misstated.
7. There is an increasing gap between a firm's income reported on its financial statements and its taxable income. In general, the relationship between book and tax accounting is likely to remain constant over time unless there are changes in tax rules or accounting standards.
8. Unexpected large asset write-offs may reflect management inertia in incorporating changing business circumstances into its accounting estimates.
9. Extensive use of related party transactions may not be subject to the same discipline and high standards of integrity as unrelated party transactions.
10. There are changes in auditing firms that are not well justified. The firm may be seeking a firm that will accept its problematic accounting positions.

Pro forma accounting

Pro forma financial statements (also referred to as adjusted financial statements) present financial data in a way that may describe more accurately a firm's current or projected performance. Because there are no accepted standards, pro forma statements may deviate substantially from GAAP statements. Most public firms supplement their GAAP statements with pro forma statements that are "adjusted" to reflect factors that firms argue more accurately represent their business. Pro forma statements are used to show what an acquirer's and target's combined financial performance would look like if they were merged.[2]

Although pro forma statements serve a useful purpose, such liberal accounting can easily hide a company's poor performance, contributing to subsequent revision of reported financial statements and higher audit fees.[3] Exhibit 9.1 suggests some ways in which an analyst can tell if a firm is using inappropriate accounting practices.

Common financial model linkages

The income statement, balance sheet, and cash flow statements are interrelated (Fig. 9.1). All items on the income statement affect the calculation of net income, which measures how well the assets and liabilities listed on the

[2] The Securities and Exchange Commission's (SEC's) Regulation G (introduced in 2003) requires public firms disclosing non-GAAP measures to the public to also present comparable GAAP financial measures and to reconcile the GAAP and non-GAAP metrics. In 2010, the SEC issued new Compliance and Disclosure Interpretations (C&DIs) giving firms more discretion in how they adjust for non-GAAP financial indicators, somewhat offsetting the rigor introduced by Regulation G.

[3] Chen and Gong, 2019

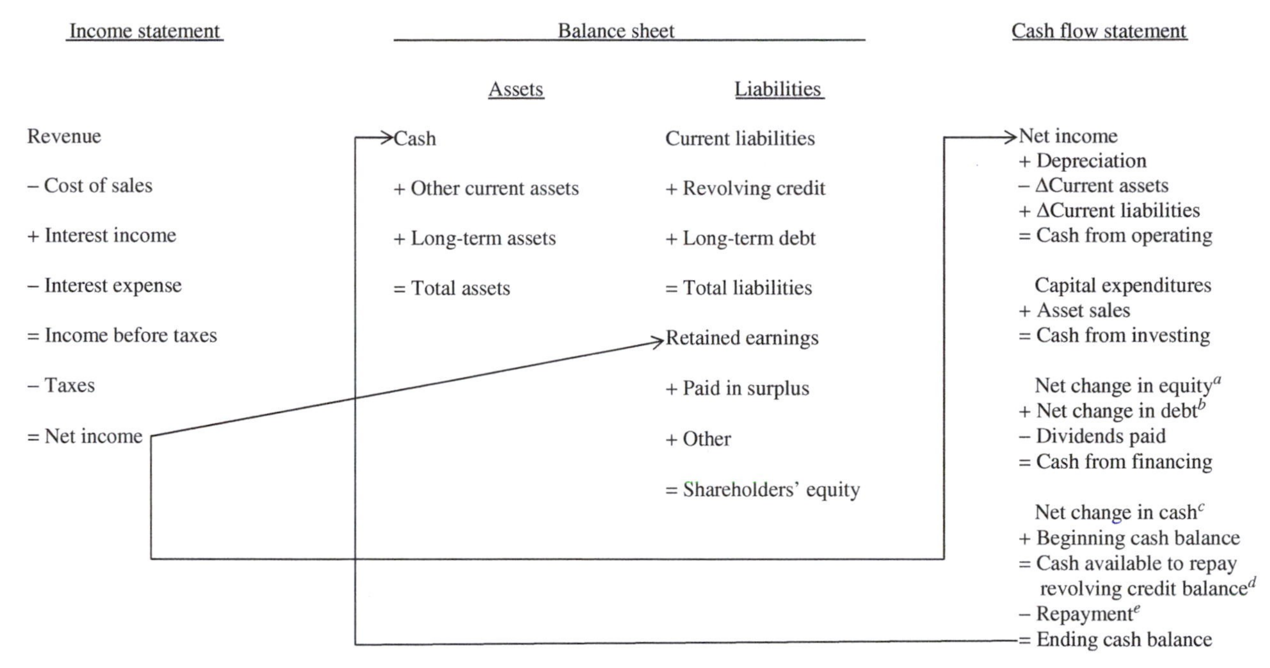

FIGURE 9.1 Interrelationships between a firm's financial statements. [a]New equity issues less repurchases. [b]New borrowing less debt repayment. [c]Sum of cash from operating, investing, and financing activities. [d]Cash available to repay outstanding revolving credit balance in excess of the firm's desired minimum cash balance. [e]Payment made to reduce outstanding revolving credit balance in excess of the firm's desired minimum cash balance.

balance sheet were used. Net income flows from the income statement to retained earnings (i.e., cumulative income or losses) on the balance sheet and also is shown as the first line of the cash flow statement. The cash flow statement shows cash from operating, investing, and financing activities. It describes the source of cash inflows and the uses for cash outflows and the amount of cash the firm reports on its balance sheet at the end of an accounting period.

Firms maintain minimum cash balances to meet short-term working capital needs such as payroll. Cash from operating and investing activities above that are required to maintain the firm's desired minimum cash balance may be used to repay any outstanding debt. Accordingly, the firm's year-ending debt balance is reduced by the amount of excess cash used to repay debt.

In building financial models, the previously described linkages among the financial statements introduce circular logic known as circular references in spreadsheet software programs. *Circular references* are a series of cell references in which the last cell reference refers to the first resulting in a closed loop. For example, increases in interest expense reduce net income, which decreases cash flow to repay borrowing, resulting in higher debt outstanding and higher interest expense. Figure 9.2 illustrates this circularity.

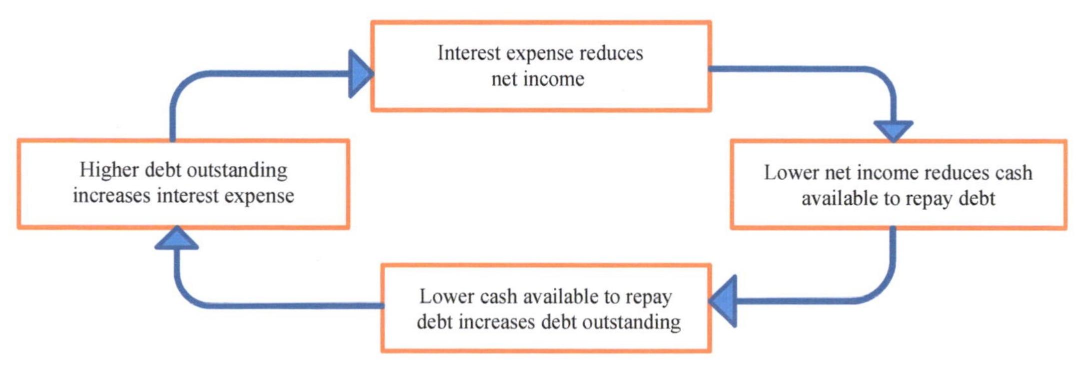

FIGURE 9.2 Financial model circularity.

Such circular references could result in the financial model becoming unstable with Microsoft's Excel software showing any of the following error messages: REF!, #Value, or Div/0!. To resolve circular references using Microsoft's Excel, turn on the iteration command for Windows 7, 8, or 10 as follows:

- On the ribbon bar, click on File >>> Options >>> Formulas.
- Set workbook calculation to Automatic and enable Iterative Calculation.
- Set the maximum number of iterations to 100 and the maximum amount of change to 0.001.

An alternative means of resolving circular references is to use "toggle buttons," which indicate a state such as yes/no or on/off. "Toggle buttons" are used in the models accompanying this textbook on the income statement (interest income and expense rows) and debt repayment (revolving credit facility row) worksheets. Such buttons are triggered by switching the interest income or expense or revolving credit "toggle button" on and off and on (i.e., from 1 to 0 to 1 and may be expressed as 1 >> enter 0 >> enter 1). This often restores model stability just as turning a wireless modem on and off and on can restore an internet connection. "Toggle buttons" are displayed on the worksheets as follows:

1 0 = circ off

1 = circ on

Modeling changes in US corporate tax laws

The Tax Cuts and Jobs Act of 2017 capped net interest expense deductions at 30% of earnings before interest and taxes (EBIT) after 2022. Figure 9.3 illustrates the decision rule that determines the extent to which net interest expense can be deducted for tax purposes based on EBIT.[4] If net interest expense is less than or equal to 30% of EBIT, 100% of net interest expense is deductible; otherwise, only the amount of net interest expense equal to 30% of EBIT is deductible. EBT and i are earnings before taxes and net interest expense, respectively.

See Equation 9.1 for the Excel formula for modeling this decision rule.

$$\text{EBT} = \text{IF}[i \leq .3\ \text{EBIT},\ i,\ \text{EBT} - .3\text{EBIT}] \tag{9.1}$$

Key steps in the valuation process

The modeling process used to value a firm consists of a series of steps. First, analyze the target firm's historical statements to identify the primary determinants of cash flow. Second, project 3 to 5 years (or more) of annual pro forma financial statements. This period is called the *planning period*. Third, estimate the present value (PV) of the projected pro forma cash flows, including the terminal value. These steps are discussed in detail in the following sections.

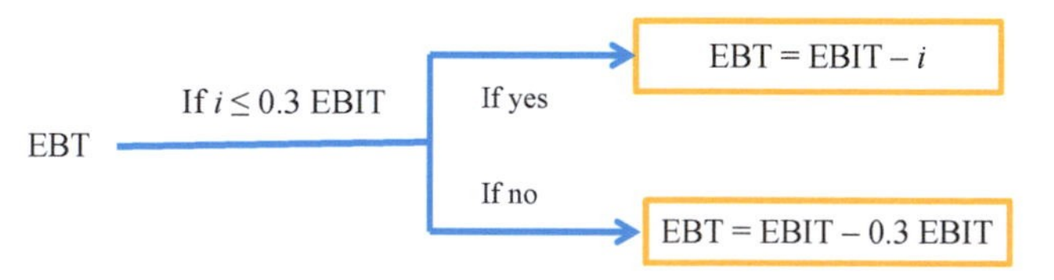

FIGURE 9.3 Limited tax deductibility of interest expense. *EBIT,* Earnings before interest and taxes; *EBT,* earnings before taxes; *i,* net interest expense.

[4] Before 2022, earnings before interest, taxes, depreciation, and amortization (EBITDA) should be used to determine the amount of net interest expense that can be deducted.

Step 1: analyze recent financial statements

Understanding how a firm made money historically is helpful in determining how it may do so in the future.[5] The analyst should look for relationships or correlation between line items on financial statements and the firm's free cash flows. Variables exhibiting strong historical correlation with cash flows and in turn firm value often are referred to as value drivers. *Value drivers* are variables exerting the greatest impact on firm value. For nonfinancial firms, they generally include the sales growth rate; the cost of sales as a percent of sales; selling, general and administrative expenses (SG&A) as a percent of sales; weighted average cost of capital (WACC) assumed during the annual cash flow growth period; and the WACC and sustainable cash flow growth rate assumed during the terminal period.[6]

Because of the difference between sales and cost of sales as a percent of sales, gross margin per dollar of sales summarizes a firm's ability to create value. A simple diagram plot of a firm's gross margin over at least one full business cycle (5–7 years) provides insight into how the firm was able to create value historically. An increase in the ratio over time indicates that the firm has been able to reduce its costs compared with sales, raise prices on items sold, or a combination. A declining ratio reflects deterioration in the firm's ability to control costs, raise prices, or both.

Normalize historical data

To ensure historical relationships can be accurately defined, *normalize* the data by removing nonrecurring changes and questionable accounting practices in order to identify longer-term trends in the data. Cash flow may be adjusted by adding back large increases in reserves[7] or deducting large decreases in reserves from free cash flow to the firm (FCFF). Similar adjustments can be made for significant nonrecurring gains on the sale of assets or losses caused by nonrecurring expenses, such as those associated with the settlement of a lawsuit or warranty claim.

Common-size financial statements are used to uncover data irregularities. They are constructed by calculating the percentage each line item of the financial statements is of annual sales for each quarter or year for which historical data are available. They are useful for comparing businesses of different sizes in the same industry at a specific moment.

Called *cross-sectional comparisons*, such analyses may indicate that the ratio of capital spending to sales for the target firm is much less than for other firms in the industry. This discrepancy may reflect "catch-up" spending at the target's competitors or suggest the target is deferring necessary spending. To determine which is true, calculate common-size statements for the target firm and its primary competitors over a number of consecutive periods.[8]

Financial ratio analysis is the calculation of performance ratios from data in a firm's financial statements to identify the firm's financial strengths and weaknesses. Such analysis helps identify potential problems to be examined during due diligence. Ratios allow the analyst to compare firms of different sizes. For example, assume we are comparing operating profits (EBIT) of two firms. EBITs for firm A are $20 million and $6 million for firm B. It is inappropriate to conclude that firm A is better managed than firm B. Firm A may have a larger dollar value of profits only because it is larger. The firms' profitability should be compared in terms of their margins (i.e., the amount of profit per dollar of sales each firm can keep). If firm A has sales of $100 million and firm B has sales of $30 million, the two firms are equally profitable (when measured in this manner) with each earning 20% of each dollar of sales.

Because ratios adjust for firm size, they enable a comparison of a firm's ratios with industry averages to discover if the company is out of line with competitors. A successful competitor's performance ratios may be used if industry average data[9] are not available. After the historical data have been normalized or smoothed, we need to understand

[5] Common sources of data for publicly traded firms include the firm's annual report and 10k filing with the SEC (available at sec.gov/edgar.shtml) or via the firm's website (see Investor Relations). Other sources of information include subscription-based services such as Standard and Poor's Compustat service (www.compustatresources.com/support/index.html), Morningstar.com, and free sources such as finance.yahoo.com or finance.google.com.

[6] Value drivers differ by type of firm. For marketing-oriented businesses such as Nike, SG&A as a percent of sales is a key determinant of firm value; for pharmaceuticals such as Pfizer, research and development is an important value driver.

[7] Reserves are charges taken on the income statement against current earnings in anticipation of future expenses. Such reserves also are entered on the firm's balance sheet as a liability item to reflect pending obligations.

[8] Large increases or decreases in these ratios from one period to the next highlight the need for further examination to explain why these fluctuations occurred.

[9] Industry data are found in such publications as *The Almanac of Business and Industrial Financial Ratios* (Prentice Hall), *Annual Statement Studies* (Robert Morris Associates), *Dun's Review* (Dun and Bradstreet), *Industry Norms and Key Business Ratios* (Dun and Bradstreet), and *Value Line Investment Survey for Company and Industry Ratios.*

the primary factors that affected changes in gross margin historically. That is, what are the primary determinants of sales growth and profit margins?

Understand determinants of revenue growth and profit margins

A suggested approach to understanding the determinants of a firm's revenue growth and profit margins is to evaluate the industry's attractiveness in terms of the intensity of competition within the industry (and in turn potential profitability) and the firm's competitive position within the industry. A convenient means of evaluating industry attractiveness is to apply the Porter Five Forces model described in Chapter 4.

The Porter model identifies a series of factors that collectively determine the potential competitiveness of an industry. Highly competitive industries tend to offer lower potential profitability than less competitive ones. These factors include the threat of new entrants, bargaining power of suppliers, bargaining power of customers, threat of substitute products, and degree of competitive rivalry within the industry. *Bargaining power* refers to the ability of customers to influence the prices of the products and services they buy and suppliers to set the prices they charge for what they sell.

Table 9.1 summarizes the factors that determine the significance of each "force" and its implication for potential profitability. These forces can be augmented to include other considerations such as the role of regulation, unions, and government as needed.

Table 9.2 generalizes the results of the Porter model by summarizing the characteristics of high-profit versus low-profit industries. In general, highly profitable industries are subject to less competition than lower-profit industries.

TABLE 9.1 Porter Five Forces model summary

Force	Implication for profit margins
Threat of new entrants into a market: Stronger when • Entry barriers are low, such as - Low capital requirements - Absence of strong brands - Access to distribution channels • Competitors use a common technology	New entrants may • Intensify rivalry or competitive environment • Compete for market share by reducing selling prices • Add to costs by stimulating innovation and boosting advertising and marketing expenses
Bargaining power of suppliers: Stronger when • Resource supplied is scarce • Switching costs are high • Customer is small relative to supplier • Few substitutes	Suppliers having substantial bargaining power can • Boost prices paid for inputs used by current customers • Impose less favorable terms such as longer delivery schedules
Bargaining power of customers: Stronger when • They are few in number relative to sellers • A customer purchases a large portion of a seller's output • They possess a credible backward integration threat (i.e., ability to enter the supplier's business) • Switching costs are low	Customers having substantial bargaining power can • Force selling prices down and squeeze supplier profit margins • Extract more favorable terms such as longer payment periods
Threat of substitute products: Impact on reducing demand for current competitor products greater when • Substitutes are close to existing products • Switching costs are low • Customers willing to switch	Many substitutes (i.e., those meeting the same customer need) can • Limit prices that can be charged • Reduce demand for product and service offerings of current industry competitors
Degree of competitive rivalry: Intensity greater when • Competitors are comparable in size and few in number (oligopoly) • Market size and growth prospects are limited (stagnant markets breed more intense competition) • Product differentiation and brand loyalty are low • Exit barriers are high • Capacity utilization is low • Fixed costs as a percent of total costs are high	Intense rivalry may • Breed competitive price reductions, innovation, and investment in new products • Intensify sales promotions and advertising campaigns • Reduce current competitor profit margins

TABLE 9.2 Characteristics of High- versus Low-Profit Industries

High industry profits are associated with	Low industry profits (all lowercase) are associated with
Weak suppliers	Strong suppliers
Weak customers	Strong customers
High entry barriers	Low entry barriers
Few substitutes	Many substitutes
Little rivalry or competition	Intense rivalry or competition

Highly competitive industries tend to experience so-called *normal profits* (i.e., a level of profits that compensates firms for the risk they have assumed). Less competitive industries often result in firms earning abnormal profits (i.e., those in excess of the risk assumed). An example of a high-profit industry is soft drinks and a low-profit industry is airlines. The terms *weak* and *strong* refer to the bargaining power of suppliers and customers relative to the firm being analyzed.

After factors affecting industry profitability are understood, the analyst can turn to analyzing firm-specific factors determining profit margins: sales and cost of sales.

Sales are the price per unit times the number of units sold. The growth in the firm's sales thus reflects the ability of the firm to raise prices without a significant decline in unit sales (i.e., pricing power), the firm's ability to gain market share, and the growth in product demand in the industry. The firm's capacity to raise prices is a measure of its pricing power. Pricing power often is less in highly competitive markets than in less competitive ones. The degree of competitiveness and in turn pricing power is affected by the ease with which new firms can enter a market, the availability of close substitutes for products or services currently offered in the market, the degree of industry concentration, and the amount of excess capacity.

Figure 9.4 provides a framework (the pricing power continuum) for assessing a firm's pricing power within its served market. Firms have significant pricing power when barriers to entry are high, there are few substitutes for its product or service offering, there is little excess capacity, the firm's market share is high relative to current competitors, and government regulation and oversight is limited. An analyst can describe subjectively the degree of a firm's pricing power by its relative position on the continuum. The farther to the right the firm is placed, the greater its perceived pricing power.

The other major component of revenue growth, unit sales, is driven by the growth in industry product demand and by gains in market share. Industry product demand often is correlated with one or two key variables. The determinants of unit sales differ by industry. For example, beer, beverage, and personal care products are heavily influenced by demographics such as population growth and changes in the age composition of the population. Sporting goods sales are directly related to advertising and marketing expenditures. Automotive sales are driven by a combination of changes in consumer purchasing power, consumer confidence, and borrowing costs. Pharmaceutical product sales are impacted by research and development spending and the aging of the population. The demand for smart phone apps is correlated with the growth in handset sales.

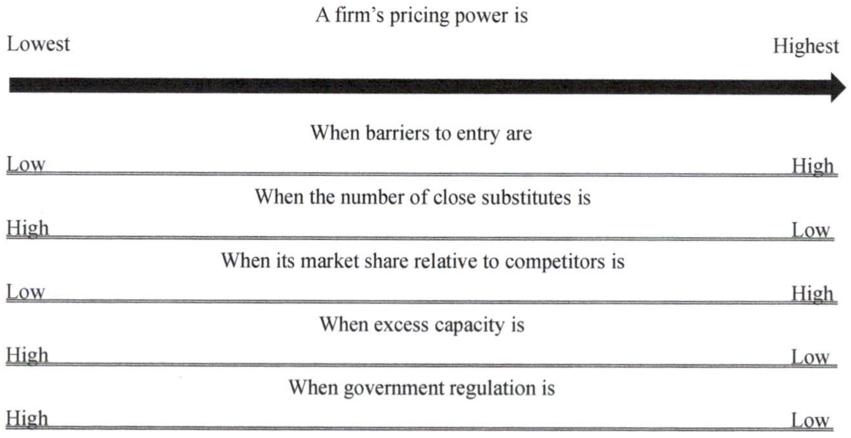

A firm's pricing power is

Lowest — Highest

When barriers to entry are

Low — High

When the number of close substitutes is

High — Low

When its market share relative to competitors is

Low — High

When excess capacity is

High — Low

When government regulation is

High — Low

FIGURE 9.4 Pricing power continuum.

After an analyst thinks that she or he understands what determines pricing power and unit sales growth historically, it is necessary to analyze the determinants of the cost of sales. Depending on the industry, the two largest components of the cost of sales are usually direct labor costs and purchased materials and services. Direct labor costs are those directly attributable to the production of goods and services. Indirect labor costs such as those affecting distribution, marketing, and sales are excluded from the calculation of cost of sales. Factors affecting direct labor cost often include the availability of labor having the requisite skills, the degree of unionization, government regulation, and productivity. Purchased material and service costs correlate with the size of purchase, the number of suppliers, product uniqueness, and substitutes. In addition to labor and capital costs, raw material costs are frequently impacted by external factors such geopolitical supply disruptions and weather.

Because current sales can be satisfied from current production or from inventory, cost of sales is affected by how a firm values its inventory. The current cost of sales is reduced by units produced currently but not sold and placed in inventory and increased by current sales that are satisfied by reducing inventory.

The two most common ways to value inventory are first in, first out (FIFO) and last in, last out (LIFO). FIFO uses inventory that is purchased earliest in the production process, resulting in lower-priced inventory used to satisfy sales in the current period. Items placed in inventory that are purchased at earlier dates are generally considered to have been purchased at a lower price because of inflation. Thus FIFO has the effect of reducing the cost of sales. In contrast, LIFO uses the most recently purchased inventory items, resulting in higher-cost inventory items, which adds to the cost of sales.

Step 2: project pro forma financial statements

If the factors affecting sales, profit, and cash flow historically are expected to exert the same influence in the future, a firm's financial statements may be projected by extrapolating historical growth rates in key variables such as revenue, with other line items on the financial statement projected as a percent of sales. If the factors affecting sales growth are expected to change because of the introduction of new products, total revenue growth may accelerate from its historical trend. In contrast, the emergence of additional competitors in the future may limit revenue growth by eroding the firm's market share and selling prices.

When a product or service lacks history, proxies can be used to project growth rates. For example, the founder of online shoe seller Zappos was able to convince early investors that people would buy shoes on the internet by drawing a parallel with catalogue sales, which at the time was the fastest growing apparel category.

Financial statements should be projected for at least 3 to 5 years and possibly more until the firm's cash flows turn positive or the growth rate slows to what is believed to be a sustainable pace. Some firms may show profit growth in excess of the industry average. Because above-average profit growth is not sustainable, cash flows for such firms should be projected until they are expected to slow to the industry average. This usually happens when new competitors are expected to enter the industry. Projections should reflect the best information about product demand growth, future pricing, technological changes, new competitors, new product and service offerings from current competitors, potential supply disruptions, raw material and labor cost increases, and possible new product or service substitutes.

Because accuracy diminishes the further the analyst projects financial statements, projections are typically made over two forecast periods: the planning period and the terminal period. Whereas the *planning period* represents the period of annual projections, the *terminal period* is the PV of all cash flows beyond the last year of the planning period.

The planning period forecast begins with an estimate of the firm's revenue using either the top-down or bottom-up approaches. The *top-down approach* projects the size of the firm's target market using macro (e.g., personal income, interest rates) or market level data (e.g., the number of customers) and then applies an estimated market share for the firm. That is, if the market is projected to grow to $800 million next year and the firm's market share is expected to be 10%, then the firm's revenue next year is expected to be $80 million. The *bottom-up approach* involves summing up forecasts made by the firm's sales force by product line and by customer. Alternatively, the analyst could extend present trends using historical growth rates or multiple regression techniques, which implicitly assumes the factors affecting growth in the past will do so in the same way in the future.

Tables 9.3 to 9.7 illustrate the output of the Microsoft Excel spreadsheet model titled Target Valuation Model found on the website accompanying this text. The cells denoted in each worksheet in bold yellow type represent *input cells*. Cells in black contain formulas. Entries into input cells change automatically the subsequent years to reflect the new data in the input cell.

TABLE 9.3 Target firm planning period assumptions

	Actual			Projections for the Period Ending December 31				
	2011	2012	2013	2014	2015	2016	2017	2018
Income Statement								
Sales growth (%)	NA	5.2	4.8	**7.5**	7.5	7.0	7.5	7.5
COGS as a percentage of sales	41.3	44.1	42.0	**41.0**	41.0	41.0	41.0	41.0
SG&A percent annual increase (decrease)	NA	(1.4)	4.5	**4.0**	4.0	4.0	4.0	4.0
Other operating expense as a percentage of sales	13.10	12.00	10.50	**11.0**	11.0	11.0	11.0	11.0
EBITDA growth (%)	NA	5.8	27.4	14.6	11.6	11.3	11.0	10.8
EBITDA margin (%)	17.10	17.20	20.80	22.20	23.10	23.90	24.70	25.40
Balance Sheet								
Receivable days	59.8	61.6	64.3	**49.0**	49.0	49.0	49.0	49.0
Inventory days	79.6	82.8	88.5	**74.0**	74.0	74.0	74.0	74.0
Other current assets percentage of sales	7.8	5.2	6.3	**5.5**	5.5	5.5	5.5	5.5
Accounts payable days	43.0	39.1	40.9	**40.0**	40.0	40.0	40.0	40.0
Other current liabilities percentage of COGS (%)	65.6	79.1	60.4	**68.0**	68.0	68.0	68.0	68.0
Working capital/sales (excluding cash and debt) (%)	1.3	(7.5)	4.0	(5.1)	(5.1)	(5.1)	(5.1)	(5.1)
Cash Flow								
Capital expenditures ($millions)	**26.70**	**13.80**	**10.03**	17.00	18.30	19.70	21.10	22.70
Capex as a percentage of sales	0.7	0.4	0.3	**0.4**	0.4	0.4	0.4	0.4
Depreciation ($millions)	**123.00**	**123.60**	**126.00**	136.20	146.40	157.40	169.20	181.90
Depreciation as a percentage of sales	3.4	3.3	3.2	**3.2**	3.2	3.2	3.2	3.2

COGS, Cost of goods sold; *EBITDA*, earnings before interest, taxes, depreciation, and amortization; *NA*, *not available;* SG&A, selling, general and administrative.

Changes to the model are made primarily by making changes in the worksheet labeled Target Assumptions (see Table 9.3), which contains the assumptions underlying the projected income statement, balance sheet, and cash flow statement. The analyst should enter cell values one at a time using small changes to assess accurately the outcome of each change on valuation. It will become evident which variables represent key value drivers.

Note that the Target Valuation Model already contains input and output data and an estimated valuation for the firm. For our purposes, consider this projection the "base case" valuation. To simulate the impact of an assumption change, change the value in the appropriate input cell.

For example, to assess the impact on valuation of an increase of one percentage point in the target's revenue growth rate, change the target's revenue growth rate assumption on the Target's Assumptions Worksheet by 1 percentage point during the planning period (2014–2018) from 5.5% to 6.5% in the yellow input cell on the Sales Growth line for the year 2014. The model will increase automatically the growth rate annually from 2014 to 2018 by one percentage point. The model also accommodates a variable growth rate forecast. For example, if the growth rate in 2015 is expected to increase by an additional one percentage point and to continue at that higher rate in subsequent years, the analyst simply increases the growth rate by from 5.5% to 6.5% in 2014 and to 7.5% in 2015.

Worksheets labeled Target Income Statement (see Table 9.4) and Target Balance Sheet (see Table 9.5) provide the input for the worksheet labeled Target Cash Flow (see Table 9.6) and reflect assumptions provided in the Target Assumptions Worksheet. If the balance sheet is balancing properly, the values in the red cells at the bottom on the Target Balance Sheet should be zero because they represent the difference between total assets and total liabilities plus shareholders' equity.

TABLE 9.4 Target Firm Planning Period Income Statement

	Actual			Projections for the Period Ending December 31				
	2011	2012	2013	2014	2015	2016	2017	2018
Sales ($millions)	3588.10	3775.70	3958.50	4255.40	4574.50	4917.60	5286.50	5682.90
Cost of goods sold ($millions)	1482.00	1665.70	1664.10	1744.70	1875.60	2016.20	2167.40	2330.00
Gross profit ($millions)	2106.10	2110.00	2294.40	2510.70	2699.00	2901.40	3119.00	3352.90
SG&A ($millions)	1023.20	1009.00	1054.60	1096.80	1140.70	1186.30	1233.70	1283.10
Other operating expenses ($millions)	470.70	453.20	414.60	468.10	503.20	540.90	581.50	625.10
Depreciation ($millions)	123.00	123.60	126.00	136.20	146.40	157.40	169.20	181.90
Amortization ($millions)	299.60	313.90	302.90	300.00	300.00	300.00	300.00	300.00
EBIT ($millions)	189.00	210.30	396.30	509.60	608.70	716.80	834.60	962.90
Unusual (gain) loss ($millions)	(37.20)	—	—	—	—	—	—	—
(Income) from affiliates ($millions)		—	—	—	—	—	—	—
Other expense (income) ($millions)	60.00	10.90	11.90	—	—	—	—	—
Interest (income) ($millions)	(4.30)	(3.90)	(2.40)	—	—	—	—	—
Interest expense ($millions)	152.30	162.10	123.90	95.50	80.50	65.50	50.50	35.00
Earnings before taxes ($millions)	18.80	41.20	262.90	414.10	528.20	651.30	784.10	927.30
Noncontrolling interest ($millions)	—	—	—	—	—	—	—	—
Taxes ($millions)	63.70	100.90	101.40	165.60	211.30	260.50	313.60	370.90
Net income before extra items ($millions)	(44.90)	(59.70)	161.50	248.50	316.90	390.80	470.40	556.40
Extraordinary items ($millions)	0.60	0.70	0.400	—	—	—	—	—
Net income after extra items ($millions)	(44.30)	(59.00)	161.90	248.50	316.90	390.80	470.40	556.40

EBIT, Earnings before interest and taxes; EBT, earnings before taxes; i, net interest expense.

Step 3: estimate the present value of the projected pro forma cash flows

This step requires the analyst to estimate the sum of the PV of the cash flows during the planning period (in this instance, 2014–2018) and the PV of those beyond the planning period. The PV of the cash flows beyond the planning period is commonly referred to as the *terminal value*, which is estimated using the constant-growth valuation method (see Chapter 7).

Calculating enterprise and equity values

Table 9.7 illustrates the calculation of the enterprise and equity values of the firm. The former is the value of the firm to all those supplying funds to the firm, and the equity value represents the value of firm to common shareholders only. The target's enterprise value is estimated on the model's Valuations Worksheet using inputs from the Target Assumptions Worksheet.

Enterprise value often is defined as the sum of the market value of a firm's equity, preferred shares, debt,[10] and noncontrolling interest less total cash and cash equivalents. Cash is commonly deducted. The amount of cash in excess of what is needed to satisfy working capital requirements is a nonoperating asset whose value is implicitly included in the market value of equity because it is owned by the shareholders. After the enterprise value has been estimated, the market value of equity is then calculated by adding cash to and deducting long-term debt and noncontrolling interests from the enterprise value.

Although this definition may approximate the takeover value of a company, it does not entail all of the significant nonequity claims on cash flow such as unfunded pension and health care obligations and loan guarantees. Thus the

[10] Effective January 1, 2019, the Financial Accounting Standards Board requires operating leases to be included in debt on the balance sheet.

TABLE 9.5 Target Firm Planning Period Balance Sheet

	Actual			Projections for the Period Ending December 31				
	2011	2012	2013	2014	2015	2016	2017	2018
Cash ($millions)	**854.90**	**882.10**	**276.30**	**1019.00**	**1480.40**	**2026.40**	**2663.80**	**3399.70**
Accounts receivable ($millions)	587.50	637.00	697.30	571.30	614.10	660.20	709.70	762.90
Inventory ($millions)	323.10	377.90	403.50	353.70	380.30	408.80	439.40	472.40
Other ($millions)	281.00	196.60	248.10	234.00	251.60	270.50	290.80	312.60
Current assets ($millions)	2046.50	2093.60	1625.20	2178.00	2726.30	3365.90	4103.70	4947.60
Property, plant, and equipment ($millions)	870.40	858.70	871.40	888.40	906.70	926.40	947.50	970.30
Accumulated depreciation ($millions)	—	—	—	(136.20)	(282.60)	(439.90)	(609.10)	(790.90)
Net property, plant, and equipment ($millions)	870.40	858.70	871.40	752.20	624.20	486.50	338.40	179.30
Goodwill ($millions)	4372.10	4366.70	4503.4	4503.40	4503.40	4503.40	4503.40	4503.40
Intangible assets ($millions)	2040.2	1746.6	1525.8	1225.80	925.80	625.80	325.80	25.80
Deferred taxes ($millions)	26.80	28.80	23.00	23.00	23.00	23.00	23.00	23.00
Other ($millions)	130.20	93.60	89.20	89.20	89.20	89.20	89.20	89.20
Total assets ($millions)	**9486.20**	**9188.00**	**8638.00**	**8771.70**	**8891.90**	**9093.70**	**9383.60**	**9768.30**
Accounts payable ($millions)	174.4	178.40	186.60	191.20	205.50	221.00	237.50	255.30
Other ($millions)	972.00	1317.90	1005.80	1186.4	1275.40	1371.00	1473.90	1584.40
Current liabilities ($millions)	1146.40	1496.30	1192.40	1377.60	1480.90	1592.00	1711.40	1839.70
Revolving credit facility ($millions)	—	—	—	—	—	—	—	—
Senior debt ($millions)	2727.60	2297.70	2060.90	1760.90	1460.90	1160.90	860.90	560.90
Subordinated debt ($millions)	—	—	—	—	—	—	—	—
Total ($millions)	2727.60	2297.70	2060.90	1760.90	1460.90	1160.90	860.90	560.90
Deferred taxes ($millions)	558.00	410.60	287.40	287.40	287.40	287.40	287.40	287.40
Other ($millions)	616.10	384.10	443.90	443.90	443.90	443.90	443.90	443.90
Total liabilities ($millions)	5048.10	4588.70	3984.60	3869.80	3673.10	3484.20	3303.60	3131.90
Common stock ($millions)	5225.00	5443.20	5733.70	5733.70	5733.70	5733.70	5733.700	5733.70
Preferred equity ($millions)	—	—	—	—	—	—	—	—
Retained earnings ($millions)	532.50	911.00	1341.8	1590.30	1907.20	2297.9	2768.4	3324.8
Treasury stock ($millions)	(1420.0)	(1820.00)	(2482.0)	(2482.00)	(2482.00)	(2482.00)	(2482.00)	(2482.00)
Other adjustments ($millions)	96.60	65.10	59.10	59.10	59.10	59.10	59.10	59.10
Noncontrolling interest ($millions)	4.00	—	0.80	0.80	0.80	0.80	0.80	0.80
Total stockholders' equity ($millions)	4438.10	4599.30	4653.40	4901.90	5218.80	5609.50	6080.00	6636.40
Total liabilities and equity ($millions)	9486.2-	9188.00	8638.00	8771.70	8891.90	9093.70	9383.60	9768.30
Reconciliation ($millions)	0.00	0.00	0.00	0.00	0.00	0.00	0.00	0.00

common definition of enterprise value may omit significant obligations that must be paid by the acquirer and whose present value (PV) should be included in estimating the target's purchase price. When calculating the ratio of enterprise to earnings before interest, taxes, depreciation, and amortization (EBITDA) as a valuation multiple, the analyst needs to add back leasing and pension expenses to EBITDA to compare the ratio for a firm with substantial amounts of such long-term obligations with other companies.

TABLE 9.6 Target Planning Period Cash Flow Statement[a]

	Actual		Projections for the Period Ending December 31				
	2012	**2013**	**2014**	**2015**	**2016**	**2017**	**2018**
Net income ($millions)	(59.00)	161.90	248.50	316.90	390.80	470.40	556.40
Depreciation and amortization ($millions)	437.50	428.90	436.20	446.40	457.40	469.20	481.90
Change in							
Accounts receivable ($millions)	(49.50)	(60.30)	126.00	(42.80)	(46.10)	(49.50)	(53.20)
Inventory ($millions)	(54.80)	(25.60)	49.80	(26.50)	(28.50)	(30.70)	(33.00)
Accounts payable ($millions)	4.00	8.20	4.60	14.30	15.40	16.60	17.80
Deferred taxes ($millions)	(149.40)	(117.40)	—	—	—	—	—
Other liabilities ($millions)	(232.00)	59.80	—	—	—	—	—
Cash flow from operating activities ($millions)	**359.70**	**97.10**	**1059.70**	**779.70**	**865.70**	**958.50**	**1058.60**
Capital expenditures ($millions)	(13.80)	(10.30)	(17.00)	(18.30)	(19.70)	(21.10)	(22.70)
Acquisitions ($millions)	**(0.10)**	**(149.00)**	—	—	—	—	—
Sale of assets ($millions)	**3.40**	**25.50**	—	—	—	—	—
Cash flow from investing activities ($millions)	**(10.50)**	**(133.80)**	**(17.00)**	**(18.30)**	**(19.70)**	**(21.10)**	**(22.70)**
Net change in equity ($millions)	(213.30)	(377.50)	—	—	—	—	—
Net change in debt ($millions)	(429.90)	(236.80)	(300.00)	(300.00)	(300.00)	(300.00)	(300.00)
Dividends paid ($millions)	—	—	—	—	—	—	—
Cash flow from financing activities ($millions)	**(643.20)**	**(614.30)**	**(300.00)**	**(300.00)**	**(300.00)**	**(300.00)**	**(300.00)**
Net change in cash ($millions)	(294.00)	(651.00)	742.70	461.40	546.10	637.40	735.90
Beginning cash balance ($millions)	854.90	882.10	276.30	1019.00	1480.40	2026.40	2663.80
Cash available for revolving credit ($millions)	**560.90**	**231.10**	**1019.00**	**1480.40**	**2026.40**	**2663.80**	**3399.70**
Beginning revolver ($millions)			—	—	—	—	—
Total repayment ($millions)			—	—	—	—	—
Ending revolving credit facility ($millions)			—	—	—	—	—
Ending cash ($millions)			1019.00	1480.40	2026.40	263.80	3399.70

[a]In the target valuation model accompanying this text, the components of working capital are calculated according to whether they represent a source or use of cash. Consequently, increasing annual accounts receivable would be shown as negative representing a use of funds as the firm's revenues grow. As a simplifying assumption, changes in working capital items other than changes in accounts receivable, inventory, and accounts payable are assumed to be zero during the forecast period.

Chapter 7 discusses ways of estimating the market value of a firm's long-term debt. Commonly used methods for modeling involve either valuing the book value of a firm's long-term debt at its current market value if it is publicly traded or book value if it is not. Alternatively, the market value of similar debt at a firm exhibiting a comparable credit rating can be used to value a target firm's debt. For example, assume the book value of the target's debt with 10 years remaining to maturity is $478 million, and its current market value or the market value of comparable publicly traded debt is 1.024 per $1000 of face value. The market value of the firm's debt can be estimated as $489.5 million (i.e., 1.024 × $478).

The market value of noncontrolling interests can be estimated by multiplying the book value of such interests by the price-to-earnings ratio for comparable firms. That is, if the book value of the noncontrolling interests in the firm is $25 million and the price-to-earnings ratio for comparable firms is 15, the market value of noncontrolling interests would be $375 million (i.e., 15 × $25 million).

TABLE 9.7 Target Firm Valuation

	2014	2015	2016	2017	2018
Free Cash Flow					
EBIT ($millions)	509.60	608.70	716.80	834.60	962.90
Taxes ($millions)	(203.90)	(243.50)	(286.70)	(333.80)	(385.10)
Depreciation and amortization ($millions)	436.20	446.40	457.40	469.20	481.90
Gross capex ($millions)	(17.00)	(18.30)	(19.70)	(21.10)	(22.70)
Δ NWC ($millions)	180.40	(55.00)	(59.20)	(63.60)	(68.40)
Free cash flow ($millions)	905.30	738.30	808.60	885.20	968.50[a]
Period[b]	1.00	1.00	1.00	1.00	1.00
Midyear convention[c]	0.50	1.50	2.50	3.50	4.50
Discount factor[d]	0.96	0.88	0.80	0.73	0.67
PV FCFF ($millions)	866.00	646.30	647.70	648.80	649.50
PV (years 1−5) ($millions)	3458.30				
PV (terminal value) ($millions)	10,453.50				
Enterprise value ($millions)	**13,911.80**				
Plus cash ($millions)	276.30				
Less debt and minimum interest ($millions)	2061.70				
Equity value ($millions)	**12,126.40**				
Equity value per share ($millions)	69.49				
Assumptions					
WACC (%)	9.3				
Target D/E (%)	**75.0**				
Target D/TC (%)	42.9				
Marginal tax rate	40.0				
k_e (%)	14.0				
R_f (%)	**2.5**				
$R_m - R_f$ (%)	**5.5**				
Beta (%)	**2.09**				
Terminal Value					
FCF 2020 ($millions)	968.50				
Terminal growth rate (%)	**3.0**				
Terminal period WACC (%)	**9.4**				

[a]Free cash flow (FCF) in the last year of the planning period is recalculated at the marginal tax rate of 40% rather than the lower effective tax rate used during the planning period and then used to estimate the terminal value using the constant growth model.
[b]Period reflects months of actual data available for first forecast year, e.g., if you have 9 months of actual data, period one equals 0.25; if you have one half year of data, period one is 0.5; and if 3 months of data are available, period one equals 0.75. If the data available are less than a full year, they must be annualized.
[c]Discounted cash flow valuation assumes that cash flows occur in a lump sum at the end of the year. What is more likely is that that they occur throughout the year. With the midyear convention, cash flows are assumed to occur in the middle of the year. Consequently, those cash flows are discounted half a year instead of a whole year.
[d]A factor that when multiplied by the period cash flow converts it into a present value.
D/E, Desired future (or target) debt-to-equity ratio set by the firm; *D/TC,* debt to total capital; *FCF, free cash flow;* *FCFF,* free cash flow to the firm; k_e, cost of equity; *NWC,* net working capital; *PV, present value;* $R_m - R_f$ = equity risk premium; *WACC,* weighted average cost of capital.

Calculating the weighted average cost of capital

Converting projected pro forma cash flows to a PV requires estimation of the WACC during the planning period and the terminal period. The data, with the exception of borrowing costs, used in estimating Equations 9.2 and 9.3 come from Table 9.7. From Chapter 7, the WACC assumed during the planning period can be expressed as follows:

$$WACC = (D/(D+E)) \times (1-T) \times i + (E/D+E) \times K_e \quad (9.2)$$

in which

D = debt
E = equity
T = corporate marginal tax rate (i.e., 40%)
R_f = risk-free rate approximated by the 10-year US Treasury Bond rate = 2.5%
R_m = return on a broad-based stock index
$R_m - R_f$ = equity risk premium = 5.5%
β_l = levered beta (from finance.yahoo.com) = 2.09
i = weighted average cost of borrowing[11] = 5%
k_e = cost of equity (estimated using the capital asset pricing model) = $R_f + \beta_l(R_m - R_f)$ = 2.5 + 2.09(5.5) = 14%
D/E = desired future (or target) debt-to-equity ratio set by the firm = 75%
D/(D + E) = target debt-to-total capital ratio = (D/E)/(1 + D/E) = 0.75/(1 + 0.75) = 0.429
E/(D + E) = 1 − [D/(D + E)] = 1 − 0.429 = 0.571

The WACC is estimated as follows:

$$WACC = 0.429 \times [(1 - 0.4) \times 5] + 0.571 \times 14 = 1.29 + 7.99 = 9.28\%$$

Calculating the terminal value

The terminal value represents the PV of all cash flows beyond the planning period (i.e., 2014–2018). Recall from Chapter 7 that the WACC, $WACC_{TV}$, used during the terminal period is assumed to equal the current industry average WACC. The terminal value, P_{TV}, is calculated using the constant growth valuation method (see Chapter 7).

$$P_{TV} = \frac{FCFF_n \times (1 + g_{TV})}{(WACC_{TV} - g_{TV})} \times \text{Discount factor}^{12} \quad (9.3)$$

in which

$FCFF_{2018}$ = FCFF in year 2018 (i.e., the last year of the planning period), must be recalculated if the marginal and effective tax rates differ)[13] = $968.50
$WACC_{TV}$ = cost of capital assumed beyond year *n* (2018) and is assumed to equal the current industry average WACC of 9.4%
g_{TV} = assumed growth rate during the terminal period = 3%
Discount factor uses the midyear convention = 0.66 (Table 9.8)

The PV of the terminal value is calculated as follows:

$$P_{TV} = [\$968.5 \times (1 + 0.03) / (0.094 - 0.03)] \times 0.66 = [\$997.56 / 0.064] \times 0.67 = \$10.4 \text{ billion}$$

[11] The weighted average borrowing cost is displayed on the Target Assumptions Worksheet but not shown on Table 9.2 because of space limitations. See the Target Assumptions Worksheet in the model on the companion site to this text.

[12] Recall that the discount factor equals $[1/(1 + WACC)^N]$ in which N is the number of time periods.

[13] The effective tax rate is the tax rate actually paid by the firm during the planning period. In this illustration, free cash flow in 2018 used in the calculation of the terminal value is the same as the last year of the 5-year planning period because the effective and marginal tax rates, at 40%, are the same.

TABLE 9.8 Calculating the Discount Factor Using the Midyear Convention[a]

	2014	2015	2016	2017	2018
Discount Factor	$1/(1 + 0.093)^{1 - 0.5}$ $= 1/(1 + 0.093)^{0.5}$ $= 0.96$	$1/(1 + 0.093)^{2 - 0.5}$ $=1/(1 + 0.093)^{1.5}$ $=0.88$	$1/(1 + 0.093)^{3 - 0.5}$ $=1/(1 + 0.093)^{2.5}$ $= 0.80$	$1/(1 + 0.093)^{4 - 0.05}$ $= 1/(1 + 0.093)^{3.5}$ $=0.73$	$1/(1 + 0.093)^{5 - 0.5}$ $= 1/(1 + 0.093)^{4.5}$ $=0.67$

[a]Using the midyear convention results in a larger discounted cash flow valuation than using full-year discounting. Why? Full-year discounting results in a larger discount rate and a smaller discount factor. For example, assume cash flow in 2014 is $100 million. Using the midyear convention, its present value would be $95 million (i.e., $[1/(1 + 0.098)^{0.5} = 0.95] \times$ $100 million), but using full-year discounting, it would be $91 million (i.e., $[1/(1 + 0.098)^{1} = 0.911] \times$ $100 million).

Model-balancing mechanisms

Financial models are said to balance when total assets equal total liabilities plus shareholders' equity. This may be done manually by inserting a value equal to the difference between the two sides of the balance sheet or automatically forcing this equality. The latter has the enormous advantage of allowing the model to simulate multiple scenarios over many years without having to stop the forecast each year to manually force the balance sheet to balance.

The mechanism in the model illustrated in this chapter for forcing automatic balance is the use of a revolving loan facility or line of credit. Such arrangements allow a firm to borrow up to a specific amount. To maintain the ability to borrow to meet unanticipated needs, firms have an incentive to pay off the loan as quickly as possible. When the maximum has been reached, the firm can no longer borrow.

If total assets exceed total liabilities plus equity, the model borrows (the "revolver" shows a positive balance). If total liabilities plus shareholders' equity exceed total assets, the model first pays off any outstanding "revolver" balances and uses the remaining excess cash flow to add to cash and short-term investments on the balance sheet.

Ending cash balances equal minimum cash if available cash is less than the loan balance. Why? Because only that portion of the loan balance greater than the minimum balance will be used to repay the loan. If available cash exceeds the loan balance, the ending cash balance equals the difference between available cash and the loan payment because the total loan balance will not be repaid unless there is cash available to cover the minimum balance.

Data sources

Financial models often require large amounts of historical data inputs to operate. For publicly traded firms, most of the financial statement data is available in the firm's annual 10k submitted to the US Securities and Exchange Commission (SEC). The 10k contains detailed income, balance sheet, and cash flow statements as well as numerous footnotes explaining these financial statements. The annual 10k provides the current year and 2 historical years. Firms often make 10ks available for many years. Consequently, by downloading past 10ks, the analyst can create an historical time series for analysis.[14]

Although the SEC mandates publicly traded firms submit certain types of information, it does not require that each firm's 10k be formatted in precisely the same way because of the differing circumstances for each firm. For example, one firm may have extraordinary or nonrecurring events that need to be displayed, but others do not. Explanations of specific line-item details are available in the Notes to the Consolidated Financial Statements. Additional data required by financial models such as industry credit ratios and firm betas often are available for free through various sources of publicly available information. What follows is a discussion of the sources of data for each financial statement and for other data inputs required by the model.

Income statement

Typically, sales, cost of sales, gross profit, SG&A, other operating expenses, extraordinary (nonrecurring) expenses, and the provision for taxes are shown in a firm's annual 10k. However, depreciation and amortization expense often are not shown as separate line items because they are frequently included in the cost of sales or in some instances such as for retailing businesses in sales, general, and administrative expenses. These data usually are broken out separately on the firm's cash flow statement.

[14] The analyst should check for revisions to the data to ensure that the historical information is recorded properly. Morningstar is a good source of selected historical data on public firms.

It is unnecessary to separate amortization expense from depreciation if they are included as one line item, but it is imperative that we add noncash expenses back to net income in the calculation of cash flow. When we include depreciation and amortization expense as a separate line item on the model's income statement, it is important to deduct such expenses from the cost of sales or SG&A if these line items taken from the firm's 10k include depreciation and amortization expense.

A discontinued operation occurs when a business unit or product line within a company's business has been sold, disposed of, or abandoned and is subsequently reported on the company's income statement as income separate from continuing operations. Discontinued operations are reported under GAAP as long as two conditions are satisfied: (1) the discontinued operation is completely removed from the financial statements and (2) the former parent has no ongoing relationship with the unit. Both current period and prior period operations are disclosed in the discontinued operations section and not under extraordinary items.[15]

Table 9.9 identifies the income statement information usually available (column 1) in a firm's 10k and shows how this information corresponds to the input data requirements (column 2) of the financial model discussed in this chapter. Column 3 indicates where data not available on the income statement may be found in the "Notes to the Consolidated Financial Statements." Brackets in column 1 indicate that multiple line items on the firm's 10k are included in a single line item in the M&A model. Similarly, brackets in column 2 indicate that multiple line items in the model are included in a single line item on the firm's 10k financial statements and that the detail is found in the Notes to the Financial Statements.

TABLE 9.9 Historical Income Statement

Typical 10k Income Statement	Financial Model Income Statement Input Requirements	Notes to Financial Statements
Revenue/sales (consolidated and by major business segment)	Sales	See note on business segment data
Cost of product/service sales (consolidated and by major business segment); may include depreciation and amortization expense	Cost of goods sold	See note on business segment data
Sales, General & Administrative Expense (consolidated and by major business segment)	SG&A	See note on business segment data
R&D expenses Restructuring and other costs, net }	Other operating expenses	
	Depreciation	See 10k's cash flow statement
	Amortization	See 10k's cash flow statement
Operating income	EBIT	
Total other expense, net Unusual (gain) loss Income from affiliates Interest (income) Interest expense	{ Unusual (gain) loss (Income) from affiliates Other expense (income) Interest (income) Interest expense	See note on other expense, net for detail on interest income and interest expense
Income from continuing operations before income taxes	Earnings before taxes	
Taxes	Taxes	
Net income (loss) before extraordinary items	Net income before extraordinary items	
Loss (income) from discontinued Operations after tax Loss (gain) from disposal of discontinued operations after tax }	Extraordinary items	
Net income after extraordinary items	Net income after extraordinary items	

R&D, Research and development; *SG&A,* selling, general and administrative.

[15] On the income statement, continuing operations are first reported followed by discontinued operations. The total gain or loss from the discontinued operations is reported followed by the relevant income taxes paid.

Balance sheet

Current assets including cash, short-term investments, accounts receivable, inventories, the current portion of deferred tax assets, and other current assets are available on 10ks. Long-term assets listed on 10ks include net property, plant, and equipment (i.e., gross property, plant, and equipment less accumulated depreciation), other assets, and goodwill (Table 9.10).

Current liabilities usually displayed on 10ks include short-term obligations and current maturities of long-term obligations (i.e., the current portion of long-term debt), accounts payable, accrued payroll and benefits, deferred

TABLE 9.10 Historical Balance Sheet

Typical 10k Balance Sheet	Financial Model Balance Sheet Input Requirements	Notes to Financial Statements
Assets		
Current assets		
Cash and cash equivalents Short-term investments	Cash (includes short-term investments)	
Accounts receivable (net of reserves)	Accounts receivable (net of reserves)	
Inventory	Inventory	
Deferred tax assets (current portion) Other current assets	Other	See note on income taxes for details
Long-Term Assets		
Net property, plant, and equipment	Property, plant, and equipment less accumulated depreciation = Net property, plant, and equipment	See note on property, plant, and equipment for accumulated depreciation
Other assets	Intangible assets Deferred taxes Other	
Goodwill	Goodwill	
Liabilities and shareholders' equity		
Current liabilities		
Accounts payable	Accounts payable	
Short-term obligations Accrued payroll and employee benefits Deferred revenue Other accrued expenses	Other	
Long-Term Liabilities		
Deferred income taxes	Deferred taxes (long-term portion)	See note on income taxes for details
Other long-term liabilities		See note on pensions
Long-term obligations	Revolving credit facility Senior debt Subordinated debt	
Shareholders' equity		See consolidated statement of shareholders' equity
Preferred stock, par value, shares authorized and issued	Preferred stock	

Continued

TABLE 9.10 Historical Balance Sheet—cont'd

Typical 10k Balance Sheet	Financial Model Balance Sheet Input Requirements	Notes to Financial Statements
Common stock, par value, shares authorized and issued	Common stock	
Retained earnings	Retained earnings	
Treasury stock (at cost)	Treasury stock	
Capital in excess of par Accumulated other comprehensive items	Other adjustments	
Noncontrolling interest (if any)	Noncontrolling interests	
Total shareholders' equity	Total stockholders' equity	
Liabilities and shareholders' equity	Liabilities and shareholders' equity	

revenue, and other accrued expenses. Long-term liabilities contain deferred income taxes (i.e., taxes owed but not paid because of timing differences), other long-term liabilities, and long-term obligations (e.g., long-term debt).

The components of shareholders' equity shown on the 10k balance sheet include preferred stock (par value and the number of shares authorized and the number issued) and common stock (par value and the number of such shares authorized and the number issued). Authorized shares have been approved by shareholders and the SEC but have not yet been issued by the firm. Capital in excess of par value (also called "additional paid in capital") shows the value of the issued shares when issued in excess of their par value when authorized. The remaining shareholders' equity items include retained earnings (i.e., accumulated historical net income after preferred dividends), treasury stock, and accumulated "other comprehensive items" (e.g., corrections made due to prior accounting errors and restatements).

The Note on Debt and Long-term Obligations describes the types of debt outstanding, maturity dates, and associated interest rates, and usually gives a 5-year projection of the annual debt repayment schedule. Principal repayments beyond the fifth year are shown as a total figure. Interest expense and principal usually can be estimated by using a weighted average of each type of debt (e.g., senior, subordinate) and applying the applicable amortization rate (i.e., annual principal repayment) for the largest amount of debt outstanding in each category.

Cash flow statement

The firm's cash flow statement (Table 9.11) typically shows the key cash inflows and outflows from operating, investing, and financing activities. This financial statement determines the ending cash balances for the firm, which is also reported on the firm's balance sheet.

Risk measures: betas and credit ratios

Historical betas for public firms and industry credit ratios are available from Yahoo Finance, Google Finance, Morningstar, Value Line Research Center, Standard & Poor's Net Advantage, One Source, and Thomson One Banker. Go to the yahoo.com/finance website and search in the "look up" block for a specific firm. The firm's beta is located below the day's closing price in the table of daily trading activity. Or go to google.com/finance and search for your firm; the firm's beta will be at the top of the page among the daily trading data.

Managing the model

Following certain protocols simplifies using the model. Save the model once historical data and forecast assumptions have been entered. Make additional changes to copies of the saved model. If errors arise and cannot be resolved, it is helpful to return to an earlier version of the model. This obviates the need to reload historical and forecast information.

TABLE 9.11 Historical Cash Flow Statement

Typical 10k Cash Flow Statement	Financial Model Cash Flow Statement Input Requirements	Notes to Financial Statements
Operating Activities		
Loss (income) from discontinued operations Loss (gain) on disposal of discontinued operations Income from continuing operations	Net income	
Depreciation and amortization	Depreciation and amortization	
Change in deferred income taxes	Deferred taxes (current portion)	See note on income taxes
Changes in Assets and Liabilities		
Accounts receivable	Accounts receivable	
Inventories	Inventory	
Other assets		
Accounts payable	Accounts payable	
Other liabilities	Other liabilities	
Net cash from operating activities	Cash flow from operating activities	
Investing Activities		
Acquisitions, net of cash acquired	Acquisition	See note on acquisitions
Purchases of property, plant, and equipment	Capital expenditures	
Proceeds from sale of property, plant, and equipment Proceeds from sale of investments Proceeds from sale of businesses Other investing activities, net	Sale of assets	
Net cash from investing activities	Cash flow from investing activities	
Financing Activities		
Net proceeds from issuance of long-term debt Redemptions and repayments of long-term debt	Net change in debt	
Purchases of company common stock Net proceeds from issuance of common stock	Net change in equity	
Dividends paid	Dividends paid	
Other financing activities, net		
Net cash from financing activities	Cash flow from financing activities	
(Decrease) increase in cash and cash equivalents	Net change in cash	
Cash and cash equivalents at beginning of period	Beginning cash balance	
Cash and cash equivalents at end of period	Ending cash balance	

Make sure the model's balance sheet "balances" because the red cells at the bottom of the balance sheet worksheet should equal zero (i.e., total assets equal total liabilities plus shareholders' equity). Do not "fine tune" the model's forecast until the model "balances." Adjusting the model's forecast should start with a focus on making small changes to model value drivers one at a time. To test the reasonableness of the model's output, check key output variables such as net present value and the trend in earnings per share, outstanding debt, and cash balance. Avoid making too many changes to the model before saving its output.

Addressing valuation issues in a near-zero interest rate environment

Chapter 7 discusses the challenges of valuation in a sustained artificially low interest rate environment. Although adjustments can be made in an attempt to offset potential underestimation in the calculation of the cost of capital and the resulting overvaluation of a target firm, they tend to be highly subjective and therefore problematic. Financial models can be used to address this problem by providing a range of valuation estimates enabling senior management to have a reasonable understanding of potential outcomes.

A model can be used to define alternative scenarios, which can be as basic as three outcomes: optimistic, pessimistic, and most likely. Alternatively, more sophisticated statistical methods can be used to estimate the most probable outcome. One method is Monte Carlo simulation. The primary advantage of a Monte Carlo simulation (which involves the random sampling of model inputs to simulate a range of outcomes) is its ability to allow the user to vary assumptions such as the cost of capital. This is also its foremost disadvantage because the outcomes are only as good as the quality of the inputs. Another major disadvantage is that Monte Carlo simulations tend to underestimate the likelihood of extreme events (so-called "black swan events") such as the 2008 to 2009 financial market crisis.

Some things to remember

Financial modeling helps the analyst understand determinants of value creation, provides a means of assessing options and risks, and identifies how firm value is affected by different economic events. The estimation of firm value involves a three-step procedure: (1) analyze the target's historical statements to determine the primary determinants of cash flow; (2) project 3 to 5 years of annual pro forma financial statements (i.e., the planning period); and (3) estimate the present value of the projected pro forma cash flows, including the terminal value.

Chapter discussion questions

9.1 What is financial modeling? How is it helpful in analyzing a firm's financial statements?
9.2 How is financial modeling applied to M&As?
9.3 What are the differences between GAAP-based and pro forma financial statements?
9.4 What are value drivers, and why are they important?
9.5 What does it mean to normalize historical financial data, and why is this an important part of the financial model building process?
9.6 What are common-size financial statements, and how might they impact the financial model building process?
9.7 A firm's financial statements are linked such that an increase in a key variable on one statement impacts other financial statements. Assuming a firm's gross margin is positive and constant, describe how an increase in revenue will impact net income and in turn the other financial statements. Assume the firm does not pay preferred dividends.
9.8 What is the appropriate number of years to project a firm's financial statement?
9.9 What is the difference between a firm's enterprise and equity values?
9.10 Financial models normally are said to balance when total assets equal total liabilities plus shareholders' equity. How can financial models be forced to balance automatically?

Answers to these Chapter Discussion Questions are available in the Online Instructor's Manual for instructors using this book.

Practice problems and answers

9.11 This exercise illustrates how a change in an input cell impacts variables on other financial statements. Using the Excel spreadsheet model in the file titled Target Firm Valuation Model on the companion website accompanying this book (see the Chapter Overview section at the beginning of this chapter for the website address), note the values for 2018 of the target's net income (Target IS Worksheet), cash balance and shareholders' equity (Target's BS Worksheet), and enterprise value and equity value (Target Valuation Worksheet).
Change the target's revenue growth rate assumption by one percentage point in 2014. On the Target's Assumptions Worksheet, increase the growth rate from 7.5% to 8.5% in the yellow input cell on the Sales Growth line for the year 2014. What are the new values in 2018 for net income, cash balance, shareholders' equity, enterprise value, and equity value following the increase in the growth rate assumption in the base case by one percentage point? Explain why these variables increased. (Hint: See Figure 9.1.)

9.12 The purpose of this exercise is to underscore how small changes in terminal value assumptions result in disproportionately large changes in firm value. Using the Excel spreadsheet model in the file folder titled Target Valuation Model found on the companion website to this book, locate the PV of the target's enterprise and equity values on the Valuation Worksheet and write them down. Increase the terminal value growth rate assumption by 1 percentage point and reduce the discount rate by one percentage point. How does this impact the firm's enterprise and equity value? Explain how this might happen. (Hint: Consider the definition of the constant growth valuation model.) Click the undo command to eliminate changes to the base case model, or close the model but do not save the results.

Solutions to these Practice Problems are available in the Online Instructor's Manual for instructors using this book.

End-of-chapter case study: Life Technologies undertakes a strategic review

Case study objectives

To illustrate how financial models

- Can be used to estimate firm value
- Allow simulation of alternative scenarios to facilitate management decision making
- Help identify the key drivers of firm value
- Focus attention on key assumptions underlying financial projections and valuation
- Facilitate executive decision making

Background

Life Technologies (Life Tech), a leading global life sciences firm, had rewarded its shareholders by almost doubling the firm's share price from its 2009 low of $26 per share to $51 by mid-2012. Despite this stellar performance, Gregory T. Lucier, Life Tech's chairman of the board and CEO since 2008, felt uneasy about the firm's future.

The life sciences industry is facing major challenges. Foremost is the increasing pressure on profit margins stemming from the escalating cost of health care because of the growth in chronic diseases, an aging population, and new therapies. Efforts to control health care costs are resulting in lower reimbursement rates for health care providers such as hospitals, testing laboratories, and physicians. These developments are driving consolidation among Life Tech's customers. Such consolidation reduces the number of potential new accounts and enables customers to increase their negotiating leverage with vendors such as Life Tech.

Customer consolidation is driving consolidation among life science companies to realize economies of scale, scope, and purchasing. Underway for several years, consolidation among Life Tech's competitors is expected to continue as they attempt to increase or hold their market share. An increasingly concentrated life sciences industry is expected to result in stronger competitors that are better able to compete as sole-source vendors for customers.

The combination of customer and competitor consolidation could put significant downward pressure on Life Tech's profit margins. Mr. Lucier and the Life Tech board faced a dilemma: whether to continue to pursue the firm's strategy of growing market share through customer-focused innovation or to consider alternative ways to maximize shareholder value, such as selling the firm or aggressively growing the firm.

Founded in 1987, Life Tech had established itself as a leading innovator of life science products and services that improve the effectiveness and efficiency of professionals in the pharmaceutical, biotechnology, agricultural, clinical, government, and academic scientific communities. The company's products also are used in forensics, food and water safety, animal health testing, and other industrial applications. Life Tech produces laboratory analytical and testing instruments; robotic systems to automate research; consumables, including glassware, plastic ware, and syringes; equipment from centrifuges to microscopes; laboratory furniture; and laboratory information management and testing systems.

On January 18, 2013, Life Tech announced that it had hired investment banks Deutsche Bank and Moelis & Co. to explore strategic options for the firm as part of the board's annual strategic review. Sensing the possibility of a sale, investors drove the share price up by 10% to $58 by the end of February. Mr. Lucier and the board's decision would be based on a continued analysis of industry trends and the firm's overall competitive position. Mr. Lucier directed his accounting and finance department to assess the impact of the results of this analysis on the value of the firm under different sets of assumptions. What follows is a discussion of these considerations.

The life sciences industry

Although biology remains the centerpiece of the life sciences, technological advances in molecular biology and biotechnology have led to a burgeoning of specializations and new interdisciplinary fields. Because of extremely high research and development (R&D) costs coupled with little revenue in the initial years of development, many life sciences firms partner with larger firms to complete product development. However, the industry tends to be dominated by a handful of big companies. Table 9.12 lists the major market segments of the industry.

The ratio of R&D spending to revenue drives new products in this industry. Successful firms achieve the proper balance between R&D spending and expense control. Because of the long R&D phase, when there is very little revenue being generated, projecting earnings requires looking at both a firm's products under development and in production. For firms already selling products, looking at sales trends makes projecting revenue growth rates easier.

Firm value in this industry is largely driven by their intellectual property and the ability to derive commercial products from their proprietary knowledge to generate future profits and cash flows. Because life sciences firms require substantial amounts of capital, they are prone to maintaining substantial amounts of cash on hand. Table 9.13 provides an overview of the factors contributing to the intensity of industry competition.

For firms to succeed in the life sciences industry, they must be able to innovate cost-effectively. Furthermore, to minimize product distribution costs and to gain access to needed R&D capabilities, firms need to be able to work collaboratively with product distributers, universities, and government agencies. Finally, because of the long lead time in developing new products and services, firms must have continuing access to financing. These three success factors ultimately drive future cash flow and firm value in this industry.

Life Technologies' business overview

Life Tech's business is described in terms of its markets; products, services, and after-sale support; R&D activities; licenses; and suppliers. These factors (in italics) are discussed next.

Life Tech's markets include life sciences, applied sciences, and medical sciences. Customers within the life sciences segment consist of laboratories generally associated with universities, medical research centers, government institutions, and other research institutions as well as biotechnology, pharmaceutical, and chemical companies. The applied sciences segment serves a diverse range of industries, with a focus in the areas of forensic analysis, quality

TABLE 9.12 Major Life Science Market Segments

Health care: drugs, vaccines, gene therapy, and tissue replacements	Research: understanding the human genome and better disease detection
Agriculture: improved foods and food production, pest control, and plant and animal disease control	Industry: oil and mineral recovery, environmental protection, waste reduction; improved detergents, chemicals, stronger textiles

TABLE 9.13 Assessing the Intensity of Life Science Industry Competition

Factor	Implications
Threat of new entrants	Limited by high barriers to entry • Substantial funding requirements are needed to finance R&D budgets • Specialized knowledge • Existing patents • Limited access to distribution channels
Power of suppliers	Limited by • Firms not generally reliant on a single supplier • Forward integration unlikely because of the specialized nature of computers, testing equipment, and materials
Power of buyers	Substantial for firms • Selling to governments, hospitals, and universities • Many firms small relative to their customers
Availability of substitutes	Depends on time horizon • Limited by existing patents • Generics emerge as patent protection expires
Competitive rivalry	Intense • Industry concentration high; ~1% of firms in industry account for most of the revenue • Industry growth slow; although the degree of rivalry varies by segment, industry size, and growth, prospects are clouded by potential cutbacks in government funding of research and health care reimbursement rates • Market share gains important to realize economies of scale, scope, and purchasing

Conclusions

- Downward pressure on selling prices
- Decelerating future unit sales growth rate during the 2014–2018 planning period
- Moderate increases in human resource costs caused by modest inflation outlook and sluggish job market

Downward pressure on gross operating margins for life science firms

R&D, Research and development.

and safety testing, animal health testing, and the commercial production of genetically engineered products. The medical services segment includes customers in clinical laboratories and medical institutions that use commercial technology for clinical and diagnostic purposes and medical researchers that use Life Tech's research-related technologies to search for new discoveries.

Life Tech's *services and support* activities provide limited warranties on equipment it sells for up to 2 years from the date of the sale. The firm also offers service contracts to customers that are generally 1 to 5 years in duration after the original warranty period. Life Tech provides both repair services and routine maintenance services under these arrangements.

Life Tech's continued growth in market share is dependent on R&D. Its core R&D skills include expertise ranging from biology to chemistry to engineering. The company invested $341.9 million, $377.9 million, and $375.5 million in R&D for the years ended December 31, 2012, 2011, and 2010, respectively. These expenditures comprise about 10.5% of annual revenue, slightly above the industry average.

Life Tech's *sales and marketing* activities include a direct sales force of 3700 employees and a presence in more than 180 countries. The company also has more than 1000 supply centers worldwide in close proximity to customers' laboratories to provide convenient access and an e-commerce website to provide easy online ordering of Life Tech products.

The firm manufactures and sells some of its existing products under the terms of *license agreements* that require it to pay royalties to the licensor based on the sales of products containing the licensed materials or technology. Although the company emphasizes its own R&D, its ability to license new technology from third parties is and will continue to be critical to Life Tech's ability to offer competitive new products.

The firm buys materials from many *suppliers* and has contracts with many third parties for the manufacturing of products sold under the firm's brand. The firm is not dependent on any one supplier as raw materials are generally available from a number of suppliers.

Life Technologies' competitor profile

Competitor profiling consists of ranking a firm against its competitors in terms of critical success factors. A common technique is to create detailed profiles on the major competitors. These profiles give an in-depth description of the competitor's background, finances, products, markets, facilities, personnel, and strategies.

Table 9.14 provides a ranking of Life Tech compared with its primary competitors by factors critical for success in the life sciences industry. These include the ability to innovate, collaborate with research and distribution partners, and finance ongoing R&D spending. The critical success factors are weighted by their presumed importance and sum to one. Each competitor is ranked on a scale of 1 to 10 with respect to each success factor. These scores are then totaled to create a competitor ranking in terms of the success factors.

The primary competitors were selected from among 20 competitors; each had a market value at year-end 2012 of $2.4 billion or more (Table 9.15). Only those having a market value greater than $9 billion were included in the comparison of Life Tech and its competitors. Thermo Fisher Scientific, Agilent Technologies, Quest Diagnostics, and Laboratory Corporation of America share many products and services in common with Life Tech. Based on this subjective ranking, Life Tech has a slight competitive edge over Thermo Fisher Scientific and Agilent Technologies, its largest competitors in terms of size.

Life Technologies' historical financial performance

Life Tech's historical performance in terms of its gross profit margin has been remarkably stable over time at about 56% (Table 9.16). The historical resiliency of the firm's gross margin caused Mr. Lucier to use the historical gross margin in valuing the firm despite anticipated future pricing pressures. The firm's revenue growth rate has averaged a 6.5% compound annual average growth rate since 2008 when the firm completed an acquisition that nearly doubled the size of the company. Mr. Lucier directed his staff to evaluate different revenue growth rate, cost reduction, and asset utilization assumptions, as well as to increase Life Tech's leverage, to assess the impact of alternative strategies on the firm's market value.

The firm's historical performance has exceeded major financial benchmarks. Life Tech's price to earnings, cash flow, and sales ratios exceeded both the life sciences industry average and the S&P 500 average as of the end of 2012 (Table 9.17). Table 9.18 shows Life Tech's historical data for selected financial metrics.

Conclusions

The Life Tech CEO, Greg Lucier, and the Life Tech Board were at a crossroads. The ongoing trend toward customer consolidation would require increased consolidation among life science companies. The strategic options available to the firm were clear: continue the firm's current strategy; acquire a sizeable competitor to achieve economies of scale, scope, and purchasing; or sell the firm to a competitor. The firm lacked the financial resources to

TABLE 9.14 Life Technologies and Primary Competitors Ranked by Critical Success Factors

Key Industry Success Factors	Weight	Life Technologies	Thermo Fisher Scientific	Agilent Technologies	Quest Diagnostics	Laboratory Corp of America
1. Ability to innovate	.4	8	8	7	4	3
2. Effective collaboration	.3	8	7	6	6	5
3. Access to capital	.3	8	7	7	4	2
Totals	**1.0**	**24**	**22**	**20**	**14**	**10**

TABLE 9.15 Life Technologies versus Peers: Financial Metrics

	Market Cap ($ Millions)	Net Income ($ Millions)	P/S	P/B	P/E	Dividend Yield (%)	5-Year Rev CAGR (%)	Net Operating Margin (%)	Interest Coverage	D/E
Thermo Fisher Scientific Inc.	34,749	1307	2.7	2.1	26.5	0.6	5.1	11.4	6.3	0.4
Agilent Technologies Inc.	16,556	938	2.6	3.5	8.7	0.9	4.8	13.3	11.3	0.6
Life Technologies Corp	**13.064**	**476**	**3.5**	**2.6**	**27.9**	—	**24.3**	**17.1**	**5.3**	**0.4**
Quest Diagnostics Inc.	9263	762	1.4	2.4	11.8	1.9	1.9	16.9	7.5	0.8
Laboratory Corporation of America Holdings	9118	567	1.7	3.6	17.2	—	6.9	18.7	11.0	1.0
Waters Corporation	8381	484	4.6	5.2	17.7	—	4.6	27.4	18.4	0.7
Mettler-Toledo International, Inc.	7336	298	3.3	9.0	25.6	—	5.5	15.1	17.8	0.5
Quintiles Transnational Holdings Inc	5679	188	1.1	-8.0	29.1	—	—	8.2	3.0	—
Idexx Laboratories	5633	187	4.4	10.5	31.6	—	7.0	18.5	68.7	0.0
Qiagen NV	5298	47	4.2	2.0	114.9	—	14.1	16.3	7.2	0.3
Covance, Inc.	4809	167	1.9	3.2	28.8	—	7.7	8.1	20.0	—
Lonza Group AG	4693	139	1.2	2.0	31.0	2.3	6.5	9.7	3.4	1.2
PerkinElmer Inc	4092	84	1.9	2.1	49.8	0.8	3.4	7.9	2.1	0.5
Eurofins Scientific Group S.A.	3556	69	2.5	7.3	40.5	—	16.0	7.2	5.6	1.2
Cepheid	2767	-2	7.2	10.1	—	—	20.7	-6.4	-144.1	0.0
Alere Inc	2721	-130	0.9	1.8	—	—	27.4	3.9	0.5	2.6
Swedish Orphan Biovitrum AB	2670	-211	8.7	3.6	—	—	8.9	-2.8	-0.7	0.2
Icon PLC	2484	80	1.5	3.1	31.2	—	19.0	7.3	35.5	—
Industry Average	**7357**	**277**	**2.3**	**3.2**	**26.9**	**0.4**	**8.9**	**11.3**	**25.4**	**0.7**

CAGR, Compound annual growth rate; desired future (or target) debt-to-equity ratio set by the firm; *D/E*, debt to equity ratio; *P/B*, price-to-book ratio; *P/E*, price-to-earnings ratio; P/S, *price per share*; Rev, *revenue*.

TABLE 9.16 Historical Gross Profit Margin

Average, 1998–2012 (%)	56.46
Average, 2003–2012 (%)	56.38
Average, 2008–2012 (%)	56.83
Regression, 1998–2012 (%)	56.73

TABLE 9.17 Life Technology Valuation Ratios (as of Year-End 2012)

	Life Technologies	Life Sciences Industry Average	S&P 500	Life Technologies 5-Year Industry
Price/earnings	27.9	26.9	17.1	42.7
Price/book	2.6	3.2	2.5	1.7
Price/sales	3.5	2.3	1.6	2.3
Price/cash flow[a]	16.1	10.4	10.7	11.5

[a]Price/cash flow = 3-year average.

acquire a major competitor. Therefore that option was dismissed. Of the remaining two options, maintaining the current strategy or selling the firm, which would maximize shareholder value? In April 2013, the firm announced that it had agreed to merge with the industry leader, Thermo Fisher Scientific. The merger, discussed in detail in Chapter 15, was completed in 2014.

Discussion questions

Use the Microsoft Excel model titled Target Firm Valuation Model Case Study Final Version on the companion site to this book to answer the following questions. Please see the Chapter Overview section of this chapter for the site's internet address.

The model already contains data and an estimate of Life Tech's enterprise and equity valuations based on this data and a set of assumptions about the planning period spanning 2014 through 2018, as well as the years beyond. In answering the following questions, assume the valuation provided in this model represents the firm's base case and reflects what the firm could do if it continued the business strategy in effect in 2012.

1. Note the enterprise and equity valuations for Life Technology in the Excel spreadsheet model titled *Life Tech Undertakes Strategic Review Financial Model* on the companion website accompanying this book. View this as the base case. The CEO Greg Lucier asks his CFO to determine the impact of plausible assumption changes on the firm's valuation. The CFO asks you as a financial analyst to estimate the impact of a change in the firm's revenue growth rate and cost of sales as a percent of sales. On the Target Assumptions Worksheet, make the following changes and note their impact on Life Tech's enterprise and equity values on the Valuation Worksheet:
   a. Increase the sales growth rate in 2014 by 2 percentage points.
   b. Retaining the assumption change made in (a), decrease the cost of sales as a percent of sales by 2 percentage points in 2014.
   What is Life Tech's enterprise and equity value resulting from these changes? How do they compare with the base case? Briefly explain why each of these changes affects firm value. Do not undo the results of your changes to the model's base case.
2. Using the model results from question 1, the CFO believes that in addition to an increase in the sales growth rate and an improving cost position, Life Tech could use its assets more effectively by better managing its receivables and inventory. Specifically, the CFO directs you as a financial analyst to make the following changes to days sales in receivables and days in inventory. On the Target Assumptions Worksheet, make the following changes and note their impact on Life Tech's enterprise and equity values on the Valuation Worksheet:
   a. Reduce receivables days by 10 days starting in 2014.
   b. Reduce inventory days by 10 days starting in 2014.

TABLE 9.18 Life Technologies Corp (12 Months Ending December)

	2003–2012	2004–2012	2005–2012	2006–2012	2007–2012	2008–2012	2009–2012	2010–2012	2011–2012	2012–2012	TTM
Revenue ($ millions)	778	1024	1198	1263	1282	1620	3280	3588	3776	3799	3842
Gross margin (%)	60.3	59.4	58.7	59.5	55.9	58.1	55.6	58.7	55.9	56.2	57.9
Operating income ($ millions)	89	136	127	-158	178	167	386	612	648	665	683
Operating margin (%)	11.5	13.3	10.6	-12.5	13.9	10.3	11.8	17.1	17.2	17.5	17.8
Net income ($ millions)	60	89	132	-191	143	31	145	378	378	431	476
Earnings per share ($s)	0.59	0.82	1.17	-1.86	1.48	0.30	0.80	1.99	2.05	2.40	2.71
Shares (Millions)	103	121	120	103	97	104	181	191	186	179	175
Book value per share ($millions)	16.64	18.67	19.32	16.95	18.96	37.43	22.36	24.33	25.76	27.17	28.79
Operating cash flow ($ millions)	168	253	309	235	324	366	714	739	809	778	826
Cap spending ($ millions)	-32	-39	-726	-70	-78	-82	-181	-131	-108	-136	-142
Free cash flow ($ millions)	136	214	-417	165	245	284	534	608	701	642	684

TTM, Trailing 12 months

What is Life Tech's enterprise and equity value resulting from these changes? How do they compare to the results in question 1? Briefly explain why each of these changes affects firm value. Do not undo the changes you have made to the model.

3. Given the results of the model from questions 1 and 2, assume Mr. Lucier and the Life Tech board raised their target debt-to-equity ratio from 30% to 60% to reduce their WACC. Such a reduction would make projects that would not have been undertaken at a higher cost of capital attractive. Recalculate the firm's WACC, assuming that none of the assumptions about the cost of capital made in the base case have changed, with the exception of the levered beta. (Hint: The levered beta needs to be unlevered and then relevered to reflect the new debt-to-equity ratio.) Without undoing the assumption changes made in questions 1 and 2, use your new estimate of the firm's WACC during the planning period to calculate Life Tech's enterprise and equity values given on the Valuation Worksheet. Explain why the change in the debt-to-equity ratio affected firm value.
4. Based on your answers to questions 1, 2, and 3, what do you believe are the most important value drivers for Life Tech based on their impact on the firm's enterprise and equity values? Which are the least important? (Hint: Calculate the percentage increase in enterprise and equity values over the base case due to each assumption change.)
5. The base case valuation reflects a constant 57% gross margin throughout the planning period. Based on the information given in the case study, do you believe that this is realistic? Why? Why not? How might this assumption have biased the estimates of enterprise and equity valuation in your answers to questions 1 to 4? If they were biased, what would be the direction of the bias?

Solutions to these case study discussion questions are available in the Online Instructor's Manual for instructors using this book.

CHAPTER

10

Analysis and valuation of privately held firms

OUTLINE

Mergers, Acquisitions, and Other Restructuring Activities, Eleventh Edition
https://doi.org/10.1016/B978-0-12-819782-0.00010-1

Maier's law: If the facts do not conform to the theory, they must be disposed of.

Inside M&A: factors impacting the success or failure of acquisitions of privately owned firms

KEY POINTS

- An outright sale of a startup accomplishes two goals: providing financing for growth opportunities and providing cash for the founders and early investors.
- Contractual arrangements often are not enough to keep founders motivated.
- Founder retention requires startup and acquirer management to have a strong shared vision of the future.

How did Nick and Elyse Oleksak find success? Through frozen mini stuffed bagels, of course! Frozen products have been resurging in popularity in recent years because of their convenience, relatively low prices, and the application of quick-freeze technology. Since New York City–based Bantam Bagels was founded in 2012, the firm's growth exploded from a single location to marketing its products nationwide through the retail, e-commerce, and food service distribution channels. Originally, the firm financed the business through funds provided by family and friends, but this prevented them from expanding beyond their New York City retail location.

Growth was jumpstarted by an appearance on the television show *Shark Tank* in 2015 when they raised $275,000 from "shark" investor Lori Greiner in return for a 25% stake in their business. Sales in 2018 exceeded $20 million, compared with annual sales of about $200,000 before their appearance on the show. Ms. Greiner, known as the "queen of QVC," (QVC is a TV shopping channel), helped the firm sell 30,000 stuffed bagels on live TV in 5 minutes. This attracted the attention of Starbucks, which was interested in stocking Bantam products in its stores nationwide. By 2018, Bantam Bagels were sold in retailers Target, Kroger, Costco, and Albertsons.

The explosive growth caught the eye of T. Marzetti Company (Marzetti), owned by publicly traded Lancaster Colony Corp (Lancaster). Lancaster had annual sales of more than $1.3 billion in 2019. Lancaster produces and markets national and regional branded food products for the food service markets. Marzetti is the firm's specialty food group. Bantam Bagels provides Lancaster with entry into the large and growing frozen breakfast category. The relationship with Starbucks in the food service channel positions Bantam for substantial future expansion.

Lancaster acquired Bantam for $34 million in early 2019, including the value of an earnout.[1] Aware of the need to keep Bantam largely independent of other operations, Lancaster operates it largely as an independent entity with the founders having a high degree of autonomy.

The Oleksaks emphasized finding the right business partner, and with Marzetti, they found the support to grow Bantam exponentially while retaining control over daily operations. The Oleksaks and their six employees were able to stay with the company to run daily operations and direct product development. Lancaster offered Bantam's founders what they were seeking: access to capital while retaining operational control. Moreover, the timing of the sale gave the initial investors such as Ms. Greiner the ability to cash out of her investment in less than 4 years.

The challenge for Lancaster is to keep the founders motivated. If sales slow, dimming the prospects of realizing the benefits of the earnout, the founders may leave. If they cannot leave because of contractual constraints, they will likely be demotivated. In either situation, the parent firm loses the talent and innovative energy that attracted them to Bantam in the first place. In addition, Lancaster could lose interest in continued investment in Bantam if the relatively small business does not contribute significantly to the firm's consolidated earnings in a comparatively short time period to satisfy its investors.

[1] Earnouts are arrangements in which a portion of the purchase price is contingent on achieving a predetermined level of future revenue and earnings. Acquirers use earnouts to shift a portion of the risk associated with future financial performance to the sellers and to keep the former owners motivated.

Chapter overview

In most mergers and acquisitions (M&As), the acquirer, the target, or both are privately held firms. Such firms are those whose securities are not registered with state or federal regulators and therefore cannot be listed on public markets.[2] The lack of "tradeable" markets makes valuing these businesses challenging. Nonetheless, the need to value such businesses may arise for a variety of reasons. Investors and small business owners may need a valuation as part of a merger or acquisition, for settling an estate, or because employees wish to exercise their stock options. Employee stock ownership plans (ESOPs) also may require periodic valuations. And shareholder disputes, court cases, divorce, or the payment of gift or estate taxes may necessitate a valuation.

This chapter discusses how to deal with problems specific to privately held firms. Because making initial contact and negotiating with private business owners are addressed in Chapter 5, this chapter focuses on the influence of family control and the difficulties of valuing such firms and adjusting firm value for control premiums (CPs), minority discounts, and liquidity discounts (LDs).

This chapter also includes a discussion of how corporate shells, created through reverse mergers, and leveraged ESOPs are used to acquire privately owned companies and how so-called private investment in public equity financing may be used to fund their ongoing operations. The chapter also discusses the mechanics of early-stage investment in embryonic firms. A review of this chapter is available in the file folder titled "Student Study Guide" on the companion site to this book (https://www.elsevier.com/books-and-journals/book-companion/9780128197820).

Ownership structure, agency conflicts, and stock market returns

Most privately held firms are owned (or controlled) by members of the same family. As such, the terms *privately held* or *family-owned* or *-controlled* are used interchangeably. Ownership tends to be more concentrated in family-owned firms than in widely held publicly traded companies.[3] Family-owned or -controlled firms often are somewhat more profitable than nonfamily companies. Furthermore, abnormal financial returns to investors in family-owned firms increase on average with the level of family ownership, consistent with the notion that family members have a strong incentive to maximize firm value. Financial returns to investors in family-owned firms tend to be higher than for investors in nonfamily firms, possibly as compensation for the risk of potential conflicts between majority and minority investors.[4] The tendency for family-controlled firms to outperform nonfamily firms occurs primarily among large publicly listed firms. Why? The higher governance and disclosure requirements for listed firms offset agency conflicts in which family members may extract benefits not available to other shareholders.[5]

How family control affects M&A activity

Because most firms are family owned, they account for most M&As. However, such firms exhibit on average a low propensity to engage in M&As, which can threaten the family's control if they dilute ownership, alter succession planning, change the founder's legacy, and impact the firm's reputation. M&As also can have adverse consequences such as layoffs that often run contrary to the family's core values. Although such factors can make family-owned firms reluctant to make acquisitions, their interest in M&As seems to vary with the degree of shareholder protections provided by a country's legal system, with such firms being more inclined to engage in takeovers in countries where shareholders are better protected.[6] Aspirational levels also play an important role in how family-dominated firms

[2] Privately owned corporations should not be confused with closely held firms whose shares are sometimes traded publicly. More than half of the value of closely held corporations is held by five or fewer investors.

[3] All family-owned firms are not small because families control the operating policies at many large, publicly traded firms. In such firms, family influence is exercised by family members in senior management positions or board seats and through holding supervoting shares. Examples of large publicly traded family businesses include Walmart, Ford Motor, Loew's, and Bechtel Group, each of which has annual revenues of more than $25 billion.

[4] Eugster and Isakov, 2019

[5] Hansen and Block, 2020

[6] Requejo et al., 2018

are managed, such that when actual performance falls below aspirational levels, they are more inclined to pursue riskier strategies such as international diversification, which can be through M&A, joint venture (JV), or start-up.[7]

When they do engage in M&As, family-controlled firms are more profitable after closing than firms in which ownership is less concentrated.[8] This may reflect more active monitoring by large shareholders of manager performance, a longer-term view for the firm, and a greater tendency to make value-enhancing investments than in public firms, where CEOs may engage in empire building. Family-owned firm CEOs also are less likely to pursue empire building or excessive pay packages as is often the case with non—family-owned firms because they are closely monitored by family members.[9] And nonfinancial goals such as sustaining the family dynasty can drive family-owned firms to diversify risk through acquisitions.[10]

Private versus public company governance

Whereas public company agency problems usually involve differences between management and shareholders, privately held firms are more often confronted by disputes involving different shareholders (or classes of shareholders) seeking to gain influence and control. In private firms, control often resides with the head of the founding family, which can be exercised as a controlling shareholder or as chairman of the board and CEO. Unlike listed firms, governance practices in private firms are often informal and undocumented and implemented by founding family members. Financial reporting and accountability are likely to be lax. Succession planning and recruitment are made more difficult by family ties, with decisions often made more on a familial relationship and less on merit. And decisions often reflect the family interests of the dominant shareholder rather than sound business principles.[11] Finally, family-dominated firms are more likely to become entrenched than nonfamily firms because of their incentive to protect private family benefits.[12]

Challenges of valuing privately held companies

The anonymity of many privately held firms, the potential for data manipulation, problems specific to small firms, and the tendency of owners of private firms to manage in a way to minimize tax liabilities create a number of significant valuation issues. These are discussed next.

Lack of externally generated information

There is generally a lack of analyses of private firms provided by sources outside of the company. Private firms provide little incentive for outside analysts to cover them because of the absence of a public market for their securities. As such, there are few forecasts of their performance other than those provided by the firm's management. Press coverage is usually quite limited, and what is available is often based on information provided by the firm's management. Even companies (e.g., Dun & Bradstreet) purporting to offer demographic and financial information on small privately held firms use infrequent telephone interviews with the management of such firms as their primary source of information.

Lack of internal controls and inadequate reporting systems

Private firms generally do not have the same level of controls and reporting systems as public firms, which are required to prepare audited financial statements and are subject to Sarbanes-Oxley. The lack of systems to monitor

[7] Xu et al., 2020

[8] Adhikari et al., 2016

[9] DeCesari et al., 2016

[10] Schierstedt et al., 2020

[11] Debellis et al. (2020) note that these issues inhibit private firms from growing through international JVs because they lack the required expertise on their boards, which are populated with family members and insiders.

[12] Ashraf et al., 2020

how money is spent invites fraud and misuse of private-firm resources. With intellectual property being a substantial portion of the value of many private firms, the lack of documentation also constitutes a key valuation issue. Often only a few individuals within the firm know how to reproduce valuable intangible assets such as software, chemical formulas, and recipes; the loss of such individuals can destroy a firm. Moreover, customer lists and the terms and conditions associated with key customer relationships also may be undocumented, creating the basis for customer disputes when a change in ownership occurs.

Firm-specific problems

Private firms may lack product, industry, and geographic diversification, as well as management talent to allow a firm to develop products for its current or new markets. Small size may restrict their influence with regulators and unions and limit access to distribution channels and leverage with suppliers and customers. Finally, these companies may have little brand recognition.

Common forms of manipulating reported income

Overwhelmingly, private firms tend to manipulate earnings more than public firms by misstating revenue, operating expenses, or both.[13] Moreover, unlisted family firms tend to engage in tax avoidance more than unlisted nonfamily businesses.[14]

Misstating revenue

Revenue may be over- or understated, depending on the owner's objectives. If the intent is tax minimization, businesses operating on a cash basis may opt to report less revenue because of the difficulty outside parties have in tracking transactions. Private-business owners intending to sell a business may be inclined to inflate revenue if the firm is to be sold. Common examples include manufacturers, which rely on others to distribute their products. These manufacturers can inflate revenue in the current accounting period by booking as revenue products shipped to resellers without adequately adjusting for probable returns. Membership or subscription businesses, such as health clubs and magazine publishers, may inflate revenue by booking the full value of multiyear contracts in the current period rather than prorating the payment received at the beginning of the contract period over the life of the contract.[15]

Manipulation of operating expenses

Owners of private businesses attempting to minimize taxes may give themselves and family members higher-than-normal salaries, benefits, and bonuses. Other examples include expenses that are really other forms of compensation for the owner, his or her family, and key employees, including the rent on the owner's summer home or hunting lodge and salaries for the pilot and captain of the owner's airplane or yacht. Current or potential customers sometimes are allowed to use these assets. Owners frequently argue that these expenses are necessary to maintain customer relationships and are therefore legitimate expenses.

Other areas commonly abused include travel and entertainment, insurance, and excessive payments to vendors supplying services to the firm. Due diligence frequently uncovers situations in which the owner or a family member is either an investor in or an owner of the vendor supplying the products or services.

If the business owner's objective is to maximize the firm's selling price, salaries, benefits, and other operating costs may be understated significantly. An examination of the historical trend in the firm's profitability may reveal that profits are being manipulated. If operating profits in the year in which the business is being offered for sale unexpectedly improve, this may suggest that expenses have historically been overstated, revenues understated, or both.

[13] Habib et al., 2018

[14] Kovermann and Wendt, 2019

[15] Such booking activity boosts current profitability because not all the costs associated with multiyear contracts, such as customer service, are incurred in the period when the full amount of revenue is booked.

Process for valuing privately held businesses

To address the challenges presented by privately owned firms, an analyst should adopt a four-step procedure. Step 1 requires adjustment of the target firm's financial data to reflect true profitability and cash flow in the current period. Step 2 entails determining the appropriate valuation methodology. Step 3 requires estimating the proper discount rate. Finally, in the fourth step, firm value is adjusted for a CP (if appropriate), an LD, and a minority discount (if an investor takes a less-than-controlling ownership stake).

Step 1: adjusting financial statements

Income statement adjustments can provide accurate estimates of the current year's net or pretax income; earnings before interest and taxes (EBIT); or earnings before interest, taxes, depreciation, and amortization (EBITDA). All measures of income should reflect costs actually incurred in generating the level of revenue, adjusted for doubtful accounts, the firm booked in the current period. They also should reflect other expenditures (e.g., training and advertising) that must be incurred in the current period to sustain the anticipated growth in revenue.

The importance of establishing accurate current or base-year data is evident when we consider how businesses are often valued. If the current year's profit data are incorrect, future projections of the dollar value would be inaccurate even if the projected growth rate is accurate. Valuations based on relative valuation methods such as price—to—current year earnings ratios would be biased to the extent estimates of the target's current income are inaccurate.

EBITDA facilitates the comparison of firms because it eliminates the potential distortion in earnings because of differences in depreciation methods and financial leverage among firms. This indicator is often more applicable in relative valuation methods than other measures of profitability because firms are more likely to display positive EBITDA than EBIT or net income figures. However, EBITDA ignores the impact on cash flow of changes in net working capital, investing, and financing activities.

Making informed adjustments

Although finding reliable current information on privately held firms is challenging, information is available. The first step for the analyst is to search the internet for references to the target firm. This search should unearth a number of sources of information on the target firm. Table 10.1 provides a partial list of websites containing information on private firms.

TABLE 10.1 Sources of information on private firms

Source and web address	Content
Research Firms	
Washington Researchers: www.washingtonresearchers.com Fuld & Company: www.fuld.com	Provide listing of sources such as local government officials, local chambers of commerce, state government regulatory bodies, credit-reporting agencies, and local citizen groups
Databases	
Dun & Bradstreet: smallbusiness.dnb.com	Information on firms' payments histories and limited financial data
Hoover: www.hoovers.com (a division of Dun & Bradstreet)	Data on 40,000 international and domestic firms, IPOs, not-for-profits, trade associations, and small businesses and limited data on 18 million other companies
Standard & Poor's NetAdvantage: www.netadvantage.standardandpoors.com	Financial data and management and directors' bibliographies on 125,000 firms
InfoUSA: www.infousa.com	Industry benchmarking and company-specific data
Forbes: www.forbes.com/list	Provides list of top privately held firms annually
Inc: www.inc.com/inc500	Provides list of 500 of fastest-growing firms annually

IPO, Initial public offering.

Salaries and benefits

Before drawing any conclusions, the analyst should determine the actual work performed by key employees and the compensation received for performing a similar job in the same industry. Comparative salary data can be obtained by employing the services of a compensation consultant familiar with the industry or simply by scanning "employee wanted" advertisements in the industry trade press and magazines and the "help wanted" pages of the local newspaper.

Depending on the industry, benefits can range from 14% to 50% of an employee's base salary. Certain employee benefits, such as Social Security and Medicare taxes, are mandated by law and therefore are an uncontrollable cost of doing business. Other types of benefits may be more controllable such as pension contributions and life insurance coverage, which are calculated as a percentage of base salary. As such, trimming salaries that appear to be excessive also reduces these types of benefits. However, benefit reductions often contribute to higher operating costs in the short run because of higher employee turnover, the need to retrain replacements, and the potential negative impact on the productivity of those who remain.

Travel, meals, and entertainment

Travel and entertainment (T&E) expenses often are the first costs cut when a buyer values a target. What may look excessive to one unfamiliar with the industry may be necessary for retaining current and acquiring new customers. Building and maintaining relationships is particularly important for personal and business services companies, such as consulting and law firms. Account management may require consultative selling at the customer's site. A complex product such as software may require onsite training. Indiscriminate reduction in the T&E budget could lead to a loss of customers after a change in ownership.

Auto expenses and personal life insurance

Ask if such expenses are critical to attract and retain key employees. This can be determined by comparing total compensation paid to employees of the target firm with compensation packages offered to employees in similar positions in the same industry in the same region. A similar review should be undertaken with respect to the composition of benefits packages.

Family members

Family members often perform real services and tend to be highly motivated because of their close affinity with the business. The loss of family members who built relationships with customers may result in a subsequent loss of key accounts and proprietary knowledge.

Rent or lease payments in excess of fair market value

Check ownership of buildings and equipment used by the business. This is a common method of transferring company funds to the business owner, who also owns the building and equipment.

Professional services fees

Professional services could include legal, accounting, personnel, and actuarial services. Again, check for any nonbusiness relationship between the business owner and the firm providing the service. Always consider special circumstances that may justify unusually high fees such as the legal and accounting expenses incurred by firms in highly regulated industries.

Depreciation expense

Accelerated depreciation methodologies may make sense for tax purposes, but they may seriously understate current earnings. For financial reporting purposes, it may be appropriate to convert depreciation schedules from accelerated to straight-line depreciation if this results in a better matching of when expenses actually are incurred and revenue actually is received.

Reserves

Current reserves may be inadequate to reflect future events. Increasing (decreasing) reserves lowers (increases) taxable income. Collection problems may be uncovered after an analysis of accounts receivable. It may be necessary to add to reserves for doubtful accounts. Similarly, the target firm may not have adequately reserved for future obligations to employees under existing pension and health care plans or for known environmental and litigation exposures.

Accounting for inventory

During periods of inflation, businesses use the last-in, first-out (LIFO) method to account for inventories. This approach results in an increase in the cost of sales that reflects the most recent and presumably highest cost inventory; therefore, it reduces gross profit and taxable income. The use of LIFO during inflationary periods tends to lower the value of inventory on the balance sheet because items in inventory are valued at the lower cost of production associated with earlier time periods. LIFO accounting makes sense when inflation is expected to remain high.

In contrast, the use of first-in, first-out (FIFO) accounting for inventory assumes that inventory is sold in the chronological order in which it was purchased. When prices are increasing, the FIFO method produces a higher ending inventory, a lower cost of goods sold, and higher gross profit. Although it may make sense for tax purposes to use LIFO, the buyer's objective for valuation purposes should be to obtain a realistic estimate of actual earnings in the current period. FIFO accounting is most logical for products that are perishable or subject to rapid obsolescence and therefore most likely to be sold in chronological order.

Areas that are commonly understated

Projected sales increases normally require more aggressive marketing efforts, more effective customer service support, and better employee training. Nonetheless, it is common for the ratio of annual advertising and training expenses to annual sales to decline during the period of highest projected growth in forecasts developed by either the seller or the buyer. The seller wants to boost the purchase price. The buyer simply may be overly optimistic about how much more effectively they can manage the business or because they want a lender to finance the deal. Other areas that are commonly understated in projections include environmental cleanup, employee safety, and pending litigation expenses.

Areas that are commonly overlooked

Intangible assets often are more valuable than tangible assets. Examples include high valuations placed on internet-related and biotechnology companies. Intangible assets may include customer lists, patents, licenses, leases, regulatory approvals, noncompete agreements, and employment contracts. To represent incremental value, these factors must reflect sources of revenue or cost reduction not already included in the target's operating cash flows.

Explaining adjustments to financial statements

Table 10.2 illustrates how historical and projected financial statements received from the target as part of the due diligence process could be restated to reflect what the buyer believes is a more accurate description of revenue and costs. Adjusting the historical financials provides insight into what the firm could have done had it been managed differently. Note that the cost of sales is divided into direct and indirect expenses. Direct cost of sales relates to those incurred directly in the production process. Indirect costs are those incurred as a result of the various functions (e.g., senior management) supporting the production process. The actual historical costs are displayed above the "explanation of adjustments" line. Some adjustments represent "add backs" to profit, while others reduce profit. The adjusted EBITDA numbers at the bottom of the table represent what the buyer believes is the most realistic estimate of the profitability. By displaying the data historically, the buyer can see trends that may be useful in projecting the firm's profitability.

In this illustration, the buyer believes inventories are more accurately valued on a FIFO rather than LIFO basis, causing a sizeable boost to profitability. Due diligence also revealed that the firm was overstaffed and that it could be operated by eliminating the full-time position held by the former owner (including fees received as a member of the firm's board of directors) and a number of part-time positions held by the owner's family members. Office space is reduced, thereby lowering rental expense as a result of the elimination of regional sales offices. However, the sales- and marketing-related portion of the travel and entertainment budget is increased to accommodate the increased travel necessary to service out-of-state customers. Advertising expenses will have to be increased to promote the firm's products in those regions. The new buyer believes the historical training budget is inadequate to sustain growth and more than doubles spending in this category.

Step 2: applying valuation methodologies to privately held companies

Methods used to value private firms are similar to those discussed elsewhere in this book. However, in the absence of public markets, alternative definitions of value often are used, and the valuation methods are subject to adjustments not commonly applied to public firms.

TABLE 10.2 Adjusting the target firm's financial statements

	Year 1	Year 2	Year 3	Year 4	Year 5
Revenue	8000.0	8400.0	8820.0	9261.0	9724.1
Less: direct COS, excluding depreciation and amortization	5440.0	5712.0	5997.6	6297.5	6612.4
Equals: gross profit	2560.0	2688.0	2822.4	2963.5	3111.7
Less: indirect COS					
Salaries and benefits	1200.0	1260.0	1323.0	1389.2	1458.6
Rent	320.0	336.0	352.8	370.4	389.0
Insurance	160.0	168.0	176.4	185.2	194.5
Advertising	80.0	84.0	88.2	92.6	97.2
Travel and entertainment	240.0	252.0	264.6	277.8	291.7
Director fees	50.0	50.0	50.0	50.0	50.0
Training	10.0	10.0	10.0	10.0	10.0
All other indirect expenses	240.0	252.0	264.6	277.8	291.7
Equals: EBITDA	260.0	276.0	292.8	310.4	329.0
Explanation of adjustments	**Add backs/(deductions)**				
LIFO direct COS is higher than FIFO cost; adjustment converts to FIFO costs	200.0	210.0	220.5	231.5	243.1
Eliminate part-time family members' salaries and benefits	150.0	157.5	165.4	173.6	182.3
Eliminate owner's salary, benefits, and director fees	125.0	131.3	137.8	144.7	151.9
Increase targeted advertising to sustain regional brand recognition	(50.0)	(52.5)	(55.1)	(57.9)	(60.8)
Increase T&E expense to support out-of-state customer accounts	(75.0)	(78.8)	(82.7)	(86.8)	(91.2)
Reduce office space (rent) by closing regional sales offices	120.0	126.0	132.3	138.9	145.9
Increase training budget	(25.0)	(26.3)	(27.6)	(28.9)	(30.4)
Adjusted EBITDA	705.0	743.3	783.4	825.6	869.9

COS, Cost of sales; *EBITDA*, earnings before interest, taxes, depreciation, and amortization; *FIFO*, first in, first out; *LIFO*, last in, first out; T&E, travel and entertainment

Defining value

Fair market value (FMV) is the cash or cash-equivalent price that a willing buyer would propose and a willing seller would accept for a business if both parties have access to all relevant information. FMV assumes neither party is obligated to buy or sell. It is easier to obtain the FMV for a public company because of the existence of public markets. The concept may be applied to privately held firms if similar publicly traded companies exist. Because finding substantially similar companies is difficult, valuation professionals have developed a related concept called fair value. *Fair value* is applied when no strong market exists for a business or it is not possible to identify the value of similar firms. Fair value is more subjective because it represents the dollar value of a business based on an appraisal of its tangible and intangible assets.[16]

Selecting the appropriate valuation methodology

Appraisers, brokers, and investment bankers generally classify valuation methodologies into four approaches: income (discounted cash flow [DCF]), relative or market-based, replacement cost, and asset oriented. These are discussed next as they apply to private businesses.

The income, or discounted cash flow approach

Factors affecting this method include the definition of income or cash flow, the timing of those cash flows, and the selection of an appropriate discount rate. Although valuation methods should be in theory robust enough to be applied to different types of asset classes (e.g., financial versus real), analysts differ as to whether this is true in practice. Some argue that DCF methodology was developed to value publicly traded companies, whose shares typically trade in a liquid market, and that it is not applicable to valuation of real estate or closely held businesses because of their general lack of liquidity. Alternative methods, they claim, should be applied in such instances.

One such alternative is the capitalization rate or simply "cap rate." An analogue to the discount rate, the cap rate often is the preferred metric used in valuing real estate and closely held firms. It represents the ratio of net operating income[17] divided by asset value. If the net operating income is $2 million and the value of an asset is $20 million, the cap rate is 10%. The reciprocal of the cap rate is analogous to a price to earnings ratio (i.e., $20 million/$2 million = 10 or the number of dollars investors are willing to pay for each dollar of earnings).

The cap and discount rate are both used to convert future earnings or cash flows to a present value (PV). The discount and cap rates should equal the rate of return earned on investments exhibiting the same level of profitability, earnings growth, and risk (i.e., the opportunity cost associated with an investment). And the benefit streams to be discounted or capitalized should be consistent: both benefit streams should be measured either in terms of before- or after-tax earnings or cash flows. If a business's earnings or cash flows are expected to be stable or grow at a constant rate over time, estimates provided by DCF and capitalization valuation methods are equivalent.

Cap rates may be converted to multiples for valuation purposes based on projected stable net operating income (or more broadly defined cash flows) or those growing at a constant growth rate (Exhibit 10.1). Note that the valuation methods used in this exhibit are the zero growth and constant growth models discussed in Chapter 7.

Cap multiples are commonly used in commercial real estate because of simplicity and ease of comparing different size assets. Such multiples (the reciprocal of cap rates) are easy to calculate and explain to the parties involved and may facilitate deal completion. Also, there is little empirical evidence that more complex methods result in more accurate valuation estimates.

The relative-value (or market-based) approach

The Internal Revenue Service (IRS) and the US tax courts have encouraged the use of market-based valuation techniques. In valuing private companies, it is always important to keep in mind what factors the IRS thinks are relevant because the IRS may contest any sale requiring the payment of estate, capital gains, or unearned-income taxes. The IRS's position on tax issues is outlined in revenue rulings. Revenue Ruling 59–60 describes the factors the IRS and tax courts consider relevant in valuing private firms. These include general economic conditions, specific industry conditions, type of business, historical industry trends, firm's performance, and book value. The IRS and tax courts also consider the firm's ability to generate earnings and pay dividends, intangibles such as goodwill, recent sales of stock, and the stock prices of companies engaged in the "same or similar" line of business.

[16] Fair value is the statutory standard applicable in cases of dissenting stockholders' appraisal rights. After a merger or corporate dissolution, shareholders in many states have the right to have their shares appraised and to receive fair value in cash. In states adopting the Uniform Business Corporation Act, fair value refers to the value of shares just before the corporate decision to which the shareholder objects, excluding any appreciation or depreciation in anticipation of the corporate decision. In contrast, according to the Financial Accounting Standards Board Statement 157 effective November 15, 2007, fair value is the price determined in an orderly transaction between market participants (Pratt and Niculita, 2008).

[17] Net operating income is total revenue less operating expenses before taxes, excluding principal and interest payments, capital outlays, and depreciation. Therefore, it is not a measure of net operating cash flows.

EXHIBIT 10.1

Applying Capitalization Multiples

Assume Firm A's and Firm B's current year cash flows are \$1.5 million and the discount rate is 8%. Firm A's cash flows are not expected to grow, but Firm B's cash flows are expected to grow at 4% in perpetuity. What is the current market value of each firm?

Answer: Firm A is valued using the zero-growth method, and Firm B the constant-growth discounted cash flow method.

Firm A: \$1.5 million × (1/0.08) = \$1.5 million × 12.5 = \$18.75 million
Firm B: \$1.5 million × (1.04)/(0.08–0.04) = \$1.5 million × 26 = \$39 million

The perpetuity and constant-growth capitalization multiples are 12.5 and 26, respectively, and imply that investors are willing to pay \$12.5 and \$26 for each dollar of cash flow.

The replacement-cost approach

This approach states that the assets of a business are worth what it costs to replace them and is most applicable to businesses that have substantial amounts of tangible assets for which the actual cost to replace them can be determined. This method is not useful in valuing a business whose assets are primarily intangible. Moreover, the replacement-cost approach ignores the value created by operating the assets as a going concern.[18]

The asset-oriented approach

Book value is not a good measure of market value because it reflects historical rather than current values. However, tangible book value (i.e., book value less intangible assets) may be a good proxy for the current market value for both financial services and product distribution companies. *Breakup value* is an estimate of what the value of a business would be if each of its primary assets were sold independently. *Liquidation value* is a reflection of a firm under duress.

Step 3: developing discount rates

Although the discount rate can be derived using a variety of methods, the focus in this chapter is on the weighted average cost of capital (WACC) or the cost of equity. The capital asset pricing model (CAPM) provides an estimate of the acquirer's cost of equity, which may be used as the discount rate when the firm is debt free. There is evidence that CAPM tends to understate financial returns for private companies. What follows is a discussion of ways to adjust CAPM to improve its accuracy in estimating the cost of equity for small privately owned firms.

Estimating a private firm's beta and cost of equity

CAPM assumes the cost of equity is determined by the marginal or incremental investor. Although both public and private firms are subject to systematic risk, nonsystematic risk associated with publicly traded firms can be eliminated by such investors holding a properly diversified portfolio of securities. This often is not true for privately held firms.[19]

[18] The replacement-cost approach sometimes is used to value intangible assets by examining the amount of historical investment associated with the asset. For example, the cumulative historical advertising spending targeted at developing a particular brand may be a reasonable proxy for its intangible value.

[19] Abudy et al. (2016) find that the cost of equity for an unlevered private firm exceeds a comparable unlevered public firm's cost of equity by between 2% and 15%, depending on the riskiness of the firm's operating cash flows and nondiversification of investors. When considering levered firms, the private firm's cost of equity can be up to 33% higher than a comparably leveraged public firm

For firms in which the owner is the only investor, the marginal investor is the current owner because of the difficultly in attracting new investors.[20] Because the owner's net worth is primarily his or her ownership stake in the business, the owner is not well diversified, and their required rate of return (cost of equity) will be higher than for better diversified investors in public firms. Why? Because a private business owner's net worth is more exposed to the firm's asset risk (i.e., the volatility of the firm's operating cash flows).

Betas for privately held firms understate their true risk, which would include both systematic and nonsystematic risk. Thus, unlike investors in publicly traded firms, owners of private firms are concerned about total risk and not just systematic risk. To approximate total risk for owners of closely held firms, the analyst may estimate the *total beta*. The total beta is calculated by dividing the CAPM market beta (β) for a security by the correlation coefficient for comparable public firms with the overall stock market.[21] Because the correlation with the overall market has been removed, the total beta captures the security's risk as a standalone asset rather than as part of a well-diversified portfolio. The correlation coefficient may be estimated by taking the square root of the average coefficient of determination (R^2) for comparable public companies, obtained from linear regressions of their share prices against the overall stock market. The total beta (β_{tot}) may be expressed as follows:

$$\beta_{tot} = \beta / \sqrt{R^2} \tag{10.1}$$

An alternative to the total beta to estimate the cost of equity is the *buildup method*, which represents the sum of the risks associated with a particular class of assets. This method assumes the firm's market beta is equal to 1 and adds to the CAPM's estimate of a firm's cost of equity an estimate of firm size, industry risk, and company-specific risk to measure nonsystematic risk.

Firm-size adjustments assume on average larger firms are less likely to default than smaller firms; the industry adjustment reflects the observation that certain industries are more cyclical (and therefore riskier) than others. Examples of company-specific risks for small privately owned firms include a lack of professional management, dependence on a single customer or supplier, lack of access to capital, and a narrow product focus. Reflecting these factors, the buildup method could be displayed as follows:

$$k_e = R_f + \text{ERP} + \text{FSP} + \text{IND} + \text{CSR} \tag{10.2}$$

in which

k_e = cost of equity
R_f = risk-free return
ERP = equity risk premium (market return on stocks less the risk-free rate)
FSP = firm-size premium (see Chapter 7)
IND = industry-risk premium
CSR = company-specific–risk premium

Assume the risk-free rate, equity risk premium, firm-size premium, industry-risk premium, and company-specific risk premium are 3%, 5.5%, 3.5%, 2%, and 1.5%, respectively, for a small privately held firm. An estimate of the firm's cost of equity using the buildup method would equal 15.5%, the sum of the risk-free rate and the risk premiums.

[20] The business owner may not want new investors because of a desire to retain control.

[21] Unlike the CAPM beta, which measures a security's volatility relative to the market and its correlation with the overall market, the total beta measures only the volatility of the security compared with market volatility. In a linear regression, $\beta = \text{Cov}(i, m)/\sigma m2$ and may be rewritten as $(\sigma_i/\sigma_m)R$ because $(\sigma_i/\sigma_m) \times [\text{Cov}(i, m)/(\sigma_i \times \sigma_m)] = \text{Cov}(i, m)/\sigma_m^2$, in which σ_i is the standard deviation (volatility) of an *i*th security, σ_m is the standard deviation of the overall stock market, and R is the correlation coefficient $[\text{Cov}(i, m)/(\sigma_i \times \sigma_m)]$ between the *i*th security and the overall stock market. By multiplying (σ_i/σ_m), a measure of systematic and nonsystematic risk, by R, which lies between zero and 1, the CAPM beta provides an estimate of the systematic portion of total risk. Note that the total beta will generally be larger than the CAPM beta because the estimated correlation coefficient is between zero and 1; the total beta and the CAPM market beta are equal only if $R = 1$.

For risk premium historical data, see Ibbotson et al. (2017) *Stocks, Bonds, Bills & Inflation (SBBI) Yearbook* and Grabowski et al. (2017) *Valuation Handbook-US Guide to Cost of Capital*.[22] Estimating company-specific-risk premiums requires qualitative analysis, usually consisting of management interviews and site visits. The magnitude of the company-specific risk premium is adjusted up or down to reflect such factors as leverage, size, and earnings or cash flow volatility. Other factors include management depth and acumen, customer concentration, product substitutes, potential new entrants, and product diversification.

Although commonly used by practitioners, the buildup method is problematic because it assumes that the size, industry and company-specific-risk premiums are additive. If so, they would have to be independent or uncorrelated. It is likely that the factors captured by the size premium also are reflected in the industry- and company-specific risk premiums, potentially resulting in "double counting" their impact in estimating the magnitude of the firm's cost of equity. Furthermore, subjective adjustments made to the company-specific risk premium based on the experience and intuition of the appraiser could also result in significant bias.

Estimating the cost of private-firm debt

Private firms seldom can access public debt markets and are usually not rated by the credit-rating agencies. Most debt is bank debt, and the interest expense on loans on the firm's books that are more than a year old may not reflect what it actually would cost the firm to borrow currently. The common solution is to assume private firms can borrow at the same rate as comparable publicly listed firms or to estimate an appropriate bond rating for the company based on financial ratios and to use the interest rate that public firms with similar ratings pay.

An analyst can identify publicly traded company bond ratings using the various internet bond-screening services (e.g., finance.yahoo.com/bonds) to search for bonds with various credit ratings. Royal Caribbean Cruise Lines LTD had a BBB rating and a 2.7 interest coverage ratio in 2009 and would have to pay 7.0% to 7.5% for bonds maturing in 7 to 10 years. Consequently, firms with similar interest-coverage ratios could have similar credit ratings. If the private firm to be valued had a similar interest-coverage ratio and wanted to borrow for a similar time period, it is likely that it would have had to pay a comparable rate of interest.[23] Other sources of information about the interest rates that firms of a certain credit rating pay often are available in publications such as the Wall Street Journal, Investors' Business Daily, and Barron's.[24]

Determining the appropriate tax rate

Throughout this book, a corporate marginal tax rate of 40% has been used in calculating the after-tax cost of debt in valuing public firms.[25] When the acquirer of a private firm is a public firm, using the 40% corporate marginal tax rate is generally correct. However, for acquirers that are private firms or individuals, the choice of the tax rate to use depends on the nature of the buyer. The right marginal tax rate could be as high as 40% (assuming a maximum corporate tax rate of 40%) if a public company is the acquirer, as low as zero if the buyer is a nonprofit entity, and the highest marginal personal income tax rate if the buyer(s) are individuals.

If the acquirer is a sole proprietorship (i.e., business income is recorded on the owner's tax return), the tax rate would be the highest marginal personal income tax rate. For partnerships, limited liability companies, and subchapter S corporations, in which all income is distributed to partners, members, and owners, respectively, the correct tax rate would be a weighted average of the owners' marginal tax rates, with weights reflecting the respective ownership percentages.

[22] Ibbotson et al. (2017) provide equity-risk premiums for 10-size deciles based on companies' market capitalizations. The 10th decile is further subdivided for firms with market caps from as low as $1.2 million. The firm also provides 500 industry-level-risk premiums. Grabowski et al. (2017) provide equity-risk premiums by grouping companies into 25 size categories based on eight different definitions of size. The definitions include market cap, book value, 5-year average net income, market value of invested capital, 5-year average EBITDA, sales, number of employees, and total assets. Analysts can use these data to benchmark the subject company without having to estimate the market value of equity.

[23] If the maturity date, coupon rate, how frequently interest is paid, and the face value of a private firm's outstanding debt are known, the market value of such debt can be estimated using the yield to maturity on comparable debt that is currently traded for firms of similar risk.

[24] Unlike the estimation of the cost of equity for small privately held firms, it is unnecessary to adjust the cost of debt for specific business risk because it is already reflected in the interest rate charged to firms of similar risk.

[25] Although the current US corporate tax rate is well below 40% because of changes made in 2017, the current rate may be subject to change in the future. Regardless of the actual tax rate, the logic remains the same.

Estimating the cost of capital

In the presence of debt, the cost-of-capital should be used to estimate the discount rate. This involves calculating a weighted average of the cost of equity and the after-tax cost of debt. The weights should reflect market rather than book values.

The market value of equity and debt are usually not available. A common solution is to use what the firm's management has set as its target debt-to-equity ratio in determining the weights to be used or to assume that the private firms will eventually adopt the industry average debt-to-equity ratio.[26] For firms growing above the industry average, the cost of capital estimated for the high-growth period can be expected to decline when the firm begins to grow at a more sustainable rate. At that point, the firm begins to take on the risk and growth characteristics of the typical firm in the industry. Thus, the discount rate may be assumed to be the industry average cost of capital during the sustainable-growth period. Exhibit 10.2 illustrates how to calculate a private firm's beta, cost of equity, and cost of capital.

Step 4: applying control premiums, liquidity, and minority discounts

The maximum purchase price an acquirer should pay for a target firm (PV_{MAX}) is defined as its current market or standalone value (i.e., the minimum price, or PV_{MIN}) plus the value of anticipated net synergies (i.e., PV_{NS}):

$$PV_{MAX} = PV_{MIN} + PV_{NS} \tag{10.3}$$

Because the acquirer must earn more than the premium paid for the target when the firms are combined to realize its required cost of capital, the purchase price paid should be less than the maximum price. Otherwise, any synergy would be transferred to the target firm's shareholders.

Equation 10.3 is a reasonable representation of the maximum offer price for firms whose shares are traded in liquid markets and where no single shareholder (i.e., block shareholder)[27] can direct the activities of the business. Examples of such firms include Microsoft, IBM, and Facebook. When markets are illiquid and there are block shareholders with the ability to influence strategic decisions made by the firm, the maximum offer price for the firm needs to be adjusted for liquidity risk and the value of control. These concepts are explored next.

Liquidity discounts

Liquidity is the ease with which investors can sell assets without a serious loss in the value of their investment. An investor in a private company may find it difficult to sell her shares quickly because of limited interest in the company. It may be necessary to sell at a large discount from what was paid for the shares. Liquidity or marketability risk may be expressed as a liquidity or marketability discount, which equals the reduction in the offer price for the target firm by an amount equal to the potential loss of value when sold.

Studies of LDs demonstrate that they exist, but there is substantial disagreement over their magnitude. Whereas pre-1992 studies found discounts as high as 50%,[28] studies since 1999 indicate more modest discounts, ranging from 5% to 35%, with an average discount of about 20%.[29] The decline in the discount since 1990 reflects a reduction in the Rule 144 holding period for restricted shares[30] and improved market liquidity. The latter is caused by better business governance practices, lower transaction costs, greater access to information via the internet, and the emergence of

[26] The firm's target D/E ratio should be consistent with the debt–to–total capital and equity–to–total capital weights used in the WACC. This consistency can be achieved simply by dividing the target D/E (or the industry D/E if that is what is used) by $(1 + D/E)$ to estimate the implied debt–to–total capital ratio. Subtracting this ratio from 1 provides the implied equity–to–total capital ratio.

[27] Insider block shareholders can negatively influence firm value if they may make decisions (e.g., making large acquisitions) not in the best interests of shareholders to retain their senior management or board positions, to increase compensation, or because of hubris. Block shareholders who are not insiders tend to have a positive impact on firm value because of their aggressive monitoring of firm performance (Basu et al., 2016).

[28] Pratt 2008

[29] Loughran and Ritter, 2002; Officer, 2007; Comment, 2012

[30] Restricted shares are those issued by public firms, with the caveat that they not be traded for a specific time period; as such, such shares can be sold only through a private placement under the provisions of the SEC's Rule 144, usually at a discount because of their lack of marketability. In 1997, the SEC reduced the holding period for restricted stock from 2 years to 1, making such shares more liquid.

EXHIBIT 10.2

Valuing Private Firms

Acuity Lighting, a regional manufacturer and distributor of custom lighting fixtures, has revenues of $10 million and an earnings before interest and taxes of $2 million in the current year (i.e., year 0). The book value of the firm's debt is $5 million. The firm's debt matures at the end of 5 years and has annual interest expense of $400,000. The firm's marginal tax rate is 40%, the same as the industry average. Capital spending equals depreciation in year 0, and both are expected to grow at the same rate. As a result of excellent working capital management, the future change in working capital is expected to be essentially zero. The firm's revenue is expected to grow 15% annually for the next 5 years and 5% per year thereafter. The firm's current operating profit margin is expected to remain constant throughout the forecast period.

As a result of the deceleration of its growth rate to a more sustainable rate, Acuity Lighting is expected to assume the risk and growth characteristics of the average firm in the industry during the sustainable-growth period. Consequently, its discount rate during this period is expected to decline to the industry average cost of capital of 11%.

The industry average beta and debt-to-equity ratio are 2 and 0.4, respectively. The R^2 associated with a linear regression of the share prices of comparable publicly traded companies with the overall stock market is .25. The 10-year US Treasury bond rate is 4.5%, and the historical equity premium on all stocks is 5.5%. Acuity Lighting's interest coverage ratio is 2.89, equivalent to a Better Business Bureau (BBB) credit rating. BBB-rated firms are currently paying a pretax cost of debt of 7.5%. Acuity Lighting's management has a target debt-to-equity ratio at 0.5 based on the firm's profitability and growth characteristics. Estimate the equity value of the firm.

Solution

Calculate Acuity's cost of equity using the methodology discussed in Chapter 7 (see Table 7.5) and the weighted average cost of capital (WACC). This requires computing the average of comparable firms' unlevered betas and relevering the average unlevered beta using the target's debt-to-equity ratio:

1. Unlevered beta for publicly traded firms in the same industry $= 2/(1 + 0.6 \times 0.4) = 1.61$, in which 2 is the industry's average levered beta, 0.6 is (1 − tax rate), and 0.4 is the average debt-to-equity ratio for firms in this industry.
2. The total beta (see Equation 10.1) is $1.61/\sqrt{.25} = 3.22$ (Note: The total beta reflects only operating and industry risk.)
3. Acuity's levered beta $= 3.22 \times (1 + 0.6 \times 0.5) = 4.19$, in which 0.5 is the target debt-to-equity ratio established by Acuity's management.
4. Acuity's cost of equity $= 4.5 + 4.19 \times 5.5 = 27.6$.
5. Acuity's after-tax cost of debt $= 7.5 \times (1 - 0.4) = 4.5$, in which 7.5 is the pretax cost of debt.
6. Acuity's WACC $= (27.6 \times 0.67) + (4.5 \times 0.33) = 19.98$, in which the firm's debt–to–total capital ratio (D/TC) is determined by dividing Acuity's debt-to-equity target (D/E) by 1 + D/E. Therefore,

$$D/TC = 0.5/(1+0.5) = 0.33, \text{ and equity to total capital} = 1 - 0.33 = 0.67$$

Value Acuity by means of the FCFF DCF model using the data provided in Table 10.3.

$$\text{Present value of FCFF} = \$1,380,000 + \$1,587,000 + \$1,825,050 + \$2,098,807 + \$2,413,628$$

$$1.1998(1.1998)^2(1.1998)^3(1.1998)^4(1.1998)^5$$

$$= \$1,150,192 + \$1,102,451 + \$1,056,692 + \$1,012,831 + \$970,792$$

$$= \$5,292,958$$

$$\text{PV of terminal value} = [\$2,534,310 / (0.11 - 0.05)]/(1.1824)^5 = \$18,276,220$$

$$\text{Total present value} = \$5,292,958 + \$18,276,220 = \$23,569,178$$

$$\text{Market value of Acuity's debt} = \$400,000 \times \left[\left(1 - (1/1.075)^5\right)\right] + \$5,000,000$$

$$0.075\ (1.075)^5$$

$$= \$1,618,354 + \$3,482,793$$

$$= \$5,101,147$$

$$\text{Value of equity} = \$23,569,178 - \$5,101,147 = \$18,468,031$$

DCF, Discounted cash flow; *D/E*, debt to equity ratio; *FCFF*, free cash flow to the firm.

TABLE 10.3 Free cash flow to the firm model

	Year					
	1	2	3	4	5	6
EBIT[a] ($)	2,300,000	2,645,000	3,041,750	3,498,012	4,022,714	4,223,850
EBIT (1 − Tax rate)[b] ($)	1,380,000	1,587,000	$1,825,050	2,098,807	2,413,628	2,534,310

[a]*Earnings before interest and taxes (EBIT) grows at 15% annually for the next 5 five years and 5% thereafter.*
[b]*Capital spending equals depreciation in year 0, and both are expected to grow at the same rate. Moreover, the change in working capital is zero. Therefore, free cash flow equals after-tax EBIT.*

markets for trading nonpublic stocks.[31] Furthermore, the secular increase in corporate cash holdings has resulted in many firms holding excess cash balances. Because such firms exhibit less liquidity risk, their shares are likely to trade at lower LDs.[32]

Purchase price premiums, control premiums, and minority discounts

For many transactions, the purchase price premium includes both a premium for anticipated synergy and for control. The value of control is different from the value of synergy, which represents revenue increases and cost savings resulting from combining two firms. The value of control provides the right to direct the activities of the target firm on an ongoing basis.

Although control is often assumed to require a greater than 50% ownership stake, effective control can be achieved at a lower figure if other shareholders own relatively smaller stakes and do not vote as a block. An investor may be willing to pay a significant premium to buy a less than 50% stake if the investor believes that effective control over key decisions can be achieved.

Control includes the ability to select management, determine compensation, set policy, liquidate assets, award contracts, make acquisitions, sell or recapitalize the company, and register the company's stock for an initial public offering (IPO). The more control a block investor has, the less influence a minority investor has and the less valuable is their stock. When controlling interests are very large, a controlling shareholder may even overpay for a target to diversify their holdings when the benefit of diversification is seen as greater than the resulting dilution in their own holdings.[33]

Reflecting these factors, a CP is the amount an investor is willing to pay to direct the activities of the firm. A *minority discount* is the reduction in the value of the investment because the minority owners have little control over the firm's operations.

Purchase price premiums reflect only CPs when a buyer acquires a target firm and manages it as an independent subsidiary. The *pure CP* is the value the acquirer believes can be created by replacing incompetent management, changing the firm's strategy, gaining a foothold in a market not currently served, or achieving unrelated diversification.[34]

Country comparison studies indicate a huge variation in median CPs from as little as 2% to 5% in countries where corporate ownership is widely dispersed and investor protections are effective to as much as 60% to 65% in countries where ownership tends to be concentrated and governance practices are poor. Median estimates across countries are 10% to 12%.[35] A recent study pegs the average premium paid by investors for a block of stock in the United States at 9.6% based on 114 publicly disclosed US acquisitions between 1990 and 2010 of blocks of more than 35% but less than 90% of the shares of a company.[36]

[31] Examples of markets for nonpublic companies include secondmarket.com, sharespost.com, and peqx.com.

[32] Huang et al., 2018

[33] Thraya and Hamza (2019) argue the threat of litigation can be mitigated when there are multiple large investors.

[34] Another example of a pure control premium is that paid for a firm going private through a leveraged buyout, in that the target firm generally is merged into a shell corporation, with no synergy being created, and managed for cash after having been recapitalized. Although the firm's management team may remain intact, the board of directors usually consists of representatives of the financial sponsor (i.e., equity or block investor).

[35] Weifeng et al., 2008

[36] Albuquerque et al., 2015

The relationship between liquidity discounts and control premiums

Market liquidity and the value of control tend to move in opposite directions—when it is easy for shareholders to sell their shares, the benefits of control diminish. Why? Shareholders who are dissatisfied with the decisions made by controlling shareholders may choose to sell their shares, thereby driving down the value of the controlling shareholder's interest.

When it is difficult for shareholders to sell without incurring significant losses (i.e., the market is illiquid), investors place a greater value on control. Minority shareholders have no easy way to dispose of their investment because they cannot force the sale of the firm, and the controlling shareholder has little incentive to acquire their shares except at a steep discount. The controlling shareholder can continue to make decisions that may not be in the best interests of the minority shareholders. The size of CPs and LDs are positively correlated because the value of control rises as market liquidity declines.

Equation 10.3 can be rewritten to reflect the interdependent relationship between the CP and the LD as follows:

$$\begin{aligned} PV_{MAX} &= (PV_{MIN} + PV_{NS})(1 + CP\%)(1 - LD\%) \\ &= (PV_{MIN} + PV_{NS})(1 - LD\% + CP\% - LD\% \times CP\%) \\ &= (PV_{MIN} + PV_{NS})[1 - LD\% + CP\%(1 - LD\%)] \end{aligned} \tag{10.4}$$

in which

$CP\%$ = CP expressed as a percentage of the maximum purchase price
$LD\%$ = LD expressed as a percentage of the maximum purchase price

The term (i.e., $LD\% \times CP\%$) in Equation 10.4 serves as an estimate of the interaction between the CP and the LD.[37] This term reflects the potential reduction in the value of control [i.e., $CP\%(1 - LD\%)$] resulting from disaffected minority shareholders' taking a more active role in monitoring the firm's performance. This could result in proxy contests to change board decisions or the composition of the board as well as litigation.[38]

Estimating liquidity discounts, control premiums, and minority discounts

There is no such thing as a standard LD or CP because the size of the discount or premium should reflect firm-specific factors. These are discussed next.

Factors affecting the liquidity discount

The median LD for empirical studies since the early 1990s is about 20%. Table 10.4 suggests a means of adjusting a private firm for liquidity risk in which an analyst starts with the median LD of 20% and adjusts for factors specific to the target firm. Such factors include firm size, liquid assets as a percent of total assets, financial returns, and cash flow growth and leverage as compared to the industry. Although not intended to be an exhaustive list, these factors were selected based on the findings of empirical studies of restricted stocks.

The LD should be smaller for highly liquid firms because liquid assets generally can be converted quickly to cash with minimal loss of value. Furthermore, firms whose financial returns significantly exceed the industry average have an easier time attracting investors and should be subject to a smaller LD than firms that are underperforming the industry. Likewise, firms with relatively low leverage and high cash flow growth should be subject to a smaller LD than more-leveraged firms with slower cash flow growth because they have a lower breakeven point and are less likely to default or become insolvent.

Factors affecting the control premium

Factors affecting the size of the CP include the ability of the target's current management, the extent to which operating expenses are discretionary, the value of nonoperating assets, and the net present value (NPV) of unexploited business opportunities. The value of replacing incompetent management is difficult to quantify. The value

[37] If control premiums and minority discounts and control premiums and liquidity discounts are positively correlated, minority discounts and liquidity discounts must be positively correlated.

[38] PV_{MAX} may also be adjusted for illiquidity and value of control by adjusting the cost of equity (ke). Assume $ke = k(1 + CP\%)(1 - LD\%)$, in which k is the cost of equity, including the effects of illiquidity and the value of control, then $k = ke/(1 + CP\%)(1 - LD\%)$. That is, k decreases with an increasing value of control (PV_{MAX} increases) and increases with increasing illiquidity (PV_{MAX} decreases).

TABLE 10.4 Estimating the size of the liquidity discount

Factor	Guideline	Adjust 20% median discount as follows:
Firm size	• Large • Small	• Reduce discount • Increase discount
Liquid assets as a percentage of total assets	• >50% • <50%	• Reduce discount • Increase discount
Financial returns	• 2 × industry median[a] • ½ × industry median	• Reduce discount • Increase discount
Cash-flow growth rate	• 2 × industry median • ½ × industry median	• Reduce discount • Increase discount
Leverage	• ½ × industry median • 2 × industry median	• Reduce discount • Increase discount
Estimated firm-specific liquidity discount		= 20% ± adjustments

[a]*Industry median financial information often is available from industry trade associations, conference presentations, Wall Street analysts' reports, Yahoo! Finance, Barron's, Investor's Business Daily, The Wall Street Journal, and similar publications and websites.*

of nonoperating assets and discretionary expenses is quantified by estimating the after-tax sale value of redundant assets and the pretax profit improvement from eliminating redundant personnel. Although relatively easy to measure, such actions may be impossible to implement without having control of the business.[39]

If the target business is to be run as currently managed, no CP should be added to the purchase price. If the acquirer intends to take actions possible only if the acquirer has control, the purchase price should include a CP sufficient to gain a controlling interest. Table 10.5 provides a methodology for adjusting a CP to be applied to a specific business. The 10% premium in the table is for illustrative purposes only and is intended to provide a starting point. The actual premium selected should reflect the analyst's perception of what is appropriate given the country's legal system and propensity to enforce laws and the extent to which the firm's ownership tends to be concentrated or widely dispersed.

The percentages applied to the discretionary expenses' share of total expenses, nonoperating assets as a percent of total assets, and the NPV of alternative strategies reflect risks inherent in cutting costs, selling assets, and pursuing other investment opportunities. These risks include a decline in morale and productivity after layoffs, the management time involved in selling assets and disruption of the business, and the potential for overestimating the NPV of other investments. In other words, the perceived benefits of these decisions should be large enough to offset the associated risks. Additional adjustments not shown in Table 10.5 may be necessary to reflect state statutes affecting the rights of controlling and minority shareholders.[40]

As a practical matter, business appraisers frequently rely on the Control Premium Study, published annually by FactSet Mergerstat. Another source is Duff and Phelps. The use of these data is problematic because the control-premium estimates provided by these firms include the estimated value of synergy as well as the amount paid to gain control.

[39] This is true because such decisions could involve eliminating the positions of members of the family owning the business or selling an asset owned by the business but used primarily by the family owning the business.

[40] In more than half of the states, major corporate actions, such as a merger, sale, liquidation, or a recapitalization of a firm, may be approved by a simple majority vote of the firm's shareholders. Other states require at least a two-thirds majority to approve such decisions. A majority of the states have dissolution statutes that make it possible for minority shareholders to force dissolution of a corporation if they can show there is a deadlock in their negotiations with the controlling shareholders or that their rights are being violated.

TABLE 10.5 Estimating the size of the control premium to reflect the value of changing the target's business strategy and operating practices

Factor	Guideline	Adjust 10% median control premium as follows[a]
Target management	• Retain • Replace	• No change in premium • Increase premium
Discretionary expenses	• Cut if potential savings >5% of total expenses • Do not cut if potential savings <5% of total expenses	• Increase premium • No change in premium
Nonoperating assets	• Sell if potential after-tax gain >10% of purchase price[b] • Defer decision if potential after-tax gain <10% of purchase price	• Increase premium • No change in premium
Alternative business opportunities	• Pursue if NPV >20% of target's standalone value • Do not pursue if NPV <20% of target's standalone value	• Increase premium • No change in premium
Estimated firm-specific control premium		= 10% + adjustments

[a]*The 10% premium represents the median estimate from the Nenova (2003) and Dyck and Zingales (2004) studies for countries perceived to have relatively stronger investor protection and law enforcement.*
[b]*The purchase price refers to the price paid for the controlling interest in the target.*
NPV, Net present value.

Factors affecting the minority discount

Minority discounts reflect the loss of influence due to the power of a controlling-block investor. Intuitively, the magnitude of the discount should relate to the size of the CP. The larger the CP, the greater the perceived value of being able to direct the activities of the business and the value of special privileges that come at the expense of the minority investor.

Reflecting the relationship between CP and minority discounts, FactSet Mergerstat estimates minority discounts using the following formula:

$$\text{Implied median minority discount} = 1 - [1 / (1 + \text{median premium paid})] \quad (10.5)$$

Equation 10.5 implies that an investor would pay a higher price for control of a company and a lesser amount for a minority stake (i.e., larger CPs are associated with larger minority discounts). Although Equation 10.5 is used routinely by practitioners to estimate minority discounts, there is little empirical support for this largely intuitive relationship.[41]

Exhibit 10.3 shows what an investor should pay for a controlling interest and for a minority interest. The example assumes that 50.1% ownership is required for a controlling interest. In practice, control may be achieved with less than a majority ownership position if there are numerous other minority investors or the investor is buying super-voting shares. Readers should note how the 20% median LD rate (based on recent empirical studies) is adjusted for the specific risk and return characteristics of the target firm. The CP is equal to what the acquirer believes is the minimum increase in value created by having a controlling interest. Observe how the direct relationship between CPs and minority discounts is used to estimate the size of the minority discount. Finally, see how median estimates of LDs and CPs can serve as guidelines in valuation analyses.

[41] Minority rights are protected in some states by requiring two-thirds voting approval of certain major corporate decisions, implying that minority ownership interests may be subject to a smaller discount in such states.

EXHIBIT 10.3

Incorporating Liquidity Risk, Control Premiums, and Minority Discounts in Valuing a Private Business

Lighting Group Incorporated, a holding company, wants to acquire a controlling interest in Acuity Lighting, whose estimated standalone equity value equals \$18,468,031 (see Exhibit 10.2). LGI believes that the PV of synergies due to cost savings is \$2,250,000 (PV_{SYN}) related to bulk purchase discounts, the elimination of duplicate overhead, and combining operations.

LGI believes that the value of Acuity, including synergy, can be increased by at least 10% by applying new management methods (and implicitly by making better management decisions). To achieve these efficiencies, LGI must gain control of Acuity. LGI is willing to pay a CP of as much as 10%. The minority discount is derived from Equation 10.5. The factors used to adjust the 20% median liquidity discount are taken from Table 10.4. The magnitudes of the adjustments are the opinion of the analyst. LGI's analysts have used Yahoo! Finance to obtain the industry data in Table 10.6 for the home furniture and fixtures industry.

What is the maximum purchase price LGI should pay for a 50.1% controlling interest in the business? For a minority 20% interest in the business?

To adjust for presumed liquidity risk of the target due to lack of a liquid market, LGI discounts its offer to purchase 50.1% of the firm's equity by 16%.

Using Equation 10.4, we get:

$$PV_{MAX} = (PV_{MIN} + PV_{NS})(1 - LD\%)(1 + CP\%)$$
$$= [(\$18,468,031 + \$2,250,000)(1 - 0.16)(1 + 0.10)] \times 0.501$$
$$= \$20,718,031 \times 0.924 \times 0.501$$
$$= \$9,590,873 (\text{maximum purchase price for } 50.1\%)$$

CP, Control premium; *LD*, liquidity discount; PV_{MAX}, maximum purchase price; PV_{MIN}, minimum purchase price; PV_{NS}, PV of net synergy.

TABLE 10.6 Industry data

Industry data factor	Acuity Lighting	Home furniture and fixtures industry	Adjustments to 20% median liquidity discount
Median liquidity discount[a] (%)	NA	NA	20.0
Firm size	Small	NA	+2.0
Liquid assets as a percentage of total assets	>50	NA	−2.0
Return on equity (%)	19.7	9.7	−2.0
Cash flow growth rate (%)	15	12.6	0.0
Leverage (debt to equity)	0.22[b]	1.02	−2.0
Estimated liquidity discount for Acuity Lighting (%)			16.0

[a]*Median estimate of the liquidity discount of empirical studies (excluding pre–initial public offering studies) since 1992.*
[b]*From Exhibit 10.2: \$5,101,147/\$23,569,178 = 0.22*
NA, Not available or not applicable.

If Lighting Group Incorporated (LGI) were to acquire only a 20% stake in Acuity, it is unlikely that there would be any synergy because LGL would lack the authority to implement potential cost-saving measures without the approval of the controlling shareholders. Because it is a minority investment, there is no CP, but a minority discount for lack of control should be estimated. This is accomplished using Equation 10.5—that is, $1 - [1/(1 + 0.10)] = 9.1$.

$$PV_{MAX} = [\$18,468,873 \times (1 - 0.16)(1 - 0.091)] \times 0.2$$
$$= \$2,820,419 (\text{maximum purchase price for } 20\%)$$

EXHIBIT 10.4

Estimating the Fair Market Value of SoftBank's Minority Investment in Uber

SoftBank offered on November 28, 2017, to spend more than $6 billion for up to a 14% stake in Uber, valuing the firm at $48 billion, about a 30% discount from the post-money $69 billion valuation in its Series G round in 2016. The SoftBank proposal offered an opportunity for earlier investors to sell shares. They had been restricted to selling shares only to Uber, making them relatively illiquid. Consequently, the maximum amount SoftBank should offer Uber shareholders was subject to both a minority and liquidity discount (LD). Uber shareholders had to decide if the SoftBank offer approached the fair market value (FMV) of Uber shares at that time.

Assume the Series G round represented the FMV of Uber at the time of the SoftBank offer and no synergy is created with other SoftBank businesses. Furthermore, the 20% median LD rate used in this analysis (based on an average of various studies) is unadjusted for specific Uber risk and return characteristics. The minority discount for lack of control is estimated using Equation 10.5—that is, $1 - [1/(1 + 0.33)] = 24.8$, in which 0.33 is the long-term average control premium paid for US technology companies according to the Boston Consulting Group's report titled "The 2017 M&A Report: The Technology Takeover."

The maximum purchase price (PV_{MAX}) SoftBank should pay for a 14% stake in Uber is calculated as follows:

$$PV_{MAX} = [\$69 \text{ billion} \times (1 - 0.2) \times (1 - 0.248)] \times 0.14$$
$$= \$5.81 \text{ billion (compared with the actual amount of the SoftBank offer of \$6 billion)}$$

At more than 103% ($6.00/$5.81) of the estimated FMV of 14% of Uber, it appears that SoftBank's offer was fair to Uber shareholders at that time based on the assumptions used in this calculation.

Early-stage investment

Investment in emerging businesses consists of a series of *funding rounds* starting with seed financing and extending to series A, series B, series C, and so on. The letters in the series refer to the stages of development of firms and their need for capital. Before each round, the firm is valued based on the quality of management, track record, growth potential, and risk. The firm's valuation in the most recent funding round is the starting point for valuation in the next round.

Pre- and post-money valuations

Valuations in this context are referred to as *pre-money* or *post-money. Pre-money* is the firm's valuation before it receives its financing or its value in the latest financing round; *post-money* is the firm's value including both its pre-money valuation plus capital raised in the current round.

Assume an investor agrees that a start-up is worth $2 million and is willing to inject $.5 million into the firm. Pre-money, the firm is valued at $2 million, and post-money, its value is $2.5 million. Ownership percentages vary depending on whether the valuation is pre- or post-money: pre-money, the investor will own 25% of the firm ($0.5/$2), and post-money ($0.5/$2.5), it will own 20%.

Series A funding runs from $2 million to $15 million and is intended to pay for market research, build a management team and infrastructure, and launch their products. Funding at this stage often comes from venture capitalists who invest in "good" stories and are less data-driven than later-stage investors. The series B round focuses on growing market share and expanding into new and larger markets. Series C rounds attract investors to already successful businesses intent on accelerating growth. Likely investors at this stage include private equity firms, hedge funds, and investment banks.

Ride-hailing firm Uber Technologies Inc. (Uber) has shown meteoric growth since its 2009 inception. The firm engaged in frequent cash infusions to sustain rapid growth. By mid-2016, the firm entered its series G funding round, which valued the business at an eye-popping (post-money) $69 billion. However, the firm stumbled because of sexual harassment scandals and intellectual property lawsuits. The firm also failed to report a computer hack for more than 1 year that resulted in the loss of personal data on thousands of drivers and millions of customers.

Although investor confidence had been shaken, interest in Uber remained high because of its game-changing potential. Exhibit 10.4 illustrates how Japanese conglomerate SoftBank along with other investors showed interest in buying a portion of Uber's outstanding shares in late 2017.

The rise of the unicorn

In the past, most successful VC-backed firms (firms backed by venture capital) went public within 3 to 8 years after receiving their initial funding. Recently, VC-backed firms have remained private for longer periods during which they have become very large. Examples include Uber, Airbnb, and Pinterest, which have multibillion valuations. Such VC-financed firms are called "unicorns" and have valuations exceeding $1 billion. Once considered rare, there were more than 100 unicorns in the United States and another 100 in other developed countries as of 2020. How such firms are valued is largely a mystery because of the difficulty in valuing high-growth firms with opaque capital structures.[42] Determining the fair value of such firms has proved highly challenging. Post-money valuations typically overvalue unicorns. However, the extent of the overvaluation varies widely. On average, unicorns tend to be overvalued by about 48%, with the least overvalued averaging about 13% and the most overvalued averaging approximately 145%.[43]

Taking private companies public

IPOs represent the traditional way of taking a private firm public and refer to the first time a private firm offers shares to the public. Usually an investment bank (underwriter) is hired by the firm wishing to sell the shares to determine the number of shares to be offered and at what price. The investment bank collects data for a registration statement to be filed with the Securities and Exchange Commission (SEC). This statement provides information about the offering and company including financial statements, managers' backgrounds, how the money raised is to be used, and who owns the firm's pre-IPO stock.

During the past decade, private firms were more likely to be acquired than to go public through an IPO. Many small firms chose to be acquired, believing they can more rapidly achieve scale within the infrastructure of a larger firm. And there is evidence that selling to a strategic buyer can result in valuations superior to IPOs.[44] For firms choosing not to go public through a merger, other options exist: reverse mergers and special-purpose acquisition companies.

Reverse mergers

In a reverse merger, a private firm merges with a publicly traded target (often a corporate shell) in a statutory merger in which the public firm survives. Even though the private firm becomes a wholly owned subsidiary of the public firm, the former private firm shareholders have a majority ownership stake in the public firm and control of the board. This is the reverse of mergers in which surviving firm shareholders have a majority interest in the combined firms.

Merging with an existing corporate shell of a publicly traded company may be a reasonable alternative for a firm wanting to go public that does not have the 2 years of audited financial statements required by the SEC or is unwilling to incur the costs of an IPO. The new firm must have a minimum of 300 shareholders to be listed on the NASDAQ Small Cap Market.

Shell corporations usually are of two types. The first type is a failed public company whose shareholders want to recover some of their losses. The second type is a shell that has been created to engage in a reverse merger. The latter typically carries less risk of having unknown liabilities. (See the case study at the end of this chapter for an example of a reverse merger.)

[42] Understanding capital structure is challenging because investors in these companies are given convertible preferred shares that have both downside protections (if they were issued in early financing rounds) and upside potential having an option to convert into common shares. Different classes of shares have different dividend and control rights depending on the round in which they were issued.

[43] Gornall and Strebulaev, 2019

[44] Signori, 2018

Reverse mergers typically cost about $100,000, a fraction of the expense of an IPO, and can be completed in about 60 days, or one third of the time to complete a typical IPO.[45] Firms undertaking IPOs incur underwriting fees equal to 4% to 7% of gross proceeds, plus offering costs associated with the IPO of $3 to $5 million. Despite their initial cost advantage, reverse mergers may take as long as IPOs and are sometimes more complex.

The acquiring company must still perform due diligence on the target and communicate information on the shell corporation to the exchange on which its stock will be traded and prepare a prospectus. It can often take months to settle outstanding claims against the shell corporation. Public exchanges often require the same level of information for companies going through reverse mergers as those undertaking IPOs. The principal concern is that the shell company may contain unseen liabilities, such as unpaid bills or pending litigation, which can make the reverse merger more costly than an IPO.[46]

To reduce the potential for fraud, the SEC prohibits reverse-merger firms from applying to list on major exchanges until they have completed a 1-year "seasoning period" by trading on the OTC Bulletin Board or on another regulated US or foreign exchange. The firm also must file all required reports with the SEC and maintain a minimum share price for at least 30 of the 60 trading days before its listing application can be submitted to an exchange.

Financing reverse mergers

Private investment in public equities (PIPEs) is a common means of financing reverse mergers. In a PIPE offering, a firm with publicly traded shares sells, usually at a discount, newly issued but unregistered securities, typically stock or convertible debt, directly to investors in a private deal. The issuing firm is required to file a shelf registration statement, Form S-3, with the SEC as quickly as possible (usually between 10 and 45 days after issuance) and to use its "best efforts" to complete registration within 30 days after filing. PIPEs also are used in conjunction with a reverse merger to provide companies financing once they are listed on the public exchange.[47]

Special-purpose acquisition corporations

Less common than reverse mergers, special-purpose acquisition corporations (SPACs), or so-called "blank check" companies, represent another means of taking a firm public. SPACs are shell companies that raise funds through an IPO to acquire private firms. Unlike an IPO, which issues shares in a privately held operating company, SPACs raise money through an IPO before acquiring operating companies. The money raised is placed in a trust fund until the SPAC identifies a target firm. SPACs usually have 24 months to complete a deal. If unsuccessful, the money raised is returned to investors. Capping a record year for SPACs in 2020, United Wholesale Mortgage, the largest wholesale mortgage originator in the United States, merged with a SPAC late in the year in a deal valued at $16 billion, the largest SPAC deal on record.

Like reverse mergers, SPACs offer some advantages over IPOs for the firm seeking a public listing. SPACs have substantial cash on hand, making them less dependent on stock market conditions. SPACs also can offer target firm shareholders cash, stock, or a combination for their shares. Like reverse mergers, SPACs deals can be completed in a few months compared with a traditional IPO that takes longer, exposing a firm to market fluctuations.[48] Investors find SPACs attractive because of their founders' reputation and their specialized industry expertise.

SPACs do, however, have disadvantages for target firms. When the number of SPAC shareholders is large, there is the risk SPAC shareholders will not approve the deal. Firms going public through reverse mergers usually do not have this concern because there are relatively few shareholders in the shell company, making approval likely. Also, private firm shareholders' ownership can be diluted in deals in which they exchanged their shares for SPAC shares and SPAC shareholders exercise warrants to buy more shares.

[45] Sweeney, 2005

[46] Wang, 2019

[47] To issuers, PIPEs offer the advantage of being able to be completed more quickly, cheaply, and confidentially than a public stock offering, which requires registration upfront and a more elaborate investor "road show" to sell the securities to public investors. Frequently sold as private placements, PIPEs are most suitable for raising small amounts of financing, typically in the range of $5 million to $10 million.

[48] SPAC disclosure requirements are considerably less onerous than a traditional IPO for operating companies as they can qualify as "smaller reporting companies" under Item 10(f)(1) of Regulation S-K. SPACs are essentially pools of cash without operating assets and therefore are less complex than an operating company.

Firms going public through IPOs often underperform similar firms because of the excessive optimism shown by investors in bidding up the firm's price on the first day. The extent of underperformance tends to be larger for firms taken public by SPACs than for those choosing IPOs.[49] Why? Whereas firms with significant growth opportunities and less leverage use IPOs, smaller firms with limited opportunities and more leverage use SPACs. SPACs may underperform the broad stock market indices, particularly if their deals are made close to the 2-year holding period during which the SPAC sponsors are required to complete an acquisition.[50] The time crush may cause them to make bad acquisition decisions. Reverse mergers may also underperform IPOs long-term because they frequently involve lower-quality firms.

Using leveraged employee stock ownership plans to buy private companies

An ESOP is a trust established by an employer for its employees; its assets are allocated to employees and are not taxed until withdrawn by employees. ESOPs generally must invest at least 50% of their assets in employer stock. Employees frequently use leveraged ESOPs to buy out owners of private companies who have most of their net worth in the firm. For firms with ESOPs, the business owner sells at least 30% of their stock to the ESOP, which pays for the stock with borrowed funds. The owner may invest the proceeds and defer taxes if the investment is made within 12 months of the sale of the stock to the ESOP, the ESOP owns at least 30% of the firm, and neither the owner nor his or her family participates in the ESOP. The firm makes tax-deductible contributions to the ESOP in an amount sufficient to repay interest and principal. Shares held by the ESOP, which serve as collateral for the loan, are distributed to employees as the loan is repaid. As the outstanding loan balance is reduced, the shares are allocated to employees, who eventually own the firm.

Empirical studies of shareholder returns

As noted in Chapter 1, target shareholders of both public and private firms routinely experience abnormal positive returns when a bid is announced for the firm. In contrast, acquirer shareholders may experience abnormal negative returns on the announcement date, particularly when using stock to purchase large publicly traded firms. However, substantial empirical evidence shows that public acquirers using their stock to buy unlisted firms (i.e., both privately held firms and subsidiaries of publicly traded firms) experience significant abnormal positive returns around the deal announcement date.

Other studies suggest that acquirers of private firms often experience abnormal positive returns regardless of the form of payment. In general, acquirers tend to show better performance over their corporate life cycle (i.e., high growth, stable growth, and declining growth periods) when they acquire private (rather than publicly traded) firms.[51] These studies are discussed next.

Public-company shareholders earn an average positive 2.6% abnormal return when using stock rather than cash to acquire privately held firms.[52] Ownership of privately held firms tends to be highly concentrated, so an exchange of stock tends to create a few large block stockholders. Close monitoring of management may contribute to these returns. These findings are consistent with studies conducted in Canada, the United Kingdom, and Western Europe.[53]

[49] Kolb et al., 2016

[50] Dimitrov, 2016

[51] Arikan et al., 2016

[52] Chang, 1998

[53] Draper and Paudyal, 2006; Ben-Amar and Andre, 2006; Bigelli and Mengoli, 2004. These results are consistent with studies of returns to companies that issue stock and convertible debt in private placements. In private placements, large shareholders are effective monitors of managerial performance, thereby enhancing the prospects of the issuing firm. Wruck et al. (2009) argue that relationships such as board representation developed between investors and issuers contribute to improved firm performance due to increased monitoring of performance and improved corporate governance.

Firms acquiring private firms often earn excess returns regardless of the form of payment.[54] Acquirers can also earn excess returns of as much as 2.1% when buying private firms or 2.6% for subsidiaries of public companies.[55] The abnormal returns may reflect the tendency of acquirers to pay less for non-publicly traded companies because of the relative difficulty in valuing private firms or subsidiaries of public companies. In both cases, shares are not publicly traded, and access to information is limited.[56] Moreover, there may be fewer bidders for nonpublic companies, and cash-starved public firms may be forced to sell subsidiaries to gain liquidity. With few options, private firm shareholders may be forced to sell shares at a discount from true value because of their weak bargaining positions, allowing acquirers to realize more of the synergy.

Other factors contributing to positive abnormal returns for acquirers of private companies include the introduction of more professional management into the privately held firms and tax considerations. The acquirer's use of stock rather than cash may induce the seller to accept a lower price because it allows sellers to defer taxes on gains until they decide to sell their shares.

Some things to remember

Valuing private firms is more challenging than valuing public firms because of the lack of published share price data and the unique problems associated with private companies. When markets are illiquid and block shareholders exert control over the firm, the offer price for the target must be adjusted for liquidity risk and the value of control. Buyers of private firms in the United States and abroad often realize significant abnormal positive returns, particularly in share-for-share deals.

Chapter discussion questions

10.1 What is a capitalization rate? When is it used and why?
10.2 What are the common ways of estimating capitalization multiples?
10.3 What is the liquidity discount, and what are common ways of estimating this discount?
10.4 Give examples of private company costs that might be understated and explain why.
10.5 How can an analyst determine if the target's costs and revenues are under- or- overstated?
10.6 Why might shell corporations have value?
10.7 Why might succession planning be more challenging for a family firm?
10.8 What are some of the reasons a family-owned or privately owned business may want to go public? What are some of the reasons that discourage such firms from going public?
10.9 Why are family-owned firms often attractive to private equity investors?
10.10 Rank from the highest to lowest the LD you would apply if you, as a business appraiser, had been asked to value the following businesses: (a) a local, profitable hardware store; (b) a money-losing laundry; (c) a large privately owned firm with significant excess cash balances and other liquid short-term investments; and (d) a pool cleaning service whose primary tangible assets consist of a 4-year-old truck and miscellaneous equipment. Explain your ranking.

Answers to these Chapter Discussion Questions are available in the Online Instructor's Manual for instructors using this book.

Practice problems and answers

10.11 An analyst constructs a privately held firm's cost of equity using the "build-up" method. The 10-year Treasury bond rate is 4%, and the historical equity risk premium for the S&P 500 stock index is 5.5%. The risk premium

[54] Ang et al., 2001

[55] Fuller et al., 2002

[56] Madura, 2012. Jindra and Moeller (2020) document a parallel with firms having recently undergone an IPO. Premiums paid tend to increase for public target firms as the time since their IPO lengthens and the availability of public information increases.

associated with firms of this size is 3.8% and for firms within this industry is 2.4%. Based on due diligence, the analyst estimates the risk premium specific to this firm to be 2.5%. What is the firm's cost of equity based on this information? *Answer:* 18.2%

10.12 An investor is interested in making a minority equity investment in a small privately held firm. Because of the nature of the business, she concludes that it would be difficult to sell her interest in the business quickly. She believes that the discount for the lack of marketability to be 25%. She also estimates that if she were to acquire a controlling interest, the CP would be 15%. Based on this information, what should be the discount rate for making a minority investment in this firm? What should she pay for 20% of the business if she believes the value of the entire business to be $1 million? *Answer:* Discount rate = 9.78% and purchase price for a 20% interest = $180,440

10.13 Based on its growth prospects, a private investor values a local bakery at $750,000. She believes that cost savings having a PV of $50,000 can be achieved by changing staffing levels and store hours. She believes the appropriate liquidity discount is 20%. A recent transaction in the same city required the buyer to pay a 5% premium to the average price for similar businesses to gain a controlling interest in a bakery. What is the most she should be willing to pay for a 50.1% stake in the bakery? *Answer:* $336,672

10.14 You have been asked by an investor to value a restaurant. Last year, the restaurant earned pretax operating income of $300,000. Income has grown 4% annually during the past 5 years, and it is expected to continue growing at that rate into the foreseeable future. The annual change in working capital is $20,000, and capital spending for maintenance exceeded depreciation in the prior year by $15,000. Both working capital and the excess of capital spending over depreciation are projected to grow at the same rate as operating income. By introducing modern management methods, you believe the pretax operating-income growth rate can be increased to 6% beyond the second year and sustained at that rate into the foreseeable future. The 10-year Treasury bond rate is 5%, the equity-risk premium is 5.5%, and the marginal federal, state, and local tax rate is 40%. The beta and debt-to-equity ratio for publicly traded firms in the restaurant industry are 2 and 1.5, respectively. The business's target debt-to-equity ratio is 1, and its pretax cost of borrowing, based on its recent borrowing activities, is 7%. The business-specific-risk premium for firms of this size is estimated to be 6%. The liquidity-risk premium is believed to be 15%, relatively low for firms of this type because of the excellent reputation of the restaurant. Because the current chef and the staff are expected to remain when the business is sold, the quality of the restaurant is expected to be maintained. The investor is willing to pay a 10% premium to reflect the value of control.

a. What is free cash flow to the firm in year 1? *Answer*: $150,800
b. What is free cash flow to the firm in year 2? *Answer*: $156,832
c. What is the firm's cost of equity? *Answer*: 20.2%
d. What is the firm's after-tax cost of debt? *Answer*: 4.2%
e. What is the firm's target debt-to—total capital ratio? *Answer*: 0.5
f. What is the weighted average cost of capital? *Answer*: 12.2%
g. What is the business worth? *Answer:* $2,226,448

Solutions to these practice exercises and problems are available in the Online Instructor's Manual for instructors using this book.

End-of-chapter case study: "going public": reverse merger or initial public offering?

Case study objectives

To illustrate

- Alternative ways to "go public"
- The mechanics of reverse mergers
- Risks and rewards associated with reverse mergers
- Why reverse mergers may be preferable to IPOs for firms wanting to "go public"

Biotech firms research, develop, and produce a wide variety of commercial products. Most focus on medical or agricultural applications derived from living organisms. Such firms generally have very high operating expenses reflecting the cost of research and development and testing that often takes years to complete. The end result: historic breakthrough or utter failure!

Estimates of the rate at which experimental drugs fail to become commercially viable range from two thirds to more than 80%. When experimental drugs are commercially successful, firms receive patent protection for 12 years during which they can recapture their initial investments and reward their shareholders. Given the lengthy drug development cycle, biotech firms suck up cash at a mind-numbing pace. Firms needing funds to sustain development but wishing to retain control often avoid being acquired or seeking venture capital because such moves may result in changes in management and a loss of decision-making capacity. Other methods for gaining access to capital are reverse mergers and IPOs.

Whereas conventional IPOs can take months to complete, reverse mergers can take only a few weeks. Because the reverse merger is solely a mechanism to convert a private company into a public entity, the process is less dependent on financial market conditions because the company often is not proposing to raise capital. The cost of regulatory filings and approvals is less with reverse mergers than with IPOs. Finally, firms lacking in historical financial statements often find the reverse merger as the only practical option. Even if a firm has demonstrated strong financial performance, it is still subject to the vagaries of the stock market.

Using a reverse merger comes at a cost. The desire to achieve speed means that due diligence often is cut short, with significant liabilities overlooked. Also, the resources devoted to performing due diligence often limit the amount of time devoted to understanding whether a firm's experimental drugs have groundbreaking potential. Also, public shell companies into which the private firm is merged often have low trading volumes, creating liquidity problems for investors. Consequently, investors in reverse mergers are under considerable pressure to get listed on a public stock exchange so that the firm's stock can be actively traded.

In mid-2018, Aravive Inc., a clinical-stage biotech company, was at a crossroads. It did not have sufficient cash to conduct the clinical trials to prove the safety and efficacy of its promising cancer drug. The firm faced the prospect of having to curtail operations. In contrast, another biotech firm, Versartis Inc., had failed to pass clinical trials for its drugs and was facing the prospect of bankruptcy. However, the firm had about $60 million in cash left over from prior fundraising activities, down from more than $200 million 2 years earlier. Even though the firm ceased operations to slow the rate at which it was burning cash, the end was fast approaching, and its investors were looking to recover their earlier investments. The timing appeared to be right for both firms to join forces. Versartis had cash on hand but no promising drugs in development; in contrast, Aravive had promising drugs in development but little cash.

With the strength of the equity markets at the time unclear and a growing inability of each firm to sustain operations, the firms quickly reached an agreement for Aravive to merge into Versartis with Aravive surviving. The merger resulted in a clinical-stage pharmaceutical firm focused on developing Aravive's drugs that target solid tumors and hematologic malignancies.

To implement a reverse merger, Versartis created a wholly owned subsidiary shell corporation (Merger Sub) and exchanged its shares for Merger Sub shares. Merger Sub was merged with Aravive in a reverse triangular merger[57] with Aravive surviving as a wholly owned subsidiary of Versartis. The reverse triangular merger preserved licenses, contracts, and intellectual property owned by Aravive. Aravive Inc. was then merged with Versartis in a backend merger and the firm renamed Aravive, now trading as a public company.

Before the closing of the merger, Versartis filed with The Nasdaq Stock Market (Nasdaq) for the listing of its shares. Because of the large number of existing and newly issued Versartis shares exchanged for Aravive shares, a reverse split was undertaken to reduce the number of shares outstanding. The split was designed to improve earnings per share and to support the share price after closing by reducing the number of shares outstanding.

In early 2019, Aravive Inc. traded on the Nasdaq stock exchange concurrent with a 1-for-6 reverse split of common shares. The reverse split resulted in 6 shares of issued and outstanding Aravive common stock combined into 1 issued and outstanding share of common stock with no change in par value. The number of shares outstanding as a result of the split was reduced from 67.40 million to 11.23 million.

For accounting purposes, the merger is considered to be a reverse merger under the acquisition method of accounting in which Versartis is considered the acquirer and Aravive the target firm. For tax purposes, the merger

[57] See Chapter 12 for a detailed discussion of triangular mergers.

will be treated as a reorganization rather than an actual sale in accordance with the US tax code (see Chapter 12 for a more detailed discussion). Consequently, Aravive shareholders will not recognize a gain or loss upon the exchange of their shares.

Discussion questions

1. What are the common reasons for a private firm to go public? What are the advantages and disadvantages of doing so? Be specific.
2. Discuss the pros and cons of a reverse merger versus an IPO.
3. Discuss why Aravive and Versartis chose a reverse merger over an IPO?
4. What is the purpose of a private firm wanting to be listed on a major stock exchange such as Nasdaq?
5. What is a shell corporation? Which firm is the shell corporation (Versartis or Aravive) in the case study? Why is it misleading to call Versartis the acquirer and Aravive the target firm?
6. What are the auditing challenges associated with reverse mergers? How can investors protect themselves from the liabilities that may be contained in corporate shells?

Solutions to this case are provided in the Online Instructor's Manual available for instructors using this book.

P A R T I V

Deal-structuring and financing strategies

Successful negotiators spend considerable time in advance of talks identifying the objectives of all participants as well as those that if not satisfied could be considered as "deal breakers." Substantial effort also is required to identify the range of options likely to lead to agreement. Despite advance preparation, negotiations often take a series of unpredictable twists and turns.

Part IV describes various aspects of the negotiating process and how deal structuring and financing are inextricably linked, how consensus is reached during the deal-structuring (or bargaining) process, and the role of financial models in closing the deal. The output of the negotiating process is an agreement or deal structure between two parties (the acquirer and the target firms) defining the rights and obligations of the those involved. The deal structure also establishes what is being acquired (stock or assets), assumed liabilities, the amount of payment that must be financed, and the form of payment: cash, stock, or both. Whether what needs to be financed can in fact be funded determines whether the deal gets done.

Chapter 11 outlines the major facets of the deal-structuring process, including the acquisition vehicle and postclosing organization, the form of acquisition, the form of payment, and the legal form of selling entity and how changes in one area of the deal often impact significantly other parts of the agreement. Specific ways to bridge major differences on price and to manage risk are also discussed.

Chapter 12 addresses tax considerations, including alternative forms of taxable and nontaxable structures, and how they impact reaching agreement. The implications of the 2017 Tax Cuts and Jobs Act for mergers and acquisitions are addressed in detail. This chapter also discusses how business combinations are recorded for financial-reporting purposes and the impact on reported earnings.

Chapter 13 focuses on the ways in which mergers and acquisitions (M&A) transactions are financed, the role played by private equity firms and hedge funds in financing highly leveraged transactions, and the impact of recent US tax legislation on such deals. This chapter also discusses how leveraged buyouts are structured and create value.

Chapter 14 addresses the basics of valuing and modeling highly leveraged transactions, including a discussion of how investors evaluate leveraged buyout (LBO) investment opportunities and typical formats used in building LBO financial models. The cost of capital and adjusted present value (APV) methods are described in detail, as well as the strengths and weaknesses of each approach.

Chapter 15 concentrates on applying financial modeling to value and structure M&As in both stock and asset deals. The strengths and limitations of such models also are discussed, as well as how models can be used to estimate the impact on earnings per share (EPS) and credit ratios of alternative deal and financing structures.

CHAPTER

11

Structuring the deal: tax and accounting considerations

OUTLINE

Mergers, Acquisitions, and Other Restructuring Activities, Eleventh Edition
https://doi.org/10.1016/B978-0-12-819782-0.00011-3

If you can't convince them, confuse them. —*Harry S. Truman*

Inside M&A: GlaxoSmithKline undertakes a cash tender offer to acquire Tesaro

KEY POINTS

- The form of payment to Tesaro shareholders was cash.
- The form of acquisition (i.e., what was being acquired) was Tesaro stock.
- Ownership was transferred by merging Tesaro into a GlaxoSmithKline merger subsidiary.
- Minority shareholders were "squeezed out" by a backend merger.
- Shareholders had the right to have their shares appraised to determine "fair value."

In an effort to strengthen its position in cancer-fighting treatments and add to its drug development pipeline, UK-based pharmaceutical giant GlaxoSmithKline (GSK) announced that it had completed its acquisition of Tesaro on January 22, 2019. Tesaro is a US-based oncology-focused biopharmaceutical firm with a successful ovarian cancer treatment already approved for sale in the United States and Europe. The firm also had several promising oncology drugs in development. The deal valued Tesaro at $5.1 billion (£4.0 billion).

GSK reasoned that it would be cheaper to acquire rather than to develop its own cancer-fighting treatments given the time and resources to do so with no guarantee of commercial success. Large bureaucratic pharmaceutical firms have for years had difficulty in developing and marketing new treatments compared with more nimble smaller firms.

GSK created a merger subsidiary (merger sub) by transferring cash in the amount necessary to do the deal to the subsidiary in exchange for the subsidiary's stock. Merger sub then initiated a cash tender offer at $75 per share for all of the shares of Tesaro on December 14, 2018. As of the January 14, 2019, expiration date, 50.1 million Tesaro shares had been tendered, representing 82.8% of the firm's outstanding shares.

The offer price per share represented an eye-popping 110% premium to Tesaro's 30-day volume weighted average price of $35.67 before the deal's announcement date of December 4, 2018. The size of the premium could be viewed as a "preemptive bid" by GSK designed to dissuade others from bidding for Tesaro.

GSK completed the deal through a merger under Section 251(h) of Delaware's General Corporation Law, the state where Tesaro is incorporated. Ownership was transferred by having Tesoro merged into GSK's merger sub, with the merger sub as the surviving legal entity. Tesaro (from a legal standpoint) is referred to as the disappearing corporation. By acquiring Tesaro's stock, all Tesaro assets and liabilities (both known and unknown) under this merger structure transfer by law to GSK in accordance with the statutes of the state of Delaware.

Because not all Tesaro shares were tendered in the first round of the tender offer, GSK announced that it would purchase any shares of Tesaro not tendered through a two-step or backend merger at $75 per share. Minority shareholders (those not participating in the tender offer) can prove troublesome to the current board and management if they prove litigious or publicly criticize decisions made by the firm. GSK would also have had to prepare separate financial statements for reporting purposes for the minority shareholders.

Neither GSK nor Tesaro had to hold shareholder meetings to get approval for the deal. Target shareholders gave their implicit consent by tendering their shares in exchange for cash. The acquirer's board owned a majority stake in Tesaro after completion of the tender offer and therefore had the legal right to "squeeze out" the remaining Tesaro shareholders not participating in either round of the tender offer through a backend merger.

Under the merger agreement, these shareholders had the right to have their shares appraised by Delaware's Chancery Court. Although dissenting or minority shareholders are required to sell their shares as a result of the backend merger, Delaware statutes grant them the right to be paid the appraised value of their shares, which can be equal to, more than, or less than the offer price.

Chapter overview

A *deal structure* is an agreement between two parties (the acquirer and the target firms) defining their rights and obligations. The way in which this agreement is reached is called the *deal-structuring process*. In this chapter, this process is described in terms of seven interdependent components: acquisition vehicle, the postclosing organization, the form of payment, the legal form of the selling entity, form of acquisition, accounting considerations, and tax considerations.

The focus in this chapter is on the form of payment, the form of acquisition, and alternative forms of legal structures in which ownership is conveyed and how they interact to impact the overall deal. The implications of alternative tax structures, how deals are recorded for financial-reporting purposes, and how they might affect the deal-structuring process are discussed in detail in Chapter 12. A review of this chapter is available in the file folder titled "Student Study Guide" on the companion website to this book (https://www.elsevier.com/books-and-journals/book-companion/9780128197820).

The deal-structuring process

This process involves satisfying as many of the primary acquirer and target objectives as possible, determining how risk will be shared, and identifying the rights and obligations of parties to the deal. The process may involve multiple parties, approvals, forms of payment, and sources of financing. Decisions made in one area often affect other areas of the deal. Containing risk associated with a complex deal is analogous to squeezing one end of a water balloon, which simply forces the contents to shift elsewhere.

To paraphrase Peter Carnevale, deal structuring is decision making under uncertainty. And the element of time is a key aspect of that uncertainty.[1] Although various factors impact different aspects of deal structuring, the degree of time pressure is a factor throughout the process. When parties to a negotiation are not constrained by time, the selection of tactics is likely to be quite different from when either or both parties are subject to substantial time pressure.

For example, when the parties are in a hurry to close a deal, an asset purchase might be preferable to a stock purchase as it often requires less due diligence. The use of cash rather than stock may be the appropriate form of payment. Unlike acquirer stock, there is no doubt about the value of a cash offer (assuming financing is in place). Moreover, there is no need to register shares or negotiate terms (e.g., collar arrangements) to minimize fluctuations in the value of acquirer shares between signing and closing. A corporate structure as an acquisition vehicle can expedite a deal because it offers financing flexibility, continuity of ownership, and deal flexibility (e.g., option to engage in a tax-free deal). If the acquirer intends to integrate the target immediately after closing, the appropriate postclosing organization might be a corporate structure because it offers the greatest control in combining the acquirer and target.

Key components of the deal-structuring process

The process begins with addressing a set of key questions, shown on the left-hand side of Figure 11.1. Answers to these questions help define initial negotiating positions, potential risks, options for managing risk, levels of tolerance for risk, and conditions under which either party will "walk away" from the negotiations. The key components of the process are discussed next.

The *acquisition vehicle* refers to the legal structure created to acquire the target firm. The *postclosing organization*, or structure, is the organizational and legal framework used to manage the combined businesses following the consummation of the transaction. Common acquisition vehicles and postclosing organizations include the corporate, division, holding company, joint venture (JV), partnership, limited liability company (LLC), and employee stock ownership plan (ESOP) structure. Although the two structures are often the same before and after completion of the deal, the postclosing organization may differ from the acquisition vehicle.

The *form of payment*, or total consideration, may consist of cash, common stock, debt, or a combination of all three types. The payment may be fixed at a moment in time, contingent on the target's future performance, or payable over time. The *form of acquisition* reflects what is being acquired (stock or assets) and how ownership is conveyed.

[1] Carnevale, 2019

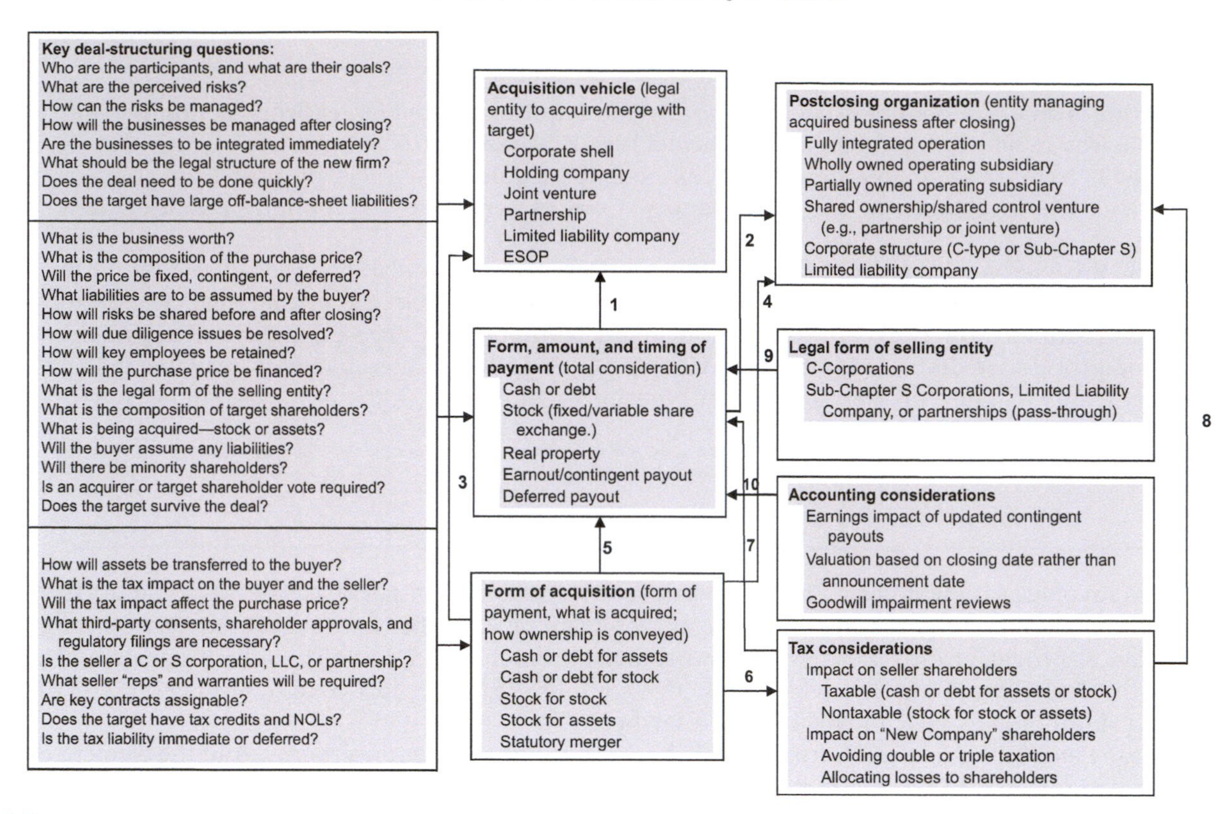

FIGURE 11.1 The mergers and acquisitions deal-structuring process. *ESOP*, Employee stock ownership plan; *LLC*, limited liability company; *NOL*, net operating loss.

Accounting considerations address the impact of reporting requirements on the future earnings of the combined businesses. *Tax considerations* determine whether a deal is taxable or nontaxable to the seller's shareholders. The *legal form of the selling entity* (i.e., the target) also has tax implications.

Common linkages

Figure 11.1 explains through examples common interactions among various components of the deal structure. These are discussed in more detail later in this chapter and in Chapter 12.

Form of payment (Fig. 11.1, **arrows 1** *and* **2)** *affects choice of acquisition vehicle and postclosing organization*

The buyer may offer a purchase price contingent on the future performance of the target and choose to acquire and operate the target as a wholly owned subsidiary within a holding company during the term of the earnout (deferred payout). This facilitates monitoring the operation's performance and minimizes possible post-earnout litigation.

Form of acquisition (Fig. 11.1, **arrows 3–6)** *affects:*

Choice of acquisition vehicle and postclosing organization: If the form of acquisition is a statutory merger, all liabilities transfer to the buyer, which may acquire and operate the target within a holding company to provide some protection from the target's liabilities.

Form, timing, and amount of payment: The assumption of all seller liabilities in a merger or stock purchase may cause the buyer to alter the terms of the deal to include more debt or installment payments, to reduce the present value (PV) of the purchase price, or both.

Tax considerations: The transaction may be tax-free to the seller if the acquirer uses its stock to acquire substantially all of the seller's assets or stock.

TABLE 11.1 Summary of common linkages within the deal-structuring process

Component of deal-structuring process	Influences choice of:
Form, amount, and timing of payment	Acquisition vehicle Postclosing organization Accounting considerations Tax structure (taxable or nontaxable)
Form of acquisition	Acquisition vehicle Postclosing organization Form, amount, and timing of payment Tax structure (taxable or nontaxable)
Tax considerations	Form, amount, and timing of payment Postclosing organization
Legal form of selling entity	Tax structure (taxable or nontaxable)

Tax considerations (Fig. 11.1, arrows 7 and 8) affect:

Amount, timing, and composition of the purchase price: If the deal is taxable to the target shareholders, the purchase price often is increased to offset the target shareholders' tax liability. The higher purchase price could alter the composition of the purchase price as the buyer defers a portion of the price or includes more debt to lower its present value.

Selection of postclosing organization: The desire to minimize taxes encourages the use of S corporations, LLCs and partnerships to eliminate double taxation; tax benefits also pass through to LLC members and partners in partnerships.

Legal form of selling entity (Fig. 11.1, arrow 9) affects form of payment

Because of the potential for deferring shareholder tax liabilities, target firms qualifying as C corporations often prefer to exchange their stock or assets for acquirer shares. Owners of S corporations, LLCs, and partnerships are largely indifferent to a deal's tax status because the proceeds of the sale are taxed at the owners' ordinary tax rate.

Accounting considerations (Fig. 11.1, arrow 10) affect form, amount, and timing of payment

The requirement to adjust more frequently the fair value of contingent payments may make earnouts less attractive as a form of payment because of the potential increase in earnings volatility. Equity as a form of payment may be less attractive because of the potential for changes in its value between the deal announcement date and closing date. The potential for future write-downs may discourage overpayment by acquirers because of the required periodic review of fair market versus book values. Table 11.1 provides a summary of these common linkages.

Form of acquisition vehicle and postclosing organization

Choosing an acquisition vehicle or postclosing organization requires consideration of the cost of establishing the organization, ease of transferring ownership, continuity of existence, management control, ease of financing, ease of integration, method of distribution of profits, extent of personal liability, and taxation. Each form of legal entity has different risk, financing, tax, and control implications for the acquirer. The selection of the appropriate entity can help to mitigate risk, maximize financing flexibility, and minimize the net cost of the acquisition.

Choosing the appropriate acquisition vehicle

The corporate structure is the most commonly used acquisition vehicle because it offers limited liability, financing flexibility, continuity of ownership, and deal flexibility (e.g., option to engage in a tax-free deal). For small privately owned firms, an ESOP may be a convenient way for transferring the owner's interest to the employees while offering tax advantages. Holding-company structures help insulate the parent from the liabilities of a subsidiary. Non-US buyers intending to make acquisitions may prefer a holding-company structure, enabling the buyer to control other companies by owning only a small portion of the company's voting stock. A partnership may be appropriate if it is important to share risk, to involve partners with special attributes, to avoid double taxation, or in special situations.[2]

Choosing the appropriate postclosing organization

The postclosing organization can be the same as that chosen for the acquisition vehicle. Common postclosing structures include divisional[3] and holding-company arrangements. Although holding companies are often corporations, they also represent a distinct way of operating the firm.

The choice of the postclosing organization depends on the acquirer's objectives. The acquirer may choose a structure that facilitates postclosing integration, minimizes risk from the target's known and unknown liabilities, minimizes taxes, passes through losses to shelter the owners' tax liabilities, preserves unique target attributes, maintains target independence during the duration of an earnout, or preserves the tax-free status of the deal.

If the acquirer intends to integrate the target immediately after closing, the corporate or divisional structure is preferred because it offers the greatest control. In JVs and partnerships, implementation is more likely to depend on close cooperation and consensus building, which may slow efforts at rapid integration. Realizing synergies may be more protracted than if management control is centralized within the parent.

Holding companies are desirable when the target has significant actual or potential liabilities. The parent may be able to isolate target liabilities within the subsidiary, which could be forced into bankruptcy without jeopardizing the parent. Holding companies may be appropriate when a deal involves an earnout, the target is a foreign firm, or the acquirer is a financial investor. When a portion of the purchase price is deferred as in an earnout, acquirers often operate the acquired unit in a separate subsidiary to limit the potential for target firm managers to complain they were unable to achieve their earnout targets because of parent interference. If the target is a foreign firm, operating it separately from the rest of the acquirer's operations may minimize disruption from cultural differences. Finally, a financial buyer may use a holding company because they have no interest in operating the target firm for any length of time, and as a legal subsidiary, the unit can be more easily sold.

A partnership or JV structure may be appropriate if the risk and the value of tax benefits are high. The acquired firm may benefit because of the expertise that the different partners or owners might provide. A partnership or LLC eliminates double taxation and passes current operating losses, tax credits, and loss carryforwards[4] to the owners.

Legal form of the selling entity

Seller concerns about the form of the transaction may depend on whether it is an S corporation, an LLC, a partnership, or a C corporation. C corporations are subject to double taxation, whereas owners of S corporations, partnerships, and LLCs are not (see Exhibit 11.1).

Form of payment

Although these percentages ebb and flow with fluctuations in the cost of borrowing and equity markets, all-stock deals, all-cash deals, and mixed deals (both stock and cash) comprised 32%, 54%, and 14%, respectively, of total 2019 US mergers and acquisitions (M&A) deals. This section addresses the different forms of payment used and the circumstances in which one form may be preferred over another.

[2] Certain situations often require specific types of partnership arrangements. For example, a *master limited partnership* (MLP) is used in industries in which cash flow is relatively predictable, such as oil and gas extraction and distribution and real estate. As with other limited partnerships, it is not subject to double taxation, and its investors are subject to limited liability; unlike other partnerships, its units can be more easily bought and sold than those of private partnerships and privately owned corporations and often trade in the same manner as shares of common stock. MLPs are considered in default if all profits are not distributed.

[3] A division is not a separate legal entity but rather an organizational unit, and it is distinguished from a legal subsidiary in that it typically will not have its own stock or board of directors that meets regularly. Because a division is not a separate legal entity, its liabilities are the responsibility of the parent.

[4] Tax losses can no longer by used to recover taxes paid in prior years under the Tax Cuts and Jobs Act of 2017.

EXHIBIT 11.1

How the Seller's Legal Form Affects Form of Payment

Assume that a business owner starting with an initial investment of $100,000 sells her business for $1 million. Different legal structures have different tax impacts:

1. After-tax proceeds of a stock sale are ($1,000,000 − $100,000) × (1 − 0.15) = $765,000. The S corporation shareholder or limited liability company (LLC) member holding shares for more than one year pays a maximum capital gains tax equal to 15% of the gain on the sale.
2. After-tax proceeds from an asset sale are ($1,000,000 − $100,000) × (1 − 0.26) × (1 − 0.15) = $900,000 × 0.63 = $566,100. A C corporation pays tax equal to 26% (i.e., 21% federal[39] and 5% state and local), and the shareholder pays a maximum capital gains tax equal to 15%, resulting in double taxation of the gain on sale.

Implications

1. C corporation shareholders generally prefer acquirer stock for their stock or assets to avoid double taxation.
2. S corporation and LLC owners often are indifferent to an asset sale or stock sale because 100% of the corporation's income passes through the corporation untaxed to the owners, who are subject to their own personal tax rates. The S corporation shareholders or LLC members still may prefer a share-for-share exchange if they are interested in deferring their tax liability or are attracted by the long-term growth potential of the acquirer's stock.

[39] The maximum marginal corporate rate under the Tax Cuts and Jobs Act of 2017 is 21%.

Cash

Acquirers may use cash if the firm has significant borrowing capacity, a high credit rating, less restrictive current loan covenants, undervalued shares, and wishes to maintain control. A cash purchase is often financed from borrowing if the firm is relatively liquid as a result of low borrowing costs.[5] However, highly leveraged acquirers are less likely to offer all-cash deals and more likely to use less cash in mixed-payment offers because of stringent loan covenants and potential credit rating downgrades.[6] When practical, firms tend to offer cash when management believes its shares are undervalued, to avoid diluting current shares and target shareholders prefer cash to acquirer shares. Furthermore, a bidder may use cash rather than shares if the voting control of its dominant shareholder is threatened because of the issuance of voting stock.[7]

Noncash

The 2020 global pandemic and the resulting economic and financial crisis reduced deal values. Acquirer stock became more widespread as a partial or total replacement for cash as a form of payment. Acquirer stock enabled buyers and sellers to more readily reach agreement because target shareholders would participate in future upside (and downside) risk.

Using stock is more complicated than cash because of the need to comply with prevailing securities laws. An acquirer having limited borrowing capacity may choose to use stock if it is believed to be overvalued and when the integration of the target firm is expected to be lengthy in order to minimize the amount of indebtedness required to complete the takeover. By maintaining the ability to borrow, the acquirer is able to finance unanticipated cash outlays during the integration period and to pursue investment opportunities that might arise.[8]

Acquirer stock may be used when the target is suspected of manipulating earnings or valuing the target firm is difficult because it has substantial intangible assets, new products, or large research and development outlays.[9] In

[5] Hu et al., 2020

[6] Hu et al., 2015

[7] Faccio and Masulis, 2005

[8] Huang et al., 2011

[9] Huang et al., 2019

accepting acquirer stock, a seller has less incentive to negotiate an overvalued purchase price if it wishes to participate in any appreciation of the stock it receives.[10] Similarly, stock is useful in cross-border deals when there is little information about the target.[11] Other forms of noncash payment include real property, rights to intellectual property, royalties, earnouts, and contingent payments.

Seller shareholders may find debt unattractive because of the acquirer's perceived high risk of default. Debt or equity securities issued by private firms may also be illiquid because of the small size of the resale market for such securities. Smaller acquirers may not have access to inexpensive debt. As such, they may finance their cash bids by issuing equity. Because equity is a higher-cost source of financing, its use to finance the cash bid can lower purchase price premiums. In contrast, acquirers with access to low-cost debt may borrow to finance their cash bids and tend to overbid for target firms.[12]

Cash and stock in combination

Offering target shareholders multiple payment options may encourage more participation in tender offers. Some target shareholders want a combination of acquirer stock and cash if they are unsure of the appreciation potential of the acquirer's stock. Others may prefer a combination of cash and stock if they need the cash to pay taxes due on the sale of their shares. Also, acquirers unable to borrow to finance an all-cash offer or unwilling to absorb the dilution in an all-stock offer may choose to offer the target firm a combination of stock and cash.

Acquirers also may be motivated to offer their shares if they believe they are overvalued, because they are able to issue fewer shares. Target shareholders may be willing to accept overvalued acquirer shares because the overvaluation may not be obvious or the acquirer stock may reduce the degree of post-merger leverage of the combined firms.[13] If investors believe the combined firms are less risky because of the reduction in leverage, the intrinsic value of the acquirer shares may rise, reflecting lower default risk. The resulting rise in their intrinsic value may reduce or eliminate the overvaluation of the acquirer shares.

The multiple-option bidding strategy creates uncertainty: the amount of cash the acquirer ultimately will have to pay to target shareholders is unclear because the number of shareholders choosing the all-cash or cash-and-stock option is not known before completion of the tender offer. Acquirers resolve this issue by including a *proration clause* in tender offers and merger agreements that allows them to fix—at the time the tender offer is initiated—the amount of cash they will ultimately have to pay out.[14]

Convertible securities

An acquirer and a target often have inadequate information about the other despite due diligence. The acquirer is anxious about overpaying, and target shareholders are concerned about the offer price reflecting the fair value of their shares. Using acquirer stock as the primary form of payment mitigates some of this concern because target shareholders hoping to participate in any future appreciation are less likely to withhold important information. However, this does not address the issue of the fairness of the purchase price to target shareholders.

Convertible securities[15] potentially resolve acquirer and target concerns when each lacks information about the other. Bidders believing their shares are undervalued are reluctant to use stock, to avoid diluting their current shareholders. Such bidders may offer convertible debt as a form of payment. Target shareholders may find such offers attractive because they provide a floor equal to the value of the debt at maturity plus accumulated interest payments

[10] Officer et al. (2007). Note that simply accepting acquirer stock does not guarantee the seller will not attempt to negotiate an overvalued purchase price if the seller intends to sell the acquirer shares immediately after closing.

[11] Cho et al., 2017

[12] Vladimirov, 2015

[13] Vermaelen and Xu, 2014

[14] Assume the acquisition cost is $100 million, the acquirer wishes to limit cash paid to target shareholders to half of that amount, and the acquirer offers the target's shareholders a choice of stock or cash. If the amount target shareholders who choose to receive cash exceeds $50 million, the proration clause enables the acquirer to pay all target shareholders tendering their shares half of the purchase price in cash and the rest in stock.

[15] Convertible bonds and preferred stock can be converted into a predetermined number of a firm's common shares if the shares exceed the price per share at which a convertible security can be converted into common stock. These types of securities are explained in more detail in Chapter 14.

as well as the potential for participating in future share appreciation. Bidders believing their shares are overvalued are inclined to offer stock rather than cash or convertible securities. If the convertible securities are unlikely to be converted because of the limited share price appreciation of the bidder's stock, the securities will remain as debt and burden the firm with substantial leverage.

Cryptocurrency: fiction versus reality

Cryptocurrencies are digital monies using cryptography (i.e., the scrambling of data to make it unreadable) to make transactions secure, verify the transfer of funds, and control the creation of additional units. Powered by blockchain technology,[16] Bitcoin is the best known cryptocurrency in existence.

Users trade Bitcoin over a network of decentralized computers, eliminating intermediaries such as governments, commercial banks, and central banks. Bitcoin enables users to avoid fees incurred if the banking system had been used to complete transactions and to eliminate currency conversion costs in international transactions, all done in relative secrecy. Bitcoin is difficult to counterfeit and may enable immediate verifiable payment in M&A deals.

Despite its potential benefits, the widespread acceptance of cryptocurrency as a form of payment remains problematic. The lack of price stability compared with government fiat currencies undermines confidence in using this form of payment in M&As without some type of a collar arrangement within which the value of the purchase price can fluctuate. Alternatively, Bitcoin, if traded on a futures exchange, could be hedged against loss of value by buying a futures contract locking in the current price. This would add to transaction costs.

There also are concerns about security, with several instances of theft of Bitcoin by hackers. Other issues include the general lack of regulation and transparency. Government taxing authorities, concerned with the accuracy of the sale price reported for tax purposes, might be quick to audit those involved in Bitcoin-financed M&A deals. Money laundering also is a potential concern to governments. Monies obtained from criminal activities can be used to buy Bitcoin, which could then be used to acquire a legitimate business.

Could there be a role for cryptocurrency as a form of payment in M&As? Yes, if concerns about security, volatility, and transparency are overcome. Until then, cash and securities will be the primary form of payment in M&As. Although cryptocurrencies could either revolutionize financial markets or become a quaint footnote in history books, they do merit watching.

Managing risk and reaching consensus on purchase price

Someone once said, "You name the price, and I will name the terms." While the purchase price is just a number, the form and the timing of the payment as well as concessions made to the other party refer to the terms. Balance-sheet adjustments and escrow accounts; earnouts; contingent value rights (CVRs); rights to intellectual property and licensing fees; and consulting agreements may be used to close the deal when the buyer and seller cannot reach agreement on price.

Postclosing balance sheet price adjustments and escrow accounts

Many M&As require some purchase price adjustment, resulting most often from a restatement of operating earnings or cash flow or working capital. Escrow or holdback accounts and adjustments to the target's balance sheet are most often used in cash rather than stock-for-stock purchases (particularly when the number of target shareholders is large). They rely on an audit of the target firm to determine its fair value and are applicable only when what is being acquired is identifiable, such as in a purchase of tangible assets. With escrow accounts, the buyer retains a portion of the purchase price until completion of a postclosing audit of the target's financial statements. Escrow accounts may also be used to cover continuing claims beyond closing.

[16] A blockchain is a database of electronic records maintained not by a central authority but by a network of users on computer servers. Consisting of records, called blocks, linked and secured using cryptography, a blockchain is an open ledger that can record transactions between parties. Copies of the entire system can be kept simultaneously on millions of computers located anywhere. When a new entry is made, the entire ledger is updated on every server. Although anyone can add a new record to the system, all changes to old entries require everyone to agree to make the changes on their servers, making historical data reliable.

TABLE 11.2 Working capital guarantee balance-sheet adjustments ($ million)

	Purchase price		Purchase price reduction	Purchase price increase
	At time of negotiation	At closing		
If working capital equals	110	100	10	
If working capital equals	110	125		15

Balance-sheet adjustments are used when the elapsed time between the agreement on price and the actual closing date is lengthy. The balance sheet may change significantly, so the purchase price is adjusted up or down. Such adjustments can be used to guarantee the value of the target firm's shareholder equity or, more narrowly, the value of working capital. With a shareholder equity guarantee, both parties agree at signing to an estimate of the target's equity value on the closing date. The purchase price is then increased or decreased to reflect changes in the book value of the target's equity between the signing and closing dates due to net profit earned (or lost) during this period.

Agreement may be reached more easily between the buyer and the seller with a working capital guarantee, which ensures against changes in the firm's net current operating assets.[17] As Table 11.2 indicates, the buyer reduces the total purchase price by an amount equal to the decrease in net working capital or shareholders' equity of the target and increases the purchase price by any increase in these measures during this period.

Earnouts and other contingent payments

Contingent payouts may be used when the value of the target is dependent of the realization of critical future events. In mid-2019, Canada-based Canopy Growth Corp (CGC) agreed to buy US marijuana grower Acreage Holdings Inc. in a deal valued at $3.4 billion. The terms of the deal required CGC to pay Acreage $300 million in cash upfront and to issue 0.5818 shares of CGC for each Acreage share outstanding contingent on cannabis production and sales becoming legal at the federal level in the United States. The deal will be suspended if legalization does not occur by 2025.

Earnouts and warrants often are used whenever the buyer and the seller cannot agree on price or when the parties involved wish to participate in the upside potential of the business. Earnout agreements may also be used to retain and motivate key target firm managers. An earnout agreement is a financial contract whereby a portion of the purchase price is to be paid in the future, contingent on realizing the future earnings level or some other performance measure agreed on earlier. A subscription warrant, or simply warrant, is a type of security—often issued with a bond or preferred stock—that entitles the holder to purchase an amount of common stock at a stipulated price. The exercise price is usually higher than the price at the time the warrant is issued. Warrants may be converted over a period of many months to many years.

The earnout typically requires that the acquired business be operated as a subsidiary of the acquiring firm under the management of the former owners or key executives. Earnouts differ substantially in terms of the performance measure on which the contingent payout is based, the period over which performance is measured, and the form of payment for the earnout.[18]

Some earnouts are payable only if a certain threshold is achieved; others depend on average performance over several periods. Still others may involve periodic payments, depending on the achievement of interim performance measures rather than a single lump-sum payment at the end of the earnout period. The value of the earnout is often capped. In some cases, the seller may have the option to repurchase the company at some predetermined percentage of the original purchase price if the buyer is unable to pay the earnout at maturity.

Earnouts consist of two parts: a payment up front and a deferred payment. The initial payment must be large enough to induce the target's shareholders to agree to the terms, and the deferred payment must be of sufficient size to keep them motivated. Relatively large deferred payments and longer earnout periods are associated with higher takeover premia paid at closing than the premia paid in comparable nonearnout deals. Why? Target firm shareholders in earnouts are compensated for sharing the post-acquisition integration risk with the acquiring

[17] It is critical to define clearly what constitutes working capital and equity in the agreement of purchase and sale because—similar to equity—what constitutes working capital may be ambiguous.

[18] Cain et al., 2014

EXHIBIT 11.2

Hypothetical Earnout as Part of the Purchase Price

Purchase price

1. Lump-sum payment at closing: the seller receives $100 million.
2. Earnout payment: the seller receives four times the excess of the actual average annual net operating cash flow over the baseline projection after 3 years, not to exceed $35 million.

	Base year (first full year of ownership)		
	Year 1	Year 2	Year 3
Baseline projection (net cash flow)	$10	$12	$15
Actual performance (net cash flow)	$15	$20	$25

Earnout at the end of 3 years:[a]

$$\frac{(\$15-\$10)+(\$20-\$12)+(\$25-\$15)}{3}\times 4=\$30.67$$

Potential increase in shareholder value:[b]

$$\left\{\frac{(\$15-\$10)+(\$20-\$12)+(\$25-\$15)}{3}\times 10\right\}-\$30.67$$

$$=\$46$$

[a] The cash flow multiple of 4 applied to the earnout is a result of negotiation before closing.
[b] The cash flow multiple of 10 applied to the potential increase in shareholder value for the buyer is the multiple the buyer anticipates that investors would apply to a 3-year average of actual operating cash flow at the end of the 3-year period.

firm by receiving a higher premium than they would have received had they received the entire payment upfront.[19]

Exhibit 11.2 illustrates how an earnout formula could be constructed reflecting these factors. The purchase price has two components. At closing, the seller receives a lump-sum payment of $100 million. The seller and the buyer agree to a baseline projection for a 3-year period and that the seller will receive a fixed multiple of the average annual performance of the acquired business in excess of the baseline projection. Thus the earnout provides an incentive for the seller to operate the business as efficiently as possible.[20] By multiplying the anticipated multiple investors will pay for operating cash flow at the end of the 3-year period by projected cash flow, it is possible to estimate the potential increase in shareholder value.[21]

Used in about 3% of US deals, earnouts are more common when the targets are small private firms or subsidiaries of larger firms rather than large public firms. Such contracts are more easily written and enforced when there are relatively few shareholders. Earnouts are most common in high-tech and service industries, when the acquirer and target firms are in different industries, when the target firm has a significant number of assets not recorded on the balance sheet, when buyer access to information is limited, and when little integration will be attempted. Earnouts are unpopular in countries that have relatively lax enforcement of contracts.[22]

Earnouts on average account for 45% of the price paid for private firms and 33% for subsidiary acquisitions, and target firm shareholders tend to realize about 62% of the potential earnout amount. In deals involving earnouts, acquirers earn abnormal returns, ranging from 1.5%[23] to 5.4%,[24] around the announcement date, much more than

[19] Barbopoulos et al., 2016

[20] The baseline projection often is what the buyer used to value the seller. Shareholder value for the buyer is created when the acquired business's actual performance exceeds the baseline projection and the multiple applied by investors at the end of the 3-year period exceeds the multiple used to calculate the earnout payment. This assumes that the baseline projection values the business accurately and that the buyer does not overpay.

[21] Earnouts may demotivate management if the acquired firm does not perform well enough to achieve any payout under the earnout formula or if the acquired firm exceeds the performance targets substantially, effectively guaranteeing the maximum payout under the plan. The management of the acquired firm may cut back on training expenses or make only those investments that improve short-term profits. To avoid such pitfalls, it may be appropriate to set multiple targets, including revenue, income, and investment.

[22] Viarengo et al., 2018

[23] Barbopoulos et al., 2016

[24] Kohers and Ang, 2000

deals not involving earnouts. Positive abnormal returns to acquirer shareholders may be a result of investor perception that, with an earnout, the buyer is less likely to overpay and more likely to retain target firm talent.

Unless properly structured, earnouts can convert today's agreement into tomorrow's litigation. To minimize this risk, make sure milestones are unambiguous and avoid implied covenants (not explicitly stated but assumed to be true). The most common example of an implied covenant is that of "good faith and fair dealing" in which it is assumed the parties to the contract will deal with each other in an honest manner.

There are several ways to minimize the risk of implied covenants overriding contract language. Contract provisions should be as inclusive as possible (e.g., the buyer should make all reasonable efforts to help the seller achieve agreed-upon milestones), examples illustrating various situations should be used, and language in the agreement should state that contract provisions supersede implied covenants.

Even when properly structured, earnouts can still fail to achieve their objectives. In a much-publicized breakup in April 2018, Jan Koum (founder of WhatsApp) quit over the placement of advertising on the messaging service. In doing so, Koum may have walked away from billions in unvested restricted stock options, although the amount is unclear. And Facebook failed to retain Koum, whom they had viewed as critical to the operation when it acquired the firm for an eye-popping $19 billion in 2014.

Contingent value rights

CVR securities issued by the acquirer commit it to pay additional cash or securities to the holder of the CVR (i.e., the seller) if the acquirer's share price falls below a specified level at some future date. And they can be traded on public exchanges. Their use suggests that the acquirer believes that its shares are unlikely to fall below their current level.

CVRs are sometimes granted when the buyer and the seller are far apart on the purchase price. A CVR is more suitable for a public company or a private firm with many shareholders than is an earnout because it can be transferred to many investors. Earnouts are more often used with sales of private firms rather than for sales of public firms because they are designed to motivate a firm's managers who have control over the firm's future performance.[25]

There are two basic types of CVRs: those offering price protection and those that are triggered by an event or achieving a milestone. *Price-protected CVRs* offer seller shareholders additional cash if the buyer's shares they received as part of the deal fail to achieve certain price levels within a certain time period. They can be used when acquirer stock is the dominant form of payment. *Event-triggered CVRs* are more common and offer additional cash if certain events are achieved. Events that can trigger the CVR include the beginning of patent testing, regulatory approval, and satisfying certain commercial sales thresholds.

An important benefit of CVRs is that they can be customized to the needs of the parties involved in the transactions. However, they have significant shortcomings because of their complexity and potential liability. Whereas the former involves the potential for multiple layers of triggers and detailed definitions, the latter reflects their significant litigation risk.

Drug companies often use CVRs as part of the payment to acquire other drug companies, whose products do not have a proven track record, to reduce the risk of overpaying. In 2016, an Irish drug manufacturer, Shire, paid US biotech firm Dyax Corp shareholders $37.30 per share in cash at closing. Dyax shareholders would also receive an additional cash payment of $4 per share if the firm's drug for hereditary angioedema received US Food and Drug Administration approval by the end of 2019. Having received approval, the payout was made to holders of the CVR in early 2020.

In 2016, conflicts of interest associated with CVRs were highlighted in a shareholder lawsuit against French pharmaceutical firm Sanofi, which acquired Genzyme, a US-based biotech firm. Genzyme had been conducting clinical trials for a multiple sclerosis treatment called Lemtrada and estimated the value of each CVR at $5.58. The merger contract did not address the potential conflict from Sanofi's developing its own multiple sclerosis drug, Aubagio, which would compete with Lemtrada. The lawsuit alleged Sanofi developed its own drug to avoid as much as $3.8 billion in payments to CVR holders. After 1 year, Lemtrada generated sales of about $37 million, less than one-fifth of the approximate $180 million realized by Aubagio in its first year on the market. By the end of 2016, the CVRs traded at $0.14.

[25] Chatterjee and Yan (2008) document that acquirers issuing CVRs realize abnormal announcement date returns of 5.4% because investors view their use as confirmation that the acquirer believes their shares are undervalued.

Rights, royalties, and fees

Intellectual property, royalties from licenses, and fee-based consulting or employment contracts are other forms of payment used to resolve price differences between the buyer and the seller. The right to use a proprietary process or technology for free or at a below-market rate may interest former owners considering other business opportunities. Such arrangements should be coupled with agreements not to compete in the same industry as their former firm. Table 11.3 summarizes the advantages and disadvantages of these various forms of payment.

TABLE 11.3 Evaluating alternative forms of payment

Form of payment	Advantages	Disadvantages
Cash (including highly marketable securities)	*Buyer:* simplicity *Seller:* ensures payment if acquirer's creditworthiness is questionable	*Buyer:* must rely solely on protections afforded in the contract to recover claims *Seller:* creates immediate tax liability
Stock • Common • Preferred • Convertible preferred	*Buyer:* high P/E relative to seller's P/E may increase the value of the combined firms if investors apply higher P/E to combined firms' earnings *Seller:* defers taxes and provides potential price increase; retains interest in the business	*Buyer:* adds complexity; potential EPS dilution *Seller:* potential decrease in purchase price if the value of equity received declines; may delay closing because of SEC registration requirements
Debt • Secured • Unsecured • Convertible	*Buyer:* interest expense is tax deductible *Seller:* defers tax liability on the principal	*Buyer:* adds complexity and increases leverage *Seller:* risk of default
Performance-related earnouts	*Buyer:* shifts some portion of the risk to the seller *Seller:* potential for a higher purchase price	*Buyer:* may limit the integration of the businesses *Seller:* increases the uncertainty of the sales price
Purchase price adjustments	*Buyer:* protection from eroding values of working capital before closing *Seller:* protection from increasing values of working capital before closing	*Buyer:* audit expense *Seller:* audit expense (Note that buyers and sellers often split the audit expense.)
Real property • Real estate • Plant and equipment • Business or product line	*Buyer:* minimizes use of cash *Seller:* may minimize tax liability	*Buyer:* opportunity cost *Seller:* real property may be illiquid
Rights to intellectual property • License • Franchise	*Buyer:* minimizes cash use *Seller:* gains access to valuable rights; spreads taxable income over time	*Buyer:* potential for setting up a new competitor *Seller:* illiquid; income taxed at ordinary rates
Royalties from • Licenses • Franchises	*Buyer:* minimizes cash use *Seller:* spreads taxable income over time	*Buyer:* opportunity cost *Seller:* income taxed at ordinary rates
Fee based • Consulting contract • Employment agreement	*Buyer:* uses seller's expertise and removes seller as a potential competitor *Seller:* augments the purchase price and allows the seller to stay with the business	*Buyer:* may involve demotivated employees *Seller:* limits ability to compete in the same business; income taxed at ordinary rates
Contingent value rights	*Buyer:* minimizes upfront payment *Seller:* provides for minimum payout guarantee	*Buyer:* commits buyer to minimum payout *Seller:* buyer may ask for purchase price reduction
Staged or distributed payouts	*Buyer:* reduces amount of upfront investment *Seller:* reduces buyer angst about certain future events	*Buyer:* may result in underfunding of needed investments *Seller:* lower present value of purchase price

EPS, Earnings per share; *P/E,* price to earnings ratio; *SEC,* Securities and Exchange Commission.

Constructing collar arrangements

Unlike all-cash deals, large fluctuations in the acquirer's share price can threaten to change the terms of the deal or lead to its termination in share exchanges. Fixed share-exchange agreements, precluding any change in the number of acquirer shares exchanged for each target share, are used in share exchanges because they involve both firms' share prices, allowing each party to share in the risk or benefit from fluctuating share prices.

The acquirer's risk is that its shares will appreciate between signing and closing, raising the cost of the deal. The seller's risk is a drop in the value of the acquirer's share price, resulting in a lower-than-expected purchase price. Although the buyer will know exactly how many shares will have to be issued to complete the deal, the acquirer and the target will be subject to significant uncertainty about the final value of the deal.

Alternatively, a fixed-value agreement fixes the value of the offer price per share by allowing the share-exchange ratio to vary. Whereas an increase in the value of the acquirer's share price results in fewer acquirer shares being issued to keep the value of the deal unchanged, a decrease would require that additional shares be issued.

Both fixed-value and fixed-share-exchange agreements sometimes include a collar arrangement. For fixed-value agreements, the share-exchange ratio is allowed to vary within a narrow range; for fixed-share-exchange agreements, the offer price per share (deal value) is allowed to fluctuate within narrow limits.[26] Collar arrangements can be constructed as follows:

$$\text{Offer price per share} = \text{Share exchange ratio (SER)} \times \text{Acquirer's share price (ASP)}$$
$$= \left\{\frac{\text{Offer price per share}}{\text{Acquirer's share price}}\right\} \times \text{Acquirer's share}$$

$$\text{Collar range: } SER_L \times ASP_L \text{ (lower limit)} \leq \text{Offer price share} \leq SER_U \times ASP_U \text{ (upper limit)}$$

in which $ASP_U > ASP_L$, $SER_U < SER_L$, and subscripts L and U refer to lower and upper limits.

Case Study 11.1 illustrates the use of both fixed-value and fixed-share exchange agreements. Within the first collar (fixed value), the purchase price is fixed by allowing the share exchange ratio to vary, giving the seller some certainty inside a narrow range within which the acquirer share price floats; the second collar (fixed share exchange) allows the acquirer's share price (and therefore deal value) to vary within a specific range with both the buyer and seller sharing the risk. Finally, if the acquirer's share price rises above a certain level, the purchase price is capped; if it falls below a floor price, the seller can walk away. Table 11.4 illustrates the effect of a 1% increase (decrease) in the acquirer's $11.73 share price on the $6.55 offer price for the target firm's shares under various collar arrangements.

If Flextronics' stock price declines by as much as 10% to $10.55, 0.6209 shares of Flextronics stock (i.e., $6.55/ $10.55) is issued for each International DisplayWorks (IDW) share.

If Flextronics' stock price increases by as much as 10% to $12.90, 0.5078 shares of Flextronics' stock (i.e., $6.55/ $12.90) is issued for each IDW share.

M&A options and warrants takeover strategies

Options and warrants confer the right but not the obligation to buy or sell a security. The price at which they can be bought or sold before a specific expiration date is called the exercise or strike price. Warrants tend to have much longer periods between issue and expiration dates than options, sometimes stretching to years rather than months.

Options and warrants can be structured as the mechanism for a takeover of another firm's shares or assets. Such deals are relatively common in the pharmaceutical, medical devices, and life sciences industries in which the value of the target firm is largely unproven or unapproved (by regulators) intellectual property. Options may be applied to acquisitions of firms at various stages of the product life cycle. Options takeover strategies tend to be more common than those using warrants because of certain potentially adverse tax consequences explained later.

[26] According to Factset MergerMetrics, about 15% of deals include collars. Merger contracts often contain "material adverse-effects clauses" allowing parties to the contract to withdraw from or renegotiate the deal. Officer (2004) argues that collars reduce the likelihood of renegotiation caused by unexpected share price changes.

CASE STUDY 11.1

Flextronics Acquires International DisplayWorks Using Multiple Collar Arrangements

Key Points

- Collar arrangements may involve fixed-share-exchange or fixed-value agreements (or both).
- Both buyers and sellers may benefit from such arrangements.

Flextronics, a camera modules producer, acquired International DisplayWorks (IDW), an LCD maker, in a share exchange valued at $300 million. The share-exchange ratio was calculated using the Flextronics average daily closing share price for the 20 trading days ending on the fifth trading day preceding the closing.[a] Transaction terms included these three collars:

1. *Fixed-value agreement:* The offer price involved an exchange ratio floating inside a 10% collar above and below a Flextronics share price of $11.73 and a fixed purchase price of $6.55 for each share of IDW common stock. The range in which the exchange ratio floats can be expressed as follows:[b]

$$(\$6.55 / \$10.55) \times \$10.55 \le (\$6.55 / \$11.73) \times \$11.73 \le (\$6.55 / \$12.90) \times \$12.90 = 0.6209 \times \$10.55 \le 0.5584 \times \$11.73 \le 0.5078 \times \$12.90$$

2. *Fixed-share-exchange agreement:* The offer price involved a fixed exchange ratio inside a collar 11% and 15% above and below $11.73, resulting in a floating purchase price if Flextronics' stock increases or decreases between 11% and 15% from $11.73 per share.
3. IDW has the right to terminate the agreement if Flextronics's share price falls by more than 15% below $11.73. If Flextronics' share price increases by more than 15% above $11.73, the exchange ratio floats based on a fixed purchase price of $6.85 per share.[c]

[a] Calculating the acquirer share price as a 20-day average ending five days before closing reduces the chance of using an aberrant price per share and provides time to update the purchase agreement.
[b] The share-exchange ratio varies within ±10% of Flextronics' $11.73 share price.
[c] IDW is protected against a "free fall" in Flextronics share price, and the purchase price is capped at $6.85.

Firms often find themselves without sufficient capital to develop new products. Other firms looking for opportunities may be willing to invest but may want to ensure that they have the exclusive right to purchase or to the benefits of the product. Selling an "option to acquire" to an investor may be sufficient to satisfy the needs of both parties. Options and warrants as takeover strategies are discussed next.

Option-based takeover strategies

"Option to acquire" deals often are used to buy start-up firms. The acquirer uses this structure to assist the start-up in developing a product and successfully bringing it to market by providing financing and other resources (e.g., intellectual property, manufacturing facilities, management expertise). For firms at a later stage of their product life cycle, a firm may see an option to acquire structure as a means of tapping into a growth opportunity or to diversify.

Such strategies are used when the acquirer is unwilling to provide financing without the assurance that it will have the exclusive right to acquire the target firm at some future date. The premium paid for an option granted by the target firm is generally nonrefundable, and the potential acquirer may also make an equity investment in the target at some point before the option expires. At the time the option is negotiated, both the acquirer and target firms' boards and management negotiate a merger agreement. Subsequently, the target shareholders' approval is solicited and obtained. Without such approval, the acquirer does not have to pay the option fees to the target firm. This source of income is critical to satisfying the target firm's financing needs.

TABLE 11.4 Flextronics–International DisplayWorks (IDW) fixed-value and fixed-share-exchange agreements[a]

	Change (%)	Offer price	Change (%)	Offer price
		(\$6.55/\$11.73) × \$11.73 = \$6.55		(\$6.55/\$11.73) × \$11.73 = \$6.55
Fixed value	1	(\$6.55/\$11.85) × \$11.85 = \$6.55	(1)	(\$6.55/\$11.61) × \$11.61 = \$6.55
	2	(\$6.55/\$11.96) × \$11.96 = \$6.55	(2)	(\$6.55/\$11.50) × \$11.50 = \$6.55
	3	(\$6.55/\$12.08) × \$12.08 = \$6.55	(3)	(\$6.55/\$11.38) × \$11.38 = \$6.55
	4	(\$6.55/\$12.20) × \$12.20 = \$6.55	(4)	(\$6.55/\$11.26) × \$11.26 = \$6.55
	5	(\$6.55/\$12.32) × \$12.32 = \$6.55	(5)	(\$6.55/\$11.14) × \$11.14 = \$6.55
	6	(\$6.55/\$12.43) × \$12.43 = \$6.55	(6)	(\$6.55/\$11.03) × \$11.03 = \$6.55
	7	(\$6.55/\$12.55) × \$12.55 = \$6.55	(7)	(\$6.55/\$10.91) × \$10.91 = \$6.55
	8	(\$6.55/\$12.67) × \$12.67 = \$6.55	(8)	(\$6.55/\$10.79) × \$10.79 = \$6.55
	9	(\$6.55/\$12.79) × \$12.79 = \$6.55	(9)	(\$6.55/\$10.67) × \$10.67 = \$6.55
Fixed SER	10	(\$6.55/\$12.90) × \$12.90 = \$6.55	(10)	(\$6.55/\$10.56) × \$10.56 = \$6.55
	11	(\$6.55/\$12.90) × \$13.02 = \$6.61	(11)	(\$6.55/\$10.56) × \$10.44 = \$6.48
	12	(\$6.55/\$12.90) × \$13.14 = \$6.67	(12)	(\$6.55/\$10.56) × \$10.32 = \$6.40
	13	(\$6.55/\$12.90) × \$13.25 = \$6.73	(13)	(\$6.55/\$10.56) × \$10.21 = \$6.33
	14	(\$6.55/\$12.90) × \$13.37 = \$6.79	(14)	(\$6.55/\$10.56) × \$10.09 = \$6.26
	15	(\$6.55/\$12.90) × \$13.49 = \$6.85	(15)	(\$6.55/\$10.56) × \$9.97 = \$6.18
	>15	SER floats based on fixed \$6.85	>(15)	IDW may terminate agreement

[a]Offer price changes based on a 1% change from \$11.73.
SER, Share exchange ratio.

Warrant-based takeover strategies

Because warrants are issued by the target firm, an acquirer purchases a warrant from the target to acquire a newly created special class of target preferred shares at some future date. The acquirer pays the target firm the purchase price of the warrant. The target firm must change its charter documents to provide that all of its shares other than a newly issued special class of preferred stock will be redeemed by the target at some future point for a previously determined price if the acquirer exercises the warrant. When all other classes of target stock are redeemed, the only remaining shares would be the special class of preferred shares. If the acquirer chooses to exercise their warrants, it automatically owns the target firm.

Disadvantages of option and warrant takeover strategies

A major drawback of using either options or warrants is that they are very difficult to value. As noted in Chapter 8, the Black-Scholes model or some variation may be used to value these types of securities. Using this model requires knowing the volatility of the underlying stock or asset, which is unavailable for privately held stock. Under current tax laws, no tax is due on the receipt of the option premium or warrant consideration, but if they cannot be valued, the value of any increase in the shares or asset on which they are based may be taxed as ordinary income.

Form of acquisition

What acquirers purchase (target stock or assets) and how ownership is transferred from the target to the acquirer is called the form of acquisition. Each form affects the deal structure differently.[27]

An *asset purchase* involves the sale of all or a portion of the assets of the target to the buyer or its subsidiary in exchange for buyer stock, cash, debt, or some combination. The buyer may assume all, some, or none of the target's

[27] For more information on this topic, see DePamphilis (2010b), Chapter 11.

liabilities. The purchase price is paid directly to the target firm. A *stock purchase* involves the sale of the outstanding stock of the target to the buyer or its subsidiary by the target's shareholders. Unlike an asset purchase, the purchase price is paid to the target firm's shareholders. This is the biggest difference between the two methods, and it has significant tax implications for the seller's shareholders (see Chapter 12). A *statutory or direct merger* involves the combination of the target with the buyer or a subsidiary formed to complete the merger. One corporation survives the merger, and the other disappears. The surviving corporation can be the buyer, the target, or the buyer's subsidiary.

Merger terminology usually refers to the bidder as the *surviving corporation* and to the target as the *disappearing corporation*. Knowing which company is to survive is critical under merger law because of *successor liability*. This legal principle states that the surviving corporation receives by operation of law all rights and liabilities of both the bidder company and the target company in accordance with the statutes of the state where the combined businesses will be incorporated.[28] Dissenting or minority shareholders are required to sell their shares, although some state statutes grant them the right to be paid the appraised value of their shares. *Stock-for-stock* or *stock-for-assets* deals represent alternatives to a merger.

State statutes usually require shareholder approval by both the bidder and target firms in a merger. However, no acquirer shareholder vote is required if the form of payment is cash, the number of new acquirer shares issued is less than 20% of the firm's outstanding shares, or the number of shares previously authorized is sufficient to complete the deal. These exceptions are discussed in more detail later in this chapter.

The most important difference between a merger and a stock-for-stock purchase is that the latter does not require a target shareholder vote because target shareholders are giving their assent by willingly selling their shares. By purchasing all of the target's stock for acquirer stock or at least a controlling interest, the target firm is left intact as a wholly owned (or at least controlled) subsidiary of the bidder. Table 11.5 highlights the advantages and disadvantages of these alternative forms of acquisition.

Purchase of assets

A buyer in an asset purchase acquires all rights a seller has to an asset for cash, stock, or some combination. This may be the most practical way to do a deal when the acquirer is interested only in a product line or division of the parent firm that is not organized as a separate legal subsidiary. The seller retains ownership of the shares of stock of the business. Only assets and liabilities identified in the agreement of purchase and sale are transferred to the buyer.

In a *cash-for-assets* deal, the acquirer pays cash for the seller's assets and may choose to accept some or all of the seller's liabilities.[29] Seller shareholders must approve the transaction whenever the seller's board votes to sell all or "substantially all" of the firm's assets and the firm is liquidated. After paying for any liabilities not assumed by the buyer, the assets remaining with the seller and the cash received from the acquiring firm are transferred to the seller's shareholders in a liquidating distribution.[30]

In a *stock-for-assets* transaction, after approval by the seller's board and shareholders, the seller's shareholders receive buyer stock in exchange for the seller's assets and assumed liabilities. In a second stage, the seller dissolves the corporation after shareholder ratification of such a move, leaving its shareholders with buyer stock.

Advantages and disadvantages from the buyer's perspective

Buyer advantages include being able to select which assets to purchase and not being responsible for the seller's liabilities unless assumed under the contract. However, the buyer can be held responsible for certain liabilities, such

[28] Because of successor liability, the bidder can realize cost savings by not having to transfer individual target assets and liabilities separately that would have otherwise required the payment of transfer taxes. For the creditor, all of the assets of the surviving corporation are available to satisfy its liabilities due to successor liability.

[29] In cases in which the buyer purchases most of the assets of a target firm, courts have ruled that the buyer is also responsible for the target's liabilities.

[30] Selling "substantially all" assets does not necessarily mean that most of the firm's assets have been sold; rather, it could refer to a small percentage of the firm's total assets critical to the ongoing operation of the business. The firm may be forced to liquidate if a sale of assets does not leave the firm with "significant continuing business activity"—that is, at least 25% of total pretransaction operating assets and 25% of pretransaction income or revenue. Unless required by the firm's bylaws, the buyer's shareholders do not vote to approve the transaction.

TABLE 11.5 Advantages and disadvantages of alternative forms of acquisition

Alternative forms	Advantages	Disadvantages
Cash purchase of assets	Buyer • Allows selective purchase of assets • Asset write-up • May renegotiate union and benefits agreements in the absence of a successor clause[a] in the labor agreement • May avoid the need for shareholder approval • No minority shareholders Seller • Maintains corporate existence and ownership of assets not acquired • Retains NOLs and tax credits	Buyer • Loses NOLs[b] and tax credits • Loses rights to intellectual property • May require consents to assignment of contracts • Exposed to liabilities transferring with assets (e.g., warranty claims) • Subject to taxes on any gains resulting in asset write-up • Subject to lengthy documentation of assets in the contract Seller • Potential double taxation if shell is liquidated • Subject to state transfer taxes • Necessity of disposing of unwanted residual assets • Requires shareholder approval if substantially all of the firm's assets are sold
Cash purchase of stock	Buyer • Assets and liabilities transfer automatically • May avoid the need to get consents to assignment for contracts • Less documentation • NOLs and tax credits pass to buyer • No state transfer taxes • May insulate from target liabilities if kept as a subsidiary • No shareholder approval if funded by cash or debt • Enables circumvention of target's board in hostile tender offer Seller • Liabilities generally pass to the buyer • May receive favorable tax treatment if acquirer stock received in payment	Buyer • Responsible for known and unknown liabilities • No asset write-up unless 338 election is adopted by buyer and seller[c] • Union and employee benefit agreements do not terminate • Potential for minority shareholders[d] Seller • Loss of NOLs and tax credits • Favorable tax treatment is lost if buyer and seller adopt 338 election[c]
Statutory merger	Buyer • Flexible form of payment (stock, cash, or debt) • Assets and liabilities transfer automatically, without lengthy documentation • No state transfer taxes • No minority shareholders because shareholders are required to tender shares (minority freeze-out) • May avoid shareholder approval Seller • Favorable tax treatment if the purchase price is primarily in acquirer stock • Allows for continuing interest in combined companies • Flexible form of payment	Buyer • May have to pay dissenting shareholders' appraised value of stock • May be time-consuming because of the need for target shareholder and board approvals, which may delay closing Seller • May be time-consuming • Target firm often does not survive • May not qualify for favorable tax status
Stock-for-stock transaction	Buyer • May operate target company as a subsidiary • See purchase of stock above Seller • See purchase of stock above	Buyer • May postpone realization of synergies • See purchase of stock above Seller • See purchase of stock above
Stock-for-assets transaction	Buyer • See purchase of assets above	Buyer • May dilute buyer's ownership position • See purchase of assets above

TABLE 11.5 Advantages and disadvantages of alternative forms of acquisition—cont'd

Alternative forms	Advantages	Disadvantages
	Seller • See purchase of assets above	Seller • See purchase of assets above
Staged transactions	• Provides greater strategic flexibility	• May postpone realization of synergies

[a]If the labor bargaining agreement includes a "successor clause" covering the workforce in the target firm, the terms of the agreement may still apply to the workforce of the new business.
[b]Net operating loss carryforwards.
[c]In a Section 338 deal, the acquirer in a purchase of 80% or more of the target's stock may elect to treat the acquisition as if it were an acquisition of the target's assets. The seller must agree with the election.
[d]Minority shareholders in a subsidiary may be eliminated by a "backend" merger after the initial purchase of target stock. As a result, minority shareholders are required to abide by the majority vote of all shareholders and to sell their shares to the acquirer. If the acquirer owns more than 90% of the target's shares, it may be able to use a short-form merger, which does not require any shareholder vote.
NOL, Net operating loss.

as environmental claims, property taxes, and, in some states, pension liabilities and product liability claims. To protect themselves, buyers insist on indemnification that holds the seller responsible for damages resulting from such claims.[31]

Another advantage is that asset purchases enable buyers to revalue acquired assets to market value under the purchase method of accounting (see Chapter 12). This increase in the tax basis to fair market value provides for higher depreciation and amortization expense deductions for tax purposes. Absent successor clauses in the contract, the asset purchase results in the termination of union agreements if less than 50% of the workforce in the new firm is unionized, thereby providing an opportunity to renegotiate agreements viewed as too restrictive.

Among the disadvantages to an asset purchase is that the buyer loses the seller's net operating losses and tax credits as well as rights to assets such as licenses, franchises, and patents, which are viewed as owned by the target shareholders. The buyer often must seek the consent of customers and vendors to transfer existing contracts to the buyer. The deal is more complex and costly because acquired assets must be identified and listed in appendices to the definitive agreement, the sale of and titles to each asset transferred must be recorded, and state title *transfer taxes* must be paid. Finally, a lender's consent is required if the assets sold are being used as collateral for loans.

Advantages and disadvantages from the seller's perspective

Among the advantages, sellers are able to maintain their corporate existence and thus ownership of assets not acquired by the buyer. The seller retains the right to use all tax credits and accumulated net operating losses to shelter future income from taxes. Disadvantages include potential double taxation of the seller. If the tax basis in the assets is low, the seller may experience a sizeable gain on the sale; if the corporation subsequently is liquidated, the seller may be responsible for the recapture of taxes deferred as a result of the use of accelerated rather than straight-line depreciation. If the number of assets transferred is large, the amount of state transfer taxes may become onerous. Whether the seller or the buyer actually pays the transfer taxes or they are shared is negotiable.

Purchase of stock

In cash-for-stock or stock-for-stock deals, the buyer purchases the seller's stock directly from the seller's shareholders. For a public company, the acquirer would make a tender offer because public-company shareholders are likely to be too numerous to deal with individually. A purchase of stock is the approach most often taken in hostile takeovers. If the buyer is unable to convince all of the seller's shareholders to tender their shares, then a minority of seller shareholders remains. The target firm would then be viewed as a partially owned subsidiary of the acquiring company. No seller shareholder approval is required in such transactions because the seller's shareholders are expressing approval by tendering their shares.

Advantages and disadvantages from the buyer's perspective

Advantages include the automatic transfer of all assets with the target's stock, the avoidance of state asset transfer taxes, and the transfer of net operating losses and tax credits to the buyer. The purchase of the seller's stock provides

[31] Note that in most purchase agreements, buyers and sellers agree to indemnify each other from claims for which they are directly responsible. Liability under such arrangements is subject to a specific dollar limit and time period.

for the continuity of contracts and corporate identity. However, the consent of some customers and vendors may be required before a contract is transferred if it is stipulated in the contract. Although the acquirer's board normally approves any major acquisition, approval by shareholders is not required if the purchase is financed with cash or debt. If stock that has not yet been authorized is used, shareholder approval is required.

Among the disadvantages, the buyer is liable for all unknown, undisclosed, or contingent liabilities. The seller's tax basis is carried over to the buyer at historical cost[32]; therefore there is no step-up in the cost basis of assets, and no tax shelter is created. Dissenting shareholders in many states have the right to have their shares appraised, with the option of being paid the appraised value of their shares, or to remain minority shareholders. The purchase of stock does not terminate existing union agreements or employee benefit plans. The existence of minority shareholders creates significant administrative costs and practical concerns.[33]

Advantages and disadvantages from the seller's perspective

Sellers often prefer a stock purchase to an asset purchase because the seller is free of future obligations, because all liabilities transfer to the buyer, and the seller is able to defer paying taxes if payment is mostly buyer stock. Disadvantages for the seller include the inability to retain certain assets and the loss of net operating losses, tax credits, and intellectual property rights.

Mergers

In a merger, two or more firms combine, with only one surviving. Unlike purchases of target stock, mergers require approval of both the target's and acquirer's boards and are subsequently submitted to both firms' shareholders for approval. There are some exceptions for acquirers, which are addressed later in this chapter. Usually, a simple majority of all the outstanding voting shares must ratify the proposal, which is then registered with the appropriate state authority. Such deal structures are sometimes called one-step or long-form mergers.

Statutory and subsidiary mergers

In a statutory merger, the acquiring company assumes the assets and liabilities of the target in accordance with the statutes of the state in which the combined firms will be incorporated. A subsidiary merger involves the target becoming a subsidiary of the parent. To the public, the target firm may be operated under its brand name but will be owned and controlled by the acquirer. Most mergers are structured as subsidiary mergers in which the acquiring firm creates a new corporate subsidiary that merges with the target.

Statutory consolidations

Unlike a merger in which the target or acquirer survives, a statutory consolidation requires all legal entities to be consolidated into a new company, usually with a new name. The new company assumes ownership of the assets and liabilities of the consolidated organizations. Stockholders in merged companies exchange their shares for shares in the new company.

Mergers of equals

A merger of equals is a deal structure usually applied whenever the participants are comparable in size, competitive position, profitability, and market capitalization—which can make it unclear whether one party is ceding control to the other and which party provides the greater synergy. Consequently, target firm shareholders rarely receive any significant premium for their shares. The new firm often is managed by the CEOs of the merged firms as co-equals and for the new firm's board to have equal representation from the boards of the merged firms. It is uncommon for the ownership split to be equally divided. In mergers of equals, each firm's shareholders exchange their shares for new shares in the combined firms. The number of new company shares each shareholder receives depends on the desired pro forma ownership distribution in the new company after closing and the relative contribution to potential synergy by each firm.

Mergers of equals are rare. To reach agreement, one firm will acquire another and in the merger agreement stipulate the takeover as a merger of equals even when the target is in reality ceding control to the acquirer. Why the

[32] This is true unless the seller consents to take a Section 338 tax code election, which can create a tax liability for the seller. See Chapter 12 for more detail.

[33] The parent incurs significant additional expenses to submit annual reports, hold annual shareholder meetings, and conduct a formal board election process. Furthermore, implementing strategic decisions may be inhibited by lawsuits initiated by disaffected minority shareholders.

charade? Being taken over often has negative connotations. So, making it appear that both firms are equal "partners" makes the deal more acceptable to the target's board and senior managers. From a legal perspective, no change of control has taken place.

Tender offers

An alternative to a traditional one-step (or long-form) merger is the two-step merger. In the first step, the acquirer buys through a stock purchase the majority of the target's outstanding stock from its shareholders in a tender offer. The second step involves a squeeze-out, freeze-out merger, or backend merger approved by the acquirer as majority shareholder. Minority shareholders are required to tender their shares.

The two-step merger usually is faster (if the buyer can get enough votes in the tender offer to qualify for a short-form merger) than the more traditional one-step merger, which requires shareholder approval (with some exceptions) by both acquirer and target shareholders. The one-step merger process may take several months to close as a proxy statement must be prepared and reviewed by the Securities and Exchange Commission (SEC) and mailed to shareholders, and a shareholder vote must be obtained. The lengthy process creates uncertainty due to possible competing bids.

In the past, if the buyer failed to own 90% of the target's stock after the tender, the buyer was not permitted to use a short-form merger, which requires a target board but not shareholder approval. In 2013, Delaware General Corporation Law was amended to include Section 251(h) permitting backend mergers under certain conditions[34] to be completed after a tender offer enabling the buyer to acquire at least enough target shares to approve the merger (but less than the 90% required to use a short-form merger). This means that backend mergers can now be implemented without the lengthy process required by the SEC.

Although Section 251(h) of Delaware General Corporate Law makes the two-step merger more attractive for M&A deals involving public companies, one-step (long-form) mergers may still make sense in other instances. Deals subject to extensive regulatory review and delay may benefit from the one-step process in which shareholder approval is obtained as soon as possible rather than allowing a tender offer to be subject to the receipt of regulatory approval. The shareholder approval eliminates the ability of the target's board to accept a competing bid. With a tender offer contingent on receiving approval by regulators, the target's board could accept competing bids. Other instances include the target's charter requiring a shareholder vote on all merger deals and when the target's shares are not publicly traded.

Shareholder approvals

Target shareholders must give consent if all or "substantially all" of the firm's assets are being acquired.[35] Although no acquirer shareholder vote is mandatory when the form of payment is cash because there is no dilution of current shareholders, there are certain instances in which no vote is required by the acquirer's shareholders in share exchanges.

The first, the so-called small-scale merger exception, involves a deal not considered material.[36] The second, a short-form merger or the parent-submerger exception, occurs when a subsidiary is merged into the parent and the parent owns a substantial majority (more than 90% in some states) of the subsidiary's stock before the deal. The third exception involves use of a triangular merger, in which the acquirer establishes a merger subsidiary in which it is the sole shareholder. The only approval required is that of the subsidiary's board, which may be the

[34] The target must be listed on a national public exchange with at least 2000 shareholders and the buyer must be a corporation, the target's certificate of incorporation must not require shareholder approval for mergers, and the merger agreement must stipulate a provision requiring a backend merger as soon as practicable after the tender offer. After the tender offer, the buyer must own at least the number of target shares required to adopt the merger agreement, usually a simple majority; the consideration in the second step must be in the same amount and form as paid to shareholders in the first step; and no single target shareholder when the merger agreement is approved by the target's board may own 15% or more of the target's shares.

[35] "Substantially all" refers to asset sales critical to the ongoing operation of the business. Target shareholders do not get approval rights in short-form mergers in which the parent owns more than 90% of a subsidiary's stock.

[36] Acquiring firm shareholders cannot vote unless their ownership in the acquiring firm is diluted by more than one sixth, or 16.67% (i.e., acquirer owns at least 83.33% of the firm's voting shares after closing). This effectively limits the acquirer to issuing no more than 20% of its total shares outstanding. For example, if the acquirer has 80 million shares outstanding and issues 16 million new shares (i.e., 0.2×80 million), its current shareholders are not diluted by more than one-sixth [i.e., 16/(16 million + 80 million) equals one sixth, or 16.67%]. Issuing more than 16 million new shares would violate the small-scale merger exception.

same as the parent or acquirer.[37] Finally, no shareholder approval is needed if the number of shares previously authorized under the firm's articles of incorporation is sufficient to complete the deal.

Top-up options and dual-track deal structures

Such options are granted by the target to the bidding firm, whose tender offer is less than the 90% threshold to qualify as a short-form merger, to buy up newly issued target shares to reach the threshold. Because the option ensures that the merger will be approved, the bidder benefits by avoiding the delay associated with backend mergers requiring a shareholder vote. The target firm benefits by eliminating potential changes in the value of the bidder's shares that are offered in exchange for target shares that could occur between signing and closing.

Dual-track deal structures include a two-step tender offer and the filing of preliminary proxy materials for a one-step merger. The intent is to minimize the risk of a delayed backend merger if the tender offer does not reach 90%. The dual track can be just as time-consuming and expensive as using a tender offer in the first step and a long-form merger in the second step.

Special applications of basic structures

The two-step merger is popular in *leveraged buyouts* because of the potential for faster closing. A financial sponsor (equity investor) creates a shell corporation funded by equity from the sponsor. After raising additional cash by borrowing from banks and selling debt to institutional investors, the shell corporation buys at least 90% of the target's stock for the deal to qualify as a short-form merger, squeezing out minority shareholders with a backend merger.[38]

Single-firm recapitalizations are used by controlling shareholders to squeeze out minority shareholders. To do so, a firm creates a wholly owned shell corporation and merges itself into the shell in a statutory merger. Stock in the original firm is cancelled, with the majority shareholders receiving stock in the surviving firm and minority shareholders receiving cash or debt.

Staged transactions involve an acquirer's completing a takeover in stages spread over an extended period. They may be used to structure an earnout, enable the target to complete the development of a technology or process, or await regulatory approval of a license or patent.

Some things to remember

Deal-structuring entails satisfying the key objectives of the parties involved and how risk will be shared. The process defines initial negotiating positions, risks, options for managing risk, levels of risk tolerance, and conditions under which the buyer or seller will "walk away" from the deal.

Chapter discussion questions

11.1 What are the advantages and disadvantages of a purchase of assets from the perspective of the buyer and the seller?
11.2 What are the advantages and disadvantages of a purchase of stock from the perspective of the buyer and the seller?
11.3 What are the advantages and disadvantages of a statutory merger?
11.4 What are the reasons acquirers choose to undertake a staged or multistep takeover?
11.5 What forms of acquisition represent common alternatives to a merger? When would these alternative structures be employed?

[37] The listing requirements of all major US stock exchanges may still force acquirer shareholder approval if the number of new shares issued to finance the transaction is greater than or equal to 20% of the acquirer's common shares outstanding before the deal. Such deals are deemed to be material.

[38] Alternatively, the buyout firm could negotiate with the board of the target firm for a top-up option to be exercised if 90% of the target's shares cannot be acquired in the first step tender offer.

11.6 Comment on the following statement: A premium offered by a bidder over a target's share price is not necessarily a fair price; a fair price is not necessarily an adequate price.

11.7 In a year marked by turmoil in the global credit markets, Mars Corporation was able to negotiate a reverse breakup fee structure in its acquisition of Wrigley Corporation. This structure allowed Mars to walk away from the transaction at any time by paying a $1 billion fee to Wrigley. Speculate as to the motivation behind Mars' and Wrigley's negotiating such a fee.

11.8 Despite disturbing discoveries during due diligence, Mattel acquired The Learning Company (TLC), a leading developer of software for toys, in a stock exchange valued at $3.5 billion. Mattel had determined that TLC's receivables were overstated because product returns from distributors were not deducted from receivables and its allowance for bad debt was inadequate. Also, a $50 million licensing deal also had been prematurely put on the balance sheet. Nevertheless, driven by the appeal of becoming a big player in the children's software market rapidly, Mattel closed on the transaction, aware that TLC's cash flows were overstated. Despite being aware of extensive problems, Mattel proceeded to acquire TCL. Why? What could Mattel have done to protect its interests better? Be specific.

11.9 Describe the conditions under which an earnout may be most appropriate.

11.10 Deutsche Bank announced that it would buy the commercial banking assets (including a number of branches) of the Netherlands' ABN Amro for $1.13 billion. What liabilities, if any, would Deutsche Bank have to (or want to) assume? Explain your answer.

Solutions to these Chapter Discussion Questions are found in the Online Instructor's Manual for instructors using this book.

End-of-chapter case study: Disney's bold move in the direct-to-consumer video business

Case study objectives

To illustrate

- How M&As can be used to respond to emerging strategic threats
- The role of "collar arrangements" in deal structuring
- The use of form of payment and acquisition as a bidding strategy
- How competitive bidding can drive up purchase prices when targets are considered critical to a bidder's business strategy

The Walt Disney Company (Disney) watched as viewership to its cable channels, including its one-time powerhouse ESPN, dropped as consumers "cut the cord." Many consumers have opted for subscriptions to Netflix or Amazon, which offered more diverse video at a fraction of the cost of cable. In a daring move, Disney announced a major media takeover in late 2017 but was unable to seal the deal until early 2019 because of a bewildering array of twists and turns.

Disney's board and chairman and CEO, Bob Iger, recognized the need for bold action. They reasoned that by building up an impressive array of programming the firm could ward off efforts by these competitors' to penetrate the content market. With enough material, so the thinking goes, Disney could develop a streaming service that would win over customers who would have otherwise moved away from Disney products.

Rupert Murdoch, chairman and CEO of 21st Century Fox (Fox), a Disney competitor, was dealing with challenges similar to those confronting Disney. After AT&T's takeover of Time Warner, the value of entertainment assets had exploded. The timing was right for Fox to sell off its entertainment assets and focus on its news businesses. Fox News and Fox Business were included as part of most basic cable bundles and were vulnerable to consumer cord-cutting. The major threats to Fox are free-access platforms such as Facebook, which have become a common source of news for many people. Murdoch hoped that by offering live news and sports and a strong broadcast network, Fox could remain competitive in the changing media landscape.

American telecommunications conglomerate Comcast Corp's (Comcast) strategy involved accumulating content for resale to consumers. The firm had been in discussions with Fox in early 2017 to acquire its entertainment assets. But interest in Fox would soon heat up as Comcast's negotiation with Fox attracted Disney as an alternative bidder.

After several rounds of bidding, Disney announced on December 14, 2017, that it had reached an agreement to acquire the majority of the Fox's entertainment assets. As part of the all-stock deal, Disney would also acquire

Fox's 30% stake in Hulu (a website offering video streaming to consumers), a group of US cable stations, several powerhouse international satellite channels (Star India and Sky Italia), and a host of US regional sports outlets. Disney agreed to pay $52.8 billion for Fox, excluding the firm's news broadcast networks, the Fox News Channel and Fox Business channel, the Fox studio lot in Los Angeles, and several national sports channels. These assets would be retained by Fox chairman Rupert Murdoch and his family. The combined annual revenue of the two firms' exceeded $75 billion, with one-third coming from Fox.

Disney's bid for Fox hit a snag when on June 12, 2018, Comcast reentered the fray, making a $65 billion counteroffer for Fox, after AT&T's $81 billion takeover of Time Warner was approved by regulators, making it clear that Comcast's bid could receive approval. A week later, Disney raised its bid to $71.3 billion, consisting of both cash and stock, forcing Comcast to back out. The changed composition of the purchase price was intended to broaden its appeal to more Fox shareholders. And the size of the eye-popping bid was intended to force the debt-laden Comcast out of the bidding because Disney believed Comcast would not be able to match it.

After all the regulatory bodies approved the deal, closing was imminent. Disney announced on March 19, 2019, that the value of the cash and stock merger was $51.73 per Fox share for a total purchase price of $71.3 billion. The acquisition was effective on March 20, 2019. The stock portion of the total consideration was subject to a collar and would be tax-free to Fox shareholders. Disney also acquired about $19.8 billion in cash and assumed $19.2 billion of Fox debt, resulting in an enterprise value of $70.7 billion (i.e., $71.3 plus $19.2 billion less $19.8 billion). The deal was expected to yield $2 billion in cost savings by 2021.

Disney's share price had been flat or down since the deal was unveiled, but it had been trending up since mid-February 2019 in anticipation of the deal closing. The collar on the stock consideration ensured that Fox shareholders would receive a number of (or fraction of) Disney shares equal to $38 if the average Disney stock price at closing was between $93.53 and $114.32. Fox shareholders would receive an exchange ratio of 0.3324 shares of Disney common stock if the average price of Disney stock during the 20 trading days before closing was above $114.32 and 0.4063 shares of Disney common if the average Disney share price at closing was below $95.53. At closing, Disney's average share price topped the upper limit of the collar.

Figure 11.2 illustrates how 21st Century Fox split in two: New Fox (containing news assets excluded from the transaction) and Old Fox (containing entertainment assets included in the deal). New Fox became a publicly traded firm owned by former 21st Century Fox shareholders, and Old Fox was sold to Disney.

The Disney holding company (New Disney) owned two subsidiaries: 21st Century Merger Sub and Old Disney (a subsidiary which owned preclosing Disney assets). Immediately before closing, 21st Century Fox (the parent) initiated a "separation agreement" to transfer certain news assets to New Fox which paid the parent a dividend of $8.5 billion. The dividend reflected repayment of money transfers between the parent and its news subsidiaries in the

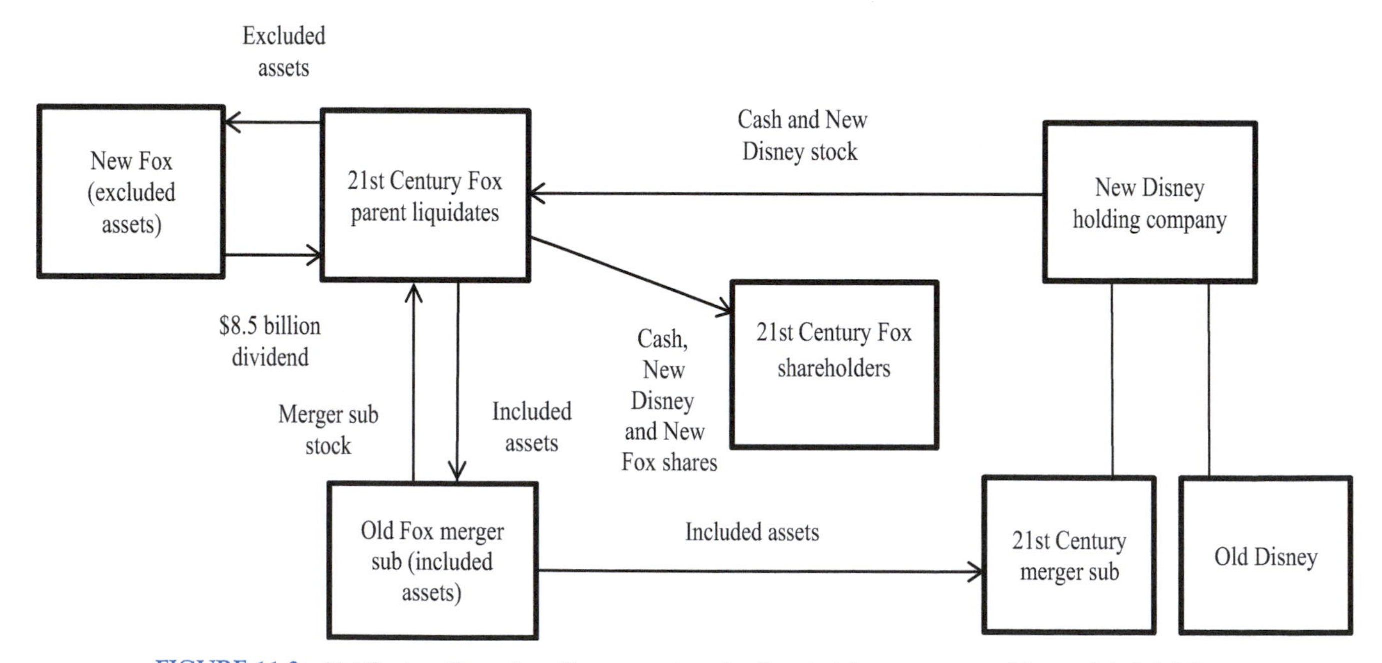

FIGURE 11.2 21st Century Fox spins off news assets and sells entertainment assets to Disney. *Sub*, Subsidiary.

form of intercompany loans and dividends, adjusted at closing based on the final estimate of transaction related taxes paid. The parent's liquidation involved the distribution on a pro rata basis to 21st Century Fox shareholders New Fox stock and newly issued Disney shares and cash paid to the parent to acquire Old Fox. At closing, Old Fox Merger Sub was merged into 21st Century Merger Sub, with the latter surviving. Old Disney and 21st Century Merger Sub were then merged into New Disney. Upon completion of the merger into New Disney, both Old Disney and New Fox shares were converted into New Disney shares.

Discussion questions

1. What is the form of acquisition used in this deal? What are the advantages and disadvantages of this deal structure?
2. What is the form of payment used to acquire the Fox entertainment assets? Speculate why this form may have been used in this instance.
3. Would you consider Disney's purchase of Fox's entertainment assets as a vertical or horizontal takeover? Explain your answer.
4. What is the purpose of a collar arrangement? Is the collar used by Disney a fixed share-exchange ratio or a fixed-value agreement? How does the collar arrangement used in this deal impact Disney and Fox shareholders?

Solutions to these questions are provided in the Online Instructor's Manual for instructors using this book.

CHAPTER

12

Structuring the deal: tax and accounting considerations

OUTLINE

Mergers, Acquisitions, and Other Restructuring Activities, Eleventh Edition
https://doi.org/10.1016/B978-0-12-819782-0.00012-5

When people find they can vote themselves money, that will herald the end of the republic. —***Benjamin Franklin***

Inside M&A: megamerger creates the world's second-largest aerospace and defense contractor

KEY POINTS

- Deal structures can avoid shareholder votes and ensure that valuable rights are transferred to the acquirer.
- The form of payment determines the tax status of a deal for target shareholders.
- Acquirer stock is commonly used if the deal cannot be financed through borrowing.

Pressure from the Defense Department to cut costs is driving consolidation in the US defense industry. In response, United Technologies Corp. (UT) and Raytheon Co. (Raytheon) agree to merge their operations in mid-2019 in an all-stock deal valued at more than $100 billion. Structured as a merger of equals, the deal will create the second-largest aerospace and defense company ranked by revenue, behind Boeing Corp. The new firm will be named Raytheon Technologies Corp and does not include a takeover premium. The scale achieved in combining the two firms provides greater negotiating leverage with suppliers, opportunities to cut overhead, and cash flow to invest in advanced technologies.

The "merger of equals" moniker is critical to achieving a merger agreement. Why? Neither board has to concede publicly that they are the target because shareholders often see this as a failure of the board's strategy. From a legal standpoint, one of the two parties must be designated as the acquirer and the other the target because the acquirer buying the target's equity is subject to successor liability. That is, the acquirer is responsible for the target's current and future liabilities.

As a practical matter, the acquirer is usually the one who gains control. Because UT shareholders will own 57% of the new company, it is cited as the acquirer in the merger agreement. Because it is difficult to determine which firm is providing the most synergy, Raytheon shareholders do not receive a premium. UT appoints 8 of the 15 board members, with the remainder former Raytheon board members. UT's current CEO will serve as the CEO of the merged firms.

To transfer ownership, UT creates a wholly owned subsidiary, Merger Sub, which is merged with Raytheon at closing, with Raytheon surviving. Known as a reverse triangular merger, this structure eliminates the need for UT shareholder approval because UT is the sole shareholder in Merger Sub. As the survivor, Raytheon retains franchise, lease, and other valuable contract rights that otherwise may have required permission from owners of such rights to transfer them to UT.

Acquired Raytheon assets and assumed liabilities are recorded at their fair values on the combined firms' balance sheet using the acquisition method of accounting. The excess of the purchase price (PP) over the value of acquired assets less assumed liabilities is recorded as goodwill on the balance sheet. Goodwill is the value perceived by the buyer of synergy, brand name, contracts, and so on. Structured as a share exchange, the deal is tax free to Raytheon shareholders: taxes on capital gains are not due until the shares are sold. If the shares have been held more than 1 year, gains will be treated at the more favorable capital gains tax rate.

Chapter overview

Do taxes and accounting considerations affect mergers and acquisitions (M&A) valuation, deal structuring, and financing? The answer is a resounding yes! Despite the importance of taxes and accounting, the main theme of this chapter is that the fundamental economics of a transaction should always be the deciding factor in whether or not to do a deal. A review of this chapter (including practice questions and answers) is available in the file folder titled "Student Study Guide" on the companion website to this book (https://www.elsevier.com/books-and-journals/book-companion/9780128197820).

Understanding tax authority communications

An Internal Revenue Service (IRS) *regulation* provides guidance for new laws or issues arising from the existing sections of the Internal Revenue Code (IRC). Final regulations are published in the *Federal Register* after public commentary. A *revenue ruling* is an IRS interpretation of the IRC representing how it believes the law should be applied. A *private letter ruling* is a written statement issued to a taxpayer interpreting how the laws should be applied in their situation. A *technical advice memorandum* is guidance from the Office of Chief Counsel in response to specific technical questions.

Alternative tax structures

Tax considerations generally are less important for buyers than for sellers. Buyers are concerned primarily with determining the basis of the acquired assets and avoiding any liability for tax problems the target may have, as well as gaining access to the target's tax credits and loss carryforwards. The tax basis determines future taxable gains for the buyer in the event such assets are sold and also the level from which they may be depreciated. In contrast, the seller usually is concerned about how to structure the deal to defer the payment of any taxes owed. Table 12.1 summarizes the most commonly used taxable and tax-free structures. The implications of these alternative structures are explored in detail in the following sections.

Taxable transactions

A deal is taxable to target shareholders if it involves purchasing the target's stock or assets using mostly cash, debt, or nonequity consideration.[1] Taxable deals include a cash purchase of target assets, a cash purchase of target stock, or a statutory cash merger or consolidation, which commonly includes direct cash mergers and triangular forward and reverse cash mergers.

TABLE 12.1 Alternative taxable and nontaxable structures

Taxable transactions: immediately taxable to target shareholders	Nontaxable transactions: tax deferred to target shareholders
1. Purchase of assets with cash[a]	**1.** Type A reorganization
2. Purchase of stock with cash	**a.** Statutory stock merger or consolidation (mostly acquirer stock for stock)[b]
3. Statutory cash mergers and consolidations	**b.** Forward triangular merger (asset purchase)
a. Direct merger (cash for stock)	**c.** Reverse triangular merger (stock purchase)
b. Forward triangular merger (cash for assets)	**2.** Type B reorganization (stock for stock)
c. Reverse triangular merger (cash for stock)	**3.** Type C reorganization (stock for assets)
	4. Type D divisive merger

[a]The form of payment consists mostly of consideration other than acquirer stock. Such consideration sometimes is called *boot* and could consist of cash, debt, or other nonequity compensation.
[b]Acquirer stock usually comprises 50% or more of the total consideration. The exception for type A reorganizations is for reverse triangular mergers.

[1] *Nonequity, cash,* and *boot* are terms used to describe forms of payment other than acquirer equity.

Taxable mergers

In a direct statutory cash merger (i.e., the form of payment is cash), the acquirer and target boards reach a negotiated settlement; and both firms, with certain exceptions, must receive approval from their respective shareholders. The target is then merged into the acquirer or the acquirer into the target, with only one surviving. Assets and liabilities on and off the balance sheet automatically transfer to the surviving firm. To protect themselves from target liabilities, acquirers use so-called triangular mergers: the target is merged into an acquirer's operating or shell merger subsidiary, with the subsidiary surviving (forward triangular cash merger), or the subsidiary is merged into the target, with the target surviving (reverse triangular cash merger). Direct cash and forward triangular mergers are treated as a taxable purchase of assets, with cash and reverse triangular mergers treated as a taxable purchase of stock with cash.

Taxable purchase of target assets with cash

If a deal involves a cash purchase of target assets, the target's tax cost or basis in the acquired assets is increased, or "stepped up," to its fair market value (FMV), equal to the purchase price (less any assumed liabilities) paid by the acquirer. The additional depreciation in future years reduces the present value (PV) of the tax liability of the combined firms. The target realizes an immediate gain or loss on assets sold equal to the difference between the asset's FMV and net book value.

The target's shareholders could be taxed twice—once when the firm pays taxes on any gains and again when the proceeds from the sale are paid to the shareholders as either a dividend or a distribution following liquidation of the corporation. A liquidation of the target firm may occur if a buyer acquires enough of the assets of the target to cause it to cease operations.[2] Taxable transactions have become somewhat more attractive to acquiring firms since 1993, when a change in legislation allowed acquirers to amortize certain intangible assets for tax purposes.[3]

Taxable purchase of target stock with cash

Taxable transactions involve the purchase of the target's voting stock to avoid double taxation of gains to the target's shareholders. An asset purchase automatically triggers a tax on any gain on the sale by the target firm and another tax on any payment of the after-tax proceeds to shareholders. Taxable stock purchases avoid double taxation because the transaction takes place between the acquirer and the target firm's shareholders. Target shareholders may realize a gain or loss on the sale of their stock. Assets may not be stepped up to their FMV in these types of transactions. Because from the IRS's viewpoint the target firm continues to exist, the target's investment tax credits and net operating losses (NOLs) may be used by the acquirer, but their use may be limited by Sections 382 and 383 of the IRC. These are explained in more detail later in this chapter. Table 12.2 summarizes the features of various forms of taxable deals.

Section 338 election

The acquirer and target can jointly elect Section 338 of the IRC, allowing the buyer to record acquired assets and liabilities at their FMV for tax purposes. This allows a buyer of 80% or more of the voting stock and market value of the target to treat the acquisition of stock as an asset purchase. The target's net acquired assets (i.e., acquired assets

[2] The IRS views deals resulting in the liquidation of the target as actual sales rather than reorganizations, in which the target shareholders have an ongoing interest in the combined firms. Thus the target's tax attributes (e.g., tax credits) may not be used by the acquirer following closing because they cease to exist along with the target.

[3] Intangible assets are addressed under Section 197 of the IRC. Such assets include goodwill, going concern value, books and records, customer lists, licenses, permits, franchises, and trademarks and must be amortized over 15 years for tax purposes. Although no immediate loss on goodwill can be recognized for tax purposes, the basis of other intangible assets purchased in the same transaction giving rise to goodwill must be increased by the amount of the goodwill write-down. The resulting write-up of these intangible assets is then amortized over their remaining amortizable lives. Moreover, changes to the US tax code in 2017 allow operating losses to be used to reduce future tax liabilities for an indefinite period.

TABLE 12.2 Key characteristics of alternative transaction structures that are taxable (to target shareholders)

Transaction structure	Form of payment	Acquirer retains tax attributes of target	Target survives?	Parent exposure to target liabilities	Shareholder vote required?		Minority freeze out?	Automatic transfer of contracts?[b]
					Acquirer	Target		
Cash purchase of stock	Mostly cash, debt, or other nonequity payment	Yes, assuming no asset step-up because of 338 election[a]	Yes	High	No[d]	No, but shareholders may not sell shares	No	Yes
Cash purchase of assets	Mostly cash, debt, or other nonequity payment	No, but can step up assets (tax attributes used to offset taxable gains)	Perhaps[c]	Low, except for assumed liabilities	No[d]	Yes, if sale of assets is substantial	No minority created	No
Statutory cash merger or consolidation	Mostly cash, debt, or other nonequity payment	Yes, but no step-up in assets	No, if target merged into acquirer	High, if target merged into acquirer	Yes	Yes	Yes[e]	Yes
Forward triangular cash merger (IRS views as asset purchase)	Mostly cash, debt, or other nonequity payment	No, but can step up assets (tax attributes used to offset taxable gains)	No	Low—limited by subsidiary relationship	No[d]	Yes	Yes	No
Reverse triangular cash merger (IRS views as stock purchase)	Mostly cash, debt, or other nonequity payment	Yes	Yes	Low—limited by subsidiary relationship	No[d]	Yes	Yes	Yes

[a]An acquirer may treat a stock purchase as an asset purchase if it and the target agree to invoke a Section 338 election. Such an election would allow a step-up in net acquired assets and result in the loss of the target's tax attributes because the target is viewed by the Internal Revenue Service (IRS) as having been liquidated.
[b]Contracts, leases, licenses, and rights to intellectual property automatically transfer unless contracts stipulate that consent to assignment is required.
[c]The target may choose to liquidate if the sale of assets is substantial and to distribute the proceeds to its shareholders or to continue as a shell.
[d]May be required by public stock exchanges or by legal counsel if deemed material to the acquiring firm or if the parent needs to authorize new stock. In practice, most big mergers require shareholder approval.
[e]Target shareholders must accept terms because of a merger, although in some states, dissident shareholders have appraisal rights for their shares.

less assumed target liabilities) are increased to their FMV, triggering a taxable gain when the deal is completed.[4] For legal purposes, the sale of target stock under a 338 election still is treated as a purchase of stock by the buyer, allowing target shareholders to defer the payment of taxes on any gains until they sell their shares. Section 338 elections are rare as the tax liability triggered by the transaction often exceeds the PV of the tax savings. A 338 election is most useful when the target has substantial NOLs or tax credit carryovers that the acquirer can use to offset any taxable gain triggered by the transaction.

Tax-free transactions

A deal is tax free if the form of payment is mostly acquirer stock and may be partially taxable if target shareholders receive something other than equity. This nonequity consideration is taxable as ordinary income. Tax-free deals do not allow for a step-up of net acquired assets to FMV.

Qualifying a transaction for tax-free treatment

To qualify as tax free, a deal must satisfy certain conditions: continuity of ownership interests, continuity of business enterprise, valid business purpose, and the step-transaction doctrine. To demonstrate *continuity of ownership interests*, target shareholders must own a substantial part of the value of the combined firms, which requires the purchase price to consist mostly of acquirer stock. *Continuity of business enterprise* requires the acquirer to use a significant portion of the target's "historic business assets" in a business[5] to demonstrate a long-term commitment by the acquirer to the target. This usually means an acquirer must buy "substantially all" of the target's assets. Furthermore, the transaction must have a *valid business purpose*, such as maximizing acquirer profits, rather than only for tax avoidance. Finally, under the *step-transaction doctrine*, the deal cannot be part of a larger plan that would have resulted in a taxable deal.[6] Tax-free deals are also called tax-free reorganizations. Failure to satisfy these conditions prevents transactions that more closely resemble a sale from qualifying as a tax-free reorganization.

Alternative tax-free reorganizations

The most common is the type A reorganization used in direct statutory mergers or consolidations (mostly acquirer stock for target stock), forward triangular mergers (asset purchases), and reverse triangular mergers (stock purchases). Type B reorganizations are stock-for-stock acquisitions, and type C reorganizations are stock-for-assets acquisitions. Type D reorganizations may be applied to acquisitions or restructuring.[7]

For a *type A statutory merger* (Fig. 12.1) or *consolidation* (Fig. 12.2), payment can include cash, voting or nonvoting common or preferred stock, notes, or some combination. At least 50% of the purchase price must be acquirer stock to satisfy the IRS requirement of continuity of interests. Type A reorganizations are widely used because there is no requirement to use voting stock, and acquirers avoid dilution by issuing nonvoting shares. The buyer may acquire less than 100% of the target's net assets. Finally, there is no limit on the amount of cash used in the purchase price, as is true of Type B and C reorganizations. Because some target shareholders will want cash, some stock, and some both, the acquirer is better able to satisfy the different needs of the target shareholders than in other types of reorganizations.

With a *type A forward triangular stock merger*, the parent funds the shell corporation by buying stock issued by the shell with its own stock (Fig. 12.3). All of the target's stock is acquired by the subsidiary with the parent's stock,

[4] Benefits to the acquirer of a 338 election include not having to transfer assets and obtain consents to assignment of contracts (as would be required in a direct purchase of assets) while still benefiting from asset write-ups. Asset transfer, sales, and use taxes are avoided. Either the acquirer or target must pay the taxes on any gain on the sale.

[5] The acquirer must purchase assets critical to continuing the target's business. Acquirers often purchase at least 80% of the target's assets to ensure that they are in compliance with IRS guidelines.

[6] The step-transaction doctrine might be applied by the IRS as follows: firm A buys the stock or assets of firm B with its stock and describes it as a tax-free deal. A year later, it sells firm B. The IRS may disallow the original deal as tax free, arguing that the merger and subsequent sale were part of a larger plan to postpone the payment of taxes.

[7] A type D reorganization requires that the acquirer receive at least 80% of the target's stock in exchange for the acquirer's voting stock. Divisive type D reorganizations are used in spin-offs, split-offs, and split-ups and involve a firm's transferring all or some of its assets to a subsidiary it controls in exchange for subsidiary stock or securities.

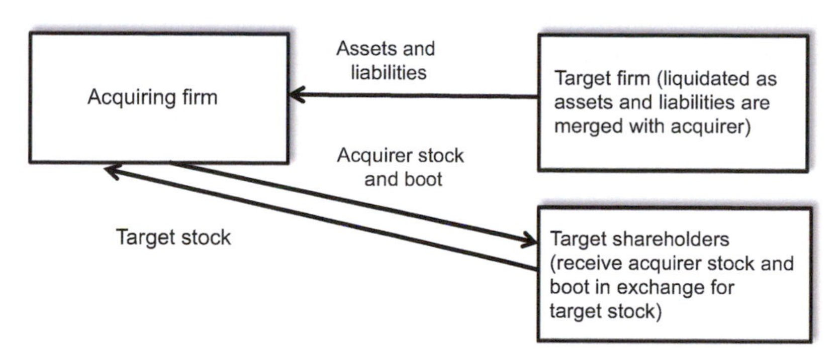

FIGURE 12.1 Direct statutory stock merger (type A reorganization). Note: This figure depicts the acquirer surviving. In practice, either the acquirer or the target could survive the merger.

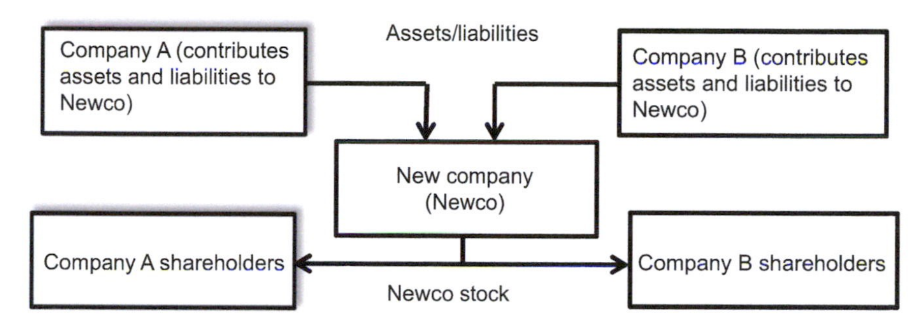

FIGURE 12.2 Statutory stock consolidation (type A reorganization).

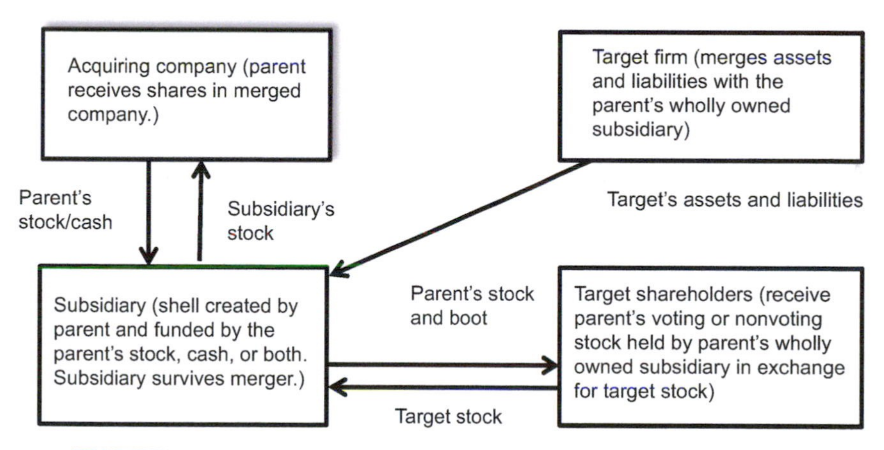

FIGURE 12.3 A forward triangular stock merger (type A reorganization).

the target's stock is cancelled, the acquirer subsidiary survives, and the target's assets and liabilities are merged into the subsidiary. The IRS views such deals as an asset purchase because the target does not survive. The parent's stock may be voting or nonvoting, and the acquirer must purchase "substantially all" of the target's assets and liabilities (defined as at least 70% and 90% of the FMV of the target's gross and net assets, respectively).[8] At least 50% of the purchase price must consist of acquirer stock.

The advantages of the forward triangular merger include the flexible form of payment and avoidance of approval by the parent firm's shareholders. Public exchanges still may require shareholder approval if the amount of the parent stock used to acquire the target exceeds 20% of the parent's voting shares outstanding. Other advantages

[8] Target asset sales before the deal threaten the tax-free status if it is viewed as a violation of the step doctrine. Tax-free deals such as spin-offs are often disallowed within 2 years before or after the merger.

include the possible insulation of the parent from target liabilities, which remain in the subsidiary, and the avoidance of asset transfer taxes because the target's assets go directly to the parent's wholly owned subsidiary. The target's tax attributes that transfer to the buyer are subject to limitation. Because the target disappears, contract rights do not automatically transfer to the acquirer, which must obtain the consent of the other parties to the contracts to reassign them to the buyer.

With a *type A reverse triangular stock merger*, the acquirer forms a shell subsidiary, which is merged into the target (Fig. 12.4). As the survivor, the target becomes the acquirer's wholly owned subsidiary. The target's shares are cancelled, and target shareholders receive the parent's shares. The parent, who owned all of the subsidiary stock, now owns all of the new target stock and, indirectly, all of the target's assets and liabilities. At least 80% of the total consideration paid to the target must be acquirer voting common or preferred stock for the transaction to be tax free to target shareholders. The IRS views reverse triangular mergers as a purchase of stock because the target survives the transaction.

The reverse triangular merger may eliminate the need for parent firm shareholder approval because the parent is the sole shareholder in the subsidiary. Because the target survives, it retains any nonassignable franchise, lease, or other valuable contract rights. By not dissolving the target, the acquirer avoids accelerating[9] the repayment of loans outstanding. Insurance, banking, and public utility regulators may require the target to remain in existence. The major drawback is the need to use acquirer voting shares to buy at least 80% of the target's outstanding shares.

In a *type B stock-for-stock reorganization*, the acquirer must use voting common or preferred stock to buy at least 80% of the target's voting and nonvoting stock in a tender offer (Fig. 12.5). Any cash or debt disqualifies the deal as a type

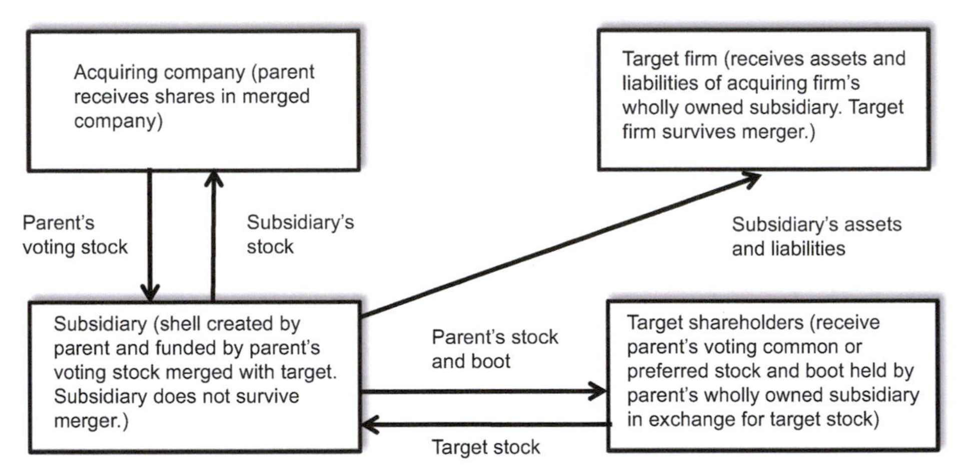

FIGURE 12.4 Type A reverse triangular stock merger (type A reorganization).

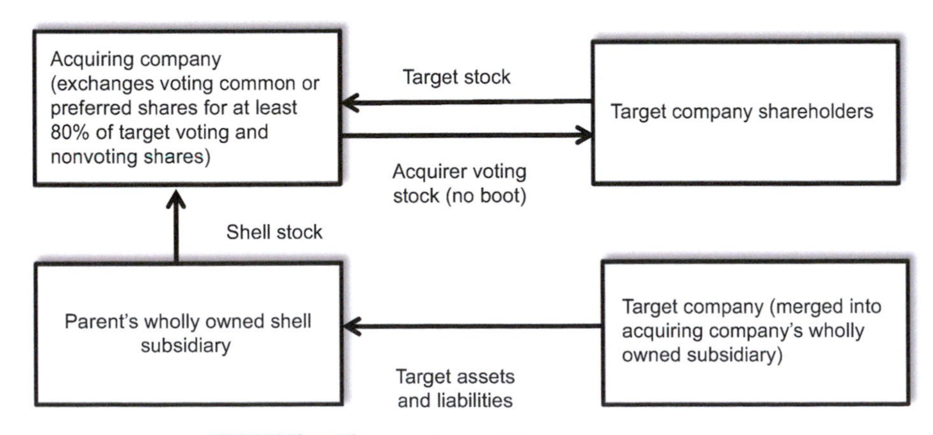

FIGURE 12.5 Type B stock-for-stock reorganization.

[9] Loan agreements often require the repayment of loans if a change of control of the borrower takes place.

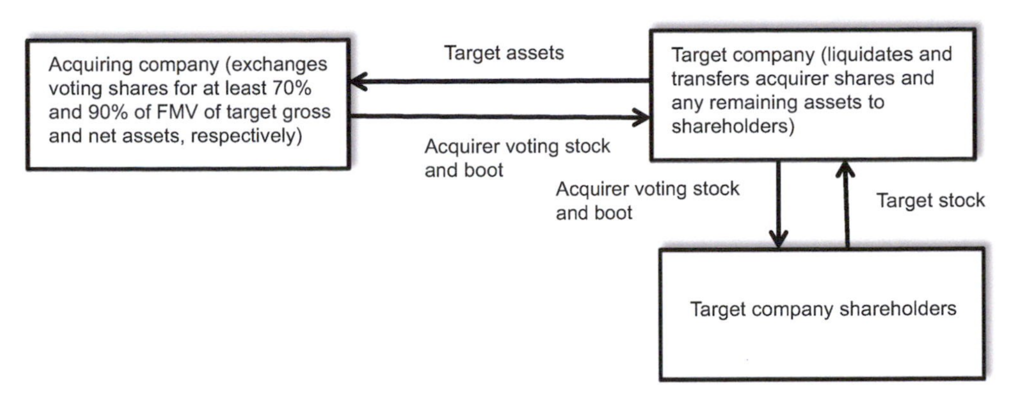

FIGURE 12.6 Type C stock-for-assets reorganization. *FMV*, Fair market value

B structure.[10] Type B deals are used as an alternative to a merger or consolidation.[11] Such reorganizations are useful if the acquirer wishes to conserve cash or borrowing capacity. Because shares are acquired from shareholders, there is no need for a target shareholder vote. Finally, contracts and licenses transfer with the stock, which obviates the need to receive consent to assignment, unless specified in contracts. The target firm is either retained as a subsidiary or merged into the parent.[12]

The *type C stock-for-assets reorganization* is used when the acquirer does not want to assume any undisclosed liabilities (Fig. 12.6). It requires that at least 70% and 90% of the FMV of the target's gross and net assets, respectively, be acquired for acquirer voting stock. Consideration paid in cash cannot exceed 20% of the FMV of the target's assets; any liabilities assumed by the acquirer must be deducted from the 20%. Because assumed liabilities frequently exceed 20% of the FMV of the acquired assets, the form of payment generally is all stock. The target dissolves and distributes the acquirer's stock to the target's shareholders. The requirement to use only voting stock discourages the use of type C reorganizations. Table 12.3 summarizes the key characteristics of alternative tax-free deal structures.

Treatment of target tax attributes in M&A deals

Tax attributes, such as NOL carryforwards, capital loss carryovers, excess credit carryovers, tax basis in company assets, and tax basis in subsidiary companies, can represent considerable value to acquiring firms in terms of tax savings. The IRS allows acquirers to realize tax savings from additional depreciation resulting from the revaluation of net acquired target assets to their FMV or from the target's other tax attributes, but not both. Thus acquirers can use a target's tax attributes in tax-free reorganizations and in taxable purchases of stock without a Section 338 election because net acquired assets are not revalued to their FMV. Acquirers cannot use the target's tax attributes in taxable purchases of assets and taxable purchases of stock undertaken as a 338 election because net acquired assets are revalued to their FMV.[13]

[10] Cash may be used to purchase fractional shares.

[11] The target's stock does not have to be purchased all at once, allowing for a "creeping merger" as the target's stock may be purchased over 12 months or less as part of a formal acquisition plan.

[12] A type B stock-for-stock deal is equivalent to a reverse triangular merger because the target firm becomes the acquirer's subsidiary. The primary difference between a reverse triangular merger and a type B stock-for-stock deal is the requirement to use at least 80% acquirer voting or preferred stock to buy target shares, in contrast to the need to use 100% acquirer voting common or preferred stock in a type B share-for-share reorganization.

[13] When tax attributes do survive and carry over (transfer) to the acquirer, their use is limited by Sections 382 (net operating losses) and 383 (tax credit and capital loss carryforwards) of the tax code. When tax attributes do not survive, they may still be used to offset gains on the sale of target assets.

TABLE 12.3 Key characteristics of alternative transaction structures that are tax free (to target shareholders)[a]

Transaction structure (type of reorganization)	Form of payment	Limitation[b]	Acquirer retains target tax attributes	Target survives?	Parent exposure to target liabilities	Shareholder vote required?		Minority freeze out?	Automatic transfer of contracts?[c]
						Acquirer	Target		
Statutory merger or consolidation (type A reorganization)	At least 50% parent voting or nonvoting stock	Assets and liabilities pass automatically to buyer	Yes, but no asset step-up	No	High	Yes	Yes	Yes	No because target is liquidated
Forward triangular merger (type A reorganization)	At least 50% parent voting or nonvoting stock	Must purchase at least 70% and 90% of FMV of gross and net assets unless LLC acquiring subsidiary	Yes, but no asset step-up	No	Low, limited by subsidiary[d]	No[f,g]	Yes	Yes	No because target is liquidated
Reverse triangular merger (type A reorganization)	At least 80% parent voting stock (common or preferred)	Must purchase at least 80% of voting and of nonvoting shares	Yes, but no asset step-up	Yes	Low, limited by subsidiary[d]	No[f,g]	Yes	Yes	Yes, target retains nonassignable contracts and so on.
Purchase of stock—without a merger (type B reorganization)	100% parent voting stock (common or preferred)	Must purchase at least 80% of voting and of nonvoting shares	Yes, but no asset step-up	Yes	Low, limited by subsidiary[d]	No[f]	No, because shares bought directly from shareholders	No	Yes
Purchase of assets (type C reorganization)	100% voting stock[h]	Must purchase at least 70% and 90% of FMV of gross and net assets	Yes, but no asset step-up	No	Low,[e] except for assumed liabilities	No[f]	Yes, if sale of assets substantial	No minority created	No

[a]Target shareholders are taxed at ordinary rates on any "boot" received (i.e., anything other than acquiring company stock).
[b]Asset sales or spin-offs 2 years prior (may reflect effort to reduce size of purchase) or subsequent to (violates continuity requirement) closing may invalidate tax-free status. Forward triangular mergers do not require any limitations on purchase of target net assets if a so-called "disregarded unit," such as a limited liability corporation (LLC), is used as the acquiring entity and the target is a C corporation that ceases to exist as a result of the transaction. Disregarded units are businesses that are pass-through entities and include LLCs or Subchapter S corporations.
[c]Contracts, leases, licenses, and rights to intellectual property automatically transfer with the stock unless contracts stipulate that consent to assignment is required. Moreover, target retains any nonassignable franchise, lease, or other contract rights as long as the target is the surviving entity as in a reverse triangular merger.
[d]Acquirer may be insulated from a target's liabilities as long as it is held in a subsidiary, except for liabilities such as unpaid taxes, unfunded pension obligations, and environmental liabilities.
[e]The parent is responsible for those liabilities conveying with the assets, such as warranty claims.
[f]May be required by public stock exchanges or by legal counsel if deemed material to the acquiring firm or if the parent needs to authorize new stock.
[g]Mergers are generally ill suited for hostile transactions because they require approval of both the target's board and target shareholders.
[h]Although cash may be used to pay for up to 20% of the fair market value (FMV) of net assets, it must be offset by assumed liabilities, making the purchase price usually 100% stock.

Tax-free transactions arising from 1031 "like-kind" exchanges

The prospect of being able to defer taxable gains is often associated with 1031 exchanges of real estate property or other income-producing properties. By postponing tax payments, investors have more money to reinvest in new assets. Assume a property was purchased 10 years ago for $5 million and is now worth $15 million. If the property were sold with no subsequent purchase of a similar property within the required period, the federal capital gains tax bill would be $1.5 million [i.e., ($15 − $5) × 0.15], assuming a capital gains tax rate of .15. This ignores the potential for state taxes or depreciation recapture taxes owed if the owner took deductions for depreciation. However, by entering into a 1031 exchange, the owner could use the entire $15 million from the sale of the property as a down payment on a more expensive property. If the investor acquires a property of a lesser value, taxes are owed on the difference. Under the Tax Cuts and Jobs Act (TCJA) of 2017, 1031 exchanges completed after January 1, 2018, apply only to real and not personal property. The implications of this change are explored later in this chapter.

Tax Cuts and Jobs Act of 2017

The TCJA allows faster deductions for capital spending, limits interest expense and operating loss deductions, provides partnership tax breaks, and requires minimum taxes on foreign income. Changes in various provisions of the tax code could offset some of the benefit of the reduction in the corporate tax rate. The tax cuts help stimulate business start-ups, leading to an increase in the demand for labor and, in time, higher wage rates.[14] Critics argue that the tax cuts are not revenue neutral because they do not generate enough future revenue to offset the lower tax rates.[15] The extent to which the new tax code stimulates M&A activity is likely to depend on the circumstances of the acquirer and target firms. Each of the key provisions affecting M&As is listed in Table 12.4 and discussed in more detail later in this section.

Corporate tax rates

Beginning on January 1, 2018, the corporate income tax rate on earnings was lowered to 21%. Prior corporate tax rates consisted of eight brackets ranging from a low of 15% of taxable income of less than or equal to $50,000 to a high of 35% of taxable income greater than $18.3 million. The lower corporate rate can stimulate greater M&A activity because of the potential for higher future economic growth and after-tax financial returns[16] and increase the quality of takeovers measured by higher acquirer returns and overall synergies in cash-financed deals, particularly for acquirers having limited access to capital.[17]

Pass-through income

Known as the Section 199A deduction, the new law adopts a standard deduction of 20% for pass-through income limited to the greater of 50% of wage income or 25% of wage income plus 2.5% of the cost of tangible depreciable property. Coupled with the reduction in the maximum personal income tax rate to 37%, the 20% deduction creates an effective top tax rate on pass-through income of 29.6% (i.e., .37 × (1 − .20)).[18] This provision expires on December 31, 2025. The extent to which the changes in the tax law will impact pass-through entities varies by industry, profession, and size of business. This is discussed in more detail in Chapter 16.

To avoid double taxation, firms having switched from a pass-through structure (e.g., partnerships) to a C corporation must wait 5 years after making the switch to sell the business, to avoid gains resulting from the sale from being taxed twice: once when the sale is completed and again when the proceeds are paid to owners. This waiting period is

[14] Sedlacek and Sterk, 2019

[15] Zeida, 2019

[16] Shevlin et al. (2019) found that lower effective corporate tax rates stimulate future macroeconomic growth and that mixed results in prior studies were attributable to their use of statutory rather than effective tax rates.

[17] Blouin et al., 2020

[18] The limitations are intended to discourage the improper classification of wage income as business income. This deduction excludes short-term capital gains, dividends, interest income not allocable to a business, certain other passive income, and income from investment management services.

TABLE 12.4 US tax law changes potentially impacting M&As

Tax code provision	Pre-2018	Post-2018
Corporate tax rates	Multiple income tax brackets with a top rate of 35%	Single 21% corporate income tax rate
Pass-through income	Subject to individual income brackets and tax rates	Adopts a 20% standard deduction for pass-through income with certain limitations
Investment in capital	Allows 50% depreciation of machinery and equipment through 2020 and Section 179 small-business expensing capped at $500,000	Allows full (100%) expensing of machinery and equipment for 5 years without a cap; cap on Section 179 expensing raised to $1 million
Alternative minimum tax (AMT)	Applies a 20% tax rate to a broader definition of income	AMT repealed for corporations
Deductibility of interest expense	Full deductibility of interest expense	Caps net interest deduction at 30% of EBITDA for 4 years, and 30% of EBIT thereafter.
Dividends (from other corporations) received deduction	If two corporations in same affiliated group, deduction is 100%; if corporate ownership stake in paying firm ≥20%, deduction is 80%; if stake <20%, deduction is 70%	Deduction is reduced depending on ownership stake
Net operating loss (NOLs)	NOLs could be carried back 2 years or forward 20 years with no limits on taxable income	NOL carrybacks eliminated but can be carried forward indefinitely; limited to 80% of taxable income after 2022
Carried interest	Taxed at long-term capital gains tax rates after a 1-year holding period	Qualifies for long-term capital gains tax treatment if held 3 years
Foreign earnings	Income earned anywhere in world subject to US tax rate less any taxes paid in country where income earned (so-called "worldwide" tax system)	Moved to "territorial" system in which firms pay rate of 5% of modified taxable income over an amount equal to regular tax liability for the first year, then 10% through 2025 and 12.5% thereafter.
Deemed repatriation	Not applicable	Repatriated currently deferred foreign profits taxed at a rate of 15.5% for cash and equivalents and 8% for reinvested earnings[a]
1031 "like-kind" exchanges	Like-kind exchanges tax free for both real and personal property	Like-kind exchanges tax free but only for real property

[a]Reinvested earnings in this context refer to investments in illiquid assets such as plant and equipment with foreign earnings previously untaxed by US tax authorities. *EBIT*, Earnings before interest and taxes; *EBITDA*, earnings before interest, taxes, depreciation, and amortization.

intended to discourage C corporations from switching to a pass-through entity immediately before they sell to avoid double taxation.

Investment in capital

Investment in capital can be depreciated over their useful lives for tax purposes. Whereas the straight-line method allows for assets to be depreciated evenly, the accelerated methods allow for a larger portion of depreciation to be deducted immediately. Designed to benefit small businesses, Section 179 of the US tax code allows for the immediate expensing of qualifying assets such as cars, office equipment, business machinery, and computers, subject to a cap. Accelerated depreciation under the new tax law could encourage acquirers to structure deals as asset purchases and encourage more acquisitions of pass-through entities. Why? Takeovers of partnerships are treated as asset purchases. For example, hospitality company Aramark's takeover of two hotel management firms, both partnerships, were treated as asset purchases. The total purchase price was $2.35 billion; however, after the immediate expensing of qualified assets, the net cost of the purchases was $1.86 billion.

The TCJA allows full expensing of short-lived capital investment such as machinery and equipment through 2022. The provision is then phased out between 2023 and 2026: 80%, 60%, 40%, and 20%. The cap on Section 179 business expensing is raised to $1 million from its prior $500,000 limit. The full cost of investment in certain tangible property and computer software will be immediately deductible if acquired and placed in service after September 27, 2017, and before January 1, 2023, even if it is used.

Although stock acquisitions do not benefit from the immediate expensing of revalued net acquired assets, the acquisition of a division of a firm can be structured as an asset purchase to take advantage of the new tax law. Alternatively, a transaction could be structured as a 338 exchange in which both the buyer and seller agree to treat a share exchange as an asset sale.

Alternative minimum corporate income tax

The 2017 tax law completely eliminates the alternative minimum tax (AMT) for corporations so as not to offset the reduction in corporate tax rates. Banks, restaurants, and other companies with operations mostly in the United States that have been paying close to the previous 35% statutory tax rate are likely to benefit the most from the elimination of the 20% AMT.

Deductibility of interest expense

The new law limits the tax deductibility of net interest expense to 30% of earnings before interest and taxes (EBIT) after January 1, 2022. Interest on debt incurred before the new tax law will be limited in the same way as debt incurred after the law was passed.[19] Interest expense in excess of the limitations is deductible indefinitely in future years.[20] Acquirers with high interest expense and low EBIT may seek targets with little debt and high EBIT because such targets enable the acquirer (when combined with the target) to deduct a larger percentage of interest expense from pretax income. Firms with large excess cash balances that would allow highly leveraged acquirers to deleverage could become more attractive as targets. Furthermore, the cap on interest expense deduction could make preferred stock more common as a form of payment as it exhibits some of the characteristics of debt: dividends paid before common shareholders in liquidation.

Several deal structures make spinoffs more attractive. Spinoffs, if properly structured, enable firms to transfer corporate assets to their shareholders tax free. Spinoffs followed by an initial public offering (IPO) could be structured to allow the former parent to keep much of the proceeds of the newly issued shares enabling the parent to deleverage. Reverse Morris Trust deals provide a means of increasing the interest rate cap for acquirers. Such deals involve spinning or splitting off assets to be combined with a merger partner into a new public company, with the new company combining with the merger partner tax free to shareholders. The merger partner can increase its ability to deduct interest expense if the spun-off or split-off firm has significant EBIT and little debt.

Dividends received deduction

The size of the deduction depends on the size of the receiving corporation's ownership stake in the paying corporation. The deduction is equal to 100% of the dividend if the two firms are in the same affiliated group (i.e., parent has a controlling interest in its dividend-paying subsidiary). If the receiving corporation owns more than 20% of the paying firm, then the deduction is 80%; if it is less than 20%, the deduction is 70%. The new tax law lowers the 80% deduction to 65% and the 70% deduction to 50%, making minority investments less attractive.

[19] The new rules do not apply to taxpayers with average annual gross revenue for the 3-taxable-year period ending with the prior taxable year of less than $25 million.

[20] The cap on interest expense deductibility encourages equipment leasing and sale-leaseback arrangements, making it more important than ever to include leasing expenses in assessing a firm's ability to finance its ongoing operations.

Net operating losses

For federal tax purposes, NOLs are created when firms lose money. Before 2018, such losses could be carried back 2 years to get refunds on prior tax payments and forward 20 years to reduce future tax liabilities without income limits. The new law scraps NOL carrybacks[21] and caps carryforwards at 90% of taxable income, falling to 80% after 2022. NOLs arising in taxable years ending after December 31, 2017, and not deductible in a taxable year can be carried forward indefinitely. How states treat NOLs varies widely. Targets with large accumulated losses are less attractive because the value of loss carryforwards is reduced. However, NOLs created after January 1, 2018, still represent potential value for acquirers. When acquired net assets are stepped up for tax purposes, the target's NOLs may be used immediately by the acquirer to offset the gain on an asset sale. For deals not resulting in an asset write-up, the target's NOLs may be used by the acquirer in future years, subject to the limitation specified in Section 382 of the IRC.[22] Loss carryforwards alone rarely justify an acquisition.[23]

Carried interest

Carried interest is that portion of profits general partners of private equity and hedge funds receive regardless of their having contributed their own money to the fund. Historically, general partners have received a management fee equal to 2% of the fund's assets plus 20% of any profit generated when the fund is terminated. The management fee is intended to cover the costs of managing the fund. Under the new law, carried interest will be subject to a 3-year holding period to qualify as a long-term capital gain for tax years beginning after December 31, 2017. Previously, carried interest was subject to a 1-year holding period to be treated as a long-term gain. Because most private equity deals are held longer than 3 years, this change in the holding period has little impact on private equity investors.

Foreign earnings

Under the prior "worldwide" tax system, overseas taxes were subject to a statutory 35% tax rate less any taxes paid in the country where the profits were earned. The United States allowed the payment of taxes on these earnings to be deferred until they were repatriated. To avoid a current tax bill, multinational firms allowed their cash balances held abroad to accumulate. The new tax law moves to a "territorial" system in which only domestic profits are taxed. To discourage firms from shifting income earned in the United States to lower-tax countries, two new rules were introduced: the Base Erosion Anti-Abuse Tax (BEAT) and the Global Intangible Low-Taxed Income Tax (GILTI).[24]

BEAT applies to large firms with at least $500 million in gross receipts and significant cross-border payments to related parties. Firms subject to BEAT must calculate their tax liabilities with and without cross-border payments to foreign affiliates. If such payments reduce a firm's tax liability below what it would have been without the payments, the firm must pay the BEAT tax equal to 10% of the difference through 2025 and 12.5% thereafter.

GILTI sets a floor on taxes paid on foreign income, whether to US or foreign tax authorities. Firms paying less than 10.5% of foreign income to foreign tax authorities must pay the difference to the IRS. That minimum tax is applied to foreign income over a threshold based on the firm's foreign tangible assets, with income over that threshold assumed to have been generated by intangible assets held in low-tax countries.[25] GILTI reduces tax on foreign income from

[21] The Coronavirus Aid, Relief, and Economic Security Act of 2020 allowed for a 5-year carryback on losses incurred before January 1, 2021.

[22] Section 382 was created to prevent acquisitions of firms with substantial NOLs to reduce the acquirer's taxable income simply to avoid taxes. An acquirer's ability to use NOLs to offset current income may be limited if the firm has a 50% change in ownership. The acquirer could still use the target's NOLs in existence before the change in ownership, but their value would be limited to a percentage of the firm's market value on the date of the change in ownership equal to the target's market value times the IRS long-term tax-exempt interest rate.

[23] To discourage a change in ownership from jeopardizing their NOLs, firms may adopt a poison pill takeover defense, which, when paired with a staggered board, substantially reduces the likelihood of a takeover.

[24] US multinational firms make payments to foreign affiliates in countries with favorable tax rates for many reasons, including interest on debt borrowed from a foreign affiliate, payments made for back-office services supplied in another country, or royalties paid for patents held abroad. These payments represent income to the foreign affiliates subject to lower tax rates and are deductible from taxable income earned in the United States.

[25] Historically, firms attributed a large portion of the value of their products to patents and trademarks. The firms would then assign some of their intellectual property as a percent of overseas sales to subsidiaries in countries with low tax rates and assess patent royalties on sales. Such royalties would be subject to the country's low tax rate.

goods produced in the US using intellectual property (IP) to 13.1% until the end of 2025 and 16.4% thereafter. Multinational firms have less incentive to hold IP outside the United States.[26]

Multinational firms are now more likely to repatriate foreign profits. Before the new tax law, firms borrowed at historically low interest rates to avoid the tax bill on repatriating foreign earnings in order to pay dividends, repurchase shares, and invest (including M&As) in the United States. Now these firms can reduce leverage and use more of their future cash flow for these purposes. Companies likely to benefit most from the movement to a territorial system are those that have maintained large cash balances abroad such as large pharmaceutical, technology, industrial, financial, and consumer product firms. During the 2 years after the passage of the new tax legislation, US multinational enterprises have repatriated $1 trillion in past overseas earnings that were previously invested abroad.[27]

Deemed repatriation

Foreign profits on which taxes had been previously deferred are under the new law subject to a one-time tax of 15.5% of cash and cash equivalents and 8% of reinvested foreign earnings when such profits are repatriated to the United States. Although firms are not required to repatriate the cash, they are viewed as having done so even if they allow cash to remain abroad. Firms may pay the tax over 8 years. Reinvested earnings are foreign earnings not yet taxed but that have been invested in illiquid assets such as plant and equipment. Future foreign earnings are treated as described in the previous section. Multinational firms can now more efficiently manage their global cash position, disbursing cash based on returns rather than on the desire to defer tax payments. There is significant empirical evidence that multinational corporations are more likely to engage in domestic acquisitions if the tax cost of repatriation is lower.[28]

1031 "like-kind" exchanges

Used for decades to defer capital gains in real estate deals, like-kind exchanges expanded to apply to exchanges of income-producing businesses. The loss of tax revenue prompted tax code changes such that such transfers apply only to real property exchanges occurring after January 1, 2018. Personal property assets that no longer qualify as tax-free exchanges include broadband spectrums, fast-food restaurant franchise licenses and patents, aircraft, vehicles, machinery and equipment, railcars, boats, artwork, and collectibles. So-called "self-created property" such as patents, inventions, models or designs (patented or otherwise), and proprietary formulas or processes held by the taxpayer who created the property are included in the definition of personal property. As a result of the new law, 1031 exchanges will be focused on real estate deals.

State and local tax issues

In the United States, the magnitude and type of corporate levy varies widely by state. In 2018, 44 states had corporate income taxes ranging from 3% in North Carolina to 12% in Iowa. Nevada, Ohio, Texas, and Washington impose gross receipts (revenue) taxes rather than corporate income taxes. Six states—Alaska, Illinois, Iowa, Minnesota, New Jersey, Pennsylvania—and the District of Columbia impose top marginal corporate income tax rates of 9% or more. Seven states—Arizona, Colorado, Mississippi, North Carolina, North Dakota, South Carolina, and Utah—have maximum rates of 5% or less. Only South Dakota and Wyoming do not levy a corporate income or gross receipts tax.[29] Issues surrounding state and local taxes go far beyond the magnitude and type of corporate taxes levied. These are discussed next.

[26] Revisions implemented on December 2, 2019, by the US Treasury allowed for more generous rules for calculating tax credits as multinationals with higher foreign tax rates found that existing limits on such credits meant they were subject to GILTI even if they were paying foreign tax rates near or above US rates.

[27] US Council of Economic Advisors, December 20, 2019

[28] Chen et al., 2019

[29] Scarboro, 2018

Preclosing, due diligence, and postclosing issues

When the form of the transaction (i.e., asset or stock purchase) is determined, the buyer should consider state and local "transfer taxes" (i.e., applicable when asset ownership changes) and whether they are to be paid by the acquirer, target, or shared. During due diligence, the buyer must determine what, if any, taxes owed by the target are unpaid. Such tax liabilities must be paid by the acquirer and can include income, sales, use, and employment taxes when the buyer buys all or substantially all of the target's assets. Moreover, some states impose limitations on the use of NOLs, which may affect the value of target NOLs. Finally, the combined acquirer and target firms may have expanded their geographic coverage in more tax jurisdictions than before the deal, resulting in additional future tax liabilities.

Potentially unforeseen tax liabilities

A common problem in takeovers is the likelihood that the target firm is not filing tax returns in all states in which it should. Each state has different rules for when companies are liable for taxes, and many firms often unknowingly create potential tax liabilities in multiple states. States such as Washington and Texas tax gross receipts, others such as Ohio have occupancy taxes, and still others such as Delaware and California have franchise taxes. These taxes are not based on income; as such, firms can still owe taxes even though they are incurring losses.

Pressure on states to raise revenue

Amid shrinking tax bases and increased spending, states are seeking new revenue sources. States and local authorities were limited historically on what they could tax. However, this changed when the US Supreme Court ruled on June 20, 2018, that states could tax online commerce in the *Wayfair vs. South Dakota* decision, reversing the "physical presence rule" in the US Constitution's "commerce clause." This allowed tax authorities to collect sales taxes on businesses not physically present in the state. Acquirers must now determine during due diligence if the target firm has satisfied its obligations to pay taxes that might be owed on sales to customers located in states in which they do not have a physical presence. This also includes past years because of a lack of a statute of limitations.

International taxes

When the target has foreign operations, the acquirer needs to determine whether the target is in compliance with its foreign tax filings. Tax jurisdictions enforce compliance by requiring increasing levels of transparency into foreign-owned assets and operations and levy substantial fines for firms found to be noncompliant. Common problems arising from takeovers include the target failing to report foreign-held assets to tax authorities, to pay value-added taxes, to disclose cross-border payments, and being unable to justify intracompany pricing. In addition, the target firm may not have qualified for tax holidays[30] or reduced tax rates on foreign earnings or have improperly taken foreign tax credits to offset US taxes owed.

Tax inversions

Before new US tax legislation in 2017, the average combined US federal and state corporate statutory tax rate of 38.91% was the fourth highest in the world, behind only United Arab Emirates, Comoros, and Puerto Rico. The combined US rate exceeded 40% for companies domiciled in some states. Worldwide, the average statutory corporate rate is about 23%.[31]

The 2017 US tax law, by lowering US corporate tax rates, appears to have deterred any new US corporate inversions in which firms relocate overseas to more favorable tax jurisdictions. Since the new law took effect, some "inverted firms" returned to the United States. In late 2019, Allergan PLC, which had been based in Dublin, Ireland, moved its address to the United States through a sale to AbbieVie Inc. Drug manufacturer Mylan Labs moved its

[30] Tax holidays are temporary reductions or eliminations of taxes owed offered by tax authorities as an incentive to attract business investment.

[31] Jahnsen et al., 2017

corporate address to the Netherlands in 2015. But the firm returned to the United States through a merger with Pfizer in 2020.

Although generally not the main motivation for takeovers, US firms have for years tried to reduce their tax liabilities by reincorporating through a process called *tax inversion* in low-tax areas such as Bermuda, the Cayman Islands, or Ireland. More recently, firms have reduced their tax liabilities by buying a foreign firm and subsequently restructuring such that the foreign firm becomes the parent of the US firm.

There is evidence that reducing taxes in this manner, which increases funds available to reward shareholders, can provide abnormal positive returns of between 2% and 5% in the short run. However, agency issues may reduce firm value by as much as a cumulative 21% in the long run.[32] Why? Inversions may be undertaken if the firm's CEO stands to benefit by pumping up the stock price in the short run, enabling them to exercise their equity options at a higher share price. In the longer term, firm value may decline because of the costs associated with the inversion such as loss of domestic tax credits and NOLs and political and reputational costs because inverting firms can be viewed as unpatriotic.[33]

Master limited partnerships, real estate investment trusts, and yield cos

All three legal structures are designed to provide a predictable dividend stream to investors. Master limited partnerships (MLPs) use oil and gas pipeline income, real estate investment trusts (REITS) use commercial real estate income, and yield cos use income generated from renewable energy assets.

MLPs are limited partnerships whose shares or units are publicly traded, whose investors are subject to limited liability, and whose ownership units trade like common stocks. Not subject to double taxation, the MLP is treated like any other partnership for which income is allocated proportionately to the partners. MLP distributions may be tax free; where tax-deductible expenses exceed the amount of the MLP's cash distribution, the excess may be applied to shelter the investor's other pretax income.[34] Unlike corporate dividends, quarterly payouts to investors in MLPs are mandatory. In MLPs, a missed mandatory quarterly payment constitutes an event of default. Because of these mandatory payments, MLPs are common in industries having predictable cash flows, such as natural resources and real estate.[35]

Despite their significant tax advantages, the MLP structure may limit the ability of the partnership to grow. In late 2014, Kinder Morgan, the huge North American oil and gas pipeline MLP, announced it would reorganize into a corporate structure. Because the MLP structure requires the distribution of profits to shareholders, it becomes difficult for the MLP to acquire new assets large enough to increase annual payouts. Despite its less favorable tax structure, Kinder Morgan believes that as a corporation, it can finance more acquisitions and make the capital outlays required to develop new oil and gas reserves to fund future dividend increases.

Similar to MLPs, REITs allow investors to own and operate commercial properties including apartment complexes, shopping malls, warehouses, and office buildings. REITs must by law distribute at least 90% of profits to avoid taxation. REIT investors must pay taxes on the dividends they receive based on their personal tax rate.

Yield cos use completed renewable energy projects with long-term power purchase agreements in place to provide dividends to investors. After they are formed, these yield cos are spun off in IPOs to become publicly traded companies. The parent is able to raise capital from the project immediately and to reinvest the proceeds in new projects.

Financial reporting of business combinations

What are the key differences between business combinations and asset acquisitions? Transaction costs are capitalized in an asset acquisition but expensed in a business combination. Identifiable assets, assumed liabilities, and

[32] Laing et al., 2019

[33] Cortes et al., 2020

[34] Unit holders receive their proportionate share of tax-deductible expenses such as depletion and depreciation expenses as well as investment tax credits attributable to the partnership's operations.

[35] MLPs are structured as two entities: a limited partnership that sells shares to the public and a general partnership controlled by the founders. Initially, the general partnership receives a 2% quarterly distribution paid by the company, but if distributions increase, the general partnership can receive a greater percentage of the profits.

noncontrolling interests are recognized and measured as of the date they are acquired at their fair value in a business combination. For an asset acquisition, the purchase price is allocated to the assets acquired according to a set of rules.

Unlike an asset acquisition in which assets are valued when acquired, an acquirer in a business combination has up to 1 year to accumulate facts existing on the acquisition date to finalize its financial reporting. In business combinations, contingent considerations (e.g., earnouts) are recognized at the acquisition date's fair value, but for asset acquisitions, their value is recognized when actually paid. These considerations are discussed in more detail next.

Acquisition method of accounting

A firm maintaining its financial statements under International Financial Reporting Standards (IFRS) or generally accepted accounting principles (GAAP) needs to account for business combinations using the acquisition method.[36] Accordingly, the purchase price or acquisition cost is determined, and then, using a cost-allocation approach, assigned first to tangible and then to intangible net assets and recorded on the books of the acquiring company.

Net assets (or net acquired assets) refer to acquired assets less assumed liabilities. Any excess of the purchase price over the fair value[37] of the acquired net assets is recorded as goodwill. Goodwill is an asset representing future economic benefits arising from acquired assets that were not identified individually. Current accounting standards stipulated in Statements of Financial Accounting Standards (SFAS) 141 R require an acquirer to recognize acquired assets, assumed liabilities, and any noncontrolling interest in the target to be measured at fair value as of the acquisition date, which generally corresponds to the closing date.[38] According to Calcbench, the total amount of goodwill for all US publicly traded firms at the end of 2019 was $5.5 trillion.

Who is the acquirer?

The acquirer is the firm having effective control of decision making in the combined firms. Determining which firm is the acquirer defines which firm's assets and liabilities will be revalued on the acquisition date, whether positive or negative goodwill is created, and the impact on the combined firm's future earnings. According to SFAS 141 R, the acquirer usually is the firm retaining the largest share of voting rights after closing and is significantly larger measured in terms of assets, revenue, and earnings. The acquirer also is the firm whose former board members make up the largest share of the new board and whose former management dominates senior management of the combined firms and in an equity exchange is the firm paying a premium for the other firm's shares.

Determining the acquirer is sometimes ambiguous. Take, for example, the 2008 merger between regional telecom firms CenturyTel and Embarq. Several factors suggested that Century Tel should be viewed as the acquirer because it issued new shares in exchange for Embarq shares and paid a premium to Embarq shareholders, and its former board members and senior managers made up a majority of the board and senior management of the combined firm. Yet other factors suggested Embarq should be considered the acquirer because its shareholders had the largest percentage of voting rights, and it was the much larger firm. Based on these factors, Century Tel was determined to be the acquirer for financial reporting purposes. This resulted in a larger increase in net acquired assets and lower future reported earnings for the combined firms because of larger depreciation expenses than if Embarq had been viewed as the acquirer.

Recognizing acquired net assets and goodwill at fair value

To compare different deals, current accounting rules require recognizing 100% of the assets acquired and liabilities assumed even if the acquirer buys less than 100% of the target. This results in the recognition of the target's business in its entirety, regardless of whether 51%, 100%, or any percentage in between is acquired. Thus the portion

[36] See IFRS 3 and SFAS (Statements of Financial Accounting Standards) 141, respectively. In the past, purchase accounting was used to record business combinations. The acquisitions method was later adopted because of its focus on the determination of the fair value of net acquired assets by relating them to prevailing market values and its inclusion of noncontrolling interests and contingencies that were not addressed under the purchase method.

[37] According to SFAS 157, fair value is the price that would be received in selling an asset or paid to transfer a liability between willing participants on the date an asset or liability is estimated.

[38] According to IFRS 38, whereas goodwill arising from business combinations can be recognized for financial reporting, "internally generated" goodwill, such as brands, copyrights, patents, and customer lists, created within the firm cannot.

of the target that was not acquired (i.e., the noncontrolling, or minority interest) is also recognized, causing the buyer to account for the goodwill attributable to both it as well as to the noncontrolling interest.

Noncontrolling or minority interest is reported in the consolidated balance sheet within the equity account, separately from the parent's equity. Moreover, the revenues, expenses, gains, losses, net income or loss, and other income associated with the noncontrolling interest should be reported on the consolidated income statement.

For example, if firm A were to buy 50.1% of firm B, reflecting its effective control, firm A must add 100% of firm B's acquired assets and assumed liabilities to its assets and liabilities and record the value of the 49.9% noncontrolling, or minority, interest in shareholders' equity. This treats the noncontrolling interest as simply another form of equity and recognizes that firm A is responsible for managing all of the acquired assets and assumed liabilities. Similarly, 100% of firm B's earnings are included in firm A's income statement less that portion attributable to the 49.9% minority owner and added to the retained earnings of the consolidated firms.[39]

Recognizing and measuring net acquired assets in step (or stage) transactions

Staged transactions are required to recognize the acquired net assets as well as the noncontrolling interest in the target firm at their fair values. Net acquired assets at each step must be revalued to the current FMV. The acquirer must disclose on the income statement gains or losses caused by the re-estimation of the formerly noncontrolling interests.

Recognizing contingent considerations

Contingencies are uncertainties—such as potential legal, environmental, and warranty claims about which the future may not be fully known at the time a transaction is consummated—that may result in future assets or liabilities. The acquirer must report an asset or liability arising from a contingency to be recognized at its acquisition-date fair value. As new information becomes available, the acquirer must revalue the asset or liability and record the impact of changes in their fair values on earnings, thereby contributing to potential earnings volatility.

In-process research and development assets

An acquirer must recognize separately from goodwill the acquisition-date fair values of research and development (R&D) assets acquired. Such assets will remain on the books as an asset with an indefinite life until the project's outcome is known. If the project is a success, the firm will amortize the asset over the estimated useful life; if the research project is abandoned, the R&D asset will be expensed.

Expensing deal costs

Transaction-related costs such as legal, accounting, and investment banking fees are recorded as an expense on the closing date and charged against current earnings. Firms need to explain the nature of the costs incurred in closing a deal and the impact of such costs on the earnings of the combined firms. Financing costs, such as expenses incurred as a result of new debt and equity issues, will continue to be capitalized and amortized over time.

Impact of acquisition accounting on business combinations

A long-term asset is impaired if its fair value falls below its book or carrying value. Impairment could occur because of customer attrition, loss of key personnel, obsolescence of technology, patent expiration, and so on. Measuring the degree of impairment can be challenging when the extent and duration of the issue are uncertain such as the 2020 global coronavirus pandemic.

When assets are impaired, the firm must report a loss equal to the difference between the asset's fair value and its carrying value (e.g., for machinery the carrying value would be its original cost less accumulated depreciation).

[39] On a nonconsolidated basis, firm B will be operated within firm A as a majority-owned subsidiary, with firm A's investment in firm B shown at cost, according to the equity method of accounting. The value of this investment will increase with firm B's net income and decrease with dividends paid to firm A.

Although publicly traded companies filing with the US Securities and Exchange Commission (SEC) are required under GAAP to check goodwill for impairment annually, private companies have a choice as of December 15, 2014: either check goodwill annually or amortize goodwill equally over 10 years using the straight-line method.[40] If a private firm chooses to amortize goodwill, goodwill must only be tested if there is a "triggering event" indicating impairment.[41]

But goodwill write-downs simply represent one type of the larger category of "restructuring" charges. Viewed as a one-time expense paid by the firm when it reorganizes, such charges are incurred when employees are laid off, manufacturing plants closed, or assets sold at below book value. If investors view such charges as a result of management's implementation of a new and more effective business strategy, the firm's share price might increase after the announcement. However, if investors view such charges as a reflection of current management's incompetence, their announcement may increase the likelihood of a subsequent takeover bid. Why? Because substantial charges signal a poorly performing firm and represent the potential for value creation if the firm's current management is removed.

Firms may incur restructuring charges for reasons other than impairment. Those wishing to change their business strategy may divest businesses that they no longer consider important to their business portfolios. These actions can result in accounting restructuring gains or losses. Large firms are more likely to divest assets or businesses on which they will experience a gain on the sale in the year of or immediately after an acquisition. Their motivation may be the desire to streamline their complex business portfolios as quickly as possible or to use the proceeds of the sale to finance the acquisition.

SEC guidance encourages management to alert investors whenever so-called "big R" historical earnings restatements ($\geq$5%) occur. Such events often are associated with significant declines in a firm's share price as investors question management's credibility and competence. Moreover, managers may be subject to "claw backs" that allow firms to recoup compensation from executives after outsized financial revisions. Aware of such consequences, there is some evidence that management has been less inclined to report publicly substantial earnings revisions in recent years. According to Audit Analytics, the number of "big R" restatements fell from a peak of 973 in 2005 to 119 in 2018.[42] Firms such as Papa John's International responded to SEC inquiries about their failure to alert investors despite revisions exceeding 5% by noting that they use the 5% rule of thumb as a first step before applying their own 10% measure to decide if alerting investors is warranted.

Balance-sheet considerations

For financial-reporting purposes, the purchase price paid[43] for the target company consists of the FMV of total identifiable acquired tangible and intangible assets (FMV_{TA}) less total assumed liabilities (FMV_{TL}) plus goodwill (FMV_{GW}). The difference between FMV_{TA} and FMV_{TL} is called net asset value. PP is the total consideration (e.g., cash, stock, etc.) transferred to target shareholders for net acquired assets less any interest not owned by the acquirer (i.e., noncontrolling interest). These relationships can be summarized as follows:

$$\text{PP(total consideration)}:\ PP = FMV_{TA} - FMV_{TL} + FMV_{GW} - FMV_{NCI} \quad (12.1)$$

$$\text{Goodwill}:\ FMV_{GW} = PP + FMV_{NCI} - FMV_{TA} + FMV_{TL} = (PP + FMV_{NCI}) - (FMV_{TA} - FMV_{TL}) \quad (12.2)$$

From Equation 12.2, as net asset value increases, FMV_{GW} decreases, for a given PP. Therefore goodwill can be either positive (i.e., PP > net asset value) or negative (i.e., PP < net asset value). Negative goodwill arises if the

[40] Companies with less than 300 shareholders for a class of securities or 500 shareholders for a class of securities and less than $10 million in total assets are exempt from SEC filings.

[41] Amortizing goodwill impacts a firm's annual earnings. Although private firms do not have to worry about public shareholders, the reduction in earnings because of amortization could cause them to be in violation of certain loan covenants. If the private firm goes public, it will incur the cost of having to restate its historical earnings to show what it would look like had it been a public firm.

[42] Eaglesham, December 5, 2019

[43] This includes the fair value of any noncontrolling interest (FMV_{NCI}) in the target at the acquisition date.

TABLE 12.5 Example of the acquisition method of accounting

	Column 1: acquirer preacquisition book value[a]	Column 2: target preacquisition book value[a]	Column 3: target fair market value[a]	Column 4: acquirer postacquisition value[a]
Current assets	12,000	1200	1200	13,200
Long-term assets	7000	1000	1400	8400
Goodwill				100[d]
Total assets	19,000	2200	2600	21,700
Current liabilities	10,000	1000	1000	11,000
Long-term debt	3000	600	700	3700
Common equity	2000	300	1000[b]	3000
Retained earnings	4000	300		4000
Equity + liabilities	19,000	2200	2700[c]	21,700

[a]*Millions of dollars.*
[b]*The FMV of the target's equity is equal to the purchase price. Note that the value of the target's retained earnings is implicitly included in the purchase price paid for the target's equity.*
[c]*The difference of $100 million between the fair market value of the target's equity plus liabilities less total assets represents the unallocated portion of the purchase price.*
[d]*Goodwill = Purchase price − FMV of net acquired assets = $1000 − ($2600 − $1000 − $700).*

acquired assets are purchased at a discount to their FMV and is referred to under SFAS 141R as a "bargain purchase."[44]

Table 12.5 shows how acquisition accounting can be applied in business combinations. Assume the acquirer buys 100% of the target's equity for $1 billion in cash at year end. Columns 1 and 2 present the preacquisition book values on the two firms' balance sheets. Column 3 reflects the restatement of the book value of the target's balance sheet in column 2 to their FMV. As the sum of columns 1 and 3, column 4 presents the acquirer's postacquisition balance sheet. This includes the acquirer's book value of the preacquisition balance sheet plus the FMV of the target's balance sheet. In column 3, total assets are less than shareholders' equity plus total liabilities by $100 million, reflecting the unallocated portion of the PP, or goodwill. This $100 million is shown in column 4 as goodwill on the postacquisition acquirer balance sheet to equate total assets with equity plus total liabilities. Note that the difference between the acquirer's pre- and postacquisition equity is equal to the $1 billion purchase price.

Exhibit 12.1 shows the calculation of goodwill in a transaction in which the acquirer purchases less than 100% of the target's outstanding shares but is still required to account for all of the target's net acquired assets, including 100% of goodwill. Exhibit 12.2 lists valuation guidelines for each major balance-sheet category.

Table 12.6 illustrates the balance-sheet impacts of acquisition accounting on the acquirer's balance sheet and the effects of impairment subsequent to closing. Assume that Acquirer Inc. purchases Target Inc. on December 31, 2020 (the acquisition or closing date), for $500 million. Identifiable acquired assets and assumed liabilities are shown at their fair value on the acquisition date. The excess of the purchase price over the fair value of net acquired assets is shown as goodwill. The fair value of the "reporting unit" (i.e., Target Inc.) is determined annually to ensure that its fair value exceeds its carrying (book) value. As of December 31, 2021, it is determined that the fair value of Target Inc. has fallen below its carrying value, largely because of the loss of a number of key customers.

The process for valuing goodwill impairment under GAAP is calculated as the amount by which a business unit's carrying value exceeds its fair value. The treatment of impaired goodwill according to international accounting standards is different in that some portion of an asset may be recoverable if sold and that the asset may still have some value if used in the firm's operations. The recoverable amount of an asset is either the asset's fair value less costs to sell or its value in use, whichever is greater.

[44] A "bargain" purchase is a business combination in which the total acquisition-date fair value of the acquired net assets exceeds the fair value of the purchase price plus the fair value of any noncontrolling interest in the target. Such a purchase may arise because of forced liquidation or distressed sales. SFAS 141R requires the acquirer to recognize that excess on the consolidated income statement as a gain attributable to the acquisition.

EXHIBIT 12.1

Estimating goodwill

On the closing date, Acquirer Inc. purchased 80% of Target Inc.'s 1 million shares outstanding at $50 per share, for a total value of $40 million (i.e., 0.8 × 1,000,000 shares outstanding × $50/share). On that date, the fair value of the net assets acquired from Target was estimated to be $42 million. Acquirer paid a 20% control premium, which was already included in the $50-per-share purchase price. The implied minority discount of the noncontrolling (minority) shares is 16.7% [i.e., 1 − (1/(1 + 0.2)].[a] What is the value of the goodwill shown on Acquirer's consolidated balance sheet? What portion of that goodwill is attributable to the noncontrolling interest retained by Target's shareholders? What is the fair market value (FMV) of the 20% noncontrolling interest per share reflecting the minority discount?

Goodwill shown on Acquirer's balance sheet: From Equation 12.2, goodwill (FMV_{GW}) can be estimated as follows:

$$\begin{aligned} FMV_{GW} &= (PP + FMV_{NCI}) - (FMV_{TA} - FMV_{TL}) \\ &= (\$40,000,000 + \$10,000,000) - \$42,000,000 \\ &= \$8,000,000 \end{aligned}$$

Goodwill attributable to the noncontrolling interest: Note that 20% of the total shares outstanding equals 200,000 shares, with a market value of $10 million ($50/share × 200,000). The amount of goodwill attributable to the noncontrolling interest is calculated as follows:

Fair value of noncontrolling interest: $10,000,000

Less: 20% fair value of net acquired assets (0.2 × $42,000,000): $8,400,000

Equals goodwill attributable to noncontrolling interest: $1,600,000

Fair value of the noncontrolling interest per share: Because the fair value of Acquirer's interest in Target and Target's retained interest are proportional to their respective ownership interest, the value of the ownership distribution of the controlling (majority) and noncontrolling (minority) owners is as follows:

Acquirer interest (0.8 × 1,000,000 × $50/share): $40,000,000

Target noncontrolling interest (0.2 × 1,000,000 × $50/share): $10,000,000

Total market value: $50,000,000

The FMV per share of the noncontrolling interest is $41.65 [i.e., ($10,000,000/200,000) × (1 − 0.167)]. The noncontrolling interest share value is less than the share price of the controlling shareholders (i.e., $50/share) because it must be discounted for the relative lack of influence of noncontrolling or minority shareholders on the firm's decision-making process.

[a] See Chapter 10 for how to calculate control premiums and noncontrolling or minority discounts.

Income statement and cash flow considerations

For reporting purposes, an upward valuation of tangible and intangible assets, other than goodwill, raises depreciation and amortization expenses, which lowers operating and net income. For tax purposes, goodwill created after July 1993 may be amortized up to 15 years and is tax deductible. Goodwill booked before July 1993 is not tax deductible. Cash flow benefits from the tax deductibility of additional depreciation and amortization expenses that are written off over the useful lives of the assets. If the purchase price paid is less than the target's net asset value, the acquirer records on its income statement a one-time gain equal to the difference. If the carrying value of the net asset value subsequently falls below its FMV, the acquirer records a one-time loss equal to the difference.

Rule changes affecting the balance sheet

Beginning in 2019, operating leases must be shown on a firm's balance sheet.[45] Although the change does not create new obligations, some firms will look more leveraged than currently when evaluated in terms of debt-to-equity ratios. For purposes of financial analysis, these ratios are generally looked at in terms of the market value of debt and equity. As such, the value of a firm relying heavily on operating leases may show a large increase in the value of its debt

[45] Previously, operating leases were discussed in footnotes to the balance sheet.

EXHIBIT 12.2

Guidelines for valuing acquired assets and liabilities

1. Cash and accounts receivable, reduced for bad debt and returns, are valued at their values on the books of the target on the acquisition or closing date.
2. Marketable securities are valued at their realizable value after transaction costs.
3. Inventories are broken down into finished goods and raw materials. Finished goods are valued at their liquidation value; raw material inventories are valued at their current replacement cost. Target last-in, first-out inventory reserves are eliminated.
4. Property, plant, and equipment are valued at the FMV on the acquisition or closing date.
5. Accounts payable and accrued expenses are valued at the levels stated on the target's books on the acquisition or closing date.
6. Notes payable and long-term debt are valued at their net present value of the future cash payments discounted at the current market rate of interest for similar securities.
7. Pension fund obligations are booked at the excess or deficiency of the PV of the projected benefit obligations over the PV of pension fund assets.
8. All other liabilities are recorded at their net present value of future cash payments.
9. Intangible assets are booked at their appraised values on the acquisition or closing date.
10. Goodwill is the difference between the purchase price and the FMV of the target's net asset value. Whereas positive goodwill is recorded as an asset, negative goodwill (i.e., a bargain purchase) is shown as a gain on the acquirer's consolidated income statement.

TABLE 12.6 Balance-sheet impacts of acquisition accounting

Target Inc. December 31, 2020, purchase price (total consideration)		**$500,000,000**
Fair values of Target Inc.'s Net assets on December 31, 2020		
Current assets ($)	40,000,000	
Plant and equipment ($)	200,000,000	
Customer list ($)	180,000,000	
Copyrights ($)	120,000,000	
Current liabilities ($)	(35,000,000)	
Long-term debt ($)	(100,000,000)	
Value assigned to identifiable net assets ($)		405,000,000
Value assigned to goodwill ($)		95,000,000
Carrying value as of December 31, 2020 ($)		500,000,000
Fair values of Target Inc.'s net assets on December 31, 2021 ($)		400,000,000[a]
Current assets ($)	30,000,000	
Plant and equipment ($)	175,000,000	
Customer list ($)	100,000,000	
Copyrights ($)	120,000,000	
Current liabilities ($)	(25,000,000)	
Long-term debt ($)	(90,000,000)	
Fair value of identifiable net assets ($)		310,000,000
Value of goodwill ($)		90,000,000
Carrying value after impairment on December 31, 2021 ($)		400,000,000
Impairment loss (difference between December 31, 2021, and December 31, 2020, carrying values) ($)		(100,000,000)

[a]*The December 31, 2021, carrying value is estimated based on the discounted value of projected cash flows of the reporting unit and represents the fair market value of the unit on that date. The fair value is composed of the sum of the fair values of identifiable net assets plus goodwill.*

relative to equity. The value of equity should be relatively unaffected because the addition of operating leases on the balance sheet has no impact on the firm's cash flow generation capability and in turn the market value of its equity.

International accounting standards

The objective of the International Accounting Standards Board (IASB) is the convergence of accounting standards worldwide and the establishment of global standards, sometimes referred to as "global GAAP." The IASB issues IFRS, and, since 2005, firms in the European Union have had to conform to IFRS directives. Nevertheless, many countries do not adhere strictly to standardized accounting practices, making comparing companies in different countries a daunting challenge for firms wishing to engage in cross-border deals.[46] In the United States, concerns about moving to international standards from GAAP include higher taxes (if the conversion results in increases in reported earnings), increased implementation costs, and litigation. The SEC has indicated that if the United States decides to shift to international rules, it will use a hybrid structure incorporating certain IFRS rules into the US system of accounting standards.[47]

International environmental, social, and governance standards

Companies are under pressure to report metrics that purport to estimate their environmental, social, and governance (ESG) risk. Because these risks vary by industry and country, investors are faced with a variety of differing, incomplete and often inconsistent standards. Without common standards analogous to GAAP and IFRS, investors cannot accurately estimate company-level ESG risk. But with different organizations supported by diverse constituencies competing to establish a global reporting standard, consensus is lacking. The larger organizations include the Sustainable Accounting Standards Board (SASB), the IFRS, and the World Economic Forum's International Business Council, in concert with the "big four" accounting firms. Companies also follow the reporting guidelines of the Task Force on Climate-Related Financial Disclosures (TCFD). One way to achieve convergence is for these organizations to consolidate. And in late 2020, SASB merged with the International Integrated Reporting Council to create the Value Reporting Foundation.

Recapitalization ("recap") accounting

Recap accounting is designed to record restructuring actions reflecting changes in a firm's capital structure without having any impact on the firm's assets and liabilities and triggering any tax liabilities. It applies to firms engaging in reorganizations, repurchasing their own stock, undertaking leveraged buyouts (LBOs), or executing reverse mergers. The SEC views such activities as not having a material impact on the firm's assets and liabilities. Each scenario is discussed next.

When two entities have the same parent, transfers of assets between them are viewed as reorganizations internal to the firm not resulting in a change in control impacting the value of the operating assets and liabilities of the firm. Such transfers do not require any revaluation of the firm's assets and liabilities. Recap accounting also applies when a firm buys its own stock; the repurchased shares, valued at the price paid for the stock, are included in treasury stock, which is deducted from the firm's shareholders' equity. The transaction does not have any impact on the value of the firm's assets or liabilities, and it does not require any change in the book value of the firm's assets or liabilities. The full impact of the transaction is on shareholders' equity.

Recap accounting also may be used for the financial reporting of LBOs. In LBOs, the buyout firm often creates a shell subsidiary and merges it into the target, with the target surviving. Target firm assets and liabilities are shown at their pretransaction book values. Because there is no write-up (or write-down) to FMV, there is no additional depreciation and amortization that would reduce the firm's net income. The LBO buyout firm may use recap accounting

[46] Pineiro-Chousa et al., 2019

[47] Companies from China and other countries not complying with US accounting standards will be delisted from US stock exchanges as of the end of 2021.

rather than acquisition accounting if it anticipates exiting the firm through an IPO, because reported earnings are higher than they would have been under acquisition accounting and no goodwill is created.[48] To qualify for recap accounting, the shareholders of the firm undergoing the LBO (the target) must retain an interest in the recapitalized firm of 5% to 20%. The SEC views that merger of the LBO buyout firm's sub into the target, with the target surviving, as a recapitalization of the target rather than as a business combination in which the survivor gained valuable assets.

Finally, recap accounting is used to record reverse mergers. Such mergers involve a private firm's merging into a public shell corporation with nominal net assets, with the public company surviving. The owners of the private firm typically have effective control of the surviving company at closing, with the former public shell shareholders having an ongoing noncontrolling interest in the recapitalized firm. The SEC views reverse mergers as changes in the acquiring firm's capital structure rather than as a business combination in which the shell corporation had significant pretransaction assets whose value was impacted by the transaction.

Putting it all together: takeover and deal-structuring strategies

From a legal perspective, there are two basic strategies: a takeover and a deal structure strategy. After what is being acquired (stock or assets) is identified, the former strategy describes the means for acquiring control of the target, and the latter deals with how assets and liabilities are transferred and the tax and due diligence implications of the deal.

Acquirers must decide what they want to buy. If they want to purchase a product line or subsidiary of a target firm, an asset purchase often is the preferred approach. Acquirers can select only assets they want and to accept only certain liabilities. However, asset deals can be cumbersome because of the lengthy due diligence that is required to determine exactly what assets the buyer wants and which liabilities it is willing to assume. If the acquirer wants to ensure that it is buying all known and unknown assets, a purchase of stock is relevant. In a stock deal, all target assets and liabilities transfer to the acquirer.

Takeover strategy: A target firm can generally be acquired via a one-step merger or a two-step tender offer followed by a backend squeeze-out merger. Two-step deals in which a tender offer is followed by a short form or statutory squeeze-out merger are completed much faster than one-step transactions. Why? One-step deals require target shareholder approval. In a two-step process, target shareholders express their approval of the deal if they tender their shares.

Deal structure strategy: The most common merger form is the forward or reverse triangular merger. Such mergers involve three parties: acquirer, acquirer merger subsidiary, and target. A forward merger entails a target firm being acquired by an acquirer subsidiary with the subsidiary surviving; a reverse triangular merger involves the target firm buying an acquirer subsidiary with the target surviving. Which form is selected depends on the objectives of the acquirer and target firms. If having flexibility in determining the form of payment is critical, acquirers often choose a forward merger. When preservation of target intellectual property and rights are paramount, the reverse triangular merger is preferred as the target firm is viewed as having maintained its legal existence throughout the process.

Implications of the Biden Administration's tax policy for M&As

The Biden tax plan doubles the tax rate on long-term gains from 20% to 39.6% for those whose adjusted gross income exceeds $1 million and eliminates the qualified income deduction for partnerships and S corporations. The plan calls for a new 12.4% payroll tax on income above $400,000. The top individual tax rate would rise to 39.6% from 37% for incomes greater than $400,000. Also, the corporate tax rate would jump from 21% to 28%, with a minimum tax on book income for firms with profits greater than $100 million. And the tax rate on global intangible income would increase from 10.5% to 21%. Federal tax hikes also raise state income taxes as some state tax codes conform to federal statutes. The middle class will be hurt by eliminating the "step-up" in the cost basis in inherited

[48] The target's shareholders' equity usually is negative because the repurchased stock is shown as treasury stock, which is deducted from shareholders' equity.

investments, which had eliminated capital gains taxes. This provision also covers family-owned businesses. Even if the new Biden Administration is unable to roll back Trump-era corporate tax cuts, corporate taxes can still go up by changing regulations put in place to implement the TCJA of 2017.

The net effect of Biden's tax plan is to reduce corporate cash flow and valuations. The effective tax rate will also rise for firms with a number of employees earning more than $400,000 because the employer pays 50% of the payroll tax liability. For pass-through entities such as S corporations, the phasing out of the qualified income deduction increases investors' taxable income. Currently, financial sponsors must hold their interests for at least 3 years to achieve favorable long-term capital gains treatment. But the increase in the long-term capital gains tax rate for those earning more than $1 million eliminates this preferential treatment for high earners. The change would hurt returns at private equity firms, whose profits are taxed as capital gains rather than regular income.

With higher taxes on corporate profits for both C and S corporations and increased payroll taxes, founding shareholders or partners in partnerships or private equity firms may sell before changes take effect. For owners of pass-through entities, increasing capital gains tax rates will be a major factor in considering whether or when to sell. Higher tax rates will make debt more costly because of limitations on interest expense deductions and change how deals are financed. Higher taxes on carried interest would change how private equity firms value businesses.

Some things to remember

Taxes are rarely the deciding factor in most M&A deals. A deal generally is tax free if mostly acquirer stock is used to buy the target's stock or assets; otherwise, it is taxable. For financial-reporting purposes, M&As (except those qualifying for recapitalization accounting) must be recorded using the acquisition method.

Chapter discussion questions

12.1 When does the IRS consider a transaction to be nontaxable to the target firm's shareholders? What is the justification for the IRS position?

12.2 What are the advantages and disadvantages of a tax-free transaction for the buyer?

12.3 Under what circumstances are the assets of the acquired firm increased to FMV when the transaction is deemed a taxable purchase of stock?

12.4 What is goodwill, and how is it created?

12.5 Under what circumstances might an asset become impaired? How might this event affect the way in which acquirers bid for target firms?

12.6 Why do boards of directors of both acquiring and target companies often obtain so-called fairness opinions from outside investment advisors or accounting firms? What valuation methodologies might be used in constructing these opinions? Should stockholders have confidence in such opinions? Why or why not?

12.7 Archer Daniel Midland (ADM) wants to acquire AgriCorp to augment its ethanol manufacturing capability. AgriCorp wants the deal to be tax free. ADM wants to preserve AgriCorp's investment tax credits and tax loss carryforwards so that they transfer in the transaction. Also, ADM plans on selling certain unwanted AgriCorp assets to help finance the transaction. How would you structure the deal so that both parties' objectives could be achieved?

12.8 Tangible assets are often increased to FMV after a transaction and depreciated faster than their economic lives. What is the potential impact on posttransaction EPS, cash flow, and balance sheet?

12.9 Discuss how the form of acquisition (i.e., asset purchase or stock deal) could affect the net present value or internal rate of return of the deal calculated postclosing.

12.10 What are some of the important tax-related issues the boards of the acquirer and target companies may need to address before entering negotiations? How might the resolution of these issues affect the form of payment and form of acquisition?

Solutions to these Chapter Discussion Questions are found in the Online Instructor's Manual for instructors using this book.

TABLE 12.7 Premerger balance sheets for companies in problem 12.14 ($ Million)

	Acquiring company	Target company
Current assets	600,000	800,000
Plant and equipment	1,200,000	1,500,000
Total assets	1,800,000	2,300,000
Long-term debt	500,000	300,000
Shareholders' equity	1,300,000	2,000,000
Shareholders' equity + total liabilities	1,800,000	2.300,000

Practice problems and answers

12.11 The target company has incurred $5 million in losses during the past 3 years. The acquiring company anticipates pretax earnings of $3 million in each of the next 3 years. What is the difference between the taxes that the acquiring company would have paid before the merger as compared with actual taxes paid after the merger, assuming a marginal tax rate of 40%? *Answer:* $2 million

12.12 The acquiring company buys 100% of the target company's equity for $5 million in cash. As an analyst, you are given the premerger balance sheets for the two companies (Table 12.7). Assuming plant and equipment are revalued upward by $500,000, what will be the combined companies' shareholders' equity plus total liabilities? What is the difference between the acquiring company's shareholders' equity and the shareholders' equity of the combined companies?

Answer: The combined companies' shareholders' equity plus total liabilities is $7.1 million, and the change between the combined companies' and the acquiring company's shareholders' equity is $5 million. Note that the change in the acquirer's equity equals the PP.

Solutions to these problems are found in the Online Instructor's Manual available to instructors using this text.

End-of-chapter case study: Bristol-Myers Squibb buys Celgene in the biggest biopharma deal in history

Case study objectives

To illustrate

- The importance of deal structure in getting a deal done
- The form of payment and form of acquisition
- Tax and accounting considerations

Bristol-Myers Squibb (Bristol) and Celgene Corp. (Celgene) entered 2019 more with a whimper than a bang. Amid setbacks on clinical drug trials required to get regulatory approval and the projected loss of exclusivity on its big money-making drugs, Bristol's shares had fallen 15.2% in 2018. Celgene saw its shares plunge almost 40% during the same period.

What was driving the poor performance of both stocks when the stock market was soaring? Bristol's most important cancer drug and growth driver, Opdivo, had lost much of its luster as Merck & Co's rival drug Keytruda became the leader in treating lung cancer, the most lucrative oncology market. Celgene suffered major clinical testing failures in its efforts to get new drugs approved, and its US patent protection on its flagship multiple myeloma drug, Revlimid, will start being phased out in 2022. With few drugs in the pipeline, investors feared new revenue would be insufficient to offset major products losing patent protection between 2022 and 2026.

Reflecting their common concerns, Bristol had been in talks with Celgene periodically about combining their firms since 2016, but the negotiations had intensified in the closing weeks of 2018. Negotiations culminated on January 3, 2019, with the announcement that they had agreed to merge the two firms in the largest biopharmaceutical combination in history.

Under the terms of the deal, Celgene would receive one Bristol share and $50 in cash for each Celgene share. Celgene shareholders would also receive a tradeable contingent value receipt (CVR) for each Celgene share they held. The CVR entitles its holder to a potential future payment of $9 per share when three specific new drugs are approved by the US Federal Drug Administration. Based on Bristol's share price on January 2, 2019, of $52.43, the total consideration offered by Bristol was valued at $102.43 per Celgene share. At closing, Bristol shareholders would own 69% of the combined firms and Celgene shareholders the remainder.

The cash and stock deal implied a 54% premium based on Celgene's closing share price on January 2, 2019. Including assumed debt, the deal's enterprise value was $95 billion, eclipsing Pfizer's $89 billion takeover of Warner-Lambert in 2000. The equity value of the deal was about $74 billion. Although Celgene's shares soared by 24%, investor concerns about the deal pushed Bristol's shares down by 14%. Critics argued that Bristol had paid too much and that the deal would not prevent the firm from losing its preeminent position in immunotherapies.

Bristol countered investor angst noting that the combined firm will have about $38 billion in annual revenue and a leading position in the $123 billion global market for cancer drugs. The combination is said to be highly complementary in terms of their drug portfolios with leading positions in oncology, immunology, and inflammation and cardiovascular disease. The tie-up also has six near-term drug launches with a combined annual revenue potential of $15 billion. The merger anticipates $2.5 billion of annual cost synergies by 2022.

Bristol's promotion of the deal failed to temper investor anxiety. In February, hedge fund Starboard Value LP voiced opposition to the deal and moved to install its own slate of directors. However, Starboard dropped its proxy fight after the deal received support from respected proxy solicitors Institutional Shareholders Services Inc. and Glass Lewis & Co. Bristol shareholders finally approved the company's acquisition of rival Celgene Corp. on April 12, 2019. The deal passed with relatively tepid support, with about 75% of shareholders approving the deal. Such deals often receive support from more than 90% of shareholders.

The merger of the two firms involved Bristol's merger subsidiary merged with Celgene, with Celgene surviving. Celgene would postclosing be a wholly owned subsidiary of Bristol. The business combination received regulatory approval in late 2019 shortly after Amgen Inc. agreed to buy Celgene's psoriasis treatment Otzela for $13.4 billion in cash. The Federal Trade Commission had expressed anticompetitive concerns about the combined firms' share of the antiinflammatory drug market.

Discussion questions

1. What is the form of payment used in this deal? Why might this form have been selected? What are the advantages and disadvantages of the form of payment used?
2. What is the form of acquisition used in this deal? Why might this form have been chosen? What are the advantages and disadvantages of the form of acquisition?
3. Would you characterize this as a reverse or forward triangular merger? Based on your answer, speculate as to why this type of reorganization was selected by Bristol-Myers Squibb.
4. How would this deal be treated for financial reporting purposes? Briefly describe how the methodology you have identified might be applied to how Celgene's financial data would be presented on Bristol-Myers Squibb's consolidated financial statements.
5. Assume it is determined by auditors during the next several years that Bristol overpaid significantly for Celgene. What is the most likely reason this determination could happen? How might this impact the firm's reported earnings per share and in turn its share price? Be specific.

Solutions to these questions are provided in the Online Instructor's Manual for instructors using this book.

CHAPTER

13

Financing the deal

private equity, hedge funds, and other sources of financing

OUTLINE

Mergers, Acquisitions, and Other Restructuring Activities, Eleventh Edition
https://doi.org/10.1016/B978-0-12-819782-0.00013-7

The only difference between you and someone you envy is that you settled for less. —*Phillip McGraw*

Inside M&As: financing megamergers and acquisitions

KEY POINTS

- Bridge financing in this context is used to satisfy immediate cash needs associated with the merger or acquisition.
- Term loans are used as a partial replacement of higher cost bridge loans and to extend maturities.
- Permanent financing consists of long-term debt issues to replace short-term financing.

Bristol-Myers Squibb's (Bristol) takeover of Celgene Corp (Celgene) in late 2019 required a complex structuring of the firm's balance sheet. Under the terms of the deal, Celgene would receive one Bristol share and $50 in cash for each Celgene share. Celgene shareholders would also receive a tradeable contingent value receipt (CVR) for each Celgene share they held. The CVR entitles its holder to a potential future payment of $9 per share when three specific new drugs are approved by the US Federal Drug Administration. Based on Bristol's share price on January 2, 2019, of $52.43, the total consideration was valued at $102.43 per Celgene share. Including assumed debt, the deal had an enterprise value of $95 billion, eclipsing Pfizer's $89 billion takeover of Warner-Lambert in 2000. The equity value of the deal was about $74 billion.

To fund the equity exchange offer, Bristol issued 701,024,507 new shares of its common and the same number of CVRs to Celgene shareholders in the merger. With interest rates at historical lows, Bristol borrowed and used excess cash to pay the cash portion of the purchase price and transaction costs. The firm entered into three types of borrowing arrangements: a bridge loan, term loans, and permanent or long-term financing.

Bridge loans represent interim financing provided by banks to allow firms to provide cash when it is needed but not yet available. Bristol entered such an arrangement at closing to finance up to $33.5 billion of the cash portion of the purchase price, repayment of a portion of Celgene's debt, and related expenses. Bridge loans are easier to obtain than traditional loans but tend to be for less than 1 year and charge higher interest rates and loan origination fees. And bridge loans do not have repayment penalties, giving borrowers the flexibility to pay off the loan early.

Term loans are bank loans for a specific amount and have a stipulated repayment schedule. They can have either fixed or variable interest rates. Bristol entered into term loan arrangements shortly after closing, consisting of a $1 billion 1-year loan, a $4 billion 3-year loan, and a $3 billion 5-year loan to spread the burden of repaying the debt over a longer period. The proceeds of the term loans reduced usage of the bridge loan facility by $8 billion to $25.5 billion.

Bristol's permanent financing entailed issuing senior unsecured bonds to raise $19 billion consisting of nine different maturity dates (or tranches). Such debt is backed by the cash generation capability of the firm and is paid off before other types of debt that have a lower priority when a firm is liquidated. The 30-year debt yielded

4.25% and was oversubscribed. Bristol was able to lock in historically low interest rates with the vast majority of its new bond issues at fixed rates, as is the existing debt for both firms. The highest rate Bristol will pay is 4.25% (1.45 percentage points more than 30-year Treasury bonds) for $3.75 billion due in 2049, extremely low by historical standards. Only $1.25 billion of Bristol's total new debt issues will be floating rate.

The maturity schedule for the firm's debt requires that $10 billion be repaid during the 3.5 years after closing. In the 10-year period after closing, Bristol will have about $30 billion to repay. The amount of such debt coming due makes the successful launch of new drugs extremely important if the firm is to be able to meet its debt service requirements.

Bristol offered to exchange Celgene's outstanding notes for up to $19.5 billion in Bristol notes and a nominal cash payment. The exchange eliminates all restrictive covenants. Another $1.5 billion in Celgene notes was paid off. Bristol said it would take on $32 billion of new debt in addition to $19.5 billion of existing Celgene debt. Its bridge loan is among the 10 largest in history. With the debt load of the combined firms at $51.5 billion—four times earnings before interest and taxes—Moody's, S&P Global Ratings, and Fitch Ratings cut Bristol's credit rating. Bristol hopes to improve its credit rating as it whittles down its outstanding debt.

Chapter overview

In theory, a deal that makes economic sense can always be financed as those providing the funds anticipate earning their cost of capital. In practice, financing a deal often is more complicated. This chapter discusses common sources of mergers and acquisitions (M&As) financing (and associated challenges) ranging from debt to equity to seller financing, the role of private and public financial markets in such financing, and the impact of the TCJA 2017 on financing strategies from the perspective of both internal and external sources of funding. Highly leveraged transactions, typically referred to as leveraged buyouts (LBOs), are discussed as a specific type of financing strategy. How LBOs create value and the key factors contributing to their success are addressed.

The terms *buyout firm, financial buyer,* and *financial sponsor* are used interchangeably (as they are in the literature) throughout this chapter to include a variety of investor groups. The companion website to this book (https://www.elsevier.com/books-and-journals/book-companion/9780128197820) contains a review of this chapter in the file folder titled "Student Study Guide."

The role of public and private financial markets

Financial markets can be global, regional, country specific, or local and consist of highly regulated standardized public or informal private markets. *Public markets* are those in which stocks or bonds are traded using standard contracts subject to disclosure rules set by exchanges and government agencies. Their standardized nature appeals to a wide array of investors, helping to ensure they are relatively liquid. *Private markets* are those in which contracts are negotiated directly—rather than on exchanges—between the parties involved.

Private placement of debt or equity with insurance companies and pension funds illustrate common private market deals. Because these deals are private, they provide more anonymity than public deals. Nonstandard contracts tend to make private markets less liquid, appealing to a narrower group of investors. Participants range from individuals to private equity and hedge funds. The decision to raise money in the public or private markets reflects the disclosure requirements of the public markets, firm size, market liquidity, and creditworthiness.

At $2.4 trillion, private market financing exceeded public market financing of $2.1 trillion in 2017.[1] Money raised privately has more than doubled during the past decade. So-called private placement deals represent about two-thirds or $1.6 trillion of total funds raised on private markets. Regulators dislike the growth in private markets because they lack oversight, and public exchanges are concerned because they view private markets as competitors.

The growth in private market financing may be a key reason why the number of initial public offerings (IPOs) has fallen since 2000. Between 1980 and 2000, the annual average of IPOs was 310; after 2000, the yearly average fell to 110.[2] Private firms face less pressure to go public to satisfy their financing needs with investors searching aggressively for higher yields offered in the private markets.

[1] Eaglesham et al., April 3, 2018

[2] University of Florida Warrington College of Business, https://site.warrington.ufl.edu/ritter/ipo-data

By borrowing in private markets, firms are able to stay private longer to achieve greater scale economies, postpone the cost of going public, and avoid investor pressure for short-term results. As traditional investors in public firms, mutual funds in particular have been increasing their investments in private firms in a search for higher returns, greater diversification, and increased IPO allotments[3] when the firms in which they invest go public.[4] Furthermore, with the decline in the number of publicly traded firms, mutual funds have fewer companies in which to invest.

The growth in the private market may undermine efforts to limit the riskiness of the financial system as commercial banks subject to regulation continue to lend to largely unregulated private lenders such as hedge funds and private equity firms. Increasing loan default rates among private lenders will adversely impact commercial banks and ultimately the taxpayer if institutions deemed "too big to fail" develop liquidity or solvency problems.

Newer forms of private funding include selling shares in emerging firms through crowdfunding.[5] Securities and Exchange Commission (SEC) rules dictate that private offerings are sold only to banks, institutional investors, and "accredited" individuals (i.e., those with net incomes of more than $200,000 or a net worth of $1 million, not counting homes).[6] Most of the private placement market is subject to SEC's Regulation D (Reg D).[7] Securities offered under Reg D must comply with state "blue sky" laws governing security issues. See Chapter 2 for a more detailed discussion of this subject. How both public and private markets are used to finance deals is described next.

How are M&A transactions commonly financed?

M&A transactions typically are financed by using cash, equity, debt, or some combination. Which source(s) of financing is chosen depends on various factors, including current capital market conditions, the liquidity and creditworthiness of the acquiring and target firms, the incremental borrowing capacity of the combined acquiring and target firms, the size of the deal, and the preference of the target shareholders for cash or acquirer shares.

Financing options: borrowing

There are two basic types of debt financing: recourse and nonrecourse loans. In recourse lending, the lender can pursue the borrower for all debt owed in the event of default. After liquidating the assets pledged to secure the loan, the lender can collect any amount of loan that exceeds the value of the collateral by filing a lawsuit and obtaining a judgment against the borrower. For nonrecourse lending, the lender must accept the proceeds generated by selling the collateral, and they cannot collect any amount owed in excess of the proceeds of the collateral. Whereas borrowers generally want nonrecourse loans, lenders favor recourse loans.[8] As explained next, an acquirer or financial sponsor may tap into an array of alternative sources of borrowing.

Asset-based (secured) lending

Under asset-based lending, the borrower pledges certain assets as collateral. These assets can be tangible or sometimes intangible assets.[9] These loans are often short-term (i.e., less than 1 year in maturity) and secured by easily liquidated assets, such as accounts receivable and inventory. Borrowers often seek *revolving lines of credit* for daily borrowing needs. Under such an arrangement, the bank agrees to make loans up to a maximum for a specified period,

[3] An allotment refers to the allocation of shares granted to a participating underwriting firm during an IPO.

[4] Kwon et al., 2019

[5] *Crowdfunding* refers to raising small amounts of money from large numbers of people to finance a new business using social media and crowdfunding websites.

[6] In 2020, the SEC expanded the definition of accredited investors to include holders of an entry-level stockbroker's license and "knowledgeable employees" of nonpublic firms.

[7] Reg D defines who is exempt from much of the disclosure requirements associated with public security issues.

[8] Lenders may be willing to grant a borrower a nonrecourse loan but only at a higher rate of interest and only when the borrower is viewed as a good credit risk.

[9] Lim et al., 2020. Goodwill is generally not acceptable to lenders as collateral. However, identifiable intangible assets (e.g., brand names, patents, in-process research and development, trademarks, noncompete agreements, and customer contracts) may be used as collateral if they are viewed as critical to generating future cash flows.

usually 1 year or more. As the borrower repays a portion of the loan, an amount equal to the repayment can be borrowed against under the terms of the agreement. In addition to interest, the bank charges a fee for the commitment to make the funds available. For a fee, the borrower may choose to convert the revolving credit line into a term loan, which has a maturity of 2 to 10 years and typically is secured by the asset that is being financed, such as new capital equipment.[10]

Loan documents define the rights and obligations of the parties to the loan. The *loan agreement* stipulates the terms and conditions under which the lender will make the loan, the *security agreement* specifies which of the borrower's assets will be pledged to secure the loan, and the *promissory note* commits the borrower to repay the loan.[11]

Loan agreements contain an *acceleration clause* allowing a lender to demand a borrower repay a loan if the contract is breached, such as failing to pay interest and principal when due or breaking a covenant. If the borrower defaults, the lender can sell the collateral to recover the value of the loan.[12] Loan agreements often have *cross-default provisions* allowing lenders to collect loans immediately if the borrower is in default on a loan to another lender.

Loan documents contain security provisions and protective affirmative and negative covenants limiting what the borrower may do as long as the loan is outstanding. Typical *security provisions* include the assignment of payments due to the lender, an assignment of a portion of receivables or inventories, and a pledge of marketable securities held by the borrower.

An *affirmative covenant* specifies actions the borrower agrees to take during the term of the loan. These include furnishing periodic financial statements, carrying insurance to cover insurable business risks, maintaining a minimum amount of net working capital, and retaining key managers. A *negative covenant* restricts a borrower's actions. They include limiting the amount of dividends paid, the level of compensation given to employees, the amount of borrower indebtedness, capital investments, and asset sales.

Debt covenants are frequently renegotiated before a firm is technically in default (i.e., in violation of a covenant). More than 60% of covenant renegotiations relax restrictive covenants. Such renegotiations occur as lenders and borrowers attempt to avoid actual default.[13] Renegotiation to remove onerous bond covenants may not be practical because of the sheer number of bondholders and the likelihood a significant number of "holdouts" would remain even if agreement can be reached with the largest bondholders. Firms may be inclined to tender for bonds, offering a significant premium to their current market price as a means of "indirectly renegotiating" with their bondholders.

Bond tender offers are often undertaken by target firms whose boards are supportive of a bidder's deal. Such tender offers reduce leverage and eliminate potentially troublesome bond characteristics such as put options or change-in-control provisions. The use of bond tender offers in M&A often increases the probability the transaction will be completed and are associated with lower takeover premiums.[14]

Cash flow (unsecured) lending

Cash flow lenders view the borrower's capability to generate cash flow as the primary means of recovering a loan and the borrower's assets as a secondary source of funds in the event of default. In the mid-1980s, LBO capital structures assumed increasing amounts of unsecured debt.

Unsecured debt that lies between senior debt and equity is called *mezzanine financing* and includes senior subordinated debt, subordinated debt, and bridge financing. It frequently consists of high-yield junk bonds, used to increase the postacquisition cash flow of the acquired entity.[15] Unsecured financing often consists of several layers of debt, each subordinate in liquidation to the next-most-senior issue. Those with the lowest level of security typically offer the highest yields to compensate for their higher level of default risk.

[10] Acquirers often prefer to borrow funds on an unsecured basis because the added administrative costs involved in pledging assets as security raise the total cost of borrowing significantly. Secured borrowing also can be onerous because the security agreements can severely limit a company's future borrowing and ability to pay dividends, make investments, and manage working capital aggressively.

[11] The security agreement is filed at a state regulatory office in the state where the collateral is located. Future lenders can check with this office to see which assets a firm has pledged and which are free to be used as future collateral. The filing of this security agreement legally establishes the lender's security interest in the collateral.

[12] The process of determining which of a firm's assets are free from liens is made easier today by commercial credit-reporting repositories, such as Dun & Bradstreet, Experian, Equifax, and Transunion.

[13] Denis and Wang, 2014

[14] Billett et al., 2016

[15] Junk bonds may include zero-coupon bonds whose interest is not paid until maturity.

Bridge financing consists of unsecured loans, often provided by investment banks or hedge funds, to supply short-term financing pending the sale of subordinated debt (i.e., long-term or "permanent" financing). Bridge financing usually is replaced 6 to 9 months after the closing date of a transaction. Borrowers tend to be able to get this type of financing more rapidly than traditional bank loans. And bridge loans do not have repayment penalties. For this convenience, bridge loans come with higher interest rates and origination fees than traditional bank loans.

Types of long-term financing

Long-term debt issues are classified as senior or junior in liquidation. Senior debt has a higher-priority claim to a firm's earnings and assets than junior debt. Unsecured debt also may be classified according to whether it is subordinated to other types of debt. In general, subordinated debentures are junior to other types of debt, including bank loans, because they are backed only by the overall creditworthiness of the borrower.

Convertible bonds convert, at some predetermined ratio (i.e., a specific number of shares per bond), into shares of stock of the issuing company. They normally offer low coupon rates. The bond buyer is compensated primarily by the ability to convert the bond to common stock at a substantial discount from the stock's market value. Current shareholders experience earnings or ownership dilution when the bondholders convert their bonds into new shares.

A debt issue is junior to other debt depending on the restrictions placed on the firm in the *indenture*, a contract between the firm that issues the long-term debt and the lenders. The indenture details the nature of the issue, specifies the way in which the principal must be repaid, and stipulates affirmative and negative covenants. Debt issues often are rated by various *credit-rating agencies* according to their relative degree of risk. The agencies consider such factors as a firm's earnings stability, interest coverage ratios, debt as a percent of total capital, the degree of subordination, and the firm's past performance in meeting its debt service requirements.[16]

Junk bonds

Junk bonds are high-yield bonds that credit-rating agencies have deemed either below investment grade or have not rated.[17] When issued, junk bonds frequently yield more than 4 percentage points above the yields on US Treasury debt of comparable maturity. Junk bond prices tend to be positively correlated with equity prices. As a firm's cash flow improves, its share price generally rises due to improving future cash flow expectations, and the firm's junk bond prices increase, reflecting the lower likelihood of default.

Junk bonds are often issued to finance LBOs and are illiquid because of inactive secondary markets. Credit spreads widen on the existing debt of a firm announcing an LBO because it is viewed by bondholders as riskier.[18] Yields on bonds without covenants such as poison puts (i.e., the right of bondholders to sell their bonds back to the issuer at par or a premium because of a change in ownership) average 21 basis points above comparable 10-year bonds with such provisions.[19] Junk bond financing exploded in the early 1980s but has become less important because of the popularity of leveraged bank loans.

Leveraged bank loans

Leveraged loans are noninvestment-grade bank loans and include second mortgages, which typically have a floating rate and give lenders less security than first mortgages. Some analysts include mezzanine or senior unsecured debt and payment-in-kind notes, for which interest is paid in the form of more debt. Leveraged loans are less costly than junk bonds because they are senior to high-yield bonds in a firm's capital structure. Such loans often are used to finance M&As, recapitalize a firm's balance sheet, refinance debt, or finance general corporate expenditures.

The syndicated loan market, including leveraged loans, senior unsecured debt, and payment-in-kind notes, is growing more rapidly than public markets for debt and equity. Syndicated loans are those issued through a consortium of institutions (including hedge funds, pension funds, and insurance companies) to individual borrowers.

[16] Rating agencies include Moody's Investors Services and Standard & Poor's Corporation. Each has its own scale for identifying the risk of an issue. For Moody's, the ratings are Aaa (the lowest risk category), Aa, A, Baa, Ba, B, Caa, Ca, and C (the highest risk). For S&P, AAA denotes the lowest risk category, and risk rises progressively through ratings AA, A, BBB, BB, B, CCC, CC, C, and D.

[17] Moody's usually rates noninvestment-grade bonds Ba or lower; for S&P, it is BB or lower.

[18] A credit spread is the difference in yield between a risk-free rate (e.g., a US Treasury bond) and another debt security of the same maturity but having a different credit quality.

[19] Eisenthal-Berkovitz et al., 2020

A *syndicated loan* is one structured, arranged, and administered by one or several commercial or investment banks, known as *arrangers*.

Increasingly, nonbank institutional lenders are taking larger roles in the corporate syndicated leveraged loan market. Examples include hedge funds, private equity funds, pension funds, mutual funds, and insurance companies. Lending along with banks, these nonbank lenders charge higher fees and interest rates than banks because they generally have higher required returns. Firms are willing to pay the higher rates if they cannot satisfy all of their financing requirements in the traditional bank loan market.

Transferring default risk from lenders to investors

Default risk can be transferred from the lender to another investor in deals involving three parties: the lender, the borrower, and an investor. Investors typically include mutual funds, pension funds, and hedge funds. By being able to transfer risk, lenders are able to engage in more problematic lending practices to finance higher-risk M&A transactions, particularly LBOs.

Collateralized debt obligations (CDOs) are asset-backed securities (secured by pooling financial assets such as mortgages, credit card receivables, auto loans, and commercial loans) sold to third-party investors. The interest and principal payments on the pooled assets are used to pay interest and principal on the securities. Called *securitization*, this process enables lenders to remove loans from their balance sheets by transferring these assets to off-balance sheet subsidiaries, called special purpose entities, while raising cash to make additional loans by selling asset-backed securities. The ability of a lender to transfer default risk to a third-party investor contributed to the 2008 to 2009 financial crisis by undermining underwriting standards. CDOs collateralized by high-yield bonds are called *collateralized bond obligations*.

Another way for lenders to transfer risk is through *credit default swaps* (CDSs). A CDS is an agreement that the seller of the CDS will compensate the buyer (the lender) if the borrower defaults. The CDS buyer pays the seller a fee for the assurance that they will be compensated if the borrower fails to repay the loan.

Financing options: common and preferred equity

Some common equity pays dividends and provides voting rights, but other common shares have multiple voting rights. When new common shares are issued, shareholders' proportional ownership in that company is reduced. Commonly referred to as *dilution*, the value of existing shares may also decline unless offset by improved earnings expectations. Dilutive situations can arise as a result of conversion of options or other convertible debt and preferred securities[20] into common shares, secondary common share issues[21] to raise capital, or share exchanges in mergers. The net effect of all three is to increase the number of new shares outstanding and, for a given level of earnings, to lower earnings per share and potentially the firm's share price.

Common shareholders sometimes receive *rights offerings* that allow them to maintain their proportional ownership in the company if the firm issues another new stock.[22] Common shareholders with rights may, but are not obligated to, acquire as many shares of new stock as needed to maintain their proportional ownership in the company. Rights are short-term instruments usually expiring within 30 to 60 days of issuance. The exercise price of rights is always set below the firm's current share price.

Although preferred stockholders receive dividends rather than interest, their shares often are considered a fixed income security. Dividends on preferred stock are generally constant over time, like interest payments on debt, but the firm is generally not obligated to pay them at a specific time.[23] In liquidation, bondholders are paid first, then

[20] See Chapter 15 for a more detailed explanation of options and other convertible securities.

[21] Secondary equity issues are those implemented after a firm has undertaken an IPO and are undertaken when the firm's equity price is at or near historical highs. If the price per share realized in the secondary issue is lower than the IPO price, the price of shares held by current shareholders will fall to that realized in the secondary issue.

[22] Preemption rights, antidilution provisions, or subscription rights are often included in contracts between a firm and those acquiring its new issue.

[23] Unpaid dividends cumulate for eventual payment by the issuer if the preferred stock is a cumulative issue.

preferred stockholders, and last, common stockholders. To conserve cash, LBOs frequently issue paid-in-kind preferred stock, in which dividends are paid in the form of more preferred stock.[24]

How shares are issued varies by country. In the United States and a few other countries, management, with some exceptions, typically needs only board approval to issue common stock.[25] In most countries, however, by law or stock exchange rules, shareholders usually vote to approve equity issuances. When shareholders approve issuances, average announcement returns tend to be positive. When managers issue stock without shareholder approval, returns on average are negative, reflecting differences between shareholder and management objectives.[26]

IPOs and equity carveouts are additional mechanisms for raising money to finance capital outlays, including M&As. In recent years, IPOs have become more of a "liquidity event" undertaken to allow founders and early investors to take cash out of the business rather than to raise money to fund capital spending. Private markets have proved to be an attractive alternative to public markets for equity financing.[27] *Equity carveouts* represent the partial sale of a business to outside investors to raise funds. Both IPOs and carveouts are discussed in detail in Chapter 17.

Firms in economies with more developed equity markets use IPOs more frequently than those in economies relying more on bank lending. Countries such as Germany where banks play a central role in corporate financing usually are characterized by close relationships between financial and nonfinancial corporations. In contrast, in the United States and the United Kingdom, which have more liquid stock markets, firms are more likely to enter the financial markets to raise capital.[28]

Seller financing

Seller financing can "close the gap" between what sellers want and what a buyer is willing to pay. It involves the seller's deferral of a portion of the purchase price until some future date—in effect, providing a loan to the buyer. A buyer may be willing to pay the seller's asking price if a portion is deferred because the buyer recognizes that the loan will reduce the present value (PV) of the purchase price. The advantages to the buyer include a lower overall transaction risk (because of the need to provide less capital at the time of closing) and the shifting of risk to the seller if the buyer ultimately defaults on the loan to the seller.[29]

Earnouts and warrants represent forms of seller financing. With the earnout, the seller defers a portion of the purchase price contingent on realizing a future earnings target or some other measure. Warrants may be issued to the seller enabling them to purchase an amount of the acquirer's stock at a certain exercise price, which is higher than the price at the time the warrant is issued. Warrants may be converted over a period of many months to many years, enabling the warrant holder to participate in the upside potential of the business. Table 13.1 summarizes the alternative forms of financing. For more detail on earnouts and warrants, see Chapter 11.

Asset sales

Acquirers with limited borrowing capacity and excess cash balance may finance a portion of the purchase price by divesting nonstrategic acquirer and target assets in a "sale-to-buy" strategy.[30] The proceeds are used to reduce leverage incurred in financing the deal, to buy back equity issued to raise funds before the takeover, or to augment

[24] To attract investors to start-ups, preferred stock may have additional benefits or preferences; for example, if a company is sold or goes public, investors get a multiple of their initial investment before common shareholders get anything; other preferences could include board seats and veto rights over important decisions. Preferred dividends paid to corporate investors receive favorable tax treatment (i.e., the dividend received deduction).

[25] In the United States, each stock exchange requires listed firms to receive shareholder approval before they can issue 20% or more of their outstanding common stock or voting power.

[26] Holderness, 2018

[27] Public markets require divulging considerable amounts of information about the firm and raise concerns about being regulated as a public company.

[28] Aktas et al., 2019

[29] Many businesses do not want to use seller financing because it requires that they accept the risk that the note will not be repaid. Such financing is necessary, though, when bank financing is not an option.

[30] Mavis et al., 2020

TABLE 13.1 Alternative financing by type of security and lending source

Type of security		Debt	
	Backed by	**Lenders loan up to**	**Lending source**
Secured debt			
Short-term (<1 year) debt Intermediate-term (1–10 years) debt	Liens generally on receivables and inventories Liens on land and equipment	50%–80%, depending on quality Up to 80% of appraised value of equipment and 50% of real estate	Banks and finance companies Life insurance companies, private equity investors, pension funds, and hedge funds
Unsecured or mezzanine debt (subordinated and junior subordinated debt, including seller financing) • First layer • Second layer • And so on Bridge financing Payment in kind	Cash-generating capabilities of the borrower	Face value of securities	Life insurance companies, pension funds, private equity, and hedge funds
Type of security		**Equity**	
Preferred stock • Cash dividends • Convertible • Payment in kind	Cash-generating capabilities of the firm		Life insurance companies, pension funds, hedge funds, private equity, and angel investors
Common stock	Cash-generating capabilities of the firm		Same

working capital for the combined firms. Firms also may deleverage by selling certain assets such as equipment and facilities with an option to lease back assets needed to continue operations.[31]

Capital structure theory and practice

Two popular theories describe how firms select the appropriate capital structure (i.e., debt versus equity): the trade-off theory and the pecking order theory.[32] The *trade-off theory* posits a trade-off between tax savings (or tax shield) and financial risk. Because interest payments are tax deductible, borrowing is initially cheaper than equity financing. By taking on more debt, the firm can lower its weighted average cost of capital (WACC) by adding debt relative to equity. But as debt increases relative to equity, so does the risk of default, which pushes up the WACC. According to the *pecking order theory,* a firm initially prefers to finance itself from internally generated funds. As cash balances are reduced below some desired minimum level, the firm chooses to finance its expenditures through borrowing. Because equity represents the highest cost source of funds, the firm issues new equity only as a last resort.

Of the two theories, the pecking order theory is better able to explain how acquirers choose to finance deals because it provides a prioritization of financing sources. As explained later, the trade-off theory seems to better explain highly leveraged transactions. Neither of these theories explains why some firms tend to hold larger excess cash balances than others and how such cash balances impact the performance of future investments, including M&As. Some argue that excess cash balances could reflect agency problems or management's desire to entrench itself. Agency problems arise when shareholders want excess cash distributed to them while managers want excess balances to make large acquisitions to gain personal prestige and increased compensation commensurate with the increased size of their firm.

[31] Elseify et al., 2019

[32] For a discussion of how to value a firm's complex capital structure, which could include convertible securities, options, warrants, finite maturity preferred stock, and sinking fund provisions, see Borochin (2019).

Others counter that excess balances reflect management taking precautions to have cash on hand to exploit future investment opportunities and to hedge against risk. Recent research seems to support the precautionary motive for large cash balances because cash-rich firms tend to exhibit higher announcement date returns than cash-poor acquirers. Excess balances seem to relate more to management having better information than investors about future investment opportunities and M&A deal synergies than a desire to protect their positions.[33]

The trade-off and pecking order theories address how capital structures are determined from the perspective of corporate managers. In practice, investors also affect such decisions. A recent survey finds that about 80% of institutional investors surveyed believe they influence capital structure decisions both directly through talks with management and indirectly through talks with the investment banks assisting with securities issuance. Among equity, convertible bond, and conventional bond investors, 75%, 83%, and 84%, respectively, indicate that they find capital structure important when making the decision to invest in a particular company. And more than 50% of respondents consider agency problems to be important. Those most likely to be influenced by investors are smaller, younger, and financially constrained firms.[34]

How capital structure can impact abnormal financial returns to acquirers

Abnormal financial returns to acquirers appear to be influenced by the way a deal is financed. How a firm raises funds often signals investors how well the firm is doing. Using internally generated funds suggests the firm is generating substantial excess cash flows. If the firm chooses to use debt, management appears to be confident that it can meet its financial obligations.

There is evidence that the level of debt can indeed affect firm value, especially for small- to medium-sized companies, if management can communicate to shareholders that they can expect the proceeds to be used in a way that will meet or exceed the firm's cost of capital.[35] Large firms are better able to increase leverage without adversely impacting firm value because of the amount of assets available for liquidation to cover their debt service requirements.[36]

Issuing new stock is generally viewed as negative as management believes its shares are overvalued and is seeking to raise money before the value of a firm's shares fall. Investors often react by selling their shares, anticipating declining future share prices. Abnormal returns to acquirers are higher when cash or debt is used to finance the deal than when equity is used.[37]

What is the role of private equity, hedge, and venture capital funds in deal financing?

These investor groups take money from large institutions such as pension funds, borrow additional cash, and buy private and public companies. Private equity funds invest for the long term, taking an active role in managing the firms they acquire. Hedge funds are more traders than long-term investors, investing in a wide variety of assets (be it stocks, commodities, or foreign currency), holding them for a short time, and then selling. Venture capital (VC) funds take money from institutional investors and make small investments in start-ups. In deal financing, these investor groups play the role of financial intermediaries and "lenders of last resort" for firms having limited access to capital. They also provide financial engineering and operational expertise, and they monitor the performance of firms in which they invest, contributing to their attractive returns and ability to manage financial distress better than other similarly leveraged firms.

[33] Gao et al., 2018

[34] Brown et al., 2019

[35] Kim et al., 2019

[36] Gong (2020) argues the threat of short-selling limits increases in leverage, particularly for firms experiencing financial distress, whose shares are relatively illiquid, and whose managers are risk-averse.

[37] Fischer, 2017

Financial intermediaries

Private equity, hedge, and VC funds represent conduits between investors or lenders and borrowers, pooling resources and investing in firms with attractive growth prospects. All three types of buyout funds limit investors' ability to withdraw funds for a number of years. Both private equity and VC funds deploy investor money within 5 years, with more than half of new investments made during the first 2 years of the average fund's lifetime.[38]

All three typically exit their investments via sales to strategic buyers, IPOs, or another buyout fund. However, their roles in financing M&A activity differ in significant ways. Private equity firms use substantial leverage to acquire firms, remain invested for up to 10 years, and often take an active operational role in firms in which they have an ownership stake. Although hedge funds also use leverage to acquire firms outright, they are more likely to provide financing for takeovers through short-term loans or minority equity stakes. Finally, VC funds' primary role is to finance emerging businesses, with limited access to capital.[39]

Private equity, hedge, and VC funds usually are limited partnerships (for US investors) or offshore investment corporations (for non-US or tax-exempt investors) in which the general partner (GP) has made a substantial personal investment, giving the GP control. Partnerships offer favorable tax benefits, a finite life, and investor liability limited to the amount of their investment. Institutional investors, such as pension funds, endowments, insurance companies, and private banks, as well as high–net worth individuals, typically invest in these types of funds as limited partners. When a partnership has reached its target size, it closes to further investment, whether from new or existing investors.

VC funds whose GPs contribute large amounts of their own money invest more rapidly, invest where they have greater expertise, and realize greater success when they sell the fund's investments. Because of their rigorous screening process, VC-financed IPOs often display superior financial performance post-IPO than non–VC-financed IPOs.[40]

Relationships matter! For example, VC firms, with directors on mature public company boards, are able to raise larger sums of money than otherwise because of their networks, visibility, and credibility, which enhances their fundraising activities. Moreover, the experience, knowledge, and expertise obtained through these directors have been shown to benefit VC company portfolios by enhancing the likelihood of successful exits of their investments.

Private equity, hedge, and VC funds' revenue has both a fixed and a variable component. GPs earn most of the private equity firm's revenue through management fees, commonly equal to 2% of assets under management[41] and as much as 6% of the equity invested by the GPs.[42] Fee income varies little over the business cycle or with the GP's performance. GPs can also earn variable revenue from so-called *carried interest*,[43] or the percentage of profits, often 20%, accruing to the GP. The carried interest percentage may be applied without the fund's having achieved any minimum return for investors or may be triggered only if a certain preset return is achieved.

Private equity funds also receive fees from their portfolio companies for completing deals, arranging financing, performing due diligence, providing advice, and monitoring business performance. There is evidence that the presence of carried interest, in which the GP is rewarded for a successful investment outcome (but not penalized for failure), encourages them to engage in excessive risk taking.[44] Moreover, GPs are rewarded less based on past investment performance and more on their status as a founder.[45] Although skill is a critical factor in the top-performing funds, the average private equity or hedge fund manager tends to mimic the strategies and portfolios of their peers or larger funds.[46]

[38] Giot et al., 2014

[39] Paglia et al., 2014

[40] Megginson et al., 2019

[41] Metrick et al., 2010

[42] Phalippou et al., 2018

[43] The TCJA of 2017 requires a fund's investment to be held for a minimum of 3 years for carried interest to receive long-term capital gains treatment. Previously, the required holding period was 1 year.

[44] Buchner et al., 2017

[45] Ivashina et al., 2019

[46] Buchner et al., 2020

Lenders and investors of last resort

Since 1995, hedge funds and private equity funds have participated in more than half of the private equity placements (i.e., sales to a select number of investors rather than the general public) in the United States. Contributing more than one-fourth of the total capital raised, hedge funds have consistently been the largest single investor group in these types of transactions.[47] Public firms using private placements tend to be small, young, and poorly performing and have trouble obtaining financing. Although representing a high-cost source of financing, such firms often undertake transactions called *private investments in public equity* (PIPES).[48]

Hedge funds investing in PIPE securities perform relatively well. Why? They buy such securities at discounts from their value in public markets, protect their investment through repricing rights[49] and selling short the firm's shares already trading on public markets, receive warrants, and hold their investments for relatively short periods. As such, hedge funds are able to serve "as investors of last resort" for firms having difficulty borrowing.

Abnormal returns to PIPE investors average almost 20% for those holding their shares for a year. Financial returns tend to decline over longer investor holding periods because most of the gain accrues to investors having bought at a discount who sell immediately after the registration of the shares.[50] Shareholders selling at a later date often do so only at lower prices because of the postregistration selling and the expected decline in the firm's longer-term performance.[51]

Providers of financial engineering and operational expertise for target firms

In this context, financial engineering describes the creation of a viable capital structure that magnifies financial returns to equity investors. The additional leverage drives the need to improve operating performance to meet debt service requirements; in turn, the anticipated improvement in operating performance enables the firm to assume greater leverage. In this manner, leverage and operating performance are inextricably linked.

Successful private equity investors manage the relationship between leverage and operating performance, realizing superior financial returns and operating performance on average relative to their peers. Private equity firms seem better able to survive financial distress than other comparably leveraged firms. These conclusions (discussed next) are supported by abnormal financial returns to both prebuyout shareholders, who benefit from the premium paid for their shares as a result of the leveraged buyout, and postbuyout shareholders.

Prebuyout returns to leveraged buyout target firm (prebuyout) shareholders

Prebuyout shareholder abnormal financial returns often exceed 40% on the announcement date for nondivisional leveraged buyouts. The outsized returns reflect the anticipated improvement in the target's operating performance because of management incentives, the discipline imposed on management to repay debt, and future tax savings.[52]

Because tax benefits are predictable for a given future earnings stream, the value of future tax savings tends to be more predictable than improvements in operating performance. Thus the impact of tax benefits often is fully reflected in premiums offered to shareholders of firms subject to LBOs, but the effects of improved operating performance are not. The failure of expected improvements in operating performance to be fully reflected in premiums helps to explain the presence of sizeable postbuyout returns to LBO shareholders.

Also contributing to the abnormal returns to prebuyout shareholders is the elimination of prebuyout inefficient decision making because of conflicts among different shareholder groups. In firms having dual-class capital structures, in which investors holding stock with multiple voting rights have control while investors holding another class of stock receive dividends, the first shareholder class has control rights, and the second class has cash flow rights.

Conflicts arise when controlling shareholders want excess cash flow reinvested in the firm but others want it disbursed as dividends or share repurchases. Controlling shareholders may see significant value in buying out

[47] Brophy et al., 2009. Other significant participants in the private placement market (i.e., direct lender market) include insurance companies, pension funds, and endowment funds.

[48] See Chapter 10 for more detail on PIPE financing.

[49] Repricing rights protect investors from a decline in the price of their holdings by requiring firms to issue more shares if the price of the privately placed shares decreases.

[50] The issuing firm is required to use its best efforts to file a shelf registration statement, Form S-3, with the SEC.

[51] Lim et al., 2019

[52] Guo et al., 2011

the other public shareholders to gain complete control over decisions about how the firm's cash flow will be used. Controlling shareholders may be willing to pay attractive premiums to take public firms private (so-called public-to-private LBOs), which are documented to average about 36% in 18 Western European countries.[53]

Postbuyout returns to leveraged buyout shareholders

Studies show public-to-private LBOs on average improve operating profits and cash flow, regardless of methodology, benchmarks, and time period. However, more recent public-to-private LBOs had a more modest impact on operating performance than those of the 1980s.[54]

Large-sample studies in the United States, the United Kingdom, and France show that companies in private equity portfolios improve their operations more than their competitors on average, as measured by their profit margins and cash flows. Private equity funds accelerate the process of creative destruction that invigorates the economy by replacing mature, often moribund, firms with more innovative, dynamic ones, tending to increase productivity by more than 2%.[55] Industry and gross domestic product growth and stock market returns also have a substantial impact on private equity financial returns.[56]

Some studies document that average private equity fund returns in the United States have exceeded those of public markets in both the short and the long terms. On average, private equity funds have earned at least 18% to 20% more over the life of their investments than the S&P 500 during the same period; private equity firms also have outperformed public equities in both good and bad markets.[57] These higher returns compensate private equity investors for the relative illiquidity of their investments as compared with more conventional investments, such as equities.[58]

Critics note that financial returns for private equity funds are self-reported and may be distorted by measurement errors, methodology, and failure to include all management fees. A widely quoted study found that financial returns to private equity limited partners (after all fees were considered) were equivalent to what they could have earned if they had invested in the S&P 500.[59] Others argue that once management fees, the illiquid nature of the investment, and the risk of losing money are taken into account, investors essentially break even.[60] Another study concludes that private equity firms' ability to achieve above-average financial returns declines over time as the industry matures and competition for target firms bids up prices.[61]

Still others find that the positive improvement in operating results after an LBO occurs in empirical studies of LBOs for which public financial statements are available because of such firms having publicly traded debt outstanding or going public again and providing historical financial statements. These researchers attribute the post-LBO operating improvement for such firms to sample bias.[62] A study of US firms using US tax data concludes that the average LBO firm shows little improvement in operating performance between the pre- and post-LBO periods.[63]

Private equity–owned firms and financial distress

Firms acquired by private equity investors do not display a higher default rate than other similarly leveraged firms. And firms financed by private equity funds are less likely to be liquidated and exit Chapter 11 sooner than

[53] Broubaker et al., 2014

[54] Cumming et al. (2007), in a summary of much of the literature on post-LBO performance, concluded that LBOs, especially management buyouts, enhance firm operating performance. However, Guo et al. (2011) find that the improvement in operating performance after public-to-private LBOs has been more modest during the period from 1990 to 2006 than during the 1980s.

[55] Alperovych et al., 2013; Davis et al., 2011; Guo et al., 2011; Kaplan and Stromberg, 2009

[56] Valkama et al., 2013

[57] Robinson, 2011; Kaplan, 2012

[58] Frazoni et al., 2012

[59] Kaplan and Schoar, 2005

[60] Sorensen et al., 2014

[61] Braun et al., 2017

[62] That is, such samples include only those firms that are superior performers in their industries because only the best performers are likely to be taken public and in general only higher-quality corporate borrowers issue public debt.

[63] Cohn et al., 2014.

comparably leveraged firms.[64] Private equity—backed firms exhibited a default rate between 1980 and 2002 of 1.2% versus Moody's Investors Services reported default rate of 1.6% for all US corporate bond issuers during the same period.[65]

Although the increased leverage associated with LBOs raises bankruptcy risk,[66] bankruptcy rates among private equity buyouts of European firms showed that experienced private equity investors were better able to manage financial distress and avoid bankruptcy than their peer companies. The success of many private equity investors in avoiding bankruptcy reflects their selection of undervalued but less financially distressed firms as buyout targets[67] and their ability to manage the additional leverage after the buyout is completed.

Listed versus unlisted fund performance

In recent years, public listings of hedge funds, such as KKR and The Blackstone Group, have increased sharply. Going public, they argue, allows them to improve investment performance by better incentivizing management through employee stock options and by investing funds raised in their IPOs in better technology and infrastructure.

Public shareholders contend that a public listing worsens agency conflicts. Owners of privately held investment firms contribute a substantial share of their net worth to the funds managed by the firm, thus aligning their interests with other investors. In going public, the owners sell out to new shareholders, who do not typically invest with those investing in the funds. This separates the interests of the owners from what is being invested. As such, hedge funds managed by publicly listed firms underperform those firms that remain private by 3% per year.[68]

On average, hedge funds achieve abnormal financial returns only during "good" times irrespective of their strategies. And small and young hedge funds tend to outperform their peers during "good times." In contrast, during "bad times," small funds underperform large funds.[69]

Venture capital—backed versus buyout firm—backed IPO performance

IPOs allow VC and buyout funds to exit their investments. Buyout-backed IPOs realize superior operating performance when compared with VC-backed IPOs. However, both VC and buyout-backed IPOs slightly underperform the major stock market indices in the long run.[70]

VCs specialize in firms in the early stages of development. Without a track record, the future cash flows of such firms are difficult to predict. VCs have an incentive to underprice their IPO shares to establish a reputation of engaging in IPOs whose share prices rise after issuance. In contrast, buyout firms use IPOs to quickly cash out of their investments; as such, they may have an incentive to not fully inform IPO investors about the true quality of the firms taken public.

The empirical evidence suggests that VC-sponsored IPOs are more likely to be underpriced compared to their true value than buyout-sponsored ones, resulting in VC-sponsored IPOs showing greater short-term performance than buyout-backed IPOs. However, during the 3 years after the IPO, share price performance of either VC- or buyout-backed IPOs is about the same. Why? Using operating performance measures such as return on assets, buyout-sponsored firms outperform VC-backed firms in the long run, offsetting the initial short-term pop in VC-backed IPO share prices because of underpricing of VC-backed firms' share prices.

Impact of tax reform on M&A financing

On balance, M&A activity should benefit from the TCJA passed in the United States in late 2017 (see Chapter 12). Improvements in operating cash flow because of a substantially lower corporate tax rate and 100% write-off of

[64] Stromberg et al., 2011

[65] Kaplan and Stromberg, 2009

[66] Ayash and Rastad (2020) estimate an 18% increase in the likelihood of bankruptcy for the average LBO.

[67] Dittmar et al. (2012) document that private equity firms excel at identifying targets with high potential for operational improvement.

[68] Sun et al., 2019

[69] Stafylas and Andrikopoulosb, 2020. "Good times" and "bad times" refer to periods of bull and bear markets.

[70] Buchner et al., 2019

certain types of short-lived tangible assets should more than compensate for the less favorable treatment of interest expense. Future M&A financing is likely to be skewed more toward using cash balances (including the target's) and equity rather than debt. The implications of that law for an acquirer's ability to finance takeovers through internal after-tax operating cash flow versus external debt and equity issues are addressed next.

Internal financing

The new law favors the use of internally generated funds by reducing the corporate tax rate and accelerating capital cost recovery. But this will be partially offset by the less favorable treatment of net operating losses (NOLs). Moreover, the move to a worldwide tax system in which only domestic profits are taxed will enable firms to better manage their overseas cash balances by financing investment opportunities (including M&As) based more on economics and less on tax concerns. Although the accelerated deduction for capital outlays remains in effect (through January 1, 2023, for most tangible property), acquirers may be more inclined to structure deals as asset acquisitions (or those deemed asset acquisitions under Section 338 of the US tax code).

Under the new tax law, NOLs existing on January 1, 2018, and those created in subsequent years lose a significant amount of their value because the applicable statutory tax rate is now 21%, 14 percentage points lower than previously. NOLs arising in taxable years ending after December 31, 2017, not deductible in a taxable year can be carried forward indefinitely. NOL carrybacks have been eliminated. NOL deductions used in tax years up to 2022 would be limited to 90% of taxable income falling to 80% thereafter. Although a target's NOLs can still sweeten a buyout, their benefit to acquirers in the future will be less than in the past.

External financing

Limitation of net interest expense deductions to 30% of earnings before interest and taxes could make debt financing less attractive. Interest on debt held on balance sheets before the enactment of the 2017 tax law will be treated in the same way. However, that portion of net interest deductions not allowed because of the cap may be carried forward indefinitely to future taxable years. The mixture of limitations on net interest expense and NOLs means that highly leveraged firms are likely to become taxpayers sooner than they would have under the earlier tax law.

Fun with acronyms: the transition from LIBOR to SOFR

US regulators have asked banks not to use the London Interbank Offer Rate (LIBOR) in any new transactions by the end of 2021.[71] However, LIBOR will not be fully phased out until June 2023 to allow existing derivative and business loans tied to the rate to mature. The phase-out was triggered by a lack of transparency into how LIBOR was determined. Promoted by US regulators, the successor to LIBOR as of this writing is expected to be the Secured Overnight Financing Rate (SOFR).[72] And the number of new floating-rate loans and investments using SOFR has risen significantly in recent years, increasing its probable wider acceptance.

The two interest rates are quite different. Calculated using actual transactions, SOFR is considered a broad measure of the overnight cost of borrowing collateralized by Treasury securities. LIBOR is determined by a panel of banks submitting subjective estimates of their borrowing costs. Whereas SOFR is an overnight borrowing rate only, LIBOR has terms ranging from overnight to 12 months. As an overnight rate, SOFR has typically traded below LIBOR on longer maturities because rates on short-term loans are typically under those on longer maturities.

Leveraged buyouts as financing strategies

LBOs are a common financing strategy used by private equity firms to buy companies using a substantial amount of debt. Table 13.2 illustrates how leverage magnifies financial returns. As a risk proxy, the debt-to-equity ratio

[71] Before 2021, LIBOR served as a "reference rate" for floating-rate notes, bank loans, and in some instances preferred stock. LIBOR also served as a benchmark for many consumer loans as well as margin loans, asset-based loans and lines of credit, and variable-rate mortgages. Fluctuations in LIBOR would trigger corresponding changes in interest rates that used it as a benchmark.

[72] Regulators in other countries are recommending other interest rates.

TABLE 13.2 Impact of leverage on return to shareholders[a]

	Column 1: all-cash purchase	Column 2: 60% cash/40% debt	Column 3: 40% cash/60% debt	Column 4: 20% cash/80% debt
Purchase price ($)	100	100	100	100
Equity (cash investment) ($)	100	60	40	20
Borrowings ($)	0	40	60	80
EBITDA ($)	20	20	20	20
Interest at 10% ($)	0	4	6	8
Tax-deductible interest ($)	0	4	6	6[b]
Depreciation and amortization ($)	2	2	2	2
Taxable income ($)	18	14	12	12
Less income taxes at 26% ($)[c]	4.7	3.6	3.1	3.1
Net income ($)	13.3	10.4	8.9	8.9
After-tax return on equity (%)	13.3	17.3	22.3	44.5
Debt-to-equity ratio	0	0.67×	1.5×	4.0×

[a]Unless otherwise noted, all numbers are in millions of dollars.
[b]Tax deductible interest expense limited to 30% of earnings before interest, taxes, depreciation, and amortization (EBITDA) under recent US tax legislation.
[c]Current US federal, state, and local tax rate.

increases with increasing leverage. In column 3, equity investors are rewarded for increasing risk by higher financial returns. In column 4, while returns to equity investors double, risk as measured by the debt-to-equity ratio almost triples.

In a typical LBO, the most liquid assets, like receivables, are used as collateral for bank financing. The firm's fixed assets are used to secure a portion of long-term senior financing. Subordinated debt, either unrated or low-rated debt, is used to raise the balance of the purchase price. When a public firm undertakes an LBO, it is said to be *going private* as the firm's equity has been purchased by an investor group and is no longer publicly traded. Firms that go private often are those whose boards are insider dominated and that have concentrated ownership because of super-voting shares.[73] LBOs comprise a larger share of total deals when credit spreads (i.e., difference between risk-free rate and rates on securities of a lower credit quality) narrow, reflecting easier access to the credit markets.[74]

The private equity market is a global phenomenon

About 10% of cross-border deals are undertaken by private equity firms, and their share of such deals has been increasing over time. Such firms are in direct competition with multinational companies, which has substantial advantages. These include larger synergistic opportunities, better access to capital markets, and typically a lower risk premium on borrowing. Despite these advantages, private equity firms have superior track records in reorganizing target firms to improve financial performance over multinational firms.[75]

Private equity investors in cross-border deals structured as LBOs come from countries with strong creditor protections and buy firms in countries with weak creditor protections where potential financial returns may be higher. Strong creditor rights include the ability to seize collateral after bankruptcy reorganization has been approved, the requirement that creditors consent before a debtor firm can enter bankruptcy, and whether secured creditors are paid first when a debtor firm is liquidated.[76]

The ease with which the majority owner can squeeze out minority shareholders is another factor affecting cross-border deals. The United States, the United Kingdom, and Ireland tend to be the least restrictive when it comes to

[73] Gogineni and Upadhyay, 2020
[74] Chiarella and Ostinelli, 2020
[75] Baziki et al., 2017
[76] Cao et al., 2015

squeezing out minority investors; Italy, Denmark, Finland, and Spain are far more restrictive.[77] Other factors such as exchange rates, a country's political environment, and the potential for asset expropriation are discussed in detail in Chapter 19.

Sales to strategic buyers represent the most common exit strategy

LBO financial sponsors and management are able to realize their expected financial returns on exiting the business. Constituting about 13% of total transactions since the 1970s, IPOs declined in importance as an exit strategy.[78] At 39% of all exits, the most common ways of exiting buyouts is through a sale to a strategic buyer[79]; the second most common method, at 24%, is a sale to another buyout or private equity firm in so-called secondary buyouts.

The choice between IPOs and secondary buyouts depends on capital market conditions. IPOs are used when the stock market is rising; secondary buyouts are popular when debt is cheap.[80] Selling to a strategic buyer often results in the best price because the buyer may be able to generate significant synergies by combining the firm with its existing business. However, selling to a private equity firm can provide an even more attractive price when the target is poorly performing and has few investment opportunities. Private equity firms often have greater expertise in managing underperforming firms and access to cheaper capital.[81]

Buyout firms sometimes remain invested in a business portfolio for up to 10 years. They may sell businesses through secondary buyouts when their holding period comes to a close, and they have to pay off investors at the highest possible price and in the shortest possible time. Pressure to sell quickly often causes them to sell at depressed cash flow multiples, making such businesses attractive to other buyout firms seeking new investment opportunities.[82]

An IPO is often less attractive because of the requirement for public disclosure, the commitment of management time, the difficulty in timing the market, and the potential for valuation errors. The original investors also can cash out through a *leveraged recapitalization*: borrowing additional funds to repurchase stock from other shareholders.

Empirical studies show that strategic buyers of private equity–backed firms experience announcement-date abnormal returns of 1% to 3%. Strategic acquirers of VC-backed firms display positive announcement-date returns of about 3%.[83]

The effects of leveraged buyouts on innovation

LBOs tend to improve the rate of innovation.[84] Private equity firms' expertise with respect to strategy development; operational, financial, and human resource management; marketing and sales; and M&As may create an innovative culture. They also play an important role in assessing incumbent management skills and those of their potential replacements.[85] Finally, LBO targets are more likely to implement innovative marketing programs (e.g., design, packaging, and promotion) to increase sales and market share.

Private firms or firms taken private through an LBO often demonstrate higher rates of unique, higher-quality innovation than public firms as measured by the number of patent citations per firm even though public firms typically generate more patents overall. Why? Private firms tend to be more focused, less bureaucratic, and consequently

[77] Wright et al., 2008

[78] After an IPO, buyout firms often retain a significant investment in the firm and undertake a secondary IPO, often at a discount to complete their exit. Secondary IPOs do not portend deteriorating operating performance but rather the expiration of lock-up periods (Dong et al., 2020).

[79] Harford and Kolasinski, 2012

[80] Jenkinson and Souza, 2015

[81] Gorbenko and Malenko, 2015

[82] Arcot et al., 2015

[83] Harford et al., 2012

[84] Lerner et al. (2011) found the rate of innovation, as measured by the quantity and generality of patents, does not change after private equity investments. In fact, the patents of private equity–backed firms applied for in the years after the private equity investment are more frequently cited, suggesting improved innovation.

[85] Meuleman et al., 2009

more attractive to the most talented innovators than are public firms, and they are less prone to interference from the less sophisticated shareholders of public firms.[86] When firms go public, they lose talent, often made rich as a result of the IPO, causing a substantial decline in the uniqueness of their innovation.[87]

The effects of leveraged buyouts on employment growth

In the post-LBO period, firms experience a decline in sales and asset growth because of the pressure to reduce leverage often at the expense of capital spending.[88] But the impact on employment is mixed. Private equity firm buyouts lead to a slightly positive increase in employment when closely held firms are bought out, but the usually larger public company buyouts lead to job losses. After a buyout, employment in existing operations tends to decline relative to other firms in the same industry, but employment in new operations tends to increase relative to other companies in the same industry, resulting in an overall modest 1% decline in employment after private equity deals. Excluding retailers, the overall net employment change (gains less losses) appears to be neutral or positive.[89]

The changing nature of private equity firm collaboration

To finance the increased average size of targets taken private, buyout firms started to bid for target firms as groups of investors.[90] Often time-consuming to set up, such transactions were referred to as club deals. Critics of such tactics argued that banding together to buy large LBO targets could result in lower takeover premiums for target firms by reducing the number of potential bidders. By mitigating risk and allowing for a pooling of complementary resources and skills,[91] supporters countered that clubbing could increase premiums.

Academic research concerning how club deals impact target shareholders is mixed. For deals involving large private equity firms and few bidders, club bidding may depress purchase premiums.[92] However, when the number of bidders is high, there is little evidence of anticompetitive activity,[93] and purchase premiums may increase,[94] particularly when joining forces enables bidders to overcome capital constraints.[95]

Despite the inconclusiveness of these studies, a class action lawsuit against major private equity firms in 2014 was successful in proving the existence of collusion in LBO bidding among such firms after years of litigation. The use of agreements among private equity firms to share capital, valuations, and sector expertise (so-called club deals) reduced the number of bidders. Bain Capital Partners, Blackstone Group, Carlyle, Goldman Sachs, Kohlberg Kravis Roberts & Co., Silver Lake Technology Management, and TPG Capital agreed to pay $590.5 million.[96]

Buyout firms have found that investing along with institutional investors who are also limited partners in the firm's existing funds enables them to raise funds more easily. Advantages to limited partners include escaping management fees they would have incurred had they invested through a new fund and retaining the share of capital gains that would have accrued to the fund's GPs. Moreover, their capital is invested more quickly than is normally the case with a new fund that raises financing in anticipation of finding new investment opportunities.

[86] Kamoto, 2016

[87] Bernstein, 2015.

[88] Ayash, 2020

[89] Davis et al., 2011

[90] Boone and Mulherin (2011) found that nearly half of all acquisitions by private equity firms between 2003 and 2007 involved clubbing. Officer et al. (2010) found similar results between 2002 and 2006.

[91] Complementary resources and skills include information, target screening and selection, and the managerial ability to make operational improvements to the target firm. Stanfield (2020) finds that more highly skilled and resource-rich private equity firms are less likely to engage in clubbing than firms with fewer resources and lower skill levels, which use clubbing as a means of approximating the success levels of the more highly skilled firms.

[92] Officer et al., 2010

[93] Boone and Mulherin, 2011

[94] Guo et al. (2008), and Marquez et al. (2013) found some evidence that "clubbing" is associated with higher target transaction prices when the number of independent bidders is large.

[95] Dasilas et al., 2018

[96] Burke et al., 2019

Returns to investors that co-invest with private equity funds have tended to underperform those that could have been earned had they invested as a limited partner in one of the private equity firm's funds. Why? Institutional investors are given the opportunity to co-invest only after the buyout funds have selected the most promising opportunities for their own investments.[97]

Leveraged buyout leverage and employee bankruptcy rights

Firms may exploit their highly leveraged position to negotiate smaller wage and benefit gains (or extract concessions), arguing that interest and principal repayments have eroded their ability to improve worker compensation. Incentive plans based on the firm's future profitability or worker productivity may be introduced to give workers the potential to earn income above what they earned previously. Workers may make concessions if they believe that the proposed incentive programs are realistic and, in the event of liquidation or reorganization, their ability to recover unpaid wages and accrued pension contributions is protected. The ability to negotiate lower wage rates in these circumstances is affected by prevailing bankruptcy laws, which vary widely from country to country.[98] Firms may be highly aggressive in their use of debt if employees are protected in liquidation but have weak rights when the firm is reorganized.[99]

What factors are critical to successful leveraged buyouts?

Although many factors contribute to the success of LBOs, studies suggest that target selection, not overpaying, and improving operating performance are among the most important.

Target selection

Private equity investors often argue that their ability to find (or "source") deals in which they have some insight not widely known in the industry provides significant value-creation potential. For every hundred firms considered, the average private equity firm investigates in detail about 15, signs a purchase agreement with 8, and actually closes on 4.[100] Attractive LBO candidates have little debt, significant tangible assets, predictable positive cash flow, and redundant assets. Competent management is always crucial to the eventual success of the LBO. Finally, firms in certain types of industries, with revenue enhancement opportunities, part of larger firms, and without change in control covenants also are attractive.

Firms with little debt, redundant assets, and predictable cash flow

Target firms likely to have significant borrowing capacity are those with cash in excess of working capital needs, relatively low leverage, and a strong performance track record. Firms with undervalued assets may use such assets as collateral for loans from asset-based lenders. Undervalued assets also provide significant tax shelter because they may be revalued after closing to their fair market value and depreciated over their allowable tax lives. Operating assets not germane to the target's core business can be divested to payoff of debt.

Firms whose management is competent and motivated

Management of the firm to be taken private is normally given an opportunity to own a significant portion of the firm's equity. On average, 17% of the firm's equity is allocated to the CEO and employees, with the CEO receiving about 8%. Unlike acquirers of public firms, which retain the target's CEO about 31% of the time, private equity acquirers do so about 60% of the time.

[97] Fang et al., 2015

[98] Failing firms may be shielded from creditors by seeking protection under a country's bankruptcy laws. If the parties to the process agree, the firm can be reorganized and emerge from bankruptcy. If not, the firm's assets may be sold to raise cash to pay creditors all or a portion of what they are owed in a process called liquidation. Creditor payments are paid in accordance with priorities set by law. For example, creditors whose loans are secured by the firm's assets are generally paid first and common shareholders last.

[99] Ellul and Pagano, 2019

[100] Gompers et al., 2016

Public company targets have layers of management and the ability to replace the CEO without disrupting the firm's postmerger performance. Private equity firms place a higher value on retaining the CEO and are willing to pay a higher premium for the target firm if the CEO (and management) is willing to stay to create greater postmerger stability.[101] Even then, turnover may be inevitable. Although private equity investors rarely recruit a new management team when they acquire a firm, about half end up doing so at some point after the takeover is completed.[102]

Firms in attractive industries

Typical targets are in mature industries such as manufacturing, retailing, and textiles. Such industries usually are characterized by large tangible book values; modest growth prospects; stable cash flow; and limited research and development, new product, or technology spending. Such industries are not dependent on technologies and production processes that are subject to rapid change.

Firms with significant revenue enhancement opportunities

The most attractive firms are those with significant revenue growth potential and that provide substantial value-added products or services.[103] *Value added* in this context refers to firms that can take products or services comparable to the competition and differentiate them by adding features and functions highly valued by their customers. This differentiation enables them to charge higher prices than their competitors.

Firms that are large-company operating divisions

The best candidates for management buyouts often are underperforming divisions of large companies in which the division is not considered critical to the parent firm's strategy. Frequently, such divisions have excessive overhead, often required by the parent. And expenses are allocated to the division by the parent for services, such as legal, auditing, and treasury functions, that could be purchased less expensively from sources outside the parent firm.

Firms without change-of-control covenants

Such covenants in bond indentures either limit the amount of debt a firm can add or require the company to buy back outstanding debt, often at a premium, whenever a change of control occurs. Firms with bonds lacking such covenants are twice as likely to be the target of an LBO.[104]

Not overpaying

Overpaying can result in excessive borrowing to finance the deal. Failure to meet debt service obligations often requires the LBO firm to renegotiate the terms of loan agreements. If the parties to the agreement cannot compromise, the firm may be forced to file for bankruptcy. Highly leveraged firms also are subject to aggressive tactics from major competitors, who understand that taking on large amounts of debt raises the break-even point for the firm. Competitors may gain market share by cutting product prices. The ability of the LBO firm to match such price cuts is limited because of the required interest and principal repayments.

Private equity acquirers appear to be particularly astute at not overpaying. Using leverage to hype financial returns, they tend to pay lower premiums for targets that are not properly valued by investors. However, they do pay higher premiums for targets that have attractive long-term growth opportunities.[105]

Improving operating performance

Ways to improve performance include negotiating employee wage and benefit concessions in exchange for a profit-sharing or stock ownership plan and outsourcing services once provided by the parent. Other options include

[101] Bargeron et al., 2017

[102] Gompers et al., 2016

[103] Block et al., 2019

[104] Billett et al., 2010

[105] Lai and Pu, 2020

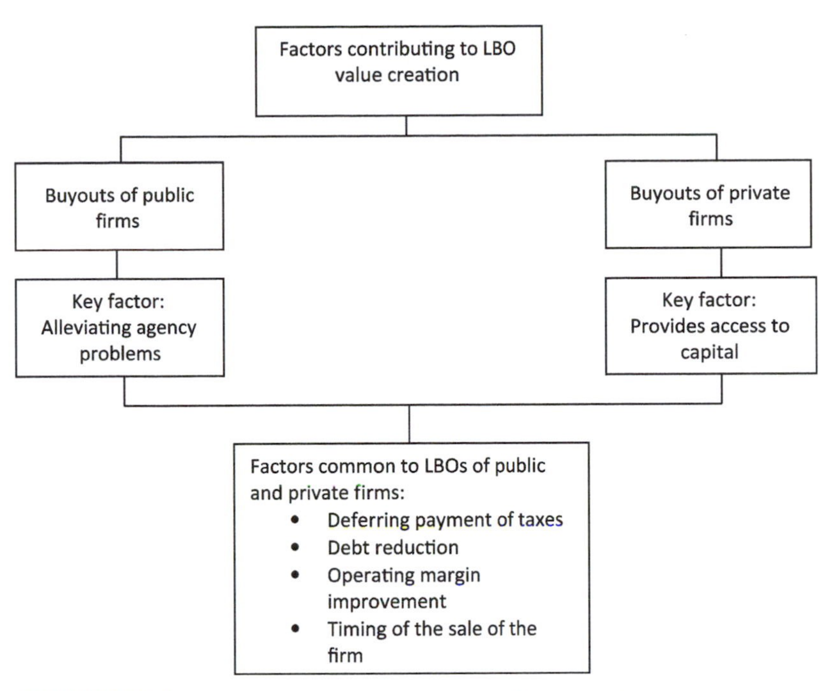

FIGURE 13.1 **Factors contributing to leveraged buyout (LBO) value creation.**

moving the corporate headquarters to a less expensive location, pruning unprofitable customers, and eliminating such perks as corporate aircraft.

Firms with private equity investor representation on their boards are more likely to display higher announcement-date returns and improved operating performance than firms without such representation.[106] Research shows that new owners choosing to retain their investment longer, such as private equity investors, have more time to put controls and reporting monitoring systems in place, enhancing the firm's competitive performance.[107] Other factors contributing to postbuyout returns include professional management and the private equity firm's reputation.[108] Research also suggests that public to private to public IPOs (so-called reverse LBOs) show greater post-IPO performance than IPOs. Why? Investors can review the firm's historical performance when it was public and benefit from any restructuring while it was private.[109]

How do leveraged buyouts create value?

A number of factors combine to create value in an LBO. Public firms do so through LBOs by reducing underperformance related to agency conflicts between management and shareholders. For private firms, LBOs improve access to capital. For both public and private firms, LBOs create value by temporarily shielding the firm from taxes, reducing debt, improving operating performance, and timing properly the sale of the business. See Figure 13.1.

For example, the Blackstone group used a combination of margin improvement, debt reduction, and fortuitous timing in converting what appeared to be a disastrous investment into a highly profitable one. As financial sponsor,

[106] Chen et al., 2014

[107] Cao and Lerner, 2006

[108] Katz (2008) reports that private equity–sponsored firms display superior performance after they go public because of tighter monitoring and the reputations of the private equity firms. Acharya and Kehoe (2010) conclude that private equity firms contribute the most to firms when their representatives on the boards of these firms have relevant industry experience. Guo et al. (2011) find that postbuyout performance improves because of the discipline that debt imposes on management and better alignment between management shareholders because of management's typically owning a large part of the firm's equity. Cornelli et al. (2013) show that, as private equity investors learn about a CEO's competence, their willingness to take corrective action adds to improved firm performance.

[109] Datta et al., 2015

Blackstone paid $26 billion to take the Hilton hotel chain private in 2007, shortly before one of the worst recessions in US history. To buy Hilton, Blackstone invested $5.5 billion and borrowed the rest. Blackstone's management improved operating performance using profits to reduce debt.

Concerns about Hilton's ability to repay its debt caused the market value of its debt to plummet. In 2010, Blackstone was able to restructure Hilton's outstanding debt, buying back some of the debt from lenders at steep discounts. Blackstone was also able to convince lenders to refinance the remaining debt at record low interest rates by investing another $1 billion into the business, bringing its total equity stake in Hilton to $6.5 billion or 76% of total equity.

In an IPO in late 2013, Hilton raised $2.4 billion, most of which was used to pay off additional debt, bringing the firm's outstanding debt to $12.5 billion. Immediately after the IPO, Hilton shares traded at $21.50 per share, giving Hilton a market capitalization of $21.2 billion and Blackstone's ownership stake a value of $16.1 billion and a $9.6 billion profit.

Alleviating public firm agency problems

Access to liquid public capital markets enables a firm to lower its cost of capital, but participating in such markets may create disagreements between management on one hand and shareholders on the other, so-called agency problems. For example, managers engaging in empire building may be in conflict with shareholders seeking higher returns.

After an LBO, these conflicts tend to be resolved as the discipline imposed by the pressure to repay debt forces management to focus on improving performance and shareholder value.[110] And public-to-private LBOs often engage in asset sales and reduced capital spending to improve performance rather than build empires.

Similar conflicts can arise when ownership is heavily concentrated. Majority shareholders may use their voting positions to make decisions inconsistent with the interests of minority shareholders. For example, the majority shareholder wants to increase dividends while minority shareholders want to pursue a more aggressive investment strategy reinvesting excess cash flow. Sometimes such conflicts can be eliminated by taking a firm private in which the majority shareholder buys out the minority shareholders. In countries where ownership often is highly concentrated, pretransaction minority shareholders often receive cumulative abnormal financial returns (the increase in the value of their shares before the deal announcement date) on their investment of 22% and a purchase price premium for their shares of 35%.[111]

Providing access to capital for private firms

Agency problems are less significant for private than public firms because of the concentration of ownership and control. Private firms often undertake LBOs to gain access to capital and to enable owners and managers to take cash out of the business.[112] Private firms having undergone LBOs tend to be more profitable and experience faster growth than their peers. Why? Because private equity investors introduce professional management methods and more aggressively monitor performance and are willing to take actions to improve firm performance to satisfy principal and interest payments. Private equity firms tending to specialize in certain industries or regions often demonstrate an ability to more readily raise capital for reinvestment in firms within their areas of expertise than more diversified buyout firms.[113]

Creating a tax shield

Tax shields refer to the reduction in income taxes resulting from allowable deductions from taxable income such as depreciation and interest expense. Such tax savings, assuming other factors remain unchanged, increase the PV of

[110] Ji et al. (2020) argue that this applies more to focused than to a diversified firm. Diversified firm managers are more likely to add debt (reducing cash available for compensating shareholders) because greater leverage lowers the likelihood of takeover.

[111] Boubaker et al., 2014

[112] Gao et al., 2010

[113] Gejadze et al., 2018

TABLE 13.3 Tax shield example

Income statement		
	Case 1: no asset write-up	Case 2: asset write-up[a]
Revenue ($)	100	100
Depreciation ($)	0	50
Income before taxes ($)	100	50
Taxes at 34% ($)	34	17
Income after taxes ($)	66	33

Key points:
1. Tax shield = $50 × 0.34 = $17
2. Case 1 operating cash flow[b] = $66
   Case 2 operating cash flow = $33 + $50 = $83
3. Case 2 operating cash flow > Case 1 by $17 or the amount of the tax shield

[a]Assumes asset write-up results in an additional depreciation expense of $50.
[b]Assumes capital spending and changes in working capital and financing activities are zero.

the firm by boosting future operating cash flows. Table 13.3 illustrates how a tax shield resulting from an increase in depreciation reduces taxable income while increasing operating cash flow.

Historically, LBOs have not paid taxes 5 to 7 years[114] after the buyout because of the deductibility of interest and the additional depreciation resulting from the write-up of net acquired assets.[115] Profits are shielded from taxes until a substantial portion of the outstanding debt is repaid and the assets depreciated. LBO investors use cumulative free cash flow to increase firm value by repaying debt and improving operating performance.[116]

Debt reduction

When debt is repaid, the equity value of the firm increases in direct proportion to the reduction in outstanding debt—equity increases by $1 for each $1 of debt repaid—assuming the financial sponsor can sell the firm for at least what it paid for the company. Debt reduction contributes to cash flow by eliminating future interest and principal payments.[117]

Improvement in operating margin

When a firm reinvests cumulative free cash flow, profit margins can increase by a combination of revenue growth and cost reduction. Private equity investors tend to concentrate more on revenue growth as they focus on industries in which they have substantial experience and proprietary knowledge rather than on cost reduction.[118] Revenue gains are achieved through new product introduction, better marketing, and acquisitions. The margin increase augments cash flow, which in turn raises the firm's equity value, if the level of risk is unchanged.

[114] Cohn et al., 2014

[115] This assumes that the LBO is recorded using purchase accounting rather than recapitalization accounting, which does not permit asset revaluation. Recap accounting may be used if the LBO is expected to be taken public through an IPO and the financial sponsor wishes to maximize reporting earnings. For more details, see Chapter 12.

[116] Recent changes in the US corporate tax rates, which reduce the value of NOLs and depreciation and cap the deductibility of net interest expense, mean LBOs may become taxpayers sooner than in the past.

[117] Cohn et al. (2014) find that some firms do not reduce their leverage even if they generate cash flow above their investment needs. Such LBOs may add to leverage to pay dividends and to acquire other businesses.

[118] Gompers et al., 2016

Timing the sale of the firm

LBOs may benefit from rising industry multiples while the firm is private. The amount of the increase in firm value depends on the valuation multiple investors place on each dollar of earnings; cash flow; or earnings before interest, taxes, depreciation, and amortization (EBITDA) when the firm is sold. LBO investors create value by timing the sale of the firm to coincide with the decline of the firm's leverage to the industry average and with favorable industry conditions. This occurs when the firm assumes the risks of the average firm in the industry and when the industry in which the business competes is most attractive to investors, a point at which valuation multiples are likely to be the highest.[119]

Table 13.4 illustrates how LBOs create value by "paying down" debt, in part using cash generated by tax savings, by improving the firm's operating margins, and by increasing the market multiple applied to the firm's EBITDA in the year in which the firm is sold.[120] Each case assumes that the sponsor group pays $500 million for the target firm and finances the transaction by borrowing $400 million and contributing $100 million in equity. The sponsor group is assumed to exit the LBO at the end of 7 years. In case 1, all cumulative free cash flow is used to reduce outstanding debt. Case 2 assumes the same exit multiple as case 1 but that cumulative free cash flow is higher due to margin improvement and lower interest and principal repayments as a result of debt reduction. Case 3 assumes the same cumulative free cash flow available for debt repayment and EBITDA as in case 2 but a higher exit multiple.

TABLE 13.4 Leveraged buyouts (LBOs) create value by reducing debt, improving margins, and increasing exit multiples

	Case 1: debt reduction	Case 2: debt reduction + margin improvement	Case 3: debt reduction + margin improvement + higher exit multiples
LBO formation year			
Total debt ($)	400,000,000	400,000,000	400,000,000
Equity ($)	100,000,000	100,000,000	100,000,000
Transaction value ($)	500,000,000	500,000,000	500,000,000
Exit-year (year 7) assumptions			
Cumulative cash available for debt repayment[a] ($)	150,000,000	185,000,000	185,000,000
Net debt[b] ($)	250,000,000	215,000,000	215,000,000
EBITDA ($)	100,000,000	130,000,000	130,000,000
EBITDA multiple (×)	7.0	7.0	8.0
Enterprise value[c] ($)	700,000,000	910,000,000	1,040,000,000
Equity value[d] ($)	450,000,000	695,000,000	825,000,000
Internal rate of return (%)	24	31.9	35.2
Cash on cash return[5] (×)	4.5	6.95	8.25

[a]Cumulative cash available for debt repayment and earnings before interest, taxes, depreciation, and amortization (EBITDA) increase between case 1 and case 2 because of improving margins and lower interest and principal repayments, reflecting the reduction in net debt.
[b]Net debt = Total debt − Cash available for debt repayment = $400 million − $185 million = $215 million
[c]Enterprise value = EBITDA in the seventh year × EBITDA multiple in the seventh year
[d]Equity value = Enterprise value in the seventh year − Net debt
[e]The equity value when the firm is sold divided by the initial equity contribution. The internal rate of return represents a more accurate financial return because it accounts for the time value of money.

[119] The annual return on equity (ROE) of the firm will decline, as the impact of leverage declines, to the industry average ROE, which usually occurs when the firm's debt−to−total capital ratio approximates the industry average ratio. At this point, the financial sponsor is unable to earn excess returns by continuing to operate the business. Table 13.2 illustrates this point. ROE is highest when leverage is highest and lowest when leverage is zero, subject to the caveat that ROE could decline because of escalating borrowing costs if lenders viewed debt as excessive.

[120] Guo et al. (2011) find that operating performance, tax benefits, and market multiples applied when the investor group exits the business each explain about one-fourth of the financial returns to buyout investors.

Estimating tax-deductible interest expense

Recall that recent US tax legislation limits the tax deductibility of net interest expense to 30% of earnings before interest and taxes (EBIT). The product of the interest rate on borrowed funds and a leverage multiple (i.e., debt to EBIT) that equals 30% or less implies that 100% of interest expense is tax deductible (see Equation 13.1). If the product exceeds 30%, the excess over 30% will not be deductible (see Equation 13.2). The requirement for full deductibility of interest expense can be expressed as follows:

$$i \times D = 0.3 \times EBIT, \text{ and}$$
$$i \times m \times EBIT = 0.3 \times EBIT; \text{ therefore,} \tag{13.1}$$
$$i \times m = 0.3$$

in which i, D, and m are the rate of interest, debt, and the ratio of debt to EBIT, respectively. If the following is true, some portion of interest expense will not be tax deductible:

$$i \times m > .3 \tag{13.2}$$

Dividing the results of Equation 13.1 by Equation 13.2 gives the share of total interest expense that will be tax deductible. For example, if a company borrows five times EBIT at 6%, then 100% of interest expense will be tax deductible. Why? Because $0.06 \times 5 = 0.30 \times 100 = 30\%$. If the firm borrows five times EBIT at 7%, total interest expense will exceed 30% of EBIT (i.e., $5 \times 0.07 = 0.35 \times 100 = 35\%$). Consequently, only 85.7% of total interest expense will be tax deductible (i.e., $0.30/0.35 = 0.857 \times 100 = 85.7\%$).

The impact on financial returns of alternative transaction strategies

Grouping LBOs by transaction strategy provides insights into factors impacting LBO sponsor financial returns.[121] "Classic LBOs" improve financial performance by reducing costs and improving efficiency. Those dubbed "entrepreneurial LBOs" attempt to create value through aggressive revenue growth. However, sponsor returns vary widely.[122] The portion of financial returns that is most directly impacted by the sponsor's skill may be the choice of transaction strategy and their ability to implement that strategy. Empirical evidence suggests that "classic LBOs" tend to underperform "entrepreneurial LBOs." Improving operating margins is less about cost cutting and more about aggressively growing revenues, often through multiple acquisitions.

Common leveraged buyout deal and capital structures

Deal structures refer to how ownership is transferred; capital structures, to how they are financed. These are discussed next.

Common deal structures

Because of the epidemic of bankruptcies in the late 1980s of LBOs based on the cash flow of a business, the most common form of LBO today is the asset-based LBO. This type of LBO can take the form of an asset sale or a direct or subsidiary merger. The target firm could sell assets to the acquiring company, with the seller using the cash received

[121] Ayash et al., 2017

[122] Caution must be used in assessing sponsor performance as reported financial returns may overstate realized returns. To measure the extent of the overstatement, it is necessary to distinguish between paper gains at the time of the exit and gains actually realized by the sponsor. Delays in liquidating companies within a sponsor's portfolio can impact actual sponsor internal rate of returns by affecting the timing of when the reported proceeds are actually received. Cognizant of this problem, sponsors have an incentive to make cash distributions in the form of dividends before exiting businesses to increase the likelihood they will achieve their financial return targets. Brown et al. (2019) find that underperforming private equity managers are prone to overstate reported returns when they are raising funds.

to pay off its outstanding liabilities. Alternatively, the target could merge into the acquiring company (direct merger) or a wholly owned subsidiary of the acquiring company (subsidiary merger).[123]

In a *direct merger*, the firm to be taken private merges with a firm controlled by the financial sponsor, with the seller receiving cash for stock. The lender will make the loan to the buyer after the security agreements are in place and the target's stock has been pledged against the loan. The target then is merged into the acquiring company, which is the surviving corporation.

In a *subsidiary merger*, the company (i.e., the parent) controlled by the financial sponsor creates a new shell subsidiary (merger sub) and contributes cash or stock in exchange for the subsidiary's stock.[124] The subsidiary raises additional funds by borrowing from lenders whose loans are collateralized by the stock of the target firm at closing. The subsidiary then makes a tender offer for the outstanding public shares and merges with the target, often with the target surviving as a wholly owned subsidiary of the parent. This may be done to avoid any negative impact that the new company might have on existing customer or creditor relationships. If 90% of the target firm's shares can be acquired in the tender offer, the remaining shareholders can be squeezed out in a backend merger.[125]

Common capital structures

LBOs tend to have complicated capital structures consisting of bank debt, high-yield debt, mezzanine debt, and equity provided primarily by the financial sponsor. Figure 13.2 illustrates a typical LBO capital structure. The degree of leverage used in LBOs is determined by borrowing costs, the reputation of the financial sponsor, tax benefits, and the potential for financial distress if the firm were unable to meet its debt obligations.

Collateralized bank debt is the most senior in the capital structure in the event of liquidation. Such loans usually mature within 5 to 7 years. Bank credit facilities consist of revolving-credit and term loans. A revolving-credit facility is used to satisfy daily liquidity requirements, secured by the firm's most liquid assets such as receivables and inventory. Term loans are usually secured by the firm's longer-lived assets and are granted in tranches (or slices), denoted as A, B, C, and D, with A the most senior and D the least of all bank financing. Whereas bank debt in the A tranche usually must be paid off before other forms of debt can be paid, the remaining tranches generally involve little or no amortization and are repaid at maturity. Whereas lenders in the A tranche often sell such loans to other commercial banks, loans in the B, C, and D tranches usually are sold to hedge funds and mutual funds. Loans in B, C, and D tranches commonly are referred to as leveraged loans, reflecting their risk relative to loans in the A tranche.

The next layer of LBO capital structure consists of unsecured subordinated debt, also referred to as *junk bonds*. Interest is fixed and represents a constant percentage over the US Treasury bond rate. The amount depends on the credit quality of the debt. Often callable at a premium, this debt usually has a 7- to 10-year maturity range. As an alternative to high-yield publicly traded junk bonds, second mortgage or lien loans became popular between 2003 and mid-2007. Often called *mezzanine debt*, such loans are privately placed with hedge funds and collateralized loan obligation (CLO) investors. They are secured by the firm's assets but are subordinated to the bank debt in liquidation. By pooling large numbers of first and second mortgage loans (so-called noninvestment-grade, or leveraged, loans) and subdividing the pool into tranches, CLO investors sell tranches to institutional investors such as pension funds. Such debt may be issued with warrants to buy equity in the firm.[126]

The final layer consists of equity (common and preferred) contributed by the financial sponsor and management. Preferred stock offers a greater chance of recovering some of the sponsor's investment in bankruptcy because holders of such equity are paid before common shareholders. Convertible preferred shares (or convertible debt) are used to provide investors with some minimum rate of return as well as the opportunity to participate in any

[123] For small companies, a reverse stock split may be used to take the firm private by reducing the number of shareholders to below 300 enabling the public firm to delist from public stock exchanges.

[124] The parent contributes equity rather than making a loan, usually in cash to avoid leveraging the merger sub.

[125] The financial sponsor may negotiate a top-up option (i.e., an option to buy as many shares as necessary to reach the 90% threshold) with the target firm's board if there is concern the 90% figure cannot be reached in the tender offer. If the merger qualifies under Delaware General Corporation Law, a backend merger involving a publicly traded target firm is possible with only a simple majority of shares purchased through the tender offer.

[126] Warrants are long-term instruments allowing shareholders or bondholders to purchase shares at a discounted price, with an exercise price above the market value of the firm's current share price. Warrants cannot be exercised for a period ranging from 6 months to 1 year, giving the stock price time to exceed the exercise price.

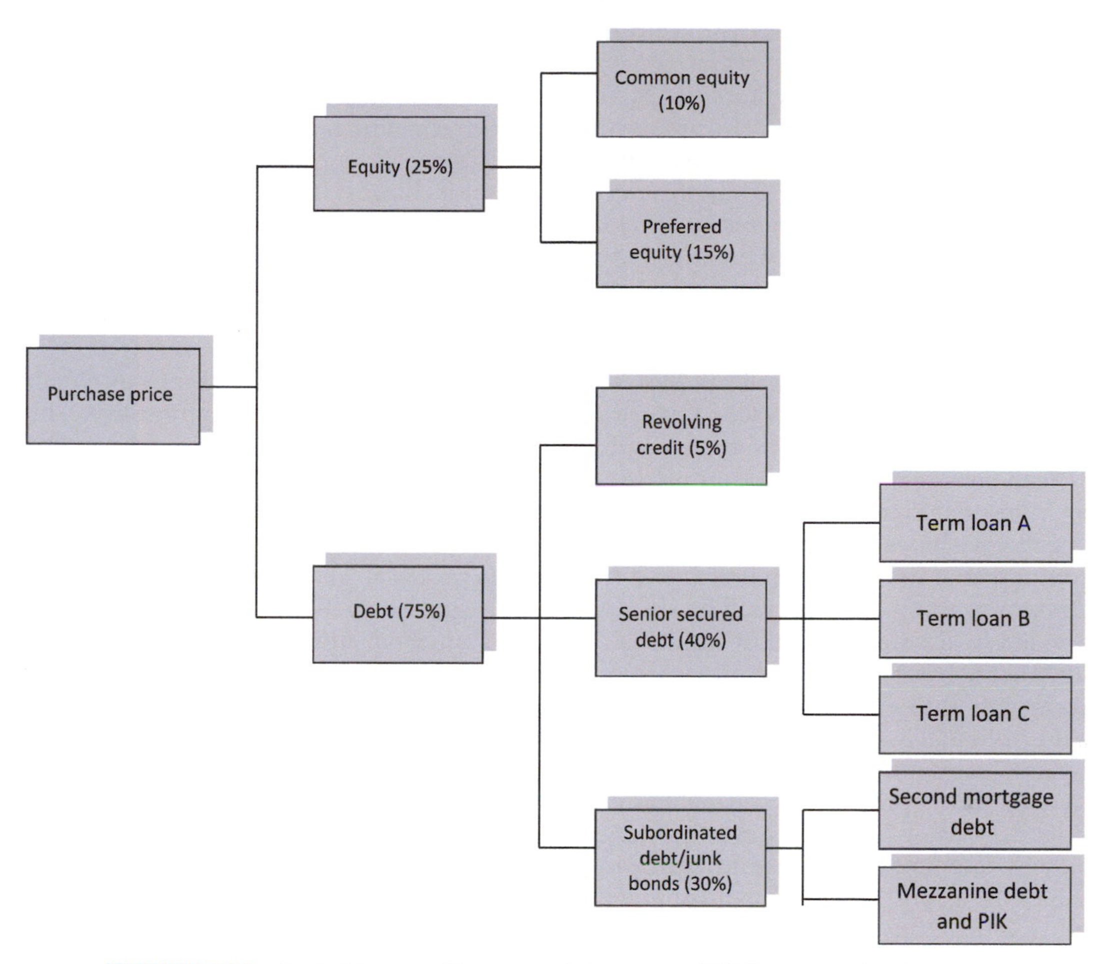

FIGURE 13.2 **Typical leveraged buyout capital structure.** *PIK,* Payment-in-kind securities

future appreciation of the common shares. Convertible securities include an option for the holder to convert such shares (or debt) into a fixed number of common shares any time after a predetermined date. Convertible securities also are used to minimize agency problems arising between investors and managers: investors want dividends or interest, and management wants to reinvest cash flow.

Some things to remember

M&As typically are financed by cash, equity, debt, or some combination, with funding sources ranging from cash on hand to commercial bank loans to seller financing. Highly leveraged transactions, or LBOs, often are structured by financial sponsors such as private equity firms, hedge funds, and venture capitalists.

Chapter discussion questions

13.1 What are the primary ways in which an LBO is financed?

13.2 How do loan and security covenants affect the way in which an LBO is managed? Note the differences between positive and negative covenants.

13.3 Describe common strategies LBO firms use to exit their investment. Discuss the circumstances under which some methods of "cashing out" are preferred to others.

13.4 Hospital chain HCA relied heavily on revenue growth in its effort to take the firm private. On July 24, 2006, management announced that it would "go private" in a deal valued at $33 billion, including the assumption of

$11.7 billion in existing debt. Would you consider a hospital chain a good or bad candidate for an LBO? Explain your answer.

13.5 Seven private investment firms acquired 100% of the outstanding stock of SunGard Data Systems Inc. (SunGard). SunGard is a financial-software firm known for providing application and transaction software services and creating backup data systems in the event of disaster. The company's software manages 70% of the transactions made on the NASDAQ stock exchange, but its biggest business is creating backup data systems in case a client's main systems are disabled by a natural disaster, blackout, or terrorist attack. Its large client base for disaster recovery and backup systems provides a substantial and predictable cash flow. The firm had substantial amounts of unencumbered current assets. The deal left SunGard with a nearly 5-to-1 debt-to-equity ratio. Why do you believe lenders might have been willing to finance such a highly leveraged transaction?

13.6 Cox Enterprises announced on August 3, 2004, a proposal to buy the remaining 38% of Cox Communications' shares that it did not already own. Cox Enterprises stated that the increasingly competitive cable industry environment makes investment in the cable industry best done through a private company structure. Why might the firm believe that increasing future levels of investment would be best done as a private company?

13.7 After Cox Enterprises' announcement on August 3, 2004, of its intent to buy the remaining 38% of Cox Communications' shares that it did not already own, the Cox Communications board of directors formed a special committee of independent directors to consider the proposal. Why? Be specific.

13.8 Qwest Communications agreed to sell its slow but steadily growing yellow pages business, QwestDex, to a consortium led by the Carlyle Group and Welsh, Carson, Anderson, and Stowe for $7.1 billion. Why do you believe the private equity groups found the yellow pages business attractive? Explain the following statement: "A business with high growth potential may not be a good candidate for an LBO."

13.9 Describe the potential benefits and costs of LBOs to stakeholders, including shareholders, employers, lenders, customers, and communities, in which the firm undergoing the buyout may have operations. Do you believe that on average LBOs provide a net benefit or cost to society? Explain your answer.

13.10 Sony's long-term vision has been to create synergy between its consumer electronics products business and its music, movies, and games. A consortium consisting of Sony Corp. of America, Providence Equity Partners, Texas Pacific Group, and DLJ Merchant Banking Partners agreed to acquire MGM for $4.8 billion. In what way do you believe that Sony's objectives might differ from those of the private equity investors making up the remainder of the consortium? How might such differences affect the management of MGM? Identify possible short-term and long-term effects.

Answers to these Chapter Discussion Questions are available in the Online Instructor's Manual for instructors using this book.

End-of-chapter case study: implications of a credit rating downgrade after a merger or acquisition

Case study objectives

To illustrate how a credit downgrade can

- Impact the firm's cost of capital
- Subject a firm to more restrictive loan covenants
- Limit its ability to pursue future attractive investment opportunities

Although more expensive to locate and develop, offshore wells tend to be more productive and longer lasting than onshore finds. Notwithstanding the recent slide in drilling activity, offshore production remained a major contributor to global oil and gas production, accounting for almost 30% in 2019. But major threats to offshore drilling remain, including the inherent complexity and high cost of finding new oil and gas reserves in what is often a very inhospitable environment.

The past slump in offshore drilling put great pressure on the profits of firms whose primary business was to support such activity. Firms that owned drilling rigs and rented them to oil and gas exploration and development companies had billions of dollars invested in rigs. They made money when the number of rigs in operation rose but were brutalized when offshore drilling activity plummeted. Such firms often borrowed large sums of money to build and maintain drilling rigs and to remain liquid throughout the industry's "boom and bust" cycle.

Beset by plunging profits and excessive leverage, London-based Ensco Plc (Ensco) with $5.5 billion in debt outstanding merged with less-leveraged Rowan Company (Rowan) with $2.2 billion in debt in 2019. Ensco's objective was to diversify its product offering by type of rig and across different geographic areas to stabilize and improve cash flow. Ensco anticipated that the combined firms would have greater borrowing capacity than if they remained separate.

The deal, in which Rowan shareholders received 2.75 Ensco shares for each Rowan share, was completed on April 11, 2019, and was valued at $2.38 billion. Ensco and Rowan shareholders own approximately 55% and 45%, respectively, of the outstanding common shares of the new firm, which has been renamed EnscoRowan. At closing, EnscoRowan had the capacity to borrow under its unsecured revolving credit line up to $2.3 billion through September 2019 and about $1.7 billion between October 2019 and September 2022. The interest rate paid on borrowings under the credit line would be the LIBOR plus 4.25%.

The firm also had $7.7 billion in unsecured debt on its consolidated balance sheet of which $1.1 billion was maturing between 2020 and 2024; the remaining $6.6 billion is repayable in varying amounts between 2025 and 2044. The weighted average coupon rate on its outstanding debt is 7.2%.

The new firm had a contract backlog to rent rigs of $3.4 billion and $1.63 billion in cash at closing. According to Computstat data, the new company also had a debt-to-equity ratio of 0.64 (compared with the industry average of 0.47), a current ratio of 2.52 (compared with 2.09 for the industry), and a negative price-to-earnings ratio on forward 12-month earnings of $(1.56). Although EnscoRowan was more leveraged than other firms, its revolving credit line made it more liquid.

The transaction created the largest offshore drilling company in the world and is expected to create $150 million in annual cost savings. These synergies are a result of closure of overlapping regional offices, elimination of redundant employees, systems standardization, and supply chain efficiencies. Postclosing, EnscoRowan prioritized creditors after the Rowan acquisition by providing corporate guarantees on assumed debt rather than allowing a lower priority layer of debt to exist within its capital structure.[127]

Since the deal was announced in October 2018, Ensco's share price had fallen from $35 to $7.61 at closing. Immediately after closing, the credit rating agencies downgraded the outlook for the new firm's ability to repay its indebtedness, potentially impacting its access to capital and the cost of borrowing.[128] Because of the credit downgrade, future financings or refinancing could be done only at a higher cost of borrowing and require more restrictive covenants.

Although the new company will have one of the largest, most diversified, and technologically advanced fleets in the offshore drilling industry, the rating agencies argued that daily rig rental rates and global rig utilization were expected to remain weak at least through 2020. As such, EnscoRowan's debt to EBITDA (a proxy for cash flow) ratio was expected to remain above 20 times during the same period, meaning the firm had $20 dollars in debt for each dollar of cash flow with which to repay principal and interest.

Questions abound! Will the recovery in offshore come soon enough and be strong enough for EnscoRowan to meet its substantial debt repayments due after 2022? If not, what are its best options (asset sales, renegotiating the terms of its debt, bankruptcy, or some combination)? Will EnscoRowan be able to finance future attractive investment opportunities that might arise?

The cost of a postmerger credit rating downgrade can be substantial and enduring. Credit downgrades represent a series of costs: the additional cost of new borrowing and of refinancing current debt, the likelihood of more restrictive covenants limiting management flexibility in decision making, and the opportunity cost (foregone financial returns) associated with the inability to make opportunistic investments.

The merger was a calculated bet that offshore drilling activity would rebound sharply before 2022 and that the new firm's revolving credit line would provide enough liquidity to meet its cash needs until then. Critical to the firm's future ability to meet the substantial required interest and principal repayments on a timely basis is the strength and sustainability of the projected rebound in the number of offshore rigs in operation and the daily rental rates for such rigs. Given the cyclical nature of this industry, this may prove to be a highly risky bet.

[127] The term describing this status is *pari-passu* or *equal footing* such that in bankruptcy the court regards all creditors equally and the trustee would repay them the same fractional amount as other creditors at the same time.

[128] Credit-rating agencies perform independent analyses when assigning credit ratings, which include an analysis of a firm's business operations and market and operational risks, as well as various financial tests.

Discussion questions and answers

1. What are positive (or affirmative) and negative covenants? How can such covenants affect EnscoRowan's future investment decisions? Be specific.
2. What is a revolving credit line? What does it mean that EnscoRowan's revolving credit line was unsecured? Why is this important?
3. EnscoRowan has high fixed costs in terms of its investments in shallow- and deep-water rigs and their maintenance. As such, the firm has substantial operating leverage when the market for offshore drilling recovers. What is operating leverage, and how can it boost the firm's financial returns? (Hint: See Chapter 7.)
4. What factors do you believe a lender would consider in determining how much to lend to EnscoRowan? Be specific.
5. Why was the form of payment stock and not cash or cash and stock? Explain your answer.

Solutions to these case study discussion questions are available in the Online Instructor's Manual for instructors using this book.

CHAPTER

14

Highly leveraged transactions
leveraged buyout valuation and modeling basics

OUTLINE

No one spends other people's money as carefully as they spend their own. —*Milton Friedman*

Inside M&As: private equity firms partner to acquire Johnson Controls' power solutions business

KEY POINTS

- Firms that have stable cash flows and relatively low capital requirements because of modest growth potential often are good candidates for leveraged buyouts (LBOs).
- Leverage offers the prospect of outsized financial returns for investors and shelters some portion of profits from taxes.
- The timing of LBO deals is influenced by equity and credit market conditions.

Mergers, Acquisitions, and Other Restructuring Activities, Eleventh Edition
https://doi.org/10.1016/B978-0-12-819782-0.00014-9

Brookfield Business Partners L.P. (Brookfield), Caisse dedepot et placement du Quebec (CPDQ), and other institutional investors who invested with the private equity funds announced in late 2018 an agreement to acquire 100% of Johnson Controls' Power Solutions business (Power Solutions). The total purchase price was $13.2 billion. To avoid high fees, increasingly institutional investors such as pension funds and endowments invest along with private equity funds rather than as limited partners in the investment funds they manage.

Power Solutions, the global leader in automotive batteries, generates consistent cash flows and profitability. Why? Batteries need to be replaced regardless of the state of the economy. The largely noncyclical after-market sales contribute 75% of the firm's profit, underpinning its ability to pay interest and principal on debt. In 2018, Power Solutions recorded $8 billion in revenue and $1.68 billion in earnings before interest, taxes, depreciation, and amortization (EBITDA). The purchase price represented a multiple of 7.9 times trailing 12-month EBITDA.

At closing in June 2019, Power Solutions' parent, Johnson Controls, received net proceeds of $11.4 billion. The divestiture increased the parent's focus and enabled the firm to strengthen its balance sheet by reducing outstanding debt by $3.5 billion and returning capital to shareholders through share repurchases. With the divestiture, Johnson Controls became a "pure play" building technologies and solutions provider focused on controls and related instrumentation for commercial heating and air conditioning, security, and fire detection applications.

The leveraged buyout (LBO) was funded with about $3 billion in equity and $10.2 billion in long-term financing, consisting of both dollar and euro-dollar denominated debt. The deal has more debt and less equity than 2018's buyouts because investors anticipating a rising interest rate environment were hungry for floating rate debt. Brookfield and CPDQ each provided 30% of equity at closing, with the remainder provided by institutional investors. The equity contribution comprised just 22.7% of the purchase price, considerably less than the average equity contribution for LBOs of 31% in 2018 and 41% in 2017.

Junk bonds and leveraged loans are common sources of financing for LBOs. Junk bonds are those that credit-rating agencies have deemed below investment grade or have not rated.[1] They cannot be easily traded because of inactive secondary markets. Leveraged loans are unrated or noninvestment-grade bank loans and include second mortgages.

In early 2019, borrowers were more easily able to tap the high-yield bond market than that of leveraged loans. The initial financing mix for Power Solutions was to be $8 billion in leveraged loans and $2 billion in junk bonds. However, changing credit market conditions dictated a reduction in the loan portion of the total financing to $5.45 billion in favor of additional high-yield debt when underwriters attempted to market the debt. High-yield bonds were viewed more favorably than leveraged loans at the time of the financing because of less stringent covenants and the possibility of issuing subordinated debt.

Chapter overview

This chapter addresses the basics of valuing and modeling highly leveraged transactions. Transactions involving large amounts of debt to finance the purchase price generally are described as LBOs (see Chapter 13 for more details).

In an LBO, borrowed funds, often secured by assets of the target firm, are used to pay for most of the purchase price, with the remainder provided by a financial sponsor, such as a private equity investor group or hedge fund. LBOs can be of an entire company or divisions of a company. LBO targets can be private or public firms. As in prior chapters, the terms *buyout firm* and *financial sponsor* are used interchangeably throughout this chapter to include the variety of investor groups, such as private equity investors and hedge funds, that commonly engage in LBO transactions.

The cost of capital (CC) and adjusted present value (APV) methods are described in detail along with the strengths and weaknesses of each approach. The chapter also addresses how investors may evaluate LBO investment opportunities and illustrates a basic format for an LBO financial model. Such models may be used to determine the maximum amount of leverage that can be supported by the target firm consistent with the investor's desired financial returns. A Microsoft Excel-based LBO valuation and structuring model is available on the companion site to this book (https://www.elsevier.com/books-and-journals/book-companion/9780128197820). The companion site also contains a review of this chapter in the file folder titled "Student Study Guide."

[1] Moody's usually rates noninvestment-grade bonds Ba or lower; for S&P, it is BB or lower.

How are leveraged buyouts valued?

An LBO can be valued from the perspective of common equity investors only or all those who supply funds, including common and preferred investors and lenders. Conventional capital budgeting procedures may be used to evaluate the LBO.

The transaction makes sense from the viewpoint of all investors if the present value of the cash flows to the firm (PV_{FCFF}) or enterprise value, discounted at the weighted average cost of capital (WACC), equals or exceeds the total investment consisting of debt, common equity, and preferred equity ($I_{D+E+PFD}$) required to buy the outstanding shares of the target company:

$$PV_{FCFF} - I_{D+E+PFD} \geq 0 \tag{14.1}$$

Equation 14.1 implies that the target firm can earn its cost of capital and return sufficient cash flow to all investors and lenders, enabling them to meet or exceed their required returns. However, it is possible for an LBO to make sense to common equity investors but not to other investors, such as pre-LBO debt holders and preferred stockholders.[2]

What follows is a discussion of two methods for valuing LBOs. The cost of capital or CC method adjusts future cash flows for changes in the cost of capital as the firm reduces its outstanding debt. The second method, adjusted present value (APV), sums the value of the firm without debt plus the value of future tax savings resulting from the tax-deductibility of interest.

The cost of capital method

If the debt-to-equity (D/E) ratio is expected to be constant, discounting future cash flows with a constant WACC is appropriate. However, assuming a constant D/E ratio for highly leveraged deals is inconsistent with actual practice. Many firms reduce their outstanding debt relative to equity, and such changes in the capital structure distort valuation estimates based on traditional discounted cash flow (DCF) methods.[3]

The high leverage associated with LBOs increases the riskiness of cash flows available to equity investors because of the increase in fixed obligations to lenders. The cost of equity (COE) should be adjusted for the increased leverage of the firm. Because the debt is to be paid off over time, the COE will decrease. Therefore, in valuing an LBO, the analyst must project free cash flows and adjust the discount rate to reflect changes in the capital structure. Instead of discounting the cash flows at a constant discount rate, the discount rate must decline with the firm's declining D/E ratio. A four-step methodology for adjusting the discount rate to reflect a firm's declining leverage is discussed next.

Step 1: project annual cash flows until the target debt-to-equity ratio is achieved

Step 1 involves projecting free cash flow to equity (FCFE)—the cash flow available for common equity holders—annually until the LBO reaches its target D/E ratio. The target D/E ratio often is the industry average ratio or one that would appear acceptable to strategic buyers or IPO investors or the point at which the firm resumes paying taxes.

Step 2: project debt-to-equity ratios

The decline in D/E ratios depends on known debt repayment schedules and the projected growth in the market value of shareholders' equity.[4] The latter can be assumed to grow in line with the anticipated growth in net income.

[2] After the LBO has been consummated, the firm's ability to meet its obligations to current debt holders and preferred stockholders may deteriorate. The firm's pre-LBO debt and preferred stock may be revalued in the market by investors to reflect this higher perceived risk, resulting in a significant reduction in the market value of both debt and preferred equity owned by pre-LBO investors. Although there is little evidence to show that this is typical of LBOs, this revaluation may characterize large LBOs, such as RJR Nabisco in 1989, HCA in 2006, and TXU Corp in 2007.

[3] Oded et al., 2011

[4] New Financial Accounting Standards Board accounting standards effective in 2019 require firms to report operating leases as debt on the balance sheet and not in footnotes. This will inflate D/E ratios and other leverage metrics as well as financial return measures, making them inconsistent with historical data.

Step 3: adjust the discount rate to reflect changing risk

The high leverage associated with an LBO increases the risk of the cash flows available for equity investors. As the LBO's high debt level is reduced, the COE needs to be adjusted to reflect declining risk, as measured by the firm's levered beta (β_{FL}). This adjustment may be estimated starting with the firm's levered beta in period 1 (β_{FL1}) as follows:

$$\beta_{FL1} = \beta_{IUL1}(1 + (D/E)_{F1}(1 - t_F)) \tag{14.2}$$

β_{IUL1} is the comparable firm unlevered β in period 1; $(D/E)_{F1}$ and t_F are the firm's D/E ratio and marginal tax rate, respectively; and $\beta_{IUL1} = \beta_{IL1}/[1 + (D/E)_{I1}(1 - t_I)]$, in which β_{IL1},$(D/E)_{I1}$,and t_I are the comparable firm's levered β, D/E ratio, and tax rate, respectively. The firm's β in each successive period should be recalculated using the target firm's projected D/E ratio for that period. The target firm's COE (k_e) must be recalculated each period using that period's estimated β determined by Equation 14.2.[5]

Because the firm's COE changes over time, the firm's cumulative COE is used to discount projected cash flows.[6] This reflects the fact that each period's cash flows generate a different rate of return. The cumulative COE is represented as follows:

$$\begin{aligned} PV_1 &= FCFE_1/(1 + k_{e1}) \\ PV_2 &= FCFE_2/[(1 + k_{e1})(1 + k_{e\,2})] \\ PV_n &= FCFE_n/[(1 + k_{e\,1})(1 + k_{e\,2}) \ldots (1 + k_{e\,n-1})(1 + k_{en})] \end{aligned} \tag{14.3}$$

Step 4: determine if the deal makes sense

Making sense of the deal requires calculating the present value (PV) of FCFE discounted by the cumulative COE generalized by Equation 14.3, including the terminal value. Calculate the terminal value of equity (TVE) and of the firm in year *t*:

$$TVE = FCFE_{t+1}/(k_e - g) \tag{14.4}$$

Note that k_e and g represent the COE and the sustainable cash flow growth rate during the terminal period. TVE represents the PV of the dollar proceeds available to the firm at time *t*, generated by selling equity to the public, to a strategic buyer, or another LBO firm. A similar calculation would be made for the terminal value of the firm using the appropriate weighted average cost of capital for the terminal period, which would then be converted to a present value and added to the PV of free cash flows to the firm. Table 14.1 shows how to calculate the value of an LBO using the cost of capital method. The deal makes sense to common equity investors if the total PV exceeds the value of the equity investment in the deal and to lenders and preferred equity investors if the total PV of free cash flow to the firm (FCFF) is greater than the total cost of the deal.

Adjusted present value method

Some analysts suggest that the bias from a variable discount rate is avoidable by separating the value of a firm's operations into two components: the firm's value as if it were debt free and the value of interest tax savings or tax shield. The total value of the firm is the PV of the firm's free cash flows to equity investors (i.e., unlevered cash flows) plus the PV of future tax savings discounted at the firm's unlevered COE.[7] The unlevered COE is the appropriate

[5] Interest rates and betas appear to be independent as long as rates are above zero. Although a reduction in interest rates does not generally appear to impact betas, risk-taking and implicitly betas may increase significantly when interest rates become negative (Baars et al., 2020). Consequently, the analyst may want to slow the reduction in beta by taking into account the firm's repayment schedule and the restrictiveness of its loan covenants. Why? Large near-term principal repayments may be difficult to meet, triggering potentially cross-default clauses in loan covenants.

[6] Recall that the future value of \$1 (FV\$1) in 2 years invested at a 5% return in the first year and 8% in the second year is \$1 × [(1 + 0.05)(1 + 0.08)] = \$1.13; the present value of \$1 received in 2 years earning the same rates of return (PV\$1) is \$1/[(1 + 0.05)(1 + 0.08)] = \$0.88.

[7] Additional tax savings could be realized by writing up the target's assets to their fair market value resulting in additional depreciation expense. Some analysts also add the PV of these tax savings to the unlevered firm value.

TABLE 14.1 Present value of equity cash flow using the cost of capital method

	Forecast period						
Process steps	2013	2014	2015	2016	2017	2018	2019
Step 1: project annual cash flows ($ millions)[a]	0.30	0.20	1.80	7.40	7.70	8.10	8.50
Step 2: project D/E ratio[a]	1.46	1.02	0.68	0.48	0.32	0.18	0.05
Step 3: adjust discount rate to reflect changing risk							
Assumptions:							
Comparable firm							
Leveraged beta (β_l)	2.40						
D/E ratio	0.30						
Unlevered beta (βu)[b]	2.03						
Marginal tax rate (%)	0.40						
10-year US Treasury bond rate (%)	0.05						
Risk premium on stocks (%)	0.055						

Year	D/E ratio	Leveraged Beta[c]	Cost of Equity (k_e)[d]	Cumulative cost of equity
2013	1.46	3.81	25.96	1/(1 + 0.2596) = 0.7939
2014	1.02	3.27	22.99	1/(1 + 0.2596)(1 + 0.2299) = 0.6455
2015	0.68	2.86	20.73	1/(1 + 0.2596)(1 + 0.2299)(1 + 0.2073) = 0.5347
2016	0.48	2.61	19.36	1/(1 + 0.2596)(1 + 0.2299)(1 + 0.2073)(1 + 0.1936) = 0.4479
2017	0.32	2.42	18.31	1/(1 + 0.2596)(1 + 0.2299)(1 + 0.2073)(1 + 0.1936)(1 + 0.1831) = 0.3786
2018	0.18	2.25	17.38	1/(1 + 0.2596)(1 + 0.2299)(1 + 0.2073)(1 + 0.1936)(1 + 0.1831)(1 + 0.1738) = 0.3226
2019	0.05	2.09	16.50	1/(1 + 0.2596)(1 + 0.2299)(1 + 0.2073)(1 + 0.1936)(1 + 0.1831)(1 + 0.1738)(1 + 0.1650) = 0.2769

Step 4: determine if the deal makes sense	
Assumptions:	
Terminal period growth rate (%)	0.05
Terminal period cost of equity (%)[e]	0.10

Continued

TABLE 14.1 Present value of equity cash flow using the cost of capital method—cont'd

PV of annual cash flows (2013–2019, $ millions)[f]	0.24	0.13	0.96	3.31	2.92	2.61	2.35
Sum of annual cash flows (2013–2019)							12.53
Terminal value ($ millions)							44.72
Total PV ($ millions)							57.25
The deal makes sense for equity investors if the NPV ≥ 0.							

[a]Projections come from the Excel-Based Leveraged Buyout Valuation and Structuring Model available on the website accompanying this book. Assumes firm's target debt-to-equity (D/E) ratio is zero. When achieved, the financial sponsor will exit the business.
[b]$\beta u = (\beta_l)/(1 + (D/E)(1 - t)) = 2.4/(1 + 0.3 \times .6) = 2.03$.
[c]For 2013, $\beta_l = (\beta_u)(1 + (D/E)(1 - t)) = 2.03 \times (1 + (1.46)(1 - 0.4)) = 3.81$, in which 2.03 is the unlevered comparable firm beta.
For 2014, $\beta i = 2.03 \times (1 + (1.02)(1 - 0.4)) = 3.27$.
For 2015, $\beta i = 2.03 \times (1 + (0.68)(1 - 0.4)) = 2.86$, and so on.
[d]For 2013, $k_e = 0.05 + 3.81(0.055) = 0.2596 \times 100 = 25.96$.
For 2014, $k_e = 0.05 + 3.27(0.055) = 0.2299 \times 100 = 22.99$.
For 2015, $k_e = 0.05 + 2.86(0.055) = 0.20.73 \times 100 = 20.73$, and so on.
[e]Industry average cost of equity.
[f]Present value (PV) is calculated by multiplying each year's cash flow by the cumulative cost of equity for that year, e.g., for 2013, $0.7939 \times \$0.30 = \$0.24$.
NPV, Net present value.

discount rate rather than the cost of debt or a risk-free rate, because tax savings are subject to risk as the firm may be unable to use the tax savings due to continuing operating losses.[8]

The justification for the APV method reflects the theory that firm value is unaffected by the way in which it is financed.[9] However, studies suggest that for LBOs, the availability and cost of financing does indeed impact financing and investment decisions.[10] In the presence of taxes, firms may be less leveraged than they should be, given the potentially large tax benefits associated with debt.[11] Firms can increase market value by increasing leverage to the point at which the additional contribution of the tax shield to the firm's market value begins to decline.[12] However, management's decision to increase leverage affects and is affected by the firm's credit rating. Consequently, the tax benefits of higher leverage may be partially or entirely offset by the higher probability of default because of an increase in leverage.[13]

For the APV method to be applicable in highly leveraged transactions, the analyst needs to introduce the cost of financial distress (FD). In general, leverage is higher when the cost of FD is lower.[14] The direct cost of FD includes the costs associated with reorganization in bankruptcy and ultimately liquidation (see Chapter 18). Direct costs include legal and accounting fees. FD can also have an indirect cost even on firms that are able to avoid bankruptcy or liquidation.[15] Consequently, in applying the APV method, the PV of a highly leveraged transaction (PV_{HL}) would reflect the firm's PV without leverage (PV_{UL}) plus the PV of tax savings (i.e., interest expense, i, times the firm's marginal tax rate, t, or tax shield PV_{ti}) less the PV of expected FD (PV_{FD}).

$$PV_{HL} = PV_{UL} + PV_{ti} - PV_{FD} \tag{14.5}$$

in which $PV_{FD} = \mu FD$.

FD is the expected cost of financial distress, and μ is the probability of FD. Unfortunately, FD and μ cannot be easily or reliably estimated and often are ignored by analysts using the APV method. Failure to include an estimate of the cost and probability of FD is likely to result in an overestimate of the value of the firm using the APV method. Despite these concerns, many analysts continue to apply the APV method because of its relative simplicity, as illustrated in the following four-step process.

Step 1: estimate the present value of the target firm's unlevered cash flows

For the period during which the debt–to–total capital ratio is changing, the analyst should project free cash flows to equity (i.e., unlevered cash flows). During the firm's terminal period, the debt–to–total capital structure is assumed to be stable and the free cash flows are projected to grow at a constant rate. Estimate the unlevered COE for discounting cash flows during the period when the capital structure is changing and the WACC for discounting during the terminal period. The WACC is estimated using the proportions of debt and equity that make up the firm's capital structure in the final year of the period when the capital structure is changing.

[8] Brigham and Ehrhardt (2005), p. 597

[9] This theory assumes investors have access to perfect information, the firm is not growing and no new borrowing is required, and there are no taxes and transaction costs and implicitly that the firm is free of default risk. Under these assumptions, the decision to invest is affected by the earning power and risk associated with the firm's assets and not by the way the investment is financed.

[10] Axelson et al. (2013) argue that buyouts' capital structure has a different impact on investment decisions than that of public firms. For LBOs, the availability of financing impacts the decision to invest in LBOs, which is consistent with the widely held view among buyout practitioners that the size and frequency of LBOs are driven by the availability and cost of financing.

[11] Elkamhi et al., 2012. Many firms such as Intel and Exxon appear to have far less leverage than could be justified based on potential tax savings. However, such firms often choose to limit leverage to retain the flexibility to pursue unanticipated opportunities when they arise.

[12] Graham (2000) argues that many firms would benefit by adding additional debt; however, this notion is disputed by Blouin et al. (2012), who document that the tax savings associated with increased leveraged often are substantially overstated.

[13] Almeida and Philippon (2007) show that the risk-adjusted costs of distress can be so large as to totally offset the tax benefits derived from debt. This is particularly true during periods of economic downturns.

[14] Pires and Pereira, 2020

[15] Indirect costs include the loss of customers, employee turnover, less favorable terms from suppliers, higher borrowing costs, management distraction costs, higher operating expenses, and reduced overall competitiveness.

TABLE 14.2 Bond rating and probability of default

Rating	Cumulative probability of distress (%)	
	5 Years	10 Years
AAA	0.04	0.07
AA	0.44	0.51
A+	0.47	0.57
A	0.20	0.66
A-	3.00	5.00
BBB	6.44	7.54
BB	11.90	19.63
B+	19.20	28.25
B	27.50	36.80
B-	31.10	42.12
CCC	46.26	59.02
CC	54.15	66.60
C+	65.15	75.16
C	72.15	81.03
C-	80.00	87.16

Source: Altman, 2007.

Step 2: estimate the present value of anticipated tax savings

Project the annual tax savings resulting from the tax deductibility of interest. Discount projected tax savings at the firm's unlevered COE because it reflects a higher level of risk than either the WACC or after-tax cost of debt. Tax savings are subject to risk comparable to the firm's cash flows in that a highly leveraged firm may default or the tax savings go unused.

Step 3: estimate the potential cost of financial distress

The magnitude of the cost of financial distress can range from 10% to 30% of a firm's predistressed market value.[16] The probability of financial distress can be estimated by analyzing bond ratings[17] and the cumulative probabilities of default for bonds in different ratings classes over 5- and 10-year periods (Table 14.2).[18]

Step 4: determine if the deal makes sense

The total value of the firm is the sum of the PV of the firm's cash flows to equity, interest tax savings, and terminal value discounted at the firm's unlevered COE less the anticipated cost of FD (see Equation 14.5). Note that the

[16] Branch (2002) concluded that the impact of bankruptcy on a firm's predistressed value falls within a range of 12% to 20%. More recently, Korteweg (2010) estimated that the impact falls within a range of 15% to 30%.

[17] Although the failure of the credit-rating agencies to anticipate the financial distress in the credit markets in 2008 and 2009 casts doubt on the use of credit ratings to assess financial distress, there are few more reliable alternatives.

[18] Altman, 2007. Cumulative probability estimates reflect the likelihood of an outcome based on previous outcomes or events. They are used when reductions in cash flows due to financial distress in earlier years impact cash flows in subsequent years as the firm may be forced to underinvest. Assume that the probability of a firm experiencing financial distress in year 1 is 20%. If the firm ceases to exist at the end of the first year because of financial distress, there will not be any cash flows in year 2. If we assume that the likelihood of distress in year 2 is again 20%, the likelihood of the firm producing cash flows in the third year is only 64% (i.e., $(1 - 0.2)(1 - 0.2)$) and so on.

terminal value is calculated using WACC but that it is discounted to the present using the unlevered COE because it represents the present value of cash flows in the final year of the period when the firm's capital structure is changing and beyond. For the deal to make sense, the PV of Equation 14.5 less the value of equity invested in the transaction (i.e., net present value) must be greater than or equal to 0.

Table 14.3 illustrates the APV method with assumptions consistent with the valuation of the target firm using the CC method in Table 14.1. Assuming the firm has a C minus credit rating, the PV of the expected cost of bankruptcy is

TABLE 14.3 Present value of equity cash flows using the adjusted present value method

Process steps	2013	2014	2015	2016	2017	2018	2019
Step 1: Estimate PV of target firm's unlevered cash flows							
Assumptions:							
Annual equity cash flows	0.30	0.20	1.80	7.40	7.70	8.10	8.50
Marginal tax rate	0.40						
Comparable firm unlevered beta	2.03						
10-year US Treasury bond rate (%)	0.05						
Risk premium on stocks (%)	0.055						
Terminal period growth rate (%)	0.045						
2013–2019 unlevered cost of equity (%)[a]	0.162						
Terminal period WACC (%)[b]	0.159						
PV of 2013–2019 annual cash flows							15.51
Plus: PV of terminal value							67.05
Equals: total PV excluding tax and cost of financial distress							82.56
Step 2: estimate PV of anticipated tax savings							
Assumptions:							
Annual interest expense	3.00	2.66	2.17	1.67	1.33	1.00	0.67
Interest tax savings (tax shield)[c]	1.80	1.60	1.30	1.00	0.80	0.60	0.40
PV of tax shield at 16.2%							4.87
Step 3: estimate the potential cost of financial distress							
Assumptions:							
Target firm credit rating	C-						
Cumulative default probability for a C- rated firm over 10 years (see Table 14.2)	0.8716						
Expected cost of financial distress per Andrade and Kaplan (1998) and Korteweg (2010) as a percentage of firm value	0.30						
Potential cost of financial distress							21.59
Step 4: determine if the deal makes sense							
Total PV excluding tax shield and cost of financial distress							82.56
Plus: PV of tax shield							4.87
Less: expected cost of financial distress							21.59
Equals: total PV, including tax shield and financial distress							65.85

[a] $k_e = 0.05 + 2.03\ (.055) = 0.162 \times 100 = 16.2\%$.
[b] The discount rate in the terminal period reflects the presence of debt. The target debt-to-equity (D/E) ratio is taken from Table 14.1, which shows the D/E ratio in 2019 at 5%. Recall the proportion debt is of total capital can be determined by dividing the target D/E ratio by (1 + D/E) or 0.05/1.05. Therefore debt is 5% of total capital, and equity is 95% during the terminal period. If the borrowing rate for this firm is 10%, weighted average cost of capital (WACC) = $0.05 \times 0.10 + 0.95 \times 0.162 = 15.9\%$.
[c] Tax shield equals 0.4 times annual interest expense.
PV, Present value.

$21.59 million and is calculated as the cumulative probability of default over 10 years for a C minus–rated company (i.e., 0.8716 per Table 14.2 times the expected cost of bankruptcy, i.e., 0.30 × $82.56 million). Note that the estimate provided by the APV method is $87.43 million (i.e., $82.56 + $4.87 million) before the adjustment for FD. This is 44.2% (i.e., ($82.56/$57.25) − 1) more than the estimate provided using the CC method shown in Table 14.1. After adjusting for FD, the estimate declines to $65.85 million versus $57.25 million, estimated using the CC method, a difference of about 15%.

Comparing the cost of capital and adjusted present value methods

The CC method adjusts future cash flows for changes in the cost of capital as the firm reduces its outstanding debt. The second method, APV, sums the value of the firm without debt plus the value of tax savings resulting from the tax deductibility of interest.

The CC approach has the advantage of specifically attempting to adjust the discount rate for changes in risk, but it is more cumbersome to calculate than the APV scheme. Although the APV method is relatively simple to calculate, it relies on highly problematic assumptions. It ignores the impact of leverage on the discount rate as debt is repaid, implying that adding debt will always increase firm value by increasing the tax shield. Incorporating the effects of leverage into the APV method requires the estimation of the cost and probability of FD for highly leveraged firms, often a highly subjective undertaking. Finally, it is unclear whether the true discount rate that should be used for the APV approach is the cost of debt, unlevered k_e, or somewhere between the two.

Leveraged buyout valuation and structuring model basics

An LBO model determines what a firm is worth in a highly leveraged deal and is applied when there is the potential for a financial buyer to acquire the business. The model helps define the amount of debt a firm can support, given its assets and cash flows. Investment bankers use such analyses in addition to DCF and relative valuation methods to value firms they wish to sell. The intent is to provide financial buyers with an LBO opportunity offering a return in excess of their desired rate of return.

The following sections discuss a template for evaluating LBO opportunities. The Excel-based spreadsheets underlying these sections, found in a file folder titled Financial Models and Solutions on the companion site to this book, are called the Excel-Based LBO Valuation and Structuring Model and Excel-Based Model to Estimate Borrowing Capacity.

Evaluating leveraged buyout opportunities

LBO models are similar to DCF valuations in that they require projected cash flows, terminal values, present values, and discount rates. However, whereas the DCF analysis solves for the PV of the firm, the LBO model solves for the internal rate of return (IRR). Although the DCF approach often is more theoretically sound than the IRR approach (which can have multiple solutions), IRR is more widely used in LBO analyses because investors find it easier to understand.

The IRR is the discount rate that equates projected cash flows and terminal value with the initial equity investment[19] and enables investors to compare easily their expected return with their desired return (often 20%–30%). The LBO model also requires the determination of whether there is sufficient cash flow to operate the target firm while meeting interest and principal repayments and potentially paying dividends to private equity investors. Financial buyers often attempt to determine the highest amount of debt possible (i.e., the borrowing capacity[20] of the target firm) to minimize their equity investment to maximize the IRR.

[19] $NPV = CF_0 + CF_1/(1+IRR) + CF_2/(1+IRR)^2 + \ldots\ldots\ldots\ldots + CF_N/(1+IRR)^N = 0$.

[20] Borrowing capacity is defined as the amount of debt a firm can borrow without materially increasing its cost of borrowing or violating loan covenants on existing debt.

Although analysts differ on the measure of cash flow to use in evaluating LBO opportunities, EBITDA is commonly used despite its shortcomings.[21] The target's enterprise value or purchase price commonly is estimated by multiplying an enterprise value multiple for comparable recent transactions by the target's EBITDA.[22] This equation can be expressed as follows:

$$EV_{TF} = (EV / EBITDA) \times EBITDA_{TF} \quad (14.6)$$

in which

EV_{TF} = enterprise value (purchase price) of the target firm
$EBITDA_{TF}$ = target firm's earnings before interest, taxes, depreciation, and amortization
EV/EBITDA = recent comparable LBO transaction enterprise value to EBITDA multiple

After being estimated, how the enterprise value (EV_{TF}) is financed in terms of debt and equity contributed by the financial sponsor can be shown as follows:

$$EV_{TF} = (D_{TF} + E_{TF}) \quad (14.7)$$

in which

D_{TF} = net debt (i.e., total debt less cash and marketable securities held by the target firm)
E_{TF} = financial sponsor's equity contribution to the target firm's enterprise value

For a given enterprise value and level of net debt, we estimate the financial sponsor's initial equity contribution by solving equation 14.7 for E_{TF}. Net debt includes both the target firm's preacquisition debt (often refinanced after the buyout) and debt borrowed by the financial sponsor to finance the purchase price. Note how the target's cash and marketable securities can be used to pay for a portion of the deal. In summary, equation 14.6 estimates the enterprise value (purchase price), and equation 14.7 shows how it will be financed.

What follows is a simple five-step process to assess the attractiveness of a firm as a potential LBO target. The deal would make sense to the financial sponsor if the resulting IRR is equal to or greater than their target IRR.

Step 1: project cash flows

To determine cash available for financing a target's future debt obligations, the analyst projects the firm's income statement, balance sheet, and cash flow statement. Projected cash flow in excess of the firm's operating requirements is used to satisfy principal and interest repayments.

Step 2: determine the firm's borrowing capacity

The firm's maximum borrowing capacity reflects both projected cash flows and assets that may be used for collateral and confirmed in discussions with potential lenders. Table 14.4 illustrates a simple model to estimate a firm's borrowing capacity using the information developed in step 1. The estimate of borrowing capacity is expressed as a multiple of EBITDA.

The model is divided into three panels: assumptions, estimating cash available for debt reduction, and estimating borrowing capacity. Year 0 represents the year before the closing date (i.e., the beginning of year 1). The beginning debt figures are shown as of December 31 in year 0. Assume that based on similar transactions, the analyst believes that a buyout firm will be able to borrow about 5.5 times EBITDA of $200 million (i.e., about $1.1 billion), and the buyout firm has a target debt mix consisting of 75% senior and 25% subordinated debt. Assume investors in the buyout firm wish to exit the business within 8 years after the senior debt has been repaid. The investors intend to

[21] Some analysts use EBITDA as a proxy for cash flow. EBITDA supporters argue that it represents a convenient proxy for the cash available to meet the cost (i.e., interest, depreciation, and amortization) of long-term assets. EBITDA provides a simple way of determining how long the firm can continue to service its debt without additional financing. EBITDA is not affected by the method the firm uses in depreciating its assets. EBITDA can be misleading because it ignores changes in working capital and implicitly assumes that capital expenditures needed to maintain the business are equal to depreciation. FCFF may be a better measure of how much cash a company is generating because it includes changes in working capital and capital expenditures.

[22] By using the comparable recent transactions method to value the target firm, the analyst is implicitly including a purchase price premium in estimating the purchase price.

TABLE 14.4 Determining borrowing capacity

	Year 0	Year 1	Year 2	Year 3	Year 4	Year 5	Year 6	Year 7	Year 8
Assumptions									
Sales growth (%)	0	1.05	1.05	1.05	1.05	1.05	1.05	1.05	1.05
COS as a percentage of sales	0.5	0.5	0.5	0.5	0.5	0.5	0.5	0.5	0.5
Sales, general and administrative expenses as a percentage of sales	0.1	0.1	0.1	0.1	0.1	0.1	0.1	0.1	0.1
Depreciation as a percentage of sales	0.03	0.03	0.03	0.03	0.03	0.03	0.03	0.03	0.03
Amortization as a percentage of sales	0.01	0.01	0.01	0.01	0.01	0.01	0.01	0.01	0.01
Interest on cash and marketable securities (%)	0.03	0.03	0.03	0.03	0.03	0.03	0.03	0.03	0.03
Interest on senior debt (%)	0.07	0.07	0.07	0.07	0.07	0.07	0.07	0.07	0.07
Interest on subordinated debt (%)	0.09	0.09	0.09	0.09	0.09	0.09	0.09	0.09	0.09
Tax rate	0.4	0.4	0.4	0.4	0.4	0.4	0.4	0.4	0.4
Cash and marketable securities as a percentage sales	0.01	0.01	0.01	0.01	0.01	0.01	0.01	0.01	0.01
Change in working capital as a percentage of sales	0.02	0.02	0.02	0.02	0.02	0.02	0.02	0.02	0.02
Capital expenditures as a percentage sales	0.03	0.03	0.03	0.03	0.03	0.03	0.03	0.03	0.03
Cash available for debt reduction ($ millions)									
Sales	500.0	525.0	551.3	578.8	607.8	638.1	670.0	703.6	738.7
Less: COS	250.0	262.5	275.6	289.4	303.9	319.1	335.0	351.8	369.4
Less: sales, general and administrative expenses	50.0	52.5	55.1	57.9	60.8	63.8	67.0	70.4	73.9
Equals: EBITDA	200.0	210.0	220.5	231.5	243.1	255.3	268.0	281.4	295.5
Less: depreciation	15.0	15.8	16.5	17.4	18.2	19.1	20.1	21.1	22.2
Less: amortization	5.0	5.3	5.5	5.8	6.1	6.4	6.7	7.0	7.4
Plus: interest income	0.2	0.2	0.2	0.2	0.2	0.2	0.2	0.2	0.2
Less: interest expense									
Senior debt		52.2	47.9	43.1	37.7	31.7	24.9	17.4	9.1
Subordinated debt		27.0	27.0	27.0	27.0	27.0	27.0	27.0	27.0
Total interest expense		79.2	74.9	70.1	64.7	58.7	51.9	44.4	36.1
Equals: income before tax		110.0	123.7	138.4	154.3	171.3	189.5	209.1	230.0
Less: taxes paid		44.0	49.5	55.4	61.7	68.5	75.8	83.6	92.0
Equals: net income after tax		66.0	74.2	83.1	92.6	102.8	113.7	125.4	138.0
Plus: depreciation and amortization expense		21.0	22.1	23.2	24.3	25.5	26.8	28.1	29.5
Less change in working capital		10.5	11.0	11.6	12.2	12.8	13.4	14.1	14.8
Less capital expenditures		15.8	16.5	17.4	18.2	19.1	20.1	21.1	22.2
Equals: cash available for debt reduction		60.7	68.7	77.3	86.5	96.4	107.0	118.4	130.6
Borrowing capacity									
Cash balance	5.0	5.3	5.5	5.8	6.1	6.4	6.7	7.0	7.4
Senior debt outstanding at year end[a]	745.6	684.8	616.1	538.9	452.4	356.0	249.0	130.6	0.0
Subordinated debt outstanding at year end[b]	300.0	300.0	300.0	300.0	300.0	300.0	300.0	300.0	300.0

TABLE 14.4 Determining borrowing capacity—cont'd

	Year 0	Year 1	Year 2	Year 3	Year 4	Year 5	Year 6	Year 7	Year 8
Total debt	1045.6	984.8	916.1	838.9	752.4	656.0	549.0	430.6	300.0
Net debt-to-EBITDA ratio	5.20	4.66	4.13	3.60	3.07	2.55	2.02	1.51	0.99
Interest coverage (EBITDA/net interest expenses)	0.00	2.66	2.95	3.31	3.77	4.37	5.18	6.36	8.23

[a] Assumes 100% of cash available for debt reduction is used to pay off senior debt.
[b] Subordinated debt payable as a balloon note in year 10.
COS, Cost of sales; *EBITDA*, earnings before interest, taxes, depreciation, and amortization.

use 100% of cash available for debt reduction to pay off senior debt, and the subordinated debt is payable as a balloon note beyond year 8.

Using a trial-and-error method, insert a starting value for senior debt of $800 million in year 0. This $800 million starting number is in line with the firm's assumed target debt mix (i.e., 0.75 × total potential borrowing of $1.1 billion is about equal to $800 million). Senior debt outstanding at the end of the eighth year is $75.7 million. If we now try $700 million in senior debt in year 0, the amount of senior debt outstanding at the end of the eighth year is $(63.3). Using the midpoint between $700 and $800 million, we insert $750 million for senior debt in year 0, resulting in $6.2 million in remaining debt at the end of the eighth year. Additional fine-tuning results in a zero balance at the end of year 8 if we use a starting value of $745.6 million for senior debt. Consequently, the firm's maximum total debt (i.e., borrowing capacity) based on the assumptions underlying Table 14.4 is estimated at $1,045.6 million.

Step 3: estimate the target's enterprise value (purchase price)

Equation 14.6 provides an estimate of the target firm's enterprise value. Multiples may be adjusted up or down, depending on the perceived riskiness of future cash flows. Assume the financial sponsor believes that the appropriate enterprise to EBITDA multiple for the target firm's EBITDA following a review of recent comparable LBO deals is 7. From Equation 14.6, the enterprise value for the target firm (EVTF) can be estimated as 7 × $210 (year 1 EBITDA in Table 14.4) or $1470 million.

Step 4: estimate the financial sponsor's initial equity contribution

Using the target firm's maximum borrowing capacity of $1045.6 million determined in step 2 and the $1470 million enterprise value estimated in step 3, we can solve Equation 14.7 to estimate the financial sponsor's initial equity contribution at $424.4 million (i.e., $1470 − $1045.6).

Step 5: analyze financial returns

The IRR calculation considers the initial equity investment in the firm and additional capital contributions as cash outflows and any dividends as cash inflows plus the exit or residual value of the business when sold. The financial multiple applied to the equity value on the exit date is usually the same as used by the financial sponsor when determining the target firm's preliminary valuation. The firm's equity value is the sale value on the exit date less the value of debt repaid and any transaction fees. Because of their high sensitivity to the multiple applied to exit-year cash flows and the number of years the investment is to be held, financial returns are usually displayed as a range reflecting different assumptions about exit multiples. If the calculated IRR is less than the target IRR, the financial sponsor can substitute lower enterprise values (purchase prices) into Equation 14.7 as described in step 3, resulting in lower initial capital contributions, and recalculate the IRR until it exceeds the target IRR or walk away from the target firm.

Leveraged buyout model template

After an attractive LBO candidate is found, the target's financial statements are restated to reflect the firm's new capital structure. Table 14.5 summarizes the key elements of the analysis.

The Sources and uses of funds section of Table 14.5 shows how the deal is to be financed. Representing total funds required, the Uses of funds section shows where the cash will go and includes payments to the target's owners,

TABLE 14.5 Leveraged buyout model output summary

Sources (cash inflows) and uses (cash outflows) of funds								Pro forma capital structure			
Sources of funds	**Amount ($)**	**Interest rate (%)**		**Uses of funds**		**Amount ($)**		**Form of debt and equity**		**Market value ($)**	**Percent of total capital**
Cash from balance sheet	0.0	0.0		Cash to owners		70.0		Revolving loan		12.0	16.7
New revolving loan	12.0	9.0		Seller's equity		0.0		Senior debt		20.0	27.8
New senior debt	20.0	9.0		Seller's note		0.0		Subordinated debt		15.0	20.8
New subordinated debt	15.0	12.0		Excess cash		0.0		Total debt		47.0	65.3
New preferred stock (PIK)	22.0	12.0		Paid to owners		70.0		Preferred equity		22.0	30.6
New common stock	3.0	0.0		Debt repayment		0.0		Common equity		3.0	4.2
				Buyer expenses		2.0		Total equity		25.0	34.7
Total sources	72.0			Total uses		72.0		Total capital		72.0	
Equity investment	**Ownership distribution ($)**				**Percent distribution**			**Fully diluted ownership distribution ($)**			
	Common	**Preferred**		**Total**	**Common**	**Preferred**	**Common**	**Warrants**	**Preoption ownership**	**Performance options**	**Fully diluted ownership**
Equity investor	1.5	22.0		23.5	50.0	100.0	50.0	0.0	50.0	0.0	50.0
Management	1.5	0.0		1.5	50.0	0.0	50.0	0.0	50.0	0.0	50.0
Total equity investment	3.0	22.0		25.0	100.0	100.0	100.0	0.0	100.0	0.0	100.0
Internal rates of return	**Total investor return (%)**					**Equity investor investment gain ($)**			**Management investment gain ($)**		
	2017	**2018**	**2019**			**2017**	**2018**	**2019**	**2017**	**2018**	**2019**
Multiple of adjusted equity cash flow for 5-, 6-, and 7-year holding periods	5 years	6 years	7 years			5 years	6 years	7 years	5 years	6 years	7 years
8× terminal year CF	0.42	0.35	0.33			66.6	78.9	96.0	4.3	5.0	6.1
9× terminal year CF	0.46	0.39	0.35			73.8	86.6	104.5	4.7	5.5	6.7
10× terminal year CF	0.51	0.42	0.37			81.0	94.2	113.0	5.2	6.0	7.2
	Historical period							**Forecast period**			
Financial projections and analysis	**2010**	**2011**	**2012**		**2013**	**2014**	**2015**	**2016**	**2017**	**2018**	**2019**
Net sales ($)	177.6	183.5	190.4		197.1	205.0	214.2	223.8	233.9	244.4	255.4
Annual growth rate (%)	4.2	3.3	3.8		3.5	4.0	4.5	4.5	4.5	4.5	4.5
EBIT as percentage of net revenue	5.5	1.3	5.1		8.5	9.5	10.2	11.2	11.4	11.4	11.4
Adjusted enterprise cash flow[a] ($)	4.2	0.2	0.1		9.5	9.6	10.8	13.0	13.4	14.2	14.9

Adjusted equity cash flow[b] ($)	4.2	0.2	0.1	0.3	0.2	1.8	7.4	7.7	8.1	8.5
Total debt outstanding ($)	0	0	47.0	39.5	31.5	23.8	19.2	14.3	8.8	2.7
Total debt/adjusted enterprise cash flow	0.0	0.0	NA	4.1	3.3	2.2	1.5	1.1	0.6	0.2
EBIT/interest expense	0	0	0	3.6	4.9	6.6	10.1	13.3	18.6	30.9
PV of adjusted equity cash flow at 26% ($)	57.2									
PV of 2004–2010 adjusted equity CF/terminal value ($)	28.1									

[a] EBIT$(1 - t)$ + Depreciation and amortization − Gross capital spending − Change in working capital − Change in investments available for sale.
[b] Net income + Depreciation and amortization − Gross capital spending − Change in working capital − Principal repayments − Change in investments available for sale (i.e., increases in such investments are a negative cash flow entry but represent cash in excess of normal operating needs).
CF, Cash flow; *EBIT*, earnings before interest and taxes; *NA*, not applicable; *PV*, present value.

including cash, any equity retained by the seller, any seller's notes, and any excess cash retained by the sellers. The Uses section also contains the refinancing of any existing debt on the balance sheet of the target firm and any transaction fees. The Sources section describes various sources of financing, including new debt, any existing cash that is being used to finance the transaction, and the common and preferred equity being contributed by the financial sponsor. The equity contribution represents the difference between uses and all other sources of financing. It is a "plug" adjustment and represents the amount the financial sponsor must contribute in addition to the borrowed funds to fully finance the purchase price.

The Pro forma capital structure section provides the percent distribution of the firm's capital structure among the various types of debt and equity. The Equity investment section illustrates the distribution of ownership between the financial sponsor and management. The Internal rates of return section provides the projected financial returns in both percentages and dollar amounts for 3 potential exit years, as well as the multiple applied to the exit year's cash flow. Finally, income, cash flow, and balance sheet data are summarized in the section titled Financial projections and analysis.

The pro forma Excel-based balance sheet contained in the LBO model on the companion website accompanying this text reflects changes to the existing balance sheet of the target firm altered to reflect the new capital structure of the firm. Shareholders' equity is reduced after closing because of the large reduction in paid in capital.[23] The new balance sheet also reflects the goodwill resulting from the excess of the purchase price over the fair market value of the net acquired assets and any interest expense that can be capitalized under current accounting rules.

The balance sheet projections are based on the pro forma balance sheet, with the debt outstanding and interest expense reflecting the repayment schedules associated with each type of debt. The model also reflects a projected sale value on the assumed exit date. The IRRs represent the average annual compounded rate at which the financial sponsor's equity investment grows, assuming no dividend payments or additional equity contributions.

Some things to remember

Common ways of valuing highly leveraged deals include the cost of capital and adjusted present value methods. While the first method is more complicated, APV requires the estimation of the cost and probability of FD for highly leveraged firms. LBO models often are employed when there is the potential for a financial buyer to acquire a business.

Chapter discussion questions

14.1 The APV model is based on the notion that the value of a firm can be divided into PV of the firm's cash flows to equity investors plus the PV of the tax shield. What is the critical assumption underlying this premise? In your view, under what circumstances might this assumption not be practical?

14.2 How should the APV method be modified when it is applied to highly leveraged transactions? Why?

14.3 What is the cost of financial distress? Be specific.

14.4 What does the APV valuation implicitly assume that makes its results highly problematic in valuing highly leveraged businesses?

14.5 What is a firm's tax shield, and how can it be estimated?

14.6 What are the primary advantages and disadvantages of using the CC and APV methods to value highly leveraged transactions?

14.7 Investment bankers sometimes value firms using LBO analyses in addition to conventional DCF and relative valuation methods. Under what circumstances does it make sense use employ an LBO analysis as one means of valuing a firm?

14.8 In what way is a conventional DCF analysis similar to an LBO analysis of a target, and in what ways are they different?

14.9 How may a firm's borrowing capacity be defined?

[23] The target firm's shareholders' equity often becomes negative after an LBO because the buyout of the firm's shareholders increases treasury stock, which is deducted from shareholders' equity for financial reporting purposes.

14.10 The IRR is a crucial decision variable for LBO investors. What are the critical assumptions that must be made in its calculation?

Answers to these Chapter Discussion Questions are available in the Online Instructor's Manual for instructors using this book.

Practice problems

14.11 Assume that based on similar transactions, an analyst believes that a buyout firm will be able to borrow about 5.5 times first-year EBITDA of $200 million (i.e., about $1.1 billion) and that the buyout firm has a target senior-to-subordinated debt split of 75% to 25%. Further assume that investors in the buyout firm wish to exit the business within 8 years after having repaid all of the senior debt. To accomplish this objective, the investors intend to use 100% of cash available for debt reduction to pay off senior debt, and the subordinated debt is payable as a balloon note beyond year 8. Using the scenario in the template "Excel-Based Model to Estimate Firm Borrowing Capacity" on the companion site as the base case, answer the following questions:

a. Will the buyout firm be able to exit its investment by the eighth year if sales grow at 3% rather than the 5% assumed in the base case and still satisfy the assumptions in the base case scenario? After rerunning the model using the lower sales growth rate, what does this tell you about the model's sensitivity to relatively small changes in assumptions?

b. How does this slower sales growth scenario affect the amount the buyout firm could borrow initially if the investors still want to exit the business by the eighth year after paying off 100% of the senior debt and maintain the same senior-to-subordinated debt split?

14.12 By some estimates, as many as one fourth of the LBOs between 1987 and 1990 (the first mega-LBO boom) went bankrupt. The data in Table 14.6 illustrate the extent of the leverage associated with the largest completed LBOs of 2006 and 2007 (the most recent mega-LBO boom). Equity Office Properties and Alltel have been sold. Use the data given in Table 14.7 to calculate the equity contribution made by the buyout firms as a percent of enterprise value and the dollar value of their equity contribution. What other factors would you want to know in evaluating the likelihood that these LBOs will end up in bankruptcy?

Solutions to these problems are available in the Online Instructor's Manual for instructors using this book

TABLE 14.6 Ten completed buyouts ranked by deal enterprise value

Target	Bidder(s)	Enterprise value (EV)	Net debt	Equity	Value of equity	Interest coverage[a]
		($ billion)	% of EV	% of EV	($ billion)	Ratio
TXU	KKR, TPG, Goldman Sachs	43.8	89.5	?	?	1.0
Equity Office Properties	Blackstone	38.9	Sold	NA	NA	Sold
HCA	Bain, KKR, Merrill Lynch	32.7	82.4	?	?	1.6
Alltel	TPG, Goldman Sachs	27.9	Sold	NA	NA	Sold
First Data	KKR	27.7	79.2	?	?	1.0
Harrah's Entertainment	TPG, Apollo	27.4	83.7	?	?	0.8
Hilton Hotels	Blackstone	25.8	75.9	?	?	1.1
Alliance Boots	KKR	20.8	83.5	?	?	1.1
Freescale Semiconductor	Blackstone, Permira, Carlyle, TPG	17.6	49.6	?	?	1.6
Intelsat	BC Partners	16.4	88.9	?	?	1.0
Average		27.9	81	?	?	1.0

[a] Earnings before interest, taxes, depreciation, and amortization less capital expenditures divided by estimated interest expense.
EV, Enterprise value.
Source: The Economist, *July 2008, p. 85*

End-of-chapter case study: investor group takes Dun & Bradstreet private in a leveraged buyout

Case study objectives

To illustrate how

- "Going private" offers the opportunity for businesses to undertake aggressive restructuring strategies without interference from impatient public shareholders
- Private investment in public equities (PIPE) investments often are viewed as a capital infusion into a business to finance a restructuring strategy and are negotiated in a "side letter" to the merger agreement
- PIPE investors usually receive special protections in exchange for their investment

The Dun & Bradstreet (D&B) saga features a firm with a 177-year history of assisting businesses in making credit decisions and more recently in increasing response rates for target marketing programs. This highly recognizable brand provided business credit payment histories and risk assessment software to help businesses evaluate the creditworthiness of their customers. Assisting businesses in making credit decisions has provided the bulk of the firm's revenues and profits for most of its lengthy history. Although this market offered steady growth, it did not offer the potential to achieve the growth needed to boost the firm's share price.

Pairing credit information with demographic data to get a more complete picture of individual consumers offered the prospect of tapping into the supercharged growth in online advertising. This combination could in theory boost the response rate for business-to-business (B-to-B) marketers better than tools that relied on credit or demographic data only. Although D&B had substantial credit information on businesses, it lacked similar data on consumers. Although B-to-B marketing was growing, the real opportunity existed on assisting direct marketing to consumers.

Firms such as Facebook and Google have amassed much larger, more diverse, and current demographic data than D&B on both consumers and small businesses. These firms could sell this information to direct marketing vendors or provide more targeted advertising on their own sites. The end result is that D&B has been unable to participate significantly in the fast-growing consumer direct marketing business.

D&B's product offering had changed little in recent years despite quantum changes in technology. Creditors demanded faster, more accurate tools to determine whether to grant credit to clients and to improve their ability to make more effective marketing decisions. Although providing credit histories and risk assessment tools remained D&B's primary business, the growth in this area has been modest. Consequently, the firm's revenue and profit growth stalled, and its share price flatlined.

To expand their databases to include more diverse marketing data and to develop artificial intelligence–based risk assessment decision tools would take time and hundreds of millions of dollars. Because data acquisition and software development costs must be expensed in the current period, the board and management knew that the firm's reported earnings would suffer. Struggling to resolve these issues, D&B undertook a comprehensive review of the firm's business portfolio. After assessing a range of strategic options in an effort to reinvigorate growth, D&B announced on August 18, 2018, that it had entered into a definitive agreement to be acquired in an all-cash deal by an investor group led by CC Capital, Cannae Holdings, and funds affiliated with Thomas H. Lee Partners along with other investors.

D&B shareholders would receive $145 in cash for each common share held in a deal valued at $7.17 billion, including the assumption of $1.5 billion of D&B net debt and pension obligations. The purchase price represented a premium of 17% over the closing price on the prior trading day and approximately 30% over D&B 's closing share price of $111.63 on February 12, 2018, the last day of trading before D&B's announcement of a strategic review.

D&B had a 45-day go shop provision as part of the agreement during which it was able to seek other bids. As many as 22 potential strategic bidders, 35 potential financial sponsor bidders, and 1 special-purpose acquisition corporation submitted bids. Two financial sponsors and one strategic firm signed confidentiality agreements and were permitted to perform due diligence.

The merger agreement gave the investor group a right of first refusal (the right to match other bids) and the right to receive a termination fee of $81.4 million if D&B accepted another bid. D&B had a reverse termination deal totaling $380 million if the investor group backed out.

To transfer ownership, the investor group (also commonly known as the financial sponsor group) created a shell corporation referred to as Merger Sub Parent and its wholly owned subsidiary, Merger Sub, in accordance with the merger agreement. Upon consummation of the merger, Merger Sub merged with D&B, with D&B the surviving firm. The new firm's assets serve as collateral for the senior secured notes, and all its subsidiaries will guarantee

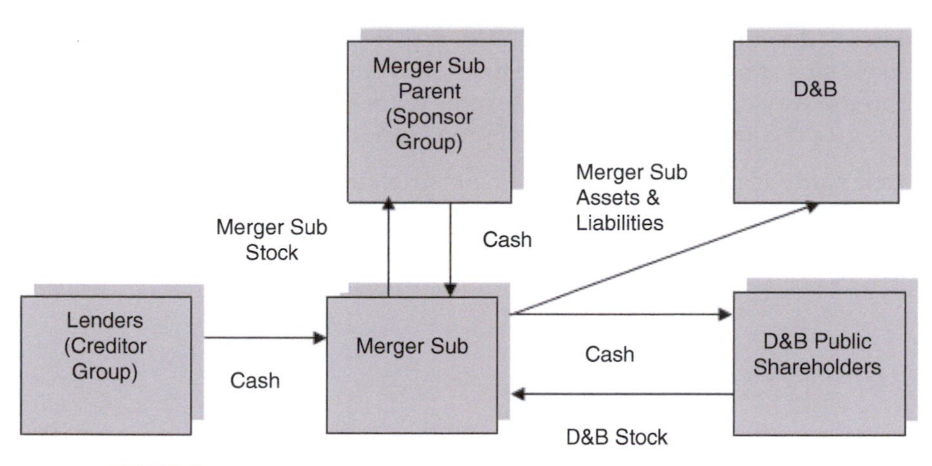

FIGURE 14.1 **Merger and financing structure.** *D&B,* Dun & Bradstreet.

repayment of other outstanding debt. Total cash required for the purchase was provided by the financial sponsor group and lenders (creditor group) to the merger sub (Fig. 14.1).

The $7.17 billion purchase price consisted of $4.18 billion in debt and the remainder in sponsor-contributed equity. The deal was initially financed with a bank bridge loan consisting of $3.33 billion senior secured loan facility and a $.85 billion senior unsecured bridge loan facility. On January 23, 2019, D&B refinanced its bridge bank loan facility. The new debt structure consisted of $.3 billion in senior secured long-term debt, $2.63 billion term loan, $.4 billion in senior secured notes, and $.85 billion in senior unsecured notes.

To refinance the bridge loan facilities, D&B had to accept stricter bond covenants, which limited its ability to issue more debt or pay the investor group dividends. Common equity financing from the investor group totaled $1.94 billion. Another $1.05 billion was invested by the investor group in liquidation preference stock, bringing total equity financing to $2.99 billion. The firm's debt-to-equity ratio increased from its pre-LBO level and was expected to remain high through at least 2020. So, credit-rating agencies downgraded the firm to a B- from a BB+.

This combination of borrowing and cash equity contributions were used to finance the merger and other transactions outlined in the merger agreement. The cash also was used to repay D&B's existing bank credit facilities, redeem D&B's existing senior notes, and pay related fees, costs, premiums and expenses in connection with these transactions. In a "side letter," private equity investor Cannae agreed to use "reasonable efforts" to raise at least $600 to $900 million from other investors in so-called private equity in public investment (or PIPE) financing. Cannae was able to raise $.75 billion, which was to be used to restructure the firm.[24]

The PIPE "side letter" gave Cannae the right to redeem its shares upon the seventh anniversary of the investment[25] and to receive dividends accruing at a rate of 6% per annum payable in cash or in kind at the option of D&B until the fourth anniversary of the investment and thereafter in kind. Cannae also had veto rights over M&A deals with a value in excess of $250 million and over which candidate the search committee of the board would recommend to be the next CEO, as well as a right to appoint its representatives to occupy two board seats, including the co-chair of the board.

Discussion questions

1. Speculate why the D&B board and management chose an LBO over alternative strategies.
2. Why did the sponsor group contribute cash from Merger Sub Parent to Merger Sub rather than lend the money to Merger Sub?
3. Why is D&B merged with Merger Sub and not directly with Merger Sub Parent?
4. What is the purpose of the bridge loan facilities?

[24] A side letter is an agreement that is not part of the merger contract in which some of the parties to the merger contract agree to do something that does not involve other parties to the merger contract.

[25] Cannae could redeem its shares at a premium of 5% to 10% over the volume-weighted average share price for the 20 trading days before announcement of the investment.

5. What type of a merger is described in Figure 14.1? Why was it structured in this manner?
6. Is this transaction likely to be taxable or nontaxable to pre-buyout D&B shareholders? Is D&B post-buyout likely to be paying much in the way of taxes during the several years after closing? Explain your answer.
7. Why did the sponsor group choose to purchase preferred stock as well as common?

A solution to this case study is provided in the Online Instructors Manual for instructors using this book.

CHAPTER

15

Applying financial models
to value, structure, and negotiate stock and asset purchases

OUTLINE

Mergers, Acquisitions, and Other Restructuring Activities, Eleventh Edition
https://doi.org/10.1016/B978-0-12-819782-0.00015-0

"He who lives by the crystal ball soon learns to eat ground glass." —*Edgar R. Fiedler*

Inside M&As: the role of financial models in getting to yes on price

KEY POINTS

M&A financial models:

- Help assess the impact of acquisitions and divestitures on a firm's "baseline" forecast.
- Address valuation, deal structuring, and financing issues.
- Help define risks associated with specific options in "real time."

The stakes were high for both firms. Bristol-Myers Squibb (BMS) and Celgene Corporation (Celgene) share prices had fallen during 2018 amid the failure to get regulatory approval for key treatments and the pending loss of patent protection for certain highly profitable drugs. Under the gun, the two firms were able to reach an agreement in early 2019 in less than 4 months, something they had been unable to do in the prior 2 years.

Financial models are commonly used to project a "baseline" forecast or reference projection of cash flow to estimate a firm's current valuation if it pursues a specific business strategy. Both BMS and Celgene were able to compare their valuations based on their baseline strategies with the valuation based on pro forma financial statements of the merged firms. Celgene, which had previously shown little interest in merging, concluded that the "going it alone" option did not make sense, laying the groundwork for many weeks of intense negotiation.

The BMS board authorized Chairman Giovanni Caforio to approach Mark Alles, chairman of Celgene, to propose a cash and stock deal on September 21, 2018. At that time, the deal was valued at $110 per Celgene share, with an implied premium of 25%. In mid-October, Celgene's board rejected the bid, saying that the proposal undervalued Celgene. Dr. Caforia informed Mr. Alles that BMS would revise its initial bid if the firm could do additional due diligence.

Celgene proceeded to sign a confidentiality agreement containing a joint standstill provision that would terminate discussions if either firm were to enter into a buyout agreement with another party. BMS's revised proposal consisted of $55 in cash ($5 more than the previous bid) and 0.93 of a BMS common share for each Celgene common share, subject to further due diligence and the negotiation of a purchase agreement. Running financial models with the new terms enabled the BMS board to determine the best financing strategy.

Within 3 days, Celgene's board looked at various model-generated scenarios and concluded that the revised proposal was still not sufficient. The second rejection by Celgene prompted a face-to-face meeting on December 10, 2018, between the two chairmen, who were able to reach a verbal agreement to acquire Celgene for an aggregate value of $108 per share.

Total consideration now consisted of one share of BMS (up from a 0.93 exchange ratio in the previous offer) and $55 in cash. The revised verbal offer was subject to BMS board approval and further due diligence performed by both firms. The purpose of the mutual due diligence was to assess the potential for synergy and the share of synergy provided by each party. The aggregate value of the offer was lower than the initial offer of $110 per Celgene share because BMS's share price had fallen in value since the start of negotiations in September.

On December 17, 2018, BMS introduced a convertible value receipt (CVR) to bridge the remaining gap in valuation between the two sides. On December 30, 2018, Celgene accepted BMS's "best and final offer," which consisted of $50 in cash, one share of BMS stock, and a CVR paying up to $9 per share if certain milestones were achieved after closing.

Throughout the negotiation, financial models allowed both parties to construct and evaluate alternative offers. For Celgene, models provided a baseline projection reflecting its current strategy and a means of assessing various bids. For BMS, financial models helped determine an appropriate offer price that it could finance and still earn its cost of capital.

Chapter overview

The emphasis in Chapter 9 is on using financial modeling to estimate the standalone value of a single firm. In this chapter, the focus is on the application of models to value and structure mergers and acquisitions (M&As). A detailed discussion of how to construct M&A models is beyond the scope of this book. Rather, the intent here is to provide readers with an appreciation of the general aspects of such models, their data requirements, and how they may be used to address questions relating to valuation, deal structuring, and financing (Table 15.1).

The acquiring firm, target firm, and combined firms are referred to throughout the chapter as Acquirer, Target, and Newco, respectively. The end-of-chapter case study provides an illustration of how models could have been applied during negotiation using a completed deal. See Appendix A to this chapter for a listing of potential sources of data inputs required to run the financial model discussed in this chapter. The Excel worksheets of the detailed M&A model discussed in this chapter are available on the companion site to this book in a Microsoft Excel file titled M&A Valuation and Deal Structuring Model (https://www.elsevier.com/books-and-journals/book-companion/9780128197820). A review of this chapter is available in the file folder titled "Student Study Guide" on the companion site.

Understanding and applying M&A financial models

The logic underlying the Excel-based M&A model found on the companion site follows the four-step process outlined in (Table 15.2). Key model outputs for a purchase of stock deal are displayed on the Acquirer Transaction Summary Worksheet (Table 15.3). This table allows for a quick review of deal terms and their implications based on specific assumptions. The cells highlighted in yellow are called "input cells" and require the analyst to input data. The remaining cells have formulas using these inputs to calculate their values automatically.

Common elements of M&A models

M&A models commonly require the estimation of the standalone value of Target and Acquirer. The standalone value is what the firm would be worth if it were an independent entity, revenue is valued at current market prices, and costs incurred in generating these revenues are known. The standalone value of Target is theoretically what the business would be worth in the absence of any takeover bid; Acquirer's standalone value represents a reference point against which the value of the combined businesses (Newco) must be compared.

TABLE 15.1 Key deal questions commonly addressed by M&A models

Key questions:

- Valuation (see Chapters 7 to 9)
  - What are the key drivers of firm value?
  - How much is Target worth without the effects of synergy (i.e., standalone value)? How much is Acquirer worth on a standalone basis? Will the combination of the two businesses create value for Acquirer's shareholders?
  - What is the value of expected synergy?
  - What is the maximum price Acquirer should pay for Target?
- Financing (see Chapter 13)
  - Can the proposed purchase price be financed?
  - What combination of potential sources of funds provides the lowest cost of funds for Acquirer, subject to existing loan covenants and credit ratios Acquirer hopes to maintain or achieve?
  - What is the acquisition's impact on Acquirer's fully diluted earnings per share?
  - Are existing loan covenants violated?
  - Is the firm's credit rating in jeopardy?
  - Will the firm's ability to finance future opportunities be impaired?
- Deal structuring (see Chapters 11 and 12)
  - What is the impact on financial performance and valuation if Acquirer is willing to assume certain Target liabilities?
  - What is the impact on Acquirer's earnings per share of alternative forms of payment?
  - What are the implications of a purchase of stock versus a purchase of assets?
  - What is the distribution of ownership of the combined businesses between Acquirer and Target shareholders following closing?
  - What is the impact on Acquirer's financial performance of a tax-free deal?

TABLE 15.2 M&A model building process steps

Step 1: Construct historical financials for Acquirer and Target; determine key value drivers.
a. Collect and analyze historical data to understand the key determinants ("key value drivers") of each firm's historical financial performance.
b. "Normalize" (i.e., remove anomalies) historical data for forecasting purposes.
c. Build historical income statement, balance sheet, and cash flow statements.

Step 2: Project Target and Acquirer financials and estimate standalone values.
a. Determine assumptions for each key input variable to the model.
b. Input assumptions into the model to project financials.
c. Select WACC and terminal period assumptions to estimate standalone values.

Step 3: Estimate value of Newco, including synergy and deal terms.
a. Estimate synergy and investment required to realize synergy.
b. Project Newco financials, including the impact of synergy and deal terms.
c. Select WACC and terminal period assumptions to value Newco.

Step 4: Determine Target offer price and Newco's posttransaction capital structure.
a. Compare the offer price with the value of synergy and recent comparable deals.
b. Compare projected credit ratios with industry average ratios.
c. Determine impact of the deal on Newco's EPS.
d. Determine if the deal allows Newco to meet or exceed required financial returns.

EPS, Earnings per share; *WACC,* weighted average cost of capital.

It makes sense for Acquirer shareholders to do the deal if the value of Newco exceeds the value of Acquirer as a standalone business. The combined business valuation should reflect not only the sum of their standalone values but also the incremental value of synergy and deal terms. The offer price is appropriate if the net present value (NPV) of the investment is greater than or equal to zero. In this context, NPV is defined as the difference between the present value (PV) of Target plus anticipated synergy and the offer price including any transaction-related expenses. Acquirer's posttransaction capital structure is suitable only if it can be supported by the future cash flows, if it does not result in a violation of current loan covenants or desired credit ratios, if it does not jeopardize the firm's credit rating, and, for public companies, if earnings per share (EPS) is not subject to sizeable or sustained dilution.

Value drivers are variables that exert the greatest impact on firm value and often include the revenue growth rate; cost of sales as a percent of sales; sales, general and administrative (SG&A) expenses as a percent of sales; weighted average cost of capital (WACC) assumed during annual cash flow growth and terminal periods; and the cash flow growth rate assumed during terminal period.[1] These variables are changed to simulate different scenarios.

Key data linkages and model balancing mechanism

Figure 15.1 displays data linkages underlying the four process steps within the model. The Acquirer Transaction Summary Worksheet plays a dual role: summarizing deal terms and performance metrics while also providing key inputs for steps 3 and 4 of the modeling process. Figure 15.2 illustrates the model's balancing mechanism. Financial models normally are said to be in balance when total assets (TAs) equal total liabilities plus shareholders' equity. This may be done manually by inserting a "plug" value whenever the two sides of the balance sheet are not equal or automatically by building a mechanism for forcing equality. The latter has the enormous advantage of allowing the model to simulate alternative scenarios over many years without having to stop the forecast each year to manually force it to balance.

The mechanism for forcing balance involves a revolving loan facility or line of credit, which allow firms to borrow up to a specific amount. When the maximum is reached, the firm can no longer borrow. To maintain the ability to borrow to meet unexpected needs, firms pay off the loan as quickly as possible. If total assets exceed total liabilities plus equity, the model borrows (i.e., the "revolver" shows a positive balance on the liability side of the balance sheet)

[1] The constant growth method described in Chapter 7 is used in this chapter to approximate the PV of cash flows beyond the annual forecast period. However, practitioners often use so-called "exit multiples" for this purpose. This involves using a multiple of some income or cash flow measure, such as net income, FCFF, or EBITDA. The multiple is estimated by examining how comparable firms are valued by the market. For example, assume an analyst projects free cash flow to the firm of $10 million and a projected price-to-cash flow multiple of 8 in the fifth year. Multiplying these figures suggests that investors would be willing to pay $80 million in the fifth year for all cash flows generated in perpetuity by the firm beyond the fifth year.

TABLE 15.3 Acquirer transaction summary worksheet (stock purchase)

Transaction value	
Price per share	$ 82.0
Target shares outstanding	174.5
Dilutive effect: Stock options/security conv	2.3
Equity consideration	$ 14,494.8
Less: Cash	$ 276.3
Less: Equity in affilates	–
Plus: Total debt	2060.9
Plus: Noncontrolling interests	0.8
Less other adjustments	–
Enterprise value	$ 16,280.2

Form of payment	Shares	%
% Stock		50.0%
% Cash		50.0%
Target preannouncement share price		$ 60.75
Implied purchase price premium		35.0%
Current shares outstanding	358.1	71.1%
Shares issued to target	94.0	18.6%
New common shares issued	51.9	10.3%
Convertible preferred shares	–	–
New warrants issued	–	–
Total shares	503.9	100.0%

Sources and uses		
Excess cash		$ 1000.0
Common shares issued to target shareholders		7247.4
New common shares issued		4000.0
Convertible preferred equity	–	–
Revolving credit facility	4.40%	–
Senior debt	4.90%	2882.4
Subordinated debt	8.00%	–
Total Sources		$ 15,129.8
Equity Consideration		$ 14,494.8
Transaction Expenses	10 yrs	635.0
Total Uses		$ 15,129.8

Goodwill	
Target tangible book value	$ 4653.4
Adjustments	–
Adjusted book value	4653.4
Equity consideration	14,494.8
Goodwill	$ 9841.4
Transaction exp amortization	$ 19.1
% of transaction expenses amortized	30.0%

Debt	
5-Year treasury rate	1.30%
Swap rate (Bps)	60
Revolving credit facility (Bps over treasury)	250
Senior debt (Bps over treasury)	300
Senor debt amortization (Years)	10.0
Unsecured debt amortization (Years)	15.0

Performance fundamentals-Acquirer	Current	2020
Price per share	77.12	38.74
Shares outstanding	94.0	503.9
Market capitalization	$ 7247.4	$ 19,524.3
Net debt and preferred equity	6175.9	4338.4
Enterprise value	$ 13,423.3	$ 23,862.6
LTM EBITDA	$ 1482.1	$ 2634.7
Enterprise value/LTM EBITDA	9.1x	9.1x

SG&A synergies	$'s
2016	3.0
2017	5.0
2018	8.0
2019	8.0
2020	8.0

Gross margin improvement	%	$'s
2016	0.0%	5.0
2017	0.1%	10.0
2018	0.1%	15.0
2019	0.1%	15.0
2020	0.1%	15.0

Incremental sales synergy	COGS % Sales	$'s
2016	45.8%	$ 25.0
2017	46.2%	75.0
2018	46.5%	150.0
2019	46.5%	150.0
2020	46.5%	150.0

Earnings per share	Acquirer	Newco
2016P	$ 0.52	$ (0.47)
2017P	$ 0.43	$ 0.68
2018P	$ 0.32	$ 0.98
2019P	$ 0.19	$ 1.03
2020P	$ 0.03	$ 1.05

Cash EPS	Acquirer	Newco
2016P	$ 4.26	$ 7.08
2017P	$ 3.63	$ 4.77
2018P	$ 3.66	$ 5.23
2019P	$ 3.67	$ 5.48
2020P	$ 3.66	$ 5.68

Accretion/(dilution)	EPS	Cash EPS
2016P	(191.6%)	66.1%
2017P	57.1%	31.4%
2018P	204.7%	42.8%
2019P	447.3%	49.3%
2020P	4092.9%	55.1%

Valuation	Present value $'s
Target	$ 16,570.9
Acquirer	33,454.4
Newco	57,412.8
Synergies	7387.5
Net present value	8828.7

Total debt to total capital	Industry average	Newco
2016P	37.8	29.5%
2017P	37.8	27.1%
2018P	37.8	24.6%
2019P	37.8	21.9%
2020P	37.8	19.2%

Interest coverage (EBITDA to interest expense)	Industry average	Newco
2016P	3.8	3.9x
2017P	3.8	4.6x
2018P	3.8	5.6x
2019P	3.8	6.4x
2020P	3.8	7.5x

to provide the cash needed to finance the increase in assets. If total liabilities plus equity exceed total assets, the model first pays off any outstanding "revolver" balances and then uses the remaining excess cash flow to add to cash on the balance sheet.

How does the model determine the size of the loan repayment when the loan balance is positive? Firms consider the amount of available cash and the minimum cash balance they wish to maintain. If available cash less the loan balance is less than the desired minimum cash balance, the loan payment equals the difference between available cash and minimum cash. Loan payments greater than this amount cause the firm's ending cash to be less than the desired minimum balance. To illustrate, consider the following:

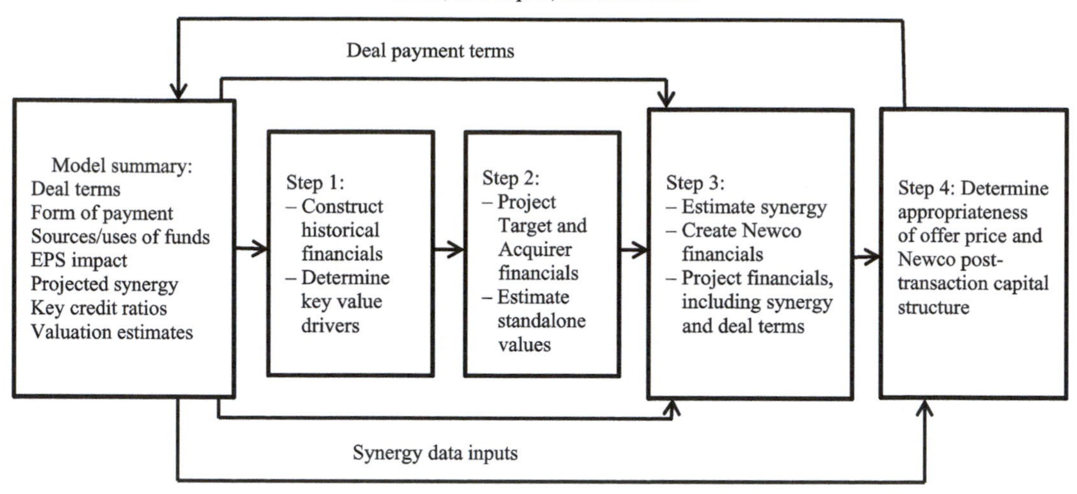

FIGURE 15.1 **Mergers and acquisitions model worksheet flow diagram.** *EPS*, Earnings per share.

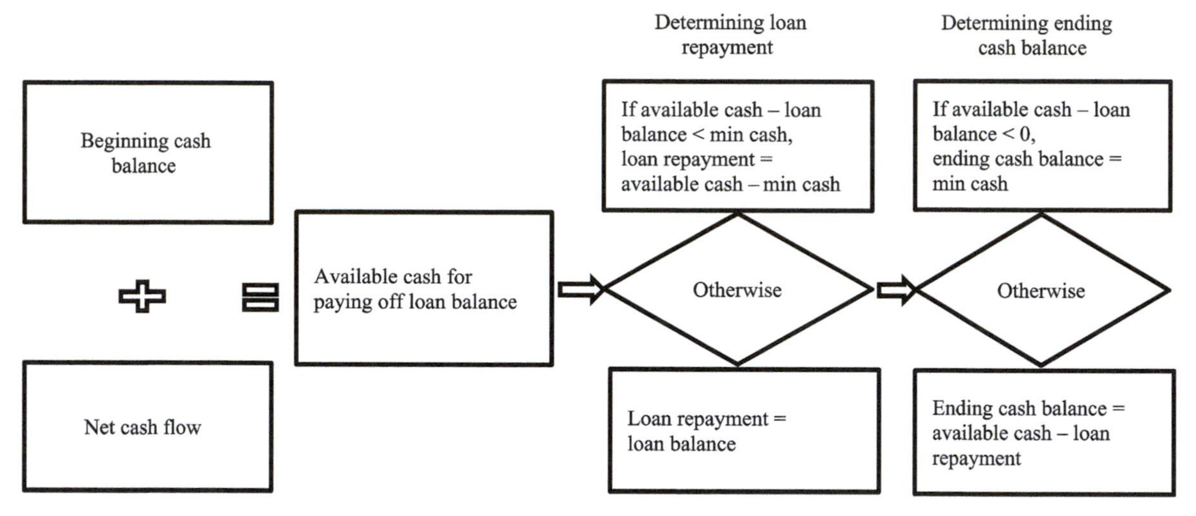

Definitions: Min cash = minimum cash balance required by firm
Loan balance = outstanding balance on the revolving loan credit facility
Available cash = cash available for paying off any loan balance owed on the revolving loan credit facility

FIGURE 15.2 **Mergers and acquisitions model balancing mechanism.**

If available cash = \$80 million

Beginning loan balance = \$75 million

Minimum cash = \$10 million

Then

Available cash − Loan balance = \$80 million − \$75 million < \$10 million (minimum cash) and

Loan payment = \$80 − \$10 = \$70 million

Ending loan balance = \$75 million − \$70 million = \$5 million

TABLE 15.4 Determining Newco's ending cash balances

	Projections ($)		
	2016	2017	2018
Cash from operating, investing, and financing activities	1899.0	229.3	363.1
Beginning cash balance	131.6	100.0	259.9
Cash available for revolving credit facility[a]	2030.6	329.3	623.0
Beginning revolving credit facility balance	2000.0	69.4[b]	0.0
Repayment of revolving credit facility loan balance[c]	1930.6	69.4	0.0
Ending revolving credit facility balance[d]	69.4	0.0	0.0
Ending cash balance	100.0	259.9[e]	623.0

[a]Cash from operating, investing, and financing activities plus the beginning cash balance.
[b]Ending revolver balance.
[c]Cash available less minimum balance if cash available less beginning revolver balance is less than minimum cash; otherwise, total repayment equals beginning revolver balance.
[d]Beginning revolver balance less total repayment.
[e]Minimum cash if cash available is less than the beginning revolver balance and minimum cash; otherwise, ending cash equals cash available less total loan repayment.

However, if available cash less the loan balance exceeds the desired minimum cash balance, the loan repayment equals the loan balance because there is more than enough cash to repay the loan and still maintain the desired minimum cash balance. Consider the following example:

If available cash = $85 million

Beginning loan balance = $75 million

Minimum cash = $10 million

Then

Available cash − Loan balance = $85 million − $75 million = $10 million (minimum cash)

Loan payment = $85 million − $75 million = $10 million

Ending loan balance = 0

Ending cash balances will always equal minimum cash if available cash is less than the loan balance. Why? Because only that portion of the loan balance greater than minimum balance will be used to repay the loan. Conversely, if available cash exceeds the loan balance, the ending cash balance equals the difference between available cash and the loan payment because the loan balance will not be repaid unless there is sufficient cash available to cover the minimum balance. Table 15.4 provides a numerical example of how the firm's ending cash balance is determined assuming the revolving credit facility balance in the Sources and Uses section of Table 15.3 is $2 billion and that the firm requires a minimum operating cash balance of $100 million. See the table's footnotes for a definition of each line item.

M&A models: stock purchases

The three basic legal forms of M&A deals include a merger, stock purchase, and purchase of assets (see Chapter 11). What follows is a discussion of an M&A model that applies to either a merger or stock purchase. Such models are generally more complex than asset purchase models.

A *merger* transaction is similar to a stock purchase in that the buyer will acquire all of Target company's assets, rights, and liabilities (known and unknown)[2] and will be unable to specifically identify which assets and liabilities it wishes to assume. In contrast, in an *asset purchase* (discussed later in this chapter), the seller retains ownership of

[2] Known liabilities are those shown on Target's balance sheet, and unknown liabilities are those not recorded.

TABLE 15.5 M&A model worksheets[a]

Acquirer transaction summary (includes deal terms, form of payment, sources and uses of funds, synergy estimates, EPS impact, and key credit ratios)

Step 1: Construct historical financials and determine key value drivers.

- Target and Acquirer assumptions (historical period only)
- Target and Acquirer IS (historical period only)
- Target and Acquirer BS (historical period only)
- Target and Acquirer CF (historical period only)

Step 2: Project Target's and Acquirer's financials and estimate standalone value.

- Acquirer assumptions (includes key value drivers)
- Acquirer IS
- Acquirer BS
- Acquirer CF

Step 3: Estimate value of combined firms (Newco), including synergy and deal terms.

- Newco assumptions (includes key value drivers)
- Newco IS
- Newco BS
- Newco CF

Step 4: Determine appropriateness of offer price and Newco post-closing capital or financing structure.

- Debt repayment (includes repayment schedule for Target debt assumed by Acquirer, Acquirer's pretransaction debt, and new debt issued to finance the deal)
- Options: convertibles (estimates the number of new Target shares that must be acquired because of the conversion of options as well as convertible debt and preferred equity)
- Valuation (includes the valuation of Target, Acquirer, and Newco enterprise value, equity value, and price per share)

[a]Each bulleted item describes a specific worksheet.
BS, Balance sheet; *CF*, cash flow; *EPS*, earnings per share; *IS*, income statement.

the firm's shares, and only assets and liabilities that are stipulated in the purchase agreement are transferred to the buyer. All other assets and liabilities remain with the seller.

A *merger* involves the mutual decision of two companies to combine to become a single legal entity and generally involves two firms relatively equal in size, with one disappearing. All Target assets and liabilities, known and unknown, automatically transfer to Acquirer. Target shareholders usually have their shares exchanged for Acquirer shares at some negotiated share exchange ratio, for cash, or some combination.

A *stock purchase* usually involves the purchase of all the shares of another entity for cash or stock. Acquirer may purchase less than 100% of Target's outstanding shares because all shareholders may not agree to sell their shares. As in a merger, Target's assets and liabilities effectively transfer to Acquirer without interruption. However, unlike a merger, Acquirer may be left with minority Target shareholders, and Target may continue to exist as a legal subsidiary of Acquirer.

The M&A model discussed in this chapter consists of a series of linked worksheets, each reflecting either a financial statement or related activity. Table 15.5 illustrates how the 17 worksheets fit into each of the four process steps described in Table 15.2. IS, BS, and CF refer to income statement, balance sheet, and cash flow statement, respectively. The following sections reflect the process steps and the activities within each process step.

Step 1: construct historical financials and determine key value drivers

Although public firms must file their financial statements with the Securities and Exchange Commission (SEC) in accordance with generally accepted accounting principles (GAAP), so-called *pro forma financial statements* are used to represent what the combined firms would look like in the future and what they could have looked like in the past based on the assumptions of the analyst who constructed the financial statements.

Step 1a: collect and analyze required historical data to understand key value drivers

A valuation's accuracy depends on understanding the historical competitive dynamics of the industry and of the firm within the industry, as well as the reliability of data used in the valuation. Competitive dynamics are factors within the industry that determine industry profitability and cash flow. An examination of historical information provides insights into key relationships among various operating variables. Examples of relevant historical relationships include seasonal or cyclical movements in the data, the relationship between fixed and variable expenses, and the impact on revenue of changes in product prices and unit sales.[3] For a more detailed discussion of value drivers in the context of model building, see Chapter 9.

Step 1b: normalize historical data for forecasting purposes

To define historical relationships accurately, *normalize* the data by removing nonrecurring changes (e.g., the 2020 COVID-19 pandemic) and questionable accounting practices. Cash flow may be adjusted by adding back unusually large increases in reserves or deducting large decreases from free cash flow to the firm (FCFF). An example of reserves is accounting entries established in anticipation of a pending expense such as employee layoffs in the year after a merger. The effect of the reserve would be to lower income in the current year. However, the actual cash outlay would not occur until the following year when the layoffs actually occur.

Similar adjustments can be made for significant nonrecurring gains or losses on the sale of assets or nonrecurring expenses, such as those associated with the settlement of a lawsuit or warranty claim. Monthly revenue may be aggregated into quarterly or even annual data to minimize distortions in earnings or cash flow resulting from inappropriate accounting practices.

Step 1c: build historical financial statements

After they have been collected, input all historical financial data for both Target and Acquirer into the historical input cells in the income statement, balance sheet, and cash flow statements worksheets. Note the reconciliation line at the bottom on the balance sheet worksheet. This represents the difference between total assets and total liabilities plus shareholders' equity and should be equal to zero if the model is balancing properly.

Step 2: project Acquirer and Target financials and estimate standalone values

If the factors affecting sales, profit, and cash flow historically are expected to exert the same influence in the future, a firm's financial statements may be projected by extrapolating normalized historical growth rates in key variables such as revenue. If the factors affecting sales growth are expected to change because of the introduction of new products, total revenue growth may accelerate from its historical trend. In contrast, the emergence of additional competitors may limit revenue growth by eroding the firm's market share and selling prices.

Key normalized financial data should be projected for at least 5 years or more until cash flow turns positive or the growth rate slows to what appears to be sustainable. Projections should include product demand growth, future pricing, technological changes, new competitors, new product and service offerings from current competitors, potential supply disruptions, raw material and labor cost increases, and new product substitutes. Projections also should include the revenue and costs associated with known new product introductions and capital expenditures, as well as expenses required to maintain or expand operations by the acquiring and target firms.

Step 2a: determine assumptions for each key input variable

Cash flow forecasts commonly involve the projection of revenue and the various components of cash flow as a percent of revenue. For example, cost of sales, depreciation, gross capital spending, and the change in working capital often are projected as a percent of future revenue.[4]

[3] For public companies, data are commonly obtained from the firm's 10Ks and 10Qs to value firms before signing a nondisclosure with Target. See Chapters 4 and 5 for additional data sources for both public and private firms.

[4] The major risk in applying historical ratios to projected revenues is that they may not reflect accurately future improvements in productivity and working capital management. Boisjoly et al. (2020) document gains in asset management in recent decades because of continuous improvement programs and aggressive working capital practices on accounts receivable turnover, inventory turnover, days payables outstanding, and cash conversion cycle.

What percentage is applied to projected revenue for these components of FCFF may be determined by calculating their historical ratio to revenue. In this simple model, revenue drives cash-flow growth. Revenue is projected by forecasting unit growth and selling prices, the product of which provides estimated revenue. Common projection methods include *trend extrapolation* and *scenario analysis*.[5]

Line-item analysis of a firm's financial statements also provides clues to near-term and longer-term revenue, profitability, and cash flow. For example, firm profitability is inversely related to changes in accruals[6] because of measurement errors, declining investment returns, conservative accounting, and costs of adjusting to future growth. In the short term, an increase in input costs raises the firm's current production and inventory costs and reduces the firm's future profitability when the inventory is sold. Moreover, accelerating sales growth often is accompanied by even faster growth in expenses as managers build inventory and add workers in anticipation of a sustained sales growth. The longer-term decline in earnings reflects increased competition from existing competitors and future industry entrants.[7]

Step 2b: input assumptions into the model and project financials

The Target Assumptions Worksheet in Table 15.6 is an example of the financial statements used in the model. Each input cell (denoted in yellow) may be changed with the subsequent years changed automatically to reflect the new entry. Changes to the model are made primarily by making changes in the worksheets labeled Target Assumptions and Acquirer Assumptions. The analyst should input cell values one at a time using only small changes in such values to assess accurately the outcome of each change on performance metrics such as net income, EPS, and NPV. It will become evident which variables are key value drivers. See the practice exercise in Exhibit 15.1 for an illustration of how to change revenue growth, a key value driver.

Step 2c: select appropriate discount rate and terminal period assumptions to estimate standalone values

The actual valuation of Target and Acquirer is done on the Valuation Worksheet using inputs from Target and Acquirer Assumptions Worksheets. See Chapter 7 for a discussion of how to estimate the appropriate WACC and terminal period assumptions for Target and Acquirer.

Step 3: estimate value of Newco, including synergy and deal terms

This step involves adjusting the sum of Target and Acquirer financial statements to create combined company pro forma statements showing what Newco would look like adjusted for synergy and deal terms. In practice, the combination of businesses can create or destroy value measured in terms of cash flows. In this chapter, we discuss the notion of net synergy, that is, the difference between sources and destroyers of value. Sources of value *add* to the economic value (i.e., ability to generate future cash flows) of the combined firms; destroyers of value *reduce* cash flows. To determine if cash flows result from synergy, ask if they can be generated only if the businesses are combined. If the answer is yes, then the cash flow in question is due to synergy.

Deal terms refer to the amount and composition of the form of payment (usually cash, stock, or some combination) for Target, whether Acquirer is purchasing the stock or assets of Target (form of acquisition), the number of shares being acquired, and how it is being financed. The amount of the purchase price will affect what has to be financed by borrowing, using excess cash balances, or issuing some form of equity consideration (EQC; i.e., common stock, preferred stock, or warrants). Such factors impact interest expense on the income statement and goodwill, cash balances, and shareholders' equity on the balance sheet.

When cash is the primary form of payment, its value is clear. In stock deals, the value of the acquirer shares depends on the accuracy of acquirer's pro forma projections. Acquirers with a strong record of accurate forecasting are associated with increased deal completion rates and lower acquisition premiums. Why? Target investors are more confident of the value of acquirer shares they receive in exchange for their shares and are more likely to vote in

[5] Trend extrapolation entails extending present trends into the future using historical growth rates or multiple regression techniques. Scenario analysis projects multiple outlooks, with each differing in terms of key variables (e.g., growth in gross domestic product, industry sales growth, fluctuations in exchange rates) or issues (e.g., competitive new product introductions, new technologies, and new regulations).

[6] Accruals are earned revenues not yet received (e.g., accounts receivable) and incurred expenses not yet paid (e.g., accounts payable).

[7] Lewellen et al., 2019

TABLE 15.6 Target assumptions worksheet

Target **Assumptions**

($Millions, except per share data)

	Actual			Projections for the period ending December 31				
	2013	2014	2015	2016	2017	2018	2019	2020
Income statement								
Sales growth	NA	5.2%	4.8%	5.5%	5.5%	5.5%	5.5%	5.5%
COGS as a % of sales	41.3%	44.1%	42.0%	43.0%	43.0%	43.0%	43.0%	43.0%
SG&A % annual increase (decrease)	NA	(1.4%)	4.5%	4.0%	4.0%	4.0%	4.0%	4.0%
Other operating expense as a % of sales	13.1%	12.0%	10.5%	11.0%	11.0%	11.0%	11.0%	11.0%
EBITDA growth	NA	5.8%	27.4%	(0.1%)	7.5%	7.4%	7.4%	7.3%
EBITDA margin	17.1%	17.2%	20.8%	19.7%	20.1%	20.5%	20.8%	21.2%
Balance sheet								
Receivable days	59.8	61.6	64.3	59.0	59.0	59.0	59.0	59.0
Inventory days	79.6	82.8	88.5	84.0	84.0	84.0	84.0	84.0
Other current assets % of sales	7.8%	5.2%	6.3%	5.5%	5.5%	5.5%	5.5%	5.5%
Accounts payable days	43.0	39.1	40.9	40.0	40.0	40.0	40.0	40.0
Other current liabilities % of COGS	65.6%	79.1%	60.4%	68.0%	68.0%	68.0%	68.0%	68.0%
Working capital/sales (Excl cash and debt)	1.3%	(7.5%)	4.0%	(2.4%)	(2.4%)	(2.4%)	(2.4%)	(2.4%)
Cash flow								
Capital expenditures	26.7	13.8	10.3	16.7	17.6	18.6	19.6	20.7
Capex as a % of sales	0.7%	0.4%	0.3%	0.4%	0.4%	0.4%	0.4%	0.4%
Depreciation	123.0	123.6	126.0	133.6	141.0	148.7	156.9	165.6
Depreciation as a % of sales	3.4%	3.3%	3.2%	3.2%	3.2%	3.2%	3.2%	3.2%
Goodwill amortization (Pre-6/2001)	–	–	–	–	–	–	–	–
Amortization of intangibles	299.6	313.9	302.9	300.0	300.0	300.0	300.0	300.0
Retirement of senior debt	2,320.2	350.4	450.0	300.0	300.0	300.0	300.0	300.0
Retirement of subordinated debt	–	–	–	–	–	–	–	–
Chg in deferred taxes—asset	NA	2.0	(5.8)	–	–	–	–	–
Chg in deferred taxes—liab	NA	(147.4)	(123.2)	–	–	–	–	–
Dividend from affiliates	–	–	–	–	–	–	–	–
Payout ratio of affiliates	–	–	–	–	–	–	–	–
Dividends per share	–	–	–	–	–	–	–	–
Dividend payout ratio	–	–	–	–	–	–	–	–
Dividends paid	–	–	–	–	–	–	–	–
Effective tax rate	338.8%	244.9%	38.6%	40.0%	40.0%	40.0%	40.0%	40.0%
Other								
Shares outstanding—basic	–	–	170.8	170.8	170.8	170.8	170.8	170.8
Shares outstanding—diluted	–	–	174.5	174.5	174.5	174.5	174.5	174.5
Revolving credit facility rate	–	–	–	2.00%	2.00%	2.00%	2.00%	2.00%
Senior debt rate	–	–	–	5.00%	5.00%	5.00%	5.00%	5.00%
Subordinated debt	–	–	–	8.00%	8.00%	8.00%	8.00%	8.00%
Average interest rate	NA	6.45%	5.69%	5.00%	5.00%	5.00%	5.00%	5.00%
Marketable securities rate	–	–	–	–	–	–	–	–

COGS, Cost of goods sold; *EBITDA*, earnings before interest, taxes, depreciation, and amortization; *NA*, not applicable; *SG&A*, sales, general and administrative expense.

EXHIBIT 15.1

Practice Exercise: Changing Target Revenue Growth

Using the Excel spreadsheet model in the file titled M&A Valuation and Structuring Model on the companion website accompanying this book (see the beginning of this chapter for website address), change Target's revenue growth rate assumption. On Target's Assumptions Worksheet, to raise Target's revenue growth rate by 1 percentage point during the annual forecast period (2016–2020), increase the growth rate from 5.5% to 6.5% in the yellow input cell on the Sales Growth line for the year 2016. The model will increase automatically the growth rate annually from 2016 to 2020 by 1 percentage point. The model also accommodates a variable growth rate forecast. For example, if the growth rate in 2017 is expected to increase by an additional 1 percentage point and to continue at that higher rate in subsequent years, the analyst simply increases the growth rate from 5.5% to 6.5% in 2016 and to 7.5% in 2017.

support of the deal. They are also willing to accept lower premiums to exchange their shares for acquirer shares because of greater confidence that the earnings forecast will be realized.[8]

Step 3a: estimate synergy and investment required to realize synergy

Common sources of value include cost savings resulting from shared overhead, elimination of duplicate facilities, better use of existing facilities, and minimizing overlapping distribution channels (e.g., direct sales forces, websites, agents). Synergy related to cost savings generally is more easily realized than synergy from other sources.

Other sources include cross-selling of Acquirer's products to Target's customers and vice versa. Potential sources of value can include land and "obsolete" inventory and equipment whose value has been written down to zero. Such inventory can still be discounted and sold to raise cash, and fully depreciated equipment can still be useful. Underused borrowing capacity or significant excess cash balances also can make an acquisition target more attractive. The addition of Target's assets, low level of indebtedness, and strong cash flow from operations could enable the buyer to increase substantially the borrowing levels of the combined companies.[9] Intellectual property, new technologies, and new customer groups also contribute to value. Likewise, income tax losses and tax credits also may represent an important source of value by reducing the combined firms' current and future tax liability.

Factors destroying value include poor product quality, excessive wage and benefit levels, low productivity, high employee turnover, and customer attrition. Badly written contracts often result in customer disputes about terms, conditions, and amounts owed. Environmental issues, product liabilities, and unresolved lawsuits are also major destroyers of value for the buyer.

In calculating synergy, it is important to include the costs associated with recruiting and training employees, achieving productivity improvements, layoffs, and exploiting revenue opportunities. Employee attrition after closing will add to recruitment and training costs. Cost savings because of layoffs frequently are offset in the early years by severance expenses. Realizing productivity gains requires more spending in new structures and equipment or redesigning workflow. Exploiting revenue-raising opportunities may require training the sales force of the combined firms in selling each firm's products and additional advertising.

Step 3b: project Newco financials, including effects of synergy and deal terms

Table 15.7 displays the key deal terms found on the Acquirer Transaction Summary Worksheet. These include the form of acquisition (stock or asset) and the amount and form of payment (Acquirer stock, cash, or some combination), as well as the timing of payment. In some transactions, some portion of the purchase price may be deferred. See the practice exercise in Exhibit 15.2 for an illustration of how to change payment terms.

TABLE 15.7 Acquirer transaction summary worksheet: deal terms (stock purchase)

Acquirer — **Transaction summary**

($Millions, except per share data)

Transaction value	
Price Per share	$ 82.0
Target shares outstanding	174.5
Dilutive effect: stock options/security conv	2.3
Equity consideration	$ 14,494.8
Less: Cash	$ 276.3
Less: Equity in affilates	–
Plus: Total debt	2060.9
Plus: Noncontrolling interests	0.8
Less other adjustments	–
Enterprise value	$ 16,280.2

Form of payment		
% Stock		50.0%
% Cash		50.0%
Target preannouncement share price		$ 60.75
Implied purchase price premium		35.0%
	Shares	%
Current shares outstanding	358.1	71.1%
Shares issued to target	94.0	18.6%
New common shares issued	51.9	10.3%
Convertible preferred shares	–	–
New warrants issued	–	–
Total shares	503.9	100.0%

Sources and uses		
Excess cash		$ 1000.0
Common shares issued to target shareholders		7247.4
New common shares issued		4000.0
Convertible preferred equity	–	–
Revolving credit facility	4.40%	–
Senior debt	4.90%	2882.4
Subordinated debt	8.00%	–
Total sources		$ 15,129.8
Equity consideration		$ 14,494.8
Transaction expenses	10 yrs	635.0
Total uses		$ 15,129.8

[8] Amel-Zadeh and Meeks, 2019

[9] The incremental borrowing capacity can be approximated by comparing the combined firms' current debt-to-total capital ratio with the industry average. For example, assume Firm A's acquisition of Firm B results in a reduction in the combined firms' debt-to-total capital ratio to 0.25 (e.g., debt represents $250 million of the new firm's total capital of $1 billion). If the same ratio for the industry is 0.5, the new firm may be able to increase its borrowing by $250 million, raising its debt-to-total capital ratio to the industry average.

EXHIBIT 15.2

Practice Exercise: Setting Payment Terms

Using the Excel spreadsheet model in the file folder titled M&A Valuation and Structuring Model on the companion website accompanying this book, change the payment terms on the Summary Worksheet. Input the percentage of the total payment that is Acquirer stock in the Form of Payment Section and the model automatically treats the remaining portion of the payment as cash. For example, an all-cash deal would require setting the percentage of the total payment that is stock to zero; for a deal that is 30% stock and 70% cash, set the percentage of the total payment that is stock to 30%.

TABLE 15.8 Acquirer transaction summary worksheet: synergy assumptions (stock purchase)

SG&A synergies		Gross margin improvement			Incremental sales synergy		
	$'s		%	$'s		Margin	$'s
2016	3.0	2016	0.0%	5.0	2016	45.8%	$ 25.0
2017	5.0	2017	0.1%	10.0	2017	46.2%	75.0
2018	8.0	2018	0.1%	15.0	2018	46.5%	150.0
2019	8.0	2019	0.1%	15.0	2019	46.5%	150.0
2020	8.0	2020	0.1%	15.0	2020	46.5%	150.0

SG&A, Sales, general and administrative.

The Transaction Summary Worksheet also displays the synergy inputs as shown in Table 15.8. These include profit margin increases, lower SG&A as a percent of revenue, and additional revenue from combining the firms. Margin improvements reflect both improvements in cost of goods sold (COGS) and selling price increases. Rising sales often reflect cross-selling one firm's products to the other's customers. The model presumes that the SG&A associated with the incremental sales is less than the historical ratio of SG&A as a percent of revenue. Assuming the two firms are similar, the existing sales and administrative infrastructure often can support a substantial portion of the additional revenue without having to add personnel.

The additional SG&A as a percent of revenue assumed to support the incremental revenue is shown in an input cell at the bottom of the Transaction Summary Worksheet (See Model's Acquirer Transaction Summary Worksheet). Note the synergies are phased in over time, reflecting delays in realizing savings and revenue growth, and when fully realized, they are sustained at that level during the remainder of the forecast period.

Newco's Income Statement Worksheet (Table 15.9) displays, in the Transaction Adjustments column between the historical and projected financial data, the effects of anticipated synergy, costs incurred to realize synergy, and other acquisition-related costs in 2016. The purpose of these adjustments is to create a pro forma income statement to illustrate what the combined firms would have looked like had they been operated jointly for the entire year.

The incremental revenue due to synergy in 2016 of $25 million generates an additional $13.6 million in COGS.[10] The net increase in COGS (i.e., additional cost to support the increase in sales less the improvement in operating margin) is $8.5 million and represents 34% of incremental sales (i.e., $8.5/$25) compared with its 58.4% historical average during the prior 3 years.[11] The improvement in the COGS ratio reflects a $5 million increase in the operating margin caused by a better utilization of existing capacity and savings associated with purchases of raw materials and services.[12]

The model assumes that the ratio of SG&A to incremental sales is 10%, resulting in an increase of SG&A of $2.5 million. However, this increase in SG&A is expected to be offset by a $3 million reduction in SG&A overhead caused

[10] (1 − Gross margin) × $25 million = (1 − 0.458) × $25 million = $13.6 million. See Table 15.8.

[11] See the Acquirer Transaction Worksheet in the M&A Model accompanying this book. The 10% figure is located in a blue input cell immediately below the last line of the worksheet.

[12] See the Gross Margin Improvement section of Table 15.8.

TABLE 15.9 Newco income statement worksheet adjustments: stock purchase

Newco **Pro forma income statement**
($Millions, except per share data)

	Actual	Projected 2016		Trans	Pro forma	Projections			
	2015	Acquirer	Target	Adj	2016	2017	2018	2019	2020
Sales	$ 12,509.9	$ 13,160.4	$ 4176.2	$ 25.0	$ 17,361.6	$ 18,325.7	$ 19,362.9	$ 20,375.9	$ 21,442.4
Integration expenses				100.0	100.0	50.0	–	–	–
Cost of goods sold	7214.4	7501.4	1795.8	8.5	9405.8	9866.4	10,365.9	10,907.5	11,477.7
Gross profit	5295.5	5659.0	2380.4		7855.9	8409.2	8997.0	9468.4	9964.7
SG&A	3354.9	3619.9	1096.8	(0.5)	4716.2	5049.1	5407.8	5788.2	6196.8
Other operating expense	458.5	460.6	459.4		920.0	969.2	1021.1	1075.7	1133.3
Depreciation	983.7	987.0	133.6		1120.7	1179.3	1241.1	1306.1	1374.5
Amortization	–	–	300.0	19.1	319.1	319.1	319.1	319.1	319.1
EBIT	**498.4**	**591.4**	**390.6**		**779.9**	**892.6**	**1008.0**	**979.4**	**941.2**
Unusual (gain) loss	–	–	–	444.5	444.5	–	–	–	–
(Income) from affiliates	–	–	–		–	–	–	–	–
Other expense (income)	212.7	–	–		–	–	–	–	–
Interest (income)	–	–	–	–	–	–	–	–	–
Interest expense	–	339.1	95.5	134.2	568.8	514.7	460.5	406.4	352.3
Earnings before taxes	285.7	252.3	295.1		(233.3)	377.9	547.5	573.0	588.9
Noncontrolling interest	–	–	–		–	–	–	–	–
Taxes	11.0	65.6	118.0	(177.0)	6.6	98.3	142.3	149.0	153.1
Net income before extra items	**$ 274.7**	**$ 186.7**	**$ 177.1**		**$ (240.0)**	**$ 279.6**	**$ 405.1**	**$ 424.0**	**$ 435.8**
Extraordinary items	(19.2)	–	–		–	–	–	–	–
Net income after extra items	$ 194.2	$ 186.7	$ 177.1		$ (240.0)	$ 279.6	$ 405.1	$ 424.0	$ 435.8
EPS—Basic	**$ 0.77**	**$ 0.52**	**$ 1.04**		**$ (0.48)**	**$ 0.55**	**$ 0.80**	**$ 0.84**	**$ 0.86**
EPS—Diluted	**$ 0.76**	**$ 0.52**	**$ 0.49**		**$ (0.47)**	**$ 0.68**	**$ 0.98**	**$ 1.03**	**$ 1.05**
Other financial data									
Depreciation and amortization	983.7	987.0	433.6	19.1	1439.7	1498.4	1560.1	1625.1	1693.5
Capital expenditures	1083.4	855.4	16.7		872.1	917.5	965.3	1015.5	1068.4
EBITDA	**1482.1**	**1578.4**	**824.3**		**2219.7**	**2391.0**	**2568.2**	**2604.5**	**2634.7**
EPS (excluding unusual items)	$ 0.76	$ 0.52	$ 1.01		$ 0.18	$ 0.68	$ 0.98	$ 1.03	$ 1.05
Cash EPS	$ (0.24)	$ 4.26	$ 4.97		$ 7.08	$ 4.77	$ 5.23	$ 5.48	$ 5.68
Dividends per share	$ –	$ –	$ –		$ –	$ –	$ –	$ –	$ –
Dividend-adjusted cash EPS	$ (0.24)	$ 4.26	$ 4.97		$ 7.08	$ 4.77	$ 5.23	$ 5.48	$ 5.68

EBIT, Earnings before interest and taxes; *EBITDA*, earnings before interest, taxes, depreciation, and amortization; *EPS*, earnings per share; *SG&A*, sales, general and administrative.

by the elimination of duplicate sales, market, and administrative functions. Integration expense incurred in the first full year of Newco operations is estimated at $100 million and includes severance expense, lease buyouts, retraining expenses, and so on. Interest expense is up by $134.2 million, reflecting additional borrowing costs associated with closing the deal. Taxes decrease by $151 million because of expensing of non–financing-related transaction closing expenses of $444.5 million.[13]

Transaction adjustments for Newco's balance sheet (Table 15.10) illustrate how the transaction purchase price is financed. This data comes from the Transaction Summary Worksheet Sources and Uses section of Table 15.7. The EQC or purchase price of $14,494.8 million (excluding transaction expenses [TEs]) is 50% cash, with the remainder paid in newly issued Acquirer shares valued at $7,247.4. The cash portion of the purchase price including transactions expenses is $7,882.4 million[14] and is financed through a combination of reducing cash on the balance sheet by $1000 million, borrowing $2882.4 million in senior debt, and issuing new acquirer common shares to the public valued at $4000 million.

[13] Note that financing fees can be capitalized on the Newco balance sheet and amortized over the life of the loan.

[14] $7882.4 = 0.5 × $14,494.8 million in equity consideration + $635 million in transaction fees.

TABLE 15.10 Newco balance sheet worksheet adjustments

Newco — **Pro forma balance sheet**

($Millions, except per share data)

	Actual 2015		Pre-trans	Trans	Pro forma	Projections				
	Acquirer	Target	Adj	Adj	2015	2016	2017	2018	2019	2020
Cash	$ 855.3	$ 276.3		$ (1000.0)	$ 131.6	$ 1862.9	$ 1868.6	$ 1977.4	$ 2140.7	$ 2331.9
Accounts receivable	1804.9	697.3			2502.2	2517.5	2657.5	2808.2	2955.3	3110.3
Inventory	1443.3	403.5	–		1846.8	142.5	149.5	157.1	165.3	173.9
Other	731.3	248.1			979.4	915.4	966.2	1020.9	1074.4	1130.6
Current assets	4834.8	1625.2			5460.0	5438.3	5641.9	5963.6	6335.7	6746.7
Property, plant, and equipment	1726.4	871.4	–		2597.8	3469.9	4387.5	5352.8	6368.3	7436.7
Accumulated depreciation	–	–	–		–	(1120.7)	(2300.0)	(3541.1)	(4847.2)	(6221.7)
Net property, plant, and equipment	1726.4	871.4			2597.8	2349.3	2087.4	1811.7	1521.1	1215.1
Goodwill	12,474.5	4503.4	–	9841.4	26,819.3	26,819.3	26,819.3	26,819.3	26,819.3	26,819.3
Intangible assets	7804.5	1525.8			9330.3	9030.3	8730.3	8430.3	8130.3	7830.3
Deferred financing expenses	–	–		190.5	190.5	171.5	152.4	133.4	114.3	95.3
Deferred taxes	–	23.0			23.0	23.0	23.0	23.0	23.0	23.0
Equity in affiliates	–	–			–	–	–	–	–	–
Other	604.4	89.2			693.6	693.6	693.6	693.6	693.6	693.6
Total assets	**$ 27,444.6**	**$ 8638.0**			**$ 45,114.5**	**$ 44,525.1**	**$ 44,147.9**	**$ 43,874.7**	**$ 43,637.3**	**$ 43,423.2**
Accounts payable	641.4	186.6			828.0	885.2	928.7	975.8	1026.8	1080.6
Other	1451.9	1005.8			2457.7	2829.1	2969.7	3122.2	3287.6	3461.9
Current liabilities	2093.3	1192.4			3285.7	3714.3	3898.4	4098.0	4314.5	4542.5
Revolving credit facility	–	–		–	–	–	–	–	–	–
Senior debt	7031.2	2060.9		2882.4	11,974.5	10,886.2	9798.0	8709.8	7621.5	6533.3
Subordinated debt	–	–		–	–	–	–	–	–	–
Total	7031.2	2060.9			11,974.5	10,886.2	9798.0	8709.8	7621.5	6533.3
Deferred taxes	2047.2	287.4			2334.6	2544.9	2755.2	2965.5	3175.8	3386.1
Other	808.2	443.9			1252.1	1252.1	1252.1	1252.1	1252.1	1252.1
Total liabilities	**11,979.9**	**3984.6**			**18,846.9**	**18,397.5**	**17,703.7**	**17,025.3**	**16,363.9**	**15,714.0**
Common stock	413.5	5733.7		5513.7	11,660.9	11,660.9	11,660.9	11,660.9	11,660.9	11,660.9
Preferred equity	–	–		–	–	–	–	–	–	–
Retained earnings	7697.3	1341.8		(1341.8)	7697.3	7557.3	7874.0	8279.1	8703.1	9138.9
Treasury stock	(2996.8)	(2482.0)		2482.0	(2996.8)	(2996.8)	(2996.8)	(2996.8)	(2996.8)	(2996.8)
Other adjustments	10,350.7	59.1		(503.6)	9906.2	9906.2	9906.2	9906.2	9906.2	9906.2
Noncontrolling interest	–	0.8		(0.8)	–	–	–	–	–	–
Total stockholders equity	**15,464.7**	**4653.4**			**26,267.6**	**26,127.6**	**26,444.2**	**26,849.4**	**27,273.4**	**27,709.2**
Total liabilities and equity	**$ 27,444.6**	**$ 8638.0**			**$ 45,114.5**	**$ 44,525.1**	**$ 44,147.9**	**$ 43,874.7**	**$ 43,637.3**	**$ 43,423.2**

The adjustment entry in Table 15.10 for common stock of $5513.7 million equals the sum of $7247.4 million in new acquirer common stock exchanged for target shares plus $4000 million in new shares issued to help finance the cash portion of the purchase price less $5733.7 in Target common stock.[15] Target retained earnings are eliminated because they are implicit in the purchase price. Goodwill, representing the difference between the purchase price and the book value of net acquired assets, totals $9841.4 million.[16] Pretransaction adjustments to the balance sheet refer to reductions in receivables for those deemed uncollectable, inventory to reflect damaged and obsolete items, obsolete equipment, and impaired goodwill.[17]

Step 3c: select appropriate discount rate and terminal period assumptions to value Newco

Newco's enterprise value is estimated on the Model's Valuations Worksheet (as are Target and Acquirer) using inputs from the Newco Assumptions Worksheet. Enterprise value is defined as the sum of the market value of a firm's equity, preferred shares, debt, and noncontrolling interest less total cash and cash equivalents. Cash in excess

[15] When Target shareholders exchange their shares for Acquirer stock or cash, they are cancelled.

[16] Note that the model assumes that book value equals fair value. This assumption may be changed after the acquirer has completed full due diligence.

[17] Goodwill is said to be impaired when its book value exceeds its current fair market value. The book value of such goodwill must be reduced by the difference between its book value and fair market value.

of working capital is deducted because it is viewed as unimportant to the ongoing operation of the business and can be used by Acquirer to finance the deal.[18]

After the enterprise value has been estimated, the market value of equity is then calculated by adding cash to and deducting long-term debt and noncontrolling interests from the enterprise value.[19] The marginal rather than the effective tax rate is used because the enterprise value is calculated before financing concerns.[20]

Although enterprise value approximates the takeover value of a firm, it does not include all nonequity claims on cash flow such as unfunded pension and health care obligations and loan guarantees.[21] Thus the common definition of enterprise value may omit significant obligations that must be paid by Acquirer and whose PV should be included in estimating Target's purchase price. When calculating the ratio of enterprise to earnings before interest, taxes, depreciation, and amortization (EBITDA) as a valuation multiple, the analyst needs to add back leasing and pension expenses to EBITDA to compare the ratio for a firm with substantial long-term obligations with other companies.

Chapter 7 discusses alternative ways of estimating the market value of a firm's long-term debt. Commonly used methods for modeling purposes involve either valuing the book value of a firm's long-term debt at its current market value if it is publicly traded or book value if it is not. Alternatively, the market value of similar debt at a firm exhibiting a comparable credit rating can be used to value a target firm's debt. For example, assume the book value of Target's debt with 10 years remaining to maturity is $478 million and its current market value or the market value of comparable publicly traded debt is 1.024 per $1000 of face value. The market value of the firm's debt can be estimated as $489.5 million (i.e., 1.024 × $478). The market value of noncontrolling interests can be estimated by multiplying the book value of such interests by the price-to-earnings (P/E) ratio for comparable firms.

Step 4: determine the appropriateness of offer price and postdeal capital structure

The Sources and Uses section of the Acquirer Transaction Summary Worksheet displayed in Table 15.7 shows how the transaction is financed. Because the form of payment in this example is 50% equity and 50% cash, the model automatically finances the equity portion of the purchase price by exchanging Acquirer for Target shares in an amount equal to half of the purchase price. The financing of the cash portion of the purchase price requires the analyst to input values for the amount of excess cash to be used and new common or preferred equity issues, as well as any increases in subordinated debt. After these inputs are provided, the model assumes that any additional cash to be financed will come from increase in senior debt. These inputs determine the capital structure proposed for financing the deal. See the practice exercise in Exhibit 15.3 for an illustration of how to change how a transaction is financed.

This process step is a reality check. Is the offer price for Target reasonable? Is Newco's proposal sustainable? Does the financial return on the deal meet or exceed Acquirer's cost of capital? Is the capital structure consistent with the desired credit rating?

The first question can be answered by comparing the offer price to recent comparable deals and to the "maximum" offer price. Although recent comparable deal values were explained in detail in Chapter 8, the notion of a maximum price has not been discussed in this context. The maximum offer price, if the target is not misvalued, is equal to the sum of the standalone value (or minimum price) plus 100% of net synergy. The PV of net synergy is equal to the PV of sources of value less the PV of destroyers of value. The presumption is that no rational seller will sell at below the minimum price and no rational buyer will pay more than the maximum price. Thus a reasonable offer price is one between the minimum and maximum prices.

Step 4a: compare offer price with estimated maximum offer price and recent comparable deals

In a stock purchase deal,[22] the minimum price is Target's standalone present value (PV_T) or its current market value (MV_T) (i.e., Target's current stock price times its shares outstanding). The maximum price is the sum of the

[18] It is useful to deduct other assets not germane to the ongoing operation of the combined businesses from the enterprise value if they can be easily sold for cash and subsequently used to finance the transaction.

[19] Noncontrolling interests are deducted from the enterprise value in calculating the market value of the firm's equity because they represent that portion of the consolidated financial statements not owned by the firm.

[20] Using the lower effective tax rate is impacted by interest expense associated with borrowing to finance the deal.

[21] Effective 2019, operating leases are included in debt on the balance sheet.

[22] Calculating the minimum and maximum offer price in an asset purchase is discussed later in this chapter.

EXHIBIT 15.3

Practice Exercise: Changing How the Deal is Financed

Using the Excel spreadsheet model in the file folder titled M&A Valuation and Structuring Model accompanying this book, change the financing structure on the Summary Worksheet. Once the portion of the purchase price to be paid in Acquirer stock is input into the model, it is necessary to determine how the remaining cash portion of the purchase price will be financed. The model subtracts from the amount paid for Target's equity (i.e., equity consideration [ECQ]) plus transaction expenses (TEs) the dollar value of Acquirer shares exchanged for Target shares and finances the remainder of the purchase price by some combination of other financing sources. Any amount of the cash portion of the purchase price that is not funded is financed by an increase in senior debt. That is, total EQC + TEs − dollar value of Acquirer equity exchanged for Target equity − excess cash − new common shares issues − preferred equity issued − revolving loan balance − subordinated debt = senior debt issued.

To change the financing structure shown on the Summary Worksheet to one including only Acquirer shares exchanged for Target shares and new senior debt, set the yellow input cells for excess cash and new common shares issued to zero. The model would subtract the $7247.4 million (i.e., dollar value of Acquirer shares exchanged for Target shares) from $15,129.8 million (i.e., EQC including TEs of $635 million) and finance the difference of $7882.4 million by issuing senior debt equal to that amount. As the equity portion of the purchase price is increased, senior debt can become negative. Because this is meaningless, the analyst should manually increase some other source of funds by the amount of the negative senior debt figure.

minimum price plus the PV of net synergy (PV_{NS}). The initial offer price (PV_{IOP}) is the sum of the minimum purchase price and a percentage, α between 0 and 1, of PV_{NS}. See Exhibit 15.4. Note α is that portion of net synergy shared with target shareholders and not the purchase price premium. The purchase price premium may be estimated by comparing the offer price to Target's preannouncement share price. The offer price should be compared with similar deals to determine if it is excessive.[23]

To determine α, Acquirer may estimate the portion of net synergy supplied by Target. Cash flows due to synergy are those resulting from combining the firms. The percentage of net synergy contributed by Target can be calculated as the contribution to incremental operating profit attributable to cross-selling or to cost savings resulting from a reduction in the number of Target employees or elimination of other Target-related overhead such as leased facilities. Additional Target-related synergy could include intellectual property whose value is represented by the potential profit generated by selling such property to others or from new products based on Target copyrights or patents. Ultimately, what fraction of synergy is negotiated successfully by Target depends on its leverage or influence relative to Acquirer.[24]

If it is determined that Target would contribute 30% of net synergy, Acquirer may share up to that amount with Target's shareholders. Acquirer may share less if it is concerned that realizing synergy on a timely basis is problematic. To discourage potential bidders, Acquirer might make a preemptive bid so attractive that Target's board could not reject the offer for fear of possible shareholder lawsuits, resulting in more than 30% of net synergy shared with Target.

The notion of a minimum price should be viewed as a starting point for determining an offer price. It does not preclude scenarios in which the acquirer could buy a target at a discount to its intrinsic value. For small, privately

[23] The percent difference between purchase price multiples of the target's earnings, cash flow, sales, book value, and so on can be compared with similar multiples of recent comparable transactions to determine the relative magnitude of the price paid for the target versus those of comparable deals. If the price-to-earnings ratio paid for the target firm is 12 versus 10 paid for comparable recent deals, the implicit *relative* purchase premium paid for the target is 20%.

[24] The contribution to the creation of synergy by each party to the deal is often subjective. For example, Target may argue that it should receive full credit for the increase in operating earnings resulting from the shutdown of their underused plant and the movement of its output to Acquirer's plant increasing its average operating rate. However, Acquirer could counter that the synergy would not have been realized had it not had a similar underutilized facility and further that its operation was more efficient.

EXHIBIT 15.4
Determining the Offer Price (PV_{OP}) Purchase of Stock

a. $PV_{MIN} = PV_T$ or MV_T, whichever is greater. MV_T is Target's current share price times the number of shares outstanding
b. $PV_{MAX} = PV_{MIN} + PV_{NS}$, where PV_{NS} = PV (sources of value) − PV (destroyers of value)
c. $PV_{OP} = PV_{MIN} + \alpha\, PV_{NS}$, in which $0 \leq \alpha \leq 1$
d. Offer price range for Target = (PV_T or MV_T) < PV_{OP} < (PV_T or MV_T) + PV_{NS}

After the dollar value of the offer price has been determined, the offer price per share, premium and offer price multiple can be determined as follows:

Assumptions:

Target's predeal price per share = \$18

Target shares outstanding = 5 million

Target's current earnings per share = \$2.20

Target's minimum (standalone or market) value = \$100 million

PV of net synergy = \$20 million

Alpha (α) = 50%

Solution:

Offer price per share =

(Target's minimum value + $\alpha \times PV_{NS}$)

× /Target shares outstanding

= (\$100 million + 0.5 × \$20 million)/5 million = \$22

Offer price premium = \$22/\$18 = 22.2%

Offer price multiple = \$22/\$2.20 = 10[a]

[a]Offer price multiple, in this instance measured as a price-to-earnings (P/E) ratio, can be compared with P/E ratios for recent comparable transactions to determine the reasonableness of the premium.

MV, Market value; *PV*, present value.

owned firms, either the buyer or seller may not have access to all relevant information about the economic value of the target. Markets for private firms may also be illiquid; sellers seeking to "cash out" quickly may be willing to sell at a discount to the firm's true value. The cost of performing due diligence and the risks associated with buying nonpublic firms often are significant and encourage the buyer to offer less than true value.

If a publicly traded target is not fairly valued, it may be appropriate to define the maximum price as PV_T plus PV_{NS}. Why? If the target is overvalued, adding the PV of net synergy to the target's market value would mean the buyer would be overpaying. Whether an acquirer defines the maximum offer price based on MV_T or PV_T depends on answers to the following questions. Is the overvaluation expected to be temporary? If the deal is a share exchange and the acquirer and target are competitors, is the acquirer's stock more overvalued than the target's?[25] Because M&As tend to occur in waves, is the acquirer's bid early or late in the cycle?[26] How confident is the acquirer in its ability to measure accurately the extent of the overvaluation? Is the risk of overpaying greater than the risk of losing the target to a competitor?

When the target is fairly valued, the offer price should fall between the minimum and maximum prices for three reasons. First, it is unlikely that Target can be purchased at the minimum price, because Acquirer normally has to pay a premium to induce Target's shareholders to sell their shares. In an asset purchase, the rational seller would not sell at a price below the after-tax liquidation value of acquired assets less assumed liabilities, because this represents what the seller could obtain by liquidating rather than selling the assets. Second, at the maximum end of the range, Acquirer would be ceding all of the net synergy created to Target's shareholders. Finally, it often is prudent to pay significantly less than the maximum price because of the uncertainty of realizing estimated synergy on a timely basis.

[25] If one firm in the same industry is "overvalued," it is reasonable that other firms in the industry will also be overvalued if the factors impacting overvaluation are viewed as affecting the entire industry.

[26] Firms pursuing attractive deals early in cycles pay lower prices for targets than followers (Faud, 2019).

TABLE 15.11 Transaction summary worksheet: credit ratios and earnings per share impact (stock purchase)

Earnings per share	Acquirer	Newco
2016P	$ 0.52	$ (0.47)
2017P	$ 0.43	$ 0.68
2018P	$ 0.32	$ 0.98
2019P	$ 0.19	$ 1.03
2020P	$ 0.03	$ 1.05

Cash EPS	Acquirer	Newco
2016P	$ 4.26	$ 7.08
2017P	$ 3.63	$ 4.77
2018P	$ 3.66	$ 5.23
2019P	$ 3.67	$ 5.48
2020P	$ 3.66	$ 5.68

Accretion/(dilution)	EPS	Cash EPS
2016P	(191.6%)	66.1%
2017P	57.1%	31.4%
2018P	204.7%	42.8%
2019P	447.3%	49.3%
2020P	4092.9%	55.1%

Valuation	Present value $'s
Target	$ 16,570.9
Acquirer	33,454.4
Newco	57,412.8
Synergies	7387.5
Net present value	8828.7

Total debt to total capital	Industry average	Newco
2016P	37.8	29.5%
2017P	37.8	27.1%
2018P	37.8	24.6%
2019P	37.8	21.9%
2020P	37.8	19.2%

Interest coverage (EBITDA to interest expense)	Industry average	Newco
2016P	3.8	3.9x
2017P	3.8	4.6x
2018P	3.8	5.6x
2019P	3.8	6.4x
2020P	3.8	7.5x

EBITDA, Earnings before interest, taxes, depreciation, and amortization; *EPS*, earnings per share.

Step 4b: compare projected credit ratios with industry average ratios

Table 15.11 shows the impact of borrowing on Newco's projected credit ratios in comparison with current industry averages. This table measures the magnitude of Newco's projected debt burden (debt-to-total capital ratio) and ability to repay its debt (interest coverage ratio). The higher the debt-to-total capital ratio relative to the industry average, the more investors will become concerned about the potential insolvency of the firm. Investors could view the liquidity of a firm with a low interest coverage ratio compared with the industry as problematic.

Assume that the current industry average credit ratios will prevail during the forecast period. Does Newco's projected debt-to-total capital ratio significantly exceed the average for the industry? Does the firm's projected interest coverage fall substantially below the industry average because of the increase in the firm's indebtedness? Will Newco be noncompliant with pre-deal loan covenants? Is the firm's credit rating in jeopardy? If the answer to these questions is yes, it may be impractical to finance the deal under the proposed capital structure.

One method for determining an appropriate financing or postclosing capital structure is to establish a target credit rating for Newco. Firms often desire at least an investment-grade rating to limit an increase in borrowing costs. Achieving a specific credit rating requires the firm to achieve certain credit ratios such as debt-to-total capital (capital structure) and interest coverage ratios. The magnitude of these ratios will be affected by the size of the firm and the industry in which it competes. Larger firms are expected to be better able to repay their debts in liquidation because of their greater asset value. Firms with stable cash flows are considered less risky than those whose cash flows are cyclical and therefore less predictable. In an effort to reach their desired credit ratings, firms move quickly to achieve their target capital structures, reducing the difference between actual and target capital structures on average by half in less than 1 year.[27]

Step 4c: determine the impact of the deal on Newco's EPS

Newco's EPS will be impacted by Acquirer's and Target's projected earnings plus the contribution to future earnings from net synergy. EPS will also be affected by the number of Acquirer shares exchanged for each Target share plus any Acquirer shares issued to raise cash to finance the cash portion of the purchase price. In addition to credit ratios, Table 15.11 also displays Newco's projected EPS and how it compares with what Acquirer would have earned per share had it not completed the deal. Despite the issuance of a large number of Acquirer shares to complete the deal, Newco EPS and cash flow per share are sharply higher after deal completion than they would have been had the transaction not been undertaken.

[27] Frank and Shen, 2019

EXHIBIT 15.5

Applying Share Exchange Ratios

Assume the following information:
Offer price per share = \$82
Pretransaction Acquirer share price = \$77.12
Pretransaction Acquirer shares outstanding: 358.1 million
Pretransaction Target shares outstanding = 176.8 million
Target shares outstanding: 174.5 million + 2.3 million (because of options exercised) = 176.8

What is the number of Acquirer shares exchanged for each Target share, the number of new Acquirer shares issued, and what are the total shares outstanding of the combined firms (i.e., Newco)?

Solution:
Share exchange ratio: \$82/\$77.12 = 1.0633 (i.e., 1.0633 Acquirer shares exchanged for each Target share)
New acquirer shares issued to Target shareholders: 1.0633 × 176.8 million = 188.0
Total Newco shares outstanding: (Target shares are cancelled) 358.1 + 188.0 = 546.1 million

Acquirers often adjust or normalize EPS during the first full year in which they operate Target for that portion of transaction-related expenses that cannot be amortized and for integration expenditures. Consistent with GAAP, such expenses would be deducted from consolidated earnings before determining EPS and reporting such figures to the SEC. So-called *adjusted EPS* (i.e., before transaction-related and integration-related expenses) may be calculated to show what the consolidated performance would be without these nonrecurring expenses.

To calculate Newco's postclosing EPS, estimate the number of new Acquirer shares issued to complete the deal. The exchange of Acquirer's shares for Target's shares requires the calculation of the share-exchange ratio (SER). The SER can be negotiated as a fixed number of shares of Acquirer's stock to be exchanged for each share of Target's stock. Alternatively, SER can be defined in terms of the dollar value of the negotiated offer price per share of Target stock (P_{OP}) to the dollar value of Acquirer's share price (P_A). The SER is calculated as follows:

$$SER = P_{OP} / P_A$$

The SER can be less than, equal to, or greater than 1, depending on the value of Acquirer's shares relative to the offer price on the date set during the negotiation for valuing the transaction. Exhibit 15.5 illustrates how share exchange ratios are used to estimate the number of Acquirer shares that must be issued in a share-for-share exchange and the resulting ownership distribution between Acquirer and former Target shareholders.

The number of new Acquirer shares issued to complete a deal also is affected by such derivative securities as options issued to Target's employees and warrants, as well as convertible securities. Such securities derive their value from the firm's common stock into which they may be converted. The number of common shares a shareholder receives upon conversion of convertible securities is called the conversion ratio. Upon conversion, these securities result in additional common shares that must be purchased by a buyer wishing to avoid minority shareholders after a takeover.

Such securities are commonly assumed to have been converted in calculating *fully diluted shares outstanding*, that is, the number of Target's "basic" shares outstanding (i.e., pre-deal shares outstanding) plus the number of shares represented by the firm's "in the money" options, warrants, and convertible debt and preferred securities. Basic shares are found on the cover of a firm's most recent 10Q or 10K submission to the SEC. Options and convertible securities information are found in the firm's most recent 10K.

Granted to employees, *stock options* represent noncash compensation and offer the holder the right to buy (call) shares of the firm's common equity at a predetermined "exercise" price. Option holders are said to be vested when the required holding period expires, and their options can be converted into shares of the firm's common equity. An option is considered to be "in the money" whenever the firm's common share price exceeds the option's exercise price; otherwise, they are "out of the money." Warrants are securities often issued along with debt and entitle holders of the debt to buy the firm's common shares at a preset price during a given time period. It is common to assume that only "in-the-money" options and warrants will be converted as a result of a takeover. However, all

TABLE 15.12 Dilutive impact of target options, warrants, and convertible securities

Target options schedule				
Potential options (millions of shares)	Strike price	In the money	Include	Proceeds
4.045	$37.46	Yes	4.045	$151.53
–	–	NA	–	–
–	–	NA	–	–
–	–	NA	–	–
–	–	NA	–	–
–	–	NA	–	–
4.045			4.045	$151.53
Weighted average exercise price				37.46
Value of options				180.16
New shares outstanding				2.1971

Target convertible preferred schedule ($millions)					
Balance	Par value	CV ratio	CV price	Convert	Shares
$ 3.40	100	1.75	$57.14	Yes	0.0595
0	100	0	0	NA	–
0	100	0	0	NA	–
0	100	0	0	NA	–
0	100	0	0	NA	–
0	100	0	0	NA	–
$ 3.40	New shares outstanding				0.0595

Target convertible debt schedule ($Millions)					
Principal	Par value	CV ratio	CV price	Convert	Shares
$.44	$1000	20.00	$50	Yes	0.0088
0	1000	0	0	NA	–
0	1000	0	0	NA	–
0	1000	0	0	NA	–
0	1000	0	0	NA	–
0	1000	0	0	NA	–
$.44	New shares outstanding				0.0088

Notes: in-the-money options and warrants
Current target share price = Acquirer offer price = $82
Value of options = ($82 – $37.46) x 4.045 = $180.16
New target shares = $180.16/$82 = 2.1971

Notes: Target convertible debt
Conversion ratio (CV) = number of target common shares when debt converted at par value = 20.00

CV price = par value/CV ratio = $1000/20 = $50
New target shares = ($.44/$1000) x 20 = 0.0088

Notes: Target convertible preferred
Conversion ratio (CV) = number of target common shares when converted at par value = 1.75
CV price = $100 / 1.75 = $57.14
New target shares = ($3.40/$100) x 1.75 = 0.0595

CV, Conversion ratio; *NA*, not applicable.

options and warrants can be exercised, regardless of vesting status (i.e., vested or not vested) and exercise price, in the event of a hostile takeover if they include change-of-control provisions.[28]

The *treasury method* assumes all in-the-money options and warrants, because they are issued at different times and prices, are exercised at their weighted average exercise price,[29] and option proceeds are assumed used to repurchase outstanding Target shares at the company's current share price. Because the exercise price is less than the current price of target shares (which has risen to approximately the level of the offer price), the dollar proceeds received by the firm when holders exercise their options and warrants enable the firm to repurchase fewer shares than had been exercised. Therefore the number of shares outstanding will increase by the difference between the number of options exercised and those repurchased.[30]

In Table 15.12, 4.045 options, whose weighted average exercise price is $37.46, are assumed to be converted as they are well below the offer price of $82 per Target share. The net increase in the value of shares outstanding resulting from the exercise of options equals the dollar value of such shares valued at the firm's current share price less the value of option proceeds expressed at the weighted average exercise price of $180.16 million, that is, ($82 – $37.46) × 4.045. This figure represents the value of shares the firm is unable to repurchase with the proceeds received from

[28] Options not currently vested may fully vest upon a change in control thereby increasing the number of options that could be converted to common shares. Such options should be added to the number of "in-the-money" options in calculating the number of fully diluted shares outstanding.

[29] The weights are the number of options issued at each exercise price as a percent of total options issued.

[30] The treasury stock method is based on the notion that when employees exercise options, the firm has to issue the appropriate number of new shares but also receives the exercise price of the options in cash. Implicitly, the firm can use the cash to offset the cost of issuing new shares. The dilutive effect of exercising an option is not one full share but rather a fraction of a share equal to what the firm does not receive in cash divided by the share price.

exercised options. Therefore the net increase in shares outstanding resulting from the exercising of options equals 2.1971 (i.e., $180.16/$82).[31]

If convertible securities are present, it is necessary to add to Target's basic shares outstanding the number of new shares issued after the conversion of such securities. Convertible securities include preferred stock and debt. Data on the number of options outstanding, vesting periods, and their exercise prices, as well as convertible securities, are available in the footnotes to Target's financial statements. It is reasonable to assume that such securities will be converted to common equity when the conversion price is less than the offer price per share.

Convertible preferred stock can be exchanged for common stock at a specific price at the discretion of the shareholder. The value of the common stock for which the preferred stock is exchanged is called the *conversion price*. If the preferred stock is convertible into 1.75 common shares and is issued at a par value of $100, the price at which it can be converted (i.e., its conversion price) is $57.14 (i.e., $100/1.75). That is, the preferred shareholder would receive 1.75 shares of common stock if the preferred shareholder choses to convert when the common share price exceeds $57.14. Similarly, *convertible debt* can be converted into a specific number of common shares and is normally denominated in units of $1000. If "when issued" buyers of such debt were given the right to convert each $1000 of debt they held into 20 common shares, the implied conversion price would be $50 (i.e., $1000/20).

Table 15.12 also illustrates the additional common shares created due to the conversion of in-the-money options and warrants as well as convertible preferred stock and debt. After conversion, the total number of new shares into common shares that must be added to the number of basic target shares is 2.2654 million shares (i.e., 2.1971 + 0.0088 + 0.0595). This will add $185.75 million (i.e., 2.2654 × $82) to the purchase price for 100 percent of Target's shares.

Unless addressed during negotiation, executive stock options exercised because of a takeover can result in a larger valuation discount from their true value than if exercised voluntarily. Why? Target firm executives forfeit more of the option's time value than might have been the case if voluntarily exercised. Most option valuation methodologies are based on voluntary valuation.[32]

Step 4d: determine if the deal will allow Newco to satisfy or exceed required returns

Newco's minimum required financial return is its WACC. Standard capital budgeting theory tells us that a firm will meet or exceed its cost of capital as long as the NPV of a discrete investment is greater than or equal to zero.

Acquirer's investment in Target is not only the EQC but also any transaction expenses (TE) associated with closing the deal. EQC refers to what Acquirer pays for Target's equity. Therefore the challenge for Acquirer is to create sufficient value by combining the two firms such that the following is true:

$$\left(PV_{Target} + PV_{NetSynergy}\right) - (EQC + TE) \geq 0 \tag{15.1}$$

PV_{Target} and $PV_{NetSynergy}$ are the PVs of Target as a standalone business and the net synergy resulting from combining Target and Acquirer.

The valuation section of the Acquirer Transaction Summary Worksheet (see Table 15.3) indicates that about $7.4 billion in incremental value or net synergy is created by Acquirer's takeover of Target. This implies that the financial return on the purchase of Target is well in excess of Acquirer's WACC or minimum required rate of return on assets.

Depending on size and deal complexity, as well as how they are financed, transaction expenses approximate 3% to 5% of the purchase price, with this percentage decreasing for larger deals. To estimate such expenses, distinguish between financing-related and non–financing-related expenses. Financing-related expenses for M&As can equal 1% to 2% of the dollar value of bank debt and include fees for arranging the loan and for establishing a line of credit. Fees for underwriting nonbank debt can average 2% to 3% of the value of the debt. Non–financing-related fees represent as much as 2% of the purchase price and include investment banking, legal, accounting, and other consulting fees. Whereas non–financing-related expenses are expensed in the year when the deal closes, those related to deal financing are capitalized on the balance sheet and amortized over the life of the loan.

[31] The net increase in the number of shares outstanding can be summarized as follows: [($82 × 4.045) – ($37.46 × 4.045)]/$82 = ($82 – $37.46) × 4.045/$82 = 2.1971.

[32] See Klein (2018) for a more detailed discussion of these issues.

M&A models: asset purchases

As with a stock purchase model, asset purchases begin with the estimation of Target's enterprise value. Viewed in this context as total Target assets, the enterprise value is then adjusted by subtracting Target assets excluded from the deal (A_{excl})[33] and Target liabilities included in the deal (L_{inc}) (i.e., assumed by the buyer).[34] The end result is referred to as *net acquired assets*[35].

$$\text{Net acquired assets} = TA - A_{excl} - L_{inc} - A_{incl} - L_{inc} \quad (15.2)$$

A_{incl} equals Target assets included in the deal (i.e., assumed by the buyer).

The purchase price is what Acquirer pays for net acquired assets and can be expressed as a multiple of net book assets. This multiple should be compared with recent comparable deals to determine its reasonableness. The purchase price should lie between the minimum (i.e., after-tax liquidation value of the assets less liabilities) and the maximum price (i.e., minimum price plus net synergy assuming the target firm is not overvalued).

Buyers commonly purchase selected assets and assume responsibility for short-term seller operating liabilities, including payables, accrued vacation, employee benefits, bonuses, commissions, and so on, to ensure a smoother transition for Target employees transferring to Acquirer. Acquirer may also accept other liabilities such as product warranty claims that have not been satisfied, to ensure they are paid in order to retain customer loyalty.

Assume that Acquirer pays $90 million to purchase $75 million in net acquired assets, consisting of $100 million of Target net property, plant, and equipment (i.e., net PP&E) less assumed Target current liabilities of $25 million and that the book values of Target assets and liabilities are equal to their fair market value.[36] The implied purchase price multiple is 1.2 times net acquired assets (i.e., $90 million/$75 million), a 20% premium.

Sales, cost of sales, and operating income associated with the net acquired assets, as well as any additional interest expense incurred to finance the purchase and expenses incurred to integrate the acquired assets, are added to Acquirer's income statement (Table 15.13). For this illustration, the adjustments column shows the addition of Target's sales, cost of sales, additional interest expense, and taxes to Acquirer's income statement.

TABLE 15.13 Acquirer income statement: asset purchase

($Millions)	Acquirer pre-deal	Adjustments	Acquirer post-deal
Sales ($)	1750.0	200.0	1950.0
Cost of sales integration ($)	1488.0	190.0	1678.0
Expense ($)		15.0	15.0
EBIT ($)	262.0		257.0
Other income ($)	0.0	10.0	10.0
Net interest ($)	30.0	7.0	37.0
EBT ($)	232.0		230.0
Tax at 0.40	92.8	(0.8)	92.0
Net income ($)	139.2		138.0

EBIT, Earnings before interest and taxes; *EBT*, earnings before taxes.

[33] Excluded assets are those the Target retains or the Acquirer does not want.

[34] Recall that enterprise value can be viewed from either the asset side (total assets) or the liability side (total liabilities plus equity) of the balance sheet.

[35] $TA = A_{excl} + A_{incl} = L_{excl} + L_{incl} + EQ$ and $A_{incl} - L_{incl} = L_{excl} - A_{excl} + EQ$, in which EQ = Target shareholders' equity and $A_{incl} - L_{incl}$ = Net acquired assets by Acquirer.

[36] If the net acquired assets are revalued up to their fair market value, any additional depreciation expense would impact both the income statement and in turn the cash flow statement. The assumption that the book value of net acquired assets equals its fair market value implies no incremental depreciation related to this asset purchase. Efforts to assume the magnitude of potential asset write-ups (write-downs) before completing a full due diligence on Target is highly questionable, potentially seriously distorting projected financial performance.

TABLE 15.14 Acquirer balance sheet: asset purchase

	Actual 2015	Transaction Adjustments	Pro forma 2016
Cash	$125.00	($20.00)	$105.00
Current assets (Excl. cash)	550.00		550.00
Net property, plant and equipment	1250.00	100.00	1350.00
Goodwill		15.00	15.00
Other long-term assets	450.00		450.00
Total assets	$2375.00		$2470.00
Current liabilities	550.00	25.00	575.00
Long-term debt	450.00	70.00	520.00
Other long-term liabilities	375.00		375.00
Total liabilities	1375.00		1470.00
Common stock	500.00		500.00
Preferred equity	50.00		50.00
Retained earnings	400.00		400.00
Other adjustments	50.00		50.00
Total shareholders' equity	1000.00		1000.00
Total liabilities and equity	$2375.00		$2470.00

Incremental revenue generated by selling Acquirer products to Target's customers is assumed to be $200 million. Target's cost of sales before the deal was $195 million, which is reduced by anticipated cost-related synergy of $5 million. Expenditures related to integrating Target assets are $15 million. A one-time $10 million noncash gain is added to Acquirer's income statement because it is buying Target's assets at a discount from their book value (i.e., paying $90 million for $100 million in net PP&E).

Acquirer is able to negotiate the favorable purchase of net PP&E because of its willingness to assume certain Target liabilities. Incremental interest expense related to financing the deal is $7 million. Taxes paid are calculated at the firm's marginal tax rate of 40%. The additional assets are expected to increase Acquirer's net income in future years because of cost savings from productivity improvements and incremental revenue from cross-selling former Target products to Acquirer's customers. In consolidation, the dollar value of net acquired assets is recorded on Acquirer's balance sheet by adding the purchased assets to Acquirer's assets and assumed liabilities to Acquirer's liabilities. Entries are made to the liability/equity side of Acquirer's balance sheet to show how the purchase is to be financed.

Table 15.14 illustrates Acquirer's balance sheet adjustments made to reflect the purchase of specific Target assets and the assumption of certain Target liabilities. Goodwill equals $15 million (i.e., $90 million less $75 million). The purchase is financed by using $20 million in Acquirer pretransaction cash balances and by borrowing $70 million in long-term debt at a 10% interest rate. Consequently, the entries in the adjustments column include a $20 million reduction in cash and an increase of $100 million in net PP&E, $15 million in goodwill, $25 million for assumed current liabilities, and $70 million in new debt.

Table 15.15 shows the cash flow statement for the purchase of the previously described net acquired assets. Ending cash balances in 2015 are reduced by $20 million to partially finance the purchase of the $100 million in Target net PP&E. Acquirer net income of ($1.2) million represents the difference between pre-deal net income of $139.2 and post-deal net income of $138.0 million.[37] The one-time gain of $10 million because of the purchase of net PP&E at a discount is eliminated in the calculation of cash flow because it does not involve the actual receipt

[37] Negative net income during the first full year of operation (including the net acquired assets) resulted from integration expenses and incremental interest expense exceeding the positive contribution of operating income and the one-time gain.

TABLE 15.15 Statement of cash flows: asset purchase

2015 Ending cash	$125.00
Cash used to finance PP&E purchase	(20.00)
2016 Beginning cash balance	$105.00
Cash from operations	
Net income	(1.20)
Depreciation	0.00
(Gain)/loss	(10.00)
Current assets	0.00
Current liabilities	25.00
Net cash flow from operations	13.80
Cash from investing	
PP&E acquisition	(90.00)
Net cash flow from investing	(90.00)
Cash from financing	
Increase in debt	70.00
Net cash flow from financing	70.00
Net cash flow	(6.20)
Ending cash balance	$98.80

PP&E, Property, plant, and equipment.

of cash. Current liabilities increase cash flow from operations by the amount of assumed Target liabilities. Whereas cash flow from investing activities decreases by the amount paid for net PP&E, cash flow from financing activities increases by what is borrowed.

Quantifying synergy

Acquirer managers often succumb to confirmation bias (i.e., give more importance to data supporting their beliefs) because they are "mentally committed" to doing a deal, contributing to a tendency to overestimate synergy. Consequently, substantial effort should be given to being as objective as possible when estimating the value created by combining firms.

There are five general categories of synergy: revenue-related, cost-related, operating- and asset-related, financing-related, and productivity-related synergy. These are discussed next.

Revenue-related synergy

Achieving revenue-related synergies is critical for driving and sustaining growth in firm value. Cost savings are important for the acquirer to earn back any premium paid for the target, but they often are not sustainable as the discipline of the postmerger integration period dissipates.

The customer base for the target and acquiring firms can be segmented into three categories: (1) those served only by the target, (2) those served only by the acquirer, and (3) those served by both firms. The first two segments may represent revenue enhancement opportunities by enabling the target or the acquirer to sell their current products into the other's customer base. The third segment could represent a net increase or decrease in revenue for the new firm. Incremental revenue may result from new products that could be offered only as a result of exploiting the capabilities of the target and acquiring firms in combination. However, revenue may be lost because some customers choose to have more than one source of supply.

The analysis of incremental revenue opportunities is simplified by focusing on the largest customers because it often is true that 80% of a company's revenue comes from about 20% of its customers. Incremental revenue can be assessed by having the sales force provide estimates of the potential revenue generated from having access to new customers and offering current customers new products. In general, such revenue can be realized over time as Target's and Acquirer's sales forces are trained to sell each other's products.

Target firms with strong customer relationships receive higher premiums than those that do not because acquirers assume they can retain the accounts.[38] As such, acquirers may overpay. Later they discover they are unable to retain the accounts, resulting in a loss of revenue. Paying a premium for strong customer relationships may only make sense when the target has long-term, profitable contracts in place with its largest customers.

Cost savings—related synergies

Cost savings are greatest between firms with overlapping employees with similar skills because the acquirer is able to negotiate lower wage and benefit packages with target firm employees and retain only the most productive employees.[39] However, not offering sufficient compensation to target firm employees contributes to labor turnover, costs incurred hiring new employees, work stoppages, lawsuits, lower productivity, and resistance to the takeover.[40]

Direct labor refers to employees directly involved in the production of goods and services. *Indirect labor* refers to supervisory and administrative support staff. A distinction needs to be made because of likely differences in average compensation for direct and indirect labor. SG&A may be reduced by the elimination of redundant jobs and the closure of unneeded sales offices, resulting in lease expense savings.[41]

To illustrate how to quantify revenue-related synergy, gross margin improvement, and SG&A synergy, see Table 15.16. The projected data serve as inputs into the synergy section of the Summary Worksheet of the model. Headcount figures shown in 2018 are held constant in subsequent years reflecting ongoing savings until terminated employees are replaced.

Operating- and asset-related synergies

Additional cash can be generated by better managing the combined firms' net operating assets, both fixed assets and working capital. With respect to fixed assets such as plant and equipment, production can be centralized in a single facility to take advantage of economies of scale because the facility may be used more fully. Economies of scope can be realized by having a single department support multiple product lines or by combining regional sales offices.

The combined firms may be able to reduce the amount of money tied up in working capital by deferring payment of bills and shortening the time required to convert products into cash. The time it takes to convert inventory to cash is the average length of time in days required to produce and sell finished goods. The receivables collection period is the average length of time in days required to collect receivables. The payables deferral period is the average time in days between the purchase of and payment for materials and labor. By reducing the time it takes to generate cash and by deferring payables, profits and cash flow increase and, in turn, firm value.

Financing-related synergies

Firms with limited cash on hand and excessive debt can enhance their borrowing capacity by buying targets with limited leverage.[42] Furthermore, acquirers with excellent access to capital because of modest leverage can create synergies with target firms lacking capital but rich in investment opportunities. The combined firms are able to pursue investment opportunities at lower overall financing costs than they would have had the two firms remained separate.[43]

Productivity-related synergy

Productivity gains often are realized in horizontal mergers in which only the best employees are retained, better use of previously underused facilities is achieved, and "best practices" are applied throughout the combined

[38] Krolikowski et al., 2017

[39] Lee et al., 2018

[40] Liang et al., 2020

[41] Leased space may be eliminated before the lease expiration date by paying off the balance of what is owed.

[42] Ang et al., 2019

[43] Cornaggia et al., 2019

TABLE 15.16 Quantifying anticipated synergy

	2016 ($ millions)	2017	2018	2019	2020
Revenue-related synergy					
New customers for acquirer products	15,000,000	30,000,000	50,000,000	50,000,000	50,000,000
New customers for target products	20,000,000	25,000,000	40,000,000	40,000,000	40,000,000
New product revenue	0	25,000,000	60,000,000	60,000,000	60,000,000
Loss from customer attrition	-10,000,000	-5,000,000	0	0	0
Total incremental sales	25,000,000	75,000,000	150,000,000	150,000,000	150,000,000
Gross margin improvement					
Cost of sales					
Headcount reduction: direct labor	40	77	109	109	109
Average salary and benefits	69,000	69,515	69,910	69,910	69,910
Direct labor savings	2,760,000	5,352,655	7,620,190	7,620,190	7,620,190
Headcount reduction: indirect labor	28	57	90	90	90
Average salary and benefits	80,000	81,535	82,000	82,000	82,000
Indirect labor savings	2,240,000	4,647,495	7,380,000	7,380,000	7,380,000
Total direct and indirect labor savings	5,000,000	10,000,150	15,000,190	15,000,190	15,000,190
SG&A savings					
Headcount reduction: direct sales	16	21	38	38	38
Average salary and benefits	90,000	91,500	92,000	92,000	92,000
Selling expense savings	1,440,000	1,921,500	3,496,000	3,496,000	3,496,000
Headcount reduction: administrative	20	36	52	52	52
Average salary and benefits	78,000	79,000	80,000	80,000	80,000
General and administrative savings	1,560,000	2,844,000	4,160,000	4,160,000	4,160,000
Total SG&A savings	3,000,000	4,765,500	7,656,000	7,656,000	7,656,000
Leased space savings (net of buyout)	0	234,500	344,000	344,000	344,000
Total SG&A savings	3,000,000	5,000,000	8,000,000	8,000,000	8,000,000

SG&A, sales, general and administrative.

companies. Because the postmerger firm can over time use each firm's best practices and resources, productivity gains are more likely to be sustained and become predictable. Even without significant cost reduction, the sustained and more predictable productivity increases can result in profit improvements.[44] Why? Output per worker increases thereby reducing labor costs per unit of output unless offset by wage increases.

Things to remember

M&A modeling facilitates deal valuation, structuring, and financing. Acquirers use models to estimate the value of targets before making a bid and the proper financing structure. Targets use models to estimate the value of the combined businesses and their contribution to synergy. Both acquirers and targets use models to review the implications of proposals and counterproposals.

[44] Yuan et al., 2020

Chapter discussion questions

15.1 Why should a target company be valued as a standalone business? Give examples of the types of adjustments that might have to be made if Target is part of a larger company.
15.2 Why should "in-the-money" options, warrants, and convertible preferred stock and debt be included in the calculation of the purchase price to be paid for Target?
15.3 What are value drivers? How can they be misused in M&A models?
15.4 Can the offer price ever exceed the maximum purchase price? If yes, why? If no, why not?
15.5 Why is it important to clearly state assumptions underlying a valuation?
15.6 Assume two firms have little geographic overlap in terms of sales and facilities. If they were to merge, how might this affect the potential for synergy?
15.7 Dow Chemical, a leading manufacturer of chemicals, in announcing that it had an agreement to acquire competitor Rohm and Haas, said it expected to broaden its current product offering by offering the higher-margin Rohm and Haas products. What would you identify as possible synergies between these two businesses? In what ways could the combination of these two firms erode combined cash flows?
15.8 Dow Chemical's acquisition of Rohm and Haas included a 74% premium over the firm's preannouncement share price. What is the possible process Dow used in determining the stunning magnitude of this premium?
15.9 For most transactions, the full impact of net synergy will not be realized for many months. Why? What factors could account for the delay?
15.10 How does the presence of management options and convertible securities affect the calculation of the offer price for Target?

Answers to these Chapter Discussion Questions are available in the Online Instructor's Manual for instructors using this book.

Practice problems and answers

15.11 Acquiring Company is considering the acquisition of Target Company in a share-for-share transaction in which Target Company would receive the share equivalent of $50.00 for each share of its common stock. Acquiring Company does not expect any change in its P/E multiple after the merger.

	Acquiring Co.	Target Co.
Earnings available for common stock ($)	150,000	30,000
Number of shares of common stock outstanding	60,000	20,000
Market price per share ($)	60.00	40.00

Using the preceding information about these two firms, and showing your work, calculate the following:
a. Purchase price premium. *Answer*: 25%
b. SER. *Answer*: 0.8333
c. New shares issued by Acquiring Company. *Answer*: 16,666.
d. Total shares outstanding of the combined companies. *Answer*: 76,666
e. Postmerger EPS of the combined companies. *Answer:* $2.35
f. Premerger EPS of Acquiring Company. *Answer*: $2.50
g. Postmerger share price. *Answer*: $56.40, compared with $60.00 premerger
h. Postmerger ownership distribution. *Answer*: Target shareholders = 21.7% and Acquirer shareholders = 78.3%

15.12 Acquiring Company is considering buying Target Company. Target Company is a small biotechnology firm that develops products licensed to the major pharmaceutical firms. Development costs are expected to generate negative cash flows during the first 2 years of the forecast period of $(10) million and $(5) million, respectively. Licensing fees are expected to generate positive cash flows during years 3 through 5 of the forecast period of $5 million, $10 million, and $15 million, respectively. Because of the emergence of competitive products, cash flow is expected to grow at a modest 5% annually after the fifth year. The discount rate for the first 5 years is estimated to be 20% and then drop to the industry average rate of 10% beyond the fifth year. Also, the PV of the estimated net synergy created by combining Acquiring and Target companies is $30 million. Calculate the minimum and maximum purchase prices for Target Company. Show your work.

Answer: Minimum price: $128.5 million; maximum price: $158.5 million.

15.13 Using the information given below, calculate fully diluted shares. Assume the firm uses proceeds received from the conversion of options to common shares to repurchase as many of these new shares as possible. Select the correct answer from a through e.

Calculating Fully Diluted Shares Outstanding	
$ Million, except per share data, shares in millions	
Current share price	30.00
Basic shares outstanding	200.00
Options that can be exercised	40.00
Weighted average exercise price	20.00

a. 224.52
b. 263.59
c. 213.33
d. 256.87
e. 233.47

Answer: C

15.14 What is the fully diluted offer price (equity value) for a tender offer made to acquire a target whose pretender shares are trading for $1.50 per share? The tender offer includes a 30% premium to the target's pretender share price. The target has basic shares outstanding of 70 million and 5 million options, which may be converted into common shares at $1.60 per share.

Answer: $138.25 million

15.15 Using the M&A Valuation & Deal Structuring Model on the website accompanying this text (see the website address in the Chapter Overview section at the beginning of this chapter) and the data contained in the cells as a starting point, complete the following:

a. What is the enterprise and equity value of Target on the Valuation Worksheet?
b. Increase the sales growth rate by one percentage point (i.e., to 6.5%) on the Target Assumptions Worksheet. What is the impact on the Target's enterprise and equity values? (Hint: See Valuation Worksheet.) Undo the change or close the model but do not save results in order to restore the model's original data.

Answers:

a. Before change to revenue growth assumption by 1 percentage point:
1. Target enterprise value: $11,582.2
2. Target equity value: $9,796.8

b. After change in revenue growth assumption by 1 percentage point
1. Target enterprise value: $12,356.3
2. Target equity value: $10,570.9

15.16 Using the M&A Valuation & Deal Structuring Model accompanying this text (see the website address in the Chapter Overview section at the beginning of this chapter) and the data contained in the cells as a starting point, complete the following:

a. What is the enterprise and equity value of Target on the Valuation Worksheet?
b. On the worksheet named Target Assumptions, increase COGS as a percent of sales by one percentage point (i.e., 0.43 to 0.44). What is the impact on the Target's enterprise and equity values? (Hint: See Valuation worksheet.) Undo the change or close the model but do not save the results in order to restore the model's original data.

Answers:

a. Before change to COGS ratio by 1 percentage point:
1. Target enterprise value: $11,582.2
2. Target equity value: $9,796.8

b. After change in COGS ratio by 1 percentage point:
1. Target enterprise value: $11,104.8
2. Target equity value: $9,319.4

15.17 Using the M&A Valuation & Deal Structuring Model accompanying this text (see the website address in the Chapter Overview section at the beginning of this chapter):

a. In the Valuation worksheet, note the enterprise and equity values for Newco.

b. On the Summary worksheet under Incremental Sales Synergy, change incremental revenue to $200 million in the first year, $250 million in the second year, and $350 in the third year. What is the impact on Newco's enterprise and equity values? (Hint: See Valuation worksheet.) Undo changes or close the model but do not save the results.

Answers:

a. Before incremental sales growth:
1. Newco enterprise value: $32,813.7
2. Newco equity value: $20,970.8

b. After change in incremental sales:
1. Newco enterprise value: $33,766.5
2. Newco equity value: $21,923.6

15.18 Using the M&A Valuation & Deal Structuring Model accompanying this text (see the website address in the Chapter Overview section of this chapter):

a. On the Transaction Summary Worksheet, under the heading Form of Payment, change the composition of the purchase price to 100% cash. Assume the purchase price is partially financed by reducing Acquirer excess cash by $1 billion and by raising $4 billion by issuing new Acquirer equity. Under the Sources and Uses heading, how is the remainder of the purchase price financed?

b. Change the composition of the purchase price to 100% equity. What is the impact on how the purchase price is financed? Close the model but do not save the results.

Answers:

a. Form of payment = 100% cash. Senior debt is increased by $10,129.8 million.

b. Form of payment = 100% equity. Senior debt shows a negative $4,365 million, which does not make sense. Set excess cash and new common shares issued to public equal to zero. Senior debt automatically increases by $635 million.

Solutions to these Practice Problems are available in the Online Instructor's Manual for instructors using this book.

End-of-chapter case study: Thermo Fisher acquires Life Technologies

Case study objectives

To illustrate how acquirers use financial models to

- Evaluate the impact of a range of offer prices for the target firm.
- Determine which financing structures are consistent with maintaining or achieving a desired credit rating.
- Investigate the implications of different payment structures (form and composition of the purchase price).
- Identify the impact of changes in operating assumptions on firm value.

Nine months after an agreement to combine their firms, the merger between Life Technologies Corporation (Life Tech) and Thermo Fisher Scientific Inc. (Thermo Fisher) was completed on January 14, 2014. Thermo Fisher is the largest provider by market value of analytical instruments, equipment, reagents and consumables, software, and services for scientific research, analysis, discovery, and diagnostics applications. Life Tech is the second largest by market value provider of similar products and services.

Life Tech had been evaluating strategic options for the firm since mid-2012, concluding that selling itself would maximize shareholder value (See the Case Study at the end of Chapter 9 titled "Life Tech Undertakes a Strategic Review" for more detail.) This case study uses the publicly announced terms of the merger of Life Tech into a wholly owned subsidiary of Thermo Fisher, with Life Tech surviving. The terms were used to develop pro forma financial statements for the combined firms. These statements are viewed as a "base case."[45]

The financial model discussed in this chapter is used to show how changes in key deal terms and financing structures impacted the base case scenario. The discussion questions following the case address how the maximum offer price for Life Tech could be determined, what the impact of an all-debt or all-equity deal would have on the combined firms' financial statements, and the implications of failing to achieve synergy targets.

Such scenarios represent the limits of the range within which the appropriate capital structure could fall and could have been part of Thermo Fisher's pre-deal evaluation. As announced by Thermo Fisher, the appropriate capital structure is that which maintains an investment-grade credit rating after the merger. Thermo Fisher's senior management could have tested various capital structures between the two extremes of all-debt and all-equity before reaching agreement on the form of payment. As such, the form of payment and how the deal was financed were instrumental to the deal getting done.

According to the terms of the deal, Thermo Fisher acquired all of Life Tech's common shares, including all outstanding stock options, at a price of $76 per share in cash, with the Life Tech shares cancelled at closing. The purchase price consisted of an EQC of $13.6 billion plus the assumption of $2.2 billion of Life Tech's outstanding debt. The purchase price was funded by a combination of new debt, equity, and cash on Thermo Fisher's balance sheet.

Thermo Fisher executed a commitment letter, dated April 14, 2013, with JPMorgan Chase Bank, N.A.; J.P. Morgan Securities LLC; and Barclays Bank PLC for a $12.5 billion 364-day unsecured bridge loan facility. The facility enabled the firm to pay for much of the purchase price before arranging permanent financing by issuing new debt and equity in late 2013.

In an effort to retain an investment-grade credit rating[46] by limiting the amount of new borrowing, Thermo Fisher issued new common equity and equity-linked securities such as convertible debt and convertible preferred totaling $3.25 billion to finance about one-fourth of the $13.6 billion EQC. The $3.25 billion consisted of $2.2 billion of common stock sold in connection with its public offering before closing and up to a maximum of $1.05 billion of additional equity to be issued at a later date in the form of convertible debt and preferred shares. Thermo Fisher financed the remaining $10.35 billion of the purchase price with the proceeds of subsequent borrowings and $1 billion in cash on its balance sheet.

Thermo Fisher and Life Tech compete in the medical laboratory and research industry. The average debt-to-total capital ratio for firms in this industry is 44.6%,[47] and the average interest coverage ratio is 4.0.[48] Thermo Fisher expects that available free cash flow will allow for a rapid reduction in its debt. The firm expects to be below the industry average debt-to-total capital ratio by the end of the third full year after closing and about 12 percentage points below it within 5 years after closing. The firm's interest coverage ratio is expected to be equal to the industry average by the second year and well above it by the third year and beyond. These publicly stated goals established metrics shareholders and analysts could use to track Thermo Fisher's progress in integrating Life Tech.

[45] Although this case study investigates the role of financial modeling in business combinations, the case study at the end of Chapter 9 titled "Life Technologies Corporation Undertakes a Strategic Review" discusses the application of financial modeling to assess the impact of alternative strategic options for a single firm, Life Tech.

[46] According to Bonds Online, Thermo Fisher Scientific had a BBB (the low end of the investment grade range).

[47] Yahoo Finance Industry Center

[48] pages.stern.nyu.edu/~adamodar/pc/datasets/covratio.xls

Consistent with management's commitment to make deals that immediately increase EPS, Thermo Fisher expects the deal to raise adjusted EPS during the first full year of operation by as much as $0.70 to $1.00 per share. Adjusted EPS exclude the impact on earnings of transaction-related expenses and expenses incurred in integrating the two businesses. Including these expenses in the calculation of EPS is expected to result in a $(0.16) per share during the first full year after closing, but excluding these expenses will result in $0.99 per share.[49]

Synergies anticipated by Thermo Fisher include additional gross margin of $75 million and $20 million in SG&A savings in 2014, the first full year after closing. Gross margin improvement and SG&A savings are projected to grow to $225 million and $100 million, respectively, by 2016, and to be sustained at these levels indefinitely. Most of the cost savings are expected to come from combining global overhead operations. Revenue-related synergy is expected to reach $300 million annually from cross-selling by the third year, up from $25 million in the first year.

Mark Fisher, CEO of Thermo Fisher, knew that the key to increasing shareholder value was realizing synergy on a timely basis. However, rationalizing facilities by reducing redundant staff, improving gross margins, and increasing revenue was fraught with risk. Eliminating staff had to be done so as not to demoralize employees, and increasing revenue could only be achieved if the loss of existing customers caused by attrition could be kept to a minimum.

At the time of closing, many questions remained. What if synergy were not realized as quickly and in the amount expected? What if expenses and capital outlays would be required in excess of what had been anticipated? How patient would shareholders be if the projected impact on EPS was not realized? Only time would tell.

Discussion questions

Answer questions 1 to 4 using as the base case the firm valuation and deal structure data in the Microsoft Excel model available on the companion site to this book titled Thermo Fisher Acquires Life Technologies Financial Model. Please see the Chapter Overview section of this chapter for the site's internet address. Assume that the base case assumptions were those used by Thermo Fisher in its merger with Life Tech. The base case reflects the input data described in this case study. To answer each question, you must change selected input data in the base case, which will change significantly the base case projections. *After answering a specific question, either undo the changes made or close the model and do not save the model results.* This will cause the model to revert back to the base case. In this way, it will be possible to analyze each question in terms of how it is different from the base case.

1. Thermo Fisher paid $76 per share for each outstanding share of Life Tech. What is the maximum offer price Thermo Fisher could have made without ceding all of the synergy value to Life Tech shareholders? (Hint: Using the Transaction Summary Worksheet, increase the offer price until the NPV in the section titled Valuation turns negative.) Why does the offer price at which NPV turns negative represent the maximum offer price for Life Tech? Undo changes to the model before answering subsequent questions.
2. Thermo Fisher designed a capital structure for financing the deal that would retain its investment-grade credit rating. To do so, it targeted a debt-to-total capital and interest coverage ratio consistent with the industry average for these credit ratios. What is the potential impact on Thermo Fisher's ability to retain an investment-grade credit rating if it had financed the takeover using 100% senior debt? Explain your answer. (Hint: In the Sources and Uses section of the Acquirer Transaction Summary Worksheet, set excess cash, new common shares issued, and convertible preferred shares to zero. Senior debt will automatically increase to 100% of the equity consideration plus transaction expenses.)[50] Undo changes to the model before answering subsequent questions.
3. Assuming Thermo Fisher would have been able to purchase the firm in a share-for-share exchange, what would have happened to the EPS in the first year? (Hint: In the Form of Payment section of the Acquirer Transaction Summary Worksheet, set the percentage of the payment denoted by "% Stock" to 100%. In the Sources and Uses

[49] Per the Summary Transaction Worksheet of the Thermo Fisher Buys Life Technologies Financial Model on the website accompanying this textbook, transaction-related expenses impacting first-year earnings consists of total expenses less that portion that is amortizable divided by total shares outstanding ($494 × (1 − 0.2))/386.6) and equals $1.02 per share. Integration expenses per share equal $50 million (see Newco Assumptions Worksheet) divided by total shares outstanding or $0.13 per share (i.e., $50/386.6). Note that $494 million, $50 million, 386.6 million, and 0.2% are transaction-related expenses, integration expenses, total Thermo Fisher shares outstanding, and that portion of transaction expenses that are amortized. Therefore adjusted earnings per share equals the pre-adjustment loss plus transaction expense per share plus integration expense per share (i.e., $(0.16) + $1.02 + $0.13 = $0.99).

[50] Other combinations of financing could have been used. For example, transaction expenses could have been paid out of excess cash balances. If this had been done, there would have been no increase in senior debt outstanding.

section, set excess cash, new common shares issued, and convertible preferred shares to zero.) Undo changes made to the model before answering the remaining question.

4. Mark Fisher, CEO of Thermo Fisher, asked rhetorically: What if synergy were not realized as quickly and in the amount expected? Assume that the integration effort is far more challenging than anticipated and that only one-fourth of the expected SG&A savings, margin improvement, and revenue synergy are realized. Furthermore, assume that actual integration expenses (shown on Newco's Assumptions Worksheet) due to the unanticipated need to upgrade and co-locate R&D facilities and to transfer hundreds of staff are $150 million in 2014, $150 million in 2015, $100 million in 2016, and $50 million in 2017. The model output resulting from these assumption changes is called the Impaired Integration Case.
What is the impact on Thermo Fisher's earning per share (including Life Tech) and the NPV of the combined firms? Compare the difference between the model "Base Case" and the model output from the "Impaired Integration Case" resulting from making the changes indicated in this question. (Hints: In the Synergy section of the Acquirer (Thermo Fisher) Worksheet, reduce the synergy inputs for each year between 2014 and 2016 by 75% and allow them to remain at those levels through 2018. On the Newco Assumptions Worksheet, change the integration expense figures to reflect the new numbers for 2014, 2015, 2016, and 2017.).

Answers to these questions are found in the Online Instructor's Manual Available to instructors using this book.

Appendix A: debt repayment schedule, convertible securities, interest rates, and betas

What follows is a listing of possible data sources for key data inputs in M&A financial models. These include the calculation of scheduled debt repayments; options, warrants, and convertible securities; betas; interest rates; and industry credit ratios.

Debt repayment schedule

Principal repayment schedules are shown for the Acquirer's debt and Target's debt (assumed by the Acquirer) and any debt that is used to finance the deal in the Acquirer's and Target's 10ks. In Notes to Consolidated Financial Statements, see the Note on Debt and Other Long-term Obligations for the repayment terms associated with Acquirer and Target debt assumed by the Acquirer at the close. Debt incurred to finance the deal and related terms are required data input (see Summary worksheet) and the repayment schedule is calculated by the model.

The Note on Debt and Other Long-term Obligations describes the types of debt outstanding, maturity dates, and associated interest rates and usually gives a 5-year projection of a total annual debt repayment schedule. Principal repayments beyond the fifth year are shown as an aggregate figure. Interest expense and principal are estimated by using a weighted average of each type of debt (i.e., senior, subordinate) and applying the applicable amortization rate (i.e., principal repayment rate) for the largest amount of debt outstanding in each category.

Options, warrants, and convertible securities

Under Notes to Consolidated Financial Statements, see the Note on Stock Options for the dollar value of outstanding options, exercise prices, and expiration dates. If the firm has convertible preferred, see the Note on Consolidated Shareholders' Equity to get the par value and amount issued. If convertible debt exists, see the Note on Debt and Other Long-term Obligations to determine the amount issued and the conversion price.

Betas

Historical betas for public firms are available from a number of sources: Yahoo Finance, Value Line Research Center, Standard & Poor's Net Advantage, One Source, and Thomson One Banker. Go to the Yahoo.com/finance website and search in the "look up" block for the company in which you are interested.

Interest rates

Information on Treasury bond rates and yield curve (i.e., interest rates on Treasury debt that varies in maturity from 1 month to 30 years) may be found at the US Department of Treasury Resource Center (http://www.treasury.gov/resource-center/data-chart-center/interest-rates/Pages/TextView.aspx?data=yield).

"Swap rates" arise as a result of an interest rate swap in which one party agrees to exchange a fixed interest payment stream they are paying for a variable or floating rate another party is paying. Such deals result from different perceptions about the future direction of interest rates. The "swap rate" is the fixed interest rate (calculated on the notational or estimated face value of the loan) that the party in an interest rate swap demands in exchange for the uncertainty of having to pay the short-term floating London Interbank Offered Rate (LIBOR) over time.[51] The market's forecast of what LIBOR will be is reflected in the forward LIBOR curve.[52] See http://www.global-rates.com/interest-rates/libor/american-dollar/american-dollar.aspx.

Swaps are typically quoted as a fixed rate or alternatively in the "swap spread," which is the difference between the swap rate and the US Treasury bond yield (or equivalent local government bond yield for non-US swaps) for the same maturity. Swap rate data may be found at the following website: http://www.barchart.com/economy/swaps.php.

Revolving credit facility interest rates equal the sum of the risk-free rate plus the default risk premium (i.e., the number of basis points[53] over the Treasury bond rate) plus interest rate risk premium (i.e., the potential for interest rate fluctuations). If we assume the 5-year US Treasury bond rate is 1.3%, the default risk premium is 250 basis points, and the swap rate is 60 basis points. The revolving credit facility rate is calculated as follows:

$$1.3\% \times 100 + 60/100 + 250/100 = 440$$

Dividing both sides by 100 results in the following expression

$$1.3 + 60/(100 \times 100) + 250/(100 \times 100) = 440/100$$

and

$$1.3 + 60/10,000 + 250/10,000 = 4.40\%$$

Finally, the default risk associated with senior debt is estimated as the difference in basis points between the interest rate on senior debt and the risk-free Treasury bond rate.

Industry credit ratios

Go to Yahoo.com/finance, click on premium and then research reports. Industry Statistics include the industry debt-to-total capital ratio required by the M&A model. Industry interest coverage ratios may be found by going to the following website: http://pages.stern.nyu.edu/~adamodar/New_iHome_Page/data.html.

[51] Note that the LIBOR rate is expected to be phased out by the end of 2021. At the time of this writing, the Secured Overnight Financing Rate published by the US Federal Reserve System is expected to be the likely replacement. See Chapter 13 for more detail on the phase out of LIBOR and its implications for M&A financing.

[52] At the time of the swap agreement, the total value of the swap's fixed rate interest payments will be equal to the value of expected floating rate payments implied by the forward LIBOR curve (i.e., expected LIBOR rates). As forward expectations for LIBOR change, so will the fixed rate that investors demand to enter into new swaps.

[53] Forty basis points equal four tenths of 1 percentage point.

PART V

Alternative business and restructuring strategies

Part V addresses strategic growth options as alternatives to domestic mergers and acquisitions (M&As), including corporate restructuring programs, business alliances, and cross-border M&A deals. This section also discusses what can be done if corporations believe more value can be created by exiting certain businesses or product lines or by reorganizing or liquidating either outside of or under bankruptcy court protection.

Restructuring strategies in this context involve selling, shutting down, or spinning off money-losing operations or those not fitting with the firm's core business strategy rather than organizational (i.e., revamping a firm's internal processes) or financial restructuring (i.e., altering a firm's capital structure). Restructuring often is a response to intensified competition or technological change and frequently causes firms to be acquired, reorganized in bankruptcy, or liquidated, resulting in their elimination as independent corporate entities.

Chapter 16 describes the common motives for entering business alliances, ranging from minority investments to joint ventures, as well as the critical success factors for establishing alliances. Reasons for using alternative legal forms, ways of resolving common deal-structuring issues, and the implications of the recent changes in US tax laws for business alliances also are addressed. The advantages and disadvantages of the various types of alliances are discussed in detail as well as what a manager should consider in choosing the type of business alliance most appropriate for the circumstances.

Chapter 17 discusses the myriad motives for exiting businesses, the various restructuring strategies for doing so, and why firms select one strategy over other options. The range of restructuring strategies considered includes divestitures, spin-offs, split-ups, equity carve-outs, and split-offs to improve shareholder value.

Chapter 18 focuses on failing firms that may attempt to preserve shareholder value by negotiating voluntarily with creditors to restructure their debt outside of bankruptcy court. Alternatively, such firms may choose or be compelled to seek the protection of the court system. The strengths and weaknesses of various strategic options for failing firms are also addressed.

Finally, Chapter 19 addresses the future of global M&As in the context of an increasingly regionalized world and the impact of tariffs and changing supply chains on cross-border deals. At the outset, the chapter describes motives for international expansion, widely used international market–entry strategies, and how to value, structure, and finance cross-border deals. This chapter carefully notes the adjustments that should be made when valuing a target firm in an emerging or developed country. Important tax considerations (including the 2017 US tax legislation) and their potential impact on cross-border deals also are addressed.

CHAPTER

16

Domestic and cross-border business alliances

joint ventures, partnerships, strategic alliances, and licensing

OUTLINE

Mergers, Acquisitions, and Other Restructuring Activities, Eleventh Edition
https://doi.org/10.1016/B978-0-12-819782-0.00016-2

Humility is not thinking less of you. It is thinking less about you. —***Rick Warren***

Inside M&As: Altria makes a big bet on cannabis

KEY POINTS

- Alliances enable firms to leverage their resources by gaining access to skills, technologies, and assets they do not currently possess.
- Alliances allow cost and risk sharing in implementing business strategies.
- Alliances require participants to cede some amount of control to the other parties.
- An alliance can be a precursor to a takeover.

Although all categories of consumer products are maturing, tobacco sales are showing a long-term decline. Countries are moving aggressively to restrict cigarette smoking because of its adverse health effects. Cannabis may be an attractive opportunity for tobacco firms because of its growing popular support, legalization in many states, and recent backlash against e-cigarettes as a tobacco substitute. The synergy between tobacco firms and cannabis growers is their knowledge of how to cultivate the crop, expertise in brand management, and dealing with regulators.

Marking "big tobacco's" first entry into the cannabis market, UK-based Imperial Brands in 2018 invested in marijuana research firm Oxford Cannabinoid Technologies, which focused on identifying new applications for cannabis. More recently, in a major alliance between a mega-tobacco company and a marijuana company, US-based Altria Group (Altria), announced in early 2019 a $1.8 billion investment in the Canadian cannabis company Cronos Group Inc.

Altria has seen a continuous decline in its cigarette sales, which fell by 20% in 2018. Finding new revenue has become a strategic imperative for the firm. By acquiring 45% of Cronos, Altria becomes Cronos's exclusive partner in the global cannabis market. The investment allows Altria to diversify beyond traditional smokers both in the United States and globally. Altria also has call options to acquire a majority of Cronos at a later date, potentially setting the stage for a future takeover.

The investments by Constellation Brands and Altria have boosted investor confidence that the projected meteoric growth in the cannabis market is more than just hype. Owing to the Altria investment, Cronos has the funds to accelerate its growth in this market, and it expects to gain a foothold in the United States through the alliance. Investors approved of the move, sending Altria's share price up by 2% on the announcement when the overall market was declining by more than 1%.

Chapter overview

What all business alliances have in common is that they generally involve sharing the risk, reward, and control among participants. The term *business alliance* is used throughout this chapter to describe the forms of cooperative relationships common in business today: joint ventures (JVs), partnerships, strategic alliances, equity partnerships, licensing agreements, and franchise alliances. The primary theme of this chapter is that business alliances often represent viable alternatives to mergers and acquisitions for achieving business objectives.

The principal differences in the various types of alliances are discussed in some detail in Chapter 1 and are therefore only summarized in Table 16.1. This chapter discusses the wide variety of motives for business alliances and the factors common to successful alliances. Also addressed are the advantages and disadvantages of alternative legal structures, important deal-structuring issues, empirical studies of business alliances shareholder wealth creation, and the implications of recent US tax legislation. A review of this chapter (including practice questions and answers) is available in the file folder titled "Student Study Guide" on the companion website (https://www.elsevier.com/books-and-journals/book-companion/9780128197820) to this book.

TABLE 16.1 Key differences among business alliances

Type	Key characteristics
Joint venture	Independent legal entity involving two or more parties May be organized as a corporation, partnership, or other legal or business organization selected by the parties Ownership, duties, risks, and rewards allocated to parties Each party retains corporate identity and autonomy Created by parties contributing assets for a specific purpose and for a limited duration
Strategic alliance (e.g., technology transfer, R&D sharing, and cross-marketing)	Does not involve the formation of separate legal entities May be precursor to a joint venture, partnership, or acquisition Generally not passive but involves cross-training, coordinated product development, and long-term contracts based on performance metrics such as product quality rather than price
Equity partnership	Has all the characteristics of an alliance Involves making minority investment in the other party Minority investor may have an option to buy a larger stake in the other party
Licensing • Product • Process • Merchandise and trademark	Patent, trademark, or copyright licensed in exchange for a royalty or fee Generally no sharing of risk or reward Generally stipulates what is being sold, how and where it can be used, and for how long Payments usually consist of an initial fee and royalties based on a percentage of future license sales
Franchising alliance	System of alliances in which partners are linked by licensing agreements (e.g., fast-food chains, hardware stores) Often grants exclusive rights to sell or distribute goods or services in specific geographic areas or markets Licensees may be required to purchase goods and services from other firms in the alliance
Network alliance	Interconnecting alliance among companies crossing international and industrial boundaries (e.g., airlines) May involve companies collaborating in one market while competing in others (e.g., computers, airlines, cellular telephones) Most often formed to access skills from different but increasingly interconnected industries
Exclusive agreement	Usually involves rights for manufacturing- or marketing-specific products or services Each party benefits from the specific skills or assets the other party brings to the relationship

R&D, Research and development.

Motivations for business alliances

Money alone rarely provides for a successful business alliance. A partner often can obtain funding from a variety of sources but may be able to obtain access to a set of skills or intellectual property only from another party. Motivations for an alliance vary widely and are discussed next.

Risk sharing

Risk is greater the more resources a firm has committed to an effort and the less certain the outcome. To mitigate risk, firms enter into alliances to reduce their resource commitment below that required to do it on their own and to limit losses if the effort proves unsuccessful. Unable to produce its antiviral drug remdesivir for COVID-19 patients in the quantities needed, Gilead Sciences signed a multiyear agreement with US drug maker Pfizer in 2020 to manufacture the drug in one of its underused facilities. In late 2018, Japanese automaker Honda agreed to take a 5.7% equity interest in General Motors' self-driving car business, Cruise LLC, by providing $.75 billion up front and $2.0 billion over 12 years to defray future development costs.

Sharing proprietary knowledge

Given the pace at which technology changes, the risk is high that a competitor will be able to develop a superior technology before a firm can bring its own new technology to market. High-tech firms with specific know-how often combine their efforts with a firm with complementary know-how to reduce the risk of failing to develop the "right" technology. Automakers Ford, Daimler, and Renault-Nissan announced that each firm would invest equally in an alliance to accelerate the development of a common hydrogen fuel cell technology to power their own cars.

The payoff is high for the firm (or firms) able to establish new standards for rapidly growing markets. One such market involves the virtual digital assistant, a software app capable of understanding natural language to perform requests for users. To coordinate development of their voice assistants, Microsoft and Amazon agreed to integrate Amazon's Echo line of virtual digital assistants powered by its voice recognition system Alexa with Microsoft's Cortana digital assistant. By enabling their software to work together on answering users' questions, they moved closer to establishing a standard operating system for voice-activated devices. The alliance is an effort to counter efforts by Google and Apple in this market.

Sharing management skills, information, and resources

Firms often lack the skills and resources to solve complex projects. These deficiencies can be remedied by aligning with other firms that possess the requisite know-how or assets. Amid the 2020 COVID-19 pandemic, pharmaceutical powerhouse GlaxoSmithKline purchased a $250 million stake in Vir Biotechnology, a small infectious disease research firm, and contributed an ingredient to boost the effectiveness of vaccines in exchange for access to the firm's research.

Sharing substantial capital outlays

Cellular phone carriers join forces to achieve the scale necessary to support the creation of national networks. Vodafone and Verizon joined forces in 1999 to form Verizon Wireless, with Verizon eventually buying out Vodafone in early 2014. Microsoft agreed in 2012 to invest $600 million over 5 years in Barnes & Noble's (B&H) e-book business to develop and market the firm's e-book reader in exchange for a 16.8% stake in B&H.

Securing sources of supply

The chemical industry is vulnerable to swings in raw material costs. Firms such as Dow, Hercules, and Olin have used JVs to build new plants throughout the world. When shortages of raw materials threaten future production, these firms commonly form JVs to secure future sources of supply. Similarly, CNOOC, the large Chinese oil concern, has been busily investing in oil and natural gas assets in highly diverse geographic areas to obtain reliable sources of supply.

Cost reduction

In the 1980s and 1990s, retailers and financial services firms outsourced such back-office activities as information processing to IBM and EDS. Others outsourced payroll processing and benefits management to such firms as ADP. More recently, package carrier FedEx and the US Post Office created an alliance covering both transportation and warehousing services. Firms may also combine their operations to meet the production requirements of all parties involved to gain economies of scale. Examples include Hitachi and Mitsubishi's forming an $8 billion-a-year semiconductor JV and Canon and Toshiba's spending a combined $1.8 billion to create a joint manufacturing operation to satisfy their requirements for complex TV displays.

Gaining access to new markets, customers, and products

Such efforts can be highly expensive, involving substantial initial marketing costs, such as advertising, promotion, warehousing, and distribution expenses, as well as complementary skills and operating assets. The cost may be prohibitive unless suitable partners can be found.

A firm may enter into an alliance to sell its products through another firm's sales force, telemarketing unit, retail outlets, or website, with the firm whose distribution channel is used receiving a portion of the revenue. Firms may also use a "cross-marketing" relationship, in which they agree to sell the other firm's products through their channels and to share revenue. For instance, eBay granted Google the exclusive right to display text advertisements on eBay's auction websites outside the United States, with eBay sharing in the revenue generated by the ads.

A firm may also simply buy the right to market to another firm's customers. In 2020, telecom companies Avaya Holdings and RingCentral entered into a partnership giving RingCentral access to Avaya's 100 million customers spread over 180 countries. RingCentral paid Avaya $375 million in advance sales commissions and licensing rights. Firms having different skills and assets may collaborate to develop new products. During the 2020 pandemic, automakers with underused facilities collaborated with 3M and General Electric, whose know-how enabled them to produce ventilators, respirators, and protective health care equipment.

Firms may take minority investments in other companies to broaden their product offering, better understand markets, offer customers a new way of accessing their products, and keep current with new technologies. In 2020, US media company ViacomCBS acquired a 49% stake in movie producer Miramax to broaden its movie offering. The Microsoft—Walgreens JV intends to develop new healthcare delivery methods in the fast-growing health care market. The alliance helps Microsoft learn how its technology can improve the delivery of medical care and helps Walgreens by cutting costs while increasing the quality of care.

Globalization

The dizzying pace of international competition increased the demand for alliances and JVs to enable companies to enter markets in which they lack production or distribution channels or in which laws prohibit 100% foreign ownership of a business. Cross-border corporate investment strategies are far more likely to involve business alliances than mergers and acquisitions (M&As), with alliances constituting the preferred investment strategy almost two-thirds of the time.[1] Many firms, such as General Motors and Ford, take minority equity positions in other companies within the industry to gain access to foreign markets. By aligning with Lenovo Group as a strategic partner in 2007, IBM hoped to grow its market share in China. More recently, Nissan and Daimler announced in 2010 the formation of a partnership in which the firms would share the cost of developing engines and small-car technologies with projected cumulative savings totaling $5.3 billion.

A prelude to acquisition or exit

A firm may make a minority investment in another company. In exchange, the investing firm may receive board representation, preferred access to proprietary technology, and greater strategic flexibility through put and call options. The investing firm is able to assess the quality of management, cultural compatibility, and the viability of the other firm's technology without having to acquire a controlling interest in the firm.

In 2019, activist Starboard Value LP invested $200 million in Papa John's Inc. hoping to turn around declining same-store sales. In exchange, Starboard received two board seats, one of which included Starboard's CEO becoming the chairman of the US pizza chain. To gain access to proprietary electric arc furnace technology, US Steel acquired 49.9% of competitor Big River in 2020 for $700 million in cash and a call option to purchase the remainder before

[1] Bodnaruk et al., 2016

2024.[2] GE had negotiated a put option with Comcast in 2010 when it contributed NBCUniversal to a JV corporation in which Comcast and GE owned 51% and 49%, respectively. In early 2013, Comcast acquired GE's entire stake, enabling GE to exit a nonstrategic business.

Favorable regulatory treatment

The Department of Justice looks at JVs far more favorably than M&As, which reduce the number of firms in an industry. JVs increase the number of firms because the parents continue to operate while another firm is created. Although partnerships enabling airlines to extend their networks have been around for decades, JVs involving revenue sharing also are gaining regulatory approval.[3] Project-oriented JVs often are viewed favorably by regulators, especially if they involve collaborative research, which is shared among all the parties to the JV.[4]

Learning

Business alliances can be conduits for acquiring new technology and know-how. The pace of a firm's knowledge accumulation increases with the number of alliances formed but tends to diminish if the types of alliances tend to be similar. Rapid knowledge accumulation can result from a high-level interaction between alliance participants and exchanging or co-locating personnel. The growth of knowledge accumulation slows and subsequently declines as the available knowledge is transferred from one party to the other, the cost required to accumulate incremental knowledge increases, and the partners' ability to coordinate activities diminishes.[5]

Product alliances among competitors provide access to similar industrial know-how, helping the alliance participants to apply industry "best practices." Product alliances with suppliers offer access to similar industry knowledge but do not appear to significantly improve a firm's manufacturing capability.[6] Research-focused JVs tend to be viewed as most successful by sharing firms when knowledge overlap (e.g., sources of knowledge and areas of application) and the intensity of collaboration are greatest.[7]

Automakers formed a number of new business alliances in 2019 and 2020 to cope with future uncertainties by learning through collaboration. Electric cars, autonomous driving vehicles, and ride-hailing services threaten to change radically the way people use cars. Some alliances involve direct investment in new products, such as Honda's $2.75 billion investment in General Motors' autonomous vehicle operation. Others such as Ford and Volkswagen involve the joint development of electrically powered autonomous cars. Still others such as BMW and Daimler represent a joint effort to develop a range of "mobility services."

What makes business alliances successful?

Success reflects synergy; clarity of purpose, roles, and responsibilities; accountability; cooperation and cultural compatibility; a "win–win" situation; compatible timeframes and financial expectations for the partners; and support from top management.[8]

Synergy

Successful alliances are those in which partners either complement existing strengths or offset significant weaknesses. Examples include partners providing opportunities for realizing economies of scale and scope, access to new products, distribution channels, and proprietary knowledge. Multiple firms may exploit economies of scale by

[2] A *call option* gives the holder the right to purchase an asset, and the *put option* gives the holder the right to sell an asset to another party at a preset price.

[3] Bilotkach et al., 2019

[4] Samano et al., 2017

[5] Lin, 2017

[6] Ozdemir et al., 2017

[7] Muller and Zaby, 2019

[8] Kantor, 2002; Lynch, 1993

centralizing production of a specific product in a single operating facility. Other firms may choose to realize economies of scope by creating a marketing alliance in which their products are sold through another partner's more effective sales force. The scope of the one partner's sales force has been expanded to include the other company's products as well as their own. Research JVs often combine the research and development (R&D) functions of multiple partners to gain access to proprietary knowledge, processes, and equipment as well as the potential boost to innovation resulting from cross-fertilization of ideas.

Clarity of purpose, roles, and responsibilities

Early on, parties to the alliance must agree to a well-understood purpose or mission for the alliance, which must be communicated to all those responsible for achieving the mission. The roles and responsibilities of the alliance partners in realizing the mission should be clearly established. How the mission is achieved is defined by specific goals, milestones for achieving the goals, and commitments to a timetable.

Accountability

Performance goals established for individual managers should be tied directly to the primary goals for the alliance. Incentives should be in place to reward good performance with respect to realizing their goals on a timely basis, and those failing to perform should be held accountable.

Cooperation and cultural compatibility

Generally speaking, alliance partners whose countries are more culturally and institutionally similar are more likely to perform better than those that are substantially dissimilar. Why? Similarity breeds familiarity and understanding, enabling alliance partners to engage in effective communication and cooperation.

Firms with similar philosophies, goals, rewards, operating practices, and ethics are more likely to cooperate over the long run. Although it often is convenient for small start-ups to align with industry leading companies, cultural differences sometimes prove intractable. In 2011, Toyota bought a $50 million stake in Tesla Motors Inc.; sold the firm a shuttered Fremont, California, auto assembly plant for only $42 million; and agreed to retrofit the Toyota RAV4 utility vehicle using Tesla technology. Tesla's motivation was a cash infusion, gaining access to a factory at a bargain price, and the credibility that comes from working with an industry leader. By late 2014, the partnership was unraveling swiftly largely because of differences between the firms' engineering approaches and difficulties in sharing proprietary technologies. Moreover, Toyota distanced itself from Tesla's core electric vehicle technology and embraced fuel cells, a technology that Tesla's founder Elon Musk has ridiculed publicly. Toyota allowed the alliance to expire in 2015.

Win—win situation

Alliance partners must believe they are benefiting from the activity for it to be successful. Johnson & Johnson's (J&J's) alliance with Merck & Company in the marketing of Pepcid AC is a classic win—win situation. Merck contributed its prescription drug Pepcid AC to the alliance so that J&J could market it as an over-the-counter drug. With Merck as the developer of the upset-stomach remedy and J&J as the marketer, the product became the leader in this drug category. In contrast, FedEx let its contract to deliver packages for Amazon.com expire in 2019 because of Amazon.com emerging as a formidable competitor in the package delivery business.

Compatible management styles, timeframes, and financial expectations

The length of time an alliance agreement remains in force depends on the partners' objectives, the availability of resources, the accuracy of the assumptions on which the alliance's plans are based, and external events. Incompatible timeframes are a recipe for disaster. The management of a small Internet business may want to "cash out" within the next 18 to 24 months, whereas a larger firm may wish to gain market share over a number of years.

Support from the top

Top management of the parents of a business alliance must involve themselves aggressively and publicly. Tepid support filters down to lower-level managers and proves to be demotivating. When this happens, managers may divert their attention to other matters.

Partner selection

Whereas choosing the wrong partner can lead to alliance dissolution, selecting the right one can heighten the prospect of success. Partners with compatible cultures and management styles are most likely to cooperate effectively.[9] Although selection criteria can vary widely, some factors are commonly considered. Does the prospective partner possess the needed skills and resources, unique (or hard to find) capabilities, successful alliance experience, and compatible expectations and organizational culture? For international JVs, the compatibility of a country's culture, language, and legal system should also be considered.

The partner selection due diligence relies heavily on publicly available information (see Chapter 6 for public information sources). However, private information sources often are critical to confirming public information.[10] Yet it is often imprudent to survey a prospective partner's customers and suppliers because of the likelihood that competitors would become aware that an alliance was under consideration. Due diligence can become even more challenging if the prospective partner is withholding information to gain an advantage in negotiating ownership share, governance structure, and filling key management positions.

Alternative legal forms of business alliances

The legal form of an alliance should follow the creation of a business strategy. Alliances may assume a variety of legal structures: corporate, partnership, franchise, equity partnership, and written contract.[11] Each has implications for taxation, control, trading ownership shares, limitations on liability, duration, and ease of raising capital (Table 16.2).

Corporate structures

A corporation is a legal entity created under state law in the United States with an unending life and limited financial liability for its owners. The *doctrine of corporate personhood* holds that corporations, as groups of people, may exercise certain rights under the US Constitution or under common law. For example, corporations may make contracts with other parties and sue or be sued in court. Such structures include a generalized corporate form (also called a C-type corporation) and the Subchapter S (S-type) corporation.

C-type corporations

A JV corporation normally involves a standalone business whose income is taxed at the prevailing corporate tax rates. Corporations other than S-type corporations are subject to "double" taxation. Taxes are paid by the corporation when profits are earned and again by the shareholders when the corporation issues dividends. Setting up a corporate legal structure may be more time consuming and costly than for other legal forms because of legal expenses incurred in drafting a corporate charter and bylaws. Advantages of this corporate form include managerial autonomy, continuity of ownership, ease of transferring ownership and raising money, and limited liability. These benefits are discussed next.

Managerial autonomy refers to a high level of discretionary authority granted by owners to those managing the organization and is used when the JV is large or complex enough to require a separate or decentralized management structure. The C-type structure works best when the JV requires some operational autonomy to be effective. The parent firms would set strategy, but the JV's management would manage the day-to-day operations.

[9] Chang et al., 2020

[10] Welcher (2019) provides a useful methodology for unlocking private information sources.

[11] Technically, a "handshake" agreement is also an option. Given the risk associated with the lack of documentation, such agreements should be avoided. However, in some cultures, insistence on a written agreement may be offensive.

TABLE 16.2 Alternative legal forms applicable to business alliances

Legal form	Advantages	Disadvantages
Corporate structures		
Corporation	Continuity of ownership Limited liability Provides operational autonomy Provides for flexible financing Facilitates tax-free merger	Double taxation Inability to pass losses on to shareholders Relatively high setup costs, including charter and bylaws
Subchapter S	Avoids double taxation Limited liability	Maximum of 100 shareholders Excludes corporate shareholders Must distribute all earnings Allows only one class of stock Lacks continuity of C corporation Difficult to raise large sums of money
Limited liability company (LLC)	Limited liability Owners can be managers without losing limited liability Avoids double taxation Allows an unlimited number of members (i.e., owners) Allows corporate shareholders to own more than 80% of another company Allows flexibility in allocating investment, profits, losses, and operational responsibilities among members Duration set by owners Can sell shares to "members" without SEC registration Allows foreign corporations as investors	Owners also must be active participants in the firm Lacks continuity of a corporate structure State laws governing LLC formation differ, making it difficult for LLCs doing business in multiple states Member shares are often illiquid because the consent of members is required to transfer ownership
Partnership structures		
General partnership	Avoids double taxation Allows flexibility in allocating investment, profits, losses, and operational responsibilities Life set by general partner	Partners have unlimited liability Lacks continuity of corporate structure Partnership interests illiquid Partners jointly and severally liable Each partner has authority to bind the partnership to contracts
Private limited liability partnership[a]	Limits partner liability (except for general partner) Avoids double taxation State laws consistent (covered under the Uniform Limited Partnership Act)	Partnership interests are illiquid Partnership is dissolved if a partner leaves Private partnerships are limited to 35 partners
Master limited partnership	Same as previous Units or shares are publicly traded and more liquid than in other types of partnership interests	Unlike corporate dividends, failure to make quarterly distributions constitutes default
Franchise alliance	Allows repeated application of a successful business model Minimizes start-up expenses Facilitates communication of common brand and marketing strategy	Success depends on quality of franchise sponsor support Royalty payments (3%–7% of revenue)
Equity partnership	Facilitates close working relationship Potential prelude to merger May preempt competition	Limited tactical and strategic control
Written contract	Facilitates start-up Potential prelude to merger	Limited control Lacks close coordination Potential for limited commitment

[a]Public limited partnerships may have an unlimited number of investors and must be registered with the Securities and Exchange Commission (SEC).

Unlike other legal forms, the C-type structure provides *continuity of ownership* because it has an indefinite life. It does not have to be dissolved because of the death of the owners or if an owner wishes to liquidate her ownership stake. This structure may be warranted if the JV's goals are long term and the parties choose to contribute cash directly to the JV. In return for the cash contribution, the JV partners receive stock in the new company, enabling a partner to "cash out" by selling her shares.[12] A corporate structure also facilitates a tax-free merger because the stock of the acquiring firm can be exchanged for the stock or assets of another firm.

Under a C-type structure, the *ease of transferring ownership* facilitates raising money. Shares, legal claims on the assets, liabilities, cash flows, and earnings of a corporation can be transferred from one owner to another without disrupting business operations. Such structures provide a broader array of financing options than other legal forms, including the ability to sell shares and issue corporate debentures and mortgage bonds. Selling new shares enables the corporation to raise funds while still retaining control if less than 50.1% of the corporation's shares are sold.

Finally, C-type corporations provide for *limited liability* in that a shareholder's obligation is limited to the extent of their investment and creditors cannot go after their personal assets. Although it mostly affects closely held corporations, the "corporate veil" (i.e., limited liability protection) is pierced by the courts only in instances of serious misconduct. For example, an owner can be held personally liable if she or he injures someone or personally guarantees a bank loan or a business debt on which the firm defaults. Other limited liability exceptions include failing to deposit taxes withheld from employees' wages, capitalize the corporation adequately, and hold regular directors and shareholders meetings. The corporate veil also may be pierced if an owner comingles personal and corporate funds or withholds information from other owners.

Subchapter S corporations

A firm having 100 or fewer principal shareholders may qualify as an S-type corporation and be taxed as if it were a partnership and thus avoid double taxation. The members of a single family may be considered a single shareholder.[13] An employee stock ownership plan (ESOP) maintained by an S corporation is not in violation of the requirement regarding the maximum number of shareholders because the S corporation contributes stock to the ESOP. The major disadvantages to S-type corporations are the exclusion of any corporate shareholders, the requirement to issue only one class of stock, the necessity of distributing all earnings to shareholders each year, and that no more than 25% of the corporation's gross income may be derived from passive income.

C corporations may convert to S corporations, eliminating double taxation on dividends. Asset sales within 10 years of the conversion are subject to capital gains taxes at the prevailing corporate tax rate. After 10 years, such gains are tax free to the S corporation but are taxable when distributed to shareholders, at their personal tax rates. Sales of assets acquired by an S corporation or after a 10-year period after conversion from one form of legal entity to an S corporation are taxed at the capital gains tax rate.[14]

As discussed next, the limited liability company offers its owners the significant advantage of greater flexibility in allocating profits and losses and is not subject to the many restrictions of the S corporation. Consequently, the popularity of the S corporation has declined.

Limited liability companies

Like a corporation, a limited liability company (LLC) limits the liability of its owners (called *members*) to the extent of their investment. Like a limited partnership, the LLC passes through all of its profits and losses to its owners without itself being taxed. To obtain this favorable tax status, the Internal Revenue Service (IRS) requires that the LLC adopt an organization agreement eliminating the characteristics of a C corporation: management autonomy, continuity of ownership or life, and free transferability of shares.

Management autonomy is limited by placing decisions about major issues pertaining to the management of the LLC (e.g., mergers or asset sales) in the hands of all its members. LLC agreements require that they be dissolved in

[12] Alternatively, the partner–shareholder can withdraw from active participation in the JV but remain a passive shareholder, anticipating potential appreciation of the stock.

[13] A husband and wife would be treated as a single shareholder. *Family members* refer to those with a common ancestor, lineal descendants of the ancestor, and the spouses of such lineal descendants or common ancestor.

[14] The 10-year "built-in-gains" period is designed by the IRS to discourage C corporations from converting to S corporations to benefit from more favorable capital gains tax rates on gains realized by selling corporate assets. Gains on the sale of assets by C corporations are taxed at the prevailing corporate income tax rate rather than a more favorable capital gains tax rate.

case of the death, retirement, or resignation of any member, thereby eliminating continuity of ownership or life. Free transferability is limited by making a transfer of ownership subject to the approval of all members.

Unlike S corporations, LLCs can own more than 80% of another corporation and have an unlimited number of members. Also, corporations as well as non-US residents can own LLC shares. Equity capital is obtained through offerings to members. The LLC can sell shares or interests to members without registering them with the Securities and Exchange Commission (SEC), which is required for corporations that sell their securities to the public. LLC shares are not traded on public exchanges, which is well suited for corporate JVs and subsidiary or affiliate projects. The parent can separate a JV's risk from its other businesses while getting favorable tax treatment and flexibility in the allocation of revenues and losses among owners. Finally, LLCs can incorporate before an initial public offering, tax free.

The LLC's drawbacks are evident if an owner leaves. All other owners must agree to continue the firm. All the LLC's owners must take active roles in managing the firm. LLC interests are illiquid because transfer of ownership is subject to the approval of other members. LLCs must be set for a limited time, typically 30 years.[15] The most common types of firms to form LLCs are family-owned businesses, professional services firms, and companies with foreign investors.

Partnership structures

Frequently used as an alternative to a corporation, partnership structures include general partnerships and limited partnerships.

General partnerships

Under this legal structure, investment, profits, losses, and operational responsibilities are allocated to the partners. Because profits and losses are allocated to partners, the partnership is not subject to tax. The partnership structure also offers substantial flexibility in how the profits and losses are allocated to the partners.

Typically, a corporate partner forms a special-purpose subsidiary to hold its interest. This limits liability and facilitates disposition of the JV interest in the future. The partnership structure is preferable to the other options when the business alliance is expected to have short (3–5 years) duration and if high levels of commitment and management interaction are necessary.

The primary disadvantage of the general partnership is that partners have unlimited liability. Each partner is said to be jointly and severally liable for the partnership's debts. If one partner negotiates a contract resulting in a loss, each partner must pay for a portion of the loss based on a previously determined agreement on the distribution of profits and losses. Because each partner has unlimited liability for the firm's debts, creditors of the partnership may claim assets from one or more of the partners if the remaining partners are unable to cover their share of the loss.

Another disadvantage is the ability of any partner to bind the business to a contract or other business deal. If one partner purchases inventory at a price the partnership cannot afford, the partnership is still obligated to pay. Partnerships also lack continuity, in that they must be dissolved if a partner dies or withdraws unless a new partnership agreement can be drafted. To avoid this possibility, a partnership agreement should include a buy–sell condition or right of first refusal, allowing the partners to buy out a departing partner's interest so the business can continue. Finally, partnership interests are illiquid because of the lack of a public market.

Limited liability partnerships

In a limited liability partnership (LLP), one or more of the partners can be designated as having limited liability as long as at least one partner has unlimited liability. Those who are responsible for the day-to-day operations of the partnership's activities, whose individual acts are binding on the other partners, and who are personally liable for the partnership's total liabilities are called *general partners*. Those who contribute only money and are not involved in management decisions are called *limited partners*. Usually limited partners receive income, capital gains, and tax benefits, whereas the general partner collects fees and a percentage of the capital gain and income.

Typical limited partnerships are in real estate, oil and gas, and equipment leasing, but they also are used to finance movies, R&D, and other projects. Public limited partnerships are sold through brokerage firms, financial planners, and other registered securities representatives. Public partnerships may have an unlimited number of investors, and

[15] Each state has different laws about LLC formation and governance, so an LLC that does business in several states might not meet the requirements in every state.

their partnership plans must be filed with the SEC. Private limited partnerships have fewer than 35 limited partners, who each invest more than $20,000. Their plans do not have to be filed with the SEC. The sources of equity capital for limited partnerships are the funds supplied by the general and limited partners. LLPs are very popular for accountants, physicians, attorneys, and consultants.

Master limited partnerships

Master limited partnerships (MLPs) are partnerships whose interests are separated into units that trade like shares of stock. Unlike common stock dividends paid by corporations, the failure to make quarterly payouts to investors is an act of default. Because of these mandatory payments, MLPs are used in industries with predictable cash flows, such as natural resources and real estate. To avoid being taxed as a corporation, an MLP can have only two of the four characteristics of a corporation: managerial autonomy, limited liability, an unlimited life, and freely traded shares. Generally, MLPs have freely traded shares and managerial autonomy but do not have unlimited life or unlimited liability for *all* owners, in that at least one partner has unlimited liability.

Franchise alliances

Franchises involve a franchisee's making an investment to purchase a license, plus additional capital investment for real estate, machinery, and working capital. For this investment, the franchisor (the one providing the license) provides training, site-selection assistance, and discounts resulting from bulk purchasing. Royalty payments for the license typically run 3% to 7% of annual franchisee revenue. Franchise success rates exceed 80% over a 5-year period as compared with other types of start-ups, which have 5-year success rates of less than 10%.

The franchise alliance is preferred when a given business format can be replicated many times. Moreover, franchise alliances are also appropriate when there needs to be a common, recognizable identity presented to customers and close operational coordination is required. A franchise alliance also may be desirable when a common marketing program needs to be coordinated and implemented by a single partner.

The franchisor and franchisee operate as separate entities, usually as corporations or LLCs. The four types of franchises are distributor (auto dealerships), processing (bottling plants), chain (restaurants), and area franchises (a geographic region is licensed to a new franchisee to subfranchise to others).

Franchising offers the prospect of converting assets owned and operated by a firm to those owned and operated by someone else. By moving toward franchising, a firm can reduce its capital expenditures and achieve a more stable revenue stream based on franchise fees. In late 2018, US-based fast-food restaurant chain Denny's announced its intention to franchise as much as 97% of their restaurants by selling most of its company-owned stores.

Equity partnerships

Equity partnerships involve a company's purchase of stock (resulting in a less-than-controlling interest) in another company or a two-way exchange of stock by the two firms.[16] This is referred to as a partnership because of the equity ownership exchanged. Equity partnerships are used in purchaser–supplier relationships, technology development, and marketing alliances and when a larger firm makes an investment in a smaller firm to ensure its continued financial viability. In exchange for an equity investment, a firm often receives a seat on the board and possibly an option to buy a controlling interest in the company. The equity partnership is most effective when there is a need to have a long-term relationship, to preempt a competitor from making an alliance or acquisition, or as a prelude to a takeover.[17]

The choice of the way in which an alliance will be organized to achieve its objectives and how the parties involved will be protected (i.e., its governance structure) is affected by a partner's experience with a particular type of governance structure. Firms having extensive experience with non-equity alliances are more likely to choose non-equity alliances in subsequent business alliances to reduce the costs of negotiating and managing the partnership. Firms

[16] Such exchanges keep both parties committed to the success of the partnership. If the partnership fails, the value of each party's partnership interest declines, as could the ownership stake each partner has in the other firm.

[17] Alternatively, an equity partnership can mean a partnership structure in which both partners contribute equity capital as opposed to a contractual partnership. The latter involves one in which the parties are contractually bound to performing certain obligations but generally does not require the contribution of equity capital by the partners.

with substantial experience in equity alliances are more likely to use the same governance structure in future business alliances. As firms accumulate experience with a particular form of governance, they are better able to implement such structures.[18]

Written contracts

This is the simplest legal structure and is used most often with strategic alliances because it maintains an independent relationship between the parties to the contract. The contract stipulates how the revenue is divided, the responsibilities of each party, alliance duration, and confidentiality requirements. No separate business entity is established for legal or tax purposes. The written contract most often is used when the alliance is expected to last less than 3 years, frequent close coordination is not required, capital investments are made independently by each party to the agreement, and the parties have had little previous contact.

Bilateral versus multilateral alliances

Bilateral alliances consist of two parties; multilateral alliances consist of three or more firms. The most common form of multilateral alliance is the three-party partners' arrangement. Studies show that multilateral alliances comprise between 27% and 55% of all alliances. Their greater complexity tends to make them more difficult to manage. Alliances involving more than two parties tend to engage in larger and riskier projects. Having more partners involved means that investment risk can be spread over more investors, and they tend to offer greater advantages to the partners in terms of access to complementary resources, market information, and investment opportunities. Their larger scale makes them more complex than bilateral arrangements. Multilateral alliances tend to be more successful when they have shared ownership based on each partner's equity contribution.[19]

Strategic and operational plans

Before any deal-structuring issues are addressed, the parties must agree on the basic strategic direction and purpose of the alliance as defined in the alliance's strategic plan, as well as the financial and nonfinancial goals established in the operation's plan. The strategic plan identifies the primary purpose of the alliance; communicates specific quantifiable targets, such as financial returns or market share and milestones; and analyzes its strengths and weaknesses, opportunities, and threats relative to the competition. The operations plan (i.e., annual budget) should reflect the specific needs of the proposed business alliance and be written by those responsible for its implementation. The operations plan is typically a 1-year plan that outlines for managers what is to be achieved, when it is to be accomplished, and what resources are required.

Resolving business alliance deal-structuring issues

A business alliance deal structure allocates risks, rewards, resource requirements, and responsibilities among participants. Table 16.3 summarizes the key issues and related questions that need to be addressed as part of the deal-structuring process. This section discusses how these issues most often are resolved.

Scope

A basic question in setting up a business alliance involves which of the partners' products are included and which are excluded from the alliance. This question deals with defining how broadly the alliance will be applied in pursuing its purpose. For example, an alliance whose purpose is to commercialize products developed by the partners could be broadly or narrowly defined in specifying what products or services are to be offered, to whom, in what

[18] Niesten et al., 2017

[19] Li et al., 2017

TABLE 16.3 Business alliance deal-structuring issues

Issue	Key questions
Scope	What products are included and what are excluded? Who receives rights to distribute, manufacture, acquire, or license technology or purchase future products or technology?
Duration	How long is the alliance expected to exist?
Legal form	What is the appropriate legal structure—standalone entity or contract?
Governance	How are the interests of the parent firms to be protected? Who is responsible for specific accomplishments?
Control	How are strategic decisions to be addressed? How are day-to-day operational decisions to be handled?
Resource contributions and ownership determination	Who contributes what and in what form? Cash? Assets? Guarantees or loans? Technology, including patents, trademarks, copyrights, and proprietary knowledge? How are contributions to be valued? How is ownership determined?
Financing ongoing capital requirements	What happens if additional cash is needed?
Distribution	How are profits and losses allocated? How are dividends determined?
Performance criteria	How is performance to the plan measured and monitored?
Dispute resolution	How are disagreements resolved?
Revision	How will the agreement be modified?
Termination	What are the guidelines for termination? Who owns the assets on termination? What are the rights of the parties to continue the alliance activities after termination?
Transfer of interests	How are ownership interests to be transferred? What are the restrictions on the transfer of interests? How will new alliance participants be handled? Will there be rights of first refusal, drag-along, tag-along, or put provisions?
Tax	Who receives tax benefits? What type of structure minimizes tax liabilities?
Management and organization	How is the alliance to be managed?
Confidential information	How is confidential information handled? How are employees and customers of the parent firms protected?
Regulatory restrictions and notifications	What licenses are required? What regulations need to be satisfied? What agencies need to be notified?

geographic areas, and for what time period. Failure to define scope adequately can lead to the alliance competing with the parent firms. With respect to both current and future products, the alliance agreement should identify who receives the rights to market or distribute products, manufacture products, acquire or license technology, or purchase products from the venture.

Duration

The participants need to agree on how long the business alliance is to remain in force. And participant expectations must be compatible because the alliance's expected longevity is an important determinant in the choice of a legal form. Unlike a partnership, the corporate structure readily provides for a continuous life more so than a partnership because it is easier to transfer ownership interests. Most business alliances have a finite life, which corresponds to the time required to achieve their original objectives.

Legal form

Businesses that are growth oriented or intend to go public generally become C corporations because of their financing flexibility, unlimited life, continuity of ownership, and ability to combine on a tax-free basis with other firms. With certain exceptions concerning frequency, firms may convert from one legal structure to a C corporation before going public. The nature of the business greatly influences the legal form chosen (Table 16.4).

TABLE 16.4 Key factors affecting choice of legal entity

Determining factors: businesses with	Should select
High liability risks	C corporation, LLP, or LLC
Large capital or financing requirements	C corporation
Desire for continuity of existence	C corporation
Desire for managerial autonomy	C corporation
Desire for growth through M&As	C corporation
Owners who are also active participants	LLC
Foreign corporate investors	LLC
Desire to allocate investments, profits, losses, and operating responsibilities among owners	LLC and LLP
High pretax profits	LLC and LLP
Project focus or expected limited existence	LLP
Owners who want to remain inactive	LLP and C corporation
Large marketing expenses	Franchise
Strategies that are easily replicated	Franchise
Close coordination among participants not required	Written "arms-length" agreement
Low risk and low capital requirements	Sole proprietorship or partnership

LLC, Limited liability corporation; *LLP,* limited liability partnership; *M&As,* mergers and acquisitions.

Governance

In the context of an alliance, *governance* may be defined broadly as an oversight function providing for efficient communication between two or more parent firms. The primary responsibilities of this oversight function are to protect the interests of the parents, approve changes to strategy and annual operating plans, allocate resources needed to make the alliance succeed, and arbitrate conflicts among lower levels of management. Historically, governance of business alliances has followed either a quasi-corporate or a quasi-project approach. For example, the oil industry traditionally has managed alliances by establishing a board of directors to provide oversight of managers and to protect the interests of nonoperating owners. In contrast, in the pharmaceutical and automotive industries, in which nonequity alliances are common, firms treat governance like project management by creating a steering committee that allows all participants to comment on issues confronting the alliance.

No matter how well written, alliance agreements often fail to address or lack sufficient clarity in addressing important subjects. Previous working relationships between partners involved in alliance activities facilitate the renegotiation of agreements to resolve issues as they arise.[20]

Resource contributions and ownership determination

The participants must agree on a fair value for all tangible and intangible assets contributed to the business alliance. The ownership shares of the corporation or the interests in the partnership are distributed among the owners in accordance with the value contributed by each participant. The partner with the largest risk, the largest contributor of cash, or who contributes critical tangible or intangible assets generally is given the greatest equity share in a JV. Exhibit 16.1 illustrates how the distribution of ownership between General Electric and Vivendi Universal Entertainment may have been determined in the formation of NBCUniversal.

[20] Duplat et al. (2020)

EXHIBIT 16.1
Determining Ownership Distribution in A Joint Venture

Vivendi Universal Entertainment (VUE) contributed film and television assets valued at $14 billion to create NBCUniversal, a JV with TV station NBC, which was wholly owned by General Electric at that time. NBCUniversal was valued at $42 billion at closing. NBCUniversal's EBITDA was estimated to be $3 billion, of which GE contributed two-thirds; VUE accounted for the remainder. EBITDA multiples for TV media deals averaged 14 times EBITDA at that time. GE provided VUE an option to buy $4 billion in GE stock, assumed $1.6 billion in VUE debt, and paid the remainder of the $14 billion purchase price in the form of NBCUniversal stock. At closing, VUE converted the option to buy GE stock into $4 billion in cash. GE owned 80% of NBCUniversal and VUE 20%. How might this ownership distribution have been determined?

Solution

Step 1: Estimate the total value of the joint venture.

$$\$3 \text{ billion} \times 14 = \$42 \text{ billion}$$

Step 2: Estimate the value of assets contributed by each partner.

Reflecting the relative contribution of each partner to EBITDA (two-thirds from GE and one-third from VUE), GE's contributed assets were valued at $28 billion (i.e., two-thirds of $42 billion) and VUE's at $14 billion (i.e., one-third of $42 billion).

Step 3: Determine the form of payment.

$4.0 billion (GE stock)

$1.6 billion (assumed Vivendi debt)

$8.4 billion (value of VUE's equity position in NBCUniversal = $14 − $4.0 − $1.6)

$14.0 billion (purchase price paid by GE to Vivendi for VUE assets)

Step 4: Determine the ownership distribution.

At closing, Vivendi chose to receive a cash infusion of $5.6 billion (i.e., $4 billion in cash in lieu of GE stock + $1.6 billion in assumed VUE debt). Thus,

VUE's ownership of NBCUniversal

$= (\$14 \text{ billion} - \$5.6 \text{ billion})/\$42 \text{ billion}$

$= \$8.4 \text{ billion}/\$42 \text{ billion}$

$= 0.2$

GE's ownership of NBCUniversal $= 1 - 0.2 = 0.8$

EBITDA, Earnings before interest, taxes, depreciation, and amortization; *JV*, joint venture.

It is relatively easy to value tangible contributions (e.g., cash, promissory notes, contingent commitments, stock of existing corporations, and assets and liabilities associated with an ongoing business) in terms of actual dollars or their present values. A party that contributes "hard" assets, such as a production facility, may want it valued in terms of the value of increased production rather than its replacement cost or lease value. The contribution of a fully operational, modern facility to a venture interested in being first to market with a particular product may provide far greater value than if the venture attempted to build a new facility because of the delay inherent in making the facility fully operational.

Intangible contributions (e.g., intellectual property) are often more difficult to value. Partners providing services may be compensated by having the business alliance pay a market-based royalty or fee for such services. Or contributors of intellectual property may receive rights to future patents or technologies developed by the alliance. Alliance participants contributing brand names may require assurances that they can purchase a certain amount of the product or service, at a guaranteed price, for a specific time period.

Financing ongoing capital requirements

Alliances may fund capital needs that cannot be financed internally by requiring participants to make a capital contribution, issuing additional equity or partnership interests, or borrowing. If it is decided that the alliance should borrow, the participants must agree on an appropriate financial structure (i.e., debt-to-equity ratio) for the enterprise.

Alliances established through a written contract do not require stipulation of a capital structure, because each party to the contract finances its own commitments to the alliance. Project-based JVs, particularly those that create a separate corporation, sometimes sell equity directly to the public or through a private placement.

Owner or partner financing

The equity owners may agree to contribute capital in addition to their initial investments in the enterprise. The contributions usually are made in direct proportion to their equity or partnership interests. If one party fails to make a capital contribution, the ownership interest of those making the contribution increases while the interest of those not contributing decreases proportionately.

Equity and debt financing

JVs formed as a corporation may issue different classes of common or preferred stock. JVs established as partnerships raise capital through the issuance of limited partnership units to investors, with the sponsoring firms becoming general partners. When a larger company aligns with a smaller firm, it may make an equity investment in the smaller firm to ensure it remains solvent or to benefit from potential equity appreciation. Such investments often include an option to purchase the remainder of the shares or at least a controlling interest at a predetermined price if the smaller firm or the JV satisfies certain financial targets.

Control

Control is distinguishable from ownership by the use of agreements among investors or voting rights or by issuing different classes of shares.[21] In some instances, the majority owner may not have effective control of the alliance because of the need to get approval from other shareholders to do certain things. Effective control can be held by minority investors if the class of stock they hold or if clauses stipulated in the alliance agreement provide them with certain veto rights over key aspects of the business.[22] Such rights may be given to minority shareholders to get a cash infusion or access to a critical resource such as proprietary software or brand name.

The most successful JVs are those in which one party is responsible for most routine decisions, with the other parties participating only when the decisions are major. The alliance agreement must define what issues are to be considered major and address how they are to be resolved, either by majority votes or by veto rights given to one or more of the parties. Operational control should be placed with the owner best able to manage the JV. The owner who has the largest equity share but not operational control is likely to insist on having a seat on the board of directors, as well as some veto rights.

About three-fourths of international JVs involving US partners have equal ownership with the rest having a dominant owner. Although stipulation of partnership rights and different classes of equity suggest that equal ownership need not imply equal control, researchers have found that JVs with dominant partners tended to show greater value creation.[23] Why? Majority ownership (and possibly control) may reduce potential indecision and missed opportunities that arise in JVs whose ownership and control are shared equally. Other research suggests that an ownership power imbalance does not necessarily have a significant impact on value creation unless the partners have had a long-standing relationship during a which trust and cooperation developed.[24]

Minority partners must assess whether their share of the additional value creation for the JV resulting from having a dominant partner offsets the potential for the majority partner taking actions that hurt the minority partner. Such actions could include selling products at below-market prices to firms that are owned by the majority partner or buying from suppliers owned by the majority partner at prices above those prevailing in the marketplace.

[21] How control is exercised by the alliance partners can impact significantly international joint venture performance and the pace of innovation. For a discussion of appropriate control "strategies," see Nguyen et al. (2020).

[22] A minority shareholder could have veto rights over such issues as changes in the alliance's purpose and scope, strategy, capital expenditures, key management promotions, salary increases applying to individual managers or to the general employee population, the amount and timing of dividend payments, buyout conditions, and restructuring.

[23] Aguir et al., 2017

[24] Lebedev et al., 2020

Distribution issues

Such issues relate to dividend policies and how profits and losses are allocated among the owners. The dividend policy determines the cash return each partner should receive. How the cash flows of the venture will be divided generally depends on the initial equity contribution of each partner, ongoing equity contributions, and noncash contributions in the form of technical and managerial resources. Profits and losses are allocated according to ownership interests.[25]

Performance criteria

The lack of adequate performance measurement criteria can result in disputes among the partners. Such criteria should be measurable and simple enough to be understood and used by the partners and managers at all levels and spelled out clearly in the business alliance agreement.

Dispute resolution

How disputes are resolved reflects the choice of law provision, the definition of what constitutes an impasse, and the arbitration clause provided in the alliance agreement. The *choice of law provision* indicates which states or country's laws have jurisdiction in settling disputes. This provision should be drafted with an understanding of the likely outcome of litigation in any of the participants' home countries or states and the attitude of these countries' or states' courts in enforcing choice-of-law provisions. The *impasse clause* defines events triggering dispute-resolution procedures. Such events should not be defined so narrowly that minor disagreements are subject to the dispute mechanism. Finally, an *arbitration clause* addresses disagreements by defining the type of dispute subject to arbitration and how the arbitrator will be selected.

Revision

If one party to the agreement wishes to withdraw, the participants should have agreed in advance how the withdrawing party's ownership interest would be divided among the remaining parties. Moreover, a product or technology may be developed that was not foreseen when the alliance first was conceived. The alliance agreement should indicate that the rights to manufacture and distribute the product or technology might be purchased by a specific alliance participant.

Termination

An alliance may be terminated because of the completion of a project, successful operations resulting in merger of the partners, diverging partner objectives, or failure of the alliance to achieve objectives. Termination provisions in the alliance agreement should include buyout clauses enabling one party to purchase another's ownership interests, prices of the buyout, and how assets and liabilities are to be divided if the partners elect to dissolve the operation.[26]

Transfer of interests

Alliance agreements often limit how and to whom parties to the agreements can transfer their interests. In agreements that permit transfers under certain conditions, the partners or the JV itself may have *right of first refusal* (i.e., the party wishing to leave the JV first must offer its interests to other JV participants). Partners may have the right to "put" (or sell) their interests to the venture, and the venture may have a call option to purchase partners' interests.

There also may be tag-along and drag-along provisions, which have the effect of a third-party purchaser's acquiring not only the interest of the JV party whose interest it seeks to acquire but also the interests of other parties.

[25] Royalties are used to compensate parties contributing intellectual property rights. When profits are attributable to distribution or marketing efforts of a partner, commissions can be used to compensate the partners. Similarly, rental payments can be used to allocate profits attributable to specific equipment or facilities contributed by a partner.

[26] Ott et al. (2019) provide a framework for assessing various termination scenarios.

A *drag-along* provision *requires* a party not otherwise interested in selling its ownership interest to the third party to do so. A *tag-along* provision gives a party to the alliance who was not originally targeted by the third party the option to join the targeted party in selling its interest to the third party.

Taxes

A partnership structure can allow some partners to receive a larger share of the profits, whereas others receive a larger share of the losses. This flexibility in tax planning is an important factor stimulating the use of partnerships and LLCs. These entities can allocate to each JV partner a portion of a particular class of revenue, income, gain, loss, or expense.[27]

In a JV structured as a corporation, if one partner owns less than 80%, the JV's financial results cannot be included in its consolidated income tax return. This has two effects. First, when earnings are distributed, they are subject to intercorporate dividend taxes. Second, JV losses cannot be used to offset other income earned by the participant. For tax purposes, the preferred alternative to a corporate structure is a pass-through structure, such as a partnership or LLC.

Under the 2017 Tax Cuts and Jobs Act, the IRS requires that pass-through entities give up valuable attributes of a C corporation to avoid double taxation: corporate profits are taxed when earned and again when they are paid to shareholders. LLCs do not allow for management autonomy, continuity of ownership, and the free transferability of shares. Owners of pass-through entities can under the new law deduct up to 20% of their business income from their taxable income until the end of 2025. When coupled with the reduction in the maximum individual tax rate to 37%, qualified pass-through entities have an effective top tax rate of 29.6% (i.e., $.37 \times (1.0 - 0.2)$). This narrowed substantially the difference between the tax benefits of pass-through versus corporate structures for those that qualify for the 20% deduction (Table 16.5).

The extent to which the changes in the tax law will impact pass-through entities varies by profession, filing status, and taxable earnings. Under the new law, if the owner's taxable income is below the threshold ($157,500 for those filing individually and $315,000 for joint filers), the amount that may be deducted from a noncorporate owner's taxable income is 20% of the noncorporate owner's qualified business income (QBI). With certain exclusions, QBI includes all revenues produced by the business less costs incurred in generating those revenues. If the owner is above the threshold, they are subject to limitations and exceptions (see Chapter 12).

How will the new law impact conversions into pass-through organizations or corporations? Those that can take full advantage of the 20% deduction and that are currently incorporated are likely to change to some form of a pass-through entity. Those that cannot because they are in an excluded profession or exceed the income thresholds and are currently a partnership or LLC are likely to incorporate.

TABLE 16.5 Tax advantages of pass-through entities versus corporations before and after the Tax Cuts and Jobs Act of 2017

Old law	Owner-retained profits per $100 of pretax profits[a]	Assumptions
Corporation	$100(1 − 0.35)(1 − 0.396) = $39.26	Corporation distributes 100% of after-tax profits No state taxes
Pass-through entity	$100(1 − 0.396) = $60.40	
New law		
Corporation	$100(1 − 0.21)(1 − 0.37) = $49.77	Corporation distributes 100% of after-tax profits No state taxes 20% business income deduction
Pass-through entity	$100(1 − 0.2)(1 − 0.37) = $50.40[b]	

[a]Maximum federal corporate and individual tax rate under the old law were 35% and 39.6%, respectively. Under the new law, the maximum federal corporate and individual rates are 21% and 37%, respectively.
[b]The maximum effective tax rate for qualified pass-through entities is [($80.0 − $50.40)/$100.00] × 1.00 = 29.6%.

[27] Services provided to the JV, such as accounting, auditing, and so on, are not viewed by the IRS as being "at risk" if the JV fails. The JV should pay prevailing market fees for such services; otherwise such services may be taxable.

Management and organizational issues

Business alliances are most often managed through a steering committee, which has the authority for keeping the venture focused on the strategic objectives agreed to by the partners. To maintain good communication, coordination, and teamwork, the committee should meet at least monthly. The committee should provide operations managers with sufficient autonomy so that they can take responsibility for their actions and be rewarded for their initiative.

One method of control is the *majority–minority* framework, which relies on identifying a dominant partner, usually the one having at least a 50.1% ownership stake. In this scenario, the equity, control, and distribution of rewards reflect the majority–minority relationship. This type of structure promotes the ability to make rapid corrections, defines who is in charge, and is most appropriate for high-risk ventures, in which quick decisions often are required. The major disadvantage is that the minority partner may feel powerless and become passive or alienated.

Another method of control is the *equal division of power* framework, which means equity is split equally. The initial contribution, distribution, decision making, and control are also split equally. This approach helps keep the partners actively engaged and is best suited for partners sharing a common vision and possessing similar corporate cultures. But this approach can lead to deadlocks and the eventual dissolution of the alliance when intractable disagreements arise.

Under the *majority rules* framework, the equity distribution may involve three partners. Whereas two of the partners have large equal shares, the third partner may have less than 10%. The minority partner is used to break deadlocks. This approach enables the primary partners to remain engaged in the enterprise without stalemating the decision-making process.

In the *multiple party* framework, no partner has control; instead, control resides with the venture's management. Decision making can be nimble and made by those who understand the issues best. This framework is well suited for international ventures, in which a country's laws may prohibit a foreign firm from having a controlling interest in a domestic firm. It is common for a domestic company to own the majority of the equity but for the operational control of the venture to reside with the foreign partner. In addition to a proportional split of the dividends paid, the foreign company may receive additional payments in the form of management fees and bonuses.

Regulatory restrictions and notifications

JVs may be subject to Hart-Scott-Rodino filing requirements because the parties to the JV are viewed as acquirers and the JV as a target. For JVs between competitors, to get regulatory approval, competitors should be able to do something together that they could not do alone. Competitors can be relatively confident that a partnership will be acceptable to regulators if, in combination, they control no more than 20% of the market. Project-oriented ventures are looked at most favorably. Collaborative research is encouraged, particularly when the research is shared among all the parties to the alliance. Alliances among competitors are likely to spark a review by the regulators because they have the potential to result in price fixing.

Challenges of cross-border joint ventures

JVs with international partners include challenges not found with alliances involving domestic partners. For most international JVs, a separate legal entity is established with parties to the alliance owning shares or partnership interests. Whether a JV is structured as a corporation or partnership differs from one country to the next. For example, in the United Kingdom, a partnership is not considered a separate legal entity.[28] In France, partnerships generally are corporate structures having a separate legal status. The controlling partner often must be a local resident. Local laws may define how JV managers and board members can be appointed and removed and if intellectual property is protected. Often each party to the JV wants their home country's laws to apply in the event of any dispute. A normal compromise is to select the governing law in a neutral country.

[28] A partnership under English law is not a separate legal entity; therefore the partners and not the partnership would be jointly and severally liable for borrowing and other liabilities.

Governance issues

What is the right size and composition of an international JV board? The answer varies by country, backgrounds of the JV participants, and JV complexity. German boards tend to be the largest in the world followed closely by Swiss, Danish, and Dutch boards. The median size of boards by country ranges from 16.2 in Germany to 10.3 members in the United Kingdom.[29] Boards in the Western European countries are two-tiered, consisting of supervisory and management committees. In contrast, US and UK boards are among the smallest in the world. US boards are dominated by a large number of independent directors. US and UK boards differ with respect to dual chair–CEO positions. Whereas the United Kingdom is dominated by the separation of these positions, in the United States about half of publicly traded firms have separate chair and CEO positions.

The purpose of a board can also be strikingly different across countries. In the United States, the fundamental purpose of the board is generally to promote and protect shareholder interests. In Germany, Japan, and China, boards represent a broader array of constituents including shareholders, employees, the community, and the public.

These differences reflect the degree of ownership concentration, the nature of bank involvement, and state ownership. In Germany, Sweden, and Japan, ownership tends to be heavily concentrated. Consequently, boards tend to be dominated by the largest shareholders. In Germany, large commercial banks through proxy voting often control more than one-fourth of the director positions and board votes at major companies and may have additional influence by having an ownership interest in the business as direct shareholders or lenders. US firms tend to have widely dispersed shareholders; as such, boards do not reflect the major shareholders but are rather selected by individual investors from a slate of candidates put up by the board.

Complex JV boards are likely to be larger and to monitor management more aggressively than in simpler ones. Why? They have higher informational needs. Some JV boards have government involvement, especially in places such as the Middle East, Africa, and China. In some cross-border JVs, the owners are from one country and the managers are from the country where the JV is located, sometimes creating serious communication problems. State involvement can create demands on the JV that have more to do with politics than economics.[30]

Cultural issues

Cultural differences also impact decision making in cross-border JVs. In the United States, individualism and focus on short-term performance are widely accepted principles. Consequently, corporate boards tend to be smaller and delegate more power to the CEO than do European and Asian boards. Smaller boards often are more nimble than larger boards, where decision making tends to be slower because they are subject to more exhaustive discussion. In cross-border JVs, directors on the same board often hold widely divergent cultural perspectives on governance. These include the extent of delegation of decision making to JV management, director involvement in daily operations, fiduciary responsibility to the JV and partners, and how to manage conflicts.

Cultural diversity between alliance partners can have a largely negative impact on the rate of innovation. Why? The complexity of cultural differences between host and home country personnel can create barriers to communication and trust. The situation can be even more complicated when it involves foreign subsidiaries of multinational firms because not only do we have country cultural differences but also differences in organizational styles. Research shows that for technology alliances, these differences can be more readily overcome if the intent is to develop new rather than improve existing technologies because diverse backgrounds and viewpoints seem to have a greater positive impact on the rate of innovation.[31]

Fuji Xerox: the demise of a 57-year-old international joint venture

As the world's longest running JV between a US and a Japanese company, Fuji Xerox was 75% owned by Japan's Fujifilm, a business document solutions firm, and 25% owned by American document processing company Xerox. The JV sold printing and document-related products and services in the Asia-Pacific region. After the 2008 to 2009 global recession, Xerox began to lose money as the market for document processing became increasingly

[29] Spencer Stuart Board Index, 2015; GCC Board of Directors Institute; and Wall Street Partners

[30] Klijn et al., 2019. JV complexity is related to its scope (i.e., number of different products, customers, operations, and geographic diversity).

[31] Elia et al., 2019

competitive. Fujifilm managed to maintain modest revenue growth by diversifying into faster-growing markets and remained profitable, as did Fuji Xerox.

When a series of accounting and management scandals at the JV made headlines in 2017, Xerox tried to make board and management changes in the JV. However, the two partners could not agree on how to govern the JV and on its strategic direction. When these efforts failed, Xerox and Fujifilm reached an agreement in 2018 to create a new company consisting of Fuji Xerox and Xerox. The deal's complexity alienated Xerox shareholders, and Xerox backed out. When their differences proved irreconcilable, dissolution of the JV was inevitable. Fujifilm purchased Xerox's 25% stake in the JV in 2020 for $2.5 billion and allowed its sales partnership between the two companies to lapse in March 2021. At that point, the former partners became rivals in Asia, the United States, and Europe.

Potential impediments to cross-border alliances and minority investments

Known as the Committee on Foreign Investment in the United States (CFIUS), CFIUS reviews foreign acquisitions of American firms for potential security threats. CFIUS was last updated more than a decade ago, and President Donald Trump signed the Foreign Investment Risk Review Modernization Act in mid-2018 with widespread bipartisan support expanding CIFIUS's review authority. Among other things, it covers foreign entities owning a minority position in an acquirer buying a controlling or minority interest in US firms. The new legislation was prompted by complaints that foreign firms were using JVs with US firms or minority interests in such ventures to gain access to technology and proprietary information critical to US security. The new statute gives CFIUS authority to block deals that might result in the loss of sensitive personal data and to initiate investigations instead of waiting for a buyer to seek approval. The expanded authority of CFIUS is likely to lengthen the approval process for certain JV and minority investments and discourage others. See Chapter 2 for more detail on CFIUS.

Recent actions taken in the United Kingdom and Germany in late 2018 suggest similar laws may be put in place covering various types of alliances. Concerns about national security caused the German government to block a proposed purchase of a German power company by a Chinese firm. A proposed Chinese takeover of an engineering company was withdrawn when authorities expressed national security concerns. In the United Kingdom, the government proposed a new law expanding its power to block foreign acquisitions that pose security concerns, and it would also apply to deals involving a foreign buyer acquiring as little as 25% of a UK firm.

Empirical findings

Empirical evidence shows that alliances often create value for their participants, with average announcement-date positive abnormal returns varying from 1% to 3%.[32] However, many alliances do stumble. Despite rapid growth in part reflecting a loosening of antitrust regulatory policies,[33] more than half of all alliances fail to meet expectations.[34]

Although there is substantial evidence that business alliances can create shareholder value for the participating firms, bondholders also benefit. JVs and strategic alliances have been documented to realize positive abnormal returns for bondholders of almost one percent.[35] Why? Because they alleviate cash constraints when partners contribute cash or make a loan or when the alliance has sufficient assets to serve as collateral to borrow on its own. Synergy between partners to the alliance or JV also reduces cost and increases operating cash flow to cover the repayment of interest and principal. Finally, JVs and alliances often provide an array of "real" options (see Chapter 8), giving the participants the flexibility to manage the rate at which they invest in (or exit) the JV.

[32] Johnson et al. (2000); Kale et al. (2002)

[33] Robinson, 2002a

[34] Klein (2004) reports that 55% of alliances fall apart within 3 years of their formation.

[35] Chen et al., 2015

Experience counts

Firms with greater alliance experience enjoy a greater likelihood of success and superior wealth creation than those with little experience.[36] Having engaged in many alliances, a firm creates a greater ability to assimilate and commercialize new information, enabling them to evaluate and screen potential target firms more effectively. Post-acquisition performance can be improved significantly when the target firm has a significant number of alliances because the acquirer's alliance expertise can contribute to better managing the combined firms' alliance portfolios.[37]

Some types of experience can be more valuable than others. What often is most valuable is experience with diverse governance arrangements that vary by level of complexity (e.g., 50/50 JVs; majority-or minority-controlled). This varied experience enables managers of JVs to adapt to specific circumstances rather than simply apply a specific format learned from the past to an entirely new situation.[38]

Impact of alliances on suppliers, customers, and competitors

Strategic alliances can have a salutary effect on the share prices of their suppliers and customers and a negative impact on the share prices of competitors. For alliances created to share technologies or develop new technical capabilities, suppliers benefit from increased sales to the alliance, and customers benefit from using the enhanced technology developed by the alliance in their products. Competitors' share prices decline because of lost sales and earnings to the alliance.[39]

Some things to remember

Business alliances may offer attractive alternatives to M&As. Motivations for alliances include risk sharing, access to new markets, new-product introduction, technology sharing, globalization, a desire to acquire (or exit) a business, and the perception that they are often more acceptable to regulators than M&As. Business alliances may assume a variety of legal structures: corporate, LLCs, partnership, franchise, equity partnership, and written contract. Key deal-structuring issues include the alliance's scope, duration, legal form, governance, and control mechanism.

Chapter discussion questions

16.1 What is an LLC? What are its advantages and disadvantages?
16.2 Why is defining the scope of a business alliance important?
16.3 Discuss ways of valuing tangible and intangible contributions to a JV.
16.4 What are the advantages and disadvantages of the various organizational structures that could be used to manage a business alliance?
16.5 What are the common reasons for the termination of a business alliance?
16.6 Google invested $1 billion for a 5% stake in America Online (AOL) as part of a partnership that expands the firm's existing search engine deal to include collaboration on advertising, instant messaging, and video. Under the deal, Google would have the customary rights afforded a minority investor. What rights or terms do you believe Google would have negotiated in this transaction? What rights do you believe AOL might want?
16.7 Conoco Phillips announced the purchase of 7.6% of Lukoil's (a largely government-owned Russian oil and gas company) stock for $2.36 billion during a government auction of Lukoil's stock. Conoco would have one seat on Lukoil's board. As a minority investor, how could Conoco protect its interests?
16.8 Johnson & Johnson sued Amgen over their 14-year alliance to sell a blood-enhancing treatment called erythropoietin. The partners ended up squabbling over sales rights and a spin-off drug and could not agree on future products for the JV. Amgen won the right in arbitration to sell a chemically similar medicine that can be taken weekly rather than daily. What could these companies have done before forming the alliance to have

[36] Kale et al., 2002

[37] Cho et al., 2018

[38] Piaskowska et al., 2019

[39] Chang, 2008.

mitigated the problems that arose after the alliance was formed? Why do you believe they may have avoided addressing these issues at the outset?

16.9 General Motors, a US-based global auto manufacturer, agreed to purchase 20% of Japan's Fuji Heavy Industries, Ltd., the manufacturer of Subaru vehicles, for $1.4 billion. Why do you believe that General Motors initially may have wanted to limit its investment to 20%?

16.10 Through its alliance with Best Buy, Microsoft is selling its products—including Microsoft Network (MSN) Internet access services and handheld devices, such as digital telephones, handheld organizers, and WebTV, that connect to the web—through kiosks in Best Buy's 354 stores nationwide. In exchange, Microsoft has invested $200 million in Best Buy. What do you believe were the motivations for this strategic alliance?

Answers to these Discussion Questions are available in the Online Instructor's Manual for instructors using this book.

End-of-chapter case study: Disney creates order out of chaos

Case study objectives

To illustrate

- How multiple shareholders and partners in business alliances can contribute to indecision and missed opportunities because of conflicting objectives
- Why exit strategies should be negotiated by each party to the alliance when it is created
- When partners can become direct competitors as their alliance expectations change

Video streaming provider Hulu formed in 2008 is an example of how not to organize a JV. To appreciate why, we need to understand the reasons for its inception. Hulu is an American subscription video-on-demand service providing consumer access to a diverse set of popular TV series. Founding investors included News Corp (owner of 21st Century Fox), TV and theme park owner NBCUniversal, and private equity investor Providence Equity Partners. Later, entertainment and media giant Disney acquired a 10% ownership stake in 2009, and TV and film producer Time Warner bought a 10% stake in 2016 seeing Hulu as an additional distribution channel for its content. Their interest also reflected the belief that Hulu represented a way of reducing the loss of revenue to pirated content viewed by millions on YouTube. Providence Equity, whose role had been to serve as an independent voice amid the media company investors, sold its interest in 2012.

The ownership distribution underwent a sea change in March 2019 when Disney acquired 21st Century Fox from News Corp, giving it a 60% majority stake in Hulu. AT&T, which had acquired Time Warner in 2018, sold back its roughly 10% stake in April 2019, valuing Hulu at $15 billion. On May 14, 2019, ownership and control became more firmly ensconced in Disney's hands when it reached an agreement with the last remaining minority owner, Comcast. The agreement ceded control of Hulu to Disney effective immediately and provided a path for Disney to buy Comcast's 33% ownership position in Hulu as early as 2024.

The deal ends the long and chaotic history for Hulu. When Hulu had multiple owners, its mission was unclear, leading to conflicts as some owners wanted to launch their own streaming video channels to exploit this increasingly popular way of accessing content. Nevertheless, Hulu managed to grow its subscriber base from 6 million in 2014 to more than 26 million by the end 2018. How? By moving aggressively into both original content and offering a pay-TV distributor service called Hulu Plus, a much cheaper alternative to traditional cable and satellite TV.

With the purchase of AT&T's stake, Disney increased its proportionate share from 60% to 66% (i.e., Disney was entitled to 60% of AT&T's 10% share) with Comcast (owner of NBCUniversal) retaining a 33% ownership position. But because NBCUniversal was a founding shareholder, Comcast retained control over certain major decisions about how to operate the business. It also had three board seats that will be vacated as part of the new deal with Disney.

Under the agreement, Disney can require Comcast to sell its one-third ownership position as early as January 2024 through a so-called "put/call" arrangement. Comcast can require Disney to buy (put option) NBCUniversal's interest at fair market value at the time of the sale, giving the firm some flexibility in timing when to sell. Disney can require NBCUniversal to sell (call option) its interest to Disney at fair market value at the time of the sale.

In either case, Disney would own 100% of Hulu. However, Disney has guaranteed a sale price for Comcast that represents a minimum total equity value of Hulu of $27.5 billion. This provides for Comcast to receive a minimum price of at least $9.1 billion (i.e., .33 × $27.5 billion) when the sale is completed assuming Comcast's ownership share remains at 33%.

Comcast will have the option but not obligation to fund its proportionate share of Hulu's future capital requirements (so-called capital calls). If Comcast chooses not to fund its share, its ownership stake will be diluted as Disney's share increases as it satisfies the total capital requirement. Disney has agreed that only $1.5 billion of any year's capital call can be funded through further equity investments. Any capital expenditures in excess of that annual amount would be financed by borrowing, which would not dilute Comcast's position. The agreement calls for Comcast's ownership interest in Hulu to never fall below 21% regardless of whether Comcast funds its share of capital calls. If Comcast's share falls to 21%, Comcast is guaranteed to receive at least $5.8 billion under the put/call agreement (i.e., 0.21 times $27.5 billion).

Hulu, reliant on next-day and library programming from a number of networks, has a new deal to license NBCUniversal programming for both its on-demand and live services through 2024. But NBCUniversal can terminate most of its content licensing agreements with Hulu in 3 years. After NBCUniversal launches its own streaming service, it has the right to stream programming it currently licenses exclusively to Hulu on its own service in exchange for reducing Hulu's license fee.

Disney, which launched its own direct-to-consumer streaming service called Disney Plus, has ambitious plans for Hulu. Whereas the firm has said its own streaming service would focus on content for families and children, Hulu is expected to be an outlet for shows aimed at adults. After buying most of the entertainment assets of 21st Century Fox, Disney now owns the Twentieth Century Fox film and program library, as well as the FX cable channel. Owning Hulu will allow Disney to integrate Hulu into its direct-to-consumer business and to sell bundles of services under the Disney brand.

Hulu's operating losses in 2019 exceeded $1.5 billion. The JV is projected to remain in the red until 2023 or 2024. Comcast, interested in starting its own video streaming business, will be able to exit Hulu without having to sell its interest immediately because it sees Hulu's valuation appreciating substantially over the next 5 years.

Discussion questions

1. What were the primary motivations for Disney and Comcast to reach an agreement allowing Disney to take full ownership of Hulu by 2024?
2. What were the primary assumptions underlying Disney and Comcast's strategies with respect to Hulu?
3. How did Hulu's original objectives conflict with its organizational arrangement?
4. What alternatives to a JV did the original investors in Hulu have? Why was the JV structure chosen?

Solutions to these case study questions are found in the Online Instructor's Manual for instructors using this book.

CHAPTER

17

Alternative exit and restructuring strategies

divestitures, spin-offs, carve-outs, split-offs, and tracking stocks

OUTLINE

Mergers, Acquisitions, and Other Restructuring Activities, Eleventh Edition
https://doi.org/10.1016/B978-0-12-819782-0.00017-4

Experience is the name everyone gives to their mistakes. —*Oscar Wilde*

Inside M&As: reducing leverage through restructuring

KEY POINTS

- Excessive leverage limits a firm's ability to reinvest in their most attractive businesses and to pay dividends thereby creating investor angst.
- Reducing leverage enables a firm to invest as attractive opportunities arise.
- To reduce leverage, firms often resort to selling "nonstrategic" assets.

It wasn't until early 2019 that American icon General Electric's (GE's) share price rebounded after having plummeted for more than 3 years. Why? Responding to investor pressure, the firm took action to allay investor concerns by raising $24.3 billion in asset sales ($21.4 billion for its BioPharma business and $2.9 billion for its transportation business). Under the bone-crushing weight of $100 billion in debt, impatient investors concerned about the firm's ability to maintain its current dividend and debt service amid shrinking operating cash flow drove the firm's share price down by 90% from its level at the beginning of 2018. And the collapse in the share price accelerated late in 2018 when GE discontinued paying a dividend.

Investors applauded the asset sales by bidding up the firm's share price by 25% after the announcement that it had reached an agreement to sell its biopharma business. No longer appearing desperate, the sale gave GE time to negotiate higher prices for other nonstrategic assets. But the pressure was by no means off. GE faced the dual challenge of further reducing its debt while articulating an exciting growth strategy to reignite investor enthusiasm. Even if investors could be convinced that the firm's view of the future would push its share price to new heights, GE had to reduce debt sufficiently to reinvest for future growth.

An additional benefit of divesting assets was the increased focus on fewer businesses. GE had long been viewed as an unnecessarily complex holding company. Its diverse set of businesses not only made it difficult for investors to value the consolidated firm but also for managers to fully understand and properly prioritize investment opportunities. Fewer businesses could make the firm easier to manage and less opaque to outside investors.

GE's ballooning debt resulted from a series of missteps made by the firm during the previous decade. GE had viewed the oil and gas industry and power generation businesses as attractive investment opportunities to replace the growth that had formerly come from GE Capital. The latter had pushed the firm to the brink of bankruptcy during the 2008 to 2009 recession, when it became embroiled in the collapsing global financial markets. GE had built up its oil and gas business just as oil prices plunged. The power-generation business also proved vulnerable to the downturn in the market for smaller and replacement generating equipment as renewable power sources (and energy conservation programs) curbed the demand for new gas turbines.

Investors had shown little patience with GE's efforts to climb out of its financial hole. John Flannery, who took over as the firm's CEO in August 2017, saw GE as a smaller, simpler, and more efficient firm. However, he failed to communicate a strategic direction for the firm that proved compelling to investors. They saw his early cost-cutting moves as too little and became frustrated when he suspended dividend payments. Mr. Flannery was replaced by Larry Culp, former CEO of Danaher Inc. (Danaher) in October 2018.

Danaher had approached GE about selling its Life Sciences business with annual revenue of more than $20 billion in early 2018 but was rebuffed as GE was unwilling to part with the profitable and fast-growing unit. With annual revenue of $3 billion, the biopharma business had been part of the life sciences unit. Danaher again approached GE about buying its life sciences business late in 2018 and found Mr. Culp and the GE board more receptive. Although unwilling to sell the entire life sciences unit, GE parted with the biopharma business to demonstrate to investors that it was making progress in reducing its indebtedness.

Although the sale of GE's Transportation unit to Webtec closed in February 2019, the sale of the biopharma business was not completed until late 2019. GE continues to consider an initial public offering (IPO) for its remaining health care businesses, which appear not to be a critical part of the firm's emerging focus on jet engines and power-generation equipment.

Chapter overview

Most businesses, particularly large, highly diversified firms, are constantly looking for ways they can enhance shareholder value by changing the composition of their assets, liabilities, equity, and operations. These activities generally are referred to as restructuring strategies. Restructuring may embody both growth strategies and exit strategies. Growth strategies have been discussed elsewhere in this book. The focus in this chapter is on strategic options allowing the firm to maximize shareholder value by redeploying assets through downsizing or refocusing the parent company. As such, this chapter discusses the myriad motives for exiting businesses, the various restructuring strategies for doing so, and why firms select one strategy over other options.

In this context, equity carve-outs, spin-offs, divestitures, split-offs and split-ups are discussed separately rather than as a specialized form of a carve-out.[1] The chapter concludes with a discussion of what empirical studies say are the primary determinants of financial returns to shareholders resulting from undertaking the various restructuring strategies. Voluntary and involuntary restructuring and reorganization (both inside and outside the protection of bankruptcy court) also represent exit strategies for firms and are discussed in detail in Chapter 18. A review of the current chapter (including practice questions with answers) is available in the file folder titled "Student Study Guide" on the companion website to this book (https://www.elsevier.com/books-and-journals/book-companion/9780128197820).

Why do firms exit businesses?

Theories abound! Although not an exhaustive list, some of the most common are discussed next.

Increasing corporate focus

Firms often choose to simplify their business portfolio by focusing on units with the highest growth potential and by exiting units not germane to the firm's core business strategy. Such firms can reduce cost by eliminating layers of management that existed at the corporate level. Increasing focus often improves firm value by allocating limited resources better and by reducing competition for such resources within multidivisional firms.

[1] In some accounting texts, divestitures (sometimes referred to as *sell-offs*), spin-offs, and split-offs are all viewed as different forms of equity carve-outs and discussed in terms of how they affect the parent firm's shareholders' equity for financial-reporting purposes. Alternatively, some analysts describe these restructuring activities as separation strategies in which the parent is able to separate from itself all or a portion of an operating business.

Underperforming businesses

Parent firms often exit businesses failing to meet or exceed the parent's required returns. Drugmaker Merck spun off 90 slow-growing products that had lost patent protection into a new company in 2020 so that it could focus on faster-growing cancer drugs. Amid plummeting readership and advertising revenues, Gannett, Tribune Company, and E.W. Scripps, firms that had historically grown as print newspapers but that had expanded into other forms of media, dumped their print businesses in 2015 through spin-offs.

Regulatory concerns

A firm with substantial market share purchasing a direct competitor may create antitrust concerns. The combination of such firms may be viewed as anticompetitive if the combined firms' market share exceeds some threshold. Regulatory agencies still may approve the merger if the acquirer divests some of its operations, the target's, or some combination of the two to establish other competitors in the industry. To receive regulatory approval for its acquisition of 21st Century Fox in 2019, Walt Disney Co. sold 21 regional sports networks it had acquired as part of the deal to TV-station giant Sinclair Broadcast Group Inc. for $10 billion. Antitrust regulators were concerned that Disney already held an 80% stake in sports network ESPN.

Lack of fit

Synergies anticipated by the parent among its businesses may not materialize. TRW's decision to sell its commercial and consumer information services businesses came after years of trying to find a significant fit with its space and defense operations.

Tax considerations

Tax benefits may be realized through a restructuring of the business. Nursing home operator Sun Healthcare Systems (Sun) contributed its nursing home real estate operations to a real estate investment trust (REIT) through a spin-off. Because REITs do not pay taxes on income that is distributed to shareholders, Sun was able to enhance shareholder value by eliminating the double taxation of income, once by the parent and again by investors when dividends are paid.

The type of taxes levied also can impact a restructuring strategy. When dividends are taxed significantly higher than capital gains, shareholders may prefer to have the firm in which they are invested sold rather than to receive dividends from the firm.[2] This is particularly true for privately held companies in which investors do not have ready access to a liquid public market in which they can sell their shares.

Raising funds

Parent firms may fund new initiatives or reduce leverage through the sale or partial sale of units no longer considered strategic. In late 2019, Anheuser-Busch Inbev sold its slow-growing Australian beer assets for $11.3 billion to Japan's Asahi Group Holdings to whittle away at the $100 billion-plus debt on its balance sheet incurred in its acquisition of US brewer SABMiller.

Worth more to others

Others may view a firm's operating assets as more valuable than the parent firm. In 2017, toolmaker Stanley Black & Decker (Stanley) acquired financially ailing retailer Sears' Craftsman tool trademark for $900 million. Sears used the money to reduce indebtedness, and Stanley expanded sales in the United States under the widely recognized Craftsman brand.

Rupert Murdoch, after having spent decades building his media empire 21st Century Fox, reached a deal to divest the firm's entertainment assets to Disney in December 2017 for $51 billion. The remaining 21st Century's assets were to be spun off to its shareholders. However, Comcast Cable Company entered with a more attractive offer

[2] Ohrna and Seegert, 2019

immediately after the announcement of 21st Century's deal with Disney. It would be another 7 months before Disney was able to close the deal in mid-2018 with a stunning $71.3 billion, 40% higher than what it had offered 7 months earlier.

Risk reduction

A firm may reduce risk associated with a unit by selling or spinning off the business. For example, major tobacco companies have been under pressure for years to divest or spin off their food businesses because of the litigation risk associated with their tobacco subsidiaries. Altria bowed to such pressure with the spin-off of its Kraft Food operations.

Discarding unwanted businesses from prior acquisitions

Acquirers often find themselves with certain target firm assets that do not fit their primary strategy. Such assets may be divested to raise funds to help pay for the acquisition and to enable management to focus on integrating the remaining businesses into the parent without the distraction of having to manage nonstrategic assets. When Northrop Grumman acquired TRW, it announced it would retain TRW's space and defense businesses and divest operations not pertinent to Northrop's core defense business.

Avoiding conflicts with customers

For years, many of the regional Bell operating companies (i.e., RBOCs) that AT&T spun off in 1984 have been interested in competing in the long-distance market, which would put them in direct competition with their former parent. Similarly, AT&T sought to penetrate the regional telephone markets by gaining access to millions of households by acquiring cable TV companies. In preparation for the implementation of these plans, AT&T announced in 1995 that it would divide the company into three publicly traded global companies to avoid conflicts between AT&T's former equipment manufacturer and its main customers, the RBOCs.

Increasing transparency

Firms may be opaque to investors due to their diverse operations. GE is an example, operating dozens of separate businesses in many countries. Even with access to financial and competitive information on each business, it is challenging for any investor to value properly such a diversified firm. By reducing its complexity, a firm may make it easier for investors to assess accurately its true value. In an effort to restore profitability and achieve greater focus, GE announced a series of far-reaching restructuring programs in 2019.

Divestitures

A divestiture is the sale of a portion of a firm's assets to an outside party, generally resulting in a cash infusion to the parent. Such assets may include a product line, a subsidiary, or a division.

Motives for divestitures

Divestitures often represent a way of raising cash. A firm may choose to sell an undervalued or underperforming operation that it determined to be nonstrategic or unrelated to the core business and to use the proceeds of the sale to fund investments in potentially higher-return opportunities, including paying off debt. Alternatively, the firm may choose to divest the undervalued business and return the cash to shareholders through either a liquidating dividend[3] or share repurchase.

[3] A liquidating dividend is a type of payment made by a corporation to its shareholders during its partial or full liquidation. They represent a return of capital to shareholders since such payments exceed the firm's net income and as a return of capital are typically not taxable to shareholders. This distinguishes a liquidating dividend from regular dividends, which are issued from the company's operating profits or retained earnings.

Corporate portfolio reviews

Parent firms often conduct strategic analyses to determine if its businesses are worth more to shareholders if they are sold and the proceeds are returned to the shareholders or reinvested in more profitable opportunities. In the United States, about three-fourths of divestitures result from portfolio reviews.[4] This process is best done at the corporate level without involvement of personnel from the firm's business units, to ensure that decision making is objective. After the decision to divest has been made, involving business unit–level managers is critical to a successful selling process because of their intimate knowledge of the business and their involvement in providing information during buyer due diligence.

To sell or not to sell

An analysis undertaken to determine if a business should be sold involves a multistep process. These steps include determining the after-tax cash flows generated by the unit, an appropriate discount rate reflecting the risk of the business, the after-tax market value (MV) of the business, and the after-tax value of the business to the parent. The decision to sell or retain the business depends on a comparison of the after-tax value of the business to the parent with the after-tax proceeds from the sale of the business. These steps are outlined in more detail next.

Step 1: calculating after-tax cash flows

To decide if a business is worth more to the shareholder if sold, the parent must first estimate the after-tax cash flows of the business viewed on a standalone basis. This requires adjusting the cash flows for intercompany sales and the cost of services (e.g., legal, treasury, and audit) provided by the parent. Intercompany sales refer to operating-unit revenue generated by selling products or services to another unit owned by the same parent. Intercompany sales should be restated to ensure they are valued at market prices.[5] Moreover, services provided by the parent to the business may be subsidized or at a markup over actual cost. Operating profits should be reduced by the amount of any subsidies and increased by any markup over what the business would have to pay if it purchased comparable services outside of the parent firm.

Step 2: estimating the discount rate

After cash flows have been determined, a discount rate should be estimated that reflects the risk characteristics of the industry in which the business competes. The cost of capital of other firms in the same industry (or firms in other industries exhibiting similar profitability, growth, and risk characteristics) is often a good proxy for the discount rate of the business being analyzed.

Step 3: estimating the after-tax market value of the business

The discount rate from step 2 then is used to estimate the MV of the projected after-tax cash flows of the business determined in step 1. Step 3 also requires the estimation of an appropriate terminal value for the business (see Chapter 7).

Step 4: estimating the value of the business to the parent

The after-tax equity value (EV) of the business as part of the parent is estimated by subtracting the MV of the business's liabilities (L) from its after-tax MV as a standalone operation. This relationship can be expressed as follows:

$$EV = MV - L$$

EV is a measure of the after-tax MV of the shareholder equity of the business, in which the shareholder is the parent firm.

[4] Gordon, March 2, 2019

[5] In vertically integrated firms such as steelmakers, much of the revenue generated by a firm's iron ore and coal operations comes from sales to the parent firm's steelmaking unit. The parent may value this revenue for financial-reporting purposes using transfer prices. If such prices do not reflect market prices, intercompany revenue may be artificially high or low, depending on whether the transfer prices are higher or lower than market prices.

Step 5: deciding to sell

The decision to sell or retain the business is made by comparing the EV with the after-tax sale value (SV) of the business. Assuming other considerations do not outweigh any after-tax gain on the sale of the business, the decision to sell or retain can be summarized as follows:

$$\text{If SV} > \text{EV, divest.}$$

$$\text{If SV} < \text{EV, retain.}$$

Although the SV may exceed the EV of the business, the parent may choose to retain the business for strategic reasons. The parent may believe that the business's products facilitate the sale of other products the firm offers. For example, Amazon.com breaks even on the sale of Kindle e-book readers while expecting to make money on electronic books that will be downloaded via the Kindle. In another instance, the divestiture of one subsidiary of a diversified parent may increase operating expenses for other parent operations. One reason given for Hewlett-Packard's (HP's) decision not to sell its personal computer (PC) unit after publicly announcing its intention to do so was the potential for a one-time increase in expenses after the sell-off of the unit.[6]

Timing of the sale

Obviously, the best time to sell a business is when the owner does have to sell or the demand for the business is greatest. Indeed, firms with more divestiture experience tend to sell during merger waves.[7] Selling when business confidence is high, stock prices are rising, and interest rates are low can fetch a higher price for the unit. If the business to be sold is highly cyclical, the sale should be timed, if possible, to coincide with the firm's peak-year earnings.

The selling process

Selling firms choose a process that best serves their objectives and influences the types of buyers that are attracted (e.g., strategic versus private equity). The selling process may be reactive or proactive (Fig. 17.1).

Reactive sales occur when the parent is unexpectedly approached by a buyer, either for the entire firm or for a portion of the firm such as a product line or subsidiary. If the bid is attractive, the parent firm may choose to reach a negotiated settlement with the bidder without investigating other options. This may occur if the parent is concerned about potential degradation of its business, or that of a subsidiary, if its interest in selling becomes public knowledge. In contrast, proactive sales may be characterized as public or private solicitations.

In a public sale or auction, a firm announces publicly that it is putting itself, a subsidiary, or a product line up for sale. Potential buyers contact the seller. This is a way to identify easily interested parties; however, this approach can attract unqualified bidders or those seeking to obtain proprietary information through the due diligence process.

In a private or controlled sale, the parent firm may hire an investment banker or undertake on its own to identify potential buyers. After a preferred potential buyer or list of qualified buyers has been compiled, contact is made.[8] In late 2019, Swiss confectioner Nestlé reached an agreement to sell its mature skin-health business for $10.1 billion after having entered into exclusive talks with private equity firm EQT and the Abu Dhabi Investment Authority. The buyers fit Nestlé's criteria for evaluating qualified buyers: they had cash and substantial acquisition experience and were highly motivated. They were under pressure by their investors to invest their growing cash hoards in a business that required little continuing investment.

In either a public or a private sale, interested parties sign confidentiality agreements before being given access to proprietary information, which can include a financial forecast provided by the selling firm. Experienced buyers know such forecasts tend to be optimistic and often discount them by 25% to 30%. The challenge for the seller is to manage this information, which can grow into thousands of pages of documents and spreadsheets, and to provide

[6] Such expenses included the need to establish new infrastructure and systems for information technology, support, sales, and distribution channels for other businesses that had been using the PC unit's infrastructure. In addition, other HP operating businesses would lose volume discounts on purchases of components enjoyed as a result of the huge volume of such purchases made by the PC business.

[7] Humphrey-Jenner et al., 2019

[8] See the discussion of the screening and contacting process (deal sourcing) in Chapter 5 for more details.

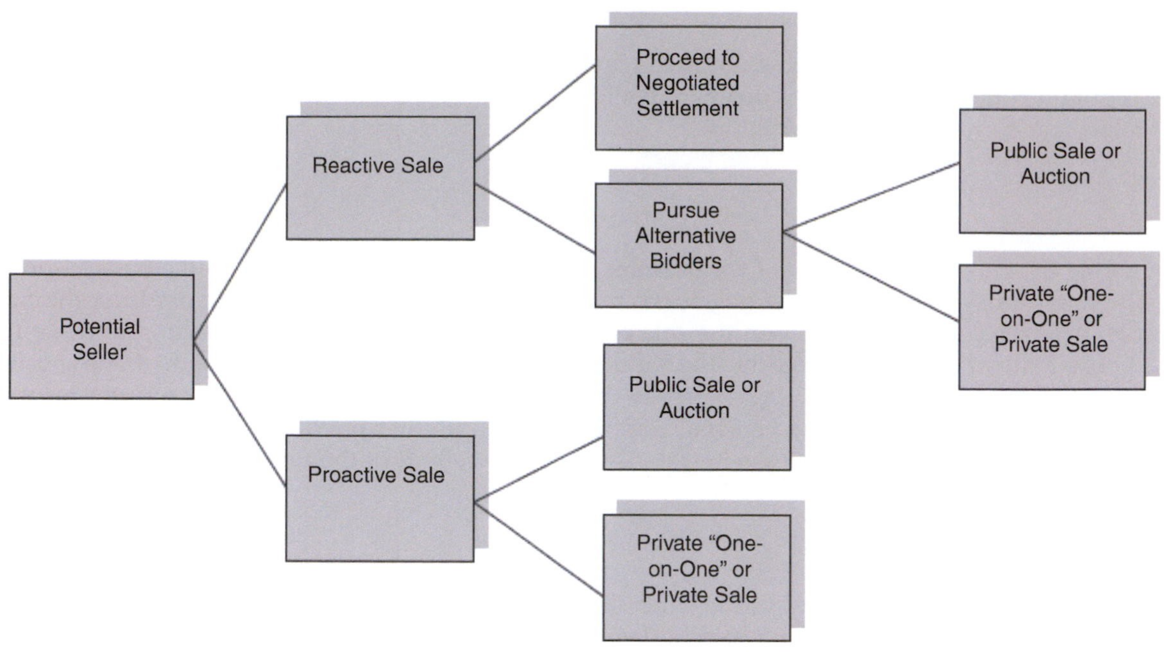

FIGURE 17.1 **The selling process.**

easy and secure access to all interested parties. This may be accomplished online through *virtual data rooms* (VDRs), particularly when the seller is represented by an investment bank.[9]

Because so much data are released, there is a significant cost to the selling firm if a sale does not take place. That is, even though they are required according to the confidentiality agreement to return any proprietary information they possess and not to use it for competitive purposes, competitors have knowledge that they can (and often do) use to gain a competitive advantage.

In private sales, bidders may be asked to sign a standstill agreement requiring them not to make an unsolicited bid. Parties signing these agreements then submit preliminary, nonbinding "indications of interest" (i.e., a single number or a bid within a range). Parties submitting such bids are ranked by the selling company by bid size, form of payment, the ability of the bidder to finance the transaction, form of acquisition, and anticipated ease of doing the deal. A small number of those submitting preliminary bids are then asked to submit a legally binding best and final offer. At this point, the seller may choose to initiate an auction among the most attractive bids or to go directly into negotiating a purchase agreement with a single party.

Choosing the right selling process

Early board involvement in developing a divestiture strategy tends to result in higher premiums paid to selling firm shareholders. Why? The board actively contributes to the selection of the appropriate selling process and monitors the actions of the CEO throughout the process.[10] Selling firms may choose to negotiate with a single firm, to control the number of potential bidders, or to engage in a public auction (Table 17.1). Large firms often choose to sell themselves, major product lines, or subsidiaries through "one-on-one" negotiations with a single bidder deemed to have the greatest synergy with the selling firm.

An auction is often used when selling smaller firms that are difficult to value in an effort to attract more bidders. Also, money-losing units that are perceived as potential threats to current competitors may initiate an auction because an existing competitor may bid for the unit to prevent others from acquiring the operation. Examples

[9] The VDR is intended to replace the paper-based data room and the challenges of keeping such information current and secure. Because the VDR is searchable electronically, bidders have easier and more rapid access to the specific information they are seeking. Because multiple parties can access the information simultaneously from anywhere in the world unaware of the presence of others, the VDR provides for more efficient and thorough due diligence. VDRs also allow for online questions and answers. The major limitations of the VDR are the expense and technical expertise required and the inability to meet in person the management of the unit to be sold.

[10] Demirtas, 2017

TABLE 17.1 Choosing the right selling process

Selling process	Advantages and disadvantages
One-on-one negotiations (single bidder)	Enables the seller to select the buyer with the greatest synergy Minimizes disruptive due diligence Limits the potential for loss of proprietary information to competitors May exclude potentially attractive bidders
Public auction (no limit on number of bidders)	Most appropriate for small, private, or hard-to-value firms May discourage bidders concerned about undisciplined bidding by uninformed bidders Potentially disruptive because of multiple due diligence activities
Controlled auction (limited number of bidders)	Enables the seller to select potential buyers with the greatest synergy Sparks competition without the disruptive effects of public auctions May exclude potentially attractive bidders

include Facebook's $1 billion takeover of Instagram, Yahoo's $1.1 billion purchase of Tumblr, and eBay's $2.6 billion buyout of Skype.

The mix of bidders in an auction can impact premiums paid for the target firm. Bids made by strategic buyers reflect their perceived synergy with the target firm; in contrast, financial buyers base their bids on a desired target rate of return. Financial buyers cannot pay as much as a strategic buyer because they do not rely on synergy for value creation. Whereas premiums paid by strategic buyers in auctions average about 28% of the current value of the target, financial buyers' premiums paid average about 19%.[11] However, for large divisional buyouts in which information about the unit is widely known, private equity firms often outbid strategic buyers based on their perceived ability to restructure the division, improve efficiency, and increase revenue.[12]

When public auctions fail to produce a bid acceptable to the seller, negotiating leverage often shifts to buyers willing to enter into direct negotiations with the seller after the auction has been completed. These negotiations frequently result in the acquirer paying lower premiums and earning higher financial returns compared with both successful auctions and negotiations with a single bidder that could have been undertaken at the outset.[13]

Public auctions may discourage some firms from bidding because of the potential for overly aggressive bidding by relatively uninformed bidders boosting the price to excessive levels. The private or controlled sale among a small number of carefully selected bidders may spark competition to boost the selling price while minimizing the deleterious effects of public auctions.

Pfizer's 2012 auction of its baby food business is an example of a controlled auction. Pfizer sought bids from those it knew could benefit from the unit's exposure to emerging markets and had the financial wherewithal to pay a substantial premium. The auction process involving Swiss-based Nestlé and France's Groupe Danone went through several rounds before Nestlé's $11.85 billion bid was accepted by Pfizer. At 19.8 times earnings before interest, taxes, depreciation, and amortization (EBITDA), the bid was considerably higher than that of the 15.7 multiple Nestlé paid for Gerber's baby food operations in 2007.

About half of corporate mergers and acquisitions (M&A) transactions involve "one-on-one" negotiations. The remaining deals involve public or controlled auctions in which the sellers contacted an average of 10 potential bidders, with some contacting as many as 150. The financial returns to the selling firm's shareholders appear to be about the same regardless of the way in which the business is sold, although auctions are more often used when uncertainty is high.[14]

For larger target firms, one-on-one negotiation is more common because there are fewer potential buyers, often resulting in a higher purchase price.[15] This is because of the selling firm's being able to share more proprietary information with potential buyers. In an auction involving many bidders, the likelihood that such information could leak to competitors is much higher.

[11] Gorbenko, 2018

[12] Hege et al., 2018

[13] Chira et al., 2017

[14] Gentry et al., 2019

[15] Boone and Mulherin, 2009

These findings seem at odds with conventional wisdom: auctions should result, on average, in higher returns for selling-company shareholders, assuming that more bidders are usually better than fewer bidders. Conventional wisdom presumes all bidders have access to the same information and have the financial ability to finance their bids. As previously noted, some qualified bidders may choose to refrain from bidding in an auction, concerned about overpaying for the target firm. Another risk to a seller of an auction is that it may attract a single viable bidder. If the potential buyer becomes aware that there are no other interested parties, negotiating leverage shifts from the seller to the buyer. This usually results in a lower premium paid for the target firm than may have been achieved had the seller undertaken a one-on-one negotiation.[16]

The fact that most deals involve few bidders does not suggest that the bidding process is not competitive.[17] The seller must maintain the perception throughout a one-on-one negotiation that other potential bidders exist but were not included in the process for reasons ranging from their exhibiting less potential synergy to concerns about loss of competitive data to worries about not receiving regulatory approval. Often the threat of rival bids is enough to raise bids. Such latent competition influences bid prices the most when market liquidity is greatest such that potential bidders have relatively inexpensive access to funds through borrowing or new equity issues.

Ultimately, premiums are affected by many factors relating to deal and industry attributes. Premiums are defined in the media as the excess of the offer price over the target's share price immediately before the deal announcement date. A more accurate estimate includes the sum of the increase in the target's share price in the weeks before the announcement (i.e., the run-up) plus the excess of the offer price over the run-up (i.e., the mark-up). The run-up reflects anticipated synergy from combining the target and acquiring firms. The bidder may be willing to mark up the offer price above the run-up if it believes the preannouncement-date target price increase did not fully reflect anticipated synergies. Table 17.2 provides a summary of factors found to be determinants of purchase price premiums grouped by financial market considerations as well as target and acquirer characteristics.

The results shown in this Table 17.2 are based on deals initiated by outside bidders, but in fact about 15% to 20% of sales are initiated by the selling company. Seller-initiated deals are highly correlated with CEO equity ownership. A combination of lucrative stock, stock option grants, and golden parachutes can motivate CEOs to promote deal negotiations. Such deals are correlated with higher takeover premiums.[18]

Tax and accounting considerations for divestitures

The divesting firm posts a gain or loss for financial-reporting purposes equal to the difference between the fair value of the payment received for the divested operation and its book value. For tax purposes, the gain or loss is the difference between the proceeds and the parent's tax basis in the stock or assets.[19] Capital gains are taxed at the same rate as other business income.

Spin-offs

A spin-off is a stock dividend paid by a firm to its current shareholders consisting of shares in an existing or newly created subsidiary. No shareholder approval is required because only the board of directors may decide the amount, type, and timing of dividends. Such distributions are made in direct proportion to the shareholders' current holdings of the parent's stock. As such, the proportional ownership of shares in the subsidiary is the same as the stockholders' proportional ownership of shares in the parent firm. The new entity has its own management and operates independent of the parent company. Unlike the divestiture or equity carve-out (explained later in this chapter), the spin-off does not result in a cash infusion to the parent. After the spin-off, shareholders own both parent company shares and shares in the unit involved in the spin-off.

Although spin-offs may be less cumbersome than divestitures, their execution is challenging. The parent must ensure that the unit to be spun off is viable and disentangled from other parent operations, and that the parent has no ongoing liabilities associated with the spun-off unit. If the unit goes into bankruptcy shortly after the

[16] Volkov, 2016

[17] Aktas et al., 2010

[18] Fidrmuc et al., 2017

[19] Book and tax basis can be quite different. For example, depreciation expense reduces the book value of a tangible asset for financial reporting purposes. However, for tax purposes, the value of the asset may be increased because of depreciation recapture.

TABLE 17.2 Factors affecting purchase price premiums

Factor	Description
Financial market considerations	
Run-up in preannouncement target share price	Although the run-up may cause bidders unsure of having adequate information to increase their offer price, there is little evidence that bidders pay for anticipated synergies twice (i.e., when the target's share price increases in advance of the deal's announcement plus the excess of the offer price over the run-up.)[76]
Credit rating	Rated firms on average pay a 3.3% higher premium, reflecting their lower cost of capital than nonrated acquirers. Bidders tend to pay lower premiums when the target firm has bonds that are rated, as the target is more transparent and more easily valued.[77]
Investor consensus around target share price	Acquisition premiums tend to be higher whenever there is considerable disagreement among bidders as to the value of the target, possibly reflecting more active bidding for the target firm.[78]
Media coverage	Media pessimism about a deal can force the acquirer to pay a higher premium to compensate target shareholders for their higher risk level.[79]
Target characteristics	
Net synergy potential	Purchase premiums are likely to increase the greater the perceived net synergy. Net synergy often is greatest in related firms.[80] Premiums are likely larger if most of the synergy is provided by the target.
Growth potential	Targets displaying greater growth potential relative to competitors generally command higher premiums.[81]
Target size	Buyers pay more for smaller targets because of the likely ease of integration.[82]
Target's eagerness to sell	Targets with a strong desire to sell typically receive lower premiums because of their relatively weak negotiating positions.[83]
Industry growth prospects	The magnitude of premiums varies substantially across industries, reflecting differences in expected growth rates.[84]
Target innovativeness	Highly innovative targets are more likely to receive higher premiums.[85]
Industry structure	Targets in industries undergoing consolidation command higher premiums than other industries as acquirers attempt to eliminate industry excess capacity.[86]
Acquirer characteristics	
Desire for control	Buyers pay more for control of firms with weak financial performance because of potential gains from making better business decisions.
Hubris	Excessive confidence may lead bidders to overpay.[87]
Financial leverage (debt/equity)	Highly leveraged buyers are disciplined by their lenders not to overpay; relatively unleveraged buyers often are prone to pay excessive premiums.[88] However, overleveraged acquirers are willing to pay higher premiums for targets which would increase their debt capacity.[89]
Value of potential target tax attributes (e.g., NOLs)	Acquirers are willing to pay more for target tax attributes if they believe the potential tax savings can be realized relatively quickly.[90]
Customer–supplier relationships	In vertical mergers, buyers substantially reliant on a target that is either a customer or a supplier and that has few alternatives will be forced to pay higher premiums than otherwise.[91]
Preemption concerns	Acquirers often are willing to pay more for a target at an earlier stage of development to prevent others from acquiring it.[92]
Information asymmetry	Informed bidders are likely to pay lower premiums because less informed bidders fear overpaying and either withdraw from or do not participate in the bidding process.[93]
Deal characteristics	
Type of payment	Cash purchases usually require an increased premium to compensate target shareholders for the immediate tax liability they incur.[94] Bidders using overvalued shares often overpay for target firms.
Type of purchase	Hostile transactions (or the credible threat of such transactions) tend to command higher premiums than friendly transactions.[95]
Board connections	Acquirers realize higher announcement-date returns in transactions in which the target and the acquirer's boards share a common director, perhaps reflecting more consistent and candid communication.[96]

spin-off, the parent may be held responsible for its liabilities. Moreover, after the spin-off has been implemented, the former parent often continues to provide "transitional" services. More than 1 year after Baxter International completed its spin-off of biopharmaceutical business Baxalta, Inc., the parent was still managing many of Baxalta's back-office operations such as finance and information technology (IT). Although receiving $100 million annually for such services, the former parent is limited in its ability to make other changes in its ongoing operations because it needs to maintain this support infrastructure.

Motives for spin-offs

In addition to the motives for exiting businesses discussed earlier, spin-offs reward shareholders with a nontaxable dividend. Parent firms with a low tax basis in a business may choose to spin off a unit as a tax-free distribution to shareholders rather than sell the business and incur a large tax liability. Independent of the parent, the unit has its own stock for possible acquisitions without interference from the parent's board. The managers of the spun-off unit have a greater incentive to improve the unit's performance if they own stock in the unit. Now more focused and transparent to investors, the unit can become an attractive takeover opportunity. Spin-offs also represent an easy alternative to divesting a difficult-to-sell business.

Disadvantages of spin-offs include the loss of both revenue and synergies associated with the unit. For publicly traded firms, the elimination of a large portion of a firm through a spin-off to shareholders can result in less stock-analyst coverage, removal from stock indices, and an increased likelihood of takeover of the former parent if the spin-off substantially reduces the size of the parent. Finally, the costs associated with separating a unit from the parent can become substantial if the unit is well integrated into other parts of the firm.

Tax and accounting considerations for spin-offs

If properly structured, a corporation can make a tax-free distribution to its shareholders of stock in a subsidiary in which it holds a controlling interest. Neither the parent nor its shareholders recognize any taxable gain or loss on the distribution. Such distributions can involve a spin-off, a split-up (a series of corporate spin-offs), or a split-off (an exchange of subsidiary stock for parent stock). Split-ups and split-offs are explained in more detail later in this chapter.

To be tax free to both the parent and its shareholders, spin-offs must satisfy certain conditions stipulated in Section 355 of the Internal Revenue Tax Code. These conditions apply to the separation of two operating businesses and not to transactions involving the distribution of cash or liquid assets or those resembling sales (a spin-off followed by an immediate acquisition of the unit). These conditions include the following:

1. The parent must control the subsidiary(ies) to be spun off, split up, or split off by owning at least 80% of each class of the unit's voting and nonvoting stock.[20]
2. The distributing firm must issue all of the stock of the controlled subsidiary.
3. The transaction must be for a sound business purpose (i.e., to improve profitability, increase capital market access for the parent or the unit to be spun off, or enhance management focus by reducing the number of lines of business) and not for tax avoidance.[21]
4. Both the parent and the controlled subsidiary must remain in the same business after the distribution in which they were actively engaged for the 5 years before the distribution. Any acquisition either 2 years before or after the spin-off may trigger an Internal Revenue Service (IRS) determination that the spin-off was actually a "disguised sale" intended to avoid taxes, with the IRS removing the tax-free status of the spin-off.

For financial-reporting purposes, the parent firm should account for the spin-off of a subsidiary's stock to its shareholders at book value, with no gain or loss recognized other than any reduction in value because of impairment.[22] The reason for this treatment is that the ownership interests are essentially the same before and after the spin-off.

[20] In 2017, the IRS in a private letter ruling stated that firms could spin off operations in which they own as little as 40% to creditors if the transaction is related to bankruptcy reorganization.

[21] A spin-off cannot be used to avoid the payment of taxes on capital gains that might have been incurred if the parent had chosen to sell a subsidiary in which it had a low tax basis.

[22] Impairment in an accounting context refers to degradation of the value of assets due to loss of key customers, patent or copyright protection, product obsolescence, and so on.

Equity carve-outs

Equity carve-outs exhibit characteristics similar to spin-offs. Both result in the subsidiary's stock being traded separately from the parent's stock. They also are similar to divestitures and IPOs in that they provide cash to the parent. However, unlike the spin-off or the divestiture, the parent generally retains control of the subsidiary in a carve-out transaction. A significant drawback to the carve-out is the creation of minority shareholders.

Motives for equity carve-outs

Like divestitures, equity carve-outs provide an opportunity to raise funds for reinvestment in the subsidiary, paying off debt, or paying a dividend to the parent firm. Carve-outs also may be used if the parent has significant contractual obligations, such as supply agreements, with its subsidiary.[23] Moreover, a carve-out frequently precedes a divestiture because it provides an opportunity to value the business by selling stock on a public stock exchange. The stock created for a carve-out often is used in incentive programs for the unit's management and as an acquisition currency (i.e., form of payment) if the parent later decides to grow the subsidiary. By creating a market for the formerly largely illiquid subsidiary shares, the carve-out provides a market in which shareholders can more easily sell their shares. The two basic forms of an equity carve-out are the IPO and the subsidiary equity carve-out.

Initial public offerings and subsidiary equity carve-outs

An IPO is the first offering to the public of common stock of a private firm. The sale of the stock provides cash to the parent and an opportunity for pre-IPO shareholders to convert their shares to cash. The cash proceeds from the IPO may be retained by the parent or returned to shareholders. In 2019, Saudi Aramco in a record-setting IPO raised more than $29 billion to diversify the Saudi Arabia economy away from dependence on oil. Alibaba, the Chinese e-commerce giant, went public in late 2014, raising more than $25 billion and valuing the firm at more than $200 billion. The proceeds of the Alibaba IPO were used to allow investors to cash out, to make acquisitions, and to build brand awareness outside of China.

How an IPO is structured and their post-IPO share performance can be predictive of whether a firm will engage in M&A activity.[24] Firms with particularly large cash infusions tend to grow through acquisition. And firms that go public and significantly underprice[25] their securities are also more likely to be acquirers. Why? Because these firms attract a broader array of investors, issue extra shares via the overallotment option,[26] create dispersed ownership, and have a liquid acquisition currency. Post-IPO share performance reduces uncertainty concerning what the firm is worth and allows the firm to have more confidence in share-for-share exchanges.

Table 17.3 illustrates a timeline associated with a typical IPO, which involves hiring one or more investment banks in an advisory and marketing capacity to guide the firm through the entire process. Alternatively, the investment bank can buy the entire issue and resell it to the public. The bank buys the shares at a substantial discount from fair value to compensate for the risk that they will not be able to resell the shares to the public at a profit.[27] As discussed later, a less common practice is for the issuing firm to directly list their shares on a public exchange.

Before issuing shares to the public, the parent estimates the size of the post-IPO float. *Float* represents unrestricted shares trading on exchanges held both by institutions and individuals. It excludes restricted shares or those issued by a firm that cannot be bought or sold for a certain period of time without permission by the Securities and Exchange Commission (SEC).[28] Why is float important? Because its size affects the degree of the parent's post-IPO

[23] By retaining a controlling interest in the subsidiary, a parent can better manage its contractual commitments. For example, for supply contracts, as the controlling owner in the subsidiary, the parent represents both sides of the contract, as supplier and buyer.

[24] Anderson et al., 2017

[25] IPO shares are underpriced when issued such that their prices rise immediately after the initial offering to encourage investor participation because investors are likely to have less information than the underwriting firm.

[26] An "overallotment option" is one enabling underwriters to sell more shares in a secondary or follow-up offering.

[27] Gao et al. (2020) find evidence that the IPO discount arises because the issue price is based on the average opinion of institutional investors while the aftermarket price is set by a minority of optimistic investors.

[28] Restricted stock is a type of stock given to insiders as part of their compensation.

TABLE 17.3 The traditional initial public offering timeline

Steps	Comments
Step 1: Decide to go public.	To raise money to grow the firm, allow early investors to cash out, reduce indebtedness, make acquisitions, to recruit talented managers, etc.
Step 2: Hire an investment bank(s) to guide and to market the equity issue.	Investment banks: • Create legal documents and satisfy regulatory requirements. • Advise the client through the process of marketing, pricing, and conducting IPOs. • Stand ready to buy IPO shares if they fall after issue, to limit volatility.
Step 3: Register with the SEC.	Requires filing an S-1 form with the SEC, which entails listing the company's plans for the funds raised, its business model, the competition, its corporate governance, and executive compensation.[a]
Step 4: "Road show" (or book-building process).	The offering is promoted to potential investors, as soon as 21 days after the S-1 is approved. Before the "road show," the number of shares offered and the price per share (often within a narrow range) are announced.[b] "Road show" attendees include hedge funds, mutual funds, banks, pension funds, endowments, and individuals.[c]
Step 5: Issue equity.	Based on precommitments to buy shares made during the "road show," a final price (or reference price) and deal size are announced. Investors, having submitted final bids, find out if they can buy the stock.

[a]*Many firms are uncomfortable with a public filing since it makes sensitive data available to their competition. Now, under the JOBS Act of 2012, many firms can file confidentially. See Chapter 2 for more detail.*
[b]*Firms often issue 10% to 25% of their stock to ensure a liquid market for the stock.*
[c]*Investment bankers conducting the "road show" record pre-issue offers made for the stock at various prices and adjust the price depending on demand before the sale of the stock.*
IPO, Initial public offering; *SEC*, Securities and Exchange Commission.

control, its ability to consolidate the unit for tax purposes, the parent's cost to reacquire its subsidiary if it chooses, and the value of the shares issued.

Although investment banks are normally hired to manage the IPO process, some firms offer their shares directly on a public exchange in a so-called *direct listing*. Such listings allow firms to issue shares for existing shareholders only. Unlike a conventional IPO, direct listings do not dilute ownership because the firm is not issuing new shares and saves millions of dollars in underwriting fees. In late 2020, the SEC approved the NYSE's proposal to enable firms undertaking direct listings to issue new shares to raise money. In addition to saving fees, the process avoids lockup periods when insiders cannot sell their shares. Direct listings can result in more volatile share prices because underwriters do not buy shares to stabilize prices.[29]

The *subsidiary carve-out* is a transaction in which the parent creates a wholly owned, independent subsidiary, with stock and a management team that are different from the parent's, and issues a portion of the subsidiary's stock to the public. Usually, only a minority share of the parent's ownership in the subsidiary is issued to the public. Although the parent retains control, the subsidiary's shareholder base may be different than that of the parent because of the public sale of equity. The cash raised may be retained in the subsidiary or transferred to the parent as a dividend, a stock repurchase, or an intercompany loan. An example of a subsidiary carve-out is the sale to the public by Phillip Morris of 15% of its wholly owned Kraft subsidiary. Phillip Morris' voting power over Kraft was reduced only to 97.7% because Kraft had a dual-class share structure in which only low-voting shares were issued in the public stock offering.

Tax and accounting considerations for equity carve-outs

Retention of at least 80% of the unit enables consolidation for tax purposes, and retention of more than 50% enables consolidation for financial-reporting purposes.[30] If the parent owns less than 50% but more than 20%, it must use the equity method for financial reporting. Below 20%, it must use the cost method.[31] For a spin-off of the

[29] The NASDAQ exchange is seeking approval of a similar plan, except it would allow a firm's shares to start trading within a wider price range than would be allowed by the NYSE.

[30] Vijh (2002) found a median ownership stake of 72%.

[31] When the equity method is used to account for ownership in a company, the investor records the initial investment at cost and periodically adjusts the value to reflect its proportionate share of the firm's income or losses. The cost method requires recording the investment at cost, and dividends received are included in investment income.

remaining stock after an IPO to be tax free, the parent must have retained at least 80% of the voting power of the shares of the subsidiary. The proceeds of an IPO distributed to the parent are tax free if the cash distributed is less than the value of the parent's investment in the stock of the controlled subsidiary, because it is considered a return of capital.

Split-offs and split-ups

A *split-off* involves the parent firm making an offer to shareholders to exchange their parent stock for all or a portion of the shares of the firm's subsidiary. It is equivalent to a share repurchase by the parent of its stock using stock in the subsidiary instead of cash. Like a spin-off, the split-off results in the parent's subsidiary becoming an independent firm; the parent does not generate any new cash. Unlike spin-offs, which result in the same proportionate ownership distribution before and after the spin-off, split-offs generally result in disproportionate changes in the ownership of parent shares.

Split-offs normally are non–pro rata stock distributions, in contrast to spin-offs, which generally are pro rata (or proportional) distributions of shares. In a pro rata distribution, a shareholder owning 10% of the outstanding parent company stock would receive 10% of the subsidiary shares. A non–pro rata distribution takes the form of a tender or exchange offer in which shareholders can accept or reject the distribution, generally resulting in a disproportionate change in the ownership of parent shares outstanding. For example, if 50% of the parent shareholders exchange their parent shares for subsidiary shares, the remaining half of parent shareholders will hold 100% of whatever parent shares remain outstanding.

A *split-up* is a restructuring strategy in which a single company splits into two or more separately managed firms. Through a series of split-offs or spin-offs, shareholders of the original or parent firm may choose to exchange their shares in the parent firm for shares in the new companies. After the split, the original firm's shares are cancelled, and it ceases to exist.

Recent examples include industrial conglomerate Pentair Plc. and US aluminum company Alcoa Inc. In an admission of a lack of synergy between their business units, Pentair split into two parts in mid-2018: one that provides fluid-processing and water-filtration technologies while retaining the businesses selling protective enclosures for electrical equipment. Alcoa split the firm into separate entities in late 2016 to isolate the firm's more profitable "value-added" upstream fabrication operations from its floundering downstream raw aluminum operations.

When circumstances change, split-ups are sometimes reversed. Media giants CBS and Viacom, having split up in 2006 to cleave Viacom's then booming cable business from CBS's more mature TV business, merged in early 2020. Why? They believed they needed the scale to improve profitability in the increasingly competitive entertainment industry.

Motives for split-offs

A split-off is most appropriate when the parent firm owns less than 100% of a subsidiary's stock. This may occur when the parent fails to buy all of the outstanding shares of another firm or when the parent undertakes an IPO of a portion of the stock of a controlled subsidiary. Divestiture may not be an option for disposing of businesses in which the parent owns less than 100% of outstanding shares because potential buyers often want to acquire all of a firm's outstanding stock. By buying only a portion of another firm's shares, a buyer inherits minority shareholders, who may disagree with the new owner's future business decisions.

Split-offs are commonly undertaken after a portion of the shares in a controlled subsidiary have been issued to the public in an IPO so that the value of the subsidiary's shares can be determined. After their trading value has been established, it is used in determining the exchange ratio between subsidiary and parent shares (i.e., the split-off exchange ratio), that is, the number of subsidiary shares (which could be less than one if the trading value of the subsidiary shares exceeds that of the parent's shares) to be exchanged for each parent share.

Typically, the parent offers to purchase parent stock at a premium compared with the subsidiary's trading price established after the IPO of a portion of the subsidiary's stock as an incentive for parent shareholders to exchange their shares for subsidiary shares. Split-offs are most successful when parent shareholders show a preference for the subsidiary's stock over the parent's stock. Any subsidiary shares not tendered during the exchange offer period may be distributed to parent shareholders through a spin-off, making the subsidiary totally independent.

A split-off reduces the pressure on the spun-off firm's share price because shareholders who exchange their stock are less likely to sell the new stock. A shareholder willing to make the exchange believes the stock in the subsidiary

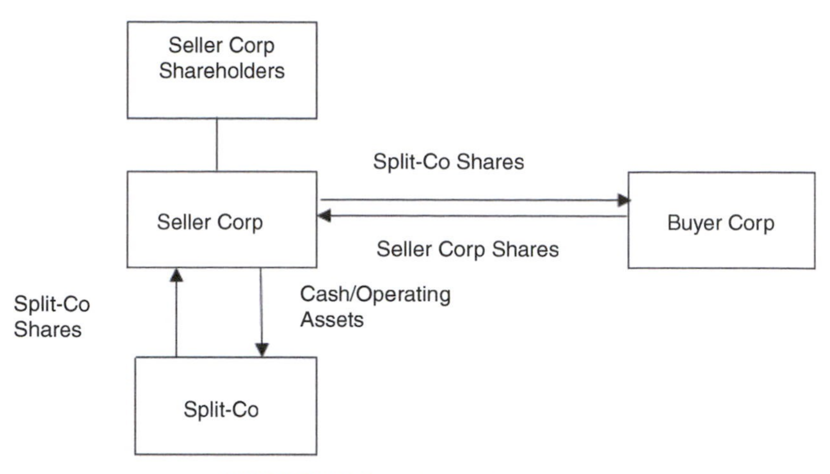

FIGURE 17.2 **"Cash-rich" split-off.**

has greater appreciation potential than the parent's. The exchange also increases the earnings per share of the parent firm by reducing the number of its shares outstanding, if the reduction in the number of shares outstanding exceeds the loss of the subsidiary's earnings. A split-off is generally tax free to shareholders if it conforms to the IRS requirements previously described for spin-offs.

Cash-rich split-offs

As variations of conventional split-offs, cash-rich split-offs commonly occur when a firm wants to reacquire stock from a large shareholder. The parent creates a new subsidiary and contributes an operating unit the parent has owned and operated for at least 5 years to the subsidiary as well as cash. The business must comprise at least 5% to 10% of the subsidiary's enterprise value, and the subsidiary cannot contain more than 66% cash or other investment securities. Assuming the there is a valid business purpose for the deal, the parent can then exchange stock in the new subsidiary for the parent's stock held by the large investor in a deal that is tax free.

How a cash-rich split-off may be structured is illustrated in Figure 17.2. Assume Buyer Corp owns stock in Seller Corp, and Seller Corp wishes to buy back its stock. To do so in a tax-free transaction, Seller Corp forms a new subsidiary (Split-Co) and transfers operating assets and liabilities and cash into the subsidiary in exchange for subsidiary stock. The subsidiary's assets can consist of up to 66% cash and 34% operating assets.

The fair MV of the subsidiary must be about equal to the market value of Seller Corp's stock held by Buyer Corp. Seller Corp enters into a split-off in which it exchanges Split-Co stock for Seller stock held by Buyer Corp. After the deal, Split-Co becomes a wholly owned subsidiary of Buyer Corp. The transaction is tax free to both Seller Corp shareholders and Buyer Corp shareholders. The disadvantages of this deal are that it is complicated to execute and Buyer Corp must operate the acquired business for at least 2 years after closing. In 2015, Warren Buffett's Berkshire Hathaway bought Proctor & Gamble's (P&G's) Duracell battery business in a deal valued at about $3 billion and structured as a tax-free cash rich split-off. P&G received shares of its own stock held by Berkshire Hathaway with a MV of $4.7 billion. To make the fair MV of the P&G stock and the Duracell business equal, P&G contributed $1.7 billion in cash to the Duracell business before closing.[32]

Spin-offs combined with M&A transactions

Spin-offs may be combined with a concurrent merger deal. Called "Morris Trust" and "Reverse Morris Trusts," these structures allow the parent to transfer a business to another firm (i.e., merger partner) in a stock deal that is tax free. In a Morris Trust deal, all of the parent's assets, except those to be combined with the merger partner, are spun off or split off into a new public company, and then the parent merges with the merger partner. In a Reverse Morris

[32] Other recent "cash-rich" split-offs include Comcast/Time Warner Cable, Comcast/Liberty, KeySpanG/Houston Exploration, Cox/Discovery Communications, and DST Systems/Janus Capital Group.

Trust, all assets to be combined with the merger partner are spun off or split off into a new public company, with the new company combining with the merger partner.[33]

To be tax free, the Morris and Reverse Morris Trust structures require the merger partner to be smaller than the business to be combined with the partner resulting in the shareholders of the parent owning a majority of the stock of the combined firms. That is, the spun-off subsidiary is the "buyer" if its shareholders (the original parent shareholders who received the stock spun off by the parent) own more than 50% the merged firms. The former subsidiary usually has a bigger market value than the target into which it is merged. This effectively reduces the number of potential merger partners. This limitation was imposed by the IRS to make such structures less attractive.

An advantage the Reverse Morris Trust is that it does not require approval by the parent shareholders. This is so because the spin-off firm is combining with the merger partner, and the parent approves this merger at the time the parent is the sole shareholder of the subsidiary to be spun off. In contrast, the Morris Trust requires approval by the parent's shareholders because the merging party (i.e., the parent) is already a public firm owned by its public shareholders at the time the merger is proposed. The major drawback of these types of deals is their complexity because each deal is dependent on the completion of the other.

In 2020, pharmaceutical giant Pfizer combined its expired patent drug operations with generic drug producer Mylan Labs in an all-stock deal structured as a Reverse Morris Trust. After the transfer of all of its off-patent drugs to its Upjohn unit, Pfizer separated the unit in a tax-free spin-off and simultaneously combined with Mylan. As part of the deal, the new company, with pro forma annual sales of $19 billion, issued new debt to pay $12 billion to Pfizer for the drugs transferred to the Upjohn before closing. At closing, Pfizer shareholders owned 57% of the new company with Mylan shareholders owning the remainder. Compliant with Reverse Morris Trust requirements, the deal was tax free to both Pfizer and Mylan shareholders.

The outcome was different for GE's shareholders. In March 2018, GE had originally agreed to spin off its transportation unit to its shareholders and subsequently merge it with Wabtec. The deal called for GE to sell Wabtec certain transportation assets for $2.9 billion in cash and 9.9% of the combined firms, while GE shareholders would receive 40.2%, leaving Wabtec shareholders with 49.9%. However, a decline in the unit's operating performance since the merger agreement was signed caused Wabtec to renegotiate the deal in early 2019. The deteriorating operating performance caused the value of the unit's shares that were to be exchanged for Wabtec shares to decline, causing Wabtec to demand a more favorable exchange ratio for its shares. As a result, GE still received $2.9 billion in cash, but Wabtec will be the majority owner with 50.8%. The spin-off will be taxable to GE shareholders because GE is now the minority owner, and the deal no longer qualifies as a Reverse Morris Trust structure.

Tracking, targeted, and letter stocks

Such stocks are separate classes of common stock of the parent firm. The parent divides its operations into two or more subsidiaries and assigns a common stock to each. Tracking stock is a class of common stock that links the shareholders' return to the subsidiary's operating performance. Tracking stock dividends rise or fall with the subsidiary's performance. Such stock represents an ownership interest in the parent rather than in the subsidiary. For voting purposes, holders of tracking stock with voting rights may vote their shares on issues related to the parent and not the subsidiary. The parent's board of directors retains control of the subsidiary because it is still legally part of the parent. Tracking stocks may be issued to current parent shareholders as a dividend, used as payment for an acquisition, or issued in a public offering.

Motives for tracking stocks

Tracking stock enables investors to value the different operations within a corporation based on their own performance. However, there is little empirical evidence that issuing a tracking stock for a subsidiary creates pure-play investment opportunities because the tracking stock tends to be correlated more with the parent's other outstanding stocks than with the stocks in the industry in which the subsidiary competes.[34]

[33] Reverse Morris Trusts originated as a result of a 1966 ruling in a lawsuit against the US IRS dealing with avoiding the payment of taxes when selling unwanted assets.

[34] D'Souza et al., 2000

Tracking stocks provide the parent with another way of raising capital for a specific operation by selling a portion of the stock to the public and an alternative "currency" for making acquisitions. Stock-based incentive programs to attract and retain key managers also can be implemented for each operation with its own tracking stock.

Firms that have created disparate asset structures sometimes use a combination of spin-offs and tracking stocks in an attempt to boost shareholder value. In 2016, Liberty Interactive Corporation, known for its digital commerce businesses, spun off two units: Commerce Hub and Liberty Expedia Holdings. The firm also reclassified its common stock into three tracking stocks: The Liberty Braves Group, which owns the Atlanta Braves baseball team; the Liberty Sirius group, which includes the satellite radio provider Sirius XM Holdings; and the Liberty Media Group, which contains the firm's remaining assets. Intended to give investors greater choice in which assets they wanted to invest, the transactions were tax free to the firm's shareholders.

Tax and accounting considerations for tracking stocks

For financial-reporting purposes, tracking stock divides the parent firm's equity structure into separate classes of stock. Unlike spin-offs, the IRS does not require that the business for which the tracking stock is created be at least 5 years old and that the parent retain a controlling interest in the business for the stock to be exempt from capital gains taxes. Unlike a spin-off or a carve-out, the parent retains ownership of the business. In general, a proportionate distribution by a company to its shareholders of the company's stock is tax free to shareholders.

Problems with tracking stocks

Few tracking stocks have been issued in recent years because of inherent governance issues and poor long-term performance. Conflicts among the parent's operating units arise in determining how the parent's overhead expenses are allocated to business units and what price one business unit is paid for selling products to other units. Tracking stocks can stimulate shareholder lawsuits. The parent's board approves overall operating unit and capital budgets. Decisions made in support of one operating unit may appear to be unfair to those holding a tracking stock in another unit. Tracking stocks also may not have voting rights. The chances of a hostile takeover of a firm with a tracking stock are virtually zero because the firm is controlled by the parent. Holders of tracking stock usually do not receive dividends and in liquidation typically do not have a claim on the parent's assets.

Tracking stocks can be particularly problematic when issued by private firms, such as Dell Inc.'s use of tracking shares as part of the compensation paid to shareholders in its 2016 takeover of storage company EMC. Why? Because governance issues can be greater when ownership is heavily concentrated, and financial reporting may be more opaque.

Restructuring implementation issues

What follows is a partial list of some of the more important issues that should be addressed early in the process in the context of a spin-off, to illustrate how they are commonly resolved. The unit to be separated from the parent will be referred to as the "spin-off company." After a unit has been identified for separation, the parent must determine what assets will be retained and what will go with the unit. Finance-related issues include determining the desired debt-to-total capital ratio, deciding which non-long-term, debt-related liabilities will go with the spin-off company and which will be retained, and how to maintain the solvency of the spin-off unit. Other critical execution issues are determining the appropriate governance mechanism for the new unit and how best to address human resource issues. These issues are discussed next.

What stays and what goes

For a subsidiary operated as a standalone unit, separating the business from the parent may be straightforward because the assets and liabilities associated with the business are easily identified. Complexities arise when the parent's staff functions provide support such as finance, human resources, accounting, and IT. These will have to be divided, reproduced, or provided by the parent to the spin-off company on an interim or transitional basis before the unit will be ready to operate as a standalone, publicly traded company.

Spinning off a portion of business through an equity carve-out may be far more complicated because the assets to be retained by the parent must be clearly identified and a means established for transferring them from the spin-off company to the parent. Such mechanisms could include a merger with or sale of assets to another business owned by the parent or an internal spin-off of selected spin-off company assets to other parent operating units.

Target capital structure

In this context, *target capital structure* refers to the spin-off company's and parent's mix of debt and equity immediately after the spin-off. The parent generally wants to reallocate its existing cash and debt between itself and the spin-off company and to raise additional cash if possible. A common strategy is for the spin-off company to issue new debt before the spin-off with the cash proceeds distributed to the parent, which can be used to reduce its debt.[35] The mechanism for transferring the cash to the parent may involve the spin-off company's making a cash distribution to the parent, buying back some of its own shares held by the parent for cash, paying off intercompany loans owed to the parent, or buying assets owned by the parent for cash. Alternatively, the spin-off company may assume some of the parent's outstanding debt.

Allocation of other liabilities

Which liabilities belong with the parent or the spin-off company? Warranty claims relating to spin-off company sales and pension fund obligations would be liabilities of the spin-off company. General corporate liabilities not relating specifically to the parent or the spin-off company, such as shareholder litigation, could remain with the parent. Indemnification clauses in the separation and distribution agreement define the rights and obligations of the parties to the separation. Such clauses require that the party assuming responsibility for a liability is to be reimbursed by the other party if the future actual cash cost of the liability exceeds the amount of the liability at the time it was assumed.

Solvency

If a spin-off quickly becomes financially nonviable, the parent may have to cover the firm's liabilities because of *fraudulent conveyance* or transfer. That is, the parent may be accused of attempting to avoid its obligations. In 2013, a judge ruled that Kerr-McGee had fraudulently transferred profitable oil and gas assets from its Tronox subsidiary to the parent in 2004, leaving the subsidiary unable to pay outstanding environmental claims. In 2014, Andarko, which had acquired Kerr-McGee's oil and gas assets, had to pay $5.2 billion to settle these claims.

Board governance

In structuring a spin-off, directors of a solvent corporation have a fiduciary responsibility to the shareholders of the pre-spin company (not to the spin-off company) and may structure the transaction to maximize value for the parent shareholders. The parent board may unilaterally allocate assets and liabilities between the parent and spin-off company before executing the spin-off, subject to insolvency and tax considerations. Such decisions often are honored by the courts as long as the board's decision was made for legitimate business purposes.

Human resource management

When a subsidiary has been operated as a standalone business, its current management usually becomes the management team after the spin-off, and its employees remain with the spin-off company. In spin-offs of divisions operated on a standalone basis, management issues are more challenging. Existing managers of the spin-off company often have responsibilities that overlap with businesses to be retained by the parent or are valuable to both the parent and the spin-off company. In determining the roles of such managers, it is critical to consider their desires in assigning them to the parent or to the spin-off company. Other challenges in separating employee populations involve the division of pension and benefit plans and assets funding such plans, the treatment of stock options, and the impact of

[35] Hewlett-Packard Enterprise raised $14.6 billion just before its being spun off by its parent Hewlett-Packard Co. in late 2015, with the cash transferred to the parent. The parent used the proceeds to redeem $8.85 billion in debt and the remainder to refinance other obligations at lower interest rates.

union contracts, which may restrict how employees and benefit plan assets are assigned between the parent and the spin-off company.

Key restructure legal documents

Key documents include a separation and distribution agreement, a transition agreement, and a tax matters agreement negotiated between the parent and spin-off companies. Additional agreements may include patent, trademark, and other intellectual property license arrangements.

Separation and distribution agreement

Outlining how the separation of the spin-off unit from the parent will be implemented, this document identifies assets to be transferred, liabilities to be assumed, and contracts to be assigned to the spin-off firm and the parent. It also explains how and when transfers, liability assignments, and contract assignments will occur and governs the rights and obligations of the parent and the spin-off company regarding the distribution of the spin-off company's shares.

Transition agreement

This agreement covers services shared by the parent and the spin-off unit, which may include legal, payroll, accounting, IT, or benefits. These may have to be continued on an interim basis after separation. The services may be provided by the parent to the spin-off company, the spin-off company to the parent, or both.

Tax matters agreement

This agreement defines the rights and obligations of the parent and the spin-off company if tax liabilities are created because of transactions undertaken to implement the spin-off (e.g., sale of specific spin-off company assets to other parent subsidiaries). This agreement also allocates tax liabilities between the parent and the spin-off company, often by making the parent responsible for all taxes incurred before closing and the spin-off company responsible for taxes after closing.

To protect the spin-off's tax-free status during the subsequent 2-year period, the agreement restricts the spin-off company's ability to merge with another firm, liquidate, sell a large share of its assets, and buy back large amounts of its stock.

Comparing alternative exit and restructuring strategies

Table 17.4 summarizes the primary characteristics of the restructuring strategies discussed in this chapter. Note that whereas divestitures and carve-outs provide cash to the parent, spin-offs and split-ups do not. The parent remains in existence in all restructuring strategies. A new legal entity generally is created with each restructuring strategy. With the exception of the carve-out, the parent generally loses control of the division involved in the restructuring strategy. Only spin-offs, split-ups, and split-offs are generally not taxable to shareholders, if properly structured.

Choosing among divestiture, carve-out, and spin-off restructuring strategies

Parent firms undertaking divestitures often are diversified in unrelated businesses and desire to achieve greater focus or to raise cash.[36] Those using carve-out strategies operate businesses with some synergy, have contractual obligations to the business, and want to raise cash. The parent may pursue a carve-out, rather than a divestiture

[36] Bergh et al., 2007

TABLE 17.4 Key characteristics of alternative exit and restructuring strategies

	Alternative strategies					
Characteristics	**Divestitures**	**Equity carve-outs and IPOs**	**Spin-offs**	**Split-ups**	**Split-offs**	**Tracking stocks**
Cash infusion to parent	Yes	Yes	No	No	No	Yes
Parent ceases to exist	No	No	No	Yes	No	No
New legal entity created	Sometimes	Yes	Yes	Yes	No	No
New shares issued	Sometimes	Yes	Yes	Yes	Yes	Yes
Parent remains in control	No	Generally	No	No	No	Yes
Taxable to shareholders	Yes	Yes	No	No	No	No

IPO, Initial public offering.

TABLE 17.5 Characteristics of parent company operating units that undergo divestiture, carve-out, or spin-off

Exit or restructuring strategy	Characteristics of operating unit subject to exit or restructuring strategy
Divestitures	Usually unrelated to other businesses owned by the parent Operating performance generally worse than the parent's performance Slightly underperform peers in the year before the announcement date Generally sell at a lower market to book ratio than carve-outs
Carve-outs	More profitable and faster growing than spun-off or divested businesses Operating performance often exceeds parent's Operate in industries with a high ratio of market to book values Generally outperform peers in the year before the announcement date
Spin-offs	Generally faster growing and more profitable than divested businesses Operating performance worse than parent's Slightly underperform peers in the year before the announcement date

Sources: *Hand et al. (1997), Kang et al. (1997), Powers (2001, 2003), Chen et al. (2005), Bergh (2007), and Prezas et al. (2015).*

or spin-off, to retain synergy. The timing of the carve-out is influenced by when management sees its subsidiary's assets as overvalued.[37] Firms engaging in spin-offs often are diversified but less so than those that are prone to pursue divestiture strategies and have little need to raise cash. Table 17.5 identifies characteristics of parent firm operating units that are subject to certain types of restructuring activities.

Divestitures, carve-outs, and spin-offs are commonly used when a parent corporation is considering exiting a business partially or entirely. Which strategy to use is influenced by the parent firm's need for cash, the degree of synergy between the business to be divested or spun off and the parent's other operating units, and the potential selling price of the division.

Parent firms needing cash are more likely to divest or engage in an equity carve-out for operations exhibiting high selling prices relative to their synergy value. Parent firms not needing cash are more likely to spin off units exhibiting low selling prices and synergy with the parent. Parent firms with moderate cash needs are likely to engage in equity carve-outs when the unit's selling price is low relative to perceived synergy.

Unlike a spin-off, a divestiture or carve-out generates a cash infusion to the firm. However, a spin-off may create greater shareholder wealth for several reasons. First, a spin-off is tax free if it is properly structured. The cash proceeds from an outright sale may be taxable to the parent if a gain is realized. Also, management must be able to reinvest the after-tax proceeds at or above the firm's cost of capital. If management chooses to return the cash proceeds to shareholders, the shareholders incur a tax liability. Second, a spin-off enables the shareholders to decide when to sell their shares. Third, a spin-off may be less traumatic than a divestiture for an operating unit.[38]

[37] Powers, 2003; Chen et al., 2005

[38] The divestiture process can degrade value if it is lengthy: employees leave, worker productivity suffers, and customers may not renew contracts.

TABLE 17.6 Returns to shareholders of firms undertaking restructuring strategies

Restructuring strategy	Average preannouncement abnormal returns (%)
Divestitures[a]	1.5
Spin-offs[b]	3.8
Tracking stocks[c]	3.0
Equity carve-outs[d]	3.9

[a] *Allen (2000), Mulherin et al. (2000), Clubb et al. (2002), Ditmar et al. (2002), Bates (2005), Slovin et al. (2005), Borisova et al. (2013), Kengelbach et al. (2014), and Prezas et al. (2015).*
[b] *Loh et al. (1995), J.P. Morgan (1995), Mulherin et al. (2000), Maxwell et al. (2003), Veld (2004), McNeil et al. (2005), Harris et al. (2007), Khorana et al. (2011), Kengelbach et al. (2014), and Prezas et al., (2015).*
[c] *Logue et al. (1996), D'Souza et al. (2000), Elder et al. (2000), Chemmanur et al. (2000), Haushalter et al. (2001), and Billet et al. (2004).*
[d] *Vijh (1999), Mulherin et al. (2000), Prezas et al. (2000), Hulbert et al. (2002), Hogan et al. (2004), and Kengelbach et al. (2014).*

Determinants of returns to shareholders resulting from restructuring strategies

Restructuring strategies can create value by increasing parent firm focus, transfer assets to those who can operate them more efficiently, and mitigate agency conflicts and financial distress. The empirical support for this statement is discussed next in terms of pre- and postannouncement financial returns to shareholders by type of strategy.

Preannouncement abnormal returns

Studies indicate that restructuring strategies generally provide positive abnormal returns to the shareholders of the firm implementing the strategy (Table 17.6). Why? Because such actions are undertaken to correct problems associated with highly diversified firms, such as having invested in underperforming businesses, having failed to link executive compensation to performance, and being too difficult for investors to evaluate. Strategies involving divisional or asset sales may create value simply because the asset is worth more to another investor.

Divestitures

Positive abnormal returns around the announcement date of the restructure strategy average 1.5% for sellers. Buyers average positive abnormal returns of about 0.5%.[39] Although both sellers and buyers gain from a divestiture, most of the gain appears to accrue to the seller. How the total gain is divided depends on the relative bargaining strength and negotiating skills of the seller and the buyer. Selling-firm CEOs are less likely to divest businesses with which they are most familiar. When they do, their greater familiarity seems to give them an edge in negotiating with buyers because they tend to earn above-average positive abnormal financial returns for seller shareholders.[40] When domestic capital markets are illiquid, domestic firms may find selling assets to foreign firms more lucrative than selling them to local firms. Foreign firms often pay a higher price if they have access to cheaper financing or a stronger currency or view the purchase as a means of entering the domestic market.[41]

Increasing focus of the divesting firm

In late 2015, Google Inc. unveiled a sweeping reorganization separating its highly profitable search and advertising business from its fledgling research and development investments, including robotics and self-driving cars. The resulting holding company was named Alphabet Inc. The search and advertising operations contribute almost 90% of the firm's total revenue and all of its profits. The so-called "moon-shot" investments are intended to identify the "next big thing" to propel the firm's future growth. Although billed as an effort to give investors greater visibility into the cost of these investments and to facilitate managing the increasingly complex firm, the new structure allows the firm to divest or spin off the noncore businesses in the future.

[39] Hanson et al., 2000

[40] Ang et al., 2014

[41] Borisova et al., 2013

Abnormal returns to shareholders of a firm divesting a business result largely from improved management of the assets that remain after the divestiture.[42] Divesting firms often improve their investment decisions in their remaining businesses after divestitures by achieving levels of investment in core businesses comparable to those of their more-focused peers.[43] However, poorly managed firms may be inclined to misuse the proceeds received from asset sales. Firms experiencing cash windfalls are prone to make value-destroying acquisitions after experiencing the cash inflow because they are more likely to overpay for the target firm.[44]

Some firms seem to prosper despite the growing complexity of their business portfolio. Berkshire Hathaway is a prime example. The firm has successfully managed for decades a highly diverse portfolio ranging from cowboy boots and Ginsu knives to ear-piercing tools and refrigerated trailers to ketchup and insurance products. The firm's success is perhaps a testimony more to the superb investment and management skills of Warren Buffett and the firm's management culture than to the conglomerate as a sustainable business model. Few have been able to even come close to Berkshire Hathaway's success in managing highly diverse firms. After years of superior stock market performance under the guidance of CEO Jack Welch, GE floundered shortly after Welch retired in the early 2000s. In the past decade, the firm has sold off hundreds of billions of dollars in underperforming assets.

Transferring assets to those who can use them more efficiently

Divestitures result in productivity gains by transferring assets from poorly managed sellers to acquirers that are on average better managed. Investors thus have a reasonable expectation that the acquirer can generate a higher financial return and bid up its share price.[45]

Resolving management and shareholder differences (agency conflicts)

Conflicts arise when management and shareholders disagree about major corporate decisions. What to do with the proceeds of the sale of assets can result in such a conflict because they can be reinvested in the seller's remaining operations, distributed to shareholders, or used to reduce the firm's outstanding debt. Abnormal returns on divestiture announcement dates tend to be positive when the proceeds are used to pay off debt[46] or are distributed to the shareholders.[47] Such results suggest shareholders mistrust management's ability to invest intelligently.

Mitigating financial distress

Not surprisingly, empirical studies indicate that firms sell assets when they need cash. The period before a firm announces asset sales often is characterized by deteriorating operating performance.[48] Firms that divest assets often have lower cash balances, cash flow, and bond credit ratings than firms exhibiting similar growth, risk, and profitability characteristics.[49] Firms experiencing financial distress are more likely to use divestitures as part of their restructuring programs than other options, because they generate cash.

Spin-offs

At 3.8%, the average excess return to parent shareholders associated with spin-off announcements is double that of divestitures. The gap between abnormal returns to shareholders from spin-offs versus divestitures may be attributable to tax considerations. Spin-offs generally are tax free, while any gains on divested assets can be subject to double taxation. With spin-offs, shareholder value is created by increasing the focus of the parent by spinning off unrelated units, providing greater transparency, and transferring wealth from bondholders to shareholders.

[42] Petty et al., 1993

[43] Dittmar et al., 2003

[44] Beschwitz, 2018

[45] Using Tobin q-ratios (i.e., the ratio of the market value of a firm to the cost of replacing the firm's assets) as a proxy for better-managed firms, Datta et al. (2003) found that announcement-period returns are highest for transactions in which the buyer's q-ratio is higher than the seller's. This implies that the assets are being transferred to a better-managed firm. Maksimovic and Phillips' (2001) findings also support this conclusion.

[46] Lang et al., 1995; Kaiser et al., 2001

[47] Slovin et al., 2005

[48] Schlingemann et al., 2003

[49] Officer, 2007

Increasing focus

Spin-offs increasing parent focus improve excess financial returns more than spin-offs that do not.[50] There is also a reduction in the diversification discount when a spin-off increases corporate focus but not for those that do not.[51] Spin-offs of subsidiaries that are in the same industry as the parent firm do not result in positive announcement-date returns because they do not enhance corporate focus.[52] Like divestitures, spin-offs contribute to better investment decisions by eliminating the tendency to use the cash flows of efficient businesses to finance investment in less efficient business units.[53]

Achieving greater transparency (eliminating information asymmetries)

Divestitures and spin-offs tending to reduce a firm's complexity help to improve investors' ability to evaluate the firm's operating performance. By reducing complexity, financial analysts are better able to forecast earnings accurately.[54] Analysts tend to revise upward their earnings forecasts of the parent in response to a spin-off.[55]

Wealth transfers

Evidence shows that spin-offs transfer wealth from bondholders to parent stockholders, for several reasons.[56] First, spin-offs reduce the assets available for liquidation in the event of business failure: investors may view the firm's existing debt as riskier.[57] Second, the loss of the cash flow generated by the spin-off may result in less total parent cash flow to cover interest and principal repayments on the parent's current debt. In contrast, stockholders benefit from holding shares in the parent firm and shares in the unit spun off by the parent, with the latter now separate from the parent, having the potential to appreciate in value.

Equity carve-outs

Investors view the announcement of a carve-out as the beginning of a series of restructuring activities, such as a reacquisition of the unit by the parent, a spin-off, a secondary offering, or an M&A. The sizeable announcement-date abnormal returns to parent firm shareholders averaging 3.9% reflect investor-anticipated profit from these subsequent events. These abnormal positive returns are realized when the parent firm retains a controlling interest after a carve-out, allowing the parent to initiate these secondary actions.[58] Furthermore, these returns tend to increase with the size of the carve-out.[59] Announcement-date returns are significant for both parent firm stock[60] and bond[61] investors when the parent indicates that the majority of the proceeds resulting from the carve-out will be used to redeem debt.[62]

Although most studies of equity carve-outs have focused on the United States, a recent study of European equity carve-outs was consistent with the performance of American equity carve-outs. The magnitude of the

[50] Desai et al., 1997

[51] Burch et al., 2001; Seoungpil et al., 2004

[52] Daley et al., 1997

[53] Gertner et al., 2002

[54] Gilson et al., 2001

[55] Huson et al., 2003

[56] Maxwell et al. (2003) note that bondholders on average suffer a negative abnormal return of 0.8% in the month of the spin-off announcement. Stockholders experience an increase of about 3.6% during the same period.

[57] Assets actually pledged as collateral to current debt may not be spun off without violating loan covenants.

[58] Otsubo, 2009

[59] Vijh, 2002

[60] Otsubo, 2013

[61] The carve-out proceeds boost bondholder returns as current debt is repurchased. The reduction in outstanding debt means less interest expense is incurred, and more cash is available for dividend payments and share repurchases of stock held by current shareholders. See Thompson et al. (2009).

[62] Mashwani et al. (2019) argue that the impact of a carve-out on the parent's shares can be predicted during the road show or book-building process in which potential investors are asked to indicate what they would be willing to pay for a partial offering of shares in a subsidiary in which the parent retains a significant interest. The impact on the parent's shares is greater when the value of the subsidiary undergoing the carve-out represents a significant portion of the firm's market value.

positive abnormal announcement-date financial returns for the parent and the subsidiary undergoing a carve-out were greatest in those countries with the highest shareholder protections, especially for minority shareholders.[63]

Value is created through equity carve-outs by increased parent focus, providing a source of financing, and resolving agency issues. These are discussed next.

Increasing focus

Positive announcement-date returns tend to be higher for carve-outs of unrelated subsidiaries. This is consistent with the common observation that carve-outs are undertaken for businesses that do not fit with the parent's business strategy.

Providing a source of financing

Equity carve-outs can help to finance the needs of the parent or the subsidiary. Firms choose equity carve-outs and divestitures over spin-offs when the ratio of MV to book value and revenue growth of the carved-out unit are high, to maximize the amount of cash raised.[64]

Resolving management and shareholder differences (agency conflicts)

Investor reaction to carve-outs is determined by how the proceeds are used. Firms announcing that the proceeds will be used to repay debt or pay dividends earn a 7% abnormal return, compared with minimal returns for those announcing the reinvestment of the proceeds.

Tracking stocks

Reflecting initial investor enthusiasm, a number of studies show that tracking stocks experience significant positive abnormal returns around their announcement date. Studies addressing the issue of whether the existence of publicly listed tracking shares increases the demand for other stock issued by the parent give mixed results.[65] However, there is some evidence that investors become disenchanted with tracking stocks over time, with excess shareholder returns averaging 13.9% around the date of the announcement that firms would eliminate their target stock issues.[66]

Post carve-out, spin-off, and tracking stock returns to shareholders

It is unclear if operating performance improves after equity carve-outs.[67] There is some evidence that both parents and carved-out subsidiaries tend to improve their operating performance relative to their industry peers in the year after the carve-out.[68] However, other studies have shown that operating performance deteriorates.[69]

Carve-outs and spin-offs are more likely to outperform stock market indices because their share prices reflect speculation that they will be acquired rather than an improvement in the operating performance. One-third of spin-offs are acquired within 3 years after the unit is spun off by the parent. After those that have been acquired are removed from the sample, the remaining spin-offs generally perform no better than their peers.[70] Spin-offs may create value by simply providing an efficient method of transferring assets to acquiring companies.[71]

[63] Dasilas et al., 2018

[64] Chen and Guo, 2005

[65] Clayton and Qian (2004) found evidence that parent shares rise after the issuance of tracking stocks. Elder et al. (2000) find no evidence that tracking shares leads to greater interest in the parent's and other subsidiary shares.

[66] Billet et al., 2004

[67] Vijh, 2002

[68] Hulbert et al., 2002

[69] Dasilas et al., 2018; Powers et al., 2003; Boone et al., 2003

[70] Cusatis et al., 1993

[71] McConnell et al., 2001

There is some evidence that spun-off units show productivity gains because of a reduction in total wage costs and employment, perhaps reflecting improved management attention and discipline. Such gains start immediately after the spin-off and tend to persist for as long as 5 years.[72] Carve-outs that are largely independent of the parent (i.e., in which the parent tended to own less than 50% of the equity) tended to outperform the S&P 500 significantly.[73] The evidence for the long-term performance of tracking stocks is mixed.[74]

Some things to remember

Divestitures, spin-offs, equity carve-outs, split-ups, and split-offs are commonly used restructuring strategies to redeploy assets by returning cash or noncash assets through a special dividend to shareholders or to use cash proceeds to pay off debt. On average, these restructuring strategies create positive abnormal financial returns for shareholders around the announcement date, but the longer-term performance of spin-offs, carve-outs, and tracking stocks is problematic.

Chapter discussion questions

17.1 What are the advantages and disadvantages of tracking stocks to investors and the firm?

17.2 How would you decide when to sell a business?

17.3 What factors influence a parent firm's decision to undertake a spin-off rather than a divestiture or equity carve-out?

17.4 How might the form of payment affect the abnormal return to sellers and buyers?

17.5 How might spin-offs result in a transfer of wealth from bondholders to shareholders?

17.6 Explain how executing successfully a large-scale divestiture can be highly complex. This is especially true when the divested unit is integrated with the parent's functional departments and other units operated by the parent. Consider the challenges of timing, interdependencies, regulatory requirements, and customer and employee perceptions.

17.7 In an effort to increase shareholder value, USX announced its intention to split US Steel and Marathon Oil into two separately traded firms. The breakup gives holders of Marathon Oil stock an opportunity to participate in the ongoing consolidation within the global oil and gas industry. Holders of USX−US Steel Group common stock (target stock) would become holders of newly formed Pittsburgh-based United States Steel Corporation. What alternatives could USX have pursued to raise shareholder value? Why do you believe they pursued the breakup strategy rather than some of the alternatives?

17.8 HP announced in 1999 the spin-off of its Agilent Technologies unit to focus on its main business of computers and printers. HP retained a controlling interest until mid-2000, when it spun off the rest of its shares in Agilent to HP shareholders as a tax-free transaction. Discuss the reasons why HP may have chosen a staged transaction rather than an outright divestiture or spin-off of the business.

17.9 After months of trying to sell its 81% stake in Blockbuster Inc., Viacom undertook a spin-off in mid-2004. Why might Viacom have chosen to spin off rather than divest its Blockbuster unit? Explain your answer.

17.10 Since 2001, GE, the world's largest conglomerate, had been underperforming the S&P 500 stock index. In late 2008, the firm announced it would spin off its consumer and industrial unit. What do you believe are GE's motives for this restructuring? Why do you believe they chose a spin-off rather than an alternative restructuring strategy?

Answers to these Chapter Discussion Questions are found in the Online Instructor's Manual for instructors using this book.

[72] Chemmanur et al., 2014

[73] Annema et al., 2002

[74] Chemmanur et al. (2000) found the stock of parent firms underperform the major stock indices, but the average tracking stock outperforms its industry stock index. However, Billett et al. (2004) found negative financial returns after the issue date for tracking stocks and positive but statistically insignificant returns for parents.

End-of-chapter case study: Gardner Denver and Ingersoll Rand's industrial segment merge in a Reverse Morris Trust

Key points

- Greater shareholder value may be created by exiting rather than operating a business.
- How? By increasing the focus of the parent firm.
- The deal structure also can create shareholder value.

Desirous of exiting its investment in Gardner Denver (Gardner)—a leading provider of flow controls—after having held it for more than 6 years, private equity firm Kohlberg Kravis & Roberts (KKR) reviewed a full range of options. They considered retaining the business, undertaking an IPO, exiting the business through a Reverse Morris Trust transaction, and selling the business for cash. KKR had acquired Gardner in 2013 for $3.9 billion, including assumed debt. Investors in its limited partnerships were disappointed in the financial returns provided by the investment, and KKR was under pressure to exit the business.

After an extensive review, KKR decided to exit Gardner through a Reverse Morris Trust transaction to minimize the tax impact on financial returns. If structured properly, a firm can spin off a business and subsequently merge it with an appropriately sized company on a tax-free basis. The challenge was to find the right merger partner.

Gardner announced on April 30, 2019, that it had reached an agreement with Ingersoll Rand (Ingersoll) to combine its industrial products operations (IndustrialCo) in a deal with an enterprise value of $15 billion. To consummate the agreement, Ingersoll would spin off its industrial unit to the firm's shareholders, which would in turn be merged with Gardner. After the closing of the merger, IndustrialCo would become a wholly owned subsidiary of Gardner (Merger Sub). The merger sub could then be combined with the parent through a backend merger without requiring a shareholder vote. The new company (NewCo) formed by merging Gardner and IndustrialCo would be renamed Ingersoll Rand.[75]

[75] Had Ingersoll sold IndustrialCo for cash, the firm would have been subject to an immediate tax liability on the difference between the sale and book values. If the proceeds of the sale had been distributed to shareholders as a special dividend, the shareholders would have been required to pay taxes on the dividend at their personal tax rates resulting in double taxation on any gains on the sale: once by Ingersoll and again by the firm's shareholders.

[76] Betton et al., 2009

[77] Harford and Uysal, 2014

[78] Chatterjee et al., 2012

[79] Yang et al., 2016

[80] Betton et al. 2009

[81] Betton et al., 2008

[82] Moeller, 2005

[83] Atkas et al., 2010

[84] Madura et al., 2012

[85] Wu and Chung, 2019

[86] Simonyan, 2014

[87] Hayward et al., 1997

[88] Gondhalekar et al. (2004) argue that highly leveraged buyers are monitored closely by their lenders and are less likely to overpay. Morellec and Zhdanov (2008) find that relatively unleveraged buyers often pay more for targets.

[89] Ang et al., 2019

[90] Chiang et al., 2014

[91] Ahern, 2012

[92] Tarsalewska, 2018

[93] Dionne et al., 2010

[94] Betton et al., 2008

[95] Calcagno et al., 2014; Moeller, 2005

[96] Cai et al., 2012. Having a board connection often improves the information flow such that the acquirer is less likely to overpay for the target firm.

Ingersoll would retain 100% ownership of its remaining operations referred to as ClimateCo, which was faster growing than IndustrialCo. ClimateCo includes Ingersoll's heating as well as ventilation and air- and temperature-controlled transport businesses. At closing, Ingersoll shareholders would receive $5.8 billion in NewCo stock, giving them a 50.1% controlling interest. The remaining 49.9% would go to existing Gardner shareholders. ClimateCo would receive a $1.9 billion cash payment financed by newly issued debt to be assumed by Gardner. IndustrialCo would finance the $1.9 billion payment to ClimateCo through bank loans. Figure 17.3 illustrates the stages of a Reverse Morris Trust transaction: premerger structure, premerger separation structure, and postmerger structure.

NewCo's CEO will be Vincente Reynal, the Gardner CEO. Senior management will consist of managers from both firms. And NewCo's Chairman will be Gardner's Chairman Peter Stavros and include seven Gardner and three Ingersoll directors. Ingersoll's chairman and CEO, Michael Lamach, and the current senior executive team will continue to lead ClimateCo, which is expected to be renamed.

NewCo is projected to have 2020 revenue of $6.6 billion and an EBITDA of $1.6 billion on a pro forma basis. EBITDA estimates include annual cost savings of $250 million by the end of the third year after closing. The combination is expected to drive revenue growth by leveraging a broader portfolio of technologies and service capabilities. ClimateCo will have pro forma revenue of $12.9 billion and EBITDA of $2 billion. The heating, ventilation, and air conditioning assets of ClimateCo would become a "pure play" in climate control solutions for buildings, homes,

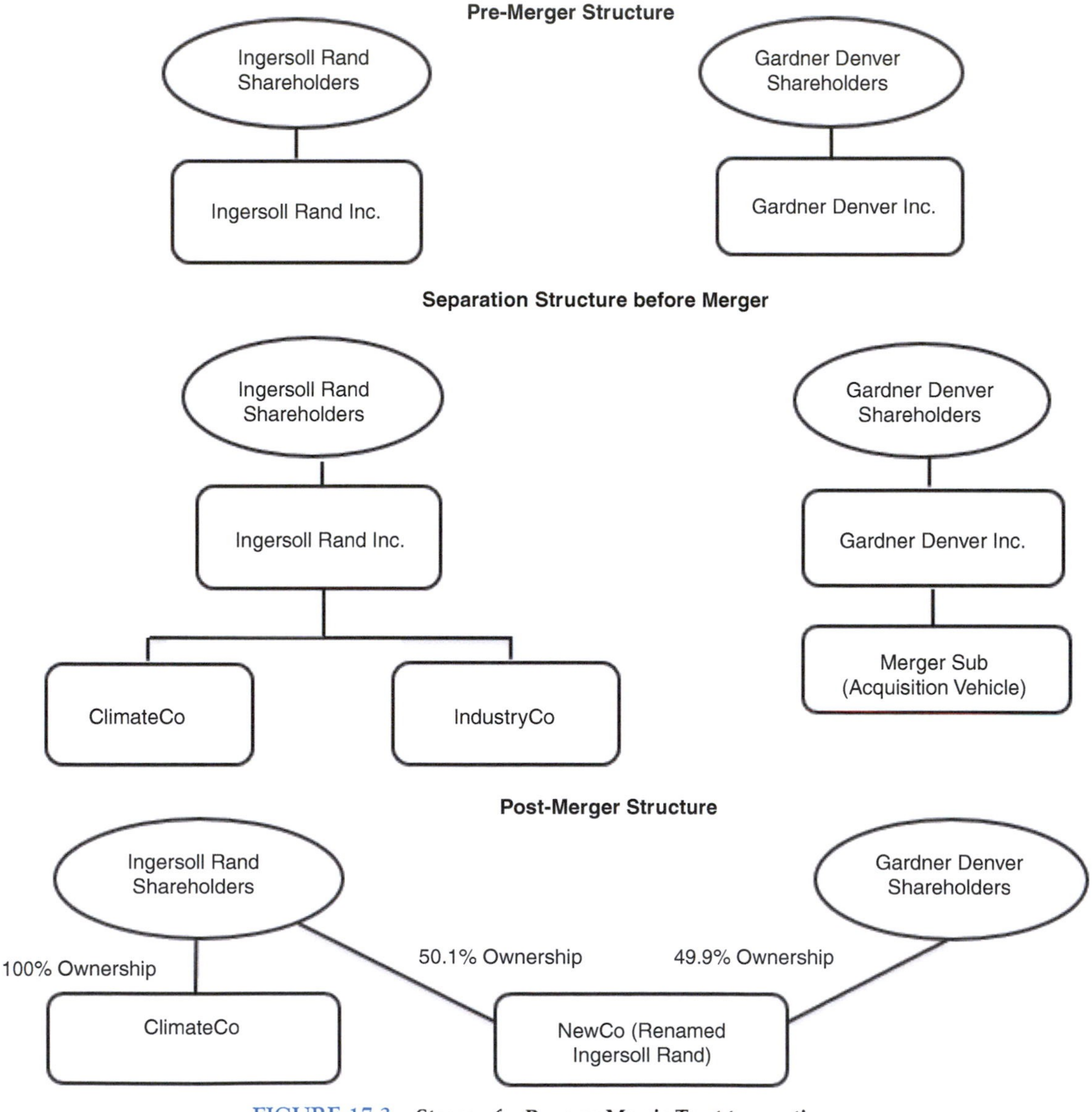

FIGURE 17.3 Stages of a Reverse Morris Trust transaction.

and transportation. As such, it could become an acquisition target shortly after closing. Acquirers prefer to acquire focused firms to avoid having to divest or spin off portions of a target firm not germane to their strategy.

Discussion questions

1. The merger of Gardner Denver and Ingersoll Rand's IndustrialCo segment could have been achieved as a result of a split-off of IndustrialCo. Explain the details of how this might happen.
2. Speculate as to why Ingersoll chose to spin-off rather than split-off IndustrialCo as part of its plan to merge Gardner and IndustrialCo. Be specific.
3. What are the Morris Trust tax regulations? How did they affect how this deal was structured? Why was the final ownership distribution of NewCo (the merger of Gardner and IndustrialCo) renamed Ingersoll Rand important?
4. How is value created for Gardner and Ingersoll shareholders in this type of a transaction?
5. What are the advantages and disadvantages of a Reverse Morris Trust structure?
6. Is KKR actually exiting its investment in Gardner? Explain your answer.
7. Speculate as to why the postmerger governance structure may have played a role in getting the parties to agree on a final deal?

Solutions to this case study are found in the Online Instructors Manual for instructors using this book.

CHAPTER

18

Alternative exit and restructuring strategies

bankruptcy, reorganization, and liquidation

OUTLINE

Mergers, Acquisitions, and Other Restructuring Activities, Eleventh Edition
https://doi.org/10.1016/B978-0-12-819782-0.00018-6

Success breeds disregard for the possibility of failure.—*Hyman P. Minsky*

Inside M&As: iHeartMedia rises from the ashes

KEY POINTS

- Chapter 11 of the US Bankruptcy Code provides an opportunity for debtor firms to reorganize, restructure their liabilities, and emerge as financially viable firms.
- Creditors often use debt-for-equity swaps to recover all or part of what they are owed.
- Imaginative bankruptcy exit strategies can offer creditors the potential to recover more than what they are owed.

Considered "dead" by creditors in early 2018, iHeartMedia (IHRT) was given new life after filing for bankruptcy on March 15, 2018. Formerly known as Clear Channel, the radio station changed its name to iHeartMedia in 2014. The firm owned 850 stations, a music streaming service, a concert business, an 89% stake in Clear Channel Outdoor, and a billboard advertising company. Only Clear Channel Outdoor was profitable.

IHRT's strategy going back to the 1990s, when it was known as Clear Channel, had been to buy stations, slash costs, and replace on-air talent with music feeds. With the rise of digital media firms such as Sirius XM and later Pandora, radio became more a national than a local market. Unable to compete with digital media firms, IHRT switched its focus to satisfying local radio markets by hiring local talent and tailoring content to local tastes. To eliminate shareholder pressure, the firm implemented a leveraged buyout, but the firm borrowed more debt than it could repay because the strategy was taking far longer to execute than originally anticipated.

In a "prearranged bankruptcy," IHRT had been negotiating with creditors and investors for months before reaching an agreement in May 2018 to restructure its debt with the firm's major creditors. As part of the deal, IHRT would sell underperforming radio stations and spin off Clear Channel Outdoor Holdings as a separate company. The firm needed to file for Chapter 11 to reach agreement with its largest creditors without the fear of being forced to cease operations and liquidate the firm by creditors not participating in the agreement. Clear Channel Outdoor Holdings was not part of the filing.

IHRT received court approval of its Chapter 11 bankruptcy plan on January 22, 2019, and reduced its debt from $16.1 billion to $5.75 billion and separated Clear Channel Outdoor Holdings from IHRT, creating two independent public companies. The debt reduction was a result of an agreement with several major creditors before the Chapter 11 filing to swap their debt for equity in the new IHRT and Clear Channel Outdoor Holdings Inc.

IHRT emerged from Chapter 11 in June 2019. Normally, prearranged bankruptcies are much faster than IHRT's deal, but time was required to implement the spin-off of Clear Channel Outdoor Holdings. The exit from bankruptcy protection had envisioned an IHRT initial public offering (IPO) to raise additional funds to satisfy creditors, but the firm settled instead for a Nasdaq listing with the approval of its creditors. With both IHRT and Clear Channel Outdoor Holdings independent firms, creditors reasoned they would become takeover targets, which offered the potential to recover more than what they were owed.

Chapter overview

Bankruptcy and liquidation can be viewed as alternative restructuring and exit strategies for failing firms. The purpose of this chapter is to explore the mechanics of this process and when and how it may be used to restructure firms. How reorganization and liquidation take place both inside and outside the protection of the bankruptcy court are examined in detail. This chapter also discusses common strategic options for failing firms, the current state of bankruptcy prediction models, and empirical studies of the performance of firms experiencing financial distress. A review of this chapter (including practice questions with answers) is available in the file folder titled "Student Study Guide" on the companion website to this book (https://www.elsevier.com/books-and-journals/book-companion/9780128197820).

Business failure

Failing firms may be subject to financial distress, as measured by declining asset values, liquidity, and cash flow. The term *financial distress* does not have a strict definition but applies to a firm unable to meet its obligations or to a security on which the issuer has defaulted.[1] *Technical insolvency* arises when a firm is unable to pay its liabilities when due. *Legal insolvency* occurs when a firm's liabilities exceed the fair market value of its assets. A federal legal proceeding designed to protect the technically or legally insolvent firm from lawsuits by its creditors until a decision can be made to close or continue to operate the firm is called *bankruptcy*. A firm is not bankrupt until it or its creditors file a petition for reorganization or liquidation with the federal bankruptcy courts.

To illustrate these definitions, consider retailer Toys "R" Us, which filed for bankruptcy in the United States and Canada on September 18, 2017. With total debt of $4.9 billion, the retailer had interest payments due in 2018 of more than $400 million and maturing debt of $1.7 billion in 2019. The firm was technically insolvent before filing for bankruptcy because it was unable to service its outstanding debt, but it was not considered in bankruptcy until it actually filed a petition in the US bankruptcy court. And the firm was not legally insolvent because the fair market value of its assets (mostly real estate) exceeded its total liabilities.

Receivership is an alternative to bankruptcy in which a court- or government-appointed individual (i.e., a receiver) manages a firm's assets according to the court's or government's directives. The purpose of a receiver may be to serve as a custodian while disputes between officers, directors, or stockholders are settled or to liquidate the firm's assets. Under no circumstances can the firm's debt be discharged without the approval of the bankruptcy court. In most states, receivership cannot take effect unless a lawsuit is underway and the court has determined that receivership is appropriate. *Conservatorship* represents a less restrictive alternative to receivership. Whereas a receiver is expected to terminate the rights of shareholders and managers, a conservator is expected to assume these rights temporarily.

A failing firm and its creditors may choose to reach a negotiated settlement outside of bankruptcy, within the protection of the court, or through a prepackaged or prearranged bankruptcy. The following sections discuss these options.

Voluntary settlements outside of bankruptcy court

An insolvent firm and its creditors may agree to restructure the firm's obligations out of court to avoid the costs of bankruptcy proceedings. This usually offers the best chance for creditors to recover the largest percentage of what they are owed and shareholders some portion of their investment. This process involves the debtor firm's requesting a meeting with its creditors. A creditor committee is selected to analyze the debtor firm's financial position and recommend a course of action: whether the firm continues to operate or is liquidated.

Voluntary settlements resulting in continued operation

Plans to restructure a debtor firm developed in concert with creditors are called *workouts*. *Debt restructuring* involves concessions by creditors that lower an insolvent firm's payments so that it may remain in business. Restructuring normally is accomplished in three ways: via an extension, a composition, or a debt-for-equity swap. An *extension* occurs when creditors agree to lengthen the debtor firm's repayment period. Creditors often agree to suspend temporarily both interest and principal repayments. A *composition* is an agreement in which creditors agree to receive less than the full amount they are owed. A *debt-for-equity swap* occurs when creditors surrender a portion of their claims in exchange for an ownership position in the firm. Such actions increase the likelihood a debtor firm will survive.[2]

[1] *Default* is defined by Moody's Credit Rating Agency as any delinquent payment of interest or principal, bankruptcy, receivership, or an exchange that reduces the value of what is owed (e.g., the issuer might offer bondholders a new security or combination of securities worth less than what they are owed).

[2] Cepec and Grajzl, 2020

Exhibit 18.1 depicts a debt-for-equity restructure. Although the firm Survivor Inc. has positive earnings before interest and taxes, they are not enough to meet its interest payments. When principal payments are considered, cash flow becomes negative, rendering the firm technically insolvent. As a result of the debt restructure, Survivor Inc. is able to continue to operate, but the firm's lenders now have a controlling interest. Note that the same type of restructuring could take place either voluntarily outside the courts or as a result of reorganizing under the protection of the bankruptcy court.

EXHIBIT 18.1

Survivor Inc. Restructures its Debt

Survivor Inc. currently has 400,000 shares of common equity outstanding at a par value of $10 per share. The current rate of interest on its debt is 8%, and the debt is amortized over 20 years. The combined federal, state, and local tax rate is 40%. The firm's cash flow and capital position are shown in Table 18.1. Assume that bondholders are willing to convert $5 million of debt to equity at the current par value of $10 per share. This necessitates that Survivor Inc. issue 500,000 new shares. These actions result in positive cash flow, a substantial reduction in the firm's debt-to-total capital ratio, and a transfer of control to the bondholders. The former stockholders now own only 44.4% (4 million/9 million) of the company. The revised cash flow and capital position are shown in Table 18.2. In addition to debt restructuring, creditors may require the divestiture of noncore operations and productivity improvement actions across all operations, often forcing firms to reduce their labor forces by as much as 5%. The debtor firm's shareholders are most likely to benefit from creditor intervention when the creditor has in-depth knowledge of the industry in which the firm competes.[3]

[3] Ersahin et al., 2020

TABLE 18.1 Cash flow and capital position

Income and cash flow		Total capital	
Earnings before interest and taxes	$500,000	Debt	$10,000,000
Interest	$800,000	Equity	$4,000,000
Earnings before taxes	$(300,000)	Total	$14,000,000
Taxes	$120,000		
Earnings after taxes	$(180,000)	Debt/total capital	71.4%
Depreciation	$400,000		
Principal repayment	$(500,000)		
Cash flow	$(280,000)		

TABLE 18.2 Revised cash flow and capital position

Income and cash flow		Total capital	
Earnings before interest and taxes	$500,000	Debt	$5,000,000
Interest	$400,000	Equity	$9,000,000
Earnings before taxes	$100,000	Total	$14,000,000
Taxes	$40,000		
Earnings after taxes	$60,000	Debt/total capital	35.7%
Depreciation	$400,000		
Principal repayment	$(250,000)		
Cash flow	$210,000		

Voluntary settlements resulting in liquidation

If the creditors conclude that the insolvent firm's situation cannot be resolved, liquidation may be the only acceptable course of action. Liquidation can be conducted outside the court in a private liquidation or through the US bankruptcy court. If the insolvent firm is willing to accept liquidation and all creditors agree, legal proceedings are not necessary. Creditors normally prefer private liquidations to avoid lengthy and costly litigation. Through a process called an *assignment*, a committee representing creditors grants the power to liquidate the firm's assets to a third party, called an *assignee* or *trustee*. The assignee's task is to sell the assets quickly while obtaining the best possible price. The assignee distributes the proceeds of the asset sales to the creditors and to the firm's owners if any monies remain.

Reorganization and liquidation in bankruptcy

In the absence of a voluntary settlement out of court, the debtor firm may seek protection from its creditors by initiating bankruptcy or may be forced into bankruptcy by its creditors. When the debtor firm files the petition with the bankruptcy court, the bankruptcy is said to be *voluntary*. When creditors do the filing, the action is said to be *involuntary*.

When a bankruptcy petition is filed, the debtor firm is protected from any further legal action related to its debts until the bankruptcy proceedings are completed. The filing of a petition triggers an *automatic stay* after the court accepts the request, which provides a period suspending all judgments, collection activities, foreclosures, and repossessions of property by the creditors on any debt or claim that arose before the filing of the bankruptcy petition. Whether a firm in bankruptcy is reorganized or liquidated depends on the reorganization plan's viability, the relative leverage of the constituent groups having claims on the firm's assets, and the perceived competence of the firm's management.

The evolution of US bankruptcy laws and practices

US bankruptcy laws focus on reorganizing debtors in distress. Modern bankruptcy laws have a number of objectives: to create a mechanism for creditors to recover what they are owed, to provide an opportunity for debtors to start over, and to preserve the going concern value of the distressed firm by reorganizing rather than liquidating to the extent possible. These laws attempt to balance the rights of creditors and borrowers in a manner that treats both parties in a uniform and fair manner. Creditor rights include the ability of a lender to file a lawsuit in the court system to recover what they are owed as prescribed by law. Borrower rights include full disclosure of their legal protections from unfair treatment by creditors.

The fair treatment of both creditors and borrowers impacts the availability and cost of credit. Giving borrowers equal access to credit can fuel economic growth by stimulating consumption and business investment. Providing creditors with the right to recover at least a portion of what they are owed through the court system lowers loan rates by reducing lender risk. Such creditor protections also influence the amount of debt used by corporate borrowers.

Rules and practices governing bankruptcy before the 20th century generally favored the creditor and were more severe with respect to the bankrupt party. More recent bankruptcy laws and practices emphasize rehabilitating debtors in distress by requiring them to reorganize with less emphasis on punishing the debtor.

Article I, Section 8, of the US Constitution authorizes Congress to enact laws pertaining to bankruptcy. Based on this authority, Congress passed the "bankruptcy code" in 1978, which is codified as Title 11 of the United States Legal Code. This law is the uniform federal law that governs all bankruptcy cases. Since 1978, this law has been amended several times.[4]

The Bankruptcy Reform Act of 1978 changed bankruptcy laws by adding a strong business reorganization mechanism, referred to as Chapter 11 of the US Bankruptcy Code. The 1978 law also broadened the conditions under

[4] Except for Chapter 12, all the chapters of the present Bankruptcy Code are odd-numbered. Chapters 1, 3, and 5 cover matters of general application, and Chapters 7, 9, 11, 12, and 13 concern liquidation (business or nonbusiness), municipality bankruptcy, business reorganization, family farm debt adjustment, and wage-earner or personal reorganization, respectively. Chapter 15 applies to international cases.

which companies could file so that a firm could declare bankruptcy without waiting until it was insolvent. The Bankruptcy Reform Act of 1994 contained provisions to expedite bankruptcy proceedings and to encourage individual debtors to use Chapter 13 to reschedule their debts rather than use Chapter 7 to liquidate.

On April 19, 2005, the Bankruptcy Abuse Prevention and Consumer Protection Act (BAPCPA) became law. Although the new legislation affects primarily consumer filings, BAPCPA affects business filers as well, with the heaviest influence on smaller businesses (i.e., those with less than $2 million in debt). BAPCPA changed the commercial bankruptcy process by (1) reducing the maximum length of time during which debtors have an exclusive right to submit a plan, (2) shortening the time that debtors have to accept or reject leases, and (3) limiting compensation under key employee retention programs.

Before BAPCPA, a debtor corporation had the opportunity to request a bankruptcy judge to extend the period for submission of the plan of reorganization as long as it could justify its request. After the judge ruled that the debtor has been given sufficient time, any creditor could submit a reorganization plan. The new law caps the exclusivity period at 18 months from the day of the bankruptcy filing. The debtor then has an additional 2 months to win the creditors' acceptance of the plan, thereby providing a debtor-in-possession (DIP) a maximum of 20 months before creditors can submit their reorganization plans.

Finally, Chapter 15 was added to the US Bankruptcy Code by BAPCPA to reflect the adoption of the Model Law on Cross-Border Insolvency passed by the United Nations Commission on International Trade Law (UNCITRAL) in 1997. The purpose of UNCITRAL is to provide for better coordination among legal systems for cross-border bankruptcy cases. Chapter 15 is discussed in more detail later in this chapter.

Filing for Chapter 11 reorganization

Chapter 11 reorganization may involve a corporation, a sole proprietorship, or a partnership. Because a corporation is viewed as separate from its owners, Chapter 11 does not put the personal assets of the stockholders at risk, other than the value of their investment in the firm's stock. In contrast, sole proprietorships and owners are not separate. A bankruptcy case involving a sole proprietorship includes the owner's business and personal assets. Like a corporation, a partnership exists as an entity separate from its partners. In a general partnership bankruptcy, because the partners are personally responsible for the debts and obligations of the partnership, they may be sued such that their personal assets are used to pay creditors, forcing the partners to file for bankruptcy.

Figure 18.1 summarizes the process for filing for Chapter 11 reorganization. The process begins by filing in a federal bankruptcy court. In the case of an involuntary petition, a hearing must be held to determine whether the firm is insolvent. If the firm is found to be insolvent, the court enters an *order for relief*, which initiates the bankruptcy proceedings. On the filing of a reorganization petition, the filing firm becomes the DIP of all the assets and is responsible for convincing creditors to accept its reorganization plan within the time allowed by law. After that, creditors can submit their own proposal. In the case of fraud, creditors may request that the court appoints a trustee instead of the debtor to run the firm.

The US Trustee (the bankruptcy department of the US Justice Department) appoints one or more committees to represent the interests of creditors and shareholders. These committees work with the DIP to develop a reorganization plan for exiting Chapter 11. Creditors and shareholders are grouped according to the similarity of claims. For creditors, the plan must be approved by holders of at least two-thirds of the dollar value of the claims as well as by a simple majority of the creditors in each group. For shareholders, two-thirds of those in each group (e.g., common and preferred shareholders) must approve the plan.

After acceptance by creditors, bondholders, and stockholders, the bankruptcy court must approve the reorganization plan. Even if creditors or shareholders reject the plan, the court is empowered to ignore the vote and approve

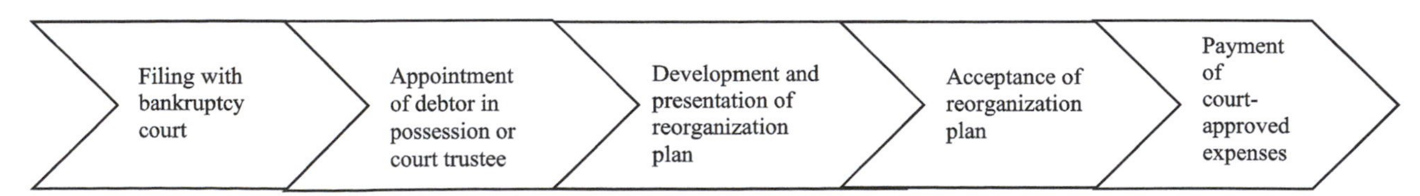

FIGURE 18.1 **Process for reorganizing during bankruptcy.**

the plan if it finds it fair to creditors and shareholders as well as feasible. The DIP must pay expenses approved by the court of all parties whose services were required to complete the bankruptcy process.

Implementing Chapter 7 liquidation

If the bankruptcy court determines that reorganization is infeasible, the failing firm may be forced to liquidate. According to the Administrative Office of US Courts, about 70% of bankruptcy filings are for Chapter 7 liquidation rather than Chapter 11 reorganization. The prevalence of Chapter 7 liquidations may be a result of the tendency of secured creditors to force debtor firms into liquidation to recover what they are owed by selling off the collateral underlying their loans, often at the expense of unsecured creditors and equity investors.

Under Chapter 7, a trustee is given the responsibility to liquidate the firm's assets, keep records, examine creditors' claims, disburse the proceeds, and submit a final report on the liquidation. The priority in which the claims are paid is stipulated in Chapter 7 of the Bankruptcy Reform Act, which must be followed by the trustee when the firm is liquidated.[5] All secured creditors are paid when the firm's assets that were pledged as collateral are liquidated.[6] If the proceeds of the sale of these assets are inadequate to satisfy all of the secured creditors' claims, they become unsecured (general) creditors for the amount that was not recovered. If the proceeds of the sale of pledged assets exceed secured creditors' claims, the excess proceeds are used to pay general creditors.

Liquidation under Chapter 7 does not mean all employees lose their jobs. When a large firm enters Chapter 7 bankruptcy, a division of the company may be sold intact to other companies. This often results in much of the firm's workforce being given the option to work for the acquiring firm, although not necessarily at the same levels of compensation.

Exhibit 18.2 describes how a legally bankrupt company could be liquidated. In this illustration, the bankruptcy court, owners, and creditors could not agree on an appropriate reorganization plan for DOA Inc. Consequently, the court ordered that the firm be liquidated in accordance with Chapter 7. Note that this illustration would differ from a private or voluntary out-of-court liquidation in two important respects. First, the expenses associated with conducting the liquidation would be lower because the liquidation would not involve extended legal proceedings. Second, the distribution of proceeds could reflect the priority of claims negotiated between the creditors and the owners that differs from that set forth in Chapter 7 of the Bankruptcy Reform Act.

EXHIBIT 18.2

Liquidation of DOA Inc. Under Chapter 7

DOA has the balance sheet in Table 18.3. The only liability that is not shown on the balance sheet is the cost of the bankruptcy proceedings, which is treated as an expense and is not capitalized (i.e., not shown as a balance sheet item). The sale of DOA's assets generates $5.4 million in cash. The distribution of the proceeds is displayed in Table 18.4. Note that the proceeds are distributed in accordance with the priorities stipulated in the current commercial bankruptcy law and that the cost of administering the bankruptcy totals 18% (i.e., $972,000/ $5,400,000) of the proceeds from liquidation. After all prior claims have been satisfied, the remaining proceeds are distributed to the unsecured creditors. The pro rata (proportional) settlement percentage of 27.64% is calculated by dividing funds available for unsecured creditors by the amount of unsecured creditor claims (i.e., $1,368/ $4,950). The shareholders receive nothing because not all unsecured creditor claims have been satisfied (Table 18.5).

[5] Chapter 7 distributes liquidation proceeds according to the following priorities: (1) administrative claims (e.g., lawyers' fees, court costs, accountants' fees, trustees' fees); (2) statutory claims (e.g., tax obligations, rent, consumer deposits, and unpaid wages and benefits owed before the filing, up to some threshold); (3) secured creditors' claims; (4) unsecured creditors' claims; and (5) equity claims.

[6] Fully secured creditors, such as bondholders and mortgage lenders, have a legally enforceable right to the collateral securing their loans or the equivalent value. A creditor is fully secured if the value of the collateral for its loan to the debtor equals or exceeds the amount of the debt. For this reason, fully secured creditors are not entitled to participate in any distribution of liquidated assets that the bankruptcy trustee might make.

TABLE 18.3 DOA balance sheet

Assets		Liabilities	
Cash	$35,000	Accounts payable	$750,000
Accounts receivable	$2,300,000	Bank notes payable	$3,000,000
Inventories	$2,100.000	Accrued salaries	$720,000
Total current assets	$4,435,000	Unpaid benefits	$140,000
Land	$1,500,000	Unsecured customer deposits	$300,000
Net plant and equipment	2,000,000	Taxes payable	400,000
Total fixed assets	$3,500,000	Total current liabilities	$5,310,000
Total assets	$7,935,000	First mortgage	$2,500,000
		Unsecured debt	$200,000
		Total long-term debt	$2,700,000
		Preferred stock	$50,000
		Common stock	$100,000
		Paid in surplus	$500,000
		Retained earnings	$(725,000)
		Total stockholders' equity	$(75,000)
		Total shareholders' equity and total liabilities	$7,935,000

TABLE 18.4 Distribution of liquidation proceeds

Proceeds from liquidation	$5,400,000
Expenses of administering bankruptcy	$972,000
Salaries owed employees	$720,000
Unpaid employee benefits	$140,000
Unsecured customer deposits	$300,000
Taxes	$400,000
Funds available for creditors	$2,868,000
First mortgage (from sale of fixed assets)	$1,500,000
Funds available for unsecured creditors	$1,368,000

TABLE 18.5 Pro rata distribution of funds among unsecured creditors

Unsecured creditor claims	Amount	Settlement at 27.64%
Unpaid balance from first mortgage	$1,000,000	$276,400
Accounts payable	$750,000	$207,300
Notes payable	$3,000,000	$829,200
Unsecured debt	$200,000	$55,280
Total	$4,950,000	$1,368,000

The Small Business Reorganization Act of 2019

Passed fortuitously in 2019, this legislation streamlined the process to restructure small business debt. The Act allows debtors to retain ownership of their business as long as secured creditors are paid the value of their collateral. To do so, the debtor has to commit all profits from the business to creditors for up to 5 years. To qualify, a debtor's total obligations cannot exceed $2.7 million.

"Section 363 sales" from Chapter 11

So-called 363 sales have become popular in recent years when time is critical. Section 363 bankruptcies allow a firm to enter a court-supervised sale of assets—usually an auction—as the best means of protecting the value of such assets. Unlike typical bankruptcies, firms may emerge in as little as 30 to 60 days. The auction process starts with a prospective buyer's setting the initial purchase price and terms as well as negotiating a *topping fee* to be paid if it is not successful in buying the assets. Often referred to as a *stalking horse*, the identity of the initial bidder may be concealed. The purpose of the stalking horse is to set a value for the business and to generate interest in the coming auction.

Credit bids occur when secured creditors propose to buy the assets. Such bidders can bid up to the amount of the debt they are owed before offering any cash. Creditors opposing the sale have only 10 to 20 days to file objections to the court, although the period may be shortened to as little as a few days by the bankruptcy judge. The bankruptcy judge decides how the proceeds of the auction are distributed among secured creditors. After filing for bankruptcy because of the 2020 pandemic, US-based regional hamburger chain Krystal was acquired by Fortress Investment Group, which cancelled the $27 million it was owed.

Chapter 15: dealing with cross-border bankruptcy

The purpose of Chapter 15 of the US Bankruptcy Code is to provide mechanisms for resolving insolvency cases involving assets, lenders, and other parties in various countries. A Chapter 15 case is secondary to the primary proceeding brought in another country, which is typically the debtor's home country. As an alternative to Chapter 15, the debtor may proceed with a Chapter 7 or Chapter 11 case in the United States. As part of a Chapter 15 proceeding, the US Bankruptcy Court may authorize a trustee to act in a foreign country on its behalf.

The foreign trustee has the right to petition the US court system for resolving insolvency issues. The petition gives the court the authority to issue an order recognizing the foreign proceeding as either a "foreign main proceeding" or a "foreign non-main proceeding." A *foreign main proceeding* is a proceeding in a country where the debtor's main interests are located; a *foreign non-main proceeding* is one in a country where the debtor has a business not representing their primary holdings. If the proceeding is recognized as a foreign main proceeding, the court imposes an automatic stay on assets in dispute in the United States and authorizes the foreign representative to operate the debtor's business.[7]

Motivations for filing for bankruptcy

Most companies file for bankruptcy because of their deteriorating financial position. Some firms seek bankruptcy protection to shed or limit exposure to acquisition-related liabilities, enhance negotiating leverage, break onerous contracts, or limit risk from pending litigation.

While in bankruptcy, Steelmaker LTV sold its plants to W.L. Ross and Company, which restarted the plants in a new company named the International Steel Group. By buying assets, ISI eliminated its obligation to pay pension, health care, and insurance liabilities, which remained with LTV. Auto parts manufacturer Delphi used its bankruptcy to threaten to rescind union contracts to gain wage and benefit reductions from employees. A bankruptcy court judge allowed Sabine Oil and Gas to shed expensive contracts made with oil and gas pipeline firms when energy prices were booming.

[7] Chapter 15 also gives foreign creditors the right to participate in US bankruptcy cases and prohibits discrimination against foreign creditors. Chapter 15 proceeding attempts to promote collaboration between US and foreign courts because the participants in the proceeding must cooperate fully.

Pending asbestos claims were resolved when a settlement enabling two subsidiaries of the energy giant Halliburton to emerge from bankruptcy limiting their exposure to potential litigation by establishing a $4.2 billion trust fund to pay such claims. In early 2019, mega utility Pacific Gas & Electric filed for Chapter 11 reorganization in the wake of potential liabilities from hundreds of lawsuits after the firm's alleged negligence in northern California wildfires. Later that same year, Talc supplier Imerys Talc America filed for bankruptcy protection against lawsuits alleging its talc supplied to Johnson & Johnson to make baby powder caused ovarian cancer. OxyContin maker Purdue Pharma also filed for bankruptcy protection in late 2019, succumbing to pressure from more than 2600 lawsuits alleging the firm powered the US opioid epidemic.

The high cost of bankruptcy

Efforts to contain costs have prompted greater use of market-based techniques. These include *prepackaged or prearranged bankruptcies* with a reorganization plan in place at the time of the bankruptcy filing, acquisition of distressed debt by investors willing to support the proposed plan of reorganization, and voluntary auction-based sales while a firm is in Chapter 11. Despite these innovations, the cost of professional services remains high. Although large and complex, fees paid to bankruptcy advisors (e.g., appraisers, investment bankers, and lawyers) since the Lehman Brothers liquidation began in 2008 totalled more than $6 billion by the time the process was completed.[8]

Preparing for Chapter 11: prepackaged bankruptcies

Under a prepackaged bankruptcy, the debtor negotiates with creditors to create a reorganization plan and solicits their votes before filing for Chapter 11 bankruptcy. Because there is general approval of the plan before the filing, the formal Chapter 11 reorganization that follows generally averages only a few months and results in substantially lower legal and administrative expenses. Prepackaged bankruptcies are often a result of major creditors' willingness to make concessions before the debtor filing for bankruptcy if they anticipate the debtor firm being liquidated at "fire or distressed sale" prices as a result of the bankruptcy process.[9] For larger ownership positions, distressed sales require substantially larger discounts. In a study of minority equity sales with a 3.7% ownership share, the size of the discount is about 8% in distressed sales. For ownership stakes in excess of 5%, the size of the average discount if forced to sell is approximately 14%.[10]

In a true prepackaged bankruptcy, creditors approve a reorganization plan before filing for bankruptcy. The bankruptcy court then approves the plan, and the company emerges from bankruptcy quickly. Minority creditors often are required by the court to accept a plan of reorganization. The confirmation of such a plan over the objections of one or more classes of creditors sometimes is referred as a *cram down*.

On November 4, 2010, US movie studio Metro-Goldwyn-Mayer filed a prepackaged Chapter 11 bankruptcy in New York that had the approval of nearly all of its creditors. The week before, creditors had approved a plan to forgive more than $4 billion in debt for ownership stakes in the restructured studio and to replace existing management. The bankruptcy was approved the following month, with the reorganized firm emerging from court protection having raised $600 million in new financing.

Preparing for Chapter 11: prearranged bankruptcies

Such bankruptcies occur when firms achieve near consensus in prebankruptcy negotiations over a reorganization plan without soliciting creditor votes (unlike prepackaged bankruptcies) before filing for Chapter 11 bankruptcy. They are often used when there is ongoing litigation among parties to the bankruptcy and the debtor lacks the liquidity needed to finance its operations during the period required to solicit creditor votes.

[8] Ferek, January 16, 2019.

[9] Fire sale prices refer to the liquidation of a firm's assets at prices far below their fair market value to achieve a rapid sale. Creditors must infer the values of assets that could be sold at distressed prices without the benefit of prices from a market in which such assets are frequently traded.

[10] Dinc et al., 2017

TABLE 18.6 Alternative strategies for failing firms

Assumptions	Options: failing firm	Outcome: failing firm
Selling price is greater than the going-concern or liquidation value	Is acquired by or merges with another firm	Continues as subsidiary of acquirer Merged into acquirer and ceases to exist
Going-concern value is greater than the sale or liquidation value	Reaches out-of-court settlement with creditors Seeks bankruptcy protection under Chapter 11 Seeks prepackaged settlement with primary creditors before entering Chapter 11	Continues with debt-for-equity swap, extension, and composition Continues in reorganization
Liquidation value is greater than the sale or going-concern value	Reaches out-of-court settlement with creditors Liquidates under Chapter 7	Ceases to exist; assignee liquidates assets and distributes proceeds, reflecting the terms of the negotiated settlement with creditors Ceases to exist; trustee supervises liquidation and distributes proceeds according to statutory priorities

The 2020 COVID-19 pandemic's impact on the bankruptcy process

The challenges of the 2020 pandemic-induced recession were more pervasive than in the 2008 to 2009 economic downturn because entire industries were ordered to close. Many creditors were slow to declare borrowers in default or to force firms into bankruptcy to avoid liquidation of assets serving as collateral in "fire sales," which generally destroy asset value. Prepackaged bankruptcies and prearranged bankruptcies were widely used, and in some instances, when businesses were totally without revenue, Section 363 sales were used to liquidate assets at auction. Contributing to a rise in Chapter 11 filings, the Small Business Reorganization Act made filing for bankruptcy easier and less expensive under Chapter 11. Companies were more likely to file under Chapter 11 than Chapter 7 because the primary reason for filing was insufficient cash flow rather than the fair market value of their assets exceeding liabilities.

Alternative options for failing firms

A failing firm's strategic options are to merge with another firm, reach an out-of-court voluntary settlement with creditors, or file for Chapter 11 bankruptcy.[11] Note that the prepackaged and prearranged bankruptcies discussed earlier in this chapter constitute a blend of the second and third options. The firm may liquidate voluntarily as part of an out-of-court settlement or be forced to liquidate under Chapter 7 of the Bankruptcy Code.

Table 18.6 summarizes the implications of each option. The choice of which option to pursue is critically dependent on which provides the greatest net present value for creditors and shareholders. To evaluate these options, the firm's management needs to estimate the going-concern, selling price, and liquidation values of the firm.[12]

Merging with another firm

If the failing firm's management estimates that the sale price of the firm is greater than the going-concern or liquidation value, management should seek to merge with another firm. In an essentially "make versus buy" decision,[13]

[11] Kang et al. (2020) discuss strategic options for failing firms in the context of real options. The value of Chapter 11 reorganization can be viewed as a call option on the postbankruptcy value of the firm's assets and the sale or liquidation value as a put option, with the preferred option the higher of the two values.

[12] Antill and Grenadier (2019) discuss how creditors anticipate a range of bargaining options available to equity investors in financially distressed firms and build those into the cost of funds when lending to such firms.

[13] "Make versus buy" decisions reflect the option of a firm to develop an asset on its own or to obtain it by acquiring another firm that already owns the desired asset.

firms in the same industry may be inclined to acquire the failing firm, especially if they are able to acquire assets at distressed prices (i.e., below their intrinsic value) that can be used in their operations. Such deals represent a transfer of wealth from bankrupt firm's debt holders to the acquiring firm's shareholders.[14]

The size of the discount from book or fair market value of assets acquired from a failing firm is likely to be greater if there are industry and economy-wide liquidity problems.[15] If the seller's direct competitors are unable to bid for the assets to be divested, nontraditional buyers such as private equity firms are likely to express interest. Such buyers generally do not value assets based on potential synergy but rather on their eventual sale value. Consequently, they often are looking to buy assets only at bargain prices.

Distressed firms in illiquid industries tend to sell at a discount of as much as 18.3% compared with distressed firms in liquid industries.[16] The problem is exacerbated when the economy is depressed because there are likely to be few potential buyers, and the assets to be sold cannot be easily used in other industries.

When the target's assets are highly specialized and cannot be readily used by firms outside of the target's industry, the target firm's announcement date returns are reduced by about 5%. The target's returns can be reduced by an additional 21% when other firms in the industry and the target are financially distressed because of the absence of buyers and the target's weak bargaining position.[17]

If there is a strategic buyer, management must convince the firm's creditors that they will be more likely to receive what they are owed, and shareholders are more likely to preserve share value if the firm is acquired rather than liquidated or allowed to remain independent. In some instances, buyers are willing to acquire failing firms only if their liabilities are reduced through the bankruptcy process. Hence, it may make sense to force the firm into bankruptcy to have some portion of its liabilities discharged during the process of Chapter 11 reorganization.[18] Alternatively, the potential buyer could reach agreement in advance of bankruptcy reorganization with the primary creditors and use the bankruptcy process to achieve compliance from the minority creditors.

Sales within the protection of Chapter 11 reorganization may be accomplished either by a negotiated private sale to a particular purchaser or through a public auction. The latter is often favored by the court because the purchase price is more likely to reflect the true market value of the assets. Generally, a public auction can withstand any court challenge by creditors questioning whether the purchaser has paid fair market value for the failing firm's assets. Time Warner Inc. and Comcast Corp reached an agreement to buy bankrupt cable operator Adelphia Communications Corp while in Chapter 11 for nearly $18 billion. They paid Adelphia bondholders and other creditors in cash and warrants for stock in a new company formed by combining Time Warner's cable business and Adelphia.

Reaching an out-of-court voluntary settlement with creditors

The going-concern value of the firm may exceed the sale or liquidation value. Management must be able to demonstrate to creditors that a restructured or downsized firm is able to repay its debts if creditors were willing to accept less, extend the maturity of the debt, or exchange debt for equity. In what is known as the *holdout problem*, smaller creditors have an incentive to attempt to hold up the agreement unless they receive special treatment, making an out-of-court voluntary settlement difficult to achieve. Consensus may be accomplished by paying all small creditors 100% of what they are owed and the larger creditors an agreed-on percentage. In contrast to bank debt, which is comparatively easy to renegotiate outside the protection of bankruptcy court, publicly traded debt (which is widely held) is very difficult to renegotiate without a formal bankruptcy proceeding. Some financially ailing firms engage in tender offers to exchange their current debt for debt with longer maturity dates or lower interest rates, for equity, or both. Others use asset sales whose proceeds are used to buy back debt. Still others use a combination of all of these methods. Firms with modest cash flow growth rates under pressure to sell assets and subject to low corporate tax rates are most inclined to use equity in their efforts to renegotiate publicly traded debt.[19]

[14] Nishihara and Shibata, 2019

[15] Finlay et al., 2016

[16] Oh, 2018

[17] Kim, 2018

[18] To protect it from litigation, Washington Construction Group required Morrison Knudsen Corporation to file for bankruptcy as a closing condition in the agreement of purchase and sale.

[19] Silaghi, 2018

Voluntary and involuntary liquidations

The failing firm's management, shareholders, and creditors may agree that the firm is worth more in liquidation than in sale or as a continuing operation. If management cannot reach agreement with creditors on a private liquidation, the firm may seek Chapter 7 liquidation. The proceeds of a private liquidation are distributed in accordance with the agreement negotiated with creditors, while the order in which claimants are paid is set by statute.

The increasing role of hedge funds in the bankruptcy process

Debtor-in-Position, or DIP, financing refers to loans made to a firm in Chapter 11 to satisfy working capital needs while being reorganized. Such financing is senior in liquidation to all other forms of debt held by the bankrupt firm. Bank lenders are more likely to provide such financing for firms in Chapter 11 when their prebankruptcy loans to the firm are at risk, the firm has the potential to reorganize, and the firm has long-standing relationships with the lender. They usually have little interest in taking an equity stake in the firm. In contrast, activist lenders such as hedge funds are more likely to provide DIP financing when debtor firms are small and their existing loans are overcollateralized. Their motive is to loan in order to own the firm.[20] According to data provider Preqin Ltd., hedge funds raised a record $67 billion in 2020 to lend to distressed firms ravaged by the pandemic-induced recession.

Hedge funds pursue activist strategies because of their focus on achieving high financial returns and because they are not limited by having business relationships with the debtor firm. Banks, mutual funds, and pension funds often have potential conflicts of interest with the debtor firm ranging from meeting their capital needs to managing the firm's pension fund assets. Unlike pension and mutual funds, hedge funds also are able to hold large amounts of illiquid investments that strengthen their influence in negotiating with secured creditors.

Hedge funds play a key role in financing debtor firms in Chapter 11 by providing DIP financing and acquiring equity stakes in such businesses. They use the offer of DIP financing to bargain for seats on the debtor firm's board of directors and for receiving an ownership stake when the firm emerges from bankruptcy. DIP loans often convert to equity because they allow for debt-for-equity swaps. Hedge funds also can acquire a controlling interest through so-called "loan-to-own" strategies and by acquiring unsecured debt in order to serve on the unsecured creditor or equity committees.

Under a "loan-to-own" strategy, a hedge fund acquires the debt of a failing firm and converts the debt into a controlling equity stake. That is, the hedge fund buys the debt at depressed prices, forces the distressed firm into Chapter 11, and converts the debt at book value to equity in a debt-for-equity swap, resulting in a controlling stake in the firm when the firm emerges from bankruptcy. The emergence from Chapter 11 is accomplished under Section 363(k) of the Bankruptcy Code, which gives debtors the right to bid on the firm in a public auction sale. During the auction, the firm's debt is valued at face value rather than market value, discouraging bidders other than the hedge fund that acquired the debt before bankruptcy at distressed levels.

By buying unsecured debt, hedge funds play an important role in affecting the balance of power between the debtor firm and secured creditors. Reorganizations in which hedge funds have substantial representation on unsecured creditor committees exhibit higher recovery rates for unsecured creditors and equity owners because of the ability of hedge funds to offset the tendency of secured creditors to push for liquidation.[21]

Failing firms and systemic risk

In response to the meltdown in global financial markets in 2008 and 2009, the US Congress passed the Dodd–Frank Wall Street Reform and Consumer Protections Act of 2010 (Dodd–Frank). This act was revised in 2018 to increase the asset threshold from $50 billion to $250 billion for banks to be classified as systematically risky (or "too big to fail"), reducing the number of banks in this category to the nation's top 10 banks.

[20] Li et al., 2016

[21] Jiang et al., 2012

Efforts to limit systemic risk

Among other things, the Dodd–Frank Act created a new government authority to dismantle financial services firms whose demise would endanger the US financial system and economy. The objectives of this new authority, called the Orderly Liquidation Authority (OLA), are to ensure that losses resulting from the speedy liquidation of a firm are borne primarily by the firm's shareholders and creditors, minimize the loss of taxpayer funds, and penalize current management. The OLA is solely a liquidation remedy and, unlike Chapter 11 of the US Bankruptcy Code, does not allow for reorganization or rehabilitation.[22]

The OLA applies to US bank holding companies and nonbank financial firms supervised by the Federal Reserve Board of Governors (the Fed). The OLA also applies to companies engaged predominantly in activities that the Fed determines are financial in nature, subsidiaries of such companies (other than insured depository institutions or insurance companies), and brokers and dealers registered with the Securities and Exchange Commission and a member of the Securities Investor Protection Corporation (SIPC).[23] The liquidation of insured depository institutions remains the responsibility of the Federal Deposit Insurance Corporation (FDIC). Although insurance companies will continue to be subject to state regulation, their holding companies are covered by the OLA.

The advantages of the OLA are that it provides government with both the authority and a clear process for winding down failing firms deemed a risk to the financial system. However, the resolution process for dealing with failing systemically risky firms can itself destabilize the financial system because the process could panic investors and lenders. Furthermore, the OLA is applicable only to firms whose operations are domestic because there is currently no cross-border mechanism for resolving issues involving banks operating in multiple countries. Consequently, large multinational banks will be unaffected by the OLA.

In late 2015, the Fed adopted a rule stopping it from bailing out individual firms. The rule stemmed from the controversial decision in 2008 to rescue American International Group and others, while deciding not to bail out Lehman Brothers, during the 2008 to 2009 financial crises. The rule is intended to end the notion of individual financial companies being too big to fail by allowing the Fed to rescue only the broader financial system rather than individual companies.[24] Under the rule, the Fed can make emergency loans available that can potentially be used by at least five companies, but it cannot selectively choose which firms to save individually.

Have these risk mitigation efforts been successful?

Recent evidence suggests that despite the Dodd–Frank legislation passed in 2010, increasing bank capital requirements, and periodic "stress testing" of banks to determine the degree of financial distress they can withstand, the big financial institutions are no safer today than before the 2008 financial market meltdown.[25] Because banks are better capitalized today, measures of risk and financial returns on their common and preferred stock required by investors and interest rates on their debt should be lower than before 2008 because they are less likely to experience financial distress and bankruptcy.[26] In fact, required returns and measures of risk such as share price volatility are higher. Why? The increase in bank capital requires banks to concentrate a larger share of their cash in low-earning investments such as Treasury securities reducing profitability, operating cash flow, dividend paying capability, interest coverage ratios, and ability to reinvest in current operations.

Severe loan losses in an economic downturn could push already-stretched operating cash flow into the red, straining bank liquidity and potentially bank solvency. Consequently, although banks have more liquid assets on hand to weather financial turmoil, their ability to generate cash from operations is lessened, leaving their perceived current risk about the same as before the 2008 financial crisis. A more recent study comes to similar

[22] The order in which claimants are paid during liquidation is similar to that defined under Chapter 7, except that the government puts itself first.

[23] The SIPC is a fund designed to insure brokerage firm clients against broker and dealer fraud.

[24] Zhu et al. (2017) argue that banks have an incentive to merge even when scale economies are lacking because of the "too big to fail" designation. The benefits of this designation provide banks with an insurance policy against default from taxpayers and enables senior management to undertake riskier activities and reap higher returns for the bank (and bonuses for themselves) while shifting the risk of default to taxpayers.

[25] Sarin et al., 2016.

[26] Increased capital requirements relative to debt should in theory reduce a bank's levered beta resulting in a reduction in investor-required returns estimated using the capital asset pricing model (see Chapter 7) and share price volatility relative to overall stock market changes.

conclusions: Dodd–Frank resulted in a redistribution of wealth from small to larger financial institutions without reducing the overall risk of the financial system.[27]

The response by equity investors and bondholders to the passage of the Dodd–Frank bill suggested they were doubtful the legislation would make the financial system safer.[28] By some measures, the danger of systemic risk could even be greater if the financial markets show signs of investor panic. The top five US banks controlled 45% of total US banking assets in 2016 compared with 25% in 2000, making such banks more likely to be bailed out by taxpayers as "too big to fail."[29]

Protected by an implied government safety net, bank managers may be prone to making risky bets unseen by regulators unable to monitor all aspects of the diversity and complexity of these megabanks. Moreover, banks continue to lend to lightly regulated hedge funds and private equity firms that have increased their share of lending to riskier borrowers unable to get bank loans. Increasing default rates on hedge fund and private equity loans would impact bank liquidity, potentially jeopardizing the entire financial system. Regulators still have an incomplete picture of the estimated $600 trillion derivatives market, widely considered a major factor in the 2008 to 2009 financial crisis. Derivatives are financial instruments whose value depends on the prices of underlying assets such as mortgage portfolios and commodities. Although derivatives serve to manage risk, they also can be used by traders to engage in extreme speculation. They are not traded on public exchanges and banks are not required to disclose derivative data (unless specifically requested to do so) to US regulators held by certain types of foreign entities as long as the subsidiary's US parent is not contractually responsible for its subsidiary's liabilities. Therefore regulators have little visibility into a US bank's risk exposure to foreign entities.

Predicting corporate default and bankruptcy

Data-mining software allows model builders to churn large quantities of data to identify patterns relevant to bankruptcy prediction. Analysts with substantial knowledge in specialized disciplines, such as accounting and finance, add value in interpreting relevant data. However, neither data mining nor specialized knowledge has proved consistently superior in forecasting accurately default. Both are backward looking, generally relying on historical data. And each new credit cycle tends to be somewhat different from past cycles.

What has proved to be the most useful is the judicious application of both data mining software and specialized knowledge.[30] The latter allows the analyst to determine whether data patterns uncovered through data mining are an anomaly or do actually improve model predictive accuracy. Although the different methodologies for developing default prediction models are too numerous to summarize here, it is likely that there is no "one-size-fits-all approach" that is definitively better than others in all situations.[31]

Model accuracy

Developed in the late 1960s, the most common statistical tool used to develop bankruptcy prediction models is multiple discriminant analysis, commonly known as the Z model. The earliest quantitative efforts to predict bankruptcy involved so-called *credit scoring models*, which relied on discriminant analysis to distinguish between bankrupt and nonbankrupt firms.

Discriminant analysis uses a combination of independent variables to assign a score (i.e., a Z score) to a particular firm. This score then is used to distinguish between bankrupt and nonbankrupt firms by using a cut-off point. The likelihood of bankruptcy for firms with low Z scores is less than for firms with high Z scores. The limitation is that it captures a firm's financial health at a moment in time and does not reflect changes in a company's financial ratios over time. Tests of this methodology applied to more recent samples found that the earlier model's ability to classify bankrupt companies correctly fell from 83.5% to 57.8%.[32]

[27] Andriosopoulos et al., 2017

[28] Gao et al., 2018

[29] *The Economist*, The Superstar Company: A Giant Problem, September 17, 2016

[30] Zhou et al., 2015

[31] Alaka et al., 2018

[32] Grice and Ingram, 2001

By the 1980s, modelling shifted from discriminant to logit analysis (probability-based predictions) and neural networks. *Neural networks* use artificial intelligence that attempts to mimic the way a human brain works and are particularly effective when a large database of prior examples exists. In analyzing model accuracy, multivariate discriminant analysis and neural networks seem to be the most promising.[33] The predictive accuracy of the various types of models tends to be similar, correctly identifying failing firms about 80% of the time when applied to firms used in the historical sample (in-sample predictions) to estimate the models. However, accuracy drops substantially (to as low as 50%–60%) in predicting failing firms not used in constructing the models (out-of-sample predictions).[34] Documenting potential problems with bankruptcy prediction models, researchers have found that accuracy not only declines when applied to out-of-sample predictions but results often vary widely by industry and time period.

Factors affecting financial distress and default rate predictions

Of the many numeric or structured variables used to predict default rates, financial or accounting measures of liquidity, solvency, leverage, profitability, asset composition, firm size, and growth rate are the best predictors of the incidence of default[35] followed by market-based variables such as interest rates and credit default swap rates.[36] Market-based variables are more important during periods of high financial market distress such as the 2008 to 2009 financial crisis.[37] Of these variables, those most common to international models of financial distress include measures solvency and profitability.[38] However, because financial ratios reflect industry[39] and country[40] characteristics, financial ratios that improve the predictive accuracy of models may differ across industries.

Various indicators of corporate governance also seem to improve the predictive accuracy of traditional models. These indicators include board structure, ownership structure, cash flow rights, and retention of key personnel. Different board structures could include one in which the chairman of the board and the chief executive officer are the same person versus a structure in which they are kept separate. Examples of ownership structure could include the existence of various classes of stock with different voting rights. Cash flow rights refer to stock whose owner is entitled to receive dividends.[41]

Firms that engage intensively in research and development spending and labor force training are less likely to fail than those that do not during or immediately after recessions. Firms more resistant to business downturns also are more likely to have developed significant proprietary knowledge as well as to engage in collaboration and information sharing with their suppliers and customers. Such firms tend to be more adaptive to changes in their environment and are likely to command greater loyalty from suppliers and customers.[42]

Machine learning models combine multiple layers of neural networks to learn how to use data available in multiple formats such as images, text, and numbers. Such models using both textual and numeric inputs have improved prediction accuracy over models using a single type of input.[43] Machine learning models tend to be more accurate than logistic regression and linear discriminant analysis in predicting the likelihood of default.[44]

[33] Hosaka, 2019

[34] Statistical methodologies used to construct bankruptcy models settle on a set of variables that exhibit the highest correlation with failing firms during the historical period used to estimate such models. The degree of model reliability is tested severely when such models are used to predict failing firms not used in constructing the models. The significant drop in accuracy of out-of-sample predictions raises serious concerns about the reliability of such models (Aziz et al., 2006).

[35] D. Liang et al., 2016.

[36] Gao et al. (2021) find evidence consistent with the notion that banks have an information advantage in assessing credit quality, with higher borrowing costs associated with lower postacquisition performance.

[37] Li and Faff, 2019

[38] Laitinen et al., 2016.

[39] Sayari et al., 2017

[40] Tian et al., 2017

[41] Liang et al., 2017; Li et al., 2020

[42] Martinez et al., 2019

[43] Mai et al., 2019

[44] Moscatelli et al., 2020

Empirical studies of financial distress

Studies of firms in financial distress analyze investor returns on firms emerging from bankruptcy and on financially distressed stocks, business failure by stage of maturity, and the extent to which one firm's financial distress can be transmitted to other firms.

Attractive returns to firms emerging from bankruptcy are often temporary

When firms emerge from bankruptcy, they often cancel the old stock and issue new common stock. Empirical studies show that such firms often experience attractive financial returns to holders of the new stock immediately after the announcement that the firm is emerging from bankruptcy. However, long-term performance often deteriorates with some studies showing that 40% of the firms studied showed operating losses in 3 years after emerging from Chapter 11. Almost one-third subsequently filed for bankruptcy or had to restructure their debt. After 5 years, about one-quarter of all firms that reorganized were liquidated or merged or refiled for bankruptcy.[45] The most common reason for firms having to file for bankruptcy again is excessive debt. As such, critics expressed doubt about the long-term viability of Pacific Gas & Electric when it emerged from bankruptcy in 2020 with a financing plan requiring it to borrow the $40 billion needed to improve its electrical grid.

Returns to financially distressed stocks are unexpectedly low

As a class, distressed stocks offer low financial rates of return despite their high risk of business failure.[46] In theory, one would expect such risky assets to offer financial returns commensurate with risk. The low financial return for distressed stocks tends to be worse for stocks with low analyst coverage, institutional ownership, and price per share. Factors potentially contributing to these low returns could include unexpected events, valuation errors by uninformed investors, and the characteristics of distressed stocks.

Unexpected events include the economy's being worse than expected. Valuation errors include investors not understanding the true risk of failure of distressed firms and not fully discounting the value of these stocks to reflect this risk. The characteristics of failing firms are such that some investors may have an incentive to hold such stocks despite their low returns. For example, majority owners of distressed stocks can benefit by having other firms in which they have an ownership stake buy the firm's output or assets at bargain prices or sell to the firm at above-market prices. Consequently, the low financial returns for these majority investors in distressed firms are more than offset by the returns on their investments in other firms that are either customers of or suppliers to the distressed firm.

Low returns to financially distressed stocks also may be related to the future potential for asset recovery. If expected recovery rates are high, the distressed firm's shareholders may trigger default by missing payments if they believe they can recover a significant portion of the value of their shares through renegotiation of credit terms with lenders. Consequently, the lower perceived risk of such shares would result in commensurately lower financial returns.[47]

Initial public offerings are more likely to experience bankruptcy than established firms

Firms that have recently undergone IPOs tend to experience a much higher incidence of financial distress and bankruptcy than more established firms.[48] These findings are consistent with other studies showing that a portfolio of IPOs performs well below the return on the S&P 500 stock index for up to 5 years after the firms go public.[49] Some observers attribute this underperformance to the limited amount of information available on these firms.[50]

[45] France, 2002

[46] Campbell et al., 2008

[47] Garlappi et al., 2011

[48] Beneda, 2007

[49] Loughran et al., 1994

[50] Grinblatt et al., 2002

Financially ailing firms can be contagious

A contagion in this context describes the spread of financial distress of one firm to others in the same industry. A declaration of bankruptcy by one firm can impact rival firms and suppliers negatively. The extent to which this may happen depends on whether the factors contributing to financial distress affect all firms or a specific firm.

The impact of financial distress may also differ depending on how much the industry is concentrated. Studies show that stock prices of peers react negatively to a competitor's bankruptcy as lender concern about competitors' financial health increases; however, peer share prices may rise whenever a competitor declares bankruptcy in concentrated industries. The latter reflects the likelihood that the remaining rivals, particularly those with strong balance sheets, will gain market share by accelerating new investment enabling them to benefit from increased economies of scale and pricing power.[51]

Furthermore, firms experiencing financial distress or in Chapter 11 are likely to experience declining sales and in turn to reduce their demand for raw materials and services from suppliers. When such firms represent important customers, suppliers often experience significant financial distress for as long as 2 years after the customer's sales and profits first falter. The impact on the supplier is directly related to the intensity of the customer's problems and the uniqueness of the supplier's products.[52]

How much a firm's bankruptcy impacts competitors also depends on what happens to its long-term competitiveness and growth prospects compared with the size of bankruptcy costs (i.e., costs resulting from disrupted operations, lost customers, or weakened worker productivity). When prospects are favorable and bankruptcy costs are small, the firm can emerge from Chapter 11 as a stronger competitor and can negotiate favorable terms with creditors hoping to recover a larger portion of what they are owed. This can reduce competitor profitability and increase the likelihood they will enter bankruptcy.[53]

Some things to remember

Bankruptcy is designed to protect the technically or legally insolvent firm from lawsuits by its creditors until a decision is made to liquidate or reorganize the firm. Absent a voluntary settlement out of court, the debtor firm may voluntarily seek protection from its creditors by initiating bankruptcy or be forced involuntarily into bankruptcy by its creditors.

Chapter discussion questions

18.1 Why would creditors make concessions to a debtor firm? Give examples of common types of concessions. Describe how these concessions affect the debtor firm.

18.2 Although most companies that file for bankruptcy do so because of their deteriorating financial position, companies increasingly are seeking bankruptcy protection to avoid litigation. Give examples of how bankruptcy can be used to avoid litigation.

18.3 What are the primary options available to a failing firm? What criteria might the firm use to select a particular option? Be specific.

18.4 Describe the probable trend in financial returns to shareholders of firms that emerge from bankruptcy. To what do you attribute these trends? Explain your answer.

18.5 Identify at least two financial or nonfinancial variables that have been shown to affect firm defaults and bankruptcies. Explain how each might affect the likelihood the firm will default or seek Chapter 11 protection.

18.6 On June 25, 2008, JHT Holdings, Inc., a Wisconsin-based package delivery service, filed for bankruptcy. The firm had annual revenues of $500 million. What would the firm have to demonstrate for its petition to be accepted by the bankruptcy court?

[51] Garcia-Appendini, 2018

[52] Lian, 2008

[53] Baranchuk et al., 2018

18.7 Dura Automotive emerged from Chapter 11 protection in mid-2008. The firm obtained exit financing consisting of a $110 million revolving-credit facility, a $50 million European first-lien term loan, and an $84 million US second-lien loan. The reorganization plan specified how a portion of the proceeds of these loans would be used. What do you believe might be typical stipulations in reorganization plans for using such funds? Be specific.

18.8 What are the primary factors contributing to business failure? Be specific.

18.9 In recent years, hedge funds engaged in so-called loan-to-own prebankruptcy investments, in which they acquired debt from distressed firms at a fraction of face value. Subsequently, they moved the company into Chapter 11, intent on converting the acquired debt to equity in a firm with sharply reduced liabilities. The hedge fund also provided financing to secure its interest in the business. The emergence from Chapter 11 was typically accomplished under Section 363(k) of the Bankruptcy Code, which gives debtors the right to bid on the firm in a public auction sale. During the auction, the firm's debt was valued at face value rather than market value, discouraging bidders other than the hedge fund, which acquired the debt before bankruptcy at distressed levels. Without competitive bidding, there was little chance of generating additional cash for the general creditors. Is this an abuse of the Chapter 11 bankruptcy process? Explain your answer.

18.10 American Home Mortgage Investments filed for Chapter 11 bankruptcy in late 2008. The company indicated that it chose this course of action because it represented the best means of preserving the firm's assets. W.L. Ross and Company agreed to provide the firm $50 million in DIP financing to meet its anticipated cash needs while in Chapter 11. Comment on the statement that bankruptcy provides the best means of asset preservation. Why would W.L. Ross and Company lend money to a firm that had just filed for bankruptcy?

End-of-chapter case study: American icon survives Chapter 11 filing

Case study objectives

To illustrate

- Conditions giving rise to business failure
- How bankruptcy is an important strategic option for failing firms
- The interplay between creditors, investors, and the bankrupt firm
- Possible outcomes in Chapter 11

Major American retailers have filed for bankruptcy in recent years, unable to compete effectively with the shift to online shopping and the emergence of discount stores. Few bankruptcies received more notoriety than American retailing icon Sears, which filed for bankruptcy under Chapter 11 on October 18, 2018, after 126 years in business. Within days of the filing, Sears Holdings Corp shares were delisted from the Nasdaq for having violated the exchange rule that shares could not trade below one dollar for more than 30 trading days. At the time of delisting, the firm's common shares traded at $0.36 per share.

Having shuttered hundreds of stores and recording seven straight annual losses, the firm could not meet its financial obligations. With few financial resources, the firm had limited options: the status quo was not sustainable, alliance opportunities were few, and being acquired was unlikely as Sears was losing market share to competitors. Restructuring under the protection of the bankruptcy court appeared to be the only viable alternative.

Sears' fall from grace did not happen overnight. At its peak in 2006, the year after Edward Lampert's ESL hedge fund took control by merging Sears and Kmart, the firm operated in excess of 2300 stores. When it filed for Chapter 11 12 years later, it operated less than 700 with annual sales having fallen to $16.7 billion from its high of $49 billion in 2005.

Sears has been closing stores and selling brands such as the Lands' End clothing chain and Craftsman tools for years. Online revenue comprised only a small percentage of the firm's sales. Lampert's strategy had been to make Sears profitable by becoming an "asset light" competitor, focusing only on the most profitable locations and brands. However, the shrinking asset base would not generate enough cash to finance an aggressive marketing program and scale to negotiate lower prices with suppliers. In contrast, brick and mortar retailers such as Walmart and Target have been able to take advantage of economies of scale to cover fixed costs and to shift more of their business online.

In late December 2018, Lampert offered to pay $5.15 billion for 500 Sears and Kmart stores, real estate holdings, receivables, and inventory and to employ its 50,000 employees. The asset bid included a financing commitment from three banks. Creditors argued that the purchase price would not provide sufficient cash to cover the costs incurred in the bankruptcy process and to compensate them fairly. They also argued that Lampert had undervalued inventory, receivables, and other assets compared with what they were worth in liquidation.

After the bid was rejected, Sears prepared for liquidation. At the last moment, Lampert was able to sway the bankruptcy court judge to allow the sale by increasing his original bid to $5.3 billion, including forgiving $1.3 billion of debt owed to his ESL hedge fund. The latter is called a "credit bid" in which a lender can include the face value of what it owed as part of a bid to acquire a bankrupt firm. Some argued that Lampert overstated what was owed ESL.

Lampert reasoned that a restructured Sears with fewer stores and substantially less debt could survive if he could gain full control. Why? Although the firm had difficulty in attracting new customers, a downsized and more focused company could survive by doing more business with existing shoppers. He also expected to win back suppliers after the firm exited Chapter 11 and was in better financial health. The firm's balance sheet would be much stronger after it shed $4 billion in debt and pension obligations as a consequence of the bankruptcy process, including money owed to Lampert's ESL hedge fund.

Could Sears survive as a smaller retailer? It lacked the scale to compete against larger national competitors. Moreover, the brand lost its luster, having been badly tarnished by going-out-of-business sales at 200 stores since the firm filed for bankruptcy. Many of its stores had serious maintenance problems. Mall owners are hoping to rent the former Sears space to more successful retailers such as Costco to drive mall foot traffic.

Conversely, Sears does have significant market share in certain local markets. Most of the profits on appliances are made on the servicing side, and Sears still has a good service business. In addition to the retail stores and brands, the restructured company includes Sears Auto Centers, Sears Home Services, and a logistics company Innovel Solutions Inc., which operates 11 warehouses, a fleet of trucks, and specializes in delivering appliances.

The planned sale of Sears to its chairman, Eddie Lampert, was criticized by the US government Pension Benefit Guaranty Corporation (PBGC) because it argued that Sears had failed to fully fund its pension plan by $1.7 billion. As the federal backstop for private retirement plans, the PBGC often takes over underfunded pension plans when their sponsors go under. In early 2019, it assumed responsibility for a pair of Sears' defined-benefit pension plans, which covered 90,000 people, making the PBGC Sears' largest single unsecured creditor.

Sears has a cumulative $5 billion in net operating losses (NOLs) over the years and has been unable to use more than $1 billion in investment tax credits. At current tax rates, the operating losses and unused tax credits are worth about $2 billion. The desire to recover what his firm ESL is owed gives Lampert a valid business purpose for wanting to buy the firm.

Any owner of Sears other than Lampert faced limits on how much of the NOLs could be used because their purchase of the Sears assets would reflect a change in ownership triggering limitations of the use of acquired NOLs. The current annual limit is about 2.4% (see Chapter 12 for limits on tax loss carry-forwards). By contrast, Lampert, as the original owner, can use those losses without restriction. Although Sears is unlikely to generate future pretax profits to allow it to fully use this tax shelter, it could buy profitable businesses and use its NOLs to shelter the acquired businesses' profits.[54]

Under the restructuring plan, assets acquired and liabilities assumed by ESL were labeled "New Sears." The remaining assets and liabilities were retained by so-called "Old Sears" under the court's protection. A trustee appointed by the court was responsible for selling the remaining assets and distributing the cash proceeds to unsecured creditors for what is likely to be a small fraction of what they were originally owed.

Ironically, Edward Lampert, the man who put Sears into bankruptcy, also owned the firm when it emerged from the protection of the court on February 7, 2019, after a federal judge approved the sale of selected assets of the firm to its former CEO and controlling shareholder. Although on paper, the move preserved 50,000 jobs, many observers remained skeptical that a smaller Sears would be able to compete successfully in today's retailing marketplace, particularly with the onset of the COVID-19–induced 2020 recession.

[54] Section 382 of the Internal Revenue Code prevents acquisitions of firms with substantial NOLs to reduce the acquirer's taxable income, without having a valid business purpose other than tax avoidance. An acquirer of a controlling interest could still use NOLs in existence before the change in ownership, but their annual value would be limited to a percentage of the firm's market value on the date of the change in ownership equal to the market value of the stock times the IRS long-term tax-exempt interest rate. As the original owner, Lampert was acquiring the Sears assets out of bankruptcy, which did not reflect a change in ownership.

Discussion questions

1. What is the purpose of a Chapter 11 bankruptcy filing?
2. What is the purpose of Chapter 7 of the US bankruptcy code?
3. What factors do you believe the federal judge considered in approving Edward Lampert's takeover of Sears?
4. Do you believe Edward Lampert abused the bankruptcy process? Explain your answer.

Answers to these Chapter Discussion Questions are found in the Online Instructor's Manual for instructors using this book.

CHAPTER

19

Cross-border mergers and acquisitions

analysis and valuation

OUTLINE

Mergers, Acquisitions, and Other Restructuring Activities, Eleventh Edition
https://doi.org/10.1016/B978-0-12-819782-0.00019-8

Courage is not the absence of fear. It is doing the thing we fear the most. —*Rick Warren*

Inside M&As: regulatory risk rises amid growing global trade tensions

KEY POINT

- This case illustrates how growing trade turmoil and national security concerns threaten to discourage cross-border tech deals.

The combination of increasing demand for complex chips at lower prices pushed semiconductor makers to acquire rivals to gain increased production scale. By bulking up, firms spread fixed expenses over greater output, increase research and development spending, and achieve greater bargaining leverage with customers and suppliers. But by 2016, the buyout momentum among semiconductor firms was beginning to stall. US regulators expressed concern about the loss of proprietary technology to foreign firms and governments that could threaten national security. Gaining regulatory approval for cross-border tech takeovers was becoming more problematic. And growing trade frictions among the world's major trading partners undermined global economic growth.

As the number of attractive targets shrank, semiconductor firms that had been on the sidelines had to either achieve greater scale through acquisitions or to become vulnerable to takeover. Having shown only limited interest in mergers and acquisitions (M&As) for the previous 5 years, Germany's largest chip maker Infineon Technologies AG (Infineon) saw its share price fall by more than one-third in 2018 because of declining sales. Long viewed as a world leader in the design and manufacture of flash memory chips and microcontrollers (i.e., chips used for powering small electronic devices), Infineon has been trying to broaden its product offering by acquiring certain technologies.

Toward this end, Infineon offered in early 2019 to buy US-based Cypress Semiconductor (Cypress) for $23.85 per share in a deal valued at $8.7 billion. The offer constituted an eye-popping multiple of 4.5 times Cypress's annual sales. Cypress is the leader in advanced chips embedded in automotive, industrial, smart home appliances, consumer electronics, and medical devices. The combination created the eighth largest chip maker in the world and offers customers the most complete chip offering for linking devices through the internet.

Expressing their dismay, investors hammered Infineon's shares, with the share price losing 9% in a single day. Investors fretted that Infineon was overpaying and that the financing of 30% of the purchase price by issuing new shares would dilute current shareholders. The remainder would be funded by a combination of debt and excess cash on the balance sheet. In contrast, Cypress shares soared 27% to $22.74, but at that level, it was 5% below Infineon's offer price. Why? It was unclear at that time if the deal would be approved by Infineon shareholders and by regulators in the United States and China. Despite investor skepticism, the deal closed on April 16, 2020.

Chapter overview

How will international businesses deal with the new realities of the 21st century? How will the backlash against globalization, growing protectionism, and national security concerns impact cross-border M&A deals? Can we manage the risk associated with such deals? What does it take to realize a successful cross-border M&A in this new environment? How should such deals be structured, financed, and valued? What are the differences between entering a developed and an emerging economy? These are only a few of the questions addressed in this chapter.

Throughout the chapter, the term *local country* and *home country* refer to the target's and acquirer's, respectively, country of residence. *Developed countries* are those having significant and sustainable per capita economic growth, globally integrated capital markets, and a well-defined legal system. Moreover, such countries tend to follow the rule of law more often than not and have transparent financial company statements, currency convertibility, and a comparatively stable government. According to the World Bank, *emerging countries* have a growth rate in per capita gross domestic product significantly below that of developed countries and often lack many of the characteristics of developed countries. A chapter review (including practice questions with answers) is available in the file folder titled "Student Study Guide" on the companion website to this book (https://www.elsevier.com/books-and-journals/book-companion/9780128197820).

Is globalization giving way to reduced capital flows, regionalism, and slower economic growth?

Globalization refers to the economic integration of the world economy characterized by the increasingly unfettered flow of products, services, and capital among countries. Since World War II, multilateral trade agreements have resulted in a reduction in barriers to entering both developed and emerging economies and in the subsequent increase in global trade. Financial markets have displayed similar global integration such that fluctuations in financial returns in one country's equity and bond markets impact returns in similar markets in other countries. Although not dead, the nature of globalization is changing. Global merchandise trade was among the first sector to rebound after the 2020 global downturn. And the magnitude of the recovery was greater than the aftermath of the 2008 to 2009 financial recession. However, in the longer term, a slowdown in international capital flows and growing regionalism are likely to depress the pace of global growth and the degree of international integration.

Slowing foreign direct investment

Globally integrated capital markets provide foreigners with access to local capital markets and local residents with access to foreign capital markets. When capital markets are globally integrated, countries with well-functioning legal systems, investor protections (e.g., strong insider trading laws and transparent financial reporting), and active institutional monitoring tend to have costs of capital lower than the global average.[1] *Segmented capital markets* exhibit different bond and equity prices in different geographic areas for identical assets in terms of risk and maturity.[2] Segmentation arises when investors are unable to move capital from one market to another because of capital controls, prefer local markets, or have better information about local than remote firms. Investors bear higher risk by holding a disproportionately large share of their investments in their local market rather than if they invested in a globally diversified portfolio. As such, the cost of capital for firms in segmented markets is higher than the global average.

[1] Kwabi et al., 2018

[2] Arbitrage should drive the prices in different markets to be the same (differing only by transaction and hedging costs) because investors sell those assets that are overvalued to buy those that are undervalued.

Impediments to trade and capital flows, such as tariff (and nontariff)[3] barriers, and restrictions on capital flows, such as currency convertibility, threaten to disrupt global economic growth and worldwide integrated capital markets. The resulting increase in product and capital market segmentation (as domestic markets become less correlated with global markets) contributes to a rising cost of capital and slower global economic growth. As relative risk-adjusted financial returns among countries become less attractive, the volume of foreign direct investment (including M&As) could decline significantly, reversing the upward trend of the past 6 decades.

The rise of regionalism

The least damaging outcome from a splintering of global trading patterns would be one in which trade and investment is conducted between regions. This outcome perhaps best describes what is happening now. According to the World Trade Organization (WTO), regional trade agreements (RTAs) cover more than half of international trade, with more than 300 in force at the end of 2020.

A more concerning form of regionalism is that the world could fracture into multiple spheres of influence dominated by the United States, China, and Europe. This would likely hinder global trade and capital flows because of limitations on foreign investment; increasing trade barriers, travel restrictions, and border enforcement; and the rise of regional currencies.[4] The end result: slower global growth caused by limited technology transfer, slower labor force growth, higher prices caused by lessened competition, and a reduction in living standards within the various trading blocks.

Reflecting these changes, the global M&A market could move more toward a series of regional markets rather than a global one. How likely this is depends on the proliferation of bilateral trade agreements and capital restrictions and how long such impediments to direct investment flows and sourcing restrictions remain in place. Recent examples include phase 1 of the bilateral trade agreement between China and the United States and the United States, Mexico, and Canada (United States–Mexico–Canada Agreement [USMCA]) free trade pact replacing the North American Free Trade Agreement (NAFTA), which had been in effect since January 1994. Other major bilateral trade deals signed in recent years between the United States and major trading partners include those with Japan and South Korea.[5]

Motives for international expansion

Although some are similar to those motivating domestic M&As (see Chapter 1), factors contributing to cross-border M&As in some instances are quite different.

Geographic, industrial, and product diversification

Firms diversify by investing in different industries in the same country, the same industries in different countries, or different industries in different countries. Firms investing in industries or countries whose economic cycles are not highly correlated may lower the overall volatility (i.e., risk) in their consolidated cash flows and in turn may reduce their cost of capital and default risk.[6] This is something that a firm may not be able to achieve by diversifying within its home country. In an effort to diversify away from higher carbon fuels and into natural gas, France's Total SA acquired Occidental's West African natural gas properties from Occidental in 2020 for $8.8 billion. The purchase provides both geographic and product diversification.

[3] Nontariff barriers include quotas, import licensing, packaging and labeling requirements, sanitary requirements, subsidies, local content requirements, antidumping laws, company bailouts, and other restrictions serving to increase the cost of imports. Grundke and Moser (2019) discuss such barriers in detail.

[4] In 2020, China proposed a digital currency backed by the Japanese yen, Korean won, Hong Kong dollar, and Chinese yuan that would be convertible into a weighted average of the underlying currencies.

[5] Although excluding autos, the 2019 Japanese agreement eliminates tariffs on farm, industrial, and ecommerce products. In 2018, South Korea agreed to give US automakers greater access to its domestic car market.

[6] Studies show that diversified international firms often exhibit a lower cost of capital than do firms whose investments are not well diversified (Stulz, 1995a, 1995b).

Accelerating growth

Foreign markets represent an opportunity for domestic firms to grow. Large firms experiencing slower growth in their home markets are more likely to make foreign acquisitions, particularly in rapidly growing emerging markets. Despite having limited success in foreign markets, Walmart in mid-2018 undertook its largest acquisition ever when it acquired a 77% interest in India's e-commerce retailer Flipkart for $16 billion. The move reflected the firm's effort to improve its online retail sales volume as it competed with Amazon.com.

Industry consolidation

Industries, global in scope, often require cross-border M&As to consolidate. Excess capacity in many industries often drives M&A activity, as firms strive to achieve greater economies of scale and scope as well as pricing power with customers and suppliers. Global consolidation is common in the metals, financial services, media, oil and gas, telecom, and drug industries.

Utilization of lower raw material and labor costs

Labor cost differences are likely to be larger between countries and regions because labor and other resources often tend to be less mobile across political boundaries. Emerging markets offer low labor costs, access to inexpensive raw materials, and low levels of regulation. Shifting production overseas allows firms to reduce operating expenses and become more competitive globally. The benefit of lower labor costs is overstated because worker productivity in emerging countries tends to be significantly lower than in more developed countries. Increases in regulations in some countries that limit layoffs inhibit the realization of labor-related synergy by as much as half, resulting in a reduction in the number and value of cross-border deals.[7]

Leveraging intangible assets

Domestic firms with valuable intangible assets often grow by exploiting these advantages in emerging markets. Firms with a reputation for superior products in their home markets might find that they can apply this reputation successfully in foreign markets (e.g., Coke and McDonald's). Firms seeking to leverage their capabilities are likely to acquire controlling interests in foreign firms in countries that have strong intellectual property protections.

Minimizing tax liabilities

Firms in high-tax countries may shift production and reported profits by building or acquiring operations in nations with more favorable tax laws. Firms in nations whose tax rates are less than those of an acquirer's home country are more likely to become targets of foreign takeovers.[8] Changes in US tax laws at the end of 2017, which dropped the maximum corporate tax rate from 35% to a flat rate of 21%, reduced significantly the incentive for US firms to relocate abroad (see "corporate inversions" in Chapter 12).

Seeking more management-friendly environments

Although corporate tax inversions are driven by potential tax savings, management may see other benefits of changing the country in which the firm is incorporated. Dutch politicians have been touting the benefits of Dutch corporate law to global corporations in an effort to turn the Netherlands into a management-friendly environment. Mylan Labs set up a Dutch foundation known as a "stichting," which is a takeover defense comparable to a US-style poison pill. The foundation has the right to receive preferred shares with multiple voting rights that allow it to block any deal by outvoting other shareholders. Mylan's board triggered the foundation's special voting rights to oppose an unwanted takeover bid by Israel's Teva Corp in 2015. Cable firm Altice switched its domicile in 2015 through a merger from Luxembourg to the Netherlands so that it could introduce a dual class share structure (which is barred in Luxembourg). This gave the firm's chairman 92% of the firm's voting power while owning 58.5% of the firm.

[7] Dessaint et al., 2017

[8] Arulampalam et al., 2019

Avoiding tariffs and other entry barriers

Tariffs and quotas on imports imposed by governments to protect domestic industries often stimulate foreign direct investment. Foreign firms may acquire existing facilities, start new operations, or seek new sources of supply in the country imposing the quotas and tariffs to circumvent such measures. In other instances, they may move their sources of supply to countries not affected by the trade restrictions rather than to the country imposing such measures.

Fluctuating exchange rates

Firms from countries whose currencies have appreciated are more likely to acquire firms from countries whose currencies have depreciated because the appreciated currencies are worth more in terms of depreciated currencies. Depending on what happens to future exchange rates, the impact on M&A financial returns is uncertain. It is exchange-rate volatility that matters more than the current exchange rate in assessing the impact of exchange rates on acquirer financial returns.[9] If the acquirer's home currency remains strong, the expected future cash flows from the target would have a lower discounted value when profits are repatriated to the acquirer's home country. Acquirers are better off if their home country currency depreciates at the time of repatriating profits. Therefore, the financial returns to acquirers depend not only on the current value of the currency at the time of the takeover but also on future changes in exchange rates.

Following customers

Often suppliers are encouraged to invest abroad to satisfy better the immediate needs of their customers. For example, auto parts suppliers worldwide have set up operations next to large auto manufacturing companies in China to serve the huge and growing Chinese car market.

Gaining access to intellectual property and resources

International expansion can reflect the desire to access intangible assets ranging from brand and names to advanced technology to production processes. The acquisition of advanced technology through M&A can stimulate substantial innovation as it is improved or applied in new ways.[10]

Common international market entry strategies

The method of market entry chosen by a firm may reflect the firm's risk tolerance, competitive conditions, overall resources, and degree of CEO overconfidence. Common entry strategies include M&As, solo ventures, joint ventures (JVs), export, and licensing.

In a solo venture, a foreign firm starts a new business in the local country, enabling the firm to control production, marketing, and distribution. However, the firm's total investment is at risk. M&As can provide quick access to a new market and avoid the risk of a start-up when the foreign firm is unfamiliar with the local country,[11] but they are often expensive, complex to negotiate, subject to myriad regulatory requirements, and beset by cultural issues.

JVs allow firms to share the risks and costs of international expansion, develop new capabilities, and gain access to resources, but they often fail because of conflict between partners. Multinational firms may choose a JV over an acquisition as the preferred market strategy when the risk of loss of intellectual property to a partner is less than the potential for expropriation by the local country's government.[12] And such firms are likely to take a majority control of the JV because ties between the JV and local suppliers and distributors and the greater use of local employees boost future growth.[13]

[9] Shetty et al., 2019

[10] Christofi et al., 2019

[11] Norback et al., 2019

[12] Bodnaruk et al., 2016

[13] Song, 2020

Exporting does not require establishing local operations; however, exporters must establish some means of marketing and distributing their products at the local level. Disadvantages include high transportation costs, exchange-rate fluctuations, and local country tariffs.

Licensing allows a firm to purchase the right to manufacture and sell another firm's products within a specific country or set of countries, with the licensor paid an upfront sum plus a royalty on each unit sold. The licensee takes the risks and makes the investments in facilities for manufacturing, marketing, and distribution of goods and services, making licensing possibly the least costly form of international expansion. It is a popular entry mode for smaller firms with limited capital and brand recognition. Disadvantages include the lack of control over the manufacture and marketing of the firm's products in other countries. Licensing often is the least profitable entry strategy because the profits must be shared. Finally, the licensee may learn the technology and sell a similar competitive product after the license expires.

Navigating cross-border deals amid trade frictions and "black swan" events

In 2017, the United States withdrew from the Trans Pacific Partnership (TPP).[14] Tariffs were imposed on steel and aluminum under Section 232 of the Trade Expansion Act in March 2018 and on certain imports from China beginning in July 2019 under Section 301 of the Trade Act of 1974. China retaliated, and the magnitude and coverage of tariffs expanded in late 2019.

Some argue global growth will be lower than it would have been if the events of the past several years had not occurred.[15] Others are more sanguine. Countries, they argue, will expand their market share through regional trade agreements. As such, total global trade volume will not change. However, the composition will change with the United States losing market share.[16] Although the long-term consequences are difficult to predict, a protracted trade war would likely impact global trade, economic growth, and international capital flows (including cross-border M&As).[17] In this section, we look at factors that are likely to impact international mergers for years to come: the rise of populism and nationalism, continued China–United States trade friction, the disruption of supply chains, and the new realities of cross-border M&As.

The rise of populism and nationalism

The income redistribution between and within countries resulting from globalization sparked a resurgence of populism and nationalism. *Populism* states that elites exploit common people. *Nationalism* is extreme patriotism that promotes one nation's (or culture's) interests over all others. The two are often intertwined. Both appear to have been driving forces behind the outcome of the 2016 US presidential election. And similar patterns have emerged elsewhere. The percentage of seats in the European Parliament now held by populists, whether left, right, or not easily defined (e.g., the five Star Movement in Italy), reached new highs in recent years. The political parties most successful in gaining power are those appealing to both populism and nationalism: from The League in Italy to National Rally in France, Vox in Spain, and the Sweden Democrats. These parties all seek to advance what they see as their country's interests.

A manifestation of these developments is the hostile reaction in the United States to what had become traditional trading patterns in which the United States had large and continuing trade deficits, particularly with China. An even larger concern was the loss of intellectual capital by firms doing business in China to their Chinese partners. The stage was set for economic confrontation.

[14] The TPP is a defunct trade agreement between Australia, Brunei, Canada, Chile, Japan, Malaysia, Mexico, New Zealand, Peru, Singapore, Vietnam, and the United States signed on February 4, 2016. After the United States withdrew its signature, the agreement could not take effect. The remaining nations negotiated a new trade agreement called Comprehensive and Progressive Agreement for Trans-Pacific Partnership, which incorporates most of the earlier agreement's terms and took effect on December 30, 2018, without US involvement.

[15] Bekkers, 2019

[16] Robinson and Thierfelder, 2019

[17] Linde and Pescatori, 2019

The emergence of China–United States trade frictions

After several rounds of tariff hikes in 2018, frictions between the United States and China in trade and investment highlighted their high level of economic interdependence. Both nations are seeking to reduce that level: the United States by finding multiple sources of supply and reducing its investment in China; and China by diversifying its sources of raw materials, through seeking new export markets, and through the Regional Comprehensive Economic Partnership (RCEP). RCEP took effect in November 2020 and included 14 other Asia-Pacific nations, accounting for about 30% of the world's gross domestic product (GDP). RCEP reduced tariffs on many products from its member nations and intentionally excluded the United States. This is the second major regional trade agreement signed in recent years that did not include the United States. After the United States withdrew from the Trans-Pacific Partnership agreement, the remaining 11 nations signed The Comprehensive and Progressive Agreement for Trans-Pacific Partnership in 2018.

Are regional trade agreements consistent with promoting multilateral trade according to the rules established by the 165-member WTO?[18] Yes, if they facilitate trade among their members without raising trade barriers to nonparticipating nations. However, given the intensified competition between the two largest economies on the globe, how these recent regional trade agreements will impact future trade and capital flows is highly uncertain. One illustration of this uncertainty is the rejiggering of global supply chains currently underway.

Supply chains, tariffs, and "black swan" events

Supply chains describe the process of getting products to the customer, including the conversion of raw materials into finished products and transporting them to the end user. How tariffs impact supply chains depends on the magnitude of the tariff, the length of time the tariffs will be in effect, and the markets affected. Similarly, so-called "black swan" events (i.e., unpredictable but potentially catastrophic developments) can be even more disruptive as they are totally unexpected and often poorly understood (e.g., the 2020 COVID-19 virus).[19] Although diversification of supply chains may reduce risk, it does not eliminate it. Why? Tariffs can be imposed on any country's exports, and viruses have the potential to become global pandemics at any time.

Impediments to moving supply chains abound. Finished goods for which there is excess capacity outside a country can be moved in 6 months or less for firms with excellent documentation on production and assembly methods. Component supply lines are far more challenging to change because developing countries often do not have the infrastructure to produce, warehouse, and distribute such items, especially where the quality requirements are high, such as for smartphones and appliances. If the tariffs are high and the duration uncertain, efforts to diversify supply chains add to their complexity and, at least in the short run, to the potential for product quality problems as the new suppliers learn how to meet product requirements. Purchasing agents must compare the costs including the higher tariffs of a reliable single source with the cost associated with untested and more complicated multiple sourcing.[20]

The beneficiaries of moving supply chains out of China are likely to be Mexico, India, Vietnam, Indonesia, and the Philippines. Many manufacturers will not move out altogether given the size of the Chinese domestic market. Those that produce in China for export elsewhere could move all or some of their production to other countries. Although a shift in supply chains back to the United States is problematic because of cost concerns, products such as pharmaceuticals or their ingredients are likely to move to the United States as insurance against future "black swan" events.

Foreign businesses that rely on Chinese manufacturers as a critical link in their supply chains have been diversifying their sources of supply for years, reflecting rising Chinese labor and land costs and an aging labor force. But with the convergence of trade disputes and the spread of COVID-19, this process has accelerated. However, the lure of 1.4 billion consumers is likely to sustain foreign investment by those wishing to gain or expand their presence in that market. For example, Walmart announced in 2020 that it intends to double its operations in China.

Although developed countries can negotiate trade arrangements given their wealth and resources, developing countries lacking in many critical resources are likely to suffer. Rising prices of items such as medical supplies

[18] The WTO represents the only internationally recognized organization in which trade disputes can be adjudicated with the power to compel its members to abide by its rulings.

[19] Nicola et al. (2020) discuss the pervasive global impact of the COVID-19 pandemic.

[20] Chae et al., 2019

will make it difficult for less developed nations to pay for them, particularly as the demand for their exports declines. Poorer countries will be confronted with growing balance of payments deficits, currency devaluations, and soaring domestic inflation.

The new realities of cross-border M&A deals

The global environment for cross-border M&A transactions is likely to become less favorable. The number of such deals could slow as tariffs cause global trade growth and in turn economic growth to slow (or contract). Why? Financial capital flows (including M&As) are highly correlated with trade flows, with capital flowing to those countries exhibiting the most attractive investment opportunities. If global growth slows, so will international capital flows.

Tariffs promote the inefficient use of resources by discouraging takeovers of less inefficient domestic firms by more efficient foreign firms and impact the types of mergers undertaken.[21] Tariffs encourage horizontal mergers (i.e., between competitors) and discourage vertical mergers (i.e., between customers and suppliers). Foreign firms acquire competitors in horizontal mergers in countries protected by tariffs as their products are not subject to tariffs. In contrast, tariffs on imports of raw materials and intermediate products from countries whose exports are subject to tariffs make vertical deals less attractive. Countries that increase the protection of intellectual capital within their borders because of tariffs (or the threat of tariffs) imposed on their exports may become more attractive to foreign investment, including M&As.[22]

Deals that target countries' technologically and culturally sensitive industries are likely to become more challenging because countries have become more protective of firms in such industries. In 2019, Germany announced its intention to take equity stakes in "strategically significant" industries to insulate these firms from foreign takeovers. The policy also called for changing national and European antitrust rules to encourage the creation of European "national champions" to compete against US and Chinese multinationals. Similar concerns have been voiced by the French. In 2020, the European Union proposed greater scrutiny of foreign acquirers receiving subsidies from their governments seeking to buy EU businesses, further complicating such deals.

China announced a new growth model in late 2020, citing its main drivers of growth as domestic consumption, markets, and companies. Foreign investment (including M&As) and technologies would play a supporting role. Doing deals in China will require a willingness to cede greater control to the government, which is demanding executives manage their businesses to achieve its goals and is channeling capital to those who comply while starving others.[23]

Future cross-border deals could be smaller on average than in the past to avoid government scrutiny. Smaller countries may represent more attractive investment opportunities because they are less likely to be involved in geopolitics. As firms alter their supply chains, they are likely to source from several countries to reduce the political, economic, and logistical risks of relying too heavily on a single source. Countries that have been ignored in the past because of a lack of infrastructure and skilled labor must be considered as potential sources of supply. In such instances, acquirers should be prepared to make investments in the local labor force and infrastructure. Finally, the China-initiated Regional Comprehensive Economic Partnership could encourage more takeovers of firms within the trade area to take advantage of lower tariffs.

Cross-border M&As, institutional voids, and human rights

Since World War II, global governance has undergone a revolutionary change. Some country governments have seen a reduction in their influence (e.g., the European Union), while the role of international organizations expanded (e.g., the United Nations and the International Monetary Fund). Record numbers of people were removed from poverty, and populations boomed in the wake of improved nutrition, health care, and relative political stability. Although difficult to measure, improving the human rights (e.g., the right to life, liberty, and equal opportunity) of an expanding global population seems to have achieved significant success. Media headlines boldly proclaimed at the outset of the 21st century that these developments were irreversible.

[21] Srinivasan, 2020

[22] Mandelmann and Waddle, 2020

[23] L. Wei, Dec. 10, 2020, China's Xi Ramps Up Control of Private Sector, *Wall Street Journal*

What was thought to be irreversible is being reversed

The nation state is again rising in prominence while relatively unfettered trade is showing signs of fatigue. International organizations' influence is waning, reflecting political infighting and reduced funding. Governments, originally thought to hold the exclusive authority in addressing human rights issues, are withdrawing from that role as measured by funding levels for international organizations and foreign aid. This has left a vacuum in terms of global governance and to a greater extent in governance and human rights issues in emerging nations.

Underdeveloped institutions contribute to uneven global development

Institutions can be viewed as significant practices, relationships, or organizations in a society or culture. To varying degrees, all nations have both formal and informal institutions providing the basis for political, economic, and social interaction. Examples of *formal institutions* include a country's constitution conferring rights to its citizens, laws defining acceptable behaviors and an impartial court system to enforce them, and property rights defining legal ownership of resources and how they can be used in market-based economies. *Informal institutions* are the norms, customs, and traditions that represent behaviors accepted by a country's population. Formal institutions often are an outgrowth of behavioral norms or codes of conduct.[24] The lack of formal institutions in some emerging nations to support economic growth has created an institutional void. Underdeveloped institutions hamstring growth by limiting both domestic and foreign investment and contribute to uneven economic growth across the globe.

Can cross-border M&As strengthen weak national institutions?

Foreign investment (including M&As) is attracted by a nation's resources and by government efforts to lower investment risk because of property expropriation and lack of a mechanism for earnings repatriation. But laws governing the property rights of shareholders and bondholders, more transparent accounting, and a legal system to enforce such laws do not ensure that domestic firms will improve their own governance practices accordingly. Corporate behaviors of engaging in fraud and bribery to improve profitability become engrained in corporate cultures. And sometimes an external catalyst is needed to change the status quo.

Cross-border deals can in some instances be that catalyst. How? Foreign acquirers from countries with good governance practices can acquire firms in emerging countries with poor governance practices and over time improve the effectiveness of such governance at the target firm and potentially among competitor firms. Improved governance helps to attract more foreign investment to stimulate economic development. Such results are well documented and are discussed in detail later in this chapter. And as cross-border transactions proliferate, corporate governance systems in developing nations can become more like those in developed countries.[25]

Structuring cross-border deals

Cross-border deals encounter obstacles atypical of domestic acquisitions. These include investment and exchange control approvals, regulatory approval, and unusual due diligence issues. Other problems involve agreeing on an allocation of the purchase price among assets located in various jurisdictions and compliance with local laws. As such, domestic bidders earn slightly higher positive announcement-date returns than cross-border acquirers.[26] Acquirers having significant prior experience in cross-border deals[27] and greater familiarity with the target's home country are more likely to earn their required returns than those that do not.[28] Why? Familiarity with a country's culture breeds greater trust and provides better communication between the parties, reducing the time to complete the deal.[29]

[24] See Wettstein et al. (2019) for an excellent overview of the literature on this subject.

[25] Drobetz et al., 2020

[26] Mateev et al., 2016

[27] Agyei-Boapeah, 2018

[28] Aybar et al., 2015

[29] Breuer et al., 2018

Friendly versus hostile deals

Cross-border takeovers are most often friendly transactions, reflecting a combination of factors, including cultural antipathy toward hostile takeovers and government protectionism. Government intervention in hostile deals is more likely if a foreign bidder is involved, it is a large transaction, and the target firm's country is experiencing high unemployment.

Bidding strategies

As with domestic deals, international mergers and acquisitions commonly use toehold investment tactics and termination fees to reduce the likelihood of competition in bidding for a target. If a bidding contest does occur, the use of these tactics increases the probability that the initial bidder will be successful. The winner in a bidding contest is generally the one who includes the most cash in the offer price. Serial acquirers are more likely not to participant in bidding contests but are more likely to complete deals.[30] Finally, US bidders tend to offer lower purchase price premiums when they are relatively unfamiliar with the culture of the target firm's country. Why? Because realizing anticipated synergies on a timely basis (or at all) because of cultural factors reduces the acquirer's confidence it can earn back the premium paid. However, this uncertainty does not appear present when foreign firms acquire US targets.[31]

Acquisition vehicles

Non-US firms seeking to acquire US companies often use C corporations rather than limited liability companies (LLCs) or partnerships to acquire the shares or assets of US targets. They are relatively easy to organize quickly because all states permit such structures, and no prior government approval is required. There is no limitation on non-US persons or entities acting as shareholders in US corporations, except for certain regulated industries.

An LLC is attractive for JVs in which the target would be owned by two or more unrelated parties, corporations, or nonresident investors. Although not traded on public stock exchanges, LLC shares can be sold freely to members. This facilitates the parent firm's operating the acquired firm as a subsidiary or JV. A partnership may have advantages for investors from certain countries (e.g., Germany), where income earned from a US partnership is not subject to taxation. A holding company structure enables a foreign parent to offset gains from one subsidiary with losses generated by another, serves as a platform for future acquisitions, and provides the parent with additional legal protection in the event of lawsuits.

Laws governing foreign firms have an important impact on the choice of acquisition vehicle because the buyer must organize a local company to hold acquired shares or assets to meet local-country law. In common law countries (the United Kingdom, Canada, Australia, India, Pakistan, Hong Kong, Singapore, and other former British colonies), the acquisition vehicle is a corporation-like structure, which is similar to those in the United States. In civil law countries (Western Europe, South America, Japan, and Korea), the acquisition is in the form of a share company or LLC.[32] *Civil law* is synonymous with *codified law, continental law,* or the *Napoleonic Code*. Practiced in some Middle Eastern Muslim countries and some countries in Southeast Asia (e.g., Indonesia and Malaysia), Islamic law is based on the Koran.

In the European Union, corporate law is the responsibility of each member nation. There is evidence that differences in corporate law across member nations have hindered progress toward a more active European M&A market because both individual country and EU-level laws must be considered.[33] To adapt to this complexity, smaller enterprises often use an LLC, but larger enterprises, particularly those with public shareholders, use so-called *share companies*. The rules applicable to LLCs tend to be flexible and are useful for wholly owned subsidiaries. In contrast, share companies are subject to numerous restrictions and securities laws, but their shares trade freely on public exchanges.

[30] Bessler et al., 2015

[31] Lim et al., 2016

[32] In common law countries, case law, in the form of accumulated judicial opinions, is of primary importance in settling disputes; under civil law systems, rules and regulations predominate.

[33] Moschieri et al., 2014

Share companies are more regulated than US corporations. They must register with the commercial registrar in the location of their principal place of business. Bureaucratic delays from several weeks to several months between the filing of the appropriate documents and the organization of the company may occur. Most civil law countries require more than one shareholder. And there is no limitation on foreigners acting as shareholders. An LLC typically is required to have more than one quota holder (i.e., investor). Either domestic or foreign corporations or individuals may be quota holders.[34]

Form of payment

US target shareholders often receive cash rather than shares in cross-border deals. Shares and other securities require registration with the Securities and Exchange Commission (SEC) and compliance with state and local securities laws if they are resold in the United States. Acquirer shares often are less attractive to target shareholders because of the lack of a liquid resale market or acquirer familiarity. In buying non-US firms, public target shareholders usually receive cash, but equity is more commonly paid to private firm shareholders because of the difficulty in valuing such firms.[35] Target shareholders provide more accurate information because the eventual value of their acquirer shares reflects the acquirer's success or failure. In addition to understanding the objectives of the parties involved, determining the proper form of payment in cross-border deals requires understanding cultural and religious differences. For example, earnouts, some observers argue, run counter to Islamic beliefs, making structuring the form of payment challenging.[36]

Form of acquisition

Share acquisitions are the simplest form of acquisition in cross-border deals because all target assets and liabilities transfer to the acquirer by "rule of law." Acquirers tend to buy 100% of the target's equity when the target is in a related industry and the acquirer is familiar with the country where the target resides.[37] The major disadvantage of a share purchase is that all the target's known and unknown liabilities transfer to the buyer. When the target is in a foreign country, full disclosure of liabilities is limited, and some target assets transfer with tax liens or other liabilities.

Asset purchases result in transferring all or some of the target's assets to the acquirer and are more complicated when local law requires that the target's employees automatically transfer to the acquirer. Mergers are not legal or practical in all countries. The protections afforded to minority shareholders often are stronger in some countries than in others. In some instances, for a merger to be implemented, minority shareholders must agree with the will of the majority.

Choosing an ownership stake

Investors often perceive cross-border M&As as more risky than domestic deals. As such, an acquirer must choose early on in the M&A process to acquire a partial, controlling, or full ownership position in the target firm. The positive and negative implications of different ownership stakes in the context of acquiring domestic firms have been discussed elsewhere in this book. In cross-border deals, the choice of what percent of a target firm to purchase is more complicated because the attributes of the target firm's home country must also be considered.

Bidders, with access to cheap financing, a desire for control, and a flexible ownership structure (e.g., holding company), are more inclined to select a level of target ownership ranging from controlling to 100%. A controlling or higher ownership stake also is more likely if the target's country has strong investor protections; strict law enforcement; is culturally similar to the bidder's home country; and has a growing economy, liquid capital markets, and few trade barriers.[38] Acquirers are also more likely to fully acquire targets that are highly leveraged and are located in countries with poorly developed capital markets.[39] Such targets often can be purchased at a discount from their true

[34] For an excellent discussion of corporate structures in common law and civil law countries, see Truitt (2006).

[35] Bae et al., 2013

[36] Elnahas et al., 2017

[37] Chiara Di Guardo et al., 2017

[38] Dang et al., 2018

[39] Alquist et al., 2019

value, and the acquirer can provide access to lower-cost financing. When the acquirer and target countries are different in terms of culture and religions, partial ownership allows the acquirer's management to adjust to these differences while less money is at risk.[40]

Tax strategies

Tax-free reorganizations are often used by foreign acquirers of US firms. The target firm merges with a US subsidiary of the foreign acquirer in a statutory merger under state laws. To qualify as a US corporation for tax purposes, the foreign firm must own at least 80% of the stock of the domestic subsidiary. As such, the transaction can qualify as a Type-A tax-free reorganization (see Chapter 12).

Another form of deal structure is the *taxable purchase*, which involves the purchase by one firm of the shares or assets of another, usually in exchange for a predominately nonequity form of payment. Target firm shareholders recognize a taxable gain or loss on the exchange. The forward triangular merger is the most common form of taxable deal. The target company merges with a US subsidiary of the foreign acquirer, with shareholders of the target firm receiving mostly cash and some acquirer shares. This structure is useful when some target company shareholders want shares while others want cash.

Hybrid transactions represent a third form of transaction used in cross-border deals and afford the US target and its shareholders tax-free treatment while avoiding the issuance of shares of the foreign acquirer. A hybrid transaction may be taxable to some target shareholders and tax free to others. To structure such deals, some target company shareholders may exchange their common shares for a nonvoting preferred stock while the foreign acquirer or its US subsidiary buys the remaining common stock for cash. This transaction is tax free to target company shareholders taking preferred stock and taxable to those receiving cash.[41]

Financing cross-border deals

Debt is most often used to finance cross-border deals. Financing sources exist in capital markets in the acquirer's home, the target's local country, or some third country. Domestic sources available to cross-border acquirers include banks, bond markets, and equity markets.

Debt markets

Eurobonds are debt expressed in terms of US dollars or other currencies and sold to investors outside the country in whose currency they are denominated. A typical Eurobond deal could be a dollar-denominated bond issued by a French firm through an underwriting group. The underwriting group could include the overseas affiliate of a New York commercial bank, a German commercial bank, and a consortium of London banks.[42]

Equity markets

The American Depository Receipt (ADR) market enables foreign firms to raise funds in US equity markets. ADRs represent the receipt for the shares of a foreign-based firm held in a US bank. The Euroequity market reflects equity issues by a foreign firm tapping a larger investor base than the firm's home equity market.[43]

[40] Prasadh and Thenmozhi, 2019

[41] For an excellent discussion of the different tax laws in various countries, see PriceWaterhouseCoopers (2015).

[42] Bonds of a non-US issuer registered with the SEC for sale in the US public bond markets are called Yankee bonds. A US company issuing a bond in Japan would be issuing a "samurai" bond.

[43] If the acquirer is not well known in the target's home market, target shareholders may be able to sell the shares only at a discount in their home market. The buyer may have to issue shares in its home market or possibly in the international equities market and use the proceeds to acquire the target for cash. Alternatively, the acquirer may issue shares in the target's market to create a resale market for target shareholders or offer target shareholders the opportunity to sell the shares in the buyer's home market through an investment banker.

Sovereign wealth funds

Sovereign wealth funds (SWFs) are government-backed entities which invest foreign currency reserves. Although visibility into their investments has improved, many remain opaque compared with other institutional investors. Countries in which SWFs are actively investing often prefer investments made by transparent SWFs from democratic countries because they are more likely to be independent of their government's influence.[44] Target firms show a 1.2% increase in abnormal returns around the announcement date of a takeover by an SWF.[45] However, the announcement date increase for SWF-owned firms tends to be short-lived. The government guarantee implied by SWF ownership protects firms experiencing financial distress, which lowers the firm's risk and cost of equity. But such ownership also discourages potential acquirers and encourages managers to engage in excessive risk taking, thereby boosting the firm's cost of financing.[46]

Planning and implementing cross-border transactions in emerging countries

Entering emerging economies poses challenges not found in developed countries. What follows is a discussion of how to deal with the inherent political and economic risks in such endeavors.

Political and economic risks

Examples include excessive local government regulation, confiscatory tax policies, restrictions on cash remittances, currency inconvertibility, restrictive employment policies, expropriation of assets, civil war or local insurgencies, and corruption. Another, sometimes overlooked, challenge is the failure of the legal system to honor contracts. Unexpected changes in exchange rates can influence the competitiveness of goods produced in the local market for export to the global marketplace. Changes in exchange rates alter the value of assets invested in the local country and earnings repatriated from the local operations to the parent firm in the home country.

Greater economic and political freedom usually encourages more foreign direct investment. When property rights are respected, foreigners are inclined to invest in the local country. But when they are weak, investment both by foreign and domestic firms is discouraged. The value of multinational firms with subsidiaries in countries experiencing expropriations declines by 3.2% in the year after the expropriation, reflecting the loss of assets. The impact of expropriation also negatively affects the value of firms in the same industry in which the expropriation occurs even if they have not experienced any loss of assets to the local country government. Expropriation in neighboring countries also decreases the value of firms in the same industry.[47]

Sources of information for assessing political and economic risks

Information sources include local country consultants, JV partners, a local legal counsel, or appropriate government agency, such as the US Department of State. Other sources include the major credit-rating agencies, such as Standard & Poor's (S&P), Moody's, and Fitch IBCA. Trade magazines, such as *Euromoney* and *Institutional Investor*, provide overall country-risk ratings. The Economic Intelligence Unit also provides country risk scores. The *International Country Risk Guide*, published by the Political Risk Services Group, offers overall numerical risk scores for individual countries as well as separate scores for political, financial, and economic risks.

Risk management

Postacquisition risk is managed in a variety of ways: insurance, political connections, options, and contract language and by considering factors known to impact significantly total risk.

[44] Megginson et al., 2019

[45] Boubakri et al., 2017

[46] Boubaker et al., 2018

[47] Lin et al., 2019

Insurance coverage can be obtained from the export credit agency in a variety of countries, such as Export Import Bank (United States), SACE (Italy), and Hermes (Germany), which may offer coverage for companies based within their jurisdictions. Whereas the Overseas Private Investment Corporation is available to US-based firms, the World Bank's Multilateral Investment Guarantee Agency is available to all firms.

Politically connected firms may experience a lower cost of equity because of their access to better information than less connected firms. Superior information offers insights into which policies will become law and how existing laws will affect their operating environment enabling them to hedge against such changes, thereby reducing risk.[48]

When adequate due diligence is impractical, acquirers may include a put option in the purchase agreement, enabling the buyer to require the seller to repurchase shares from the buyer at a predetermined price under certain circumstances. Alternatively, the agreement could include a clause requiring a purchase price adjustment if certain events occur.

Finally, total risk can be managed by incorporating certain factors into the target selection process. Such factors could include the following: industry relatedness, degree of cultural similarity, and institutional strength.[49] *Industry relatedness* refers to the acquirer's ability to understand the target firm's industry. *Cultural similarity* refers to how close the target and acquirer countries are in terms of customs and ethics, thereby decreasing the likelihood that the acquirer makes culturally insensitive decisions. *Institutional strength* describes the extent to which a foreign country has strong legal protections and a history of fair law enforcement.

Consider the following example to illustrate how risk can be mitigated using these three factors. Although an acquisition of a target in the same industry can add to cyclical risk, total postacquisition risk can be attenuated by buying firms in culturally similar countries with viable legal systems, thus limiting threats caused by cultural incompatibility and contract infractions.

How are cross-border transactions valued?

Cross-border deals require converting cash flows from one currency to another. Also, discount rates may be adjusted for risks not found when the acquirer and target are in the same country.

Converting foreign target cash flows to acquirer domestic cash flows

Target cash flows can be expressed in its own currency, including expected inflation (i.e., nominal terms), its own currency without inflation (i.e., real terms), or the acquirer's currency. Real cash flow valuation adjusts all cash flows for inflation and uses real discount rates. M&A practitioners use nominal cash flows, except when inflation rates are high. Under these circumstances, real cash flows are preferable. They are determined by dividing the nominal cash flows by the country's gross domestic product deflator or some other broad measure of inflation. Future real cash flows are estimated by dividing future nominal cash flows by the current GDP deflator,[50] increased by the expected rate of inflation. Real discount rates are determined by subtracting the expected rate of inflation from nominal discount rates.[51]

It is simpler to project the target's aggregate cash flows (rather than each component) in its own currency and then convert the cash flows into the acquirer's currency. This requires estimating future exchange rates between the target (local) and the acquirer's (home) currencies, which are affected by interest rates and expected inflation in the two countries.

The current rate at which one currency can be exchanged for another is called the *spot exchange rate*. Conversion to the acquirer's currency can be achieved by using future spot exchange rates, estimated either from relative interest rates (*interest rate parity theory*) in each country or by the relative rates of expected inflation (*purchasing power parity theory*).

[48] Pham, 2019

[49] Lewis and Bozos, 2019

[50] The GDP deflator is the ratio of current dollar GDP to real or constant-dollar GDP and measures the percent change in prices between the current period and some prior "base" period.

[51] Nominal (real) cash flows should give the same net present values (NPVs) if the expected rate of inflation used to convert future cash flows to real terms is the same inflation rate used to estimate the real discount rate.

When target firms are in developed (globally integrated) capital market countries

For developed countries, the interest rate parity theory provides a framework for estimating forward currency exchange rates (i.e., future spot exchange rates). Consider a US acquirer's valuation of a firm in the European Union, with projected cash flows expressed in terms of euros. The target's cash flows can be converted into dollars by using a forecast of future dollar-to-euro spot rates. The interest rate parity theory relates forward (future) spot exchange rates to differences in interest rates between two countries adjusted by the spot rate. Therefore the dollar/euro exchange rate $(\$/€)_n$ (i.e., the future, or forward, exchange rate), n periods into the future, is expected to appreciate (depreciate) according to the following relationship:

$$(\$/€)_n = \{(1+R_{\$n})^n / (1+R_{€n})^n\} \times (\$/€)_0 \quad (19.1)$$

Similarly, the euro-to-dollar exchange rate $(€/\$)_n$, n periods into the future, would be expected to appreciate (depreciate) according to the following relationship:

$$(€/\$)_n = \{(1+R_{€n})^n/(1+R_{\$n})^n\} \times (€/\$)_0 \quad (19.2)$$

Note that $(\$/€)_0$ and $(€/\$)_0$ represent the spot rate for the dollar-to-euro and euro-to-dollar exchange rates, respectively; $R_{\$n}$ and $R_{€n}$ represent the interest rate in the United States and the European Union, respectively. Equations 19.1 and 19.2 imply that if US interest rates rise relative to those in the European Union, investors will buy dollars with euros at the current spot rate and sell an equivalent amount of dollars for euros in the forward (future) market n periods into the future in anticipation of converting their dollar holdings back into euros. According to this theory, the dollar-to-euro spot rate will appreciate, and the dollar-to-euro forward rate will depreciate until any profit because the difference in interest rates is eliminated.[52]

Exhibit 19.1 illustrates how to convert a target company's nominal free cash flows to the firm (FCFF) expressed in euros (i.e., the local country or target's currency) to those expressed in dollars (i.e., home country or acquirer's currency). Note that Target's dollar-denominated FCFF is calculated by multiplying its projected euro-denominated FCFF by the projected \$/€ spot rate.

EXHIBIT 19.1

Converting Euro-Denominated Into Dollar-Denominated Free Cash Flows (FCFF) to the Firm Using the Interest Rate Parity Theory[a]

	Forecast period		
	2012	2013	2014
Target's euro-denominated FCFF (€ millions)	124.5	130.7	136.0
Target country's interest rate (%)	4.50	4.70	5.30
US interest rate (%)	4.25	4.35	.55
Current spot rate (\$/€) = 1.2044			
Projected spot rate (\$/€)	1.2015	1.1964	1.1788
Target's dollar-denominated FCFF (\$ millions)[b]	149.59	156.37	160.32

[a]Calculating the projected spot rate using Equation 19.1:
$(\$/€)_{2012} = \{(1.0425)/(1.0450)\} \times 1.2044 = 1.2015$
$(\$/€)_{2013} = \{(1.0435)^2/(1.0470)^2\} \times 1.2044 = 1.1964$
$(\$/€)_{2014} = \{(1.0455)^3/(1.0530)^3\} \times 1.2044 = 1.1788$
[b]Equal to Target's euro-denominated FCFF × projected spot rate (\$/€).

[52] Equilibrium between forward exchange rates and spot rates adjusted for the ratio of US interest rates to those in eurozone countries will in practice be restored by a combination of appreciating dollar-to-euro spot rates, depreciating dollar-to-euro forward rates, and declining US interest rates and increasing eurozone interest rates. Interest rates on US bonds decline as the investors bid up their prices, and interest rates on comparable eurozone bonds increase as investors sell these bonds and invest the proceeds in the United States.

When target firms are in emerging (segmented) capital market countries

Cash flows are converted, as before, using the interest rate parity theory or the purchasing power parity theory. The latter is used if there is insufficient information about interest rates in the emerging market. The purchasing power parity theory states that the percentage difference in the forward rate relative to the spot rate should over time equal the difference in expected inflation rates between countries. That is, one currency appreciates (depreciates) with respect to another currency according to the expected relative rates of inflation between the two countries such that an identical good in each country will have the same price. To illustrate, the dollar/Mexican peso exchange rate, $(\$/\text{Peso})_n$, and the Mexican peso/dollar exchange rate, $(\text{Peso}/\$)_n$, *n* periods from now (i.e., future exchange rates) is expected to change according to the following relationships:

$$(\$/\text{Peso})_n = [(1+P_{us})^n / (1+P_{mex})^n] \times (\$/\text{Peso})_0 \quad (19.3)$$

and

$$(\text{Peso}/\$)_n = [(1+P_{mex})^n/(1+P_{us})^n] \times (\text{Peso}/\$)_0 \quad (19.4)$$

in which P_{us} and P_{mex} are the expected inflation rates in the United States and Mexico, respectively, and $(\$/\text{Peso})_0$ and $(\text{Peso}/\$)_0$ are the dollar-to-peso and peso-to-dollar spot exchange rates, respectively. Assume prices in the United States are expected to rise faster than those in Mexico for the same goods and services. Other things equal, holders of pesos will buy dollars to purchase US goods and services before they rise in price and sell an equivalent amount of dollars for pesos in the forward exchange market before the dollar depreciates. This causes the dollar/peso spot rate to decline (i.e., the dollar to appreciate against the peso) and the forward dollar/peso exchange rate to increase (i.e., the dollar to depreciate against the peso).

See Exhibit 19.2 for an illustration of how this might work in practice. Note that Target's dollar denominated FFCF is calculated by multiplying its peso denominated projected FFCF by the projected are multiplied by the projected $/Peso spot rate.

Selecting the correct marginal tax rate

Global businesses generally pay taxes using either the worldwide or territorial tax regimes. The *worldwide/global tax system* taxes businesses on income earned in their home country and on the income they earn in foreign countries. The *territorial tax system* taxes profits earned by both domestic and foreign firms operating within a country's borders only on what they earn in that country and excludes most foreign-earned income. Instead of a pure territorial

EXHIBIT 19.2

Converting Peso-Denominated Into Dollar-Denominated Free Cash Flows to the Firm (FCFF) Using the Purchasing Power Parity Theory[a]

	Forecast period		
	2012	2013	2014
Target's peso-denominated FCFF (millions of pesos)	P1,050.5	P1,124.7	P1,202.7
Current Mexican expected inflation rate = 6%			
Current US expected inflation rate = 4%			
Current spot rate ($/peso) = 0.0877			
Projected spot rate ($/peso)	0.0860	0.0844	0.0828
Target's dollar-denominated FCFF ($ millions)[b]	$90.34	$94.92	$99.58

[a]Calculating the projected spot rate using Equation 19.3:
$(\$/\text{Peso})_{2012} = \{(1.04)/(1.06)\} \times 0.0877 = 0.0860$
$(\$/\text{Peso})_{2013} = \{(1.04)^2/(1.06)^2\} \times 0.0877 = 0.0844$
$(\$/\text{Peso})_{2014} = \{(1.04)^3/(1.06)^3\} \times 0.0877 = 0.0828$
[b]Equal to Target's peso-denominated FCFF × Projected spot rate ($/peso).

system, most countries use a system under which foreign income is mostly excluded from taxation. The exemption is typically 95% of foreign earnings such that most multinational firms in foreign countries pay only a token tax if they repatriate earnings back to their home country.

The Tax Cuts and Jobs Reform Act of 2017 changed the United States from a global to a territorial tax system. Before the new tax law, at nearly 40% the United States had the highest combined (federal and state) statutory corporate tax rate among the 38 industrialized countries comprising the Organization for Economic Cooperation and Development (OECD). Under the new tax law, the combined United States and state average tax rate dropped to 25.7%, slightly above the OECD average.[53] For more detail on the US territorial tax system, see Chapter 12.

The selection of the right marginal tax rate for valuation purposes depends on where most of the taxes are actually paid. If the acquirer's country exempts foreign income from further taxes (or applies only a token tax rate) after being taxed in the foreign country, the correct tax rate would be the marginal tax rate in the foreign country because that is where taxes are paid. If the marginal rate in the acquirer's country is higher than the target's country rate and taxes paid in a foreign country are deductible from the taxes owed by the acquirer in its home country, the correct tax rate would be the acquirer's effective marginal rate, that is, the difference between the acquirer's marginal tax rate in its home country and the tax rate paid in a foreign country.

Estimating the cost of equity in cross-border transactions

The capital asset pricing model (CAPM) or a multifactor model (e.g., CAPM plus a firm-size adjustment) often are used in developed countries with liquid capital markets. For emerging nations, estimating the cost of equity is more complex, with at least 12 separate approaches used.[54] Each method attempts to adjust the discount rate for potential capital market segmentation and specific country risks. Still other methods attempt to include emerging-country risk by adjusting projected cash flows. In either case, the adjustments often appear arbitrary.

Developed economies exhibit little differences in the cost of equity because of the integration of their capital markets into the global capital market. Adjusting the cost of equity for specific country risk does not seem to make any significant difference. For emerging-market countries, the existence of segmented capital markets, political instability, limited liquidity, currency fluctuations, and currency inconvertibility makes adjusting the target firm's cost of equity for these factors desirable but often impractical.

The following discussion incorporates the basic elements of valuing cross-border deals, distinguishing between the different adjustments made when investing in developed and emerging countries. Nonetheless, considerable debate exists about the "best" approach.

Estimating the cost of equity in developed (globally integrated) countries

What follows is a discussion of how to adjust basic CAPM for valuing cross-border deals when the target is located in a developed country. The CAPM discussion is similar to that outlined in Chapter 7, except for the use of either national or globally diversified stock market indices in estimating beta and calculating the equity market risk premium.

Estimating the risk-free rate of return (developed countries)

The risk-free rate generally is the local country's government (or sovereign) bond rate whenever the projected cash flows for the target firm are expressed in local currency. Risk-free rates usually are US Treasury bond rates if projected cash flows are in dollars.

Adjusting CAPM for risk (developed countries)

The equity premium is the extra yield required by investors to buy stock. Although estimates should be forward-looking, obtaining accurate projections of future market returns is very difficult. Analysts often look to historical data to calculate risk premiums[55] despite results that vary because of time periods selected and whether returns are calculated as arithmetic or geometric averages.

Beta (β) measures the extent to which a firm's financial return changes are caused by changes in the stock market's return. Although all stocks are impacted by stock market fluctuations, the extent of the impact on each stock will differ. When capital markets are fully integrated, equity investors hold globally diversified portfolios, resulting in

[53] Pomerleau, February 12, 2018

[54] Harvey, 2005

[55] See Chapter 7 for a more detailed discussion of estimating risk premiums. For estimates of risk premiums by country, see Fernandez et al. (2018) and Damodaran (http://www.stern.nyu.edu/~adamodar/pc/datasets/ctryprem.xls).

a high correlation between individual country equity indices and global indices. Betas can be estimated by regressing the percent change in the total return on a specific stock against the percent change in a well-diversified portfolio of US equities, another developed country's equity portfolio, or a global equity portfolio.[56]

The CAPM also should be adjusted for the size of the firm, which serves as a proxy for factors such as smaller firms being subject to higher default risk and generally being less liquid than large capitalization firms. See Table 7.1 in Chapter 7 for estimates of the amount of the adjustment to the cost of equity to correct for firm size, as measured by market value.

Global CAPM formulation (developed countries)

In globally integrated markets, systematic risk is defined relative to the rest of the world. An asset has systematic risk only to the extent that the performance of the asset correlates with the overall world economy. When using a global equity index, the CAPM often is called the global or international CAPM. If the target firm's risk is similar to that faced by the acquirer, the acquirer's cost of equity may be used to discount the target's cash flows.

The global CAPM for the target firm may be expressed as follows:

$$k_{e,\text{dev}} = R_f + \beta_{\text{devfirm.global}}\left(R_m - R_f\right) + \text{FSP} \tag{19.5}$$

in which

$k_{e,\text{dev}}$ = required return on equity for a firm operating in a developed country
R_f = local country's risk-free financial rate of return if cash flows are measured in the local country's currency or the US Treasury bond rate if in dollars
$(R_m - R_f)$ = difference between the expected return on the global market portfolio (i.e., Morgan Stanley Capital International World Index [MSCI]), the US equity index (S&P 500), or a broadly defined index in the target's local country and R_f. This difference is the equity premium, which should be about the same when expressed in the same currency for countries with globally integrated capital markets.
$\beta_{\text{devfirm,global}}$ = measure of nondiversifiable risk with respect to a globally diversified equity portfolio or a well-diversified country portfolio highly correlated with the global index. Alternatively, $\beta_{\text{devfirm,global}}$ may be estimated indirectly (see Equation 19.7).
FSP = firm size premium, reflecting the additional return smaller firms must earn relative to larger firms to attract investors

An analyst may wish to value the target's future cash flows in both the local and home currencies. The Fisher effect allows the analyst to convert a nominal cost of equity from one currency to another. Assuming the expected inflation rates in the two countries are accurate, the real cost of equity should be the same in both countries.

Applying the Fisher effect

The so-called Fisher effect states that nominal interest rates can be expressed as the sum of the real interest rate (i.e., interest rates excluding inflation) and the anticipated rate of inflation. The Fisher effect can be shown for the United States and Mexico as follows:

$$(1+i_{us}) = (1+r_{us})(1+P_{us}) \text{ and } (1+r_{us}) = (1+i_{us})/(1+P_{us})$$
$$(1+i_{mex}) = (1+r_{mex})(1+P_{mex}) \text{ and } (1+r_{mex}) = (1+i_{mex})/(1+P_{mex})$$

If real interest rates are constant among all countries, nominal interest rates among countries will vary only by the difference in the anticipated inflation rates. Therefore,

$$(1+i_{us})/(1+\text{P}_{us}) = (1+i_{mex})/(1+\text{P}_{mex}) \tag{19.6}$$

in which

i_{us} and i_{mex} = nominal interest rates in the United States and Mexico, respectively
r_{us} and r_{mex} = real interest rates in the United States and Mexico, respectively
P_{us} and P_{mex} = anticipated inflation rates in the United States and Mexico, respectively

[56] In the United States, an example of a well-diversified portfolio is the S&P stock index (S&P 500); in the global capital markets, the MSCI is commonly used as a proxy for a well-diversified global equity portfolio.

EXHIBIT 19.3

Calculating the Target Firm's Cost of Equity in Both Home and Local Currencies

Acquirer, a US multinational firm, is interested in purchasing Target, a small UK-based competitor, with a market value of £550 million, or about $1 billion. The current risk-free rate of return for UK 10-year government bonds is 4.2%. The anticipated inflation rates in the United States and the United Kingdom are 3% and 4%, respectively. The size premium is estimated at 1.2%. The historical equity risk premium in the United States is 5.5%.[a] Acquirer estimates Target's ß to be 0.8 by regressing Target's historical financial returns against the Standard & Poor's 500. What is the cost of equity ($k_{e,\text{uk}}$) that should be used to discount Target's projected cash flows when they are expressed in terms of British pounds (i.e., local currency)? What is the cost of equity ($k_{e,\text{us}}$) that should be used to discount Target's projected cash flows when they are expressed in terms of US dollars (i.e., home currency)?[b]

$$k_{e,\text{uk}} \text{ (see Equation 19.5)} = 0.042 + 0.8 \times (0.055) + 0.012 = 0.098 = 9.80\%$$

$$k_{e,\text{us}} \text{ (see Equation 19.6)} = [(1+0.098)] \times (1 + 0.03) \times /(1+0.04) - 1 = 0.0875 \times 100 = 8.75\%$$

[a]The US equity premium or the UK equity premium could have been used because equity markets in either country are highly correlated.
[b]The real rate of return is the same in the UK (r_{uk}) and the US (r_{us}). $r_{\text{uk}} = 9.8\% - 4.0\% = 5.8\%$, and $r_{\text{us}} = 8.8\% - 3.0\% = 5.8\%$.

If the analyst knows the Mexican interest rate and the anticipated inflation rates in Mexico and the United States, solving Equation 19.6 provides an estimate of the US interest rate (i.e., $i_{\text{us}} = [(1 + i_{\text{mex}}) \times (1 + P_{\text{us}})/(1 + P_{\text{mex}})] - 1$). Exhibit 19.3 illustrates how the cost of equity estimated in one currency is converted easily to the cost of equity in another using Equation 19.6. Although the historical equity premium in the United States is used in calculating the cost of equity, the historical UK or MSCI premium also could have been used.

Estimating the cost of equity in emerging (segmented) capital market countries

If capital markets are segmented, the global CAPM must reflect the tendency of investors in individual countries to hold local country rather than globally diversified equity portfolios. Thus, equity premiums differ among countries, reflecting the nondiversifiable risk associated with each country's equity market index. What follows is a discussion of how to adjust the basic CAPM for valuing cross-border deals when the target is located in an emerging country.

Estimating the risk-free rate of return (emerging countries)

Data limitations and the absence of a legal procedure to deal with sovereign debt (i.e., government-issued debt) in default often preclude using the local country's government bond rate as the risk-free rate. There is no court to approve a debt restructuring plan to reduce, wipe out, or convert debt to equity for commercial bankruptcies. Troubled countries negotiate directly with lenders to restructure debt by reducing the amount owed, lowering the interest rate, extending the maturity of the debt, or some combination of the three.

Countries defaulting on their sovereign debt do pay a price, but the impact is limited in duration. The increase in their borrowing costs after default tends to shrink such that it becomes negligible within 5 years after the countries return to the bond market. The default risk premium paid by these countries is higher for countries that take a long time to settle with creditors and is much higher for countries that have a history of defaulting on their bonds. These "penalties" explain why government debt defaults are infrequent, and when they occur, governments typically try to settle quickly with creditors.[57]

As an alternative to the local country government bond rate, the US Treasury bond rate often is used to estimate the risk-free rate if the target firm's cash flows are in terms of local currency. To create a local nominal interest rate,

[57] Catao et al., 2017

the Treasury bond rate should be adjusted for the difference in the anticipated inflation rates in the two countries using Equation 19.6. Alternatively, the risk-free rate can be estimated using the buildup method as the sum of the expected inflation rate and the expected real rate. The analyst can add the expected inflation rate for the country to the US Treasury inflation-adjusted bond rate (i.e., Treasury inflation-protected securities, [TIPS]). For example, the expected inflation rate for Angola in June 2012 was 12%, and the 5-year rate on US treasury inflation-indexed securities (the real rate) was 2.38%. Therefore, the estimated risk-free rate for Angolan government bonds at that time was 14.38%.

Adjusting CAPM for risk (emerging countries)

Systematic risk for a firm operating primarily in its emerging country's home market (whose capital market is segmented[58]) is measured mainly with respect to the country's equity market index ($\beta_{emfirm,country}$) and to a lesser extent with respect to a globally diversified equity portfolio ($\beta_{country,global}$). The emerging-country firm's global beta ($\beta_{emfirm,global}$) can be adjusted to reflect the relationship with the global capital market as follows:

$$\beta_{emfirm,global} = \beta_{emfirm,country} \times \beta_{country,global} \quad (19.7)$$

The value of $\beta_{emfirm,country}$ is estimated by regressing historical returns for the local firm against returns for the country's equity index.[59] The value of $\beta_{country,global}$ can be estimated by regressing the financial returns for the local-country equity index (or for an index in a similar country) against the historical financial returns for a global equity index.[60] Because of the absence of historical data in many emerging economies, the equity risk premium often is estimated using the "prospective method" implied in the constant-growth valuation model. As shown in Equation 7.4 in Chapter 7, this formulation provides an estimate of the present value of dividends growing at a constant rate in perpetuity. That is, dividends paid in the current period (d_0) are grown at a constant rate of growth (g) such that d_1 equals $d_0(1 + g)$.

Assuming the stock market values stocks correctly and we know the present value of a broadly defined index in the target firm's country ($P_{country}$) or in a similar country, dividends paid annually on this index in the next period (d_1), and the expected dividend growth (g), we can estimate the expected return ($R_{country}$) on the stock index as follows:

$$P_{country} = d_1/(R_{country} - g) \text{ and } R_{country} = (d_1 / P_{country}) + g \quad (19.8)$$

From Equation 19.8, the equity risk premium for the local country's equity market is $R_{country} - R_f$, in which R_f is the local country's risk-free rate. Exhibit 19.4 illustrates how to calculate the cost of equity for an emerging country firm in the absence of perceived significant country or political risk not captured in the beta or equity risk premium. Note the local country's risk-free rate is estimated using the US Treasury bond rate adjusted for expected inflation in the local country relative to the United States. This converts the US Treasury bond rate into a local-country nominal rate.

Adjusting the CAPM for country or political risk (emerging countries)

A country's equity premium may not capture all the events that could jeopardize a firm's ability to operate, such as political instability, limits on repatriation of earnings, capital controls, and the levying discriminatory taxes. Such factors could increase the firm's likelihood of default. Unless the analyst includes the risk of default in projecting a local firm's cash flows, the expected cash flow stream would be overstated in that it does not reflect the costs of financial distress.

If the US Treasury bond rate is used as the risk-free rate in calculating the CAPM, adding a country risk premium (CRP) to the basic CAPM estimate is appropriate. The CRP often is measured as the difference between the yield on

[58] An analyst can determine if a country's equity market is segmented from the global equity market if the two markets are relatively uncorrelated. This implies that the local country's equity premium differs from the global equity premium, reflecting the local country's systematic risk.

[59] Absent sufficient data, $\beta_{emfirm,country}$ may be estimated using the beta for a similar local or foreign firm.

[60] Alternatively, a more direct approach is to regress the local firm's historical returns against the financial returns for a globally diversified portfolio of stocks to estimate $\beta_{emfirm,global}$. Furthermore, the β between a similar local or foreign firm and the global index could be used for this purpose.

EXHIBIT 19.4
Calculating the Target Firm's Cost of Equity for Firms in Emerging Countries

Assume next year's dividend yield on an emerging country's stock market is 5%, and earnings for the companies in the stock market index are expected to grow by 6% annually in the foreseeable future. The country's global beta ($\beta_{country,global}$) is 1.1. The US Treasury bond rate is 4%, and the expected inflation rate in the emerging country is 4% compared with 3% in the United States. Estimate the country's risk-free rate (R_f), the return on a diversified portfolio of equities in the emerging country ($R_{country}$), and the country's equity risk premium ($R_{country} - R_f$). What is the cost of equity in the local currency for a local firm ($k_{e,em}$) whose country beta ($\beta_{emfirm,country}$) is 1.3?

Solution

$$R_f = [(1+0.04)((1+0.04)/(1+0.03)) - 1] = 0.0501 \times 100 = 5.01\%$$

$$R_{country} \text{ (see Equation 19.8)} = 5.00 + 6.00 = 11.00\%$$

$$R_{country} - R_f = 11.00 - 5.01 = 5.99\%$$

$$\beta_{emfirm,global} \text{(see Equation 19.7)} = 1.3 \times 1.1 = 1.43$$

$$k_{e,em} = 5.01 + 1.43(5.99) = 13.58\%$$

the country's sovereign or government bonds and the US Treasury bond rate of the same maturity. The difference, or "spread," is the additional risk premium that investors demand for holding the emerging country's debt rather than US Treasury bonds.[61] S&P (www.standardardandpoors.com), Moody's Investors Service (www.moodys.com), and Fitch IBCA (www.fitchibca.com) provide sovereign bond spreads. In practice, the sovereign bond spread is computed from a bond with the same maturity as the US benchmark 10-year Treasury bond used to compute the risk-free rate for calculating the cost of equity.

Although political risk has traditionally been linked with emerging countries, instances in the recent past illustrate political risk associated with equities and sovereign bonds in developed countries. The sovereign bond crisis in Spain and Italy following the global recession in 2008 to 2009 caused government bond rates to rise and stock prices to fall until it became clear that the eurozone would remain intact. Similarly, the decision by the United Kingdom to exit the European Union in 2016 triggered concern about the long-term health of the British economy. Consequently, the adjustments for political risk suggested in this section also can apply to developed countries.

Global CAPM formulation (emerging countries)

To estimate the cost of equity for a firm in an emerging economy ($k_{e,em}$), Equation 19.5 can be modified for specific country risk as follows:

$$k_{e,em} = R_f + \beta_{emfirm,global}\left(R_{country} - R_f\right) + FSP + CRP \tag{19.9}$$

in which

R_f = local risk-free rate or the US Treasury bond rate converted to a local nominal rate if cash flows are in the local currency (see Equation 19.6) or to the US Treasury bond rate if cash flows are in dollars
($R_{country} - R_f$) = difference between expected return on a well-diversified equity index in the local country or a similar country and the risk-free rate
$\beta_{emfirm,global}$ = emerging country firm's global beta (see Equation 19.7)
FSP = firm size premium, reflecting the additional return that smaller firms must earn relative to larger firms to attract investors

[61] A country risk premium should not be added to the cost of equity if the risk-free rate is the country's sovereign or government bond rate because the effects of specific country or political risk would already be reflected.

CRP = specific country risk premium, expressed as the difference between the local country's (or a similar country's) government bond rate and the US Treasury bond rate of the same maturity. Add to the CAPM estimate only if the US Treasury bond rate is used as a proxy for the local country's risk-free rate.

Estimating the local firm's cost of debt in emerging markets

The cost of debt for an emerging market firm (i_{emfirm}) should be adjusted for default risk because of country- and firm-specific factors. When a local corporate bond rate is not available, the cost of debt for a local firm may be estimated by using an interest rate in the home country (i_{home}) that reflects a level of creditworthiness similar to the firm in the emerging country. The CRP is added to the appropriate home country interest rate to reflect the impact of such factors as political instability on i_{emfirm}. Therefore the cost of debt can be expressed as follows:

$$i_{emfirm} = i_{home} + CRP \tag{19.10}$$

Most firms in emerging markets are not rated; to determine which home-country interest rate to select, it is necessary to assign a credit rating to the local firm. This "synthetic" credit rating is obtained by comparing financial ratios for the target firm with those used by US rating agencies. The estimate of the unrated firm's credit rating may be obtained by comparing interest coverage ratios used by S&P with the firm's interest coverage ratio to determine how S&P would rate the firm. Exhibit 19.5 illustrates how to calculate the cost of emerging-market debt.

Exhibit 19.6 illustrates the calculation of weighted average cost of capital (WACC) in cross-border transactions. Note the adjustments made to the estimate of the cost of equity for firm size and country risk. Note also the adjustment made to the local borrowing cost for country risk. The risk-free rate of return is the US Treasury bond rate converted to a local nominal rate of interest.

Table 19.1 summarizes methods commonly used for valuing cross-border M&As for developed-country and emerging-country firms. The WACC calculation assumes that the firm uses only common equity and debt financing. The CRP is added to both the cost of equity and the after-tax cost of debt in calculating the WACC for a target firm in an emerging country if the US Treasury bond rate is used as the risk-free rate of return. The analyst should avoid adding the CRP to the cost of equity if the risk-free rate used to estimate the cost of equity is the local country's government bond rate. References to home and local countries in Table 19.1 refer to the acquirer's and the target's countries, respectively.[62]

EXHIBIT 19.5
Estimating the Cost of Debt in Emerging Market Countries

Assume that a firm in an emerging market has annual operating income before interest and taxes of $550 million and annual interest expenses of $18 million. This implies an interest coverage ratio of 30.6 (i.e., $550 ÷ $18). For S&P, this corresponds to an AAA rating. According to Standard & Poor's, default spreads for AAA firms are 0.85 currently. The current interest rate on US triple A −rated bonds is 6.0 %. Assume further that the country's government bond rate is 10.3% and that the US Treasury bond rate is 5%. Assume that the firm's marginal tax rate is 0.4. What is the firm's cost of debt before and after tax?

Solution

Cost of debt before taxes (see Equation 19.10) = 6.0 + (10.3 − 5.0) = 11.3%

After−tax cost of debt = 11.3 × (1 − 0.4) = 6.78%

[62] Zurita et al. (2019) illustrate how to adjust common valuation formulas for the effects of inflation on depreciation and interest expense tax shields when taxable earnings are measured in both real and nominal terms.

EXHIBIT 19.6

Estimating the Weighted Average Cost of Capital (WACC) in Cross-Border Transactions

Acquirer Inc., a US-based corporation, wants to purchase Target Inc. Acquirer's management believes that the country in which Target is located is segmented from global capital markets because the beta estimated by regressing the financial returns on the country's stock market with those of a global index is significantly different from 1.

Assumptions: The current US Treasury bond rate (R_{us}) is 5%. The expected inflation rate in the target's country is 6% annually, as compared to 3% in the US. The country's risk premium (CRP) provided by S&P is estimated to be 2%. Based on Target's interest coverage ratio, its credit rating is estimated to be AA. The current interest rate on AA-rated US corporate bonds is 6.25%. Acquirer Inc. receives a tax credit for taxes paid in a foreign country. Because its marginal tax rate is higher than Target's, Acquirer's marginal tax rate of 0.4 is used in calculating WACC. Acquirer's pretax cost of debt is 6%. The firm's total capitalization consists only of common equity and debt. Acquirer's projected debt—to—total capital ratio is 0.3.

Target's beta and the country beta are estimated to be 1.3 and 0.7, respectively. The equity premium is estimated to be 6% based on the spread between the prospective return on the country's equity index and the estimated risk-free rate of return. Given Target Inc.'s current market capitalization of $3 billion, the firm's size premium (FSP) is estimated at 1.0 (see Table 7.1 in Chapter 7). What is the appropriate WACC Acquirer should use to discount Target's projected annual cash flows, expressed in its own local currency?

Solution

$k_{e,em}$(see Equation 19.9)

$$= \{[(1+0.05)\times(1+0.06)/(1+0.03)]-1\}\times 100^{a} + 1.3\times 0.7\,(6.0)+1.0+2.0 = 16.52\%$$

$$i_{local}(\text{see Equation 19.10}) = 6.25+2.0 = 8.25\%$$

$$wacc_{em}(\text{see Equation 7.4}) = 16.52\times(1-0.3)+8.25\times(1-0.4)\times 0.3 = 13.05\%$$

[a]Note that the expression $\{[(1+0.05)\times(1+0.06)/(1+0.03)]-1\}\times 100$ represents the conversion of the US Treasury bond rate to a local nominal rate of interest using Equation 19.6. Also note that 1.3×0.7 provides the target's global beta, as indicated in Equation 19.7.

Evaluating risk using scenario planning

An alternative to adjusting the target's cost of capital is for acquirers to consider different scenarios. Variables defining alternative scenarios include GDP growth, inflation rates, interest rates, and foreign exchange rates. A best-case scenario can reflect projected cash flows, assuming the emerging market's economy grows at a real growth rate of 3% per annum for the next 5 years. Alternative scenarios could assume a 1- to 2-year recession. A third scenario could assume a dramatic devaluation of the country's currency and the potential impact on the country's economy. The NPVs are weighted by subjectively determined probabilities. The actual valuation of the target firm is the expected value of the three scenarios.[63] This approach forces the analyst to evaluate a wider range of possible outcomes. Major disadvantages include the amount of additional effort required and the degree of subjectivity in estimating probabilities.

Empirical studies of financial returns on cross-border transactions

International diversification can reduce firm risk and boost returns. Such diversification may be achieved through start-ups, JVs, and M&As. As is true of domestic M&As, target shareholders are the greatest beneficiaries of cross-border takeovers, but acquirer shareholders also often benefit. Reflecting the correlation between risk and return, acquirer returns tend to be highest in M&As in the riskiest countries. Detailed country knowledge is a key success

[63] If a scenario approach is used to incorporate risk in the valuation, there is no need to modify the discount rate for perceived political and economic risk in the local country.

TABLE 19.1 Common methodologies for valuing cross-border transactions

Developed countries (integrated capital markets)	Emerging countries (segmented capital markets)
Step 1. Project and convert cash flows. **a.** Project target's cash flows in local currency. **b.** Convert local cash flows into acquirer's home currency using forward exchange rates projected using interest rate parity theory.	Step 1. Project and convert cash flows. **a.** Project target's cash flows in local currency. **b.** Convert local cash flows into acquirer's home currency using forward exchange rates. Project exchange rates using purchasing power parity theory if little reliable data on interest rates are available.
Step 2. Adjust discount rates. $k_{e,\text{dev}} = R_f + \beta_{devfirm,\text{global}}{}^{a}(R_m - R_f) + \text{FSP}$ $i = \text{cost of debt}^{c}$ $\text{WACC} = k_e W_e + i(1 - t) \times W_d$ **a.** R_f is the long-term government bond rate in the home country. **b.** $\beta_{\text{devfirm,global}}$ is nondiversifiable risk associated with a well-diversified global, US, or local-country equity index. **c.** R_m is the return on a well-diversified US, local, or global equity index. **d.** FSP is the firm size premium. **e.** t is the appropriate marginal tax rate. **f.** W_e is the acquirer's target equity—to—total capital ratio, and W_d is $1 - W_e$.	Step 2. Adjust discount rates. $k_{e,em} = R_f + \beta_{\text{emfirm,global}}{}^{a}$ $(R_{\text{country}} - R_f)^{b} + \text{FSP} + \text{CRP}$ $i_{\text{local}} = i_{\text{home}} + \text{CRP}$ $\text{WACC} = k_e W_e + i_{\text{local}}\,(1 - t) \times W_d$ **a.** R_f is the long-term government bond rate in the local country or the US Treasury bond rate converted to a local nominal rate if cash flows in local currency; or if cash flows in dollars, the US Treasury bond rate. Note that if the local risk-free rate is used, do *not* add CRP. **b.** $\beta_{\text{emfirm,global}}$ is nondiversifiable risk associated with target's local-country β and local country's global β. **c.** R_{country} is the return on a diversified local equity index or a similar country's index. **d.** CRP is the country risk premium. **e.** i_{home} is the home-country cost of debt. **f.** i_{local} is the local-country cost of debt.

[a] β may be estimated directly for firms whose business is heavily dependent on exports or operating in either developing or emerging countries by regressing directly the firm's historical financial returns against returns on a well-diversified global equity index. For firms operating primarily in their home markets, β may be estimated indirectly by using Equation 19.7.
[b] $(R_{\text{country}} - R_f)$ also could be the equity premium for well-diversified US or global equity indices if the degree of local segmentation is believed to be small.
[c] For developed countries, either the home-country or local-country cost of debt may be used. There is no need to add a country risk premium as would be the case in estimating a local emerging country's cost of debt.
WACC, Weighted average cost of capital.

factor in many international M&A deals. Specific deal characteristics also substantially impact returns. These include form of payment, deals resulting in improved governance, and deals in highly competitive markets. Each of these factors is discussed next.

International diversification contributes to higher financial returns

International diversification increases returns by reducing risk if economies are relatively uncorrelated.[64] Higher returns from global diversification may also reflect scale and scope economies, being nearer customers, increasing the firm's served market, and learning new technologies. How much the target contributes to postmerger performance also may reflect its size relative to the parent and its alliance affiliations with other businesses.[65]

Although most M&A gains go to target shareholders, acquirer shareholders on average also benefit

A massive study consisting of 263,461 domestic and cross-border deals (both public and private)[66] in 47 countries between 1992 and 2011 documents positive abnormal announcement date returns to target shareholders averaging 6.9% (13% for public targets) and 1.4% for acquirer shareholders.[67] These conclusions are consistent with similar findings of earlier extensive global studies.[68] Acquirer financial returns can be even larger when the target is in

[64] There is significant controversy about whether returns are higher for multinational companies that diversify across countries or across industries.

[65] Batsakis et al., 2018

[66] Because the number of private firms far exceeds the number of public firms, most cross-border deals involve private acquirers, private target firms, or both.

[67] Yilmaz et al., 2016

[68] Erel et al., 2012; Netter et al., 2011; Ellis et al., 2011

an emerging country, with positive abnormal returns of 1.65% to 3.1%, well in excess of the average cross-border or domestic deal. This improvement may be due to gaining control, improved governance, the elimination of minority shareholders, and more investment in the target by the parent.[69]

A more recent study finds that publicly traded developed country acquirers experience higher positive abnormal returns when announcing cross-border deals than on announcing domestic transactions. The opposite is true for emerging market public company acquirers.[70] Also, acquirer abnormal financial returns tend to be higher for a firm's initial cross-border deal than for successive ones because investors see the firm using previously unexploited capabilities.[71]

M&As in "frontier economies" may result in the highest acquirer returns

"Frontier economies" are those whose stage of economic development precedes emerging economies as described earlier in this chapter. Examples include such economies as Albania, Bangladesh, Botswana, Cyprus, Estonia, Lithuania, Romania, and Sri Lanka. Their financial markets are viable but tend to be smaller and less liquid than emerging or developed economies. And they exhibit higher risk because of frequent political unrest, currency risk, and limited shareholder protections. However, they do offer acquirers the potential for higher returns because of above-average growth, a greater ability to dominate markets, the potential for transferring their competitive advantage from their home countries, and relatively low takeover premiums.[72] Emerging market acquirers appear to be better able to share complementary resources and knowledge with target firms because of their greater cultural familiarity.[73]

Country familiarity contributes to higher acquirer financial returns

Firms located in countries that commonly trade with one another and are close geographically are more likely to engage in cross-border M&As. These factors contribute to the acquirer's familiarity with the language,[74] legal institutions, customs, and values of the country where the target is located; and they contribute to higher announcement-date returns in cross-border deals.[75]

Form of payment impacts acquirer financial returns

Cross-border deals involving publicly traded acquirers in which the form of payment is primarily equity frequently underperform cash-financed transactions.[76] This is consistent with domestic public acquirers using overvalued stock to overpay for the target firm, resulting in zero to negative announcement-date returns. Acquirer announcement-date returns also tend to be poor regardless of the form of payment in cross-border deals involving complex targets such as conglomerates, which tend to be difficult to value and integrate.[77]

The use of acquirer stock in cross-border deals may be appropriate when the target firm's governance practices are problematic (i.e., the target firm's financial statements are suspect, and the target is only willing to allow the acquirer to perform limited due diligence) and the local country's shareholder protections are limited or poorly enforced. Offering to exchange acquirer shares for target shares gives target shareholders choosing to retain their shares in the combined firms an incentive not to overvalue their shares. Why? Both the acquirer and target firm shareholders will share in any postclosing losses if the acquirer overpays.[78]

[69] Barbopoulos et al., 2013

[70] Otto et al., 2020

[71] Dandapani et al., 2020

[72] Vagenas-Nanos, 2016

[73] Nkiwane Nkiwane et al., 2019

[74] Kedia et al., 2016

[75] Ahern et al., 2013. Boateng et al. (2019) argue that the lack of familiarity can be overcome by large acquirers with significant experience in cross-border deals and substantial resources.

[76] Dutta et al., 2013

[77] Chkir et al., 2019

[78] Huang et al., 2017; Cho et al., 2017

Improving corporate governance creates significant shareholder value

Controlling as well as partial takeovers[79] can improve governance and firm value when countries practice good governance.[80] Country governance includes the existence of laws governing property rights,[81] transparent accounting practices, and the extent to which the court systems in these countries enforce the laws. The existence of laws protecting shareholder and bondholder rights reduces the risk of expropriation by the emerging country's government and attracts more patient investors willing to give the acquirer time for its strategy to unfold. This can lower the firm's cost of financing, increase acquirer willingness to pay higher takeover premiums,[82] and improve postmerger performance.[83]

Foreign institutional ownership also is a significant factor in encouraging acquirers and target firms in cross-border deals to adopt better governance practices. They do so by acquiring firms located in countries with weak corporate governance or legal institutions.[84] Foreign institutional investors facilitate change-of-control deals by serving as intermediaries between buyers and sellers and by supplying information not publicly available. In doing so, institutional investors augment the value of investments they may have in firms with subpar governance by forcing them to adopt more demanding governance practices because of the change in control.

Competitive product markets often boost acquirer returns in cross-border deals

Gains to acquirer shareholders are greater when the target firm is located in countries with competitive product markets and tend to disappear in less competitive markets.[85] When competition is greatest, shareholders of underperforming firms are more receptive to takeover bids giving them an opportunity to exit their investment. Skilled acquirers may be able to acquire such firms at an attractive price and improve firm performance through better management.

Financial returns earned by competitors in emerging markets after the foreign acquisition of a domestic rival tend to improve by intensifying competition in domestic markets and breaking up business group competition.[86] Foreign acquirers may be particularly effective in stimulating competition in concentrated industries and within business groups. And institutional reforms can embolden activist shareholders to remove incompetent management.[87]

Some things to remember

Motives for international corporate expansion include a desire to accelerate growth, diversify, consolidate industries, and exploit natural resources and lower labor costs available elsewhere. Other motives include applying a firm's brand name or intellectual property in new markets, minimizing tax liabilities, following customers, and avoiding tariffs and import barriers. Alternative entry strategies include exporting, licensing, alliances or JVs, and solo ventures, as well as M&As. The basic differences between within-country and cross-border valuation methods is that the latter involves converting cash flows from one currency to another and adjusting the discount

[79] Polovina and Peasnell (2020) argue that minority investors can influence governance when shareholder rights are protected such that they can demand visibility into related third-party deals and other instances in which board members and managers are profiting at the expense of shareholders.

[80] Xie et al., 2017; Hartwell and Malinowska (2020) argue firm valuation in an unstable institutional environment is mostly caused by developments in informal property rights and other factors external to the firm.

[81] Cao et al. (2019) argue that such laws are particularly important for highly leveraged deals such as leveraged buyouts because of the high frequency of bankruptcy.

[82] Maung et al., 2019

[83] Breuer et al., 2020

[84] Adriosopoulos et al., 2015

[85] Lee et al., 2019

[86] In many emerging economies, groups of businesses are affiliated by having made investments in each other or by sharing common directors on their boards. Historically, such arrangements have contributed to collusion among the firms within a business group to limit competition.

[87] Elango et al., 2019

rate for risks common in cross-border deals. Although cross-border deals reward mostly target shareholders, acquirer shareholders on average also benefit. These results are consistent with the results of domestic transactions.

Chapter discussion questions

19.1 Discuss the circumstances under which a non-US buyer may choose as its acquisition vehicle a US corporate structure, an LLC , or a partnership.
19.2 What factors influence the selection of which tax rate to use (i.e., the target's or the acquirer's) in calculating the WACC in cross-border deals?
19.3 Discuss adjustments commonly made in estimating the cost of debt in emerging countries.
19.4 Find an example of a recent cross-border transaction. Discuss the challenges an analyst might face in valuing the target firm.
19.5 Discuss the various types of adjustments for risk that might be made to the global CAPM before valuing a target firm in an emerging country. Be specific.
19.6 Do you see the growth in sovereign wealth funds as important sources of capital to the M&A market or as a threat to the sovereignty of the countries in which they invest?
19.7 What factors contribute to the increasing integration of the global capital markets? What factors could derail continued globalization?
19.8 Give examples of economic and political risk that you could reasonably expect to encounter in acquiring a firm in an emerging economy. Be specific.
19.9 During the 1980s and 1990s, changes in the S&P 500 were about 50% correlated with the MSCI EAFE (Europe, Australasia, Far East) Index. In recent years, the correlation has increased to more than 90%. Why? If an analyst wishes to calculate the cost of equity, which index should he or she use in estimating the equity risk premium?
19.10 Comment on the following statement: "The conditions for foreign buyers interested in US targets are highly auspicious. The dollar is weak, M&A financing is harder to come by for financial sponsors (private equity firms), and many strategic buyers in the US are hard-pressed to make acquisitions at a time when earnings targets are being missed."

Answers to these Chapter Discussion Questions are found in the Online Instructor's Manual for instructors using this book.

End-of-chapter case study: Takeda's high-risk bet to change its strategy and corporate culture

Case study objectives

To illustrate

- How acquisitions can be used to change an acquirer's corporate culture to support the realignment of its strategic direction
- The risks involved in such a maneuver

Investors and analysts viewed the takeover of Dublin-based Shire Plc (Shire) by Japan's Takeda Pharmaceutical Company Ltd. (Takeda) with shock and awe! It was shock in that Takeda, Japan's largest pharmaceutical company, was paying a 60% premium to acquire the larger Shire in a deal valued at $80 billion, including assumed debt. And it was awe at the audaciousness of Takeda's management, which in a single stroke catapulted Takeda into the ninth position among the top global drug companies. It was also the first Japanese firm to be counted among that elite group.

Potential synergy between the two firms was significant. Shire and Takeda have complementary positions in gastroenterology and neuroscience, with leading positions in treating certain rare diseases and oncology. Acquiring Shire would give Takeda expanded market share in the lucrative US drug market because about two-thirds of Shire's sales are in the US market. Together they will market medicines in about 80 countries. With total annual revenue exceeding $30 billion, the combined firms will be able to better fund research and development in four areas: oncology, gastroenterology, neuroscience, and rare diseases.

The risks to the deal were also clear. The combined firms faced a punishing debt load, huge cultural differences between the two firms (one Japanese and one Irish), and an uphill battle to earn the cost of capital on their investment because of the size of the premium. With a lengthy postmerger integration likely, the tasks ahead for the two firms seemed daunting.

Also, Shire's drugs for attention deficit hyperactivity disorder have been a major cash generator for years. They were soon to lose patent protection and be subject to increased price competition from generic drug firms. And pressure to reduce drug prices is intense in many markets such as the United States. Paying off the firm's bone crushing debt level will be a major challenge. Moody's downgraded the firm's credit rating from A2 to Baa2 in December 2018. Investors were concerned Takeda was paying too much and borrowing too much to finance the deal. They were also concerned that the dividend (currently at 3.42%) may be cut if the firm has trouble servicing the debt.

Although the synergy potential between the two firms was significant, Takeda's management and board were looking for ways to convert the firm's culture from one that was largely insular to one with a global perspective. To understand this motivation, it is necessary to review Takeda's recent history. Five years ago, the 237-year-old Takeda was facing a domestic market whose population was declining and that contributed about half of its revenue. Patent protection for its best-selling diabetes drug Actos was set to expire in the near future. Despite previous overseas acquisitions, Millennium in the United States in 2008 and Nucomed (with operations in Europe and Latin America) in 2011, the firm's culture and focus continued to be distinctly Japanese. The board reasoned that bold action was necessary to grow sales and earnings.

In 2014, Takeda hired the firm's first foreign CEO, Christophe Weber. Because smaller acquisitions had failed to change the firm materially, Weber pushed for a large foreign acquisition. Shire, he and the Takeda board believed, would achieve the goal of fundamentally transforming the firm. How? After the acquisitions, the share of foreign employees would increase from less than 70% to more than 82% of total. And the majority of the firm's revenue would come from outside Japan. Finally, because half of Shire's purchase price would consist of new Takeda shares, foreign ownership of Takeda would grow substantially. Greater and more diverse investor interest in Takeda was expected to make the firm's shares more liquid.

After Takeda expressed publicly an interest in the acquiring Shire, the firm had a month to make a formal offer as required by UK law. Shire rejected the initial bid, saying it undervalued the firm. Takeda made five public bids for Shire. In the final bid, Shire agreed to be acquired for $62.2 billion or $66.22 per share, consisting of $30.33 per share in cash and 0.839 shares of Takeda stock or 1.6278 ADSs.[88] At closing, Takeda shareholders would own about half of the combined firms and Shire's the remainder. Takeda expected pretax synergies to reach an annualized rate of $1.4 billion by the end of the third year after closing.

Investor reaction was swift. Since March 2018, when Takeda first publicly displayed interest in Shire, Takeda's shares dropped 26% as investors fretted about the perceived risks rather than the potential. By the time an agreement was signed, Shire's valuation exceeded Takeda's. Takeda had at that time a $33 billion market capitalization compared with Shire's of $49 billion. But when the deal closed in January 2019, Takeda's shares jumped 7.5%, its biggest gain in 3 years. Investors seemed to be warming up to the deal.

Discussion questions

1. What are the key assumptions implicit in Takeda's takeover of Shire? Which do you believe are the most critical? Be specific.
2. What alternatives to acquisition could Takeda have pursued to achieve its strategic objectives? Speculate as to why a takeover was the preferred option.
3. Which investor reaction do you think was more accurate: the immediate negative reaction when the deal was announced or the more positive one when the deal closed?
4. Speculate as to why the initial Takeda offer for Shire was all cash and the final offer was a combination of cash and stock. Explain your answer.

Solutions to these questions are found in the Online Instructor's Manual available to instructors using this book.

[88] An ADS (or American depository share) is a US dollar–denominated equity share of a foreign-based firm that can be bought on a US stock exchange.

References

Aaldering, L., Leker, J., Song, C., 2019. Recommending untapped M&A opportunities: a combined approach using principal component analysis and collaborative filtering. Expert Systems with Applications 125, 221–232.

Abeysekera, A., Fernando, C., 2020. Corporate social responsibility versus corporate shareholder responsibility: a family firm perspective. Journal of Corporate Finance 61, 101370.

Abudy, M., Benninga, S., Shust, E., 2016. The cost of equity for private firms. Journal of Corporate Finance 37, 431–443.

Acharya, V., Franks, J., Servaes, H., 2007. Private equity: boom or bust? Journal of Applied Corporate Finance 19, 44–53.

Acharya, V., Kehoe, C., 2010. Board directors and experience: a lesson from private equity. Perspectives on Corporate Finance 35.

Acuña-Carvajal, F., Pinto-Tarazona, L., Lopez-Ospina, H., Barros-Castro, R., Quezada, L., Palacio, K., 2019. An integrated method to plan, structure, and validate a business strategy using fuzzy DEMATEL and the balanced scorecard. Expert Systems with Applications 122, 351–368.

Adams, R., Ferreira, D., 2007. A theory of friendly boards. Journal of Finance 62, 217–250.

Adams, R., Akyol, A., Verwijmeren, P., 2018. Director skill sets. Journal of Financial Economics 130, 641–662.

Adegoke, Y., 2008. YouTube rolls out sponsored videos in revenue drive. Reuters.

Adhikari, H., Sutton, N., 2016. All in the family: the effect of family ownership on acquisition performance. Journal of Economics and Business 88, 65–78.

Adolph, G., 2006. Mergers: back to happily ever after. In: Strategy and Business. Booz Allen Hamilton, New York.

Adra, S., Barbopoulos, L., 2019. Do corporations learn from mispricing? Evidence from takeovers and corporate performance. International Review of Financial Analysis 61, 91–107.

Adra, S., Barbopoulos, L., Saunders, A., 2020. The impact of monetary policy on M&A outcomes. Journal of Corporate Finance 62 article 101529.

Aggarwal, R., Dahiya, S., Prabhal, N., 2019. The power of shareholder votes: evidence from uncontested director elections. Journal of Financial Economics 133, 134–153.

Aggarwal, R., Erel, I., Stulz, R., Williamson, R., 2007. Differences in Governance Practices between U.S. and Foreign Firms: Measurement, Causes, and Consequences. NBER Working Paper 13288. http://www.aggdata.com/business/fortune_500.

Aggarwal, R., Jindal, V., Seth, R., 2019. Board diversity and firm performance: the role of business group affiliation. International Business Review 28 article 11600.

Aggarwal, R., Schloetzer, J., Williamson, R., 2019. Do corporate mandates impact long-term firm value and governance culture? Journal of Corporate Finance 59, 202–217.

Agliardi, E., Amel-Zadeh, A., Koussis, N., 2016. Leverage changes and growth options in mergers and acquisitions. Journal of Empirical Finance 37, 37–58.

Agrawal, A., Nasser, T., 2012. Insider trading in takeover targets. Journal of Corporate Finance 18, 598–625.

Aguir, I., Misra, L., 2017. Ownership level and value creation in international joint ventures: the role of investor protections. International Review of Economics and Finance 49, 515–535.

Agyei-Boapeah, H., 2019. Foreign acquisitions and firm performance: the moderating role of prior foreign experience. Global Finance Journal 42 article 100415.

Ahern, K., Harford, J., 2014. The importance of industry links in merger waves. Journal of Finance 69, 527–576.

Ahern, K., Daminelli, D., Fracassi, C., 2015. Lost in translation? The effect of cultural values on mergers around the world. Journal of Financial Economics 17, 165–189.

Ahmad, M., Lambert, T., 2019. Collective bargaining and mergers and acquisitions around the world. Journal of Banking and Finance 99, 21–44.

Akbulut, M., 2013. Do overvaluation-driven stock acquisitions really benefit acquirer shareholders? Journal of Financial and Quantitative Analysis 48, 637–668.

Akbulut, M., Matsusaka, J., 2010. 50+ years of diversification announcements. Financial Review 45, 231–262.

Aktas, N., Andries, K., Croci, E., Ozdakak, A., 2019b. Stock market development and the financing role of IPOs in acquisitions. Journal of Banking and Finance 98, 25–38.

Aktas, N., Croci, E., Petmezas, D., 2015. Is working capital management value-enhancing? Evidence from firm performance and investments. Journal of Corporate Finance 30, 98–113.

Aktas, N., de Bodt, E., Roll, R., 2010. Negotiations under the threat of an auction. Journal of Financial Economics 98, 241–255.

Aktas, N., de Bodt, E., Roll, R., 2013. Learning from repetitive acquisitions: evidence from the time between deals. Journal of Financial Economics 108, 99–117.

Aktas, N., Louca, C., Petmezas, D., 2019a. CEO overconfidence and the value of corporate cash holdings. Journal of Corporate Finance 54, 85–106.

Alaka, H., Oyedele, L., Owolabi, H., Kumar, V., Ajayi, S., Akinade, O., Bilal, M., 2018. Systematic review of bankruptcy prediction models: towards a framework for tool selection. Expert Systems with Applications 94, 164–184.

Albring, S., Huang, S., Pereira, R., Xu, X., 2020. Disclosure and liquidity management: evidence from regulation fair disclosure. Journal of Contemporary Accounting and Economics 16 article 100201.

Albuquerque, R., Schroth, E., 2015. The value of control and the costs of illiquidity. Journal of Finance 70, 1405–1455.

Al Dah, B., Michael, A., Dixon, R., 2017. Antitakeover provisions and CEO monetary benefits: revisiting the E-index authors. Research in International Business and Finance 42, 992–1004.

Alderson, M., Halford, J., Sibilkov, V., 2020. An examination of the wealth effects of share repurchases on bondholders. Journal of Corporate Finance article 101499, forthcoming.

Alexandridis, G., Antypas, N., Travlos, N., 2017. Value creation from M&As: new evidence. Journal of Corporate Finance 45, 632–650.

Alexandridis, G., Fuller, K., Terhaar, L., Travlos, N., 2013. Deal size, acquisition premia, and shareholder gains. Journal of Corporate Finance 20, 1–13.

Alhenawi, Y., Krishnaswami, S., 2015. The long-term impact of merger synergies on performance and value. Journal of Quarterly Economics and Finance 58, 93–118.

Allen, J., 2001. Private information and spin-off performance. Journal of Business 74, 281–306.

Allen, P., 2000. Corporate equity ownership, strategic alliances, and product market relationships. Journal of Finance 55, 2791–2816.

Alli, K., Thompson, D., 1991. The value of the resale limitation on restricted stock: an option theory approach. Valuation 36, 22–34.

Almeida, H., Philippon, T., 2007. The risk-adjusted cost of financial distress. Journal of Finance 62, 2557–2586.

Alperovych, Y., Amess, K., Wright, M., 2013. Private equity firm experience and buyout vendor source: what is the impact on efficiency? European Journal of Operational Research 228, 601–611.

Alquist, R., Berman, N., Mukherjee, R., Tesar, L., 2019. Financial constraints, institutions, and foreign ownership. Journal of International Economics 118, 63–83.

Altman, E.I., 2007. Global debt markets in 2007: a new paradigm or great credit bubble. Journal of Applied Corporate Finance summer, 17–31.

Altman, E.I., Brady, B., Resti, A., Sironi, A., 2005. The link between default and recovery rates: theory, empirical evidence and implications. Journal of Business 78, 2203–2227.

Amankwah-Amoaha, J., Adomako, S., 2019. Big data analytics and business failures in data-rich environments: an organizing framework. Computers in Industry 105, 204–212.

Amel-Zadeh, A., Meeks, G., 2019. Bidder earnings forecasts in mergers and acquisitions. Journal of Corporate Finance 58, 373–392.

American Bar Association, 2006. In: Mergers and Acquisitions: Understanding Antitrust Issues, 2nd ed. American Bar Association, Chicago.

Amihud, Y., Stoyanov, S., 2017. Do staggered boards harm shareholders? Journal of Financial Economics 123, 432–439.

Amin, A., Chourou, L., Kamal, S., Malik, M., Zhao, Y., 2020. It's who you know that counts: board connectedness and CSR performance. Journal of Corporate Finance 64 article 101662.

Anderson, W., Huang, J., Torna, G., 2018. Can investors anticipate post-IPO mergers and acquisitions? Journal of Corporate Finance 83, 160–172.

Andriosopoulos, D., Yang, S., 2015. The impact of institutional investors on mergers and acquisitions in the United Kingdom. Journal of Banking & Finance 50, 547–561.

Andriosopoulos, D., Yang, S., Li, W., 2015. The market valuation of M&A announcements in the United Kingdom. International Review of Financial Analysis 48, 350–366.

Andriosopoulos, K., Chan, K., Dontis-Charitos, P., Staikouras, S., 2017. Wealth and risk implications of the Dodd-Frank Act on the U.S. financial intermediaries. Journal of Financial Stability 33, 366–379.

Ang, J., Daher, M., Ismail, A., 2019. How do firms value debt capacity? Evidence from mergers and acquisitions. Journal of Banking & Finance 98, 95–107.

Ang, J., Ismail, A., 2015. What premiums do target shareholders expect? Explaining negative returns upon offer announcements. Journal of Corporate Finance 30, 245–256.

Annema, A., Fallon, W.C., Goedhart, M.H., 2002. When carve-outs make sense. McKinsey Quarterly.

Annema, A., Goedhart, M.H., 2006. Betas: back to normal. McKinsey Quarterly.

Antill, S., Grenadier, S., 2019. Optimal capital structure and bankruptcy choice: dynamic bargaining versus liquidation. Journal of Financial Economics 133, 198–224.

Antoni, M., Maug, E., Obernberger, S., 2019. Private equity and human capital risk. Journal of Financial Economics 133, 634–657.

Arcot, S., Fluck, Z., Gaspar, J., Hege, U., 2015. Fund managers under pressure: rationale and determinants of secondary buyouts. Journal of Financial Economics 115, 102–135.

Arikan, A., Stulz, R., 2016. Corporate acquisitions, diversification, and the firm's life cycle. Journal of Finance 71, 139–194.

Armstrong, C., Core, J.E., Guay, W.R., 2014. Do independent directors cause improvements in firm transparency? Journal of Financial Economics 113, 383–403.

Arocena, P., Saal, D., Urakami, T., Urakami, M., Zschille, M., 2020. Measuring and decomposing change in the presence of mergers. European Journal of Operational Research 282, 319–333.

Arouri, M., Gomes, M., Pukthuanthong, K., 2019. Corporate social responsibility and M&A uncertainty. Journal of Corporate Finance 56, 176–198.

Arslanalp, S., Lee, J., Rawat, U., 2019. Demographics and interest rates in Asia. Japan and the World Economy 50, 14–24.

Arulampalama, W., Devereux, M., Liberini, F., 2019. Taxes and the location of targets. Journal of Public Economics 176, 161–178.

Ashraf, R., Li, H., Ryan, H., 2020. Dual agency problems in family firms: evidence from director elections. Journal of Corporate Finance 62 article 101556.

Asker, J., Farre-Mensa, J., Ljungqvist, A., 2015. Corporate investment and stock market listing: a puzzle? Review of Financial Studies 28, 342–390.

Aspatore staff, 2006. M&A Negotiations: Leading Lawyers on Negotiating Deals: Structuring Contracts and Resolving Merger and Acquisition Disputes. Aspatore Books, Boston.

Association for Financial Professionals, March 2011. AFP Survey of Current Trends in Estimating and Applying the Cost of Capital. Report of Survey Results. Association for Financial Professionals, Bethesda, MD.

Atanasov, V., Boone, A., Haushalter, D., 2010. Is there shareholder expropriation in the U.S.? An analysis of publicly traded subsidiaries. Journal of Financial and Quantitative Analysis 5, 1–26.
Axelson, U., Jenkinson, T., Stromberg, P., Weisbach, M., 2013. The determinants of leverage and pricing in buyouts: an empirical analysis. Journal of Finance 68, 2223–2267.
Ayash, B., 2020. The origin, ownership, and use of cash flows in leveraged buyouts. The Quarterly Review of Economics and Finance 77, 286–295.
Ayash, B., Bartlett, R., Poulsen, A., 2017. The determinants of buyout returns: does transaction strategy matter? Journal of Corporate Finance 46, 342–360.
Ayash, B., Rastad, M., 2020. Leveraged buyouts and financial distress. Finance Research Letters article 101452, forthcoming.
Aziz, M.A., Dar, H.A., 2006. Predicting corporate bankruptcy: where we stand. Corporate Governance 6, 18–33.
Baars, M., Cordes, H., Mohrschladt, H., 2020. How negative interest rates affect the risk taking of individual investors: experimental evidence. Finance Research Letters 32 article 1011172.
Bae, K., El Ghoul, S., Guedhami, O., Kwok, C., Zheng, Y., 2019. Does corporate social responsibility reduce the costs of high leverage? Evidence from capital structure and product market interactions. Journal of Banking and Finance 100, 135–150.
Bae, S., Chang, K., Kim, D., 2013. Determinants of target selection and acquirer returns: evidence from cross-border acquisitions. International Review of Economics and Finance 27, 552–565.
Baker, E., Niederman, F., 2014. Integrating the IS functions after mergers and acquisitions: analyzing business-IT alignment. Journal of Strategic Information Systems 23 (2), 112–127.
Baranchuk, N., Rebello, M., 2018. Spillovers from good news and other bankruptcies: real effects and price responses. Journal of Financial Economics 129, 228–249.
Barbopoulos, L., Adra, S., 2016. The earnout structure matters: takeover premia and acquirer gains in earnout financed M&As. International Review of Financial Analysis 45, 283–294.
Barbopoulos, L., Adra, S., Saunders, A., 2020. Macroeconomic news and acquirer returns in M&As. Journal of Corporate Finance 64 article 101583.
Barbopoulos, L., Cheng, Y., Cheng, A. Marshall, 2019. The role of real options in the takeover premia in mergers. International Review of Economics and Finance 61, 91–107.
Barbopoulos, L., Marshall, A., Macinnes, C., McColgan, P., 2013. Foreign direct investment in emerging markets and acquirer's value gains. International Business Review 23, 604–619.
Barbopoulos, L., Molyneux, P., Wilson, J., 2016. Earnout financing in the financial services industry. International Review of Financial Analysis 47, 119–132.
Bardos, K., Ertugrul, M., Gao, L., 2020. Corporate social responsibility, product market perception, and firm value. Journal of Corporate Finance 62 article 101588.
Bargeron, L., Lehn, K., Moeller, S., Schlingemann, F., 2014. Disagreement and the information of stock returns: the case of acquisition announcements. Journal of Corporate Finance 25, 155–172.
Bargeron, L., Lehn, K., Smith, J., 2015. Employee–management trust and M&A activity. Journal of Corporate Finance 35, 389–406.
Bargeron, L., Schlingemann, F., Stulz, R., Zutter, C., 2017. What is the shareholder wealth impact of target CEO retention in private equity deals? A review of past research and an agenda for the future. Journal of Corporate Finance 46, 186–206.
Bartlett, R., Talley, E., 2017. Law and corporate governance. The Handbook of the Economics of Corporate Governance 1, 177–234.
Basnet, A., Davis, F., Walker, T., Zhao, K., 2020. The effect of securities class action lawsuits on mergers and acquisitions. Global Finance Journal, forthcoming.
Basso, L., Ross, T., 2019. On the harm from mergers in input markets. Economic Letters 178, 70–76.
Basu, N., Paeglis, I., Rahnamaei, M., 2016. Multiple block holders, power, and firm value. Journal of Banking and Finance 66, 66–78.
Basuil, D., Datta, D., 2017. Value creation in cross-border acquisitions: the role of outside directors' human and social capital. Journal of Business Research 80, 35–44.
Bates, T., 2005. Asset sales, investment opportunities, and the use of proceeds. Journal of Finance 60, 105–135.
Bates, T., Becher, D., 2017. Bid resistance by takeover targets: managerial bargaining or bad faith. Journal of Financial and Quantitative Analysis 52, 837–866.
Batsakis, G., Wood, G., Azarb, G., Singh, S., 2018. International diversification and firm performance in the post-acquisition period: a resource dependence perspective. Journal of Business Research 93, 151–159.
Baulkaran, V., 2014. Management entrenchment and the valuation discount of dual class firms. The Quarterly Review of Economics and Finance 54, 70–81.
Baziki, S., Norback, P., Persson, L., 2017. Cross-border acquisition and restructuring: multinational enterprises and private equity firms. European Economic Review 94, 166–184.
Bebchuk, L., Brav, A., Jiang, W., 2015. The long-term effects of hedge fund activism. Columbia Law Review 115, 1085–1156.
Bebchuk, L., Coates, J., Subramanian, G., 2002. The powerful anti-takeover force of staggered boards: theory, evidence, and policy. Stanford Law Review 54, 887–951.
Bebchuk, L., Coates, J.C.I.V., Subramanian, G., 2003. The powerful antitakeover force of staggered boards. Stanford Law Review 54, 887–951.
Bebchuk, L., Cohen, A., Wang, C., 2014. Golden parachutes and the wealth of shareholders. Journal of Corporate Finance 25, 140–154.
Bebchuk, L., Cohen, A., 2017. Recent board declassifications: a response to Cremers and Sepe. https://ssrn.com/abstract=2970629 or https://doi.org/10.2139/ssrn.2970629.
Bebchuk, L., Cohen, A., Ferrell, A., 2009. What matters in corporate governance. Review of Financial Studies 22, 783–827.
Bebchuk, L., Cohen, A., Wang, C., 2010. Learning and the disappearing association between governance and returns. Journal of Financial Economics 102, 199–221.
Bebchuk, L., Hirst, S., 2019. The Specter of the Giant Three. National Bureau of Economic Research, Working Paper Series. Working Paper 25914.
Bekier, M., Bogardus, A., Oldham, T., 2001. Why mergers fail. McKinsey Quarterly 4, 3.

Bekkers, E., 2019. Challenges to the trade system: the potential impact of changes in future trade policy. Journal of Policy Modeling 41, 489–506.

Ben-Amar, W., Andre, P., 2006. Separation of ownership from control and acquiring firm performance: the case of family ownership in Canada. Journal of Business Finance and Accounting 33, 517–543.

Benamraoui, A., Jory, S., Mazouz, K., Shah, N., Gough, O., 2019. The effect of block ownership on future firm value and performance. North American Journal of Economics and Finance 50, 100–122.

Beneda, N., 2007. Performance and distress indicators of new public companies. Journal of Asset Management 8, 24–33.

Benlemlih, M., 2019. Corporate social responsibility and dividend policy. Research in International Business and Finance 47, 114–138.

Benmelech, E., Bergman, N., 2011. Bankruptcy and the collateral channel. Journal of Finance 66, 337–378.

Bergh, D., Johnson, R., Dewitt, R.L., 2007. Restructuring through spin-off or sell-off: transforming information asymmetries into financial gain. Strategic Management Journal 29, 133–148.

Berman, D., Sender, H., 2006. Backstory of Kinder LBO underscores web of ethical issues such deals face. Wall Street Journal, A6.

Bernard, D., Blackburne, T., Thornock, J., 2020. Information flows among rivals and corporate investment. Journal of Financial Economics 136, 760–779.

Bernard, V., Healy, P., Palepu, K.G., 2000. In: Business Analysis and Valuation, 2nd ed. Southwestern College Publishing Company, Georgetown, TX.

Bernile, G., Bhagwat, V., Yonker, S., 2018. Board diversity, firm risk, and corporate policies. Journal of Financial Economics 127, 588–612.

Bernstein, S., 2015. Does going public affect innovation? Journal of Finance 70, 1365–1403.

Betton, S., Eckbo, B., Thorburn, K., 2008. Corporate takeovers. In: Eckbo, B. (Ed.), Handbook of Corporate Finance: Empirical Corporate Finance, Vol. 2. Elsevier, North-Holland, pp. 291–430.

Betton, S., Eckbo, B., Thorburn, K., 2009. Merger negotiations and the toehold puzzle. Journal of Financial Economics 91, 158–178.

Betton, S., Eckbo, B., Thompson, R., Thorburn, K., 2015. Merger negotiations with stock market feedback. Journal of Finance 69, 1705–1745.

Bhagat, S., Bolton, B., 2019. Corporate governance and firm performance: the sequel. Journal of Corporate Finance 58, 142–168.

Bhagat, S., Dong, M., Hirshleifer, D., Noah, R., 2005. Do tender offers create value? New methods and evidence. Journal of Financial Economics 76, 3–60.

Bhargava, R., Faircloth, S., Khimic, H., 2017. Takeover protection and stock price crash risk: evidence from state antitakeover laws. Journal of Business Research 70, 177–184.

Bhattacharya, D., Hsu, S., Li, W., Liu, C., 2019. A combined firm's decision to hire the target's financial advisor after acquisition: does "service excellence" pay off? Finance Research Letters 29, 297–302.

Bianconi, M., Tan, C., 2019. Evaluating the instantaneous and medium-run impact of mergers and acquisitions on firm values. International Review of Economics and Finance 59, 71–87.

Bigelli, M., Mengoli, S., 2004. Sub-optimal acquisition decision under a majority shareholder system. Journal of Management Governance 8, 373–403.

Billett, M., Jiang, Z., Lie, E., 2010. The effect of change in control covenants on takeovers: evidence from leveraged buyouts. Journal of Corporate Finance 16, 1–15.

Billett, M., King, T., Mauer, D., 2004. Bondholder wealth effects in mergers and acquisitions: new evidence from the 1980s and 1990s. Journal of Finance 59, 107–135.

Billett, M.T., Vijh, A.M., 2004. The wealth effects of tracking stock restructurings. Journal of Financial Research 27, 559–583.

Billett, M., Yang, K., 2016. Bond tender offers in mergers and acquisitions. Journal of Corporate Finance 40, 128–141.

Bilotkach, V., Huschelrath, K., 2019. Balancing competition and cooperation: evidence from transatlantic airline markets. Transportation Research Part A 120, 1–16.

Binns, R., Bietti, E., 2020. Dissolving privacy one merger at a time: competition, data, and third party tracking. Computer, Law, and Security Review 36 article 105369.

Birollo, G., Teerikangas, S., 2019. Integration projects as relational spaces: a closer look at acquired managers' strategic role recovery in cross-border acquisitions. International Journal of Project Management 37, 1003–1016.

Block, J., Fisch, C., Vismarac, S., Andres, R., 2019. Private equity investment criteria: an experimental conjoint analysis of venture capital, business angels, and family offices. Journal of Corporate Finance 58, 329–352.

Blouin, J., Core, J., Guay, W., 2010. Have the tax benefits of debt been overestimated? Journal of Financial Economics 98, 195–213.

Blouin, J., Fich, E., Rice, E., Tran, A., 2020. Corporate tax cuts, merger activity, and shareholder wealth. Journal of Accounting and Economics, forthcoming.

Blume, M., Keim, D., 2017. The changing nature of institutional stock investing. Critical Finance Review 6, 1–41.

Boateng, A., Du, M., Bi, X., Lodorfos, G., 2019. Cultural distance and value creation of cross-border M&A: the moderating role of acquirer characteristics. International Review of Financial Analysis 63, 285–295.

Bodnaruk, A., Manconi, A., Massi, M., 2016. Cross border alliances and risk management. Journal of International Economics 102, 22–49.

Bodnaruk, A., Rossi, M., 2016. Dual ownership, returns, and voting in mergers. Journal of Financial Economics 120, 58–80.

Boisjoly, R., Conine, T., McDonald, M., 2020. Working capital management: financial and valuation impacts. Journal of Business Research 108, 1–8.

Boone, A., Haushalter, D., Mikkelson, W., 2003. An investigation of the gains from specialized equity claims. Financial Management 32, 67–83.

Boone, A., Mulherin, J.H., 2007. How are firms sold? Journal of Finance 62, 847–875.

Boone, A., Mulherin, J.H., 2009. Is there one best way to sell a firm? Auctions versus negotiations and controlled sales. Journal of Applied Corporate Finance 21, 28–37.

Boone, A., Mulherin, J.H., 2011. Do private equity consortiums facilitate collusion in takeover bidding? Journal of Corporate Finance 17, 1475–1495.

Boone, A., Uysal, V., 2019. Reputational concerns in the market for corporate control. Journal of Corporate Finance 61 article 101399.

Borochin, P., Kopeliovich, Y., Shea, K., 2020. A general method for valuing complex capital structures. Finance Research Letters 35 article 101304.

Borochin, P., Yang, J., 2017. The effects of institutional investor objectives on firm valuation and governance. Journal of Financial Economics 126, 171–199.

Boubaker, S., Boubakri, N., Grira, J., Guizanid, A., 2018. Sovereign wealth funds and equity pricing: evidence from implied cost of equity of publicly traded targets. Journal of Corporate Finance 53, 202–224.

Boubaker, S., Cellier, A., Manita, R., Saeed, A., 2020. Does corporate social responsibility reduce financial distress risk? Economic Modelling 91, 835–851.

Boubaker, S., Cellier, A., Rouatbi, W., 2014. The sources of shareholder wealth gains from going private transactions: the role of controlling shareholders. Journal of Banking and Finance 43, 226–246.

Boubakri, N., Cosset, J., Grira, J., 2017. Sovereign wealth funds investment effects on target firms' competitors. Emerging Markets Review 30, 96–112.

Boulton, T., Smart, S., Zutter, J., 2010. Acquisition activity and IPO underpricing. Financial Management 39, 1521–1546.

Braggion, F., Giannetti, M., 2019. Changing corporate governance norms: evidence from dual class shares in the UK. Journal of Financial Intermediation 37, 15–27.

Branch, B., 2002. The costs of bankruptcy: a review. International Review of Financial Analysis 11, 39–57.

Braun, R., Jenkinson, T., Stoff, I., 2017. How persistent is private equity performance? Evidence from deal-level data. Journal of Financial Economics 123, 273–291.

Brav, A., Jiang, W., Partnoy, F., Thomas, R., 2008. Hedge fund activism, corporate governance, and firm performance. Journal of Finance 63, 1729–1775.

Breuer, W., Ghufran, B., Salzmann, A., 2018. National culture, managerial preferences, and takeover performance. International Business Review 27, 1270–1289.

Breuer, W., Ghufran, B., Salzmann, A., 2020. Investors' time preferences and takeover performance. International Review of Financial Analysis 67 article 101435.

Brigham, E., Ehrhardt, M., 2005. Financial Management: Theory and Practice. Thomson-Southwestern Publishing, Mason, OH.

Brillinger, A., Els, C., Schafer, B., Bender, B., 2020. Business model risk and uncertainty factors: toward building and maintaining profitable and sustainable business models. Business Horizons 63, 121–130.

Bris, A., Cabolis, C., 2008. Adopting better corporate governance: evidence from cross-border mergers. Journal of Corporate Finance 14, 214–240.

Brooks, C., Chen, Z., Zeng, Y., 2017. Institutional cross-ownership and corporate strategy: the case of mergers and acquisitions. Journal of Corporate Finance 48, 187–216.

Brooks, C., Chen, Z., Zeng, Y., 2018. Institutional cross-ownership, and corporate strategy: the case of mergers and acquisitions. Journal of Corporate Finance 48, 187–216.

Brophy, D., Ouimet, P., Sialm, C., 2009. Hedge funds as investors of last resort. The Review of Financial Studies 22, 541–574.

Brown, G., Gredil, O., Kaplan, S., 2019a. Do private equity funds manipulate reported returns? Journal of Financial Economics 132, 262–297.

Brown, S., Dutordoir, M., Veld, C., Veld-Merkoulova, Y., 2019b. What is the role of institutional investors in corporate capital structure decisions? Journal of Corporate Finance 58, 270–286.

Brunnermeier, M., 2009. Deciphering the liquidity and credit crunch of 2007–2008. Journal of Economic Perspectives 23, 77–100.

Bruyland, E., Lasfer, M., DeMaeseneire, W., Song, W., 2019. The performance of acquisitions by high default risk bidders. Journal of Banking and Finance 101, 37–58.

Bryan-Low, C., 2005. European telecoms vie for emerging markets. Wall Street Journal B2.

Buchner, A., Mohamed, A., Schwienbacher, A., 2020. Herd behavior in buyout investments. Journal of Corporate Finance 60 article 101503.

Buchner, A., Mohamed, A., Wagner, N., 2019. Are venture capital and buyout backed IPOs any different? Journal of International Financial Markets, Institutions, & Money 60, 39–49.

Buchner, A., Wagner, N., 2017. Rewarding risk-taking or skill? The case of private equity fund managers. Journal of Banking and Finance 80, 14–32.

Burke, C., Hackett, S., Mitchell, D., Wilke, S., Williams, M., Williams, M.S., Zhao, W., 2019. Masters of the universe: bid rigging by private equity firms in multibillion dollar LBOs. University of Cincinnati Law Review 29, 28–48.

Bygrave, W.D., Timmons, J.A., 1992. Venture Capital at the Crossroads. Harvard Business School Press, Boston.

Cai, X., Gao, N., Garrett, I., Xu, Y., 2020. Are CEOs judged on their companies' social reputation? Journal of Corporate Finance 64 article 101621.

Cai, Y., Sevilir, M., 2012. Board connections and M&A connections. Journal of Financial Economics 103, 327–349.

Cain, M., Denis, D.J., Denis, D.K., 2014. Earnouts: a study of financial contracting in acquisition agreements. Journal of Accounting and Economics 51, 151–170.

Cain, M., McKeon, S., Solomon, S., 2017. Do takeover laws matter? Evidence from five decades of hostile takeovers. Journal of Financial Economics 124, 464–485.

Caixe, D., Kalatzis, A., Castro, L., 2019. Controlling shareholders and investment sensitivity in an emerging economy. Emerging Markets 39, 133–153.

Calcagno, R., Falconieri, S., 2014. Competition and dynamics of takeover contests. Journal of Corporate Finance 26, 36–56.

Calluzzo, P., Kedia, S., 2019. Mutual fund board connections and proxy voting. Journal of Financial Economics 134, 669–688.

Campbell, J.Y., Hilscher, J., Szilagyi, J., 2008. In search of distress risk. Journal of Finance 63, 2899–2939.

Cao, J., Cumming, D., Qian, M., Wang, X., 2015. Cross-border LBOs. Journal of Banking and Finance 50, 69–80.
Cao, X., Cumming, D., Goh, J., Wang, X., 2019. The impact of investor protection law on global takeovers: LBO versus non-LBO transactions. Journal of International Financial Markets, Institutions, and Money 59, 1–18.
Capron and Shen, 2007.
Carleton, J., Lineberry, C., 2004. Achieving Post-Merger Success. Wiley, New York.
Carlton, D., Israel, M., MacSwain, I., Orlov, E., 2019. Are legacy airline mergers pro- or anti-competitive? Evidence from recent airline mergers. International Journal of Industrial Organization 62, 58–95.
Carnevale, P., 2019. Strategic time in negotiation. Current Opinion in Psychology 26, 106–112.
Catao, L., Mano, R., 2017. Default premium. Journal of International Economics 107, 91–110.
CCH Tax Law Editors, 2005. U.S. Master Tax Code. Commerce Clearinghouse, New York.
Cepeca, J., Grajzl, P., 2020. Debt-to-equity conversion in bankruptcy reorganization and post-bankruptcy firm survival. International Review of Law and Economics 61 article 105878.
Chae, S., Menab, C., Polyviouc, M., Rogers, Z., Wiedmer, R., 2019. The effects of tariff increases on supply base complexity: a conceptual framework. Journal of Purchasing and Supply Management 25, 105–156.
Chaffee, D.B., 1993. Option pricing as a proxy for discount for lack of marketability in private company valuation. Business Valuation Review 20, 182–188.
Chague, F., De-Losso, R., Giovannetti, B., 2019. The short-skilling skill of institutions and individuals. Journal of Banking and Finance 101, 77–91.
Chakrabarti, A., 1990. Organizational factors in post-acquisition performance. IEEE Transactions in Engineering Management EM-37 135, 259–266.
Chakrabarti, R., Jayaraman, N., Mukherjee, S., 2009. Mars–Venus marriages: culture and cross-border M&A. Journal of International Business Studies 40, 216–236.
Chan, K., Karolyi, G., Stulz, R., 1992. Global financial markets and the risk premium of U.S. equity. Journal of Financial Economics 32, 137–167.
Chance, D., Cicon, J., Ferris, S., 2015. Poor performance and the value of corporate honesty. Journal of Corporate Finance 33, 1–18.
Chang, E., Lin, T., Ma, X., 2019. Does short-selling threat discipline managers in mergers and acquisitions decisions? Journal of Accounting and Economics 68 article 101233.
Chang, J., Wang, J., Bai, X., 2020. Good match matters: knowledge co-creation in international joint ventures. Industrial Marketing Management 84, 138–150.
Chang, S., 1998. Takeovers of privately held targets, methods of payment, and bidder returns. Journal of Finance 53, 773–784.
Chang, S., 2008. How do strategic alliances affect suppliers, customers, and rivals? Social Science Research Network. Working Paper Series, February 1.
Chao, Y., 2018. Organizational learning and acquirer performance: how do serial acquirers learn from acquisition experience? Asia Pacific Management Review 23, 161–168.
Chaplinsky, S., Ramchand, L., 2000. The impact of global equity offers. Journal of Finance 55, 2767–2789.
Chari, A., Ouiment, P., Tesar, L., 2010. The value of control in emerging markets. Review of Financial Studies 23, 1741–1770.
Chatterjee, R., Aw, M., 2004. The performance of UK: firms acquiring large cross-border and domestic takeover targets. Applied Financial Economics 14, 337–349.
Chatterjee, S., John, K., Yan, A., 2012. Takeovers and divergence of investor opinion. Review of Financial Studies 25, 227–276.
Chatterjee, S., Yan, A., 2008. Using innovative securities under asymmetric information: why do some firms pay with contingent value rights? Journal of Financial and Quantitative Analysis 43, 1001–1035.
Chemmanur, T., Krishnan, K., Nandy, D., 2014. The effects of corporate spin-offs on productivity. Journal of Corporate Finance 27, 72–98.
Chemmanur, T., Paeglis, I., 2001. Why issue tracking stock? Insights from a comparison with spin-offs and carve-outs. Journal of Applied Corporate Finance 14, 102–114.
Chen, A., Chub, H., Hung, P., Chen, M., 2020. Financial risk and acquirers' stockholder wealth in mergers and acquisitions. North American Journal of Economics and Finance, forthcoming.
Chen, C., Gong, J., 2019. Accounting comparability, financial reporting quality, and the pricing of accruals. Advances in Accounting 45, 112–127.
Chen, F., Ramaya, K., Wu, W., 2020. The wealth effects of merger and acquisition announcements on bondholders: new evidence from the over-the-counter market. Journal of Economics and Business 107 article 105862.
Chen, G., Kang, J., Kim, J., Na, H., 2014. Sources of value gains in minority equity investments by private equity funds: evidence from block share acquisitions. Journal of Corporate Finance 29, 449–474.
Chen, H., Ho, K., Weng, P., Yeh, C., 2021. The role of equity underwriting relationships in mergers and acquisitions. Pacific Basin Finance Journal, forthcoming.
Chen, H.L., Guo, R.J., 2005. On corporate divestitures. Review of Quantitative Finance and Accounting 25, 399–421.
Chen, J., King, T.H.D., Wen, M., 2015. Do joint ventures and strategic alliances create value for bondholders? Journal of Banking and Finance 58, 247–267.
Chen, J., Leun, W., Song, W., Goergen, M., 2019a. Why female board representation matters: the role of female directors in reducing male CEO overconfidence. Journal of Empirical Finance 53, 70–90.
Chen, N., Shevlin, T., 2019. US worldwide taxation and domestic mergers and acquisitions. Journal of Accounting and Economics 66, 439–447.
Chen, S., Lin, C., 2017. Managerial ability and acquirer returns. Quarterly Review of Economics and Finance 68, 171–182.
Chen, T., Dong, H., Lin, C., 2020a. Institutional shareholders and corporate social responsibility. Journal of Financial Economics 135, 483–504.
Chen, T., Zhang, G., Zhou, Y., 2018. Enforceability of non-compete covenants, discretionary investments, and financial reporting practices: evidence from a natural experiment. Journal of Accounting and Economics 65, 41–60.

Chen, V., Hobdari, B., Zhang, Y., 2019b. Blockholder heterogeneity and conflicts in cross-border acquisitions. Journal of Corporate Finance 57, 86–101.

Chen, Y., Gayle, P., 2019. Evidence from the airline industry. International Journal of Industrial Organization 62, 96–135.

Chen, Z., Ross, T., 2020. Buffer joint ventures. International Journal of Industrial Organization article 102613, forthcoming.

Chiang, W., Stammerjohan, W., Englebrecht, T., 2014. Pricing target NOLs in mergers and acquisitions from the participating firms' perspective. Advances in Accounting 30, 32–42.

Chiara Di Guardo, M., Marrocu, E., Paci, R., 2016. The effect of local corruption on ownership strategy in cross-border mergers and acquisitions. Journal of Business Research 69, 4225–4241.

Chiarella, C., Ostinelli, D., 2020. Financial or strategic buyers: who is at the gate? International Review of Economics and Finance 67, 393–407.

Child, J., Faulkner, D., Pitkethley, R., 2001. The Management of International Acquisitions. Oxford University Press, Oxford, UK.

Chira, I., Volkov, N., 2017. The choice of sale method and its consequences in mergers and acquisitions. The Quarterly Review of Economics and Finance 63, 170–184.

Chircop, J., Johan, S., Tarsalewska, M., 2017. Common auditors and cross-country M&A transactions. Journal of International Financial Markets, Institutions, & Money 54, 34–58.

Chiu, J., Chen, C., Cheng, C., Hung, S., 2020. Knowledge capital, CEO power, and firm value: evidence from the IT industry. North American Journal of Economics and Finance, forthcoming.

Chkir, I., Dutta, D., Hassan, B., 2019. Does target geographical complexity impact acquisition performance? Finance Research Letters 33 article 101196.

Cho, H., Ahn, H., 2017. Stock payment and the effects of institutional and cultural differences. International Business Review 26, 461–475.

Cho, S., Arthurs, J., 2018. The influence of alliance experience on acquisition premiums and postacquisition performance. Journal of Business Research 88, 1–10.

Choi, W., 2020. Disclosure tone of the spin-off prospectus and insider trading. Journal of Accounting and Public Policy 39 article 106692.

Chourou, L., Hossain, A., Kryzanowski, L., 2019. Dual-class firms, M&As, and SOX. The Quarterly Review of Economics and Finance 71, 176–187.

Christofi, M., Vrontis, D., Thrassou, A., Shams, S., 2019. Triggering technological innovation through cross-border mergers and acquisitions: a micro-foundational perspective. Technological Forecasting and Social Change 146, 148–166.

Chung, C., Kim, I., Rabarison, M., To, T., Wu, W., 2020. Shareholder litigation rights and corporate acquisitions. Journal of Corporate Finance 62 article 101599.

Clifford, C., 2008. Value creation or destruction: hedge funds as shareholder activists. Journal of Corporate Finance 14, 323–336.

Clubb, C., Stouraitis, A., 2002. The significance of sell-off profitability in explaining the market reaction to divestiture announcements. Journal of Banking and Finance 26, 671–688.

Cohen, A., Wang, C., 2017. Reexamining staggered boards and shareholder value. Journal of Financial Economics 125, 637–647.

Cohn, J., Mills, L., Towery, E., 2014. The evolution of capital structure and operating performance after leveraged buyouts: evidence from US corporate tax returns. Journal of Financial Economics 111, 469–494.

Col, B., Erriumza, V., 2015. Corporate governance and state expropriation risk. Journal of Corporate Finance 33, 71–84.

Colak, G., Whited, T., 2007. Spin-offs, divestitures, and conglomerate investment. The Review of Financial Studies 20, 557–595.

Colman, H., 2020. Facilitating integration and maintaining autonomy: the role of managerial action and interaction in post-acquisition capability transfer. Journal of Business Research 109, 148–160.

Comment, R., 2012. Revisiting the illiquidity discount for private companies: a new (and "skeptical") restricted stock study. Journal of Applied Corporate Finance 23, 80–92.

Corkery, M., 2012. Pension funds increasing their ties. Wall Street Journal February 12, C1–C2.

Cornaggia, J., Li, J., 2019. The value of access to finance: evidence from M&As. The Journal of Financial Economics 131, 232–250.

Cornelli, F., Kominek, Z., Ljungqvist, A., 2013. Monitoring managers: does it matter? Journal of Finance 68, 431–481.

Corte-Real, N., Ruivo, P., Oliveira, T., Popovic, A., 2019. Unlocking the drivers of big data analytics value in firms. Journal of Business Research 97, 160–173.

Cortes, F., Gomes, A., Gopalan, R., 2020. Corporate inversions and governance. Journal of Financial Intermediation, forthcoming.

Corum, A., Levit, D., 2019. Corporate control activism. Journal of Financial Economics 133, 1–17.

Cosset, J., Meknassi, S., 2013. Does cross-listing in the US foster mergers and acquisition and increase target shareholder wealth? Journal of Multinational Financial Management 23, 54–73.

Cremers, M., Ferrell, A., 2014. Thirty years of shareholders rights. Journal of Finance 69, 1167–1196.

Cremers, M., Litov, L., Sepe, S., 2017. Staggered boards and long-term value, revisited. Journal of Financial Economics 1–23.

Creswell, J., 2001. Would you give this man your company? Fortune May 28, 127–129.

Cronqvist, H., Nilsson, M., 2003. Agency costs of controlling minority shareholders. Journal of Financial and Quantitative Analysis 38, 695–719.

Cui, H., Leung, J., 2020. The long-run performance of acquiring firms in mergers and acquisitions: does managerial ability matter? Journal of Contemporary Accounting and Economics 16 article 100185.

Culpan, T., 2019. A little hostility is just what Japanese tech needs. Bloomberg December 19. https://finance.yahoo.com/news/little-hostility-just-japanese-tech-050303816.html.

Cumming, D., Hafs, L., Schweizer, D., 2014. The fast track IPO—success factors for taking firms public with SPACs. Journal of Banking and Finance 47, 198–213.

Cumming, D., Meoli, M., Vismara, S., 2019. Investors' choices between cash and voting rights: evidence from dual-class equity crowdfunding. Research Policy 48, 103–127.

Cusatis, P., Miles, J., Woolridge, J., 1993. Restructuring through spin-offs. Journal of Financial Economics 33, 293–311.

Custodio, 2014.

Daher, M., Ismail, A., 2018. Debt covenants and corporate acquisitions. Journal of Corporate Finance 53, 174–201.

Dahiya, S., Hallak, S., Matthys, T., 2020. Targeted by an activist hedge fund, do the lender's care? Journal of Corporate Finance 62 article 101600.

Dahya, J., Golubov, A., Petmezas, D., Travlos, N., 2019. Governance mandates, outside directors, and acquisition performance. Journal of Corporate Finance 59, 218–238.

Daley, L., Mehrotra, V., Sivakumar, R., 1997. Corporate focus and value creation, evidence from spin-offs. Journal of Financial Economics 45, 257–281.

Dalton, D., Dalton, C.M., 2007. Sarbanes-Oxley and the guideline of the listing exchanges: what have we wrought? Business Horizons 50, 93–100.

Damodaran, A., 2001. The Dark Side of Valuation. Prentice-Hall, New York.

Damodaran, A., 2002. In: Investment Valuation: Tools and Techniques for Determining the Value of Any Asset, 2nd ed. Wiley, New York.

Damodaran, A. Financial Data. http://www.stern.nyu.edu/~adamodar/pc/datasets/ctryprem.xls.

Dandapani, K., Hibbert, A., Lawrence, E., 2020. The shareholder response to a firm's first international acquisition. Journal of Banking and Finance 118 article 105852.

Dang, M., Henry, D., Hoang, V., 2017. Target CEO age, ownership decisions, and takeover outcomes. Research in International Business and Finance 42, 769–783.

Dang, M., Henry, D., Nguyen, M., Hoang, V., 2018. Cross-country determinants of ownership choices in cross-border acquisitions. Journal of Multinational Financial Management 44, 14–35.

Dasilas, A., Grose, C., 2018. The wealth effects of public to private LBOs: evidence from Europe. International Review of Financial Analysis 58, 179–194.

Dasilas, A., Leventis, S., 2018. The performance of European equity carve-outs. The Journal of Financial Stability 34, 121–125.

Datta, D., Basuil, D., Agarwal, A., 2020. Effects of board characteristics on post-acquisition performance: a study of cross-border acquisitions by firms in the manufacturing sector. International Business Review 29 article 101674.

Datta, S., Gruskin, M., Iskandar-Datta, M., 2015. On post-IPO stock price performance: a comparative analysis of RLBOs and IPOs. Journal of Banking and Finance 5, 187–203, 5.

Datta, S., Iskandar-Datta, M., Raman, K., 2003. Value creation in corporate asset sales: the role of managerial performance and lender monitoring. Journal of Banking and Finance 27, 351–375.

Davidoff, S., Lund, A., Schonlau, R., 2014. Do outside directors face labor market consequences? A natural experiment from the financial crisis. Harvard Business Law Review 4, 53.

Davis, G., Kim, H., 2007. Business ties and proxy voting by mutual funds. Journal of Financial Economics 85, 552–570.

Davis, S., Haltiwanger, J., Jarmin, R., Lerner, J., Miranda, J., 2011. Private Equity and Employment. National Bureau of Economic Research. Working Paper 17399.

Davis, S., Madura, J., 2017. Premium, announcement returns and desperation in high tech mergers: a growth options analysis. Journal of High Technology Management Research 28, 61–78.

Debellis, A., De Massis, A., Petruzzelli, Frattini, F., Del Giudice, M., 2020. Strategic agility and international joint ventures: the willingness ability paradox of family firms. Journal of International Management, forthcoming.

de Bodt, E., Cousin, J., Roll, R., 2019. Improved method for detecting acquirer fixed effects. Journal of Empirical Finance 50, 20–42.

DeCesari, A., Gonenc, H., Ozkan, H., 2016. The effects of corporate acquisition on CEO compensation and CEO turnover of family firms. Journal of Corporate Finance 38, 294–317.

Degbey, W., Rodgers, P., Kromah, M., Weber, Y., 2020. The impact of psychological ownership on employee retention in mergers and acquisitions. Human Resource Management Review article 100745, forthcoming.

de Groote, J., Kleindienst, I., Hoegl, M., Schweizer, D., Laamanen, T., 2020. Similarity perceptions in investor reactions to acquisition announcements. Long Range Planning, forthcoming.

Del Negro, M., Giannone, D., Giannoni, M., Tambalotti, A., 2019. Global trends in interest rates. Journal of International Economics 118, 248–262.

De La Merced, M., 2011. Dealbook. The New York Times May 6.

De Smedt, S., Hoey, M., 2008. Integrating steel giants: an interview with the Arcelor-Mittal post-merger managers. McKinsey Quarterly 2, 94.

Demirtas, G., 2017. Board involvement in the M&A negotiation process. International Review of Financial Analysis 50, 27–43.

Demirtas, G., Simsir, S., 2016. The effect of CEO departure on target firm's post-takeover performance: evidence from non-delisting target firms. Finance Research Letters 16, 55–65.

Denes, M., Karpoff, J., McWillims, V., 2017. Thirty years of shareholder activism: a survey of empirical research. Journal of Corporate Finance 44, 405–424.

Denicolo, V., Polo, M., 2018. Duplicative research, mergers and innovation. Economic Letters 166, 56–59.

Denis, D., Wang, J., 2014. Debt covenant renegotiations and creditor control rights. Journal of Financial Economics 113, 348–367.

DePamphilis, D., 2001. Managing growth through acquisition: time-tested techniques for the entrepreneur. International Journal of Entrepreneurship and Innovation 2, 195–205.

DePamphilis, D., 2010a. M&A Basics: All You Need to Know. Elsevier, Boston.

DePamphilis, D., 2010b. M&A Negotiations and Deal Structuring: All You Need to Know. Elsevier, Boston.

DePamphilis, D., 2011. Upstart graphics: mergers and acquisitions issues. In: Westhead, P., Wright, M., McElwee, G. (Eds.), Entrepreneurship: Perspectives and Cases. Prentice Hall, London, pp. 401–410.

Desai, H., Jain, P., 1997. Firm performance and focus: long-run stock market performance following spin-offs. Journal of Financial Economics 54, 75–101.

Dessaint, O., Golubov, A., Volpin, P., 2017. Employment protection and takeovers. Journal of Financial Economics 125, 369–388.

De Visscher, F., Arnoff, C., Ward, J., 1995. Financing Transitions: Managing Capital and Liquidity in the Family Business. Business Owner Resources, Marietta, GA.

Dichev, I., 1998. Is the risk of bankruptcy a systematic risk? Journal of Finance 53, 1141–1148.

Dichev, I., Gaham, J., Harvey, C., Rajgopal, S., 2013. Earnings quality: evidence from the field. Journal of Accounting and Economics 56, 1–33.

Di Guili, A., 2013. The effect of stock misvaluation and investment opportunities on the method of payment in mergers. Journal of Corporate Finance 21, 196–215.

Dimitrova, L., 2017. Perverse incentives of special purpose acquisition companies, the "poor man's private equity funds." Journal of Accounting and Economics 63, 99–120

Dimopoulos, T., Sacchetto, S., 2014. Preemptive bidding, target resistance, and takeover premiums. Journal of Financial Economics 114, 444–480.

Dimson, E., March, P., Staunton, M., 2002. Triumph of the Optimists. Princeton University Press, Princeton, NJ.

Dimson, E., March, P., Staunton, M., 2003. Global evidence on the equity risk premium. Journal of Applied Corporate Finance 15, 27–38.

Dinc, S., Erel, I., Liao, R., 2017. Fire sale discount: evidence from the sale of minority equity stakes. Journal of Financial Economics 125, 475–490.

Dionne, G., La Haye, M., Bergeres, A., 2010. Does Asymmetric Information Affect the Premium in Mergers and Acquisitions? Interuniversity Research Center on Enterprise Networks. Logistics and Transportation and Department of Finance, HEC Montreal.

Dissanaike, G., Drobetz, W., Momtaz, P., 2020. Competition policy and the profitability of corporate acquisitions. Journal of Corporate Finance 62 article 101510.

Dittmar, A., Li, D., Nain, A., 2012. It pays to follow the leader: acquiring targets picked by private equity. Journal of Financial and Quantitative Analysis 47, 901–931.

Dittmar, A., Shivdasani, A., 2003. Divestitures and divisional investment policies. Journal of Finance 58, 2711–2744.

Doan, T., Sahib, P., van Witteloostuijn, A., 2018. Lessons from the flipside: how do acquirers learn from divestitures to complete acquisitions. Long Range Planning 51, 256–262.

Dong, J., Yang, C., 2020. Business value of big data analytics: a systems-theoretic approach and empirical test. Information and Management 57 article 103124.

Dong, Q., Slovin, M., Sushka, M., 2020. Private equity exits after IPOs. Journal of Corporate Finance 64 article 101696.

Draper, P., Paudyal, K., 2006. Acquisitions: private versus public. European Financial Management 12, 57–80.

Drobetz, W., Momtaz, P., 2020. Antitakeover provisions and firm value: new evidence. Journal of Corporate Finance 62 article 101594.

Drobetz, W., Momtaz, P., 2020. Corporate governance convergence in the European M&A market. Finance Research Letters 32 article 101091.

Drobetz, W., Mussbach, E., Westheide, C., 2020. Corporate insider trading and return skewness. Journal of Corporate Finance 60 article 101485.

Drobetz, W., von Meyerinck, F., Oesch, D., Schmid, M., 2018. Industry expert directors. Journal of Banking & Finance 92, 195–215.

Drucker, J., Silver, S., 2006. Alcatel stands to reap tax benefits on merger. Wall Street Journal April 26, C3.

D'Souza, J., Jacob, J., 2000. Why firms issue targeted stock. Journal of Financial Economics 56, 459–483.

Duan, Y., Edwards, J., Dwivedi, Y., 2019. Artificial intelligence for decision making in the era of big data—evolution, challenges, and research agenda. International Journal of Information Management 48, 63–71.

Duarte, F., Rosa, C., 2015. The equity risk premium: a review of models. Federal Reserve Bank of New York Staff Report 714.

Duchin, R., Schmidt, B., 2013. Riding the merger wave: uncertainty, reduced monitoring, and bad acquisitions. Journal of Financial Economics 107, 69–88.

Duff, X., Phelps, Y., 2010. Risk premium report—risk study. In: Pratt, S., Grabowski, R. (Eds.), Cost of Capital: Applications and Examples, 4th ed. John Wiley & Sons, New York.

Duplat, V., Klijn, E., Reuer, J., Dekker, H., 2020. Renegotiation of joint ventures and prior ties as alternative governance mechanisms. Long Range Planning 53, 101856.

Dutta, S., Iskandar-Dutta, M., Raman, K., 2001. Executive compensation and corporate acquisition decisions. Journal of Finance 56, 2299–2396.

Dutta, S., Saadi, S., Zhu, P., 2013. Does payment matter in cross-border acquisitions? International Review of Economics and Finance 25, 91–107.

Dutta, S., Shantanu, X., Vijay Jog, Y., 2009. The long-term performance of acquiring firms: a re-examination of an anomaly. Journal of Banking and Finance 33, 1400–1412.

Dyck, A., Lins, K., Roth, L., Wagner, R., 2019. Do institutional investors drive corporate social responsibility? International evidence. Journal of Financial Economics 131, 693–714.

Eaglesham, J., 2019. Shh! Companies are fixing accounting errors quietly. Wall Street Journal December 5. https://www.wsj.com/articles/shh-companies-are-fixing-accounting-errors-quietly-11575541981.

Eaglesham, J., Jones, C., 2018. The fuel powering corporate America: $2.4 trillion in private fundraising. Wall Street Journal April 3. https://www.wsj.com/articles/stock-and-bond-markets-dethroned-private-fundraising-is-now-dominant-1522683249.

Eckbo, E., Makaew, T., Thorburn, K., 2018. Are stock-financed takeovers opportunistic? Journal of Financial Economics 128, 443–465.

Eckbo, E., Thorburn, K.S., March, 2000. Gains to bidder firms revisited: domestic and foreign acquisitions in Canada. Journal of Financial and Quantitative Analysis 35, 1–25.

The Economist, 2006a. Battling for corporate America. March 9, 69–71.

The Economist, 2006b. A survey of the world economy, September 14, 12.

The Economist, 2011. Why global stock markets have become more correlated. September 22.

The Economist, 2014. From dodo to phoenix. January 11.

The Economist, 2016. The superstar company: a giant problem. September 17.

Eisenthal-Berkovitz, Y., Feldhutter, P., Vig, V., 2020. Leveraged buyouts and bond credit spreads. Journal of Financial Economics 135, 577–601.

Elango, B., Dhandapani, K., Giachetti, C., 2019. Impact of institutional reforms and industry structural factors on market returns of emerging market rivals during acquisitions by foreign firms. International Business Review 28 article 101493.

Elder, J., Westra, P., 2000. The reaction of security prices to tracking stock announcements. Journal of Economics and Finance 24, 36–55.

Elia, S., Petruzzelli, A., Piscitello, L., 2019. The impact of cultural diversity on innovation performance of MNC subsidiaries in strategic alliances. Journal of Business Research 98, 204–213.

Elkamhi, R., Ericsson, J., Parsons, C., 2012. The cost of financial distress and the timing of default. Journal of Financial Economics 105, 62–81.

Ellis, J., Moeller, S.B., Schlingemann, F.P., Stulz, R.M., 2011. Globalization, Governance, and the Returns to Cross-Border Acquisitions. NBER Working Paper No. 16676.

Ellison, S., 2006. Clash of cultures exacerbates woes for Tribune Co. Wall Street Journal 1.
Ellul, A., Pagano, M., 2019. Corporate leverage and employees' rights in bankruptcy. Journal of Financial Economics 133, 685–707.
Elnahas, A., Hassan, M., Ismail, G., 2017. Religion and mergers and acquisitions contracting: the case of earnout agreements. Journal of Corporate Finance 42, 221–246.
Elnahas, A., Kim, D., 2017. CEO political ideology and mergers and acquisitions decisions. Journal of Corporate Finance 45, 162–175.
Elsiefy, E., AbdElaal, M., 2019. The firm value in case of deleveraging using leasing and the optimal restructuring level. Quarterly Review of Economics and Finance 72, 141–151.
Emory, J.D., 2001. The value of marketability as illustrated in initial public offerings of common stock. Business Valuation Review 20, 21–24.
Enwemeka, Z., 2017. Consumers really don't want self-driving cars, MIT study finds. Bostonomix. May 25. http://www.wbur.org/bostonomix/2017/05/25/mit-study-self-driving-cars.
Erel, I., Jang, Y., Weisbach, M., 2015. Do acquisitions relieve target firms' financial constraints? Journal of Finance 70, 289–28.
Erel, I., Liao, R., Weisbach, M., 2012. Determinants of cross-border mergers and acquisitions. Journal of Finance 67, 1045–1082.
Ersahin, N., Irani, R., Le, H., 2020. Creditor control rights and resource allocation within firms. The Journal of Finance 139, 186–208.
Esfahani, H., 2019. Profitability of horizontal mergers in the presence of price stickiness. European Journal of Operation Research 279, 941–950.
Etro, F., 2019. Mergers of complements and entry in innovative industries. International Journal of Industrial Organizations 65, 302–326.
Eugster, N., Isakov, D., 2019. Founding family ownership, stock market returns, and agency problems. Journal of Banking and Finance 107 article 105600.
Ewenstein, B., Smith, W., Sologar, A., 2015. Changing change management. Insights. July.
Faccio, M., Lang, L., Young, L., 2001. Dividends and expropriation. American Economic Review 91, 54–78.
Faccio, M., Masulis, R., 2005. The choice of payment method in European mergers and acquisitions. Journal of Finance 60, 1345–1388.
Faccio, M., McConnell, J., Stolin, D., 2006. Returns to acquirers of listed and unlisted companies. Journal of Financial and Quantitative Analysis 47, 197–220.
Factset Mergerstat Review, 2011. http://www.bvresources.com/bvstore/selectbook.asp?pid=PUB259.
Faleye, O., 2004. Cash and corporate control. Journal of Finance 59, 2041–2060.
Fama, E., French, K., 2015. A five-factor asset pricing model. Journal of Financial Economics 116, 1–22.
Fama, E., French, K., 2018. Choosing factors. Journal of Financial Economics 128, 234–252.
Fang, L., Ivashina, V., Lerner, J., 2015. The disintermediation of financial markets: direct investing in private equity. Journal of Financial Economics 116, 160–178.
Fang, Y., Xu, H., Perc, M., Tan, Q., 2019. Dynamic evolution of economic networks under the influence of mergers and acquisitions. Physica A 524, 89–99.
Farzad, R., 2006. Fidelity's divided loyalties. Business Week 12.
Fauver, L., McDonald, M., Taboada, A., 2018. Does it pay to treat employees well? International evidence on the value of employee culture. Journal of Corporate Finance 50, 84–108.
Federal Reserve Bulletin, 2003. Board of Governors. US Federal Reserve System, December.
Federal Trade Commission, 1999a. Merger Guidelines. http://www.ftc.com.
Federal Trade Commission, Bureau of Competition, 1999b. A Study of the Commission's Divestiture Process.
Fee, C., Subramaniam, V., Wang, M., Zhang, Y., 2019. Bank lenders as matchmakers? Evidence from when acquirers and targets share a common lender. Pacific Basis Finance Journal 56, 248–272.
Feito-Ruiz, I., Renneboog, L., 2017. Takeovers and (excess) CEO compensation. Journal of International Financial Markets, Institutions, and Money 50, 156–181.
Ferek, K., 2019. Fed says Lehman Brothers Chapter 11 case is the most costly in history, January 16. https://www.morningstar.com/news/dow-jones/TDJNDN_201901168693/fed-says-lehman-brothers-chapter-11–case-is-costliest-in-history.html.
Fernandes, J., 2019. Developing viable, adjustable strategies for planning and management—a methodological approach. Land Use Policy 82, 563–572.
Fernandez, P., 2014. CAPM: an absurd model. November 13. http://ssrn.com/abstract=2505597.
Fernandez, P., Pershn, V., Acin, I., 2018. Market risk premium and risk-free rate used for 59 countries in 2018. A survey. IESE Business School. https://papers.ssrn.com/sol3/papers.cfm?abstract_id=3155709.
Ferreira, M., Santos, J., Almeida, M., Reis, N., 2014. Mergers and acquisitions research: a bibliometric study of top strategy and international business journals, 1980–2010. Journal of Business Research 67, 2550–2558.
Ferri, R., 2012. The total economy portfolio. Forbes June 25, 174–175.
Ferris, S., Houston, R., Javakhadze, D., 2016. Friends in the right places: the impact of political connections on corporate merger activity. Journal of Corporate Finance 41, 81–102.
Ferris, S., Jayaraman, N., Liao, M., 2020. Better directors or distracted directors? An international analysis of busy boards. Global Finance Journal 44 article 100437.
Fich, E., Nguyen, T., 2020. The value of CEO's supply chain experience: evidence from mergers and acquisitions. Journal of Corporate Finance 60 article 101525.
Fich, E., Rice, E., Tran, A., 2016. Contractual revisions in compensation: evidence of merger bonuses to target CEOs. Journal of Accounting and Economics 61, 338–368.
Fich, E., Starks, L., Yore, A., 2014. CEO deal making activities and CEO compensation. Journal of Financial Economics 114, 471–492.
Fidrmuc, J., Roosenboom, P., Zhang, E., 2018. Antitrust merger review costs and acquirer lobbying. Journal of Corporate Finance 51, 72–97.
Fidrmuc, J., Xia, C., 2019. Deal initiation and management motivation. Journal of Corporate Finance 59, 320–343.

Field, L., Mkrtchyan, A., 2017. The effect of director experience on acquisition performance. Journal of Financial Economics 123, 488–511.

Finlay, W., Marshall, A., McColgan, P., 2016. Financing, fire sales, and the shareholders' wealth effects of asset fire sales. Journal of Corporate Finance 22, 320–344.

Fischer, M., 2017. The source of financing in mergers and acquisitions. The Quarterly Review of Economics and Finance 65, 227–239.

Flor, C., Mortizen, M., 2020. Entering a new market: market profitability and first mover advantage. Journal of Corporate Finance 62, 101604.

Flugum, R., Howe, J., 2020. Hedge fund activism and analyst uncertainty. International Review of Economics and Finance 66, 206–227.

Forte, G., Gianfrate, G., Rossi, E., 2020. Does relative valuation work for banks? Global Finance Journal 44 article 100449.

France, M., 2002. Bankruptcy reform won't help telecom. Business Week 40.

Francis, B., Hasan, I., Sun, X., 2014a. Does relationship matter? The choice of financial advisors. Journal of Economics and Business 73, 22–47.

Francis, B., Hasan, I., Sun, X., Waisman, M., 2014b. Can firms learn by observing? Evidence from cross-border M&As. Journal of Corporate Finance 25, 202–215.

Franco, S., Caroli, M., Cappa, F., Del Chiappa, G., 2020. Are you good enough? CSR, quality management and corporate financial performance in the hospitality industry. International Journal of Hospitality Management 88 article 102395.

Frank, M., Shen, T., 2019. Corporate capital structure actions. Journal of Banking and Finance 106, 384–402.

Frattaroli, M., 2020. Does protectionist anti-takeover legislation lead to managerial entrenchment? Journal of Financial Economics 136, 106–136.

Frazoni, F., Nowak, E., Phalippou, L., 2012. Private equity performance and liquidity risk. Journal of Finance 67, 2341–2373.

Friberg, R., 2020. All the bottles in one basket? Evaluating the effect of intra-industry diversification on risk. Long-Range Planning article 101573, forthcoming.

Frick, K., Torres, A., 2002. Learning from high-tech deals. McKinsey Quarterly 1, 2.

Fu, F., Lin, L., Officer, M., 2013. Acquisitions driven by stock overvaluation: are they good deals? Journal of Financial Economics 109, 24–39.

Fuad, M., Gaur, A., 2019. Merger waves, entry-timing, and cross-border acquisition completion: a frictional lens perspective. Journal of World Business 54, 107–118.

Fuller, C., Pusateri, N., 2018. A holistic approach to merger models with an emphasis on heterogeneity. The Quarterly Review of Economics and Finance 69, 260–273.

Gan, H., Park, M., Suh, S., 2020. Non-financial performance measures, CEO compensation, and firms' future value. Journal of Business Research 110, 213–227.

Gantchev, N., 2013. The costs of shareholder activism: evidence from a sequential decision model. Journal of Financial Economics 107, 610–631.

Gantchev, N., Sevilir, M., Shivdasani, A., 2020. Activism and empire building. Journal of Financial Economics 138, 526–548.

Gao, N., Hua, C., Khurshed, A., 2021. Loan price in mergers and acquisitions. Journal of Corporate Finance, forthcoming.

Gao, N., Mohamed, A., 2018. Cash-rich acquirers do not always make bad acquisitions: new evidence. Journal of Corporate Finance 50, 243–264.

Gao, N., Peng, N., Strong, N., 2017. What determines horizontal merger antitrust case selection? Journal of Corporate Finance 46, 51–76.

Gao, S., Brockman, P., Meng, Q., Yan, X., 2020. Differences of opinion, institutional bids and underpricing. Journal of Corporate Finance 60 article 101540.

Gao, Y., Liao, S., Wang, X., 2018. Capital markets' assessment of the economic impact of the Dodd-Frank Act on systematically financial firms. Journal of Banking and Finance 86, 204–223.

Garcia-Appendini, E., 2018. Financial distress and competitors' investment. Journal of Corporate Finance 51, 182–209.

Garcia-Feijoo, L., Madura, J., Ngo, T., 2012. Impact of industry characteristics on the method of payment in mergers. Journal of Economics and Business 64, 261–274.

Garlappi, L., Yan, H., 2011. Financial distress and the cross section of equity returns. Journal of Finance 66, 789–822.

Gaspara, J., Massa, P., 2005. Shareholder investment horizons and the market for corporate control. Journal of Financial Economics 76, 135–165.

Gejadze, M., Giot, P., Schwienbacher, A., 2018. Private equity fundraising and firm specialization. The Quarterly Review of Economics and Finance 64, 259–274.

Gentry, M., Stroup, C., 2019. Entry and competition in takeover auctions. Journal of Financial Economics 132, 298–324.

Gertner, R., Powers, E., Scharfstein, D., 2002. Learning about internal capital markets from corporate spin-offs. Journal of Finance 57, 2479–2506.

Ghannam, S., Matolesy, Z., Spiropoulos, H., Thai, N., 2019. The influence of powerful non-executive chairs in mergers and acquisitions. Journal of Contemporary Accounting and Economics 15, 87–104.

Ghosh, P., 2019. Machine learning causing science crisis. BBC News. February 16. https://www.bbc.com/news/science-environment-47267081.

Gillan, S., Starks, L., 2007. The evolution of shareholder activism in the United States. Journal of Applied Corporate Finance 19, 55–73.

Gillette, F., 2011. The rise and inglorious fall of MySpace. Bloomberg Businessweek July 3, 54–57.

Gilson, S., Healy, P., Noe, C., Palepu, L., 2001. Analyst specialization and conglomerate stock breakups. Journal of Accounting Research 39, 565–582.

Gine, M., Moussawi, R., Sedunov, J., 2017. Governance mechanisms and effective activism: evidence from shareholder proposals on poison pills. Journal of Empirical Finance 43, 185–202.

Giot, P., Hege, U., Schwienacher, A., 2014. Are novice private equity funds risk-takers? Evidence from a comparison with established firms. Journal of Corporate Finance 27, 55–71.

Glambosky, M., Jory, R., Ngoc Ngo, T., 2020. The wealth effects of mergers and acquisitions by dividend payers. Quarterly Review of Economics and Finance 78, 154–165.

Globner, S., 2019. Investor horizons, long-term blockholders, and corporate social responsibility. Journal of Banking and Finance 103, 78–97.

Glozer, S., Morsing, M., 2020. Helpful hypocrisy? Investigating double-talk and irony in CSR marketing. Journal of Business Research 114, 363–375.

Goergen, M., Limbach, P., Scholz-Daneshgari, M., 2020. Firms' rationales for CEO duality: evidence from a mandatory disclosure regulation. Journal of Corporate Finance 65 article 101770.

Gogineni, S., Puthenpurackal, J., 2017. The impact of go-shop provisions in merger agreements. Financial Management 46, 275–315.

Gogineni, S., Upadhyay, A., 2020. Target governance provisions and acquisition types. Journal of Business Research 110, 160–172.

Goktan, M., Kieschnick, R., 2012. A target's perspective on the effects of ATPs in takeovers after recognizing its choice in the process. Journal of Corporate Finance 18, 1088–1103.

Golbe, D., Nyman, I., 2013. How do share repurchases affect ownership concentration? Journal of Corporate Finance 20, 22–40.

Goldblatt, H., 1999. Merging at internet speed. Fortune November 8, 164–165.

Golubov, A., Petmezas, D., Travlos, N., 2012. When it pays to pay your investment banker: new evidence on the role of financial advisors in M&As. Journal of Finance 67, 271–312.

Golubov, A., Yawson, A., Zhang, H., 2015. Extraordinary acquirers. Journal of Financial Economics 116, 314–330.

Golubov, A., Petmezas, D., Travlos, N., 2012. When it pays to pay your investment banker: new evidence on the role of financial advisors in M&As. Journal of Finance 67, 271–312.

Golubov, A., Xiong, N., 2020. Post-acquisition performance of private acquirers. Journal of Corporate Finance 60 article 101545.

Gomes, M., 2019. Does CSR influence target choices? Finance Letters 30, 153–159.

Gomes, M., Marsat, S., 2019. Does CSR impact premiums in M&A transactions? Finance Letters 26, 71–80.

Gompers, P., Gornall, W., Kaplan, S., Strebulaev, L., 2020. How do venture capitalists make decisions? Journal of Financial Economics 135, 169–190.

Gompers, P., Ishii, J., Metrick, A., 2010. Extreme governance: an analysis of U.S. dual-class companies in the United States. Review of Financial Studies 23, 1051–1088.

Gompers, P., Kaplan, S., Mukharlyamov, V., 2016. What do equity firms say they do? Journal of Financial Economics 121, 449–476.

Gondhalekar, V., Sant, R., Ferris, S., 2004. The price of corporate acquisition: determinants of takeover premia. Applied Economics Letters 11, 735–739.

Gong, R., 2020. Short selling threat and corporate financing decisions. Journal of Corporate Finance 118 article 105853.

Gorbenko, A., 2019. How do valuations impact outcomes of asset sales with heterogeneous bidders? Journal of Financial Economics 131, 88–117.

Gordon, P., 2019. Creating value beyond the deal. Keys to Creating Maximum Deal Value. PriceWaterhouseCoopers and Mergermarket Survey. March 2.

Gornall, W., Strebulaev, I., 2020. Squaring venture capital valuations with reality. Journal of Financial Economics 135, 120–143.

Gottschalg, O., 2012. Bain or blessing? The Economist January 28, 73–74.

Goyal, V., Park, C., 2002. Board leadership structure and CEO turnover. Journal of Corporate Finance 8, 49–66.

Grabowski, R., Nunes, C., Harrington, J., Duff, Phelps, 2017. Valuation Handbook: US Guide to Cost of Capital. John Wiley & Sons, New York.

Graham, J., 2000. How big are the tax benefits of debt? Journal of Finance 55, 1901–1941.

Graham, M., Walter, T., Yawson, A., Zhang, H., 2018. The value-added role of industry specialist advisors in M&As. Journal of Banking and Finance 81, 81–104.

Grice, S., Ingram, R., 2001. Tests of the generalizability of Altman's bankruptcy prediction model. Journal of Business Research 54, 53–61.

Grinblatt, M., Titman, S., 2002. In: Financial Markets and Corporate Strategy, 2nd ed. McGraw-Hill, New York.

Groh, A., Gottschalg, O., 2006. The risk-adjusted performance of US buyouts. HEC, Paris.

Grundke, R., Moser, C., 2019. Hidden protectionism? Evidence from non-tariff barriers to trade in the United States. Journal of International Economics 117, 143–157.

Guidi, M., Sogiakas, V., Vagenas-Nanosa, E., Verwijmeren, P., 2020. Spreading the sin: an empirical assessment from corporate takeovers. International Review of Financial Analysis 71 article 101535.

Guj, P., Chandra, A., 2019. Comparing different real option valuation approaches as applied to a copper mine. Resources Policy 61, 180–189.

Gul, F., Krishnamurti, C., Shams, S., Chowdhury, H., 2020. Corporate social responsibility, overconfident CEOs, and empire building: agency and stakeholder theoretic perspectives. Journal of Business Research 111, 52–68.

Gunter, A., van Dijk, M., 2016. The impact of European antitrust policy: evidence from the stock market. International Review of Law and Economics 46, 20–33.

Guo, J., Li, Y., Wang, C., Xing, X., 2020. The role of investment bankers in M&As: new evidence on acquirers' financial conditions. Journal of Banking and Finance 119 article 105298.

Guo, J., Lia, X., Seeger, N., Vagenas-Nanos, E., 2019b. Social connections, reference point and acquisition premium. The British Accounting Review 51, 46–71.

Guo, J., Lu, L., Hu, N., Wang, X., 2019a. Do managers keep their word? The disclosure of merger intention at pre-merger issuance and M&A performance. Finance Research Letters 28, 20–31.

Guo, R., Kruse, T.A., Nohel, T., 2008. Undoing the powerful anti-takeover force of staggered boards. Journal of Corporate Finance 14, 274–288.

Guo, S., Hotchkiss, E.S., Song, W., 2011. Do buyouts (still) create value? Journal of Finance 66, 479–517.

Guthrie, K., Sokolowsky, J., Wan, K., 2012. Compensation and board structure revisited. Journal of Finance 67, 1149–1169.

Haapanen, L., Hurmelinna-Laukkanen, P., Nikkila, S., Paakkolanvaara, P., 2019. The function-specific microfoundations of dynamic capabilities in cross-border mergers and acquisitions. International Business Review 28, 766–784.

Habib, A., Ranasinghe, D., Huang, H., 2018. A literature survey of financial reporting in private firms. Research in Accounting Regulation 30, 31–37.

Hackbarth, D., Morellec, E., 2008. Stock returns in mergers and acquisitions. Journal of Finance 63, 1213–1252.

Hall, L., Polacek, T., 1994. Strategies for obtaining the largest valuation discounts. Estate Planning January/February, 38–44.

Hamel, G., Prahalad, C., 1994. Competing for the Future. Harvard Business School Press, Cambridge, MA.

Hansen, C., Block, J., 2020. Exploring the relation between family involvement and firms' financial performance: a replication and extension meta-analysis. Journal of Business Venturing Insights 13 article e00158.

Hanson, R., Song, M., 2000. Managerial ownership, board structure, and the division of gains. Journal of Corporate Finance 6, 55–70.

Harford, J., Kecskes, A., Mansi, S., 2018. Do long-term investors improve corporate decision making? Journal of Corporate Finance 50, 424–452.
Harford, J., Stanfield, F., Zhang, 2019. Do insiders time management buyouts and freezeouts to buy undervalued targets? Journal of Financial Economics 131, 206–231.
Harford, J., Uysal, V., 2014. Bond market access and investment. Journal of Financial Economics 112, 147–163.
Harper, N., Schneider, A., 2004. Where mergers go wrong. McKinsey Quarterly 2.
Harris, O., Glegg, C., 2007. The wealth effects of cross-border spin-offs. Journal of Multinational Financial Management 18, 461–476.
Harris, R., Jenkinson, T., Kaplan, S.N., 2014. Private equity performance: what do we know? Journal of Finance 113, 1851–1882.
Hartwell, C., Malinowska, A., 2019. Informal institutions and firm valuation. Emerging Market Review 40 article 100603.
Harvey, T., 2005. Twelve Ways to Calculate the International Cost of Capital. Duke University and National Bureau of Economic Research Working Paper. October 14.
Hasan, I., Khurshed, A., Mohamed, A., Wang, F., 2018. Do venture capital firms benefit from a presence on boards of directors of mature public companies? Journal of Corporate Finance 49, 125–140.
Haucap, J., Rasch, A., Stiebale, J., 2019. How mergers affect innovation: theory and evidence. International Journal of Industrial Organization 63, 283–325.
Hauser, R., 2018. Busy directors and firm performance: evidence from mergers. Journal of Financial Economics 128, 16–37.
Hayes, R., 1979. The human side of acquisitions. Management Review 41, 41–46.
Hayward, M., Hambrick, D., 1997. Explaining the premiums paid for large acquisitions: evidence of CEO hubris. Administrative Science Quarterly 35, 621–633.
Hegde, S., Mishra, D., 2017. Strategic risk-taking and value creation: evidence from the market for corporate control. International Review of Economics & Finance 48, 212–234.
Hege, U., Lovo, S., Slovin, M., Sushka, M., 2018. Divisional buyouts by private equity and the market for divested assets. Journal of Corporate Finance 53, 21–37.
Hennart, J., Park, Y., 1993. Location, governance, and strategic determinants of Japanese manufacturing investment in the United States. Journal of Strategic Management 15, 419–436.
Heron, R., Lie, E., 2015. The effect of poison pill adoptions and court rulings on firm entrenchment. Journal of Corporate Finance 35, 286–296.
Hillyer, C., Smolowitz, I., 1996. Why do mergers fail to achieve synergy? Director's Monthly January 13.
Hogan, K., Olson, G.T., 2004. The pricing of equity carve-outs during the 1990s. Journal of Financial Research 27, 521–537.
Holderness, C., 2018. Equity issuances and agency costs: the telling story of shareholder approval around the world. Journal of Financial Economics 129, 415–439.
Holthausen, R., Larker, D.F., 1996. The financial performance of reverse leveraged buyouts. Journal of Financial Economics 42, 293–332.
Hosaka, T., 2019. Bankruptcy prediction using imaged financial ratios and convolutional neural networks. Expert Systems with Applications 117, 287–299.
Hossain, M., Heaney, R., Yu, J., 2020. The information content of director trading: evidence from acquisition announcements in Australia. Global Finance Journal 44 article 100448.
Hossain, M., Javakhadze, D., 2020. Corporate media connections and merger outcomes. Journal of Corporate Finance 65 article 101736.
Hovakimian, G., 2016. Excess value and restructuring by diversified firms. Journal of Banking and Finance 71, 1–19.
Howell, J., 2017. The survival of the U.S. dual class share structure. Journal of Corporate Finance 44, 440–450.
Hsu, S., Lin, S., Chen, W., Huang, J., 2020. CEO duality, information costs, and firm performance. The North American Journal of Economics and Finance, forthcoming.
Hu, J., Kim, J., 2019. The relative usefulness of cash flows versus accrual earnings for CEO turnover decisions across countries: the role of investor protection. The Journal of International Accounting, Auditing, and Taxation 34, 91–107.
Hu, M., Mou, J., Tuilautala, M., 2020a. How trade credit affects mergers and acquisitions. International Review of Economics and Finance 67, 1–12.
Hu, M., Yang, J., 2016. The role of leverage in cross-border mergers and acquisitions. International Review of Economics and Finance 43, 170–199.
Hu, N., Li, L., Li, H., Wang, X., 2020b. Do mega-mergers create value? The acquisition experience and mega-deals outcomes. Journal of Empirical Finance 55, 119–142.
Huang, J., Jain, B., Torn, G., 2018. Anticipating loss from proxy contests. Journal of Business Research 83, 160–172.
Huang, P., Officer, M., Powell, R., 2017. Method of payment and risk mitigation in cross-border mergers and acquisitions. Journal of Corporate Finance 40, 216–234.
Huang, W., Goodell, J., Zhang, H., 2019. Pre-merger management in developing markets: the role of earnings glamor. International Review of Financial Analysis 65 article 101375.
Huang, W., Mazouz, K., 2018. Excess cash, trading continuity, and liquidity risk. Journal of Corporate Finance 48, 275–291.
Hughes, A., Park, A., Kietzmann, J., Archer-Brown, C., 2019. Beyond Bitcoin: what blockchain and distributed ledger technologies mean for firms. Business Horizons 62, 273–281.
Hulburt, H., Miles, J., Wollridge, J., 2002. Value creation from equity carve-outs. Financial Management 31, 83–100.
Humphery-Jenner, M., Powell, R., Zhang, E.J., 2019. Practice makes progress: evidence from divestitures. Journal of Banking and Finance 105, 1–19.
Hunt, P., 2003. Structuring Mergers and Acquisitions: A Guide to Creating Shareholder Value Aspen, New York.
Hurter, W.H., Petersen, J.R., Thompson, K.E., 2005. Merger, Acquisitions, and 1031 Tax Exchanges. Lorman Education Services, New York.
Huson, M.R., MacKinnon, G., 2003. Corporate spin-offs and information asymmetry between investors. Journal of Economics and Management Strategy 9, 481–501.

Ibbotson, R., Grabowski, R., Harrington, J., Nunes, C., 2017. Stock, Bonds, Bills, and Inflation (SBBI) Yearbook. Wiley, New York.
Imbruno, M., 2020. Importing under trade policy uncertainty: evidence from China. Journal of Comparative Economics 47, 806–826.
Ioulianou, S., Trigeorgis, L., Driouch, T., 2017. Multinationality and firm value: the role of real options. Journal of Corporate Finance 46, 77–96.
Ishii, J., Xuan, Y., 2014. Acquirer-target social ties and merger outcomes. Journal of Financial Economics 112, 344–363.
Ismail, A., Khalil, S., Safieddine, A., Titman, S., 2019. Smart investments by smart money: evidence from acquirer's projected synergies. Journal of Corporate Finance 56, 343–363.
Ivashina, V., Lerner, J., 2019. Pay now or pay later? The economics within the private equity partnership. Journal of Financial Economics 131, 61–87.
Jacobsen, S., 2014. The death of the deal: are withdrawn acquisition deals informative of CEO quality? Journal of Financial Economics 114, 54–83.
Jandik, T., Lallemand, J., 2015. Value impact of debt issuances by targets of withdrawn takeovers. Journal of Corporate Finance 29, 475–494.
Jandik, T., Lallemand, J., McCumber, W., 2017. The value implications of target debt issuance in withdrawn takeovers: what role do country specific M&A regulations play? Journal of Multinational Financial Management 40, 14–32.
Jahnsen, K., Pomerleau, K., September 7, 2017. Corporate income tax rates around the world: 2017. Tax Foundation. https://taxfoundation.org/corporate-income-tax-rates-around-the-world-2017.
Jansen, I., Stuart, N., 2014. How to predict the market's reaction when you announce an acquisition. Journal of Corporate Accounting and Finance 25, 43–49.
Jarzemsky, M., 2016. How bad is retail? Look at the bonds. Wall Street Journal January 25. http://www.wsj.com/articles/how-bad-is-retail-look-at-the-bonds-1453752646.
Jenkinson, T., Souza, M., 2015. What determines the exit decision of leveraged buyouts? Journal of Banking and Finance 59, 399–408.
Jensen, M., 1986. Agency costs of free cash flow, corporate finance, and takeovers. American Economic Association Papers and Proceedings 76, 323–329.
Jensen, M., 2005. Agency costs of overvalued equity. Financial Management 34, 5–19.
Jenter, D., Lewellen, K., 2015. CEO preferences and acquisitions. Journal of Finance 70, 2815–2832.
Jeon, J., Ligonb, J.A., 2011. How much is reasonable? The size of termination fees in mergers and acquisitions. Journal of Corporate Finance 17, 959–981.
Jha, A., Kim, Y., Gutierrez-Wirsching, S., 2019. Formation of cross-border corporate strategic alliances: the roles of trust and cultural, institutional, and geographical distances. Journal of Behavioral and Experimental Finance 21, 22–38.
Ji, S., Mauer, D., Zhang, Y., 2020. Managerial entrenchment and capital structure: the effect of diversification. Journal of Corporate Finance, forthcoming.
Jia, W., Redigolo, G., Shu, S., Zhao, J., 2020. Can social media distort price discovery? Evidence from merger rumors. Journal of Accounting and Economics 70 article 101334.
Jiang, W., 2016. Reforming the Delaware law to address appraisal arbitrage. Harvard Law School Forum on Corporate Governance and Regulation May 12. https://corpgov.law.harvard.edu/2016/05/12/reforming-the-delaware-law-to-address-appraisal-arbitrage.
Jiang, W., Li, K., Wang, W., 2012. Hedge funds and Chapter 11. Journal of Finance 67, 513–560.
Jiang, W., Li, T., Mei, D., 2019. Activist arbitrage in M&A acquirers. Finance Research Letters 29, 156–161.
Jindra, J., Moeller, T., 2020. Time since target's initial public offering, asymmetric information uncertainty, and acquisition pricing. Journal of Banking and Finance 118 article 105896.
Jindra, J., Walkling, R., 2004. Arbitrage spreads and the market pricing of proposed acquisitions. Journal of Corporate Finance 10, 495–526.
Johnson, S., Houston, M., 2000. A re-examination of the motives and gains in joint ventures. Journal of Financial and Quantitative Analysis 35, 67–85.
Johnson, W., Karpoff, J., Yi, S., 2015. The bonding hypothesis of takeover defenses: evidence from IPO firms. Journal of Financial Economics 117, 307–332.
Jones, S., Hensher, D., 2008. Advances in Credit Risk Modeling and Corporate Bankruptcy Prediction. Cambridge University Press, Cambridge, England.
Jordan, B., Kim, S., Liu, M., 2016. Growth opportunities, short-term market pressure, and dual class shares. Journal of Corporate Finance 41, 304–328.
Jory, S., Ngo, T., Susnjara, J., 2017. The effect of shareholder activism on bondholders and stockholders. The Quarterly Review of Economics and Finance 66, 328–344.
Jory, S., Ngo, T., Wang, D., 2016. Credit ratings and the premiums paid in mergers and acquisitions. Journal of Empirical Finance 39, 93–104.
Jurich, S., Walker, M., 2019. What drives merger outcomes? North American Journal of Economics and Finance 48, 757–775.
Kahle, K., Walkling, R., 1996. The impact of industry classification on financial research. Journal of Financial and Quantitative Analysis 31, 309–335.
Kaiser, K., Stouraitis, A., 2001. Revering corporate diversification and the use of the proceeds from asset sales: the case of Thorn Emi. Financial Management 30, 63–101.
Kale, P., Dyer, J.H., Singh, H., 2002. Alliance capability, stock market response, and long-term alliance success: the role of the alliance function. Strategic Management Journal 23, 747–767.
Kalodimos, J., Lundberg, C., 2017. Shareholder rights in mergers and acquisitions: are appraisal rights being abused? Finance Research Letters 22, 53–57.
Kamoto, S., 2016. Managerial innovation incentives, management buyouts, and shareholders' intolerance of failure. Journal of Corporate Finance 42, 55–74.
Kang, J., Shivdasani, A., 1997. Corporate restructuring during performance declines in Japan. Journal of Financial Economics 46, 29–65.
Kang, T., James, S., Fabian, F., 2020. Real options and strategic bankruptcy. Journal of Business Research 117, 152–162.
Kantor, R., 2002. Collaborative advantage: the art of alliances. Harvard Business Review on Strategic Alliances. Harvard Business School Press, Cambridge, MA.
Kaplan, S., 1989. The effects of management buyouts on operating performance and value. Journal of Financial Economics 24, 217–254.
Kaplan, S., 1991. The staying power of leveraged buyouts. Journal of Financial Economics 29, 287–313.

Kaplan, S., 1997. The evolution of U.S. corporate governance: we are all Henry Kravis now. Journal of Private Equity fall, 7–14.
Kaplan, S., 2012. How to think about private equity. The Journal of the American Enterprise Institute.
Kaplan, S., Schoar, A., 2005. Returns, persistence and capital flows. Journal of Finance 60, 1791–1823.
Kaplan, S., Stromberg, P., 2009. Leveraged buyouts and private equity. Journal of Economic Perspectives 23, 121–146.
Karolyi, G., Taboada, A., 2015. Regulatory arbitrage and cross border acquisitions. Journal of Finance 70, 2395–2450.
Karpoff, J., Malatesta, P.H., 1989. The wealth effects of second-generation state takeover legislation. Journal of Financial Economics 25, 291–322.
Karpoff, J., Wittry, M., 2018. Institutional and legal context in natural experiments: the case of state antitakeover laws. Journal of Finance 73, 657–714.
Katz, M., 2020. Big tech mergers: innovation, competition for the market, and the acquisition of emerging competitors. Information, Economics, and Policy, forthcoming.
Katz, S., 2008. Earnings Quality and Ownership Structure: The Role of Private Equity Sponsors. NBER Working Paper No. W14085.
Kedia, B., Reddy, R., 2017. Language and cross-border acquisitions: an exploratory study. International Business Review 25, 1321–1332.
Kengelbach, J., Roos, A., Keienburg, G., 2014. Maximizing value: choose the exit strategy. BCG Perspectives, Boston Consulting Group. www.bcgperspectives.com/content/articles/mergers_acquisitions_divestitures_maximizing_value_choose_right_exit_route/Right Exit Route.
Khalifa, M., Zouaoui, H., Ben Othmand, H., Hussainey, K., 2019. Exploring the nonlinear effect of conditional conservatism on the cost of equity capital: evidence from emerging markets. Journal of International Accounting, Auditing, and Taxation 36 article 100272.
Khan, Z., Soundararajan, V., Wood, G., Ahammad, M., 2020. Employee emotional resilience during post-merger integration across national boundaries: rewards and the mediating role of fairness norms. Journal of World Business 55 article 100888.
Khimich, N., 2017. A comparison of alternative cash flow and discount rate news proxies. Journal of Empirical Finance 41, 31–52.
Kim, H., Liao, R., Wang, Y., 2015. Active block investors and corporate governance around the world. Journal of International Markets, Institutions and Money 39, 181–194.
Kim, J., 2018. Asset specificity and firm value: evidence from mergers. Journal of Corporate Finance 48, 375–412.
Kim, K., Oler, D., Sanchez, J., 2020. Examining the stock performance of acquirers where the acquirer or target hold patents. Review of Quantitative Finance and Accounting 54, 1163–1193.
Kim, S., Bae, J., Oh, H., 2019. Financing strategically: the moderating effect of marketing activities on the bifurcated relationship between debt level and firm valuation of small and medium enterprises. North American Journal of Economics and Finance 48, 663–681.
Kim, Y., Su, L., Zhou, G., Zhu, X., 2020. PCAOB international inspections and merger and acquisition outcomes. Journal of Accounting and Economics 70 article 101318.
Kirsch, A., 2018. The gender composition of corporate boards: a review and research agenda. The Leadership Quarterly 29, 346–364.
Kisgen, D., Qian, J., Wiehong, S., 2009. Are fairness opinions fair? The case of mergers and acquisitions. Journal of Financial Economics 91, 178–207.
Klein, K., 2004. Urge to merge? Take care to beware. Business Week July 1, 68.
Klein, A., Zur, E., 2009. Entrepreneurial shareholder activism: hedge funds and other private investors. Journal of Finance 64, 187–229.
Klein, D., 2018. Executive turnover and the valuation of stock options. Journal of Corporate Finance 48, 76–93.
Klijn, E., Reuer, J., Volberda, H., van den Bosch, F., 2019. Ex-post governance in JVs: determinants of monitoring by JV boards of directors. Long Range Planning 52, 72–85.
Knauer, T., Silge, L., Sommer, F., 2018. The shareholder value effects of using value-based performance measures: evidence from acquisitions and divestments. Management Accounting Research 41, 43–61.
Koeplin, J., Sarin, A., Shapiro, A.C., 2000. The private equity discount. Journal of Applied Corporate Finance 12, 94–101.
Kohers, N., Ang, J., 2000. Earnouts in mergers: agreeing to disagree and agreeing to stay. Journal of Finance 73, 445–476.
Kolb, J., Tykvova, T., 2016. Going public via special purpose acquisition companies: frogs do not turn into princes. Journal of Corporate Finance 40, 80–96.
Kolev, K., McNamara, G., 2020. Board demography and divestitures: the impact of gender and racial diversity on divestiture rate and divestiture returns. Long Range Planning 53 article 101881.
Koller, T., Goedart, M., Wessels, D., 2010. Valuation: Measuring and Managing the Value of Companies. John Wiley & Sons, New York.
Korteweg, A., 2010. The net benefits of leverage. The Journal of Finance 65, 213–2170.
Kovermann, J., Wendt, M., 2019. Tax avoidance in family firms: evidence from large private firms. Journal of Contemporary Accounting and Economics 15, 145–157.
Krolikowski, M., 2017. Incentive pay and acquirer returns - the impact of Sarbanes-Oxley. The Quarterly Review of Economics and Finance 59, 99–111.
KPMG, 2006. Mergers and acquisitions. 2006 M&A Outlook Survey.
KPMG, 2006. When hedge funds start to look like private equity firms. Global M&A Spotlight Spring.
Kranhold, K., 2006. GE's water unit remains stagnant as it struggles to integrate acquisitions. Wall Street Journal August 23, C2.
Krishnamurti, C., Shams, S., Pensiero, D., Velayutham, E., 2020. Socially responsible firms and mergers and acquisitions: Australian evidence. Pacific Basin Finance Journal 57 article 101193.
Krishnan, C., Partnoy, F., Thomas, R., 2016. The second wave of hedge fund activism: the importance of reputation, clout, and expertise. Journal of Corporate Finance 40, 296–314.
Krishnan, C., Solomon, S., Thomas, R., 2017. The impact on shareholder value of top defense counsel in mergers and acquisitions litigation. Journal of Corporate Finance 45, 480–495.

Krolikowski, W., Adhikari, H., Malm, J., Sah, N., 2017. Inter-firm linkages and M&A returns. Quarterly Review of Economics and Finance 63, 135–146.

Kruger, P., Landier, A., Thesmar, D., 2015. The WACC fallacy: the real effects of using a unique discount rate. Journal of Finance 70, 1253–1285.

Kryzanowski, L., Nie, Y., 2019. M&A price pressure revisited. Finance Letters 28, 299–308.

Kuipers, D., Miller, D., Patel, A., 2009. The legal environment and corporate valuation: evidence from cross-border mergers. International Review of Economics and Finance 18, 552–567.

Kwabi, F., Boateng, A., Adegbite, E., 2018. The impact of stringent insider trading laws and institutional quality on cost of capital. International Review of Financial Analysis 60, 127–137.

Kwon, S., Lowry, M., Qian, Y., 2019. Mutual fund investments in private firms. Journal of Financial Economics 136, 407–443.

Lahlou, I., Navatte, P., 2017. Director compensation incentives and acquisition performance. International Review of Financial Analysis 53, 1–11.

Lai, J., Lin, W., Chen, L., 2017. The influence of CEO overconfidence on ownership choice in foreign market entry decisions. International Business Review 26, 774–785.

Lai, S., Pu, X., 2020. Mispricing or growth? An empirical analysis of acquisition. Finance Research Letters 37 article 101359.

Laing, E., Gurdgiev, C., Durand, R., Boermans, B., 2019. U.S. tax inversions and shareholder wealth effects. International Review of Financial Analysis 62, 35–52.

Laitinen, K., Suvas, A., 2016. Financial distress prediction in an international context: moderating effects of Hofstede's original cultural dimensions. Journal of Behavioral and Experimental Finance 9, 98–118.

Lajoux, A., 1998. The Art of M&A Integration. McGraw-Hill, New York.

Lamoreaux, P., Litov, L., Mauler, L., 2019. Lead independent directors: good governance or window dressing? Journal of Accounting Literature 43, 47–69.

Larkin, Y., Lyandres, E., 2019. Inefficient mergers. Journal of Banking and Finance 108 article 105648.

Larrain, B., Tapia, M., Urzua, F., 2017. Investor protection and corporate control. Journal of Corporate Finance 47, 174–190.

Lattman, P., de la Merced, M.J., 2010. Old GM being sold in parts. The New York Times September 1, 23.

Launhardt, P., Miebs, F., 2019. Aggregate implied cost of capital, option-implied information and equity premium predictability. Finance Research Letters 35 article 101305.

Lauterbach, B., Pajuste, A., 2015. The long-term valuation effects of voluntary dual class share unifications. Journal of Corporate Finance 31, 171–185.

Lebedev, S., Lin, Z., Peng, M., 2020. Power imbalance and value creation in joint ventures. Long Range Planning, forthcoming.

Lee, G., Cho, S., Arthurs, J., Lee, E., 2019a. CEO pay equity, CEO-TMS pay gap, and acquisition premiums. Journal of Business Research 98, 105–116.

Lee, J., Byun, H., Park, K., 2019b. How does product market competition affect corporate takeovers in an emerging economy? International Review of Economics and Finance 60, 26–45.

Lee, K., Mauer, D., Xu, E., 2018. Human capital relatedness and mergers and acquisitions. Journal of Financial Economics 129, 111–135.

Leeth, J., Rody Borg, J., 2000. The impact of takeovers on shareholders' wealth during the 1920s merger wave. Journal of Financial and Quantitative Analysis 35, 29–38.

Lehn, M., Zhao, K., 2006. CEO turnover after acquisitions: are bad bidders fired? Journal of Finance 61, 1383–1412.

Leung, H., Tse, J., Westerholm, J., 2019. CEO traders and corporate acquisitions. Journal of Corporate Finance 54, 107–127.

Levine, D., Berenson, M., Stephan, D., 1999. Statistics for Managers, 2nd ed. Prentice-Hall, New York.

Levit, D., 2017. Advising shareholders in takeovers. Journal of Financial Economics 126, 614–634.

Lewellen, J., Resutek, R., 2019. Why do accruals predict earnings? Journal of Accounting and Economics 67, 336–356.

Lewis, Y., Bozos, K., 2019. Mitigating post-acquisition risk: the interplay of cross-border uncertainties. Journal of World Business 54 article 100996.

Li, K., Wang, W., 2016. Debtor-in-possession financing: loan-to-loan and loan-to-own. Journal of Corporate Finance 39, 121–138.

Li, D., Chen, Z., An, M., Murong, Z., 2017a. Do financial analysts play a role in shaping the rival response of target firms? International evidence. Journal of Corporate Finance 45, 84–103.

Li, D., Eden, L., Josefy, M., 2017b. Agent and task complexity in multilateral alliances: the safeguarding role of equity governance. Journal of International Management 23, 227–241.

Li, D., Taylor, L., Wang, W., 2018. Inefficiencies and externalities from opportunistic acquirers. Journal of Financial Economics 130, 265–290.

Li, J., 2012. Prediction of corporate bankruptcy from June 2008 through 2011. Journal of Accounting and Finance 12, 31–42.

Li, J., Ali Haider, Z., Jin, X., Yuan, W., 2019. Corporate controversy, social responsibility, and market performance: international evidence. Journal of International Financial Markets, Institutions, and Money 60, 1–18.

Li, K., 2020. Does information asymmetry impede market efficiency? Evidence from analyst coverage. Journal of Banking and Finance 118 article 105856.

Li, K., Wang, W., 2016. Debtor-in-possession financing: loan-to-loan and loan-to-own. Journal of Corporate Finance 39, 121–138.

Li, L., Faff, R., 2019. Predicting bankruptcy: what matters? International Review of Economics and Finance 62, 1–19.

Li, L., Tong, W., 2018. Information uncertainty and target valuation in mergers and acquisitions. Journal of Empirical Finance 45, 84–107.

Li, T., Zaiata, N., 2017. Information environment and earnings management of dual class firms around the world. Journal of Banking and Finance 74, 1–123.

Li, Y., 2018. Dissecting bidder security returns on payment methods. Journal of Banking and Finance 96, 207–219.

Li, Z., Crook, J., Andreeva, G., Tang, Y., 2020. Predicting the risk of financial distress using corporate governance measures. Pacific Basin Journal article 101334, forthcoming.

Lian, Y., 2017. Financial distress and customer-supplier relationships. Journal of Corporate Finance 43, 397–406.

Liang, D., Lu, C., Tsai, C., Shih, G., 2016. Financial ratios and corporate governance indicators in bankruptcy prediction: a comprehensive study. European Journal of Operational Research 252, 561–572.

Liang, D., Lub, C., Tsai, C., Shiha, G., 2017. Financial ratios and corporate governance indicators in bankruptcy prediction: a comprehensive study. European Journal of Operations Research 252, 561–572.

Liang, H., Renneboog, L., Vansteenkiste, C., 2020. Cross-border acquisitions and employment policies. Journal of Corporate Finance 62 article 101575.

Laitinen, K., Suvas, A., 2016. Financial distress prediction in an international context: moderating effects of Hofstede's original cultural dimensions. Journal of Behavioral and Experimental Finance 9, 98–118.

Lim, A.S., Macias, A., Moeller, T., 2020a. Intangible assets and capital structure. Journal of Banking and Finance 118 article 105873.

Lim, J., Schwert, M., Weisbach, M., 2020b. The economics of PIPES. Journal of Financial Intermediation article 10832, forthcoming.

Lim, M., Lee, J., 2016. The effects of industry relatedness and takeover motives in cross-border acquisition completion. Journal of Business Research 69, 4787–4792.

Lin, J., 2017. Knowledge creation through joint venture investments: the contingent role of organizational slack. Journal of Engineering and Technology Management 46, 1–25.

Lin, L., Mihov, A., Sanz, L., Stoyanova, D., 2019. Property rights institutions, foreign investment, and the valuation of multinational firms. Journal of Financial Economics 134, 214–235.

Lin, W., Law, S., Ho, J., Sambasivan, M., 2019. The causality direction of the corporate social responsibility–corporate financial performance nexus: application of panel vector autoregression approach. North American Journal of Economics and Finance 48, 401–418.

Linck, J., Netter, J., Yang, T., 2009. The effects and unintended consequences of the Sarbanes-Oxley Act on the supply and demand for directors. The Review of Financial Studies 22, 3287–3328.

Linde, J., Pescatori, A., 2019. The macroeconomic effects of trade tariffs: revisiting the Lerner symmetry. Journal of International Money and Finance 95, 52–69.

Listokin, Y., 2009. Corporate voting versus market price setting. American Law and Economics Review 11, 608–637.

Liu, Q., Sun, X., Wu, H., 2019. Premier advisory services for VIP acquirers. Journal of Corporate Finance 54, 1–25.

Liu, T., Mulherin, J., 2018. How has takeover competition changed over time? Journal of Corporate Finance 49, 104–119.

Liu, T., Wu, J., 2014. Merger arbitrage short selling and price pressure. Journal of Corporate Finance 27, 36–54.

Loertscher, S., Marx, L., 2019a. Merger review with intermediate buyer power. International Journal of Industrial Organization 67 article 102531.

Loertscher, S., Marx, L.M., 2019b. Merger review for markets with buyer power. Journal of Political Economy 127, 346–366.

Logue, D., Seward, J.K., Walsh, J.W., 1996. Rearranging residual claims: a case for targeted stock. Financial Management 25, 43–61.

Loh, C., Bezjak, J.R., Toms, H., 1995. Voluntary corporate divestitures as an anti-takeover mechanism. Financial Review 30, 21–24.

Longstaff, F., 1995. How can marketability affect security values? Journal of Finance 50, 1767–1774.

López-Robles, J., Otegi-Olaso, J., Porto Gomez, I., Cobo, M., 2019. Thirty years of intelligence models in management and business: a bibliometric review. International Journal of Information Management 48, 22–38.

Lou, K., Lu, Y., Shiu, C., 2020. Monitoring role of institutional investors and acquisition performance: evidence from East Asian markets. Pacific-Basin Finance Journal 59 article 101244.

Loughran, T., Anand, M., Vijh, A., 1997. Do long-term shareholders benefit from corporate acquisitions? Journal of Finance 22, 321–340.

Loughran, T., Ritter, J., 2002. Why don't issuers get upset about leaving money on the table in IPOs? Review of Financial Studies 15, 413–443.

Loughran, T., Ritter, J., Rydqvist, K., 1994. Initial public offerings: international insights. Pacific Basin Finance Journal 2, 165–199.

Lynch, R., 1993. Business Alliance Guide: The Hidden Competitive Weapon. Wiley, New York, pp. 189–205.

Ma, M., 2019. Three ways to fight bias in machines. Wall Street Journal May 30. https://www.wsj.com/articles/three-ways-to-fight-bias-in-machines-11559231701.

Ma, Q., Whidbee, D., Zhang, W., 2019. Acquirer reference prices and acquisition performance. Journal of Financial Economics 132, 175–199.

Madura, J., Ngo, T., 2012. Determinants of the medium of payment used to acquire privately held targets. Journal of Economics and Finance 36, 424–442.

Mai, F., Tian, S., Lee, C., Ma, L., 2019. Deep learning models for bankruptcy prediction using textual disclosures. European Journal of Operation Research 278, 743–758.

Maksimovic, V., Phillips, G., Yang, L., 2013. Private and public merger waves. Journal of Finance 68, 2177–2217.

Malatesta, P., Walkling, R., 1988. Poison pills securities: stockholder wealth, profitability and ownership structure. Journal of Financial Economics 20, 347–376.

Malenko, A., Malenko, N., 2015. A theory of LBO activity based on repeated debt-equity conflicts. Journal of Financial Economics 117, 607–627.

Malmendier, U., Tate, G., Yan, J., 2011. Overconfidence and early-life experiences: the impact of managerial traits on corporate financial policies. Journal of Finance 66, 1687–1733.

Mandelman, F., Waddle, A., 2020. Intellectual property, tariffs, and international trade dynamics. Journal of Monetary Economics 109, 86–103.

Marcus, D., Schneider, F., 2019. Appraisal litigation in Delaware: trends in petitions and opinions (2006–2018). Harvard Law School Forum on Corporate Governance and Financial Regulation March 1.

Markides, C., Oyon, D., 1998. International acquisitions: do they create value for shareholders? European Management Journal 16, 125–135.

Marquez, R., Singh, R., 2013. The economics of club bidding and value creation. Journal of Financial Economics 108, 275294.

Martinez, G., Zouaghib, F., Garcia-Marco, T., Robinson, C., 2019. What drives business failure? Exploring the role of internal and external knowledge capabilities during the global financial crisis. Journal of Business Research 98, 441–449.

Mashwani, A., Dereepera, S., Dowling, M., Aziz, S., 2019. Learning the wealth effects from equity carve-outs. Finance Research Letters 33 article 101191.

Maskara, K., Miller, L., 2018. Do golden parachutes matter? Evidence from firms that ultimately filed for bankruptcy. The Quarterly Review of Economics and Finance 67, 63–78.
Masulis, R., Wang, C., Xie, F., 2009. Agency problems in dual-class companies. Journal of Finance 64, 1697–1727.
Masulis, R., Zhang, E., 2019. How valuable are independent directors? Evidence from external distractions. Journal of Financial Economics 132, 226–256.
Mateev, M., 2017. Is the M&A announcement effect different across Europe? More evidence from continental Europe and the UK. Research in International Business and Finance 40, 190–216.
Mateev, M., Andonov, K., 2016. Do cross-border and domestic bidding firms perform differently? New evidence from continental Europe and the UK. Research in International Business and Finance 37, 327–349.
Maung, M., Shedden, M., Wang, Y., Wilson, C., 2019. The investment environment and cross-border merger and acquisition premiums. Journal of International Financial Markets, Institutions, & Money 59, 19–35.
Maung, M., Wilson, C., Yu, W., 2020. Does reputation risk matter? Evidence from cross-border mergers and acquisitions. Journal of International Financial Markets, Institutions & Money 66 article 101204.
Maurer, M., 2019. Companies appear to avoid hiring auditors with a history of critical audits, new research shows. The Wall Street Journal August 12. https://www.wsj.com/articles/companies-appear-to-avoid-hiring-auditors-with-a-history-of-critical-audits-new-research-shows-11565647355.
Mavis, C., McNamee, N., Petmezas, D., 2020. Selling to buy: asset sales and acquisitions. Journal of Corporate Finance 62 article 101587.
Maxwell, W.F., Rao, R.P., 2003. Do spin-offs expropriate wealth from bondholders? Journal of Finance 58, 2087–2108.
Mazboudi, M., Khalil, S., 2017. The attenuation effect of social media: evidence from acquisitions by large firms. Journal of Financial Stability 28, 115–124.
McConnell, J., Nantell, T., 1985. Corporate combinations and common stock returns: the case of joint ventures. Journal of Finance 40, 519–536.
McConnell, J., Ozbilgin, M., Wahal, S., 2001. Spin-offs: ex ante. Journal of Business 74, 245–280.
McCoy, K., Chu, K., 2011. Merger of U.S. and Chinese firms is a cautionary tale. USA Today December 26, 6.
McNeil, C., Moore, W.T., 2005. Dismantling internal capital markets via spin-off: effects on capital allocation efficiency and firm valuation. Journal of Corporate Finance 11, 253–275.
Megginson, W., Gao, X., 2019. The state of research on sovereign wealth funds. Global Finance Journal 44 article 100466.
Megginson, W., Meles, A., Sampagnaro, G., Verdoliva, V., 2019. Financial distress risk in initial public offerings: how much do venture capitals matter? Journal of Corporate Finance 59, 10–30.
Meglio, O., King, D., Risberg, A., 2017. Speed in acquisitions: a managerial framework. Business Horizons 60, 415–425.
Meier, O., Schier, G., 2014. Family firm succession: lessons from failures in external party takeovers. Journal of Family Business Strategy 5, 372–383.
Mercer, C., 1997. The Management Panning Study: Quantifying Marketability Discounts. Peabody, New York.
Merendino, A., Dibb, S., Meadows, M., Quinn, L., Wilson, D., Simkin, L., Canhoto, A., 2019. Big data, big decisions: the impact on big data on board level decision making. Journal of Business Research 93, 67–78.
Metrick, A., Yasuda, A., 2010. The economics of private equity funds. The Review of Financial Studies 23, 2303–2341.
Meuleman, M., Amess, K., Wright, M., Scholes, L., 2009. Agency, strategic entrepreneurship, and the performance of private equity-backed buyouts. Entrepreneurship Theory and Practice 33, 213–239.
Mikalef, P., Boura, M., Lekakos, G., Krogsie, J., 2019. Big data analytics and firm performance: findings from a mixed method approach. Journal of Business Research 98, 261–276.
Miller, M., 2012. The rich get richer. The Deal May 12, 38.
Mishra, C., 2020. Are frequent acquirers more entrenched? International Review of Financial Analysis 70 article 101508.
Mitchell, M., Pulvino, T., Stafford, E., 2004. Price pressure around mergers. Journal of Finance 59, 31–63.
Mittoo, U., Ng, D., Yan, M., 2020. Managerial ownership, credit market conditions, undervaluation and offer premiums in management and leveraged buyouts. Journal of International Financial Markets, Institutions, and Money 65 article 101189.
Moeller, S., Schlingemann, P., 2005. Global diversification and bidder gains: a comparison between cross-border and domestic acquisitions. Journal of Banking and Finance 29, 533–564.
Moeller, S., Schlingemann, F.P., Stulz, R.M., 2004. Firm size and the gains from acquisitions. Journal of Financial Economics 73, 201–228.
Moeller, S., Schlingemann, F.P., Stulz, R.M., 2005. Wealth destruction on a massive scale? A study of the acquiring firm returns in the recent merger wave. Journal of Finance 60, 757–782.
Moeller, S., Schlingemann, F.P., Stulz, R.M., 2007. How do diversity of opinion and information asymmetry affect acquirer returns? Review of Financial Studies 20, 2047–2078.
Moeller, T., 2005. Let's make a deal! How shareholder control impacts merger payoffs. Journal of Financial Economics 76, 167–190.
Morkunas, V., Paschen, J., Boon, E., 2019. How blockchain technologies impact your business model. Business Horizons 62, 295–306.
Moscatelli, M., Parlapiano, F., Narizzano, S., Viggiano, G., 2020. Corporate default forecasting with machine learning. Experts Systems with Applications 16 article 113567.
Moschieri, C., Campa, J., 2014. New trends in mergers and acquisitions: idiosyncrasies of the European market. Journal of Business Research 67, 1478–1485.
Moskowitz, S., 2017. Cybercrime and Business: Strategies for Global Corporate Security. Butterworth-Heinemann, London, pp. 99–120.
Mukherji, A., Mukherji, J., Dibrell, C., Francis, J., 2015. Overbidding in cross-border acquisitions: misperceptions in assessing and valuing knowledge. Journal of World Business 48, 39–46.
Mulherin, J., Netter, J., Poulsen, A., 2017. The evidence on mergers and acquisitions: a historical and modern report. In: Hermalin, B., Weisbach, M. (Eds.), The Handbook of the Economics of Corporate Governance. North Holland Press.
Muller, A., Zaby, A., 2019. Research joint ventures and technological proximity. Research Policy 48, 1187–1200.
Mun, J., 2006. Modeling Risk: Applying Monte Carlo Simulation, Real Option Analysis, Forecasting, and Optimization. Wiley, New York.
Nadauld, T., Sensoy, B., Vorknk, K., Weisbach, M., 2019. The liquidity cost of private equity investments: evidence from secondary market transactions. Journal of Financial Economics 132, 158–181.

Navarro, E., 2005. In: Merger Control in the EU: Law, Economics, and Practice, 2nd ed. Oxford University Press, Oxford, UK.

Netter, J., Stegemoller, M., Wintoki, M., 2011. Implications of data screens on merger and acquisition analysis: a large sample study of mergers and acquisitions. Review of Financial Studies 24, 2316–2357.

Neyland, J., Shekhar, C., 2018. How much is too much? Large termination fees and target distress. Journal of Banking and Finance 88, 97–112.

Nguyen, H., Larimo, J., Wang, Y., 2019. Control, innovation, and international joint venture performance: the moderating role of internal and external environments. International Business Review 28 article 101591.

Nguyen, N., Phan, H., Phan, H., Tran, D., Vo, H., 2020. Tournament-based incentives and mergers and acquisitions. International Review of Financial Analysis 71 article 101548.

Ni, X., 2020. Does stakeholder orientation matter for earnings management: evidence from non-shareholder constituency statutes. Journal of Corporate Finance 62 article 101606.

Nicola, M., Alsafi, Z., Sohrabi, C., Kerwan, A., Al-Jabir, A., Losifidis, C., Aghae, M., Agha, R., 2020. The socio-economic implications of the coronavirus pandemic (COVID-19): a review. International Journal of Surgery 78, 185–193.

Niesten, E., Jolink, A., 2017. Alliance governance choices: disentangling the effects of uncertainty and alliance experience. Long Range Planning 50, 1–14.

Nishihara, M., Shibata, T., 2019. Liquidation, fire sales, and acquirers' private information. Journal of Economic Dynamics and Control 108, 103769.

Nkiwane, P., Chipeta, C., 2019. The performance of cross-border acquisitions targeting African firms. Emerging Markets Review 39, 68–82.

Norback, P., Persson, L., 2019. Stock market impact of cross-border acquisitions in emerging markets. North American Journal of Economics and Finance 48, 346–363.

Norback, P., Persson, L., Tag, J., 2014. Acquisitions, entry, and innovation in oligopolistic network industries. International Journal of industrial Organization 37, 1–12.

Oded, A., Michel, A., Weinstein, S., 2011. Distortion in corporate valuation: implications for capital structure changes. Managerial Finance 37, 681–696.

Offenberg, D., Pirinsky, C., 2015. How do acquirers choose between mergers and tender offers? Journal of Financial Economics 116, 331–348.

Officer, M., 2004. Collars and renegotiation in mergers and acquisitions. Journal of Finance 59, 2719–2743.

Officer, M., 2007. The price of corporate liquidity: acquisition discounts for unlisted targets. Journal of Financial Economics 83, 571–593.

Officer, M., Ozbas, O., Sensoy, B.A., 2008. Club deals in leveraged buyouts. Journal of Financial Economics 98, 214–240.

Officer, M., Poulsen, A.B., Stegemoller, M., 2009. Information asymmetry and acquirer returns. Review of Finance 13, 467–493.

Oh, S., 2018. Fire sale acquisitions and intra-industry contagion. Journal of Corporate Finance 50, 265–293.

Ohrn, E., Seeger, N., 2019. The impact of investor-level taxation on mergers and acquisitions. Journal of Public Economics 177, 104–138.

Ongsakul, V., Treepongkaruna, S., Jiraporn, P., Uyar, A., 2020. Do firms adjust corporate governance in response to policy uncertainty: evidence from board size. Finance Research Letters article 101613, forthcoming.

Ordóñez-Calafia, G., Thanassoulis, J., 2020. Stock selling during takeovers. Journal of Corporate Finance 60 article 101550.

Otsubo, M., 2009. Gains from equity carve-outs and subsequent events. Journal of Business 62, 1207–1213.

Otsubo, M., 2013. Value creation from financing in equity carve-outs: evidence from Japan. Journal of Economics and Business 68, 52–69.

Ott, U., Williams, D., Saker, J., Staley, L., 2019. A configurational analysis of the termination scenarios of international joint ventures: all is well that ends well. Journal of Knowledge and Innovation 4, 202–210.

Otto, F., Sampaio, J., Silva, V., 2020. Domestic and cross-border effect of acquisition announcements: a short-term study for developed and emerging countries. Finance Research Letters article 101501, forthcoming.

Ouyang, W., Zhu, P., 2016. An international study of shareholder protection in freeze-out M&A transactions. International Review of Financial Analysis 45, 157–171.

Ozdemir, S., Kandemir, D., Eng, T., 2017. The role of horizontal and vertical new product alliances in responsive and proactive market orientations and performance of industrial manufacturing firms. Industrial Marketing and Management 64, 25–35.

Paglia, J., Harjoto, M., 2014. The effects of private equity and venture capital on sales and employment growth in small and medium-sized businesses. Journal of Banking and Finance 47, 177–197.

Palter, R., Srinivasan, D., 2006. Habits of the busiest acquirers. McKinsey Quarterly.

Parfomak, P., 2011. Keeping American pipelines safe and secure: key issues in Congress. Congressional Research Service 7–5700.

Park, K., Meglio, O., Schriber, S., 2019. Building a global corporate social responsibility program via mergers and acquisitions: a management framework. Business Horizons 62, 395–407.

Pasal, F., Instefjord, N., 2013. Corporate governance and the cost of borrowing. Journal of Business, Finance, and Accounting 40, 918–948.

Pehrsson, A., 2008. Strategy antecedents of mode of entry into foreign markets. Journal of Business Research 61, 132–140.

Pérez-Calero, L., Hurtado-Gonzalez, J., Lopez-Iturriaga, F., 2019. Do the institutional environment and types of owners influence the relationship between ownership concentration and board of director independence? An international meta-analysis. International Review of Financial Analysis 61, 233–244.

Pergola, T., 2005. Management entrenchment: can it negate the effectiveness of recently legislated governance reforms? Journal of American Academy of Business 6, 177–185.

Phalippou, L., Rauch, C., Umber, M., 2018. Private equity portfolio company fees. Journal of Financial Economics 129, 559–585.

Pham, A., 2019. Political risk and cost of equity: the mediating role of political connections. Journal of Corporate Finance 56, 64–87.

Piaskowska, D., Nadolska, A., Barkema, H., 2019. Embracing complexity: learning from minority, 50-50, and majority joint venture experience. Long-Range Planning 52, 134–153.

Pineiro-Chousa, J., Vizaino-Gonzalez, M., Caby, J., 2019. Financial development and standardized reporting: a comparison among developed, emerging, and frontier markets. Journal of Business Research 101, 797–802.

Pires, M., Pereira, P., 2020. Leverage, premium, and timing in corporate acquisitions. Economic Letters 188 article 108933.
Poldolski, J., Truong, C., Veeraraghavan, M., 2016. Cash holdings and bond returns around takeovers. International Review of Financial Analysis 46, 1–11.
Polovina, N., Peasnell, K., 2020. Do minority acquisitions transfer better corporate governance practices? An analysis of UK cross-border minority investments. The British Accounting Review 52, 100897.
Pomerleau, K., February 12, 2018. The United States' corporate income tax rate is now more in line with those levied by other major nations. Tax Foundation. https://taxfoundation.org/us-corporate-income-tax-more-competitive/.
Porter, R., 2020. Mergers and coordinated effects. International Journal of Industrial Organization 73 article 102583.
Povel, P., Sertsios, G., 2014. Getting to know each other: the role of toeholds in acquisitions. Journal of Corporate Finance 26, 201–224.
Powers, E., 2003. Deciphering the motives for equity carve-outs. Journal of Financial Research 26, 31–50.
Prasadh, R., Thenmozhi, M., 2019. Does religion affect cross-border acquisitions? Finance Research Letters 31, 300–312.
Pratt, S., Niculita, A., 2008. Valuing a Business: The Analysis and Appraisal of Closely Held Businesses. McGraw-Hill, New York.
Prezas, A., Simmonyan, K., 2015. Corporate divestitures: spin-offs v. sell-offs. Journal of Corporate Finance 34, 83–107.
Prezas, A., Tarmicilar, M., Vasudevan, G., 2000. The pricing of equity carve-outs. Financial Review 35, 123–138.
PriceWaterhouseCoopers, 2015. PriceWaterhouseCoopers, Mergers and Acquisitions 2015: A Global Tax Guide. Wiley, New York.
PriceWaterhouseCoopers, 2017. Mergers and acquisitions. PriceWaterhouseCoopers, Mergers and Acquisitions 2015: A Global Tax Guide. Wiley, New York.
Ransbotham, S., Khodabandeh, S., Fehling, R., LaFountain, B., Kiron, D., 2019. Winning with AI: pioneers combine strategy, organizational behavior, and technology. Findings from the 2019 artificial intelligence global executive study and research project. MIT Sloan Management Review October 15.
Rao, U., Mishra, T., 2020. Posterior analysis of mergers and acquisitions in the international financial market: a re-appraisal. Research in International Business and Finance 51 article 101062.
Rappaport, A., 1990. The staying power of the public corporation. Harvard Business Review 76, 1–4.
Rehm, W., Uhlaner, R., West, A., January, 2012. Taking a longer-term look at M&A value creation. McKinsey Quarterly. http://www.mckinseyquarterly.com/article_print.aspx?L2=5&L3=4&ar=2916.
Renneboog, L., Szilagyi, P., 2007. Corporate restructuring and bondholder wealth. European Financial Management 14, 792–819.
Renneboog, L., Zhao, Y., 2013. Director networks and takeovers. Journal of Corporate Finance 17, 1068–1077.
Renneboog, L., Vansteenkiste, C., 2019. Failure and success in mergers and acquisitions. Journal of Corporate Finance 58, 650–699.
Requejo, I., Reyes-Reina, F., Sanchez-Bueno, M., Suarez-Gonzalez, I., 2018. European family firms and acquisition propensity: a comprehensive analysis of the legal system's role. Journal of Family Business Strategy 9, 44–58.
Robinson, D., Sensoy, B., 2011. Cyclicality, Performance Measurement, and Cash Flow Liquidity in private equity. National Bureau of Economic Research. NBER Working Paper 17428.
Robinson, A., 2002. Is corporate governance the solution or the problem? Corporate Board 23, 12–16.
Robinson, S., Thierfelder, K., 2019. Global adjustment to US disengagement from the world trading system. Journal of Policy Modeling 41, 522–536.
Robson, M., Katsikeas, C., Schlegelmilch, B., Prambock, B., 2019. Alliance capabilities, interpartner attributes, and performance outcomes in international strategic alliances. Journal of World Business 54, 137–153.
Romano, R., 2001. Less is more: making institutional investor activism a valuable mechanism of corporate governance. Yale Journal of Regulation 18, 174–251.
Rouzies, A., Loe Colman, H., Angwin, D., 2019. Recasting the dynamics of post-acquisition integration: an embeddedness perspective. Long-Range Planning 52, 271–282.
RSM McGladrey, Inc., 2011. Maximizing investments in an evolving market. Managing Portfolio Investments Survey, Los Angeles.
Rzakhanov, Z., Jetley, G., 2019. Competition, scale, and hedge fund performance: evidence from merger arbitrage. Journal of Economics and Business 105, 358–376.
Safhi, H., Frikh, B., Ouhbi, B., 2019. Assessing reliability of big data knowledge discovery process. Procedia Computer Science 148, 30–36.
Samano, M., Santugini, M., Zacour, G., 2017. Dynamics in research joint ventures and R&D collaborations. Journal of Economic Dynamics and Control 77, 70–92.
Sandler, L., 2013. Lehman bankruptcy advisory fees top $2 billion. Bloomberg News January 31. http://www.bloomberg.com/news/2013–01–31/lehman-bankruptcy-fees-expenses-top-2–billion.html.
Sarala, R., Vaara, E., Junni, P., 2019. Beyond merger syndrome and cultural differences: new avenues for research on the "human side" of global mergers and acquisitions. Journal of World Business 54, 307–321.
Sarin, N., Summers, L., 2016. Have big banks gotten safer? Brookings Papers on Economic Activity fall issue.
Sayari, N., Mugan, C., 2017. Industry specific financial distress modeling. Business Research Quarterly 20, 45–62.
Scarboro, M., 2017. Net operating loss carryback and carryforward provisions by state. Tax Foundation. August 31. https://taxfoundation.org/net-operating-loss-carryforward-carryback-2017.
Scarboro, M., 2018. State Corporate Income Tax Rates and Brackets for 2018, 571. Tax Foundation Fiscal Fact, February.
Scherreik, S., 2002. Gems among the trash. Business Week XX, 112–113.
Schierstedt, B., Henn, M., Lutz, E., 2020. Diversified acquisitions in family firms: restricted versus extended family priorities. Journal of Family Business Strategy 11 article 100357.
Schultes, R., 2010. AB InBev shines in tough times. Wall Street Journal November 12, C7.

Schwarz, J., Ram, C., Rohrbeck, R., 2019. Combining scenario planning and business war gaming to better anticipate future competitive dynamics. Future 105, 133–142.

Schweiger, D., 2002. M&A Integration: Framework for Executives and Managers. McGraw-Hill, New York.

Sedlacek, P., Sterk, V., 2019. Reviving American entrepreneurship? Tax reform and business dynamism. Journal of Monetary Economics 105, 94–108.

Sender, H., 2006. High-risk debt still has allure for buyout deals. Wall Street Journal C2.

Seoungpil, A., Denis, D.J., 2004. Internal capital market and investment policy: evidence of corporate spin-offs. Journal of Financial Economics 71, 489–516.

Seth, A., Song, K.P., Petit, R., 2000. Synergy, managerialism or hubris: an empirical examination of motives for foreign acquisitions of U.S. firms. Journal of International Business Studies 31, 387–405.

Sheikh, S., 2018. Is corporate social responsibility a value-increasing investment? Evidence from antitakeover provisions. Global Finance Journal 38, 1–12.

Sheikh, S., 2019. Corporate social responsibility and firm leverage: the impact of market competition. Research in International Business and Finance 48, 496–510.

Sherman, A., 2018. In: Mergers and Acquisitions from A to Z, 4th ed. AMACOM, New York.

Sherman, D., Young, S.D., 2001. Tread lightly through these accounting minefields. Harvard Business Review July-August 129–137.

Shetty, A., Manley, J., Kyaw, N., 2019. The impact of exchange rate movements on mergers and acquisitions. Journal of Multinational Financial Management 53 article 100594.

Shevlin, T., Shivakumar, L., Urcan, O., 2019. Macroeconomic effects of corporate tax policy. Journal of Accounting and Economics 68 article 101233.

Shin, H., Stulz, R., 1998. Are internal capital markets efficient? Quarterly Journal of Economics 113, 531–552.

Signori, A., Vismara, S., 2018. M&A synergies and trends in IPOs. *Technological* Forecasting and Social Change 127, 141–153.

Silaghi, F., 2018. The use of equity financing in debt renegotiation. Journal of Economic Dynamics and Control 86, 123–143.

Simonyan, K., 2014. What determines takeover premia: an empirical analysis. Journal of Economics and Business 75, 93–125.

Siraj, I., Hassan, M., Maroney, N., 2020. Product demand sensitivity and the corporate diversification discount. Journal of Financial Stability 48 article 100748.

Slovin, M., Sushka, M., Polonchek, J.A., 2005. Methods of payment in asset sales: contracting with equity versus cash. Journal of Finance 60, 2385–2407.

Smith, G., Coy, J., Spieler, A., 2019. Cross-border transactions, mergers and the inconsistency of international reference points. Journal of Behavioral and Experimental Finance 22, 14–21.

Song, S., 2020. Actualization of growth potential in international joint ventures: the moderating effects of localization strategies. Journal of World Business 55 article 101124.

Sorensen, M., Wang, N., Yang, J., 2014. Valuing Private Equity. NBER Working Paper No. 19612. http://ssrn.com/abstract=2352129.

Souther, M., 2016. The effects of takeover defenses: evidence from closed end funds. The Journal of Financial Economics 119, 420–440.

Srinivasan, S., 2020. Foreign competition and acquisitions. Journal of Corporate Finance 60 article 101484.

Stafylas, D., Andrikopoulos, A., 2020. Determinants of hedge fund performance during "good" and "bad" economic periods. Research in International Business and Finance 52 article 101130.

Stanfield, J., 2020. Skill, syndication and performance: evidence from leveraged buyouts. Journal of Corporate Finance article 101496, forthcoming.

Stromberg, P., 2008. The new demography of private equity. Globalization of Alternative Investments Project. The Global Economic Impact of Private Equity Report. World Economic Forum 1, 3–26. Working Paper.

Stulz, R., 1995a. Globalization of the capital markets and the cost of capital: the case of Nestle. Journal of Applied Corporate Finance 8, 30–38.

Stulz, R., 1995b. The cost of capital in internationally integrated markets: the case of Nestle, 1. European Financial Management, pp. 11–22.

Sun, L., Teo, M., 2019. Public hedge funds. Journal of Financial Economics 131, 44–60.

Surbakti, F., Wang, W., Indulska, M., Sadiq, S., 2019. Factors influencing effective use of big data: a research framework. Information and Management 57 article 103146.

Sweeney, P., 2005. Gap. Financial Executives Magazine 33–40.

Tabesh, P., Mousavidin, E., Hasani, S., 2019. Implementing big data strategies: a managerial perspective. Business Horizons 62, 347–358.

Tampakoudis, I., Anagnostopoulou, E., 2020. The effect of mergers and acquisitions on environmental, social and governance performance and market value. Business Strategy and the Environment 71, 114–13.

Tang, Q., Li, W., 2018. Identifying M&A targets and the information content of VC/PEs. China Journal of Accounting Research 11, 33–50.

Tar, H., Harford, J., Li, K., 2010. Determinants of Corporate Cash Policy: A Comparison of Private and Public Firms. University of Washington Working Paper.

Tarsalewska, M., 2015. The timing of mergers along the production chain, capital structure, and risk dynamics. Journal of Banking and Finance 57, 51–64.

Tarsalewska, M., 2018. Buyouts under the threat of preemption. Journal of Banking and Finance 89, 39–58.

Teerikangas, S., Thanos, I., 2017. Looking into the black box—unlocking the effect of integration on acquisition performance. European Management Journal 23, 1–15.

Thompson, T., Apilado, V., 2009. An examination of the impact of equity carve-outs on stockholder and bondholder wealth. Journal of Economics and Business 61, 376–391.

Thraya, M., Hamza, T., 2019b. Bidder excess control, target overpayment, and control contestability: evidence from France. Quarterly Review of Economics and Finance 72, 178–190.

Thraya, M., Lichy, J., Louizi, A., Rzem, M., 2019a. High-tech acquirers and the moderating role of corporate governance. Journal of High Technology Management Research 30 article 100354.
Tian, S., Yu, Y., 2017. Financial ratios and bankruptcy predictions: international evidence. International Review of Economics and Finance 51, 510–526.
Ting, P., 2020. Do large firms just talk corporate social responsibility? The evidence. Finance Research Letters article 101476, forthcoming.
Titman, S., Martin, J., 2010. Valuation: The Art and Science of Corporate Investment Decisions, 2nd ed. Prentice-Hall, Boston, pp. 144–147.
Todtenhaupt, M., Voget, J., Feld, L., Ruf, M., Schreiber, U., 2020. Taxing away M&A: capital gains taxation and acquisition activity. European Economic Review 128 article 103505.
Trigeorgis, L., Tsekrekos, A., 2018. Real options in operations research. European Journal of Operational Research 270, 1–24.
Truitt, W., 2006. The Corporation. Greenwood Press, Westport, CT.
Tsui-Auch, L., Chow, D., 2019. MNEs' agency within institutional contexts: a study of Walmart's post-acquisition practices in Mexico, Germany, and Japan. Journal of International Management 25, 100–125.
Tunyi, A., Ntim, C., Danbolt, J., 2019. Decoupling management inefficiency: myopia, hyperopia, and takeover likelihood. International Review of Financial Analysis 62, 1–20.
United States v. Primestar, L.P. (Proposed Final Judgment and Competitive Impact Study), 58 Fed Register 33944, June 22, 1993.
Unsal, O., Brodmann, J., 2020. The impact of employee relations on the reputation of the board of directors and CEO. The Quarterly Review of Economics and Finance 78, 372–388.
US Attorney General, 2000. Global antitrust regulation: issues and solutions. In: Final Report of the International Competition Policy Advisory Committee.
US Council of Economic Advisors, 2019. Two Years On, Tax Cuts Continue Boosting the United States Economy, December 20. https://www.whitehouse.gov/articles/two-years-tax-cuts-continue-boosting-united-states-economy/.
US Department of Justice, 1999. Antitrust division. http://www.usdoj.gov.
US Securities and Exchange Commission, 2012. Work Plan for the Consideration of Incorporating International Financial Reporting Standards in the Financial Reporting System for U.S. Issuers, Final Staff Report. Office of the Chief Accountant. July 13.
US Small Business Administration, 1999. Financial Difficulties of Small Businesses and Reasons for Their Failure Office of Advocacy. RS 188.
Vafeas, N., Vlittis, A., 2019. Board executive committees, board decisions, and firm value. Journal of Corporate Finance 58, 43–63.
Vagenas-Nanos, E., 2016. Mergers and acquisitions in frontier markets: a comparative analysis. In: Andrikopoulos, P., Gregoriou, G., Kallinterakis, V. (Eds.), Handbook of Frontier Markets: Evidence from the Middle East, North Africa, and International Comparative Studies, vol. 2. Academic Press, Cambridge, MA.
Valkama, P., Maula, M., Nikoskelainen, E., Wright, M., 2013. Driver of holding period firm-level returns in private equity-backed buyouts. Journal of Banking and Finance 37, 2378–2391.
Veld, C., Veld-Merkoulova, Y., 2004. Do spin-offs really create value? Journal of Banking and Finance 28, 1111–1135.
Vermaelen, T., Xu, M., 2014. Acquisition finance and market timing. Journal of Corporate Finance 25, 73–91.
Viarengo, L., Gatti, S., Prencipe, A., 2018. Enforcement quality and the use of earnouts in M&A transactions: international evidence. Journal of Business Finance & Accounting 45, 437–481.
Vijh, A., 1999. Long-term returns from equity carve-outs. Journal of Financial Economics 51, 273–308.
Vijh, A., 2002. The positive announcement period returns of equity carve-outs: asymmetric information or divestiture gains. Journal of Business 75, 153–190.
Vijh, A., Yang, K., 2013. Are small firms less vulnerable to overpriced stock offers? Journal of Financial Economics 110, 61–86.
Vladimirov, V., 2015. Financing bidders in takeover contests. Journal of Financial Economics 117, 534–557.
Volkov, I., 2016. The choice of sale method and its consequences in mergers and acquisitions. The Quarterly Review of Economics and Finance 63, 170–184.
von Beschwitz, B., 2018. Cash windfalls and acquisitions. Journal of Financial Economics 128, 287–319.
von Lilienfeld-Toal, U., Schnitzler, J., 2020. The anatomy of block accumulations by activist shareholders. Journal of Corporate Finance 62 article 101620.
Wang, D., Hain, D., Larimo, J., Dao, L., 2020. Cultural differences and synergy realization in cross-border acquisitions: the moderating effect of the acquisition process. International Business Review 29 article 101675.
Wang, L., 2019. Do investors care about earnings quality? The case of Chinese reverse mergers. Pacific Basin Finance Journal 55, 82–94.
Wang, W., 2018. Bid anticipation, information revelation, and merger gains. Journal of Financial Economics 128, 320–343.
Wang, W., Wu, Y., 2020. Managerial control benefits and takeover market efficiency. Journal of Financial Economics 136, 857–878.
Wang, Y., 2019. Executive migration and international mergers and acquisitions. International Business Review 28, 284–293.
Warrick, D., 2016. Leadership: A High Impact Approach. Bridgepoint Education, San Diego.
Warrick, D., 2017. What leaders need to know about culture. Business Horizons 60, 395–404.
Wei, L., 2020. China's Xi ramps up control of private sector. Wall Street Journal December 10.
Weifeng, W., Guo, Z., Shasa, Z., 2008. Ownership structure and the private benefits of control: an analysis of Chinese firms. Corporate Governance 8, 286–298.
Welch, X., Pavicevic, S., Keil, T., 2020. The pre-deal phase of mergers and acquisitions: a review and research agenda. Journal of Management 46, 3011–3038.
Welcher, T., 2019. A new way to look at an old problem: international joint venture partner selection via constrained systematic search. Business Horizons 62, 199–205.
Wettstein, F., Giuliani, E., Santangelo, G., Stahld, G., 2019. International business and human rights: a research agenda. Journal of World Business 54, 54–65.
White, E., 2007. Companies trim executive perks to avoid glare. Wall Street Journal 13, A1.
Wiltbank, R., Boeker, W., 2007. Returns to Angel Investors in Groups. Marian Ewing Foundation and Angel Capital Education Foundation, November.

Wiltermuth, S., Raja, M., Wood, A., 2018. How perceived power influences the consequences of dominance expressions in negotiations. Organizational Behavior and Human Decision Processes 146, 14–30.

Wruck, K., Yilin, W., 2009. Relationships, corporate governance, and performance: evidence from private placements of common stock. Journal of Corporate Finance 15, 30–47.

Wu, C., Reuer, J., 2020. The impact of industry IPOs on acquisitions of new ventures: an information spillovers perspective. Long-Range Planning article 101945, forthcoming.

Wu, C., Yu, X., Zheng, Y., 2020. The spillover effect of financial information in mergers and acquisitions. The British Accounting Review 52 article 100879.

Wu, S., Chung, K., 2019. Corporate innovation, likelihood to be acquired, and takeover premiums. Journal of Banking and Finance 108 article 105634.

Wursthorn, M., Zuckerman, G., 2018. Fewer listed companies: is that good or bad for stock markets? Wall Street Journal January 4.

Xiao, X., Xu, L., 2019. What do mean impacts miss? Distributional effects of corporate diversification. Journal of Econometrics 213, 92–120.

Xie, E., Reddy, K., Liang, J., 2017. Country-specific determinants of cross-border mergers and acquisitions: a comprehensive review and future research directions. Journal of World Business 52, 127–183.

Xu, E., 2017a. Cross-border merger waves. Journal of Corporate Finance 46, 207–231.

Xu, J., 2017b. Growing through merger and acquisition. Journal of Economic Dynamics & Control 80, 54–74.

Xu, K., Hitt, M., Dai, L., 2020. International diversification of family-dominant firms: integrating socioemotional wealth and behavioral theory of the firm. Journal of World Business 55 article 101071.

Yang, B., Sun, J., Guo, J., Fu, J., 2019. Can financial media sentiment predict merger and acquisition performance? Economic Modelling 80, 121–129.

Yen, T., Andre, P., 2019. Market reaction to the effect of corporate social responsibility on mergers and acquisitions: evidence on emerging markets. The Quarterly Review of Economics and Finance 71, 114–131.

Yen, T., Chou, S., Andre, P., 2013. Operating performance of emerging market acquirers: corporate governance issues. Emerging Markets Finance and Trade 49, 20–34.

Yilmaz, I., Tanyeri, B., 2016. Global mergers and acquisition activity: 1992-2011. Finance Research Letters 17, 1–9.

Yuan, Z., Chen, F., Yana, X., Yua, Y., 2020. Operational implications of yield uncertainty in mergers and acquisitions. International Journal of Production Economics 219, 248–258.

Zeida, T., 2019. On the corporate tax reform: coordination and trade-offs. Journal of Macroeconomics 62 article 103156.

Zhang, Z., Lyles, M., Wu, C., 2020. The stock market performance of exploration-oriented and exploitation-oriented cross-border mergers and acquisitions: evidence from emerging market enterprises. International Business Review 29 article 101707.

Zhou, B., Dutta, S., Zhu, P., 2020. CEO tenure and mergers and acquisitions. Finance Research Letters 34 article 101277.

Zhou, L., Lu, D., Fujita, H., 2015. The performance of corporate financial distress prediction models guided by domain knowledge and data mining approaches. Knowledge Based Systems 85, 52–61.

Zhu, J., Li, G., Li, J., 2017. Merge to be too big to fail: a real option approach. International Review of Economics and Finance 51, 342–353.

Zingales, L., 1995. What determines the value of corporate control? Quarterly Journal of Economics 110, 1047–1073.

Zola, M., Meier, D., 2008. What is M&A performance? Academy of Management Perspectives 22, 55–77.

Zurita, S., Castillo, A., Nino, J., 2019. Inflation, tax integration, and company valuation: the Latin American case. Journal of Business Research 105, 370–380.

Glossary

Abnormal return The return to shareholders due to nonrecurring events that differs from what would have been predicted by the market. It is the return due to an event such as a merger or acquisition.

Acquirer A firm that attempts to acquire a controlling interest in another company.

Acquisition The purchase by one company of a controlling ownership interest in another firm, a legal subsidiary of another firm, or selected assets of another firm.

Acquisition vehicle The legal structure used to acquire another company.

Advance ruling An Internal Revenue Service ruling sought by acquirers and targets planning to enter into a tax-free transaction. A favorable ruling is often a condition of closing.

Affirmative covenant A portion of a loan agreement that specifies the actions the borrowing firm agrees to take during the term of the loan.

Antigreenmail provisions Amendments to corporate charters restricting the firm's ability to repurchase shares from specific shareholders at a premium.

Antitakeover amendments Amendments to corporate charters designed to slow or make more expensive efforts to take control of the firm.

Antitrust laws Federal laws prohibiting individual corporations from assuming too much market power.

Appraisal rights Rights to seek "fair value" for their shares in court given to target company shareholders who choose not to tender shares in the first or second tier of a tender offer.

Arbitrageurs ("arbs") In the context of mergers and acquisitions, speculators who attempt to profit from the difference between the bid price and the target firm's current share price.

Asset-based lending A type of lending in which the decision to grant a loan is based largely on the quality of the assets collateralizing the loan.

Asset impairment An asset is said to be impaired according to the Financial Accounting Standards Board Statement 142 if its fair value falls below its book or carrying value.

Asset purchases Transactions in which the acquirer buys all or a portion of the target company's assets and assumes all, some, or none of the target's liabilities.

Assignment The process through which a committee representing creditors grants the power to liquidate a firm's assets to a third party, called an *assignee* or *trustee*.

Asymmetric information Information about a firm that is not equally available to both managers and shareholders.

Automatic stay The requirement for a period of time after the submission of a petition for bankruptcy in which all judgments, collection activities, foreclosures, and repossessions of property are suspended and may not be pursued by the creditors on any debt or claim that arose before the filing of the bankruptcy petition.

Back-end merger The merger after either a single- or two-tier tender offer consisting of either a long- or short-form merger, with the latter not requiring a target firm shareholder vote.

Bankruptcy A federal legal proceeding designed to protect the technically or legally insolvent firm from lawsuits by its creditors until a decision can be made to shut down or continue to operate the firm.

Bear hug A takeover tactic involving the mailing of a letter containing an acquisition proposal to the board of directors of a target company without prior warning and demanding a rapid decision.

Beta A measure of nondiversifiable risk or the extent to which a firm's (or asset's) return changes because of a change in the market's return.

Bidder See *acquirer.*

Boot The nonequity portion of the purchase price.

Breakup fee A fee paid to the potential acquirer if the target firm decides to accept an alternative bid. Also called a *termination fee.*

Bridge financing Temporary unsecured short-term loans provided by investment banks to pay all or a portion of the purchase price and meet immediate working-capital requirements until permanent or long-term financing is found.

Business alliance A generic term referring to all forms of business combinations other than mergers and acquisitions.

Business-level strategies Strategies pertaining to a specific operating unit or product line within a firm.

Business strategy or model The portion of a business plan detailing the way the firm intends to achieve its vision.

Buyout Change in controlling interest in a corporation.

Capital asset pricing model A framework for measuring the relationship between expected risk and return.

Capitalization multiple The multiple estimated by dividing 1 by the estimated discount that can be used to estimate the value of a business by multiplying it by an indicator of value such as free cash flow.

Capitalization rate (cap rate) The ratio of net operating income divided by asset value. Net operating income is total revenue less operating expenses. It is before taxes and excludes principal and interest payments on loans, capital expenditures, depreciation, and amortization.

Cash-for-assets An acquisition in which the acquirer pays cash for the seller's assets and may choose to accept some or all of the seller's liabilities.

Cash-out statutory merger A merger in which the shareholders of the selling firm receive cash or some form on nonvoting investment (e.g., debt, nonvoting preferred or common stock) for their shares.

Certificate of incorporation A document received from the state after the articles of incorporation have been approved.

Classified board election An antitakeover defense involving the separation of a firm's board into several classes, only one of which is up for election at any one point in time. Also called a *staggered board.*

Closing The phase of the acquisition process in which ownership is transferred from the target to the acquiring firm in exchange for some agreed-on consideration after the receipt of all necessary shareholder, regulatory, and third-party approvals.

Closing conditions Stipulations that must be satisfied before closing can take place.

Collar agreement An arrangement providing for certain changes in the share exchange ratio contingent on the level of the acquirer's share price around the effective date of the merger.

Common-size financial statements Valuation calculated by taking each line item as a percentage of revenue.

Composition An agreement in which creditors consent to settling for less than the full amount they are owed.

Confidentiality agreement A mutually binding accord defining how information exchanged among the parties may be used and the circumstances under which the discussions may be made public. Also known as a *nondisclosure agreement.*

Conglomerate discount The share prices of conglomerates often trade at a discount from focused firms or their value if they were broken up and sold in pieces.

Conglomerate mergers Transactions in which the acquiring company purchases firms in largely unrelated industries.

Consent decree Requires the merging parties to divest overlapping businesses or restrict anticompetitive practices.

Consent solicitation A process enabling dissident shareholders in certain states to obtain shareholder support for their proposals by simply obtaining their written consent.

Consolidation A business combination involving two or more companies joining to form a new company, in which none of the combining firms survive.

Constant growth model A valuation method that assumes that cash flow will grow at a constant rate.

Contingent value rights (CVRs) Commitments by the issuing company to pay additional cash or securities to the holder of the CVRs if the share price of the issuing company falls below a specified level at some future date.

Control premium The excess over the target's current share price the acquirer is willing to pay to gain a controlling interest. A pure control premium is one in which the anticipated synergies are small and the perceived value of the purchase is in gaining control to direct the activities of the target firm.

Corporate bylaws Rules governing the internal management of the corporation, which are determined by the corporation's founders.

Corporate charter A state license defining the powers of the firm and the rights and responsibilities of its shareholders, board of directors, and managers. The charter consists of articles of incorporation and a certificate of incorporation.

Corporate governance The systems and controls in place to protect the rights of corporate stakeholders.

Corporate restructuring Actions taken to expand or contract a firm's basic operations or fundamentally change its asset or financial structure.

Cost leadership A strategy designed to make a firm the cost leader in its market by constructing efficient production facilities, tightly controlling overhead expense, and eliminating marginally profitable customer accounts.

Covenants Promises made by the borrower that certain acts will be performed and others will be avoided.

Cram down A legal reorganization occurring whenever one or more classes of creditors or shareholders approve even though others may not.

Cumulative voting rights In an election for a board of directors, each shareholder is entitled to as many votes as equal the number of shares the shareholder owns multiplied by the number of directors to be elected. Furthermore, the shareholder may cast all of these votes for a single candidate or any two or more of them.

Deal-structuring process The process focused on satisfying as many of the primary objectives of the parties involved and determining how risk will be shared.

Debt-for-equity swap Creditors surrender a portion of their claims on the firm in exchange for an ownership position in the firm.

Debtor-in-possession On the filing of a reorganization petition, the firm's current management remains in place to conduct the ongoing affairs of the firm.

Debt restructuring Involves concessions by creditors that lower an insolvent firm's payments so that it may remain in business.

Definitive agreement of purchase and sale The legal document indicating all of the rights and obligations of the parties both before and after closing.

Destroyers of value Factors that can reduce the future cash flow of the combined companies.

Discounted cash flow The conversion of future to current cash flows by applying an appropriate discount rate.

Discount rate The opportunity cost associated with investment in the firm used to convert the projected cash flows to present values.

Dissident shareholders Those who disagree with a firm's incumbent management and attempt to change policies by initiating proxy contests to gain representation on the board of directors.

Diversifiable risk The risk specific to an individual firm, such as strikes and lawsuits.

Diversification A strategy of buying firms outside of the company's primary line of business.

Divestiture The sale of all or substantially all of a company or product line to another party for cash or securities.

Divisional organization An organizational structure in which groups of products are combined into independent divisions or "strategic business units."

Dual-class recapitalization A takeover defense in which a firm issues multiple classes of stock in which one class has voting rights that are 10 to 100 times those of another class. Such stock is also called *supervoting stock*.

Due diligence The process by which the acquirer seeks to determine the accuracy of the target's financial statements, evaluate the firm's operations, validate valuation assumptions, determine fatal flaws, and identify sources and destroyers of value.

Earnouts Payments to the seller based on the acquired business achieving certain profit or revenue targets.

Economic value The present value of a firm's projected cash flows.

Economies of scale The spreading of fixed costs over increasing production levels.

Economies of scope The use of a specific set of skills or an asset currently used to produce a specific product to produce related products.

Effective control Control achieved when one firm has purchased another firm's voting stock, it is not likely to be temporary, there are no legal restrictions on control such as from a bankruptcy court, and there are no powerful minority shareholders.

Employee stock ownership plan (ESOP) A trust fund or plan that invests in the securities of the firm sponsoring the plan on behalf of the firm's employees. Such plans are generally defined contribution employee retirement plans.

Enterprise cash flow Cash available to shareholders and lenders after all operating obligations of the firm have been satisfied.

Enterprise value Viewed from the liability side of the balance sheet, it is the sum of the market or present value of a firm's common equity plus preferred stock and long-term debt. For simplicity, other long-term liabilities are often excluded from the calculation. From the perspective of the asset side of the balance sheet, it is equal to cash plus the market value of current operating and nonoperating assets less current liabilities plus long-term assets.

Equity beta A measure of the risk of a stock's financial returns compared with the risk of the financial returns to the general stock market, which in turn is affected by the overall economy.

Equity carve-out A transaction in which the parent firm issues a portion of its stock or that of a subsidiary to the public.

Equity cash flow Cash available to common shareholders after all operating obligations of the firm have been satisfied.

Equity premium The rate of return in excess of the risk-free rate investors require to invest in equities.

Excess returns See *abnormal returns*.

Exchange offer A tender offer involving a share-for-share exchange.

Exit strategy A strategy enabling investors to realize their required returns by undertaking an initial public offering or selling to a strategic buyer.

Extension Creditor agreement to lengthen the period during which the debtor firm can repay its debt and, in some cases, to temporarily suspend both interest and principal repayments.

Fair market value The cash or cash-equivalent price a willing buyer would propose and a willing seller would accept for a business if both parties have access to all relevant information.

Fairness opinion letter A written and signed third-party assertion certifying the appropriateness of the price of a proposed deal involving a tender offer, merger, asset sale, or leveraged buyout.

Fair value An estimate of the value of an asset when no strong market exists for a business or it is not possible to identify the value of substantially similar firms.

Financial buyer Acquirers that focus on relatively short to intermediate financial returns.

Financial restructuring Actions by the firm to change its total debt and equity structure.

Financial sponsor An investor group providing equity financing in leveraged buyout transactions.

Financial synergy The reduction in the cost of capital as a result of more stable cash flows, financial economies of scale, or a better matching of investment opportunities with available funds.

Fixed or constant share-exchange agreement An exchange agreement in which the number of acquirer shares exchanged for each target share is unchanged between the signing of the agreement of purchase and sale and closing.

Fixed value agreement The value of the price per share is fixed by allowing the number of acquirer shares issued to vary to offset fluctuations in the buyer's share price.

Flip-in poison pill A shareholders' rights plan in which the shareholders of the target firm can acquire stock in the target firm at a substantial discount.

Flip-over poison pill A shareholders' rights plan in which target firm shareholders may convert such rights to acquire stock of the surviving company at a substantial discount.

Form of acquisition The determination of what is being acquired (i.e., stock or assets).

Form of payment A means of payment: cash, common stock, debt, or some combination. Some portion of the payment may be deferred or dependent on the future performance of the acquired entity.

Forward triangular merger The acquisition subsidiary being merged with the target and the acquiring subsidiary surviving.

Fraudulent conveyance Laws governing the rights of shareholders if the new company created following an acquisition or leveraged buyout is inadequately capitalized to remain viable.

Free cash flow The difference between cash inflows and cash outflows, which may be positive, negative, or zero.

Friendly takeover Acquisition when the target's board and management are receptive to the idea and recommend shareholder approval.

Functional strategies Description in detail of how each major function (e.g., manufacturing, marketing, and human resources) within the firm will support the business strategy.

Generally accepted accounting principles (GAAP) Accounting guidelines established by the Financial Accounting Standards Board.

General partner An individual responsible for the daily operations of a limited partnership.

Global capital asset pricing model A version of the capital asset pricing model in which a global equity index is used in calculating the equity risk premium.

Globally integrated capital markets Capital markets providing foreigners with unfettered access to local capital markets and local residents to foreign capital markets.

Going concern value The value of a company defined as the firm's value in excess of the sum of the value of its parts.

Going private The purchase of the publicly traded shares of a firm by a group of investors.

Golden parachutes Employee severance arrangements that are triggered whenever a change in control takes place.

Goodwill The excess of the purchase price over the fair value of the acquired net assets on the acquisition date.

Go-shop provision A provision allowing a seller to continue to solicit other bidders for a specific time period after an agreement has been signed but before closing. However, the seller that accepts another bid must pay a breakup fee to the bidder with which it had a signed agreement.

Greenmail The practice of a firm buying back its shares at a premium from an investor threatening a takeover.

Hedge fund Private investment limited partnerships (for US investors) or off-shore investment corporations (for non-US or tax-exempt investors) in which the general partner has made a substantial personal investment.

Herfindahl–Hirschman Index The measure of industry concentration used by the Federal Trade Commission as one criterion in determining when to approve mergers and acquisitions.

Highly leveraged transactions Transactions involving a substantial amount of debt relative to the amount of equity invested.

Holding company A legal entity often having a controlling interest in one or more companies.

Holdout problem Tendency for smaller creditors to hold up the agreement among creditors during reorganization unless they receive special treatment.

Horizontal merger A combination of two firms within the same industry.

Hostile takeover Acquisition when the initial bid was unsolicited, the target was not seeking a merger at the time of the approach, the approach was contested by the target's management, and control changed hands.

Hostile tender offer A tender offer that is unwanted by the target's board.

Hubris An explanation for takeovers that attributes a tendency to overpay to excessive optimism about the value of a deal's potential synergy or excessive confidence in management's ability to manage the acquisition.

Impaired asset As defined by the Financial Accounting Standards Board, a long-term asset whose fair value falls below its book or carrying value.

Implementation strategy The way in which the firm chooses to execute the business strategy.

Indemnification A common contractual clause requiring the seller to indemnify or absolve the buyer of liability in the event of misrepresentations or breaches of warranties or covenants. Similarly, the buyer usually agrees to indemnify the seller. In effect, it is the reimbursement to the other party for a loss for which it was not responsible.

Initial offer price A price that lies between the estimated minimum and maximum offer prices for a target firm.

Insider trading Individuals buying or selling securities based on knowledge not available to the general public.

Interest rate parity theory A theory that relates forward or future spot exchange rates to differences in interest rates between two countries adjusted by the spot rate.

Investment bankers Advisors who offer strategic and tactical advice and acquisition opportunities, screen potential buyers and sellers, make initial contact with a seller or buyer, and provide negotiation support, valuation, and deal structuring advice.

Involuntary bankruptcy A situation in which creditors force a debtor firm into bankruptcy.

Joint venture A cooperative business relationship formed by two or more separate entities to achieve common strategic objectives.

Junk bonds High-yield bonds either rated by the credit-rating agencies as below investment grade or not rated at all.

Legal form of the selling entity Whether the seller is a C or subchapter S corporation, a limited liability company, or a partnership.

Legal insolvency When a firm's liabilities exceed the fair market value of its assets.

Letter of intent Preliminary agreement between two companies intending to merge that stipulates major areas of agreement between the parties.

Leveraged buyout Purchase of a company financed primarily by debt.

Leveraged loans Unrated or noninvestment-grade bank loans whose interest rates are equal to or greater than the London Inter Bank Rate plus 150 basis points.

Liquidating dividend Proceeds left to shareholders after company is liquidated and outstanding obligations to creditors are paid off.

Liquidation The value of a firm's assets sold separately less its liabilities and expenses incurred in breaking up the firm.

Liquidity discount The discount or reduction in the offer price for the target firm made by discounting the value of the target firm estimated by examining the market values of comparable publicly traded firms to reflect the potential loss in value when sold caused by the illiquidity of the market for similar types of investments. The liquidity discount also is referred to as a *marketability discount*.

Liquidity risk See *marketability risk*.

Management buyout A leveraged buyout in which managers of the firm to be taken private are also equity investors in the transaction.

Management entrenchment theory A theory that managers use a variety of takeover defenses to ensure their longevity with the firm.

Management integration team Senior managers from the two merged organizations charged with delivering on sales and operating synergies identified during the preclosing due diligence.

Management preferences The boundaries or limits that senior managers of the acquiring firm place on the acquisition process.

Managerialism theory A theory espousing that managers acquire companies to increase the acquirer's size and their own remuneration.

Market power A situation in which the merger of two firms enables the resulting combination to profitably maintain prices above competitive levels for a significant period.

Market power hypothesis A theory that firms merge to gain greater control over pricing.

Marketability discount See *liquidity discount*.

Marketability risk The risk associated with an illiquid market for the specific stock. Also called *liquidity risk*.

Maximum offer price The sum of the minimum price plus the present value of net synergy.

Merger A combination of two or more firms in which all but one legally cease to exist.

Merger acquisition plan A specific type of implementation strategy that describes in detail the motivation for the acquisition and how and when it will be achieved.

Merger arbitrage An investment strategy that attempts to profit from the spread between a target firm's current share price and a pending takeover bid.

Merger of equals A merger framework usually applied whenever the merger participants are comparable in size, competitive position, profitability, and market capitalization.

Mezzanine financing Capital that in liquidation has a repayment priority between senior debt and common stock.

Minimum offer price The target's standalone or present value or its current market value.

Minority discount The reduction in the value of their investment in a firm because the minority investors cannot direct the activities of the firm.

Minority investment A less-than-controlling interest in another firm.

Negative covenant Restriction found in loan agreements on the actions of the borrower.

Negotiating price range The difference between the minimum and maximum offer prices.

Net asset value The difference between the fair market value of total identifiable acquired assets and the value of acquired liabilities.

Net debt The market value of debt assumed by the acquirer less cash and marketable securities on the books of the target firm.

Net operating loss carryforward and carrybacks Provisions in the tax laws allowing firms to use accumulated net tax losses to offset income earned over a specified number of future years or recover taxes paid during a limited number of prior years.

Net purchase price The total purchase price plus other assumed liabilities less the proceeds from the sale of discretionary or redundant target assets.

Net synergy The difference between estimated sources of value and destroyers of value.

Nondiversifiable risk Risk generated by factors that affect all firms, such as inflation and war.

Nonrecourse financing Loans granted to a venture without partner guarantees.

No-shop agreement That which prohibits the takeover target from seeking other bids or making public information not currently readily available while in discussions with a potential acquirer.

One-tiered offer A bidder announces the same offer to all target shareholders.

Open market share repurchase The act of a corporation buying its shares in the open market at the prevailing price as any other investor, as opposed to a tender offer for shares or a repurchase resulting from negotiation such as with an unwanted investor.

Operating synergy Increased value resulting from a combination of businesses caused by such factors as economies of scale and scope.

Operational restructuring The outright or partial sale of companies or product lines or downsizing by closing unprofitable or nonstrategic facilities.

Payment-in-kind (PIK) notes Equity or debt that pays dividends or interest in the form of additional equity or debt.

Permanent financing Financing usually consisting of long-term unsecured debt.

Poison pills A new class of securities issued as a dividend by a company to its shareholders, giving shareholders rights to acquire more shares at a discount.

Portfolio companies Companies in which the hedge or private equity fund has made investments.

Postclosing organization The organizational and legal framework used to manage the combined businesses following the completion of the transaction.

Prepackaged bankruptcies A situation in which the failing firm starts negotiating with its creditors well in advance of filing for a Chapter 11 bankruptcy to reach agreement on major issues before formally filing for bankruptcy.

Private corporation A firm whose securities are not registered with state or federal authorities.

Private equity fund Limited partnerships in which the general partner has made a substantial personal investment.

Private placements The sale of securities to institutional investors, such as pension funds and insurance companies, for investment rather than for resale. Such securities do not have to be registered with the Securities and Exchange Commission.

Private solicitation A firm hires an investment banker or undertakes on its own to identify potential buyers to be contacted as potential buyers for the entire firm or a portion of the firm.

Pro forma financial statements A form of accounting that presents financial statements in a way that purports to more accurately describe a firm's current or projected performance.

Proxy contest An attempt by dissident shareholders to obtain representation on the board of directors or to change a firm's bylaws.

Public solicitation Public announcement by a firm that it is putting itself, a subsidiary, or a product line up for sale.

Purchase accounting A form of accounting for financial reporting purposes in which the acquired assets and assumed liabilities are revalued to their fair market value on the date of acquisition and recorded on the books of the acquiring company.

Purchase premium The excess of the offer price over the target's current share price, which reflects both the value of expected synergies and the amount necessary to obtain control.

Purchasing power parity theory The theory stating that one currency will appreciate (depreciate) with respect to another currency according to the expected relative rates of inflation between the two countries.

Pure control premium The value the acquirer believes can be created by replacing incompetent management or changing the strategic direction of the firm.

Pure play A firm whose products or services focus on a single industry or market.

Real options Management's ability to adopt and later revise corporate investment decisions.

Receivership Court appointment of an individual to administer the assets and affairs of a business in accordance with its directives.

Retention bonuses Incentives granted key employees of the target firm if they remain with the combined companies for a specific period following completion of the transaction.

Revenue ruling An official interpretation by the Internal Revenue Service of the Internal Revenue Code, related statutes, tax treaties, and regulations.

Reverse breakup fee Fee paid to a target firm in the event the bidder wants to withdraw from a signed contract.

Reverse leverage buyouts Public companies that are taken private and later are taken public again. The second effort to take the firm public is called a *secondary public offering*.

Reverse merger Process by which a private firm goes public by merging with a public firm with the public firm surviving.

Reverse triangular merger The merger of the target with a subsidiary of the acquiring firm, with the target surviving.

Right of first refusal A contract clause requiring that a party wishing to leave a joint venture or partnership to first offer its interests to other participants in the joint venture or partnership.

Risk-free rate of return The return on a security with an exceedingly low probability of default, such as US Treasury securities, and minimal reinvestment risk.

Risk premium The additional rate of return in excess of the risk-free rate that investors require to purchase a firm's equity. Also called the *equity premium*.

Secondary public offering A stock offering by a private company that had previously been a public company.

Secured debt Debt backed by the borrower's assets.

Security agreement A legal document stipulating which of the borrower's assets are pledged to secure the loan.

Segmented capital markets Capital markets exhibiting different bond and equity prices in different geographic areas for identical assets in terms of risk and maturity.

Self-tender offer A tender offer used when a firm seeks to repurchase its stock from its shareholders.

Share-exchange ratio The number of shares of the acquirer's stock to be exchanged for each share of the target's stock.

Shareholders' interest theory The presumption that management resistance to proposed takeovers is a good bargaining strategy to increase the purchase price for the benefit of the target firm shareholders.

Shark repellents Specific types of takeover defenses that can be adopted by amending either a corporate charter or its bylaws.

Shell corporation One that is incorporated but has no significant assets or operations.

Sources of value Factors increasing the cash flow of the combined companies.

Spin-off A transaction in which a parent creates a new legal subsidiary and distributes shares it owns in the subsidiary to its current shareholders as a stock dividend.

Split-off A variation of a spin-off in which some parent company shareholders receive shares in a subsidiary in return for relinquishing their parent company shares.

Split-up A transaction in which a parent firm splits its assets between two or more subsidiaries and the stock of each subsidiary is offered to its shareholders in exchange for their parent firm shares.

Staggered board election A takeover defense involving the division of the firm's directors into a number of different classes, with no two classes up for reelection at the same time. Also called a *classified board*.

Stakeholders Groups having interests in a firm, such as customers, shareholders, employees, suppliers, regulators, and communities.

Standalone business One whose financial statements reflect all the costs of running the business and all the revenues generated by the business.

Standstill agreement A contractual arrangement in which the acquirer agrees not to make any further investments in the target's stock for a stipulated period.

Statutory consolidation Involves two or more companies joining to form a new company.

Statutory merger The combination of the acquiring and target firms, in which one firm ceases to exist, in accordance with the statutes of the state in which the combined businesses will be incorporated.

Stock-for-stock statutory merger A merger in which the seller receives acquirer shares in exchange for its shares (with the seller shares subsequently canceled); also called a *stock swap merger*.

Stock purchases The exchange of the target's stock for cash, debt, or the stock of the acquiring company.

Strategic buyer An acquirer primarily interested in increasing shareholder value by realizing long-term synergies.

Subsidiary carve-out A transaction in which the parent creates a wholly owned independent legal subsidiary, with stock and a management team different from the parent's, and issues a portion of the subsidiary's stock to the public.

Subsidiary merger A transaction in which the target becomes a subsidiary of the parent.

Supermajority rules A takeover defense requiring a higher level of approval for amending the charter or for certain types of transactions, such as a merger or acquisition.

Supervoting stock A class of voting stock having voting rights many times those of other classes of stock.

Syndicate An arrangement in which a group of investment banks agrees to purchase a new issue of securities from the acquiring company for sale to the investing public.

Synergy The notion that the value of the combined enterprises will exceed the sum of their individual values.

Takeover Generic term referring to a change in the controlling ownership interest of a corporation.

Takeover defenses Protective devices put in place by a firm to frustrate, slow down, or raise the cost of a takeover.

Target company The firm that is being solicited by the acquiring company.

Taxable transaction Transactions in which the form of payment is primarily something other than acquiring company stock.

Tax considerations Structures and strategies determining whether a transaction is taxable or nontaxable to the seller's shareholders.

Tax-free reorganization Nontaxable transactions usually involving mergers, with the form of payment primarily acquirer stock exchanged for the target's stock or assets.

Tax-free transactions Transactions in which the form of payment is primarily acquiring company stock. Also called *tax-free reorganizations*.

Tax shield The reduction in the firm's tax liability caused by the tax deductibility of interest.

Technical insolvency A situation in which a firm is unable to pay its liabilities as they come due.

Tender offer The offer to buy shares in another firm, usually for cash, securities, or both.

Terminal growth value The discounted value of the cash flows generated during the stable growth period. Also called the *sustainable, horizon,* or *continuing growth value.*

Term loan A loan usually having a maturity of 2 to 10 years and secured by the asset being financed, such as new capital equipment.

Term sheet A document outlining the primary areas of agreement between the buyer and the seller, which is often used as the basis for a more detailed letter of intent.

Total capitalization The sum of a firm's debt and all forms of equity.

Total consideration A commonly used term in legal documents to reflect the different types of remuneration received by target company shareholders.

Total purchase price The total consideration plus the market value of the target firm's debt assumed by the acquiring company. Also referred to as *enterprise value.*

Tracking stocks Separate classes of common stock of the parent corporation whose dividend payouts depend on the financial performance of a specific subsidiary. Also called *target* or *letter stocks.*

Transfer taxes State taxes paid whenever titles to assets are transferred, as in an asset purchase.

Two-tiered offer A tender offer in which target shareholders receive an offer for a specific number of shares. Immediately following this offer, the bidder announces its intentions to purchase the remaining shares at a lower price or using something other than cash.

Type A reorganization A tax-free merger or consolidation in which target shareholders receive cash, voting or nonvoting common or preferred stock, or debt for their shares. At least 40% of the purchase price must be in acquirer stock.

Type B stock-for-stock reorganization A tax-free transaction in which the acquirer uses its voting common stock to purchase at least 80% of the voting power of the target's outstanding voting stock and at least 80% of each class of nonvoting shares. Used as an alternative to a merger.

Type C stock-for-assets reorganization A tax-free transaction in which acquirer voting stock is used to purchase at least 80% of the fair market value of the target's net assets.

Valuation cash flows Restated generally accepted accounting principles cash flows used for valuing a firm or a firm's assets.

Variable growth valuation model A valuation method that assumes that a firm's cash flows will experience periods of high growth followed by a period of slower, more sustainable growth.

Vertical merger Merger in which companies that do not own operations in each major segment of the value chain choose to backward integrate by acquiring a supplier or to forward integrate by acquiring a distributor.

Voluntary bankruptcy A situation in which the debtor firm files for bankruptcy.

Voluntary liquidation Sale by management, which concludes that the sale of the firm in parts could realize greater value than the value created by a continuation of the combined corporation.

Weighted average cost of capital A broader measure than the cost of equity that represents the return that a firm must earn to induce investors to buy its stock and bonds.

White knight A potential acquirer that is viewed more favorably by a target firm's management and board than the initial bidder.

Winner's curse The tendency of the auction winners to show remorse, believing that they may have paid too much.

Zero-growth valuation model A valuation model that assumes that free cash flow is constant in perpetuity.

Index

Note: Page numbers followed by "f" indicate figures, "t" indicate tables, and "b" indicate boxes.

B

C